The Best of the Bard

The Best of the Bard

A Midsummer Night's Dream
Hamlet
Romeo and Juliet
Macbeth
Twelfth Night
As You Like It
Much Ado About Nothing
The Tempest
The Comedy of Errors
Julius Caesar

The Taming of the Shrew
Othello
King Lear
The Winter's Tale
Richard III
The Merry Wives of Windsor
Love's Labour's Lost
Henry V
Measure for Measure
The Merchant of Venice

William Shakespeare's

TOP TWENTY

Edited by PlayShakespeare.com

Waking Lion Press

ISBN 978-1-4341-0465-6

© 2005–2021 PlayShakespeare.com. Permission is granted to copy, distribute and/or modify this information under the terms of the GNU Free Documentation License, Version 1.3 or any later version published by the Free Software Foundation. Terms at http://www.playshakespeare.com/license

Published by Waking Lion Press, an imprint of the Editorium. Waking Lion Press is not endorsed by or affiliated with PlayShakespeare.com.

Waking Lion Press™ and Editorium™ are trademarks of:

The Editorium, LLC
West Jordan, UT 84081-6132
www.editorium.com

The views expressed in this book are the responsibility of the author and do not necessarily represent the position of Waking Lion Press. The reader alone is responsible for the use of any ideas or information provided by this book.

This book is a work of fiction. The characters, places, and incidents in it are the products of the author's imagination or are represented fictitiously. Any resemblance of characters to actual persons is coincidental.

Contents

Foreword	vii
Publisher's Preface	xi
A Midsummer Night's Dream	1
Hamlet	37
Romeo and Juliet	107
Macbeth	162
Twelfth Night	207
As You Like It	257
Much Ado About Nothing	304
The Tempest	353
The Comedy of Errors	394
Julius Caesar	428
The Taming of the Shrew	475
Othello	524
King Lear	590
The Winter's Tale	655
Richard III	709
The Merry Wives of Windsor	775
Love's Labour's Lost	828
Henry V	881
Measure for Measure	934
The Merchant of Venice	986

Foreword

The proliferation of editions of Shakespeare's works is a great thing. When PlayShakespeare.com started, it was difficult to find them in digital form—primarily because there were really only two or three editions in the public domain. Now there is a larger selection (including the PlayShakespeare.com editions), enabling students, teachers, scholars, theatre professionals, computer programmers, and even the average fan to rework the Bard in new ways.

Thinking Makes it So

In the spring of 2005 at Marin Shakespeare, I was rehearsing Beaumont's *Knight of the Burning Pestle*, which was written at the same time Shakespeare was working on *Pericles*. I searched for parallels between the two works (and other works, there are many), which meant carrying around the Globe Edition of the complete works (a fat tome I'd also lugged around Europe in my travels). I spent many hours looking for lines, cross-referencing against glosses, and consulting the other editions my fellow thespians were using (Folger, Riverside, Arden, and so on). I had a Palm Treo at the time (this was a pre-iPhone world) with really slow access to the Internet, and I thought I could find a website that made this easier (in spite of the slow 3G speeds that were just starting to become available). The internet was in full swing, but Shakespeare resources online were rare, with badly mangled or incomplete texts. They were exercises in technology rather than textual or scholarly works. The more I looked, the more disappointed I became.

After a few months and discussions with actor/director/scholar Julian López-Morillas, a fellow actor in *Pestle*, I decided to start a new website. I explored options for an open-source content management system to handle the large amount of text more efficiently, and by the end of summer 2005, the basic structure of the first PlayShakespeare.com website was up and running. But it was far from my original vision of making quality editions of the complete works available online and searchable—a much more convenient alternative to carrying around a big book.

I researched editions of Shakespeare's works that I could use for the website and found that all except the poor versions I'd found online were heavily copyrighted. None offered any flexible usage terms by which I could use them for my website, let alone build a powerful search engine on. That meant I had to create my own, and it also meant a lot of work. I had a few discussions with actor/dramaturg Barry Kraft (longtime dramaturg at the Oregon Shakespeare Festival) about the best approach to creating a new set of editions, and we came up with the matrix of sources (*www.playshakespeare.com/text-sources*) on the website as a starting point.

I recruited a few other people to help with the editing, but I did most of the "grunt" work of formatting, organizing, leading debates on various passages, and modernizing the spelling. I created scripts to manipulate the text and save us a ton of time in modernizing Elizabethan spellings and comparing multiple sources in an efficient way. I also consulted with many people on specific problem areas of the canon to understand the best approach. The overarching principles in how the editions were approached were:

Clarity: If the playwright's intent was clear, reinforce it. If ambiguous, clarify the ambiguity. In some ambiguous cases (for example, "solid" vs. "sullied"), we made editorial decisions that reflected the other criteria. Clarity means approachability.

Modern: Use modern spellings with a light touch and modern scholarly interpretations.

Playability: Is the line performable by an actor? As actors ourselves, this sometimes helped make things clearer and strengthen how meter and verse vs. prose might be interpreted. The works were meant to be performed, not just read.

Integrity: Stay as faithful as possible to the source material and commonly accepted scholarly interpretations.

Inclusive: In cases where one edition was missing text another had, and vice-versa, we included both texts (for example, the *Richard II* deposition scene or *Taming of A Shrew*).

Additionally, we preserved the blank-verse meter, and that meant including text indentations where characters speak partial lines. This aids the speaker in finding the rhythm and makes scansion a little easier—a feature usually found only in proprietary editions.

As print and online editions of Shakespeare's plays proliferate, the need for "through line numbers" (Charlton Hinman's system from the Norton First Folio) becomes obsolete because of the need for flexibility of systems for viewing and printing—it didn't make sense to recreate a printed page on an iPhone screen, where a "reflowable" layout was more suitable. Additionally, in a classroom where students have their own editions from different publishers, line numbers of a play are not consistent from one edition to another (none of which have the "correct" numbers anyway). The "old school" method actors and directors use to indicate a location in the text (act, scene, number of lines, and so on) works best to refer and navigate, and therefore we've chosen to number lines in a way most appropriate for the digital age—that is, not at all.

Open Source Drives the Vision

At PlayShakespeare.com, we believe strongly in the philosophy of open source. When intellectual property is released to the world using an open-source license, it fosters creativity and innovation when building upon those ideas, creating new works and making them better. When open source is supported, everyone benefits, and that idea combined with creating high-quality digital editions was a driving principle in 2005 when the first version of our editions was created.

What's the difference between "free" and "free"? This is a point of confusion for most. Often the word "free" is used when promoting open-source material. But free can mean several things, and it's very important to distinguish the difference:

"Free of charge" means you don't have to pay for it. You can download it with no cost to you at all.

"Freedom to use" means you can do whatever you want with it—adapt it, give it away, sell it, and so on.

Just because you have the first doesn't automatically mean you have the second (and vice versa). The definition of "open source" comes from the Open Source Initiative (OSI) and the Freedom Software Foundation (FSF). In short, the definition doesn't mean the source code is freely available to download (a common misconception). Open source defines the *conditions of usage* of that source code. If that usage is restricted (especially commercially), it's not open source.

Existing editions like Arden, Riverside, and Folger are all proprietary. There are a few "free" editions of Shakespeare's works available on the Internet because they're now in the public domain. Here are the three most popular:

The Globe Edition

The Globe edition was published in 1866 and based on Cambridge texts from the same decade. It was groundbreaking in its time, but Shakespeare scholarship has evolved by leaps and bounds in the past 150 years, so this edition is sorely outdated, with many errors.

The Moby Edition

This edition, created by The Moby Project, is essentially a minor derivative of the Globe Edition with even more errors. It was available online until the project was later absorbed into Project Gutenberg.

The Oxford Shakespeare

This edition was published in 1914 by W. J. Craig for Oxford University Press. It is a somewhat improved edition over the Globe and Moby editions but definitely shows its age at 100 years old.

Because all of these editions are in the public domain, they are not technically "open source" by definition, but since they are "free of charge" and "free to use", they are widely copied in spite of their age and textual errors. They are not maintained in any way and are essentially "snapshots" of the times in which they were released many years ago.

To further illustrate the point, there are other sources which claim to have either "free" or "open source" editions available:

MIT

This site uses the public domain Moby Edition. Ironically, MIT is the creator of the popular MIT license for many kinds of open-source software, but these texts are not released under it.

Folger Digital Texts

The well-respected Folger Shakespeare Library launched their digital texts in December 2012 under the CC-ANC 3.0 license. Their site says:

"The full source code of the texts may be downloaded by researchers and developers at no cost for noncommercial use."

According to the definition of open source, the texts should be unencumbered for use in *any* project, commercial or not. No Creative Commons licenses qualify as open source as they all come with restrictions that go against the spirit of it. So while the texts are being called "free", they are "free of charge", not free to use as you wish.

Open Source Shakespeare

Despite its domain name, this website uses the public domain Globe Edition. The license page doesn't mention any particular open-source license but states:

"You may download the OSS code and/or the database and use them in your personal, non-commercial projects without charge, as long as you give us credit and provide a link somewhere to www.opensourceshakespeare.org. Commercial use is not authorized without the permission from George Mason University."

According to the definition of open source, anyone should be able to use the content in any project, for commercial use or not. In open source, no special permission is needed because it is, by definition, open. So, like the Folger Digital Texts, Open Source Shakespeare is "free of charge", not "free to use". Therefore, neither the site software nor the content is actually open source as the name of the website implies.

Why This Matters

These are just a few examples of digital editions in use by people who might inadvertently be breaking the law because the terms are either unclear or restrictive. What is a "non-commercial project"? Isn't a theatrical performance where I charge an admission fee considered a commercial project? There are many questions like these when an open-source license isn't used. I question whether George Mason University or The Folger is going to send the "Shakespeare Police" after anyone, but are you sure? In some cases, you could be violating their copyright and not even know it.

We continue to publicly maintain our open-source editions on GitHub and encourage feedback and contributions. We are proud to have created the first truly open-source editions of Shakespeare's plays with an emphasis on quality. To us, the term "open source" isn't just a buzzword to attract people looking for free stuff. It's a different way of looking at copyright with the goal of fostering innovation and free thinking.

The Future of Shakespeare

Since the creation of these editions in 2005, we've taken many suggestions from scholars, teachers, theatre professionals, and aficionados all over the world to improve them. We consider them "living" documents that have been "forked", reused, edited, hacked, and much more. They're used as the basis for performances at theatres like the Oregon Shakespeare Festival, Prague Shakespeare Company, and in countless classrooms. They're also used in the popular Shakespeare Pro apps for Apple and Android devices, which have currently been downloaded more than 15 million times. They've even been used in various open-source technology projects to search, analyze, and visualize Shakespeare's works in new ways. The possibilities are limitless.

As for the future? It's anyone's guess. It's been more than fifteen years since this project's inception, but I can say we've accomplished much more than what we originally intended. What started as a website project to replace a heavy book has become an incredible way to empower Shakespeare lovers all over the world and impact millions more using only the words of the Bard.

Ron Severdia
San Anselmo, California
March 2021

Publisher's Preface

How does one decide which of Shakespeare's plays should be included in his "top twenty"? The answer has been provided by Bard on the Boards, "What's Playing Where," which has ranked the plays according to how frequently they were produced from 2012 through May 25, 2020, at more than 200 theater companies in Australia, Canada, the United Kingdom, Denmark, and the United States. (You can learn more at shakespeareances.com.) Here is their ranking, which is followed in this book:

1. *A Midsummer Night's Dream* (180 productions)
2. *Hamlet* (143)
3. *Romeo and Juliet* (143)
4. *Macbeth* (137)
5. *Twelfth Night* (132)
6. *As You Like It* (122)
7. *Much Ado About Nothing* (122)
8. *The Tempest* (111)
9. *The Comedy of Errors* (95)
10. *Julius Caesar* (91)
11. *The Taming of the Shrew* (91)
12. *Othello* (78)
13. *King Lear* (76)
14. *The Winter's Tale* (73)
15. *Richard III* (73)
16. *The Merry Wives of Windsor* (72)
17. *Love's Labour's Lost* (65)
18. *Henry V* (60)
19. *Measure for Measure* (57)
20. *The Merchant of Venice* (55)

The text of the plays used in this book was produced by PlayShakespeare.com, which has made expertly edited versions of Shakespeare's works freely available under the only truly open-source license for those works. Please lend your support through donations or assistance, and be sure to get the Shakespeare Pro app, which actor and producer Kenneth Branagh has rightly characterized as "really great," and award-winning playwright Ken Ludwig has said is "simply terrific!" You can learn more and find play summaries, plot overviews, character descriptions, and many other useful aids at www.playshakespeare.com.

But enough of this; the play's the thing!

A Midsummer Night's Dream

Act 1

Scene 1

Athens. A room in the palace of Theseus.

(Theseus; Hippolyta; Philostrate; Egeus; Hermia; Lysander; Demetrius; Helena)

Duke Theseus orders Philostrate to stir up merriment in the streets of Athens before his wedding to Hippolyta, the Queen of the Amazons he defeated in battle. Egeus brings in his daughter Hermia in order to ask the Duke to force her to marry Demetrius, his choice for her husband. Hermia is insisting on marrying Lysander instead, and Egeus begs permission to either force her to wed Demetrius or to have her killed, as is his right by the law. Theseus gives Hermia until his own wedding date to either give in or become a nun. Lysander argues his case, pointing out that he is in all ways equal to Demetrius and that the latter had earlier promised to marry Helena, but Theseus will not go against the law. Left alone, the two lovers lament their fate. Lysander comes up with a plan to flee to an aunt of his, who lives outside the boundaries of Athens and where they could therefore be safely married. They tell this plan to Helena, who is lovesick for Demetrius. Learning that the two runaways will be meeting in the wood that night, she decides to tell Demetrius, in the hopes of winning his favor.

Enter Theseus, Hippolyta, Philostrate, with others.

Theseus, Duke of Athens.
Now, fair Hippolyta, our nuptial hour
Draws on apace. Four happy days bring in
Another moon; but O, methinks, how slow
This old moon wanes! She lingers my desires,
Like to a step-dame, or a dowager,
Long withering out a young man's revenue.

Hippolyta.
Four days will quickly steep themselves in night;
Four nights will quickly dream away the time;
And then the moon, like to a silver bow
New bent in heaven, shall behold the night
Of our solemnities.

Theseus, Duke of Athens.
            Go, Philostrate,
Stir up the Athenian youth to merriments,
Awake the pert and nimble spirit of mirth,
Turn melancholy forth to funerals:
The pale companion is not for our pomp.

Exit Philostrate.

Hippolyta, I woo'd thee with my sword,
And won thy love doing thee injuries;
But I will wed thee in another key,
With pomp, with triumph, and with reveling.

Enter Egeus and his daughter Hermia and Lysander and Demetrius.

Egeus.
Happy be Theseus, our renowned Duke!

Theseus, Duke of Athens.
Thanks, good Egeus. What's the news with thee?

Egeus.
Full of vexation come I, with complaint
Against my child, my daughter Hermia.
Stand forth, Demetrius. My noble lord,
This man hath my consent to marry her.
Stand forth, Lysander. And, my gracious Duke,
This man hath bewitch'd the bosom of my child.
Thou, thou, Lysander, thou hast given her rhymes,
And interchang'd love-tokens with my child;

Thou hast by moonlight at her window sung
With faining voice verses of faining love,
And stol'n the impression of her fantasy
With bracelets of thy hair, rings, gawds, conceits,
Knacks, trifles, nosegays, sweetmeats—messengers
Of strong prevailment in unhardened youth.
With cunning hast thou filch'd my daughter's heart,
Turn'd her obedience (which is due to me)
To stubborn harshness. And, my gracious Duke,
Be it so she will not here before your Grace
Consent to marry with Demetrius,
I beg the ancient privilege of Athens:
As she is mine, I may dispose of her;
Which shall be either to this gentleman,
Or to her death, according to our law
Immediately provided in that case.

Theseus, Duke of Athens.
What say you, Hermia? Be advis'd, fair maid.
To you your father should be as a god;
One that compos'd your beauties; yea, and one
To whom you are but as a form in wax,
By him imprinted, and within his power,
To leave the figure, or disfigure it.
Demetrius is a worthy gentleman.

Hermia.
So is Lysander.

Theseus, Duke of Athens.
                     In himself he is;
But in this kind, wanting your father's voice,
The other must be held the worthier.

Hermia.
I would my father look'd but with my eyes.

Theseus, Duke of Athens.
Rather your eyes must with his judgment look.

Hermia.
I do entreat your Grace to pardon me.
I know not by what power I am made bold,
Nor how it may concern my modesty,
In such a presence here to plead my thoughts;
But I beseech your Grace that I may know
The worst that may befall me in this case,
If I refuse to wed Demetrius.

Theseus, Duke of Athens.
Either to die the death, or to abjure
Forever the society of men.
Therefore, fair Hermia, question your desires,
Know of your youth, examine well your blood,
Whether (if you yield not to your father's choice)
You can endure the livery of a nun,
For aye to be in shady cloister mew'd,
To live a barren sister all your life,
Chaunting faint hymns to the cold fruitless moon.
Thrice blessed they that master so their blood
To undergo such maiden pilgrimage;
But earthlier happy is the rose distill'd,
Than that which withering on the virgin thorn
Grows, lives, and dies in single blessedness.

Hermia.
So will I grow, so live, so die, my lord,
Ere I will yield my virgin patent up
Unto his lordship, whose unwished yoke
My soul consents not to give sovereignty.

Theseus, Duke of Athens.
Take time to pause, and by the next new moon—
The sealing-day betwixt my love and me
For everlasting bond of fellowship—
Upon that day either prepare to die
For disobedience to your father's will,
Or else to wed Demetrius, as he would,
Or on Diana's altar to protest
For aye austerity and single life.

Demetrius.
Relent, sweet Hermia, and, Lysander, yield
Thy crazed title to my certain right.

Lysander.
You have her father's love, Demetrius,
Let me have Hermia's; do you marry him.

Egeus.
Scornful Lysander, true, he hath my love;
And what is mine, my love shall render him.
And she is mine, and all my right of her
I do estate unto Demetrius.

Lysander.
I am, my lord, as well deriv'd as he,
As well possess'd; my love is more than his;
My fortunes every way as fairly rank'd
(If not with vantage) as Demetrius';
And (which is more than all these boasts can be)

I am belov'd of beauteous Hermia.
Why should not I then prosecute my right?
Demetrius, I'll avouch it to his head,
Made love to Nedar's daughter, Helena,
And won her soul; and she, sweet lady, dotes,
Devoutly dotes, dotes in idolatry,
Upon this spotted and inconstant man.

Theseus, Duke of Athens.
I must confess that I have heard so much,
And with Demetrius thought to have spoke thereof;
But, being over-full of self-affairs,
My mind did lose it. But, Demetrius, come,
And come, Egeus, you shall go with me;
I have some private schooling for you both.
For you, fair Hermia, look you arm yourself
To fit your fancies to your father's will;
Or else the law of Athens yields you up
(Which by no means we may extenuate)
To death, or to a vow of single life.
Come, my Hippolyta; what cheer, my love?
Demetrius and Egeus, go along;
I must employ you in some business
Against our nuptial, and confer with you
Of something nearly that concerns yourselves.

Egeus.
With duty and desire we follow you.

Exeunt. Manent Lysander and Hermia.

Lysander.
How now, my love? Why is your cheek so pale?
How chance the roses there do fade so fast?

Hermia.
Belike for want of rain; which I could well
Beteem them from the tempest of my eyes.

Lysander.
Ay me! For aught that I could ever read,
Could ever hear by tale or history,
The course of true love never did run smooth;
But either it was different in blood—

Hermia.
O cross! Too high to be enthrall'd to low.

Lysander.
Or else misgraffed in respect of years—

Hermia.
O spite! Too old to be engag'd to young.

Lysander.
Or else it stood upon the choice of friends—

Hermia.
O hell, to choose love by another's eyes!

Lysander.
Or if there were a sympathy in choice,
War, death, or sickness did lay siege to it,
Making it momentany as a sound,
Swift as a shadow, short as any dream,
Brief as the lightning in the collied night,
That, in a spleen, unfolds both heaven and earth;
And ere a man hath power to say "Behold!"
The jaws of darkness do devour it up:
So quick bright things come to confusion.

Hermia.
If then true lovers have been ever cross'd,
It stands as an edict in destiny.
Then let us teach our trial patience,
Because it is a customary cross,
As due to love as thoughts and dreams and sighs,
Wishes and tears, poor fancy's followers.

Lysander.
A good persuasion; therefore hear me, Hermia:
I have a widow aunt, a dowager,
Of great revenue, and she hath no child.
From Athens is her house remote seven leagues;
And she respects me as her only son.
There, gentle Hermia, may I marry thee;
And to that place the sharp Athenian law
Cannot pursue us. If thou lovest me, then
Steal forth thy father's house tomorrow night;
And in the wood, a league without the town
(Where I did meet thee once with Helena
To do observance to a morn of May),
There will I stay for thee.

Hermia.
              My good Lysander,
I swear to thee, by Cupid's strongest bow,
By his best arrow with the golden head,
By the simplicity of Venus' doves,
By that which knitteth souls and prospers loves,
And by that fire which burn'd the Carthage queen
When the false Troyan under sail was seen,
By all the vows that ever men have broke

(In number more than ever women spoke),
In that same place thou hast appointed me
Tomorrow truly will I meet with thee.

Lysander.
Keep promise, love. Look, here comes Helena.

Enter Helena.

Hermia.
God speed fair Helena! Whither away?

Helena.
Call you me fair? That fair again unsay.
Demetrius loves your fair, O happy fair!
Your eyes are lodestars, and your tongue's sweet air
More tuneable than lark to shepherd's ear
When wheat is green, when hawthorn buds appear.
Sickness is catching; O, were favor so,
Yours would I catch, fair Hermia, ere I go;
My ear should catch your voice, my eye your eye,
My tongue should catch your tongue's sweet melody.
Were the world mine, Demetrius being bated,
The rest I'll give to be to you translated.
O, teach me how you look, and with what art
You sway the motion of Demetrius' heart.

Hermia.
I frown upon him; yet he loves me still.

Helena.
O that your frowns would teach my smiles such skill!

Hermia.
I give him curses; yet he gives me love.

Helena.
O that my prayers could such affection move!

Hermia.
The more I hate, the more he follows me.

Helena.
The more I love, the more he hateth me.

Hermia.
His folly, Helena, is no fault of mine.

Helena.
None but your beauty; would that fault were mine!

Hermia.
Take comfort; he no more shall see my face;
Lysander and myself will fly this place.
Before the time I did Lysander see,
Seem'd Athens as a paradise to me;
O then, what graces in my love do dwell,
That he hath turn'd a heaven unto a hell!

Lysander.
Helen, to you our minds we will unfold:
Tomorrow night, when Phoebe doth behold
Her silver visage in the wat'ry glass,
Decking with liquid pearl the bladed grass
(A time that lovers' flights doth still conceal),
Through Athens gates have we devis'd to steal.

Hermia.
And in the wood, where often you and I
Upon faint primrose beds were wont to lie,
Emptying our bosoms of their counsel sweet,
There my Lysander and myself shall meet;
And thence from Athens turn away our eyes,
To seek new friends and stranger companies.
Farewell, sweet playfellow, pray thou for us;
And good luck grant thee thy Demetrius!
Keep word, Lysander; we must starve our sight
From lovers' food till morrow deep midnight.

Lysander.
I will, my Hermia.

Exit Hermia.

                         Helena, adieu:
As you on him, Demetrius dote on you!

Exit Lysander.

Helena.
How happy some o'er other some can be!
Through Athens I am thought as fair as she.
But what of that? Demetrius thinks not so;
He will not know what all but he do know;
And as he errs, doting on Hermia's eyes,
So I, admiring of his qualities.
Things base and vile, holding no quantity,
Love can transpose to form and dignity.
Love looks not with the eyes but with the mind;
And therefore is wing'd Cupid painted blind.
Nor hath Love's mind of any judgment taste;
Wings, and no eyes, figure unheedy haste;
And therefore is Love said to be a child,

Because in choice he is so oft beguil'd.
As waggish boys in game themselves forswear,
So the boy Love is perjur'd every where;
For ere Demetrius look'd on Hermia's eyne,
He hail'd down oaths that he was only mine;
And when this hail some heat from Hermia felt,
So he dissolv'd, and show'rs of oaths did melt.
I will go tell him of fair Hermia's flight;
Then to the wood will he tomorrow night
Pursue her; and for this intelligence
If I have thanks, it is a dear expense.
But herein mean I to enrich my pain,
To have his sight thither and back again.

Exit.

Scene 2

Athens. A room in Quince's house.

(Quince; Snug; Bottom; Flute; Snout; Starveling)

A group of craftsmen meet to rehearse the play they hope to be asked to perform at Theseus's wedding. Quince the carpenter, who has written the play, assigns the various roles, having to keep down Bottom the weaver, who wants to play everything. They plan to meet the next night in the wood so that no one will see them rehearse.

Enter Quince the carpenter and Snug the joiner and Bottom the weaver and Flute the bellows-mender and Snout the tinker and Starveling the tailor.

Quince.
Is all our company here?

Bottom.
You were best to call them generally, man by man, according to the scrip.

Quince.
Here is the scroll of every man's name, which is thought fit, through all Athens, to play in our enterlude before the Duke and the Duchess, on his wedding-day at night.

Bottom.
First, good Peter Quince, say what the play treats on; then read the names of the actors; and so grow to a point.

Quince.
Marry, our play is The most lamentable comedy and most cruel death of Pyramus and Thisbe.

Bottom.
A very good piece of work, I assure you, and a merry. Now, good Peter Quince, call forth your actors by the scroll. Masters, spread yourselves.

Quince.
Answer as I call you. Nick Bottom the weaver.

Bottom.
Ready. Name what part I am for, and proceed.

Quince.
You, Nick Bottom, are set down for Pyramus.

Bottom.
What is Pyramus? A lover, or a tyrant?

Quince.
A lover, that kills himself most gallant for love.

Bottom.
That will ask some tears in the true performing of it. If I do it, let the audience look to their eyes. I will move storms; I will condole in some measure. To the rest—yet my chief humor is for a tyrant. I could play Ercles rarely, or a part to tear a cat in, to make all split.
"The raging rocks
And shivering shocks
Shall break the locks
Of prison gates;
And Phibbus' car
Shall shine from far,
And make and mar
The foolish Fates."
This was lofty! Now name the rest of the players. This is Ercles' vein, a tyrant's vein; a lover is more condoling.

Quince.
Francis Flute the bellows-mender.

Flute.
Here, Peter Quince.

Quince.
Flute, you must take Thisbe on you.

Flute.
What is Thisbe? A wand'ring knight?

Quince.
It is the lady that Pyramus must love.

Flute.
Nay, faith; let not me play a woman; I have a beard coming.

Quince.
That's all one; you shall play it in a mask, and you may speak as small as you will.

Bottom.
And I may hide my face, let me play Thisbe too. I'll speak in a monstrous little voice, "Thisne! Thisne!" "Ah, Pyramus, my lover dear! Thy Thisbe dear, and lady dear!"

Quince.
No, no, you must play Pyramus; and, Flute, you Thisbe.

Bottom.
Well, proceed.

Quince.
Robin Starveling the tailor.

Starveling.
Here, Peter Quince.

Quince.
Robin Starveling, you must play Thisbe's mother. Tom Snout the tinker.

Snout.
Here, Peter Quince.

Quince.
You, Pyramus' father; myself, Thisbe's father; Snug the joiner, you the lion's part. And I hope here is a play fitted.

Snug.
Have you the lion's part written? Pray you, if it be, give it me, for I am slow of study.

Quince.
You may do it extempore, for it is nothing but roaring.

Bottom.
Let me play the lion too. I will roar, that I will do any man's heart good to hear me. I will roar, that I will make the Duke say, "Let him roar again; let him roar again."

Quince.
And you should do it too terribly, you would fright the Duchess and the ladies, that they would shriek; and that were enough to hang us all.

All.
That would hang us, every mother's son.

Bottom.
I grant you, friends, if you should fright the ladies out of their wits, they would have no more discretion but to hang us; but I will aggravate my voice so that I will roar you as gently as any sucking dove; I will roar you and 'twere any nightingale.

Quince.
You can play no part but Pyramus; for Pyramus is a sweet-fac'd man; a proper man as one shall see in a summer's day; a most lovely gentleman-like man: therefore you must needs play Pyramus.

Bottom.
Well; I will undertake it. What beard were I best to play it in?

Quince.
Why, what you will.

Bottom.
I will discharge it in either your straw-color beard, your orange-tawny beard, your purple-in-grain beard, or your French-crown-color beard, your perfit yellow.

Quince.
Some of your French crowns have no hair at all; and then you will play barefac'd. But, masters, here are your parts, and I am to entreat you, request you, and desire you, to con them by tomorrow night; and meet me in the palace wood, a mile without the town, by moonlight; there will we rehearse; for if we meet in the city, we shall be dogg'd with company, and our devices known. In the meantime I will draw a bill of properties, such as our play wants. I pray you fail me not.

Bottom.
We will meet, and there we may rehearse most obscenely and courageously. Take pains, be perfit; adieu.

Quince.
At the Duke's oak we meet.

Bottom.
Enough; hold, or cut bow-strings.

Exeunt.

Act 2

Scene 1

In the woods near Athens.

(Fairy; Puck; King Oberon; Queen Titania; Demetrius; Helena)

The next night, Robin Goodfellow, the Puck, meets a fairy and learns that Titania, Queen of the Fairies, is coming to the very place where Oberon, the King, is planning to hold his revels. He explains that there is a great quarrel between the two over a changeling boy. The two monarchs enter and meet, immediately renewing the quarrel, accusing each other of infidelity with Theseus and Hippolyta respectively. Titania absolutely refuses to hand over the changeling to Oberon, explaining that the boy's mother was one of her votaresses. Furious, Oberon decides on revenge, and sends Puck to fetch a flower that will enable him to make Titania fall in love with an animal until she gives up the changeling. At this point he sees Demetrius, who is searching through the woods for Lysander and Hermia and is being dogged by Helena, who absolutely refuses to leave him no matter how badly he treats her. Oberon decides that he will use some of the juice from the flower to make Demetrius love her. When Puck returns with the flower, Oberon gives him some of the juice and orders him to find the Athenian man and drip it in his eyes.

Enter a Fairy at one door and Robin Goodfellow (Puck) at another.

Puck.
How now, spirit, whither wander you?

A Fairy.
Over hill, over dale,
Thorough bush, thorough brier,
Over park, over pale,
Thorough flood, thorough fire,
I do wander every where,
Swifter than the moon's sphere;
And I serve the Fairy Queen,
To dew her orbs upon the green.
The cowslips tall her pensioners be,
In their gold coats spots you see:
Those be rubies, fairy favors,
In those freckles live their savors.
I must go seek some dewdrops here,
And hang a pearl in every cowslip's ear.
Farewell, thou lob of spirits; I'll be gone.
Our Queen and all her elves come here anon.

Puck.
The King doth keep his revels here tonight;
Take heed the Queen come not within his sight;
For Oberon is passing fell and wrath,
Because that she as her attendant hath
A lovely boy stolen from an Indian king;
She never had so sweet a changeling.
And jealous Oberon would have the child
Knight of his train, to trace the forests wild;
But she, perforce, withholds the loved boy,
Crowns him with flowers, and makes him all her joy.
And now they never meet in grove or green,
By fountain clear, or spangled starlight sheen,
But they do square, that all their elves for fear
Creep into acorn-cups, and hide them there.

A Fairy.
Either I mistake your shape and making quite,
Or else you are that shrewd and knavish sprite
Call'd Robin Goodfellow. Are not you he
That frights the maidens of the villagery,
Skim milk, and sometimes labor in the quern,
And bootless make the breathless huswife churn,
And sometime make the drink to bear no barm,
Mislead night-wanderers, laughing at their harm?
Those that Hobgoblin call you, and sweet Puck,
You do their work, and they shall have good luck.
Are not you he?

Puck.
        Thou speakest aright;
I am that merry wanderer of the night.
I jest to Oberon and make him smile
When I a fat and bean-fed horse beguile,
Neighing in likeness of a filly foal;
And sometime lurk I in a gossip's bowl,
In very likeness of a roasted crab,
And when she drinks, against her lips I bob,
And on her withered dewlop pour the ale.
The wisest aunt, telling the saddest tale,
Sometime for three-foot stool mistaketh me;
Then slip I from her bum, down topples she,
And "tailor" cries, and falls into a cough;

And then the whole quire hold their hips and loff,
And waxen in their mirth, and neeze, and swear
A merrier hour was never wasted there.
But room, fairy! Here comes Oberon.

A Fairy.
And here my mistress. Would that he were gone!

Enter the King of Fairies Oberon at one door with his Train, and the Queen Titania at another with hers.

Oberon.
Ill met by moonlight, proud Titania.

Titania.
What, jealous Oberon? Fairies, skip hence—
I have forsworn his bed and company.

Oberon.
Tarry, rash wanton! Am not I thy lord?

Titania.
Then I must be thy lady; but I know
When thou hast stolen away from fairy land,
And in the shape of Corin sat all day,
Playing on pipes of corn, and versing love,
To amorous Phillida. Why art thou here
Come from the farthest steep of India?
But that, forsooth, the bouncing Amazon,
Your buskin'd mistress, and your warrior love,
To Theseus must be wedded, and you come
To give their bed joy and prosperity.

Oberon.
How canst thou thus for shame, Titania,
Glance at my credit with Hippolyta,
Knowing I know thy love to Theseus?
Didst not thou lead him through the glimmering night
From Perigenia, whom he ravished?
And make him with fair Aegles break his faith,
With Ariadne, and Antiopa?

Titania.
These are the forgeries of jealousy;
And never, since the middle summer's spring,
Met we on hill, in dale, forest, or mead,
By paved fountain or by rushy brook,
Or in the beached margent of the sea,
To dance our ringlets to the whistling wind,
But with thy brawls thou hast disturb'd our sport.
Therefore the winds, piping to us in vain,
As in revenge, have suck'd up from the sea
Contagious fogs; which, falling in the land,
Hath every pelting river made so proud
That they have overborne their continents.
The ox hath therefore stretch'd his yoke in vain,
The ploughman lost his sweat, and the green corn
Hath rotted ere his youth attain'd a beard.
The fold stands empty in the drowned field,
And crows are fatted with the murrion flock;
The nine men's morris is fill'd up with mud,
And the quaint mazes in the wanton green,
For lack of tread, are undistinguishable.
The human mortals want their winter here;
No night is now with hymn or carol blest.
Therefore the moon (the governess of floods),
Pale in her anger, washes all the air,
That rheumatic diseases do abound.
And thorough this distemperature, we see
The seasons alter: hoary-headed frosts
Fall in the fresh lap of the crimson rose,
And on old Hiems' thin and icy crown
An odorous chaplet of sweet summer buds
Is, as in mockery, set; the spring, the summer,
The childing autumn, angry winter, change
Their wonted liveries; and the mazed world,
By their increase, now knows not which is which.
And this same progeny of evils comes
From our debate, from our dissension;
We are their parents and original.

Oberon.
Do you amend it then; it lies in you.
Why should Titania cross her Oberon?
I do but beg a little changeling boy,
To be my henchman.

Titania.
           Set your heart at rest;
The fairy land buys not the child of me.
His mother was a vot'ress of my order,
And in the spiced Indian air, by night,
Full often hath she gossip'd by my side,
And sat with me on Neptune's yellow sands,
Marking th' embarked traders on the flood;
When we have laugh'd to see the sails conceive
And grow big-bellied with the wanton wind;
Which she, with pretty and with swimming gait,
Following (her womb then rich with my young squire)
Would imitate, and sail upon the land
To fetch me trifles, and return again,

As from a voyage, rich with merchandise.
But she, being mortal, of that boy did die,
And for her sake do I rear up her boy;
And for her sake I will not part with him.

Oberon.
How long within this wood intend you stay?

Titania.
Perchance till after Theseus' wedding-day.
If you will patiently dance in our round,
And see our moonlight revels, go with us;
If not, shun me, and I will spare your haunts.

Oberon.
Give me that boy, and I will go with thee.

Titania.
Not for thy fairy kingdom. Fairies, away!
We shall chide downright, if I longer stay.

Exeunt Titania and her Train.

Oberon.
Well; go thy way. Thou shalt not from this grove
Till I torment thee for this injury.
My gentle Puck, come hither. Thou rememb'rest
Since once I sat upon a promontory,
And heard a mermaid on a dolphin's back
Uttering such dulcet and harmonious breath
That the rude sea grew civil at her song,
And certain stars shot madly from their spheres,
To hear the sea-maid's music?

Puck.
                I remember.

Oberon.
That very time I saw (but thou couldst not),
Flying between the cold moon and the earth,
Cupid all arm'd. A certain aim he took
At a fair vestal throned by the west,
And loos'd his love-shaft smartly from his bow,
As it should pierce a hundred thousand hearts;
But I might see young Cupid's fiery shaft
Quench'd in the chaste beams of the wat'ry moon,
And the imperial vot'ress passed on,
In maiden meditation, fancy-free.
Yet mark'd I where the bolt of Cupid fell.
It fell upon a little western flower,
Before milk-white, now purple with love's wound,
And maidens call it love-in-idleness.
Fetch me that flow'r; the herb I showed thee once.
The juice of it on sleeping eyelids laid
Will make or man or woman madly dote
Upon the next live creature that it sees.
Fetch me this herb, and be thou here again
Ere the leviathan can swim a league.

Puck.
I'll put a girdle round about the earth
In forty minutes.

Exit.

Oberon.
                Having once this juice,
I'll watch Titania when she is asleep,
And drop the liquor of it in her eyes;
The next thing then she waking looks upon
(Be it on lion, bear, or wolf, or bull,
On meddling monkey, or on busy ape),
She shall pursue it with the soul of love.
And ere I take this charm from off her sight
(As I can take it with another herb),
I'll make her render up her page to me.
But who comes here? I am invisible,
And I will overhear their conference.

Enter Demetrius, Helena following him.

Demetrius.
I love thee not; therefore pursue me not.
Where is Lysander and fair Hermia?
The one I'll slay; the other slayeth me.
Thou toldst me they were stol'n unto this wood;
And here am I, and wode within this wood,
Because I cannot meet my Hermia.
Hence, get thee gone, and follow me no more.

Helena.
You draw me, you hard-hearted adamant;
But yet you draw not iron, for my heart
Is true as steel. Leave you your power to draw,
And I shall have no power to follow you.

Demetrius.
Do I entice you? Do I speak you fair?
Or rather do I not in plainest truth
Tell you I do not nor I cannot love you?

Helena.
And even for that do I love you the more;
I am your spaniel; and, Demetrius,
The more you beat me, I will fawn on you.
Use me but as your spaniel; spurn me, strike me,
Neglect me, lose me; only give me leave,
Unworthy as I am, to follow you.
What worser place can I beg in your love
(And yet a place of high respect with me)
Than to be used as you use your dog?

Demetrius.
Tempt not too much the hatred of my spirit,
For I am sick when I do look on thee.

Helena.
And I am sick when I look not on you.

Demetrius.
You do impeach your modesty too much,
To leave the city and commit yourself
Into the hands of one that loves you not;
To trust the opportunity of night,
And the ill counsel of a desert place,
With the rich worth of your virginity.

Helena.
Your virtue is my privilege. For that
It is not night when I do see your face,
Therefore I think I am not in the night,
Nor doth this wood lack worlds of company,
For you in my respect are all the world.
Then how can it be said I am alone,
When all the world is here to look on me?

Demetrius.
I'll run from thee, and hide me in the brakes,
And leave thee to the mercy of wild beasts.

Helena.
The wildest hath not such a heart as you.
Run when you will; the story shall be chang'd:
Apollo flies, and Daphne holds the chase;
The dove pursues the griffin; the mild hind
Makes speed to catch the tiger—bootless speed,
When cowardice pursues and valor flies.

Demetrius.
I will not stay thy questions. Let me go;
Or if thou follow me, do not believe
But I shall do thee mischief in the wood.

Helena.
Ay, in the temple, in the town, the field,
You do me mischief. Fie, Demetrius!
Your wrongs do set a scandal on my sex.
We cannot fight for love, as men may do.
We should be woo'd, and were not made to woo.

Exit Demetrius.

I'll follow thee and make a heaven of hell,
To die upon the hand I love so well.

Exit.

Oberon.
Fare thee well, nymph. Ere he do leave this grove,
Thou shalt fly him, and he shall seek thy love.

Enter Puck.

Hast thou the flower there? Welcome, wanderer.

Puck.
Ay, there it is.

Oberon.
                    I pray thee give it me.
I know a bank where the wild thyme blows,
Where oxlips and the nodding violet grows,
Quite over-canopied with luscious woodbine,
With sweet musk-roses and with eglantine;
There sleeps Titania sometime of the night,
Lull'd in these flowers with dances and delight;
And there the snake throws her enamell'd skin,
Weed wide enough to wrap a fairy in;
And with the juice of this I'll streak her eyes,
And make her full of hateful fantasies.
Take thou some of it, and seek through this grove:
A sweet Athenian lady is in love
With a disdainful youth; anoint his eyes,
But do it when the next thing he espies
May be the lady. Thou shalt know the man
By the Athenian garments he hath on.
Effect it with some care, that he may prove
More fond on her than she upon her love;
And look thou meet me ere the first cock crow.

Puck.
Fear not, my lord! Your servant shall do so.

Exeunt.

Act 2, Scene 2

Scene 2

Another part of the woods near Athens.

(Titania; Fairies; Oberon; Lysander; Hermia; Puck; Demetrius; Helena; Fairy Chorus)

Titania lies herself down to sleep, lulled by the charms sung by her attendant fairies. When they leave, Oberon sneaks up on his Queen and pours the love-juice into her eyes. The weary Lysander and Hermia appear, and exhaustedly decide to sleep. Hermia insists that Lysander lie a little away from her for decency's sake. They fall asleep and Puck, passing by, believes that he has finally found the Athenian he has been ordered to enchant and puts his love-juice on Lysander's eyes. Demetrius, still searching, is distracted by still being followed by Helena, and misses his prey as he shakes her off. She sees Lysander, who is sleeping so deeply she is afraid he is dead. Finally, she manages to wake him, and, under the charm of the love-juice, he instantly falls head over heels in love with her. She is convinced that he is mocking her and is deeply hurt. She leaves, and he pursues her, abandoning Hermia, who awakes to find herself alone and decides to seek for him.

Enter Titania, Queen of Fairies, with her Train.

Titania.
Come, now a roundel and a fairy song;
Then, for the third part of a minute, hence,
Some to kill cankers in the musk-rose buds,
Some war with rere-mice for their leathren wings
To make my small elves coats, and some keep back
The clamorous owl, that nightly hoots and wonders
At our quaint spirits. Sing me now asleep;
Then to your offices, and let me rest.

Fairies sing.

First Fairy.
You spotted snakes with double tongue,
Thorny hedgehogs, be not seen,
Newts and blind-worms, do no wrong,
Come not near our fairy queen.

Fairy Chorus.
Philomele, with melody,
Sing in our sweet lullaby,
Lulla, lulla, lullaby, lulla, lulla, lullaby.
Never harm,
Nor spell, nor charm,
Come our lovely lady nigh.
So good night, with lullaby.

First Fairy.
Weaving spiders, come not here;
Hence, you long-legg'd spinners, hence!
Beetles black, approach not near;
Worm nor snail, do no offense.

Fairy Chorus.
Philomele, with melody, etc.

Second Fairy.
Hence, away! Now all is well.
One aloof stand sentinel.

Exeunt Fairies. Titania sleeps.
Enter Oberon and squeezes the flower on Titania's eyelids.

Oberon.
What thou seest when thou dost wake,
Do it for thy true-love take;
Love and languish for his sake.
Be it ounce, or cat, or bear,
Pard, or boar with bristled hair,
In thy eye that shall appear
When thou wak'st, it is thy dear:
Wake when some vile thing is near.

Exit.
Enter Lysander and Hermia.

Lysander.
Fair love, you faint with wand'ring in the wood;
And to speak troth I have forgot our way.
We'll rest us, Hermia, if you think it good,
And tarry for the comfort of the day.

Hermia.
Be't so, Lysander. Find you out a bed;
For I upon this bank will rest my head.

Lysander.
One turf shall serve as pillow for us both,
One heart, one bed, two bosoms, and one troth.

Hermia.
Nay, good Lysander; for my sake, my dear,
Lie further off yet; do not lie so near.

Lysander.
O, take the sense, sweet, of my innocence!
Love takes the meaning in love's conference:
I mean, that my heart unto yours is knit,
So that but one heart we can make of it;

Two bosoms interchained with an oath,
So then two bosoms and a single troth.
Then by your side no bed-room me deny;
For lying so, Hermia, I do not lie.

Hermia.
Lysander riddles very prettily.
Now much beshrew my manners and my pride,
If Hermia meant to say Lysander lied.
But, gentle friend, for love and courtesy,
Lie further off, in humane modesty;
Such separation as may well be said
Becomes a virtuous bachelor and a maid,
So far be distant; and good night, sweet friend.
Thy love ne'er alter till thy sweet life end!

Lysander.
Amen, amen, to that fair prayer, say I,
And then end life when I end loyalty!
Here is my bed; sleep give thee all his rest!

Hermia.
With half that wish the wisher's eyes be press'd!

They sleep.
Enter Puck.

Puck.
Through the forest have I gone,
But Athenian found I none,
On whose eyes I might approve
This flower's force in stirring love.
Night and silence—Who is here?
Weeds of Athens he doth wear:
This is he, my master said,
Despised the Athenian maid;
And here the maiden, sleeping sound,
On the dank and dirty ground.
Pretty soul, she durst not lie
Near this lack-love, this kill-courtesy.
Churl, upon thy eyes I throw
All the power this charm doth owe.
When thou wak'st, let love forbid
Sleep his seat on thy eyelid.
So awake when I am gone,
For I must now to Oberon.

Exit.
Enter Demetrius and Helena, running.

Helena.
Stay—though thou kill me, sweet Demetrius.

Demetrius.
I charge thee hence, and do not haunt me thus.

Helena.
O, wilt thou darkling leave me? Do not so.

Demetrius.
Stay, on thy peril; I alone will go.

Exit.

Helena.
O, I am out of breath in this fond chase!
The more my prayer, the lesser is my grace.
Happy is Hermia, wheresoe'er she lies,
For she hath blessed and attractive eyes.
How came her eyes so bright? Not with salt tears;
If so, my eyes are oft'ner wash'd than hers.
No, no; I am as ugly as a bear;
For beasts that meet me run away for fear.
Therefore no marvel though Demetrius
Do, as a monster, fly my presence thus.
What wicked and dissembling glass of mine
Made me compare with Hermia's sphery eyne!
But who is here? Lysander! On the ground?
Dead, or asleep? I see no blood, no wound.
Lysander, if you live, good sir, awake.

Lysander.

Awaking.

And run through fire I will for thy sweet sake.
Transparent Helena, nature shows art,
That through thy bosom makes me see thy heart.
Where is Demetrius? O, how fit a word
Is that vile name to perish on my sword!

Helena.
Do not say so, Lysander, say not so.
What though he love your Hermia? Lord, what though?
Yet Hermia still loves you; then be content.

Lysander.
Content with Hermia? No; I do repent
The tedious minutes I with her have spent.
Not Hermia, but Helena I love.
Who will not change a raven for a dove?
The will of man is by his reason sway'd;

And reason says you are the worthier maid.
Things growing are not ripe until their season,
So I, being young, till now ripe not to reason;
And touching now the point of human skill,
Reason becomes the marshal to my will,
And leads me to your eyes, where I o'erlook
Love's stories written in Love's richest book.

Helena.
Wherefore was I to this keen mockery born?
When at your hands did I deserve this scorn?
Is't not enough, is't not enough, young man,
That I did never, no, nor never can,
Deserve a sweet look from Demetrius' eye,
But you must flout my insufficiency?
Good troth, you do me wrong (good sooth, you do)
In such disdainful manner me to woo.
But fare you well; perforce I must confess
I thought you lord of more true gentleness.
O that a lady, of one man refus'd,
Should of another therefore be abus'd!

Exit.

Lysander.
She sees not Hermia. Hermia, sleep thou there,
And never mayst thou come Lysander near!
For as a surfeit of the sweetest things
The deepest loathing to the stomach brings,
Or as the heresies that men do leave
Are hated most of those they did deceive,
So thou, my surfeit and my heresy,
Of all be hated, but the most of me!
And, all my powers, address your love and might
To honor Helen and to be her knight.

Exit.

Hermia.

Starting up.

Help me, Lysander, help me! Do thy best
To pluck this crawling serpent from my breast!
Ay me, for pity! What a dream was here!
Lysander, look how I do quake with fear.
Methought a serpent ate my heart away,
And you sat smiling at his cruel prey.
Lysander! What, remov'd? Lysander! Lord!
What, out of hearing gone? No sound, no word?
Alack, where are you? Speak, and if you hear;
Speak, of all loves! I swoon almost with fear.

No? Then I well perceive you are not nigh:
Either death, or you, I'll find immediately.

Exit.

Act 3
Scene 1

In the woods.

(*Quince; Snug; Bottom; Flute; Snout; Starveling; Puck; Peaseblossom; Cobweb; Moth; Mustardseed; Titania*)

Bottom and the others meet to rehearse, not knowing that they are near Titania's bower, and begin to work out difficulties in the script. Fearful of offending or scaring the ladies at court, they decide to add a prologue to the play, explaining that the lion is not a real one. Likewise, parts for Moonshine and the Wall are added and assigned. As they begin to go through the play, Puck happens upon them, and is vastly amused. Seeing a chance to play mischief, he waits until Bottom exits and changes his head into a donkey's; when Bottom returns, the others fly in fear, pushed on by Puck. Bottom stolidly believes that they are playing a practical joke on him, not even noticing his transformation. Refusing to play along, he sits down and sings to himself making a racket that wakes Titania — who seeing him, instantly falls in love with him. She begins to woo him, while he, with great common sense, declines to see any truth in her flowery compliments. She calls in fairies to attend on him, and has him led into her bower.

Enter the Clowns: Quince, Snug, Bottom, Flute, Snout, and Starveling. Titania still sleeps.

Bottom.
Are we all met?

Quince.
Pat, pat; and here's a marvail's convenient place for our rehearsal. This green plot shall be our stage, this hawthorn brake our tiring-house, and we will do it in action as we will do it before the Duke.

Bottom.
Peter Quince!

Quince.
What sayest thou, bully Bottom?

Bottom.
There are things in this comedy of Pyramus and Thisbe that will never please. First, Pyramus must draw a sword to kill himself; which the ladies cannot abide. How answer you that?

Snout.
By'r lakin, a parlous fear.

Starveling.
I believe we must leave the killing out, when all is done.

Bottom.
Not a whit! I have a device to make all well. Write me a prologue, and let the prologue seem to say we will do no harm with our swords, and that Pyramus is not kill'd indeed; and for the more better assurance, tell them that I Pyramus am not Pyramus, but Bottom the weaver. This will put them out of fear.

Quince.
Well; we will have such a prologue, and it shall be written in eight and six.

Bottom.
No; make it two more; let it be written in eight and eight.

Snout.
Will not the ladies be afeard of the lion?

Starveling.
I fear it, I promise you.

Bottom.
Masters, you ought to consider with yourselves, to bring in (God shield us!) a lion among ladies, is a most dreadful thing; for there is not a more fearful wild-fowl than your lion living; and we ought to look to't.

Snout.
Therefore another prologue must tell he is not a lion.

Bottom.
Nay; you must name his name, and half his face must be seen through the lion's neck, and he himself must speak through, saying thus, or to the same defect: "Ladies," or "Fair ladies, I would wish you," or "I would request you," or "I would entreat you, not to fear, not to tremble: my life for yours. If you think I come hither as a lion, it were pity of my life. No! I am no such thing; I am a man as other men are"; and there indeed let him name his name, and tell them plainly he is Snug the joiner.

Quince.
Well; it shall be so. But there is two hard things: that is, to bring the moonlight into a chamber; for you know, Pyramus and Thisbe meet by moonlight.

Snout.
Doth the moon shine that night we play our play?

Bottom.
A calendar, a calendar! Look in the almanac. Find out moonshine, find out moonshine.

Quince.
Yes; it doth shine that night.

Bottom.
Why then may you leave a casement of the great chamber window (where we play) open; and the moon may shine in at the casement.

Quince.
Ay; or else one must come in with a bush of thorns and a lantern, and say he comes to disfigure, or to present, the person of Moonshine. Then, there is another thing: we must have a wall in the great chamber; for Pyramus and Thisbe (says the story) did talk through the chink of a wall.

Snout.
You can never bring in a wall. What say you, Bottom?

Bottom.
Some man or other must present Wall; and let him have some plaster, or some loam, or some rough-cast about him, to signify wall; or let him hold his fingers thus, and through that cranny shall Pyramus and Thisbe whisper.

Quince.
If that may be, then all is well. Come, sit down, every mother's son, and rehearse your parts. Pyramus, you begin. When you have spoken your speech, enter into that brake; and so every one according to his cue.

Enter Puck, behind.

Puck.
What hempen home-spuns have we swagg'ring here,
So near the cradle of the Fairy Queen?
What, a play toward? I'll be an auditor,
An actor too perhaps, if I see cause.

Act 3, Scene 1

Quince.
Speak, Pyramus. Thisbe, stand forth.

Bottom.
"Thisbe, the flowers of odious savors sweet"—

Quince.
Odorous, odorous.

Bottom.
 —"odors savors sweet;
So hath thy breath, my dearest Thisbe dear.
But hark; a voice! Stay thou but here a while,
And by and by I will to thee appear."

Exit.

Puck.
A stranger Pyramus than e'er played here.

Exit.

Flute.
Must I speak now?

Quince.
Ay, marry, must you; for you must understand he goes but to see a noise that he heard, and is to come again.

Flute.
"Most radiant Pyramus, most lily-white of hue,
Of color like the red rose on triumphant brier,
Most brisky juvenal, and eke most lovely Jew,
As true as truest horse, that yet would never tire,
I'll meet thee, Pyramus, at Ninny's tomb."

Quince.
"Ninus' tomb," man. Why, you must not speak that yet. That you answer to Pyramus. You speak all your part at once, cues and all. Pyramus, enter. Your cue is past; it is "never tire."

Flute.
O—"As true as truest horse, that yet would never tire."

Enter Puck, and Bottom with an ass's head.

Bottom.
"If I were fair, Thisbe, I were only thine."

Quince.
O monstrous! O strange! We are haunted.
Pray, masters, fly, masters! Help!

Exeunt Quince, Snug, Flute, Snout, and Starveling.

Puck.
I'll follow you, I'll lead you about a round,
Through bog, through bush, through brake, through brier:
Sometime a horse I'll be, sometime a hound,
A hog, a headless bear, sometime a fire,
And neigh, and bark, and grunt, and roar, and burn,
Like horse, hound, hog, bear, fire, at every turn.

Exit.

Bottom.
Why do they run away? This is a knavery of them to make me afeard.

Enter Snout.

Snout.
O Bottom, thou art chang'd! What do I see on thee?

Bottom.
What do you see? You see an ass-head of your own, do you?

Exit Snout.
Enter Quince.

Quince.
Bless thee. Bottom, bless thee! Thou art translated.

Exit.

Bottom.
I see their knavery. This is to make an ass of me, to fright me, if they could; but I will not stir from this place, do what they can. I will walk up and down here, and I will sing, that they shall hear I am not afraid.

Sings.

The woosel cock so black of hue,
With orange-tawny bill,
The throstle with his note so true,
The wren with little quill—

Titania.

Awaking.

What angel wakes me from my flow'ry bed?

Bottom.

Sings.

The finch, the sparrow, and the lark,
The plainsong cuckoo grey,
Whose note full many a man doth mark,
And dares not answer nay—
For indeed, who would set his wit to so foolish a bird?
Who would give a bird the lie, though he cry "cuckoo" never so?

Titania.
I pray thee, gentle mortal, sing again.
Mine ear is much enamored of thy note;
So is mine eye enthralled to thy shape;
And thy fair virtue's force (perforce) doth move me
On the first view to say, to swear, I love thee.

Bottom.
Methinks, mistress, you should have little reason for that. And yet, to say the truth, reason and love keep little company together now-a-days. The more the pity that some honest neighbors will not make them friends. Nay, I can gleek upon occasion.

Titania.
Thou art as wise as thou art beautiful.

Bottom.
Not so, neither; but if I had wit enough to get out of this wood, I have enough to serve mine owe turn.

Titania.
Out of this wood do not desire to go;
Thou shalt remain here, whether thou wilt or no.
I am a spirit of no common rate;
The summer still doth tend upon my state;
And I do love thee; therefore go with me.
I'll give thee fairies to attend on thee;
And they shall fetch thee jewels from the deep,
And sing while thou on pressed flowers dost sleep.
And I will purge thy mortal grossness so,
That thou shalt like an aery spirit go.
Peaseblossom! Cobweb! Moth! And Mustardseed!

Enter four Fairies—Peaseblossom, Cobweb, Moth, and Mustardseed.

Peaseblossom.
Ready.

Cobweb.
And I.

Moth.
And I.

Mustardseed.
And I.

All Fairies.
Where shall we go?

Titania.
Be kind and courteous to this gentleman,
Hop in his walks and gambol in his eyes;
Feed him with apricots and dewberries,
With purple grapes, green figs, and mulberries;
The honey-bags steal from the humble-bees,
And for night-tapers crop their waxen thighs,
And light them at the fiery glow-worm's eyes,
To have my love to bed and to arise;
And pluck the wings from painted butterflies,
To fan the moonbeams from his sleeping eyes.
Nod to him, elves, and do him courtesies.

Peaseblossom.
Hail, mortal!

Cobweb.
Hail!

Moth.
Hail!

Mustardseed.
Hail!

Bottom.
I cry your worships mercy, heartily. I beseech your worship's name.

Cobweb.
Cobweb.

Bottom.
I shall desire you of more acquaintance, good Master Cobweb. If I cut my finger, I shall make bold with you. Your name, honest gentleman?

Peaseblossom.
Peaseblossom.

Bottom.
I pray you commend me to Mistress Squash, your mother, and to Master Peascod, your father. Good Master Peaseblossom, I shall desire you of more acquaintance too. Your name, I beseech you, sir?

Mustardseed.
Mustardseed.

Bottom.
Good Master Mustardseed, I know your patience well. That same cowardly, giant-like ox-beef hath devour'd many a gentleman of your house. I promise you your kindred hath made my eyes water ere now. I desire you of more acquaintance, good Master Mustardseed.

Titania.
Come wait upon him; lead him to my bower.
The moon methinks looks with a wat'ry eye;
And when she weeps, weeps every little flower,
Lamenting some enforced chastity.
Tie up my lover's tongue, bring him silently.

Exeunt.

Scene 2

Another part of the woods.

(Oberon; Puck; Demetrius; Hermia; Lysander; Helena)

Puck reports to Oberon that Titania has fallen for a half-man-half-ass, and Oberon is delighted with this development. Puck also claims to have fulfilled the order to charm the Athenian, but as Demetrius and Hermia enter, it becomes apparent that he got the wrong man. Demetrius begs Hermia to grant him her favor, but Hermia can only think of Lysander. She leaves him and, disconsolate, he lies down to sleep. Oberon is furious and suspects that Puck has done this deliberately, but Puck points out that Oberon didn't exactly describe Demetrius very well. Oberon tells him to find Helena and while he is gone, puts love-juice on Demetrius's eyes. Lysander and Helena enter, he wooing her loudly, she rejecting him, and the noise wakes Demetrius who, seeing her, is instantly enamored. Helena is even more convinced that a cruel prank is being played on her. As the two men quarrel, Hermia enters searching for Lysander and is appalled to find him rejecting her. Helena immediately believes that Hermia is in on the prank, while Hermia soon comes to believe that Helena has seduced Lysander and a general fight breaks out. Lysander and Demetrius exit to duel, while the ladies go their separate ways. Oberon orders Puck to make things right by distracting the men during their fight and finding an occasion to use an antidote to the love-juice on Lysander. Imitating both their voices, Puck keeps them from meeting each other until they are exhausted and lie down to sleep. The ladies too come and lie down nearby, and Puck applies the antidote to Lysander's eyes.

Enter King of Fairies Oberon.

Oberon.
I wonder if Titania be awak'd;
Then what it was that next came in her eye,
Which she must dote on in extremity.

Enter Puck.

Here comes my messenger. How now, mad spirit?
What night-rule now about this haunted grove?

Puck.
My mistress with a monster is in love.
Near to her close and consecrated bower,
While she was in her dull and sleeping hour,
A crew of patches, rude mechanicals,
That work for bread upon Athenian stalls,
Were met together to rehearse a play
Intended for great Theseus' nuptial day.
The shallowest thick-skin of that barren sort,
Who Pyramus presented, in their sport,
Forsook his scene, and ent'red in a brake;
When I did him at this advantage take,
An ass's nole I fixed on his head.
Anon his Thisbe must be answered,
And forth my mimic comes. When they him spy,
As wild geese that the creeping fowler eye,
Or russet-pated choughs, many in sort
(Rising and cawing at the gun's report),
Sever themselves and madly sweep the sky,
So, at his sight, away his fellows fly;
And at our stamp, here o'er and o'er one falls;
He murder cries, and help from Athens calls.
Their sense thus weak, lost with their fears thus strong,
Made senseless things begin to do them wrong,
For briers and thorns at their apparel snatch;
Some sleeves, some hats, from yielders all things catch.
I led them on in this distracted fear,
And left sweet Pyramus translated there;
When in that moment (so it came to pass)
Titania wak'd, and straightway lov'd an ass.

Oberon.
This falls out better than I could devise.
But hast thou yet latch'd the Athenian's eyes
With the love-juice, as I did bid thee do?

Puck.
I took him sleeping (that is finish'd too)
And the Athenian woman by his side;
That when he wak'd, of force she must be ey'd.

Enter Demetrius and Hermia.

Oberon.
Stand close; this is the same Athenian.

Puck.
This is the woman; but not this the man.

Demetrius.
O, why rebuke you him that loves you so?
Lay breath so bitter on your bitter foe.

Hermia.
Now I but chide; but I should use thee worse,
For thou (I fear) hast given me cause to curse.
If thou hast slain Lysander in his sleep,
Being o'er shoes in blood, plunge in the deep,
And kill me too.
The sun was not so true unto the day
As he to me. Would he have stolen away
From sleeping Hermia? I'll believe as soon
This whole earth may be bor'd, and that the moon
May through the center creep, and so displease
Her brother's noontide with th' Antipodes.
It cannot be but thou hast murd'red him;
So should a murderer look—so dead, so grim.

Demetrius.
So should the murdered look, and so should I,
Pierc'd through the heart with your stern cruelty.
Yet you, the murderer, look as bright, as clear,
As yonder Venus in her glimmering sphere.

Hermia.
What's this to my Lysander? Where is he?
Ah, good Demetrius, wilt thou give him me?

Demetrius.
I had rather give his carcass to my hounds.

Hermia.
Out, dog, out, cur! Thou driv'st me past the bounds
Of maiden's patience. Hast thou slain him then?
Henceforth be never numb'red among men!
O, once tell true; tell true, even for my sake!
Durst thou have look'd upon him being awake?
And hast thou kill'd him sleeping? O brave touch!
Could not a worm, an adder, do so much?
An adder did it! For with doubler tongue
Than thine, thou serpent, never adder stung.

Demetrius.
You spend your passion on a mispris'd mood.
I am not guilty of Lysander's blood;
Nor is he dead, for aught that I can tell.

Hermia.
I pray thee, tell me then that he is well.

Demetrius.
And if I could, what should I get therefore?

Hermia.
A privilege never to see me more.
And from thy hated presence part I so:
See me no more, whether he be dead or no.

Exit.

Demetrius.
There is no following her in this fierce vein.
Here therefore for a while I will remain.
So sorrow's heaviness doth heavier grow
For debt that bankrupt sleep doth sorrow owe;
Which now in some slight measure it will pay,
If for his tender here I make some stay.

Lie down and sleep.

Oberon.
What hast thou done? Thou hast mistaken quite,
And laid the love-juice on some true-love's sight.
Of thy misprision must perforce ensue
Some true love turn'd, and not a false turn'd true.

Puck.
Then fate o'errules, that one man holding troth,
A million fail, confounding oath on oath.

Act 3, Scene 2

Oberon.
About the wood go swifter than the wind,
And Helena of Athens look thou find.
All fancy-sick she is and pale of cheer
With sighs of love, that costs the fresh blood dear.
By some illusion see thou bring her here.
I'll charm his eyes against she do appear.

Puck.
I go, I go, look how I go,
Swifter than arrow from the Tartar's bow.

Exit.

Oberon.
Flower of this purple dye,
Hit with Cupid's archery,
Sink in apple of his eye.
When his love he doth espy,
Let her shine as gloriously
As the Venus of the sky.
When thou wak'st, if she be by,
Beg of her for remedy.

Enter Puck.

Puck.
Captain of our fairy band,
Helena is here at hand,
And the youth, mistook by me,
Pleading for a lover's fee.
Shall we their fond pageant see?
Lord, what fools these mortals be!

Oberon.
Stand aside. The noise they make
Will cause Demetrius to awake.

Puck.
Then will two at once woo one;
That must needs be sport alone.
And those things do best please me
That befall prepost'rously.

Enter Lysander and Helena.

Lysander.
Why should you think that I should woo in scorn?
Scorn and derision never come in tears.
Look when I vow, I weep; and vows so born,
In their nativity all truth appears.
How can these things in me seem scorn to you,
Bearing the badge of faith to prove them true?

Helena.
You do advance your cunning more and more;
When truth kills truth, O devilish-holy fray!
These vows are Hermia's. Will you give her o'er?
Weigh oath with oath, and you will nothing weigh.
Your vows to her and me, put in two scales,
Will even weigh; and both as light as tales.

Lysander.
I had no judgment when to her I swore.

Helena.
Nor none, in my mind, now you give her o'er.

Lysander.
Demetrius loves her; and he loves not you.

Demetrius.

Awaking.

O Helen, goddess, nymph, perfect, divine!
To what, my love, shall I compare thine eyne?
Crystal is muddy. O, how ripe in show
Thy lips, those kissing cherries, tempting grow!
That pure congealed white, high Taurus' snow,
Fann'd with the eastern wind, turns to a crow
When thou hold'st up thy hand. O, let me kiss
This princess of pure white, this seal of bliss!

Helena.
O spite! O hell! I see you all are bent
To set against me for your merriment.
If you were civil and knew courtesy,
You would not do me thus much injury.
Can you not hate me, as I know you do,
But you must join in souls to mock me too?
If you were men, as men you are in show,
You would not use a gentle lady so;
To vow, and swear, and superpraise my parts,
When I am sure you hate me with your hearts.
You both are rivals, and love Hermia;
And now both rivals, to mock Helena.
A trim exploit, a manly enterprise,
To conjure tears up in a poor maid's eyes
With your derision! None of noble sort
Would so offend a virgin, and extort
A poor soul's patience, all to make you sport.

Lysander.
You are unkind, Demetrius; be not so;
For you love Hermia; this you know I know.
And here, with all good will, with all my heart,
In Hermia's love I yield you up my part;
And yours of Helena to me bequeath,
Whom I do love, and will do till my death.

Helena.
Never did mockers waste more idle breath.

Demetrius.
Lysander, keep thy Hermia; I will none.
If e'er I lov'd her, all that love is gone.
My heart to her but as guest-wise sojourn'd,
And now to Helen is it home return'd,
There to remain.

Lysander.
                  Helen, it is not so.

Demetrius.
Disparage not the faith thou dost not know,
Lest, to thy peril, thou aby it dear.
Look where thy love comes; yonder is thy dear.

Enter Hermia.

Hermia.
Dark night, that from the eye his function takes,
The ear more quick of apprehension makes;
Wherein it doth impair the seeing sense,
It pays the hearing double recompense,
Thou art not by mine eye, Lysander, found;
Mine ear, I thank it, brought me to thy sound.
But why unkindly didst thou leave me so?

Lysander.
Why should he stay, whom love doth press to go?

Hermia.
What love could press Lysander from my side?

Lysander.
Lysander's love, that would not let him bide—
Fair Helena! Who more engilds the night
Than all yon fiery oes and eyes of light.
Why seek'st thou me? Could not this make thee know,
The hate I bare thee made me leave thee so?

Hermia.
You speak not as you think. It cannot be.

Helena.
Lo! She is one of this confederacy.
Now I perceive, they have conjoin'd all three
To fashion this false sport, in spite of me.
Injurious Hermia, most ungrateful maid!
Have you conspir'd, have you with these contriv'd
To bait me with this foul derision?
Is all the counsel that we two have shar'd,
The sisters' vows, the hours that we have spent,
When we have chid the hasty-footed time
For parting us—O, is all forgot?
All school-days friendship, childhood innocence?
We, Hermia, like two artificial gods,
Have with our needles created both one flower,
Both on one sampler, sitting on one cushion,
Both warbling of one song, both in one key,
As if our hands, our sides, voices, and minds
Had been incorporate. So we grew together,
Like to a double cherry, seeming parted,
But yet an union in partition,
Two lovely berries moulded on one stem;
So with two seeming bodies, but one heart,
Two of the first, like coats in heraldry,
Due but to one, and crowned with one crest.
And will you rent our ancient love asunder,
To join with men in scorning your poor friend?
It is not friendly, 'tis not maidenly.
Our sex, as well as I, may chide you for it,
Though I alone do feel the injury.

Hermia.
I am amazed at your passionate words.
I scorn you not; it seems that you scorn me.

Helena.
Have you not set Lysander, as in scorn,
To follow me and praise my eyes and face?
And made your other love, Demetrius
(Who even but now did spurn me with his foot),
To call me goddess, nymph, divine and rare,
Precious, celestial? Wherefore speaks he this
To her he hates? And wherefore doth Lysander
Deny your love (so rich within his soul)
And tender me (forsooth) affection,
But by your setting on, by your consent?
What though I be not so in grace as you,
So hung upon with love, so fortunate
(But miserable most, to love unlov'd)?
This you should pity rather than despise.

Hermia.
I understand not what you mean by this.

Helena.
Ay, do! Persever, counterfeit sad looks,
Make mouths upon me when I turn my back,
Wink each at other, hold the sweet jest up;
This sport, well carried, shall be chronicled.
If you have any pity, grace, or manners,
You would not make me such an argument.
But fare ye well; 'tis partly my own fault,
Which death, or absence, soon shall remedy.

Lysander.
Stay, gentle Helena; hear my excuse,
My love, my life, my soul, fair Helena!

Helena.
O excellent!

Hermia.
              Sweet, do not scorn her so.

Demetrius.
If she cannot entreat, I can compel.

Lysander.
Thou canst compel no more than she entreat.
Thy threats have no more strength than her weak prays.
Helen, I love thee, by my life I do!
I swear by that which I will lose for thee,
To prove him false that says I love thee not.

Demetrius.
I say I love thee more than he can do.

Lysander.
If thou say so, withdraw, and prove it too.

Demetrius.
Quick, come!

Hermia.
              Lysander, whereto tends all this?

Lysander.
Away, you Ethiop!

Demetrius.
              No, no; he'll
Seem to break loose—take on as you would follow,
But yet come not. You are a tame man, go!

Lysander.
Hang off, thou cat, thou bur! Vile thing, let loose;
Or I will shake thee from me like a serpent!

Hermia.
Why are you grown so rude? What change is this,
Sweet love?

Lysander.
              Thy love? Out, tawny Tartar, out!
Out, loathed med'cine! O hated potion, hence!

Hermia.
Do you not jest?

Helena.
              Yes, sooth; and so do you.

Lysander.
Demetrius, I will keep my word with thee.

Demetrius.
I would I had your bond, for I perceive
A weak bond holds you. I'll not trust your word.

Lysander.
What? Should I hurt her, strike her, kill her dead?
Although I hate her, I'll not harm her so.

Hermia.
What? Can you do me greater harm than hate?
Hate me, wherefore? O me, what news, my love!
Am not I Hermia? Are not you Lysander?
I am as fair now as I was erewhile.
Since night you lov'd me; yet since night you left me:
Why then, you left me (O, the gods forbid!)
In earnest, shall I say?

Lysander.
              Ay, by my life;
And never did desire to see thee more.
Therefore be out of hope, of question, of doubt;
Be certain! Nothing truer; 'tis no jest
That I do hate thee, and love Helena.

Hermia.
O me, you juggler, you canker-blossom,
You thief of love! What, have you come by night
And stol'n my love's heart from him?

Helena.
              Fine, i' faith!
Have you no modesty, no maiden shame,
No touch of bashfulness? What, will you tear

Impatient answers from my gentle tongue?
Fie, fie, you counterfeit, you puppet, you!

Hermia.
"Puppet"? Why so? Ay, that way goes the game.
Now I perceive that she hath made compare
Between our statures: she hath urg'd her height,
And with her personage, her tall personage,
Her height, forsooth, she hath prevail'd with him.
And are you grown so high in his esteem,
Because I am so dwarfish and so low?
How low am I, thou painted maypole? Speak!
How low am I? I am not yet so low
But that my nails can reach unto thine eyes.

Helena.
I pray you, though you mock me, gentlemen,
Let her not hurt me. I was never curst;
I have no gift at all in shrewishness;
I am a right maid for my cowardice.
Let her not strike me. You perhaps may think,
Because she is something lower than myself,
That I can match her.

Hermia.
              "Lower"? Hark again.

Helena.
Good Hermia, do not be so bitter with me.
I evermore did love you, Hermia,
Did ever keep your counsels, never wrong'd you;
Save that, in love unto Demetrius,
I told him of your stealth unto this wood.
He followed you; for love I followed him.
But he hath chid me hence, and threat'ned me
To strike me, spurn me, nay, to kill me too.
And now, so you will let me quiet go,
To Athens will I bear my folly back,
And follow you no further. Let me go.
You see how simple and how fond I am.

Hermia.
Why, get you gone. Who is't that hinders you?

Helena.
A foolish heart, that I leave here behind.

Hermia.
What, with Lysander?

Helena.
              With Demetrius.

Lysander.
Be not afraid; she shall not harm thee, Helena.

Demetrius.
No, sir; she shall not, though you take her part.

Helena.
O, when she is angry, she is keen and shrewd!
She was a vixen when she went to school;
And though she be but little, she is fierce.

Hermia.
"Little" again? Nothing but "low" and "little"?
Why will you suffer her to flout me thus?
Let me come to her.

Lysander.
              Get you gone, you dwarf;
You minimus, of hind'ring knot-grass made;
You bead, you acorn.

Demetrius.
              You are too officious
In her behalf that scorns your services.
Let her alone; speak not of Helena,
Take not her part. For if thou dost intend
Never so little show of love to her,
Thou shalt aby it.

Lysander.
              Now she holds me not;
Now follow, if thou dar'st, to try whose right,
Of thine or mine, is most in Helena.

Demetrius.
Follow? Nay; I'll go with thee, cheek by jowl.

Exeunt Lysander and Demetrius.

Hermia.
You, mistress, all this coil is long of you.
Nay, go not back.

Helena.
              I will not trust you, I,
Nor longer stay in your curst company.
Your hands than mine are quicker for a fray;
My legs are longer though, to run away.

Exit.

Hermia.
I am amaz'd, and know not what to say.

Exit.

Oberon.
This is thy negligence. Still thou mistak'st,
Or else commit'st thy knaveries willfully.

Puck.
Believe me, king of shadows, I mistook.
Did not you tell me I should know the man
By the Athenian garments he had on?
And so far blameless proves my enterprise,
That I have 'nointed an Athenian's eyes;
And so far am I glad it so did sort,
As this their jangling I esteem a sport.

Oberon.
Thou seest these lovers seek a place to fight;
Hie therefore, Robin, overcast the night;
The starry welkin cover thou anon
With drooping fog as black as Acheron,
And lead these testy rivals so astray
As one come not within another's way.
Like to Lysander sometime frame thy tongue;
Then stir Demetrius up with bitter wrong;
And sometime rail thou like Demetrius;
And from each other look thou lead them thus,
Till o'er their brows death-counterfeiting sleep
With leaden legs and batty wings doth creep.
Then crush this herb into Lysander's eye;
Whose liquor hath this virtuous property,
To take from thence all error with his might,
And make his eyeballs roll with wonted sight.
When they next wake, all this derision
Shall seem a dream and fruitless vision,
And back to Athens shall the lovers wend
With league whose date till death shall never end.
Whiles I in this affair do thee employ,
I'll to my queen and beg her Indian boy;
And then I will her charmed eye release
From monster's view, and all things shall be peace.

Puck.
My fairy lord, this must be done with haste,
For Night's swift dragons cut the clouds full fast,
And yonder shines Aurora's harbinger,
At whose approach, ghosts, wand'ring here and there,
Troop home to churchyards. Damned spirits all,
That in crossways and floods have burial,
Already to their wormy beds are gone.
For fear lest day should look their shames upon,
They willfully themselves exile from light,
And must for aye consort with black-brow'd Night.

Oberon.
But we are spirits of another sort.
I with the Morning's love have oft made sport,
And like a forester, the groves may tread
Even till the eastern gate, all fiery red,
Opening on Neptune with fair blessed beams,
Turns into yellow gold his salt green streams.
But notwithstanding, haste, make no delay;
We may effect this business yet ere day.

Exit.

Puck.
Up and down, up and down,
I will lead them up and down;
I am fear'd in field and town.
Goblin, lead them up and down.
Here comes one.

Enter Lysander.

Lysander.
Where art thou, proud Demetrius? Speak thou now.

Puck.
Here, villain, drawn and ready. Where art thou?

Lysander.
I will be with thee straight.

Puck.
                    Follow me then
To plainer ground.

Exit Lysander, as following the voice.
Enter Demetrius.

Demetrius.
                    Lysander, speak again!
Thou runaway, thou coward, art thou fled?
Speak! In some bush? Where dost thou hide thy head?

Puck.
Thou coward, art thou bragging to the stars,
Telling the bushes that thou look'st for wars,
And wilt not come? Come, recreant, come, thou child,
I'll whip thee with a rod. He is defil'd
That draws a sword on thee.

Demetrius.
                    Yea, art thou there?

Puck.
Follow my voice; we'll try no manhood here.

Exeunt.
Enter Lysander.

Lysander.
He goes before me, and still dares me on.
When I come where he calls, then he is gone.
The villain is much lighter-heel'd than I;
I followed fast, but faster he did fly,
That fallen am I in dark uneven way,
And here will rest me.

Lie down.

                   Come, thou gentle day!
For if but once thou show me thy grey light,
I'll find Demetrius and revenge this spite.

Sleeps.
Enter Puck and Demetrius.

Puck.
Ho, ho, ho! Coward, why com'st thou not?

Demetrius.
Abide me, if thou dar'st; for well I wot
Thou run'st before me, shifting every place,
And dar'st not stand, nor look me in the face.
Where art thou now?

Puck.
                 Come hither; I am here.

Demetrius.
Nay then thou mock'st me. Thou shalt buy this dear,
If ever I thy face by daylight see.
Now, go thy way. Faintness constraineth me
To measure out my length on this cold bed.
By day's approach look to be visited.

Lies down and sleeps.
Enter Helena.

Helena.
O weary night, O long and tedious night,
Abate thy hours! Shine, comforts, from the east,
That I may back to Athens by daylight,
From these that my poor company detest.
And sleep, that sometimes shuts up sorrow's eye,
Steal me a while from mine own company.

Sleep.

Puck.
Yet but three? Come one more;
Two of both kinds makes up four.

Enter Hermia.

Here she comes, curst and sad.
Cupid is a knavish lad,
Thus to make poor females mad.

Hermia.
Never so weary, never so in woe,
Bedabbled with the dew and torn with briers,
I can no further crawl, no further go;
My legs can keep no pace with my desires.
Here will I rest me till the break of day.
Heavens shield Lysander, if they mean a fray!

Lies down and sleeps.

Puck.
On the ground,
Sleep sound;
I'll apply,
To your eye,
Gentle lover, remedy.

Squeezing the juice on Lysander's eyes.

When thou wak'st,
Thou tak'st
True delight
In the sight
Of thy former lady's eye;
And the country proverb known,
That every man should take his own,
In your waking shall be shown.
Jack shall have Jill;
Nought shall go ill:
The man shall have his mare again, and all shall be well.

Exit.

Act 4

Scene 1

Another part of the woods.

Act 4, Scene 1

(Titania; Bottom; Peaseblossom; Cobweb; Moth; Mustardseed; Oberon; Puck; Theseus; Hippolyta; Egeus; Hermia; Lysander; Demetrius; Helena; Attendants)

Titania continues to make Bottom as comfortable as she can, having food brought to him and any sort of music he cares for. They lie down and sleep, and Puck and Oberon approach. Oberon reveals that he easily gained custody of the changeling from the distracted Titania, and is now ready to remove the enchantment from her, which he does. The couple are reconciled, and plan to bless Theseus's house after his wedding, while Puck removes the ass-head from Bottom. The fairies leave, and the lovers are discovered sleeping on the ground by Theseus and his court, who are out hunting. Waking the four with hunting horns, Theseus mocks them before asking how it is that they are now all in amity. The four cannot explain, feeling that everything that has passed was simply a dream, but Demetrius insists he is now in love with Helena, and Theseus rejects Egeus's call for punishment on Lysander. The four reassure each other that they are awake now and follow the court. Bottom wakes, and considers the dream he thinks he had, which he cannot explain in words, and then makes plans to have Quince make a ballad out of it all the same.

Enter Queen of Fairies Titania and Clown Bottom, and Fairies Peaseblossom, Cobweb, Moth, Mustardseed, and others, attending, and the King Oberon behind them unseen. Lysander, Demetrius, Helena, and Hermia still asleep.

Titania.
Come sit thee down upon this flow'ry bed,
While I thy amiable cheeks do coy,
And stick musk-roses in thy sleek smooth head,
And kiss thy fair large ears, my gentle joy.

Bottom.
Where's Peaseblossom?

Peaseblossom.
Ready.

Bottom.
Scratch my head, Peaseblossom. Where's mounsieur Cobweb?

Cobweb.
Ready.

Bottom.
Mounsieur Cobweb, good mounsieur, get you your weapons in your hand, and kill me a red-hipp'd humble-bee on the top of a thistle; and, good mounsieur, bring me the honey-bag. Do not fret yourself too much in the action, mounsieur; and, good mounsieur, have a care the honey-bag break not, I would be loath to have you overflowen with a honey-bag, signior. Where's mounsieur Mustardseed?

Mustardseed.
Ready.

Bottom.
Give me your neaf, mounsieur Mustardseed. Pray you, leave your curtsy, good mounsieur.

Mustardseed.
What's your will?

Bottom.
Nothing, good mounsieur, but to help Cavalery Cobweb to scratch. I must to the barber's, mounsieur; for methinks I am marvail's hairy about the face; and I am such a tender ass, if my hair do but tickle me, I must scratch.

Titania.
What, wilt thou hear some music, my sweet love?

Bottom.
I have a reasonable good ear in music. Let's have the tongs and the bones.

Music. Tongs. Rural music.

Titania.
Or say, sweet love, what thou desirest to eat.

Bottom.
Truly, a peck of provender; I could munch your good dry oats. Methinks I have a great desire to a bottle of hay. Good hay, sweet hay, hath no fellow.

Titania.
I have a venturous fairy that shall seek
The squirrel's hoard, and fetch thee new nuts.

Bottom.
I had rather have a handful or two of dried peas. But, I pray you, let none of your people stir me; I have an exposition of sleep come upon me.

Titania.
Sleep thou, and I will wind thee in my arms.
Fairies, be gone, and be all ways away.

Exeunt Fairies.

So doth the woodbine the sweet honeysuckle
Gently entwist; the female ivy so
Enrings the barky fingers of the elm.
O, how I love thee! How I dote on thee!

They sleep.
Enter Puck.

Oberon.

Advancing.

Welcome, good Robin. Seest thou this sweet sight?
Her dotage now I do begin to pity.
For meeting her of late behind the wood,
Seeking sweet favors for this hateful fool,
I did upbraid her, and fall out with her.
For she his hairy temples then had rounded
With coronet of fresh and fragrant flowers;
And that same dew which sometime on the buds
Was wont to swell like round and orient pearls,
Stood now within the pretty flouriets' eyes,
Like tears that did their own disgrace bewail.
When I had at my pleasure taunted her,
And she in mild terms begg'd my patience,
I then did ask of her her changeling child;
Which straight she gave me, and her fairy sent
To bear him to my bower in fairy land.
And now I have the boy, I will undo
This hateful imperfection of her eyes.
And, gentle Puck, take this transformed scalp
From off the head of this Athenian swain,
That he, awaking when the other do,
May all to Athens back again repair,
And think no more of this night's accidents
But as the fierce vexation of a dream.
But first I will release the Fairy Queen.

Touching her eyes.

Be as thou wast wont to be;
See as thou wast wont to see.
Dian's bud o'er Cupid's flower
Hath such force and blessed power.
Now, my Titania, wake you, my sweet queen.

Titania.
My Oberon, what visions have I seen!
Methought I was enamor'd of an ass.

Oberon.
There lies your love.

Titania.
How came these things to pass?
O, how mine eyes do loathe his visage now!

Oberon.
Silence a while. Robin, take off this head.
Titania, music call, and strike more dead
Than common sleep of all these five the sense.

Titania.
Music, ho, music, such as charmeth sleep!

Music, still.

Puck.
Now, when thou wak'st, with thine own fool's eyes peep.

Oberon.
Sound, music!

Louder music.

Come, my queen, take hands with me,
And rock the ground whereon these sleepers be.
Now thou and I are new in amity,
And will tomorrow midnight solemnly
Dance in Duke Theseus' house triumphantly,
And bless it to all fair prosperity.
There shall the pairs of faithful lovers be
Wedded, with Theseus, all in jollity.

Puck.
Fairy King, attend and mark;
I do hear the morning lark.

Oberon.
Then, my queen, in silence sad,
Trip we after night's shade.
We the globe can compass soon,
Swifter than the wand'ring moon.

Titania.
Come, my lord, and in our flight,
Tell me how it came this night
That I sleeping here was found,
With these mortals on the ground.

Exeunt. Wind horn within.
Enter Theseus, Hippolyta, Egeus, and all his Train.

Act 4, Scene 1

Theseus, Duke of Athens.
Go, one of you, find out the forester,
For now our observation is perform'd,
And since we have the vaward of the day,
My love shall hear the music of my hounds.
Uncouple in the western valley, let them go.
Dispatch, I say, and find the forester.

Exit an Attendant.

We will, fair queen, up to the mountain's top,
And mark the musical confusion
Of hounds and echo in conjunction.

Hippolyta.
I was with Hercules and Cadmus once,
When in a wood of Crete they bay'd the bear
With hounds of Sparta. Never did I hear
Such gallant chiding; for besides the groves,
The skies, the fountains, every region near
Seem all one mutual cry. I never heard
So musical a discord, such sweet thunder.

Theseus, Duke of Athens.
My hounds are bred out of the Spartan kind;
So flew'd, so sanded; and their heads are hung
With ears that sweep away the morning dew;
Crook-knee'd, and dewlapp'd like Thessalian bulls;
Slow in pursuit; but match'd in mouth like bells,
Each under each. A cry more tuneable
Was never hollow'd to, nor cheer'd with horn,
In Crete, in Sparta, nor in Thessaly.
Judge when you hear. But soft! What nymphs are these?

Egeus.
My lord, this' my daughter here asleep,
And this Lysander, this Demetrius is,
This Helena, old Nedar's Helena.
I wonder of their being here together.

Theseus, Duke of Athens.
No doubt they rose up early to observe
The rite of May; and hearing our intent,
Came here in grace of our solemnity.
But speak, Egeus, is not this the day
That Hermia should give answer of her choice?

Egeus.
It is, my lord.

Theseus, Duke of Athens.
Go, bid the huntsmen wake them with their horns.

Exit an Attendant. Shout within. Wind horns. They all start up.

Good morrow, friends. Saint Valentine is past;
Begin these wood-birds but to couple now?

Lysander.
Pardon, my lord.

They kneel.

Theseus, Duke of Athens.
                I pray you all, stand up.
I know you two are rival enemies.
How comes this gentle concord in the world,
That hatred is so far from jealousy
To sleep by hate and fear no enmity?

Lysander.
My lord, I shall reply amazedly,
Half sleep, half waking; but, as yet, I swear,
I cannot truly say how I came here.
But, as I think—for truly would I speak,
And now I do bethink me, so it is—
I came with Hermia hither. Our intent
Was to be gone from Athens, where we might,
Without the peril of the Athenian law—

Egeus.
Enough, enough, my lord; you have enough.
I beg the law, the law, upon his head.
They would have stol'n away, they would, Demetrius,
Thereby to have defeated you and me:
You of your wife, and me of my consent,
Of my consent that she should be your wife.

Demetrius.
My lord, fair Helen told me of their stealth,
Of this their purpose hither to this wood,
And I in fury hither followed them,
Fair Helena in fancy following me.
But, my good lord, I wot not by what power
(But by some power it is), my love to Hermia
(Melted as the snow) seems to me now
As the remembrance of an idle gaud,
Which in my childhood I did dote upon;
And all the faith, the virtue of my heart,
The object and the pleasure of mine eye,
Is only Helena. To her, my lord,
Was I betrothed ere I saw Hermia;

But like a sickness did I loathe this food;
But, as in health, come to my natural taste,
Now I do wish it, love it, long for it,
And will forevermore be true to it.

Theseus, Duke of Athens.
Fair lovers, you are fortunately met;
Of this discourse we more will hear anon.
Egeus, I will overbear your will;
For in the temple, by and by, with us
These couples shall eternally be knit.
And, for the morning now is something worn,
Our purpos'd hunting shall be set aside.
Away with us to Athens. Three and three,
We'll hold a feast in great solemnity.
Come, Hippolyta.

Exeunt Theseus, Hippolyta, Egeus, and Train.

Demetrius.
These things seem small and undistinguishable,
Like far-off mountains turned into clouds.

Hermia.
Methinks I see these things with parted eye,
When every thing seems double.

Helena.
                    So methinks;
And I have found Demetrius like a jewel,
Mine own, and not mine own.

Demetrius.
                         Are you sure
That we are awake? It seems to me
That yet we sleep, we dream. Do not you think
The Duke was here, and bid us follow him?

Hermia.
Yea, and my father.

Helena.
                    And Hippolyta.

Lysander.
And he did bid us follow to the temple.

Demetrius.
Why then, we are awake. Let's follow him,
And by the way let's recount our dreams.

Exeunt Lovers.

Bottom.
Awaking.

When my cue comes, call me, and I will answer. My next is, "Most fair Pyramus." Heigh-ho! Peter Quince! Flute the bellows-mender! Snout the tinker! Starveling! God's my life, stol'n hence, and left me asleep! I have had a most rare vision. I have had a dream, past the wit of man to say what dream it was. Man is but an ass, if he go about t' expound this dream. Methought I was—there is no man can tell what. Methought I was, and methought I had—but man is but a patch'd fool, if he will offer to say what methought I had. The eye of man hath not heard, the ear of man hath not seen, man's hand is not able to taste, his tongue to conceive, nor his heart to report, what my dream was. I will get Peter Quince to write a ballet of this dream. It shall be call'd "Bottom's Dream," because it hath no bottom; and I will sing it in the latter end of a play, before the Duke. Peradventure, to make it the more gracious, I shall sing it at her death.

Exit.

Scene 2

Athens. A room in Quince's house.

(Quince; Flute; Snout; Starveling; Snug; Bottom)

The actors are anxious about Bottom's whereabouts, as they cannot put on their play without him. As they sink into despair, Bottom joins them, and tells them that they have indeed been chosen to present their play for the newlyweds.

Enter Quince, Thisbe Flute, and the rabble Snout, Starveling.

Quince.
Have you sent to Bottom's house? Is he come home yet?

Starveling.
He cannot be heard of. Out of doubt he is transported.

Flute.
If he come not, then the play is marr'd. It goes not forward, doth it?

Quince.
It is not possible. You have not a man in all Athens able to discharge Pyramus but he.

Flute.
No, he hath simply the best wit of any handicraft man in Athens.

Quince.
Yea, and the best person too; and he is a very paramour for a sweet voice.

Flute.
You must say "paragon." A paramour is (God bless us!) a thing of naught.

Enter Snug the joiner.

Snug.
Masters, the Duke is coming from the temple, and there is two or three lords and ladies more married. If our sport had gone forward, we had all been made men.

Flute.
O sweet bully Bottom! Thus hath he lost sixpence a day during his life; he could not have scap'd sixpence a day. And the Duke had not given him sixpence a day for playing Pyramus, I'll be hang'd. He would have deserv'd it. Sixpence a day in Pyramus, or nothing.

Enter Bottom.

Bottom.
Where are these lads? Where are these hearts?

Quince.
Bottom! O most courageous day! O most happy hour!

Bottom.
Masters, I am to discourse wonders; but ask me not what; for if I tell you, I am no true Athenian. I will tell you every thing, right as it fell out.

Quince.
Let us hear, sweet Bottom.

Bottom.
Not a word of me. All that I will tell you is, that the Duke hath din'd. Get your apparel together, good strings to your beards, new ribands to your pumps; meet presently at the palace; every man look o'er his part; for the short and the long is, our play is preferr'd. In any case, let Thisbe have clean linen; and let not him that plays the lion pare his nails, for they shall hang out for the lion's claws. And, most dear actors, eat no onions nor garlic, for we are to utter sweet breath; and I do not doubt but to hear them say, it is a sweet comedy. No more words. Away, go, away!

Exeunt.

Act 5

Scene 1

Athens. A room in the palace of Theseus.

(Theseus; Hippolyta; Philostrate; Lords; Attendants; Lysander; Demetrius; Hermia; Helena; Quince; Bottom; Flute; Snout; Snug; Starveling; Puck; Oberon; Titania)

Theseus and Hippolyta discuss the story they have heard from the lovers, though Theseus dismisses its truth. The lovers, now married like their rulers, come in and Theseus asks to find out what entertainment they shall have before bedtime. He dismisses many of the options, finally choosing the artisans' play, despite Philostrate's insistence that it is unworthy. Hippolyta wonders at Theseus's choice, since Philostrate insists that the men can't act, but the Duke argues that their humble willingness to try will outweigh their inadequacy. As the play begins, the audience begins to comment. Overwrought and overacted, and endlessly interrupted by the actors' apologies to the audience, the play is unintentionally hilarious, to the delight of Theseus's court. The comments grow crueler and crueler, but the actors are undeterred. Once the actors finish the dance that ends the play, it is midnight and Theseus orders all to go to bed. Once the humans have left, the fairies enter, blessing the house and promising a quiet night to all its occupants. Left alone, Puck begs the audience's forgiveness for any offense.

Enter Theseus, Hippolyta, and Philostrate, Lords, and Attendants.

Hippolyta.
'Tis strange, my Theseus, that these lovers speak of.

Theseus, Duke of Athens.
More strange than true. I never may believe
These antic fables, nor these fairy toys.
Lovers and madmen have such seething brains,
Such shaping fantasies, that apprehend
More than cool reason ever comprehends.

The lunatic, the lover, and the poet
Are of imagination all compact.
One sees more devils than vast hell can hold;
That is the madman. The lover, all as frantic,
Sees Helen's beauty in a brow of Egypt.
The poet's eye, in a fine frenzy rolling,
Doth glance from heaven to earth, from earth to heaven;
And as imagination bodies forth
The forms of things unknown, the poet's pen
Turns them to shapes, and gives to aery nothing
A local habitation and a name.
Such tricks hath strong imagination,
That if it would but apprehend some joy,
It comprehends some bringer of that joy;
Or in the night, imagining some fear,
How easy is a bush suppos'd a bear!

Hippolyta.
But all the story of the night told over,
And all their minds transfigur'd so together,
More witnesseth than fancy's images,
And grows to something of great constancy;
But howsoever, strange and admirable.

Enter lovers, Lysander, Demetrius, Hermia, and Helena.

Theseus, Duke of Athens.
Here come the lovers, full of joy and mirth.
Joy, gentle friends, joy and fresh days of love
Accompany your hearts!

Lysander.
                More than to us
Wait in your royal walks, your board, your bed!

Theseus, Duke of Athens.
Come now; what masques, what dances shall we have,
To wear away this long age of three hours
Between our after-supper and bed-time?
Where is our usual manager of mirth?
What revels are in hand? Is there no play
To ease the anguish of a torturing hour?
Call Philostrate.

Philostrate.
            Here, mighty Theseus.

Theseus, Duke of Athens.
Say, what abridgment have you for this evening?
What masque? What music? How shall we beguile
The lazy time, if not with some delight?

Philostrate.
There is a brief how many sports are ripe.
Make choice of which your Highness will see first.

Giving a paper.

Theseus, Duke of Athens.

Reads.

"The battle with the Centaurs, to be sung
By an Athenian eunuch to the harp."
We'll none of that: that have I told my love,
In glory of my kinsman Hercules.
"The riot of the tipsy Bacchanals,
Tearing the Thracian singer in their rage."
That is an old device; and it was play'd
When I from Thebes came last a conqueror.
"The thrice three Muses mourning for the death
Of Learning, late deceas'd in beggary."
That is some satire, keen and critical,
Not sorting with a nuptial ceremony.
"A tedious brief scene of young Pyramus
And his love Thisbe; very tragical mirth."
Merry and tragical? Tedious and brief?
That is hot ice and wondrous strange snow.
How shall we find the concord of this discord?

Philostrate.
A play there is, my lord, some ten words long,
Which is as brief as I have known a play;
But by ten words, my lord, it is too long,
Which makes it tedious; for in all the play
There is not one word apt, one player fitted.
And tragical, my noble lord, it is;
For Pyramus therein doth kill himself;
Which when I saw rehears'd, I must confess,
Made mine eyes water; but more merry tears
The passion of loud laughter never shed.

Theseus, Duke of Athens.
What are they that do play it?

Philostrate.
Hard-handed men that work in Athens here,
Which never labor'd in their minds till now;
And now have toiled their unbreathed memories
With this same play, against your nuptial.

Act 5, Scene 1

Theseus, Duke of Athens.
And we will hear it.

Philostrate.
                No, my noble lord,
It is not for you. I have heard it over,
And it is nothing, nothing in the world;
Unless you can find sport in their intents,
Extremely stretch'd, and conn'd with cruel pain,
To do you service.

Theseus, Duke of Athens.
                I will hear that play;
For never any thing can be amiss,
When simpleness and duty tender it.
Go bring them in; and take your places, ladies.

Exit Philostrate.

Hippolyta.
I love not to see wretchedness o'ercharged,
And duty in his service perishing.

Theseus, Duke of Athens.
Why, gentle sweet, you shall see no such thing.

Hippolyta.
He says they can do nothing in this kind.

Theseus, Duke of Athens.
The kinder we, to give them thanks for nothing.
Our sport shall be to take what they mistake;
And what poor duty cannot do, noble respect
Takes it in might, not merit.
Where I have come, great clerks have purposed
To greet me with premeditated welcomes;
Where I have seen them shiver and look pale,
Make periods in the midst of sentences,
Throttle their practic'd accent in their fears,
And in conclusion dumbly have broke off,
Not paying me a welcome. Trust me, sweet,
Out of this silence yet I pick'd a welcome;
And in the modesty of fearful duty
I read as much as from the rattling tongue
Of saucy and audacious eloquence.
Love, therefore, and tongue-tied simplicity
In least speak most, to my capacity.

Enter Philostrate.

Philostrate.
So please your Grace, the Prologue is address'd.

Theseus, Duke of Athens.
Let him approach.

Flourish trumpet.
Enter Quince for the Prologue.

Prologue.
If we offend, it is with our good will.
That you should think, we come not to offend,
But with good will. To show our simple skill,
That is the true beginning of our end.
Consider then, we come but in despite.
We do not come, as minding to content you,
Our true intent is. All for your delight
We are not here. That you should here repent you,
The actors are at hand; and, by their show,
You shall know all, that you are like to know.

Theseus, Duke of Athens.
This fellow doth not stand upon points.

Lysander.
He hath rid his prologue like a rough colt; he knows not the stop. A good moral, my lord: it is not enough to speak, but to speak true.

Hippolyta.
Indeed he hath play'd on this prologue like a child on a recorder—a sound, but not in government.

Theseus, Duke of Athens.
His speech was like a tangled chain; nothing impair'd, but all disorder'd. Who is next?

Enter with a Trumpet before them Pyramus and Thisbe and Wall and Moonshine and Lion.

Prologue.
Gentles, perchance you wonder at this show;
But wonder on till truth make all things plain.
This man is Pyramus, if you would know;
This beauteous lady Thisbe is certain.
This man, with lime and rough-cast, doth present
Wall, that vile Wall, which did these lovers sunder;
And through Wall's chink, poor souls, they are content
To whisper. At the which let no man wonder.
This man, with lantern, dog, and bush of thorn,
Presenteth Moonshine; for if you will know,
By moonshine did these lovers think no scorn
To meet at Ninus' tomb, there, there to woo.
This grisly beast, which Lion hight by name,

The trusty Thisbe, coming first by night,
Did scare away, or rather did affright;
And as she fled, her mantle she did fall,
Which Lion vile with bloody mouth did stain.
Anon comes Pyramus, sweet youth and tall,
And finds his trusty Thisbe's mantle slain;
Whereat, with blade, with bloody blameful blade,
He bravely broach'd his boiling bloody breast;
And Thisbe, tarrying in mulberry shade,
His dagger drew, and died. For all the rest,
Let Lion, Moonshine, Wall, and lovers twain
At large discourse, while here they do remain.

Exit with Pyramus, Thisbe, Lion, and Moonshine.

Theseus, Duke of Athens.
I wonder if the lion be to speak.

Demetrius.
No wonder, my lord; one lion may, when many asses do.

Wall.
In this same enterlude it doth befall
That I, one Snout by name, present a wall;
And such a wall, as I would have you think,
That had in it a crannied hole or chink,
Through which the lovers, Pyramus and Thisbe,
Did whisper often, very secretly.
This loam, this rough-cast, and this stone doth show
That I am that same wall; the truth is so;
And this the cranny is, right and sinister,
Through which the fearful lovers are to whisper.

Theseus, Duke of Athens.
Would you desire lime and hair to speak better?

Demetrius.
It is the wittiest partition that ever I heard discourse, my lord.

Enter Pyramus.

Theseus, Duke of Athens.
Pyramus draws near the wall. Silence!

Pyramus.
O grim-look'd night! O night with hue so black!
O night, which ever art when day is not!
O night, O night! Alack, alack, alack,
I fear my Thisbe's promise is forgot!
And thou, O wall, O sweet, O lovely wall,
That stand'st between her father's ground and mine!
Thou wall, O wall, O sweet and lovely wall,
Show me thy chink, to blink through with mine eyne!

Wall holds up his fingers.

Thanks, courteous wall; Jove shield thee well for this!
But what see I? No Thisbe do I see.
O wicked wall, through whom I see no bliss!
Curs'd be thy stones for thus deceiving me!

Theseus, Duke of Athens.
The wall methinks, being sensible, should curse again.

Pyramus.
No, in truth, sir, he should not. "Deceiving me" is Thisbe's cue. She is to enter now, and I am to spy her through the wall. You shall see it will fall pat as I told you. Yonder she comes.

Enter Thisbe.

Thisbe.
O wall, full often hast thou heard my moans,
For parting my fair Pyramus and me!
My cherry lips have often kiss'd thy stones,
Thy stones with lime and hair knit up in thee.

Pyramus.
I see a voice! Now will I to the chink,
To spy and I can hear my Thisbe's face.
Thisbe!

Thisbe.
My love thou art, my love I think.

Pyramus.
Think what thou wilt, I am thy lover's grace;
And, like Limander, am I trusty still.

Thisbe.
And I, like Helen, till the Fates me kill.

Pyramus.
Not Shafalus to Procrus was so true.

Thisbe.
As Shafalus to Procrus, I to you.

Pyramus.
O, kiss me through the hole of this vild wall!

Act 5, Scene 1

Thisbe.
I kiss the wall's hole, not your lips at all.

Pyramus.
Wilt thou at Ninny's tomb meet me straightway?

Thisbe.
'Tide life, 'tide death, I come without delay.

Exeunt Pyramus and Thisbe.

Wall.
Thus have I, Wall, my part discharged so;
And being done, thus Wall away doth go.

Exit.

Theseus, Duke of Athens.
Now is the moon used between the two neighbors.

Demetrius.
No remedy, my lord, when walls are so willful to hear without warning.

Hippolyta.
This is the silliest stuff that ever I heard.

Theseus, Duke of Athens.
The best in this kind are but shadows; and the worst are no worse, if imagination amend them.

Hippolyta.
It must be your imagination then, and not theirs.

Theseus, Duke of Athens.
If we imagine no worse of them than they of themselves, they may pass for excellent men. Here come two noble beasts in, a man and a lion.

Enter Lion and Moonshine.

Lion.
You, ladies, you, whose gentle hearts do fear
The smallest monstrous mouse that creeps on floor,
May now, perchance, both quake and tremble here,
When lion rough in wildest rage doth roar.
Then know that I as Snug the joiner am
A lion fell, nor else no lion's dam,
For, if I should, as lion, come in strife
Into this place, 'twere pity on my life.

Theseus, Duke of Athens.
A very gentle beast, and of a good conscience.

Demetrius.
The very best at a beast, my lord, that e'er I saw.

Lysander.
This lion is a very fox for his valor.

Theseus, Duke of Athens.
True; and a goose for his discretion.

Demetrius.
Not so, my lord; for his valor cannot carry his discretion, and the fox carries the goose.

Theseus, Duke of Athens.
His discretion, I am sure, cannot carry his valor; for the goose carries not the fox. It is well; leave it to his discretion, and let us listen to the Moon.

Moonshine.
This lantern doth the horned moon present—

Demetrius.
He should have worn the horns on his head.

Theseus, Duke of Athens.
He is no crescent, and his horns are invisible within the circumference.

Moonshine.
This lantern doth the horned moon present;
Myself the man i' th' moon do seem to be.

Theseus, Duke of Athens.
This is the greatest error of all the rest. The man should be put into the lantern. How is it else the man i' th' moon?

Demetrius.
He dares not come there for the candle; for, you see, it is already in snuff.

Hippolyta.
I am a-weary of this moon. Would he would change!

Theseus, Duke of Athens.
It appears, by his small light of discretion, that he is in the wane; but yet in courtesy, in all reason, we must stay the time.

Lysander.
Proceed, Moon.

Moonshine.
All that I have to say is to tell you that the lantern is the moon, I the man i' th' moon, this thorn-bush my thorn-bush, and this dog my dog.

Demetrius.
Why, all these should be in the lantern; for all these are in the moon. But silence! Here comes Thisbe.

Enter Thisbe.

Thisbe.
This is old Ninny's tomb. Where is my love?

Lion.
O!

The Lion roars. Thisbe runs off.

Demetrius.
Well roar'd, Lion.

Theseus, Duke of Athens.
Well run, Thisbe.

Hippolyta.
Well shone, Moon. Truly, the moon shines with a good grace.

The Lion shakes Thisbe's mantle.

Theseus, Duke of Athens.
Well mous'd, Lion.

Enter Pyramus.

Demetrius.
And then came Pyramus.

Exit Lion.

Lysander.
And so the lion vanish'd.

Pyramus.
Sweet Moon, I thank thee for thy sunny beams;
I thank thee, Moon, for shining now so bright;
For by thy gracious, golden, glittering gleams,
I trust to take of truest Thisbe sight.
But stay! O spite!
But mark, poor knight,
What dreadful dole is here!
Eyes, do you see?
How can it be?
O dainty duck! O dear!
Thy mantle good,
What, stain'd with blood?
Approach, ye Furies fell!
O Fates, come, come,
Cut thread and thrum,
Quail, crush, conclude, and quell!

Theseus, Duke of Athens.
This passion, and the death of a dear friend, would go near to make a man look sad.

Hippolyta.
Beshrew my heart, but I pity the man.

Pyramus.
O, wherefore, Nature, didst thou lions frame?
Since lion vild hath here deflow'r'd my dear;
Which is—no, no—which was the fairest dame
That liv'd, that lov'd, that lik'd, that look'd with cheer.
Come, tears, confound,
Out, sword, and wound
The pap of Pyramus;
Ay, that left pap,
Where heart doth hop.

Stabs himself.

Thus die I, thus, thus, thus.
Now am I dead,
Now am I fled;
My soul is in the sky.
Tongue, lose thy light,
Moon, take thy flight,

Exit Moonshine.

Now die, die, die, die, die.

Dies.

Demetrius.
No die, but an ace, for him; for he is but one.

Lysander.
Less than an ace, man; for he is dead, he is nothing.

Theseus, Duke of Athens.
With the help of a surgeon he might yet recover, and yet prove an ass.

Hippolyta.
How chance Moonshine is gone before Thisbe comes back and finds her lover?

Enter Thisbe.

Theseus, Duke of Athens.
She will find him by starlight. Here she comes, and her passion ends the play.

Hippolyta.
Methinks she should not use a long one for such a Pyramus. I hope she will be brief.

Demetrius.
A mote will turn the balance, which Pyramus, which Thisbe, is the better: he for a man. God warr'nt us; she for a woman. God bless us.

Lysander.
She hath spied him already with those sweet eyes.

Demetrius.
And thus she means, videlicet—

Thisbe.
Asleep, my love?
What, dead, my dove?
O Pyramus, arise!
Speak, speak! Quite dumb?
Dead, dead? A tomb
Must cover thy sweet eyes.
These lily lips,
This cherry nose,
These yellow cowslip cheeks,
Are gone, are gone!
Lovers, make moan;
His eyes were green as leeks.
O Sisters Three,
Come, come to me,
With hands as pale as milk;
Lay them in gore,
Since you have shore
With shears his thread of silk.
Tongue, not a word!
Come, trusty sword,
Come, blade, my breast imbrue!

Stabs herself.

And farewell, friends;
Thus Thisbe ends;
Adieu, adieu, adieu.

Dies.

Theseus, Duke of Athens.
Moonshine and Lion are left to bury the dead.

Demetrius.
Ay, and Wall too.

Bottom.

Starting up.

No, I assure you, the wall is down that parted their fathers. Will it please you to see the epilogue, or to hear a Bergomask dance between two of our company?

Theseus, Duke of Athens.
No epilogue, I pray you; for your play needs no excuse. Never excuse; for when the players are all dead, there need none to be blam'd. Marry, if he that writ it had play'd Pyramus, and hang'd himself in Thisbe's garter, it would have been a fine tragedy; and so it is, truly, and very notably discharg'd. But come, your Bergomask; let your epilogue alone.

A dance.

The iron tongue of midnight hath told twelve.
Lovers, to bed, 'tis almost fairy time.
I fear we shall outsleep the coming morn
As much as we this night have overwatch'd.
This palpable-gross play hath well beguil'd
The heavy gait of night. Sweet friends, to bed.
A fortnight hold we this solemnity,
In nightly revels and new jollity.

Exeunt.
Enter Puck.

Puck.
Now the hungry lion roars,
And the wolf behowls the moon;
Whilst the heavy ploughman snores,
All with weary task foredone.
Now the wasted brands do glow,
Whilst the screech owl, screeching loud,
Puts the wretch that lies in woe
In remembrance of a shroud.
Now it is the time of night
That the graves, all gaping wide,
Every one lets forth his sprite,
In the church-way paths to glide.
And we fairies, that do run

By the triple Hecat's team
From the presence of the sun,
Following darkness like a dream,
Now are frolic. Not a mouse
Shall disturb this hallowed house.
I am sent with broom before,
To sweep the dust behind the door.

Enter King and Queen of Fairies, Oberon and Titania, with all their Train.

Oberon.
Through the house give glimmering light
By the dead and drowsy fire,
Every elf and fairy sprite
Hop as light as bird from brier,
And this ditty, after me,
Sing, and dance it trippingly.

Titania.
First, rehearse your song by rote,
To each word a warbling note.
Hand in hand, with fairy grace,
Will we sing, and bless this place.

Song and dance.

Oberon.
Now, until the break of day,
Through this house each fairy stray.
To the best bride-bed will we,
Which by us shall blessed be;
And the issue, there create,
Ever shall be fortunate.
So shall all the couples three
Ever true in loving be;
And the blots of Nature's hand
Shall not in their issue stand;
Never mole, hare-lip, nor scar,
Nor mark prodigious, such as are
Despised in nativity,
Shall upon their children be.
With this field-dew consecrate,
Every fairy take his gait,
And each several chamber bless,
Through this palace, with sweet peace,
And the owner of it blest
Ever shall in safety rest.
Trip away; make no stay;
    Meet me all by break of day.

Exeunt Oberon, Titania, and Train.

Puck.
If we shadows have offended,
Think but this, and all is mended,
That you have but slumb'red here
While these visions did appear.
And this weak and idle theme,
No more yielding but a dream,
Gentles, do not reprehend.
If you pardon, we will mend.
And, as I am an honest Puck,
If we have unearned luck
Now to scape the serpent's tongue,
We will make amends ere long;
Else the Puck a liar call.
So, good night unto you all.
Give me your hands, if we be friends,
And Robin shall restore amends.

Exit.

Hamlet

Act 1

Scene 1

Elsinore. A platform before the castle.

(Barnardo; Francisco; Horatio; Marcellus; Ghost)

For two nights Bernardo and Marcellus have seen a ghost in the form of the late King appear on the battlements. They have called on the scholar Horatio to join them on the third night, in the hopes he will know what to do. Horatio is skeptical, as he does not believe in ghosts, but he is shaken when the ghost appears just as predicted. They discuss the preparations for war occupying the Danish court, and Horatio explains that young Fortinbras of Norway is threatening to take back the lands that his father lost to old Hamlet, the dead King whose ghost they have seen. The ghost reappears, and Horatio tries to get it to speak, suggesting every explanation for its appearance that he can think of; but the ghost remains silent and vanishes as the morning rises. The three agree to tell young Hamlet, the dead man's son, about the event.

Enter Barnardo and Francisco, two sentinels, meeting.

Barnardo.
Who's there?

Francisco.
Nay, answer me. Stand and unfold yourself.

Barnardo.
Long live the King!

Francisco.
Barnardo.

Barnardo.
He.

Francisco.
You come most carefully upon your hour.

Barnardo.
'Tis now struck twelve. Get thee to bed, Francisco.

Francisco.
For this relief much thanks. 'Tis bitter cold,
And I am sick at heart.

Barnardo.
Have you had quiet guard?

Francisco.
                 Not a mouse stirring.

Barnardo.
Well, good night.
If you do meet Horatio and Marcellus,
The rivals of my watch, bid them make haste.

Enter Horatio and Marcellus.

Francisco.
I think I hear them. Stand ho! Who is there?

Horatio.
Friends to this ground.

Marcellus.
                 And liegemen to the Dane.

Francisco.
Give you good night.

Marcellus.
                 O, farewell, honest soldier.
Who hath reliev'd you?

Francisco.
                      Barnardo hath my place.
Give you good night.

Exit Francisco.

Marcellus.
                      Holla, Barnardo!

Barnardo.
                      Say—
What, is Horatio there?

Horatio.
                      A piece of him.

Barnardo.
Welcome, Horatio, welcome, good Marcellus.

Horatio.
What, has this thing appear'd again tonight?

Barnardo.
I have seen nothing.

Marcellus.
Horatio says 'tis but our fantasy,
And will not let belief take hold of him
Touching this dreaded sight twice seen of us;
Therefore I have entreated him along,
With us to watch the minutes of this night,
That if again this apparition come,
He may approve our eyes and speak to it.

Horatio.
Tush, tush, 'twill not appear.

Barnardo.
Sit down a while,
And let us once again assail your ears,
That are so fortified against our story,
What we have two nights seen.

Horatio.
                    Well, sit we down,
And let us hear Barnardo speak of this.

Barnardo.
Last night of all,
When yond same star that's westward from the pole
Had made his course t' illume that part of heaven
Where now it burns, Marcellus and myself,
The bell then beating one—

Enter Ghost.

Marcellus.
Peace, break thee off! Look where it comes again!

Barnardo.
In the same figure like the King that's dead.

Marcellus.
Thou art a scholar, speak to it, Horatio.

Barnardo.
Looks 'a not like the King? Mark it, Horatio.

Horatio.
Most like; it harrows me with fear and wonder.

Barnardo.
It would be spoke to.

Marcellus.
                    Speak to it, Horatio.

Horatio.
What art thou that usurp'st this time of night,
Together with that fair and warlike form
In which the majesty of buried Denmark
Did sometimes march? By heaven I charge thee speak!

Marcellus.
It is offended.

Barnardo.
                    See, it stalks away!

Horatio.
Stay! Speak, speak, I charge thee speak!

Exit Ghost.

Marcellus.
'Tis gone, and will not answer.

Barnardo.
How now, Horatio? You tremble and look pale.
Is not this something more than fantasy?
What think you on't?

Horatio.
Before my God, I might not this believe
Without the sensible and true avouch
Of mine own eyes.

Marcellus.
                    Is it not like the King?

Horatio.
As thou art to thyself.
Such was the very armor he had on
When he the ambitious Norway combated.
So frown'd he once when in an angry parle
He smote the sledded Polacks on the ice.
'Tis strange.

Marcellus.
Thus twice before, and jump at this dead hour,
With martial stalk hath he gone by our watch.

Horatio.
In what particular thought to work I know not,
But in the gross and scope of mine opinion,
This bodes some strange eruption to our state.

Marcellus.
Good now, sit down, and tell me, he that knows,
Why this same strict and most observant watch
So nightly toils the subject of the land,
And why such daily cast of brazen cannon,
And foreign mart for implements of war,
Why such impress of shipwrights, whose sore task
Does not divide the Sunday from the week,
What might be toward, that this sweaty haste
Doth make the night joint-laborer with the day:
Who is't that can inform me?

Horatio.
                    That can I,
At least the whisper goes so: our last king,
Whose image even but now appear'd to us,
Was, as you know, by Fortinbras of Norway,
Thereto prick'd on by a most emulate pride,
Dar'd to the combat; in which our valiant Hamlet
(For so this side of our known world esteem'd him)
Did slay this Fortinbras, who, by a seal'd compact
Well ratified by law and heraldy,
Did forfeit (with his life) all those his lands
Which he stood seiz'd of, to the conqueror;
Against the which a moi'ty competent
Was gaged by our king, which had return'd
To the inheritance of Fortinbras,
Had he been vanquisher; as by the same comart
And carriage of the article design'd,
His fell to Hamlet. Now, sir, young Fortinbras,
Of unimproved mettle hot and full,
Hath in the skirts of Norway here and there
Shark'd up a list of lawless resolutes
For food and diet to some enterprise

That hath a stomach in't, which is no other,
As it doth well appear unto our state,
But to recover of us, by strong hand
And terms compulsatory, those foresaid lands
So by his father lost; and this, I take it,
Is the main motive of our preparations,
The source of this our watch, and the chief head
Of this post-haste and romage in the land.

Barnardo.
I think it be no other but e'en so.
Well may it sort that this portentous figure
Comes armed through our watch so like the King
That was and is the question of these wars.

Horatio.
A mote it is to trouble the mind's eye.
In the most high and palmy state of Rome,
A little ere the mightiest Julius fell,
The graves stood tenantless and the sheeted dead
Did squeak and gibber in the Roman streets.
As stars with trains of fire, and dews of blood,
Disasters in the sun; and the moist star
Upon whose influence Neptune's empire stands
Was sick almost to doomsday with eclipse.
And even the like precurse of fear'd events,
As harbingers preceding still the fates
And prologue to the omen coming on,
Have heaven and earth together demonstrated
Unto our climatures and countrymen.

Enter Ghost.

But soft, behold! Lo where it comes again!

It spreads his arms.

I'll cross it though it blast me. Stay, illusion!
If thou hast any sound or use of voice,
Speak to me.
If there be any good thing to be done
That may to thee do ease, and grace to me,
Speak to me.
If thou art privy to thy country's fate,
Which happily foreknowing may avoid,
O speak!
Or if thou hast uphoarded in thy life
Extorted treasure in the womb of earth,
For which, they say, your spirits oft walk in death,
Speak of it, stay and speak!

The cock crows.

Stop it, Marcellus.

Marcellus.
Shall I strike it with my partisan?

Horatio.
Do, if it will not stand.

Barnardo.
                              'Tis here!

Horatio.
                              'Tis here!

Marcellus.
'Tis gone!

Exit Ghost.

We do it wrong, being so majestical,
To offer it the show of violence,
For it is as the air, invulnerable,
And our vain blows malicious mockery.

Barnardo.
It was about to speak when the cock crew.

Horatio.
And then it started like a guilty thing
Upon a fearful summons. I have heard
The cock, that is the trumpet to the morn,
Doth with his lofty and shrill-sounding throat
Awake the god of day, and at his warning,
Whether in sea or fire, in earth or air,
Th' extravagant and erring spirit hies
To his confine; and of the truth herein
This present object made probation.

Marcellus.
It faded on the crowing of the cock.
Some say that ever 'gainst that season comes
Wherein our Saviour's birth is celebrated,
This bird of dawning singeth all night long,
And then they say no spirit dare stir abroad,
The nights are wholesome, then no planets strike,
No fairy takes, nor witch hath power to charm,
So hallowed, and so gracious, is that time.

Horatio.
So have I heard and do in part believe it.
But look, the morn in russet mantle clad
Walks o'er the dew of yon high eastward hill.
Break we our watch up, and by my advice
Let us impart what we have seen tonight
Unto young Hamlet, for, upon my life,
This spirit, dumb to us, will speak to him.
Do you consent we shall acquaint him with it,
As needful in our loves, fitting our duty?

Marcellus.
Let's do't, I pray, and I this morning know
Where we shall find him most convenient.

Exeunt.

Scene 2

Elsinore. A room of state in the castle.

(Claudius; Gertrude; Polonius; Laertes; Hamlet; Voltemand; Cornelius; Horatio; Marcellus; Barnardo)

King Claudius explains that he has married his brother's widow; he then moves on to matters of state and sends Voltemand and Cornelius to Fortinbras's uncle Norway, detailing the young man's movements and warning Norway to restrain him. Claudius then gives Laertes permission to return to Parism since Polonius has agreed. Claudius then turns to his stepson Hamlet's endless mourning for his father. Gertrude attempts to persuade her son to cheer up, but he is unresponsive. At Claudius and Gertrude's urging, he accepts not to return to university in Wittenberg. Left alone, Hamlet laments his mother's remarriage, especially as it came within three months of his father's death; he is disgusted that she married her brother-in-law. Horatio and the soldiers appear and tell him their story; he is disbelieving and tests them, but quickly grows suspicious, and agrees to watch with them that night.

Flourish. Enter Claudius, King of Denmark, Gertrude the Queen; Council: as Polonius; and his son Laertes, Hamlet, cum aliis including Voltemand and Cornelius.

Claudius, King of Denmark.
Though yet of Hamlet our dear brother's death
The memory be green, and that it us befitted
To bear our hearts in grief, and our whole kingdom
To be contracted in one brow of woe,
Yet so far hath discretion fought with nature
That we with wisest sorrow think on him
Together with remembrance of ourselves.
Therefore our sometime sister, now our queen,
Th' imperial jointress to this warlike state,
Have we, as 'twere with a defeated joy,
With an auspicious, and a dropping eye,

With mirth in funeral, and with dirge in marriage,
In equal scale weighing delight and dole,
Taken to wife; nor have we herein barr'd
Your better wisdoms, which have freely gone
With this affair along. For all, our thanks.
Now follows that you know young Fortinbras,
Holding a weak supposal of our worth,
Or thinking by our late dear brother's death
Our state to be disjoint and out of frame,
Co-leagued with this dream of his advantage,
He hath not fail'd to pester us with message
Importing the surrender of those lands
Lost by his father, with all bands of law,
To our most valiant brother. So much for him.
Now for ourself, and for this time of meeting,
Thus much the business is: we have here writ
To Norway, uncle of young Fortinbras—
Who, impotent and bedrid, scarcely hears
Of this his nephew's purpose—to suppress
His further gait herein, in that the levies,
The lists, and full proportions are all made
Out of his subject; and we here dispatch
You, good Cornelius, and you, Voltemand,
For bearers of this greeting to old Norway,
Giving to you no further personal power
To business with the King, more than the scope
Of these delated articles allow.

Giving a paper.

Farewell, and let your haste commend your duty.

Both Cornelius and Voltemand.
In that, and all things, will we show our duty.

Claudius, King of Denmark.
We doubt it nothing; heartily farewell.

Exeunt Voltemand and Cornelius.

And now, Laertes, what's the news with you?
You told us of some suit, what is't, Laertes?
You cannot speak of reason to the Dane
And lose your voice. What wouldst thou beg, Laertes,
That shall not be my offer, not thy asking?
The head is not more native to the heart,
The hand more instrumental to the mouth,
Than is the throne of Denmark to thy father.
What wouldst thou have, Laertes?

Laertes.
                    My dread lord,
Your leave and favor to return to France,
From whence though willingly I came to Denmark
To show my duty in your coronation,
Yet now I must confess, that duty done,
My thoughts and wishes bend again toward France,
And bow them to your gracious leave and pardon.

Claudius, King of Denmark.
Have you your father's leave? What says Polonius?

Polonius.
H'ath, my lord, wrung from me my slow leave
By laborsome petition, and at last
Upon his will I seal'd my hard consent.
I do beseech you give him leave to go.

Claudius, King of Denmark.
Take thy fair hour, Laertes, time be thine,
And thy best graces spend it at thy will!
But now, my cousin Hamlet, and my son—

Hamlet.

Aside.

A little more than kin, and less than kind.

Claudius, King of Denmark.
How is it that the clouds still hang on you?

Hamlet.
Not so, my lord, I am too much in the sun.

Getrude, Queen of Denmark.
Good Hamlet, cast thy nighted color off,
And let thine eye look like a friend on Denmark.
Do not forever with thy vailed lids
Seek for thy noble father in the dust.
Thou know'st 'tis common, all that lives must die,
Passing through nature to eternity.

Hamlet.
Ay, madam, it is common.

Getrude, Queen of Denmark.
                    If it be,
Why seems it so particular with thee?

Hamlet.
Seems, madam? Nay, it is, I know not "seems."
'Tis not alone my inky cloak, good mother,
Nor customary suits of solemn black,
Nor windy suspiration of forc'd breath,

No, nor the fruitful river in the eye,
Nor the dejected havior of the visage,
Together with all forms, moods, shapes of grief,
That can denote me truly. These indeed seem,
For they are actions that a man might play,
But I have that within which passes show,
These but the trappings and the suits of woe.

Claudius, King of Denmark.
'Tis sweet and commendable in your nature, Hamlet,
To give these mourning duties to your father.
But you must know your father lost a father,
That father lost, lost his, and the survivor bound
In filial obligation for some term
To do obsequious sorrow. But to persever
In obstinate condolement is a course
Of impious stubbornness, 'tis unmanly grief,
It shows a will most incorrect to heaven,
A heart unfortified, or mind impatient,
An understanding simple and unschool'd:
For what we know must be, and is as common
As any the most vulgar thing to sense,
Why should we in our peevish opposition
Take it to heart? Fie, 'tis a fault to heaven,
A fault against the dead, a fault to nature,
To reason most absurd, whose common theme
Is death of fathers, and who still hath cried,
From the first corse till he that died today,
"This must be so." We pray you throw to earth
This unprevailing woe, and think of us
As of a father, for let the world take note
You are the most immediate to our throne,
And with no less nobility of love
Than that which dearest father bears his son
Do I impart toward you. For your intent
In going back to school in Wittenberg,
It is most retrograde to our desire,
And we beseech you bend you to remain
Here in the cheer and comfort of our eye,
Our chiefest courtier, cousin, and our son.

Getrude, Queen of Denmark.
Let not thy mother lose her prayers, Hamlet,
I pray thee stay with us, go not to Wittenberg.

Hamlet.
I shall in all my best obey you, madam.

Claudius, King of Denmark.
Why, 'tis a loving and a fair reply.
Be as ourself in Denmark. Madam, come.
This gentle and unforc'd accord of Hamlet
Sits smiling to my heart, in grace whereof,
No jocund health that Denmark drinks today,
But the great cannon to the clouds shall tell,
And the King's rouse the heaven shall bruit again,
Respeaking earthly thunder. Come away.

Flourish. Exeunt all but Hamlet.

Hamlet.
O that this too too solid flesh would melt,
Thaw, and resolve itself into a dew!
Or that the Everlasting had not fix'd
His canon 'gainst self-slaughter! O God, God,
How weary, stale, flat, and unprofitable
Seem to me all the uses of this world!
Fie on't, ah fie! 'Tis an unweeded garden
That grows to seed, things rank and gross in nature
Possess it merely. That it should come to this!
But two months dead, nay, not so much, not two.
So excellent a king, that was to this
Hyperion to a satyr, so loving to my mother
That he might not beteem the winds of heaven
Visit her face too roughly. Heaven and earth,
Must I remember? Why, she should hang on him
As if increase of appetite had grown
By what it fed on, and yet, within a month—
Let me not think on't! Frailty, thy name is woman!—
A little month, or ere those shoes were old
With which she followed my poor father's body,
Like Niobe, all tears—why, she, even she—
O God, a beast that wants discourse of reason
Would have mourn'd longer—married with my uncle,
My father's brother, but no more like my father
Than I to Hercules. Within a month,
Ere yet the salt of most unrighteous tears
Had left the flushing in her galled eyes,
She married—O most wicked speed: to post
With such dexterity to incestuous sheets,
It is not, nor it cannot come to good,
But break my heart, for I must hold my tongue.

Enter Horatio, Marcellus, and Barnardo.

Horatio.
Hail to your lordship!

Hamlet.
                    I am glad to see you well.
Horatio—or I do forget myself.

Horatio.
The same, my lord, and your poor servant ever.

Hamlet.
Sir, my good friend—I'll change that name with you.
And what make you from Wittenberg, Horatio?
Marcellus.

Marcellus.
My good lord.

Hamlet.
I am very glad to see you.

To Barnardo.

Good even, sir.—
But what, in faith, make you from Wittenberg?

Horatio.
A truant disposition, good my lord.

Hamlet.
I would not hear your enemy say so,
Nor shall you do my ear that violence
To make it truster of your own report
Against yourself. I know you are no truant.
But what is your affair in Elsinore?
We'll teach you to drink deep ere you depart.

Horatio.
My lord, I came to see your father's funeral.

Hamlet.
I prithee do not mock me, fellow student,
I think it was to see my mother's wedding.

Horatio.
Indeed, my lord, it followed hard upon.

Hamlet.
Thrift, thrift, Horatio, the funeral bak'd-meats
Did coldly furnish forth the marriage tables.
Would I had met my dearest foe in heaven
Or ever I had seen that day, Horatio!
My father—methinks I see my father.

Horatio.
Where, my lord?

Hamlet.
                In my mind's eye, Horatio.

Horatio.
I saw him once, 'a was a goodly king.

Hamlet.
'A was a man, take him for all in all,
I shall not look upon his like again.

Horatio.
My lord, I think I saw him yesternight.

Hamlet.
Saw, who?

Horatio.
My lord, the King your father.

Hamlet.
                The King my father?

Horatio.
Season your admiration for a while
With an attent ear, till I may deliver,
Upon the witness of these gentlemen,
This marvel to you.

Hamlet.
                For God's love let me hear!

Horatio.
Two nights together had these gentlemen,
Marcellus and Barnardo, on their watch,
In the dead waste and middle of the night,
Been thus encount'red: a figure like your father,
Armed at point exactly, cap-a-pe,
Appears before them, and with solemn march
Goes slow and stately by them; thrice he walk'd
By their oppress'd and fear-surprised eyes
Within his truncheon's length, whilst they, distill'd
Almost to jelly with the act of fear,
Stand dumb and speak not to him. This to me
In dreadful secrecy impart they did,
And I with them the third night kept the watch,
Where, as they had delivered, both in time,
Form of the thing, each word made true and good,
The apparition comes. I knew your father,
These hands are not more like.

Hamlet.
                But where was this?

Marcellus.
My lord, upon the platform where we watch.

Hamlet.
Did you not speak to it?

Horatio.
                My lord, I did,
But answer made it none. Yet once methought
It lifted up it head and did address
Itself to motion like as it would speak;
But even then the morning cock crew loud,
And at the sound it shrunk in haste away
And vanish'd from our sight.

Hamlet.
                        'Tis very strange.

Horatio.
As I do live, my honor'd lord, 'tis true,
And we did think it writ down in our duty
To let you know of it.

Hamlet.
Indeed, indeed, sirs. But this troubles me.
Hold you the watch tonight?

Both Barnardo and Marcellus.
                        We do, my lord.

Hamlet.
Arm'd, say you?

Both Barnardo and Marcellus.
Arm'd, my lord.

Hamlet.
From top to toe?

Both Barnardo and Marcellus.
                    My lord, from head to foot.

Hamlet.
Then saw you not his face.

Horatio.
O yes, my lord, he wore his beaver up.

Hamlet.
What, look'd he frowningly?

Horatio.
                  A countenance more
In sorrow than in anger.

Hamlet.
                Pale, or red?

Horatio.
Nay, very pale.

Hamlet.
                And fix'd his eyes upon you?

Horatio.
Most constantly.

Hamlet.
              I would I had been there.

Horatio.
It would have much amaz'd you.

Hamlet.
Very like, very like. Stay'd it long?

Horatio.
While one with moderate haste might tell a hundred.

Both Barnardo and Marcellus.
Longer, longer.

Horatio.
Not when I saw't.

Hamlet.
                His beard was grisl'd, no?

Horatio.
It was, as I have seen it in his life,
A sable silver'd.

Hamlet.
                I will watch tonight,
Perchance 'twill walk again.

Horatio.
                I warr'nt it will.

Hamlet.
If it assume my noble father's person,
I'll speak to it though hell itself should gape
And bid me hold my peace. I pray you all,
If you have hitherto conceal'd this sight,
Let it be tenable in your silence still,
And whatsomever else shall hap tonight,
Give it an understanding but no tongue.
I will requite your loves. So fare you well.
Upon the platform 'twixt eleven and twelve
I'll visit you.

Horatio, Marcellus, and Barnardo.
                      Our duty to your honor.

Hamlet.
Your loves, as mine to you; farewell.

Exeunt all but Hamlet.

My father's spirit—in arms! All is not well,
I doubt some foul play. Would the night were come!
Till then sit still, my soul. Foul deeds will rise,
Though all the earth o'erwhelm them, to men's eyes.

Exit.

Scene 3

Elsinore. A room in Polonius' house.

(Laertes; Ophelia; Polonius)

Laertes, on the verge of leaving for Paris, warns his sister Ophelia not to take Hamlet's courting too seriously and to be certain to guard her chastity against him. She cautions him not to offer hypocritical moralizing. Polonius enters to hurry Laertes along, offering him some fatherly precepts before he leaves. Discovering that Hamlet has been paying court to Ophelia, he orders her to cease seeing him. She promises to obey.

Enter Laertes and Ophelia, his sister.

Laertes.
My necessaries are inbark'd. Farewell.
And, sister, as the winds give benefit
And convey is assistant, do not sleep,
But let me hear from you.

Ophelia.
                    Do you doubt that?

Laertes.
For Hamlet, and the trifling of his favor,
Hold it a fashion and a toy in blood,
A violet in the youth of primy nature,
Forward, not permanent, sweet, not lasting,
The perfume and suppliance of a minute—
No more.

Ophelia.
                    No more but so?

Laertes.
                    Think it no more:

For nature crescent does not grow alone
In thews and bulk, but as this temple waxes,
The inward service of the mind and soul
Grows wide withal. Perhaps he loves you now,
And now no soil nor cautel doth besmirch
The virtue of his will, but you must fear,
His greatness weigh'd, his will is not his own,
For he himself is subject to his birth:
He may not, as unvalued persons do,
Carve for himself, for on his choice depends
The safety and health of this whole state,
And therefore must his choice be circumscrib'd
Unto the voice and yielding of that body
Whereof he is the head. Then if he says he loves you,
It fits your wisdom so far to believe it
As he in his particular act and place
May give his saying deed, which is no further
Than the main voice of Denmark goes withal.
Then weigh what loss your honor may sustain
If with too credent ear you list his songs,
Or lose your heart, or your chaste treasure open
To his unmast'red importunity.
Fear it, Ophelia, fear it, my dear sister,
And keep you in the rear of your affection,
Out of the shot and danger of desire.
The chariest maid is prodigal enough
If she unmask her beauty to the moon.
Virtue itself scapes not calumnious strokes.
The canker galls the infants of the spring
Too oft before their buttons be disclos'd,
And in the morn and liquid dew of youth
Contagious blastments are most imminent.
Be wary then, best safety lies in fear:
Youth to itself rebels, though none else near.

Ophelia.
I shall the effect of this good lesson keep
As watchman to my heart. But, good my brother,
Do not, as some ungracious pastors do,
Show me the steep and thorny way to heaven,
Whiles, like a puff'd and reckless libertine,
Himself the primrose path of dalliance treads,
And recks not his own rede.

Laertes.
O, fear me not.

Enter Polonius.

I stay too long—but here my father comes.
A double blessing is a double grace,

Occasion smiles upon a second leave.

Polonius.
Yet here, Laertes? Aboard, aboard, for shame!
The wind sits in the shoulder of your sail,
And you are stay'd for. There—

Laying his hand on Laertes' head.

My blessing with thee!
And these few precepts in thy memory
Look thou character. Give thy thoughts no tongue,
Nor any unproportion'd thought his act.
Be thou familiar, but by no means vulgar:
Those friends thou hast, and their adoption tried,
Grapple them unto thy soul with hoops of steel,
But do not dull thy palm with entertainment
Of each new-hatch'd, unfledg'd courage. Beware
Of entrance to a quarrel, but being in,
Bear't that th' opposed may beware of thee.
Give every man thy ear, but few thy voice,
Take each man's censure, but reserve thy judgment.
Costly thy habit as thy purse can buy,
But not express'd in fancy, rich, not gaudy,
For the apparel oft proclaims the man,
And they in France of the best rank and station
Are of a most select and generous chief in that.
Neither a borrower nor a lender be,
For loan oft loses both itself and friend,
And borrowing dulleth th' edge of husbandry.
This above all: to thine own self be true,
And it must follow, as the night the day,
Thou canst not then be false to any man.
Farewell, my blessing season this in thee!

Laertes.
Most humbly do I take my leave, my lord.

Polonius.
The time invests you, go, your servants tend.

Laertes.
Farewell, Ophelia, and remember well
What I have said to you.

Ophelia.
                'Tis in my memory lock'd,
And you yourself shall keep the key of it.

Laertes.
Farewell.

Exit Laertes.

Polonius.
What is't, Ophelia, he hath said to you?

Ophelia.
So please you, something touching the Lord Hamlet.

Polonius.
Marry, well bethought.
'Tis told me, he hath very oft of late
Given private time to you, and you yourself
Have of your audience been most free and bounteous.
If it be so—as so 'tis put on me,
And that in way of caution—I must tell you,
You do not understand yourself so clearly
As it behooves my daughter and your honor.
What is between you? Give me up the truth.

Ophelia.
He hath, my lord, of late made many tenders
Of his affection to me.

Polonius.
Affection, puh! You speak like a green girl,
Unsifted in such perilous circumstance.
Do you believe his tenders, as you call them?

Ophelia.
I do not know, my lord, what I should think.

Polonius.
Marry, I will teach you: think yourself a baby
That you have ta'en these tenders for true pay,
Which are not sterling. Tender yourself more dearly,
Or (not to crack the wind of the poor phrase,
Wringing it thus) you'll tender me a fool.

Ophelia.
My lord, he hath importun'd me with love
In honorable fashion.

Polonius.
Ay, fashion you may call it. Go to, go to.

Ophelia.
And hath given countenance to his speech, my lord,
With almost all the holy vows of heaven.

Polonius.
Ay, springes to catch woodcocks. I do know,
When the blood burns, how prodigal the soul
Lends the tongue vows. These blazes, daughter,
Giving more light than heat, extinct in both
Even in their promise, as it is a-making,
You must not take for fire. From this time

Be something scanter of your maiden presence,
Set your entreatments at a higher rate
Than a command to parle. For Lord Hamlet,
Believe so much in him, that he is young,
And with a larger teder may he walk
Than may be given you. In few, Ophelia,
Do not believe his vows, for they are brokers,
Not of that dye which their investments show,
But mere implorators of unholy suits,
Breathing like sanctified and pious bonds,
The better to beguile. This is for all:
I would not, in plain terms, from this time forth
Have you so slander any moment leisure
As to give words or talk with the Lord Hamlet.
Look to't, I charge you. Come your ways.

Ophelia.
I shall obey, my lord.

Exeunt.

Scene 4

Elsinore. A platform before Elsinore castle.

(Hamlet; Horatio; Marcellus; Ghost)

Hamlet, Horatio, and Marcellus are on watch. Hamlet discourses against the heavy drinking of the Danes. The ghost appears. Hamlet begs it to speak, but it beckons him to come on alone. The others urge him not to go, afraid that the ghost may be a demon seeking to drive Hamlet mad, and attempt to forcibly restrain the prince, but he breaks free, threatening their lives. He goes after the ghost, and the others follow.

Enter Hamlet, Horatio, and Marcellus.

Hamlet.
The air bites shrewdly, it is very cold.

Horatio.
It is a nipping and an eager air.

Hamlet.
What hour now?

Horatio.
            I think it lacks of twelve.

Marcellus.
No, it is struck.

Horatio.
Indeed? I heard it not. It then draws near the season
Wherein the spirit held his wont to walk.

A flourish of trumpets, and two pieces goes off within.

What does this mean, my lord?

Hamlet.
The King doth wake tonight and takes his rouse,
Keeps wassail, and the swagg'ring up-spring reels;
And as he drains his draughts of Rhenish down,
The kettle-drum and trumpet thus bray out
The triumph of his pledge.

Horatio.
            Is it a custom?

Hamlet.
Ay, marry, is't,
But to my mind, though I am native here
And to the manner born, it is a custom
More honor'd in the breach than the observance.
This heavy-headed revel east and west
Makes us traduc'd and tax'd of other nations.
They clip us drunkards, and with swinish phrase
Soil our addition, and indeed it takes
From our achievements, though perform'd at height,
The pith and marrow of our attribute.
So, oft it chances in particular men,
That for some vicious mole of nature in them,
As in their birth, wherein they are not guilty
(Since nature cannot choose his origin),
By their o'ergrowth of some complexion
Oft breaking down the pales and forts of reason,
Or by some habit, that too much o'er-leavens
The form of plausive manners—that these men,
Carrying, I say, the stamp of one defect,
Being nature's livery, or fortune's star,
His virtues else, be they as pure as grace,
As infinite as man may undergo,
Shall in the general censure take corruption
From that particular fault: the dram of ev'l
Doth all the noble substance of a doubt
To his own scandal.

Enter Ghost.

Horatio.
            Look, my lord, it comes!

Hamlet.
Angels and ministers of grace defend us!
Be thou a spirit of health, or goblin damn'd,
Bring with thee airs from heaven, or blasts from hell,
Be thy intents wicked, or charitable,
Thou com'st in such a questionable shape
That I will speak to thee. I'll call thee Hamlet,
King, father, royal Dane. O, answer me!
Let me not burst in ignorance, but tell
Why thy canoniz'd bones, hearsed in death,
Have burst their cerements; why the sepulchre,
Wherein we saw thee quietly inurn'd,
Hath op'd his ponderous and marble jaws
To cast thee up again. What may this mean,
That thou, dead corse, again in complete steel
Revisits thus the glimpses of the moon,
Making night hideous, and we fools of nature
So horridly to shake our disposition
With thoughts beyond the reaches of our souls?
Say why is this? Wherefore? What should we do?

Ghost beckons Hamlet.

Horatio.
It beckons you to go away with it,
As if it some impartment did desire
To you alone.

Marcellus.
           Look with what courteous action
It waves you to a more removed ground,
But do not go with it.

Horatio.
           No, by no means.

Hamlet.
It will not speak, then I will follow it.

Horatio.
Do not, my lord.

Hamlet.
           Why, what should be the fear?
I do not set my life at a pin's fee,
And for my soul, what can it do to that,
Being a thing immortal as itself?
It waves me forth again, I'll follow it.

Horatio.
What if it tempt you toward the flood, my lord,
Or to the dreadful summit of the cliff
That beetles o'er his base into the sea,
And there assume some other horrible form
Which might deprive your sovereignty of reason,
And draw you into madness? Think of it.
The very place puts toys of desperation,
Without more motive, into every brain
That looks so many fathoms to the sea
And hears it roar beneath.

Hamlet.
           It waves me still.—
Go on, I'll follow thee.

Marcellus.
You shall not go, my lord.

Hamlet.
           Hold off your hands.

Horatio.
Be rul'd, you shall not go.

Hamlet.
           My fate cries out,
And makes each petty artere in this body
As hardy as the Nemean lion's nerve.
Still am I call'd. Unhand me, gentlemen.
By heaven, I'll make a ghost of him that lets me!
I say away!—Go on, I'll follow thee.

Exeunt Ghost and Hamlet.

Horatio.
He waxes desperate with imagination.

Marcellus.
Let's follow. 'Tis not fit thus to obey him.

Horatio.
Have after. To what issue will this come?

Marcellus.
Something is rotten in the state of Denmark.

Horatio.
Heaven will direct it.

Marcellus.
           Nay, let's follow him.

Exeunt.

Scene 5

Elsinore. Another part of the platform before Elsinore castle.

(Ghost; Hamlet; Horatio; Marcellus)

Hamlet refuses to go any further. The ghost finally speaks, confirming that it is indeed Old Hamlet's spirit, which has been condemned to tortures in the afterlife until its sins are washed away. The ghost reveals the Old Hamlet was murdered, and by Claudius — who now has his crown and wife. It charges Hamlet to revenge the crime, though insisting that he not harm Gertrude. As the morning arrives, the ghost vanishes. Horatio and Marcellus arrive and plead with hamlet to tell them what the ghost said, but the prince, in a wild mood, refuses. Seconded by the ghost's voice, he makes them swear on his sword never to speak of the apparition again, and tells them that he may decide to act mad in the future, and that they are in no way to let anyone suspect it might not be genuine.

Enter Ghost and Hamlet.

Hamlet.
Whither wilt thou lead me? Speak, I'll go no further.

Ghost of Hamlet's Father.
Mark me.

Hamlet.
      I will.

Ghost of Hamlet's Father.
      My hour is almost come
When I to sulph'rous and tormenting flames
Must render up myself.

Hamlet.
      Alas, poor ghost!

Ghost of Hamlet's Father.
Pity me not, but lend thy serious hearing
To what I shall unfold.

Hamlet.
      Speak, I am bound to hear.

Ghost of Hamlet's Father.
So art thou to revenge, when thou shalt hear.

Hamlet.
What?

Ghost of Hamlet's Father.
I am thy father's spirit,
Doom'd for a certain term to walk the night,
And for the day confin'd to fast in fires,
Till the foul crimes done in my days of nature
Are burnt and purg'd away. But that I am forbid
To tell the secrets of my prison-house,
I could a tale unfold whose lightest word
Would harrow up thy soul, freeze thy young blood,
Make thy two eyes like stars start from their spheres,
Thy knotted and combined locks to part,
And each particular hair to stand an end,
Like quills upon the fearful porcupine.
But this eternal blazon must not be
To ears of flesh and blood. List, list, O, list!
If thou didst ever thy dear father love—

Hamlet.
O God!

Ghost of Hamlet's Father.
Revenge his foul and most unnatural murder.

Hamlet.
Murder!

Ghost of Hamlet's Father.
Murder most foul, as in the best it is,
But this most foul, strange, and unnatural.

Hamlet.
Haste me to know't, that I with wings as swift
As meditation, or the thoughts of love,
May sweep to my revenge.

Ghost of Hamlet's Father.
      I find thee apt,
And duller shouldst thou be than the fat weed
That roots itself in ease on Lethe wharf,
Wouldst thou not stir in this. Now, Hamlet, hear:
'Tis given out that, sleeping in my orchard,
A serpent stung me, so the whole ear of Denmark
Is by a forged process of my death
Rankly abus'd; but know, thou noble youth,
The serpent that did sting thy father's life
Now wears his crown.

Hamlet.
      O my prophetic soul!
My uncle?

Ghost of Hamlet's Father.
Ay, that incestuous, that adulterate beast,
With witchcraft of his wits, with traitorous gifts—
O wicked wit and gifts that have the power
So to seduce!—won to his shameful lust
The will of my most seeming virtuous queen.
O Hamlet, what a falling-off was there
From me, whose love was of that dignity
That it went hand in hand even with the vow
I made to her in marriage, and to decline
Upon a wretch whose natural gifts were poor
To those of mine!
But virtue, as it never will be moved,
Though lewdness court it in a shape of heaven,
So lust, though to a radiant angel link'd,
Will sate itself in a celestial bed
And prey on garbage.
But soft, methinks I scent the morning air,
Brief let me be. Sleeping within my orchard,
My custom always of the afternoon,
Upon my secure hour thy uncle stole,
With juice of cursed hebona in a vial,
And in the porches of my ears did pour
The leperous distillment, whose effect
Holds such an enmity with blood of man
That swift as quicksilver it courses through
The natural gates and alleys of the body,
And with a sudden vigor it doth posset
And curd, like eager droppings into milk,
The thin and wholesome blood. So did it mine,
And a most instant tetter bark'd about,
Most lazar-like, with vile and loathsome crust
All my smooth body.
Thus was I, sleeping, by a brother's hand
Of life, of crown, of queen, at once dispatch'd,
Cut off even in the blossoms of my sin,
Unhous'led, disappointed, unanel'd,
No reck'ning made, but sent to my account
With all my imperfections on my head.
O, horrible, O, horrible, most horrible!
If thou hast nature in thee, bear it not,
Let not the royal bed of Denmark be
A couch for luxury and damned incest.
But howsomever thou pursues this act,
Taint not thy mind, nor let thy soul contrive
Against thy mother aught. Leave her to heaven,
And to those thorns that in her bosom lodge
To prick and sting her. Fare thee well at once!
The glow-worm shows the matin to be near,
And gins to pale his uneffectual fire.

Adieu, adieu, adieu! Remember me.

Exit.

Hamlet.
O all you host of heaven! O earth! What else?
And shall I couple hell? O fie, hold, hold, my heart,
And you, my sinews, grow not instant old,
But bear me stiffly up. Remember thee!
Ay, thou poor ghost, whiles memory holds a seat
In this distracted globe. Remember thee!
Yea, from the table of my memory
I'll wipe away all trivial fond records,
All saws of books, all forms, all pressures past
That youth and observation copied there,
And thy commandment all alone shall live
Within the book and volume of my brain,
Unmix'd with baser matter. Yes, by heaven!
O most pernicious woman!
O villain, villain, smiling, damned villain!
My tables—meet it is I set it down
That one may smile, and smile, and be a villain!
At least I am sure it may be so in Denmark.

He writes.

So, uncle, there you are. Now to my word:
It is "Adieu, adieu! Remember me."
I have sworn't.

Horatio.

Within.

                                    My lord, my lord!

Marcellus.

Within.

                                    Lord Hamlet!

Enter Horatio and Marcellus.

Horatio.

                                    Heavens secure him!

Hamlet.
So be it!

Marcellus.
Illo, ho, ho, my lord!

Hamlet.
Hillo, ho, ho, boy! Come, bird, come.

Marcellus.
How is't, my noble lord?

Horatio.
                    What news, my lord?

Hamlet.
O, wonderful!

Horatio.
Good my lord, tell it.

Hamlet.
                    No, you will reveal it.

Horatio.
Not I, my lord, by heaven.

Marcellus.
                    Nor I, my lord.

Hamlet.
How say you then, would heart of man once think it?—
But you'll be secret?

Both Barnardo and Marcellus.
                    Ay, by heaven, my lord.

Hamlet.
There's never a villain dwelling in all Denmark
But he's an arrant knave.

Horatio.
There needs no ghost, my lord, come from the grave
To tell us this.

Hamlet.
                Why, right, you are in the right,
And so, without more circumstance at all,
I hold it fit that we shake hands and part,
You, as your business and desire shall point you,
For every man hath business and desire,
Such as it is, and for my own poor part,
I will go pray.

Horatio.
These are but wild and whirling words, my lord.

Hamlet.
I am sorry they offend you, heartily,
Yes, faith, heartily.

Horatio.
                There's no offense, my lord.

Hamlet.
Yes, by Saint Patrick, but there is, Horatio,
And much offense too. Touching this vision here,
It is an honest ghost, that let me tell you.
For your desire to know what is between us,
O'ermaster't as you may. And now, good friends,
As you are friends, scholars, and soldiers,
Give me one poor request.

Horatio.
What is't, my lord, we will.

Hamlet.
Never make known what you have seen tonight.

Both Barnardo and Marcellus.
My lord, we will not.

Hamlet.
                    Nay, but swear't.

Horatio.
                    In faith,
My lord, not I.

Marcellus.
                    Nor I, my lord, in faith.

Hamlet.
Upon my sword.

Marcellus.
                    We have sworn, my lord, already.

Hamlet.
Indeed, upon my sword, indeed.

Ghost cries under the stage.

Ghost of Hamlet's Father.
Swear.

Hamlet.
Ha, ha, boy, say'st thou so? Art thou there, truepenny?
Come on, you hear this fellow in the cellarage,
Consent to swear.

Horatio.
                    Propose the oath, my lord.

Hamlet.
Never to speak of this that you have seen,
Swear by my sword.

Ghost of Hamlet's Father.

Beneath.

Swear.

Hamlet.
Hic et ubique? Then we'll shift our ground.
Come hither, gentlemen,
And lay your hands again upon my sword.
Swear by my sword
Never to speak of this that you have heard.

Ghost of Hamlet's Father.

Beneath.

Swear by his sword.

Hamlet.
Well said, old mole, canst work i' th' earth so fast?
A worthy pioner! Once more remove, good friends.

Horatio.
O day and night, but this is wondrous strange!

Hamlet.
And therefore as a stranger give it welcome.
There are more things in heaven and earth, Horatio,
Than are dreamt of in your philosophy.
But come—
Here, as before, never, so help you mercy,
How strange or odd some'er I bear myself—
As I perchance hereafter shall think meet
To put an antic disposition on—
That you, at such times seeing me, never shall,
With arms encumb'red thus, or this headshake,
Or by pronouncing of some doubtful phrase,
As "Well, well, we know," or "We could, and if we would,"
Or "If we list to speak," or "There be, and if they might,"
Or such ambiguous giving out, to note
That you know aught of me—this do swear,
So grace and mercy at your most need help you.

Ghost of Hamlet's Father.

Beneath.

Swear.

They swear.

Hamlet.
Rest, rest, perturbed spirit! So, gentlemen,
With all my love I do commend me to you,
And what so poor a man as Hamlet is
May do t' express his love and friending to you,
God willing, shall not lack. Let us go in together,
And still your fingers on your lips, I pray.
The time is out of joint—O cursed spite,
That ever I was born to set it right!
Nay, come, let's go together.

Exeunt.

Act 2

Scene 1

Elsinore. A room in Polonius' house.

(Polonius; Reynaldo; Ophelia)

Polonius sends Reynaldo to spy on Laertes in Paris. Ophelia rushes in to tell her father that Hamlet came to visit her, not speaking a word but completely under-dressed and disheveled. Polonius is certain that Hamlet has gone mad for love, and regrets having told Ophelia to cease seeing him, as the prince's love is clearly stronger than he thought.

Enter old Polonius with his man, Reynaldo.

Polonius.
Give him this money and these notes, Reynaldo.

Reynaldo.
I will, my lord.

Polonius.
You shall do marvell's wisely, good Reynaldo,
Before you visit him, to make inquire
Of his behavior.

Reynaldo.
              My lord, I did intend it.

Polonius.
Marry, well said, very well said. Look you, sir,
Inquire me first what Danskers are in Paris,
And how, and who, what means, and where they keep,
What company, at what expense; and finding

By this encompassment and drift of question
That they do know my son, come you more nearer
Than your particular demands will touch it.
Take you as 'twere some distant knowledge of him,
As thus, "I know his father and his friends,
And in part him." Do you mark this, Reynaldo?

Reynaldo.
Ay, very well, my lord.

Polonius.
"And in part him—but," you may say, "not well.
But if't be he I mean, he's very wild,
Addicted so and so," and there put on him
What forgeries you please: marry, none so rank
As may dishonor him, take heed of that,
But, sir, such wanton, wild, and usual slips
As are companions noted and most known
To youth and liberty.

Reynaldo.
                As gaming, my lord.

Polonius.
Ay, or drinking, fencing, swearing, quarreling,
Drabbing—you may go so far.

Reynaldo.
My lord, that would dishonor him.

Polonius.
Faith, as you may season it in the charge:
You must not put another scandal on him,
That he is open to incontinency—
That's not my meaning. But breathe his faults so quaintly
That they may seem the taints of liberty,
The flash and outbreak of a fiery mind,
A savageness in unreclaimed blood,
Of general assault.

Reynaldo.
                But, my good lord—

Polonius.
Wherefore should you do this?

Reynaldo.
                Ay, my lord,
I would know that.

Polonius.
                Marry, sir, here's my drift,
And I believe it is a fetch of wit:
You laying these slight sallies on my son,
As 'twere a thing a little soil'd wi' th' working,
Mark you,
Your party in converse, him you would sound,
Having ever seen in the prenominate crimes
The youth you breathe of guilty, be assur'd
He closes with you in this consequence:
"Good sir," or so, or "friend," or "gentleman,"
According to the phrase or the addition
Of man and country.

Reynaldo.
                Very good, my lord.

Polonius.
And then, sir, does 'a this—'a does—what was I
About to say?
By the mass, I was about to say something.
Where did I leave?

Reynaldo.
                At "closes in the consequence."

Polonius.
At "closes in the consequence," ay, marry.
He closes thus: "I know the gentleman.
I saw him yesterday, or th' other day,
Or then, or then, with such or such, and as you say,
There was 'a gaming, there o'ertook in 's rouse,
There falling out at tennis"; or, perchance,
"I saw him enter such a house of sale,"
Videlicet, a brothel, or so forth. See you now,
Your bait of falsehood take this carp of truth,
And thus do we of wisdom and of reach,
With windlasses and with assays of bias,
By indirections find directions out;
So by my former lecture and advice
Shall you my son. You have me, have you not?

Reynaldo.
My lord, I have.

Polonius.
                God buy ye, fare ye well.

Reynaldo.
Good my lord.

Polonius.
Observe his inclination in yourself.

Reynaldo.
I shall, my lord.

Polonius.
And let him ply his music.

Reynaldo.
                      Well, my lord.

Polonius.
Farewell.

Exit Reynaldo.
Enter Ophelia.

How now, Ophelia, what's the matter?

Ophelia.
O my lord, my lord, I have been so affrighted!

Polonius.
With what, i' th' name of God?

Ophelia.
My lord, as I was sewing in my closet,
Lord Hamlet, with his doublet all unbrac'd,
No hat upon his head, his stockins fouled,
Ungart'red, and down-gyved to his ankle,
Pale as his shirt, his knees knocking each other,
And with a look so piteous in purport
As if he had been loosed out of hell
To speak of horrors—he comes before me.

Polonius.
Mad for thy love?

Ophelia.
                My lord, I do not know,
But truly I do fear it.

Polonius.
                      What said he?

Ophelia.
He took me by the wrist, and held me hard,
Then goes he to the length of all his arm,
And with his other hand thus o'er his brow,
He falls to such perusal of my face
As 'a would draw it. Long stay'd he so.
At last, a little shaking of mine arm,
And thrice his head thus waving up and down,
He rais'd a sigh so piteous and profound
As it did seem to shatter all his bulk
And end his being. That done, he lets me go,
And with his head over his shoulder turn'd,
He seem'd to find his way without his eyes,
For out a' doors he went without their helps,
And to the last bended their light on me.

Polonius.
Come, go with me. I will go seek the king.
This is the very ecstasy of love,
Whose violent property fordoes itself,
And leads the will to desperate undertakings
As oft as any passions under heaven
That does afflict our natures. I am sorry—
What, have you given him any hard words of late?

Ophelia.
No, my good lord, but as you did command
I did repel his letters, and denied
His access to me.

Polonius.
                  That hath made him mad.
I am sorry that with better heed and judgment
I had not coted him. I fear'd he did but trifle
And meant to wrack thee, but beshrew my jealousy!
By heaven, it is as proper to our age
To cast beyond ourselves in our opinions,
As it is common for the younger sort
To lack discretion. Come, go we to the king.
This must be known, which, being kept close, might move
More grief to hide, than hate to utter love.
Come.

Exeunt.

Scene 2

Elsinore. A room in Elsinore castle.

(King; Queen; Hamlet; Rosencrantz; Guildenstern; Polonius; Voltemand; Cornelius; Attendants; First Player (Player King); Player Queen; Player Prologue; Player Lucianus)

Claudius and Gertrude welcome Hamlet's childhood friends Guildenstern and Rosencrantz to the court, asking them to find out what lies behind Hamlet's strange behavior. The crawling young men agree. The ambassadors from Norway return, reporting that Fortinbras has been pulled over the coals by his uncle and ordered to attack the Polacks instead. Norway seeks free passage for its army through Denmark. Polonius explains to the King and Queen about the relationship between his daughter and Hamlet, quoting from a letter the prince sent the girl, and expounds his belief that it is this unrequited love that has driven Hamlet mad. He suggests arranging a meeting between the two young people and spying on them with Claudius. Hamlet enters reading, and Polonius attempts to make him speak sense; the old man realizes that Hamlet's talk is not entirely senseless. Rosencrantz and Guildernstern accost Hamlet, who is delighted to see them, but he soon realizes that they must have been summoned by the King and Queen, and is disappointed that they do not admit it outright. They two are confounded and do not know how to react, but mention that a troupe of traveling players will soon arrive at Elsinore. Hamlet, who loves theatre, is thrilled. Polonius announces the actors' arrival. Hamlet welcomes them all by name, as he knows them well. He is so excited that he begins reciting one of his favorite speeches, asking the lead player to complete it. The tale, of a son avenging his father, moves him greatly. He arranges to have a play performed the next day and to add a few lines to it. Alone, he rails against his own procrastination in exacting revenge. Wanting to be certain that the ghost's story is true, he decides that the players will act a play showing a very similar murder the next day; if Claudius shows signs of guilt, Hamlet will be convinced the ghost spoke true.

Flourish. Enter King and Queen, Rosencrantz and Guildenstern cum aliis.

Claudius, King of Denmark.
Welcome, dear Rosencrantz and Guildenstern!
Moreover that we much did long to see you,
The need we have to use you did provoke
Our hasty sending. Something have you heard
Of Hamlet's transformation; so call it,
Sith nor th' exterior nor the inward man
Resembles that it was. What it should be,
More than his father's death, that thus hath put him
So much from th' understanding of himself,
I cannot dream of. I entreat you both
That, being of so young days brought up with him,
And sith so neighbored to his youth and havior,
That you vouchsafe your rest here in our court
Some little time, so by your companies
To draw him on to pleasures, and to gather
So much as from occasion you may glean,
Whether aught to us unknown afflicts him thus,
That, open'd, lies within our remedy.

Getrude, Queen of Denmark.
Good gentlemen, he hath much talk'd of you,
And sure I am two men there is not living
To whom he more adheres. If it will please you
To show us so much gentry and good will
As to expend your time with us a while
For the supply and profit of our hope,
Your visitation shall receive such thanks
As fits a king's remembrance.

Rosencrantz.
                    Both your Majesties
Might, by the sovereign power you have of us,
Put your dread pleasures more into command
Than to entreaty.

Guildenstern.
                    But we both obey,
And here give up ourselves, in the full bent,
To lay our service freely at your feet,
To be commanded.

Claudius, King of Denmark.
Thanks, Rosencrantz and gentle Guildenstern.

Getrude, Queen of Denmark.
Thanks, Guildenstern and gentle Rosencrantz.
And I beseech you instantly to visit
My too much changed son. Go some of you
And bring these gentlemen where Hamlet is.

Guildenstern.
Heavens make our presence and our practices
Pleasant and helpful to him!

Getrude, Queen of Denmark.
                    Ay, amen!

Exeunt Rosencrantz and Guildenstern with some Attendants.
Enter Polonius.

Polonius.
Th' ambassadors from Norway, my good lord,
Are joyfully return'd.

Claudius, King of Denmark.
Thou still hast been the father of good news.

Polonius.
Have I, my lord? I assure my good liege
I hold my duty as I hold my soul,
Both to my God and to my gracious king;
And I do think, or else this brain of mine

Hunts not the trail of policy so sure
As it hath us'd to do, that I have found
The very cause of Hamlet's lunacy.

Claudius, King of Denmark.
O, speak of that, that do I long to hear.

Polonius.
Give first admittance to th' ambassadors;
My news shall be the fruit to that great feast.

Claudius, King of Denmark.
Thyself do grace to them, and bring them in.

Exit Polonius.

He tells me, my dear Gertrude, he hath found
The head and source of all your son's distemper.

Getrude, Queen of Denmark.
I doubt it is no other but the main,
His father's death and our o'erhasty marriage.

Enter Polonius with Voltemand and Cornelius, the Ambassadors.

Claudius, King of Denmark.
Well, we shall sift him.—Welcome, my good friends!
Say, Voltemand, what from our brother Norway?

Voltemand.
Most fair return of greetings and desires.
Upon our first, he sent out to suppress
His nephew's levies, which to him appear'd
To be a preparation 'gainst the Polack;
But better look'd into, he truly found
It was against your Highness. Whereat griev'd,
That so his sickness, age, and impotence
Was falsely borne in hand, sends out arrests
On Fortinbras, which he, in brief, obeys,
Receives rebuke from Norway, and in fine,
Makes vow before his uncle never more
To give th' assay of arms against your Majesty.
Whereon old Norway, overcome with joy,
Gives him threescore thousand crowns in annual fee,
And his commission to employ those soldiers,
So levied, as before, against the Polack,
With an entreaty, herein further shown,

Giving a paper.

That it might please you to give quiet pass
Through your dominions for this enterprise,
On such regards of safety and allowance
As therein are set down.

Claudius, King of Denmark.
       It likes us well,
And at our more considered time we'll read,
Answer, and think upon this business.
Mean time, we thank you for your well-took labor.
Go to your rest, at night we'll feast together.
Most welcome home!

Exeunt Ambassadors and Attendants.

Polonius.
       This business is well ended.
My liege, and madam, to expostulate
What majesty should be, what duty is,
Why day is day, night night, and time is time,
Were nothing but to waste night, day, and time;
Therefore, since brevity is the soul of wit,
And tediousness the limbs and outward flourishes,
I will be brief. Your noble son is mad:
Mad call I it, for to define true madness,
What is't but to be nothing else but mad?
But let that go.

Getrude, Queen of Denmark.
More matter with less art.

Polonius.
Madam, I swear I use no art at all.
That he's mad, 'tis true, 'tis true 'tis pity,
And pity 'tis 'tis true—a foolish figure,
But farewell it, for I will use no art.
Mad let us grant him then, and now remains
That we find out the cause of this effect,
Or rather say, the cause of this defect,
For this effect defective comes by cause:
Thus it remains, and the remainder thus.
Perpend.
I have a daughter—have while she is mine—
Who in her duty and obedience, mark,
Hath given me this. Now gather, and surmise.

Reads the salutation of the letter.

"To the celestial and my soul's idol, the most beautified
Ophelia"—
That's an ill phrase, a vile phrase, "beautified" is a vile
phrase. But you shall hear. Thus:
"In her excellent white bosom, these, etc."

Act 2, Scene 2

Getrude, Queen of Denmark.
Came this from Hamlet to her?

Polonius.
Good madam, stay awhile. I will be faithful.

Reads the letter.

"Doubt thou the stars are fire,
Doubt that the sun doth move,
Doubt truth to be a liar,
But never doubt I love.
O dear Ophelia, I am ill at these numbers. I have not art to reckon my groans, but that I love thee best, O most best, believe it. Adieu.
Thine evermore, most dear lady,
whilst this machine is to him, Hamlet."
This in obedience hath my daughter shown me,
And more above, hath his solicitings,
As they fell out by time, by means, and place,
All given to mine ear.

Claudius, King of Denmark.
                    But how hath she
Receiv'd his love?

Polonius.
                    What do you think of me?

Claudius, King of Denmark.
As of a man faithful and honorable.

Polonius.
I would fain prove so. But what might you think,
When I had seen this hot love on the wing—
As I perceiv'd it (I must tell you that)
Before my daughter told me—what might you,
Or my dear Majesty your queen here, think,
If I had play'd the desk or table-book,
Or given my heart a winking, mute and dumb,
Or look'd upon this love with idle sight,
What might you think? No, I went round to work,
And my young mistress thus I did bespeak:
"Lord Hamlet is a prince out of thy star;
This must not be"; and then I prescripts gave her,
That she should lock herself from his resort,
Admit no messengers, receive no tokens.
Which done, she took the fruits of my advice;
And he repell'd, a short tale to make,
Fell into a sadness, then into a fast,
Thence to a watch, thence into a weakness,
Thence to a lightness, and by this declension,
Into the madness wherein now he raves,
And all we mourn for.

Claudius, King of Denmark.
                  Do you think 'tis this?

Getrude, Queen of Denmark.
It may be, very like.

Polonius.
Hath there been such a time—I would fain know that—
That I have positively said, "'Tis so,"
When it prov'd otherwise?

Claudius, King of Denmark.
                  Not that I know.

Polonius.

Points to his head and shoulder.

Take this from this, if this be otherwise.
If circumstances lead me, I will find
Where truth is hid, though it were hid indeed
Within the centre.

Claudius, King of Denmark.
                  How may we try it further?

Polonius.
You know sometimes he walks four hours together
Here in the lobby.

Getrude, Queen of Denmark.
                  So he does indeed.

Polonius.
At such a time I'll loose my daughter to him.
Be you and I behind an arras then,
Mark the encounter: if he love her not,
And be not from his reason fall'n thereon,
Let me be no assistant for a state,
But keep a farm and carters.

Claudius, King of Denmark.
                  We will try it.

Enter Hamlet reading on a book.

Getrude, Queen of Denmark.
But look where sadly the poor wretch comes reading.

Polonius.
Away, I do beseech you, both away.
I'll board him presently.

Exeunt King and Queen.

                        O, give me leave,
How does my good Lord Hamlet?

Hamlet.
Well, God-a-mercy.

Polonius.
Do you know me, my lord?

Hamlet.
Excellent well, you are a fishmonger.

Polonius.
Not I, my lord.

Hamlet.
Then I would you were so honest a man.

Polonius.
Honest, my lord?

Hamlet.
Ay, sir, to be honest, as this world goes, is to be one man pick'd out of ten thousand.

Polonius.
That's very true, my lord.

Hamlet.
For if the sun breed maggots in a dead dog, being a good kissing carrion—Have you a daughter?

Polonius.
I have, my lord.

Hamlet.
Let her not walk i' th' sun. Conception is a blessing, but as your daughter may conceive, friend, look to't.

Polonius.

Aside.

How say you by that? Still harping on my daughter. Yet he knew me not at first, 'a said I was a fishmonger. 'A is far gone. And truly in my youth I suff'red much extremity for love—very near this. I'll speak to him again.—What do you read, my lord?

Hamlet.
Words, words, words.

Polonius.
What is the matter, my lord?

Hamlet.
Between who?

Polonius.
I mean, the matter that you read, my lord.

Hamlet.
Slanders, sir; for the satirical rogue says here that old men have grey beards, that their faces are wrinkled, their eyes purging thick amber and plum-tree gum, and that they have a plentiful lack of wit, together with most weak hams; all which, sir, though I most powerfully and potently believe, yet I hold it not honesty to have it thus set down, for yourself, sir, shall grow old as I am, if like a crab you could go backward.

Polonius.

Aside.

Though this be madness, yet there is method in't.—Will you walk out of the air, my lord?

Hamlet.
Into my grave.

Polonius.
Indeed that's out of the air.

Aside.

How pregnant sometimes his replies are! A happiness that often madness hits on, which reason and sanity could not so prosperously be deliver'd of. I will leave him, and suddenly contrive the means of meeting between him and my daughter.—My lord, I will take my leave of you.

Hamlet.
You cannot take from me any thing that I will not more willingly part withal—except my life, except my life, except my life.

Polonius.
Fare you well, my lord.

Hamlet.
These tedious old fools!

Enter Guildenstern and Rosencrantz.

Polonius.
You go to seek the Lord Hamlet, there he is.

Rosencrantz.

To Polonius.

God save you, sir!

Exit Polonius.

Guildenstern.
My honor'd lord!

Rosencrantz.
My most dear lord!

Hamlet.
My excellent good friends! How dost thou, Guildenstern? Ah, Rosencrantz! Good lads, how do you both?

Rosencrantz.
As the indifferent children of the earth.

Guildenstern.
Happy, in that we are not over-happy, on Fortune's cap we are not the very button.

Hamlet.
Nor the soles of her shoe?

Rosencrantz.
Neither, my lord.

Hamlet.
Then you live about her waist, or in the middle of her favors?

Guildenstern.
Faith, her privates we.

Hamlet.
In the secret parts of Fortune? O, most true, she is a strumpet. What news?

Rosencrantz.
None, my lord, but the world's grown honest.

Hamlet.
Then is doomsday near. But your news is not true. Let me question more in particular. What have you, my good friends, deserv'd at the hands of Fortune, that she sends you to prison hither?

Guildenstern.
Prison, my lord?

Hamlet.
Denmark's a prison.

Rosencrantz.
Then is the world one.

Hamlet.
A goodly one, in which there are many confines, wards, and dungeons, Denmark being one o' th' worst.

Rosencrantz.
We think not so, my lord.

Hamlet.
Why then 'tis none to you; for there is nothing either good or bad, but thinking makes it so. To me it is a prison.

Rosencrantz.
Why then your ambition makes it one. 'Tis too narrow for your mind.

Hamlet.
O God, I could be bounded in a nutshell, and count myself a king of infinite space—were it not that I have bad dreams.

Guildenstern.
Which dreams indeed are ambition, for the very substance of the ambitious is merely the shadow of a dream.

Hamlet.
A dream itself is but a shadow.

Rosencrantz.
Truly, and I hold ambition of so airy and light a quality that it is but a shadow's shadow.

Hamlet.
Then are our beggars bodies, and our monarchs and outstretch'd heroes the beggars' shadows. Shall we to th' court? For, by my fay, I cannot reason.

Both Rosencrantz and Guildenstern.
We'll wait upon you.

Hamlet.
No such matter. I will not sort you with the rest of my servants; for to speak to you like an honest man, I am most dreadfully attended. But in the beaten way of friendship, what make you at Elsinore?

Rosencrantz.
To visit you, my lord, no other occasion.

Hamlet.
Beggar that I am, I am even poor in thanks—but I thank you, and sure, dear friends, my thanks are too dear a halfpenny. Were you not sent for? Is it your own inclining? Is it a free visitation? Come, come, deal justly with me. Come, come—nay, speak.

Guildenstern.
What should we say, my lord?

Hamlet.
Any thing but to th' purpose. You were sent for, and there is a kind of confession in your looks, which your modesties have not craft enough to color. I know the good King and Queen have sent for you.

Rosencrantz.
To what end, my lord?

Hamlet.
That you must teach me. But let me conjure you, by the rights of our fellowship, by the consonancy of our youth, by the obligation of our ever-preserv'd love, and by what more dear a better proposer can charge you withal, be even and direct with me, whether you were sent for or no!

Rosencrantz.
Aside to Guildenstern.
What say you?

Hamlet.
Aside.
Nay then I have an eye of you!—If you love me, hold not off.

Guildenstern.
My lord, we were sent for.

Hamlet.
I will tell you why, so shall my anticipation prevent your discovery, and your secrecy to the King and Queen moult no feather. I have of late—but wherefore I know not—lost all my mirth, forgone all custom of exercises; and indeed it goes so heavily with my disposition, that this goodly frame, the earth, seems to me a sterile promontory; this most excellent canopy, the air, look you, this brave o'erhanging firmament, this majestical roof fretted with golden fire, why, it appeareth nothing to me but a foul and pestilent congregation of vapors. What a piece of work is a man, how noble in reason, how infinite in faculties, in form and moving, how express and admirable in action, how like an angel in apprehension, how like a god! The beauty of the world; the paragon of animals; and yet to me what is this quintessence of dust? Man delights not me—nor women neither, though by your smiling you seem to say so.

Rosencrantz.
My lord, there was no such stuff in my thoughts.

Hamlet.
Why did ye laugh then, when I said, "Man delights not me"?

Rosencrantz.
To think, my lord, if you delight not in man, what lenten entertainment the players shall receive from you. We coted them on the way, and hither are they coming to offer you service.

Hamlet.
He that plays the king shall be welcome—his Majesty shall have tribute on me, the adventurous knight shall use his foil and target, the lover shall not sigh gratis, the humorous man shall end his part in peace, the clown shall make those laugh whose lungs are tickle a' th' sere, and the lady shall say her mind freely, or the blank verse shall halt for't. What players are they?

Rosencrantz.
Even those you were wont to take such delight in, the tragedians of the city.

Hamlet.
How chances it they travel? Their residence, both in reputation and profit, was better both ways.

Rosencrantz.
I think their inhibition comes by the means of the late innovation.

Hamlet.
Do they hold the same estimation they did when I was in the city? Are they so follow'd?

Rosencrantz.
No indeed are they not.

Hamlet.
How comes it? Do they grow rusty?

Rosencrantz.
Ay, their endeavor keeps in the wonted pace; but there is, sir, an aery of children, little eyases, that cry out on the top of question, and are most tyrannically clapp'd for't. These are now the fashion, and so berattle the common stages—so they call them—that many wearing rapiers are afraid of goose-quills and dare scarce come thither.

Hamlet.
What, are they children? Who maintains 'em? How are they escoted? Will they pursue the quality no longer than they can sing? Will they not say afterwards, if they should grow themselves to common players (as it is most like, if their means are no better), their writers do them wrong, to make them exclaim against their own succession?

Rosencrantz.
Faith, there has been much to do on both sides, and the nation holds it no sin to tarre them to controversy. There was for a while no money bid for argument, unless the poet and the player went to cuffs in the question.

Hamlet.
Is't possible?

Guildenstern.
O, there has been much throwing about of brains.

Hamlet.
Do the boys carry it away?

Rosencrantz.
Ay, that they do, my lord—Hercules and his load too.

Hamlet.
It is not very strange, for my uncle is King of Denmark, and those that would make mouths at him while my father liv'd, give twenty, forty, fifty, a hundred ducats a-piece for his picture in little. 'Sblood, there is something in this more than natural, if philosophy could find it out.

A flourish for the Players.

Guildenstern.
There are the players.

Hamlet.
Gentlemen, you are welcome to Elsinore. Your hands, come then: th' appurtance of welcome is fashion and ceremony. Let me comply with you in this garb, lest my extent to the players, which, I tell you, must show fairly outwards, should more appear like entertainment than yours. You are welcome; but my uncle-father and aunt-mother are deceiv'd.

Guildenstern.
In what, my dear lord?

Hamlet.
I am but mad north-north-west. When the wind is southerly I know a hawk from a hand-saw.

Enter Polonius.

Polonius.
Well be with you, gentlemen!

Hamlet.

Aside to them.

Hark you, Guildenstern, and you too—at each ear a hearer—that great baby you see there is not yet out of his swaddling-clouts.

Rosencrantz.
Happily he is the second time come to them, for they say an old man is twice a child.

Hamlet.
I will prophesy, he comes to tell me of the players, mark it.

Aloud.

You say right, sir, a' Monday morning, 'twas then indeed.

Polonius.
My lord, I have news to tell you.

Hamlet.
My lord, I have news to tell you. When Roscius was an actor in Rome—

Polonius.
The actors are come hither, my lord.

Hamlet.
Buzz, buzz!

Polonius.
Upon my honor—

Hamlet.
"Then came each actor on his ass"—

Polonius.
The best actors in the world, either for tragedy, comedy, history, pastoral, pastoral-comical, historical-pastoral, tragical-historical, tragical-comical-historical-pastoral scene individable, or poem unlimited; Seneca cannot be too heavy, nor Plautus too light, for the law of writ and the liberty: these are the only men.

Hamlet.
O Jephthah, judge of Israel, what a treasure hadst thou!

Polonius.
What a treasure had he, my lord?

Hamlet.
Why—
"One fair daughter, and no more,
    The which he loved passing well."

Polonius.

Aside.

Still on my daughter.

Hamlet.
Am I not i' th' right, old Jephthah?

Polonius.
If you call me Jephthah, my lord, I have a daughter that I love passing well.

Hamlet.
Nay, that follows not.

Polonius.
What follows then, my lord?

Hamlet.
Why—
"As by lot, God wot,"
And then, you know,
"It came to pass, as most like it was"—
The first row of the pious chanson will show you more, for look where my abridgement comes.

Enter the Players, four or five.

You are welcome, masters, welcome all. I am glad to see thee well. Welcome, good friends. O, old friend! Why, thy face is valanc'd since I saw thee last; com'st thou to beard me in Denmark? What, my young lady and mistress! By' lady, your ladyship is nearer to heaven than when I saw you last, by the altitude of a chopine. Pray God your voice, like a piece of uncurrent gold, be not crack'd within the ring. Masters, you are all welcome. We'll e'en to't like French falc'ners—fly at any thing we see; we'll have a speech straight. Come give us a taste of your quality, come, a passionate speech.

First Player (Player King).
What speech, my good lord?

Hamlet.
I heard thee speak me a speech once, but it was never acted, or if it was, not above once; for the play, I remember, pleas'd not the million, 'twas caviary to the general, but it was—as I receiv'd it, and others, whose judgments in such matters cried in the top of mine—an excellent play, well digested in the scenes, set down with as much modesty as cunning. I remember one said there were no sallets in the lines to make the matter savory, nor no matter in the phrase that might indict the author of affection, but call'd it an honest method, as wholesome as sweet, and by very much more handsome than fine. One speech in't I chiefly lov'd, 'twas Aeneas' tale to Dido, and thereabout of it especially when he speaks of Priam's slaughter. If it live in your memory, begin at this line—let me see, let me see:
"The rugged Pyrrhus, like th' Hyrcanian beast—"
'Tis not so, it begins with Pyrrhus:
"The rugged Pyrrhus, he whose sable arms,
Black as his purpose, did the night resemble
When he lay couched in th' ominous horse,
Hath now this dread and black complexion smear'd

Act 2, Scene 2

With heraldry more dismal: head to foot
Now is he total gules, horridly trick'd
With blood of fathers, mothers, daughters, sons,
Bak'd and impasted with the parching streets,
That lend a tyrannous and a damned light
To their lord's murder. Roasted in wrath and fire,
And thus o'er-sized with coagulate gore,
With eyes like carbuncles, the hellish Pyrrhus
Old grandsire Priam seeks."
So proceed you.

Polonius.
'Fore God, my lord, well spoken, with good accent and good discretion.

First Player (Player King).
"Anon he finds him
Striking too short at Greeks. His antique sword,
Rebellious to his arm, lies where it falls,
Repugnant to command. Unequal match'd,
Pyrrhus at Priam drives, in rage strikes wide,
But with the whiff and wind of his fell sword
Th' unnerved father falls. Then senseless Ilium,
Seeming to feel this blow, with flaming top
Stoops to his base, and with a hideous crash
Takes prisoner Pyrrhus' ear; for lo his sword,
Which was declining on the milky head
Of reverent Priam, seem'd i' th' air to stick.
So as a painted tyrant Pyrrhus stood
And, like a neutral to his will and matter,
Did nothing.
But as we often see, against some storm,
A silence in the heavens, the rack stand still,
The bold winds speechless, and the orb below
As hush as death, anon the dreadful thunder
Doth rend the region; so after Pyrrhus' pause,
A roused vengeance sets him new a-work,
And never did the Cyclops' hammers fall
On Mars's armor forg'd for proof eterne
With less remorse than Pyrrhus' bleeding sword
Now falls on Priam.
Out, out, thou strumpet Fortune! All you gods,
In general synod take away her power!
Break all the spokes and fellies from her wheel,
And bowl the round nave down the hill of heaven
As low as to the fiends!"

Polonius.
This is too long.

Hamlet.
It shall to the barber's with your beard. Prithee say on, he's for a jig or a tale of bawdry, or he sleeps. Say on, come to Hecuba.

First Player (Player King).
"But who, ah woe, had seen the mobled queen"—

Hamlet.
"The mobled queen"?

Polonius.
That's good, "mobled queen" is good.

First Player (Player King).
"Run barefoot up and down, threat'ning the flames
With bisson rheum, a clout upon that head
Where late the diadem stood, and for a robe,
About her lank and all o'er-teemed loins,
A blanket, in the alarm of fear caught up—
Who this had seen, with tongue in venom steep'd,
'Gainst Fortune's state would treason have pronounc'd.
But if the gods themselves did see her then,
When she saw Pyrrhus make malicious sport
In mincing with his sword her husband's limbs,
The instant burst of clamor that she made,
Unless things mortal move them not at all,
Would have made milch the burning eyes of heaven,
And passion in the gods."

Polonius.
Look whe'er he has not turn'd his color and has tears in 's eyes. Prithee no more.

Hamlet.
'Tis well, I'll have thee speak out the rest of this soon. Good my lord, will you see the players well bestow'd? Do you hear, let them be well us'd, for they are the abstract and brief chronicles of the time. After your death you were better have a bad epitaph than their ill report while you live.

Polonius.
My lord, I will use them according to their desert.

Hamlet.
God's bodkin, man, much better: use every man after his desert, and who shall scape whipping? Use them after your own honor and dignity—the less they deserve, the more merit is in your bounty. Take them in.

Polonius.
Come, sirs.

Exit.

Hamlet.
Follow him, friends, we'll hear a play tomorrow.

Exeunt all the Players but the First.

Dost thou hear me, old friend? Can you play "The Murder of Gonzago"?

First Player (Player King).
Ay, my lord.

Hamlet.
We'll ha't tomorrow night. You could for need study a speech of some dozen lines, or sixteen lines, which I would set down and insert in't, could you not?

First Player (Player King).
Ay, my lord.

Hamlet.
Very well. Follow that lord, and look you mock him not.

Exit First Player.

My good friends, I'll leave you till night. You are welcome to Elsinore.

Rosencrantz.
Good my lord!

Hamlet.
Ay so, God buy to you.

Exeunt Rosencrantz and Guildenstern.

                Now I am alone.
O, what a rogue and peasant slave am I!
Is it not monstrous that this player here,
But in a fiction, in a dream of passion,
Could force his soul so to his own conceit
That from her working all the visage wann'd,
Tears in his eyes, distraction in his aspect,
A broken voice, an' his whole function suiting
With forms to his conceit? And all for nothing,
For Hecuba!
What's Hecuba to him, or he to Hecuba,
That he should weep for her? What would he do
Had he the motive and the cue for passion
That I have? He would drown the stage with tears,
And cleave the general ear with horrid speech,
Make mad the guilty, and appall the free,
Confound the ignorant, and amaze indeed
The very faculties of eyes and ears. Yet I,
A dull and muddy-mettled rascal, peak
Like John-a-dreams, unpregnant of my cause,
And can say nothing; no, not for a king,
Upon whose property and most dear life
A damn'd defeat was made. Am I a coward?
Who calls me villain, breaks my pate across,
Plucks off my beard and blows it in my face,
Tweaks me by the nose, gives me the lie i' th' throat
As deep as to the lungs? Who does me this?
Hah, 'swounds, I should take it; for it cannot be
But I am pigeon-liver'd, and lack gall
To make oppression bitter, or ere this
I should 'a' fatted all the region kites
With this slave's offal. Bloody, bawdy villain!
Remorseless, treacherous, lecherous, kindless villain!
Why, what an ass am I! This is most brave,
That I, the son of a dear father murdered,
Prompted to my revenge by heaven and hell,
Must like a whore unpack my heart with words,
And fall a-cursing like a very drab,
A stallion. Fie upon't, foh!
About, my brains! Hum—I have heard
That guilty creatures sitting at a play
Have by the very cunning of the scene
Been struck so to the soul, that presently
They have proclaim'd their malefactions:
For murder, though it have no tongue, will speak
With most miraculous organ. I'll have these players
Play something like the murder of my father
Before mine uncle. I'll observe his looks,
I'll tent him to the quick. If 'a do blench,
I know my course. The spirit that I have seen
May be a dev'l, and the dev'l hath power
T' assume a pleasing shape, yea, and perhaps,
Out of my weakness and my melancholy,
As he is very potent with such spirits,
Abuses me to damn me. I'll have grounds
More relative than this—the play's the thing
Wherein I'll catch the conscience of the king.

Exit.

Act 3
Scene 1

Elsinore. A room in Elsinore castle.

(King; Queen; Polonius; Ophelia; Rosencrantz; Guildenstern; Lords; Hamlet)

Guildenstern and Rosencrantz report on their activity to the King and Queen and Polonius, but cannot give them an explanation for his behavior. The King and Polonius have sent for Hamlet, and they hide behind a tapestry while leaving Ophelia supposedly reading a prayer-book, to observe the encounter. The King is hiding an uneasy conscience. Hamlet enters, thinking on death, suicide and the afterlife. He fears that conscience turns people into cowards. Seeing Ophelia, he approaches her. She tries to give him back all the letters and gifts he sent her. He turns cold and begins questioning her honesty, and soon whips himself into a rage, insulting her dreadfully, accusing her of hypocrisy, and telling her that he never loved her. He rails against marriage. Ophelia is distraught. Polonius still thinks that love is at the root of his behavior, but Claudies spies something darker, and resolves to send him to England as an ambassador to collect tribute, in the hopes that the change will do him good. Polonius suggests that Hamlet should have a talk with his mother, in the hopes that he may tell her what is troubling; Polonius offers to spy on that meeting, too.

Enter King, Queen, Polonius, Ophelia, Rosencrantz, Guildenstern, Lords.

Claudius, King of Denmark.
And can you by no drift of conference
Get from him why he puts on this confusion,
Grating so harshly all his days of quiet
With turbulent and dangerous lunacy?

Rosencrantz.
He does confess he feels himself distracted,
But from what cause 'a will by no means speak.

Guildenstern.
Nor do we find him forward to be sounded,
But with a crafty madness keeps aloof
When we would bring him on to some confession
Of his true state.

Getrude, Queen of Denmark.
     Did he receive you well?

Rosencrantz.
Most like a gentleman.

Guildenstern.
But with much forcing of his disposition.

Rosencrantz.
Niggard of question, but of our demands
Most free in his reply.

Getrude, Queen of Denmark.
     Did you assay him
To any pastime?

Rosencrantz.
Madam, it so fell out that certain players
We o'erraught on the way; of these we told him,
And there did seem in him a kind of joy
To hear of it. They are here about the court,
And as I think, they have already order
This night to play before him.

Polonius.
     'Tis most true,
And he beseech'd me to entreat your Majesties
To hear and see the matter.

Claudius, King of Denmark.
With all my heart, and it doth much content me
To hear him so inclin'd.
Good gentlemen, give him a further edge,
And drive his purpose into these delights.

Rosencrantz.
We shall, my lord.

Exeunt Rosencrantz and Guildenstern.

Claudius, King of Denmark.
     Sweet Gertrude, leave us two,
For we have closely sent for Hamlet hither,
That he, as 'twere by accident, may here
Affront Ophelia. Her father and myself,
We'll so bestow ourselves that, seeing unseen,
We may of their encounter frankly judge,
And gather by him, as he is behav'd,
If't be th' affliction of his love or no
That thus he suffers for.

Getrude, Queen of Denmark.
     I shall obey you.
And for your part, Ophelia, I do wish
That your good beauties be the happy cause

Of Hamlet's wildness. So shall I hope your virtues
Will bring him to his wonted way again,
To both your honors.

Ophelia.
                              Madam, I wish it may.

Exit Queen.

Polonius.
Ophelia, walk you here.—Gracious, so please you,
We will bestow ourselves.

To Ophelia.

Read on this book,
That show of such an exercise may color
Your loneliness. We are oft to blame in this—
'Tis too much prov'd—that with devotion's visage
And pious action we do sugar o'er
The devil himself.

Claudius, King of Denmark.

Aside.

                            O, 'tis too true!
How smart a lash that speech doth give my conscience!
The harlot's cheek, beautied with plast'ring art,
Is not more ugly to the thing that helps it
Than is my deed to my most painted word.
O heavy burden!

Polonius.
I hear him coming. Withdraw, my lord.

Exeunt King and Polonius.
Enter Hamlet.

Hamlet.
To be, or not to be, that is the question:
Whether 'tis nobler in the mind to suffer
The slings and arrows of outrageous fortune,
Or to take arms against a sea of troubles,
And by opposing, end them. To die, to sleep—
No more, and by a sleep to say we end
The heart-ache and the thousand natural shocks
That flesh is heir to; 'tis a consummation
Devoutly to be wish'd. To die, to sleep—
To sleep, perchance to dream—ay, there's the rub,
For in that sleep of death what dreams may come,
When we have shuffled off this mortal coil,
Must give us pause; there's the respect
That makes calamity of so long life:
For who would bear the whips and scorns of time,
Th' oppressor's wrong, the proud man's contumely,
The pangs of despis'd love, the law's delay,
The insolence of office, and the spurns
That patient merit of th' unworthy takes,
When he himself might his quietus make
With a bare bodkin; who would fardels bear,
To grunt and sweat under a weary life,
But that the dread of something after death,
The undiscover'd country, from whose bourn
No traveler returns, puzzles the will,
And makes us rather bear those ills we have,
Than fly to others that we know not of?
Thus conscience does make cowards of us all,
And thus the native hue of resolution
Is sicklied o'er with the pale cast of thought,
And enterprises of great pitch and moment
With this regard their currents turn awry,
And lose the name of action.—Soft you now,
The fair Ophelia. Nymph, in thy orisons
Be all my sins rememb'red.

Ophelia.
                          Good my lord,
How does your honor for this many a day?

Hamlet.
I humbly thank you, well, well, well.

Ophelia.
My lord, I have remembrances of yours
That I have longed long to redeliver.
I pray you now receive them.

Hamlet.
                          No, not I,
I never gave you aught.

Ophelia.
My honor'd lord, you know right well you did,
And with them words of so sweet breath compos'd
As made these things more rich. Their perfume lost,
Take these again, for to the noble mind
Rich gifts wax poor when givers prove unkind.
There, my lord.

Hamlet.
Ha, ha! Are you honest?

Ophelia.
My lord?

Hamlet.
Are you fair?

Ophelia.
What means your lordship?

Hamlet.
That if you be honest and fair, your honesty should admit no discourse to your beauty.

Ophelia.
Could beauty, my lord, have better commerce than with honesty?

Hamlet.
Ay, truly, for the power of beauty will sooner transform honesty from what it is to a bawd than the force of honesty can translate beauty into his likeness. This was sometime a paradox, but now the time gives it proof. I did love you once.

Ophelia.
Indeed, my lord, you made me believe so.

Hamlet.
You should not have believ'd me, for virtue cannot so inoculate our old stock but we shall relish of it. I lov'd you not.

Ophelia.
I was the more deceiv'd.

Hamlet.
Get thee to a nunn'ry, why wouldst thou be a breeder of sinners? I am myself indifferent honest, but yet I could accuse me of such things that it were better my mother had not borne me: I am very proud, revengeful, ambitious, with more offenses at my beck than I have thoughts to put them in, imagination to give them shape, or time to act them in. What should such fellows as I do crawling between earth and heaven? We are arrant knaves, believe none of us. Go thy ways to a nunn'ry. Where's your father?

Ophelia.
At home, my lord.

Hamlet.
Let the doors be shut upon him, that he may play the fool no where but in 's own house. Farewell.

Ophelia.
O, help him, you sweet heavens!

Hamlet.
If thou dost marry, I'll give thee this plague for thy dowry: be thou as chaste as ice, as pure as snow, thou shalt not escape calumny. Get thee to a nunn'ry, farewell. Or if thou wilt needs marry, marry a fool, for wise men know well enough what monsters you make of them. To a nunn'ry, go, and quickly too. Farewell.

Ophelia.
Heavenly powers, restore him!

Hamlet.
I have heard of your paintings, well enough. God hath given you one face, and you make yourselves another. You jig and amble, and you lisp, you nickname God's creatures and make your wantonness your ignorance. Go to, I'll no more on't, it hath made me mad. I say we will have no more marriage. Those that are married already (all but one) shall live, the rest shall keep as they are. To a nunn'ry, go.

Exit.

Ophelia.
O, what a noble mind is here o'erthrown!
The courtier's, soldier's, scholar's, eye, tongue, sword,
Th' expectation and rose of the fair state,
The glass of fashion and the mould of form,
Th' observ'd of all observers, quite, quite down!
And I, of ladies most deject and wretched,
That suck'd the honey of his music vows,
Now see that noble and most sovereign reason
Like sweet bells jangled out of time, and harsh;
That unmatch'd form and stature of blown youth
Blasted with ecstasy. O, woe is me
T' have seen what I have seen, see what I see!

Ophelia withdraws.
Enter King and Polonius.

Claudius, King of Denmark.
Love? His affections do not that way tend,
Nor what he spake, though it lack'd form a little,
Was not like madness. There's something in his soul
O'er which his melancholy sits on brood,
And I do doubt the hatch and the disclose
Will be some danger; which for to prevent,
I have in quick determination
Thus set it down: he shall with speed to England
For the demand of our neglected tribute.

Haply the seas, and countries different,
With variable objects, shall expel
This something-settled matter in his heart,
Whereon his brains still beating puts him thus
From fashion of himself. What think you on't?

Polonius.
It shall do well; but yet do I believe
The origin and commencement of his grief
Sprung from neglected love.

Ophelia comes forward.

       How now, Ophelia?
You need not tell us what Lord Hamlet said,
We heard it all. My lord, do as you please,
But if you hold it fit, after the play
Let his queen-mother all alone entreat him
To show his grief. Let her be round with him,
And I'll be plac'd (so please you) in the ear
Of all their conference. If she find him not,
To England send him, or confine him where
Your wisdom best shall think.

Claudius, King of Denmark.
       It shall be so.
Madness in great ones must not unwatch'd go.

Exeunt.

Scene 2

Elsinore. A hall in Elsinore castle.

(Hamlet; Polonius; Guildenstern; Rosencrantz; Horatio; King; Queen; Polonius; Ophelia; Rosencrantz; Guildenstern; Lords; Guard; First Player (Player King); Player Queen; Prologue; Lucianus)

As the players prepare for the play, Hamlet gives them advice. He explains the plan behind his choice of play to Horatio, and asks him to keep an eye on the King as well. The court enters for the performance. Hamlet refuses to sit by his mother, preferring to sit by Ophelia and speak lewdly to her. The play opens with a dumb show with a King and Queen protesting love before he settles down for a nap and is poisoned in his sleep, his murderer winning the Queen's love with gifts. The play itself follows the same plot. When it reaches the poisoning, which mirrors the one the ghost spoke of, Claudius rises and leaves, bringing an end to the production. Hamlet and Horatio are convinced that the ghost's story of murder is true and that Claudius is guilty. Guildenstern and Rosencrantz brings Hamlet an order to go visit his mother, and ask him once again to tell them what the matter is, but he refuses, accusing them of attempting to play him like an instrument. Polonius appears, reinforcing the summons to the Queen. Hamlet promises he will go. He realizes that he is in a bloodthirsty mood, and forces himself to promise that he will not use any violence against his mother.

Enter Hamlet and three of the Players.

Hamlet.
Speak the speech, I pray you, as I pronounc'd it to you, trippingly on the tongue, but if you mouth it, as many of our players do, I had as lief the town-crier spoke my lines. Nor do not saw the air too much with your hand, thus, but use all gently, for in the very torrent, tempest, and, as I may say, whirlwind of your passion, you must acquire and beget a temperance that may give it smoothness. O, it offends me to the soul to hear a robustious periwig-pated fellow tear a passion to totters, to very rags, to spleet the ears of the groundlings, who for the most part are capable of nothing but inexplicable dumb shows and noise. I would have such a fellow whipt for o'erdoing Termagant, it out-Herods Herod, pray you avoid it.

First Player (Player King).
I warrant your honor.

Hamlet.
Be not too tame neither, but let your own discretion be your tutor. Suit the action to the word, the word to the action, with this special observance, that you o'erstep not the modesty of nature: for any thing so o'erdone is from the purpose of playing, whose end, both at the first and now, was and is, to hold as 'twere the mirror up to nature: to show virtue her feature, scorn her own image, and the very age and body of the time his form and pressure. Now this overdone, or come tardy off, though it makes the unskillful laugh, cannot but make the judicious grieve; the censure of which one must in your allowance o'erweigh a whole theatre of others. O, there be players that I have seen play—and heard others praise, and that highly—not to speak it profanely, that, neither having th' accent of Christians nor the gait of Christian, pagan, nor man, have so strutted and bellow'd that I have thought some of Nature's journeymen had made men, and not made them well, they imitated humanity so abominably.

Act 3, Scene 2

First Player (Player King).
I hope we have reform'd that indifferently with us, sir.

Hamlet.
O, reform it altogether. And let those that play your clowns speak no more than is set down for them, for there be of them that will themselves laugh to set on some quantity of barren spectators to laugh too, though in the mean time some necessary question of the play be then to be consider'd. That's villainous, and shows a most pitiful ambition in the fool that uses it. Go make you ready.

Exeunt Players.
Enter Polonius, Guildenstern, and Rosencrantz.

How now, my lord? Will the King hear this piece of work?

Polonius.
And the Queen too, and that presently.

Hamlet.
Bid the players make haste.

Exit Polonius.

Will you two help to hasten them?

Rosencrantz.
Ay, my lord.

Exeunt they two.

Hamlet.
What ho, Horatio!

Enter Horatio.

Horatio.
Here, sweet lord, at your service.

Hamlet.
Horatio, thou art e'en as just a man
As e'er my conversation cop'd withal.

Horatio.
O my dear lord—

Hamlet.
              Nay, do not think I flatter,
For what advancement may I hope from thee
That no revenue hast but thy good spirits
To feed and clothe thee? Why should the poor be flatter'd?
No, let the candied tongue lick absurd pomp,
And crook the pregnant hinges of the knee
Where thrift may follow fawning. Dost thou hear?
Since my dear soul was mistress of her choice
And could of men distinguish her election,
Sh' hath seal'd thee for herself, for thou hast been
As one in suff'ring all that suffers nothing,
A man that Fortune's buffets and rewards
Hast ta'en with equal thanks; and blest are those
Whose blood and judgement are so well co-meddled,
That they are not a pipe for Fortune's finger
To sound what stop she please. Give me that man
That is not passion's slave, and I will wear him
In my heart's core, ay, in my heart of heart,
As I do thee. Something too much of this.
There is a play tonight before the King,
One scene of it comes near the circumstance
Which I have told thee of my father's death.
I prithee, when thou seest that act afoot,
Even with the very comment of thy soul
Observe my uncle. If his occulted guilt
Do not itself unkennel in one speech,
It is a damned ghost that we have seen,
And my imaginations are as foul
As Vulcan's stithy. Give him heedful note,
For I mine eyes will rivet to his face,
And after we will both our judgements join
In censure of his seeming.

Horatio.
              Well, my lord.
If 'a steal aught the whilst this play is playing,
And scape detecting, I will pay the theft.

Sound a flourish. Danish march. Enter Trumpets and Kettle-drums, King, Queen, Polonius, Ophelia, Rosencrantz, Guildenstern, and other Lords attendant, with his Guard carrying torches.

Hamlet.
They are coming to the play. I must be idle; Get you a place.

Claudius, King of Denmark.
How fares our cousin Hamlet?

Hamlet.
Excellent, i' faith, of the chameleon's dish: I eat the air, promise-cramm'd—you cannot feed capons so.

Claudius, King of Denmark.
I have nothing with this answer, Hamlet, these words are not mine.

Hamlet.
No, nor mine now.

To Polonius.

My lord, you play'd once i' th' university, you say?

Polonius.
That did I, my lord, and was accounted a good actor.

Hamlet.
What did you enact?

Polonius.
I did enact Julius Caesar. I was kill'd i' th' Capitol; Brutus kill'd me.

Hamlet.
It was a brute part of him to kill so capital a calf there. Be the players ready?

Rosencrantz.
Ay, my lord, they stay upon your patience.

Getrude, Queen of Denmark.
Come hither, my dear Hamlet, sit by me.

Hamlet.
No, good mother, here's metal more attractive.

Lying down at Ophelia's feet.

Polonius.

To the King.

O ho, do you mark that?

Hamlet.
Lady, shall I lie in your lap?

Ophelia.
No, my lord.

Hamlet.
I mean, my head upon your lap?

Ophelia.
Ay, my lord.

Hamlet.
Do you think I meant country matters?

Ophelia.
I think nothing, my lord.

Hamlet.
That's a fair thought to lie between maids' legs.

Ophelia.
What is, my lord?

Hamlet.
Nothing.

Ophelia.
You are merry, my lord.

Hamlet.
Who, I?

Ophelia.
Ay, my lord.

Hamlet.
O God, your only jig-maker. What should a man do but be merry, for look you how cheerfully my mother looks, and my father died within 's two hours.

Ophelia.
Nay, 'tis twice two months, my lord.

Hamlet.
So long? Nay then let the dev'l wear black, for I'll have a suit of sables. O heavens, die two months ago, and not forgotten yet? Then there's hope a great man's memory may outlive his life half a year, but, by'r lady, 'a must build churches then, or else shall 'a suffer not thinking on, with the hobby-horse, whose epitaph is, "For O, for O, the hobby-horse is forgot."

The trumpets sound.
Dumb show follows. Enter a King and a Queen very lovingly, the Queen embracing him and he her. She kneels and makes show of protestation unto him. He takes her up and declines his head upon her neck. He lies him down upon a bank of flowers. She, seeing him asleep, leaves him. Anon come in another man, takes off his crown, kisses it, pours poison in the sleeper's ears, and leaves him. The Queen returns, finds the King dead, makes passionate action. The pois'ner with some three or four mutes come in again, seem to condole with her. The dead body is carried away. The pois'ner woos the Queen with gifts; she seems harsh and unwilling awhile, but in the end accepts love.
Exeunt.

Ophelia.
What means this, my lord?

Hamlet.
Marry, this' miching mallecho, it means mischief.

Ophelia.
Belike this show imports the argument of the play.

Enter Player Prologue.

Hamlet.
We shall know by this fellow. The players cannot keep counsel, they'll tell all.

Ophelia.
Will 'a tell us what this show meant?

Hamlet.
Ay, or any show that you will show him. Be not you asham'd to show, he'll not shame to tell you what it means.

Ophelia.
You are naught, you are naught. I'll mark the play.

Player Prologue.
For us, and for our tragedy,
Here stooping to your clemency,
We beg your hearing patiently.

Exit.

Hamlet.
Is this a prologue, or the posy of a ring?

Ophelia.
'Tis brief, my lord.

Hamlet.
As woman's love.

Enter two Players, King and Queen.

First Player (Player King).
Full thirty times hath Phoebus' cart gone round
Neptune's salt wash and Tellus' orbed ground,
And thirty dozen moons with borrowed sheen
About the world have times twelve thirties been,
Since love our hearts and Hymen did our hands
Unite comutual in most sacred bands.

Player Queen.
So many journeys may the sun and moon
Make us again count o'er ere love be done!
But woe is me, you are so sick of late,
So far from cheer and from your former state,
That I distrust you. Yet though I distrust,
Discomfort you, my lord, it nothing must,
For women's fear and love hold quantity,
In neither aught, or in extremity.
Now what my love is, proof hath made you know,
And as my love is siz'd, my fear is so.
Where love is great, the littlest doubts are fear;
Where little fears grow great, great love grows there.

First Player (Player King).
Faith, I must leave thee, love, and shortly too;
My operant powers their functions leave to do,
And thou shalt live in this fair world behind,
Honor'd, belov'd, and haply one as kind
For husband shalt thou—

Player Queen.
                O, confound the rest!
Such love must needs be treason in my breast.
In second husband let me be accurs'd!
None wed the second but who kill'd the first.

Hamlet.

Aside.

That's wormwood!

Player Queen.
The instances that second marriage move
Are base respects of thrift, but none of love.
A second time I kill my husband dead,
When second husband kisses me in bed.

First Player (Player King).
I do believe you think what now you speak,
But what we do determine, oft we break.
Purpose is but the slave to memory,
Of violent birth, but poor validity,
Which now, the fruit unripe, sticks on the tree,
But fall unshaken when they mellow be.
Most necessary 'tis that we forget
To pay ourselves what to ourselves is debt.
What to ourselves in passion we propose,
The passion ending, doth the purpose lose.
The violence of either grief or joy
Their own enactures with themselves destroy.
Where joy most revels, grief doth most lament;

Grief joys, joy grieves, on slender accident.
This world is not for aye, nor 'tis not strange
That even our loves should with our fortunes change:
For 'tis a question left us yet to prove,
Whether love lead fortune, or else fortune love.
The great man down, you mark his favorite flies,
The poor advanc'd makes friends of enemies.
And hitherto doth love on fortune tend,
For who not needs shall never lack a friend,
And who in want a hollow friend doth try,
Directly seasons him his enemy.
But orderly to end where I begun,
Our wills and fates do so contrary run
That our devices still are overthrown,
Our thoughts are ours, their ends none of our own:
So think thou wilt no second husband wed,
But die thy thoughts when thy first lord is dead.

Player Queen.
Nor earth to me give food, nor heaven light,
Sport and repose lock from me day and night,
To desperation turn my trust and hope,
An anchor's cheer in prison be my scope!
Each opposite that blanks the face of joy
Meet what I would have well and it destroy!
Both here and hence pursue me lasting strife,
If once I be a widow, ever I be a wife!

Hamlet.
If she should break it now!

First Player (Player King).
'Tis deeply sworn. Sweet, leave me here a while,
My spirits grow dull, and fain I would beguile
The tedious day with sleep.

Sleeps.

Player Queen.
                    Sleep rock thy brain,
And never come mischance between us twain!

Exit.

Hamlet.
Madam, how like you this play?

Getrude, Queen of Denmark.
The lady doth protest too much, methinks.

Hamlet.
O but she'll keep her word.

Claudius, King of Denmark.
Have you heard the argument? Is there no offense in't?

Hamlet.
No, no, they do but jest, poison in jest—no offense i' th' world.

Claudius, King of Denmark.
What do you call the play?

Hamlet.
"The Mouse-trap." Marry, how? Tropically: this play is the image of a murder done in Vienna; Gonzago is the duke's name, his wife, Baptista. You shall see anon. 'Tis a knavish piece of work, but what of that? Your Majesty, and we that have free souls, it touches us not. Let the gall'd jade winch, our withers are unwrung.

Enter Player Lucianus.

This is one Lucianus, nephew to the king.

Ophelia.
You are as good as a chorus, my lord.

Hamlet.
I could interpret between you and your love, if I could see the puppets dallying.

Ophelia.
You are keen, my lord, you are keen.

Hamlet.
It would cost you a groaning to take off mine edge.

Ophelia.
Still better, and worse.

Hamlet.
So you mistake your husbands. Begin, murderer, leave thy damnable faces and begin. Come, the croaking raven doth bellow for revenge.

Player Lucianus.
Thoughts black, hands apt, drugs fit, and time agreeing,
Confederate season, else no creature seeing,
Thou mixture rank, of midnight weeds collected,
With Hecat's ban thrice blasted, thrice infected,
Thy natural magic and dire property
On wholesome life usurps immediately.

Pours the poison in his ears.

Act 3, Scene 2

Hamlet.
'A poisons him i' th' garden for his estate. His name's Gonzago, the story is extant, and written in very choice Italian. You shall see anon how the murderer gets the love of Gonzago's wife.

Ophelia.
The King rises.

Hamlet.
What, frighted with false fire?

Getrude, Queen of Denmark.
How fares my lord?

Polonius.
Give o'er the play.

Claudius, King of Denmark.
Give me some light. Away!

Polonius.
Lights, lights, lights!

Exeunt all but Hamlet and Horatio.

Hamlet.
"Why, let the strucken deer go weep,
　　　　The hart ungalled play,
For some must watch while some must sleep,
　　　　Thus runs the world away."
Would not this, sir, and a forest of feathers—if the rest of my fortunes turn Turk with me—with two Provincial roses on my raz'd shoes, get me a fellowship in a cry of players?

Horatio.
Half a share.

Hamlet.
A whole one, I.
"For thou dost know, O Damon dear,
　　　　This realm dismantled was
Of Jove himself, and now reigns here
　　　　A very, very"—pajock.

Horatio.
You might have rhym'd.

Hamlet.
O good Horatio, I'll take the ghost's word for a thousand pound. Didst perceive?

Horatio.
Very well, my lord.

Hamlet.
Upon the talk of the pois'ning?

Horatio.
I did very well note him.

Hamlet.
Ah, ha! Come, some music! Come, the recorders!
For if the King like not the comedy,
Why then belike he likes it not, perdy.
Come, some music!

Enter Rosencrantz and Guildenstern.

Guildenstern.
Good my lord, vouchsafe me a word with you.

Hamlet.
Sir, a whole history.

Guildenstern.
The King, sir—

Hamlet.
Ay, sir, what of him?

Guildenstern.
Is in his retirement marvelous distemp'red.

Hamlet.
With drink, sir?

Guildenstern.
No, my lord, with choler.

Hamlet.
Your wisdom should show itself more richer to signify this to the doctor, for for me to put him to his purgation would perhaps plunge him into more choler.

Guildenstern.
Good my lord, put your discourse into some frame, and start not so wildly from my affair.

Hamlet.
I am tame, sir. Pronounce.

Guildenstern.
The Queen, your mother, in most great affliction of spirit, hath sent me to you.

Hamlet.
You are welcome.

Guildenstern.
Nay, good my lord, this courtesy is not of the right breed. If it shall please you to make me a wholesome answer, I will do your mother's commandment; if not, your pardon and my return shall be the end of my business.

Hamlet.
Sir, I cannot.

Rosencrantz.
What, my lord?

Hamlet.
Make you a wholesome answer—my wit's diseas'd. But, sir, such answer as I can make, you shall command, or rather, as you say, my mother. Therefore no more, but to the matter: my mother, you say—

Rosencrantz.
Then thus she says: your behavior hath struck her into amazement and admiration.

Hamlet.
O wonderful son, that can so 'stonish a mother! But is there no sequel at the heels of this mother's admiration? Impart.

Rosencrantz.
She desires to speak with you in her closet ere you go to bed.

Hamlet.
We shall obey, were she ten times our mother. Have you any further trade with us?

Rosencrantz.
My lord, you once did love me.

Hamlet.
And do still, by these pickers and stealers.

Rosencrantz.
Good my lord, what is your cause of distemper? You do surely bar the door upon your own liberty if you deny your griefs to your friend.

Hamlet.
Sir, I lack advancement.

Rosencrantz.
How can that be, when you have the voice of the King himself for your succession in Denmark?

Hamlet.
Ay, sir, but "While the grass grows"—the proverb is something musty.

Enter the Players with recorders.

O, the recorders! Let me see one.—To withdraw with you—why do you go about to recover the wind of me, as if you would drive me into a toil?

Guildenstern.
O my lord, if my duty be too bold, my love is too unmannerly.

Hamlet.
I do not well understand that. Will you play upon this pipe?

Guildenstern.
My lord, I cannot.

Hamlet.
I pray you.

Guildenstern.
Believe me, I cannot.

Hamlet.
I do beseech you.

Guildenstern.
I know no touch of it, my lord.

Hamlet.
It is as easy as lying. Govern these ventages with your fingers and thumbs, give it breath with your mouth, and it will discourse most eloquent music. Look you, these are the stops.

Guildenstern.
But these cannot I command to any utt'rance of harmony. I have not the skill.

Hamlet.
Why, look you now, how unworthy a thing you make of me! You would play upon me, you would seem to know my stops, you would pluck out the heart of my mystery, you would sound me from my lowest note to the top of my compass; and there is much music, excellent voice, in this little organ, yet cannot you make it speak. 'Sblood, do you think I am easier to be play'd

Act 3, Scene 3

on than a pipe? Call me what instrument you will, though you fret me, yet you cannot play upon me.

Enter Polonius.

God bless you, sir.

Polonius.
My lord, the Queen would speak with you, and presently.

Hamlet.
Do you see yonder cloud that's almost in shape of a camel?

Polonius.
By th' mass and 'tis, like a camel indeed.

Hamlet.
Methinks it is like a weasel.

Polonius.
It is back'd like a weasel.

Hamlet.
Or like a whale.

Polonius.
Very like a whale.

Hamlet.
Then I will come to my mother by and by.

Aside.

They fool me to the top of my bent.—I will come by and by.

Polonius.
I will say so.

Exit.

Hamlet.
"By and by" is easily said. Leave me, friends.

Exeunt all but Hamlet.

'Tis now the very witching time of night,
When churchyards yawn and hell itself breathes out
Contagion to this world. Now could I drink hot blood,
And do such bitter business as the day
Would quake to look on. Soft, now to my mother.
O heart, lose not thy nature! Let not ever
The soul of Nero enter this firm bosom,
Let me be cruel, not unnatural;

I will speak daggers to her, but use none.
My tongue and soul in this be hypocrites—
How in my words somever she be shent,
To give them seals never my soul consent!

Exit.

Scene 3

Elsinore. A room in Elsinore castle.

(King; Rosencrantz; Guildenstern; Polonius; Hamlet)

Claudius has prepared Hamlet's commission for England, and instructs Rosencrantz and Guildenstern to leave with him and keep an eye on him. Polonius passes by and tells Claudius that he is on his way to hide in the Queen's closet to spy on her meeting with Hamlet. Alone, Claudius reflects on his crime, and is stricken with remorse. He attempts to pray, but cannot bring himself to ask forgiveness while he still enjoys everything he gained by committing the murder. Hamlet, passing by, sees him at prayer and almost kills him, but reflects that if killed at prayer, Claudius will go to heaven, so he decides to wait until Claudius is doing something sinful, in the hopes of sending him straight to hell. Claudius realizes that his prayers are going nowhere — ironically, Hamlet's caution was useless.

Enter King, Rosencrantz, and Guildenstern.

Claudius, King of Denmark.
I like him not, nor stands it safe with us
To let his madness range. Therefore prepare you.
I your commission will forthwith dispatch,
And he to England shall along with you.
The terms of our estate may not endure
Hazard so near 's as doth hourly grow
Out of his brows.

Guildenstern.
                We will ourselves provide.
Most holy and religious fear it is
To keep those many many bodies safe
That live and feed upon your Majesty.

Rosencrantz.
The single and peculiar life is bound
With all the strength and armor of the mind
To keep itself from noyance, but much more
That spirit upon whose weal depends and rests
The lives of many. The cess of majesty

Dies not alone, but like a gulf doth draw
What's near it with it. Or it is a massy wheel
Fix'd on the summit of the highest mount,
To whose huge spokes ten thousand lesser things
Are mortis'd and adjoin'd, which when it falls,
Each small annexment, petty consequence,
Attends the boist'rous ruin. Never alone
Did the King sigh, but with a general groan.

Claudius, King of Denmark.
Arm you, I pray you, to this speedy voyage,
For we will fetters put about this fear,
Which now goes too free-footed.

Rosencrantz.
                    We will haste us.

Exeunt Gentlemen, Rosencrantz and Guildenstern.
Enter Polonius.

Polonius.
My lord, he's going to his mother's closet.
Behind the arras I'll convey myself
To hear the process. I'll warrant she'll tax him home,
And as you said, and wisely was it said,
'Tis meet that some more audience than a mother,
Since nature makes them partial, should o'erhear
The speech, of vantage. Fare you well, my liege,
I'll call upon you ere you go to bed,
And tell you what I know.

Claudius, King of Denmark.
                    Thanks, dear my lord.

Exit Polonius.

O, my offense is rank, it smells to heaven,
It hath the primal eldest curse upon't,
A brother's murder. Pray can I not,
Though inclination be as sharp as will.
My stronger guilt defeats my strong intent,
And, like a man to double business bound,
I stand in pause where I shall first begin,
And both neglect. What if this cursed hand
Were thicker than itself with brother's blood,
Is there not rain enough in the sweet heavens
To wash it white as snow? Whereto serves mercy
But to confront the visage of offense?
And what's in prayer but this twofold force,
To be forestalled ere we come to fall,
Or pardon'd being down? Then I'll look up.
My fault is past, but, O, what form of prayer
Can serve my turn? "Forgive me my foul murder"?
That cannot be, since I am still possess'd
Of those effects for which I did the murder:
My crown, mine own ambition, and my queen.
May one be pardon'd and retain th' offense?
In the corrupted currents of this world
Offense's gilded hand may shove by justice,
And oft 'tis seen the wicked prize itself
Buys out the law, but 'tis not so above:
There is no shuffling, there the action lies
In his true nature, and we ourselves compell'd,
Even to the teeth and forehead of our faults,
To give in evidence. What then? What rests?
Try what repentance can. What can it not?
Yet what can it, when one can not repent?
O wretched state! O bosom black as death!
O limed soul, that struggling to be free
Art more engag'd! Help, angels! Make assay,
Bow, stubborn knees, and heart, with strings of steel,
Be soft as sinews of the new-born babe!
All may be well.

He kneels.
Enter Hamlet.

Hamlet.
Now might I do it pat, now 'a is a-praying;
And now I'll do't—and so 'a goes to heaven,
And so am I reveng'd. That would be scann'd:
A villain kills my father, and for that
I, his sole son, do this same villain send
To heaven.
Why, this is hire and salary, not revenge.
'A took my father grossly, full of bread,
With all his crimes broad blown, as flush as May,
And how his audit stands who knows save heaven?
But in our circumstance and course of thought
'Tis heavy with him. And am I then revenged,
To take him in the purging of his soul,
When he is fit and season'd for his passage?
No!
Up, sword, and know thou a more horrid hent:
When he is drunk asleep, or in his rage,
Or in th' incestuous pleasure of his bed,
At game a-swearing, or about some act
That has no relish of salvation in't—
Then trip him, that his heels may kick at heaven,
And that his soul may be as damn'd and black
As hell, whereto it goes. My mother stays,
This physic but prolongs thy sickly days.

Exit.

Claudius, King of Denmark.

Rising.

My words fly up, my thoughts remain below:
Words without thoughts never to heaven go.

Exit.

Scene 4

Elsinore. The Queen's room in Elsinore castle.

(Queen Gertrude; Polonius; Hamlet; Ghost)

Polonius advises the Queen before hiding behind a tapestry to spy on the meeting. Gertrude attempts to berate Hamlet, but he answers as strongly, even more so, attacking her for marrying his unworthy uncle. He is so wild that she cries out in fear; Polonius calls for help, and Hamlet, thinking it may be the King, kills the man behind the tapestry. He gives Polonius a cold farewell before returning to his attack on the Queen, asking her how she could marry Claudius after having been Old Hamlet's wife, and accuses his uncle of murder. Gertrude tries to get him to stop, but is unsuccessful. The ghost enters to stop Hamlet from harming his mother and to tell him to get a move on with the revenge business. Gertrude cannot see the ghost, and is convinced that Hamlet is truly insane. He begs her to repent and to stop sleeping with Claudius. They recall that he must go to England. Hamlet drags Polonius's body out.

Enter Queen Gertrude and Polonius.

Polonius.
'A will come straight. Look you lay home to him.
Tell him his pranks have been too broad to bear with,
And that your Grace hath screen'd and stood between
Much heat and him. I'll silence me even here;
Pray you be round with him.

Getrude, Queen of Denmark.
I'll warr'nt you, fear me not. Withdraw,
I hear him coming.

Polonius hides behind the arras.
Enter Hamlet.

Hamlet.
Now, mother, what's the matter?

Getrude, Queen of Denmark.
Hamlet, thou hast thy father much offended.

Hamlet.
Mother, you have my father much offended.

Getrude, Queen of Denmark.
Come, come, you answer with an idle tongue.

Hamlet.
Go, go, you question with a wicked tongue.

Getrude, Queen of Denmark.
Why, how now, Hamlet?

Hamlet.
                    What's the matter now?

Getrude, Queen of Denmark.
Have you forgot me?

Hamlet.
                    No, by the rood, not so:
You are the Queen, your husband's brother's wife,
And would it were not so, you are my mother.

Getrude, Queen of Denmark.
Nay, then I'll set those to you that can speak.

Hamlet.
Come, come, and sit you down, you shall not budge;
You go not till I set you up a glass
Where you may see the inmost part of you.

Getrude, Queen of Denmark.
What wilt thou do? Thou wilt not murder me?
Help ho!

Polonius.

Behind.

What ho, help!

Hamlet.

Drawing.

How now? A rat? Dead, for a ducat, dead!

Kills Polonius through the arras.

Polonius.

Behind.

O, I am slain.

Getrude, Queen of Denmark.
                        O me, what hast thou done?

Hamlet.
Nay, I know not, is it the King?

Getrude, Queen of Denmark.
O, what a rash and bloody deed is this!

Hamlet.
A bloody deed! Almost as bad, good mother,
As kill a king, and marry with his brother.

Getrude, Queen of Denmark.
As kill a king!

Hamlet.
                Ay, lady, it was my word.

Parts the arras and discovers Polonius.

Thou wretched, rash, intruding fool, farewell!
I took thee for thy better. Take thy fortune;
Thou find'st to be too busy is some danger.—
Leave wringing of your hands. Peace, sit you down,
And let me wring your heart, for so I shall
If it be made of penetrable stuff,
If damned custom have not brass'd it so
That it be proof and bulwark against sense.

Getrude, Queen of Denmark.
What have I done, that thou dar'st wag thy tongue
In noise so rude against me?

Hamlet.
              Such an act
That blurs the grace and blush of modesty,
Calls virtue hypocrite, takes off the rose
From the fair forehead of an innocent love
And sets a blister there, makes marriage vows
As false as dicers' oaths, O, such a deed
As from the body of contraction plucks
The very soul, and sweet religion makes
A rhapsody of words. Heaven's face does glow
O'er this solidity and compound mass
With heated visage, as against the doom;
Is thought-sick at the act.

Getrude, Queen of Denmark.
                  Ay me, what act,
That roars so loud and thunders in the index?

Hamlet.
Look here upon this picture, and on this,
The counterfeit presentment of two brothers.
See what a grace was seated on this brow:
Hyperion's curls, the front of Jove himself,
An eye like Mars, to threaten and command,
A station like the herald Mercury
New lighted on a heaven-kissing hill,
A combination and a form indeed,
Where every god did seem to set his seal
To give the world assurance of a man.
This was your husband. Look you now what follows:
Here is your husband, like a mildewed ear,
Blasting his wholesome brother. Have you eyes?
Could you on this fair mountain leave to feed,
And batten on this moor? Ha, have you eyes?
You cannot call it love, for at your age
The heyday in the blood is tame, it's humble,
And waits upon the judgment, and what judgment
Would step from this to this? Sense sure you have,
Else could you not have motion, but sure that sense
Is apoplex'd, for madness would not err,
Nor sense to ecstasy was ne'er so thrall'd
But it reserv'd some quantity of choice
To serve in such a difference. What devil was't
That thus hath cozen'd you at hoodman-blind?
Eyes without feeling, feeling without sight,
Ears without hands or eyes, smelling sans all,
Or but a sickly part of one true sense
Could not so mope. O shame, where is thy blush?
Rebellious hell,
If thou canst mutine in a matron's bones,
To flaming youth let virtue be as wax
And melt in her own fire. Proclaim no shame
When the compulsive ardor gives the charge,
Since frost itself as actively doth burn,
And reason panders will.

Getrude, Queen of Denmark.
                  O Hamlet, speak no more!
Thou turn'st my eyes into my very soul,
And there I see such black and grained spots
As will not leave their tinct.

Hamlet.
                  Nay, but to live
In the rank sweat of an enseamed bed,
Stew'd in corruption, honeying and making love
Over the nasty sty!

Getrude, Queen of Denmark.
                    O, speak to me no more!
These words like daggers enter in my ears.
No more, sweet Hamlet!

Hamlet.
                    A murderer and a villain!
A slave that is not twentith part the tithe
Of your precedent lord, a Vice of kings,
A cutpurse of the empire and the rule,
That from a shelf the precious diadem stole,
And put it in his pocket—

Getrude, Queen of Denmark.
                    No more!

Enter Ghost in his night-gown.

Hamlet.
A king of shreds and patches—
Save me, and hover o'er me with your wings,
You heavenly guards! What would your gracious figure?

Getrude, Queen of Denmark.
Alas, he's mad!

Hamlet.
Do you not come your tardy son to chide,
That, laps'd in time and passion, lets go by
Th' important acting of your dread command?
O, say!

Ghost of Hamlet's Father.
Do not forget! This visitation
Is but to whet thy almost blunted purpose.
But look, amazement on thy mother sits,
O, step between her and her fighting soul.
Conceit in weakest bodies strongest works,
Speak to her, Hamlet.

Hamlet.
                    How is it with you, lady?

Getrude, Queen of Denmark.
Alas, how is't with you,
That you do bend your eye on vacancy,
And with th' incorporal air do hold discourse?
Forth at your eyes your spirits wildly peep,
And as the sleeping soldiers in th' alarm,
Your bedded hair, like life in excrements,
Start up and stand an end. O gentle son,
Upon the heat and flame of thy distemper
Sprinkle cool patience. Whereon do you look?

Hamlet.
On him, on him! Look you how pale he glares!
His form and cause conjoin'd, preaching to stones,
Would make them capable.—Do not look upon me,
Lest with this piteous action you convert
My stern effects, then what I have to do
Will want true color—tears perchance for blood.

Getrude, Queen of Denmark.
To whom do you speak this?

Hamlet.
                    Do you see nothing there?

Getrude, Queen of Denmark.
Nothing at all, yet all that is I see.

Hamlet.
Nor did you nothing hear?

Getrude, Queen of Denmark.
                    No, nothing but ourselves.

Hamlet.
Why, look you there, look how it steals away!
My father, in his habit as he lived!
Look where he goes, even now, out at the portal!

Exit Ghost.

Getrude, Queen of Denmark.
This is the very coinage of your brain,
This bodiless creation ecstasy
Is very cunning in.

Hamlet.
                    Ecstasy?
My pulse as yours doth temperately keep time,
And makes as healthful music. It is not madness
That I have utt'red. Bring me to the test,
And I the matter will reword, which madness
Would gambol from. Mother, for love of grace,
Lay not that flattering unction to your soul,
That not your trespass but my madness speaks;
It will but skin and film the ulcerous place,
Whiles rank corruption, mining all within,
Infects unseen. Confess yourself to heaven,
Repent what's past, avoid what is to come,
And do not spread the compost on the weeds
To make them ranker. Forgive me this my virtue,
For in the fatness of these pursy times

Virtue itself of vice must pardon beg,
Yea, curb and woo for leave to do him good.

Getrude, Queen of Denmark.
O Hamlet, thou hast cleft my heart in twain.

Hamlet.
O, throw away the worser part of it,
And live the purer with the other half.
Good night, but go not to my uncle's bed—
Assume a virtue, if you have it not.
That monster custom, who all sense doth eat,
Of habits devil, is angel yet in this,
That to the use of actions fair and good
He likewise gives a frock or livery
That aptly is put on. Refrain tonight,
And that shall lend a kind of easiness
To the next abstinence, the next more easy;
For use almost can change the stamp of nature,
And either lodge the devil or throw him out
With wondrous potency. Once more good night,
And when you are desirous to be blest,
I'll blessing beg of you. For this same lord,

Pointing to Polonius.

I do repent; but heaven hath pleas'd it so
To punish me with this, and this with me,
That I must be their scourge and minister.
I will bestow him, and will answer well
The death I gave him. So again good night.
I must be cruel only to be kind.
This bad begins and worse remains behind.
One word more, good lady.

Getrude, Queen of Denmark.
                What shall I do?

Hamlet.
Not this, by no means, that I bid you do:
Let the bloat king tempt you again to bed,
Pinch wanton on your cheek, call you his mouse,
And let him, for a pair of reechy kisses,
Or paddling in your neck with his damn'd fingers,
Make you to ravel all this matter out,
That I essentially am not in madness,
But mad in craft. 'Twere good you let him know,
For who that's but a queen, fair, sober, wise,
Would from a paddock, from a bat, a gib,
Such dear concernings hide? Who would do so?
No, in despite of sense and secrecy,
Unpeg the basket on the house's top,
Let the birds fly, and like the famous ape,
To try conclusions in the basket creep,
And break your own neck down.

Getrude, Queen of Denmark.
Be thou assur'd, if words be made of breath,
And breath of life, I have no life to breathe
What thou hast said to me.

Hamlet.
I must to England, you know that?

Getrude, Queen of Denmark.
                Alack,
I had forgot. 'Tis so concluded on.

Hamlet.
There's letters seal'd, and my two schoolfellows,
Whom I will trust as I will adders fang'd,
They bear the mandate, they must sweep my way
And marshal me to knavery. Let it work,
For 'tis the sport to have the enginer
Hoist with his own petar, an't shall go hard
But I will delve one yard below their mines,
And blow them at the moon. O, 'tis most sweet
When in one line two crafts directly meet.
This man shall set me packing;
I'll lug the guts into the neighbor room.
Mother, good night indeed. This counsellor
Is now most still, most secret, and most grave,
Who was in life a foolish prating knave.
Come, sir, to draw toward an end with you.
Good night, mother.

Exeunt severally, Hamlet tugging in Polonius.

Act 4

Scene 1

Elsinore. A room in Elsinore castle.

(King; Queen; Rosencrantz; Guildenstern)

Gertrude tells Claudius that Hamlet has killed Polonius. The King sends Guildenstern and Rosencrantz to find the body and bring it to the chapel, while he goes to announce the old man's death. He worries that he himself will be blamed, for not having restrained Hamlet enough.

Enter King and Queen with Rosencrantz and Guildenstern.

Claudius, King of Denmark.
There's matter in these sighs, these profound heaves—
You must translate, 'tis fit we understand them.
Where is your son?

Getrude, Queen of Denmark.
Bestow this place on us a little while.

Exeunt Rosencrantz and Guildenstern.

Ah, mine own lord, what have I seen tonight!

Claudius, King of Denmark.
What, Gertrude? How does Hamlet?

Getrude, Queen of Denmark.
Mad as the sea and wind when both contend
Which is the mightier. In his lawless fit,
Behind the arras hearing something stir,
Whips out his rapier, cries, "A rat, a rat!"
And in this brainish apprehension kills
The unseen good old man.

Claudius, King of Denmark.
                      O heavy deed!
It had been so with us had we been there.
His liberty is full of threats to all,
To you yourself, to us, to every one.
Alas, how shall this bloody deed be answer'd?
It will be laid to us, whose providence
Should have kept short, restrain'd, and out of haunt
This mad young man; but so much was our love,
We would not understand what was most fit,
But like the owner of a foul disease,
To keep it from divulging, let it feed
Even on the pith of life. Where is he gone?

Getrude, Queen of Denmark.
To draw apart the body he hath kill'd,
O'er whom his very madness, like some ore
Among a mineral of metals base,
Shows itself pure: 'a weeps for what is done.

Claudius, King of Denmark.
O Gertrude, come away!
The sun no sooner shall the mountains touch,
But we will ship him hence, and this vile deed
We must with all our majesty and skill
Both countenance and excuse. Ho, Guildenstern!

Enter Rosencrantz and Guildenstern.

Friends both, go join you with some further aid:
Hamlet in madness hath Polonius slain,
And from his mother's closet hath he dragg'd him.
Go seek him out, speak fair, and bring the body
Into the chapel. I pray you haste in this.

Exeunt Rosencrantz and Guildenstern.

Come, Gertrude, we'll call up our wisest friends
And let them know both what we mean to do
And what's untimely done. So envious slander,
Whose whisper o'er the world's diameter,
As level as the cannon to his blank,
Transports his pois'ned shot, may miss our name,
And hit the woundless air. O, come away!
My soul is full of discord and dismay.

Exeunt.

Scene 2

Elsinore. Another room in Elsinore castle.

(Hamlet; Rosencrantz; Guildenstern)

Hamlet refuses to tell Guildenstern and Rosencrantz where the body is, calling them sponges who soak up the words and rewards of the King. They do not understand. He runs away from them, and they and others hunt after him.

Enter Hamlet.

Hamlet.
Safely stow'd.

Gentleman.

Within.

Hamlet! Lord Hamlet!

Hamlet.
But soft, what noise? Who calls on Hamlet? O, here they come.

Enter Rosencrantz and Guildenstern.

Rosencrantz.
What have you done, my lord, with the dead body?

Hamlet.
Compounded it with dust, whereto 'tis kin.

Rosencrantz.
Tell us where 'tis, that we may take it thence,
And bear it to the chapel.

Hamlet.
Do not believe it.

Rosencrantz.
Believe what?

Hamlet.
That I can keep your counsel and not mine own. Besides, to be demanded of a sponge, what replication should be made by the son of a king?

Rosencrantz.
Take you me for a sponge, my lord?

Hamlet.
Ay, sir, that soaks up the King's countenance, his rewards, his authorities. But such officers do the King best service in the end: he keeps them, like an ape an apple, in the corner of his jaw, first mouth'd, to be last swallow'd. When he needs what you have glean'd, it is but squeezing you, and, sponge, you shall be dry again.

Rosencrantz.
I understand you not, my lord.

Hamlet.
I am glad of it, a knavish speech sleeps in a foolish ear.

Rosencrantz.
My lord, you must tell us where the body is, and go with us to the king.

Hamlet.
The body is with the King, but the King is not with the body. The King is a thing—

Guildenstern.
A thing, my lord?

Hamlet.
Of nothing, bring me to him. Hide fox, and all after.

Exeunt.

Scene 3

Elsinore. Another room in Elsinore castle.

(King; Attendants; Rosencrantz; Hamlet; Guildenstern)

Claudius considers that he cannot punish Hamlet too severely due to his popularity with the commoners. Rosencrantz and Guildenstern admit their inability to get Hamlet to tell where Polonius's body is. The prince refuses to answer the question when Claudius asks it to, instead pointing out how everybody, even emperors, will be food for worms one day. Finally he tells them that they will be able to find Polonius by smell in the lobby if they wait long enough. Claudius orders Hamlet to leave for England more quickly than planned. Hamlet mockingly bids him farewell as his mother, seeing as man and wife are one flesh. The King orders Rosencrantz and Guildenstern to see to it that Hamlet sails immediately. He reveals that the letters being carried to England order the English to execute the prince.

Enter King and two or three.

Claudius, King of Denmark.
I have sent to seek him, and to find the body.
How dangerous is it that this man goes loose!
Yet must not we put the strong law on him.
He's lov'd of the distracted multitude,
Who like not in their judgment, but their eyes,
And where 'tis so, th' offender's scourge is weigh'd,
But never the offense. To bear all smooth and even,
This sudden sending him away must seem
Deliberate pause. Diseases desperate grown
By desperate appliance are reliev'd,
Or not at all.

Enter Rosencrantz.

How now, what hath befall'n?

Rosencrantz.
Where the dead body is bestow'd, my lord,
We cannot get from him.

Claudius, King of Denmark.
But where is he?

Rosencrantz.
Without, my lord, guarded, to know your pleasure.

Claudius, King of Denmark.
Bring him before us.

Rosencrantz.
Ho, bring in the lord.

They, Hamlet and Guildenstern, enter.

Claudius, King of Denmark.
Now, Hamlet, where's Polonius?

Hamlet.
At supper.

Claudius, King of Denmark.
At supper? Where?

Hamlet.
Not where he eats, but where 'a is eaten; a certain convocation of politic worms are e'en at him. Your worm is your only emperor for diet: we fat all creatures else to fat us, and we fat ourselves for maggots; your fat king and your lean beggar is but variable service, two dishes, but to one table—that's the end.

Claudius, King of Denmark.
Alas, alas!

Hamlet.
A man may fish with the worm that hath eat of a king, and eat of the fish that hath fed of that worm.

Claudius, King of Denmark.
What dost thou mean by this?

Hamlet.
Nothing but to show you how a king may go a progress through the guts of a beggar.

Claudius, King of Denmark.
Where is Polonius?

Hamlet.
In heaven, send thither to see; if your messenger find him not there, seek him i' th' other place yourself. But if indeed you find him not within this month, you shall nose him as you go up the stairs into the lobby.

Claudius, King of Denmark.

To Attendants.

Go seek him there.

Hamlet.
'A will stay till you come.

Exeunt Attendants.

Claudius, King of Denmark.
Hamlet, this deed, for thine especial safety—
Which we do tender, as we dearly grieve
For that which thou hast done—must send thee hence
With fiery quickness; therefore prepare thyself,
The bark is ready, and the wind at help,
Th' associates tend, and every thing is bent
For England.

Hamlet.
                For England.

Claudius, King of Denmark.
                Ay, Hamlet.

Hamlet.
                Good.

Claudius, King of Denmark.
So is it, if thou knew'st our purposes.

Hamlet.
I see a cherub that sees them. But come, for England!
Farewell, dear mother.

Claudius, King of Denmark.
Thy loving father, Hamlet.

Hamlet.
My mother: father and mother is man and wife, man and wife is one flesh—so, my mother. Come, for England!

Exit.

Claudius, King of Denmark.
Follow him at foot, tempt him with speed aboard.
Delay it not, I'll have him hence tonight.
Away, for every thing is seal'd and done
That else leans on th' affair. Pray you make haste.

Exeunt Rosencrantz and Guildenstern.

And, England, if my love thou hold'st at aught—
As my great power thereof may give thee sense,
Since yet thy cicatrice looks raw and red
After the Danish sword, and thy free awe
Pays homage to us—thou mayst not coldly set
Our sovereign process, which imports at full,
By letters conguring to that effect,
The present death of Hamlet. Do it, England,
For like the hectic in my blood he rages,
And thou must cure me. Till I know 'tis done,
How e'er my haps, my joys were ne'er begun.

Exit.

Scene 4

Near Elsinore. A plain in Denmark.

(Fortinbras; Captain; Hamlet; Rosencrantz; Guildenstern)

Fortinbras's army waits for its safe-conduct to pass over Danish territory. Hamlet asks a Norwegian captain where they are going, and is told that they are going to fight in Poland for a completely worthless patch of land. Hamlet considers that such a great army should be moving so resolutely for nothing, while he, with great reason, can't bring himself to do anything about his revenge. He resolves to move to action.

Enter Fortinbras with his army over the stage.

Fortinbras.
Go, captain, from me greet the Danish king.
Tell him that by his license Fortinbras
Craves the conveyance of a promis'd march
Over his kingdom. You know the rendezvous.
If that his Majesty would aught with us,
We shall express our duty in his eye,
And let him know so.

Norwegian Captain.
                    I will do't, my lord.

Fortinbras.
Go softly on.

Exeunt all but the Captain.
Enter Hamlet, Rosencrantz, Guildenstern, etc.

Hamlet.
Good sir, whose powers are these?

Norwegian Captain.
They are of Norway, sir.

Hamlet.
How purpos'd, sir, I pray you?

Norwegian Captain.
Against some part of Poland.

Hamlet.
Who commands them, sir?

Norwegian Captain.
The nephew to old Norway, Fortinbras.

Hamlet.
Goes it against the main of Poland, sir,
Or for some frontier?

Norwegian Captain.
Truly to speak, and with no addition,
We go to gain a little patch of ground
That hath in it no profit but the name.
To pay five ducats, five, I would not farm it;
Nor will it yield to Norway or the Pole
A ranker rate, should it be sold in fee.

Hamlet.
Why then the Polack never will defend it.

Norwegian Captain.
Yes, it is already garrison'd.

Hamlet.
Two thousand souls and twenty thousand ducats
Will not debate the question of this straw.
This is th' imposthume of much wealth and peace,
That inward breaks, and shows no cause without
Why the man dies. I humbly thank you, sir.

Norwegian Captain.
God buy you, sir.

Exit.

Rosencrantz.
                    Will't please you go, my lord?

Hamlet.
I'll be with you straight—go a little before.

Exeunt all but Hamlet.

How all occasions do inform against me,
And spur my dull revenge! What is a man,
If his chief good and market of his time
Be but to sleep and feed? A beast, no more.
Sure He that made us with such large discourse,
Looking before and after, gave us not
That capability and godlike reason
To fust in us unus'd. Now whether it be
Bestial oblivion, or some craven scruple
Of thinking too precisely on th' event—
A thought which quarter'd hath but one part wisdom
And ever three parts coward—I do not know
Why yet I live to say, "This thing's to do,"
Sith I have cause, and will, and strength, and means
To do't. Examples gross as earth exhort me:
Witness this army of such mass and charge,
Led by a delicate and tender prince,

Whose spirit with divine ambition puff'd
Makes mouths at the invisible event,
Exposing what is mortal and unsure
To all that fortune, death, and danger dare,
Even for an egg-shell. Rightly to be great
Is not to stir without great argument,
But greatly to find quarrel in a straw
When honor's at the stake. How stand I then,
That have a father kill'd, a mother stain'd,
Excitements of my reason and my blood,
And let all sleep, while to my shame I see
The imminent death of twenty thousand men,
That for a fantasy and trick of fame
Go to their graves like beds, fight for a plot
Whereon the numbers cannot try the cause,
Which is not tomb enough and continent
To hide the slain? O, from this time forth,
My thoughts be bloody, or be nothing worth!

Exit.

Scene 5

Elsinore. A room in Elsinore castle.

(Horatio; Queen Gertrude; Gentleman; Ophelia; King; Messenger; Laertes; Laertes's Followers)

Gertrude tries to avoid seeing the distracted Ophelia, but is finally persuaded to let her in. She enters, speaking senselessly, singing snatches of old songs relating to her abandonment and her father's death. Claudius witnesses this, and, moved, orders that a close watch be kept on her. He reveals that Laertes has returned to Denmark and that the people are muttering because of Polonius's death. Suddenly there is a noise, and the monarchs are told that a mob led by Laertes is attacking the palace, and that the commoners are yelling that Laertes should be King. Laertes breaks in, demanding to know where his father is. The Queen tries to protect the King, but she is pushed away by Claudius, who faces Laertes fearlessly. Laertes swears he will have vengeance whatever the consequences, and the King approves him. Ophelia enters, still singing. Laertes's rage turns to grief at the sight of his sister having lost her wits. Claudius insists on his own grief, and begs Laertes to listen to him. He offers to explain everything that has happened, and to offer any redress Laertes might call for.

Enter Horatio, Queen Gertrude, and a Gentleman.

Getrude, Queen of Denmark.
I will not speak with her.

Gentleman.
She is importunate, indeed distract.
Her mood will needs be pitied.

Getrude, Queen of Denmark.
    What would she have?

Gentleman.
She speaks much of her father, says she hears
There's tricks i' th' world, and hems, and beats her heart,
Spurns enviously at straws, speaks things in doubt
That carry but half sense. Her speech is nothing,
Yet the unshaped use of it doth move
The hearers to collection; they yawn at it,
And botch the words up fit to their own thoughts,
Which as her winks and nods and gestures yield them,
Indeed would make one think there might be thought,
Though nothing sure, yet much unhappily.

Horatio.
'Twere good she were spoken with, for she may strew
Dangerous conjectures in ill-breeding minds.

Getrude, Queen of Denmark.
Let her come in.

Exit Gentleman.
Aside.

To my sick soul, as sin's true nature is,
Each toy seems prologue to some great amiss,
So full of artless jealousy is guilt,
It spills itself in fearing to be spilt.

Enter Ophelia distracted, with her hair down, playing on a lute.

Ophelia.
Where is the beauteous majesty of Denmark?

Getrude, Queen of Denmark.
How now, Ophelia?

Ophelia.

She sings.

"How should I your true-love know
From another one?

By his cockle hat and staff,
And his sandal shoon."

Getrude, Queen of Denmark.
Alas, sweet lady, what imports this song?

Ophelia.
Say you? Nay, pray you mark.

Song.

"He is dead and gone, lady,
He is dead and gone,
At his head a grass-green turf,
At his heels a stone."
O ho!

Getrude, Queen of Denmark.
Nay, but, Ophelia—

Ophelia.
Pray you mark.

Sings.

"White his shroud as the mountain snow"—

Enter King.

Getrude, Queen of Denmark.
Alas, look here, my lord.

Ophelia.

Song.

"Larded all with sweet flowers,
Which bewept to the ground did not go
With true-love showers."

Claudius, King of Denmark.
How do you, pretty lady?

Ophelia.
Well, God dild you! They say the owl was a baker's daughter. Lord, we know what we are, but know not what we may be. God be at your table!

Claudius, King of Denmark.
Conceit upon her father.

Ophelia.
Pray let's have no words of this, but when they ask you what it means, say you this:

Song.

"Tomorrow is Saint Valentine's day,
All in the morning betime,
And I a maid at your window,
To be your Valentine.
Then up he rose and donn'd his clo'es,
And dupp'd the chamber-door,
Let in the maid, that out a maid
Never departed more."

Claudius, King of Denmark.
Pretty Ophelia!

Ophelia.
Indeed without an oath I'll make an end on't.

Sings.

"By Gis, and by Saint Charity,
Alack, and fie for shame!
Young men will do't if they come to't,
By Cock, they are to blame.
Quoth she, "Before you tumbled me,
You promis'd me to wed."'

He answers.

"'So would I 'a' done, by yonder sun,
And thou hadst not come to my bed.'"

Claudius, King of Denmark.
How long hath she been thus?

Ophelia.
I hope all will be well. We must be patient, but I cannot choose but weep to think they would lay him i' th' cold ground. My brother shall know of it, and so I thank you for your good counsel. Come, my coach! Good night, ladies, good night. Sweet ladies, good night, good night.

Exit.

Claudius, King of Denmark.
Follow her close, give her good watch, I pray you.

Exit Horatio.

O, this is the poison of deep grief, it springs
All from her father's death—and now behold!
O Gertrude, Gertrude,
When sorrows come, they come not single spies,
But in battalions: first, her father slain;
Next, your son gone, and he most violent author
Of his own just remove; the people muddied,

Thick and unwholesome in their thoughts and whispers
For good Polonius' death; and we have done but greenly
In hugger-mugger to inter him; poor Ophelia
Divided from herself and her fair judgement,
Without the which we are pictures, or mere beasts;
Last, and as much containing as all these,
Her brother is in secret come from France,
Feeds on this wonder, keeps himself in clouds,
And wants not buzzers to infect his ear
With pestilent speeches of his father's death,
Wherein necessity, of matter beggar'd,
Will nothing stick our person to arraign
In ear and ear. O my dear Gertrude, this,
Like to a murd'ring-piece, in many places
Gives me superfluous death.

A noise within.

Getrude, Queen of Denmark.
      Alack, what noise is this?

Claudius, King of Denmark.
Attend!
Where is my Swissers? Let them guard the door.

Enter a Messenger.

What is the matter?

Messenger.
      Save yourself, my lord!
The ocean, overpeering of his list,
Eats not the flats with more impetuous haste
Than young Laertes, in a riotous head,
O'erbears your officers. The rabble call him lord,
And as the world were now but to begin,
Antiquity forgot, custom not known,
The ratifiers and props of every word,
They cry, "Choose we, Laertes shall be king!"
Caps, hands, and tongues applaud it to the clouds,
"Laertes shall be king, Laertes king!"

A noise within.

Getrude, Queen of Denmark.
How cheerfully on the false trail they cry!
O, this is counter, you false Danish dogs!

Enter Laertes with others.

Claudius, King of Denmark.
The doors are broke.

Laertes.
Where is this king? Sirs, stand you all without.

Laertes's Followers.
No, let 's come in.

Laertes.
      I pray you give me leave.

Laertes's Followers.
We will, we will.

Laertes.
I thank you, keep the door.

Exeunt Laertes' followers.

O thou vile king,
Give me my father!

Getrude, Queen of Denmark.
      Calmly, good Laertes.

Laertes.
That drop of blood that's calm proclaims me bastard,
Cries cuckold to my father, brands the harlot
Even here between the chaste unsmirched brow
Of my true mother.

Claudius, King of Denmark.
      What is the cause, Laertes,
That thy rebellion looks so giant-like?
Let him go, Gertrude, do not fear our person:
There's such divinity doth hedge a king
That treason can but peep to what it would,
Acts little of his will. Tell me, Laertes,
Why thou art thus incens'd. Let him go, Gertrude.
Speak, man.

Laertes.
Where is my father?

Claudius, King of Denmark.
      Dead.

Getrude, Queen of Denmark.
      But not by him.

Claudius, King of Denmark.
Let him demand his fill.

Laertes.
How came he dead? I'll not be juggled with.
To hell, allegiance! Vows, to the blackest devil!
Conscience and grace, to the profoundest pit!
I dare damnation. To this point I stand,
That both the worlds I give to negligence,
Let come what comes, only I'll be reveng'd
Most throughly for my father.

Claudius, King of Denmark.
                Who shall stay you?

Laertes.
My will, not all the world's:
And for my means, I'll husband them so well,
They shall go far with little.

Claudius, King of Denmark.
                Good Laertes,
If you desire to know the certainty
Of your dear father, is't writ in your revenge
That, swoopstake, you will draw both friend and foe,
Winner and loser?

Laertes.
None but his enemies.

Claudius, King of Denmark.
                Will you know them then?

Laertes.
To his good friends thus wide I'll ope my arms,
And like the kind life-rend'ring pelican,
Repast them with my blood.

Claudius, King of Denmark.
                Why, now you speak
Like a good child and a true gentleman.
That I am guiltless of your father's death,
And am most sensibly in grief for it,
It shall as level to your judgment 'pear
As day does to your eye.

A noise within:

"Let her come in!"

Laertes.
How now, what noise is that?

Enter Ophelia.

O heat, dry up my brains! Tears seven times salt
Burn out the sense and virtue of mine eye!
By heaven, thy madness shall be paid with weight
Till our scale turn the beam. O rose of May!
Dear maid, kind sister, sweet Ophelia!
O heavens, is't possible a young maid's wits
Should be as mortal as an old man's life?
Nature is fine in love, and where 'tis fine,
It sends some precious instance of itself
After the thing it loves.

Ophelia.

Song.

"They bore him barefac'd on the bier,
Hey non nonny, nonny, hey nonny,
And in his grave rain'd many a tear"—
Fare you well, my dove!

Laertes.
Hadst thou thy wits and didst persuade revenge,
It could not move thus.

Ophelia.
You must sing, "A-down, a-down,"
And you call him a-down-a.
O how the wheel becomes it! It is the false steward, that stole his master's daughter.

Laertes.
This nothing's more than matter.

Ophelia.
There's rosemary, that's for remembrance; pray you, love, remember. And there is pansies, that's for thoughts.

Laertes.
A document in madness, thoughts and remembrance fitted.

Ophelia.

To Claudius.

There's fennel for you, and columbines.

To Gertrude.

There's rue for you, and here's some for me; we may call it herb of grace a' Sundays. You may wear your rue with a difference. There's a daisy. I would give you some violets, but they wither'd all when my father died. They say 'a made a good end—

Sings.

"For bonny sweet Robin is all my joy."

Laertes.
Thought and afflictions, passion, hell itself,
She turns to favor and to prettiness.

Ophelia.

Song.

"And will 'a not come again?
And will 'a not come again?
No, no, he is dead,
Go to thy death-bed,
He never will come again.
His beard was as white as snow,
All flaxen was his pole,
He is gone, he is gone,
And we cast away moan,
God 'a' mercy on his soul!"
And of all Christians' souls, I pray God. God buy you.

Exit.

Laertes.
Do you see this, O God?

Claudius, King of Denmark.
Laertes, I must commune with your grief,
Or you deny me right. Go but apart,
Make choice of whom your wisest friends you will,
And they shall hear and judge 'twixt you and me.
If by direct or by collateral hand
They find us touch'd, we will our kingdom give,
Our crown, our life, and all that we call ours,
To you in satisfaction; but if not,
Be you content to lend your patience to us,
And we shall jointly labor with your soul
To give it due content.

Laertes.
              Let this be so.
His means of death, his obscure funeral—
No trophy, sword, nor hatchment o'er his bones,
No noble rite nor formal ostentation—
Cry to be heard, as 'twere from heaven to earth,
That I must call't in question.

Claudius, King of Denmark.
              So you shall,
And where th' offense is, let the great axe fall.
I pray you go with me.

Exeunt.

Scene 6

Elsinore. Another room in Elsinore castle.

(Horatio; Gentleman; Sailors)

Horatio is brought a letter from Hamlet by some sailors. In it, Hamlet reveals that he was captured by pirates and is now back in Denmark.

Enter Horatio and others.

Horatio.
What are they that would speak with me?

Gentleman.
Sea-faring men, sir. They say they have letters for you.

Horatio.
Let them come in.

Exit Gentleman.

I do not know from what part of the world
I should be greeted, if not from Lord Hamlet.

Enter Sailors.

First Sailor.
God bless you, sir.

Horatio.
Let him bless thee too.

First Sailor.
'A shall, sir, and 't please him. There's a letter for you, sir—it came from th' ambassador that was bound for England—if your name be Horatio, as I am let to know it is.

Horatio.

Reads.

"Horatio, when thou shalt have overlook'd this, give these fellows some means to the King, they have letters for him. Ere we were two days old at sea, a pirate of very warlike appointment gave us chase. Finding ourselves too slow of sail, we put on a compell'd valor, and in the grapple I boarded them. On the instant they got clear of our ship, so I alone became their prisoner. They have dealt with me like thieves of mercy, but they knew what they did: I am to do a good turn for them. Let the King have the letters I have sent, and repair thou to me with as much speed as thou wouldest fly death. I have words to speak in thine ear will make thee dumb, yet

are they much too light for the bore of the matter. These good fellows will bring thee where I am. Rosencrantz and Guildenstern hold their course for England, of them I have much to tell thee. Farewell.
He that thou knowest thine, Hamlet."
Come, I will give you way for these your letters,
And do't the speedier that you may direct me
To him from whom you brought them.

Exeunt.

Scene 7

Elsinore. Another room in Elsinore castle.

(King; Laertes; Messenger; Queen)

Claudius has convinced Laertes that Hamlet is entirely to blame, and explains that he could not punish the prince because of Gertrude's love for him, as well as the esteem of the populace. He proposes that Laertes undertake a private revenge, serving them both. Learning that Hamlet has returned, they come up with a plan based on Hamlet's pride in his fencing abilities and Laertes's fame in that exercise. They plan to arrange for a match between the two young men, and leave one of the sword points unprotected, so that Laertes can deal an actual wound. Laertes takes up the plot, explaining that he will poison the blade. To be absolutely certain of success, Claudius plans to have a poisoned drink nearby as well. Gertrude comes in with the news that Ophelia has drowned. Laertes leaves, refusing to cry; Claudius fears that he will have to start all over again with calming him.

Enter King and Laertes.

Claudius, King of Denmark.
Now must your conscience my acquittance seal,
And you must put me in your heart for friend,
Sith you have heard, and with a knowing ear,
That he which hath your noble father slain
Pursued my life.

Laertes.
                It well appears. But tell me
Why you proceeded not against these feats
So criminal and so capital in nature,
As by your safety, greatness, wisdom, all things else
You mainly were stirr'd up.

Claudius, King of Denmark.
                O, for two special reasons,
Which may to you perhaps seem much unsinew'd,
But yet to me th' are strong. The Queen his mother
Lives almost by his looks, and for myself—
My virtue or my plague, be it either which—
She is so conjunctive to my life and soul,
That, as the star moves not but in his sphere,
I could not but by her. The other motive,
Why to a public count I might not go,
Is the great love the general gender bear him,
Who, dipping all his faults in their affection,
Work like the spring that turneth wood to stone,
Convert his gyves to graces, so that my arrows,
Too slightly timber'd for so loud a wind,
Would have reverted to my bow again,
But not where I have aim'd them.

Laertes.
And so have I a noble father lost,
A sister driven into desp'rate terms,
Whose worth, if praises may go back again,
Stood challenger on mount of all the age
For her perfections—but my revenge will come.

Claudius, King of Denmark.
Break not your sleeps for that. You must not think
That we are made of stuff so flat and dull
That we can let our beard be shook with danger
And think it pastime. You shortly shall hear more.
I lov'd your father, and we love ourself,
And that, I hope, will teach you to imagine—

Enter a Messenger with letters.

How now? What news?

Messenger.
                Letters, my lord, from Hamlet:
These to your Majesty, this to the queen.

Claudius, King of Denmark.
From Hamlet? Who brought them?

Messenger.
Sailors, my lord, they say, I saw them not.
They were given me by Claudio. He receiv'd them
Of him that brought them.

Claudius, King of Denmark.
                Laertes, you shall hear them.
—Leave us.

Exit Messenger.

Reads.

"High and mighty, You shall know I am set naked on your kingdom. Tomorrow shall I beg leave to see your kingly eyes, when I shall, first asking you pardon thereunto, recount the occasion of my sudden and more strange return. Hamlet."

What should this mean? Are all the rest come back?
Or is it some abuse, and no such thing?

Laertes.
Know you the hand?

Claudius, King of Denmark.
    'Tis Hamlet's character. "Naked"!
And in a postscript here he says "alone."
Can you devise me?

Laertes.
I am lost in it, my lord. But let him come,
It warms the very sickness in my heart
That I shall live and tell him to his teeth,
"Thus didst thou."

Claudius, King of Denmark.
    If it be so, Laertes—
As how should it be so? How otherwise?—
Will you be rul'd by me?

Laertes.
    Ay, my lord,
So you will not o'errule me to a peace.

Claudius, King of Denmark.
To thine own peace. If he be now returned
As checking at his voyage, and that he means
No more to undertake it, I will work him
To an exploit, now ripe in my device,
Under the which he shall not choose but fall;
And for his death no wind of blame shall breathe,
But even his mother shall uncharge the practice,
And call it accident.

Laertes.
    My lord, I will be rul'd,
The rather if you could devise it so
That I might be the organ.

Claudius, King of Denmark.
    It falls right.
You have been talk'd of since your travel much,
And that in Hamlet's hearing, for a quality
Wherein they say you shine. Your sum of parts
Did not together pluck such envy from him
As did that one, and that, in my regard,
Of the unworthiest siege.

Laertes.
    What part is that, my lord?

Claudius, King of Denmark.
A very riband in the cap of youth,
Yet needful too, for youth no less becomes
The light and careless livery that it wears
Than settled age his sables and his weeds,
Importing health and graveness. Two months since
Here was a gentleman of Normandy:
I have seen myself, and serv'd against, the French,
And they can well on horseback, but this gallant
Had witchcraft in't, he grew unto his seat,
And to such wondrous doing brought his horse,
As had he been incorps'd and demi-natur'd
With the brave beast. So far he topp'd my thought,
That I in forgery of shapes and tricks
Come short of what he did.

Laertes.
    A Norman was't?

Claudius, King of Denmark.
A Norman.

Laertes.
Upon my life, Lamord.

Claudius, King of Denmark.
    The very same.

Laertes.
I know him well. He is the brooch indeed
And gem of all the nation.

Claudius, King of Denmark.
He made confession of you,
And gave you such a masterly report
For art and exercise in your defense,
And for your rapier most especial,
That he cried out 'twould be a sight indeed
If one could match you. The scrimers of their nation
He swore had neither motion, guard, nor eye,
If you oppos'd them. Sir, this report of his
Did Hamlet so envenom with his envy
That he could nothing do but wish and beg
Your sudden coming o'er to play with you.
Now, out of this—

Laertes.
                What out of this, my lord?

Claudius, King of Denmark.
Laertes, was your father dear to you?
Or are you like the painting of a sorrow,
A face without a heart?

Laertes.
                Why ask you this?

Claudius, King of Denmark.
Not that I think you did not love your father,
But that I know love is begun by time,
And that I see, in passages of proof,
Time qualifies the spark and fire of it.
There lives within the very flame of love
A kind of week or snuff that will abate it,
And nothing is at a like goodness still,
For goodness, growing to a plurisy,
Dies in his own too much. That we would do,
We should do when we would; for this "would" changes,
And hath abatements and delays as many
As there are tongues, are hands, are accidents,
And then this 'should' is like a spendthrift's sigh,
That hurts by easing. But to the quick of th' ulcer:
Hamlet comes back. What would you undertake
To show yourself indeed your father's son
More than in words?

Laertes.
                To cut his throat i' th' church.

Claudius, King of Denmark.
No place indeed should murder sanctuarize,
Revenge should have no bounds. But, good Laertes,
Will you do this, keep close within your chamber.
Hamlet return'd shall know you are come home.
We'll put on those shall praise your excellence,
And set a double varnish on the fame
The Frenchman gave you, bring you in fine together,
And wager o'er your heads. He, being remiss,
Most generous, and free from all contriving,
Will not peruse the foils, so that with ease,
Or with a little shuffling, you may choose
A sword unbated, and in a pass of practice
Requite him for your father.

Laertes.
                I will do't,
And for that purpose I'll anoint my sword.
I bought an unction of a mountebank,
So mortal that, but dip a knife in it,
Where it draws blood, no cataplasm so rare,
Collected from all simples that have virtue
Under the moon, can save the thing from death
That is but scratch'd withal. I'll touch my point
With this contagion, that if I gall him slightly,
It may be death.

Claudius, King of Denmark.
                Let's further think of this,
Weigh what convenience both of time and means
May fit us to our shape. If this should fail,
And that our drift look through our bad performance,
'Twere better not assay'd; therefore this project
Should have a back or second, that might hold
If this did blast in proof. Soft, let me see.
We'll make a solemn wager on your cunnings—
I ha't!
When in your motion you are hot and dry—
As make your bouts more violent to that end—
And that he calls for drink, I'll have preferr'd him
A chalice for the nonce, whereon but sipping,
If he by chance escape your venom'd stuck,
Our purpose may hold there. But stay, what noise?

Enter Queen.

Getrude, Queen of Denmark.
One woe doth tread upon another's heel,
So fast they follow. Your sister's drown'd, Laertes.

Laertes.
Drown'd! O, where?

Getrude, Queen of Denmark.
There is a willow grows askaunt the brook,
That shows his hoary leaves in the glassy stream,
Therewith fantastic garlands did she make
Of crow-flowers, nettles, daisies, and long purples
That liberal shepherds give a grosser name,
But our cull-cold maids do dead men's fingers call them.
There on the pendant boughs her crownet weeds
Clamb'ring to hang, an envious sliver broke,
When down her weedy trophies and herself
Fell in the weeping brook. Her clothes spread wide,
And mermaid-like awhile they bore her up,

Which time she chaunted snatches of old lauds,
As one incapable of her own distress,
Or like a creature native and indued
Unto that element. But long it could not be
Till that her garments, heavy with their drink,
Pull'd the poor wretch from her melodious lay
To muddy death.

Laertes.
                  Alas, then she is drown'd?

Getrude, Queen of Denmark.
Drown'd, drown'd.

Laertes.
Too much of water hast thou, poor Ophelia,
And therefore I forbid my tears; but yet
It is our trick, Nature her custom holds,
Let shame say what it will; when these are gone,
The woman will be out. Adieu, my lord,
I have a speech a' fire that fain would blaze,
But that this folly drowns it.

Exit.

Claudius, King of Denmark.
                Let's follow, Gertrude.
How much I had to do to calm his rage!
Now fear I this will give it start again,
Therefore let's follow.

Exeunt.

Act 5

Scene 1

Elsinore. A churchyard.

(First Clown; Second Clown; Hamlet; Horatio; King; Queen; Laertes; Doctor of Divinity; Lords; Attendants)

Two gravediggers prepare a spot for Ophelia, though they think it wrong that a suspected suicide be given Christian burial. They suspect that it is only because she was upper-class that this is happening. Hamlet and Horatio come in as the gravedigger tosses out of bones and skulls from the grave as he makes room for the new arrival. Talking with the man, he discovers that he is holding the skull of his father's jester Yorick, a great favorite of his when he was a child. He contemplates how everyone will end up looking no prettier than that skull. The King and Queen enter with the funeral procession and a cranky priest who is only given Ophelia burial rites because of the direct orders he has received; believing her a suicide he does not think she should have any. Hamlet realizes from what Laertes says that it is Ophelia who is being buried. The Queen reveals her wish that Ophelia might have married Hamlet. When Laertes jumps into the grave in grief, Hamlet springs up and then joins him, and the two fight over who loved her most. Claudius tells Horatio to keep Hamlet calm, and tells Laertes to remember that he'll be able to get back at Hamlet soon.

Enter two Clowns with spades and mattocks.

First Clown (Gravedigger).
Is she to be buried in Christian burial when she willfully seeks her own salvation?

Second Clown (Gravedigger).
I tell thee she is, therefore make her grave straight. The crowner hath sate on her, and finds it Christian burial.

First Clown (Gravedigger).
How can that be, unless she drown'd herself in her own defense?

Second Clown (Gravedigger).
Why, 'tis found so.

First Clown (Gravedigger).
It must be se offendendo, it cannot be else. For here lies the point: if I drown myself wittingly, it argues an act, and an act hath three branches—it is to act, to do, to perform; argal, she drown'd herself wittingly.

Second Clown (Gravedigger).
Nay, but hear you, goodman delver—

First Clown (Gravedigger).
Give me leave. Here lies the water; good. Here stands the man; good. If the man go to this water and drown himself, it is, will he, nill he, he goes, mark you that. But if the water come to him and drown him, he drowns not himself; argal, he that is not guilty of his own death shortens not his own life.

Second Clown (Gravedigger).
But is this law?

First Clown (Gravedigger).
Ay, marry, is't—crowner's quest law.

Second Clown (Gravedigger).
Will you ha' the truth an't? If this had not been a gentlewoman, she should have been buried out a' Christian burial.

First Clown (Gravedigger).
Why, there thou say'st, and the more pity that great folk should have count'nance in this world to drown or hang themselves, more than their even-Christen. Come, my spade. There is no ancient gentlemen but gard'ners, ditchers, and grave-makers; they hold up Adam's profession.

Second Clown (Gravedigger).
Was he a gentleman?

First Clown (Gravedigger).
'A was the first that ever bore arms.

Second Clown (Gravedigger).
Why, he had none.

First Clown (Gravedigger).
What, art a heathen? How dost thou understand the Scripture? The Scripture says Adam digg'd; could he dig without arms? I'll put another question to thee. If thou answerest me not to the purpose, confess thyself—

Second Clown (Gravedigger).
Go to.

First Clown (Gravedigger).
What is he that builds stronger than either the mason, the shipwright, or the carpenter?

Second Clown (Gravedigger).
The gallows-maker, for that frame outlives a thousand tenants.

First Clown (Gravedigger).
I like thy wit well, in good faith. The gallows does well; but how does it well? It does well to those that do ill. Now thou dost ill to say the gallows is built stronger than the church; argal, the gallows may do well to thee. To't again, come.

Second Clown (Gravedigger).
Who builds stronger than a mason, a shipwright, or a carpenter?

First Clown (Gravedigger).
Ay, tell me that, and unyoke.

Second Clown (Gravedigger).
Marry, now I can tell.

First Clown (Gravedigger).
To't.

Second Clown (Gravedigger).
Mass, I cannot tell.

Enter Hamlet and Horatio afar off.

First Clown (Gravedigger).
Cudgel thy brains no more about it, for your dull ass will not mend his pace with beating, and when you are ask'd this question next, say "a grave-maker": the houses he makes lasts till doomsday. Go get thee in, and fetch me a sup of liquor.

Exit Second Clown.
First Clown digs.
Song.

"In youth when I did love, did love,
Methought it was very sweet,
To contract—O—the time for-a-my behove,
O, methought there-a-was nothing-a-meet."

Hamlet.
Has this fellow no feeling of his business? 'A sings in grave-making.

Horatio.
Custom hath made it in him a property of easiness.

Hamlet.
'Tis e'en so, the hand of little employment hath the daintier sense.

First Clown (Gravedigger).

Song.

"But age with his stealing steps
Hath clawed me in his clutch,
And hath shipped me into the land,
As if I had never been such."

Throws up a shovelful of earth with a skull in it.

Hamlet.
That skull had a tongue in it, and could sing once. How the knave jowls it to the ground, as if 'twere Cain's jaw-bone, that did the first murder! This might be the pate of a politician, which this ass now

o'erreaches, one that would circumvent God, might it not?

Horatio.
It might, my lord.

Hamlet.
Or of a courtier, which could say, "Good morrow, sweet lord! How dost thou, sweet lord?" This might be my Lord Such-a-one, that prais'd my Lord Such-a-one's horse when 'a meant to beg it, might it not?

Horatio.
Ay, my lord.

Hamlet.
Why, e'en so, and now my Lady Worm's, chopless, and knock'd about the mazzard with a sexton's spade. Here's fine revolution, and we had the trick to see't. Did these bones cost no more the breeding, but to play at loggats with them? Mine ache to think on't.

First Clown (Gravedigger).

Song.

"A pickaxe and a spade, a spade,
For and a shrouding sheet:
O, a pit of clay for to be made
For such a guest is meet."

Throws up another skull.

Hamlet.
There's another. Why may not that be the skull of a lawyer? Where be his quiddities now, his quillities, his cases, his tenures, and his tricks? Why does he suffer this mad knave now to knock him about the sconce with a dirty shovel, and will not tell him of his action of battery? Hum! This fellow might be in 's time a great buyer of land, with his statutes, his recognizances, his fines, his double vouchers, his recoveries. Is this the fine of his fines, and the recovery of his recoveries, to have his fine pate full of fine dirt? Will his vouchers vouch him no more of his purchases, and double ones too, than the length and breadth of a pair of indentures? The very conveyances of his lands will scarcely lie in this box, and must th' inheritor himself have no more, ha?

Horatio.
Not a jot more, my lord.

Hamlet.
Is not parchment made of sheep-skins?

Horatio.
Ay, my lord, and of calves'-skins too.

Hamlet.
They are sheep and calves which seek out assurance in that. I will speak to this fellow. Whose grave's this, sirrah?

First Clown (Gravedigger).
Mine, sir.

Sings.

"O, a pit of clay for to be made
For such a guest is meet."

Hamlet.
I think it be thine indeed, for thou liest in't.

First Clown (Gravedigger).
You lie out on't, sir, and therefore 'tis not yours; for my part, I do not lie in't, yet it is mine.

Hamlet.
Thou dost lie in't, to be in't and say it is thine. 'Tis for the dead, not for the quick; therefore thou liest.

First Clown (Gravedigger).
'Tis a quick lie, sir, 'twill away again from me to you.

Hamlet.
What man dost thou dig it for?

First Clown (Gravedigger).
For no man, sir.

Hamlet.
What woman then?

First Clown (Gravedigger).
For none neither.

Hamlet.
Who is to be buried in't?

First Clown (Gravedigger).
One that was a woman, sir, but, rest her soul, she's dead.

Hamlet.
How absolute the knave is! We must speak by the card, or equivocation will undo us. By the Lord, Horatio, this three years I have took note of it: the age is grown

so pick'd that the toe of the peasant comes so near the heel of the courtier, he galls his kibe. How long hast thou been grave-maker?

First Clown (Gravedigger).
Of all the days i' th' year, I came to't that day that our last king Hamlet overcame Fortinbras.

Hamlet.
How long is that since?

First Clown (Gravedigger).
Cannot you tell that? Every fool can tell that. It was that very day that young Hamlet was born— he that is mad, and sent into England.

Hamlet.
Ay, marry, why was he sent into England?

First Clown (Gravedigger).
Why, because 'a was mad. 'A shall recover his wits there, or if 'a do not, 'tis no great matter there.

Hamlet.
Why?

First Clown (Gravedigger).
'Twill not be seen in him there, there the men are as mad as he.

Hamlet.
How came he mad?

First Clown (Gravedigger).
Very strangely, they say.

Hamlet.
How strangely?

First Clown (Gravedigger).
Faith, e'en with losing his wits.

Hamlet.
Upon what ground?

First Clown (Gravedigger).
Why, here in Denmark. I have been sexton here, man and boy, thirty years.

Hamlet.
How long will a man lie i' th' earth ere he rot?

First Clown (Gravedigger).
Faith, if 'a be not rotten before 'a die—as we have many pocky corses, that will scarce hold the laying in—'a will last you some eight year or nine year. A tanner will last you nine year.

Hamlet.
Why he more than another?

First Clown (Gravedigger).
Why, sir, his hide is so tann'd with his trade that 'a will keep out water a great while, and your water is a sore decayer of your whoreson dead body. Here's a skull now hath lien you i' th' earth three and twenty years.

Hamlet.
Whose was it?

First Clown (Gravedigger).
A whoreson mad fellow's it was. Whose do you think it was?

Hamlet.
Nay, I know not.

First Clown (Gravedigger).
A pestilence on him for a mad rogue! 'A pour'd a flagon of Rhenish on my head once. This same skull, sir, was, sir, Yorick's skull, the King's jester.

Hamlet.
This?

Takes the skull.

First Clown (Gravedigger).
E'en that.

Hamlet.
Alas, poor Yorick! I knew him, Horatio, a fellow of infinite jest, of most excellent fancy. He hath bore me on his back a thousand times, and now how abhorr'd in my imagination it is! My gorge rises at it. Here hung those lips that I have kiss'd I know not how oft. Where be your gibes now, your gambols, your songs, your flashes of merriment, that were wont to set the table on a roar? Not one now to mock your own grinning-quite chop-fall'n. Now get you to my lady's chamber, and tell her, let her paint an inch thick, to this favor she must come; make her laugh at that. Prithee, Horatio, tell me one thing.

Horatio.
What's that, my lord?

Hamlet.
Dost thou think Alexander look'd a' this fashion i' th' earth?

Horatio.
E'en so.

Hamlet.
And smelt so? Pah!

Puts down the skull.

Horatio.
E'en so, my lord.

Hamlet.
To what base uses we may return, Horatio! Why may not imagination trace the noble dust of Alexander, till 'a find it stopping a bunghole?

Horatio.
'Twere to consider too curiously, to consider so.

Hamlet.
No, faith, not a jot, but to follow him thither with modesty enough and likelihood to lead it: Alexander died, Alexander was buried, Alexander returneth to dust, the dust is earth, of earth we make loam, and why of that loam whereto he was converted might they not stop a beer-barrel?
Imperious Caesar, dead and turn'd to clay,
Might stop a hole to keep the wind away.
O that that earth which kept the world in awe
Should patch a wall t' expel the winter's flaw!
But soft, but soft awhile, here comes the king.

Enter King, Queen, Laertes, and a Doctor of Divinity, following the corpse, with Lords attendant.

The Queen, the courtiers. Who is this they follow?
And with such maimed rites? This doth betoken
The corse they follow did with desp'rate hand
Foredo it own life. 'Twas of some estate.
Couch we a while and mark.

Retiring with Horatio.

Laertes.
What ceremony else?

Hamlet.
That is Laertes, a very noble youth. Mark.

Laertes.
What ceremony else?

Doctor of Divinity.
Her obsequies have been as far enlarg'd
As we have warranty. Her death was doubtful,
And but that great command o'ersways the order,
She should in ground unsanctified been lodg'd
Till the last trumpet; for charitable prayers,
Shards, flints, and pebbles should be thrown on her.
Yet here she is allow'd her virgin crants,
Her maiden strewments, and the bringing home
Of bell and burial.

Laertes.
Must there no more be done?

Doctor of Divinity.
              No more be done:
We should profane the service of the dead
To sing a requiem and such rest to her
As to peace-parted souls.

Laertes.
            Lay her i' th' earth,
And from her fair and unpolluted flesh
May violets spring! I tell thee, churlish priest,
A minist'ring angel shall my sister be
When thou liest howling.

Hamlet.
            What, the fair Ophelia!

Getrude, Queen of Denmark.

Scattering flowers.

Sweets to the sweet, farewell!
I hop'd thou shouldst have been my Hamlet's wife.
I thought thy bride-bed to have deck'd, sweet maid,
And not have strew'd thy grave.

Laertes.
            O, treble woe
Fall ten times treble on that cursed head
Whose wicked deed thy most ingenious sense
Depriv'd thee of! Hold off the earth a while,
Till I have caught her once more in mine arms.

Leaps in the grave.

Now pile your dust upon the quick and dead,

Till of this flat a mountain you have made
T' o'ertop old Pelion, or the skyish head
Of blue Olympus.

Hamlet.

Coming forward.

What is he whose grief
Bears such an emphasis, whose phrase of sorrow
Conjures the wand'ring stars and makes them stand
Like wonder-wounded hearers? This is I,
Hamlet the Dane!

Hamlet leaps in after Laertes.

Laertes.
The devil take thy soul!

Grappling with him.

Hamlet.
Thou pray'st not well.
I prithee take thy fingers from my throat.
For though I am not splenitive and rash,
Yet have I in me something dangerous,
Which let thy wisdom fear. Hold off thy hand!

Claudius, King of Denmark.
Pluck them asunder.

Getrude, Queen of Denmark.
Hamlet, Hamlet!

Ophelia's Pallbearers.
Gentlemen!

Horatio.
Good my lord, be quiet.

The Attendants part them, and they come out of the grave.

Hamlet.
Why, I will fight with him upon this theme
Until my eyelids will no longer wag.

Getrude, Queen of Denmark.
O my son, what theme?

Hamlet.
I lov'd Ophelia. Forty thousand brothers
Could not with all their quantity of love
Make up my sum. What wilt thou do for her?

Claudius, King of Denmark.
O, he is mad, Laertes.

Getrude, Queen of Denmark.
For love of God, forbear him.

Hamlet.
'Swounds, show me what thou't do.
Woo't weep, woo't fight, woo't fast, woo't tear thyself?
Woo't drink up eisel, eat a crocodile?
I'll do't. Dost thou come here to whine?
To outface me with leaping in her grave?
Be buried quick with her, and so will I.
And if thou prate of mountains, let them throw
Millions of acres on us, till our ground,
Singeing his pate against the burning zone,
Make Ossa like a wart! Nay, and thou'lt mouth,
I'll rant as well as thou.

Getrude, Queen of Denmark.
This is mere madness,
And thus a while the fit will work on him;
Anon, as patient as the female dove,
When that her golden couplets are disclosed,
His silence will sit drooping.

Hamlet.
Hear you, sir,
What is the reason that you use me thus?
I lov'd you ever. But it is no matter.
Let Hercules himself do what he may,
The cat will mew, and dog will have his day.

Exit Hamlet.

Claudius, King of Denmark.
I pray thee, good Horatio, wait upon him.

Exit Horatio.
To Laertes.

Strengthen your patience in our last night's speech,
We'll put the matter to the present push.—
Good Gertrude, set some watch over your son.
This grave shall have a living monument.
An hour of quiet shortly shall we see,
Till then in patience our proceeding be.

Exeunt.

Scene 2

Elsinore. A hall in Elsinore castle.

Act 5, Scene 2

(Hamlet; Horatio; Osric; Lord; King; Queen; Laertes; Fortinbras; English Ambassadors; Attendants)

Hamlet tells Horatio how he rifled through Rosencrantz and Guildenstern's luggage and found the orders for his execution, in which he substituted their names for his, with the result that if their ship has reached England, they are dead. He feels absolutely no remorse at this; he is much more regretful at having lost his temper at Laertes. The young courtier Osric comes in from the King to propose the duel with Laertes. Hamlet mocks him soundly, but accepts despite Horatio's cautioning. Hamlet tells his friend that he is ready to die, and thus fears nothing. Before the whole court, Hamlet begs Laertes's pardon, assuring him that any harms he may have done the other man were the fruits of madness. Laertes does not entirely accept the apology. They fight, and Hamlet lands the first two blows. The Queen drinks to his health from the poisoned cup, despite Claudius's plea that she not drink. Laertes wounds Hamlet during what is supposed to be a pause in the fighting, and in the ensuing scuffle they exchange swords. They fight now in earnest, and Hamlet wounds Laertes. Gertrude dies. Realizing that he is caught in his own trap and about to die, Laertes confesses to poisoning the blade, and casts all the blame on Claudius. Hamlet stabs the King, and as the court calls out 'Treason', forces him to drink the dregs of the poisoned cup. Claudius dies. Laertes absolves Hamlet of his and Polonius's deaths. Hamlet faces up to his own death. Horatio wishes to join him, but Hamlet prevents him from drinking from the poisoned cup, as he needs someone who knows to tell the story. He suggests that Fortinbras be chosen as the next king. The latter, passing by, salutes the ambassadors from England, who enter with him to confirm the deaths of Rosencrantz and Guildenstern. The newcomers are aghast at the pile of bodies and ask for an explanation. As the royal family of Denmark has been wiped out, Fortinbras claims the throne. Horatio promises to tell the story, and Fortinbras orders that Hamlet be interred with military honors, as he is convinced that given a chance, Hamlet would have been a good soldier.

Enter Hamlet and Horatio.

Hamlet.
So much for this, sir, now shall you see the other—
You do remember all the circumstance?

Horatio.
Remember it, my lord!

Hamlet.
Sir, in my heart there was a kind of fighting
That would not let me sleep. Methought I lay
Worse than the mutines in the bilboes. Rashly—
And prais'd be rashness for it—let us know
Our indiscretion sometime serves us well
When our deep plots do pall, and that should learn us
There's a divinity that shapes our ends,
Rough-hew them how we will—

Horatio.
                That is most certain.

Hamlet.
Up from my cabin,
My sea-gown scarf'd about me, in the dark
Grop'd I to find out them, had my desire,
Finger'd their packet, and in fine withdrew
To mine own room again, making so bold,
My fears forgetting manners, to unseal
Their grand commission; where I found, Horatio—
Ah, royal knavery!—an exact command,
Larded with many several sorts of reasons,
Importing Denmark's health and England's too,
With, ho, such bugs and goblins in my life,
That, on the supervise, no leisure bated,
No, not to stay the grinding of the axe,
My head should be struck off.

Horatio.
           Is't possible?

Hamlet.
Here's the commission, read it at more leisure.
But wilt thou hear now how I did proceed?

Horatio.
I beseech you.

Hamlet.
Being thus benetted round with villainies,
Or I could make a prologue to my brains,
They had begun the play. I sat me down,
Devis'd a new commission, wrote it fair.
I once did hold it, as our statists do,
A baseness to write fair, and labor'd much
How to forget that learning, but, sir, now
It did me yeman's service. Wilt thou know
Th' effect of what I wrote?

Horatio.
              Ay, good my lord.

Hamlet.
An earnest conjuration from the King,
As England was his faithful tributary,
As love between them like the palm might flourish,
As peace should still her wheaten garland wear
And stand a comma 'tween their amities,
And many such-like as's of great charge,
That on the view and knowing of these contents,
Without debatement further, more or less,
He should those bearers put to sudden death,
Not shriving time allow'd.

Horatio.
                How was this seal'd?

Hamlet.
Why, even in that was heaven ordinant.
I had my father's signet in my purse,
Which was the model of that Danish seal;
Folded the writ up in the form of th' other,
Subscrib'd it, gave't th' impression, plac'd it safely,
The changeling never known. Now the next day
Was our sea-fight, and what to this was sequent
Thou knowest already.

Horatio.
So Guildenstern and Rosencrantz go to't.

Hamlet.
Why, man, they did make love to this employment,
They are not near my conscience. Their defeat
Does by their own insinuation grow.
'Tis dangerous when the baser nature comes
Between the pass and fell incensed points
Of mighty opposites.

Horatio.
              Why, what a king is this!

Hamlet.
Does it not, think thee, stand me now upon—
He that hath kill'd my king and whor'd my mother,
Popp'd in between th' election and my hopes,
Thrown out his angle for my proper life,
And with such coz'nage—is't not perfect conscience
To quit him with this arm? And is't not to be damn'd,
To let this canker of our nature come
In further evil?

Horatio.
It must be shortly known to him from England
What is the issue of the business there.

Hamlet.
It will be short; the interim's mine,
And a man's life's no more than to say "one."
But I am very sorry, good Horatio,
That to Laertes I forgot myself,
For by the image of my cause I see
The portraiture of his. I'll court his favors.
But sure the bravery of his grief did put me
Into a tow'ring passion.

Horatio.
              Peace, who comes here?

Enter young Osric, a courtier.

Osric.
Your lordship is right welcome back to Denmark.

Hamlet.
I humbly thank you, sir.—Dost know this water-fly?

Horatio.
No, my good lord.

Hamlet.
Thy state is the more gracious, for 'tis a vice to know him. He hath much land, and fertile; let a beast be lord of beasts, and his crib shall stand at the King's mess. 'Tis a chough, but, as I say, spacious in the possession of dirt.

Osric.
Sweet lord, if your lordship were at leisure, I should impart a thing to you from his Majesty.

Hamlet.
I will receive it, sir, with all diligence of spirit. Put your bonnet to his right use, 'tis for the head.

Osric.
I thank your lordship, it is very hot.

Hamlet.
No, believe me, 'tis very cold, the wind is northerly.

Osric.
It is indifferent cold, my lord, indeed.

Hamlet.
But yet methinks it is very sultry and hot for my complexion.

Osric.
Exceedingly, my lord, it is very sultry—as 'twere—I cannot tell how. My lord, his Majesty bade me signify to you that 'a has laid a great wager on your head. Sir, this is the matter—

Hamlet.
I beseech you remember.

Hamlet moves him to put on his hat.

Osric.
Nay, good my lord, for my ease, in good faith. Sir, here is newly come to court Laertes, believe me, an absolute gentleman, full of most excellent differences, of very soft society, and great showing; indeed, to speak sellingly of him, he is the card or calendar of gentry; for you shall find in him the continent of what part a gentleman would see.

Hamlet.
Sir, his definement suffers no perdition in you, though I know to divide him inventorially would dozy th' arithmetic of memory, and yet but yaw neither in respect of his quick sail; but in the verity of extolment, I take him to be a soul of great article, and his infusion of such dearth and rareness as, to make true diction of him, his semblable is his mirror, and who else would trace him, his umbrage, nothing more.

Osric.
Your lordship speaks most infallibly of him.

Hamlet.
The concernancy, sir? Why do we wrap the gentleman in our more rawer breath?

Osric.
Sir?

Horatio.
Is't not possible to understand in another tongue? You will to't, sir, really.

Hamlet.
What imports the nomination of this gentleman?

Osric.
Of Laertes?

Horatio.
His purse is empty already: all 's golden words are spent.

Hamlet.
Of him, sir.

Osric.
I know you are not ignorant—

Hamlet.
I would you did, sir, yet, in faith, if you did, it would not much approve me. Well, sir?

Osric.
You are not ignorant of what excellence Laertes is—

Hamlet.
I dare not confess that, lest I should compare with him in excellence, but to know a man well were to know himself.

Osric.
I mean, sir, for his weapon, but in the imputation laid on him by them, in his meed he's unfellow'd.

Hamlet.
What's his weapon?

Osric.
Rapier and dagger.

Hamlet.
That's two of his weapons—but well.

Osric.
The King, sir, hath wager'd with him six Barbary horses, against the which he has impawn'd, as I take it, six French rapiers and poniards, with their assigns, as girdle, hangers, and so. Three of the carriages, in faith, are very dear to fancy, very responsive to the hilts, most delicate carriages, and of very liberal conceit.

Hamlet.
What call you the carriages?

Horatio.
I knew you must be edified by the margent ere you had done.

Osric.
The carriages, sir, are the hangers.

Hamlet.
The phrase would be more germane to the matter if we could carry a cannon by our sides; I would it might be hangers till then. But on: six Barb'ry horses against six French swords, their assigns, and three liberal-

conceited carriages; that's the French bet against the Danish. Why is this all impawn'd, as you call it?

Osric.
The King, sir, hath laid, sir, that in a dozen passes between yourself and him, he shall not exceed you three hits; he hath laid on twelve for nine; and it would come to immediate trial, if your lordship would vouchsafe the answer.

Hamlet.
How if I answer no?

Osric.
I mean, my lord, the opposition of your person in trial.

Hamlet.
Sir, I will walk here in the hall. If it please his Majesty, it is the breathing time of day with me. Let the foils be brought, the gentleman willing, and the King hold his purpose, I will win for him and I can; if not, I will gain nothing but my shame and the odd hits.

Osric.
Shall I deliver you so?

Hamlet.
To this effect, sir—after what flourish your nature will.

Osric.
I commend my duty to your lordship.

Hamlet.
Yours.

Exit Osric.

'A does well to commend it himself, there are no tongues else for 's turn.

Horatio.
This lapwing runs away with the shell on his head.

Hamlet.
'A did comply, sir, with his dug before 'a suck'd it. Thus has he, and many more of the same breed that I know the drossy age dotes on, only got the tune of the time, and out of an habit of encounter, a kind of yesty collection, which carries them through and through the most profound and winnow'd opinions, and do but blow them to their trial, the bubbles are out.

Enter a Lord.

Lord.
My lord, his Majesty commended him to you by young Osric, who brings back to him that you attend him in the hall. He sends to know if your pleasure hold to play with Laertes, or that you will take longer time.

Hamlet.
I am constant to my purposes, they follow the King's pleasure. If his fitness speaks, mine is ready; now or whensoever, provided I be so able as now.

Lord.
The King and Queen and all are coming down.

Hamlet.
In happy time.

Lord.
The Queen desires you to use some gentle entertainment to Laertes before you fall to play.

Hamlet.
She well instructs me.

Exit Lord.

Horatio.
You will lose, my lord.

Hamlet.
I do not think so; since he went into France I have been in continual practice. I shall win at the odds. Thou wouldst not think how ill all's here about my heart—but it is no matter.

Horatio.
Nay, good my lord—

Hamlet.
It is but foolery, but it is such a kind of gain-giving, as would perhaps trouble a woman.

Horatio.
If your mind dislike any thing, obey it. I will forestall their repair hither, and say you are not fit.

Hamlet.
Not a whit, we defy augury. There is special providence in the fall of a sparrow. If it be now, 'tis not to come; if it be not to come, it will be now; if it be not now, yet it will come—the readiness is all. Since no man, of aught he leaves, knows what is't to leave betimes, let be.

Act 5, Scene 2

A table prepar'd, and flagons of wine on it.
Enter Trumpets, Drums, and Officers with cushions, foils, daggers; King, Queen, Laertes, Osric, and all the State.

Claudius, King of Denmark.
Come, Hamlet, come, and take this hand from me.

The King puts Laertes' hand into Hamlet's.

Hamlet.
Give me your pardon, sir. I have done you wrong,
But pardon't as you are a gentleman.
This presence knows,
And you must needs have heard, how I am punish'd
With a sore distraction. What I have done
That might your nature, honor, and exception
Roughly awake, I here proclaim was madness.
Was't Hamlet wrong'd Laertes? Never Hamlet!
If Hamlet from himself be ta'en away,
And when he's not himself does wrong Laertes,
Then Hamlet does it not, Hamlet denies it.
Who does it then? His madness. If't be so,
Hamlet is of the faction that is wronged,
His madness is poor Hamlet's enemy.
Sir, in this audience,
Let my disclaiming from a purpos'd evil
Free me so far in your most generous thoughts,
That I have shot my arrow o'er the house
And hurt my brother.

Laertes.
                    I am satisfied in nature,
Whose motive in this case should stir me most
To my revenge, but in my terms of honor
I stand aloof, and will no reconcilement
Till by some elder masters of known honor
I have a voice and president of peace
To keep my name ungor'd. But till that time
I do receive your offer'd love like love,
And will not wrong it.

Hamlet.
                    I embrace it freely,
And will this brothers' wager frankly play.
Give us the foils. Come on.

Laertes.
                    Come, one for me.

Hamlet.
I'll be your foil, Laertes; in mine ignorance
Your skill shall like a star i' th' darkest night
Stick fiery off indeed.

Laertes.
                    You mock me, sir.

Hamlet.
No, by this hand.

Claudius, King of Denmark.
Give them the foils, young Osric. Cousin Hamlet,
You know the wager?

Hamlet.
                    Very well, my lord.
Your Grace has laid the odds a' th' weaker side.

Claudius, King of Denmark.
I do not fear it, I have seen you both;
But since he is better'd, we have therefore odds.

Laertes.
This is too heavy; let me see another.

Hamlet.
This likes me well. These foils have all a length?

Prepare to play.

Osric.
Ay, my good lord.

Claudius, King of Denmark.
Set me the stoups of wine upon that table.
If Hamlet give the first or second hit,
Or quit in answer of the third exchange,
Let all the battlements their ord'nance fire.
The King shall drink to Hamlet's better breath,
And in the cup an union shall he throw,
Richer than that which four successive kings
In Denmark's crown have worn. Give me the cups,
And let the kettle to the trumpet speak,
The trumpet to the cannoneer without,
The cannons to the heavens, the heaven to earth,
"Now the King drinks to Hamlet." Come begin;

Trumpets the while.

And you, the judges, bear a wary eye.

Hamlet.
Come on, sir.

Laertes.
                          Come, my lord.

They play and Hamlet scores a hit.

Hamlet.
                          One.

Laertes.
                          No.

Hamlet.
                          Judgment.

Osric.
A hit, a very palpable hit.

Laertes.
                          Well, again.

Claudius, King of Denmark.
Stay, give me drink. Hamlet, this pearl is thine,
Here's to thy health! Give him the cup.

Drum, trumpets sound flourish. A piece goes off within.

Hamlet.
I'll play this bout first, set it by a while.
Come.

They play again.

Another hit; what say you?

Laertes.
A touch, a touch, I do confess't.

Claudius, King of Denmark.
Our son shall win.

Getrude, Queen of Denmark.
                    He's fat, and scant of breath.
Here, Hamlet, take my napkin, rub thy brows.
The Queen carouses to thy fortune, Hamlet.

Hamlet.
Good madam!

Claudius, King of Denmark.
                    Gertrude, do not drink.

Getrude, Queen of Denmark.
I will, my lord, I pray you pardon me.

Claudius, King of Denmark.

Aside.

It is the pois'ned cup, it is too late.

Hamlet.
I dare not drink yet, madam; by and by.

Getrude, Queen of Denmark.
Come, let me wipe thy face.

Laertes.
My lord, I'll hit him now.

Claudius, King of Denmark.
                          I do not think't.

Laertes.

Aside.

And yet it is almost against my conscience.

Hamlet.
Come, for the third, Laertes, you do but dally.
I pray you pass with your best violence;
I am sure you make a wanton of me.

Laertes.
Say you so? Come on.

They play.

Osric.
Nothing, neither way.

Laertes.
Have at you now!

Laertes wounds Hamlet; then, in scuffling, they change rapiers.

Claudius, King of Denmark.
                    Part them, they are incens'd.

Hamlet.
Nay, come again.

Hamlet wounds Laertes.
The Queen falls.

Osric.
Look to the Queen there ho!

Horatio.
They bleed on both sides. How is it, my lord?

Osric.
How is't, Laertes?

Laertes.
Why, as a woodcock to mine own springe, Osric:
I am justly kill'd with mine own treachery.

Hamlet.
How does the Queen?

Claudius, King of Denmark.
                  She swoons to see them bleed.

Getrude, Queen of Denmark.
No, no, the drink, the drink—O my dear Hamlet—
The drink, the drink! I am pois'ned.

Dies.

Hamlet.
O villainy! Ho, let the door be lock'd!
Treachery! Seek it out.

Laertes.
It is here, Hamlet. Hamlet, thou art slain.
No med'cine in the world can do thee good;
In thee there is not half an hour's life.
The treacherous instrument is in thy hand,
Unbated and envenom'd. The foul practice
Hath turn'd itself on me. Lo here I lie,
Never to rise again. Thy mother's pois'ned.
I can no more—the King, the King's to blame.

Hamlet.
The point envenom'd too!
Then, venom, to thy work.

Hurts the King.

All.
Treason! Treason!

Claudius, King of Denmark.
O, yet defend me, friends, I am but hurt.

Hamlet.
Here, thou incestuous, murd'rous, damned Dane,
Drink off this potion! Is thy union here?
Follow my mother!

King dies.

Laertes.
                He is justly served,
It is a poison temper'd by himself.
Exchange forgiveness with me, noble Hamlet.
Mine and my father's death come not upon thee,
Nor thine on me!

Dies.

Hamlet.
Heaven make thee free of it! I follow thee.
I am dead, Horatio. Wretched queen, adieu!
You that look pale, and tremble at this chance,
That are but mutes or audience to this act,
Had I but time—as this fell sergeant, Death,
Is strict in his arrest—O, I could tell you—
But let it be. Horatio, I am dead,
Thou livest. Report me and my cause aright
To the unsatisfied.

Horatio.
                Never believe it;
I am more an antique Roman than a Dane.
Here's yet some liquor left.

Hamlet.
                As th' art a man,
Give me the cup. Let go! By heaven, I'll ha't!
O God, Horatio, what a wounded name,
Things standing thus unknown, shall I leave behind me!
If thou didst ever hold me in thy heart,
Absent thee from felicity a while,
And in this harsh world draw thy breath in pain
To tell my story.

A march afar off and a shot within.

What warlike noise is this?

Osric goes to the door and returns.

Osric.
Young Fortinbras, with conquest come from Poland,
To th' ambassadors of England gives
This warlike volley.

Hamlet.
                O, I die, Horatio,
The potent poison quite o'er-crows my spirit.
I cannot live to hear the news from England,
But I do prophesy th' election lights
On Fortinbras, he has my dying voice.

So tell him, with th' occurrents more and less
Which have solicited—the rest is silence.

Dies.

Horatio.
Now cracks a noble heart. Good night, sweet prince,
And flights of angels sing thee to thy rest!

March within.

Why does the drum come hither?

Enter Fortinbras with the English Ambassadors, with Drum, Colors, and Attendants.

Fortinbras.
Where is this sight?

Horatio.
               What is it you would see?
If aught of woe or wonder, cease your search.

Fortinbras.
This quarry cries on havoc. O proud death,
What feast is toward in thine eternal cell,
That thou so many princes at a shot
So bloodily hast struck?

First Ambassador.
               The sight is dismal,
And our affairs from England come too late.
The ears are senseless that should give us hearing,
To tell him his commandment is fulfill'd,
That Rosencrantz and Guildenstern are dead.
Where should we have our thanks?

Horatio.
               Not from his mouth,
Had it th' ability of life to thank you.
He never gave commandment for their death.
But since so jump upon this bloody question,
You from the Polack wars, and you from England,
Are here arrived, give order that these bodies
High on a stage be placed to the view,
And let me speak to th' yet unknowing world
How these things came about. So shall you hear
Of carnal, bloody, and unnatural acts,
Of accidental judgments, casual slaughters,
Of deaths put on by cunning and forc'd cause,
And in this upshot, purposes mistook
Fall'n on th' inventors' heads: all this can I
Truly deliver.

Fortinbras.
             Let us haste to hear it,
And call the noblest to the audience.
For me, with sorrow I embrace my fortune.
I have some rights, of memory in this kingdom,
Which now to claim my vantage doth invite me.

Horatio.
Of that I shall have also cause to speak,
And from his mouth whose voice will draw on more.
But let this same be presently perform'd
Even while men's minds are wild, lest more mischance
On plots and errors happen.

Fortinbras.
             Let four captains
Bear Hamlet like a soldier to the stage,
For he was likely, had he been put on,
To have prov'd most royal; and for his passage,
The soldiers' music and the rite of war
Speak loudly for him.
Take up the bodies. Such a sight as this
Becomes the field, but here shows much amiss.
  Go bid the soldiers shoot.

Exeunt marching; after the which a peal of ordinance are shot off.

Romeo and Juliet

Prologue

(Chorus)

The Chorus explains how an ancient family feud in Verona has sparked up again, and what tragic consequences it will have for a pair of young lovers.

Enter Chorus.

Chorus.
Two households, both alike in dignity,
In fair Verona, where we lay our scene,
From ancient grudge break to new mutiny,
Where civil blood makes civil hands unclean.
From forth the fatal loins of these two foes
A pair of star-cross'd lovers take their life;
Whose misadventur'd piteous overthrows
Doth with their death bury their parents' strife.
The fearful passage of their death-mark'd love,
And the continuance of their parents' rage,
Which, but their children's end, nought could remove,
Is now the two hours' traffic of our stage;
The which if you with patient ears attend,
What here shall miss, our toil shall strive to mend.

Exit.

Act 1

Scene 1

Verona. A public place.

(Sampson; Gregory; Abram; Balthasar; Benvolio; Tybalt; Citizens; Capulet; Lady Capulet; Montague; Lady Montague; Prince Escalus; Romeo)

Capulet's servants pick a quarrel with Montague's, which degenerates into a general brawl. Obedient to the Prince's ruling against brawling, Benvolio tries to part them, but he is attacked by Tybalt, who calls him a coward for speaking of peace. Infuriated citizens begin hitting at the brawlers on both sides, as Capulet and Montague themselves enter the fray. The anarchy only ceases when the Prince himself arrives and orders an end to the fighting, threatening both Capulet and Montague with death if another battle erupts. Montague, his wife and Benvolio are left alone as the others depart. Benvolio explains how the fight began, and is able to reassure his aunt that Romeo was not present. Romeo's parents are concerned about his melancholy, and Benvolio promises to find to what's going on. Seeing Romeo arrive, his parents leave to give Benvolio a clear field. It quickly becomes apparent from Romeo's hackneyed phrases that he believes himself to be deeply in love with a lady who has sworn to be chaste. Benvolio advises him to find some better-looking women to run after, but Romeo insists there are none.

Enter Sampson and Gregory, with swords and bucklers, of the house of Capulet.

Sampson.
Gregory, on my word, we'll not carry coals.

Gregory.
No, for then we should be colliers.

Sampson.
I mean, and we be in choler, we'll draw.

Gregory.
Ay, while you live, draw your neck out of collar.

Sampson.
I strike quickly, being mov'd.

Gregory.
But thou art not quickly mov'd to strike.

Sampson.
A dog of the house of Montague moves me.

Gregory.
To move is to stir, and to be valiant is to stand; therefore, if thou art mov'd, thou run'st away.

Sampson.
A dog of that house shall move me to stand! I will take the wall of any man or maid of Montague's.

Gregory.
That shows thee a weak slave, for the weakest goes to the wall.

Sampson.
'Tis true, and therefore women, being the weaker vessels, are ever thrust to the wall; therefore I will push Montague's men from the wall, and thrust his maids to the wall.

Gregory.
The quarrel is between our masters, and us their men.

Sampson.
'Tis all one; I will show myself a tyrant: when I have fought with the men, I will be civil with the maids; I will cut off their heads.

Gregory.
The heads of the maids?

Sampson.
Ay, the heads of the maids, or their maidenheads, take it in what sense thou wilt.

Gregory.
They must take it in sense that feel it.

Sampson.
Me they shall feel while I am able to stand, and 'tis known I am a pretty piece of flesh.

Gregory.
'Tis well thou art not fish; if thou hadst, thou hadst been poor-John. Draw thy tool, here comes two of the house of Montagues.

Enter two other servingmen: Abram and Balthasar.

Sampson.
My naked weapon is out. Quarrel, I will back thee.

Gregory.
How, turn thy back and run?

Sampson.
Fear me not.

Gregory.
No, marry, I fear thee!

Sampson.
Let us take the law of our sides, let them begin.

Gregory.
I will frown as I pass by, and let them take it as they list.

Sampson.
Nay, as they dare. I will bite my thumb at them, which is disgrace to them if they bear it.

Abram.
Do you bite your thumb at us, sir?

Sampson.
I do bite my thumb, sir.

Abram.
Do you bite your thumb at us, sir?

Sampson.

Aside to Gregory

Is the law of our side if I say ay?

Gregory.

Aside to Sampson

No.

Sampson.
No, sir, I do not bite my thumb at you, sir, but I bite my thumb, sir.

Gregory.
Do you quarrel, sir?

Abram.
Quarrel, sir? No, sir.

Sampson.
But if you do, sir, I am for you. I serve as good a man as you.

Abram.
No better?

Sampson.
Well, sir.

Enter Benvolio.

Gregory.
Say "better," here comes one of my master's kinsmen.

Sampson.
Yes, better, sir.

Abram.
You lie.

Sampson.
Draw, if you be men. Gregory, remember thy washing blow.

They fight.

Benvolio.
Part, fools!
Put up your swords, you know not what you do.

Beats down their swords.
Enter Tybalt.

Tybalt.
What, art thou drawn among these heartless hinds?
Turn thee, Benvolio, look upon thy death.

Benvolio.
I do but keep the peace. Put up thy sword,
Or manage it to part these men with me.

Tybalt.
What, drawn and talk of peace? I hate the word
As I hate hell, all Montagues, and thee.
Have at thee, coward!

They fight.
Enter three or four Citizens with clubs or partisans.

Citizens of Verona.
Clubs, bills, and partisans! Strike! Beat them down!
Down with the Capulets! Down with the Montagues!

Enter old Capulet in his gown, and his wife, Lady Capulet.

Capulet.
What noise is this? Give me my long sword ho!

Lady Capulet.
A crutch, a crutch! Why call you for a sword?

Capulet.
My sword, I say! Old Montague is come,
And flourishes his blade in spite of me.

Enter old Montague and his wife, Lady Montague.

Montague.
Thou villain Capulet!—Hold me not, let me go.

Lady Montague.
Thou shalt not stir one foot to seek a foe.

Enter Prince Escalus with his Train.

Prince Escalus.
Rebellious subjects, enemies to peace,
Profaners of this neighbor-stained steel—
Will they not hear?—What ho, you men, you beasts!
That quench the fire of your pernicious rage
With purple fountains issuing from your veins—
On pain of torture, from those bloody hands
Throw your mistempered weapons to the ground,
And hear the sentence of your moved prince.
Three civil brawls, bred of an airy word,
By thee, old Capulet, and Montague,
Have thrice disturb'd the quiet of our streets,
And made Verona's ancient citizens
Cast by"#FFFFFF" their grave beseeming ornaments
To wield old partisans, in hands as old,
Cank'red with peace, to part your cank'red hate;
If ever you disturb our streets again
Your lives shall pay the forfeit of the peace.
For this time all the rest depart away.
You, Capulet, shall go along with me,
And, Montague, come you this afternoon,
To know our farther pleasure in this case,
To old Free-town, our common judgment-place.
Once more, on pain of death, all men depart.

Exeunt all but Montague, Lady Montague, and Benvolio.

Montague.
Who set this ancient quarrel new abroach?
Speak, nephew, were you by when it began?

Benvolio.
Here were the servants of your adversary,
And yours, close fighting ere I did approach.
I drew to part them. In the instant came
The fiery Tybalt, with his sword prepar'd,
Which, as he breath'd defiance to my ears,
He swung about his head and cut the winds,
Who, nothing hurt withal, hiss'd him in scorn.
While we were interchanging thrusts and blows,
Came more and more, and fought on part and part,
Till the Prince came, who parted either part.

Lady Montague.
O, where is Romeo? Saw you him today?
Right glad I am he was not at this fray.

Benvolio.
Madam, an hour before the worshipp'd sun
Peer'd forth the golden window of the east,
A troubled mind drive me to walk abroad,
Where, underneath the grove of sycamore
That westward rooteth from this city side,
So early walking did I see your son.
Towards him I made, but he was ware of me,
And stole into the covert of the wood.
I, measuring his affections by my own,
Which then most sought where most might not be found,
Being one too many by my weary self,
Pursued my humor not pursuing his,
And gladly shunn'd who gladly fled from me.

Montague.
Many a morning hath he there been seen,
With tears augmenting the fresh morning's dew,
Adding to clouds more clouds with his deep sighs,
But all so soon as the all-cheering sun
Should in the farthest east begin to draw
The shady curtains from Aurora's bed,
Away from light steals home my heavy son,
And private in his chamber pens himself,
Shuts up his windows, locks fair daylight out,
And makes himself an artificial night.
Black and portendous must this humor prove,
Unless good counsel may the cause remove.

Benvolio.
My noble uncle, do you know the cause?

Montague.
I neither know it, nor can learn of him.

Benvolio.
Have you importun'd him by any means?

Montague.
Both by myself and many other friends,
But he, his own affections' counsellor,
Is to himself (I will not say how true)
But to himself so secret and so close,
So far from sounding and discovery,
As is the bud bit with an envious worm,
Ere he can spread his sweet leaves to the air
Or dedicate his beauty to the sun.
Could we but learn from whence his sorrows grow,
We would as willingly give cure as know.

Enter Romeo.

Benvolio.
See where he comes. So please you step aside,
I'll know his grievance, or be much denied.

Montague.
I would thou wert so happy by thy stay
To hear true shrift. Come, madam, let's away.

Exeunt Montague and Lady.

Benvolio.
Good morrow, cousin.

Romeo.
                Is the day so young?

Benvolio.
But new struck nine.

Romeo.
                    Ay me, sad hours seem long.
Was that my father that went hence so fast?

Benvolio.
It was. What sadness lengthens Romeo's hours?

Romeo.
Not having that which, having, makes them short.

Benvolio.
In love?

Romeo.
Out—

Benvolio.
Of love?

Romeo.
Out of her favor where I am in love.

Benvolio.
Alas that love, so gentle in his view,
Should be so tyrannous and rough in proof!

Romeo.
Alas that love, whose view is muffled still,
Should, without eyes, see pathways to his will!
Where shall we dine? O me! What fray was here?
Yet tell me not, for I have heard it all:
Here's much to do with hate, but more with love.
Why then, O brawling love! O loving hate!
O any thing, of nothing first create!
O heavy lightness, serious vanity,
Misshapen chaos of well-seeming forms,
Feather of lead, bright smoke, cold fire, sick health,
Still-waking sleep, that is not what it is!
This love feel I, that feel no love in this.
Dost thou not laugh?

Benvolio.
               No, coz, I rather weep.

Romeo.
Good heart, at what?

Benvolio.
               At thy good heart's oppression.

Romeo.
Why, such is love's transgression.
Griefs of mine own lie heavy in my breast,
Which thou wilt propagate to have it press'd
With more of thine. This love that thou hast shown
Doth add more grief to too much of mine own.
Love is a smoke made with the fume of sighs,
Being purg'd, a fire sparkling in lovers' eyes,
Being vex'd, a sea nourish'd with loving tears.
What is it else? A madness most discreet,
A choking gall, and a preserving sweet.
Farewell, my coz.

Benvolio.
               Soft, I will go along;
And if you leave me so, you do me wrong.

Romeo.
Tut, I have lost myself, I am not here:
This is not Romeo, he's some other where.

Benvolio.
Tell me in sadness, who is that you love?

Romeo.
What, shall I groan and tell thee?

Benvolio.
                         Groan? Why, no;
But sadly tell me, who?

Romeo.
Bid a sick man in sadness make his will—
A word ill urg'd to one that is so ill!
In sadness, cousin, I do love a woman.

Benvolio.
I aim'd so near when I suppos'd you lov'd.

Romeo.
A right good mark-man! And she's fair I love.

Benvolio.
A right fair mark, fair coz, is soonest hit.

Romeo.
Well, in that hit you miss: she'll not be hit
With Cupid's arrow, she hath Dian's wit;
And in strong proof of chastity well arm'd,
From Love's weak childish bow she lives uncharm'd.
She will not stay the siege of loving terms,
Nor bide th' encounter of assailing eyes,
Nor ope her lap to saint-seducing gold.
O, she is rich in beauty, only poor
That, when she dies, with beauty dies her store.

Benvolio.
Then she hath sworn that she will still live chaste?

Romeo.
She hath, and in that sparing makes huge waste;
For beauty starv'd with her severity
Cuts beauty off from all posterity.
She is too fair, too wise, wisely too fair,
To merit bliss by making me despair.
She hath forsworn to love, and in that vow
Do I live dead that live to tell it now.

Benvolio.
Be rul'd by me, forget to think of her.

Romeo.
O, teach me how I should forget to think.

Benvolio.
By giving liberty unto thine eyes:
Examine other beauties.

Romeo.
                              'Tis the way
To call hers (exquisite) in question more.
These happy masks that kiss fair ladies' brows,
Being black, puts us in mind they hide the fair.
He that is strucken blind cannot forget
The precious treasure of his eyesight lost.
Show me a mistress that is passing fair,
What doth her beauty serve but as a note
Where I may read who pass'd that passing fair?
Farewell, thou canst not teach me to forget.

Benvolio.
I'll pay that doctrine, or else die in debt.

Exeunt.

Scene 2

Verona. A street.

(Capulet; County Paris; Second Servingman; Benvolio; Romeo)

The Prince's kinsman Paris receives Capulet's permission to woo his daughter Juliet, though Capulet considers her still too young for marriage. He insists that he will not make her marry a man she does not love. He invites Paris to a feast that evening, and sends a servant out with a list of other people to invite. Unfortunately, the servant is illiterate. Coming upon the educated Benvolio and Romeo, he asks them to read the list to him, which they do. They thus learn that not only is Capulet giving a party, but that Romeo's love Rosaline will be there. Benvolio tells Romeo that seeing her in the company of other ladies will make it clear that she's nothing special, but Romeo insists that she will outshine them all.

Enter Capulet, County Paris, and Second Servingman, the clown.

Capulet.
But Montague is bound as well as I,
In penalty alike, and 'tis not hard, I think,
For men so old as we to keep the peace.

Paris.
Of honorable reckoning are you both,
And pity 'tis you liv'd at odds so long.
But now, my lord, what say you to my suit?

Capulet.
But saying o'er what I have said before:
My child is yet a stranger in the world,
She hath not seen the change of fourteen years;
Let two more summers wither in their pride,
Ere we may think her ripe to be a bride.

Paris.
Younger than she are happy mothers made.

Capulet.
And too soon marr'd are those so early made.
Earth hath swallowed all my hopes but she;
She's the hopeful lady of my earth.
But woo her, gentle Paris, get her heart,
My will to her consent is but a part;
And she agreed, within her scope of choice
Lies my consent and fair according voice.
This night I hold an old accustom'd feast,
Whereto I have invited many a guest,
Such as I love, and you, among the store
One more, most welcome, makes my number more.
At my poor house look to behold this night
Earth-treading stars that make dark heaven light.
Such comfort as do lusty young men feel
When well-apparell'd April on the heel
Of limping winter treads, even such delight
Among fresh fennel buds shall you this night
Inherit at my house; hear all, all see;
And like her most whose merit most shall be;
Which on more view of many, mine, being one,
May stand in number, though in reck'ning none.
Come go with me.

To Second Servingman.

Go, sirrah, trudge about
Through fair Verona, find those persons out
Whose names are written there, and to them say,
My house and welcome on their pleasure stay.

Exit with Paris.

Second Servingman.
Find them out whose names are written here! It is written that the shoemaker should meddle with his yard and the tailor with his last, the fisher with his pencil and the painter with his nets; but I am sent to find those persons whose names are here writ, and

Act 1, Scene 2

can never find what names the writing person hath here writ. I must to the learned. In good time!

Enter Benvolio and Romeo.

Benvolio.
Tut, man, one fire burns out another's burning,
One pain is less'ned by another's anguish;
Turn giddy, and be help by backward turning;
One desperate grief cures with another's languish:
Take thou some new infection to thy eye,
And the rank poison of the old will die.

Romeo.
Your plantain leaf is excellent for that.

Benvolio.
For what, I pray thee?

Romeo.
For your broken shin.

Benvolio.
Why, Romeo, art thou mad?

Romeo.
Not mad, but bound more than a madman is;
Shut up in prison, kept without my food,
Whipt and tormented, and—God-den, good fellow.

Second Servingman.
God gi' god-den. I pray, sir, can you read?

Romeo.
Ay, mine own fortune in my misery.

Second Servingman.
Perhaps you have learn'd it without book. But I pray, can you read any thing you see?

Romeo.
Ay, if I know the letters and the language.

Second Servingman.
Ye say honestly, rest you merry!

Romeo.
Stay, fellow, I can read.

He reads the letter.

"Signior Martino and his wife and daughters; County Anselme and his beauteous sisters; the lady widow of Vitruvio; Signior Placentio and his lovely nieces; Mercutio and his brother Valentine; mine uncle Capulet, his wife, and daughters; my fair niece Rosaline, and Livia; Signior Valentio and his cousin Tybalt; Lucio and the lively Helena."
A fair assembly. Whither should they come?

Second Servingman.
Up.

Romeo.
Whither? To supper?

Second Servingman.
To our house.

Romeo.
Whose house?

Second Servingman.
My master's.

Romeo.
Indeed I should have ask'd thee that before.

Second Servingman.
Now I'll tell you without asking. My master is the great rich Capulet, and if you be not of the house of Montagues, I pray come and crush a cup of wine. Rest you merry!

Exit.

Benvolio.
At this same ancient feast of Capulet's
Sups the fair Rosaline whom thou so loves,
With all the admired beauties of Verona.
Go thither, and with unattainted eye
Compare her face with some that I shall show,
And I will make thee think thy swan a crow.

Romeo.
When the devout religion of mine eye
Maintains such falsehood, then turn tears to fires;
And these, who, often drown'd, could never die,
Transparent heretics, be burnt for liars!
One fairer than my love! The all-seeing sun
Ne'er saw her match since first the world begun.

Benvolio.
Tut, you saw her fair, none else being by,
Herself pois'd with herself in either eye;
But in that crystal scales let there be weigh'd
Your lady's love against some other maid
That I will show you shining at this feast,
And she shall scant show well that now seems best.

Romeo.
I'll go along no such sight to be shown,
But to rejoice in splendor of mine own.

Exeunt.

Scene 3

Verona. A room in Capulet's house.

(Lady Capulet; Nurse; Juliet; First Servingman)

The rather flustered Lady Capulet talks with Juliet and her Nurse, a gossipy old thing with a taste for endless, vaguely indecent anecdotes. Lady Capulet finally brings herself to ask Juliet whether she thinks herself ready for marriage. She praises Paris, as does the Nurse, and instructs the girl to have a good look at him at the party that night. The obedient girl dutifully replies that she will do as her parents say. A Servingman announces the arrival of the guests.

Enter Capulet's Wife, and Nurse.

Lady Capulet.
Nurse, where's my daughter? Call her forth to me.

Nurse.
Now by my maidenhead at twelve year old,
I bade her come. What, lamb! What, ladybird!
God forbid! Where's this girl? What, Juliet!

Enter Juliet.

Juliet.
How now, who calls?

Nurse.
              Your mother.

Juliet.
              Madam, I am here,
What is your will?

Lady Capulet.
This is the matter. Nurse, give leave a while,
We must talk in secret. Nurse, come back again,
I have rememb'red me, thou s' hear our counsel.
Thou knowest my daughter's of a pretty age.

Nurse.
Faith, I can tell her age unto an hour.

Lady Capulet.
She's not fourteen.

Nurse.
            I'll lay fourteen of my teeth—
And yet, to my teen be it spoken, I have but four—
She's not fourteen. How long is it now
To Lammas-tide?

Lady Capulet.
            A fortnight and odd days.

Nurse.
Even or odd, of all days in the year,
Come Lammas-eve at night shall she be fourteen.
Susan and she—God rest all Christian souls!—
Were of an age. Well, Susan is with God,
She was too good for me. But as I said,
On Lammas-eve at night shall she be fourteen,
That shall she, marry, I remember it well.
'Tis since the earthquake now eleven years,
And she was wean'd—I never shall forget it—
Of all the days of the year, upon that day;
For I had then laid wormwood to my dug,
Sitting in the sun under the dove-house wall.
My lord and you were then at Mantua—
Nay, I do bear a brain—but as I said,
When it did taste the wormwood on the nipple
Of my dug and felt it bitter, pretty fool,
To see it tetchy and fall out wi' th' dug!
Shake, quoth the dove-house; 'twas no need, I trow,
To bid me trudge.
And since that time it is eleven years,
For then she could stand high-lone; nay, by th' rood,
She could have run and waddled all about;
For even the day before, she broke her brow,
And then my husband—God be with his soul!
'A was a merry man—took up the child.
"Yea," quoth he, "dost thou fall upon thy face?
Thou wilt fall backward when thou hast more wit,
Wilt thou not, Jule?" and by my holidam,
The pretty wretch left crying and said, "Ay."
To see now how a jest shall come about!
I warrant, and I should live a thousand years,
I never should forget it: "Wilt thou not, Jule?" quoth he;
And, pretty fool, it stinted and said, "Ay."

Lady Capulet.
Enough of this, I pray thee hold thy peace.

Nurse.
Yes, madam, yet I cannot choose but laugh
To think it should leave crying and say, "Ay."
And yet I warrant it had upon it brow
A bump as big as a young cock'rel's stone—
A perilous knock—and it cried bitterly.
"Yea," quoth my husband, "fall'st upon thy face?
Thou wilt fall backward when thou comest to age,
Wilt thou not, Jule?" It stinted and said, "Ay."

Juliet.
And stint thou too, I pray thee, nurse, say I.

Nurse.
Peace, I have done. God mark thee to his grace!
Thou wast the prettiest babe that e'er I nurs'd.
And I might live to see thee married once,
I have my wish.

Lady Capulet.
Marry, that "marry" is the very theme
I came to talk of. Tell me, daughter Juliet,
How stands your dispositions to be married?

Juliet.
It is an honor that I dream not of.

Nurse.
An honor! Were not I thine only nurse,
I would say thou hadst suck'd wisdom from thy teat.

Lady Capulet.
Well, think of marriage now; younger than you,
Here in Verona, ladies of esteem,
Are made already mothers. By my count,
I was your mother much upon these years
That you are now a maid. Thus then in brief:
The valiant Paris seeks you for his love.

Nurse.
A man, young lady! Lady, such a man
As all the world—why, he's a man of wax.

Lady Capulet.
Verona's summer hath not such a flower.

Nurse.
Nay, he's a flower, in faith, a very flower.

Lady Capulet.
What say you? Can you love the gentleman?
This night you shall behold him at our feast;
Read o'er the volume of young Paris' face,
And find delight writ there with beauty's pen;
Examine every married lineament,
And see how one another lends content;
And what obscur'd in this fair volume lies
Find written in the margent of his eyes.
This precious book of love, this unbound lover,
To beautify him, only lacks a cover.
The fish lives in the sea, and 'tis much pride
For fair without the fair within to hide.
That book in many's eyes doth share the glory,
That in gold clasps locks in the golden story;
So shall you share all that he doth possess,
By having him, making yourself no less.

Nurse.
No less! Nay, bigger: women grow by men.

Lady Capulet.
Speak briefly, can you like of Paris' love?

Juliet.
I'll look to like, if looking liking move;
But no more deep will I endart mine eye
Than your consent gives strength to make it fly.

Enter First Servingman.

First Servingman.
Madam, the guests are come, supper serv'd up, you call'd, my young lady ask'd for, the nurse curs'd in the pantry, and every thing in extremity. I must hence to wait; I beseech you follow straight.

Exit.

Lady Capulet.
We follow thee. Juliet, the County stays.

Nurse.
Go, girl, seek happy nights to happy days.

Exeunt.

Scene 4

Verona. A street.

(Romeo; Mercutio; Benvolio; Maskers; Torch-Bearers)

Romeo, Mercutio, Benvolio, and a few others approach the Capulets' house, wearing masks and intent on crashing the party. Romeo is melancholy, and uneasy, having had a premonitory dream; Mercutio takes the mention of dreams as an excuse to embark on a fantastical riff on the subject. This does not cheer Romeo up, and he still fears his premonition.

Enter Romeo, Mercutio, Benvolio, with five or six other Maskers; Torch-Bearers.

Romeo.
What, shall this speech be spoke for our excuse?
Or shall we on without apology?

Benvolio.
The date is out of such prolixity:
We'll have no Cupid hoodwink'd with a scarf,
Bearing a Tartar's painted bow of lath,
Scaring the ladies like a crow-keeper,
Nor no without-book prologue, faintly spoke
After the prompter, for our entrance;
But let them measure us by what they will,
We'll measure them a measure and be gone.

Romeo.
Give me a torch, I am not for this ambling;
Being but heavy, I will bear the light.

Mercutio.
Nay, gentle Romeo, we must have you dance.

Romeo.
Not I, believe me. You have dancing shoes
With nimble soles, I have a soul of lead
So stakes me to the ground I cannot move.

Mercutio.
You are a lover, borrow Cupid's wings,
And soar with them above a common bound.

Romeo.
I am too sore enpierced with his shaft
To soar with his light feathers, and so bound
I cannot bound a pitch above dull woe;
Under love's heavy burden do I sink.

Mercutio.
And, to sink in it, should you burden love—
Too great oppression for a tender thing.

Romeo.
Is love a tender thing? It is too rough,
Too rude, too boist'rous, and it pricks like thorn.

Mercutio.
If love be rough with you, be rough with love;
Prick love for pricking, and you beat love down.
Give me a case to put my visage in,

Puts on a mask.

A visor for a visor! What care I
What curious eye doth cote deformities?
Here are the beetle brows shall blush for me.

Benvolio.
Come knock and enter, and no sooner in,
But every man betake him to his legs.

Romeo.
A torch for me. Let wantons light of heart
Tickle the senseless rushes with their heels.
For I am proverb'd with a grandsire phrase,
I'll be a candle-holder and look on:
The game was ne'er so fair, and I am done.

Mercutio.
Tut, dun's the mouse, the constable's own word.
If thou art Dun, we'll draw thee from the mire
Of this sir-reverence love, wherein thou stickest
Up to the ears. Come, we burn daylight, ho!

Romeo.
Nay, that's not so.

Mercutio.
                I mean, sir, in delay
We waste our lights in vain, like lights by day!
Take our good meaning, for our judgment sits
Five times in that ere once in our five wits.

Romeo.
And we mean well in going to this mask,
But 'tis no wit to go.

Mercutio.
                Why, may one ask?

Romeo.
I dreamt a dream tonight.

Mercutio.
                And so did I.

Romeo.
Well, what was yours?

Mercutio.
                That dreamers often lie.

Act 1, Scene 5

Romeo.
In bed asleep, while they do dream things true.

Mercutio.
O then I see Queen Mab hath been with you.
She is the fairies' midwife, and she comes
In shape no bigger than an agot-stone
On the forefinger of an alderman,
Drawn with a team of little atomi
Over men's noses as they lie asleep.
Her chariot is an empty hazel-nut,
Made by the joiner squirrel or old grub,
Time out a' mind the fairies' coachmakers.
Her wagon-spokes made of long spinners' legs,
The cover of the wings of grasshoppers,
Her traces of the smallest spider web,
Her collars of the moonshine's wat'ry beams,
Her whip of cricket's bone, the lash of film,
Her wagoner a small grey-coated gnat,
Not half so big as a round little worm
Prick'd from the lazy finger of a maid.
And in this state she gallops night by night
Through lovers' brains, and then they dream of love;
O'er courtiers' knees, that dream on cur'sies straight;
O'er lawyers' fingers, who straight dream on fees;
O'er ladies' lips, who straight on kisses dream,
Which oft the angry Mab with blisters plagues,
Because their breath with sweetmeats tainted are.
Sometime she gallops o'er a courtier's nose,
And then dreams he of smelling out a suit;
And sometime comes she with a tithe-pig's tail
Tickling a parson's nose as 'a lies asleep,
Then he dreams of another benefice.
Sometime she driveth o'er a soldier's neck,
And then dreams he of cutting foreign throats,
Of breaches, ambuscadoes, Spanish blades,
Of healths five fathom deep; and then anon
Drums in his ear, at which he starts and wakes,
And being thus frighted, swears a prayer or two,
And sleeps again. This is that very Mab
That plats the manes of horses in the night,
And bakes the elf-locks in foul sluttish hairs,
Which, once untangled, much misfortune bodes.
This is the hag, when maids lie on their backs,
That presses them and learns them first to bear,
Making them women of good carriage.
This is she—

Romeo.
Peace, peace, Mercutio, peace!
Thou talk'st of nothing.

Mercutio.
True, I talk of dreams,
Which are the children of an idle brain,
Begot of nothing but vain fantasy,
Which is as thin of substance as the air,
And more inconstant than the wind, who woos
Even now the frozen bosom of the north,
And, being anger'd, puffs away from thence,
Turning his side to the dew-dropping south.

Benvolio.
This wind you talk of blows us from ourselves:
Supper is done, and we shall come too late.

Romeo.
I fear, too early, for my mind misgives
Some consequence yet hanging in the stars
Shall bitterly begin his fearful date
With this night's revels, and expire the term
Of a despised life clos'd in my breast
By some vile forfeit of untimely death.
But He that hath the steerage of my course
Direct my sail! On, lusty gentlemen!

Benvolio.
Strike, drum.

They march about the stage and stand to one side.

Scene 5

Verona. A hall in Capulet's house.

(Anthony; Potpan; Capulet; Lady Capulet; Old Capulet; Juliet; Tybalt; Nurse; First Servingman; Second Servingman; Third Servingman; Guests; Gentlewomen; Maskers; Romeo; Mercutio; Benvolio)

Capulet's servants bustle about. Capulet and his guests come in to greet the masked gentlemen who have just entered, and dancing begins. Capulet and a kinsman reflect on how long it's been since they last danced themselves. Romeo spots Juliet and is overcome by her beauty, but makes the mistake of commenting aloud: Tybalt overhears him and recognizes his voice. He sends for his sword, but he is interrupted by old Capulet, who refuses to see his house turned into a brawling place, especially since Romeo is an admired young man. When Tybalt persists, Capulet puts him in his place. Tybalt vows to make Romeo pay. Romeo speaks to Juliet, and their immediate understanding of one another is clear in how well she picks up and plays with the language he uses. He manages to steal two kisses from her before she is called away. When he asks, the Nurse tells Romeo that Juliet is the Capulets' daughter, and just how rich she is. Romeo is shocked that he has fallen for his great enemy. As the maskers leave, Juliet makes the Nurse find out who Romeo is, and she is equally appalled.

Servingmen come forth with napkins.

First Servingman.
Where's Potpan, that he helps not to take away? He shift a trencher? He scrape a trencher?

Second Servingman.
When good manners shall lie all in one or two men's hands, and they unwash'd too, 'tis a foul thing.

First Servingman.
Away with the join-stools, remove the court-cubbert, look to the plate. Good thou, save me a piece of marchpane, and, as thou loves me, let the porter let in Susan Grindstone and Nell.

Exit Second Servant.

Anthony and Potpan!

Enter Anthony and Potpan.

Anthony.
Ay, boy, ready.

First Servingman.
You are look'd for and call'd for, ask'd for and sought for, in the great chamber.

Potpan.
We cannot be here and there too. Cheerly, boys, be brisk a while, and the longer liver take all.

Exeunt.
Enter Capulet, Lady Capulet, Old Capulet, Juliet, Tybalt, Nurse, Servingmen, and all the Guests and Gentlewomen to the Maskers.

Capulet.
Welcome, gentlemen! Ladies that have their toes
Unplagu'd with corns will walk a bout with you.
Ah, my mistresses, which of you all
Will now deny to dance? She that makes dainty,
She I'll swear hath corns. Am I come near ye now?
Welcome, gentlemen! I have seen the day
That I have worn a visor and could tell
A whispering tale in a fair lady's ear,
Such as would please; 'tis gone, 'tis gone, 'tis gone.
You are welcome, gentlemen! Come, musicians, play.

Music plays, and they dance.

A hall, a hall! Give room! And foot it, girls.
More light, you knaves, and turn the tables up;
And quench the fire, the room is grown too hot.
Ah, sirrah, this unlook'd-for sport comes well.
Nay, sit, nay, sit, good cousin Capulet,
For you and I are past our dancing days.
How long is't now since last yourself and I
Were in a mask?

Old Capulet.
              By'r lady, thirty years.

Capulet.
What, man? 'Tis not so much, 'tis not so much:
'Tis since the nuptial of Lucentio,
Come Pentecost as quickly as it will,
Some five and twenty years, and then we mask'd.

Old Capulet.
'Tis more, 'tis more. His son is elder, sir;
His son is thirty.

Capulet.
              Will you tell me that?
His son was but a ward two years ago.

Romeo.

To Third Servingman.

What lady's that which doth enrich the hand
Of yonder knight?

Third Servingman.
I know not, sir.

Romeo.
O, she doth teach the torches to burn bright!
It seems she hangs upon the cheek of night
As a rich jewel in an Ethiop's ear—
Beauty too rich for use, for earth too dear!
So shows a snowy dove trooping with crows,
As yonder lady o'er her fellows shows.
The measure done, I'll watch her place of stand,
And touching hers, make blessed my rude hand.
Did my heart love till now? Forswear it, sight!
For I ne'er saw true beauty till this night.

Tybalt.
This, by his voice, should be a Montague.
Fetch me my rapier, boy. What dares the slave
Come hither, cover'd with an antic face,
To fleer and scorn at our solemnity?
Now, by the stock and honor of my kin,
To strike him dead I hold it not a sin.

Capulet.
Why, how now, kinsman, wherefore storm you so?

Tybalt.
Uncle, this is a Montague, our foe;
A villain that is hither come in spite
To scorn at our solemnity this night.

Capulet.
Young Romeo is it?

Tybalt.
                    'Tis he, that villain Romeo.

Capulet.
Content thee, gentle coz, let him alone,
'A bears him like a portly gentleman;
And to say truth, Verona brags of him
To be a virtuous and well-govern'd youth.
I would not for the wealth of all this town
Here in my house do him disparagement;
Therefore be patient, take no note of him;
It is my will, the which if thou respect,
Show a fair presence and put off these frowns,
An ill-beseeming semblance for a feast.

Tybalt.
It fits when such a villain is a guest.
I'll not endure him.

Capulet.
                    He shall be endured.
What, goodman boy? I say he shall, go to!
Am I the master here, or you? Go to!
You'll not endure him! God shall mend my soul,
You'll make a mutiny among my guests!
You will set cock-a-hoop! You'll be the man!

Tybalt.
Why, uncle, 'tis a shame.

Capulet.
                    Go to, go to,
You are a saucy boy. Is't so indeed?
This trick may chance to scath you, I know what.
You must contrary me! Marry, 'tis time.—
Well said, my hearts!—You are a princox, go,
Be quiet, or—More light, more light!—For shame,
I'll make you quiet, what!—Cheerly, my hearts!

Tybalt.
Patience perforce with willful choler meeting
Makes my flesh tremble in their different greeting.
I will withdraw, but this intrusion shall,
Now seeming sweet, convert to bitt'rest gall.

Exit.

Romeo.

To Juliet.

If I profane with my unworthiest hand
This holy shrine, the gentle sin is this,
My lips, two blushing pilgrims, ready stand
To smooth that rough touch with a tender kiss.

Juliet.
Good pilgrim, you do wrong your hand too much,
Which mannerly devotion shows in this:
For saints have hands that pilgrims' hands do touch,
And palm to palm is holy palmers' kiss.

Romeo.
Have not saints lips, and holy palmers too?

Juliet.
Ay, pilgrim, lips that they must use in pray'r.

Romeo.
O then, dear saint, let lips do what hands do,
They pray—grant thou, lest faith turn to despair.

Juliet.
Saints do not move, though grant for prayers' sake.

Romeo.
Then move not while my prayer's effect I take.
Thus from my lips, by thine, my sin is purg'd.

Kissing her.

Juliet.
Then have my lips the sin that they have took.

Romeo.
Sin from my lips? O trespass sweetly urg'd!
Give me my sin again.

Kissing her again.

Juliet.
                  You kiss by th' book.

Nurse.
Madam, your mother craves a word with you.

Romeo.
What is her mother?

Nurse.
                Marry, bachelor,
Her mother is the lady of the house,
And a good lady, and a wise and virtuous.
I nurs'd her daughter that you talk'd withal;
I tell you, he that can lay hold of her
Shall have the chinks.

Romeo.
                Is she a Capulet?
O dear account! My life is my foe's debt.

Benvolio.
Away, be gone, the sport is at the best.

Romeo.
Ay, so I fear, the more is my unrest.

Capulet.
Nay, gentlemen, prepare not to be gone,
We have a trifling foolish banquet towards.

They whisper in his ear.

Is it e'en so? Why then I thank you all.
I thank you, honest gentlemen, good night.
More torches here! Come on, then let's to bed.

To Second Capulet.

Ah, sirrah, by my fay, it waxes late,
I'll to my rest.

Exeunt all but Juliet and Nurse.

Juliet.
Come hither, nurse. What is yond gentleman?

Nurse.
The son and heir of old Tiberio.

Juliet.
What's he that now is going out of door?

Nurse.
Marry, that, I think, be young Petruchio.

Juliet.
What's he that follows here, that would not dance?

Nurse.
I know not.

Juliet.
Go ask his name.—If he be married,
My grave is like to be my wedding-bed.

Nurse.
His name is Romeo, and a Montague,
The only son of your great enemy.

Juliet.
My only love sprung from my only hate!
Too early seen unknown, and known too late!
Prodigious birth of love it is to me
That I must love a loathed enemy.

Nurse.
What's tis? What's tis?

Juliet.
                A rhyme I learnt even now
Of one I danc'd withal.

One calls within, "Juliet!"

Nurse.
                Anon, anon!
Come let's away, the strangers all are gone.

Exeunt.

Act 2

Prologue

(Chorus)

The Chorus comments on how Romeo has completely forgotten about Rosaline, and how both the young lovers will have difficulty meeting again.

Enter Chorus.

Chorus.
Now old desire doth in his death-bed lie,
And young affection gapes to be his heir;
That fair for which love groan'd for and would die,
With tender Juliet match'd is now not fair.
Now Romeo is belov'd and loves again,
Alike bewitched by the charm of looks;

But to his foe suppos'd he must complain,
And she steal love's sweet bait from fearful hooks.
Being held a foe, he may not have access
To breathe such vows as lovers use to swear,
And she as much in love, her means much less
To meet her new-beloved any where.
But passion lends them power, time means, to meet,
Temp'ring extremities with extreme sweet.

Exit.

Scene 1

A lane by the wall of Capulet's orchard.

(Romeo; Benvolio; Mercutio)

Romeo, feeling unable to leave, jumps over the wall to Capulet's orchard to escape Benvolio and Mercutio. Mercutio's acid mockery of Romeo's lovesickness as he calls for him for some reason does not make Romeo appear, and Benvolio convinces the wild joker to go to bed, since Romeo clearly does not wish to be found.

Enter Romeo alone.

Romeo.
Can I go forward when my heart is here?
Turn back, dull earth, and find thy center out.

Enter Benvolio with Mercutio. Romeo withdraws.

Benvolio.
Romeo! My cousin Romeo! Romeo!

Mercutio.
                He is wise,
And, on my life, hath stol'n him home to bed.

Benvolio.
He ran this way and leapt this orchard wall.
Call, good Mercutio.

Mercutio.
                Nay, I'll conjure too.
Romeo! Humors! Madman! Passion! Lover!
Appear thou in the likeness of a sigh!
Speak but one rhyme, and I am satisfied;
Cry but "Ay me!", pronounce but "love" and "dove",
Speak to my gossip Venus one fair word,
One nickname for her purblind son and heir,
Young Abraham Cupid, he that shot so trim,
When King Cophetua lov'd the beggar-maid!
He heareth not, he stirreth not, he moveth not,
The ape is dead, and I must conjure him.
I conjure thee by Rosaline's bright eyes,
By her high forehead and her scarlet lip,
By her fine foot, straight leg, and quivering thigh,
And the demesnes that there adjacent lie,
That in thy likeness thou appear to us!

Benvolio.
And if he hear thee, thou wilt anger him.

Mercutio.
This cannot anger him; 'twould anger him
To raise a spirit in his mistress' circle,
Of some strange nature, letting it there stand
Till she had laid it and conjur'd it down.
That were some spite. My invocation
Is fair and honest; in his mistress' name
I conjure only but to raise up him.

Benvolio.
Come, he hath hid himself among these trees
To be consorted with the humorous night.
Blind is his love and best befits the dark.

Mercutio.
If love be blind, love cannot hit the mark.
Now will he sit under a medlar tree,
And wish his mistress were that kind of fruit
As maids call medlars, when they laugh alone.
O, Romeo, that she were, O that she were
An open-arse, thou a pop'rin pear!
Romeo, good night, I'll to my truckle-bed,
This field-bed is too cold for me to sleep.
Come, shall we go?

Benvolio.
                Go then, for 'tis in vain
To seek him here that means not to be found.

Exit with Mercutio.

Scene 2

Capulet's orchard.

(Romeo; Juliet; Nurse)

Romeo comments scathingly on Mercutio's comments as he hears the latter leave. He is immediately distracted, though, when he sees a light at a balcony window, and sees Juliet come out into the night. Admiringly, he looks at her, finding her even more beautiful than the first time he saw her. She begins to speak to herself, and he is amazed as he hears her wish that he were not a Montague, since that is the only bar between them. Soon he can take no more and he replies to her. She is shocked, and immediately afraid for his life, but lets him stay, and they admit their mutual love. Much more practical than he is, Juliet undercuts all his flowery phrases, and moves on to the subject of marriage. The Nurse calls for Juliet to come in, but she delays again and again, unwilling to let Romeo go and always finding new details to ask of him. Finally, as the sun is soon going to come up, they manage to part.

Romeo advances.

Romeo.
He jests at scars that never felt a wound.

Enter Juliet above at her window.

But soft, what light through yonder window breaks?
It is the east, and Juliet is the sun.
Arise, fair sun, and kill the envious moon,
Who is already sick and pale with grief
That thou, her maid, art far more fair than she.
Be not her maid, since she is envious;
Her vestal livery is but sick and green,
And none but fools do wear it; cast it off.
It is my lady, O, it is my love!
O that she knew she were!
She speaks, yet she says nothing; what of that?
Her eye discourses, I will answer it.
I am too bold, 'tis not to me she speaks.
Two of the fairest stars in all the heaven,
Having some business, do entreat her eyes
To twinkle in their spheres till they return.
What if her eyes were there, they in her head?
The brightness of her cheek would shame those stars,
As daylight doth a lamp; her eyes in heaven
Would through the airy region stream so bright
That birds would sing and think it were not night.
See how she leans her cheek upon her hand!
O that I were a glove upon that hand,
That I might touch that cheek!

Juliet.
                    Ay me!

Romeo.
                    She speaks!
O, speak again, bright angel, for thou art
As glorious to this night, being o'er my head,
As is a winged messenger of heaven
Unto the white-upturned wond'ring eyes
Of mortals that fall back to gaze on him,
When he bestrides the lazy puffing clouds,
And sails upon the bosom of the air.

Juliet.
O Romeo, Romeo, wherefore art thou Romeo?
Deny thy father and refuse thy name;
Or, if thou wilt not, be but sworn my love,
And I'll no longer be a Capulet.

Romeo.

Aside.

Shall I hear more, or shall I speak at this?

Juliet.
'Tis but thy name that is my enemy;
Thou art thyself, though not a Montague.
What's Montague? It is nor hand nor foot,
Nor arm nor face, nor any other part
Belonging to a man. O, be some other name!
What's in a name? That which we call a rose
By any other word would smell as sweet;
So Romeo would, were he not Romeo call'd,
Retain that dear perfection which he owes
Without that title. Romeo, doff thy name,
And for thy name, which is no part of thee,
Take all myself.

Romeo.
                    I take thee at thy word.
Call me but love, and I'll be new baptiz'd;
Henceforth I never will be Romeo.

Juliet.
What man art thou that thus bescreen'd in night
So stumblest on my counsel?

Romeo.
                    By a name
I know not how to tell thee who I am.
My name, dear saint, is hateful to myself,
Because it is an enemy to thee;
Had I it written, I would tear the word.

Juliet.
My ears have yet not drunk a hundred words
Of thy tongue's uttering, yet I know the sound.
Art thou not Romeo, and a Montague?

Romeo.
Neither, fair maid, if either thee dislike.

Juliet.
How camest thou hither, tell me, and wherefore?
The orchard walls are high and hard to climb,
And the place death, considering who thou art,
If any of my kinsmen find thee here.

Romeo.
With love's light wings did I o'erperch these walls,
For stony limits cannot hold love out,
And what love can do, that dares love attempt;
Therefore thy kinsmen are no stop to me.

Juliet.
If they do see thee, they will murder thee.

Romeo.
Alack, there lies more peril in thine eye
Than twenty of their swords! Look thou but sweet,
And I am proof against their enmity.

Juliet.
I would not for the world they saw thee here.

Romeo.
I have night's cloak to hide me from their eyes,
And but thou love me, let them find me here;
My life were better ended by their hate,
Than death prorogued, wanting of thy love.

Juliet.
By whose direction foundst thou out this place?

Romeo.
By love, that first did prompt me to inquire;
He lent me counsel, and I lent him eyes.
I am no pilot, yet, wert thou as far
As that vast shore wash'd with the farthest sea,
I should adventure for such merchandise.

Juliet.
Thou knowest the mask of night is on my face,
Else would a maiden blush bepaint my cheek
For that which thou hast heard me speak tonight.
Fain would I dwell on form, fain, fain deny
What I have spoke, but farewell compliment!
Dost thou love me? I know thou wilt say, "Ay,"
And I will take thy word; yet, if thou swear'st,
Thou mayest prove false: at lovers' perjuries
They say Jove laughs. O gentle Romeo,
If thou dost love, pronounce it faithfully;
Or if thou thinkest I am too quickly won,
I'll frown and be perverse, and say thee nay,
So thou wilt woo, but else not for the world.
In truth, fair Montague, I am too fond,
And therefore thou mayest think my behavior light,
But trust me, gentleman, I'll prove more true
Than those that have more coying to be strange.
I should have been more strange, I must confess,
But that thou overheardst, ere I was ware,
My true-love passion; therefore pardon me,
And not impute this yielding to light love,
Which the dark night hath so discovered.

Romeo.
Lady, by yonder blessed moon I vow,
That tips with silver all these fruit-tree tops—

Juliet.
O, swear not by the moon, th' inconstant moon,
That monthly changes in her circled orb,
Lest that thy love prove likewise variable.

Romeo.
What shall I swear by?

Juliet.
            Do not swear at all;
Or if thou wilt, swear by thy gracious self,
Which is the god of my idolatry,
And I'll believe thee.

Romeo.
            If my heart's dear love—

Juliet.
Well, do not swear. Although I joy in thee,
I have no joy of this contract tonight,
It is too rash, too unadvis'd, too sudden,
Too like the lightning, which doth cease to be
Ere one can say it lightens. Sweet, good night!
This bud of love, by summer's ripening breath,
May prove a beauteous flow'r when next we meet.
Good night, good night! As sweet repose and rest
Come to thy heart as that within my breast!

Romeo.
O, wilt thou leave me so unsatisfied?

Juliet.
What satisfaction canst thou have tonight?

Romeo.
Th' exchange of thy love's faithful vow for mine.

Juliet.
I gave thee mine before thou didst request it;
And yet I would it were to give again.

Romeo.
Wouldst thou withdraw it? For what purpose, love?

Juliet.
But to be frank and give it thee again,
And yet I wish but for the thing I have.
My bounty is as boundless as the sea,
My love as deep; the more I give to thee,
The more I have, for both are infinite.

Nurse calls within.

I hear some noise within; dear love, adieu!
Anon, good nurse! Sweet Montague, be true.
Stay but a little, I will come again.

Exit above.

Romeo.
O blessed, blessed night! I am afeard,
Being in night, all this is but a dream,
Too flattering-sweet to be substantial.

Enter Juliet above.

Juliet.
Three words, dear Romeo, and good night indeed.
If that thy bent of love be honorable,
Thy purpose marriage, send me word tomorrow,
By one that I'll procure to come to thee,
Where and what time thou wilt perform the rite,
And all my fortunes at thy foot I'll lay,
And follow thee my lord throughout the world.

Nurse.

Within.

Madam!

Juliet.
I come, anon.—But if thou meanest not well,
I do beseech thee—

Nurse.

Within.

                Madam!

Juliet.
                By and by, I come—
To cease thy strife, and leave me to my grief.
Tomorrow will I send.

Romeo.
                So thrive my soul—

Juliet.
A thousand times good night!

Exit above.

Romeo.
A thousand times the worse, to want thy light.
Love goes toward love as schoolboys from their books,
But love from love, toward school with heavy looks.

Retiring.
Enter Juliet again above.

Juliet.
Hist, Romeo, hist! O, for a falc'ner's voice,
To lure this tassel-gentle back again!
Bondage is hoarse, and may not speak aloud,
Else would I tear the cave where Echo lies,
And make her airy tongue more hoarse than mine,
With repetition of my Romeo's name. Romeo!

Romeo.
It is my soul that calls upon my name.
How silver-sweet sound lovers' tongues by night,
Like softest music to attending ears!

Juliet.
Romeo!

Romeo.
                My nyas?

Juliet.
                What a' clock tomorrow
Shall I send to thee?

Romeo.
                By the hour of nine.

Juliet.
I will not fail, 'tis twenty year till then.
I have forgot why I did call thee back.

Romeo.
Let me stand here till thou remember it.

Act 2, Scene 3

Juliet.
I shall forget, to have thee still stand there,
Rememb'ring how I love thy company.

Romeo.
And I'll still stay, to have thee still forget,
Forgetting any other home but this.

Juliet.
'Tis almost morning, I would have thee gone—
And yet no farther than a wanton's bird,
That lets it hop a little from his hand,
Like a poor prisoner in his twisted gyves,
And with a silken thread plucks it back again,
So loving-jealous of his liberty.

Romeo.
I would I were thy bird.

Juliet.
    Sweet, so would I,
Yet I should kill thee with much cherishing.
Good night, good night! Parting is such sweet sorrow,
That I shall say good night till it be morrow.
Sleep dwell upon thine eyes, peace in thy breast!

Exit above.

Romeo.
Would I were sleep and peace, so sweet to rest!
Hence will I to my ghostly sire's close cell,
His help to crave, and my dear hap to tell.

Exit.

Scene 3

Friar Lawrence's cell.

(Friar Lawrence; Romeo)

Friar Lawrence picks herbs, commenting on their similarities with humans as he does so. Romeo arrives, and Lawrence quickly works out that for him to be up so early, he must simply not have gone to bed. Romeo admits it, and Lawrence fears that he spent the night with Rosaline, at which point Romeo is forced to admit he'd completely forgotten about her. The young man explains his love for Juliet and asks for Lawrence's help in marrying her; the friar upbraids him for his inconstancy and the shallowness of his doting on Rosaline, but agrees to help him in this instance in the hope of ending the enmity between the two houses.

Enter Friar Lawrence alone, with a basket.

Friar Lawrence.
The grey-ey'd morn smiles on the frowning night,
Check'ring the Eastern clouds with streaks of light,
And fleckled darkness like a drunkard reels
From forth day's path and Titan's fiery wheels.
Now ere the sun advance his burning eye,
The day to cheer and night's dank dew to dry,
I must up-fill this osier cage of ours
With baleful weeds and precious-juiced flowers.
The earth that's nature's mother is her tomb;
What is her burying grave, that is her womb;
And from her womb children of diverse kind
We sucking on her natural bosom find:
Many for many virtues excellent,
None but for some, and yet all different.
O, mickle is the powerful grace that lies
In plants, herbs, stones, and their true qualities;
For nought so vile that on the earth doth live
But to the earth some special good doth give;
Nor aught so good but, strain'd from that fair use,
Revolts from true birth, stumbling on abuse.
Virtue itself turns vice, being misapplied,
And vice sometime by action dignified.

Enter Romeo.

Within the infant rind of this weak flower
Poison hath residence and medicine power;
For this, being smelt, with that part cheers each part,
Being tasted, stays all senses with the heart.
Two such opposed kings encamp them still
In man as well as herbs, grace and rude will;
And where the worser is predominant,
Full soon the canker death eats up that plant.

Romeo.
Good morrow, father.

Friar Lawrence.
    Benedicite!
What early tongue so sweet saluteth me?
Young son, it argues a distempered head
So soon to bid good morrow to thy bed.
Care keeps his watch in every old man's eye,
And where care lodges, sleep will never lie;
But where unbruised youth with unstuff'd brain
Doth couch his limbs, there golden sleep doth reign.
Therefore thy earliness doth me assure
Thou art up-rous'd with some distemp'rature;

Or if not so, then here I hit it right—
Our Romeo hath not been in bed tonight.

Romeo.
That last is true—the sweeter rest was mine.

Friar Lawrence.
God pardon sin! Wast thou with Rosaline?

Romeo.
With Rosaline? My ghostly father, no;
I have forgot that name, and that name's woe.

Friar Lawrence.
That's my good son, but where hast thou been then?

Romeo.
I'll tell thee ere thou ask it me again.
I have been feasting with mine enemy,
Where on a sudden one hath wounded me
That's by me wounded; both our remedies
Within thy help and holy physic lies.
I bear no hatred, blessed man, for lo
My intercession likewise steads my foe.

Friar Lawrence.
Be plain, good son, and homely in thy drift,
Riddling confession finds but riddling shrift.

Romeo.
Then plainly know my heart's dear love is set
On the fair daughter of rich Capulet.
As mine on hers, so hers is set on mine,
And all combin'd, save what thou must combine
By holy marriage. When and where and how
We met, we woo'd, and made exchange of vow,
I'll tell thee as we pass, but this I pray,
That thou consent to marry us today.

Friar Lawrence.
Holy Saint Francis, what a change is here!
Is Rosaline, that thou didst love so dear,
So soon forsaken? Young men's love then lies
Not truly in their hearts, but in their eyes.
Jesu Maria, what a deal of brine
Hath wash'd thy sallow cheeks for Rosaline!
How much salt water thrown away in waste,
To season love, that of it doth not taste!
The sun not yet thy sighs from heaven clears,
Thy old groans yet ringing in mine ancient ears;
Lo here upon thy cheek the stain doth sit
Of an old tear that is not wash'd off yet.
If e'er thou wast thyself and these woes thine,
Thou and these woes were all for Rosaline.
And art thou chang'd? Pronounce this sentence then:
Women may fall, when there's no strength in men.

Romeo.
Thou chidst me oft for loving Rosaline.

Friar Lawrence.
For doting, not for loving, pupil mine.

Romeo.
And badst me bury love.

Friar Lawrence.
                    Not in a grave,
To lay one in, another out to have.

Romeo.
I pray thee chide me not. Her I love now
Doth grace for grace and love for love allow;
The other did not so.

Friar Lawrence.
                    O, she knew well
Thy love did read by rote that could not spell.
But come, young waverer, come go with me,
In one respect I'll thy assistant be;
For this alliance may so happy prove
To turn your households' rancor to pure love.

Romeo.
O, let us hence, I stand on sudden haste.

Friar Lawrence.
Wisely and slow, they stumble that run fast.

Exeunt.

Scene 4

Verona. A street.

(Benvolio; Mercutio; Romeo; Nurse; Peter)

Benvolio and Mercutio still have no idea where Romeo is, but have heard that Tybalt sent him a formal challenge. Mercutio, bantering as always, points out that Tybalt is deadly in a duel. When Romeo arrives, Mercutio is unsparing in his mockery, but Romeo manages to keep up with him, proving to Mercutio that his melancholy is gone. The Nurse enters with her servant Peter, searching for Romeo, much to the amusement of his fellows. Mercutio and Benvolio leave, and the Nurse berates Peter for not standing up to them. Romeo tells her to let Juliet know that if she goes to

Friar Lawrence's, they shall be married. He also arranges to have the Nurse pick up a rope ladder so that he can visit Juliet more easily at night. The Nurse is delighted, and goes off to tell Juliet.

Enter Benvolio and Mercutio.

Mercutio.
Where the dev'l should this Romeo be?
Came he not home tonight?

Benvolio.
Not to his father's, I spoke with his man.

Mercutio.
Why, that same pale hard-hearted wench, that Rosaline,
Torments him so, that he will sure run mad.

Benvolio.
Tybalt, the kinsman to old Capulet,
Hath sent a letter to his father's house.

Mercutio.
A challenge, on my life.

Benvolio.
Romeo will answer it.

Mercutio.
Any man that can write may answer a letter.

Benvolio.
Nay, he will answer the letter's master, how he dares, being dar'd.

Mercutio.
Alas, poor Romeo, he is already dead, stabb'd with a white wench's black eye, run through the ear with a love-song, the very pin of his heart cleft with the blind bow-boy's butt-shaft; and is he a man to encounter Tybalt?

Benvolio.
Why, what is Tybalt?

Mercutio.
More than Prince of Cats. O, he's the courageous captain of compliments. He fights as you sing prick-song, keeps time, distance, and proportion; he rests his minim rests, one, two, and the third in your bosom: the very butcher of a silk button, a duellist, a duellist; a gentleman of the very first house, of the first and second cause. Ah, the immortal passado, the punto reverso, the hay!

Benvolio.
The what?

Mercutio.
The pox of such antic, lisping, affecting phantasimes, these new tuners of accent! "By Jesu, a very good blade! A very tall man! A very good whore!" Why, is not this a lamentable thing, grandsire, that we should be thus afflicted with these strange flies, these fashion-mongers, these pardon-me's, who stand so much on the new form, that they cannot sit at ease on the old bench? O, their bones, their bones!

Enter Romeo.

Benvolio.
Here comes Romeo, here comes Romeo.

Mercutio.
Without his roe, like a dried herring: O flesh, flesh, how art thou fishified! Now is he for the numbers that Petrarch flow'd in. Laura to his lady was a kitchen wench (marry, she had a better love to berhyme her), Dido a dowdy, Cleopatra a gypsy, Helen and Hero hildings and harlots, Thisby a grey eye or so, but not to the purpose. Signior Romeo, bonjour! There's a French salutation to your French slop. You gave us the counterfeit fairly last night.

Romeo.
Good morrow to you both. What counterfeit did I give you?

Mercutio.
The slip, sir, the slip, can you not conceive?

Romeo.
Pardon, good Mercutio, my business was great, and in such a case as mine a man may strain courtesy.

Mercutio.
That's as much as to say, such a case as yours constrains a man to bow in the hams.

Romeo.
Meaning to cur'sy.

Mercutio.
Thou hast most kindly hit it.

Romeo.
A most courteous exposition.

Mercutio.
Nay, I am the very pink of courtesy.

Romeo.
Pink for flower.

Mercutio.
Right.

Romeo.
Why then is my pump well flower'd.

Mercutio.
Sure wit! Follow me this jest now, till thou hast worn out thy pump, that when the single sole of it is worn, the jest may remain, after the wearing, solely singular.

Romeo.
O single-sol'd jest, solely singular for the singleness!

Mercutio.
Come between us, good Benvolio, my wits faints.

Romeo.
Swits and spurs, swits and spurs, or I'll cry a match.

Mercutio.
Nay, if our wits run the wild-goose chase, I am done; for thou hast more of the wild goose in one of thy wits than, I am sure, I have in my whole five. Was I with you there for the goose?

Romeo.
Thou wast never with me for any thing when thou wast not there for the goose.

Mercutio.
I will bite thee by the ear for that jest.

Romeo.
Nay, good goose, bite not.

Mercutio.
Thy wit is a very bitter sweeting, it is a most sharp sauce.

Romeo.
And is it not then well serv'd in to a sweet goose?

Mercutio.
O, here's a wit of cheverel, that stretches from an inch narrow to an ell broad!

Romeo.
I stretch it out for that word "broad," which, added to the goose, proves thee far and wide a broad goose.

Mercutio.
Why, is not this better now than groaning for love? Now art thou sociable, now art thou Romeo; now art thou what thou art, by art as well as by nature, for this drivelling love is like a great natural that runs lolling up and down to hide his bable in a hole.

Benvolio.
Stop there, stop there.

Mercutio.
Thou desirest me to stop in my tale against the hair.

Benvolio.
Thou wouldst else have made thy tale large.

Mercutio.
O, thou art deceiv'd; I would have made it short, for I was come to the whole depth of my tale, and meant indeed to occupy the argument no longer.

Romeo.
Here's goodly gear!

Enter Nurse and her man, Peter.

A sail, a sail!

Mercutio.
Two, two: a shirt and a smock.

Nurse.
Peter!

Peter.
Anon!

Nurse.
My fan, Peter.

Mercutio.
Good Peter, to hide her face, for her fan's the fairer face.

Nurse.
God ye good morrow, gentlemen.

Act 2, Scene 4

Mercutio.
God ye good den, fair gentlewoman.

Nurse.
Is it good den?

Mercutio.
'Tis no less, I tell ye, for the bawdy hand of the dial is now upon the prick of noon.

Nurse.
Out upon you, what a man are you?

Romeo.
One, gentlewoman, that God hath made, himself to mar.

Nurse.
By my troth, it is well said; "for himself to mar," quoth 'a! Gentlemen, can any of you tell me where I may find the young Romeo?

Romeo.
I can tell you, but young Romeo will be older when you have found him than he was when you sought him. I am the youngest of that name, for fault of a worse.

Nurse.
You say well.

Mercutio.
Yea, is the worst well? Very well took, i' faith, wisely, wisely.

Nurse.
If you be he, sir, I desire some confidence with you.

Benvolio.
She will indite him to some supper.

Mercutio.
A bawd, a bawd, a bawd! So ho!

Romeo.
What hast thou found?

Mercutio.
No hare, sir, unless a hare, sir, in a lenten pie, that is something stale and hoar ere it be spent.

He walks by them and sings.

An old hare hoar,
And an old hare hoar,
Is very good meat in Lent;
But a hare that is hoar
Is too much for a score,
When it hoars ere it be spent.
Romeo, will you come to your father's? We'll to dinner thither.

Romeo.
I will follow you.

Mercutio.
Farewell, ancient lady, farewell,

Singing.

"lady, lady, lady."

Exeunt Mercutio and Benvolio.

Nurse.
I pray you, sir, what saucy merchant was this, that was so full of his ropery?

Romeo.
A gentleman, nurse, that loves to hear himself talk, and will speak more in a minute than he will stand to in a month.

Nurse.
And 'a speak any thing against me, I'll take him down, and 'a were lustier than he is, and twenty such Jacks; and if I cannot, I'll find those that shall. Scurvy knave, I am none of his flirt-gills, I am none of his skains-mates.

She turns to Peter, her man.

And thou must stand by too and suffer every knave to use me at his pleasure!

Peter.
I saw no man use you at his pleasure; if I had, my weapon should quickly have been out. I warrant you, I dare draw as soon as another man, if I see occasion in a good quarrel, and the law on my side.

Nurse.
Now, afore God, I am so vex'd that every part about me quivers. Scurvy knave! Pray you, sir, a word: and as I told you, my young lady bid me inquire you out; what she bid me say, I will keep to myself. But first let me tell ye, if ye should lead her in a fool's paradise, as they say, it were a very gross kind of behavior, as they say; for the gentlewoman is young; and therefore, if you should deal double with her, truly it were an ill thing

to be off'red to any gentlewoman, and very weak dealing.

Romeo.
Nurse, commend me to thy lady and mistress. I protest unto thee—

Nurse.
Good heart, and, i' faith, I will tell her as much. Lord, Lord, she will be a joyful woman.

Romeo.
What wilt thou tell her, nurse? Thou dost not mark me.

Nurse.
I will tell her, sir, that you do protest, which, as I take it, is a gentleman-like offer.

Romeo.
Bid her devise
Some means to come to shrift this afternoon,
And there she shall at Friar Lawrence' cell
Be shriv'd and married. Here is for thy pains.

Nurse.
No, truly, sir, not a penny.

Romeo.
Go to, I say you shall.

Nurse.
This afternoon, sir? Well, she shall be there.

Romeo.
And stay, good nurse—behind the abbey wall
Within this hour my man shall be with thee,
And bring thee cords made like a tackled stair,
Which to the high top-gallant of my joy
Must be my convoy in the secret night.
Farewell, be trusty, and I'll quit thy pains.
Farewell, commend me to thy mistress.

Nurse.
Now God in heaven bless thee! Hark you, sir.

Romeo.
What say'st thou, my dear nurse?

Nurse.
Is your man secret? Did you ne'er hear say,
"Two may keep counsel, putting one away"?

Romeo.
'Warrant thee, my man's as true as steel.

Nurse.
Well, sir, my mistress is the sweetest lady—Lord, Lord! When 'twas a little prating thing—O, there is a nobleman in town, one Paris, that would fain lay knife aboard; but she, good soul, had as lief see a toad, a very toad, as see him. I anger her sometimes and tell her that Paris is the properer man, but I'll warrant you, when I say so, she looks as pale as any clout in the versal world. Doth not rosemary and Romeo begin both with a letter?

Romeo.
Ay, nurse, what of that? Both with an R.

Nurse.
Ah, mocker, that's the dog's name. R is for the—no, I know it begins with some other letter—and she hath the prettiest sententious of it, of you and rosemary, that it would do you good to hear it.

Romeo.
Commend me to thy lady.

Nurse.
Ay, a thousand times.

Exit Romeo.

Peter!

Peter.
Anon!

Nurse.

Handing him her fan.

Before, and apace.

Exit after Peter.

Scene 5

Capulet's orchard.

(Juliet; Nurse; Peter)

Juliet anxiously waits for the Nurse to return. When she finally does, she takes as long as she can to actually report Romeo's message, milking every excuse she can to delay, until she finally tells Juliet to go to Friar Lawrence's and be married. Juliet is delighted, as the Nurse prepares to go fetch the rope ladder.

Act 2, Scene 5

Enter Juliet.

Juliet.
The clock struck nine when I did send the nurse;
In half an hour she promised to return.
Perchance she cannot meet him—that's not so.
O, she is lame! Love's heralds should be thoughts,
Which ten times faster glides than the sun's beams,
Driving back shadows over low'ring hills;
Therefore do nimble-pinion'd doves draw Love,
And therefore hath the wind-swift Cupid wings.
Now is the sun upon the highmost hill
Of this day's journey, and from nine till twelve
Is three long hours, yet she is not come.
Had she affections and warm youthful blood,
She would be as swift in motion as a ball;
My words would bandy her to my sweet love,
And his to me.
But old folks—many feign as they were dead,
Unwieldy, slow, heavy, and pale as lead.

Enter Nurse and Peter.

O God, she comes! O honey nurse, what news?
Hast thou met with him? Send thy man away.

Nurse.
Peter, stay at the gate.

Exit Peter.

Juliet.
Now, good sweet nurse—O Lord, why lookest thou sad?
Though news be sad, yet tell them merrily;
If good, thou shamest the music of sweet news
By playing it to me with so sour a face.

Nurse.
I am a-weary, give me leave a while.
Fie, how my bones ache! What a jaunce have I!

Juliet.
I would thou hadst my bones, and I thy news.
Nay, come, I pray thee speak, good, good nurse, speak.

Nurse.
Jesu, what haste! Can you not stay a while?
Do you not see that I am out of breath?

Juliet.
How art thou out of breath, when thou hast breath
To say to me that thou art out of breath?
The excuse that thou dost make in this delay
Is longer than the tale thou dost excuse.
Is thy news good or bad? Answer to that.
Say either, and I'll stay the circumstance.
Let me be satisfied, is't good or bad?

Nurse.
Well, you have made a simple choice, you know not how to choose a man. Romeo! No, not he. Though his face be better than any man's, yet his leg excels all men's, and for a hand and a foot and a body, though they be not to be talk'd on, yet they are past compare. He is not the flower of courtesy, but I'll warrant him, as gentle as a lamb. Go thy ways, wench, serve God. What, have you din'd at home?

Juliet.
No, no! But all this did I know before.
What says he of our marriage? What of that?

Nurse.
Lord, how my head aches! What a head have I!
It beats as it would fall in twenty pieces.
My back a' t' other side—ah, my back, my back!
Beshrew your heart for sending me about
To catch my death with jauncing up and down!

Juliet.
I' faith, I am sorry that thou art not well.
Sweet, sweet, sweet nurse, tell me, what says my love?

Nurse.
Your love says, like an honest gentleman,
An' a courteous, and a kind, and a handsome,
And, I warrant, a virtuous—Where is your mother?

Juliet.
Where is my mother! Why, she is within,
Where should she be? How oddly thou repliest!
"Your love says, like an honest gentleman,
'Where is your mother?'"

Nurse.
                O God's lady dear!
Are you so hot? Marry, come up, I trow;
Is this the poultice for my aching bones?
Henceforward do your messages yourself.

Juliet.
Here's such a coil! Come, what says Romeo?

Nurse.
Have you got leave to go to shrift today?

Juliet.
I have.

Nurse.
Then hie you hence to Friar Lawrence' cell,
There stays a husband to make you a wife.
Now comes the wanton blood up in your cheeks,
They'll be in scarlet straight at any news.
Hie you to church, I must another way,
To fetch a ladder, by the which your love
Must climb a bird's nest soon when it is dark.
I am the drudge, and toil in your delight;
But you shall bear the burden soon at night.
Go, I'll to dinner, hie you to the cell.

Juliet.
Hie to high fortune! Honest nurse, farewell.

Exeunt.

Scene 6

Friar Lawrence's cell.

(Friar Lawrence; Romeo; Juliet)

Romeo and Friar Lawrence await Juliet's arrival, the Friar attempting to calm Romeo down. Lawrence is somewhat concerned that the strength of Romeo's passion bodes ill. Juliet arrives, and the Friar takes them off to marry immediately.

Enter Friar Lawrence and Romeo.

Friar Lawrence.
So smile the heavens upon this holy act,
That after-hours with sorrow chide us not!

Romeo.
Amen, amen! But come what sorrow can,
It cannot countervail the exchange of joy
That one short minute gives me in her sight.
Do thou but close our hands with holy words,
Then love-devouring death do what he dare,
It is enough I may but call her mine.

Friar Lawrence.
These violent delights have violent ends,
And in their triumph die, like fire and powder,
Which as they kiss consume. The sweetest honey
Is loathsome in his own deliciousness,
And in the taste confounds the appetite.
Therefore love moderately: long love doth so;
Too swift arrives as tardy as too slow.

Enter Juliet.

Here comes the lady. O, so light a foot
Will ne'er wear out the everlasting flint;
A lover may bestride the gossamers
That idles in the wanton summer air,
And yet not fall; so light is vanity.

Juliet.
Good even to my ghostly confessor.

Friar Lawrence.
Romeo shall thank thee, daughter, for us both.

Juliet.
As much to him, else is his thanks too much.

Romeo.
Ah, Juliet, if the measure of thy joy
Be heap'd like mine, and that thy skill be more
To blazon it, then sweeten with thy breath
This neighbor air, and let rich music's tongue
Unfold the imagin'd happiness that both
Receive in either by this dear encounter.

Juliet.
Conceit, more rich in matter than in words,
Brags of his substance, not of ornament;
They are but beggars that can count their worth,
But my true love is grown to such excess
I cannot sum up sum of half my wealth.

Friar Lawrence.
Come, come with me, and we will make short work,
For by your leaves, you shall not stay alone
Till Holy Church incorporate two in one.

Exeunt.

Act 3

Scene 1

Verona. A street.

Act 3, Scene 1

(Mercutio; Benvolio; Mercutio's Page; Men; Tybalt; Petruchio; Romeo; Citizens; Prince Escalus; Montague; Capulet; Lady Capulet; Lady Montague)

Benvolio tries to get Mercutio to go indoors, as the day is very hot and this causes short tempers that might lead to a brawl. Tybalt and his companions appear, searching for Romeo. He speaks insultingly to Mercutio, who replies in kind, and they are on the verge of fighting, with Benvolio urging them to go somewhere private, when Romeo arrives. Tybalt calls Romeo a villain, an unforgivable insult, but Romeo, who is after all now Tybalt's kinsman though no one knows it, peacefully refuses to answer back in kind. Disgusted at seeing Romeo be such a wimp, Mercutio takes up the fight instead. Romeo tries to separate the two, referring to the Prince's decree against fighting, but as he gets between them Tybalt stabs Mercutio under Romeo's arm. Tybalt flees. Even though mortally wounded, Mercutio still manages to make bad puns about death, before cursing both Capulets and Montagues, laying his death at their doors. Romeo is horrified that his love for Juliet has caused this, and when Benvolio reports that Mercutio is dead, he bursts into a rage, seeing Tybalt return. He throws himself at Tybalt, and after a fight Romeo kills Mercutio's murderer. Benvolio forces Romeo to flee, as the citizens are roused and the law prescribes death for brawlers. The Prince, the Montagues and the Capulets all arrive. Benvolio explains how things occurred. Lady Capulet demands Romeo's death, but Montague points out that Tybalt was already doomed to die for killing Mercutio. Bearing that in mind, the Prince exiles Romeo, on pain of death; with Mercutio, his kinsman, dead, the Prince has now been touched directly by the feud, and he swears to levy a massive fine on both families to keep them quiet.

Enter Mercutio, Benvolio, Page, and Men.

Benvolio.
I pray thee, good Mercutio, let's retire.
The day is hot, the Capels are abroad,
And if we meet we shall not scape a brawl,
For now, these hot days, is the mad blood stirring.

Mercutio.
Thou art like one of these fellows that, when he enters the confines of a tavern, claps me his sword upon the table, and says, "God send me no need of thee!" and by the operation of the second cup draws him on the drawer, when indeed there is no need.

Benvolio.
Am I like such a fellow?

Mercutio.
Come, come, thou art as hot a Jack in thy mood as any in Italy, and as soon mov'd to be moody, and as soon moody to be mov'd.

Benvolio.
And what to?

Mercutio.
Nay, and there were two such, we should have none shortly, for one would kill the other. Thou? Why, thou wilt quarrel with a man that hath a hair more or a hair less in his beard than thou hast. Thou wilt quarrel with a man for cracking nuts, having no other reason but because thou hast hazel eyes. What eye but such an eye would spy out such a quarrel? Thy head is as full of quarrels as an egg is full of meat, and yet thy head hath been beaten as addle as an egg for quarreling. Thou hast quarrell'd with a man for coughing in the street, because he hath waken'd thy dog that hath lain asleep in the sun. Didst thou not fall out with a tailor for wearing his new doublet before Easter? With another for tying his new shoes with old riband? And yet thou wilt tutor me from quarreling!

Benvolio.
And I were so apt to quarrel as thou art, any man should buy the fee-simple of my life for an hour and a quarter.

Mercutio.
The fee-simple! O simple!

Enter Tybalt, Petruchio, and others.

Benvolio.
By my head, here comes the Capulets.

Mercutio.
By my heel, I care not.

Tybalt.
Follow me close, for I will speak to them. Gentlemen, good den, a word with one of you.

Mercutio.
And but one word with one of us? Couple it with something, make it a word and a blow.

Tybalt.
You shall find me apt enough to that, sir, and you will give me occasion.

Mercutio.
Could you not take some occasion without giving?

Tybalt.
Mercutio, thou consortest with Romeo—

Mercutio.
Consort! What, dost thou make us minstrels? And thou make minstrels of us, look to hear nothing but discords. Here's my fiddlestick, here's that shall make you dance. 'Zounds, consort!

Benvolio.
We talk here in the public haunt of men.
Either withdraw unto some private place,
Or reason coldly of your grievances,
Or else depart; here all eyes gaze on us.

Mercutio.
Men's eyes were made to look, and let them gaze;
I will not budge for no man's pleasure, I.

Enter Romeo.

Tybalt.
Well, peace be with you, sir, here comes my man.

Mercutio.
But I'll be hang'd, sir, if he wear your livery.
Marry, go before to field, he'll be your follower;
Your worship in that sense may call him man.

Tybalt.
Romeo, the love I bear thee can afford
No better term than this: thou art a villain.

Romeo.
Tybalt, the reason that I have to love thee
Doth much excuse the appertaining rage
To such a greeting. Villain am I none;
Therefore farewell, I see thou knowest me not.

Tybalt.
Boy, this shall not excuse the injuries
That thou hast done me, therefore turn and draw.

Romeo.
I do protest I never injured thee,
But love thee better than thou canst devise,
Till thou shalt know the reason of my love,
And so, good Capulet—which name I tender
As dearly as mine own—be satisfied.

Mercutio.
O calm, dishonorable, vile submission!
Alia stoccato carries it away.

Draws.

Tybalt, you rat-catcher, will you walk?

Tybalt.
What wouldst thou have with me?

Mercutio.
Good King of Cats, nothing but one of your nine lives; that I mean to make bold withal, and as you shall use me hereafter, dry-beat the rest of the eight. Will you pluck your sword out of his pilcher by the ears? Make haste, lest mine be about your ears ere it be out.

Tybalt.
I am for you.

Romeo.
Gentle Mercutio, put thy rapier up.

Mercutio.
Come, sir, your passado.

They fight.

Romeo.
Draw, Benvolio, beat down their weapons.
Gentlemen, for shame, forbear this outrage!
Tybalt, Mercutio, the Prince expressly hath
Forbid this bandying in Verona streets.

Romeo steps between them.

Hold, Tybalt! Good Mercutio!

*Tybalt under Romeo's arm thrusts Mercutio in.
Away Tybalt with his followers.*

Mercutio.
                          I am hurt.
A plague a' both houses! I am sped.
Is he gone and hath nothing?

Benvolio.
                          What, art thou hurt?

Mercutio.
Ay, ay, a scratch, a scratch, marry, 'tis enough.
Where is my page? Go, villain, fetch a surgeon.

Exit Page.

Romeo.
Courage, man, the hurt cannot be much.

Mercutio.
No, 'tis not so deep as a well, nor so wide as a church-door, but 'tis enough, 'twill serve. Ask for me tomorrow, and you shall find me a grave man. I am pepper'd, I warrant, for this world. A plague a' both your houses! 'Zounds, a dog, a rat, a mouse, a cat, to scratch a man to death! A braggart, a rogue, a villain, that fights by the book of arithmetic! Why the dev'l came you between us? I was hurt under your arm.

Romeo.
I thought all for the best.

Mercutio.
Help me into some house, Benvolio,
Or I shall faint. A plague a' both your houses!
They have made worms' meat of me. I have it,
And soundly too. Your houses!

Exeunt Mercutio and Benvolio.

Romeo.
This gentleman, the Prince's near ally,
My very friend, hath got this mortal hurt
In my behalf; my reputation stain'd
With Tybalt's slander—Tybalt, that an hour
Hath been my cousin! O sweet Juliet,
Thy beauty hath made me effeminate,
And in my temper soft'ned valor's steel!

Enter Benvolio.

Benvolio.
O Romeo, Romeo, brave Mercutio is dead!
That gallant spirit hath aspir'd the clouds,
Which too untimely here did scorn the earth.

Romeo.
This day's black fate on more days doth depend,
This but begins the woe others must end.

Enter Tybalt.

Benvolio.
Here comes the furious Tybalt back again.

Romeo.
He gone in triumph, and Mercutio slain!
Away to heaven, respective lenity,
And fire-ey'd fury be my conduct now!
Now, Tybalt, take the "villain" back again
That late thou gavest me, for Mercutio's soul
Is but a little way above our heads,
Staying for thine to keep him company.
Either thou or I, or both, must go with him.

Tybalt.
Thou wretched boy, that didst consort him here,
Shalt with him hence.

Romeo.
                This shall determine that.

They fight; Tybalt falls.

Benvolio.
Romeo, away, be gone!
The citizens are up, and Tybalt slain.
Stand not amazed, the Prince will doom thee death
If thou art taken. Hence be gone, away!

Romeo.
O, I am fortune's fool!

Benvolio.
                Why dost thou stay?

Exit Romeo.
Enter Citizens.

First Citizen of Verona.
Which way ran he that kill'd Mercutio?
Tybalt, that murderer, which way ran he?

Benvolio.
There lies that Tybalt.

First Citizen of Verona.
                Up, sir, go with me;
I charge thee in the Prince's name, obey.

Enter Prince, old Montague, Capulet, their Wives, and all.

Prince Escalus.
Where are the vile beginners of this fray?

Benvolio.
O noble Prince, I can discover all
The unlucky manage of this fatal brawl:
There lies the man, slain by young Romeo,
That slew thy kinsman, brave Mercutio.

Lady Capulet.
Tybalt, my cousin! O my brother's child!
O Prince! O husband! O, the blood is spill'd
Of my dear kinsman! Prince, as thou art true,
For blood of ours, shed blood of Montague.
O cousin, cousin!

Prince Escalus.
Benvolio, who began this bloody fray?

Benvolio.
Tybalt, here slain, whom Romeo's hand did slay!
Romeo that spoke him fair, bid him bethink
How nice the quarrel was, and urg'd withal
Your high displeasure; all this, uttered
With gentle breath, calm look, knees humbly bowed,
Could not take truce with the unruly spleen
Of Tybalt deaf to peace, but that he tilts
With piercing steel at bold Mercutio's breast,
Who, all as hot, turns deadly point to point,
And, with a martial scorn, with one hand beats
Cold death aside, and with the other sends
It back to Tybalt, whose dexterity
Retorts it. Romeo he cries aloud,
"Hold, friends! Friends, part!" and swifter than his tongue,
His agile arm beats down their fatal points,
And 'twixt them rushes; underneath whose arm
An envious thrust from Tybalt hit the life
Of stout Mercutio, and then Tybalt fled;
But by and by comes back to Romeo,
Who had but newly entertain'd revenge,
And to't they go like lightning, for, ere I
Could draw to part them, was stout Tybalt slain;
And as he fell, did Romeo turn and fly.
This is the truth, or let Benvolio die.

Lady Capulet.
He is a kinsman to the Montague,
Affection makes him false, he speaks not true.
Some twenty of them fought in this black strife,
And all those twenty could but kill one life.
I beg for justice, which thou, Prince, must give:
Romeo slew Tybalt, Romeo must not live.

Prince Escalus.
Romeo slew him, he slew Mercutio;
Who now the price of his dear blood doth owe?

Montague.
Not Romeo, Prince, he was Mercutio's friend;
His fault concludes but what the law should end,
The life of Tybalt.

Prince Escalus.
                    And for that offense
Immediately we do exile him hence.
I have an interest in your hearts' proceeding;
My blood for your rude brawls doth lie a-bleeding;
But I'll amerce you with so strong a fine
That you shall all repent the loss of mine.
I will be deaf to pleading and excuses,
Nor tears nor prayers shall purchase out abuses;
Therefore use none. Let Romeo hence in haste,
Else, when he is found, that hour is his last.
Bear hence this body and attend our will;
Mercy but murders, pardoning those that kill.

Exeunt.

Scene 2

Capulet's orchard.

(Juliet; Nurse)

Juliet in her garden impatiently waits for the day to end and her wedding night to begin. The Nurse returns in tears, and her speech is so jumbled that Juliet believes Romeo is dead. When the Nurse finally spills out the true tale, Juliet is torn between her love for Romeo and hatred of him for killing her cousin, but finally love for her husband is too strong. She laments Romeo's banishment, and to calm her overwrought grief, the Nurse promises to go find Romeo and work things out.

Enter Juliet alone.

Juliet.
Gallop apace, you fiery-footed steeds,
Towards Phoebus' lodging; such a wagoner
As Phaëton would whip you to the west,
And bring in cloudy night immediately.
Spread thy close curtain, love-performing night,
That th' runaway's eyes may wink, and Romeo
Leap to these arms untalk'd of and unseen!
Lovers can see to do their amorous rites
By their own beauties, or, if love be blind,

Act 3, Scene 2

It best agrees with night. Come, civil night,
Thou sober-suited matron all in black,
And learn me how to lose a winning match,
Play'd for a pair of stainless maidenhoods.
Hood my unmann'd blood, bating in my cheeks,
With thy black mantle, till strange love grow bold,
Think true love acted simple modesty.
Come, night, come, Romeo, come, thou day in night,
For thou wilt lie upon the wings of night,
Whiter than new snow upon a raven's back.
Come, gentle night, come, loving, black-brow'd night,
Give me my Romeo, and, when I shall die,
Take him and cut him out in little stars,
And he will make the face of heaven so fine
That all the world will be in love with night,
And pay no worship to the garish sun.
O, I have bought the mansion of a love,
But not possess'd it, and though I am sold,
Not yet enjoy'd. So tedious is this day
As is the night before some festival
To an impatient child that hath new robes
And may not wear them. O, here comes my nurse,

Enter Nurse wringing her hands, with the ladder of cords in her lap.

And she brings news; and every tongue that speaks
But Romeo's name speaks heavenly eloquence.
Now, nurse, what news? What hast thou there? The cords
That Romeo bid thee fetch?

Nurse.
                Ay, ay, the cords.

Throws them down.

Juliet.
Ay me, what news? Why dost thou wring thy hands?

Nurse.
Ah, weraday, he's dead, he's dead, he's dead!
We are undone, lady, we are undone!
Alack the day, he's gone, he's kill'd, he's dead!

Juliet.
Can heaven be so envious?

Nurse.
                Romeo can,
Though heaven cannot. O Romeo, Romeo!
Who ever would have thought it? Romeo!

Juliet.
What devil art thou that dost torment me thus?
This torture should be roar'd in dismal hell.
Hath Romeo slain himself? Say thou but ay,
And that bare vowel I shall poison more
Than the death-darting eye of cockatrice.
I am not I, if there be such an ay,
Or those eyes shut, that makes thee answer ay.
If he be slain, say ay, or if not, no.
Brief sounds determine my weal or woe.

Nurse.
I saw the wound, I saw it with mine eyes—
God save the mark!—here on his manly breast.
A piteous corse, a bloody piteous corse,
Pale, pale as ashes, all bedaub'd in blood,
All in gore blood; I swooned at the sight.

Juliet.
O, break, my heart, poor bankrupt, break at once!
To prison, eyes, ne'er look on liberty!
Vile earth, to earth resign, end motion here,
And thou and Romeo press one heavy bier!

Nurse.
O Tybalt, Tybalt, the best friend I had!
O courteous Tybalt, honest gentleman,
That ever I should live to see thee dead!

Juliet.
What storm is this that blows so contrary?
Is Romeo slaught'red? And is Tybalt dead?
My dearest cousin, and my dearer lord?
Then, dreadful trumpet, sound the general doom,
For who is living, if those two are gone?

Nurse.
Tybalt is gone, and Romeo banished,
Romeo that kill'd him, he is banished.

Juliet.
O God, did Romeo's hand shed Tybalt's blood?

Nurse.
It did, it did, alas the day, it did!

Juliet.
O serpent heart, hid with a flow'ring face!
Did ever dragon keep so fair a cave?
Beautiful tyrant! Fiend angelical!
Dove-feather'd raven! Wolvish ravening lamb!
Despised substance of divinest show!
Just opposite to what thou justly seem'st,

A damned saint, an honorable villain!
O nature, what hadst thou to do in hell
When thou didst bower the spirit of a fiend
In mortal paradise of such sweet flesh?
Was ever book containing such vile matter
So fairly bound? O that deceit should dwell
In such a gorgeous palace!

Nurse.
                    There's no trust,
No faith, no honesty in men, all perjur'd,
All forsworn, all naught, all dissemblers.
Ah, where's my man? Give me some aqua-vitae;
These griefs, these woes, these sorrows make me old.
Shame come to Romeo!

Juliet.
                    Blister'd be thy tongue
For such a wish! He was not born to shame:
Upon his brow shame is asham'd to sit;
For 'tis a throne where honor may be crown'd
Sole monarch of the universal earth.
O, what a beast was I to chide at him!

Nurse.
Will you speak well of him that kill'd your cousin?

Juliet.
Shall I speak ill of him that is my husband?
Ah, poor my lord, what tongue shall smooth thy name,
When I, thy three-hours wife, have mangled it?
But wherefore, villain, didst thou kill my cousin?
That villain cousin would have kill'd my husband.
Back, foolish tears, back to your native spring,
Your tributary drops belong to woe,
Which you, mistaking, offer up to joy.
My husband lives that Tybalt would have slain,
And Tybalt's dead that would have slain my husband.
All this is comfort, wherefore weep I then?
Some word there was, worser than Tybalt's death,
That murd'red me; I would forget it fain,
But O, it presses to my memory
Like damned guilty deeds to sinners' minds:
"Tybalt is dead, and Romeo banished."
That "banished," that one word "banished,"
Hath slain ten thousand Tybalts. Tybalt's death
Was woe enough if it had ended there;
Or if sour woe delights in fellowship,
And needly will be rank'd with other griefs,
Why followed not, when she said, "Tybalt's dead,"
Thy father or thy mother, nay, or both,
Which modern lamentation might have moved?
But with a rearward following Tybalt's death,
"Romeo is banished": to speak that word,
Is father, mother, Tybalt, Romeo, Juliet,
All slain, all dead: "Romeo is banished"!
There is no end, no limit, measure, bound,
In that word's death, no words can that woe sound.
Where is my father and my mother, nurse?

Nurse.
Weeping and wailing over Tybalt's corse.
Will you go to them? I will bring you thither.

Juliet.
Wash they his wounds with tears? Mine shall be spent,
When theirs are dry, for Romeo's banishment.
Take up those cords. Poor ropes, you are beguil'd,
Both you and I, for Romeo is exil'd.
He made you for a highway to my bed,
But I, a maid, die maiden-widowed.
Come, cords, come, nurse, I'll to my wedding-bed,
And death, not Romeo, take my maidenhead!

Nurse.
Hie to your chamber. I'll find Romeo
To comfort you, I wot well where he is.
Hark ye, your Romeo will be here at night.
I'll to him, he is hid at Lawrence' cell.

Juliet.
O, find him! Give this ring to my true knight,
And bid him come to take his last farewell.

Exeunt.

Scene 3

Friar Lawrence's cell.

(Friar Lawrence; Romeo; Nurse)

Romeo is distraught at being banished from Juliet, but Lawrence has little patience with his refusal to see how lucky he is not to be condemned to death. The Nurse arrives and reassures Romeo that Juliet still loves him, though she notes that both of them are just lying around crying. Romeo is still so grief-struck that he attempts to stab himself, but at this Lawrence has finally had enough. He points out all the ways in which Romeo is lucky and tells him to stop moaning. He tells the lad to go to Juliet for their wedding night, then leave for Mantua until the storm blows over and things can be explained. Seeing Romeo revived, the Nurse goes to tell Juliet that Romeo will be there that night. The Friar makes arrangements for Romeo's departure to Mantua, and for how they will communicate.

Enter Friar Lawrence.

Friar Lawrence.
Romeo, come forth, come forth, thou fearful man:
Affliction is enamor'd of thy parts,
And thou art wedded to calamity.

Enter Romeo.

Romeo.
Father, what news? What is the Prince's doom?
What sorrow craves acquaintance at my hand,
That I yet know not?

Friar Lawrence.
                  Too familiar
Is my dear son with such sour company!
I bring thee tidings of the Prince's doom.

Romeo.
What less than dooms-day is the Prince's doom?

Friar Lawrence.
A gentler judgment vanish'd from his lips—
Not body's death, but body's banishment.

Romeo.
Ha, banishment? Be merciful, say "death";
For exile hath more terror in his look,
Much more than death. Do not say "banishment"!

Friar Lawrence.
Here from Verona art thou banished.
Be patient, for the world is broad and wide.

Romeo.
There is no world without Verona walls,
But purgatory, torture, hell itself.
Hence "banished" is banish'd from the world,
And world's exile is death; then "banished"
Is death misterm'd. Calling death "banished,"
Thou cut'st my head off with a golden axe,
And smilest upon the stroke that murders me.

Friar Lawrence.
O deadly sin! O rude unthankfulness!
Thy fault our law calls death, but the kind Prince,
Taking thy part, hath rush'd aside the law,
And turn'd that black word 'death' to "banishment."
This is dear mercy, and thou seest it not.

Romeo.
'Tis torture, and not mercy. Heaven is here
Where Juliet lives, and every cat and dog
And little mouse, every unworthy thing,
Live here in heaven and may look on her,
But Romeo may not. More validity,
More honorable state, more courtship lives
In carrion flies than Romeo; they may seize
On the white wonder of dear Juliet's hand,
And steal immortal blessing from her lips,
Who, even in pure and vestal modesty,
Still blush, as thinking their own kisses sin;
But Romeo may not, he is banished.
Flies may do this, but I from this must fly;
They are free men, but I am banished:
And sayest thou yet that exile is not death?
Hadst thou no poison mix'd, no sharp-ground knife,
No sudden mean of death, though ne'er so mean,
But "banished" to kill me? "Banished"?
O friar, the damned use that word in hell;
Howling attends it. How hast thou the heart,
Being a divine, a ghostly confessor,
A sin-absolver, and my friend profess'd,
To mangle me with that word "banished"?

Friar Lawrence.
Thou fond mad man, hear me a little speak.

Romeo.
O, thou wilt speak again of banishment.

Friar Lawrence.
I'll give thee armor to keep off that word:
Adversity's sweet milk, philosophy,
To comfort thee though thou art banished.

Romeo.
Yet "banished"? Hang up philosophy!
Unless philosophy can make a Juliet,
Displant a town, reverse a prince's doom,
It helps not, it prevails not. Talk no more.

Friar Lawrence.
O then I see that madmen have no ears.

Romeo.
How should they when that wise men have no eyes?

Friar Lawrence.
Let me dispute with thee of thy estate.

Romeo.
Thou canst not speak of that thou dost not feel.
Wert thou as young as I, Juliet thy love,
An hour but married, Tybalt murdered,
Doting like me, and like me banished,
Then mightst thou speak, then mightst thou tear thy hair,
And fall upon the ground, as I do now,
Taking the measure of an unmade grave.

Enter Nurse within and knock.

Friar Lawrence.
Arise, one knocks. Good Romeo, hide thyself.

Romeo.
Not I, unless the breath of heart-sick groans
Mist-like infold me from the search of eyes.

Knock.

Friar Lawrence.
Hark how they knock!—Who's there?—Romeo, arise,
Thou wilt be taken.—Stay a while!—Stand up;

Loud knock.

Run to my study.—By and by!—God's will,
What simpleness is this?—I come, I come!

Knock.

Who knocks so hard? Whence come you? What's your will?

Nurse.

Within.

Let me come in, and you shall know my errant.
I come from Lady Juliet.

Friar Lawrence.
                Welcome then.

Unlocks the door.
Enter Nurse.

Nurse.
O holy friar, O, tell me, holy friar,
Where's my lady's lord? Where's Romeo?

Friar Lawrence.
There on the ground, with his own tears made drunk.

Nurse.
O, he is even in my mistress' case,
Just in her case. O woeful sympathy!
Piteous predicament! Even so lies she,
Blubb'ring and weeping, weeping and blubb'ring.
Stand up, stand up, stand, and you be a man.
For Juliet's sake, for her sake, rise and stand;
Why should you fall into so deep an O?

Romeo.
Nurse!

He rises.

Nurse.
Ah sir, ah sir, death's the end of all.

Romeo.
Spakest thou of Juliet? How is it with her?
Doth not she think me an old murderer,
Now I have stain'd the childhood of our joy
With blood removed but little from her own?
Where is she? And how doth she? And what says
My conceal'd lady to our cancell'd love?

Nurse.
O, she says nothing, sir, but weeps and weeps,
And now falls on her bed, and then starts up,
And Tybalt calls, and then on Romeo cries,
And then down falls again.

Romeo.
                As if that name,
Shot from the deadly level of a gun,
Did murder her, as that name's cursed hand
Murder'd her kinsman. O, tell me, friar, tell me,
In what vile part of this anatomy
Doth my name lodge? Tell me, that I may sack
The hateful mansion.

He offers to stab himself, and Nurse snatches the dagger away.

Friar Lawrence.
                Hold thy desperate hand!
Art thou a man? Thy form cries out thou art;
Thy tears are womanish, thy wild acts denote
The unreasonable fury of a beast.
Unseemly woman in a seeming man,
And ill-beseeming beast in seeming both,
Thou hast amaz'd me! By my holy order,
I thought thy disposition better temper'd.
Hast thou slain Tybalt? Wilt thou slay thyself,
And slay thy lady that in thy life lives,
By doing damned hate upon thyself?
Why railest thou on thy birth? The heaven and earth?
Since birth, and heaven, and earth, all three do meet
In thee at once, which thou at once wouldst lose.
Fie, fie, thou shamest thy shape, thy love, thy wit,
Which like a usurer abound'st in all,
And usest none in that true use indeed
Which should bedeck thy shape, thy love, thy wit.
Thy noble shape is but a form of wax,
Digressing from the valor of a man;
Thy dear love sworn but hollow perjury,
Killing that love which thou hast vow'd to cherish;
Thy wit, that ornament to shape and love,
Misshapen in the conduct of them both,
Like powder in a skilless soldier's flask,
Is set afire by thine own ignorance,
And thou dismemb'red with thine own defense.
What, rouse thee, man! Thy Juliet is alive,
For whose dear sake thou wast but lately dead:
There art thou happy. Tybalt would kill thee,
But thou slewest Tybalt: there art thou happy.
The law that threat'ned death becomes thy friend,
And turns it to exile: there art thou happy.
A pack of blessings light upon thy back,
Happiness courts thee in her best array,
But like a mishaved and sullen wench,
Thou pouts upon thy fortune and thy love.
Take heed, take heed, for such die miserable.
Go get thee to thy love as was decreed,
Ascend her chamber, hence and comfort her.
But look thou stay not till the watch be set,
For then thou canst not pass to Mantua,
Where thou shalt live till we can find a time
To blaze your marriage, reconcile your friends,
Beg pardon of the Prince, and call thee back
With twenty hundred thousand times more joy
Than thou went'st forth in lamentation.
Go before, nurse; commend me to thy lady,
And bid her hasten all the house to bed,
Which heavy sorrow makes them apt unto.
Romeo is coming.

Nurse.
O Lord, I could have sta'd here all the night
To hear good counsel. O, what learning is!
My lord, I'll tell my lady you will come.

Romeo.
Do so, and bid my sweet prepare to chide.

Nurse offers to go in, and turns again.

Nurse.
Here, sir, a ring she bid me give you, sir.
Hie you, make haste, for it grows very late.

Romeo.
How well my comfort is reviv'd by this!

Exit Nurse.

Friar Lawrence.
Go hence, good night; and here stands all your state:
Either be gone before the watch be set,
Or by the break of day disguis'd from hence.
Sojourn in Mantua. I'll find out your man,
And he shall signify from time to time
Every good hap to you that chances here.
Give me thy hand. 'Tis late; farewell, good night.

Romeo.
But that a joy past joy calls out on me,
It were a grief, so brief to part with thee.
Farewell.

Exeunt.

Scene 4

A room in Capulet's house.

(Capulet; Lady Capulet; Paris)

Paris has come to see Capulet to find out if Juliet has an answer for him, but given events he feels it is no time to speak of these matters. Capulet, however, decides to presume that Juliet will consent and arranges for she and Paris to marry in three days. He insists that it be a small wedding, so that they will not seem to be slighting Tybalt's death. He sends Lady Capulet to inform Juliet of this decision.

Enter old Capulet, his Wife, and Paris.

Capulet.
Things have fall'n out, sir, so unluckily
That we have had no time to move our daughter.
Look you, she lov'd her kinsman Tybalt dearly,
And so did I. Well, we were born to die.
'Tis very late, she'll not come down tonight.
I promise you, but for your company,
I would have been a-bed an hour ago.

Paris.
These times of woe afford no times to woo.
Madam, good night, commend me to your daughter.

Lady Capulet.
I will, and know her mind early tomorrow;
Tonight she's mewed up to her heaviness.

Paris offers to go in, and Capulet calls him again.

Capulet.
Sir Paris, I will make a desperate tender
Of my child's love. I think she will be rul'd
In all respects by me; nay more, I doubt it not.
Wife, go you to her ere you go to bed,
Acquaint her here of my son Paris' love,
And bid her—mark you me?—on We'n'sday next—
But soft, what day is this?

Paris.
                Monday, my lord.

Capulet.
Monday! Ha, ha! Well, We'n'sday is too soon,
A' Thursday let it be—a' Thursday, tell her,
She shall be married to this noble earl.
Will you be ready? Do you like this haste?
We'll keep no great ado—a friend or two,
For hark you, Tybalt being slain so late,
It may be thought we held him carelessly,
Being our kinsman, if we revel much:
Therefore we'll have some half a dozen friends,
And there an end. But what say you to Thursday?

Paris.
My lord, I would that Thursday were tomorrow.

Capulet.
Well, get you gone, a' Thursday be it then.—
Go you to Juliet ere you go to bed,
Prepare her, wife, against this wedding-day.
Farewell, my lord. Light to my chamber ho!
Afore me, it is so very late that we
May call it early by and by. Good night.

Exeunt.

Scene 5

Capulet's orchard and Juliet's chamber.

(*Romeo; Juliet; Nurse; Lady Capulet; Capulet*)

Romeo and Juliet part at the break of dawn, though Juliet wants to deny that it is that late. She almost convinces Romeo to stay, but then reality breaks in and she insists that he flee before he is caught. The Nurse announces that Lady Capulet is coming, and Romeo descends from the balcony to the garden. From her high vantage point, Juliet has a premonition that they will never meet again. He leaves. Lady Capulet comes in, and thinks that her daughter's distraction is grief over Tybalt's death. She tries to comfort her daughter by promising to have Romeo poisoned. She then tells her that she is to be married in two days, but Juliet, horrified, refuses. When Capulet hears of this, he is infuriated and swears to disown her unless she gives in, feeling she is rejecting all the efforts he has made to find her a good match. Lady Capulet refuses her daughter any sympathy. The Nurse, for her part, can see no solution other than agreeing to marry Paris, and recommends that she forget Romeo. Juliet is outraged at her suggestion, but sends her to tell her parents that she is going to Friar Lawrence's to confess. Once the Nurse has gone, Juliet curses her and decides never to trust her again. She is resolved to kill herself if Lawrence can't come up with a solution.

Enter Romeo and Juliet aloft at the window.

Juliet.
Wilt thou be gone? It is not yet near day.
It was the nightingale, and not the lark,
That pierc'd the fearful hollow of thine ear;
Nightly she sings on yond pomegranate tree.
Believe me, love, it was the nightingale.

Romeo.
It was the lark, the herald of the morn,
No nightingale. Look, love, what envious streaks
Do lace the severing clouds in yonder east.
Night's candles are burnt out, and jocund day
Stands tiptoe on the misty mountain tops.
I must be gone and live, or stay and die.

Juliet.
Yond light is not day-light, I know it, I;

Act 3, Scene 5

It is some meteor that the sun exhal'd
To be to thee this night a torch-bearer
And light thee on thy way to Mantua.
Therefore stay yet, thou need'st not to be gone.

Romeo.
Let me be ta'en, let me be put to death,
I am content, so thou wilt have it so.
I'll say yon grey is not the morning's eye,
'Tis but the pale reflex of Cynthia's brow;
Nor that is not the lark whose notes do beat
The vaulty heaven so high above our heads.
I have more care to stay than will to go.
Come, death, and welcome! Juliet wills it so.
How is't, my soul? Let's talk, it is not day.

Juliet.
It is, it is! Hie hence, be gone, away!
It is the lark that sings so out of tune,
Straining harsh discords and unpleasing sharps.
Some say the lark makes sweet division;
This doth not so, for she divideth us.
Some say the lark and loathed toad change eyes;
O now I would they had chang'd voices too,
Since arm from arm that voice doth us affray,
Hunting thee hence with hunt's-up to the day.
O now be gone, more light and light it grows.

Romeo.
More light and light, more dark and dark our woes!

Enter Nurse hastily.

Nurse.
Madam!

Juliet.
Nurse?

Nurse.
Your lady mother is coming to your chamber.
The day is broke, be wary, look about.

Exit.

Juliet.
Then, window, let day in, and let life out.

Romeo.
Farewell, farewell! One kiss, and I'll descend.

He goeth down.

Juliet.
Art thou gone so, love, lord, ay, husband, friend!
I must hear from thee every day in the hour,
For in a minute there are many days.
O, by this count I shall be much in years
Ere I again behold my Romeo!

Romeo.

From below.

       Farewell!
I will omit no opportunity
That may convey my greetings, love, to thee.

Juliet.
O, think'st thou we shall ever meet again?

Romeo.
I doubt it not, and all these woes shall serve
For sweet discourses in our times to come.

Juliet.
O God, I have an ill-divining soul!
Methinks I see thee now, thou art so low,
As one dead in the bottom of a tomb.
Either my eyesight fails, or thou lookest pale.

Romeo.
And trust me, love, in my eye so do you;
Dry sorrow drinks our blood. Adieu, adieu!

Exit.

Juliet.
O Fortune, Fortune, all men call thee fickle;
If thou art fickle, what dost thou with him
That is renowm'd for faith? Be fickle, Fortune:
For then I hope thou wilt not keep him long,
But send him back.

Lady Capulet.

Within.

       Ho, daughter, are you up?

Juliet.
Who is't that calls? It is my lady mother.
Is she not down so late, or up so early?
What unaccustom'd cause procures her hither?

She goeth down from the window.
Enter Mother, Lady Capulet.

Lady Capulet.
Why, how now, Juliet?

Juliet.
                Madam, I am not well.

Lady Capulet.
Evermore weeping for your cousin's death?
What, wilt thou wash him from his grave with tears?
And if thou couldst, thou couldst not make him live;
Therefore have done. Some grief shows much of love,
But much of grief shows still some want of wit.

Juliet.
Yet let me weep for such a feeling loss.

Lady Capulet.
So shall you feel the loss, but not the friend
Which you weep for.

Juliet.
                Feeling so the loss,
I cannot choose but ever weep the friend.

Lady Capulet.
Well, girl, thou weep'st not so much for his death,
As that the villain lives which slaughter'd him.

Juliet.
What villain, madam?

Lady Capulet.
                That same villain Romeo.

Juliet.

Aside.

Villain and he be many miles asunder.—
God pardon him! I do with all my heart;
And yet no man like he doth grieve my heart.

Lady Capulet.
That is because the traitor murderer lives.

Juliet.
Ay, madam, from the reach of these my hands.
Would none but I might venge my cousin's death!

Lady Capulet.
We will have vengeance for it, fear thou not.
Then weep no more. I'll send to one in Mantua,
Where that same banish'd runagate doth live,
Shall give him such an unaccustom'd dram
That he shall soon keep Tybalt company;
And then I hope thou wilt be satisfied.

Juliet.
Indeed I never shall be satisfied
With Romeo, till I behold him—dead—
Is my poor heart, so for a kinsman vex'd.
Madam, if you could find out but a man
To bear a poison, I would temper it,
That Romeo should, upon receipt thereof,
Soon sleep in quiet. O how my heart abhors
To hear him nam'd, and cannot come to him
To wreak the love I bore my cousin
Upon his body that hath slaughter'd him!

Lady Capulet.
Find thou the means, and I'll find such a man.
But now I'll tell thee joyful tidings, girl.

Juliet.
And joy comes well in such a needy time.
What are they, beseech your ladyship?

Lady Capulet.
Well, well, thou hast a careful father, child,
One who, to put thee from thy heaviness,
Hath sorted out a sudden day of joy,
That thou expects not, nor I look'd not for.

Juliet.
Madam, in happy time, what day is that?

Lady Capulet.
Marry, my child, early next Thursday morn,
The gallant, young, and noble gentleman,
The County Paris, at Saint Peter's Church,
Shall happily make thee there a joyful bride.

Juliet.
Now, by Saint Peter's Church and Peter too,
He shall not make me there a joyful bride.
I wonder at this haste, that I must wed
Ere he that should be husband comes to woo.
I pray you tell my lord and father, madam,
I will not marry yet, and when I do, I swear
It shall be Romeo, whom you know I hate,
Rather than Paris. These are news indeed!

Lady Capulet.
Here comes your father, tell him so yourself;
And see how he will take it at your hands.

Enter Capulet and Nurse.

Capulet.
When the sun sets, the earth doth drizzle dew,
But for the sunset of my brother's son
It rains downright.
How now, a conduit, girl? What, still in tears?
Evermore show'ring? In one little body
Thou counterfeits a bark, a sea, a wind:
For still thy eyes, which I may call the sea,
Do ebb and flow with tears; the bark thy body is,
Sailing in this salt flood; the winds, thy sighs,
Who, raging with thy tears, and they with them,
Without a sudden calm, will overset
Thy tempest-tossed body. How now, wife?
Have you delivered to her our decree?

Lady Capulet.
Ay, sir, but she will none, she gives you thanks.
I would the fool were married to her grave!

Capulet.
Soft, take me with you, take me with you, wife.
How, will she none? Doth she not give us thanks?
Is she not proud? Doth she not count her blest,
Unworthy as she is, that we have wrought
So worthy a gentleman to be her bride?

Juliet.
Not proud you have, but thankful that you have.
Proud can I never be of what I hate,
But thankful even for hate that is meant love.

Capulet.
How how, how how, chopp'd logic! What is this?
"Proud," and "I thank you," and "I thank you not,"
And yet "not proud," mistress minion you?
Thank me no thankings, nor proud me no prouds,
But fettle your fine joints 'gainst Thursday next,
To go with Paris to Saint Peter's Church,
Or I will drag thee on a hurdle thither.
Out, you green-sickness carrion! Out, you baggage!
You tallow-face!

Lady Capulet.
           Fie, fie, what, are you mad?

Juliet.
Good father, I beseech you on my knees,
Hear me with patience but to speak a word.

She kneels down.

Capulet.
Hang thee, young baggage! Disobedient wretch!
I tell thee what: get thee to church a' Thursday,
Or never after look me in the face.
Speak not, reply not, do not answer me!
My fingers itch. Wife, we scarce thought us blest
That God had lent us but this only child,
But now I see this one is one too much,
And that we have a curse in having her.
Out on her, hilding!

Nurse.
           God in heaven bless her!
You are to blame, my lord, to rate her so.

Capulet.
And why, my Lady Wisdom? Hold your tongue,
Good Prudence, smatter with your gossips, go.

Nurse.
I speak no treason.

Capulet.
           O, God-i-goden!

Nurse.
May not one speak?

Capulet.
Peace, you mumbling fool!
Utter your gravity o'er a gossip's bowl,
For here we need it not.

Lady Capulet.
           You are too hot.

Capulet.
God's bread, it makes me mad! Day, night, work, play,
Alone, in company, still my care hath been
To have her match'd; and having now provided
A gentleman of noble parentage,
Of fair demesnes, youthful and nobly lien'd,
Stuff'd, as they say, with honorable parts,
Proportion'd as one's thought would wish a man,
And then to have a wretched puling fool,
A whining mammet, in her fortune's tender,
To answer, "I'll not wed, I cannot love;
I am too young, I pray you pardon me."
But and you will not wed, I'll pardon you.
Graze where you will, you shall not house with me.
Look to't, think on't, I do not use to jest.
Thursday is near, lay hand on heart, advise.
And you be mine, I'll give you to my friend;

And you be not, hang, beg, starve, die in the streets,
For, by my soul, I'll ne'er acknowledge thee,
Nor what is mine shall never do thee good.
Trust to't, bethink you, I'll not be forsworn.

Exit.

Juliet.
Is there no pity sitting in the clouds,
That sees into the bottom of my grief?
O sweet my mother, cast me not away!
Delay this marriage for a month, a week,
Or if you do not, make the bridal bed
In that dim monument where Tybalt lies.

Lady Capulet.
Talk not to me, for I'll not speak a word.
Do as thou wilt, for I have done with thee.

Exit.

Juliet.
O God!—O nurse, how shall this be prevented?
My husband is on earth, my faith in heaven;
How shall that faith return again to earth,
Unless that husband send it me from heaven
By leaving earth? Comfort me, counsel me!
Alack, alack, that heaven should practice stratagems
Upon so soft a subject as myself!
What say'st thou? Hast thou not a word of joy?
Some comfort, nurse.

Nurse.
                    Faith, here it is.
Romeo is banished, and all the world to nothing
That he dares ne'er come back to challenge you;
Or if he do, it needs must be by stealth.
Then, since the case so stands as now it doth,
I think it best you married with the County.
O he's a lovely gentleman!
Romeo's a dishclout to him. An eagle, madam,
Hath not so green, so quick, so fair an eye
As Paris hath. Beshrew my very heart,
I think you are happy in this second match,
For it excels your first; or if it did not,
Your first is dead, or 'twere as good he were
As living here and you no use of him.

Juliet.
Speak'st thou from thy heart?

Nurse.
And from my soul too, else beshrew them both.

Juliet.
Amen!

Nurse.
What?

Juliet.
Well, thou hast comforted me marvelous much.
Go in, and tell my lady I am gone,
Having displeas'd my father, to Lawrence' cell,
To make confession and to be absolv'd.

Nurse.
Marry, I will, and this is wisely done.

Exit.

Juliet.

She looks after Nurse.

Ancient damnation! O most wicked fiend!
Is it more sin to wish me thus forsworn,
Or to dispraise my lord with that same tongue
Which she hath prais'd him with above compare
So many thousand times? Go, counsellor,
Thou and my bosom henceforth shall be twain.
I'll to the friar to know his remedy;
If all else fail, myself have power to die.

Exit.

Act 4
Scene 1

Friar Lawrence's cell.

(Friar Lawrence; County Paris; Juliet)

Paris has come to ask Friar Lawrence to officiate at his wedding. He admits that things are moving quickly, but explains that Capulet doesn't think Juliet should mourn as much as she is doing. Juliet arrives, and Paris speaks kindly if possessively to her. Juliet replies with double meanings. Paris leaves her to confess, and she begs Lawrence for a solution, threatening to kill herself if he can't find one. He suddenly finds one: if she has the courage, he can give her a sleeping potion that will make her seem dead to everyone. She will then be buried in the Capulet tomb, and he and Romeo could rescue her later. She agrees.

Enter Friar Lawrence and County Paris.

Friar Lawrence.
On Thursday, sir? The time is very short.

Paris.
My father Capulet will have it so,
And I am nothing slow to slack his haste.

Friar Lawrence.
You say you do not know the lady's mind?
Uneven is the course, I like it not.

Paris.
Immoderately she weeps for Tybalt's death,
And therefore have I little talk'd of love,
For Venus smiles not in a house of tears.
Now, sir, her father counts it dangerous
That she do give her sorrow so much sway;
And in his wisdom hastes our marriage,
To stop the inundation of her tears,
Which, too much minded by herself alone,
May be put from her by society.
Now do you know the reason of this haste.

Friar Lawrence.

Aside.

I would I knew not why it should be slowed.—
Look, sir, here comes the lady toward my cell.

Enter Juliet.

Paris.
Happily met, my lady and my wife!

Juliet.
That may be, sir, when I may be a wife.

Paris.
That may be must be, love, on Thursday next.

Juliet.
What must be shall be.

Friar Lawrence.
                    That's a certain text.

Paris.
Come you to make confession to this father?

Juliet.
To answer that, I should confess to you.

Paris.
Do not deny to him that you love me.

Juliet.
I will confess to you that I love him.

Paris.
So will ye, I am sure, that you love me.

Juliet.
If I do so, it will be of more price,
Being spoke behind your back, than to your face.

Paris.
Poor soul, thy face is much abus'd with tears.

Juliet.
The tears have got small victory by that,
For it was bad enough before their spite.

Paris.
Thou wrong'st it more than tears with that report.

Juliet.
That is no slander, sir, which is a truth,
And what I spake, I spake it to my face.

Paris.
Thy face is mine, and thou hast sland'red it.

Juliet.
It may be so, for it is not mine own.
Are you at leisure, holy father, now,
Or shall I come to you at evening mass?

Friar Lawrence.
My leisure serves me, pensive daughter, now.
My lord, we must entreat the time alone.

Paris.
God shield I should disturb devotion!
Juliet, on Thursday early will I rouse ye;
Till then adieu, and keep this holy kiss.

Exit.

Juliet.
O, shut the door, and when thou hast done so,
Come weep with me, past hope, past cure, past help!

Friar Lawrence.
O Juliet, I already know thy grief,
It strains me past the compass of my wits.
I hear thou must, and nothing may prorogue it,
On Thursday next be married to this County.

Juliet.
Tell me not, friar, that thou hearest of this,
Unless thou tell me how I may prevent it.
If in thy wisdom thou canst give no help,
Do thou but call my resolution wise,
And with this knife I'll help it presently.
God join'd my heart and Romeo's, thou our hands,
And ere this hand, by thee to Romeo's seal'd,
Shall be the label to another deed,
Or my true heart with treacherous revolt
Turn to another, this shall slay them both.
Therefore, out of thy long-experienc'd time,
Give me some present counsel, or, behold,
'Twixt my extremes and me this bloody knife
Shall play the umpire, arbitrating that
Which the commission of thy years and art
Could to no issue of true honor bring.
Be not so long to speak, I long to die,
If what thou speak'st speak not of remedy.

Friar Lawrence.
Hold, daughter! I do spy a kind of hope,
Which craves as desperate an execution
As that is desperate which we would prevent.
If rather than to marry County Paris,
Thou hast the strength of will to slay thyself,
Then is it likely thou wilt undertake
A thing like death to chide away this shame,
That cop'st with Death himself to scape from it;
And if thou darest, I'll give thee remedy.

Juliet.
O, bid me leap, rather than marry Paris,
From off the battlements of any tower,
Or walk in thievish ways, or bid me lurk
Where serpents are; chain me with roaring bears,
Or hide me nightly in a charnel-house,
O'ercover'd quite with dead men's rattling bones,
With reeky shanks and yellow chapless skulls;
Or bid me go into a new-made grave,
And hide me with a dead man in his shroud—
Things that, to hear them told, have made me tremble—
And I will do it without fear or doubt,
To live an unstain'd wife to my sweet love.

Friar Lawrence.
Hold then. Go home, be merry, give consent
To marry Paris. We'n'sday is tomorrow;
Tomorrow night look that thou lie alone,
Let not the nurse lie with thee in thy chamber.
Take thou this vial, being then in bed,
And this distilling liquor drink thou off,
When presently through all thy veins shall run
A cold and drowsy humor; for no pulse
Shall keep his native progress, but surcease;
No warmth, no breath shall testify thou livest;
The roses in thy lips and cheeks shall fade
To wanny ashes, thy eyes' windows fall,
Like death when he shuts up the day of life;
Each part, depriv'd of supple government,
Shall, stiff and stark and cold, appear like death,
And in this borrowed likeness of shrunk death
Thou shalt continue two and forty hours,
And then awake as from a pleasant sleep.
Now when the bridegroom in the morning comes
To rouse thee from thy bed, there art thou dead.
Then, as the manner of our country is,
In thy best robes, uncovered on the bier,
Thou shall be borne to that same ancient vault
Where all the kindred of the Capulets lie.
In the mean time, against thou shalt awake,
Shall Romeo by my letters know our drift,
And hither shall he come, an' he and I
Will watch thy waking, and that very night
Shall Romeo bear thee hence to Mantua.
And this shall free thee from this present shame,
If no inconstant toy, nor womanish fear,
Abate thy valor in the acting it.

Juliet.
Give me, give me! O, tell not me of fear!

Friar Lawrence.
Hold, get you gone. Be strong and prosperous
In this resolve. I'll send a friar with speed
To Mantua, with my letters to thy lord.

Juliet.
Love give me strength! And strength shall help afford.
Farewell, dear father!

Exeunt.

Scene 2

A hall in Capulet's house.

(*Capulet; Lady Capulet; Nurse; First Servingman; Second Servingman; Juliet*)

Capulet is giving orders to arrange for the wedding feast. Juliet comes in, and agrees to marry Paris,

Act 4, Scene 2

begging her father for forgiveness. Capulet is delighted — so delighted, in fact, that he changes the marriage date to the next morning. Lady Capulet complains that this gives her no time to get everything ready, but Capulet announces he'll take charge of all the domestic arrangements.

Enter Capulet, Mother Lady Capulet, Nurse, and Servingmen, two or three.

Capulet.
So many guests invite as here are writ.

Exit First Servant.

Sirrah, go hire me twenty cunning cooks.

Second Servingman.
You shall have none ill, sir, for I'll try if they can lick their fingers.

Capulet.
How canst thou try them so?

Second Servingman.
Marry, sir, 'tis an ill cook that cannot lick his own fingers; therefore he that cannot lick his fingers goes not with me.

Capulet.
Go, be gone.

Exit Second Servant.

We shall be much unfurnish'd for this time.
What, is my daughter gone to Friar Lawrence?

Nurse.
Ay forsooth.

Capulet.
Well, he may chance to do some good on her.
A peevish self-will'd harlotry it is.

Enter Juliet.

Nurse.
See where she comes from shrift with merry look.

Capulet.
How now, my headstrong, where have you been gadding?

Juliet.
Where I have learnt me to repent the sin
Of disobedient opposition
To you and your behests, and am enjoin'd
By holy Lawrence to fall prostrate here
To beg your pardon.

She kneels down.

Pardon, I beseech you!
Henceforward I am ever rul'd by you.

Capulet.
Send for the County, go tell him of this.
I'll have this knot knit up tomorrow morning.

Juliet.
I met the youthful lord at Lawrence' cell,
And gave him what becomed love I might,
Not stepping o'er the bounds of modesty.

Capulet.
Why, I am glad on't, this is well, stand up.
This is as't should be. Let me see the County;
Ay, marry, go, I say, and fetch him hither.
Now, afore God, this reverend holy friar,
All our whole city is much bound to him.

Juliet.
Nurse, will you go with me into my closet
To help me sort such needful ornaments
As you think fit to furnish me tomorrow?

Lady Capulet.
No, not till Thursday, there is time enough.

Capulet.
Go, nurse, go with her, we'll to church tomorrow.

Exeunt Juliet and Nurse.

Lady Capulet.
We shall be short in our provision,
'Tis now near night.

Capulet.
          Tush, I will stir about,
And all things shall be well, I warrant thee, wife;
Go thou to Juliet, help to deck up her.
I'll not to bed tonight; let me alone,
I'll play the huswife for this once. What ho!
They are all forth. Well, I will walk myself
To County Paris, to prepare up him
Against tomorrow. My heart is wondrous light,

Since this same wayward girl is so reclaim'd.

Exeunt.

Scene 3

Juliet's chamber.

(Juliet; Nurse; Lady Capulet)

Lady Capulet and the Nurse bid Juliet good night. She prepares to take the potion, but is frightened. Uncertain that it will work, she lays down a dagger by her side so that she can kill herself in the morning if need be. The potion worries her: she is fearful of waking up in the grave, even doubts Lawrence's intentions, is afraid the potion might be poison, and terrified of Tybalt's ghost. Nevertheless, she drinks it.

Enter Juliet and Nurse.

Juliet.
Ay, those attires are best, but, gentle nurse,
I pray thee leave me to myself tonight,
For I have need of many orisons
To move the heavens to smile upon my state,
Which, well thou knowest, is cross and full of sin.

Enter Mother, Lady Capulet.

Lady Capulet.
What, are you busy, ho? Need you my help?

Juliet.
No, madam, we have cull'd such necessaries
As are behoofeful for our state tomorrow.
So please you, let me now be left alone,
And let the nurse this night sit up with you,
For I am sure you have your hands full all,
In this so sudden business.

Lady Capulet.
                    Good night.
Get thee to bed and rest, for thou hast need.

Exeunt Lady Capulet and Nurse.

Juliet.
Farewell! God knows when we shall meet again.
I have a faint cold fear thrills through my veins,
That almost freezes up the heat of life.
I'll call them back again to comfort me.
Nurse!—What should she do here?
My dismal scene I needs must act alone.
Come, vial.
What if this mixture do not work at all?
Shall I be married then tomorrow morning?
No, no, this shall forbid it. Lie thou there.

Laying down her dagger.

What if it be a poison which the friar
Subtly hath minist'red to have me dead,
Lest in this marriage he should be dishonor'd
Because he married me before to Romeo?
I fear it is, and yet methinks it should not,
For he hath still been tried a holy man.
How if, when I am laid into the tomb,
I wake before the time that Romeo
Come to redeem me? There's a fearful point!
Shall I not then be stifled in the vault,
To whose foul mouth no healthsome air breathes in,
And there die strangled ere my Romeo comes?
Or if I live, is it not very like
The horrible conceit of death and night,
Together with the terror of the place—
As in a vault, an ancient receptacle,
Where for this many hundred years the bones
Of all my buried ancestors are pack'd,
Where bloody Tybalt, yet but green in earth,
Lies fest'ring in his shroud, where, as they say,
At some hours in the night spirits resort—
Alack, alack, is it not like that I,
So early waking—what with loathsome smells,
And shrikes like mandrakes' torn out of the earth,
That living mortals, hearing them, run mad—
O, if I wake, shall I not be distraught,
Environed with all these hideous fears,
And madly play with my forefathers' joints,
And pluck the mangled Tybalt from his shroud,
And in this rage, with some great kinsman's bone,
As with a club, dash out my desp'rate brains?
O, look! Methinks I see my cousin's ghost
Seeking out Romeo, that did spit his body
Upon a rapier's point. Stay, Tybalt, stay!
Romeo, Romeo, Romeo! Here's drink—I drink to thee.

She falls upon her bed, within the curtains.

Scene 4

A hall in Capulet's house.

(Lady Capulet; Nurse; Capulet; First Servingman; Second Servingman)

Capulet bustles about making the final arrangements for the wedding. He sends the Nurse to wake Juliet up.

Enter lady of the house Lady Capulet and Nurse with herbs.

Lady Capulet.
Hold, take these keys and fetch more spices, nurse.

Nurse.
They call for dates and quinces in the pastry.

Enter old Capulet.

Capulet.
Come, stir, stir, stir! The second cock hath crowed,
The curfew-bell hath rung, 'tis three a' clock.
Look to the bak'd meats, good Angelica,
Spare not for cost.

Nurse.
              Go, you cot-quean, go,
Get you to bed. Faith, you'll be sick tomorrow
For this night's watching.

Capulet.
No, not a whit. What, I have watch'd ere now
All night for lesser cause, and ne'er been sick.

Lady Capulet.
Ay, you have been a mouse-hunt in your time,
But I will watch you from such watching now.

Exeunt Lady Capulet and Nurse.

Capulet.
A jealous hood, a jealous hood!

Enter three or four Servingmen with spits and logs and baskets.

Now, fellow, what is there?

First Servingman.
Things for the cook, sir, but I know not what.

Capulet.
Make haste, make haste.

Exit First Servant.

                Sirrah, fetch drier logs.
Call Peter, he will show thee where they are.

Second Servingman.
I have a head, sir, that will find out logs,
And never trouble Peter for the matter.

Capulet.
Mass, and well said, a merry whoreson, ha!
Thou shalt be logger-head.

Exit Second Servant.

                Good faith, 'tis day.
The County will be here with music straight,
For so he said he would.

Play music within.

                I hear him near.
Nurse! Wife! What ho! What, nurse, I say!

Enter Nurse.

Go waken Juliet, go and trim her up,
I'll go and chat with Paris. Hie, make haste,
Make haste, the bridegroom he is come already,
Make haste, I say.

Exit.

Scene 5

Juliet's chamber.

(Nurse; Juliet; Lady Capulet; Capulet; Friar Lawrence; County Paris; First Musician; Second Musician; Third Musician; Peter)

The Nurse cheerfully attempts to wake Juliet, only to find her lying dead on the bed. Her calls for help draw the Capulets in, and all begin to lament. Friar Lawrence arrives for the wedding with Paris, and there is yet more lamentation until Lawrence quiets them and insists that Juliet is much happier now in heaven. Capulet orders that all the signs of merriment be change to mourning. The musicians are dismissed, though Peter asks them to play him a song he likes. They refuse, but hang around in the hopes of getting food and money.

Nurse.
Mistress! What, mistress! Juliet!—Fast, I warrant her, she.—
Why, lamb! Why, lady! Fie, you slug-a-bed!
Why, love, I say! Madam! Sweet heart! Why, bride!
What, not a word? You take your pennyworths now;
Sleep for a week, for the next night, I warrant,
The County Paris hath set up his rest

That you shall rest but little. God forgive me!
Marry and amen! How sound is she asleep!
I needs must wake her. Madam, madam, madam!
Ay, let the County take you in your bed,
He'll fright you up, i' faith. Will it not be?

Draws back the curtains.

What, dress'd, and in your clothes, and down again?
I must needs wake you. Lady, lady, lady!
Alas, alas! Help, help! My lady's dead!
O, weraday, that ever I was born!
Some aqua-vitae ho! My lord! My lady!

Enter Mother, Lady Capulet.

Lady Capulet.
What noise is here?

Nurse.
                    O lamentable day!

Lady Capulet.
What is the matter?

Nurse.
                    Look, look! O heavy day!

Lady Capulet.
O me, O me, my child, my only life!
Revive, look up, or I will die with thee!
Help, help! Call help.

Enter Father Capulet.

Capulet.
For shame, bring Juliet forth, her lord is come.

Nurse.
She's dead, deceas'd, she's dead, alack the day!

Lady Capulet.
Alack the day, she's dead, she's dead, she's dead!

Capulet.
Hah, let me see her. Out alas, she's cold,
Her blood is settled, and her joints are stiff;
Life and these lips have long been separated.
Death lies on her like an untimely frost
Upon the sweetest flower of all the field.

Nurse.
O lamentable day!

Lady Capulet.
                    O woeful time!

Capulet.
Death, that hath ta'en her hence to make me wail,
Ties up my tongue and will not let me speak.

Enter Friar Lawrence and the County Paris with the Musicians.

Friar Lawrence.
Come, is the bride ready to go to church?

Capulet.
Ready to go, but never to return.—
O son, the night before thy wedding-day
Hath Death lain with thy wife. There she lies,
Flower as she was, deflowered by him.
Death is my son-in-law. Death is my heir,
My daughter he hath wedded. I will die,
And leave him all; life, living, all is Death's.

Paris.
Have I thought long to see this morning's face,
And doth it give me such a sight as this?

Lady Capulet.
Accurs'd, unhappy, wretched, hateful day!
Most miserable hour that e'er time saw
In lasting labor of his pilgrimage!
But one, poor one, one poor and loving child,
But one thing to rejoice and solace in,
And cruel Death hath catch'd it from my sight!

Nurse.
O woe! O woeful, woeful, woeful day!
Most lamentable day, most woeful day
That ever, ever, I did yet behold!
O day, O day, O day, O hateful day!
Never was seen so black a day as this.
O woeful day, O woeful day!

Paris.
Beguil'd, divorced, wronged, spited, slain!
Most detestable Death, by thee beguil'd,
By cruel cruel thee quite overthrown!
O love, O life! Not life, but love in death!

Capulet.
Despis'd, distressed, hated, martyr'd, kill'd!
Uncomfortable time, why cam'st thou now
To murder, murder our solemnity?
O child, O child! My soul, and not my child!

Dead art thou! Alack, my child is dead,
And with my child my joys are buried.

Friar Lawrence.
Peace ho, for shame! Confusion's cure lives not
In these confusions. Heaven and yourself
Had part in this fair maid, now heaven hath all,
And all the better is it for the maid.
Your part in her you could not keep from death,
But heaven keeps his part in eternal life.
The most you sought was her promotion,
For 'twas your heaven she should be advanc'd,
And weep ye now, seeing she is advanc'd
Above the clouds, as high as heaven itself?
O, in this love, you love your child so ill
That you run mad, seeing that she is well.
She's not well married that lives married long,
But she's best married that dies married young.
Dry up your tears, and stick your rosemary
On this fair corse, and as the custom is,
And in her best array, bear her to church;
For though fond nature bids us all lament,
Yet nature's tears are reason's merriment.

Capulet.
All things that we ordained festival,
Turn from their office to black funeral:
Our instruments to melancholy bells,
Our wedding cheer to a sad burial feast;
Our solemn hymns to sullen dirges change;
Our bridal flowers serve for a buried corse;
And all things change them to the contrary.

Friar Lawrence.
Sir, go you in, and, madam, go with him;
And go, Sir Paris. Every one prepare
To follow this fair corse unto her grave.
The heavens do low'r upon you for some ill;
Move them no more by crossing their high will.

They all, but the Nurse and the Musicians, go forth, casting rosemary on her, and shutting the curtains.

First Musician.
Faith, we may put up our pipes and be gone.

Nurse.
Honest good fellows, ah, put up, put up,
For well you know this is a pitiful case.

Exit.

First Musician.
Ay, by my troth, the case may be amended.

Enter Peter.

Peter.
Musicians, O musicians, "Heart's ease," "Heart's ease"!
O, and you will have me live, play "Heart's ease."

First Musician.
Why "Heart's ease"?

Peter.
O musicians, because my heart itself plays "My heart is full." O, play me some merry dump to comfort me.

First Musician.
Not a dump we, 'tis no time to play now.

Peter.
You will not then?

First Musician.
No.

Peter.
I will then give it you soundly.

First Musician.
What will you give us?

Peter.
No money, on my faith, but the gleek; I will give you the minstrel.

First Musician.
Then will I give you the serving-creature.

Peter.
Then will I lay the serving-creature's dagger on your pate. I will carry no crotchets, I'll re you, I'll fa you. Do you note me?

First Musician.
And you re us and fa us, you note us.

Second Musician.
Pray you put up your dagger, and put out your wit.

Peter.
Then have at you with my wit! I will dry-beat you with an iron wit, and put up my iron dagger. Answer me like men:
"When griping griefs the heart doth wound,
And doleful dumps the mind oppress,

Then music with her silver sound"—
Why "silver sound"? Why "music with her silver sound"? What say you, Simon Catling?

First Musician.
Marry, sir, because silver hath a sweet sound.

Peter.
Pretty! What say you, Hugh Rebeck?

Second Musician.
I say, "silver sound," because musicians sound for silver.

Peter.
Pretty too! What say you, James Sound-post?

Third Musician.
Faith, I know not what to say.

Peter.
O, I cry you mercy, you are the singer; I will say for you; it is "music with her silver sound," because musicians have no gold for sounding:
"Then music with her silver sound
With speedy help doth lend redress."

Exit.

First Musician.
What a pestilent knave is this same!

Second Musician.
Hang him, Jack! Come, we'll in here, tarry for the mourners, and stay dinner.

Exeunt.

Act 5

Scene 1

Mantua. A street.

(Romeo; Balthasar; Apothecary)

Romeo has had an odd dream that leaves him convinced he is about to receive good news. Instead, his servant Balthasar arrives and tells him that Juliet is dead. Romeo immediately decides to return to Verona, buying a strong poison first from an Apothecary. He is resolved to kill himself at Juliet's grave.

Enter Romeo.

Romeo.
If I may trust the flattering truth of sleep,
My dreams presage some joyful news at hand.
My bosom's lord sits lightly in his throne,
And all this day an unaccustom'd spirit
Lifts me above the ground with cheerful thoughts.
I dreamt my lady came and found me dead—
Strange dream, that gives a dead man leave to think!—
And breath'd such life with kisses in my lips
That I reviv'd and was an emperor.
Ah me, how sweet is love itself possess'd,
When but love's shadows are so rich in joy!

Enter Romeo's man Balthasar, booted.

News from Verona! How now, Balthasar?
Dost thou not bring me letters from the friar?
How doth my lady? Is my father well?
How doth my Juliet? That I ask again,
For nothing can be ill if she be well.

Balthasar.
Then she is well and nothing can be ill:
Her body sleeps in Capel's monument,
And her immortal part with angels lives.
I saw her laid low in her kindred's vault,
And presently took post to tell it you.
O, pardon me for bringing these ill news,
Since you did leave it for my office, sir.

Romeo.
Is it e'en so? Then I defy you, stars!
Thou knowest my lodging, get me ink and paper,
And hire post-horses; I will hence tonight.

Balthasar.
I do beseech you, sir, have patience.
Your looks are pale and wild, and do import
Some misadventure.

Romeo.
                    Tush, thou art deceiv'd.
Leave me, and do the thing I bid thee do.
Hast thou no letters to me from the friar?

Balthasar.
No, my good lord.

Romeo.
                    No matter, get thee gone,
And hire those horses; I'll be with thee straight.

Exit Balthasar.

Well, Juliet, I will lie with thee tonight.
Let's see for means. O mischief, thou art swift
To enter in the thoughts of desperate men!
I do remember an apothecary—
And hereabouts 'a dwells—which late I noted
In tatt'red weeds, with overwhelming brows,
Culling of simples; meager were his looks,
Sharp misery had worn him to the bones;
And in his needy shop a tortoise hung,
An alligator stuff'd, and other skins
Of ill-shap'd fishes, and about his shelves
A beggarly account of empty boxes,
Green earthen pots, bladders, and musty seeds,
Remnants of packthread, and old cakes of roses
Were thinly scattered, to make up a show.
Noting this penury, to myself I said,
"An' if a man did need a poison now,
Whose sale is present death in Mantua,
Here lives a caitiff wretch would sell it him."
O, this same thought did but forerun my need,
And this same needy man must sell it me.
As I remember, this should be the house.
Being holiday, the beggar's shop is shut.
What ho, apothecary!

Enter Apothecary.

Apothecary.
                    Who calls so loud?

Romeo.
Come hither, man. I see that thou art poor.
Hold, there is forty ducats; let me have
A dram of poison, such soon-speeding gear
As will disperse itself through all the veins
That the life-weary taker may fall dead,
And that the trunk may be discharg'd of breath
As violently as hasty powder fir'd
Doth hurry from the fatal cannon's womb.

Apothecary.
Such mortal drugs I have, but Mantua's law
Is death to any he that utters them.

Romeo.
Art thou so bare and full of wretchedness,
And fearest to die? Famine is in thy cheeks,
Need and oppression starveth in thy eyes,
Contempt and beggary hangs upon thy back;
The world is not thy friend, nor the world's law,
The world affords no law to make thee rich;
Then be not poor, but break it, and take this.

Apothecary.
My poverty, but not my will, consents.

Romeo.
I pay thy poverty, and not thy will.

Apothecary.
Put this in any liquid thing you will
And drink it off, and if you had the strength
Of twenty men, it would dispatch you straight.

Romeo.
There is thy gold, worse poison to men's souls,
Doing more murder in this loathsome world,
Than these poor compounds that thou mayest not sell.
I sell thee poison, thou hast sold me none.
Farewell! Buy food, and get thyself in flesh.

Exit Apothecary.

Come, cordial and not poison, go with me
To Juliet's grave, for there must I use thee.

Exit.

Scene 2

Friar Lawrence's cell.

(Friar John; Friar Lawrence)

Friar John, who has been sent to Mantua bearing Friar Lawrence's letter explaining to Romeo all that is going on, return to tell Lawrence that due to an outbreak of plague he was prevented from delivering the note. Worried, Lawrence sends John to find him a crowbar, as he will have to get Juliet out of the tomb himself. He plans to keep her in his cell until he can get the news to Romeo.

Enter Friar John.

Friar John.
Holy Franciscan friar! Brother, ho!

Enter Friar Lawrence.

Friar Lawrence.
This same should be the voice of Friar John.
Welcome from Mantua! What says Romeo?
Or, if his mind be writ, give me his letter.

Friar John.
Going to find a barefoot brother out,
One of our order, to associate me,
Here in this city visiting the sick,
And finding him, the searchers of the town,
Suspecting that we both were in a house
Where the infectious pestilence did reign,
Seal'd up the doors and would not let us forth,
So that my speed to Mantua there was stay'd.

Friar Lawrence.
Who bare my letter then to Romeo?

Friar John.
I could not send it—here it is again—
Nor get a messenger to bring it thee,
So fearful were they of infection.

Friar Lawrence.
Unhappy fortune! By my brotherhood,
The letter was not nice but full of charge,
Of dear import, and the neglecting it
May do much danger. Friar John, go hence,
Get me an iron crow, and bring it straight
Unto my cell.

Friar John.
Brother, I'll go and bring it thee.

Exit.

Friar Lawrence.
Now must I to the monument alone,
Within this three hours will fair Juliet wake.
She will beshrew me much that Romeo
Hath had no notice of these accidents;
But I will write again to Mantua,
And keep her at my cell till Romeo come—
Poor living corse, clos'd in a dead man's tomb!

Exit.

Scene 3

A churchyard; before a tomb belonging to the Capulets.

(Paris; Page; Romeo; Balthasar; Friar Lawrence; Juliet; First Watchman; Second Watchman; Third Watchman; Prince Escalus; Attendants; Montague)

Paris arrives at the Capulet tomb bearing flowers. Wishing to be alone, he tells his Page to watch and whistle if anyone else approaches. Paris strews his flowers over the grave, and as he promises Juliet to do this every night, he hears the Page whistle. He hides. Romeo and Balthasar appear. Romeo orders his servant to leave him alone, but Balthasar, worried, only goes a little way off. Recognizing Romeo as he breaks into the tomb, Paris steps forward to apprehend him, persuaded that Romeo is trying to wreak some outrage on the tomb. Romeo warns Paris off, but Paris is insistent, and the two fight. The Page runs off to find the Watch, while Romeo kills Paris. Only once he is dead does Romeo find out who he is. As he was requested, he lays Paris by Juliet's side. He then bids farewell to Paris, Juliet, and Tybalt, drinks the poison, and dies. Friar Lawrence arrives and runs into Balthasar. Growing deeply worried, Lawrence rushes into the tomb, where he finds Paris and Romeo's bodies. Juliet awakes, and Lawrence tries to get her out without her seeing Romeo, but fails. Hearing the noise of the approaching watch, he loses his nerve and flees. Juliet realizes what has happened, but Romeo has drunk all the poison, and there is none left. So she takes his dagger and stabs herself. The Watch arrive and begin gathering up everyone they find in the graveyard. The Prince appears, accompanied by the Capulets and Montagues. Lawrence is brought in and explains all that has happened, shouldering the blame. The Prince refuses to accept this, and lays the blame squarely on the quarreling families, seeing that the deaths have punished everybody. Capulet and Montague unite in grief and swear friendship, promising to pay for golden statues of the lovers. The Prince leads them away to discuss the matter further and decide on punishments for those deserving of them.

Enter Paris and his Page with flowers and sweet water and a torch.

Paris.
Give me thy torch, boy. Hence, and stand aloof.
Yet put it out, for I would not be seen.
Under yond yew trees lay thee all along,
Holding thy ear close to the hollow ground,
So shall no foot upon the churchyard tread,
Being loose, unfirm, with digging up of graves,
But thou shalt hear it. Whistle then to me
As signal that thou hearest something approach.
Give me those flowers. Do as I bid thee, go.

Page to Paris.

Aside.

I am almost afraid to stand alone
Here in the churchyard, yet I will adventure.

Act 5, Scene 3

Retires. Paris strews the tomb with flowers.

Paris.
Sweet flower, with flowers thy bridal bed I strew—
O woe, thy canopy is dust and stones!—
Which with sweet water nightly I will dew,
Or wanting that, with tears distill'd by moans.
The obsequies that I for thee will keep
Nightly shall be to strew thy grave and weep.

Whistle Boy.

The boy gives warning, something doth approach.
What cursed foot wanders this way tonight,
To cross my obsequies and true love's rite?
What, with a torch? Muffle me, night, a while.

Retires.
Enter Romeo and Balthasar with a torch, a mattock, and a crow of iron.

Romeo.
Give me that mattock and the wrenching iron.
Hold, take this letter; early in the morning
See thou deliver it to my lord and father.
Give me the light. Upon thy life I charge thee,
What e'er thou hearest or seest, stand all aloof,
And do not interrupt me in my course.
Why I descend into this bed of death
Is partly to behold my lady's face,
But chiefly to take thence from her dead finger
A precious ring—a ring that I must use
In dear employment—therefore hence be gone.
But if thou, jealous, dost return to pry
In what I farther shall intend to do,
By heaven, I will tear thee joint by joint,
And strew this hungry churchyard with thy limbs.
The time and my intents are savage-wild,
More fierce and more inexorable far
Than empty tigers or the roaring sea.

Balthasar.
I will be gone, sir, and not trouble ye.

Romeo.
So shalt thou show me friendship. Take thou that;
Live and be prosperous, and farewell, good fellow.

Balthasar.

Aside.

For all this same, I'll hide me hereabout,
His looks I fear, and his intents I doubt.

Retires.

Romeo.
Thou detestable maw, thou womb of death,
Gorg'd with the dearest morsel of the earth,
Thus I enforce thy rotten jaws to open,
And in despite I'll cram thee with more food.

Romeo begins to open the tomb.

Paris.
This is that banish'd haughty Montague,
That murd'red my love's cousin, with which grief
It is supposed the fair creature died,
And here is come to do some villainous shame
To the dead bodies. I will apprehend him.

Steps forth.

Stop thy unhallowed toil, vile Montague!
Can vengeance be pursued further than death?
Condemned villain, I do apprehend thee.
Obey and go with me, for thou must die.

Romeo.
I must indeed, and therefore came I hither.
Good gentle youth, tempt not a desp'rate man.
Fly hence and leave me, think upon these gone,
Let them affright thee. I beseech thee, youth,
Put not another sin upon my head,
By urging me to fury: O, be gone!
By heaven, I love thee better than myself,
For I come hither arm'd against myself.
Stay not, be gone; live, and hereafter say
A madman's mercy bid thee run away.

Paris.
I do defy thy conjuration,
And apprehend thee for a felon here.

Romeo.
Wilt thou provoke me? Then have at thee, boy!

They fight.

Page to Paris.
O Lord, they fight! I will go call the watch.

Exit.

Paris.
O, I am slain!

Falls.

               If thou be merciful,
Open the tomb, lay me with Juliet.

Dies.

Romeo.
In faith, I will. Let me peruse this face.
Mercutio's kinsman, noble County Paris!
What said my man, when my betossed soul
Did not attend him as we rode? I think
He told me Paris should have married Juliet.
Said he not so? Or did I dream it so?
Or am I mad, hearing him talk of Juliet,
To think it was so? O, give me thy hand,
One writ with me in sour misfortune's book!
I'll bury thee in a triumphant grave.
A grave? O no, a lantern, slaught'red youth;
For here lies Juliet, and her beauty makes
This vault a feasting presence full of light.
Death, lie thou there, by a dead man interr'd.

Laying Paris in the tomb.

How oft when men are at the point of death
Have they been merry, which their keepers call
A lightning before death! O how may I
Call this a lightning? O my love, my wife,
Death, that hath suck'd the honey of thy breath,
Hath had no power yet upon thy beauty:
Thou art not conquer'd, beauty's ensign yet
Is crimson in thy lips and in thy cheeks,
And death's pale flag is not advanced there.
Tybalt, liest thou there in thy bloody sheet?
O, what more favor can I do to thee,
Than with that hand that cut thy youth in twain
To sunder his that was thine enemy?
Forgive me, cousin! Ah, dear Juliet,
Why art thou yet so fair? Shall I believe
That unsubstantial Death is amorous,
And that the lean abhorred monster keeps
Thee here in dark to be his paramour?
For fear of that, I still will stay with thee,
And never from this palace of dim night
Depart again. Here, here will I remain
With worms that are thy chambermaids; O, here
Will I set up my everlasting rest,
And shake the yoke of inauspicious stars
From this world-wearied flesh. Eyes, look your last!
Arms, take your last embrace! And, lips, O you
The doors of breath, seal with a righteous kiss
A dateless bargain to engrossing death!
Come, bitter conduct, come, unsavory guide!
Thou desperate pilot, now at once run on
The dashing rocks thy sea-sick weary bark!
Here's to my love!

Drinks.

               O true apothecary!
Thy drugs are quick. Thus with a kiss I die.

Dies.
Enter Friar Lawrence with lantern, crow, and spade.

Friar Lawrence.
Saint Francis be my speed! How oft tonight
Have my old feet stumbled at graves! Who's there?

Balthasar.
Here's one, a friend, and one that knows you well.

Friar Lawrence.
Bliss be upon you! Tell me, good my friend,
What torch is yond, that vainly lends his light
To grubs and eyeless skulls? As I discern,
It burneth in the Capels' monument.

Balthasar.
It doth so, holy sir, and there's my master,
One that you love.

Friar Lawrence.
               Who is it?

Balthasar.
               Romeo.

Friar Lawrence.
How long hath he been there?

Balthasar.
               Full half an hour.

Friar Lawrence.
Go with me to the vault.

Balthasar.
               I dare not, sir.
My master knows not but I am gone hence,
And fearfully did menace me with death
If I did stay to look on his intents.

Friar Lawrence.
Stay then, I'll go alone. Fear comes upon me.
O, much I fear some ill unthrifty thing.

Balthasar.
As I did sleep under this yew tree here,
I dreamt my master and another fought,
And that my master slew him.

Exit.

Friar Lawrence.
                    Romeo!

Friar stoops and looks on the blood and weapons.

Alack, alack, what blood is this, which stains
The stony entrance of this sepulchre?
What mean these masterless and gory swords
To lie discolor'd by this place of peace?

Enters the tomb.

Romeo, O, pale! Who else? What, Paris too?
And steep'd in blood? Ah, what an unkind hour
Is guilty of this lamentable chance!
The lady stirs.

Juliet rises.

Juliet.
O comfortable friar! Where is my lord?
I do remember well where I should be,
And there I am. Where is my Romeo?

Noise within.

Friar Lawrence.
I hear some noise, lady. Come from that nest
Of death, contagion, and unnatural sleep.
A greater power than we can contradict
Hath thwarted our intents. Come, come away.
Thy husband in thy bosom there lies dead;
And Paris too. Come, I'll dispose of thee
Among a sisterhood of holy nuns.
Stay not to question, for the watch is coming.
Come go, good Juliet,

Noise again.

                I dare no longer stay.

Exit.

Juliet.
Go get thee hence, for I will not away.
What's here? A cup clos'd in my true love's hand?
Poison, I see, hath been his timeless end.
O churl, drunk all, and left no friendly drop
To help me after? I will kiss thy lips,
Haply some poison yet doth hang on them,
To make me die with a restorative.
Thy lips are warm.

First Watchman.

Within.

                Lead, boy, which way?

Juliet.
Yea, noise? Then I'll be brief. O happy dagger,

Taking Romeo's dagger.

This is thy sheath;

Stabs herself.

                there rust, and let me die.

Falls on Romeo's body and dies.
Enter Paris' Page and Watch.

Page to Paris.
This is the place, there where the torch doth burn.

First Watchman.
The ground is bloody, search about the churchyard.
Go, some of you, whoe'er you find attach.

Exeunt some.

Pitiful sight! Here lies the County slain,
And Juliet bleeding, warm, and newly dead,
Who here hath lain this two days buried.
Go tell the Prince, run to the Capulets,
Raise up the Montagues; some others search.

Exeunt others.

We see the ground whereon these woes do lie,
But the true ground of all these piteous woes
We cannot without circumstance descry.

Enter some of the Watch with Romeo's man, Balthasar.

Second Watchman.
Here's Romeo's man, we found him in the churchyard.

First Watchman.
Hold him in safety till the Prince come hither.

Enter Friar Lawrence and another Watchman.

Third Watchman.
Here is a friar, that trembles, sighs, and weeps.
We took this mattock and this spade from him,
As he was coming from this churchyard's side.

First Watchman.
A great suspicion. Stay the friar too.

Enter the Prince and Attendants.

Prince Escalus.
What misadventure is so early up,
That calls our person from our morning rest?

Enter Capels (Capulet, Lady Capulet, and others).

Capulet.
What should it be that is so shrik'd abroad?

Lady Capulet.
O, the people in the street cry "Romeo,"
Some "Juliet," and some "Paris," and all run
With open outcry toward our monument.

Prince Escalus.
What fear is this which startles in your ears?

First Watchman.
Sovereign, here lies the County Paris slain,
And Romeo dead, and Juliet, dead before,
Warm and new kill'd.

Prince Escalus.
Search, seek, and know how this foul murder comes.

First Watchman.
Here is a friar, and slaughter'd Romeo's man,
With instruments upon them, fit to open
These dead men's tombs.

Capulet.
O heavens! O wife, look how our daughter bleeds!
This dagger hath mista'en, for lo his house
Is empty on the back of Montague,
And it mis-sheathed in my daughter's bosom!

Lady Capulet.
O me, this sight of death is as a bell
That warns my old age to a sepulchre.

Enter Montague and others.

Prince Escalus.
Come, Montague, for thou art early up
To see thy son and heir now early down.

Montague.
Alas, my liege, my wife is dead tonight;
Grief of my son's exile hath stopp'd her breath.
What further woe conspires against mine age?

Prince Escalus.
Look and thou shalt see.

Montague.
O thou untaught! What manners is in this,
To press before thy father to a grave?

Prince Escalus.
Seal up the mouth of outrage for a while,
Till we can clear these ambiguities,
And know their spring, their head, their true descent,
And then will I be general of your woes,
And lead you even to death. Mean time forbear,
And let mischance be slave to patience.
Bring forth the parties of suspicion.

Friar Lawrence.
I am the greatest, able to do least,
Yet most suspected, as the time and place
Doth make against me, of this direful murder;
And here I stand both to impeach and purge
Myself condemned and myself excus'd.

Prince Escalus.
Then say at once what thou dost know in this.

Friar Lawrence.
I will be brief, for my short date of breath
Is not so long as is a tedious tale.
Romeo, there dead, was husband to that Juliet,
And she, there dead, that Romeo's faithful wife.
I married them, and their stol'n marriage-day
Was Tybalt's dooms-day, whose untimely death
Banish'd the new-made bridegroom from this city,
For whom, and not for Tybalt, Juliet pin'd.
You, to remove that siege of grief from her,
Betroth'd and would have married her perforce
To County Paris. Then comes she to me,

Act 5, Scene 3

And with wild looks bid me devise some mean
To rid her from this second marriage,
Or in my cell there would she kill herself.
Then gave I her (so tutor'd by my art)
A sleeping potion, which so took effect
As I intended, for it wrought on her
The form of death. Mean time I writ to Romeo,
That he should hither come as this dire night
To help to take her from her borrowed grave,
Being the time the potion's force should cease.
But he which bore my letter, Friar John,
Was stayed by accident, and yesternight
Return'd my letter back. Then all alone,
At the prefixed hour of her waking,
Came I to take her from her kindred's vault,
Meaning to keep her closely at my cell,
Till I conveniently could send to Romeo.
But when I came, some minute ere the time
Of her awakening, here untimely lay
The noble Paris and true Romeo dead.
She wakes, and I entreated her come forth
And bear this work of heaven with patience.
But then a noise did scare me from the tomb,
And she, too desperate, would not go with me,
But as it seems, did violence on herself.
All this I know, and to the marriage
Her nurse is privy; and if aught in this
Miscarried by my fault, let my old life
Be sacrific'd some hour before his time,
Unto the rigor of severest law.

Prince Escalus.
We still have known thee for a holy man.
Where's Romeo's man? What can he say to this?

Balthasar.
I brought my master news of Juliet's death,
And then in post he came from Mantua
To this same place, to this same monument.
This letter he early bid me give his father,
And threat'ned me with death, going in the vault,
If I departed not and left him there.

Prince Escalus.
Give me the letter, I will look on it.
Where is the County's page that rais'd the watch?
Sirrah, what made your master in this place?

Page to Paris.
He came with flowers to strew his lady's grave,
And bid me stand aloof, and so I did.
Anon comes one with light to ope the tomb,
And by and by my master drew on him,
And then I ran away to call the watch.

Prince Escalus.
This letter doth make good the friar's words,
Their course of love, the tidings of her death;
And here he writes that he did buy a poison
Of a poor pothecary, and therewithal
Came to this vault, to die and lie with Juliet.
Where be these enemies? Capulet! Montague!
See what a scourge is laid upon your hate,
That heaven finds means to kill your joys with love.
And I for winking at your discords too
Have lost a brace of kinsmen. All are punish'd.

Capulet.
O brother Montague, give me thy hand.
This is my daughter's jointure, for no more
Can I demand.

Montague.
                    But I can give thee more,
For I will raise her statue in pure gold,
That whiles Verona by that name is known,
There shall no figure at such rate be set
As that of true and faithful Juliet.

Capulet.
As rich shall Romeo's by his lady's lie,
Poor sacrifices of our enmity!

Prince Escalus.
A glooming peace this morning with it brings,
The sun, for sorrow, will not show his head.
Go hence to have more talk of these sad things;
Some shall be pardon'd, and some punished:
For never was a story of more woe
Than this of Juliet and her Romeo.

Exeunt omnes.

Macbeth

Act 1

Scene 1

A desert place.

(First Witch; Second Witch; Third Witch)

Amid thunder and lightning, three witches agree to meet again when the battle is over, by the end of the day, and meet Macbeth.

Thunder and lightning. Enter three Witches.

First Witch.
When shall we three meet again?
In thunder, lightning, or in rain?

Second Witch.
When the hurly-burly's done,
When the battle's lost and won.

Third Witch.
That will be ere the set of sun.

First Witch.
Where the place?

Second Witch.
                  Upon the heath.

Third Witch.
There to meet with Macbeth.

First Witch.
I come, Graymalkin.

Second Witch.
Paddock calls.

Third Witch.
Anon.

Three Witches.
Fair is foul, and foul is fair,
Hover through the fog and filthy air.

Exeunt.

Scene 2

A camp near Forres.

(King Duncan; Malcolm; Donalbain; Lennox; Attendants; Sergeant; Rosse; Angus)

An injured Sergeant tells Duncan, King of Scots, of how the Thane of Glamis, Macbeth, defeated the rebel Macdonwald and killed him; the Sergeant faints as he explains that at that moment, the King of Norway began a second attack. Ross arrives to inform the King that Macbeth proceeded to beat Norway, along with the traitor Thane of Cawdor who was helping him. The defeat is complete; in recognition of Macbeth's valor, Duncan gives him Cawdor's title as he sentences the traitor to death.

Alarum within. Enter King Duncan, Malcolm, Donalbain, Lennox, with Attendants, meeting a bleeding Sergeant.

Duncan, King of Scotland.
What bloody man is that? He can report,
As seemeth by his plight, of the revolt
The newest state.

Malcolm.
                  This is the sergeant,
Who like a good and hardy soldier fought
'Gainst my captivity. Hail, brave friend!
Say to the King the knowledge of the broil
As thou didst leave it.

Act 1, Scene 2

Sergeant.
                       Doubtful it stood,
As two spent swimmers that do cling together
And choke their art. The merciless Macdonwald
(Worthy to be a rebel, for to that
The multiplying villainies of nature
Do swarm upon him) from the Western Isles
Of kerns and gallowglasses is supplied,
And Fortune, on his damned quarrel smiling,
Show'd like a rebel's whore. But all's too weak;
For brave Macbeth (well he deserves that name),
Disdaining Fortune, with his brandish'd steel,
Which smok'd with bloody execution,
(Like Valor's minion) carv'd out his passage
Till he fac'd the slave;
Which nev'r shook hands, nor bade farewell to him,
Till he unseam'd him from the nave to th' chops,
And fix'd his head upon our battlements.

Duncan, King of Scotland.
O valiant cousin, worthy gentleman!

Sergeant.
As whence the sun gins his reflection
Shipwracking storms and direful thunders break,
So from that spring whence comfort seem'd to come
Discomfort swells. Mark, King of Scotland, mark!
No sooner justice had, with valor arm'd,
Compell'd these skipping kerns to trust their heels,
But the Norweyan lord, surveying vantage,
With furbish'd arms and new supplies of men,
Began a fresh assault.

Duncan, King of Scotland.
                       Dismay'd not this
Our captains, Macbeth and Banquo?

Sergeant.
                       Yes,
As sparrows eagles; or the hare the lion.
If I say sooth, I must report they were
As cannons overcharg'd with double cracks, so they
Doubly redoubled strokes upon the foe.
Except they meant to bathe in reeking wounds,
Or memorize another Golgotha,
I cannot tell—
But I am faint, my gashes cry for help.

Duncan, King of Scotland.
So well thy words become thee as thy wounds,
They smack of honor both. Go get him surgeons.

Exit Sergeant, attended.
Enter Rosse and Angus.

Who comes here?

Malcolm.
                       The worthy Thane of Rosse.

Lennox.
What a haste looks through his eyes! So should he look
That seems to speak things strange.

Rosse.
                       God save the King!

Duncan, King of Scotland.
Whence cam'st thou, worthy thane?

Rosse.
                       From Fife, great King,
Where the Norweyan banners flout the sky
And fan our people cold.
Norway himself, with terrible numbers,
Assisted by that most disloyal traitor,
The Thane of Cawdor, began a dismal conflict,
Till that Bellona's bridegroom, lapp'd in proof,
Confronted him with self-comparisons,
Point against point, rebellious arm 'gainst arm,
Curbing his lavish spirit; and to conclude,
The victory fell on us.

Duncan, King of Scotland.
                       Great happiness!

Rosse.
                       That now
Sweno, the Norways' king, craves composition;
Nor would we deign him burial of his men
Till he disbursed at Saint Colme's inch
Ten thousand dollars to our general use.

Duncan, King of Scotland.
No more that Thane of Cawdor shall deceive
Our bosom interest. Go pronounce his present death,
And with his former title greet Macbeth.

Rosse.
I'll see it done.

Duncan, King of Scotland.
What he hath lost, noble Macbeth hath won.

Exeunt.

Scene 3

A heath near Forres.

(First Witch; Second Witch; Third Witch; Macbeth; Banquo; Rosse; Angus)

The three witches trade tales of what evils they have been up to of late. On their way back from the battle, Macbeth and his fellow general Banquo are met by the three, who greet Macbeth as Thane of Glamis, Thane of Cawdor, and King-to-be. Macbeth is incredulous, as two of these titles are not his. Banquo asks the sisters to prophesy to him, too, and they tell him that though he shall never be King himself, his children will take the throne. As Macbeth seeks to know more, the witches vanish. Ross and Angus arrive to greet Macbeth with his new title; the general is amazed to be called Thane of Cawdor, but it is explained to him. The truth of the witches' words disturbs Macbeth, and Banquo cautions him not to aim at the throne despite the fulfillment of the prophecy, as it may merely be a bait of the devil. He and Banquo agree to discuss the matter further at a better time.

Thunder. Enter the three Witches.

First Witch.
Where hast thou been, sister?

Second Witch.
Killing swine.

Third Witch.
Sister, where thou?

First Witch.
A sailor's wife had chestnuts in her lap,
And mounch'd, and mounch'd, and mounch'd. "Give me!" quoth I.
"Aroint thee, witch!" the rump-fed ronyon cries.
Her husband's to Aleppo gone, master o' th' Tiger;
But in a sieve I'll thither sail,
And like a rat without a tail,
I'll do, I'll do, and I'll do.

Second Witch.
I'll give thee a wind.

First Witch.
Th' art kind.

Third Witch.
And I another.

First Witch.
I myself have all the other,
And the very ports they blow,
All the quarters that they know
I' th' shipman's card.
I'll drain him dry as hay:
Sleep shall neither night nor day
Hang upon his penthouse lid;
He shall live a man forbid;
Weary sev'nnights, nine times nine,
Shall he dwindle, peak, and pine;
Though his bark cannot be lost,
Yet it shall be tempest-toss'd.
Look what I have.

Second Witch.
Show me, show me.

First Witch.
Here I have a pilot's thumb,
Wrack'd as homeward he did come.

Drum within.

Third Witch.
A drum, a drum!
Macbeth doth come.

Three Witches.
The weird sisters, hand in hand,
Posters of the sea and land,
Thus do go, about, about,
Thrice to thine, and thrice to mine,
And thrice again, to make up nine.
Peace, the charm's wound up.

Enter Macbeth and Banquo.

Macbeth.
So foul and fair a day I have not seen.

Banquo.
How far is't call'd to Forres? What are these
So wither'd and so wild in their attire,
That look not like th' inhabitants o' th' earth,
And yet are on't? Live you? Or are you aught
That man may question? You seem to understand me,
By each at once her choppy finger laying
Upon her skinny lips. You should be women,
And yet your beards forbid me to interpret
That you are so.

Macbeth.
                Speak, if you can: what are you?

First Witch.
All hail, Macbeth, hail to thee, Thane of Glamis!

Second Witch.
All hail, Macbeth, hail to thee. Thane of Cawdor!

Third Witch.
All hail, Macbeth, that shalt be King hereafter!

Banquo.
Good sir, why do you start, and seem to fear
Things that do sound so fair?—I' th' name of truth,
Are ye fantastical, or that indeed
Which outwardly ye show? My noble partner
You greet with present grace, and great prediction
Of noble having and of royal hope,
That he seems rapt withal; to me you speak not.
If you can look into the seeds of time,
And say which grain will grow, and which will not,
Speak then to me, who neither beg nor fear
Your favors nor your hate.

First Witch.
Hail!

Second Witch.
Hail!

Third Witch.
Hail!

First Witch.
Lesser than Macbeth, and greater.

Second Witch.
Not so happy, yet much happier.

Third Witch.
Thou shalt get kings, though thou be none.
So all hail, Macbeth and Banquo!

First Witch.
Banquo and Macbeth, all hail!

Macbeth.
Stay, you imperfect speakers, tell me more:
By Sinel's death I know I am Thane of Glamis,
But how of Cawdor? The Thane of Cawdor lives
A prosperous gentleman; and to be king
Stands not within the prospect of belief,
No more than to be Cawdor. Say from whence
You owe this strange intelligence, or why
Upon this blasted heath you stop our way
With such prophetic greeting? Speak, I charge you.

Witches vanish.

Banquo.
The earth hath bubbles, as the water has,
And these are of them. Whither are they vanish'd?

Macbeth.
Into the air; and what seem'd corporal melted,
As breath into the wind. Would they had stay'd!

Banquo.
Were such things here as we do speak about?
Or have we eaten on the insane root
That takes the reason prisoner?

Macbeth.
Your children shall be kings.

Banquo.
                You shall be king.

Macbeth.
And Thane of Cawdor too; went it not so?

Banquo.
To th' self-same tune and words. Who's here?

Enter Rosse and Angus.

Rosse.
The King hath happily receiv'd, Macbeth,
The news of thy success; and when he reads
Thy personal venture in the rebels' fight,
His wonders and his praises do contend
Which should be thine or his. Silenc'd with that,
In viewing o'er the rest o' th' self-same day,
He finds thee in the stout Norweyan ranks,
Nothing afeard of what thyself didst make,
Strange images of death. As thick as tale
Came post with post, and every one did bear
Thy praises in his kingdom's great defense,
And pour'd them down before him.

Angus.
                We are sent
To give thee from our royal master thanks,
Only to herald thee into his sight,
Not pay thee.

Rosse.
And for an earnest of a greater honor,
He bade me, from him, call thee Thane of Cawdor;
In which addition, hail, most worthy thane,
For it is thine.

Banquo.
               What, can the devil speak true?

Macbeth.
The Thane of Cawdor lives; why do you dress me
In borrow'd robes?

Angus.
               Who was the thane lives yet,
But under heavy judgment bears that life
Which he deserves to lose. Whether he was combin'd
With those of Norway, or did line the rebel
With hidden help and vantage, or that with both
He labor'd in his country's wrack, I know not;
But treasons capital, confess'd and prov'd,
Have overthrown him.

Macbeth.

Aside.
               Glamis, and Thane of Cawdor!
The greatest is behind.

To Rosse and Angus.
               Thanks for your pains.

Aside to Banquo.

Do you not hope your children shall be kings,
When those that gave the Thane of Cawdor to me
Promis'd no less to them?

Banquo.

Aside to Macbeth
               That, trusted home,
Might yet enkindle you unto the crown,
Besides the Thane of Cawdor. But 'tis strange;
And oftentimes, to win us to our harm,
The instruments of darkness tell us truths,
Win us with honest trifles, to betray 's
In deepest consequence.—
Cousins, a word, I pray you.

Macbeth.

Aside.
               Two truths are told,
As happy prologues to the swelling act
Of the imperial theme.—I thank you, gentlemen.

Aside.

This supernatural soliciting
Cannot be ill; cannot be good. If ill,
Why hath it given me earnest of success,
Commencing in a truth? I am Thane of Cawdor.
If good, why do I yield to that suggestion
Whose horrid image doth unfix my hair
And make my seated heart knock at my ribs,
Against the use of nature? Present fears
Are less than horrible imaginings:
My thought, whose murder yet is but fantastical,
Shakes so my single state of man that function
Is smother'd in surmise, and nothing is
But what is not.

Banquo.
               Look how our partner's rapt.

Macbeth.

Aside.

If chance will have me king, why, chance may crown me
Without my stir.

Banquo.
               New honors come upon him,
Like our strange garments, cleave not to their mould
But with the aid of use.

Macbeth.

Aside.
               Come what come may,
Time and the hour runs through the roughest day.

Banquo.
Worthy Macbeth, we stay upon your leisure.

Macbeth.
Give me your favor; my dull brain was wrought
With things forgotten. Kind gentlemen, your pains
Are regist'red where every day I turn
The leaf to read them. Let us toward the King.

Aside to Banquo.

Think upon what hath chanc'd; and at more time,
The interim having weigh'd it, let us speak
Our free hearts each to other.

Banquo.
                       Very gladly.

Macbeth.
Till then, enough.—Come, friends.

Exeunt.

Scene 4

Forres. A room in the palace.

(King Duncan; Lennox; Malcolm; Donalbain; Attendants; Macbeth; Banquo; Rosse; Angus)

Malcolm describes to his father Duncan how well the traitor Cawdor died; Duncan points out that people's faces do not necessarily reveal their thoughts. Macbeth and Banquo arrive, and the King greets them heartily, promising to lavish rewards on them. Duncan then immediately names Malcolm heir to the throne. Macbeth realizes that this puts Malcolm in the way to the throne. Duncan invites himself to Macbeth's castle for dinner and Macbeth leaves to prepare his household for the King's arrival.

Flourish. Enter King Duncan, Lennox, Malcolm, Donalbain, and Attendants.

Duncan, King of Scotland.
Is execution done on Cawdor? Are not
Those in commission yet return'd?

Malcolm.
                       My liege,
They are not yet come back. But I have spoke
With one that saw him die; who did report
That very frankly he confess'd his treasons,
Implor'd your Highness' pardon, and set forth
A deep repentance. Nothing in his life
Became him like the leaving it. He died
As one that had been studied in his death,
To throw away the dearest thing he ow'd,
As 'twere a careless trifle.

Duncan, King of Scotland.
                       There's no art
To find the mind's construction in the face:
He was a gentleman on whom I built
An absolute trust.

Enter Macbeth, Banquo, Rosse, and Angus.

                       O worthiest cousin!
The sin of my ingratitude even now
Was heavy on me. Thou art so far before,
That swiftest wing of recompense is slow
To overtake thee. Would thou hadst less deserv'd,
That the proportion both of thanks and payment
Might have been mine! Only I have left to say,
More is thy due than more than all can pay.

Macbeth.
The service and the loyalty I owe,
In doing it, pays itself. Your Highness' part
Is to receive our duties; and our duties
Are to your throne and state children and servants;
Which do but what they should, by doing every thing
Safe toward your love and honor.

Duncan, King of Scotland.
                       Welcome hither!
I have begun to plant thee, and will labor
To make thee full of growing. Noble Banquo,
That hast no less deserv'd, nor must be known
No less to have done so, let me infold thee
And hold thee to my heart.

Banquo.
                       There if I grow,
The harvest is your own.

Duncan, King of Scotland.
                       My plenteous joys,
Wanton in fullness, seek to hide themselves
In drops of sorrow. Sons, kinsmen, thanes,
And you whose places are the nearest, know
We will establish our estate upon
Our eldest, Malcolm, whom we name hereafter
The Prince of Cumberland; which honor must
Not unaccompanied invest him only,
But signs of nobleness, like stars, shall shine
On all deservers. From hence to Enverness,
And bind us further to you.

Macbeth.
The rest is labor, which is not us'd for you.
I'll be myself the harbinger, and make joyful
The hearing of my wife with your approach;
So humbly take my leave.

Duncan, King of Scotland.
>My worthy Cawdor!

Macbeth.

Aside.

The Prince of Cumberland! That is a step
On which I must fall down, or else o'erleap,
For in my way it lies. Stars, hide your fires,
Let not light see my black and deep desires;
The eye wink at the hand; yet let that be
Which the eye fears, when it is done, to see.

Exit.

Duncan, King of Scotland.
True, worthy Banquo! He is full so valiant,
And in his commendations I am fed;
It is a banquet to me. Let's after him,
Whose care is gone before to bid us welcome:
It is a peerless kinsman.

Flourish. Exeunt.

Scene 5

Inverness. Macbeth's castle.

(Lady Macbeth; Macbeth's Messenger; Macbeth)

Lady Macbeth reads the letter that Macbeth has sent her detailing his meeting with the witches. She immediately sees where the prophecy leads. She realizes, however, that Macbeth would rather simply become King by chance rather than play for the throne, and that he is not a natural hypocrite. She impatiently awaits his arrival so that she may convince him otherwise. Hearing that the King will be arriving that evening, she grasps the possibilities at once. She begs the spirits of the night to block all of her compassion so that she may be cruel enough to go through with her plan. Macbeth arrives, and she begins to work on him at once, offering to take care of everything; but he promises only that they shall discuss the matter further.

Enter Macbeth's Wife alone, with a letter.

Lady Macbeth.

Reads.

"They met me in the day of success; and I have learn'd by the perfect'st report, they have more in them than mortal knowledge. When I burnt in desire to question them further, they made themselves air, into which they vanish'd. Whiles I stood rapt in the wonder of it, came missives from the King, who all-hail'd me "Thane of Cawdor," by which title, before, these weird sisters saluted me, and referr'd me to the coming on of time with "Hail, King that shalt be!" This have I thought good to deliver thee, my dearest partner of greatness, that thou mightst not lose the dues of rejoicing by being ignorant of what greatness is promis'd thee. Lay it to thy heart, and farewell."
Glamis thou art, and Cawdor, and shalt be
What thou art promis'd. Yet do I fear thy nature,
It is too full o' th' milk of human kindness
To catch the nearest way. Thou wouldst be great,
Art not without ambition, but without
The illness should attend it. What thou wouldst highly,
That wouldst thou holily; wouldst not play false,
And yet wouldst wrongly win. Thou'ldst have, great Glamis,
That which cries, "Thus thou must do," if thou have it;
And that which rather thou dost fear to do
Than wishest should be undone. Hie thee hither,
That I may pour my spirits in thine ear,
And chastise with the valor of my tongue
All that impedes thee from the golden round,
Which fate and metaphysical aid doth seem
To have thee crown'd withal.

Enter Macbeth's Messenger.
>What is your tidings?

Macbeth's Messenger.
The King comes here tonight.

Lady Macbeth.
>Thou'rt mad to say it!
Is not thy master with him? Who, were't so,
Would have inform'd for preparation.

Macbeth's Messenger.
So please you, it is true; our thane is coming.
One of my fellows had the speed of him,
Who, almost dead for breath, had scarcely more
Than would make up his message.

Lady Macbeth.
>Give him tending,
He brings great news.

Exit Macbeth's Messenger.

                    The raven himself is hoarse
That croaks the fatal entrance of Duncan
Under my battlements. Come, you spirits
That tend on mortal thoughts, unsex me here,
And fill me from the crown to the toe topful
Of direst cruelty! Make thick my blood,
Stop up th' access and passage to remorse,
That no compunctious visitings of nature
Shake my fell purpose, nor keep peace between
Th' effect and it! Come to my woman's breasts,
And take my milk for gall, you murd'ring ministers,
Wherever in your sightless substances
You wait on nature's mischief! Come, thick night,
And pall thee in the dunnest smoke of hell,
That my keen knife see not the wound it makes,
Nor heaven peep through the blanket of the dark
To cry, "Hold, hold!"

Enter Macbeth.

                    Great Glamis! Worthy Cawdor!
Greater than both, by the all-hail hereafter!
Thy letters have transported me beyond
This ignorant present, and I feel now
The future in the instant.

Macbeth.
                    My dearest love,
Duncan comes here tonight.

Lady Macbeth.
                    And when goes hence?

Macbeth.
Tomorrow, as he purposes.

Lady Macbeth.
                    O, never
Shall sun that morrow see!
Your face, my thane, is as a book, where men
May read strange matters. To beguile the time,
Look like the time; bear welcome in your eye,
Your hand, your tongue; look like th' innocent flower,
But be the serpent under't. He that's coming
Must be provided for; and you shall put
This night's great business into my dispatch,
Which shall to all our nights and days to come
Give solely sovereign sway and masterdom.

Macbeth.
We will speak further.

Lady Macbeth.
                    Only look up clear:
To alter favor ever is to fear.
Leave all the rest to me.

Exeunt.

Scene 6

Before Macbeth's castle.

(*King Duncan; Malcolm; Donalbain; Banquo; Lennox; Macduff; Rosse; Angus; Attendants; Lady Macbeth*)

Duncan admires Macbeth's castle. Lady Macbeth greets the King, his sons, generals, and attendants in courteous fashion, bland and obsequious, never giving a hint of her intentions as the kind old man promises to shower favors on Macbeth.

Hoboys and torches. Enter King Duncan, Malcolm, Donalbain, Banquo, Lennox, Macduff, Rosse, Angus, and Attendants.

Duncan, King of Scotland.
This castle hath a pleasant seat, the air
Nimbly and sweetly recommends itself
Unto our gentle senses.

Banquo.
                    This guest of summer,
The temple-haunting marlet, does approve,
By his lov'd mansionry, that the heaven's breath
Smells wooingly here; no jutty, frieze,
Buttress, nor coign of vantage, but this bird
Hath made his pendant bed and procreant cradle.
Where they most breed and haunt, I have observ'd
The air is delicate.

Enter Lady Macbeth.

Duncan, King of Scotland.
                    See, see, our honor'd hostess!
The love that follows us sometime is our trouble,
Which still we thank as love. Herein I teach you
How you shall bid God 'ield us for your pains,
And thank us for your trouble.

Lady Macbeth.
                    All our service
In every point twice done, and then done double,
Were poor and single business to contend
Against those honors deep and broad wherewith

Your Majesty loads our house. For those of old,
And the late dignities heap'd up to them,
We rest your ermites.

Duncan, King of Scotland.
      Where's the Thane of Cawdor?
We cours'd him at the heels, and had a purpose
To be his purveyor; but he rides well,
And his great love, sharp as his spur, hath help him
To his home before us. Fair and noble hostess,
We are your guest tonight.

Lady Macbeth.
      Your servants ever
Have theirs, themselves, and what is theirs, in compt,
To make their audit at your Highness' pleasure,
Still to return your own.

Duncan, King of Scotland.
      Give me your hand.
Conduct me to mine host, we love him highly,
And shall continue our graces towards him.
By your leave, hostess.

Exeunt.

Scene 7

A room in Macbeth's castle.

(Sewer; Servants; Macbeth; Lady Macbeth)

Macbeth openly considers murdering the King, but the thought gnaws at his conscience, as the King is his kinsman and his guest, not to mention a good and mild King beloved by all. He realizes that he has no excuse or rationalization for the deed other than his own desire to be King. Lady Macbeth joins him and is shocked when he announces that he will not go through with the deed. She accuses him of cowardice, unmanliness, and oath-breaking, and he reveals his fear of failure. She points out how easy it will be to murder Duncan and frame his attendants. He reconciles himself to murder.

Hoboys, torches. Enter a Sewer and diverse Servants with dishes and service over the stage. Then enter Macbeth.

Macbeth.
If it were done, when 'tis done, then 'twere well
It were done quickly. If th' assassination
Could trammel up the consequence, and catch
With his surcease, success; that but this blow
Might be the be-all and the end-all—here,
But here, upon this bank and shoal of time,
We'd jump the life to come. But in these cases
We still have judgment here, that we but teach
Bloody instructions, which, being taught, return
To plague th' inventor. This even-handed justice
Commends th' ingredience of our poison'd chalice
To our own lips. He's here in double trust:
First, as I am his kinsman and his subject,
Strong both against the deed; then, as his host,
Who should against his murderer shut the door,
Not bear the knife myself. Besides, this Duncan
Hath borne his faculties so meek, hath been
So clear in his great office, that his virtues
Will plead like angels, trumpet-tongu'd, against
The deep damnation of his taking-off;
And pity, like a naked new-born babe,
Striding the blast, or heaven's cherubin, hors'd
Upon the sightless couriers of the air,
Shall blow the horrid deed in every eye,
That tears shall drown the wind. I have no spur
To prick the sides of my intent, but only
Vaulting ambition, which o'erleaps itself,
And falls on th' other—

Enter Lady Macbeth.

      How now? What news?

Lady Macbeth.
He has almost supp'd. Why have you left the chamber?

Macbeth.
Hath he ask'd for me?

Lady Macbeth.
      Know you not he has?

Macbeth.
We will proceed no further in this business:
He hath honor'd me of late, and I have bought
Golden opinions from all sorts of people,
Which would be worn now in their newest gloss,
Not cast aside so soon.

Lady Macbeth.
      Was the hope drunk
Wherein you dress'd yourself? Hath it slept since?
And wakes it now to look so green and pale
At what it did so freely? From this time
Such I account thy love. Art thou afeard
To be the same in thine own act and valor
As thou art in desire? Wouldst thou have that

Which thou esteem'st the ornament of life,
And live a coward in thine own esteem,
Letting "I dare not" wait upon "I would,"
Like the poor cat i' th' adage?

Macbeth.
                    Prithee peace!
I dare do all that may become a man;
Who dares do more is none.

Lady Macbeth.
                    What beast was't then
That made you break this enterprise to me?
When you durst do it, then you were a man;
And to be more than what you were, you would
Be so much more the man. Nor time, nor place,
Did then adhere, and yet you would make both:
They have made themselves, and that their fitness now
Does unmake you. I have given suck, and know
How tender 'tis to love the babe that milks me;
I would, while it was smiling in my face,
Have pluck'd my nipple from his boneless gums,
And dash'd the brains out, had I so sworn as you
Have done to this.

Macbeth.
                    If we should fail?

Lady Macbeth.
                    We fail?
But screw your courage to the sticking place,
And we'll not fail. When Duncan is asleep
(Whereto the rather shall his day's hard journey
Soundly invite him), his two chamberlains
Will I with wine and wassail so convince,
That memory, the warder of the brain,
Shall be a fume, and the receipt of reason
A limbeck only. When in swinish sleep
Their drenched natures lies as in a death,
What cannot you and I perform upon
Th' unguarded Duncan? What not put upon
His spungy officers, who shall bear the guilt
Of our great quell?

Macbeth.
                    Bring forth men-children only!
For thy undaunted mettle should compose
Nothing but males. Will it not be receiv'd,
When we have mark'd with blood those sleepy two
Of his own chamber, and us'd their very daggers,
That they have done't?

Lady Macbeth.
                    Who dares receive it other,
As we shall make our griefs and clamor roar
Upon his death?

Macbeth.
                    I am settled, and bend up
Each corporal agent to this terrible feat.
Away, and mock the time with fairest show:
False face must hide what the false heart doth know.

Exeunt.

Act 2

Scene 1

The court of Macbeth's castle.

(Banquo; Fleance; Macbeth; Servant)

Banquo and his son Fleance are on their way to bed after the very late end of the night's feasting. Banquo is uneasy. Met by Macbeth, Banquo hands over to him a diamond from Duncan. Banquo reveals that he has dreamt of the three weird sisters; Macbeth insists that he is not thinking of them, but asks that he and Banquo may have some further talk on the matter. Banquo agrees, while subtly making it clear that he will have no part in any action against Duncan. Left alone, preparing to go in to murder Duncan, Macbeth hallucinates a dagger in the air before him, on which he soon sees blood running. He summons up his courage, and hearing the bell toll goes in to end Duncan's life.

Enter Banquo, and Fleance with a torch before him.

Banquo.
How goes the night, boy?

Fleance.
The moon is down; I have not heard the clock.

Banquo.
And she goes down at twelve.

Fleance.
                    I take't, 'tis later, sir.

Banquo.
Hold, take my sword. There's husbandry in heaven,
Their candles are all out. Take thee that too.

Gives him his belt and dagger.

A heavy summons lies like lead upon me,
And yet I would not sleep. Merciful powers,
Restrain in me the cursed thoughts that nature
Gives way to in repose!

Enter Macbeth, and a Servant with a torch.

       Give me my sword.
Who's there?

Macbeth.
A friend.

Banquo.
What, sir, not yet at rest? The King's a-bed.
He hath been in unusual pleasure, and
Sent forth great largess to your offices.
This diamond he greets your wife withal,
By the name of most kind hostess, and shut up
In measureless content.

Macbeth.
      Being unprepar'd,
Our will became the servant to defect,
Which else should free have wrought.

Banquo.
       All's well.
I dreamt last night of the three weird sisters:
To you they have show'd some truth.

Macbeth.
      I think not of them;
Yet when we can entreat an hour to serve,
We would spend it in some words upon that business,
If you would grant the time.

Banquo.
     At your kind'st leisure.

Macbeth.
If you shall cleave to my consent, when 'tis,
It shall make honor for you.

Banquo.
      So I lose none
In seeking to augment it, but still keep
My bosom franchis'd and allegiance clear,
I shall be counsell'd.

Macbeth.
     Good repose the while!

Banquo.
Thanks, sir; the like to you!

Exit Banquo with Fleance.

Macbeth.
Go bid thy mistress, when my drink is ready,
She strike upon the bell. Get thee to bed.

Exit Servant.

Is this a dagger which I see before me,
The handle toward my hand? Come, let me clutch thee:
I have thee not, and yet I see thee still.
Art thou not, fatal vision, sensible
To feeling as to sight? Or art thou but
A dagger of the mind, a false creation,
Proceeding from the heat-oppressed brain?
I see thee yet, in form as palpable
As this which now I draw.
Thou marshal'st me the way that I was going,
And such an instrument I was to use.
Mine eyes are made the fools o' th' other senses,
Or else worth all the rest. I see thee still;
And on thy blade and dudgeon gouts of blood,
Which was not so before. There's no such thing:
It is the bloody business which informs
Thus to mine eyes. Now o'er the one half world
Nature seems dead, and wicked dreams abuse
The curtain'd sleep; witchcraft celebrates
Pale Hecat's off'rings; and wither'd Murder,
Alarum'd by his sentinel, the wolf,
Whose howl's his watch, thus with his stealthy pace,
With Tarquin's ravishing strides, towards his design
Moves like a ghost. Thou sure and firm-set earth,
Hear not my steps, which way they walk, for fear
The very stones prate of my whereabout,
And take the present horror from the time,
Which now suits with it. Whiles I threat, he lives:
Words to the heat of deeds too cold breath gives.

A bell rings.

I go, and it is done; the bell invites me.
Hear it not, Duncan, for it is a knell,
That summons thee to heaven or to hell.

Exit.

Scene 2

The court of Macbeth's castle.

(Lady Macbeth; Macbeth)

Lady Macbeth waits for Macbeth to return; she is nervous, realizing that success gives them everything, but failure will be the end of them. Macbeth comes out of Duncan's room, his hands covered in blood, nerve-racked and terrified. Lady Macbeth tries to steel him as he talks of how he tried to say "Amen" to the prayer of one of the grooms, but could not, and how he thought he heard a voice announcing that since he had killed the sleeping King, he himself would never sleep again. His wife tries to snap him out of it, sending him to wash his hands, and discovering that he brought the murder weapons with him. Incensed, she takes the daggers back into the murder chamber after Macbeth refuses to go in there again. There is a knocking at the gate that startles Macbeth as Lady Macbeth returns, her hands now bloody as well. She insists that all they need do is wash their hands, and all will be well. They retire to their room to get undressed so that the new arrivals will not guess that they have been up all night.

Enter Lady Macbeth.

Lady Macbeth.
That which hath made them drunk hath made me bold;
What hath quench'd them hath given me fire. Hark!
Peace!
It was the owl that shriek'd, the fatal bellman,
Which gives the stern'st good-night. He is about it:
The doors are open; and the surfeited grooms
Do mock their charge with snores. I have drugg'd their possets,
That death and nature do contend about them,
Whether they live or die.

Macbeth.

Within.

      Who's there? What ho?

Lady Macbeth.
Alack, I am afraid they have awak'd,
And 'tis not done; th' attempt, and not the deed,
Confounds us. Hark! I laid their daggers ready,
He could not miss 'em. Had he not resembled
My father as he slept, I had done't.

Enter Macbeth.

      My husband!

Macbeth.
I have done the deed. Didst thou not hear a noise?

Lady Macbeth.
I heard the owl scream and the crickets cry.
Did not you speak?

Macbeth.

    When?

Lady Macbeth.

    Now.

Macbeth.

    As I descended?

Lady Macbeth.
Ay.

Macbeth.
Hark! Who lies i' th' second chamber?

Lady Macbeth.
Donalbain.

Macbeth.

    This is a sorry sight.

Looking on his hands.

Lady Macbeth.
A foolish thought, to say a sorry sight.

Macbeth.
There's one did laugh in 's sleep, and one cried, "Murder!"
That they did wake each other. I stood and heard them;
But they did say their prayers, and address'd them
Again to sleep.

Lady Macbeth.

    There are two lodg'd together.

Macbeth.
One cried, "God bless us!" and "Amen!" the other,
As they had seen me with these hangman's hands.
List'ning their fear, I could not say "Amen,"
When they did say "God bless us!"

Lady Macbeth.

    Consider it not so deeply.

Macbeth.
But wherefore could not I pronounce "Amen"?
I had most need of blessing, and "Amen"
Stuck in my throat.

Lady Macbeth.
               These deeds must not be thought
After these ways; so, it will make us mad.

Macbeth.
Methought I heard a voice cry, "Sleep no more!
Macbeth does murder sleep"—the innocent sleep,
Sleep that knits up the ravell'd sleave of care,
The death of each day's life, sore labor's bath,
Balm of hurt minds, great nature's second course,
Chief nourisher in life's feast.

Lady Macbeth.
                      What do you mean?

Macbeth.
Still it cried, "Sleep no more!" to all the house;
"Glamis hath murder'd sleep, and therefore Cawdor
Shall sleep no more—Macbeth shall sleep no more."

Lady Macbeth.
Who was it that thus cried? Why, worthy thane,
You do unbend your noble strength, to think
So brain-sickly of things. Go get some water,
And wash this filthy witness from your hand.
Why did you bring these daggers from the place?
They must lie there. Go carry them, and smear
The sleepy grooms with blood.

Macbeth.
                      I'll go no more.
I am afraid to think what I have done;
Look on't again I dare not.

Lady Macbeth.
                    Infirm of purpose!
Give me the daggers. The sleeping and the dead
Are but as pictures; 'tis the eye of childhood
That fears a painted devil. If he do bleed,
I'll gild the faces of the grooms withal,
For it must seem their guilt.

Exit.
Knock within.

Macbeth.
               Whence is that knocking?
How is't with me, when every noise appalls me?
What hands are here? Hah! They pluck out mine eyes.
Will all great Neptune's ocean wash this blood
Clean from my hand? No; this my hand will rather
The multitudinous seas incarnadine,
Making the green one red.

Enter Lady Macbeth.

Lady Macbeth.
My hands are of your color; but I shame
To wear a heart so white.

Knock.

                      I hear a knocking
At the south entry. Retire we to our chamber.
A little water clears us of this deed;
How easy is it then! Your constancy
Hath left you unattended.

Knock.

                  Hark, more knocking.
Get on your night-gown, lest occasion call us
And show us to be watchers. Be not lost
So poorly in your thoughts.

Macbeth.
To know my deed, 'twere best not know myself.

Knock.

Wake Duncan with thy knocking! I would thou couldst!

Exeunt.

Scene 3

The court of Macbeth's castle.

(*Porter; Macduff; Lennox; Macbeth; Lady Macbeth; Banquo; Rosse; Malcolm; Donalbain*)

Still drunk after last night's reveling, the castle's porter comes to open the gate to the new arrivals still pounding at the gate, imagining himself the porter of hell as he does so. The noblemen Macduff and Lennox come in, having orders to meet the King early. Macbeth joins them, and as Macduff goes to wake the King, Lennox talks to Macbeth about the wild storm the previous night, and odd portents that occurred. Having

Act 2, Scene 3

discovered the murder, Macduff reenters in shock, and wildly begins to rouse the house. Lady Macbeth comes in, pretending to wonder what all the commotion is about, and expresses horror at the King being murdered in her house. Slowly the other members of the court arrive. Macbeth, who had gone in with Lennox to witness the deed, returns. He has killed the grooms and begs pardon for having done so, saying that he lost his temper at their evident guilt and executed summary justice on them. Lady Macbeth faints, or pretends to faint, before he can be pressed too far on this point. The nobles agree to get properly dressed and discuss the matter in full. Left alone, Duncan's sons Malcolm and Donalbain agree that they will not trust any of the nobles, and decide to flee the country, one to England and the other to Ireland, to escape the risk that they both be murdered as well.

Enter a Porter. Knocking within.

Porter.
Here's a knocking indeed! If a man were porter of Hell Gate, he should have old turning the key.

Knock.

Knock, knock, knock! Who's there, i' th' name of Beelzebub? Here's a farmer, that hang'd himself on th' expectation of plenty. Come in time! Have napkins enow about you, here you'll sweat for't.

Knock.

Knock, knock! Who's there, in th' other devil's name? Faith, here's an equivocator, that could swear in both the scales against either scale, who committed treason enough for God's sake, yet could not equivocate to heaven. O, come in, equivocator.

Knock.

Knock, knock, knock! Who's there? Faith, here's an English tailor come hither for stealing out of a French hose. Come in, tailor, here you may roast your goose.

Knock.

Knock, knock! Never at quiet! What are you? But this place is too cold for hell. I'll devil—porter it no further. I had thought to have let in some of all professions that go the primrose way to th' everlasting bonfire.

Knock.

Anon, anon!

Opens the gate.

I pray you remember the porter.

Enter Macduff and Lennox.

Macduff.
Was it so late, friend, ere you went to bed,
That you do lie so late?

Porter.
Faith, sir, we were carousing till the second cock; and drink, sir, is a great provoker of three things.

Macduff.
What three things does drink especially provoke?

Porter.
Marry, sir, nose-painting, sleep, and urine. Lechery, sir, it provokes, and unprovokes: it provokes the desire, but it takes away the performance. Therefore much drink may be said to be an equivocator with lechery: it makes him, and it mars him; it sets him on, and it takes him off; it persuades him, and disheartens him; makes him stand to, and not stand to; in conclusion, equivocates him in a sleep, and giving him the lie, leaves him.

Macduff.
I believe drink gave thee the lie last night.

Porter.
That it did, sir, i' the very throat on me; but I requited him for his lie, and (I think) being too strong for him, though he took up my legs sometime, yet I made a shift to cast him.

Macduff.
Is thy master stirring?

Enter Macbeth.

Our knocking has awak'd him; here he comes.

Lennox.
Good morrow, noble sir.

Macbeth.
                Good morrow, both.

Macduff.
Is the King stirring, worthy thane?

Macbeth.
                Not yet.

Macduff.
He did command me to call timely on him,
I have almost slipp'd the hour.

Macbeth.
                     I'll bring you to him.

Macduff.
I know this is a joyful trouble to you;
But yet 'tis one.

Macbeth.
The labor we delight in physics pain.
This is the door.

Macduff.
                   I'll make so bold to call,
For 'tis my limited service.

Exit Macduff.

Lennox.
Goes the King hence today?

Macbeth.
                 He does; he did appoint so.

Lennox.
The night has been unruly. Where we lay,
Our chimneys were blown down, and (as they say)
Lamentings heard i' th' air; strange screams of death,
And prophesying, with accents terrible,
Of dire combustion and confus'd events
New hatch'd to th' woeful time. The obscure bird
Clamor'd the livelong night. Some say, the earth
Was feverous, and did shake.

Macbeth.
                 'Twas a rough night.

Lennox.
My young remembrance cannot parallel
A fellow to it.

Enter Macduff.

Macduff.
O horror, horror, horror! Tongue nor heart
Cannot conceive nor name thee!

Macbeth and Lennox.
                 What's the matter?

Macduff.
Confusion now hath made his masterpiece!
Most sacrilegious murder hath broke ope
The Lord's anointed temple, and stole thence
The life o' th' building!

Macbeth.
                 What is't you say—the life?

Lennox.
Mean you his Majesty?

Macduff.
Approach the chamber, and destroy your sight
With a new Gorgon. Do not bid me speak;
See, and then speak yourselves.

Exeunt Macbeth and Lennox.
                 Awake, awake!
Ring the alarum-bell! Murder and treason!
Banquo and Donalbain! Malcolm, awake!
Shake off this downy sleep, death's counterfeit,
And look on death itself! Up, up, and see
The great doom's image! Malcolm! Banquo!
As from your graves rise up, and walk like sprites,
To countenance this horror! Ring the bell.

Bell rings.
Enter Lady Macbeth.

Lady Macbeth.
What's the business,
That such a hideous trumpet calls to parley
The sleepers of the house? Speak, speak!

Macduff.
                 O gentle lady,
'Tis not for you to hear what I can speak:
The repetition in a woman's ear
Would murder as it fell.

Enter Banquo.
                 O Banquo, Banquo,
Our royal master's murder'd!

Lady Macbeth.
                 Woe, alas!
What, in our house?

Banquo.
                              Too cruel any where.
Dear Duff, I prithee contradict thyself,
And say, it is not so.

Enter Macbeth, Lennox, Rosse.

Macbeth.
Had I but died an hour before this chance,
I had liv'd a blessed time; for from this instant
There's nothing serious in mortality:
All is but toys: renown and grace is dead,
The wine of life is drawn, and the mere lees
Is left this vault to brag of.

Enter Malcolm and Donalbain.

Donalbain.
What is amiss?

Macbeth.
                    You are, and do not know't.
The spring, the head, the fountain of your blood
Is stopp'd, the very source of it is stopp'd.

Macduff.
Your royal father's murder'd.

Malcolm.
                              O, by whom?

Lennox.
Those of his chamber, as it seem'd, had done't.
Their hands and faces were all badg'd with blood;
So were their daggers, which unwip'd we found
Upon their pillows. They star'd and were distracted;
No man's life was to be trusted with them.

Macbeth.
O, yet I do repent me of my fury,
That I did kill them.

Macduff.
                    Wherefore did you so?

Macbeth.
Who can be wise, amaz'd, temp'rate, and furious,
Loyal, and neutral, in a moment? No man.
Th' expedition of my violent love
Outrun the pauser, reason. Here lay Duncan,
His silver skin lac'd with his golden blood,
And his gash'd stabs look'd like a breach in nature
For ruin's wasteful entrance; there, the murderers,
Steep'd in the colors of their trade, their daggers
Unmannerly breech'd with gore. Who could refrain,
That had a heart to love, and in that heart
Courage to make 's love known?

Lady Macbeth.
                              Help me hence, ho!

Macduff.
Look to the lady.

Malcolm.

Aside to Donalbain

                    Why do we hold our tongues,
That most may claim this argument for ours?

Donalbain.

Aside to Malcolm

What should be spoken here, where our fate,
Hid in an auger-hole, may rush and seize us?
Let's away,
Our tears are not yet brew'd.

Malcolm.

Aside to Donalbain

                              Nor our strong sorrow
Upon the foot of motion.

Banquo.
                              Look to the lady.

Lady Macbeth is carried out.

And when we have our naked frailties hid,
That suffer in exposure, let us meet
And question this most bloody piece of work,
To know it further. Fears and scruples shake us.
In the great hand of God I stand, and thence
Against the undivulg'd pretense I fight
Of treasonous malice.

Macduff.
                              And so do I.

All.
                              So all.

Macbeth.
Let's briefly put on manly readiness,
And meet i' th' hall together.

All.
                    Well contented.

Exeunt all but Malcolm and Donalbain.

Malcolm.
What will you do? Let's not consort with them;
To show an unfelt sorrow is an office
Which the false man does easy. I'll to England.

Donalbain.
To Ireland, I; our separated fortune
Shall keep us both the safer. Where we are,
There's daggers in men's smiles; the near in blood,
The nearer bloody.

Malcolm.
                    This murderous shaft that's shot
Hath not yet lighted, and our safest way
Is to avoid the aim. Therefore to horse,
And let us not be dainty of leave-taking,
But shift away. There's warrant in that theft
Which steals itself, when there's no mercy left.

Exeunt.

Scene 4

Outside Macbeth's castle.

(Rosse; Old Man; Macduff)

Ross and an Old Man discuss the terrible portents that have occurred, including the fact that Duncan's horses have eaten one another, that the day is dark, and that a tiny owl killed a huge hunting hawk. Macduff greets Ross and tells him that Malcolm and Donalbain have fled and are therefore suspected of the murder. Ross realizes that Macbeth is the most likely heir, and decides to go to his coronation, though Macduff chooses to simply go home.

Enter Rosse with an Old Man.

Old Man.
Threescore and ten I can remember well,
Within the volume of which time I have seen
Hours dreadful and things strange; but this sore night
Hath trifled former knowings.

Rosse.
                    Ha, good father,
Thou seest the heavens, as troubled with man's act,
Threatens his bloody stage. By th' clock 'tis day,
And yet dark night strangles the traveling lamp.
Is't night's predominance, or the day's shame,
That darkness does the face of earth entomb,
When living light should kiss it?

Old Man.
                    'Tis unnatural,
Even like the deed that's done. On Tuesday last,
A falcon, tow'ring in her pride of place,
Was by a mousing owl hawk'd at, and kill'd.

Rosse.
And Duncan's horses (a thing most strange and certain),
Beauteous and swift, the minions of their race,
Turn'd wild in nature, broke their stalls, flung out,
Contending 'gainst obedience, as they would make
War with mankind.

Old Man.
                    'Tis said, they eat each other.

Rosse.
They did so—to th' amazement of mine eyes
That look'd upon't.

Enter Macduff.
                    Here comes the good Macduff.
How goes the world, sir, now?

Macduff.
                    Why, see you not?

Rosse.
Is't known who did this more than bloody deed?

Macduff.
Those that Macbeth hath slain.

Rosse.
                    Alas the day,
What good could they pretend?

Macduff.
                    They were suborned.
Malcolm and Donalbain, the King's two sons,
Are stol'n away and fled, which puts upon them
Suspicion of the deed.

Rosse.
                    'Gainst nature still!
Thriftless ambition, that will ravin up
Thine own live's means! Then 'tis most like
The sovereignty will fall upon Macbeth.

Macduff.
He is already nam'd, and gone to Scone
To be invested.

Rosse.
                    Where is Duncan's body?

Macduff.
Carried to Colmekill,
The sacred store-house of his predecessors
And guardian of their bones.

Rosse.
                    Will you to Scone?

Macduff.
No, cousin, I'll to Fife.

Rosse.
                    Well, I will thither.

Macduff.
Well, may you see things well done there: adieu,
Lest our old robes sit easier than our new!

Rosse.
Farewell, father.

Old Man.
God's benison go with you, and with those
That would make good of bad, and friends of foes!

Exeunt omnes.

Act 3

Scene 1

Forres. The palace.

(Banquo; Macbeth; Lady Macbeth; Lennox; Rosse; Lords; Attendants; Servant; Two Murderers)

Banquo sees that the witches' prophecy is fulfilled and suspects that Macbeth helped it along a little. But he cannot forget the part about his own sons becoming kings rather than Macbeth's. Macbeth enters with his train and invites Banquo to a feast that evening; Banquo says he will spend the time till then going for a ride with Fleance. Macbeth dismisses everyone, and calls for some men he spoke to the day before. As he waits for them, he ruminates on the same subject as Banquo, the insufferable idea that Banquo's sons, not his, will succeed to the throne, and that therefore Macbeth has damned himself for Banquo's good. The two men he has called for enter; they are sworn enemies of Banquo, and Macbeth brings them to agree to murder the man, explaining that he cannot do it openly himself. He lets them know where they can find them, insisting that they must kill Fleance as well.

Enter Banquo.

Banquo.
Thou hast it now: King, Cawdor, Glamis, all,
As the weird women promis'd, and I fear
Thou play'dst most foully for't; yet it was said
It should not stand in thy posterity,
But that myself should be the root and father
Of many kings. If there come truth from them—
As upon thee, Macbeth, their speeches shine—
Why, by the verities on thee made good,
May they not be my oracles as well,
And set me up in hope? But hush, no more.

Sennet sounded. Enter Macbeth as King, Lady Macbeth as Queen, Lennox, Rosse, Lords, and Attendants.

Macbeth.
Here's our chief guest.

Lady Macbeth.
                    If he had been forgotten,
It had been as a gap in our great feast,
And all-thing unbecoming.

Macbeth.
Tonight we hold a solemn supper, sir,
And I'll request your presence.

Banquo.
                    Let your Highness
Command upon me, to the which my duties
Are with a most indissoluble tie
Forever knit.

Macbeth.
Ride you this afternoon?

Banquo.
                    Ay, my good lord.

Macbeth.
We should have else desir'd your good advice
(Which still hath been both grave and prosperous)
In this day's council; but we'll take tomorrow.
Is't far you ride?

Banquo.
As far, my lord, as will fill up the time
'Twixt this and supper. Go not my horse the better,
I must become a borrower of the night
For a dark hour or twain.

Macbeth.
      Fail not our feast.

Banquo.
My lord, I will not.

Macbeth.
We hear our bloody cousins are bestow'd
In England and in Ireland, not confessing
Their cruel parricide, filling their hearers
With strange invention. But of that tomorrow,
When therewithal we shall have cause of state
Craving us jointly. Hie you to horse; adieu,
Till you return at night. Goes Fleance with you?

Banquo.
Ay, my good lord. Our time does call upon's.

Macbeth.
I wish your horses swift and sure of foot;
And so I do commend you to their backs.
Farewell.

Exit Banquo.

Let every man be master of his time
Till seven at night. To make society
The sweeter welcome, we will keep ourself
Till supper-time alone; while then, God be with you!

Exeunt Lords with Lady Macbeth and others. Manent Macbeth and a Servant.

Sirrah, a word with you. Attend those men
Our pleasure?

Servant.
They are, my lord, without the palace gate.

Macbeth.
Bring them before us.

Exit Servant.
     To be thus is nothing,
But to be safely thus. Our fears in Banquo
Stick deep, and in his royalty of nature
Reigns that which would be fear'd. 'Tis much he dares,
And to that dauntless temper of his mind,
He hath a wisdom that doth guide his valor
To act in safety. There is none but he
Whose being I do fear; and under him
My Genius is rebuk'd, as it is said
Mark Antony's was by Caesar. He chid the sisters
When first they put the name of king upon me,
And bade them speak to him; then prophet-like
They hail'd him father to a line of kings.
Upon my head they plac'd a fruitless crown,
And put a barren sceptre in my gripe,
Thence to be wrench'd with an unlineal hand,
No son of mine succeeding. If't be so,
For Banquo's issue have I fil'd my mind,
For them the gracious Duncan have I murder'd,
Put rancors in the vessel of my peace
Only for them, and mine eternal jewel
Given to the common enemy of man,
To make them kings—the seeds of Banquo kings!
Rather than so, come fate into the list,
And champion me to th' utterance! Who's there?

Enter Servant and two Murderers.

Now go to the door, and stay there till we call.

Exit Servant.

Was it not yesterday we spoke together?

Both First and Second Murderers.
It was, so please your Highness.

Macbeth.
      Well then, now
Have you consider'd of my speeches?—know
That it was he in the times past which held you
So under fortune, which you thought had been
Our innocent self? This I made good to you
In our last conference, pass'd in probation with you:
How you were borne in hand, how cross'd, the instruments,
Who wrought with them, and all things else that might
To half a soul and to a notion craz'd
Say, "Thus did Banquo."

First Murderer.
     You made it known to us.

Macbeth.
I did so; and went further, which is now
Our point of second meeting. Do you find
Your patience so predominant in your nature

That you can let this go? Are you so gospell'd,
To pray for this good man, and for his issue,
Whose heavy hand hath bow'd you to the grave,
And beggar'd yours forever?

First Murderer.
                       We are men, my liege.

Macbeth.
Ay, in the catalogue ye go for men,
As hounds and greyhounds, mongrels, spaniels, curs,
Shoughs, water-rugs, and demi-wolves are clipt
All by the name of dogs; the valued file
Distinguishes the swift, the slow, the subtle,
The house-keeper, the hunter, every one,
According to the gift which bounteous nature
Hath in him clos'd; whereby he does receive
Particular addition, from the bill
That writes them all alike: and so of men.
Now, if you have a station in the file,
Not i' th' worst rank of manhood, say't,
And I will put that business in your bosoms,
Whose execution takes your enemy off,
Grapples you to the heart and love of us,
Who wear our health but sickly in his life,
Which in his death were perfect.

Second Murderer.
                       I am one, my liege,
Whom the vile blows and buffets of the world
Hath so incens'd that I am reckless what
I do to spite the world.

First Murderer.
                       And I another,
So weary with disasters, tugg'd with fortune,
That I would set my life on any chance,
To mend it, or be rid on't.

Macbeth.
                       Both of you
Know Banquo was your enemy.

Both First and Second Murderers.
                       True, my lord.

Macbeth.
So is he mine; and in such bloody distance,
That every minute of his being thrusts
Against my near'st of life; and though I could
With barefac'd power sweep him from my sight,
And bid my will avouch it, yet I must not,
For certain friends that are both his and mine,
Whose loves I may not drop, but wail his fall
Who I myself struck down. And thence it is
That I to your assistance do make love,
Masking the business from the common eye
For sundry weighty reasons.

Second Murderer.
                       We shall, my lord,
Perform what you command us.

First Murderer.
                       Though our lives—

Macbeth.
Your spirits shine through you. Within this hour, at most,
I will advise you where to plant yourselves,
Acquaint you with the perfect spy o' th' time,
The moment on't, for't must be done tonight,
And something from the palace; always thought
That I require a clearness: and with him—
To leave no rubs nor botches in the work—
Fleance his son, that keeps him company,
Whose absence is no less material to me
Than is his father's, must embrace the fate
Of that dark hour. Resolve yourselves apart,
I'll come to you anon.

Both First and Second Murderers.
                       We are resolv'd, my lord.

Macbeth.
I'll call upon you straight; abide within.

Exeunt Murderers.

It is concluded: Banquo, thy soul's flight,
If it find heaven, must find it out tonight.

Exit.

Scene 2

Forres. The palace.

(*Lady Macbeth; Waiting Gentlewoman; Macbeth*)

Lady Macbeth is concerned about her husband, who is dark-minded and cheerless. He tells her that she does not know what he is thinking, and refuses to let her in on it. Both of them have been suffering from bad dreams night after night. She realizes he has planned something for Banquo and Fleance, but does not tell her what.

Enter Macbeth's Lady and her Waiting Gentlewoman.

Lady Macbeth.
Is Banquo gone from court?

Gentlewoman.
Ay, madam, but returns again tonight.

Lady Macbeth.
Say to the King, I would attend his leisure
For a few words.

Gentlewoman.
      Madam, I will.

Exit.

Lady Macbeth.
     Nought's had, all's spent,
Where our desire is got without content;
'Tis safer to be that which we destroy
Than by destruction dwell in doubtful joy.

Enter Macbeth.

How now, my lord, why do you keep alone,
Of sorriest fancies your companions making,
Using those thoughts which should indeed have died
With them they think on? Things without all remedy
Should be without regard: what's done, is done.

Macbeth.
We have scorch'd the snake, not kill'd it;
She'll close and be herself, whilest our poor malice
Remains in danger of her former tooth.
But let the frame of things disjoint, both the worlds suffer,
Ere we will eat our meal in fear, and sleep
In the affliction of these terrible dreams
That shake us nightly. Better be with the dead,
Whom we, to gain our peace, have sent to peace,
Than on the torture of the mind to lie
In restless ecstasy. Duncan is in his grave;
After life's fitful fever he sleeps well.
Treason has done his worst; nor steel, nor poison,
Malice domestic, foreign levy, nothing,
Can touch him further.

Lady Macbeth.
      Come on;
Gentle my lord, sleek o'er your rugged looks,
Be bright and jovial among your guests tonight.

Macbeth.
So shall I, love, and so, I pray, be you.
Let your remembrance apply to Banquo,
Present him eminence both with eye and tongue:
Unsafe the while, that we
Must lave our honors in these flattering streams,
And make our faces vizards to our hearts,
Disguising what they are.

Lady Macbeth.
     You must leave this.

Macbeth.
O, full of scorpions is my mind, dear wife!
Thou know'st that Banquo and his Fleance lives.

Lady Macbeth.
But in them nature's copy's not eterne.

Macbeth.
There's comfort yet, they are assailable.
Then be thou jocund; ere the bat hath flown
His cloister'd flight, ere to black Hecat's summons
The shard-borne beetle with his drowsy hums
Hath rung night's yawning peal, there shall be done
A deed of dreadful note.

Lady Macbeth.
     What's to be done?

Macbeth.
Be innocent of the knowledge, dearest chuck,
Till thou applaud the deed. Come, seeling night,
Scarf up the tender eye of pitiful day,
And with thy bloody and invisible hand
Cancel and tear to pieces that great bond
Which keeps me pale! Light thickens, and the crow
Makes wing to th' rooky wood;
Good things of day begin to droop and drowse,
Whiles night's black agents to their preys do rouse.
Thou marvel'st at my words, but hold thee still:
Things bad begun make strong themselves by ill.
So prithee go with me.

Exeunt.

Scene 3

Forres. A park near the palace.

(*First Murderer; Second Murderer; Third Murderer; Banquo; Fleance*)

A Third Murderer joins the first two, who are rather put out by what they see as a lack of trust on Macbeth's part. Banquo and Fleance arrive, and the Murderers set upon them, but Fleance, urged on by his father, escapes.

Enter three Murderers.

First Murderer.
But who did bid thee join with us?

Third Murderer.
                         Macbeth.

Second Murderer.
He needs not our mistrust, since he delivers
Our offices, and what we have to do,
To the direction just.

First Murderer.
                    Then stand with us.
The west yet glimmers with some streaks of day;
Now spurs the lated traveler apace
To gain the timely inn, and near approaches
The subject of our watch.

Third Murderer.
                    Hark, I hear horses.

Banquo.

Within.

Give us a light there, ho!

Second Murderer.
                    Then 'tis he; the rest
That are within the note of expectation
Already are i' th' court.

First Murderer.
                    His horses go about.

Third Murderer.
Almost a mile; but he does usually,
So all men do, from hence to th' palace gate
Make it their walk.

Enter Banquo, and Fleance with a torch.

Second Murderer.
                    A light, a light!

Third Murderer.
                         'Tis he.

First Murderer.
Stand to't.

Banquo.
It will be rain tonight.

First Murderer.
                    Let it come down.

They assault Banquo.

Banquo.
O, treachery! Fly, good Fleance, fly, fly, fly!
Thou mayst revenge. O slave!

Dies.
Fleance escapes.

Third Murderer.
Who did strike out the light?

First Murderer.
                    Was't not the way?

Third Murderer.
There's but one down; the son is fled.

Second Murderer.
                         We have lost
Best half of our affair.

First Murderer.
Well, let's away, and say how much is done.

Exeunt.

Scene 4

A room of state in the palace.

(Macbeth; Lady Macbeth; Rosse; Lennox; Lord; Lords; Attendants; First Murderer; Ghost of Banquo)

Macbeth cordially greets his guests to the banquet. One of the Murderers arrives to let Macbeth know that the deed is done; Macbeth is full of praise until he hears that Fleance escaped. Lady Macbeth calls him back to the table to toast the guests; he does so, but as he attempts to take his place, he finds the seat reserved for him occupied by Banquo's bleeding ghost, visible to him alone. As he raves at the apparently empty seat, Lady Macbeth attempts to reassure the noblemen, telling them that Macbeth occasionally suffers from fits and has done since his childhood. She drags her husband aside and urges him to stiffen his spine, insisting that it is only his overactive imagination at work. The ghost vanishes and Macbeth regains control of himself, but then it appears again and he becomes even wilder. Seeing that he will not calm down and that his speech risks giving away their guilt, Lady Macbeth dismisses the lords in a hurry. Macbeth fears that Nature itself will give away their guilt. He asks why Macduff refused to come to the feast, revealing that he keeps a spy in all of the great households of the land, and decides that he will visit the weird sisters, in the hope of finding out the worst that is to come. He feels that he has gone so far in dark practices that he might as well continue now.

Banquet prepar'd.
Enter Macbeth, Lady Macbeth, Rosse, Lennox, Lords, and Attendants.

Macbeth.
You know your own degrees, sit down. At first
And last, the hearty welcome.

Lord.
                    Thanks to your Majesty.

Macbeth.
Ourself will mingle with society,
And play the humble host.
Our hostess keeps her state, but in best time
We will require her welcome.

Lady Macbeth.
Pronounce it for me, sir, to all our friends,
For my heart speaks they are welcome.

Enter First Murderer to the door.

Macbeth.
See, they encounter thee with their hearts' thanks.
Both sides are even; here I'll sit i' th' midst.
Be large in mirth; anon we'll drink a measure
The table round.—

Goes to the door.

There's blood upon thy face.

First Murderer.
                    'Tis Banquo's then.

Macbeth.
'Tis better thee without than he within.
Is he dispatch'd?

First Murderer.
                My lord, his throat is cut;
That I did for him.

Macbeth.
              Thou art the best o' th' cut-throats,
Yet he's good that did the like for Fleance.
If thou didst it, thou art the nonpareil.

First Murderer.
Most royal sir, Fleance is scap'd.

Macbeth.
Then comes my fit again. I had else been perfect,
Whole as the marble, founded as the rock,
As broad and general as the casing air;
But now I am cabin'd, cribb'd, confin'd, bound in
To saucy doubts and fears. But Banquo's safe?

First Murderer.
Ay, my good lord; safe in a ditch he bides,
With twenty trenched gashes on his head,
The least a death to nature.

Macbeth.
                  Thanks for that:
There the grown serpent lies; the worm that's fled
Hath nature that in time will venom breed,
No teeth for th' present. Get thee gone; tomorrow
We'll hear ourselves again.

Exit Murderer.

Lady Macbeth.
                My royal lord,
You do not give the cheer. The feast is sold
That is not often vouch'd, while 'tis a-making,
'Tis given with welcome. To feed were best at home;
From thence, the sauce to meat is ceremony,
Meeting were bare without it.

Enter the Ghost of Banquo and sits in Macbeth's place.

Macbeth.
                  Sweet remembrancer!
Now good digestion wait on appetite,
And health on both!

Lennox.
                May't please your Highness sit.

Macbeth.
Here had we now our country's honor roof'd,
Were the grac'd person of our Banquo present,
Who may I rather challenge for unkindness
Than pity for mischance.

Rosse.
                    His absence, sir,
Lays blame upon his promise. Please't your Highness
To grace us with your royal company?

Macbeth.
The table's full.

Lennox.
               Here is a place reserv'd, sir.

Macbeth.
Where?

Lennox.
Here, my good lord. What is't that moves your Highness?

Macbeth.
Which of you have done this?

Lord.
                    What, my good lord?

Macbeth.
Thou canst not say I did it; never shake
Thy gory locks at me.

Rosse.
Gentlemen, rise, his Highness is not well.

Lady Macbeth.
Sit, worthy friends; my lord is often thus,
And hath been from his youth. Pray you keep seat.
The fit is momentary, upon a thought
He will again be well. If much you note him,
You shall offend him and extend his passion.
Feed, and regard him not.—Are you a man?

Macbeth.
Ay, and a bold one, that dare look on that
Which might appall the devil.

Lady Macbeth.
                    O proper stuff!
This is the very painting of your fear;
This is the air-drawn dagger which you said
Led you to Duncan. O, these flaws and starts
(Impostors to true fear) would well become
A woman's story at a winter's fire,
Authoriz'd by her grandam. Shame itself,
Why do you make such faces? When all's done,
You look but on a stool.

Macbeth.
                Prithee see there!
Behold! Look! Lo! How say you?
Why, what care I? If thou canst nod, speak too.
If charnel-houses and our graves must send
Those that we bury back, our monuments
Shall be the maws of kites.

Exit Ghost.

Lady Macbeth.
              What? Quite unmann'd in folly?

Macbeth.
If I stand here, I saw him.

Lady Macbeth.
                Fie, for shame!

Macbeth.
Blood hath been shed ere now, i' th' olden time,
Ere humane statute purg'd the gentle weal;
Ay, and since too, murders have been perform'd
Too terrible for the ear. The time has been,
That when the brains were out, the man would die,
And there an end; but now they rise again
With twenty mortal murders on their crowns,
And push us from our stools. This is more strange
Than such a murder is.

Lady Macbeth.
                My worthy lord,
Your noble friends do lack you.

Macbeth.
                I do forget.
Do not muse at me, my most worthy friends,
I have a strange infirmity, which is nothing
To those that know me. Come, love and health to all,
Then I'll sit down. Give me some wine, fill full.

Enter Ghost.

I drink to th' general joy o' th' whole table,
And to our dear friend Banquo, whom we miss;
Would he were here! To all, and him, we thirst,
And all to all.

Lord.
                    Our duties, and the pledge.

Macbeth.
Avaunt, and quit my sight! Let the earth hide thee!
Thy bones are marrowless, thy blood is cold;
Thou hast no speculation in those eyes
Which thou dost glare with!

Lady Macbeth.
                    Think of this, good peers,
But as a thing of custom. 'Tis no other;
Only it spoils the pleasure of the time.

Macbeth.
What man dare, I dare.
Approach thou like the rugged Russian bear,
The arm'd rhinoceros, or th' Hyrcan tiger,
Take any shape but that, and my firm nerves
Shall never tremble. Or be alive again,
And dare me to the desert with thy sword;
If trembling I inhabit then, protest me
The baby of a girl. Hence, horrible shadow!
Unreal mock'ry, hence!

Exit Ghost.
                    Why, so; being gone,
I am a man again. Pray you sit still.

Lady Macbeth.
You have displac'd the mirth, broke the good meeting,
With most admir'd disorder.

Macbeth.
                    Can such things be,
And overcome us like a summer's cloud,
Without our special wonder? You make me strange
Even to the disposition that I owe,
When now I think you can behold such sights,
And keep the natural ruby of your cheeks,
When mine is blanch'd with fear.

Rosse.
                    What sights, my lord?

Lady Macbeth.
I pray you speak not. He grows worse and worse,
Question enrages him. At once, good night.
Stand not upon the order of your going,
But go at once.

Lennox.
                    Good night, and better health
Attend his Majesty!

Lady Macbeth.
                    A kind good night to all!

Exeunt Lords and Attendants.

Macbeth.
It will have blood, they say; blood will have blood.
Stones have been known to move and trees to speak;
Augures and understood relations have
By maggot-pies and choughs and rooks brought forth
The secret'st man of blood. What is the night?

Lady Macbeth.
Almost at odds with morning, which is which.

Macbeth.
How say'st thou, that Macduff denies his person
At our great bidding?

Lady Macbeth.
                    Did you send to him, sir?

Macbeth.
I hear it by the way; but I will send.
There's not a one of them but in his house
I keep a servant fee'd. I will tomorrow
(And betimes I will) to the weird sisters.
More shall they speak; for now I am bent to know,
By the worst means, the worst. For mine own good
All causes shall give way. I am in blood
Stepp'd in so far that, should I wade no more,
Returning were as tedious as go o'er.
Strange things I have in head, that will to hand,
Which must be acted ere they may be scann'd.

Lady Macbeth.
You lack the season of all natures, sleep.

Macbeth.
Come, we'll to sleep. My strange and self-abuse
Is the initiate fear that wants hard use:
We are yet but young in deed.

Exeunt.

Scene 5

A heath.

(First Witch; Second Witch; Third Witch; Hecat)

Hecat, the Queen of the witches, chides the three weird sisters for daring to traffic with Macbeth without involving her. She insists in joining in.

Thunder. Enter the three Witches, meeting Hecat.

First Witch.
Why, how now, Hecat? You look angerly.

Hecat.
Have I not reason, beldams as you are?
Saucy and overbold, how did you dare
To trade and traffic with Macbeth
In riddles and affairs of death;
And I, the mistress of your charms,
The close contriver of all harms,
Was never call'd to bear my part,
Or show the glory of our art?
And which is worse, all you have done
Hath been but for a wayward son,
Spiteful and wrathful, who (as others do)
Loves for his own ends, not for you.
But make amends now. Get you gone,
And at the pit of Acheron
Meet me i' th' morning; thither he
Will come to know his destiny.
Your vessels and your spells provide,
Your charms and every thing beside.
I am for th' air; this night I'll spend
Unto a dismal and a fatal end.
Great business must be wrought ere noon:
Upon the corner of the moon
There hangs a vap'rous drop profound,
I'll catch it ere it come to ground;
And that, distill'd by magic sleights,
Shall raise such artificial sprites
As by the strength of their illusion
Shall draw him on to his confusion.
He shall spurn fate, scorn death, and bear
His hopes 'bove wisdom, grace, and fear;
And you all know, security
Is mortals' chiefest enemy.

Music, and a song. Sing within:

"Come away, come away, etc."
Hark, I am call'd; my little spirit, see,
Sits in a foggy cloud, and stays for me.

Exit.

First Witch.
Come, let's make haste, she'll soon be back again.

Exeunt.

Scene 6

Forres. The palace.

(Lennox; Lord)

Lennox and another Lord sardonically list off Macbeth's deed, leaving little doubt of their mutual conviction of his guilt. The Lord reveals that Macduff has fled to Malcolm's side in England, where Duncan's son is hoping for the help of the English King to raise an army and overthrow Macbeth.

Enter Lennox and another Lord.

Lennox.
My former speeches have but hit your thoughts,
Which can interpret farther; only I say
Things have been strangely borne. The gracious Duncan
Was pitied of Macbeth; marry, he was dead.
And the right valiant Banquo walk'd too late,
Whom you may say (if't please you) Fleance kill'd,
For Fleance fled. Men must not walk too late.
Who cannot want the thought, how monstrous
It was for Malcolm and for Donalbain
To kill their gracious father? Damned fact!
How it did grieve Macbeth! Did he not straight
In pious rage the two delinquents tear,
That were the slaves of drink and thralls of sleep?
Was not that nobly done? Ay, and wisely too;
For 'twould have anger'd any heart alive
To hear the men deny't. So that, I say,
He has borne all things well, and I do think
That had he Duncan's sons under his key
(As, and't please heaven, he shall not), they should find
What 'twere to kill a father; so should Fleance.
But peace! For from broad words, and 'cause he fail'd
His presence at the tyrant's feast, I hear
Macduff lives in disgrace. Sir, can you tell
Where he bestows himself?

Lord.
            The son of Duncan
(From whom this tyrant holds the due of birth)
Lives in the English court, and is receiv'd

Of the most pious Edward with such grace
That the malevolence of fortune nothing
Takes from his high respect. Thither Macduff
Is gone to pray the holy king, upon his aid
To wake Northumberland and warlike Siward,
That by the help of these (with Him above
To ratify the work) we may again
Give to our tables meat, sleep to our nights;
Free from our feasts and banquets bloody knives;
Do faithful homage and receive free honors;
All which we pine for now. And this report
Hath so exasperate the King that he
Prepares for some attempt of war.

Lennox.
                Sent he to Macduff?

Lord.
He did; and with an absolute "Sir, not I,"
The cloudy messenger turns me his back,
And hums, as who should say, "You'll rue the time
That clogs me with this answer."

Lennox.
                And that well might
Advise him to a caution, t' hold what distance
His wisdom can provide. Some holy angel
Fly to the court of England, and unfold
His message ere he come, that a swift blessing
May soon return to this our suffering country
Under a hand accurs'd!

Lord.
                I'll send my prayers with him.

Exeunt.

Act 4

Scene 1

A cavern.

(*First Witch; Second Witch; Third Witch; Fourth Witch; Fifth Witch; Sixth Witch; Hecat; Macbeth; First Apparition; Second Apparition; Third Apparition; Kings; Ghost of Banquo; Lennox*)

In a cavern, the Three Witches prepare a foul broth. Macbeth enters and demands from them that they answer the questions he will ask them, the consequences be damned. Given the choice between the Witches and their spirit masters, he chooses the latter. A head in armor tells him to beware of Macduff. A blood child tells him that he will never be killed by anyone born of woman. Lastly, a child with a crown on its head, holding a tree, tells him that he will never be beaten until the forest of Birnam comes to Dunsinane castle. Reassured, Macbeth still wants to know whether Banquo's descendants will take the throne, and despite warnings not to ask too much he insists on finding out. Eight kings appear, one after the other, the last showing him a mirror in which even more can be seen; Banquo's ghost follows, proudly pointing to them as his own. The apparitions and the witches vanish. Macbeth calls for Lennox, who is waiting for him, but the man has seen nothing. Hearing that Macduff has fled, Macbeth resolves to slaughter the man's family.

Thunder. Enter the three Witches.

First Witch.
Thrice the brinded cat hath mew'd.

Second Witch.
Thrice, and once the hedge-pig whin'd.

Third Witch.
Harpier cries, "'Tis time, 'tis time."

First Witch.
Round about the cauldron go;
In the poison'd entrails throw;
Toad, that under cold stone
Days and nights has thirty-one
Swelt'red venom sleeping got,
Boil thou first i' th' charmed pot.

Three Witches.
Double, double, toil and trouble;
Fire burn, and cauldron bubble.

Second Witch.
Fillet of a fenny snake,
In the cauldron boil and bake;
Eye of newt and toe of frog,
Wool of bat and tongue of dog,
Adder's fork and blind-worm's sting,
Lizard's leg and howlet's wing,
For a charm of pow'rful trouble,
Like a hell-broth boil and bubble.

Three Witches.
Double, double, toil and trouble;
Fire burn, and cauldron bubble.

Third Witch.
Scale of dragon, tooth of wolf,
Witch's mummy, maw and gulf
Of the ravin'd salt-sea shark,
Root of hemlock digg'd i' th' dark,
Liver of blaspheming Jew,
Gall of goat, and slips of yew
Sliver'd in the moon's eclipse,
Nose of Turk and Tartar's lips,
Finger of birth-strangled babe
Ditch-deliver'd by a drab,
Make the gruel thick and slab.
Add thereto a tiger's chawdron,
For th' ingredience of our cau'dron.

Three Witches.
Double, double, toil and trouble;
Fire burn, and cauldron bubble.

Second Witch.
Cool it with a baboon's blood,
Then the charm is firm and good.

Enter Hecat and the other three Witches.

Hecat.
O, well done! I commend your pains,
And every one shall share i' th' gains.
And now about the cauldron sing,
Like elves and fairies in a ring,
Enchanting all that you put in.

Music and a song: "Black spirits, etc."
Exit Hecat.

Second Witch.
By the pricking of my thumbs,
Something wicked this way comes.

Knocking.

      Open, locks,
    Whoever knocks!

Enter Macbeth.

Macbeth.
How now, you secret, black, and midnight hags?
What is't you do?

All Witches.
     A deed without a name.

Macbeth.
I conjure you, by that which you profess
(How e'er you come to know it), answer me:
Though you untie the winds, and let them fight
Against the churches; though the yesty waves
Confound and swallow navigation up;
Though bladed corn be lodg'd, and trees blown down;
Though castles topple on their warders' heads;
Though palaces and pyramids do slope
Their heads to their foundations; though the treasure
Of nature's germains tumble all together,
Even till destruction sicken; answer me
To what I ask you.

First Witch.
       Speak.

Second Witch.
       Demand.

Third Witch.
       We'll answer.

First Witch.
Say, if th' hadst rather hear it from our mouths,
Or from our masters'?

Macbeth.
      Call 'em; let me see 'em.

First Witch.
Pour in sow's blood, that hath eaten
Her nine farrow; grease that's sweaten
From the murderer's gibbet throw
Into the flame.

All Witches.
      Come high or low;
Thyself and office deftly show!

Thunder. First Apparition, an armed Head.

Macbeth.
Tell me, thou unknown power—

First Witch.
      He knows thy thought:
Hear his speech, but say thou nought.

First Apparition.
Macbeth! Macbeth! Macbeth! Beware Macduff,
Beware the Thane of Fife. Dismiss me. Enough.

He descends.

Macbeth.
What e'er thou art, for thy good caution, thanks;
Thou hast harp'd my fear aright. But one word more—

First Witch.
He will not be commanded. Here's another,
More potent than the first.

Thunder. Second Apparition, a bloody Child.

Second Apparition.
Macbeth! Macbeth! Macbeth!

Macbeth.
Had I three ears, I'ld hear thee.

Second Apparition.
Be bloody, bold, and resolute: laugh to scorn
The pow'r of man; for none of woman born
Shall harm Macbeth.

Descends.

Macbeth.
Then live, Macduff; what need I fear of thee?
But yet I'll make assurance double sure,
And take a bond of fate: thou shalt not live,
That I may tell pale-hearted fear it lies,
And sleep in spite of thunder.

Thunder. Third Apparition, a Child crowned, with a tree in his hand.

                What is this
That rises like the issue of a king,
And wears upon his baby-brow the round
And top of sovereignty?

All Witches and Apparitions.
              Listen, but speak not to't.

Third Apparition.
Be lion-mettled, proud, and take no care
Who chafes, who frets, or where conspirers are:
Macbeth shall never vanquish'd be until
Great Birnan wood to high Dunsinane hill
Shall come against him.

Descend.

Macbeth.
           That will never be.
Who can impress the forest, bid the tree
Unfix his earth-bound root? Sweet bodements! Good!
Rebellious dead, rise never till the wood
Of Birnan rise, and our high-plac'd Macbeth
Shall live the lease of nature, pay his breath
To time and mortal custom. Yet my heart
Throbs to know one thing: tell me, if your art
Can tell so much, shall Banquo's issue ever
Reign in this kingdom?

All Witches and Apparitions.
            Seek to know no more.

Macbeth.
I will be satisfied. Deny me this,
And an eternal curse fall on you! Let me know.
Why sinks that cauldron? And what noise is this?

Hoboys.

First Witch.
Show!

Second Witch.
Show!

Third Witch.
Show!

All Witches.
Show his eyes, and grieve his heart;
Come like shadows, so depart.

A show of eight Kings, the eighth with a glass in his hand, and Banquo last.

Macbeth.
Thou art too like the spirit of Banquo; down!
Thy crown does sear mine eyeballs. And thy hair,
Thou other gold-bound brow, is like the first.
A third is like the former. Filthy hags,
Why do you show me this?—A fourth? Start, eyes!
What, will the line stretch out to th' crack of doom?
Another yet? A seventh? I'll see no more.
And yet the eight appears, who bears a glass
Which shows me many more; and some I see
That twofold balls and treble sceptres carry.
Horrible sight! Now I see 'tis true,
For the blood-bolter'd Banquo smiles upon me,
And points at them for his.

Apparitions vanish.
            What? Is this so?

First Witch.
Ay, sir, all this is so. But why
Stands Macbeth thus amazedly?
Come, sisters, cheer we up his sprites,
And show the best of our delights.
I'll charm the air to give a sound,
While you perform your antic round;
That this great king may kindly say
Our duties did his welcome pay.

Music.
The Witches dance and vanish.

Macbeth.
Where are they? Gone? Let this pernicious hour
Stand aye accursed in the calendar!
Come in, without there!

Enter Lennox.

Lennox.
          What's your Grace's will?

Macbeth.
Saw you the weird sisters?

Lennox.
          No, my lord.

Macbeth.
Came they not by you?

Lennox.
          No indeed, my lord.

Macbeth.
Infected be the air whereon they ride,
And damn'd all those that trust them! I did hear
The galloping of horse. Who was't came by?

Lennox.
'Tis two or three, my lord, that bring you word
Macduff is fled to England.

Macbeth.
          Fled to England!

Lennox.
Ay, my good lord.

Macbeth.
Aside.
Time, thou anticipat'st my dread exploits:
The flighty purpose never is o'ertook
Unless the deed go with it. From this moment
The very firstlings of my heart shall be
The firstlings of my hand. And even now,
To crown my thoughts with acts, be it thought and done:
The castle of Macduff I will surprise,
Seize upon Fife, give to th' edge o' th' sword
His wife, his babes, and all unfortunate souls
That trace him in his line. No boasting like a fool;
This deed I'll do before this purpose cool.
But no more sights!—Where are these gentlemen?
Come bring me where they are.

Exeunt.

Scene 2

Fife. Macduff's castle.

(*Lady Macduff; Son; Rosse; Messenger; First and Second Murderers*)

Lady Macduff complains bitterly to Ross about her husband's desertion, though Ross insists Macduff's flight cannot be seen as such. She is not mollified. Ross takes his leave, promising to return soon. Lady Macduff chats with her Son, a highly intelligent and charming boy, but they are interrupted by the arrival of a Messenger begging them to flee. Too late, however: Lady Macduff has nowhere to go. Macbeth's underlings enter, referring to Macduff as a traitor, and when the Son denies the charge kill him, before advancing on his mother.

Enter Macduff's Wife, her Son, and Rosse.

Lady Macduff.
What had he done, to make him fly the land?

Rosse.
You must have patience, madam.

Lady Macduff.
          He had none;
His flight was madness. When our actions do not,
Our fears do make us traitors.

Rosse.
          You know not
Whether it was his wisdom or his fear.

Lady Macduff.
Wisdom? To leave his wife, to leave his babes,

His mansion and his titles, in a place
From whence himself does fly? He loves us not,
He wants the natural touch; for the poor wren,
The most diminutive of birds, will fight,
Her young ones in her nest, against the owl.
All is the fear, and nothing is the love;
As little is the wisdom, where the flight
So runs against all reason.

Rosse.
      My dearest coz,
I pray you school yourself. But for your husband,
He is noble, wise, judicious, and best knows
The fits o' th' season. I dare not speak much further,
But cruel are the times when we are traitors,
And do not know ourselves; when we hold rumor
From what we fear, yet know not what we fear,
But float upon a wild and violent sea
Each way, and move. I take my leave of you;
'Shall not be long but I'll be here again.
Things at the worst will cease, or else climb upward
To what they were before. My pretty cousin,
Blessing upon you!

Lady Macduff.
Father'd he is, and yet he's fatherless.

Rosse.
I am so much a fool, should I stay longer,
It would be my disgrace and your discomfort.
I take my leave at once.

Exit Rosse.

Lady Macduff.
     Sirrah, your father's dead,
And what will you do now? How will you live?

Son to Macduff.
As birds do, mother.

Lady Macduff.
     What, with worms and flies?

Son to Macduff.
With what I get, I mean, and so do they.

Lady Macduff.
Poor bird, thou'dst never fear the net nor lime,
The pitfall nor the gin.

Son to Macduff.
Why should I, mother? Poor birds they are not set for.
My father is not dead, for all your saying.

Lady Macduff.
Yes, he is dead. How wilt thou do for a father?

Son to Macduff.
Nay, how will you do for a husband?

Lady Macduff.
Why, I can buy me twenty at any market.

Son to Macduff.
Then you'll buy 'em to sell again.

Lady Macduff.
Thou speak'st with all thy wit, and yet, i' faith,
With wit enough for thee.

Son to Macduff.
Was my father a traitor, mother?

Lady Macduff.
Ay, that he was.

Son to Macduff.
What is a traitor?

Lady Macduff.
Why, one that swears and lies.

Son to Macduff.
And be all traitors that do so?

Lady Macduff.
Every one that does so is a traitor, and must be hang'd.

Son to Macduff.
And must they all be hang'd that swear and lie?

Lady Macduff.
Every one.

Son to Macduff.
Who must hang them?

Lady Macduff.
Why, the honest men.

Son to Macduff.
Then the liars and swearers are fools; for there are liars and swearers enow to beat the honest men and hang up them.

Lady Macduff.
Now God help thee, poor monkey! But how wilt thou do for a father?

Son to Macduff.
If he were dead, you'ld weep for him; if you would not, it were a good sign that I should quickly have a new father.

Lady Macduff.
Poor prattler, how thou talk'st!

Enter a Messenger.

Messenger.
Bless you, fair dame! I am not to you known,
Though in your state of honor I am perfect.
I doubt some danger does approach you nearly.
If you will take a homely man's advice,
Be not found here; hence with your little ones.
To fright you thus, methinks I am too savage;
To do worse to you were fell cruelty,
Which is too nigh your person. Heaven preserve you!
I dare abide no longer.

Exit Messenger.

Lady Macduff.
                    Whither should I fly?
I have done no harm. But I remember now
I am in this earthly world—where to do harm
Is often laudable, to do good sometime
Accounted dangerous folly. Why then, alas,
Do I put up that womanly defense,
To say I have done no harm?

Enter Murderers.
                    What are these faces?

First Murderer.
Where is your husband?

Lady Macduff.
I hope, in no place so unsanctified
Where such as thou mayst find him.

First Murderer.
                    He's a traitor.

Son to Macduff.
Thou li'st, thou shag-ear'd villain!

First Murderer.
                    What, you egg!

Stabbing him.
Young fry of treachery!

Son to Macduff.
                    He has kill'd me, mother:
Run away, I pray you!

Dies.
Exit Lady Macduff crying "Murder!" and pursued by the Murderers.

Scene 3

England. Before the King's palace.

(Malcolm; Macduff; English Doctor; Rosse)

Maclcolm and Macduff discuss the sufferings of Scotland under Macbeth's rule. Malcolm insists, however, that he would make a far worse king than Macbeth himself, detailing all of his various sins. Macduff brushes them all aside as irrelevant, until Malcolm convinces him that he is an appalling human being and Macduff weeps at the thought of Scotland suffering yet further. This is all Malcolm was waiting for, as he wanted to test Macduff's good faith, since Macbeth has sent many spies to him. All he has said was lies. They are interrupted by an English Doctor who informs them that the King, who has offered ten thousand men to help Malcolm overthrow Macbeth, is coming out of his palace to cure an evil plague by his touch. Ross arrives, and after temporizing, has to tell Macduff that his entire family has been killed. Macduff is broken by the news, laying all the blame on himself. Malcolm tries to console him by recommending that he use his grief as fodder for his anger as they attack Macbeth. Macduff reminds the others that Macbeth has no children himself, and cannot know what it is to lose them. He swears not to rest until he has killed Macbeth, and Malcolm urges that they go to the King of England and receive their forces.

Enter Malcolm and Macduff.

Malcolm.
Let us seek out some desolate shade, and there
Weep our sad bosoms empty.

Macduff.
                    Let us rather
Hold fast the mortal sword, and like good men

Bestride our downfall birthdom. Each new morn
New widows howl, new orphans cry, new sorrows
Strike heaven on the face, that it resounds
As if it felt with Scotland, and yell'd out
Like syllable of dolor.

Malcolm.
                          What I believe, I'll wail,
What know, believe; and what I can redress,
As I shall find the time to friend, I will.
What you have spoke, it may be so perchance.
This tyrant, whose sole name blisters our tongues,
Was once thought honest; you have lov'd him well;
He hath not touch'd you yet. I am young, but something
You may discern of him through me, and wisdom
To offer up a weak, poor, innocent lamb
T' appease an angry god.

Macduff.
I am not treacherous.

Malcolm.
                          But Macbeth is.
A good and virtuous nature may recoil
In an imperial charge. But I shall crave your pardon;
That which you are, my thoughts cannot transpose:
Angels are bright still, though the brightest fell.
Though all things foul would wear the brows of grace,
Yet grace must still look so.

Macduff.
                          I have lost my hopes.

Malcolm.
Perchance even there where I did find my doubts.
Why in that rawness left you wife and child,
Those precious motives, those strong knots of love,
Without leave-taking? I pray you,
Let not my jealousies be your dishonors,
But mine own safeties. You may be rightly just,
What ever I shall think.

Macduff.
                          Bleed, bleed, poor country!
Great tyranny, lay thou thy basis sure,
For goodness dare not check thee! wear thou thy wrongs,
The title is affeer'd! Fare thee well, lord,
I would not be the villain that thou think'st
For the whole space that's in the tyrant's grasp,
And the rich East to boot.

Malcolm.
                          Be not offended;
I speak not as in absolute fear of you.
I think our country sinks beneath the yoke:
It weeps, it bleeds, and each new day a gash
Is added to her wounds. I think withal
There would be hands uplifted in my right;
And here from gracious England have I offer
Of goodly thousands. But, for all this,
When I shall tread upon the tyrant's head,
Or wear it on my sword, yet my poor country
Shall have more vices than it had before,
More suffer, and more sundry ways than ever,
By him that shall succeed.

Macduff.
                          What should he be?

Malcolm.
It is myself I mean; in whom I know
All the particulars of vice so grafted
That, when they shall be open'd, black Macbeth
Will seem as pure as snow, and the poor state
Esteem him as a lamb, being compar'd
With my confineless harms.

Macduff.
                          Not in the legions
Of horrid hell can come a devil more damn'd
In evils to top Macbeth.

Malcolm.
                          I grant him bloody,
Luxurious, avaricious, false, deceitful,
Sudden, malicious, smacking of every sin
That has a name; but there's no bottom, none,
In my voluptuousness. Your wives, your daughters,
Your matrons, and your maids could not fill up
The cistern of my lust, and my desire
All continent impediments would o'erbear
That did oppose my will. Better Macbeth
Than such an one to reign.

Macduff.
                          Boundless intemperance
In nature is a tyranny; it hath been
Th' untimely emptying of the happy throne,
And fall of many kings. But fear not yet
To take upon you what is yours. You may
Convey your pleasures in a spacious plenty,
And yet seem cold, the time you may so hoodwink.
We have willing dames enough; there cannot be

That vulture in you to devour so many
As will to greatness dedicate themselves,
Finding it so inclin'd.

Malcolm.
                            With this, there grows
In my most ill-compos'd affection such
A stanchless avarice that, were I king,
I should cut off the nobles for their lands,
Desire his jewels, and this other's house,
And my more-having would be as a sauce
To make me hunger more, that I should forge
Quarrels unjust against the good and loyal,
Destroying them for wealth.

Macduff.
                        This avarice
Sticks deeper, grows with more pernicious root
Than summer-seeming lust; and it hath been
The sword of our slain kings. Yet do not fear,
Scotland hath foisons to fill up your will
Of your mere own. All these are portable,
With other graces weigh'd.

Malcolm.
But I have none. The king-becoming graces,
As justice, verity, temp'rance, stableness,
Bounty, perseverance, mercy, lowliness,
Devotion, patience, courage, fortitude,
I have no relish of them, but abound
In the division of each several crime,
Acting it many ways. Nay, had I pow'r, I should
Pour the sweet milk of concord into hell,
Uproar the universal peace, confound
All unity on earth.

Macduff.
                    O Scotland, Scotland!

Malcolm.
If such a one be fit to govern, speak.
I am as I have spoken.

Macduff.
                    Fit to govern?
No, not to live. O nation miserable!
With an untitled tyrant bloody-sceptred,
When shalt thou see thy wholesome days again,
Since that the truest issue of thy throne
By his own interdiction stands accus'd,
And does blaspheme his breed? Thy royal father
Was a most sainted king; the queen that bore thee,
Oft'ner upon her knees than on her feet,
Died every day she liv'd. Fare thee well,
These evils thou repeat'st upon thyself
Hath banish'd me from Scotland. O my breast,
Thy hope ends here!

Malcolm.
                Macduff, this noble passion,
Child of integrity, hath from my soul
Wip'd the black scruples, reconcil'd my thoughts
To thy good truth and honor. Devilish Macbeth
By many of these trains hath sought to win me
Into his power, and modest wisdom plucks me
From over-credulous haste. But God above
Deal between thee and me! For even now
I put myself to thy direction, and
Unspeak mine own detraction; here abjure
The taints and blames I laid upon myself,
For strangers to my nature. I am yet
Unknown to woman, never was forsworn,
Scarcely have coveted what was mine own,
At no time broke my faith, would not betray
The devil to his fellow, and delight
No less in truth than life. My first false speaking
Was this upon myself. What I am truly
Is thine and my poor country's to command:
Whither indeed, before thy here-approach,
Old Siward, with ten thousand warlike men
Already at a point, was setting forth.
Now we'll together, and the chance of goodness
Be like our warranted quarrel! Why are you silent?

Macduff.
Such welcome and unwelcome things at once
'Tis hard to reconcile.

Enter English Doctor.

Malcolm.
Well, more anon.—Comes the King forth, I pray you?

English Doctor.
Ay, sir; there are a crew of wretched souls
That stay his cure. Their malady convinces
The great assay of art; but at his touch,
Such sanctity hath heaven given his hand,
They presently amend.

Malcolm.
        I thank you, doctor.

Exit English Doctor.

Macduff.
What's the disease he means?

Malcolm.
         'Tis call'd the evil:
A most miraculous work in this good king,
Which often, since my here-remain in England,
I have seen him do. How he solicits heaven,
Himself best knows; but strangely-visited people,
All swoll'n and ulcerous, pitiful to the eye,
The mere despair of surgery, he cures,
Hanging a golden stamp about their necks,
Put on with holy prayers, and 'tis spoken,
To the succeeding royalty he leaves
The healing benediction. With this strange virtue,
He hath a heavenly gift of prophecy,
And sundry blessings hang about his throne
That speak him full of grace.

Enter Rosse.

Macduff.
        See who comes here.

Malcolm.
My countryman; but yet I know him not.

Macduff.
My ever gentle cousin, welcome hither.

Malcolm.
I know him now. Good God betimes remove
The means that makes us strangers!

Rosse.
        Sir, amen.

Macduff.
Stands Scotland where it did?

Rosse.
        Alas, poor country,
Almost afraid to know itself! It cannot
Be call'd our mother, but our grave; where nothing,
But who knows nothing, is once seen to smile;
Where sighs, and groans, and shrieks that rent the air
Are made, not mark'd; where violent sorrow seems
A modern ecstasy. The dead man's knell
Is there scarce ask'd for who, and good men's lives
Expire before the flowers in their caps,
Dying or ere they sicken.

Macduff.
        O relation!
Too nice, and yet too true.

Malcolm.
        What's the newest grief?

Rosse.
That of an hour's age doth hiss the speaker;
Each minute teems a new one.

Macduff.
        How does my wife?

Rosse.
Why, well.

Macduff.
        And all my children?

Rosse.
        Well too.

Macduff.
The tyrant has not batter'd at their peace?

Rosse.
No, they were well at peace when I did leave 'em.

Macduff.
Be not a niggard of your speech; how goes't?

Rosse.
When I came hither to transport the tidings,
Which I have heavily borne, there ran a rumor
Of many worthy fellows that were out,
Which was to my belief witness'd the rather,
For that I saw the tyrant's power afoot.
Now is the time of help; your eye in Scotland
Would create soldiers, make our women fight,
To doff their dire distresses.

Malcolm.
        Be't their comfort
We are coming thither. Gracious England hath
Lent us good Siward, and ten thousand men;
An older and a better soldier none
That Christendom gives out.

Rosse.
                    Would I could answer
This comfort with the like! But I have words
That would be howl'd out in the desert air,
Where hearing should not latch them.

Macduff.
                        What concern they?
The general cause? Or is it a fee-grief
Due to some single breast?

Rosse.
                      No mind that's honest
But in it shares some woe, though the main part
Pertains to you alone.

Macduff.
                          If it be mine,
Keep it not from me, quickly let me have it.

Rosse.
Let not your ears despise my tongue forever,
Which shall possess them with the heaviest sound
That ever yet they heard.

Macduff.
                      Humh! I guess at it.

Rosse.
Your castle is surpris'd; your wife, and babes,
Savagely slaughter'd. To relate the manner,
Were on the quarry of these murder'd deer
To add the death of you.

Malcolm.
                      Merciful heaven!
What, man, ne'er pull your hat upon your brows;
Give sorrow words. The grief that does not speak
Whispers the o'er-fraught heart, and bids it break.

Macduff.
My children too?

Rosse.
                Wife, children, servants, all
That could be found.

Macduff.
                And I must be from thence!
My wife kill'd too?

Rosse.
                    I have said.

Malcolm.
                    Be comforted.
Let's make us med'cines of our great revenge
To cure this deadly grief.

Macduff.
He has no children. All my pretty ones?
Did you say all? O hell-kite! All?
What, all my pretty chickens, and their dam,
At one fell swoop?

Malcolm.
Dispute it like a man.

Macduff.
                    I shall do so;
But I must also feel it as a man:
I cannot but remember such things were,
That were most precious to me. Did heaven look on,
And would not take their part? Sinful Macduff,
They were all struck for thee! Naught that I am,
Not for their own demerits, but for mine,
Fell slaughter on their souls. Heaven rest them now!

Malcolm.
Be this the whetstone of your sword, let grief
Convert to anger; blunt not the heart, enrage it.

Macduff.
O, I could play the woman with mine eyes,
And braggart with my tongue! But, gentle heavens,
Cut short all intermission. Front to front
Bring thou this fiend of Scotland and myself;
Within my sword's length set him; if he scape,
Heaven forgive him too!

Malcolm.
                    This tune goes manly.
Come go we to the King, our power is ready,
Our lack is nothing but our leave. Macbeth
Is ripe for shaking, and the pow'rs above
Put on their instruments. Receive what cheer you may,
The night is long that never finds the day.

Exeunt.

Act 5

Scene 1

Dunsinane. An anteroom in the castle.

(Doctor of Physic; Waiting Gentlewoman; Lady Macbeth)

The Doctor waits with Lady Macbeth's Waiting Gentlewoman for the third night in a row. She insists that what she has told him is true about Lady Macbeth sleepwalking, but refuses to repeat what she has heard the Queen say in her sleep. Lady Macbeth enters, endlessly wringing her hands as though to wash them. She begins to speak, wishing the spots on her hands away, as the Doctor notes down what she says. Her words clearly reveal her guilt over Duncan's death, and those of Macduff's family, not to mention Banquo. The Doctor is horrified, and admits that he cannot cure her.

Enter a Doctor of Physic and a Waiting Gentlewoman.

Doctor of Physic.
I have two nights watch'd with you, but can perceive no truth in your report. When was it she last walk'd?

Gentlewoman.
Since his Majesty went into the field, I have seen her rise from her bed, throw her night-gown upon her, unlock her closet, take forth paper, fold it, write upon't, read it, afterwards seal it, and again return to bed; yet all this while in a most fast sleep.

Doctor of Physic.
A great perturbation in nature, to receive at once the benefit of sleep and do the effects of watching! In this slumb'ry agitation, besides her walking and other actual performances, what, at any time, have you heard her say?

Gentlewoman.
That, sir, which I will not report after her.

Doctor of Physic.
You may to me, and 'tis most meet you should.

Gentlewoman.
Neither to you nor any one, having no witness to confirm my speech.

Enter Lady Macbeth with a taper.

Lo you, here she comes! This is her very guise, and upon my life, fast asleep. Observe her, stand close.

Doctor of Physic.
How came she by that light?

Gentlewoman.
Why, it stood by her. She has light by her continually, 'tis her command.

Doctor of Physic.
You see her eyes are open.

Gentlewoman.
Ay, but their sense are shut.

Doctor of Physic.
What is it she does now? Look how she rubs her hands.

Gentlewoman.
It is an accustom'd action with her, to seem thus washing her hands. I have known her continue in this a quarter of an hour.

Lady Macbeth.
Yet here's a spot.

Doctor of Physic.
Hark, she speaks. I will set down what comes from her, to satisfy my remembrance the more strongly.

Lady Macbeth.
Out, damn'd spot! Out, I say! One—two—why then 'tis time to do't. Hell is murky. Fie, my lord, fie, a soldier, and afeard? What need we fear who knows it, when none can call our pow'r to accompt? Yet who would have thought the old man to have had so much blood in him?

Doctor of Physic.
Do you mark that?

Lady Macbeth.
The Thane of Fife had a wife; where is she now? What, will these hands ne'er be clean? No more o' that, my lord, no more o' that; you mar all with this starting.

Doctor of Physic.
Go to, go to; you have known what you should not.

Gentlewoman.
She has spoke what she should not, I am sure of that; heaven knows what she has known.

Lady Macbeth.
Here's the smell of the blood still. All the perfumes of Arabia will not sweeten this little hand. O, O, O!

Doctor of Physic.
What a sigh is there! The heart is sorely charg'd.

Gentlewoman.
I would not have such a heart in my bosom for the dignity of the whole body.

Doctor of Physic.
Well, well, well.

Gentlewoman.
Pray God it be, sir.

Doctor of Physic.
This disease is beyond my practice; yet I have known those which have walk'd in their sleep who have died holily in their beds.

Lady Macbeth.
Wash your hands, put on your night-gown, look not so pale. I tell you yet again, Banquo's buried; he cannot come out on 's grave.

Doctor of Physic.
Even so?

Lady Macbeth.
To bed, to bed; there's knocking at the gate. Come, come, come, come, give me your hand. What's done cannot be undone. To bed, to bed, to bed.

Exit Lady.

Doctor of Physic.
Will she go now to bed?

Gentlewoman.
Directly.

Doctor of Physic.
Foul whisp'rings are abroad. Unnatural deeds
Do breed unnatural troubles; infected minds
To their deaf pillows will discharge their secrets.
More needs she the divine than the physician.
God, God, forgive us all! Look after her,
Remove from her the means of all annoyance,
And still keep eyes upon her. So good night.
My mind she has mated, and amaz'd my sight.
I think, but dare not speak.

Gentlewoman.
          Good night, good doctor.

Exeunt.

Scene 2

The country near Dunsinane.

(Menteth; Cathness; Angus; Lennox; Soldiers)

The Scottish noblemen Mentieth, Angus, Lennox, and Caithness all go with their soldiers to join Malcolm and Macduff. They discuss Macbeth, asserting that he rules only by ordering, not by love, and note that he has fortified Dunsinane against all comers.

Drum and Colors. Enter Menteth, Cathness, Angus, Lennox, Soldiers.

Menteth.
The English pow'r is near, led on by Malcolm,
His uncle Siward, and the good Macduff.
Revenges burn in them; for their dear causes
Would to the bleeding and the grim alarm
Excite the mortified man.

Angus.
          Near Birnan wood
Shall we well meet them; that way are they coming.

Cathness.
Who knows if Donalbain be with his brother?

Lennox.
For certain, sir, he is not; I have a file
Of all the gentry. There is Siward's son,
And many unrough youths that even now
Protest their first of manhood.

Menteth.
          What does the tyrant?

Cathness.
Great Dunsinane he strongly fortifies.
Some say he's mad; others that lesser hate him
Do call it valiant fury; but for certain
He cannot buckle his distemper'd cause
Within the belt of rule.

Angus.
          Now does he feel
His secret murders sticking on his hands;
Now minutely revolts upbraid his faith-breach;
Those he commands move only in command,
Nothing in love. Now does he feel his title
Hang loose about him, like a giant's robe
Upon a dwarfish thief.

Menteth.
                  Who then shall blame
His pester'd senses to recoil and start,
When all that is within him does condemn
Itself for being there?

Cathness.
                 Well, march we on
To give obedience where 'tis truly ow'd.
Meet we the med'cine of the sickly weal,
And with him pour we, in our country's purge,
Each drop of us.

Lennox.
               Or so much as it needs
To dew the sovereign flower and drown the weeds.
Make we our march towards Birnan.

Exeunt marching.

Scene 3

Dunsinane. A room in the castle.

(Macbeth; English Doctor; Attendants; Servant; Seyton)

Macbeth refuses to receive news of any more Thanes fleeing, blustering about the safety that the prophecies have promised him. He bullies the servant who comes to warn him of the approach of the English army. But he is aware that he is not loved, and realizes that he is growing old without earning respect. He prepares himself for battle, insisting that he will put on his armor even though it is not needed yet, and sending out men to hang anyone heard speaking fearfully. Macbeth asks the Doctor about Lady Macbeth, and queries whether it is possible for a physician to cure the afflictions of the mind the same way one can cure the body; but the Doctor tells him that only the patient can do that. Macbeth denounces all medicine as useless and prepares to fight, as the Doctor wishes he were well clear of the place.

Enter Macbeth, English Doctor, and Attendants.

Macbeth.
Bring me no more reports, let them fly all.
Till Birnan wood remove to Dunsinane
I cannot taint with fear. What's the boy Malcolm?
Was he not born of woman? The spirits that know
All mortal consequences have pronounc'd me thus:
"Fear not, Macbeth, no man that's born of woman
Shall e'er have power upon thee." Then fly, false thanes,
And mingle with the English epicures!
The mind I sway by, and the heart I bear,
Shall never sag with doubt, nor shake with fear.

Enter Servant.

The devil damn thee black, thou cream-fac'd loon!
Where got'st thou that goose-look?

Servant.
There is ten thousand—

Macbeth.
                     Geese, villain?

Servant.
                    Soldiers, sir.

Macbeth.
Go prick thy face, and over-red thy fear,
Thou lily-liver'd boy. What soldiers, patch?
Death of thy soul! Those linen cheeks of thine
Are counsellors to fear. What soldiers, whey-face?

Servant.
The English force, so please you.

Macbeth.
Take thy face hence.

Exit Servant.
               Seyton!—I am sick at heart
When I behold—Seyton, I say!—This push
Will cheer me ever, or disseat me now.
I have liv'd long enough: my way of life
Is fall'n into the sear, the yellow leaf,
And that which should accompany old age,
As honor, love, obedience, troops of friends,
I must not look to have; but in their stead,
Curses, not loud but deep, mouth-honor, breath,
Which the poor heart would fain deny, and dare not.
Seyton!

Enter Seyton.

Seyton.
What's your gracious pleasure?

Macbeth.
               What news more?

Seyton.
All is confirm'd, my lord, which was reported.

Macbeth.
I'll fight, till from my bones my flesh be hack'd.
Give me my armor.

Seyton.
                  'Tis not needed yet.

Macbeth.
I'll put it on.
Send out more horses, skirr the country round,
Hang those that talk of fear. Give me mine armor.
How does your patient, doctor?

English Doctor.
                  Not so sick, my lord,
As she is troubled with thick-coming fancies,
That keep her from her rest.

Macbeth.
                  Cure her of that.
Canst thou not minister to a mind diseas'd,
Pluck from the memory a rooted sorrow,
Raze out the written troubles of the brain,
And with some sweet oblivious antidote
Cleanse the stuff'd bosom of that perilous stuff
Which weighs upon the heart?

English Doctor.
                  Therein the patient
Must minister to himself.

Macbeth.
Throw physic to the dogs, I'll none of it.
Come, put mine armor on; give me my staff.
Seyton, send out. Doctor, the thanes fly from me.—
Come, sir, dispatch.—If thou couldst, doctor, cast
The water of my land, find her disease,
And purge it to a sound and pristine health,
I would applaud thee to the very echo,
That should applaud again.—Pull't off, I say.—
What rhubarb, cyme, or what purgative drug,
Would scour these English hence? Hear'st thou of them?

English Doctor.
Ay, my good lord; your royal preparation
Makes us hear something.

Macbeth.
                  Bring it after me.—
I will not be afraid of death and bane,
Till Birnan forest come to Dunsinane.

Exeunt all but the English Doctor.

English Doctor.
Were I from Dunsinane away and clear,
Profit again should hardly draw me here.

Exit.

Scene 4

Country near Birnam wood.

(Malcolm; Siward; Macduff; Siward's Son; Menteth; Cathness; Angus; Lennox; Rosse; Soldiers)

Arriving at Birnam forest, Malcolm orders that his soldiers cut down the trees and carry the branches in front of them to disguise their number and movements.

Drum and Colors. Enter Malcolm, Siward, Macduff, Siward's Son, Menteth, Cathness, Angus, Lennox, Rosse, and Soldiers, marching.

Malcolm.
Cousins, I hope the days are near at hand
That chambers will be safe.

Menteth.
                  We doubt it nothing.

Siward, Earl of Northumberland.
What wood is this before us?

Menteth.
                  The wood of Birnan.

Malcolm.
Let every soldier hew him down a bough,
And bear't before him, thereby shall we shadow
The numbers of our host, and make discovery
Err in report of us.

Soldiers.
                  It shall be done.

Siward, Earl of Northumberland.
We learn no other but the confident tyrant
Keeps still in Dunsinane, and will endure
Our setting down before't.

Malcolm.
                    'Tis his main hope;
For where there is advantage to be given,
Both more and less have given him the revolt,
And none serve with him but constrained things,
Whose hearts are absent too.

Macduff.
                    Let our just censures
Attend the true event, and put we on
Industrious soldiership.

Siward, Earl of Northumberland.
                        The time approaches
That will with due decision make us know
What we shall say we have, and what we owe.
Thoughts speculative their unsure hopes relate,
But certain issue strokes must arbitrate,
Towards which advance the war.

Exeunt marching.

Scene 5

Dunsinane. Within the castle.

(Macbeth; Seyton; Soldiers; Macbeth's Messenger)

Macbeth finalizes his preparations against a siege, certain that no enemy can get in, but his bluster is broken by women screaming, and the news that Lady Macbeth is dead. Already grown apathetic, Macbeth realizes to what an extent life is empty and meaningless. A Soldier announces that he was looking towards Birnam forest and that he saw the wood begin to move. Shocked and enraged, Macbeth begins to doubt, wondering whether the prophecies leave him as safe as he thought; still, though beginning to be weary of life, he still insists that he and his men will die fighting.

Enter Macbeth, Seyton, and Soldiers, with Drum and Colors.

Macbeth.
Hang out our banners on the outward walls,
The cry is still, "They come!" Our castle's strength
Will laugh a siege to scorn; here let them lie
Till famine and the ague eat them up.
Were they not forc'd with those that should be ours,
We might have met them dareful, beard to beard,
And beat them backward home.

A cry within of women.

                    What is that noise?

Seyton.
It is the cry of women, my good lord.

Exit.

Macbeth.
I have almost forgot the taste of fears.
The time has been, my senses would have cool'd
To hear a night-shriek, and my fell of hair
Would at a dismal treatise rouse and stir
As life were in't. I have supp'd full with horrors;
Direness, familiar to my slaughterous thoughts,
Cannot once start me.

Enter Seyton.

                    Wherefore was that cry?

Seyton.
The Queen, my lord, is dead.

Macbeth.
She should have died hereafter;
There would have been a time for such a word.
Tomorrow, and tomorrow, and tomorrow,
Creeps in this petty pace from day to day,
To the last syllable of recorded time;
And all our yesterdays have lighted fools
The way to dusty death. Out, out, brief candle!
Life's but a walking shadow, a poor player,
That struts and frets his hour upon the stage,
And then is heard no more. It is a tale
Told by an idiot, full of sound and fury,
Signifying nothing.

Enter Macbeth's Messenger.

                Thou com'st to use thy tongue;
Thy story quickly.

Macbeth's Messenger.
                Gracious my lord,
I should report that which I say I saw,
But know not how to do't.

Macbeth.
                Well, say, sir.

Macbeth's Messenger.
As I did stand my watch upon the hill,
I look'd toward Birnan, and anon methought
The wood began to move.

Act 5, Scene 6

Macbeth.
                    Liar and slave!

Macbeth's Messenger.
Let me endure your wrath, if't be not so.
Within this three mile may you see it coming;
I say, a moving grove.

Macbeth.
                    If thou speak'st false,
Upon the next tree shall thou hang alive,
Till famine cling thee; if thy speech be sooth,
I care not if thou dost for me as much.
I pull in resolution, and begin
To doubt th' equivocation of the fiend
That lies like truth. "Fear not, till Birnan wood
Do come to Dunsinane," and now a wood
Comes toward Dunsinane. Arm, arm, and out!
If this which he avouches does appear,
There is nor flying hence, nor tarrying here.
I gin to be a-weary of the sun,
And wish th' estate o' th' world were now undone.
Ring the alarum-bell! Blow wind, come wrack,
At least we'll die with harness on our back.

Exeunt.

Scene 6

Dunsinane. Before the castle.

(Malcolm; Siward; Macduff)

Considering that they have crept near enough to Dunsinane, Malcolm gives the order to toss away the branches and attack, sending Siward and his son to attack first, while he and Macduff will hang back to see where they will most be needed.

Drum and Colors. Enter Malcolm, Siward, Macduff, and their army, with boughs.

Malcolm.
Now near enough; your leavy screens throw down,
And show like those you are. You, worthy uncle,
Shall with my cousin, your right noble son,
Lead our first battle. Worthy Macduff and we
Shall take upon 's what else remains to do,
According to our order.

Siward, Earl of Northumberland.
                    Fare you well.
Do we but find the tyrant's power tonight,
Let us be beaten, if we cannot fight.

Macduff.
Make all our trumpets speak, give them all breath,
Those clamorous harbingers of blood and death.

Exeunt. Alarums continued.

Scene 7

A part of the field.

(Macbeth; Young Siward; Macduff; Malcolm; Siward)

Macbeth realizes that he is trapped, but still questions where the one not born of woman might be. Young Siward finds him and is killed by Macbeth, who sneers that the young man was born of woman. Macduff rushes in, having heard the noise, searching for Macbeth; he fears he will be haunted by his family forever if he is not the one to kill the tyrant. The battle is going so well for the English that Malcolm enters the castle.

Enter Macbeth.

Macbeth.
They have tied me to a stake; I cannot fly,
But bear-like I must fight the course. What's he
That was not born of woman? Such a one
Am I to fear, or none.

Enter Young Siward.

Young Siward.
What is thy name?

Macbeth.
                    Thou'lt be afraid to hear it.

Young Siward.
No; though thou call'st thyself a hotter name
Than any is in hell.

Macbeth.
                    My name's Macbeth.

Young Siward.
The devil himself could not pronounce a title
More hateful to mine ear.

Macbeth.
                    No; nor more fearful.

Young Siward.
Thou liest, abhorred tyrant, with my sword
I'll prove the lie thou speak'st.

Fight, and Young Siward slain.

Macbeth.
      Thou wast born of woman.
But swords I smile at, weapons laugh to scorn,
Brandish'd by man that's of a woman born.

Exit.
Alarums. Enter Macduff.

Macduff.
That way the noise is. Tyrant, show thy face!
If thou beest slain and with no stroke of mine,
My wife and children's ghosts will haunt me still.
I cannot strike at wretched kerns, whose arms
Are hir'd to bear their staves; either thou, Macbeth,
Or else my sword with an unbattered edge
I sheathe again undeeded. There thou shouldst be;
By this great clatter, one of greatest note
Seems bruited. Let me find him, Fortune!
And more I beg not.

Exit. Alarums.
Enter Malcolm and Siward.

Siward, Earl of Northumberland.
This way, my lord, the castle's gently rend'red:
The tyrant's people on both sides do fight,
The noble thanes do bravely in the war,
The day almost itself professes yours,
And little is to do.

Malcolm.
      We have met with foes
That strike beside us.

Siward, Earl of Northumberland.
      Enter, sir, the castle.

Exeunt. Alarum.

Scene 8

Another part of the field.

(Macbeth; Macduff)

Macbeth dismisses suicide as an option, just as Macduff finally finds him. Macbeth has no wish to fight him, and admits to having avoided Macduff so far, having killed too many of his family already. Macduff has no patience for words, and they fight. When Macbeth taunts him with the prophecy about how he cannot be killed, Macduff strikes right back, revealing that he was not born of woman, but ripped from his mother in a Caesarian section. Macbeth is suddenly full of fear, and curses the witches; he tries to avoid fighting any more with Macduff, but the latter calls him a coward, offering him the chance to surrender and be paraded around the country in a cage. Macbeth regains his courage, and though all the prophecies that announce his time is up have been fulfilled, he chooses to try to escape all the same, and the two begin fighting again. Macduff kills Macbeth.

Enter Macbeth.

Macbeth.
Why should I play the Roman fool, and die
On mine own sword? Whiles I see lives, the gashes
Do better upon them.

Enter Macduff.

Macduff.
      Turn, hell-hound, turn!

Macbeth.
Of all men else I have avoided thee.
But get thee back, my soul is too much charg'd
With blood of thine already.

Macduff.
      I have no words,
My voice is in my sword, thou bloodier villain
Than terms can give thee out!

Fight. Alarum.

Macbeth.
      Thou losest labor.
As easy mayst thou the intrenchant air
With thy keen sword impress as make me bleed.
Let fall thy blade on vulnerable crests,
I bear a charmed life, which must not yield
To one of woman born.

Macduff.
      Despair thy charm,
And let the angel whom thou still hast serv'd
Tell thee, Macduff was from his mother's womb
Untimely ripp'd.

Macbeth.
Accursed be that tongue that tells me so,
For it hath cow'd my better part of man!
And be these juggling fiends no more believ'd,
That palter with us in a double sense,
That keep the word of promise to our ear,
And break it to our hope. I'll not fight with thee.

Macduff.
Then yield thee, coward,
And live to be the show and gaze o' th' time!
We'll have thee, as our rarer monsters are,
Painted upon a pole, and underwrit,
"Here may you see the tyrant."

Macbeth.
      I will not yield,
To kiss the ground before young Malcolm's feet,
And to be baited with the rabble's curse.
Though Birnan wood be come to Dunsinane,
And thou oppos'd, being of no woman born,
Yet I will try the last. Before my body
I throw my warlike shield. Lay on, Macduff,
And damn'd be him that first cries, "Hold, enough!"

Exeunt fighting. Alarums.
Enter fighting, and Macbeth slain. Macduff carries off Macbeth's body.

Scene 9

Dunsinane. Within Macbeth's castle.

(Malcolm; Siward; Rosse; Thanes; Soldiers; Macduff)

The victors are assembling, the various commanders arriving and tallying up the dead. Ross informs Siward that Young Siward is dead, but the old man is not too fussed once he is reassured that the young man died fighting. Macduff, the only missing commander, enters, carrying Macbeth's head, and salutes Malcolm as King of Scotland. Malcolm is pleased, and immediately re-titles all the Scottish nobles as Earls instead of Thanes, and plans to call back all the exiles. He mentions in passing that Lady Macbeth most likely killed herself. He invites everyone to join him at his coronation.

Retreat and flourish. Enter, with Drum and Colors, Malcolm, Siward, Rosse, Thanes, and Soldiers.

Malcolm.
I would the friends we miss were safe arriv'd.

Siward, Earl of Northumberland.
Some must go off; and yet, by these I see,
So great a day as this is cheaply bought.

Malcolm.
Macduff is missing, and your noble son.

Rosse.
Your son, my lord, has paid a soldier's debt.
He only liv'd but till he was a man,
The which no sooner had his prowess confirm'd
In the unshrinking station where he fought,
But like a man he died.

Siward, Earl of Northumberland.
      Then he is dead?

Rosse.
Ay, and brought off the field. Your cause of sorrow
Must not be measur'd by his worth, for then
It hath no end.

Siward, Earl of Northumberland.
      Had he his hurts before?

Rosse.
Ay, on the front.

Siward, Earl of Northumberland.
      Why then. God's soldier be he!
Had I as many sons as I have hairs,
I would not wish them to a fairer death.
And so his knell is knoll'd.

Malcolm.
      He's worth more sorrow,
And that I'll spend for him.

Siward, Earl of Northumberland.
He's worth no more;
They say he parted well, and paid his score,
And so God be with him! Here comes newer comfort.

Enter Macduff with Macbeth's head.

Macduff.
Hail, King! For so thou art. Behold where stands
Th' usurper's cursed head: the time is free.
I see thee compass'd with thy kingdom's pearl,
That speak my salutation in their minds;
Whose voices I desire aloud with mine:
Hail, King of Scotland!

All.
                    Hail, King of Scotland!

Flourish.

King Malcolm.
We shall not spend a large expense of time
Before we reckon with your several loves,
And make us even with you. My thanes and kinsmen,
Henceforth be earls, the first that ever Scotland
In such an honor nam'd. What's more to do,
Which would be planted newly with the time,
As calling home our exil'd friends abroad
That fled the snares of watchful tyranny,
Producing forth the cruel ministers
Of this dead butcher and his fiend-like queen,
Who (as 'tis thought) by self and violent hands
Took off her life; this, and what needful else
That calls upon us, by the grace of Grace,
We will perform in measure, time, and place.
So thanks to all at once and to each one,
Whom we invite to see us crown'd at Scone.

Flourish. Exeunt omnes.

Twelfth Night

Act 1

Scene 1

Illyria. A room in Duke Orsino's palace.

(Duke of Illyria; Curio; Lords; Musicians; Valentine)

Orsino, Duke of Illyria, is deeply moved by sentimental music. His courtiers try to distract him by encouraging him to hunt, but he merely begins to prattle about his love for the Countess Olivia. His gentleman Valentine returns to inform the Duke that he was not allowed into Olivia's house to deliver the message Orsino sent her. The Countess is mourning for her dead brother and has sworn to remain veiled and alone for seven years in his memory. Orsino is only further inflamed by this, imagining how much more she could love someone if she loved a brother that much.

Enter Orsino, Duke of Illyria, Curio, and other Lords; Musicians attending.

Orsino.
If music be the food of love, play on,
Give me excess of it; that surfeiting,
The appetite may sicken, and so die.
That strain again, it had a dying fall;
O, it came o'er my ear like the sweet sound
That breathes upon a bank of violets,
Stealing and giving odor. Enough, no more,
'Tis not so sweet now as it was before.
O spirit of love, how quick and fresh art thou,
That notwithstanding thy capacity
Receiveth as the sea, nought enters there,
Of what validity and pitch soe'er,
But falls into abatement and low price
Even in a minute. So full of shapes is fancy
That it alone is high fantastical.

Curio.
Will you go hunt, my lord?

Orsino.
                What, Curio?

Curio.
                The hart.

Orsino.
Why, so I do, the noblest that I have.
O, when mine eyes did see Olivia first,
Methought she purg'd the air of pestilence!
That instant was I turn'd into a hart,
And my desires, like fell and cruel hounds,
E'er since pursue me.

Enter Valentine.

                How now, what news from her?

Valentine.
So please my lord, I might not be admitted,
But from her handmaid do return this answer:
The element itself, till seven years' heat,
Shall not behold her face at ample view;
But like a cloistress she will veiled walk,
And water once a day her chamber round
With eye-offending brine; all this to season
A brother's dead love, which she would keep fresh
And lasting in her sad remembrance.

Orsino.
O, she that hath a heart of that fine frame
To pay this debt of love but to a brother,
How will she love when the rich golden shaft
Hath kill'd the flock of all affections else
That live in her; when liver, brain, and heart,
These sovereign thrones, are all supplied and fill'd

Her sweet perfections with one self king!
Away before me to sweet beds of flow'rs,
Love-thoughts lie rich when canopied with bow'rs.

Exeunt.

Scene 2

The sea coast.

(Viola; Captain; Sailors)

Shipwrecked, Viola lands on the coast of Illyria, along with the Captain of the ship that went down and some other sailors. She hopes against hope that her brother has not drowned either, and the Captain comforts her by telling her that she saw her brother holding on to a mast. She questions him about the country; as he was born nearby, he is able to tell her that it is Orsino's land, and that rumor has it he is wooing Olivia. Viola wishes she could serve Olivia when she hears how the Countess lives in retreat, but the Captain tells her that would be impossible, as Olivia is receiving no one. She resolves instead to serve Orsino and pays the Captain to help her disguise herself as a eunuch.

Enter Viola, a Captain, and Sailors.

Viola.
What country, friends, is this?

Sea Captain.
This is Illyria, lady.

Viola.
And what should I do in Illyria?
My brother he is in Elysium.
Perchance he is not drown'd—what think you, sailors?

Sea Captain.
It is perchance that you yourself were saved.

Viola.
O my poor brother! And so perchance may he be.

Sea Captain.
True, madam, and to comfort you with chance,
Assure yourself, after our ship did split,
When you, and those poor number saved with you,
Hung on our driving boat, I saw your brother,
Most provident in peril, bind himself
(Courage and hope both teaching him the practice)
To a strong mast that liv'd upon the sea;
Where like Arion on the dolphin's back,
I saw him hold acquaintance with the waves
So long as I could see.

Viola.
For saying so, there's gold.
Mine own escape unfoldeth to my hope,
Whereto thy speech serves for authority,
The like of him. Know'st thou this country?

Sea Captain.
Ay, madam, well, for I was bred and born
Not three hours' travel from this very place.

Viola.
Who governs here?

Sea Captain.
A noble duke, in nature as in name.

Viola.
What is his name?

Sea Captain.
Orsino.

Viola.
Orsino! I have heard my father name him. He was a bachelor then.

Sea Captain.
And so is now, or was so very late;
For but a month ago I went from hence,
And then 'twas fresh in murmur (as you know
What great ones do, the less will prattle of)
That he did seek the love of fair Olivia.

Viola.
What's she?

Sea Captain.
A virtuous maid, the daughter of a count
That died some twelvemonth since, then leaving her
In the protection of his son, her brother,
Who shortly also died; for whose dear love,
They say, she hath abjur'd the company
And sight of men.

Viola.
                    O that I serv'd that lady,
And might not be delivered to the world
Till I had made mine own occasion mellow
What my estate is!

Sea Captain.
                That were hard to compass,
Because she will admit no kind of suit,
No, not the Duke's.

Viola.
There is a fair behavior in thee, captain,
And though that nature with a beauteous wall
Doth oft close in pollution, yet of thee
I will believe thou hast a mind that suits
With this thy fair and outward character.
I prithee (and I'll pay thee bounteously)
Conceal me what I am, and be my aid
For such disguise as haply shall become
The form of my intent. I'll serve this duke;
Thou shalt present me as an eunuch to him,
It may be worth thy pains; for I can sing
And speak to him in many sorts of music
That will allow me very worth his service.
What else may hap, to time I will commit,
Only shape thou thy silence to my wit.

Sea Captain.
Be you his eunuch, and your mute I'll be;
When my tongue blabs, then let mine eyes not see.

Viola.
I thank thee. Lead me on.

Exeunt.

Scene 3

A room in Olivia's house.

(Sir Toby Belch; Maria; Sir Andrew Aguecheek)

Olivia's debauched uncle Sir Toby chats with her gentlewoman Maria, who tries to convince him to be a bit less rowdy. Sir Toby cannot understand why Olivia is moaning so much about her brother. They discuss Sir Andrew Aguecheek, a foolish suitor for Olivia's hand whom Sir Toby keeps around to milk of his money. Sir Toby praises his accomplishments while Maria points out his foolishness. Sir Andrew enters and quickly proves Maria's opinion of him correct. Still, he has sense enough to suspect that Olivia will have nothing to do with him, and proposes returning home the next day. Sir Toby convinces him to stay a month longer, promising to help him, and Sir Toby therefore gets to keep his moneybags close for that much longer. He has Sir Andrew practice his dancing.

Enter Sir Toby Belch and Maria.

Sir Toby Belch.
What a plague means my niece to take the death of her brother thus? I am sure care's an enemy to life.

Maria.
By my troth, Sir Toby, you must come in earlier a' nights. Your cousin, my lady, takes great exceptions to your ill hours.

Sir Toby Belch.
Why, let her except before excepted.

Maria.
Ay, but you must confine yourself within the modest limits of order.

Sir Toby Belch.
Confine? I'll confine myself no finer than I am. These clothes are good enough to drink in, and so be these boots too; and they be not, let them hang themselves in their own straps.

Maria.
That quaffing and drinking will undo you. I heard my lady talk of it yesterday; and of a foolish knight that you brought in one night here to be her wooer.

Sir Toby Belch.
Who, Sir Andrew Aguecheek?

Maria.
Ay, he.

Sir Toby Belch.
He's as tall a man as any's in Illyria.

Maria.
What's that to th' purpose?

Sir Toby Belch.
Why, he has three thousand ducats a year.

Maria.
Ay, but he'll have but a year in all these ducats. He's a very fool and a prodigal.

Sir Toby Belch.
Fie, that you'll say so! He plays o' th' viol-de-gamboys, and speaks three or four languages word for word without book, and hath all the good gifts of nature.

Maria.
He hath indeed, almost natural; for besides that he's a fool, he's a great quarreler; and but that he hath the gift of a coward to allay the gust he hath in quarreling, 'tis thought among the prudent he would quickly have the gift of a grave.

Sir Toby Belch.
By this hand, they are scoundrels and sub-stractors that say so of him. Who are they?

Maria.
They that add moreov'r, he's drunk nightly in your company.

Sir Toby Belch.
With drinking healths to my niece. I'll drink to her as long as there is a passage in my throat, and drink in Illyria. He's a coward and a coystrill that will not drink to my niece till his brains turn o' th' toe like a parish-top. What, wench! Castiliano vulgo! For here comes Sir Andrew Agueface.

Enter Sir Andrew Aguecheek.

Sir Andrew Aguecheek.
Sir Toby Belch! How now, Sir Toby Belch?

Sir Toby Belch.
Sweet Sir Andrew!

Sir Andrew Aguecheek.
Bless you, fair shrew.

Maria.
And you too, sir.

Sir Toby Belch.
Accost, Sir Andrew, accost.

Sir Andrew Aguecheek.
What's that?

Sir Toby Belch.
My niece's chambermaid.

Sir Andrew Aguecheek.
Good Mistress Accost, I desire better acquaintance.

Maria.
My name is Mary, sir.

Sir Andrew Aguecheek.
Good Mistress Mary Accost—

Sir Toby Belch.
You mistake, knight. "Accost" is front her, board her, woo her, assail her.

Sir Andrew Aguecheek.
By my troth, I would not undertake her in this company. Is that the meaning of "accost"?

Maria.
Fare you well, gentlemen.

Sir Toby Belch.
And thou let part so, Sir Andrew, would thou mightst never draw sword again.

Sir Andrew Aguecheek.
And you part so, mistress, I would I might never draw sword again. Fair lady, do you think you have fools in hand?

Maria.
Sir, I have not you by th' hand.

Sir Andrew Aguecheek.
Marry, but you shall have—and here's my hand.

Maria.
Now, sir, thought is free. I pray you bring your hand to th' butt'ry-bar, and let it drink.

Sir Andrew Aguecheek.
Wherefore, sweetheart? What's your metaphor?

Maria.
It's dry, sir.

Sir Andrew Aguecheek.
Why, I think so. I am not such an ass but I can keep my hand dry. But what's your jest?

Maria.
A dry jest, sir.

Sir Andrew Aguecheek.
Are you full of them?

Maria.
Ay, sir, I have them at my fingers' ends. Marry, now I let go your hand, I am barren.

Exit Maria.

Sir Toby Belch.
O knight, thou lack'st a cup of canary. When did I see thee so put down?

Sir Andrew Aguecheek.
Never in your life I think, unless you see canary put me down. Methinks sometimes I have no more wit than a Christian or an ordinary man has; but I am a great eater of beef, and I believe that does harm to my wit.

Sir Toby Belch.
No question.

Sir Andrew Aguecheek.
And I thought that, I'd forswear it. I'll ride home tomorrow, Sir Toby.

Sir Toby Belch.
Pourquoi, my dear knight?

Sir Andrew Aguecheek.
What is "pourquoi"? Do, or not do? I would I had bestow'd that time in the tongues that I have in fencing, dancing, and bear-baiting. O had I but follow'd the arts!

Sir Toby Belch.
Then hadst thou had an excellent head of hair.

Sir Andrew Aguecheek.
Why, would that have mended my hair?

Sir Toby Belch.
Past question, for thou seest it will not curl by nature.

Sir Andrew Aguecheek.
But it becomes me well enough, does't not?

Sir Toby Belch.
Excellent, it hangs like flax on a distaff; and I hope to see a huswife take thee between her legs, and spin it off.

Sir Andrew Aguecheek.
Faith, I'll home tomorrow, Sir Toby. Your niece will not be seen, or if she be, it's four to one she'll none of me. The Count himself here hard by woos her.

Sir Toby Belch.
She'll none o' th' Count. She'll not match above her degree, neither in estate, years, nor wit; I have heard her swear't. Tut, there's life in't, man.

Sir Andrew Aguecheek.
I'll stay a month longer. I am a fellow o' th' strangest mind i' th' world; I delight in masques and revels sometimes altogether.

Sir Toby Belch.
Art thou good at these kickshawses, knight?

Sir Andrew Aguecheek.
As any man in Illyria, whatsoever he be, under the degree of my betters, and yet I will not compare with an old man.

Sir Toby Belch.
What is thy excellence in a galliard, knight?

Sir Andrew Aguecheek.
Faith, I can cut a caper.

Sir Toby Belch.
And I can cut the mutton to't.

Sir Andrew Aguecheek.
And I think I have the back-trick simply as strong as any man in Illyria.

Sir Toby Belch.
Wherefore are these things hid? Wherefore have these gifts a curtain before 'em? Are they like to take dust, like Mistress Mall's picture? Why dost thou not go to church in a galliard, and come home in a coranto? My very walk should be a jig.
I would not so much as make water but in a sink-a-pace. What dost thou mean? Is it a world to hide virtues in? I did think by the excellent constitution of thy leg, it was form'd under the star of a galliard.

Sir Andrew Aguecheek.
Ay, 'tis strong; and it does indifferent well in a dun-color'd stock. Shall we set about some revels?

Sir Toby Belch.
What shall we do else? Were we not born under Taurus?

Sir Andrew Aguecheek.
Taurus? That's sides and heart.

Sir Toby Belch.
No, sir, it is legs and thighs. Let me see thee caper. Ha, higher! Ha, ha, excellent!

Exeunt.

Scene 4

A room in Duke Orsino's palace.

(Valentine; Viola; Duke; Curio; Attendants)

Viola, dressed as a youth and calling herself Cesario, has become a favorite servant of Orsino's. He sends her to woo Olivia for him. She promises to do her best, though to herself she admits the task will be difficult, as she is herself in love with Orsino.

Enter Valentine, and Viola in man's attire.

Valentine.
If the Duke continue these favors towards you, Cesario, you are like to be much advanc'd; he hath known you but three days, and already you are no stranger.

Viola.
You either fear his humor or my negligence, that you call in question the continuance of his love. Is he inconstant, sir, in his favors?

Valentine.
No, believe me.

Enter Duke, Curio, and Attendants.

Viola.
I thank you. Here comes the Count.

Orsino.
Who saw Cesario, ho?

Viola.
On your attendance, my lord, here.

Orsino.
Stand you awhile aloof. Cesario,
Thou know'st no less but all. I have unclasp'd
To thee the book even of my secret soul.
Therefore, good youth, address thy gait unto her,
Be not denied access, stand at her doors,
And tell them, there thy fixed foot shall grow
Till thou have audience.

Viola.
               Sure, my noble lord,
If she be so abandon'd to her sorrow
As it is spoke, she never will admit me.

Orsino.
Be clamorous, and leap all civil bounds,
Rather than make unprofited return.

Viola.
Say I do speak with her, my lord, what then?

Orsino.
O then, unfold the passion of my love,
Surprise her with discourse of my dear faith;
It shall become thee well to act my woes:
She will attend it better in thy youth
Than in a nuntio's of more grave aspect.

Viola.
I think not so, my lord.

Orsino.
               Dear lad, believe it;
For they shall yet belie thy happy years,
That say thou art a man. Diana's lip
Is not more smooth and rubious; thy small pipe
Is as the maiden's organ, shrill and sound,
And all is semblative a woman's part.
I know thy constellation is right apt
For this affair. Some four or five attend him—
All, if you will; for I myself am best
When least in company. Prosper well in this,
And thou shalt live as freely as thy lord,
To call his fortunes thine.

Viola.
               I'll do my best
To woo your lady.

Aside.

               Yet a barful strife!
Whoe'er I woo, myself would be his wife.

Exeunt.

Scene 5

A room in Olivia's house.

(Maria; Clown Feste; Lady Olivia; Malvolio; Attendants; Sir Toby; Viola)

Feste the jester has returned after a long absence and Maria refuses to help him get back into Olivia's favor unless he tells her where he's been. He gets himself out of the dilemma by use of his wit. Olivia and her steward Malvolio pass by, and Feste salutes her. She orders that the fool be taken away, and he quickly turns the order on its head, ordering that she be taken away. He unarguably proves that Olivia is herself a fool, in a

Act 1, Scene 5

manner clever enough that Olivia is mollified, though Malvolio expresses his distaste at the fact that she enjoys the chatter of a jester, but Olivia warns him that he is too conceited for his own good. Maria announces a young man, probably from Orsino, who refuses to go away without seeing Olivia. The Countess sends Malvolio to deal with it. Toby passes through, half-drunk though it is the middle of the day. Malvolio returns to report that the young man absolutely refuses to leave unless he speaks to Olivia. The Countess decides to receive him, throwing on a veil. Viola comes in, still as Cesario. She begins to recite her set speech, but interrupts herself, and soon departs from her official text and starts to improvise. Olivia admits she knows nothing to Orsino's detriment, but that she still isn't in love with him. Viola woos passionately, as if she were courting Orsino, and Olivia finds herself rather taken with the youth. While still insisting that she'll never be able to respond to Orsino as he wishes, she makes it clear that she wouldn't mind seeing Cesario again. As "Cesario" leaves, Olivia realizes that she has fallen for "him" completely and sends Malvolio after "him" with a ring, pretending that "he" left it there.

Enter Maria and Clown Feste.

Maria.
Nay, either tell me where thou hast been, or I will not open my lips so wide as a bristle may enter, in way of thy excuse. My lady will hang thee for thy absence.

Feste.
Let her hang me! He that is well hang'd in this world needs to fear no colors.

Maria.
Make that good.

Feste.
He shall see none to fear.

Maria.
A good lenten answer. I can tell thee where that saying was born, of "I fear no colors."

Feste.
Where, good Mistress Mary?

Maria.
In the wars, and that may you be bold to say in your foolery.

Feste.
Well, God give them wisdom that have it; and those that are fools, let them use their talents.

Maria.
Yet you will be hang'd for being so long absent, or to be turn'd away—is not that as good as a hanging to you?

Feste.
Many a good hanging prevents a bad marriage; and for turning away, let summer bear it out.

Maria.
You are resolute then?

Feste.
Not so, neither, but I am resolv'd on two points—

Maria.
That if one break, the other will hold; or if both break, your gaskins fall.

Feste.
Apt, in good faith, very apt. Well, go thy way, if Sir Toby would leave drinking, thou wert as witty a piece of Eve's flesh as any in Illyria.

Maria.
Peace, you rogue, no more o' that. Here comes my lady. Make your excuse wisely, you were best.

Exit.
Enter Lady Olivia with Malvolio and Attendants.

Feste.
Wit, and't be thy will, put me into good fooling! Those wits that think they have thee do very oft prove fools; and I that am sure I lack thee, may pass for a wise man. For what says Quinapalus? "Better a witty fool than a foolish wit."—God bless thee, lady!

Olivia.
Take the fool away.

Feste.
Do you not hear, fellows? Take away the lady.

Olivia.
Go to, y' are a dry fool; I'll no more of you. Besides, you grow dishonest.

Feste.
Two faults, madonna, that drink and good counsel will amend; for give the dry fool drink, then is the fool not dry; bid the dishonest man mend himself: if he mend, he is no longer dishonest; if he cannot, let the botcher mend him. Any thing that's mended is but patch'd; virtue that transgresses is but patch'd with sin, and sin that amends is but patch'd with virtue. If that this simple syllogism will serve, so; if it will not, what remedy? As there is no true cuckold but calamity, so beauty's a flower. The lady bade take away the fool, therefore I say again, take her away.

Olivia.
Sir, I bade them take away you.

Feste.
Misprision in the highest degree! Lady, "Cucullus non facit monachum": that's as much to say as I wear not motley in my brain. Good madonna, give me leave to prove you a fool.

Olivia.
Can you do it?

Feste.
Dexteriously, good madonna.

Olivia.
Make your proof.

Feste.
I must catechize you for it, madonna. Good my mouse of virtue, answer me.

Olivia.
Well, sir, for want of other idleness, I'll bide your proof.

Feste.
Good madonna, why mourn'st thou?

Olivia.
Good fool, for my brother's death.

Feste.
I think his soul is in hell, madonna.

Olivia.
I know his soul is in heaven, fool.

Feste.
The more fool, madonna, to mourn for your brother's soul, being in heaven. Take away the fool, gentlemen.

Olivia.
What think you of this fool, Malvolio? Doth he not mend?

Malvolio.
Yes, and shall do till the pangs of death shake him. Infirmity, that decays the wise, doth ever make the better fool.

Feste.
God send you, sir, a speedy infirmity, for the better increasing your folly! Sir Toby will be sworn that I am no fox, but he will not pass his word for twopence that you are no fool.

Olivia.
How say you to that, Malvolio?

Malvolio.
I marvel your ladyship takes delight in such a barren rascal. I saw him put down the other day with an ordinary fool that has no more brain than a stone. Look you now, he's out of his guard already. Unless you laugh and minister occasion to him, he is gagg'd. I protest I take these wise men that crow so at these set kind of fools no better than the fools' zanies.

Olivia.
O, you are sick of self-love, Malvolio, and taste with a distemper'd appetite. To be generous, guiltless, and of free disposition, is to take those things for bird-bolts that you deem cannon-bullets. There is no slander in an allow'd fool, though he do nothing but rail; nor no railing in a known discreet man, though he do nothing but reprove.

Feste.
Now Mercury indue thee with leasing, for thou speak'st well of fools!

Enter Maria.

Maria.
Madam, there is at the gate a young gentleman much desires to speak with you.

Olivia.
From the Count Orsino, is it?

Maria.
I know not, madam. 'Tis a fair young man, and well attended.

Olivia.
Who of my people hold him in delay?

Maria.
Sir Toby, madam, your kinsman.

Olivia.
Fetch him off, I pray you, he speaks nothing but madman; fie on him!

Exit Maria.

Go you, Malvolio; if it be a suit from the Count, I am sick, or not at home—what you will, to dismiss it.

Exit Malvolio.

Now you see, sir, how your fooling grows old, and people dislike it.

Feste.
Thou hast spoke for us, madonna, as if thy eldest son should be a fool; whose skull Jove cram with brains! For—here he comes—

Enter Sir Toby.

One of thy kin has a most weak pia mater.

Olivia.
By mine honor, half drunk. What is he at the gate, cousin?

Sir Toby Belch.
A gentleman.

Olivia.
A gentleman? What gentleman?

Sir Toby Belch.
'Tis a gentleman here—a plague o' these pickle-herring! How now, sot?

Feste.
Good Sir Toby!

Olivia.
Cousin, cousin, how have you come so early by this lethargy?

Sir Toby Belch.
Lechery! I defy lechery. There's one at the gate.

Olivia.
Ay, marry, what is he?

Sir Toby Belch.
Let him be the devil and he will, I care not; give me faith say I. Well, it's all one.

Exit.

Olivia.
What's a drunken man like, fool?

Feste.
Like a drown'd man, a fool, and a madman. One draught above heat makes him a fool, the second mads him, and a third drowns him.

Olivia.
Go thou and seek the crowner, and let him sit o' my coz; for he's in the third degree of drink, he's drown'd. Go look after him.

Feste.
He is but mad yet, madonna, and the fool shall look to the madman.

Exit.
Enter Malvolio.

Malvolio.
Madam, yond young fellow swears he will speak with you. I told him you were sick; he takes on him to understand so much, and therefore comes to speak with you. I told him you were asleep; he seems to have a foreknowledge of that too, and therefore comes to speak with you. What is to be said to him, lady? He's fortified against any denial.

Olivia.
Tell him he shall not speak with me.

Malvolio.
H'as been told so; and he says he'll stand at your door like a sheriff's post, and be the supporter to a bench, but he'll speak with you.

Olivia.
What kind o' man is he?

Malvolio.
Why, of mankind.

Olivia.
What manner of man?

Malvolio.
Of very ill manner: he'll speak with you, will you or no.

Olivia.
Of what personage and years is he?

Malvolio.
Not yet old enough for a man, nor young enough for a boy; as a squash is before 'tis a peas-cod, or a codling when 'tis almost an apple. 'Tis with him in standing water, between boy and man. He is very well-favor'd, and he speaks very shrewishly. One would think his mother's milk were scarce out of him.

Olivia.
Let him approach. Call in my gentlewoman.

Malvolio.
Gentlewoman, my lady calls.

Exit.
Enter Maria.

Olivia.
Give me my veil; come throw it o'er my face. We'll once more hear Orsino's embassy.

Enter Viola.

Viola.
The honorable lady of the house, which is she?

Olivia.
Speak to me, I shall answer for her. Your will?

Viola.
Most radiant, exquisite, and unmatchable beauty—I pray you tell me if this be the lady of the house, for I never saw her. I would be loath to cast away my speech; for besides that it is excellently well penn'd, I have taken great pains to con it. Good beauties, let me sustain no scorn; I am very comptible, even to the least sinister usage.

Olivia.
Whence came you, sir?

Viola.
I can say little more than I have studied, and that question's out of my part. Good gentle one, give me modest assurance if you be the lady of the house, that I may proceed in my speech.

Olivia.
Are you a comedian?

Viola.
No, my profound heart; and yet (by the very fangs of malice I swear) I am not that I play. Are you the lady of the house?

Olivia.
If I do not usurp myself, I am.

Viola.
Most certain, if you are she, you do usurp yourself; for what is yours to bestow is not yours to reserve. But this is from my commission; I will on with my speech in your praise, and then show you the heart of my message.

Olivia.
Come to what is important in't. I forgive you the praise.

Viola.
Alas, I took great pains to study it, and 'tis poetical.

Olivia.
It is the more like to be feign'd, I pray you keep it in. I heard you were saucy at my gates, and allow'd your approach rather to wonder at you than to hear you. If you be not mad, be gone. If you have reason, be brief. 'Tis not that time of moon with me to make one in so skipping a dialogue.

Maria.
Will you hoist sail, sir? Here lies your way.

Viola.
No, good swabber, I am to hull here a little longer. Some mollification for your giant, sweet lady. Tell me your mind—I am a messenger.

Olivia.
Sure you have some hideous matter to deliver, when the courtesy of it is so fearful. Speak your office.

Viola.
It alone concerns your ear. I bring no overture of war, no taxation of homage; I hold the olive in my hand; my words are as full of peace as matter.

Olivia.
Yet you began rudely. What are you? What would you?

Viola.
The rudeness that hath appear'd in me have I learn'd from my entertainment. What I am, and what I would, are as secret as maidenhead: to your ears, divinity; to any other's, profanation.

Olivia.
Give us the place alone, we will hear this divinity.

Exeunt Maria and Attendants.

Now, sir, what is your text?

Viola.
Most sweet lady—

Olivia.
A comfortable doctrine, and much may be said of it. Where lies your text?

Viola.
In Orsino's bosom.

Olivia.
In his bosom? In what chapter of his bosom?

Viola.
To answer by the method, in the first of his heart.

Olivia.
O, I have read it; it is heresy. Have you no more to say?

Viola.
Good madam, let me see your face.

Olivia.
Have you any commission from your lord to negotiate with my face? You are now out of your text; but we will draw the curtain, and show you the picture. Look you, sir, such a one I was this present.

Unveiling.

Is't not well done?

Viola.
Excellently done, if God did all.

Olivia.
'Tis in grain, sir, 'twill endure wind and weather.

Viola.
'Tis beauty truly blent, whose red and white
Nature's own sweet and cunning hand laid on.
Lady, you are the cruell'st she alive
If you will lead these graces to the grave,
And leave the world no copy.

Olivia.
O, sir, I will not be so hard-hearted; I will give out diverse schedules of my beauty. It shall be inventoried, and every particle and utensil labell'd to my will: as, item, two lips, indifferent red; item, two grey eyes, with lids to them; item, one neck, one chin, and so forth. Were you sent hither to praise me?

Viola.
I see you what you are, you are too proud;
But if you were the devil, you are fair.
My lord and master loves you. O, such love
Could be but recompens'd, though you were crown'd
The nonpareil of beauty.

Olivia.
         How does he love me?

Viola.
With adorations, fertile tears,
With groans that thunder love, with sighs of fire.

Olivia.
Your lord does know my mind, I cannot love him,
Yet I suppose him virtuous, know him noble,
Of great estate, of fresh and stainless youth;
In voices well divulg'd, free, learn'd, and valiant,
And in dimension, and the shape of nature,
A gracious person. But yet I cannot love him.
He might have took his answer long ago.

Viola.
If I did love you in my master's flame,
With such a suff'ring, such a deadly life,
In your denial I would find no sense,
I would not understand it.

Olivia.
         Why, what would you?

Viola.
Make me a willow cabin at your gate,
And call upon my soul within the house;
Write loyal cantons of contemned love,
And sing them loud even in the dead of night;
Hallow your name to the reverberate hills,
And make the babbling gossip of the air
Cry out "Olivia!" O, you should not rest
Between the elements of air and earth
But you should pity me!

Olivia.
                       You might do much.
What is your parentage?

Viola.
Above my fortunes, yet my state is well:
I am a gentleman.

Olivia.
                    Get you to your lord.
I cannot love him; let him send no more—
Unless (perchance) you come to me again
To tell me how he takes it. Fare you well.
I thank you for your pains. Spend this for me.

Viola.
I am no fee'd post, lady; keep your purse;
My master, not myself, lacks recompense.
Love make his heart of flint that you shall love,
And let your fervor like my master's be
Plac'd in contempt! Farewell, fair cruelty.

Exit Viola.

Olivia.
"What is your parentage?"
"Above my fortunes, yet my state is well:
I am a gentleman." I'll be sworn thou art;
Thy tongue, thy face, thy limbs, actions, and spirit
Do give thee fivefold blazon. Not too fast! Soft, soft!
Unless the master were the man. How now?
Even so quickly may one catch the plague?
Methinks I feel this youth's perfections
With an invisible and subtle stealth
To creep in at mine eyes. Well, let it be.
What ho, Malvolio!

Enter Malvolio.

Malvolio.
                Here, madam, at your service.

Olivia.
Run after that same peevish messenger,
The County's man. He left this ring behind him,
Would I or not. Tell him I'll none of it.
Desire him not to flatter with his lord,
Nor hold him up with hopes: I am not for him.
If that the youth will come this way tomorrow,
I'll give him reasons for't. Hie thee, Malvolio.

Malvolio.
Madam, I will.

Exit.

Olivia.
I do I know not what, and fear to find
Mine eye too great a flatterer for my mind.
Fate, show thy force: ourselves we do not owe;
What is decreed must be; and be this so.

Exit.

Act 2

Scene 1

The sea coast.

(Antonio; Sebastian)

Viola's brother Sebastian, who was rescued from the shipwreck by the sea captain Antonio, reveals his true identity to his friend and insists on leaving him to search for Viola. Antonio begs him to remain, or at least to let him follow, but Sebastian refuses, not wishing to bring ill luck upon him. Antonio begs further, even offering to be his servant, but Sebastian still says no, and sets off for Orsino's court. Antonio has many enemies in Illyria, but unable to face the thought of losing Sebastian, he follows him there.

Enter Antonio and Sebastian.

Antonio.
Will you stay no longer? Nor will you not that I go with you?

Sebastian.
By your patience, no. My stars shine darkly over me. The malignancy of my fate might perhaps distemper yours; therefore I shall crave of you your leave, that I may bear my evils alone. It were a bad recompense for your love, to lay any of them on you.

Antonio.
Let me yet know of you whither you are bound.

Sebastian.
No, sooth, sir; my determinate voyage is mere extravagancy. But I perceive in you so excellent a touch of modesty, that you will not extort from me what I am willing to keep in; therefore it charges me in manners

the rather to express myself. You must know of me then, Antonio, my name is Sebastian, which I call'd Rodorigo; my father was that Sebastian of Messaline, whom I know you have heard of. He left behind him myself and a sister, both born in an hour. If the heavens had been pleas'd, would we had so ended! But you, sir, alter'd that, for some hour before you took me from the breach of the sea was my sister drown'd.

Antonio.
Alas the day!

Sebastian.
A lady, sir, though it was said she much resembled me, was yet of many accounted beautiful; but though I could not with such estimable wonder overfar believe that, yet thus far I will boldly publish her: she bore a mind that envy could not but call fair. She is drown'd already, sir, with salt water, though I seem to drown her remembrance again with more.

Antonio.
Pardon me, sir, your bad entertainment.

Sebastian.
O good Antonio, forgive me your trouble.

Antonio.
If you will not murder me for my love, let me be your servant.

Sebastian.
If you will not undo what you have done, that is, kill him whom you have recover'd, desire it not. Fare ye well at once; my bosom is full of kindness, and I am yet so near the manners of my mother, that upon the least occasion more mine eyes will tell tales of me. I am bound to the Count Orsino's court. Farewell.

Exit.

Antonio.
The gentleness of all the gods go with thee!
I have many enemies in Orsino's court,
Else would I very shortly see thee there.
But come what may, I do adore thee so
That danger shall seem sport, and I will go.

Exit.

Scene 2

Illyria. A street.

(Viola; Malvolio)

Malvolio catches up to Viola and hands her the ring Olivia gave him. Viola protests that she left no ring with Olivia, but Malvolio insists, and drops the ring in the dirt for her to pick up. Left alone, Viola considers the situation and suddenly realizes that the only explanation for Olivia's actions is that she's fallen in love with Cesario. Which is a bit of a problem, since Cesario is in fact Viola, who is in love with Orsino, on whose behalf she/he is wooing Olivia. Viola can think of no solution but to let time take care of things.

Enter Viola and Malvolio at several doors.

Malvolio.
Were you not ev'n now with the Countess Olivia?

Viola.
Even now, sir; on a moderate pace I have since arriv'd but hither.

Malvolio.
She returns this ring to you, sir. You might have sav'd me my pains, to have taken it away yourself. She adds moreover, that you should put your lord into a desperate assurance she will none of him. And one thing more, that you be never so hardy to come again in his affairs, unless it be to report your lord's taking of this. Receive it so.

Viola.
She took the ring of me, I'll none of it.

Malvolio.
Come, sir, you peevishly threw it to her; and her will is, it should be so return'd. If it be worth stooping for, there it lies, in your eye; if not, be it his that finds it.

Exit.

Viola.
I left no ring with her. What means this lady?
Fortune forbid my outside have not charm'd her!
She made good view of me; indeed so much
That methought her eyes had lost her tongue,
For she did speak in starts distractedly.
She loves me sure, the cunning of her passion
Invites me in this churlish messenger.
None of my lord's ring? Why, he sent her none.
I am the man! If it be so, as 'tis,
Poor lady, she were better love a dream.
Disguise, I see thou art a wickedness

Wherein the pregnant enemy does much.
How easy is it for the proper-false
In women's waxen hearts to set their forms!
Alas, our frailty is the cause, not we,
For such as we are made of, such we be.
How will this fadge? My master loves her dearly,
And I (poor monster) fond as much on him;
And she (mistaken) seems to dote on me.
What will become of this? As I am man,
My state is desperate for my master's love;
As I am woman (now alas the day!),
What thriftless sighs shall poor Olivia breathe!
O time, thou must untangle this, not I,
It is too hard a knot for me t' untie.

Exit.

Scene 3

A room in Olivia's house.

(*Sir Toby; Sir Andrew; Clown; Maria; Malvolio*)

Sir Toby and Sir Andrew sneak back in well after midnight on a night of drinking. Toby calls for Maria to bring them more wine. Feste joins them and the three begin to have a merry time. Toby is soon paying Feste to sing for them. Soon they are all drunkenly singing together. Maria comes in to warn them to quiet down, as they have probably woken Olivia by now, and she will have called up Malvolio. They pay absolutely no attention. Malvolio storms in to demand peace and quiet on Olivia's behalf, and threatens to have Toby kicked out of the house if he doesn't mend his ways. Toby reminds him that he is only a servant, and he takes it out on Maria, threatening to tell Olivia that Maria aids and abets Sir Toby and his company. He leaves in a huff. They decide to revenge themselves on him, using his own self-importance against him. Maria, whose handwriting looks a great deal like Olivia's, plans to con him into thinking that the Countess is in love with him, and thereby to make him act like a fool. She leaves as Sir Toby and Sir Andrew admire her. Toby tells Andrew that he'll need to send for more money; Andrew is a little worried, as if he does not win Olivia's hand he will have spent a huge amount on nothing. But Toby reassures him on that count.

Enter Sir Toby and Sir Andrew.

Sir Toby Belch.
Approach, Sir Andrew. Not to be a-bed after midnight is to be up betimes, and "deliculo surgere," thou know'st—

Sir Andrew Aguecheek.
Nay, by my troth, I know not; but I know, to be up late is to be up late.

Sir Toby Belch.
A false conclusion. I hate it as an unfill'd can. To be up after midnight and to go to bed then, is early; so that to go to bed after midnight is to go to bed betimes. Does not our lives consist of the four elements?

Sir Andrew Aguecheek.
Faith, so they say, but I think it rather consists of eating and drinking.

Sir Toby Belch.
Th' art a scholar; let us therefore eat and drink. Marian, I say, a stoup of wine!

Enter Clown.

Sir Andrew Aguecheek.
Here comes the fool, i' faith.

Feste.
How now, my hearts? Did you never see the picture of "we three"?

Sir Toby Belch.
Welcome, ass. Now let's have a catch.

Sir Andrew Aguecheek.
By my troth, the fool has an excellent breast. I had rather than forty shillings I had such a leg, and so sweet a breath to sing, as the fool has. In sooth, thou wast in very gracious fooling last night, when thou spok'st of Pigrogromitus, of the Vapians passing the equinoctial of Queubus. 'Twas very good, i' faith. I sent thee sixpence for thy leman; hadst it?

Feste.
I did impeticos thy gratillity; for Malvolio's nose is no whipstock. My lady has a white hand, and the Mermidons are no bottle-ale houses.

Sir Andrew Aguecheek.
Excellent! Why, this is the best fooling, when all is done. Now a song.

Sir Toby Belch.
Come on, there is sixpence for you. Let's have a song.

Sir Andrew Aguecheek.
There's a testril of me too. If one knight give a—

Feste.
Would you have a love-song, or a song of good life?

Sir Toby Belch.
A love-song, a love-song.

Sir Andrew Aguecheek.
Ay, ay. I care not for good life.

Feste.

Sings.

O mistress mine, where are you roaming?
O, stay and hear, your true-love's coming,
That can sing both high and low.
Trip no further, pretty sweeting;
Journeys end in lovers meeting,
Every wise man's son doth know.

Sir Andrew Aguecheek.
Excellent good, i' faith.

Sir Toby Belch.
Good, good.

Feste.

Sings.

What is love? 'Tis not hereafter;
Present mirth hath present laughter;
What's to come is still unsure.
In delay there lies no plenty,
Then come kiss me sweet and twenty;
Youth's a stuff will not endure.

Sir Andrew Aguecheek.
A mellifluous voice, as I am true knight.

Sir Toby Belch.
A contagious breath.

Sir Andrew Aguecheek.
Very sweet and contagious, i' faith.

Sir Toby Belch.
To hear by the nose, it is dulcet in contagion. But shall we make the welkin dance indeed? Shall we rouse the night-owl in a catch that will draw three souls out of one weaver? Shall we do that?

Sir Andrew Aguecheek.
And you love me, let's do't. I am dog at a catch.

Feste.
By'r lady, sir, and some dogs will catch well.

Sir Andrew Aguecheek.
Most certain. Let our catch be "Thou knave."

Feste.
"Hold thy peace, thou knave," knight? I shall be constrain'd in't to call thee knave, knight.

Sir Andrew Aguecheek.
'Tis not the first time I have constrain'd one to call me knave. Begin, fool. It begins, "Hold thy peace."

Feste.
I shall never begin if I hold my peace.

Sir Andrew Aguecheek.
Good, i' faith. Come, begin.

Catch sung.
Enter Maria.

Maria.
What a caterwauling do you keep here! If my lady have not call'd up her steward Malvolio and bid him turn you out of doors, never trust me.

Sir Toby Belch.
My lady's a Cataian, we are politicians, Malvolio's a Peg-a-Ramsey, and

Sings.

"Three merry men be we."
Am not I consanguineous? Am I not of her blood? Tilly-vally! Lady!

Sings.

"There dwelt a man in Babylon, lady, lady."

Feste.
Beshrew me, the knight's in admirable fooling.

Sir Andrew Aguecheek.
Ay, he does well enough if he be dispos'd, and so do I too. He does it with a better grace, but I do it more natural.

Sir Toby Belch.

Sings.

"O' the twelfth day of December"—

Maria.
For the love o' God, peace!

Enter Malvolio.

Malvolio.
My masters, are you mad? Or what are you? Have you no wit, manners, nor honesty, but to gabble like tinkers at this time of night? Do ye make an alehouse of my lady's house, that ye squeak out your coziers' catches without any mitigation or remorse of voice? Is there no respect of place, persons, nor time in you?

Sir Toby Belch.
We did keep time, sir, in our catches. Sneck up!

Malvolio.
Sir Toby, I must be round with you. My lady bade me tell you, that though she harbors you as her kinsman, she's nothing allied to your disorders. If you can separate yourself and your misdemeanors, you are welcome to the house; if not, and it would please you to take leave of her, she is very willing to bid you farewell.

Sir Toby Belch.

Sings.

"Farewell, dear heart, since I must needs be gone."

Maria.
Nay, good Sir Toby.

Feste.

Sings.

"His eyes do show his days are almost done."

Malvolio.
Is't even so?

Sir Toby Belch.

Sings.

"But I will never die."

Feste.
Sir Toby, there you lie.

Malvolio.
This is much credit to you.

Sir Toby Belch.

Sings.

"Shall I bid him go?"

Feste.

Sings.

"What and if you do?"

Sir Toby Belch.

Sings.

"Shall I bid him go, and spare not?"

Feste.

Sings.

"O no, no, no, no, you dare not."

Sir Toby Belch.

To Clown.

Out o' tune, sir! Ye lie.

To Malvolio.

Art any more than a steward? Dost thou think because thou art virtuous there shall be no more cakes and ale?

Feste.
Yes, by Saint Anne, and ginger shall be hot i' th' mouth too.

Sir Toby Belch.
Th' art i' th' right. Go, sir, rub your chain with crumbs. A stope of wine, Maria!

Malvolio.
Mistress Mary, if you priz'd my lady's favor at any thing more than contempt, you would not give means for this uncivil rule. She shall know of it, by this hand.

Exit.

Maria.
Go shake your ears.

Sir Andrew Aguecheek.
'Twere as good a deed as to drink when a man's a-hungry, to challenge him the field, and then to break promise with him, and make a fool of him.

Sir Toby Belch.
Do't, knight. I'll write thee a challenge, or I'll deliver thy indignation to him by word of mouth.

Maria.
Sweet Sir Toby, be patient for tonight. Since the youth of the Count's was today with my lady, she is much out of quiet. For Monsieur Malvolio, let me alone with him. If I do not gull him into an ayword, and make him a common recreation, do not think I have wit enough to lie straight in my bed. I know I can do it.

Sir Toby Belch.
Possess us, possess us, tell us something of him.

Maria.
Marry, sir, sometimes he is a kind of puritan.

Sir Andrew Aguecheek.
O, if I thought that, I'd beat him like a dog!

Sir Toby Belch.
What, for being a puritan? Thy exquisite reason, dear knight?

Sir Andrew Aguecheek.
I have no exquisite reason for't, but I have reason good enough.

Maria.
The dev'l a puritan that he is, or any thing constantly but a time-pleaser, an affection'd ass, that cons state without book, and utters it by great swarths; the best persuaded of himself, so cramm'd (as he thinks) with excellencies, that it is his grounds of faith that all that look on him love him; and on that vice in him will my revenge find notable cause to work.

Sir Toby Belch.
What wilt thou do?

Maria.
I will drop in his way some obscure epistles of love, wherein by the color of his beard, the shape of his leg, the manner of his gait, the expressure of his eye, forehead, and complexion, he shall find himself most feelingly personated. I can write very like my lady your niece; on a forgotten matter we can hardly make distinction of our hands.

Sir Toby Belch.
Excellent, I smell a device.

Sir Andrew Aguecheek.
I have't in my nose too.

Sir Toby Belch.
He shall think by the letters that thou wilt drop that they come from my niece, and that she's in love with him.

Maria.
My purpose is indeed a horse of that color.

Sir Andrew Aguecheek.
And your horse now would make him an ass.

Maria.
Ass, I doubt not.

Sir Andrew Aguecheek.
O, 'twill be admirable!

Maria.
Sport royal, I warrant you. I know my physic will work with him. I will plant you two, and let the fool make a third, where he shall find the letter; observe his construction of it. For this night, to bed, and dream on the event. Farewell.

Exit.

Sir Toby Belch.
Good night, Penthesilea.

Sir Andrew Aguecheek.
Before me, she's a good wench.

Sir Toby Belch.
She's a beagle true-bred, and one that adores me. What o' that?

Sir Andrew Aguecheek.
I was ador'd once too.

Sir Toby Belch.
Let's to bed, knight. Thou hadst need send for more money.

Sir Andrew Aguecheek.
If I cannot recover your niece, I am a foul way out.

Sir Toby Belch.
Send for money, knight; if thou hast her not i' th' end, call me cut.

Sir Andrew Aguecheek.
If I do not, never trust me, take it how you will.

Sir Toby Belch.
Come, come, I'll go burn some sack, 'tis too late to go to bed now. Come, knight, come, knight.

Exeunt.

Scene 4

A room in Duke Orsino's palace.

(Duke; Viola; Curio; Clown; Attendants)

Orsino calls for yet more music, a song he heard the other day and greatly enjoyed. Its proper singer is Feste, who is hanging around the palace, and he is sent for. In the meantime, Orsino has the music played, and listens to it with Viola. Asking "Cesario" how he likes it, Orsino soon works out that the "young man" is in love. As he questions her, Viola tries to lie as little as possible about who she's in love with. Her description of a woman resembling him amuses Orsino a great deal, and he gives the boy a great deal of advice. Feste comes in and sings the song. Orsino demands that "Cesario" return to plead to Olivia once again. Viola tries to make him see reason, but he refuses to accept that Olivia could refuse him. Orsino also cannot believe that a woman can love as deeply as a man, but Viola contradicts him, telling him of "his sister's" love for a man, in truth talking about her own feelings for Orsino. The Duke sends "him" off all the same.

Enter Duke, Viola, Curio, and others.

Orsino.
Give me some music. Now good morrow, friends.
Now, good Cesario, but that piece of song,
That old and antique song we heard last night;
Methought it did relieve my passion much,
More than light airs and recollected terms
Of these most brisk and giddy-paced times.
Come, but one verse.

Curio.
He is not here, so please your lordship, that should sing it.

Orsino.
Who was it?

Curio.
Feste the jester, my lord, a fool that the Lady Olivia's father took much delight in. He is about the house.

Orsino.
Seek him out, and play the tune the while.

Exit Curio.
Music plays.

Come hither, boy. If ever thou shalt love,
In the sweet pangs of it remember me;
For such as I am, all true lovers are,
Unstaid and skittish in all motions else,
Save in the constant image of the creature
That is belov'd. How dost thou like this tune?

Viola.
It gives a very echo to the seat
Where Love is thron'd.

Orsino.
    Thou dost speak masterly.
My life upon't, young though thou art, thine eye
Hath stay'd upon some favor that it loves.
Hath it not, boy?

Viola.
    A little, by your favor.

Orsino.
What kind of woman is't?

Viola.
    Of your complexion.

Orsino.
She is not worth thee then. What years, i' faith?

Viola.
About your years, my lord.

Orsino.
Too old, by heaven. Let still the woman take
An elder than herself, so wears she to him;
So sways she level in her husband's heart.
For, boy, however we do praise ourselves,
Our fancies are more giddy and unfirm,

Act 2, Scene 4

More longing, wavering, sooner lost and worn,
Than women's are.

Viola.
                I think it well, my lord.

Orsino.
Then let thy love be younger than thyself,
Or thy affection cannot hold the bent;
For women are as roses, whose fair flow'r
Being once display'd, doth fall that very hour.

Viola.
And so they are; alas, that they are so!
To die, even when they to perfection grow!

Enter Curio and Clown.

Orsino.
O fellow, come, the song we had last night.
Mark it, Cesario, it is old and plain.
The spinsters and the knitters in the sun,
And the free maids that weave their thread with bones,
Do use to chaunt it. It is silly sooth,
And dallies with the innocence of love,
Like the old age.

Feste.
Are you ready, sir?

Orsino.
Ay, prithee sing.

Music. The Song

Feste.
Come away, come away, death,
And in sad cypress let me be laid.
Fly away, fly away, breath,
I am slain by a fair cruel maid.
My shroud of white, stuck all with yew,
O, prepare it!
My part of death, no one so true
Did share it.
Not a flower, not a flower sweet
On my black coffin let there be strown.
Not a friend, not a friend greet
My poor corpse, where my bones shall be thrown.
A thousand thousand sighs to save,
Lay me, O, where
Sad true lover never find my grave,
To weep there.

Orsino.
There's for thy pains.

Feste.
No pains, sir, I take pleasure in singing, sir.

Orsino.
I'll pay thy pleasure then.

Feste.
Truly, sir, and pleasure will be paid, one time or another.

Orsino.
Give me now leave to leave thee.

Feste.
Now the melancholy god protect thee, and the tailor make thy doublet of changeable taffeta, for thy mind is a very opal. I would have men of such constancy put to sea, that their business might be every thing and their intent every where, for that's it that always makes a good voyage of nothing. Farewell.

Exit.

Orsino.
Let all the rest give place.

Curio and Attendants retire.

Once more, Cesario,
Get thee to yond same sovereign cruelty,
Tell her, my love, more noble than the world,
Prizes not quantity of dirty lands;
The parts that fortune hath bestow'd upon her,
Tell her, I hold as giddily as fortune;
But 'tis that miracle and queen of gems
That nature pranks her in attracts my soul.

Viola.
But if she cannot love you, sir?

Orsino.
I cannot be so answer'd.

Viola.
                Sooth, but you must.
Say that some lady, as perhaps there is,
Hath for your love as great a pang of heart
As you have for Olivia. You cannot love her;
You tell her so. Must she not then be answer'd?

Orsino.
There is no woman's sides
Can bide the beating of so strong a passion
As love doth give my heart; no woman's heart
So big, to hold so much; they lack retention.
Alas, their love may be call'd appetite,
No motion of the liver, but the palate,
That suffer surfeit, cloyment, and revolt,
But mine is all as hungry as the sea,
And can digest as much. Make no compare
Between that love a woman can bear me
And that I owe Olivia.

Viola.
                    Ay, but I know—

Orsino.
What dost thou know?

Viola.
Too well what love women to men may owe;
In faith, they are as true of heart as we.
My father had a daughter lov'd a man
As it might be perhaps, were I a woman,
I should your lordship.

Orsino.
                And what's her history?

Viola.
A blank, my lord; she never told her love,
But let concealment like a worm i' th' bud
Feed on her damask cheek; she pin'd in thought,
And with a green and yellow melancholy
She sate like Patience on a monument,
Smiling at grief. Was not this love indeed?
We men may say more, swear more, but indeed
Our shows are more than will; for still we prove
Much in our vows, but little in our love.

Orsino.
But died thy sister of her love, my boy?

Viola.
I am all the daughters of my father's house,
And all the brothers too—and yet I know not.
Sir, shall I to this lady?

Orsino.
                    Ay, that's the theme,
To her in haste; give her this jewel; say
My love can give no place, bide no denay.

Exeunt.

Scene 5

Olivia's garden.

(Sir Toby; Sir Andrew; Fabian; Maria; Malvolio)

Sir Toby and Sir Andrew have brought Fabian into the plot against Malvolio. Fabian hates the steward for having put him on Olivia's bad side. Maria enters with the fake letter and leaves it where Malvolio is sure to find it, and the conspirators hide in the hedge to spy on the steward as he arrives. Malvolio enters talking to himself, considering the possibility that he could rise in social status by marrying Olivia, which is not an unheard-of sort of circumstance. Sir Toby is outraged as Malvolio thinks through just how wonderful life would be as a count — particularly the possibility of putting Sir Toby in his place. The steward finds the letter, and, deceived by the handwriting and the seal, takes it upon himself to open it. The message is enigmatic, but Malvolio soon manages to convince himself that it is a love letter from Olivia intended for him. The hidden conspirators mock him soundly as he goes through the letter. Malvolio soon believes that Olivia wishes him to dress in cross-gartered yellow stockings and that he should smile, and runs off to dress that way. Coming forth, the men kneel before Maria in adoration for what she has managed, and she urges them to follow to see the rest, since the style she has suggested Malvolio dress in is one that Olivia particularly detests. At this stage, the men are ready to do anything Maria tells them.

Enter Sir Toby, Sir Andrew, and Fabian.

Sir Toby Belch.
Come thy ways, Signior Fabian.

Fabian.
Nay, I'll come. If I lose a scruple of this sport, let me be boil'd to death with melancholy.

Sir Toby Belch.
Wouldst thou not be glad to have the niggardly rascally sheep-biter come by some notable shame?

Fabian.
I would exult, man. You know he brought me out o' favor with my lady about a bear-baiting here.

Sir Toby Belch.
To anger him we'll have the bear again, and we will fool him black and blue, shall we not, Sir Andrew?

Sir Andrew Aguecheek.
And we do not, it is pity of our lives.

Enter Maria.

Sir Toby Belch.
Here comes the little villain. How now, my metal of India?

Maria.
Get ye all three into the box-tree; Malvolio's coming down this walk. He has been yonder i' the sun practicing behavior to his own shadow this half hour. Observe him, for the love of mockery; for I know this letter will make a contemplative idiot of him. Close, in the name of jesting!

The men hide themselves.

Lie thou there;

Throws down a letter.

for here comes the trout that must be caught with tickling.

Exit.
Enter Malvolio.

Malvolio.
'Tis but fortune, all is fortune. Maria once told me she did affect me, and I have heard herself come thus near, that should she fancy, it should be one of my complexion. Besides, she uses me with a more exalted respect than any one else that follows her. What should I think on't?

Sir Toby Belch.
Here's an overweening rogue!

Fabian.
O, peace! Contemplation makes a rare turkey-cock of him. How he jets under his advanc'd plumes!

Sir Andrew Aguecheek.
'Slight, I could so beat the rogue!

Sir Toby Belch.
Peace, I say!

Malvolio.
To be Count Malvolio!

Sir Toby Belch.
Ah, rogue!

Sir Andrew Aguecheek.
Pistol him, pistol him!

Sir Toby Belch.
Peace, peace!

Malvolio.
There is example for't: the Lady of the Strachy married the yeoman of the wardrobe.

Sir Andrew Aguecheek.
Fie on him, Jezebel!

Fabian.
O, peace! Now he's deeply in. Look how imagination blows him.

Malvolio.
Having been three months married to her, sitting in my state—

Sir Toby Belch.
O, for a stone-bow, to hit him in the eye!

Malvolio.
Calling my officers about me, in my branch'd velvet gown; having come from a day-bed, where I have left Olivia sleeping—

Sir Toby Belch.
Fire and brimstone!

Fabian.
O, peace, peace!

Malvolio.
And then to have the humor of state; and after a demure travel of regard—telling them I know my place as I would they should do theirs—to ask for my kinsman Toby—

Sir Toby Belch.
Bolts and shackles!

Fabian.
O, peace, peace, peace! Now, now.

Malvolio.
Seven of my people, with an obedient start, make out for him. I frown the while, and perchance wind up my watch, or play with my—some rich jewel. Toby approaches; curtsies there to me—

Sir Toby Belch.
Shall this fellow live?

Fabian.
Though our silence be drawn from us with cars, yet peace.

Malvolio.
I extend my hand to him thus, quenching my familiar smile with an austere regard of control—

Sir Toby Belch.
And does not Toby take you a blow o' the lips then?

Malvolio.
Saying, "Cousin Toby, my fortunes, having cast me on your niece, give me this prerogative of speech"—

Sir Toby Belch.
What, what?

Malvolio.
"You must amend your drunkenness."

Sir Toby Belch.
Out, scab!

Fabian.
Nay, patience, or we break the sinews of our plot!

Malvolio.
"Besides, you waste the treasure of your time with a foolish knight"—

Sir Andrew Aguecheek.
That's me, I warrant you.

Malvolio.
"One Sir Andrew"—

Sir Andrew Aguecheek.
I knew 'twas I, for many do call me fool.

Malvolio.
What employment have we here?

Taking up the letter.

Fabian.
Now is the woodcock near the gin.

Sir Toby Belch.
O, peace, and the spirit of humors intimate reading aloud to him!

Malvolio.
By my life, this is my lady's hand. These be her very c's, her u's, and her t's, and thus makes she her great P's. It is, in contempt of question, her hand.

Sir Andrew Aguecheek.
Her c's, her u's, and her t's: why that?

Malvolio.

Reads.

"*To the unknown belov'd, this, and my good wishes*":— Her very phrases! By your leave, wax. Soft! And the impressure her Lucrece, with which she uses to seal. 'Tis my lady. To whom should this be?

Fabian.
This wins him, liver and all.

Malvolio.

Reads.

"*Jove knows I love,
But who?
Lips, do not move;
No man must know.*"
"No man must know." What follows? The numbers alter'd! "No man must know." If this should be thee, Malvolio?

Sir Toby Belch.
Marry, hang thee, brock!

Malvolio.

Reads.

"*I may command where I adore,
But silence, like a Lucrece knife,
With bloodless stroke my heart doth gore;
M.O.A.I. doth sway my life.*"

Fabian.
A fustian riddle!

Sir Toby Belch.
Excellent wench, say I.

Malvolio.
"M.O.A.I. doth sway my life." Nay, but first let me see, let me see, let me see.

Fabian.
What dish a' poison has she dress'd him!

Sir Toby Belch.
And with what wing the staniel checks at it!

Malvolio.
"I may command where I adore." Why, she may command me: I serve her, she is my lady. Why, this is evident to any formal capacity, there is no obstruction in this. And the end—what should that alphabetical position portend? If I could make that resemble something in me! Softly! M.O.A.I.—

Sir Toby Belch.
O ay, make up that. He is now at a cold scent.

Fabian.
Sowter will cry upon't for all this, though it be as rank as a fox.

Malvolio.
M—Malvolio; M—why, that begins my name.

Fabian.
Did not I say he would work it out? The cur is excellent at faults.

Malvolio.
M—but then there is no consonancy in the sequel that suffers under probation: A should follow, but O does.

Fabian.
And O shall end, I hope.

Sir Toby Belch.
Ay, or I'll cudgel him, and make him cry O!

Malvolio.
And then I comes behind.

Fabian.
Ay, and you had any eye behind you, you might see more detraction at your heels than fortunes before you.

Malvolio.
M.O.A.I. This simulation is not as the former; and yet, to crush this a little, it would bow to me, for every one of these letters are in my name. Soft, here follows prose.

Reads.
"If this fall into thy hand, revolve. In my stars I am above thee, but be not afraid of greatness. Some are born great, some achieve greatness, and some have greatness thrust upon 'em. Thy Fates open their hands, let thy blood and spirit embrace them, and to inure thyself to what thou art like to be, cast thy humble slough and appear fresh. Be opposite with a kinsman, surly with servants; let thy tongue tang arguments of state; put thyself into the trick of singularity. She thus advises thee that sighs for thee. Remember who commended thy yellow stockings, and wish'd to see thee ever cross-garter'd: I say, remember. Go to, thou art made if thou desir'st to be so; if not, let me see thee a steward still, the fellow of servants, and not worthy to touch Fortune's fingers. Farewell. She that would alter services with thee,
The Fortunate-Unhappy."
Daylight and champian discovers not more. This is open. I will be proud, I will read politic authors, I will baffle Sir Toby, I will wash off gross acquaintance, I will be point-devise the very man. I do not now fool myself, to let imagination jade me; for every reason excites to this, that my lady loves me. She did commend my yellow stockings of late, she did praise my leg being cross-garter'd, and in this she manifests herself to my love, and with a kind of injunction drives me to these habits of her liking. I thank my stars, I am happy. I will be strange, stout, in yellow stockings, and cross-garter'd, even with the swiftness of putting on. Jove and my stars be prais'd! Here is yet a postscript.

Reads.
"Thou canst not choose but know who I am. If thou entertain'st my love, let it appear in thy smiling; thy smiles become thee well. Therefore in my presence still smile, dear my sweet, I prithee."
Jove, I thank thee. I will smile, I will do every thing that thou wilt have me.

Exit.

Fabian.
I will not give my part of this sport for a pension of thousands to be paid from the Sophy.

Sir Toby Belch.
I could marry this wench for this device—

Sir Andrew Aguecheek.
So could I too.

Sir Toby Belch.
And ask no other dowry with her but such another jest.

Enter Maria.

Sir Andrew Aguecheek.
Nor I neither.

Fabian.
Here comes my noble gull-catcher.

Sir Toby Belch.
Wilt thou set thy foot o' my neck?

Sir Andrew Aguecheek.
Or o' mine either?

Sir Toby Belch.
Shall I play my freedom at tray-trip, and become thy bond-slave?

Sir Andrew Aguecheek.
I' faith, or I either?

Sir Toby Belch.
Why, thou hast put him in such a dream, that when the image of it leaves him he must run mad.

Maria.
Nay, but say true, does it work upon him?

Sir Toby Belch.
Like aqua-vitae with a midwife.

Maria.
If you will then see the fruits of the sport, mark his first approach before my lady. He will come to her in yellow stockings, and 'tis a color she abhors, and cross-garter'd, a fashion she detests; and he will smile upon her, which will now be so unsuitable to her disposition, being addicted to a melancholy as she is, that it cannot but turn him into a notable contempt. If you will see it, follow me.

Sir Toby Belch.
To the gates of Tartar, thou most excellent devil of wit!

Sir Andrew Aguecheek.
I'll make one too.

Exeunt.

Act 3

Scene 1

Olivia's garden.

(Viola; Clown; Sir Toby; Andrew; Olivia; Gentlewoman)

Viola, returning to Olivia's on Orsino's business, runs into Feste, who converses with her until she gives him a coin. As Feste goes to fetch Olivia, Sir Toby and Sir Andrew enter. When Olivia arrives, Sir Andrew takes notes on what "Cesario" says. Olivia asks to be left alone with the messenger (Viola as Cesario), who begins to press Orsino's suit, but Olivia dismisses the Duke from her mind and begins courting "Cesario" herself. Viola tries to escape the subject, but cannot. She can only offer Olivia her pity, and insists that she loves no woman. Olivia begs "him" to come back anyway, in the hopes that she may soften "his" heart.

Enter Viola, and Clown with a tabor.

Viola.
'Save thee, friend, and thy music! Dost thou live by thy tabor?

Feste.
No, sir, I live by the church.

Viola.
Art thou a churchman?

Feste.
No such matter, sir. I do live by the church; for I do live at my house, and my house doth stand by the church.

Viola.
So thou mayst say the king lies by a beggar, if a beggar dwells near him; or the church stands by thy tabor, if thy tabor stand by the church.

Feste.
You have said, sir. To see this age! A sentence is but a chev'ril glove to a good wit. How quickly the wrong side may be turn'd outward!

Viola.
Nay, that's certain. They that dally nicely with words may quickly make them wanton.

Feste.
I would therefore my sister had had no name, sir.

Viola.
Why, man?

Feste.
Why, sir, her name's a word, and to dally with that word might make my sister wanton. But indeed, words are very rascals since bonds disgrac'd them.

Viola.
Thy reason, man?

Feste.
Troth, sir, I can yield you none without words, and words are grown so false, I am loath to prove reason with them.

Viola.
I warrant thou art a merry fellow, and car'st for nothing.

Feste.
Not so, sir, I do care for something; but in my conscience, sir, I do not care for you. If that be to care for nothing, sir, I would it would make you invisible.

Viola.
Art not thou the Lady Olivia's fool?

Feste.
No, indeed, sir, the Lady Olivia has no folly. She will keep no fool, sir, till she be married, and fools are as like husbands as pilchers are to herrings, the husband's the bigger. I am indeed not her fool, but her corrupter of words.

Viola.
I saw thee late at the Count Orsino's.

Feste.
Foolery, sir, does walk about the orb like the sun, it shines everywhere. I would be sorry, sir, but the fool should be as oft with your master as with my mistress. I think I saw your wisdom there.

Viola.
Nay, and thou pass upon me, I'll no more with thee. Hold, there's expenses for thee.

Feste.
Now Jove, in his next commodity of hair, send thee a beard!

Viola.
By my troth, I'll tell thee, I am almost sick for one—

Aside.

though I would not have it grow on my chin. Is thy lady within?

Feste.
Would not a pair of these have bred, sir?

Viola.
Yes, being kept together, and put to use.

Feste.
I would play Lord Pandarus of Phrygia, sir, to bring a Cressida to this Troilus.

Viola.
I understand you, sir. 'Tis well begg'd.

Feste.
The matter, I hope, is not great, sir—begging but a beggar: Cressida was a beggar. My lady is within, sir. I will conster to them whence you come; who you are, and what you would, are out of my welkin—I might say "element," but the word is overworn.

Exit.

Viola.
This fellow is wise enough to play the fool,
And to do that well craves a kind of wit.
He must observe their mood on whom he jests,
The quality of persons, and the time;
And like the haggard, check at every feather
That comes before his eye. This is a practice
As full of labor as a wise man's art;
For folly that he wisely shows is fit,
But wise men, folly-fall'n, quite taint their wit.

Enter Sir Toby and Andrew.

Sir Toby Belch.
'Save you, gentleman.

Viola.
And you, sir.

Sir Andrew Aguecheek.
Dieu vous garde, monsieur.

Viola.
Et vous aussi; votre serviteur.

Sir Andrew Aguecheek.
I hope, sir, you are, and I am yours.

Sir Toby Belch.
Will you encounter the house? My niece is desirous you should enter, if your trade be to her.

Viola.
I am bound to your niece, sir; I mean she is the list of my voyage.

Sir Toby Belch.
Taste your legs, sir, put them to motion.

Viola.
My legs do better understand me, sir, than I understand what you mean by bidding me taste my legs.

Sir Toby Belch.
I mean, to go, sir, to enter.

Viola.
I will answer you with gait and entrance—but we are prevented.

Enter Olivia and Gentlewoman.

Most excellent accomplish'd lady, the heavens rain odors on you!

Sir Andrew Aguecheek.
That youth's a rare courtier—"rain odors," well.

Viola.
My matter hath no voice, lady, but to your own most pregnant and vouchsafed ear.

Sir Andrew Aguecheek.
"Odors," "pregnant," and "vouchsafed"; I'll get 'em all three all ready.

Olivia.
Let the garden door be shut, and leave me to my hearing.

Exeunt all but Olivia and Viola.

Give me your hand, sir.

Viola.
My duty, madam, and most humble service.

Olivia.
What is your name?

Viola.
Cesario is your servant's name, fair princess.

Olivia.
My servant, sir? 'Twas never merry world
Since lowly feigning was call'd compliment.
Y' are servant to the Count Orsino, youth.

Viola.
And he is yours, and his must needs be yours:
Your servant's servant is your servant, madam.

Olivia.
For him, I think not on him. For his thoughts,
Would they were blanks, rather than fill'd with me.

Viola.
Madam, I come to whet your gentle thoughts
On his behalf.

Olivia.
          O, by your leave, I pray you:
I bade you never speak again of him;
But would you undertake another suit,
I had rather hear you to solicit that
Than music from the spheres.

Viola.
          Dear lady—

Olivia.
Give me leave, beseech you. I did send,
After the last enchantment you did here,
A ring in chase of you; so did I abuse
Myself, my servant, and I fear me you.
Under your hard construction must I sit,
To force that on you in a shameful cunning
Which you knew none of yours. What might you think?
Have you not set mine honor at the stake,
And baited it with all th' unmuzzled thoughts
That tyrannous heart can think? To one of your receiving
Enough is shown; a cypress, not a bosom,
Hides my heart. So let me hear you speak.

Viola.
I pity you.

Olivia.
                    That's a degree to love.

Viola.
No, not a grize; for 'tis a vulgar proof
That very oft we pity enemies.

Olivia.
Why then methinks 'tis time to smile again.
O world, how apt the poor are to be proud!
If one should be a prey, how much the better
To fall before the lion than the wolf!

Clock strikes.

The clock upbraids me with the waste of time.
Be not afraid, good youth, I will not have you,
And yet when wit and youth is come to harvest,
Your wife is like to reap a proper man.
There lies your way, due west.

Viola.
                    Then westward-ho!
Grace and good disposition attend your ladyship!
You'll nothing, madam, to my lord by me?

Olivia.
Stay!
I prithee tell me what thou think'st of me.

Viola.
That you do think you are not what you are.

Olivia.
If I think so, I think the same of you.

Viola.
Then think you right: I am not what I am.

Olivia.
I would you were as I would have you be.

Viola.
Would it be better, madam, than I am?
I wish it might, for now I am your fool.

Olivia.

Aside.

O, what a deal of scorn looks beautiful
In the contempt and anger of his lip!
A murd'rous guilt shows not itself more soon

Than love that would seem hid: love's night is noon.—
Cesario, by the roses of the spring,
By maidhood, honor, truth, and every thing,
I love thee so, that maugre all thy pride,
Nor wit nor reason can my passion hide.
Do not extort thy reasons from this clause,
For that I woo, thou therefore hast no cause;
But rather reason thus with reason fetter:
Love sought is good, but given unsought is better.

Viola.
By innocence I swear, and by my youth,
I have one heart, one bosom, and one truth,
And that no woman has, nor never none
Shall mistress be of it, save I alone.
And so adieu, good madam, never more
Will I my master's tears to you deplore.

Olivia.
Yet come again; for thou perhaps mayst move
That heart which now abhors, to like his love.

Exeunt.

Scene 2

A room in Olivia's house.

(Sir Toby; Sir Andrew; Fabian; Maria)

Sir Andrew is angry and insistent that he will leave, given that the Duke's messenger-boy was better received by Olivia than he ever has been himself. Fabian and Toby, afraid of losing his access to Andrew's money, persuades him that Olivia only acted that way to make him jealous. They convince Andrew that the only honorable thing for him to do is challenge Cesario to a duel. Andrew goes off to write it while Toby and Fabian plan the fun they'll have at the expense of the two, neither of whom appears to be particularly courageous. Maria arrives to tell them that Malvolio has dressed himself up as planned and is doing his best to smile, a sight well-worth seeing.

Enter Sir Toby, Sir Andrew, and Fabian.

Sir Andrew Aguecheek.
No, faith, I'll not stay a jot longer.

Sir Toby Belch.
Thy reason, dear venom, give thy reason.

Fabian.
You must needs yield your reason, Sir Andrew.

Sir Andrew Aguecheek.
Marry, I saw your niece do more favors to the Count's servingman than ever she bestow'd upon me. I saw't i' th' orchard.

Sir Toby Belch.
Did she see thee the while, old boy? Tell me that.

Sir Andrew Aguecheek.
As plain as I see you now.

Fabian.
This was a great argument of love in her toward you.

Sir Andrew Aguecheek.
'Slight! Will you make an ass o' me?

Fabian.
I will prove it legitimate, sir, upon the oaths of judgment and reason.

Sir Toby Belch.
And they have been grand-jurymen since before Noah was a sailor.

Fabian.
She did show favor to the youth in your sight only to exasperate you, to awake your dormouse valor, to put fire in your heart, and brimstone in your liver. You should then have accosted her, and with some excellent jests, fire-new from the mint, you should have bang'd the youth into dumbness. This was look'd for at your hand, and this was balk'd. The double gilt of this opportunity you let time wash off, and you are now sail'd into the north of my lady's opinion, where you will hang like an icicle on a Dutchman's beard, unless you do redeem it by some laudable attempt either of valor or policy.

Sir Andrew Aguecheek.
And't be any way, it must be with valor, for policy I hate. I had as lief be a Brownist as a politician.

Sir Toby Belch.
Why then build me thy fortunes upon the basis of valor. Challenge me the Count's youth to fight with him, hurt him in eleven places—my niece shall take note of it, and assure thyself, there is no love-broker in the world can more prevail in man's commendation with woman than report of valor.

Fabian.
There is no way but this, Sir Andrew.

Sir Andrew Aguecheek.
Will either of you bear me a challenge to him?

Sir Toby Belch.
Go, write it in a martial hand, be curst and brief. It is no matter how witty, so it be eloquent and full of invention. Taunt him with the license of ink. If thou thou'st him some thrice, it shall not be amiss; and as many lies as will lie in thy sheet of paper, although the sheet were big enough for the bed of Ware in England, set 'em down. Go about it. Let there be gall enough in thy ink, though thou write with a goose-pen, no matter. About it.

Sir Andrew Aguecheek.
Where shall I find you?

Sir Toby Belch.
We'll call thee at the cubiculo. Go.

Exit Sir Andrew.

Fabian.
This is a dear manikin to you, Sir Toby.

Sir Toby Belch.
I have been dear to him, lad, some two thousand strong, or so.

Fabian.
We shall have a rare letter from him; but you'll not deliver't?

Sir Toby Belch.
Never trust me then; and by all means stir on the youth to an answer. I think oxen and wain-ropes cannot hale them together. For Andrew, if he were open'd and you find so much blood in his liver as will clog the foot of a flea, I'll eat the rest of th' anatomy.

Fabian.
And his opposite, the youth, bears in his visage no great presage of cruelty.

Enter Maria.

Sir Toby Belch.
Look where the youngest wren of nine comes.

Maria.
If you desire the spleen, and will laugh yourselves into stitches, follow me. Yond gull Malvolio is turn'd heathen, a very renegado; for there is no Christian

that means to be sav'd by believing rightly can ever believe such impossible passages of grossness. He's in yellow stockings.

Sir Toby Belch.
And cross-garter'd?

Maria.
Most villainously; like a pedant that keeps a school i' th' church. I have dogg'd him like his murderer. He does obey every point of the letter that I dropp'd to betray him. He does smile his face into more lines than is in the new map, with the augmentation of the Indies; you have not seen such a thing as 'tis. I can hardly forbear hurling things at him. I know my lady will strike him. If she do, he'll smile, and take't for a great favor.

Sir Toby Belch.
Come bring us, bring us where he is.

Exeunt omnes.

Scene 3

Illyria. A street.

(Sebastian; Antonio)

Antonio has caught up with Sebastian, who cannot help but be grateful. Sebastian suggests that they play tourists and see the sights, but Antonio explains that he is in danger in Illyria due to his having taken part in a sea-battle on the opposite side and doing the Illyrians no little damage. He proposes to arrange for their lodging and to meet up at an inn, the Elephant, later. Antonio gives Sebastian his purse on the off-chance Sebastian sees a trinket he'd like to buy.

Enter Sebastian and Antonio.

Sebastian.
I would not by my will have troubled you,
But since you make your pleasure of your pains,
I will no further chide you.

Antonio.
I could not stay behind you. My desire
(More sharp than filed steel) did spur me forth,
And not all love to see you (though so much
As might have drawn one to a longer voyage)
But jealousy what might befall your travel,
Being skilless in these parts; which to a stranger,
Unguided and unfriended, often prove
Rough and unhospitable. My willing love,
The rather by these arguments of fear,
Set forth in your pursuit.

Sebastian.
              My kind Antonio,
I can no other answer make but thanks,
And thanks; and ever oft good turns
Are shuffled off with such uncurrent pay;
But were my worth as is my conscience firm,
You should find better dealing. What's to do?
Shall we go see the reliques of this town?

Antonio.
Tomorrow, sir; best first go see your lodging.

Sebastian.
I am not weary, and 'tis long to night;
I pray you let us satisfy our eyes
With the memorials and the things of fame
That do renown this city.

Antonio.
              Would you'ld pardon me.
I do not without danger walk these streets.
Once in a sea-fight 'gainst the Count his galleys
I did some service, of such note indeed,
That were I ta'en here, it would scarce be answer'd.

Sebastian.
Belike you slew great number of his people?

Antonio.
Th' offense is not of such a bloody nature,
Albeit the quality of the time and quarrel
Might well have given us bloody argument.
It might have since been answer'd in repaying
What we took from them, which for traffic's sake
Most of our city did. Only myself stood out,
For which if I be lapsed in this place
I shall pay dear.

Sebastian.
              Do not then walk too open.

Antonio.
It doth not fit me. Hold, sir, here's my purse.
In the south suburbs at the Elephant
Is best to lodge. I will bespeak our diet,
Whiles you beguile the time, and feed your knowledge
With viewing of the town. There shall you have me.

Sebastian.
Why I your purse?

Antonio.
Haply your eye shall light upon some toy
You have desire to purchase; and your store
I think is not for idle markets, sir.

Sebastian.
I'll be your purse-bearer, and leave you
For an hour.

Antonio.
To th' Elephant.

Sebastian.
                    I do remember.

Exeunt.

Scene 4

Olivia's garden.

(Olivia; Maria; Malvolio; Servant; Toby; Fabian; Sir Andrew; Viola; Antonio; First Officer; Second Officer)

Olivia is all aflutter over the thought of Cesario's return, and calls for Malvolio in the hopes that his sober demeanor will calm her down. Maria warns her, however, that Malvolio seems to have gone mad. Malvolio enters, grinning and dressed in cross-gartered yellow stockings. Olivia is astounded and a little frightened by his manner and his apparently ludicrous talk. As he quotes the letter to her, she concludes that he is ill, and likely out of his wits. Hearing that "Cesario" has returned, she tells Maria to have Malvolio taken care of by Toby, emphasizing that she does not wish Malvolio harmed. The steward takes this as a sign of favor and believes that she has sent for Toby so that he can be haughty with him, as the letter directed. The three conspirators enter and pretend to believe that he is possessed. Malvolio exits in a cloud of superiority and the trio can hardly believe how well the trick has worked. Toby proposes that they have Malvolio tied up in a dark room, the cure for madmen. At this point Andrew arrives with his ludicrous letter of challenge. Toby takes the letter and promises to deliver it to Cesario, though he has no intention of doing so; the letter is so silly that Toby realizes Cesario will pay it no attention. He decides instead to challenge Cesario on Andrew behalf verbally, and to terrify the lad with reports of Andrew's proficiency in weapons. They see Olivia and "Cesario" approaching and sneak away to wait for the lad to leave to catch him. Olivia is still wooing "Cesario", but Viola insists that the only thing she is asking is for Olivia's love for Orsino. The Countess is disappointed, but still tells "Cesario" to visit again the next day. As Viola prepares to leave, she is confronted by Sir Toby and Fabian, who explain that Sir Andrew is planning to kill "him". She cannot understand what she has done to merit this, and asks to at least be allowed to know what her fault is. As Sir Toby goes to prepare an answer, Fabian frightens her even more with tales of Sir Andrew's fierceness. Sir Toby, meanwhile, is doing the same to Sir Andrew, presenting "Cesario" to himself as a murderous opponent. Both Viola and Sir Andrew ask for a way out of the duel; Sir Toby and Fabian pretend to negotiate between them, but return to say that the other is insistent on fighting. Viola and Sir Andrew unwillingly begin to fight, when Antonio bursts in. Convinced that Viola is Sebastian, he takes up the quarrel with Sir Andrew on "his" behalf. Toby tries to intervene and Antonio threatens him, but they are interrupted by the arrival of two Officers who recognize Antonio and arrest him. Antonio realizes that there is no remedy and asks Viola for his purse. Viola is completely confused, though since she is grateful for Antonio's intervention she offers him the little money she has. Antonio is deeply injured that Sebastian, as he thinks, not only refuses to give back his money but even pretends not to know him. Viola suspects from his words that her brother might be alive. She takes off and Toby pronounces "him" a coward. Sir Andrew, heartened by this, runs after her to start the fight again. Toby and Fabian follow, convinced that it will still produce no results.

Enter Olivia and Maria.

Olivia.

Aside.

I have sent after him; he says he'll come.
How shall I feast him? What bestow of him?
For youth is bought more oft than begg'd or borrow'd.
I speak too loud.—
Where's Malvolio? He is sad and civil,
And suits well for a servant with my fortunes.
Where is Malvolio?

Maria.
He's coming, madam, but in very strange manner. He is sure possess'd, madam.

Olivia.
Why, what's the matter? Does he rave?

Act 3, Scene 4

Maria.
No, madam, he does nothing but smile. Your ladyship were best to have some guard about you, if he come, for sure the man is tainted in 's wits.

Olivia.
Go call him hither.

Enter Malvolio.

I am as mad as he,
If sad and merry madness equal be.
How now, Malvolio?

Malvolio.
Sweet lady, ho, ho.

Olivia.
Smil'st thou? I sent for thee upon a sad occasion.

Malvolio.
Sad, lady? I could be sad. This does make some obstruction in the blood, this cross-gartering, but what of that? If it please the eye of one, it is with me as the very true sonnet is, "Please one, and please all."

Olivia.
Why, how dost thou, man? What is the matter with thee?

Malvolio.
Not black in my mind, though yellow in my legs. It did come to his hands, and commands shall be executed. I think we do know the sweet Roman hand.

Olivia.
Wilt thou go to bed, Malvolio?

Malvolio.
To bed? Ay, sweet heart, and I'll come to thee.

Olivia.
God comfort thee! Why dost thou smile so, and kiss thy hand so oft?

Maria.
How do you, Malvolio?

Malvolio.
At your request! Yes, nightingales answer daws.

Maria.
Why appear you with this ridiculous boldness before my lady?

Malvolio.
"Be not afraid of greatness": 'twas well writ.

Olivia.
What mean'st thou by that, Malvolio?

Malvolio.
"Some are born great"—

Olivia.
Ha?

Malvolio.
"Some achieve greatness"—

Olivia.
What say'st thou?

Malvolio.
"And some have greatness thrust upon them."

Olivia.
Heaven restore thee!

Malvolio.
"Remember who commended thy yellow stockings"—

Olivia.
Thy yellow stockings?

Malvolio.
"And wish'd to see thee cross-garter'd."

Olivia.
Cross-garter'd?

Malvolio.
"Go to, thou art made, if thou desir'st to be so"—

Olivia.
Am I made?

Malvolio.
"If not, let me see thee a servant still."

Olivia.
Why, this is very midsummer madness.

Enter Servant.

Olivia's Servant.
Madam, the young gentleman of the Count Orsino's is return'd. I could hardly entreat him back. He attends your ladyship's pleasure.

Olivia.
I'll come to him.

Exit Servant.

Good Maria, let this fellow be look'd to. Where's my cousin Toby? Let some of my people have a special care of him. I would not have him miscarry for the half of my dowry.

Exit with Maria.

Malvolio.
O ho, do you come near me now? No worse man than Sir Toby to look to me! This concurs directly with the letter: she sends him on purpose, that I may appear stubborn to him; for she incites me to that in the letter. "Cast thy humble slough," says she; "be opposite with a kinsman, surly with servants; let thy tongue tang with arguments of state; put thyself into the trick of singularity"; and consequently sets down the manner how: as a sad face, a reverend carriage, a slow tongue, in the habit of some sir of note, and so forth. I have lim'd her, but it is Jove's doing, and Jove make me thankful! And when she went away now, "Let this fellow be look'd to"; "fellow"! Not "Malvolio," nor after my degree, but "fellow." Why, every thing adheres together, that no dram of a scruple, no scruple of a scruple, no obstacle, no incredulous or unsafe circumstance—What can be said? Nothing that can be can come between me and the full prospect of my hopes. Well, Jove, not I, is the doer of this, and he is to be thank'd.

Enter Toby, Fabian, and Maria.

Sir Toby Belch.
Which way is he, in the name of sanctity? If all the devils of hell be drawn in little, and Legion himself possess'd him, yet I'll speak to him.

Fabian.
Here he is, here he is. How is't with you, sir?

Sir Toby Belch.
How is't with you, man?

Malvolio.
Go off, I discard you. Let me enjoy my private. Go off.

Maria.
Lo, how hollow the fiend speaks within him! Did not I tell you? Sir Toby, my lady prays you to have a care of him.

Malvolio.
Ah ha, does she so?

Sir Toby Belch.
Go to, go to; peace, peace, we must deal gently with him. Let me alone. How do you, Malvolio? How is't with you? What, man, defy the devil! Consider, he's an enemy to mankind.

Malvolio.
Do you know what you say?

Maria.
La you, and you speak ill of the devil, how he takes it at heart! Pray God he be not bewitch'd!

Fabian.
Carry his water to th' wise woman.

Maria.
Marry, and it shall be done tomorrow morning if I live. My lady would not lose him for more than I'll say.

Malvolio.
How now, mistress?

Maria.
O Lord!

Sir Toby Belch.
Prithee hold thy peace, this is not the way. Do you not see you move him? Let me alone with him.

Fabian.
No way but gentleness, gently, gently. The fiend is rough, and will not be roughly us'd.

Sir Toby Belch.
Why, how now, my bawcock? How dost thou, chuck?

Malvolio.
Sir!

Sir Toby Belch.
Ay, biddy, come with me. What, man, 'tis not for gravity to play at cherry-pit with Satan. Hang him, foul collier!

Act 3, Scene 4

Maria.
Get him to say his prayers, good Sir Toby, get him to pray.

Malvolio.
My prayers, minx!

Maria.
No, I warrant you, he will not hear of godliness.

Malvolio.
Go hang yourselves all! You are idle shallow things, I am not of your element. You shall know more hereafter.

Exit.

Sir Toby Belch.
Is't possible?

Fabian.
If this were play'd upon a stage now, I could condemn it as an improbable fiction.

Sir Toby Belch.
His very genius hath taken the infection of the device, man.

Maria.
Nay, pursue him now, lest the device take air, and taint.

Fabian.
Why, we shall make him mad indeed.

Maria.
The house will be the quieter.

Sir Toby Belch.
Come, we'll have him in a dark room and bound. My niece is already in the belief that he's mad. We may carry it thus, for our pleasure and his penance, till our very pastime, tir'd out of breath, prompt us to have mercy on him; at which time we will bring the device to the bar and crown thee for a finder of madmen. But see, but see.

Enter Sir Andrew.

Fabian.
More matter for a May morning.

Sir Andrew Aguecheek.
Here's the challenge, read it. I warrant there's vinegar and pepper in't.

Fabian.
Is't so saucy?

Sir Andrew Aguecheek.
Ay, is't! I warrant him. Do but read.

Sir Toby Belch.
Give me.

Reads.

"Youth, whatsoever thou art, thou art but a scurvy fellow."

Fabian.
Good, and valiant.

Sir Toby Belch.

Reads.

"Wonder not, nor admire not in thy mind, why I do call thee so, for I will show thee no reason for't."

Fabian.
A good note, that keeps you from the blow of the law.

Sir Toby Belch.

Reads.

"Thou com'st to the Lady Olivia, and in my sight she uses thee kindly. But thou liest in thy throat, that is not the matter I challenge thee for."

Fabian.
Very brief, and to exceeding good sense—less.

Sir Toby Belch.

Reads.

"I will waylay thee going home, where if it be thy chance to kill me"—

Fabian.
Good.

Sir Toby Belch.

Reads.

"Thou kill'st me like a rogue and a villain."

Fabian.
Still you keep o' th' windy side of the law; good.

Sir Toby Belch.

Reads.

"Fare thee well, and God have mercy upon one of our souls! He may have mercy upon mine, but my hope is better, and so look to thyself. Thy friend as thou usest him, and thy sworn enemy,
Andrew Aguecheek."
If this letter move him not, his legs cannot. I'll give't him.

Maria.
You may have very fit occasion for't; he is now in some commerce with my lady, and will by and by depart.

Sir Toby Belch.
Go, Sir Andrew, scout me for him at the corner of the orchard like a burn-baily. So soon as ever thou seest him, draw, and as thou draw'st, swear horrible; for it comes to pass oft that a terrible oath, with a swaggering accent sharply twang'd off, gives manhood more approbation than ever proof itself would have earn'd him. Away!

Sir Andrew Aguecheek.
Nay, let me alone for swearing.

Exit.

Sir Toby Belch.
Now will not I deliver his letter; for the behavior of the young gentleman gives him out to be of good capacity and breeding; his employment between his lord and my niece confirms no less. Therefore this letter, being so excellently ignorant, will breed no terror in the youth; he will find it comes from a clodpole. But, sir, I will deliver his challenge by word of mouth, set upon Aguecheek a notable report of valor, and drive the gentleman (as I know his youth will aptly receive it) into a most hideous opinion of his rage, skill, fury, and impetuosity. This will so fright them both that they will kill one another by the look, like cockatrices.

Enter Olivia and Viola.

Fabian.
Here he comes with your niece. Give them way till he take leave, and presently after him.

Sir Toby Belch.
I will meditate the while upon some horrid message for a challenge.

Exeunt Sir Toby, Fabian, and Maria.

Olivia.
I have said too much unto a heart of stone,
And laid mine honor too unchary on't.
There's something in me that reproves my fault;
But such a headstrong potent fault it is
That it but mocks reproof.

Viola.
With the same havior that your passion bears
Goes on my master's griefs.

Olivia.
Here, wear this jewel for me, 'tis my picture.
Refuse it not, it hath no tongue to vex you;
And I beseech you come again tomorrow.
What shall you ask of me that I'll deny,
That honor, sav'd, may upon asking give?

Viola.
Nothing but this—your true love for my master.

Olivia.
How with mine honor may I give him that
Which I have given to you?

Viola.
                    I will acquit you.

Olivia.
Well, come again tomorrow. Fare thee well.
A fiend like thee might bear my soul to hell.

Exit.
Enter Toby and Fabian.

Sir Toby Belch.
Gentleman, God save thee!

Viola.
And you, sir.

Sir Toby Belch.
That defense thou hast, betake thee to't. Of what nature the wrongs are thou hast done him, I know not; but thy intercepter, full of despite, bloody as the hunter, attends thee at the orchard-end. Dismount thy tuck, be yare in thy preparation, for thy assailant is quick, skillful, and deadly.

Viola.
You mistake, sir, I am sure; no man hath any quarrel to me. My remembrance is very free and clear from any image of offense done to any man.

Sir Toby Belch.
You'll find it otherwise, I assure you; therefore, if you hold your life at any price, betake you to your guard; for your opposite hath in him what youth, strength, skill, and wrath can furnish man withal.

Viola.
I pray you, sir, what is he?

Sir Toby Belch.
He is knight, dubb'd with unhatch'd rapier, and on carpet consideration, but he is a devil in private brawl. Souls and bodies hath he divorc'd three, and his incensement at this moment is so implacable, that satisfaction can be none but by pangs of death and sepulchre. Hob, nob, is his word; give't or take't.

Viola.
I will return again into the house, and desire some conduct of the lady. I am no fighter. I have heard of some kind of men that put quarrels purposely on others, to taste their valor. Belike this is a man of that quirk.

Sir Toby Belch.
Sir, no; his indignation derives itself out of a very competent injury; therefore get you on, and give him his desire. Back you shall not to the house, unless you undertake that with me which with as much safety you might answer him; therefore on, or strip your sword stark naked; for meddle you must, that's certain, or forswear to wear iron about you.

Viola.
This is as uncivil as strange. I beseech you do me this courteous office, as to know of the knight what my offense to him is. It is something of my negligence, nothing of my purpose.

Sir Toby Belch.
I will do so. Signior Fabian, stay you by this gentleman till my return.

Exit Toby.

Viola.
Pray you, sir, do you know of this matter?

Fabian.
I know the knight is incens'd against you, even to a mortal arbitrement, but nothing of the circumstance more.

Viola.
I beseech you, what manner of man is he?

Fabian.
Nothing of that wonderful promise, to read him by his form, as you are like to find him in the proof of his valor. He is indeed, sir, the most skillful, bloody, and fatal opposite that you could possibly have found in any part of Illyria. Will you walk towards him? I will make your peace with him if I can.

Viola.
I shall be much bound to you for't. I am one that had rather go with sir priest than sir knight. I care not who knows so much of my mettle.

Exeunt.
Enter Toby and Andrew.

Sir Toby Belch.
Why, man, he's a very devil, I have not seen such a firago. I had a pass with him, rapier, scabbard, and all; and he gives me the stuck in with such a mortal motion that it is inevitable; and on the answer, he pays you as surely as your feet hits the ground they step on. They say he has been fencer to the Sophy.

Sir Andrew Aguecheek.
Pox on't, I'll not meddle with him.

Sir Toby Belch.
Ay, but he will not now be pacified. Fabian can scarce hold him yonder.

Sir Andrew Aguecheek.
Plague on't, and I thought he had been valiant, and so cunning in fence, I'd have seen him damn'd ere I'd have challeng'd him. Let him let the matter slip, and I'll give him my horse, grey Capilet.

Sir Toby Belch.
I'll make the motion. Stand here, make a good show on't; this shall end without the perdition of souls.

Aside.

Marry, I'll ride your horse as well as I ride you.

Enter Fabian and Viola.

To Fabian.

I have his horse to take up the quarrel. I have persuaded him the youth's a devil.

Fabian.
He is as horribly conceited of him; and pants and looks pale, as if a bear were at his heels.

Sir Toby Belch.

To Viola.

There's no remedy, sir, he will fight with you for 's oath sake. Marry, he hath better bethought him of his quarrel, and he finds that now scarce to be worth talking of; therefore draw, for the supportance of his vow. He protests he will not hurt you.

Viola.

Aside.

Pray God defend me! A little thing would make me tell them how much I lack of a man.

Fabian.
Give ground if you see him furious.

Sir Toby Belch.
Come, Sir Andrew, there's no remedy, the gentleman will for his honor's sake have one bout with you. He cannot by the duello avoid it; but he has promis'd me, as he is a gentleman and a soldier, he will not hurt you. Come on, to't.

Sir Andrew Aguecheek.
Pray God he keep his oath!

Enter Antonio.

Viola.
I do assure you, 'tis against my will.

They draw.

Antonio.
Put up your sword. If this young gentleman
Have done offense, I take the fault on me;
If you offend him, I for him defy you.

Sir Toby Belch.
You, sir? Why, what are you?

Antonio.
One, sir, that for his love dares yet do more
Than you have heard him brag to you he will.

Sir Toby Belch.
Nay, if you be an undertaker, I am for you.

They draw.
Enter Officers.

Fabian.
O good Sir Toby, hold! Here come the officers.

Sir Toby Belch.

To Antonio.

I'll be with you anon.

Steps aside to avoid the Officers.

Viola.
Pray, sir, put your sword up, if you please.

Sir Andrew Aguecheek.
Marry, will I, sir; and for that I promis'd you, I'll be as good as my word. He will bear you easily, and reins well.

First Officer.
This is the man, do thy office.

Second Officer.
Antonio, I arrest thee at the suit of Count Orsino.

Antonio.
You do mistake me, sir.

First Officer.
No, sir, no jot. I know your favor well,
Though now you have no sea-cap on your head.
Take him away, he knows I know him well.

Antonio.
I must obey.

To Viola.

       This comes with seeking you;
But there's no remedy, I shall answer it.
What will you do, now my necessity
Makes me to ask you for my purse? It grieves me
Much more for what I cannot do for you
Than what befalls myself. You stand amaz'd,
But be of comfort.

Second Officer.
Come, sir, away.

Antonio.
I must entreat of you some of that money.

Viola.
What money, sir?
For the fair kindness you have show'd me here,
And part being prompted by your present trouble,
Out of my lean and low ability
I'll lend you something. My having is not much;
I'll make division of my present with you.
Hold, there's half my coffer.

Antonio.
                    Will you deny me now?
Is't possible that my deserts to you
Can lack persuasion? Do not tempt my misery,
Lest that it make me so unsound a man
As to upbraid you with those kindnesses
That I have done for you.

Viola.
                    I know of none,
Nor know I you by voice or any feature.
I hate ingratitude more in a man
Than lying, vainness, babbling, drunkenness,
Or any taint of vice whose strong corruption
Inhabits our frail blood.

Antonio.
                    O heavens themselves!

Second Officer.
Come, sir, I pray you go.

Antonio.
Let me speak a little. This youth that you see here
I snatch'd one half out of the jaws of death,
Reliev'd him with such sanctity of love,
And to his image, which methought did promise
Most venerable worth, did I devotion.

First Officer.
What's that to us? The time goes by; away!

Antonio.
But O, how vild an idol proves this god!
Thou hast, Sebastian, done good feature shame.
In nature there's no blemish but the mind;
None can be call'd deform'd but the unkind.
Virtue is beauty, but the beauteous evil
Are empty trunks o'erflourish'd by the devil.

First Officer.
The man grows mad, away with him! Come, come, sir.

Antonio.
Lead me on.

Exit with Officers.

Viola.
Methinks his words do from such passion fly
That he believes himself; so do not I.
Prove true, imagination, O, prove true,
That I, dear brother, be now ta'en for you!

Sir Toby Belch.
Come hither, knight; come hither, Fabian; we'll whisper o'er a couplet or two of most sage saws.

Viola.
He nam'd Sebastian. I my brother know
Yet living in my glass; even such and so
In favor was my brother, and he went
Still in this fashion, color, ornament,
For him I imitate. O, if it prove,
Tempests are kind and salt waves fresh in love.

Exit.

Sir Toby Belch.
A very dishonest paltry boy, and more a coward than a hare. His dishonesty appears in leaving his friend here in necessity, and denying him; and for his cowardship, ask Fabian.

Fabian.
A coward, a most devout coward, religious in it.

Sir Andrew Aguecheek.
'Slid, I'll after him again, and beat him.

Sir Toby Belch.
Do, cuff him soundly, but never draw thy sword.

Sir Andrew Aguecheek.
And I do not—

Exit.

Fabian.
Come, let's see the event.

Sir Toby Belch.
I dare lay any money 'twill be nothing yet.

Exeunt.

Act 4

Scene 1

Illyria, A street adjoining Olivia's house.

(Sebastian; Clown; Andrew; Toby; Fabian; Olivia)

Feste, believing him to be "Cesario", is following Sebastian around, insisting that he has been sent to fetch the young man. Sebastian is quite confused, and thinking the jester a beggar, tries to pay him to go away. Just then Andrew comes in and hits Sebastian. Unfortunately for him, Sebastian is not the type to take this lying down, and beats him right back, and much worse. Toby tries to restrain him, and they end up drawing swords on each other while Feste runs to fetch Olivia. The Countess arrives and dismisses Toby from her sight in a rage before meltingly inviting "Cesario" in to hear her relate all the other fooleries that Toby has made himself guilty of over the years. Sebastian thinks he must be dreaming to have such a beautiful woman invite him in, but he is quite willing to do so.

Enter Sebastian and Clown.

Feste.
Will you make me believe that I am not sent for you?

Sebastian.
Go to, go to, thou art a foolish fellow,
Let me be clear of thee.

Feste.
Well held out, i' faith! No, I do not know you, nor I am not sent to you by my lady, to bid you come speak with her, nor your name is not Master Cesario, nor this is not my nose neither: nothing that is so is so.

Sebastian.
I prithee vent thy folly somewhere else,
Thou know'st not me.

Feste.
Vent my folly! He has heard that word of some great man, and now applies it to a fool. Vent my folly! I am afraid this great lubber the world will prove a cockney. I prithee now ungird thy strangeness, and tell me what I shall vent to my lady. Shall I vent to her that thou art coming?

Sebastian.
I prithee, foolish Greek, depart from me.
There's money for thee. If you tarry longer,
I shall give worse payment.

Feste.
By my troth, thou hast an open hand. These wise men that give fools money get themselves a good report—after fourteen years' purchase.

Enter Andrew, Toby, and Fabian.

Sir Andrew Aguecheek.
Now, sir, have I met you again? There's for you.

Strikes Sebastian.

Sebastian.
Why, there's for thee, and there, and there.

Strikes Sir Andrew.

Are all the people mad?

Draws his dagger.

Sir Toby Belch.
Hold, sir, or I'll throw your dagger o'er the house.

Seizes Sebastian's arm.

Feste.
This will I tell my lady straight; I would not be in some of your coats for twopence.

Exit.

Sir Toby Belch.
Come on, sir, hold!

Sir Andrew Aguecheek.
Nay, let him alone. I'll go another way to work with him; I'll have an action of battery against him, if there be any law in Illyria. Though I struck him first, yet it's no matter for that.

Sebastian.
Let go thy hand.

Sir Toby Belch.
Come, sir, I will not let you go. Come, my young soldier, put up your iron; you are well flesh'd. Come on.

Sebastian.
I will be free from thee.

Breaks away and draws his sword.

What wouldst thou now?
If thou dar'st tempt me further, draw thy sword.

Sir Toby Belch.
What, what? Nay then I must have an ounce or two of this malapert blood from you.

Draws.
Enter Olivia.

Olivia.
Hold, Toby, on thy life I charge thee hold!

Sir Toby Belch.
Madam—

Olivia.
Will it be ever thus? Ungracious wretch,
Fit for the mountains and the barbarous caves,
Where manners ne'er were preach'd! Out of my sight!
Be not offended, dear Cesario.
Rudesby, be gone!

Exeunt Sir Toby, Sir Andrew, and Fabian.

                      I prithee, gentle friend,
Let thy fair wisdom, not thy passion, sway
In this uncivil and unjust extent
Against thy peace. Go with me to my house,
And hear thou there how many fruitless pranks
This ruffian hath botch'd up, that thou thereby
Mayst smile at this. Thou shalt not choose but go;
Do not deny. Beshrew his soul for me,
He started one poor heart of mine, in thee.

Sebastian.
What relish is in this? How runs the stream?
Or I am mad, or else this is a dream.
Let fancy still my sense in Lethe steep;
If it be thus to dream, still let me sleep!

Olivia.
Nay, come, I prithee. Would thou'dst be rul'd by me!

Sebastian.
Madam, I will.

Olivia.
                      O, say so, and so be!

Exeunt.

Scene 2

A room in Olivia's house.

(Maria; Clown; Toby; Malvolio)

Maria dresses Feste up with a false beard as the curate Sir Topas so that he may visit Malvolio, who is locked and bound in a dark room. Feste does so, pretending to determine whether or not Malvolio is mad, but refusing to believe the steward's claims that he is not. He goes away, leaving Malvolio in his jail. Toby, worried at how much trouble he's in with Olivia, tells Feste to go back to Malvolio as himself, and to see if he can find a way to safely set Malvolio free. Feste wanders by the cell, singing, and Malvolio begs him to bring him pen and ink. Feste pretends that Sir Topas is coming, and holds a conversation with himself warning Feste to stay away from the madman. Still, in the end he agrees to help Malvolio write a letter to Olivia.

Enter Maria and Clown.

Maria.
Nay, I prithee put on this gown and this beard, make him believe thou art Sir Topas the curate, do it quickly. I'll call Sir Toby the whilst.

Exit.

Feste.
Well, I'll put it on, and I will dissemble myself in't, and I would I were the first that ever dissembled in such a gown. I am not tall enough to become the function well, nor lean enough to be thought a good student; but to be said an honest man and a good housekeeper goes as fairly as to say a careful man and a great scholar. The competitors enter.

Enter Toby and Maria.

Sir Toby Belch.
Jove bless thee, Master Parson.

Feste.
Bonos dies, Sir Toby: for as the old hermit of Prague, that never saw pen and ink, very wittily said to a niece of King Gorboduc, "That that is is"; so I, being Master Parson, am Master Parson; for what is "that" but "that," and "is" but "is"?

Sir Toby Belch.
To him, Sir Topas.

Feste.
What ho, I say! Peace in this prison!

Sir Toby Belch.
The knave counterfeits well; a good knave.

Malvolio.

Within.

Who calls there?

Feste.
Sir Topas the curate, who comes to visit Malvolio the lunatic.

Malvolio.
Sir Topas, Sir Topas, good Sir Topas, go to my lady.

Feste.
Out, hyperbolical fiend! How vexest thou this man! Talkest thou nothing but of ladies?

Sir Toby Belch.
Well said, Master Parson.

Malvolio.
Sir Topas, never was man thus wrong'd. Good Sir Topas, do not think I am mad; they have laid me here in hideous darkness.

Feste.
Fie, thou dishonest Satan! I call thee by the most modest terms, for I am one of those gentle ones that will use the devil himself with courtesy. Say'st thou that house is dark?

Malvolio.
As hell, Sir Topas.

Feste.
Why, it hath bay windows transparent as barricadoes, and the clerestories toward the south north are as lustrous as ebony; and yet complainest thou of obstruction?

Malvolio.
I am not mad, Sir Topas, I say to you this house is dark.

Feste.
Madman, thou errest. I say there is no darkness but ignorance, in which thou art more puzzled than the Egyptians in their fog.

Malvolio.
I say this house is as dark as ignorance, though ignorance were as dark as hell; and I say there was never man thus abus'd. I am no more mad than you are; make the trial of it in any constant question.

Feste.
What is the opinion of Pythagoras concerning wild-fowl?

Malvolio.
That the soul of our grandam might happily inhabit a bird.

Feste.
What think'st thou of his opinion?

Malvolio.
I think nobly of the soul, and no way approve his opinion.

Feste.
Fare thee well. Remain thou still in darkness. Thou shalt hold th' opinion of Pythagoras ere I will allow of thy wits, and fear to kill a woodcock lest thou dispossess the soul of thy grandam. Fare thee well.

Malvolio.
Sir Topas, Sir Topas!

Sir Toby Belch.
My most exquisite Sir Topas!

Feste.
Nay, I am for all waters.

Maria.
Thou mightst have done this without thy beard and gown, he sees thee not.

Sir Toby Belch.
To him in thine own voice, and bring me word how thou find'st him. I would we were well rid of this knavery. If he may be conveniently deliver'd, I would he were, for I am now so far in offense with my niece that

I cannot pursue with any safety this sport t' the upshot. Come by and by to my chamber.

Exit with Maria.

Feste.

Sings.

"Hey, Robin, jolly Robin,
Tell me how thy lady does."

Malvolio.
Fool!

Feste.
"My lady is unkind, perdie."

Malvolio.
Fool!

Feste.
"Alas, why is she so?"

Malvolio.
Fool, I say!

Feste.
"She loves another"—
Who calls, ha?

Malvolio.
Good fool, as ever thou wilt deserve well at my hand, help me to a candle, and pen, ink, and paper. As I am a gentleman, I will live to be thankful to thee for't.

Feste.
Master Malvolio?

Malvolio.
Ay, good fool.

Feste.
Alas, sir, how fell you besides your five wits?

Malvolio.
Fool, there was never man so notoriously abus'd; I am as well in my wits, fool, as thou art.

Feste.
But as well! Then you are mad indeed, if you be no better in your wits than a fool.

Malvolio.
They have here propertied me, keep me in darkness, send ministers to me, asses, and do all they can to face me out of my wits.

Feste.
Advise you what you say; the minister is here.—Malvolio, Malvolio, thy wits the heavens restore! Endeavor thyself to sleep, and leave thy vain bibble babble.

Malvolio.
Sir Topas!

Feste.
Maintain no words with him, good fellow.—Who, I, sir? Not I, sir. God buy you, good Sir Topas.—Marry, amen.—I will, sir, I will.

Malvolio.
Fool, fool, fool, I say!

Feste.
Alas, sir, be patient. What say you, sir? I am shent for speaking to you.

Malvolio.
Good fool, help me to some light and some paper. I tell thee I am as well in my wits as any man in Illyria.

Feste.
Well-a-day that you were, sir!

Malvolio.
By this hand, I am. Good fool, some ink, paper, and light; and convey what I will set down to my lady. It shall advantage thee more than ever the bearing of letter did.

Feste.
I will help you to't. But tell me true, are you not mad indeed, or do you but counterfeit?

Malvolio.
Believe me I am not, I tell thee true.

Feste.
Nay, I'll ne'er believe a madman till I see his brains. I will fetch you light and paper and ink.

Malvolio.
Fool, I'll requite it in the highest degree. I prithee be gone.

Feste.

Sings.

I am gone, sir,
And anon, sir,
I'll be with you again;
In a trice,
Like to the old Vice,
Your need to sustain;
Who with dagger of lath,
In his rage and his wrath,
Cries, ah, ha! To the devil;
Like a mad lad,
Pare thy nails, dad.
Adieu, goodman devil.

Exit.

Scene 3

Olivia's garden.

(Sebastian; Olivia; Priest)

Sebastian wanders in the garden, reassuring himself that the world is still tangible and real, and that therefore this is likely not all a dream. He wonders where the vanished Antonio has got to, and wishes he were around to offer him counsel. He comes to the conclusion that either he is mad, or else Olivia is; but seeing that she clearly manages her household well, he cannot admit the latter possibility to be very likely. Olivia enters with a priest and begs Sebastian to come and marry her, promising to keep it a secret as long as he wishes. Sebastian agrees.

Enter Sebastian.

Sebastian.
This is the air, that is the glorious sun,
This pearl she gave me, I do feel't and see't,
And though 'tis wonder that enwraps me thus,
Yet 'tis not madness. Where's Antonio then?
I could not find him at the Elephant,
Yet there he was, and there I found this credit,
That he did range the town to seek me out.
His counsel now might do me golden service,
For though my soul disputes well with my sense,
That this may be some error, but no madness,
So far exceed all instance, all discourse,
That I am ready to distrust mine eyes,
And wrangle with my reason that persuades me
To any other trust but that I am mad,
Or else the lady's mad; yet if 'twere so,
She could not sway her house, command her followers,
Take and give back affairs, and their dispatch,
With such a smooth, discreet, and stable bearing
As I perceive she does. There's something in't
That is deceivable. But here the lady comes.

Enter Olivia and Priest.

Olivia.
Blame not this haste of mine. If you mean well,
Now go with me, and with this holy man,
Into the chantry by; there, before him,
And underneath that consecrated roof,
Plight me the full assurance of your faith,
That my most jealous and too doubtful soul
May live at peace. He shall conceal it
Whiles you are willing it shall come to note,
What time we will our celebration keep
According to my birth. What do you say?

Sebastian.
I'll follow this good man, and go with you,
And having sworn truth, ever will be true.

Olivia.
Then lead the way, good father, and heavens so shine
That they may fairly note this act of mine!

Exeunt.

Act 5
Scene 1

A street before Olivia's house.

(Clown; Fabian; Duke; Viola; Curio; Lords; Antonio; First Officer; Second Officer; Olivia; Attendants; Priest; Sir Andrew; Sir Toby; Malvolio)

Fabian tries to get Feste to let him read the letter Malvolio has written to Olivia, but the jester refuses. Orsino arrives, having finally decided to visit Olivia in person. Feste jests with him until Orsino has little choice but to pay him. The Officers bring Antonio in, and Viola, who is in Orsino's train, points him out as the man who rescued her. Orsino recognizes him as the pirate who did them so much damage in the sea-battle, in which his own nephew lost a leg. Antonio protests that he was not a pirate, and explains his presence by telling the tale of how he followed Sebastian to Illyria, and how the lad denied knowing him. As Olivia comes in, Orsino tells the captain that he's mad: "Cesario" has spent the three months Antonio claims he spent with him in the Duke's own company. Olivia enters, chiding "Cesario" for not being with her and still refusing to love Orsino. The Duke soon works out that she is in love with his servant and promises to never let her see "him" again. Olivia calls on "Cesario" to stay by her, but Viola insists on following Orsino. When Olivia calls her "husband", she is utterly confused, but Orsino is enraged, convinced that "Cesario" has been acting behind his back. Viola denies having married the Countess, but Olivia calls in the priest to confirm her tale. Orsino banishes "Cesario" from his presence and Olivia reproaches "him" for perjury. Just then Sir Andrew comes in with a bleeding head, calling for a doctor. He accuses "Cesario" of the deed, though Viola, as confused as everyone else, denies this. Sir Toby arrives, his head bleeding as well. Sir Andrew offers to help him in so that they can have their wounds tended to together, but Toby turns on him and tells him to his face just what he is. Olivia sends them out. Sebastian arrives to apologize to Olivia for wounding her kinsman, to everyone's great confusion. He also greets Antonio happily and gives him back his purse. No one can tell the difference between Sebastian and "Cesario". As they look at each other, the twins realize who they must be, and test each other, asking for details that only they would know to confirm their respective identities before they will believe that they are reunited. Viola's identity as a woman is finally revealed and the confusions cleared up. Orsino, remembering her promises that she would never love a woman as much as she loved him, takes her at her word and offers to marry her. Viola offers to change back into women's clothing, but explains that the Captain who can prove her story (and who has her clothes) has been imprisoned for debt at Malvolio's request. Olivia promises that Malvolio will let him go, but then remembers that the steward is mad. Feste hands over Malvolio's letter after trying to read it aloud in a madman's voice. Olivia is impatient with foolery at this moment and has Fabian read it instead. No one thinks it is the letter of a madman. While waiting for Malvolio to be fetched in, Orsino and Olivia agree to have a double wedding, and Olivia greets Viola as her sister. Malvolio enters and pleads for justice, holding out the letter he found in the garden as an explanation for his behavior. Olivia takes it and has to tell him that she didn't write it: the handwriting's is Maria's. Fabian steps forward and admits to the whole plot against Malvolio, mentioning that to reward Maria for her ideas Toby has married her, and hoping that in the joy of a wedding day they will be forgiven. Malvolio admits to his own role and points out that he brought it on himself. The steward refuses to be reconciled, and goes out swearing that he will have his revenge on them all. Orsino requests that he be followed and persuaded to tell them about the Captain. In the meantime everyone goes indoors to sort out all the details of the story. Orsino insists they will not leave Olivia's house until everyone is happily married. Feste remains behind, singing a farewell song to the audience.

Enter Clown and Fabian.

Fabian.
Now as thou lov'st me, let me see his letter.

Feste.
Good Master Fabian, grant me another request.

Fabian.
Any thing.

Feste.
Do not desire to see this letter.

Fabian.
This is to give a dog and in recompense desire my dog again.

Enter Duke, Viola, Curio, and Lords.

Orsino.
Belong you to the Lady Olivia, friends?

Feste.
Ay, sir, we are some of her trappings.

Orsino.
I know thee well; how dost thou, my good fellow?

Feste.
Truly, sir, the better for my foes and the worse for my friends.

Orsino.
Just the contrary: the better for thy friends.

Feste.
No, sir, the worse.

Orsino.
How can that be?

Feste.
Marry, sir, they praise me, and make an ass of me. Now my foes tell me plainly I am an ass; so that by my foes, sir, I profit in the knowledge of myself, and by my friends I am abus'd; so that, conclusions to be as kisses, if your four negatives make your two affirmatives, why then the worse for my friends and the better for my foes.

Orsino.
Why, this is excellent.

Feste.
By my troth, sir, no; though it please you to be one of my friends.

Orsino.
Thou shalt not be the worse for me, there's gold.

Feste.
But that it would be double-dealing, sir, I would you could make it another.

Orsino.
O, you give me ill counsel.

Feste.
Put your grace in your pocket, sir, for this once, and let your flesh and blood obey it.

Orsino.
Well, I will be so much a sinner to be a double-dealer. There's another.

Feste.
Primo, secundo, tertio, is a good play, and the old saying is, the third pays for all. The triplex, sir, is a good tripping measure, or the bells of Saint Bennet, sir, may put you in mind—one, two, three.

Orsino.
You can fool no more money out of me at this throw. If you will let your lady know I am here to speak with her, and bring her along with you, it may awake my bounty further.

Feste.
Marry, sir, lullaby to your bounty till I come again. I go, sir, but I would not have you to think that my desire of having is the sin of covetousness; but as you say, sir, let your bounty take a nap, I will awake it anon.

Exit.
Enter Antonio and Officers.

Viola.
Here comes the man, sir, that did rescue me.

Orsino.
That face of his I do remember well,
Yet when I saw it last, it was besmear'd
As black as Vulcan in the smoke of war.
A baubling vessel was he captain of,
For shallow draught and bulk unprizable,
With which such scathful grapple did he make
With the most noble bottom of our fleet,
That very envy, and the tongue of loss,
Cried fame and honor on him. What's the matter?

First Officer.
Orsino, this is that Antonio
That took the Phoenix and her fraught from Candy,
And this is he that did the Tiger board,
When your young nephew Titus lost his leg.
Here in the streets, desperate of shame and state,
In private brabble did we apprehend him.

Viola.
He did me kindness, sir, drew on my side,
But in conclusion put strange speech upon me.
I know not what 'twas but distraction.

Orsino.
Notable pirate, thou salt-water thief!
What foolish boldness brought thee to their mercies
Whom thou in terms so bloody and so dear
Hast made thine enemies?

Antonio.
                    Orsino, noble sir,
Be pleas'd that I shake off these names you give me.
Antonio never yet was thief or pirate,
Though I confess, on base and ground enough,
Orsino's enemy. A witchcraft drew me hither:
That most ingrateful boy there by your side
From the rude sea's enrag'd and foamy mouth
Did I redeem; a wrack past hope he was.
His life I gave him, and did thereto add
My love, without retention or restraint,
All his in dedication. For his sake
Did I expose myself (pure for his love)
Into the danger of this adverse town,
Drew to defend him when he was beset;
Where being apprehended, his false cunning
(Not meaning to partake with me in danger)
Taught him to face me out of his acquaintance,
And grew a twenty years removed thing

Act 5, Scene 1

While one would wink; denied me mine own purse,
Which I had recommended to his use
Not half an hour before.

Viola.
                      How can this be?

Orsino.
When came he to this town?

Antonio.
Today, my lord; and for three months before,
No int'rim, not a minute's vacancy,
Both day and night did we keep company.

Enter Olivia and Attendants.

Orsino.
Here comes the Countess, now heaven walks on earth.
But for thee, fellow—fellow, thy words are madness.
Three months this youth hath tended upon me,
But more of that anon. Take him aside.

Olivia.
What would my lord, but that he may not have,
Wherein Olivia may seem serviceable?
Cesario, you do not keep promise with me.

Viola.
Madam—

Orsino.
Gracious Olivia—

Olivia.
What do you say, Cesario? Good my lord—

Viola.
My lord would speak, my duty hushes me.

Olivia.
If it be aught to the old tune, my lord,
It is as fat and fulsome to mine ear
As howling after music.

Orsino.
                      Still so cruel?

Olivia.
Still so constant, lord.

Orsino.
What, to perverseness? You uncivil lady,
To whose ingrate and unauspicious altars
My soul the faithfull'st off'rings have breath'd out
That e'er devotion tender'd! What shall I do?

Olivia.
Even what it please my lord, that shall become him.

Orsino.
Why should I not (had I the heart to do it),
Like to th' Egyptian thief at point of death,
Kill what I love? (a savage jealousy
That sometime savors nobly), but hear me this:
Since you to non-regardance cast my faith,
And that I partly know the instrument
That screws me from my true place in your favor,
Live you the marble-breasted tyrant still.
But this your minion, whom I know you love,
And whom, by heaven I swear, I tender dearly,
Him will I tear out of that cruel eye,
Where he sits crowned in his master's spite.
Come, boy, with me, my thoughts are ripe in mischief.
I'll sacrifice the lamb that I do love,
To spite a raven's heart within a dove.

Viola.
And I most jocund, apt, and willingly,
To do you rest, a thousand deaths would die.

Olivia.
Where goes Cesario?

Viola.
                      After him I love
More than I love these eyes, more than my life,
More by all mores than e'er I shall love wife.
If I do feign, you witnesses above
Punish my life for tainting of my love!

Olivia.
Ay me, detested! How am I beguil'd!

Viola.
Who does beguile you? Who does do you wrong?

Olivia.
Hast thou forgot thyself? Is it so long?
Call forth the holy father.

Orsino.
                      Come, away!

Olivia.
Whither, my lord? Cesario, husband, stay.

Orsino.
Husband?

Olivia.
     Ay, husband. Can he that deny?

Orsino.
Her husband, sirrah?

Viola.
     No, my lord, not I.

Olivia.
Alas, it is the baseness of thy fear
That makes thee strangle thy propriety.
Fear not, Cesario, take thy fortunes up,
Be that thou know'st thou art, and then thou art
As great as that thou fear'st.

Enter Priest.

     O, welcome, father!
Father, I charge thee by thy reverence
Here to unfold, though lately we intended
To keep in darkness what occasion now
Reveals before 'tis ripe, what thou dost know
Hath newly pass'd between this youth and me.

Priest.
A contract of eternal bond of love,
Confirm'd by mutual joinder of your hands,
Attested by the holy close of lips,
Strength'ned by interchangement of your rings,
And all the ceremony of this compact
Seal'd in my function, by my testimony;
Since when, my watch hath told me, toward my grave
I have travel'd but two hours.

Orsino.
O thou dissembling cub! What wilt thou be
When time hath sow'd a grizzle on thy case?
Or will not else thy craft so quickly grow,
That thine own trip shall be thine overthrow?
Farewell, and take her, but direct thy feet
Where thou and I (henceforth) may never meet.

Viola.
My lord, I do protest—

Olivia.
     O, do not swear!
Hold little faith, though thou hast too much fear.

Enter Sir Andrew.

Sir Andrew Aguecheek.
For the love of God, a surgeon! Send one presently to Sir Toby.

Olivia.
What's the matter?

Sir Andrew Aguecheek.
H'as broke my head across, and has given Sir Toby a bloody coxcomb too. For the love of God, your help! I had rather than forty pound I were at home.

Olivia.
Who has done this, Sir Andrew?

Sir Andrew Aguecheek.
The Count's gentleman, one Cesario. We took him for a coward, but he's the very devil incardinate.

Orsino.
My gentleman, Cesario?

Sir Andrew Aguecheek.
'Od's lifelings, here he is! You broke my head for nothing, and that that I did, I was set on to do't by Sir Toby.

Viola.
Why do you speak to me? I never hurt you.
I drew your sword upon me without cause,
But I bespake you fair, and hurt you not.

Enter Toby and Clown.

Sir Andrew Aguecheek.
If a bloody coxcomb be a hurt, you have hurt me. I think you set nothing by a bloody coxcomb. Here comes Sir Toby halting—you shall hear more. But if he had not been in drink, he would have tickled you othergates than he did.

Orsino.
How now, gentleman? How is't with you?

Sir Toby Belch.
That's all one. H'as hurt me, and there's th' end on't. Sot, didst see Dick surgeon, sot?

Feste.
O, he's drunk, Sir Toby, an hour agone; his eyes were set at eight i' th' morning.

Sir Toby Belch.
Then he's a rogue, and a passy-measures pavin. I hate a drunken rogue.

Olivia.
Away with him! Who hath made this havoc with them?

Sir Andrew Aguecheek.
I'll help you, Sir Toby, because we'll be dress'd together.

Sir Toby Belch.
Will you help?—an ass-head and a coxcomb and a knave, a thin-fac'd knave, a gull!

Olivia.
Get him to bed, and let his hurt be look'd to.

Exeunt Clown, Fabian, Sir Toby, and Sir Andrew.
Enter Sebastian.

Sebastian.
I am sorry, madam, I have hurt your kinsman,
But had it been the brother of my blood,
I must have done no less with wit and safety.
You throw a strange regard upon me, and by that
I do perceive it hath offended you.
Pardon me, sweet one, even for the vows
We made each other but so late ago.

Orsino.
One face, one voice, one habit, and two persons,
A natural perspective, that is and is not!

Sebastian.
Antonio, O my dear Antonio!
How have the hours rack'd and tortur'd me,
Since I have lost thee!

Antonio.
Sebastian are you?

Sebastian.
                    Fear'st thou that, Antonio?

Antonio.
How have you made division of yourself?
An apple, cleft in two, is not more twin
Than these two creatures. Which is Sebastian?

Olivia.
Most wonderful!

Sebastian.
Do I stand there? I never had a brother;
Nor can there be that deity in my nature
Of here and every where. I had a sister,
Whom the blind waves and surges have devour'd.
Of charity, what kin are you to me?
What countryman? What name? What parentage?

Viola.
Of Messaline; Sebastian was my father,
Such a Sebastian was my brother too;
So went he suited to his watery tomb.
If spirits can assume both form and suit,
You come to fright us.

Sebastian.
                    A spirit I am indeed,
But am in that dimension grossly clad
Which from the womb I did participate.
Were you a woman, as the rest goes even,
I should my tears let fall upon your cheek,
And say, "Thrice welcome, drowned Viola!"

Viola.
My father had a mole upon his brow.

Sebastian.
And so had mine.

Viola.
And died that day when Viola from her birth
Had numb'red thirteen years.

Sebastian.
O, that record is lively in my soul!
He finished indeed his mortal act
That day that made my sister thirteen years.

Viola.
If nothing lets to make us happy both
But this my masculine usurp'd attire,
Do not embrace me till each circumstance
Of place, time, fortune, do cohere and jump
That I am Viola—which to confirm,
I'll bring you to a captain in this town,
Where lie my maiden weeds; by whose gentle help
I was preserv'd to serve this noble count.
All the occurrence of my fortune since
Hath been between this lady and this lord.

Sebastian.

To Olivia.

So comes it, lady, you have been mistook;
But Nature to her bias drew in that.
You would have been contracted to a maid,
Nor are you therein, by my life, deceiv'd,
You are betroth'd both to a maid and man.

Orsino.
Be not amaz'd, right noble is his blood.
If this be so, as yet the glass seems true,
I shall have share in this most happy wrack.

To Viola.

Boy, thou hast said to me a thousand times
Thou never shouldst love woman like to me.

Viola.
And all those sayings will I over swear,
And all those swearings keep as true in soul
As doth that orbed continent the fire
That severs day from night.

Orsino.   Give me thy hand,
And let me see thee in thy woman's weeds.

Viola.
The captain that did bring me first on shore
Hath my maid's garments. He upon some action
Is now in durance, at Malvolio's suit,
A gentleman, and follower of my lady's.

Olivia.
He shall enlarge him; fetch Malvolio hither.
And yet, alas, now I remember me,
They say, poor gentleman, he's much distract.

Enter Clown with a letter, and Fabian.

A most extracting frenzy of mine own
From my remembrance clearly banish'd his.
How does he, sirrah?

Feste.
Truly, madam, he holds Beelzebub at the stave's end as well as a man in his case may do. H'as here writ a letter to you; I should have given't you today morning. But as a madman's epistles are no gospels, so it skills not much when they are deliver'd.

Olivia.
Open't and read it.

Feste.
Look then to be well edified when the fool delivers the madman.

Reads madly.

"By the Lord, madam"—

Olivia.
How now, art thou mad?

Feste.
No, madam, I do but read madness. And your ladyship will have it as it ought to be, you must allow vox.

Olivia.
Prithee read i' thy right wits.

Feste.
So I do, madonna; but to read his right wits is to read thus; therefore perpend, my princess, and give ear.

Olivia.

To Fabian.

Read it you, sirrah.

Fabian.

Reads.

"By the Lord, madam, you wrong me, and the world shall know it. Though you have put me into darkness, and given your drunken cousin rule over me, yet have I the benefit of my senses as well as your ladyship. I have your own letter that induc'd me to the semblance I put on; with the which I doubt not but to do myself much right, or you much shame. Think of me as you please. I leave my duty a little unthought of, and speak out of my injury. The madly-us'd Malvolio."

Olivia.
Did he write this?

Feste.
Ay, madam.

Orsino.
This savors not much of distraction.

Olivia.
See him deliver'd, Fabian, bring him hither.

Exit Fabian.

My lord, so please you, these things further thought on,
To think me as well a sister as a wife,
One day shall crown th' alliance on't, so please you,
Here at my house and at my proper cost.

Orsino.
Madam, I am most apt t' embrace your offer.

To Viola.

Your master quits you; and for your service done him,
So much against the mettle of your sex,
So far beneath your soft and tender breeding,
And since you call'd me master for so long,
Here is my hand—you shall from this time be
Your master's mistress.

Olivia.
                    A sister! You are she.

Enter Fabian with Malvolio.

Orsino.
Is this the madman?

Olivia.
                    Ay, my lord, this same.
How now, Malvolio?

Malvolio.
                    Madam, you have done me wrong,
Notorious wrong.

Olivia.
                    Have I, Malvolio? No.

Malvolio.
Lady, you have. Pray you peruse that letter.
You must not now deny it is your hand;
Write from it if you can, in hand or phrase,
Or say 'tis not your seal, not your invention.
You can say none of this. Well, grant it then,
And tell me, in the modesty of honor,
Why you have given me such clear lights of favor,
Bade me come smiling and cross-garter'd to you,
To put on yellow stockings, and to frown
Upon Sir Toby and the lighter people;
And acting this in an obedient hope,
Why have you suffer'd me to be imprison'd,
Kept in a dark house, visited by the priest,
And made the most notorious geck and gull
That e'er invention play'd on? Tell me why!

Olivia.
Alas, Malvolio, this is not my writing,
Though I confess much like the character;
But out of question 'tis Maria's hand.
And now I do bethink me, it was she
First told me thou wast mad. Then cam'st in smiling,
And in such forms which here were presuppos'd
Upon thee in the letter. Prithee be content.
This practice hath most shrewdly pass'd upon thee;
But when we know the grounds and authors of it,
Thou shalt be both the plaintiff and the judge
Of thine own cause.

Fabian.
                    Good madam, hear me speak,
And let no quarrel nor no brawl to come
Taint the condition of this present hour,
Which I have wond'red at. In hope it shall not,
Most freely I confess, myself and Toby
Set this device against Malvolio here,
Upon some stubborn and uncourteous parts
We had conceiv'd against him. Maria writ
The letter at Sir Toby's great importance,
In recompense whereof he hath married her.
How with a sportful malice it was follow'd
May rather pluck on laughter than revenge,
If that the injuries be justly weigh'd
That have on both sides pass'd.

Olivia.
Alas, poor fool, how have they baffled thee!

Feste.
Why, "some are born great, some achieve greatness, and some have greatness thrown upon them." I was one, sir, in this enterlude—one Sir Topas, sir, but that's all one. "By the Lord, fool, I am not mad." But do you remember? "Madam, why laugh you at such a barren rascal? And you smile not, he's gagg'd." And thus the whirligig of time brings in his revenges.

Malvolio.
I'll be reveng'd on the whole pack of you.

Exit.

Olivia.
He hath been most notoriously abus'd.

Orsino.
Pursue him, and entreat him to a peace;
He hath not told us of the captain yet.
When that is known, and golden time convents,
A solemn combination shall be made
Of our dear souls. Mean time, sweet sister,
We will not part from hence. Cesario, come—
For so you shall be while you are a man;
But when in other habits you are seen,
Orsino's mistress, and his fancy's queen.

Exeunt all but Clown.

Feste.

Clown sings.

When that I was and a little tiny boy,
With hey ho, the wind and the rain,
A foolish thing was but a toy,
For the rain it raineth every day.
But when I came to man's estate,
With hey ho, etc.
'Gainst knaves and thieves men shut their gate,
For the rain, etc.
But when I came, alas, to wive,
With hey ho, etc.
By swaggering could I never thrive,
For the rain, etc.
But when I came unto my beds,
With hey ho, etc.
With toss-pots still had drunken heads,
For the rain, etc.
A great while ago the world begun,
With hey ho, etc.
But that's all one, our play is done,
And we'll strive to please you every day.

Exit.

As You Like It

Act 1

Scene 1

An orchard of Oliver's house.

(Orlando; Adam; Oliver; Dennis; Charles)

Orlando complains to Adam that his brother Oliver keeps their middle brother Jacques at school, but gives him no care. Orlando asks Oliver for his patrimony and Oliver, glad to get rid of him, agrees to do it if Orlando can beat him up. Charles, the Duke's wrestler, comes in telling Oliver that there is little new at court other than the old news that the Duke has been banished by his brother, Duke Frederick, and is living with his men in the forest, while his daughter Rosalind is staying with Celia, the usurper's daughter. Charles tries to get Oliver to dissuade Orlando from wrestling with him, but Oliver tells Charles that Orlando is treacherous and will kill Charles if he is beaten, so Charles decides to do his utmost.

Enter Orlando and Adam.

Orlando.
As I remember, Adam, it was upon this fashion bequeath'd me by will but poor a thousand crowns, and, as thou say'st, charg'd my brother, on his blessing, to breed me well; and there begins my sadness. My brother Jaques he keeps at school, and report speaks goldenly of his profit. For my part, he keeps me rustically at home, or (to speak more properly) stays me here at home unkept; for call you that keeping for a gentleman of my birth, that differs not from the stalling of an ox? His horses are bred better, for besides that they are fair with their feeding, they are taught their manage, and to that end riders dearly hir'd; but I (his brother) gain nothing under him but growth, for the which his animals on his dunghills are as much bound to him as I. Besides this nothing that he so plentifully gives me, the something that nature gave me his countenance seems to take from me. He lets me feed with his hinds, bars me the place of a brother, and as much as in him lies, mines my gentility with my education. This is it, Adam, that grieves me, and the spirit of my father, which I think is within me, begins to mutiny against this servitude. I will no longer endure it, though yet I know no wise remedy how to avoid it.

Enter Oliver.

Adam.
Yonder comes my master, your brother.

Orlando.
Go apart, Adam, and thou shalt hear how he will shake me up.

Oliver.
Now, sir, what make you here?

Orlando.
Nothing. I am not taught to make any thing.

Oliver.
What mar you then, sir?

Orlando.
Marry, sir, I am helping you to mar that which God made, a poor unworthy brother of yours, with idleness.

Oliver.
Marry, sir, be better employ'd, and be naught a while.

Orlando.
Shall I keep your hogs and eat husks with them? What prodigal portion have I spent, that I should come to such penury?

Oliver.
Know you where you are, sir?

Orlando.
O, sir, very well; here in your orchard.

Oliver.
Know you before whom, sir?

Orlando.
Ay, better than him I am before knows me. I know you are my eldest brother, and in the gentle condition of blood you should so know me. The courtesy of nations allows you my better, in that you are the first born, but the same tradition takes not away my blood, were there twenty brothers betwixt us. I have as much of my father in me as you, albeit I confess your coming before me is nearer to his reverence.

Oliver.
What, boy!

Strikes him.

Orlando.
Come, come, elder brother, you are too young in this.

Collaring him.

Oliver.
Wilt thou lay hands on me, villain?

Orlando.
I am no villain; I am the youngest son of Sir Rowland de Boys. He was my father, and he is thrice a villain that says such a father begot villains. Wert thou not my brother, I would not take this hand from thy throat till this other had pull'd out thy tongue for saying so. Thou hast rail'd on thyself.

Adam.
Sweet masters, be patient, for your father's remembrance, be at accord.

Oliver.
Let me go, I say.

Orlando.
I will not till I please. You shall hear me. My father charg'd you in his will to give me good education. You have train'd me like a peasant, obscuring and hiding from me all gentleman-like qualities. The spirit of my father grows strong in me, and I will no longer endure it; therefore allow me such exercises as may become a gentleman, or give me the poor allottery my father left me by testament, with that I will go buy my fortunes.

Oliver.
And what wilt thou do? Beg, when that is spent? Well, sir, get you in. I will not long be troubled with you; you shall have some part of your will. I pray you leave me.

Orlando.
I will no further offend you than becomes me for my good.

Oliver.
Get you with him, you old dog.

Adam.
Is "old dog" my reward? Most true, I have lost my teeth in your service. God be with my old master, he would not have spoke such a word.

Exeunt Orlando, Adam.

Oliver.
Is it even so? Begin you to grow upon me? I will physic your rankness, and yet give no thousand crowns neither. Holla, Dennis!

Enter Dennis.

Dennis.
Calls your worship?

Oliver.
Was not Charles, the Duke's wrestler, here to speak with me?

Dennis.
So please you, he is here at the door, and importunes access to you.

Oliver.
Call him in.

Exit Dennis.

'Twill be a good way; and tomorrow the wrestling is.

Enter Charles.

Charles.
Good morrow to your worship.

Oliver.
Good Monsieur Charles, what's the new news at the new court?

Charles.
There's no news at the court, sir, but the old news: that is, the old Duke is banish'd by his younger brother the new Duke, and three or four loving lords have put themselves into voluntary exile with him, whose lands and revenues enrich the new Duke; therefore he gives them good leave to wander.

Oliver.
Can you tell if Rosalind, the Duke's daughter, be banish'd with her father?

Charles.
O no; for the Duke's daughter, her cousin, so loves her, being ever from their cradles bred together, that she would have follow'd her exile, or have died to stay behind her. She is at the court, and no less belov'd of her uncle than his own daughter, and never two ladies lov'd as they do.

Oliver.
Where will the old Duke live?

Charles.
They say he is already in the forest of Arden, and a many merry men with him; and there they live like the old Robin Hood of England. They say many young gentlemen flock to him every day, and fleet the time carelessly, as they did in the golden world.

Oliver.
What, you wrestle tomorrow before the new Duke?

Charles.
Marry, do I, sir; and I came to acquaint you with a matter. I am given, sir, secretly to understand that your younger brother, Orlando, hath a disposition to come in disguis'd against me to try a fall. Tomorrow, sir, I wrestle for my credit, and he that escapes me without some broken limb shall acquit him well. Your brother is but young and tender, and for your love I would be loath to foil him, as I must for my own honor if he come in; therefore out of my love to you, I came hither to acquaint you withal, that either you might stay him from his intendment, or brook such disgrace well as he shall run into, in that it is a thing of his own search, and altogether against my will.

Oliver.
Charles, I thank thee for thy love to me, which thou shalt find I will most kindly requite. I had myself notice of my brother's purpose herein, and have by underhand means labor'd to dissuade him from it; but he is resolute. I'll tell thee, Charles, it is the stubbornest young fellow of France, full of ambition, an envious emulator of every man's good parts, a secret and villainous contriver against me his natural brother; therefore use thy discretion— I had as lief thou didst break his neck as his finger. And thou wert best look to't; for if thou dost him any slight disgrace, or if he do not mightily grace himself on thee, he will practice against thee by poison, entrap thee by some treacherous device, and never leave thee till he hath ta'en thy life by some indirect means or other; for I assure thee (and almost with tears I speak it) there is not one so young and so villainous this day living. I speak but brotherly of him, but should I anatomize him to thee as he is, I must blush and weep, and thou must look pale and wonder.

Charles.
I am heartily glad I came hither to you. If he come tomorrow, I'll give him his payment. If ever he go alone again, I'll never wrestle for prize more. And so God keep your worship!

Exit.

Oliver.
Farewell, good Charles. Now will I stir this gamester. I hope I shall see an end of him; for my soul (yet I know not why) hates nothing more than he. Yet he's gentle, never school'd and yet learned, full of noble device, of all sorts enchantingly belov'd, and indeed so much in the heart of the world, and especially of my own people, who best know him, that I am altogether mispris'd. But it shall not be so long, this wrestler shall clear all. Nothing remains but that I kindle the boy thither, which now I'll go about.

Exit.

Scene 2

A lawn before the Duke's palace.

(*Rosalind; Celia; Touchstone; Le Beau; Duke Frederick; First Lord at Court; Second Lord at Court; Orlando; Charles; Attendants*)

Rosalind and Celia jest lightly with each other and with Touchstone and LeBeau about falling in love, being forsworn, and the wrestling. Rosalind and Celia try to dissuade Orlando from wrestling with Charles and when he wins, give him their congratulations. Rosalind and Orlando are visibly affected by each other. Duke Frederick grudgingly congratulates Orlando when he learns that Orlando's father was his enemy. LeBeau indicates Rosalind is under the Duke's displeasure.

Enter Rosalind and Celia.

Celia.
I pray thee, Rosalind, sweet my coz, be merry.

Rosalind.
Dear Celia—I show more mirth than I am mistress of, and would you yet I were merrier? Unless you could teach me to forget a banish'd father, you must not learn me how to remember any extraordinary pleasure.

Celia.
Herein I see thou lov'st me not with the full weight that I love thee. If my uncle, thy banish'd father, had banish'd thy uncle, the Duke my father, so thou hadst been still with me, I could have taught my love to take thy father for mine; so wouldst thou, if the truth of thy love to me were so righteously temper'd as mine is to thee.

Rosalind.
Well, I will forget the condition of my estate, to rejoice in yours.

Celia.
You know my father hath no child but I, nor none is like to have; and truly when he dies, thou shalt be his heir; for what he hath taken away from thy father perforce, I will render thee again in affection. By mine honor, I will, and when I break that oath, let me turn monster. Therefore, my sweet Rose, my dear Rose, be merry.

Rosalind.
From henceforth I will, coz, and devise sports. Let me see—what think you of falling in love?

Celia.
Marry, I prithee do, to make sport withal. But love no man in good earnest, nor no further in sport neither, than with safety of a pure blush thou mayst in honor come off again.

Rosalind.
What shall be our sport then?

Celia.
Let us sit and mock the good huswife Fortune from her wheel, that her gifts may henceforth be bestow'd equally.

Rosalind.
I would we could do so; for her benefits are mightily misplac'd, and the bountiful blind woman doth most mistake in her gifts to women.

Celia.
'Tis true, for those that she makes fair she scarce makes honest, and those that she makes honest she makes very ill-favoredly.

Rosalind.
Nay, now thou goest from Fortune's office to Nature's. Fortune reigns in gifts of the world, not in the lineaments of Nature.

Enter Clown (Touchstone).

Celia.
No; when Nature hath made a fair creature, may she not by Fortune fall into the fire? Though Nature hath given us wit to flout at Fortune, hath not Fortune sent in this fool to cut off the argument?

Rosalind.
Indeed there is Fortune too hard for Nature, when Fortune makes Nature's natural the cutter-off of Nature's wit.

Celia.
Peradventure this is not Fortune's work neither, but Nature's, who perceiveth our natural wits too dull to reason of such goddesses, and hath sent this natural for our whetstone; for always the dullness of the fool is the whetstone of the wits. How now, wit, whither wander you?

Touchstone.
Mistress, you must come away to your father.

Celia.
Were you made the messenger?

Touchstone.
No, by mine honor, but I was bid to come for you.

Rosalind.
Where learn'd you that oath, fool?

Touchstone.
Of a certain knight, that swore by his honor they were good pancakes, and swore by his honor the mustard was naught. Now I'll stand to it, the pancakes were naught, and the mustard was good, and yet was not the knight forsworn.

Celia.
How prove you that, in the great heap of your knowledge?

Rosalind.
Ay, marry, now unmuzzle your wisdom.

Touchstone.
Stand you both forth now. Stroke your chins, and swear by your beards that I am a knave.

Celia.
By our beards (if we had them) thou art.

Touchstone.
By my knavery (if I had it) then I were. But if you swear by that that is not, you are not forsworn. No more was this knight, swearing by his honor, for he never had any; or if he had, he had sworn it away before ever he saw those pancakes or that mustard.

Celia.
Prithee, who is't that thou mean'st?

Touchstone.
One that old Frederick, your father, loves.

Celia.
My father's love is enough to honor him enough. Speak no more of him, you'll be whipt for taxation one of these days.

Touchstone.
The more pity that fools may not speak wisely what wise men do foolishly.

Celia.
By my troth, thou sayest true; for since the little wit that fools have was silenc'd, the little foolery that wise men have makes a great show. Here comes Monsieur Le Beau.

Enter Le Beau.

Rosalind.
With his mouth full of news.

Celia.
Which he will put on us, as pigeons feed their young.

Rosalind.
Then shall we be news-cramm'd.

Celia.
All the better; we shall be the more marketable. Bonjour, Monsieur Le Beau. What's the news?

Le Beau.
Fair princess, you have lost much good sport.

Celia.
Sport! Of what color?

Le Beau.
What color, madam? How shall I answer you?

Rosalind.
As wit and fortune will.

Touchstone.
Or as the Destinies decrees.

Celia.
Well said—that was laid on with a trowel.

Touchstone.
Nay, if I keep not my rank—

Rosalind.
Thou losest thy old smell.

Le Beau.
You amaze me, ladies. I would have told you of good wrestling, which you have lost the sight of.

Rosalind.
Yet tell us the manner of the wrestling.

Le Beau.
I will tell you the beginning; and if it please your ladyships, you may see the end, for the best is yet to do, and here where you are, they are coming to perform it.

Celia.
Well, the beginning, that is dead and buried.

Le Beau.
There comes an old man and his three sons—

Celia.
I could match this beginning with an old tale.

Le Beau.
Three proper young men, of excellent growth and presence.

Rosalind.
With bills on their necks, "Be it known unto all men by these presents."

Le Beau.
The eldest of the three wrestled with Charles, the Duke's wrestler, which Charles in a moment threw him, and broke three of his ribs, that there is little hope of life in him. So he serv'd the second, and so the third. Yonder they lie, the poor old man, their father, making such pitiful dole over them that all the beholders take his part with weeping.

Rosalind.
Alas!

Touchstone.
But what is the sport, monsieur, that the ladies have lost?

Le Beau.
Why, this that I speak of.

Touchstone.
Thus men may grow wiser every day. It is the first time that ever I heard breaking of ribs was sport for ladies.

Celia.
Or I, I promise thee.

Rosalind.
But is there any else longs to see this broken music in his sides? Is there yet another dotes upon rib-breaking? Shall we see this wrestling, cousin?

Le Beau.
You must if you stay here, for here is the place appointed for the wrestling, and they are ready to perform it.

Celia.
Yonder sure they are coming. Let us now stay and see it.

Flourish. Enter Duke Frederick, Lords, Orlando, Charles, and Attendants.

Duke Frederick.
Come on. Since the youth will not be entreated, his own peril on his forwardness.

Rosalind.
Is yonder the man?

Le Beau.
Even he, madam.

Celia.
Alas, he is too young! Yet he looks successfully.

Duke Frederick.
How now, daughter and cousin? Are you crept hither to see the wrestling?

Rosalind.
Ay, my liege, so please you give us leave.

Duke Frederick.
You will take little delight in it, I can tell you, there is such odds in the man. In pity of the challenger's youth I would fain dissuade him, but he will not be entreated. Speak to him, ladies, see if you can move him.

Celia.
Call him hither, good Monsieur Le Beau.

Duke Frederick.
Do so; I'll not be by.

Le Beau.
Monsieur the challenger, the princess calls for you.

Orlando.
I attend them with all respect and duty.

Rosalind.
Young man, have you challeng'd Charles the wrestler?

Orlando.
No, fair princess; he is the general challenger. I come but in, as others do, to try with him the strength of my youth.

Celia.
Young gentleman, your spirits are too bold for your years. You have seen cruel proof of this man's strength. If you saw yourself with your eyes, or knew yourself with your judgment, the fear of your adventure would counsel you to a more equal enterprise. We pray you for your own sake to embrace your own safety, and give over this attempt.

Rosalind.
Do, young sir, your reputation shall not therefore be mispris'd. We will make it our suit to the Duke that the wrestling might not go forward.

Orlando.
I beseech you, punish me not with your hard thoughts, wherein I confess me much guilty to deny so fair and excellent ladies any thing. But let your fair eyes and gentle wishes go with me to my trial; wherein if I be foil'd, there is but one sham'd that was never gracious; if kill'd, but one dead that is willing to be so. I shall do my friends no wrong, for I have none to lament me; the world no injury, for in it I have nothing. Only in the world I fill up a place, which may be better supplied when I have made it empty.

Rosalind.
The little strength that I have, I would it were with you.

Celia.
And mine, to eke out hers.

Rosalind.
Fare you well; pray heaven I be deceiv'd in you!

Celia.
Your heart's desires be with you!

Charles.
Come, where is this young gallant that is so desirous to lie with his mother earth?

Orlando.
Ready, sir, but his will hath in it a more modest working.

Duke Frederick.
You shall try but one fall.

Charles.
No, I warrant your Grace, you shall not entreat him to a second, that have so mightily persuaded him from a first.

Orlando.
You mean to mock me after; you should not have mock'd me before. But come your ways.

Rosalind.
Now Hercules be thy speed, young man!

Celia.
I would I were invisible, to catch the strong fellow by the leg.

Wrestle.

Rosalind.
O excellent young man!

Celia.
If I had a thunderbolt in mine eye, I can tell who should down.

Charles is thrown. Shout.

Duke Frederick.
No more, no more.

Orlando.
Yes, I beseech your Grace, I am not yet well breath'd.

Duke Frederick.
How dost thou, Charles?

Le Beau.
He cannot speak, my lord.

Duke Frederick.
Bear him away. What is thy name, young man?

Orlando.
Orlando, my liege, the youngest son of Sir Rowland de Boys.

Duke Frederick.
I would thou hadst been son to some man else:
The world esteem'd thy father honorable,
But I did find him still mine enemy.
Thou shouldst have better pleas'd me with this deed
Hadst thou descended from another house.

But fare thee well, thou art a gallant youth.
I would thou hadst told me of another father.

Exit Duke with Train and Le Beau.

Celia.
Were I my father, coz, would I do this?

Orlando.
I am more proud to be Sir Rowland's son,
His youngest son, and would not change that calling
To be adopted heir to Frederick.

Rosalind.
My father lov'd Sir Rowland as his soul,
And all the world was of my father's mind.
Had I before known this young man his son,
I should have given him tears unto entreaties,
Ere he should thus have ventur'd.

Celia.
                Gentle cousin,
Let us go thank him, and encourage him.
My father's rough and envious disposition
Sticks me at heart. Sir, you have well deserv'd.
If you do keep your promises in love
But justly as you have exceeded all promise,
Your mistress shall be happy.

Rosalind.
                Gentleman,

Giving him a chain from her neck.

Wear this for me: one out of suits with Fortune,
That could give more, but that her hand lacks means.
Shall we go, coz?

Celia.
           Ay. Fare you well, fair gentleman.

Orlando.
Can I not say, I thank you? My better parts
Are all thrown down, and that which here stands up
Is but a quintain, a mere lifeless block.

Rosalind.
He calls us back. My pride fell with my fortunes,
I'll ask him what he would. Did you call, sir?
Sir, you have wrestled well, and overthrown
More than your enemies.

Celia.
              Will you go, coz?

Rosalind.
Have with you.—Fare you well.

Exit with Celia.

Orlando.
What passion hangs these weights upon my tongue?
I cannot speak to her, yet she urg'd conference.

Enter Le Beau.

O poor Orlando! Thou art overthrown,
Or Charles, or something weaker, masters thee.

Le Beau.
Good sir, I do in friendship counsel you
To leave this place. Albeit you have deserv'd
High commendation, true applause, and love,
Yet such is now the Duke's condition
That he misconsters all that you have done.
The Duke is humorous— what he is indeed
More suits you to conceive than I to speak of.

Orlando.
I thank you, sir; and pray you tell me this:
Which of the two was daughter of the Duke,
That here was at the wrestling?

Le Beau.
Neither his daughter, if we judge by manners,
But yet indeed the smaller is his daughter.
The other is daughter to the banish'd Duke,
And here detain'd by her usurping uncle
To keep his daughter company, whose loves
Are dearer than the natural bond of sisters.
But I can tell you that of late this Duke
Hath ta'en displeasure 'gainst his gentle niece,
Grounded upon no other argument
But that the people praise her for her virtues,
And pity her for her good father's sake;
And on my life his malice 'gainst the lady
Will suddenly break forth. Sir, fare you well.
Hereafter, in a better world than this,
I shall desire more love and knowledge of you.

Orlando.
I rest much bounden to you; fare you well.

Exit Le Beau.

Thus must I from the smoke into the smother,
From tyrant Duke unto a tyrant brother.
But heavenly Rosalind!

Exit.

Scene 3

A room in the Duke's palace.

(Celia; Rosalind; Duke Frederick; First Lord at Court; Second Lord at Court)

Celia forces the melancholy Rosalind to admit she is in love with Orlando. Duke Frederick banishes Rosalind despite Celia's pleas, convinced that she is treacherous. Together Rosalind and Celia plan to flee to the forest to find Duke Senior, Rosalind's banished father. They decide to disguise themselves as a pair of low-born people, Ganymede and Aliena, and to take Touchstone with them.

Enter Celia and Rosalind.

Celia.
Why, cousin, why, Rosalind! Cupid have mercy, not a word?

Rosalind.
Not one to throw at a dog.

Celia.
No, thy words are too precious to be cast away upon curs, throw some of them at me. Come lame me with reasons.

Rosalind.
Then there were two cousins laid up, when the one should be lam'd with reasons, and the other mad without any.

Celia.
But is all this for your father?

Rosalind.
No, some of it is for my child's father. O how full of briers is this working-day world!

Celia.
They are but burs, cousin, thrown upon thee in holiday foolery; if we walk not in the trodden paths, our very petticoats will catch them.

Rosalind.
I could shake them off my coat; these burs are in my heart.

Celia.
Hem them away.

Rosalind.
I would try, if I could cry "hem" and have him.

Celia.
Come, come, wrestle with thy affections.

Rosalind.
O, they take the part of a better wrestler than myself!

Celia.
O, a good wish upon you! You will try in time, in despite of a fall. But turning these jests out of service, let us talk in good earnest. Is it possible, on such a sudden, you should fall into so strong a liking with old Sir Rowland's youngest son?

Rosalind.
The Duke my father lov'd his father dearly.

Celia.
Doth it therefore ensue that you should love his son dearly? By this kind of chase, I should hate him, for my father hated his father dearly; yet I hate not Orlando.

Rosalind.
No, faith, hate him not, for my sake.

Celia.
Why should I not? Doth he not deserve well?

Enter Duke Frederick with Lords.

Rosalind.
Let me love him for that, and do you love him because I do. Look, here comes the Duke.

Celia.
With his eyes full of anger.

Duke Frederick.
Mistress, dispatch you with your safest haste,
And get you from our court.

Rosalind.
        Me, uncle?

Duke Frederick.
        You, cousin.
Within these ten days if that thou beest found
So near our public court as twenty miles,
Thou diest for it.

Rosalind.
                I do beseech your Grace
Let me the knowledge of my fault bear with me:
If with myself I hold intelligence,
Or have acquaintance with mine own desires;
If that I do not dream, or be not frantic
(As I do trust I am not), then, dear uncle,
Never so much as in a thought unborn
Did I offend your Highness.

Duke Frederick.
                    Thus do all traitors:
If their purgation did consist in words,
They are as innocent as grace itself.
Let it suffice thee that I trust thee not.

Rosalind.
Yet your mistrust cannot make me a traitor.
Tell me whereon the likelihood depends.

Duke Frederick.
Thou art thy father's daughter, there's enough.

Rosalind.
So was I when your Highness took his dukedom,
So was I when your Highness banish'd him.
Treason is not inherited, my lord,
Or if we did derive it from our friends,
What's that to me? My father was no traitor.
Then, good my liege, mistake me not so much
To think my poverty is treacherous.

Celia.
Dear sovereign, hear me speak.

Duke Frederick.
Ay, Celia, we stay'd her for your sake,
Else had she with her father rang'd along.

Celia.
I did not then entreat to have her stay,
It was your pleasure and your own remorse.
I was too young that time to value her,
But now I know her. If she be a traitor,
Why, so am I. We still have slept together,
Rose at an instant, learn'd, play'd, eat together,
And wheresoe'er we went, like Juno's swans,
Still we went coupled and inseparable.

Duke Frederick.
She is too subtile for thee, and her smoothness,
Her very silence, and her patience
Speak to the people, and they pity her.
Thou art a fool; she robs thee of thy name,
And thou wilt show more bright and seem more virtuous
When she is gone. Then open not thy lips:
Firm and irrevocable is my doom
Which I have pass'd upon her; she is banish'd.

Celia.
Pronounce that sentence then on me, my liege,
I cannot live out of her company.

Duke Frederick.
You are a fool. You, niece, provide yourself;
If you outstay the time, upon mine honor,
And in the greatness of my word, you die.

Exit Duke with Lords.

Celia.
O my poor Rosalind, whither wilt thou go?
Wilt thou change fathers? I will give thee mine.
I charge thee be not thou more griev'd than I am.

Rosalind.
I have more cause.

Celia.
                Thou hast not, cousin,
Prithee be cheerful. Know'st thou not the Duke
Hath banish'd me, his daughter?

Rosalind.
                That he hath not.

Celia.
No, hath not? Rosalind lacks then the love
Which teacheth thee that thou and I am one.
Shall we be sund'red? Shall we part, sweet girl?
No, let my father seek another heir.
Therefore devise with me how we may fly,
Whither to go, and what to bear with us,
And do not seek to take your change upon you,
To bear your griefs yourself, and leave me out;
For by this heaven, now at our sorrows pale,
Say what thou canst, I'll go along with thee.

Rosalind.
Why, whither shall we go?

Celia.
To seek my uncle in the forest of Arden.

Rosalind.
Alas, what danger will it be to us,
Maids as we are, to travel forth so far!
Beauty provoketh thieves sooner than gold.

Celia.
I'll put myself in poor and mean attire,
And with a kind of umber smirch my face;
The like do you. So shall we pass along
And never stir assailants.

Rosalind.
                    Were it not better,
Because that I am more than common tall,
That I did suit me all points like a man?
A gallant curtle-axe upon my thigh,
A boar-spear in my hand, and—in my heart
Lie there what hidden woman's fear there will—
We'll have a swashing and a martial outside,
As many other mannish cowards have
That do outface it with their semblances.

Celia.
What shall I call thee when thou art a man?

Rosalind.
I'll have no worse a name than Jove's own page,
And therefore look you call me Ganymede.
But what will you be call'd?

Celia.
Something that hath a reference to my state:
No longer Celia, but Aliena.

Rosalind.
But, cousin, what if we assay'd to steal
The clownish fool out of your father's court?
Would he not be a comfort to our travel?

Celia.
He'll go along o'er the wide world with me;
Leave me alone to woo him. Let's away,
And get our jewels and our wealth together,
Devise the fittest time and safest way
To hide us from pursuit that will be made
After my flight. Now go we in content
To liberty, and not to banishment.

Exeunt.

Act 2

Scene 1

The Forest of Arden.

(Duke Senior; Amiens; First Lord in Arden; Second Lord in Arden)

Duke Senior finds adversity bracing and instructive, and Amiens agrees with him. The First Lord arrives to report having seen the melancholy Jacques moralizing over a wounded deer by a stream.

Enter Duke Senior, Amiens, and two or three Lords, like foresters.

Duke Senior.
Now, my co-mates and brothers in exile,
Hath not old custom made this life more sweet
Than that of painted pomp? Are not these woods
More free from peril than the envious court?
Here feel we not the penalty of Adam,
The seasons' difference, as the icy fang
And churlish chiding of the winter's wind,
Which when it bites and blows upon my body
Even till I shrink with cold, I smile and say,
"This is no flattery: these are counsellors
That feelingly persuade me what I am."
Sweet are the uses of adversity,
Which like the toad, ugly and venomous,
Wears yet a precious jewel in his head;
And this our life, exempt from public haunt,
Finds tongues in trees, books in the running brooks,
Sermons in stones, and good in every thing.

Amiens.
I would not change it. Happy is your Grace,
That can translate the stubbornness of fortune
Into so quiet and so sweet a style.

Duke Senior.
Come, shall we go and kill us venison?
And yet it irks me the poor dappled fools,
Being native burghers of this desert city,
Should in their own confines with forked heads
Have their round haunches gor'd.

First Lord in Arden.
Indeed, my lord,
The melancholy Jaques grieves at that,
And in that kind swears you do more usurp
Than doth your brother that hath banish'd you.

Today my Lord of Amiens and myself
Did steal behind him as he lay along
Under an oak, whose antique root peeps out
Upon the brook that brawls along this wood,
To the which place a poor sequest'red stag,
That from the hunter's aim had ta'en a hurt,
Did come to languish; and indeed, my lord,
The wretched animal heav'd forth such groans
That their discharge did stretch his leathern coat
Almost to bursting, and the big round tears
Cours'd one another down his innocent nose
In piteous chase; and thus the hairy fool,
Much marked of the melancholy Jaques,
Stood on th' extremest verge of the swift brook,
Augmenting it with tears.

Duke Senior.
But what said Jaques?
Did he not moralize this spectacle?

First Lord in Arden.
O yes, into a thousand similes.
First, for his weeping into the needless stream:
"Poor deer," quoth he, "thou mak'st a testament
As worldlings do, giving thy sum of more
To that which had too much." Then being there alone,
Left and abandoned of his velvet friends
"'Tis right," quoth he, "thus misery doth part
The flux of company." Anon a careless herd,
Full of the pasture, jumps along by him
And never stays to greet him. "Ay," quoth Jaques,
"Sweep on, you fat and greasy citizens,
'Tis just the fashion. Wherefore do you look
Upon that poor and broken bankrupt there?"
Thus most invectively he pierceth through
The body of the country, city, court,
Yea, and of this our life, swearing that we
Are mere usurpers, tyrants, and what's worse,
To fright the animals and to kill them up
In their assign'd and native dwelling-place.

Duke Senior.
And did you leave him in this contemplation?

Second Lord in Arden.
We did, my lord, weeping and commenting
Upon the sobbing deer.

Duke Senior.
Show me the place.
I love to cope him in these sullen fits,
For then he's full of matter.

First Lord in Arden.
I'll bring you to him straight.

Exeunt.

Scene 2

The Duke's palace.

(Duke Frederick; First Lord at Court; Second Lord at Court)

Duke Frederick finds his daughter has gone with Touchstone the clown. Discovering that a maid overheard Celia and Rosalind commending Orlando, he sends for Oliver to seek his brother out.

Enter Duke Frederick with Lords.

Duke Frederick.
Can it be possible that no man saw them?
It cannot be. Some villains of my court
Are of consent and sufferance in this.

First Lord at Court.
I cannot hear of any that did see her.
The ladies, her attendants of her chamber,
Saw her a-bed, and in the morning early
They found the bed untreasur'd of their mistress.

Second Lord at Court.
My lord, the roynish clown, at whom so oft
Your Grace was wont to laugh, is also missing.
Hisperia, the princess' gentlewoman,
Confesses that she secretly o'erheard
Your daughter and her cousin much commend
The parts and graces of the wrestler
That did but lately foil the sinowy Charles,
And she believes, where ever they are gone,
That youth is surely in their company.

Duke Frederick.
Send to his brother; fetch that gallant hither.
If he be absent, bring his brother to me;
I'll make him find him. Do this suddenly;
And let not search and inquisition quail
To bring again these foolish runaways.

Act 2, Scene 3

Exeunt.

Scene 3

Before Oliver's house.

(Orlando; Adam)

Adam warns Orlando that Oliver plans to kill him. He gives Orlando his life savings and insists on following his young master as a servant, despite his age.

Enter Orlando and Adam, meeting.

Orlando.
Who's there?

Adam.
What, my young master? O my gentle master,
O my sweet master, O you memory
Of old Sir Rowland! Why, what make you here?
Why are you virtuous? Why do people love you?
And wherefore are you gentle, strong, and valiant?
Why would you be so fond to overcome
The bonny priser of the humorous Duke?
Your praise is come too swiftly home before you.
Know you not, master, to some kind of men
Their graces serve them but as enemies?
No more do yours. Your virtues, gentle master,
Are sanctified and holy traitors to you.
O, what a world is this, when what is comely
Envenoms him that bears it!

Orlando.
Why, what's the matter?

Adam.
                    O unhappy youth,
Come not within these doors! Within this roof
The enemy of all your graces lives.
Your brother—no, no brother, yet the son
(Yet not the son, I will not call him son)
Of him I was about to call his father—
Hath heard your praises, and this night he means
To burn the lodging where you use to lie,
And you within it. If he fail of that,
He will have other means to cut you off;
I overheard him, and his practices.
This is no place, this house is but a butchery;
Abhor it, fear it, do not enter it.

Orlando.
Why, whither, Adam, wouldst thou have me go?

Adam.
No matter whither, so you come not here.

Orlando.
What, wouldst thou have me go and beg my food?
Or with a base and boist'rous sword enforce
A thievish living on the common road?
This I must do, or know not what to do;
Yet this I will not do, do how I can.
I rather will subject me to the malice
Of a diverted blood and bloody brother.

Adam.
But do not so. I have five hundred crowns,
The thrifty hire I sav'd under your father,
Which I did store to be my foster-nurse,
When service should in my old limbs lie lame,
And unregarded age in corners thrown.
Take that, and He that doth the ravens feed,
Yea, providently caters for the sparrow,
Be comfort to my age! Here is the gold,
All this I give you, let me be your servant.
Though I look old, yet I am strong and lusty;
For in my youth I never did apply
Hot and rebellious liquors in my blood,
Nor did not with unbashful forehead woo
The means of weakness and debility;
Therefore my age is as a lusty winter,
Frosty, but kindly. Let me go with you,
I'll do the service of a younger man
In all your business and necessities.

Orlando.
O good old man, how well in thee appears
The constant service of the antique world,
When service sweat for duty, not for meed!
Thou art not for the fashion of these times,
Where none will sweat but for promotion,
And having that do choke their service up
Even with the having. It is not so with thee.
But, poor old man, thou prun'st a rotten tree,
That cannot so much as a blossom yield
In lieu of all thy pains and husbandry.
But come thy ways, we'll go along together,
And ere we have thy youthful wages spent,
We'll light upon some settled low content.

Adam.
Master, go on, and I will follow thee
To the last gasp, with truth and loyalty.
From seventeen years till now almost fourscore

Here lived I, but now live here no more.
At seventeen years many their fortunes seek,
But at fourscore it is too late a week;
Yet fortune cannot recompense me better
Than to die well, and not my master's debtor.

Exeunt.

Scene 4

The Forest of Arden.

(Rosalind; Celia; Touchstone; Corin; Silvius)

Rosalind, Celia, and Touchstone are weary from walking in the forest. They overhear Silvius tells Corin of his great love for Phebe. The trio seek food from Corin, who tells them of a churlish master with a farm for sale, which they make plans to buy.

Enter Rosalind for Ganymede, Celia for Aliena, and Clown, alias Touchstone.

Rosalind.
O Jupiter, how weary are my spirits!

Touchstone.
I care not for my spirits, if my legs were not weary.

Rosalind.
I could find in my heart to disgrace my man's apparel and to cry like a woman; but I must comfort the weaker vessel, as doublet and hose ought to show itself courageous to petticoat; therefore courage, good Aliena.

Celia.
I pray you bear with me, I cannot go no further.

Touchstone.
For my part, I had rather bear with you than bear you. Yet I should bear no cross if I did bear you, for I think you have no money in your purse.

Rosalind.
Well, this is the forest of Arden.

Touchstone.
Ay, now am I in Arden, the more fool I. When I was at home, I was in a better place, but travelers must be content.

Enter Corin and Silvius.

Rosalind.
Ay, be so, good Touchstone. Look you, who comes here, a young man and an old in solemn talk.

Corin.
That is the way to make her scorn you still.

Silvius.
O Corin, that thou knew'st how I do love her!

Corin.
I partly guess; for I have lov'd ere now.

Silvius.
No, Corin, being old, thou canst not guess,
Though in thy youth thou wast as true a lover
As ever sigh'd upon a midnight pillow.
But if thy love were ever like to mine—
As sure I think did never man love so—
How many actions most ridiculous
Hast thou been drawn to by thy fantasy?

Corin.
Into a thousand that I have forgotten.

Silvius.
O, thou didst then never love so heartily!
If thou rememb'rest not the slightest folly
That ever love did make thee run into,
Thou hast not lov'd;
Or if thou hast not sat as I do now,
Wearing thy hearer in thy mistress' praise,
Thou hast not lov'd;
Or if thou hast not broke from company
Abruptly, as my passion now makes me,
Thou hast not lov'd.
O Phebe, Phebe, Phebe!

Exit.

Rosalind.
Alas, poor shepherd, searching of thy wound,
I have by hard adventure found mine own.

Touchstone.
And I mine. I remember when I was in love, I broke my sword upon a stone, and bid him take that for coming a-night to Jane Smile; and I remember the kissing of her batler and the cow's dugs that her pretty chopp'd hands had milk'd; and I remember the wooing of a peascod instead of her, from whom I took two cods, and giving her them again, said with weeping tears, "Wear these for my sake." We that are true lovers run

into strange capers; but as all is mortal in nature, so is all nature in love mortal in folly.

Rosalind.
Thou speak'st wiser than thou art ware of.

Touchstone.
Nay, I shall ne'er be ware of mine own wit till I break my shins against it.

Rosalind.
Jove, Jove! This shepherd's passion
Is much upon my fashion.

Touchstone.
And mine, but it grows something stale with me.

Celia.
I pray you, one of you question yond man,
If he for gold will give us any food;
I faint almost to death.

Touchstone.
          Holla! You clown!

Rosalind.
Peace, fool, he's not thy kinsman.

Corin.
          Who calls?

Touchstone.
Your betters, sir.

Corin.
          Else are they very wretched.

Rosalind.
Peace, I say. Good even to you, friend.

Corin.
And to you, gentle sir, and to you all.

Rosalind.
I prithee, shepherd, if that love or gold
Can in this desert place buy entertainment,
Bring us where we may rest ourselves and feed.
Here's a young maid with travel much oppressed,
And faints for succor.

Corin.
          Fair sir, I pity her,
And wish, for her sake more than for mine own,
My fortunes were more able to relieve her;
But I am shepherd to another man,
And do not shear the fleeces that I graze.
My master is of churlish disposition,
And little reaks to find the way to heaven
By doing deeds of hospitality.
Besides, his cote, his flocks, and bounds of feed
Are now on sale, and at our sheep-cote now
By reason of his absence there is nothing
That you will feed on; but what is, come see,
And in my voice most welcome shall you be.

Rosalind.
What is he that shall buy his flock and pasture?

Corin.
That young swain that you saw here but erewhile,
That little cares for buying any thing.

Rosalind.
I pray thee, if it stand with honesty,
Buy thou the cottage, pasture, and the flock,
And thou shalt have to pay for it of us.

Celia.
And we will mend thy wages. I like this place,
And willingly could waste my time in it.

Corin.
Assuredly the thing is to be sold.
Go with me; if you like upon report
The soil, the profit, and this kind of life,
I will your very faithful feeder be,
And buy it with your gold right suddenly.

Exeunt.

Scene 5

Another part of the Forest of Arden.

(Amiens; Jaques)

Jaques listens to Amiens sing a melancholy song and asks for more. He makes mock of the other lords.

Enter Amiens, Jaques, and others.
Song.

Amiens.
Under the greenwood tree
Who loves to lie with me,
And turn his merry note
Unto the sweet bird's throat,
Come hither, come hither, come hither!

Here shall he see
No enemy
But winter and rough weather.

Jaques.
More, more, I prithee more.

Amiens.
It will make you melancholy, Monsieur Jaques.

Jaques.
I thank it. More, I prithee more. I can suck melancholy out of a song, as a weasel sucks eggs. More, I prithee more.

Amiens.
My voice is ragged, I know I cannot please you.

Jaques.
I do not desire you to please me, I do desire you to sing. Come, more, another stanzo. Call you 'em stanzos?

Amiens.
What you will, Monsieur Jaques.

Jaques.
Nay, I care not for their names, they owe me nothing. Will you sing?

Amiens.
More at your request than to please myself.

Jaques.
Well then, if ever I thank any man, I'll thank you; but that they call compliment is like th' encounter of two dog-apes; and when a man thanks me heartily, methinks I have given him a penny, and he renders me the beggarly thanks. Come, sing; and you that will not, hold your tongues.

Amiens.
Well, I'll end the song. Sirs, cover the while; the Duke will drink under this tree. He hath been all this day to look you.

Jaques.
And I have been all this day to avoid him. He is too disputable for my company. I think of as many matters as he, but I give heaven thanks, and make no boast of them. Come, warble, come.

Amiens.

Song. All together here.

Who doth ambition shun,
And loves to live i' th' sun,
Seeking the food he eats,
And pleas'd with what he gets,
Come hither, come hither, come hither!
Here shall he see
No enemy
But winter and rough weather.

Jaques.
I'll give you a verse to this note, that I made yesterday in despite of my invention.

Amiens.
And I'll sing it.

Jaques.
Thus it goes:
If it do come to pass
That any man turn ass,
Leaving his wealth and ease
A stubborn will to please,
Ducdame, ducdame, ducdame!
Here shall he see
Gross fools as he,
And if he will come to me.

Amiens.
What's that "ducdame"?

Jaques.
'Tis a Greek invocation, to call fools into a circle. I'll go sleep, if I can; if I cannot, I'll rail against all the first-born of Egypt.

Amiens.
And I'll go seek the Duke, his banquet is prepar'd.

Exeunt.

Scene 6

Another part of the Forest of Arden.

(Orlando; Adam)

Adam, weary and famished, is ready to die, but Orlando comforts him.

Enter Orlando and Adam.

Act 2, Scene 7

Adam.
Dear master, I can go no further. O, I die for food! Here lie I down, and measure out my grave. Farewell, kind master.

Orlando.
Why, how now, Adam? No greater heart in thee? Live a little, comfort a little, cheer thyself a little. If this uncouth forest yield any thing savage, I will either be food for it, or bring it for food to thee. Thy conceit is nearer death than thy powers. For my sake be comfortable, hold death a while at the arm's end. I will here be with thee presently, and if I bring thee not something to eat, I will give thee leave to die; but if thou diest before I come, thou art a mocker of my labor. Well said, thou look'st cheerly, and I'll be with thee quickly. Yet thou liest in the bleak air. Come, I will bear thee to some shelter, and thou shalt not die for lack of a dinner if there live any thing in this desert. Cheerly, good Adam!

Exeunt.

Scene 7

Another part of the Forest of Arden.

(Duke Senior; Amiens; First Lord in Arden; Second Lord in Arden; Jaques; Orlando; Adam)

Jaques comes in late to meal, bubbling over with a story about a clown he met. Discussion is interrupted when Orlando bursts in with his sword drawn, demanding food. Receiving a gentle answer, he is embarrassed at having supposed the lords to be rough fellows. Before accepting any food he insists on going back to fetch Adam. As the Duke and his men wait for Orlando's return, Jaques moralizes on the seven stages of mankind's life. When Orlando returns bearing Adam on his back, Amiens sings a song to accompany their meal. Discovering who Orlando's father was, the Duke makes him welcome.

A table set out. Enter Duke Senior, Amiens, and Lords, like outlaws.

Duke Senior.
I think he be transform'd into a beast,
For I can no where find him like a man.

First Lord in Arden.
My lord, he is but even now gone hence;
Here was he merry, hearing of a song.

Duke Senior.
If he, compact of jars, grow musical,
We shall have shortly discord in the spheres.
Go seek him, tell him I would speak with him.

Enter Jaques.

First Lord in Arden.
He saves my labor by his own approach.

Duke Senior.
Why, how now, monsieur, what a life is this,
That your poor friends must woo your company?
What, you look merrily!

Jaques.
A fool, a fool! I met a fool i' th' forest,
A motley fool. A miserable world!
As I do live by food, I met a fool,
Who laid him down, and bask'd him in the sun,
And rail'd on Lady Fortune in good terms,
In good set terms, and yet a motley fool.
"Good morrow, fool," quoth I. "No, sir," quoth he,
"Call me not fool till heaven hath sent me fortune."
And then he drew a dial from his poke,
And looking on it, with lack-lustre eye,
Says very wisely, "It is ten a' clock.
Thus we may see," quoth he, "how the world wags.
'Tis but an hour ago since it was nine,
And after one hour more 'twill be eleven,
And so from hour to hour, we ripe and ripe,
And then from hour to hour, we rot and rot;
And thereby hangs a tale." When I did hear
The motley fool thus moral on the time,
My lungs began to crow like chanticleer,
That fools should be so deep contemplative;
And I did laugh sans intermission
An hour by his dial. O noble fool!
A worthy fool! Motley's the only wear.

Duke Senior.
What fool is this?

Jaques.
O worthy fool! One that hath been a courtier,
And says, if ladies be but young and fair,
They have the gift to know it; and in his brain,
Which is as dry as the remainder biscuit
After a voyage, he hath strange places cramm'd
With observation, the which he vents
In mangled forms. O that I were a fool!
I am ambitious for a motley coat.

Duke Senior.
Thou shalt have one.

Jaques.
                It is my only suit—
Provided that you weed your better judgments
Of all opinion that grows rank in them
That I am wise. I must have liberty
Withal, as large a charter as the wind,
To blow on whom I please, for so fools have;
And they that are most galled with my folly,
They most must laugh. And why, sir, must they so?
The why is plain as way to parish church:
He that a fool doth very wisely hit
Doth very foolishly, although he smart,
Not to seem senseless of the bob; if not,
The wise man's folly is anatomiz'd
Even by the squand'ring glances of the fool.
Invest me in my motley; give me leave
To speak my mind, and I will through and through
Cleanse the foul body of th' infected world,
If they will patiently receive my medicine.

Duke Senior.
Fie on thee! I can tell what thou wouldst do.

Jaques.
What, for a counter, would I do but good?

Duke Senior.
Most mischievous foul sin, in chiding sin:
For thou thyself hast been a libertine,
As sensual as the brutish sting itself,
And all th' embossed sores, and headed evils,
That thou with license of free foot hast caught,
Wouldst thou disgorge into the general world.

Jaques.
Why, who cries out on pride
That can therein tax any private party?
Doth it not flow as hugely as the sea,
Till that the weary very means do ebb?
What woman in the city do I name,
When that I say the city-woman bears
The cost of princes on unworthy shoulders?
Who can come in and say that I mean her,
When such a one as she, such is her neighbor?
Or what is he of basest function,
That says his bravery is not on my cost,
Thinking that I mean him, but therein suits
His folly to the mettle of my speech?
There then! How then? What then? Let me see wherein
My tongue hath wrong'd him; if it do him right,
Then he hath wrong'd himself. If he be free,
Why then my taxing like a wild goose flies,
Unclaim'd of any man. But who comes here?

Enter Orlando with his sword drawn.

Orlando.
Forbear, and eat no more.

Jaques.
                Why, I have eat none yet.

Orlando.
Nor shalt not, till necessity be serv'd.

Jaques.
Of what kind should this cock come of?

Duke Senior.
Art thou thus bolden'd, man, by thy distress?
Or else a rude despiser of good manners,
That in civility thou seem'st so empty?

Orlando.
You touch'd my vein at first. The thorny point
Of bare distress hath ta'en from me the show
Of smooth civility; yet am I inland bred,
And know some nurture. But forbear, I say,
He dies that touches any of this fruit
Till I and my affairs are answered.

Jaques.
And you will not be answer'd with reason,
I must die.

Duke Senior.
What would you have? Your gentleness shall force,
More than your force move us to gentleness.

Orlando.
I almost die for food, and let me have it.

Duke Senior.
Sit down and feed, and welcome to our table.

Orlando.
Speak you so gently? Pardon me, I pray you.
I thought that all things had been savage here,
And therefore put I on the countenance
Of stern command'ment. Bur what e'er you are
That in this desert inaccessible,

Under the shade of melancholy boughs,
Lose and neglect the creeping hours of time;
If ever you have look'd on better days,
If ever been where bells have knoll'd to church,
If ever sate at any good man's feast,
If ever from your eyelids wip'd a tear,
And know what 'tis to pity, and be pitied,
Let gentleness my strong enforcement be,
In the which hope I blush, and hide my sword.

Duke Senior.
True is it that we have seen better days,
And have with holy bell been knoll'd to church,
And sat at good men's feasts, and wip'd our eyes
Of drops that sacred pity hath engend'red;
And therefore sit you down in gentleness,
And take upon command what help we have
That to your wanting may be minist'red.

Orlando.
Then but forbear your food a little while,
Whiles, like a doe, I go to find my fawn,
And give it food. There is an old poor man,
Who after me hath many a weary step
Limp'd in pure love; till he be first suffic'd,
Oppress'd with two weak evils, age and hunger,
I will not touch a bit.

Duke Senior.
                    Go find him out,
And we will nothing waste till you return.

Orlando.
I thank ye, and be blest for your good comfort!

Exit.

Duke Senior.
Thou seest we are not all alone unhappy:
This wide and universal theatre
Presents more woeful pageants than the scene
Wherein we play in.

Jaques.
                    All the world's a stage,
And all the men and women merely players;
They have their exits and their entrances,
And one man in his time plays many parts,
His acts being seven ages. At first the infant,
Mewling and puking in the nurse's arms.
Then the whining schoolboy, with his satchel
And shining morning face, creeping like snail
Unwillingly to school. And then the lover,
Sighing like furnace, with a woeful ballad
Made to his mistress' eyebrow. Then a soldier,
Full of strange oaths, and bearded like the pard,
Jealous in honor, sudden, and quick in quarrel,
Seeking the bubble reputation
Even in the cannon's mouth. And then the justice,
In fair round belly with good capon lin'd,
With eyes severe and beard of formal cut,
Full of wise saws and modern instances;
And so he plays his part. The sixth age shifts
Into the lean and slipper'd pantaloon,
With spectacles on nose, and pouch on side,
His youthful hose, well sav'd, a world too wide
For his shrunk shank, and his big manly voice,
Turning again toward childish treble, pipes
And whistles in his sound. Last scene of all,
That ends this strange eventful history,
Is second childishness, and mere oblivion,
Sans teeth, sans eyes, sans taste, sans every thing.

Enter Orlando with Adam.

Duke Senior.
Welcome. Set down your venerable burden,
And let him feed.

Orlando.
I thank you most for him.

Adam.
                    So had you need,
I scarce can speak to thank you for myself.

Duke Senior.
Welcome, fall to. I will not trouble you
As yet to question you about your fortunes.
Give us some music, and, good cousin, sing.

Song.

Amiens.
Blow, blow, thou winter wind,
Thou art not so unkind
As man's ingratitude;
Thy tooth is not so keen,
Because thou art not seen,
Although thy breath be rude.
Heigh-ho, sing heigh-ho! Unto the green holly,
Most friendship is feigning, most loving mere folly.
Then heigh-ho, the holly!
This life is most jolly.

Freeze, freeze, thou bitter sky,
That dost not bite so nigh
As benefits forgot;
Though thou the waters warp,
Thy sting is not so sharp
As friend rememb'red not.
Heigh-ho, sing, etc.

Duke Senior.
If that you were the good Sir Rowland's son,
As you have whisper'd faithfully you were,
And as mine eye doth his effigies witness
Most truly limn'd and living in your face,
Be truly welcome hither. I am the Duke
That lov'd your father. The residue of your fortune,
Go to my cave and tell me. Good old man,
Thou art right welcome as thy master is.
Support him by the arm. Give me your hand,
And let me all your fortunes understand.

Exeunt.

Act 3

Scene 1

The Duke's palace.

(Duke Frederick; First Lord at Court; Second Lord at Court; Oliver)

Duke Frederick orders Oliver to produce Orlando within a year or forfeit his lands and life.

Enter Duke Frederick, Lords, and Oliver.

Duke Frederick.
Not see him since? Sir, sir, that cannot be.
But were I not the better part made mercy,
I should not seek an absent argument
Of my revenge, thou present. But look to it:
Find out thy brother, wheresoe'er he is;
Seek him with candle; bring him dead or living
Within this twelvemonth, or turn thou no more
To seek a living in our territory.
Thy lands and all things that thou dost call thine
Worth seizure do we seize into our hands,
Till thou canst quit thee by thy brother's mouth
Of what we think against thee.

Oliver.
O that your Highness knew my heart in this!
I never lov'd my brother in my life.

Duke Frederick.
More villain thou. Well, push him out of doors,
And let my officers of such a nature
Make an extent upon his house and lands.
Do this expediently, and turn him going.

Exeunt.

Scene 2

The Forest of Arden.

(Orlando; Corin; Touchstone; Rosalind; Celia; Orlando; Jaques)

Orlando hangs love poems to Rosalind from the trees. Touchstone and Corin argue over which life is better, that of the courtier or of the shepherd, but Corin finds Touchstone's wit impossible to get around and gives up. Finding Orlando's verses, Rosalind is horrified at their dreadful quality and Touchstone quickly improvises more in the same style. Celia enters, reading yet another of Orlando's poems, and teasingly lets Rosalind know who their author is. The ladies overhear Jaques and Orlando discussing love and melancholy. Protected by her disguise, Rosalind mocks Orlando for not looking the part of a lover and offers to cure him of his affection. Orlando agrees to practice wooing Rosalind on "Ganymede", not realizing that they are one and the same.

Enter Orlando with a paper.

Orlando.
Hang there, my verse, in witness of my love,
And thou, thrice-crowned queen of night, survey
With thy chaste eye, from thy pale sphere above,
Thy huntress' name that my full life doth sway.
O Rosalind, these trees shall be my books,
And in their barks my thoughts I'll character,
That every eye which in this forest looks
Shall see thy virtue witness'd every where.
Run, run, Orlando, carve on every tree
The fair, the chaste, and unexpressive she.

Exit.
Enter Corin and Clown (Touchstone).

Corin.
And how like you this shepherd's life, Master Touchstone?

Touchstone.
Truly, shepherd, in respect of itself, it is a good life; but in respect that it is a shepherd's life, it is naught. In respect that it is solitary, I like it very well; but in respect that it is private, it is a very vild life. Now in respect it is in the fields, it pleaseth me well; but in respect it is not in the court, it is tedious. As it is a spare life (look you) it fits my humor well; but as there is no more plenty in it, it goes much against my stomach. Hast any philosophy in thee, shepherd?

Corin.
No more but that I know the more one sickens the worse at ease he is; and that he that wants money, means, and content is without three good friends; that the property of rain is to wet and fire to burn; that good pasture makes fat sheep; and that a great cause of the night is lack of the sun; that he that hath learn'd no wit by nature, nor art, may complain of good breeding, or comes of a very dull kindred.

Touchstone.
Such a one is a natural philosopher. Wast ever in court, shepherd?

Corin.
No, truly.

Touchstone.
Then thou art damn'd.

Corin.
Nay, I hope.

Touchstone.
Truly, thou art damn'd, like an ill-roasted egg, all on one side.

Corin.
For not being at court? Your reason.

Touchstone.
Why, if thou never wast at court, thou never saw'st good manners; if thou never saw'st good manners, then thy manners must be wicked, and wickedness is sin, and sin is damnation. Thou art in a parlous state, shepherd.

Corin.
Not a whit, Touchstone. Those that are good manners at the court are as ridiculous in the country as the behavior of the country is most mockable at the court. You told me you salute not at the court but you kiss your hands; that courtesy would be uncleanly if courtiers were shepherds.

Touchstone.
Instance, briefly; come, instance.

Corin.
Why, we are still handling our ewes, and their fells you know are greasy.

Touchstone.
Why, do not your courtier's hands sweat? And is not the grease of a mutton as wholesome as the sweat of a man? Shallow, shallow. A better instance, I say; come.

Corin.
Besides, our hands are hard.

Touchstone.
Your lips will feel them the sooner. Shallow again. A more sounder instance, come.

Corin.
And they are often tarr'd over with the surgery of our sheep; and would you have us kiss tar? The courtier's hands are perfum'd with civet.

Touchstone.
Most shallow man! Thou worm's-meat, in respect of a good piece of flesh indeed! Learn of the wise, and perpend: civet is of a baser birth than tar, the very uncleanly flux of a cat. Mend the instance, shepherd.

Corin.
You have too courtly a wit for me, I'll rest.

Touchstone.
Wilt thou rest damn'd? God help thee, shallow man! God make incision in thee, thou art raw.

Corin.
Sir, I am a true laborer: I earn that I eat, get that I wear, owe no man hate, envy no man's happiness, glad of other men's good, content with my harm, and the greatest of my pride is to see my ewes graze and my lambs suck.

Touchstone.
That is another simple sin in you, to bring the ewes and the rams together, and to offer to get your living by the copulation of cattle; to be bawd to a bell-wether, and to betray a she-lamb of a twelvemonth to a crooked-pated old cuckoldly ram, out of all reasonable match. If thou beest not damn'd for this, the devil

himself will have no shepherds; I cannot see else how thou shouldst scape.

Corin.
Here comes young Master Ganymede, my new mistress's brother.

Enter Rosalind with a paper, reading.

Rosalind.
"From the east to western Inde,
No jewel is like Rosalind.
Her worth, being mounted on the wind,
Through all the world bears Rosalind.
All the pictures fairest lin'd
Are but black to Rosalind.
Let no face be kept in mind
But the fair of Rosalind."

Touchstone.
I'll rhyme you so eight years together, dinners and suppers and sleeping-hours excepted. It is the right butter-women's rank to market.

Rosalind.
Out, fool!

Touchstone.
For a taste:
If a hart do lack a hind,
Let him seek out Rosalind.
If the cat will after kind,
So be sure will Rosalind.
Wint'red garments must be lin'd,
So must slender Rosalind.
They that reap must sheaf and bind,
Then to cart with Rosalind.
Sweetest nut hath sourest rind,
Such a nut is Rosalind.
He that sweetest rose will find,
Must find love's prick and Rosalind.
This is the very false gallop of verses; why do you infect yourself with them?

Rosalind.
Peace, you dull fool, I found them on a tree.

Touchstone.
Truly, the tree yields bad fruit.

Rosalind.
I'll graff it with you, and then I shall graff it with a medlar. Then it will be the earliest fruit i' th' country; for you'll be rotten ere you be half ripe, and that's the right virtue of the medlar.

Touchstone.
You have said; but whether wisely or no, let the forest judge.

Enter Celia with a writing.

Rosalind.
Peace,
Here comes my sister reading, stand aside.

Celia.

Reads.

"Why should this a desert be?
For it is unpeopled? No!
Tongues I'll hang on every tree,
That shall civil sayings show:
Some, how brief the life of man
Runs his erring pilgrimage,
That the stretching of a span
Buckles in his sum of age;
Some, of violated vows
'Twixt the souls of friend and friend;
But upon the fairest boughs,
Or at every sentence end,
Will I 'Rosalinda' write,
Teaching all that read to know
The quintessence of every sprite
Heaven would in little show.
Therefore heaven Nature charg'd
That one body should be fill'd
With all graces wide-enlarg'd.
Nature presently distill'd
Helen's cheek, but not her heart,
Cleopatra's majesty,
Atalanta's better part,
Sad Lucretia's modesty.
Thus Rosalind of many parts
By heavenly synod was devis'd,
Of many faces, eyes, and hearts,
To have the touches dearest priz'd.
Heaven would that she these gifts should have,
And I to live and die her slave."

Rosalind.
O most gentle Jupiter, what tedious homily of love have you wearied your parishioners withal, and never cried, "Have patience, good people!"

Celia.
How now? Back, friends! Shepherd, go off a little. Go with him, sirrah.

Touchstone.
Come, shepherd, let us make an honorable retreat, though not with bag and baggage, yet with scrip and scrippage.

Exit with Corin.

Celia.
Didst thou hear these verses?

Rosalind.
O yes, I heard them all, and more too, for some of them had in them more feet than the verses would bear.

Celia.
That's no matter; the feet might bear the verses.

Rosalind.
Ay, but the feet were lame, and could not bear themselves without the verse, and therefore stood lamely in the verse.

Celia.
But didst thou hear without wondering how thy name should be hang'd and carv'd upon these trees?

Rosalind.
I was seven of the nine days out of the wonder before you came; for look here what I found on a palm tree. I was never so berhym'd since Pythagoras' time, that I was an Irish rat, which I can hardly remember.

Celia.
Trow you who hath done this?

Rosalind.
Is it a man?

Celia.
And a chain, that you once wore, about his neck. Change you color?

Rosalind.
I prithee who?

Celia.
O Lord, Lord, it is a hard matter for friends to meet; but mountains may be remov'd with earthquakes, and so encounter.

Rosalind.
Nay, but who is it?

Celia.
Is it possible?

Rosalind.
Nay, I prithee now, with most petitionary vehemence, tell me who it is.

Celia.
O wonderful, wonderful, and most wonderful wonderful! And yet again wonderful, and after that, out of all hooping!

Rosalind.
Good my complexion, dost thou think, though I am caparison'd like a man, I have a doublet and hose in my disposition? One inch of delay more is a South-sea of discovery. I prithee tell me who is it quickly, and speak apace. I would thou couldst stammer, that thou mightst pour this conceal'd man out of thy mouth, as wine comes out of a narrow-mouth'd bottle, either too much at once, or none at all. I prithee take the cork out of thy mouth that I may drink thy tidings.

Celia.
So you may put a man in your belly.

Rosalind.
Is he of God's making? What manner of man? Is his head worth a hat? Or his chin worth a beard?

Celia.
Nay, he hath but a little beard.

Rosalind.
Why, God will send more, if the man will be thankful. Let me stay the growth of his beard, if thou delay me not the knowledge of his chin.

Celia.
It is young Orlando, that tripp'd up the wrestler's heels, and your heart, both in an instant.

Rosalind.
Nay, but the devil take mocking. Speak sad brow and true maid.

Celia.
I' faith, coz, 'tis he.

Rosalind.
Orlando?

Celia.
Orlando.

Rosalind.
Alas the day, what shall I do with my doublet and hose? What did he when thou saw'st him? What said he? How look'd he? Wherein went he? What makes he here? Did he ask for me? Where remains he? How parted he with thee? And when shalt thou see him again? Answer me in one word.

Celia.
You must borrow me Gargantua's mouth first; 'tis a word too great for any mouth of this age's size. To say ay and no to these particulars is more than to answer in a catechism.

Rosalind.
But doth he know that I am in this forest and in man's apparel? Looks he as freshly as he did the day he wrestled?

Celia.
It is as easy to count atomies as to resolve the propositions of a lover. But take a taste of my finding him, and relish it with good observance. I found him under a tree, like a dropp'd acorn.

Rosalind.
It may well be call'd Jove's tree, when it drops such fruit.

Celia.
Give me audience, good madam.

Rosalind.
Proceed.

Celia.
There lay he, stretch'd along, like a wounded knight.

Rosalind.
Though it be pity to see such a sight, it well becomes the ground.

Celia.
Cry "holla" to thy tongue, I prithee; it curvets unseasonably. He was furnish'd like a hunter.

Rosalind.
O ominous! He comes to kill my heart.

Celia.
I would sing my song without a burden; thou bring'st me out of tune.

Rosalind.
Do you not know I am a woman? When I think, I must speak. Sweet, say on.

Enter Orlando and Jaques.

Celia.
You bring me out. Soft, comes he not here?

Rosalind.
'Tis he. Slink by, and note him.

Jaques.
I thank you for your company, but, good faith, I had as lief have been myself alone.

Orlando.
And so had I; but yet for fashion sake I thank you too for your society.

Jaques.
God buy you, let's meet as little as we can.

Orlando.
I do desire we may be better strangers.

Jaques.
I pray you mar no more trees with writing love-songs in their barks.

Orlando.
I pray you mar no more of my verses with reading them ill-favoredly.

Jaques.
Rosalind is your love's name?

Orlando.
Yes, just.

Jaques.
I do not like her name.

Orlando.
There was no thought of pleasing you when she was christen'd.

Jaques.
What stature is she of?

Orlando.
Just as high as my heart.

Jaques.
You are full of pretty answers; have you not been acquainted with goldsmiths' wives, and conn'd them out of rings?

Orlando.
Not so; but I answer you right painted cloth, from whence you have studied your questions.

Jaques.
You have a nimble wit; I think 'twas made of Atalanta's heels. Will you sit down with me? And we two will rail against our mistress the world, and all our misery.

Orlando.
I will chide no breather in the world but myself, against whom I know most faults.

Jaques.
The worst fault you have is to be in love.

Orlando.
'Tis a fault I will not change for your best virtue. I am weary of you.

Jaques.
By my troth, I was seeking for a fool when I found you.

Orlando.
He is drown'd in the brook; look but in, and you shall see him.

Jaques.
There I shall see mine own figure.

Orlando.
Which I take to be either a fool or a cipher.

Jaques.
I'll tarry no longer with you. Farewell, good Signior Love.

Orlando.
I am glad of your departure. Adieu, good Monsieur Melancholy.

Exit Jaques.

Rosalind.

Aside to Celia.

I will speak to him like a saucy lackey, and under that habit play the knave with him.—Do you hear, forester?

Orlando.
Very well. What would you?

Rosalind.
I pray you, what is't a' clock?

Orlando.
You should ask me what time o' day; there's no clock in the forest.

Rosalind.
Then there is no true lover in the forest, else sighing every minute and groaning every hour would detect the lazy foot of Time as well as a clock.

Orlando.
And why not the swift foot of Time? Had not that been as proper?

Rosalind.
By no means, sir. Time travels in diverse paces with diverse persons. I'll tell you who Time ambles withal, who Time trots withal, who Time gallops withal, and who he stands still withal.

Orlando.
I prithee, who doth he trot withal?

Rosalind.
Marry, he trots hard with a young maid between the contract of her marriage and the day it is solemniz'd. If the interim be but a se'nnight, Time's pace is so hard that it seems the length of seven year.

Orlando.
Who ambles Time withal?

Rosalind.
With a priest that lacks Latin, and a rich man that hath not the gout; for the one sleeps easily because he cannot study, and the other lives merrily because

he feels no pain; the one lacking the burden of lean and wasteful learning, the other knowing no burden of heavy tedious penury. These Time ambles withal.

Orlando.
Who doth he gallop withal?

Rosalind.
With a thief to the gallows; for though he go as softly as foot can fall, he thinks himself too soon there.

Orlando.
Who stays it still withal?

Rosalind.
With lawyers in the vacation; for they sleep between term and term, and then they perceive not how Time moves.

Orlando.
Where dwell you, pretty youth?

Rosalind.
With this shepherdess, my sister; here in the skirts of the forest, like fringe upon a petticoat.

Orlando.
Are you native of this place?

Rosalind.
As the cony that you see dwell where she is kindled.

Orlando.
Your accent is something finer than you could purchase in so remov'd a dwelling.

Rosalind.
I have been told so of many; but indeed an old religious uncle of mine taught me to speak, who was in his youth an inland man, one that knew courtship too well, for there he fell in love. I have heard him read many lectures against it, and I thank God I am not a woman, to be touch'd with so many giddy offenses as he hath generally tax'd their whole sex withal.

Orlando.
Can you remember any of the principal evils that he laid to the charge of women?

Rosalind.
There were none principal, they were all like one another as halfpence are, every one fault seeming monstrous till his fellow-fault came to match it.

Orlando.
I prithee recount some of them.

Rosalind.
No; I will not cast away my physic but on those that are sick. There is a man haunts the forest, that abuses our young plants with carving 'Rosalind' on their barks; hangs odes upon hawthorns, and elegies on brambles; all, forsooth, deifying the name of Rosalind. If I could meet that fancy-monger, I would give him some good counsel, for he seems to have the quotidian of love upon him.

Orlando.
I am he that is so love-shak'd, I pray you tell me your remedy.

Rosalind.
There is none of my uncle's marks upon you. He taught me how to know a man in love; in which cage of rushes I am sure you are not prisoner.

Orlando.
What were his marks?

Rosalind.
A lean cheek, which you have not; a blue eye and sunken, which you have not; an unquestionable spirit, which you have not; a beard neglected, which you have not (but I pardon you for that, for simply your having in beard is a younger brother's revenue); then your hose should be ungarter'd, your bonnet unbanded, your sleeve unbutton'd, your shoe untied, and every thing about you demonstrating a careless desolation. But you are no such man; you are rather point-device in your accoustrements, as loving yourself, than seeming the lover of any other.

Orlando.
Fair youth, I would I could make thee believe I love.

Rosalind.
Me believe it? You may as soon make her that you love believe it, which I warrant she is apter to do than to confess she does. That is one of the points in the which women still give the lie to their consciences. But in good sooth, are you he that hangs the verses on the trees, wherein Rosalind is so admir'd?

Orlando.
I swear to thee, youth, by the white hand of Rosalind, I am that he, that unfortunate he.

Rosalind.
But are you so much in love as your rhymes speak?

Orlando.
Neither rhyme nor reason can express how much.

Rosalind.
Love is merely a madness, and I tell you, deserves as well a dark house and a whip as madmen do; and the reason why they are not so punish'd and cur'd is, that the lunacy is so ordinary that the whippers are in love too. Yet I profess curing it by counsel.

Orlando.
Did you ever cure any so?

Rosalind.
Yes, one, and in this manner. He was to imagine me his love, his mistress; and I set him every day to woo me. At which time would I, being but a moonish youth, grieve, be effeminate, changeable, longing and liking, proud, fantastical, apish, shallow, inconstant, full of tears, full of smiles; for every passion something, and for no passion truly any thing, as boys and women are for the most part cattle of this color; would now like him, now loathe him; then entertain him, then forswear him; now weep for him, then spit at him; that I drave my suitor from his mad humor of love to a living humor of madness, which was, to forswear the full stream of the world, and to live in a nook merely monastic. And thus I cur'd him, and this way will I take upon me to wash your liver as clean as a sound sheep's heart, that there shall not be one spot of love in't.

Orlando.
I would not be cur'd, youth.

Rosalind.
I would cure you, if you would but call me Rosalind, and come every day to my cote and woo me.

Orlando.
Now, by the faith of my love, I will. Tell me where it is.

Rosalind.
Go with me to it, and I'll show it you; and by the way, you shall tell me where in the forest you live. Will you go?

Orlando.
With all my heart, good youth.

Rosalind.
Nay, you must call me Rosalind. Come, sister, will you go?

Exeunt.

Scene 3

Another part of the Forest of Arden.

(Touchstone; Audrey; Jaques; Sir Oliver Martext)

As Jaques delightedly watches, Touchstone woos the country maid Audrey and convinces her to be married to him in the wood by the local vicar, the ill-qualified Sir Oliver Martext. Jaques spoils Touchstone's plans of having an easy-to-break wedding by forcing him to agree to a more proper, legal ceremony with a better cleric. Martext is left completely unabashed at this lack of confidence in his abilities.

Enter Clown (Touchstone), Audrey; and Jaques behind.

Touchstone.
Come apace, good Audrey; I will fetch up your goats, Audrey. And how, Audrey? Am I the man yet? Doth my simple feature content you?

Audrey.
Your features, Lord warrant us! What features?

Touchstone.
I am here with thee and thy goats as the most capricious poet, honest Ovid, was among the Goths.

Jaques.

Aside.

O knowledge ill-inhabited, worse than Jove in a thatch'd house!

Touchstone.
When a man's verses cannot be understood, nor a man's good wit seconded with the forward child, understanding, it strikes a man more dead than a great reckoning in a little room. Truly, I would the gods had made thee poetical.

Audrey.
I do not know what 'poetical' is. Is it honest in deed and word? Is it a true thing?

Touchstone.
No, truly; for the truest poetry is the most feigning, and lovers are given to poetry; and what they swear in poetry may be said as lovers they do feign.

Audrey.
Do you wish then that the gods had made me poetical?

Touchstone.
I do, truly; for thou swear'st to me thou art honest. Now if thou wert a poet, I might have some hope thou didst feign.

Audrey.
Would you not have me honest?

Touchstone.
No, truly, unless thou wert hard-favor'd; for honesty coupled to beauty is to have honey a sauce to sugar.

Jaques.

Aside.

A material fool!

Audrey.
Well, I am not fair, and therefore I pray the gods make me honest.

Touchstone.
Truly, and to cast away honesty upon a foul slut were to put good meat into an unclean dish.

Audrey.
I am not a slut, though I thank the gods I am foul.

Touchstone.
Well, prais'd be the gods for thy foulness! Sluttishness may come hereafter. But be it as it may be, I will marry thee; and to that end I have been with Sir Oliver Martext, the vicar of the next village, who hath promis'd to meet me in this place of the forest and to couple us.

Jaques.

Aside.

I would fain see this meeting.

Audrey.
Well, the gods give us joy!

Touchstone.
Amen. A man may, if he were of a fearful heart, stagger in this attempt; for here we have no temple but the wood, no assembly but horn-beasts. But what though? Courage! As horns are odious, they are necessary. It is said, "Many a man knows no end of his goods." Right! Many a man has good horns, and knows no end of them. Well, that is the dowry of his wife, 'tis none of his own getting. Horns? Even so. Poor men alone? No, no, the noblest deer hath them as huge as the rascal. Is the single man therefore bless'd? No, as a wall'd town is more worthier than a village, so is the forehead of a married man more honorable than the bare brow of a bachelor; and by how much defense is better than no skill, by so much is a horn more precious than to want.

Enter Sir Oliver Martext.

Here comes Sir Oliver. Sir Oliver Martext, you are well met. Will you dispatch us here under this tree, or shall we go with you to your chapel?

Sir Oliver Martext.
Is there none here to give the woman?

Touchstone.
I will not take her on gift of any man.

Sir Oliver Martext.
Truly, she must be given, or the marriage is not lawful.

Jaques.

Discovering himself.

Proceed, proceed. I'll give her.

Touchstone.
Good even, good Master What-ye-call't; how do you, sir? You are very well met. God 'ild you for your last company. I am very glad to see you. Even a toy in hand here, sir. Nay, pray be cover'd.

Jaques.
Will you be married, motley?

Touchstone.
As the ox hath his bow, sir, the horse his curb, and the falcon her bells, so man hath his desires; and as pigeons bill, so wedlock would be nibbling.

Jaques.
And will you (being a man of your breeding) be married under a bush like a beggar? Get you to church, and have a good priest that can tell you what marriage is. This fellow will but join you together as they join wainscot; then one of you will prove a shrunk panel, and like green timber warp, warp.

Touchstone.

Aside.

I am not in the mind but I were better to be married of him than of another, for he is not like to marry me well; and not being well married, it will be a good excuse for me hereafter to leave my wife.

Jaques.
Go thou with me, and let me counsel thee.

Touchstone.
Come, sweet Audrey,
We must be married, or we must live in bawdry.
Farewell, good Master Oliver: not
"O sweet Oliver,
O brave Oliver,
Leave me not behind thee;"
But
"Wind away,
Be gone, I say,
I will not to wedding with thee."

Exeunt Jaques, Touchstone, and Audrey.

Sir Oliver Martext.
'Tis no matter; ne'er a fantastical knave of them all shall flout me out of my calling.

Exit.

Scene 4

Another part of the Forest of Arden.

(Rosalind; Celia; Corin)

Rosalind grows very emotional as she talks with Celia about Orlando after the latter misses his appointment with her. Corin invites the ladies to watch Silvius try to win the scornful Phebe.

Enter Rosalind and Celia.

Rosalind.
Never talk to me, I will weep.

Celia.
Do, I prithee, but yet have the grace to consider that tears do not become a man.

Rosalind.
But have I not cause to weep?

Celia.
As good cause as one would desire, therefore weep.

Rosalind.
His very hair is of the dissembling color.

Celia.
Something browner than Judas's. Marry, his kisses are Judas's own children.

Rosalind.
I' faith, his hair is of a good color.

Celia.
An excellent color. Your chestnut was ever the only color.

Rosalind.
And his kissing is as full of sanctity as the touch of holy bread.

Celia.
He hath bought a pair of cast lips of Diana. A nun of winter's sisterhood kisses not more religiously, the very ice of chastity is in them.

Rosalind.
But why did he swear he would come this morning, and comes not?

Celia.
Nay certainly there is no truth in him.

Rosalind.
Do you think so?

Celia.
Yes, I think he is not a pick-purse nor a horse-stealer, but for his verity in love, I do think him as concave as a cover'd goblet or a worm-eaten nut.

Rosalind.
Not true in love?

Celia.
Yes, when he is in—but I think he is not in.

Rosalind.
You have heard him swear downright he was.

Celia.
"Was" is not "is." Besides, the oath of a lover is no stronger than the word of a tapster; they are both the confirmer of false reckonings. He attends here in the forest on the Duke your father.

Rosalind.
I met the Duke yesterday, and had much question with him. He ask'd me of what parentage I was. I told him of as good as he, so he laugh'd and let me go. But what talk we of fathers, when there is such a man as Orlando?

Celia.
O, that's a brave man! He writes brave verses, speaks brave words, swears brave oaths, and breaks them bravely, quite traverse, athwart the heart of his lover, as a puisne tilter, that spurs his horse but on one side, breaks his staff like a noble goose. But all's brave that youth mounts and folly guides. Who comes here?

Enter Corin.

Corin.
Mistress and master, you have oft inquired
After the shepherd that complain'd of love,
Who you saw sitting by me on the turf,
Praising the proud disdainful shepherdess
That was his mistress.

Celia.
    Well; and what of him?

Corin.
If you will see a pageant truly play'd
Between the pale complexion of true love
And the red glow of scorn and proud disdain,
Go hence a little, and I shall conduct you,
If you will mark it.

Rosalind.
    O, come, let us remove,
The sight of lovers feedeth those in love.
Bring us to this sight, and you shall say
I'll prove a busy actor in their play.

Exeunt.

Scene 5

Another part of the Forest of Arden.

(Silvius; Phebe; Rosalind; Celia; Corin)

Silvius tries in vain to get a soft answer from Phebe. Rosalind chides the scornful shepherdess who falls heads over heels in love with the rough, unsentimental "Ganymede". After Rosalind's departure, she speaks more kindly to Silvius, allowing him to be a hanger-on, sending him to Rosalind with a letter. He is delighted at this chance to serve, as he does not quite catch on to Phebe's new passion.

Enter Silvius and Phebe.

Silvius.
Sweet Phebe, do not scorn me, do not, Phebe;
Say that you love me not, but say not so
In bitterness. The common executioner,
Whose heart th' accustom'd sight of death makes hard,
Falls not the axe upon the humbled neck
But first begs pardon. Will you sterner be
Than he that dies and lives by bloody drops?

Enter, behind, Rosalind, Celia, and Corin.

Phebe.
I would not be thy executioner;
I fly thee for I would not injure thee.
Thou tell'st me there is murder in mine eye:
'Tis pretty, sure, and very probable,
That eyes, that are the frail'st and softest things,
Who shut their coward gates on atomies,
Should be called tyrants, butchers, murderers!
Now I do frown on thee with all my heart,
And if mine eyes can wound, now let them kill thee.
Now counterfeit to swound; why, now fall down,
Or if thou canst not, O, for shame, for shame,
Lie not, to say mine eyes are murderers!
Now show the wound mine eye hath made in thee;
Scratch thee but with a pin, and there remains
Some scar of it; lean upon a rush,
The cicatrice and capable impressure
Thy palm some moment keeps; but now mine eyes,
Which I have darted at thee, hurt thee not,
Nor I am sure there is no force in eyes
That can do hurt.

Silvius.
    O dear Phebe,

If ever (as that ever may be near)
You meet in some fresh cheek the power of fancy,
Then shall you know the wounds invisible
That love's keen arrows make.

Phebe.

                      But till that time
Come not thou near me; and when that time comes,
Afflict me with thy mocks, pity me not,
As till that time I shall not pity thee.

Rosalind.

Advancing.

And why, I pray you? Who might be your mother,
That you insult, exult, and all at once,
Over the wretched? What though you have no beauty—
As, by my faith, I see no more in you
Than without candle may go dark to bed—
Must you be therefore proud and pitiless?
Why, what means this? Why do you look on me?
I see no more in you than in the ordinary
Of nature's sale-work. 'Od's my little life,
I think she means to tangle my eyes too!
No, faith, proud mistress, hope not after it.
'Tis not your inky brows, your black silk hair,
Your bugle eyeballs, nor your cheek of cream
That can entame my spirits to your worship.
You foolish shepherd, wherefore do you follow her,
Like foggy south, puffing with wind and rain?
You are a thousand times a properer man
Than she a woman. 'Tis such fools as you
That makes the world full of ill-favor'd children.
'Tis not her glass, but you that flatters her,
And out of you she sees herself more proper
Than any of her lineaments can show her.
But, mistress, know yourself, down on your knees,
And thank heaven, fasting, for a good man's love;
For I must tell you friendly in your ear,
Sell when you can, you are not for all markets.
Cry the man mercy, love him, take his offer;
Foul is most foul, being foul to be a scoffer.
So take her to thee, shepherd. Fare you well.

Phebe.
Sweet youth, I pray you chide a year together,
I had rather hear you chide than this man woo.

Rosalind.
He's fall'n in love with your foulness— and she'll fall in love with my anger. If it be so, as fast as she answers thee with frowning looks, I'll sauce her with bitter words.—Why look you so upon me?

Phebe.
For no ill will I bear you.

Rosalind.
I pray you do not fall in love with me,
For I am falser than vows made in wine.
Besides, I like you not. If you will know my house,
'Tis at the tuft of olives here hard by.
Will you go, sister? Shepherd, ply her hard.
Come, sister. Shepherdess, look on him better,
And be not proud; though all the world could see,
None could be so abus'd in sight as he.
Come, to our flock.

Exit with Celia and Corin.

Phebe.
Dead shepherd, now I find thy saw of might,
"Who ever lov'd that lov'd not at first sight?"

Silvius.
Sweet Phebe—

Phebe.

                Hah! What say'st thou, Silvius?

Silvius.
Sweet Phebe, pity me.

Phebe.
Why, I am sorry for thee, gentle Silvius.

Silvius.
Where ever sorrow is, relief would be.
If you do sorrow at my grief in love,
By giving love, your sorrow and my grief
Were both extermin'd.

Phebe.
Thou hast my love; is not that neighborly?

Silvius.
I would have you.

Phebe.

              Why, that were covetousness.
Silvius, the time was that I hated thee;
And yet it is not that I bear thee love,

But since that thou canst talk of love so well,
Thy company, which erst was irksome to me,
I will endure; and I'll employ thee too.
But do not look for further recompense
Than thine own gladness that thou art employ'd.

Silvius.
So holy and so perfect is my love,
And I in such a poverty of grace,
That I shall think it a most plenteous crop
To glean the broken ears after the man
That the main harvest reaps. Loose now and then
A scatt'red smile, and that I'll live upon.

Phebe.
Know'st thou the youth that spoke to me yerwhile?

Silvius.
Not very well, but I have met him oft,
And he hath bought the cottage and the bounds
That the old carlot once was master of.

Phebe.
Think not I love him, though I ask for him;
'Tis but a peevish boy—yet he talks well—
But what care I for words? Yet words do well
When he that speaks them pleases those that hear.
It is a pretty youth—not very pretty—
But sure he's proud—and yet his pride becomes him.
He'll make a proper man. The best thing in him
Is his complexion; and faster than his tongue
Did make offense, his eye did heal it up.
He is not very tall—yet for his years he's tall;
His leg is but so so—and yet 'tis well;
There was a pretty redness in his lip,
A little riper and more lusty red
Than that mix'd in his cheek; 'twas just the difference
Betwixt the constant red and mingled damask.
There be some women, Silvius, had they mark'd him
In parcels as I did, would have gone near
To fall in love with him; but for my part
I love him not, nor hate him not; and yet
Have more cause to hate him than to love him,
For what had he to do to chide at me?
He said mine eyes were black and my hair black,
And, now I am rememb'red, scorn'd at me.
I marvel why I answer'd not again.
But that's all one; omittance is no quittance.
I'll write to him a very taunting letter,
And thou shalt bear it; wilt thou, Silvius?

Silvius.
Phebe, with all my heart.

Phebe.
               I'll write it straight;
The matter's in my head and in my heart.
I will be bitter with him and passing short.
Go with me, Silvius.

Exeunt.

Act 4

Scene 1

The Forest of Arden.

(Rosalind; Celia; Jaques; Orlando)

Jaques and Rosalind discuss his melancholy, though she does not take him entirely seriously. Orlando arrives and Rosalind immediately rebukes him for his tardiness. He feebly attempts to woo her and she forces him to do better. Though she is beginning to think that the joke has gone too far, Celia pretends to marry them. Orlando leaves, promising to return at two o'clock, after dinner with the Duke. Rosalind intends to spend the wait dreaming of Orlando while Celia, being more pragmatic, plans to take a nap.

Enter Rosalind and Celia and Jaques.

Jaques.
I prithee, pretty youth, let me be better acquainted with thee.

Rosalind.
They say you are a melancholy fellow.

Jaques.
I am so; I do love it better than laughing.

Rosalind.
Those that are in extremity of either are abominable fellows, and betray themselves to every modern censure worse than drunkards.

Jaques.
Why, 'tis good to be sad and say nothing.

Rosalind.
Why then 'tis good to be a post.

Jaques.
I have neither the scholar's melancholy, which is emulation; nor the musician's, which is fantastical; nor the courtier's, which is proud; nor the soldier's, which is ambitious; nor the lawyer's, which is politic; nor the lady's, which is nice; nor the lover's, which is all these: but it is a melancholy of mine own, compounded of many simples, extracted from many objects, and indeed the sundry contemplation of my travels, in which my often rumination wraps me in a most humorous sadness.

Rosalind.
A traveler! By my faith, you have great reason to be sad. I fear you have sold your own lands to see other men's; then to have seen much, and to have nothing, is to have rich eyes and poor hands.

Jaques.
Yes, I have gain'd my experience.

Enter Orlando.

Rosalind.
And your experience makes you sad. I had rather have a fool to make me merry than experience to make me sad—and to travel for it too!

Orlando.
Good day and happiness, dear Rosalind!

Jaques.
Nay then God buy you, and you talk in blank verse.

Rosalind.
Farewell, Monsieur Traveler: look you lisp and wear strange suits; disable all the benefits of your own country; be out of love with your nativity, and almost chide God for making you that countenance you are; or I will scarce think you have swam in a gundello.

Exit Jaques.

Why, how now, Orlando, where have you been all this while? You a lover! And you serve me such another trick, never come in my sight more.

Orlando.
My fair Rosalind, I come within an hour of my promise.

Rosalind.
Break an hour's promise in love! He that will divide a minute into a thousand parts, and break but a part of the thousand part of a minute in the affairs of love, it may be said of him that Cupid hath clapp'd him o' th' shoulder, but I'll warrant him heart-whole.

Orlando.
Pardon me, dear Rosalind.

Rosalind.
Nay, and you be so tardy, come no more in my sight. I had as lief be woo'd of a snail.

Orlando.
Of a snail?

Rosalind.
Ay, of a snail; for though he comes slowly, he carries his house on his head; a better jointure I think than you make a woman. Besides, he brings his destiny with him.

Orlando.
What's that?

Rosalind.
Why, horns! Which such as you are fain to be beholding to your wives for. But he comes arm'd in his fortune, and prevents the slander of his wife.

Orlando.
Virtue is no horn-maker; and my Rosalind is virtuous.

Rosalind.
And I am your Rosalind.

Celia.
It pleases him to call you so; but he hath a Rosalind of a better leer than you.

Rosalind.
Come, woo me, woo me; for now I am in a holiday humor, and like enough to consent. What would you say to me now, and I were your very very Rosalind?

Orlando.
I would kiss before I spoke.

Rosalind.
Nay, you were better speak first, and when you were gravell'd for lack of matter, you might take occasion to kiss. Very good orators when they are out, they will

spit, and for lovers lacking (God warn us!) matter, the cleanliest shift is to kiss.

Orlando.
How if the kiss be denied?

Rosalind.
Then she puts you to entreaty, and there begins new matter.

Orlando.
Who could be out, being before his belov'd mistress?

Rosalind.
Marry, that should you if I were your mistress, or I should think my honesty ranker than my wit.

Orlando.
What, of my suit?

Rosalind.
Not out of your apparel, and yet out of your suit. Am not I your Rosalind?

Orlando.
I take some joy to say you are, because I would be talking of her.

Rosalind.
Well, in her person, I say I will not have you.

Orlando.
Then in mine own person, I die.

Rosalind.
No, faith, die by attorney. The poor world is almost six thousand years old, and in all this time there was not any man died in his own person, videlicet, in a love-cause. Troilus had his brains dash'd out with a Grecian club, yet he did what he could to die before, and he is one of the patterns of love. Leander, he would have liv'd many a fair year though Hero had turn'd nun, if it had not been for a hot midsummer night; for, good youth, he went but forth to wash him in the Hellespont, and being taken with the cramp was drown'd; and the foolish chroniclers of that age found it was—Hero of Sestos. But these are all lies: men have died from time to time, and worms have eaten them, but not for love.

Orlando.
I would not have my right Rosalind of this mind, for I protest her frown might kill me.

Rosalind.
By this hand, it will not kill a fly. But come, now I will be your Rosalind in a more coming-on disposition; and ask me what you will, I will grant it.

Orlando.
Then love me, Rosalind.

Rosalind.
Yes, faith, will I, Fridays and Saturdays and all.

Orlando.
And wilt thou have me?

Rosalind.
Ay, and twenty such.

Orlando.
What sayest thou?

Rosalind.
Are you not good?

Orlando.
I hope so.

Rosalind.
Why then, can one desire too much of a good thing? Come, sister, you shall be the priest, and marry us. Give me your hand, Orlando. What do you say, sister?

Orlando.
Pray thee marry us.

Celia.
I cannot say the words.

Rosalind.
You must begin, "Will you, Orlando"—

Celia.
Go to! Will you, Orlando, have to wife this Rosalind?

Orlando.
I will.

Rosalind.
Ay, but when?

Orlando.
Why, now, as fast as she can marry us.

Rosalind.
Then you must say, "I take thee, Rosalind, for wife."

Orlando.
I take thee, Rosalind, for wife.

Rosalind.
I might ask you for your commission, but I do take thee, Orlando, for my husband. There's a girl goes before the priest, and certainly a woman's thought runs before her actions.

Orlando.
So do all thoughts, they are wing'd.

Rosalind.
Now tell me how long you would have her after you have possess'd her.

Orlando.
Forever and a day.

Rosalind.
Say "a day," without the "ever." No, no, Orlando, men are April when they woo, December when they wed; maids are May when they are maids, but the sky changes when they are wives. I will be more jealous of thee than a Barbary cock-pigeon over his hen, more clamorous than a parrot against rain, more newfangled than an ape, more giddy in my desires than a monkey. I will weep for nothing, like Diana in the fountain, and I will do that when you are dispos'd to be merry. I will laugh like a hyen, and that when thou art inclin'd to sleep.

Orlando.
But will my Rosalind do so?

Rosalind.
By my life, she will do as I do.

Orlando.
O, but she is wise.

Rosalind.
Or else she could not have the wit to do this; the wiser, the waywarder. Make the doors upon a woman's wit, and it will out at the casement; shut that, and 'twill out at the key-hole; stop that, 'twill fly with the smoke out at the chimney.

Orlando.
A man that had a wife with such a wit, he might say, "Wit, whither wilt?"

Rosalind.
Nay, you might keep that check for it, till you met your wife's wit going to your neighbor's bed.

Orlando.
And what wit could wit have to excuse that?

Rosalind.
Marry, to say she came to seek you there. You shall never take her without her answer, unless you take her without her tongue. O, that woman that cannot make her fault her husband's occasion, let her never nurse her child herself, for she will breed it like a fool!

Orlando.
For these two hours, Rosalind, I will leave thee.

Rosalind.
Alas, dear love, I cannot lack thee two hours!

Orlando.
I must attend the Duke at dinner. By two a' clock I will be with thee again.

Rosalind.
Ay, go your ways, go your ways; I knew what you would prove; my friends told me as much, and I thought no less. That flattering tongue of yours won me. 'Tis but one cast away, and so come death! Two a' clock is your hour?

Orlando.
Ay, sweet Rosalind.

Rosalind.
By my troth, and in good earnest, and so God mend me, and by all pretty oaths that are not dangerous, if you break one jot of your promise, or come one minute behind your hour, I will think you the most pathetical break-promise, and the most hollow lover, and the most unworthy of her you call Rosalind, that may be chosen out of the gross band of the unfaithful; therefore beware my censure, and keep your promise.

Orlando.
With no less religion than if thou wert indeed my Rosalind; so adieu.

Rosalind.
Well, Time is the old justice that examines all such offenders, and let Time try. Adieu.

Exit Orlando.

Celia.
You have simply misus'd our sex in your love-prate. We must have your doublet and hose pluck'd over your head, and show the world what the bird hath done to her own nest.

Rosalind.
O coz, coz, coz, my pretty little coz, that thou didst know how many fathom deep I am in love! But it cannot be sounded; my affection hath an unknown bottom, like the bay of Portugal.

Celia.
Or rather, bottomless—that as fast as you pour affection in, it runs out.

Rosalind.
No, that same wicked bastard of Venus that was begot of thought, conceiv'd of spleen, and born of madness, that blind rascally boy that abuses every one's eyes because his own are out, let him be judge how deep I am in love. I'll tell thee, Aliena, I cannot be out of the sight of Orlando. I'll go find a shadow, and sigh till he come.

Celia.
And I'll sleep.

Exeunt.

Scene 2

Another part of the Forest of Arden.

(Jaques; First Lord in Arden; Second Lord in Arden)

Jaques and the foresters sing and celebrate a forester who has killed a deer.

Enter Jaques and Lords as foresters.

Jaques.
Which is he that kill'd the deer?

First Lord in Arden.
Sir, it was I.

Jaques.
Let's present him to the Duke like a Roman conqueror, and it would do well to set the deer's horns upon his head, for a branch of victory. Have you no song, forester, for this purpose?

Second Lord in Arden.
Yes, sir.

Jaques.
Sing it. 'Tis no matter how it be in tune, so it make noise enough.

Music.
Song.

Second Lord in Arden.
What shall he have that kill'd the deer?
His leather skin and horns to wear.
Then sing him home.
The rest shall bear this burden.
Take thou no scorn to wear the horn,
It was a crest ere thou wast born;
Thy father's father wore it,
And thy father bore it.
The horn, the horn, the lusty horn
Is not a thing to laugh to scorn.

Exeunt.

Scene 3

Another part of the Forest of Arden.

(Rosalind; Celia; Silvius; Oliver)

Silvius brings Phebe's love letter to Rosalind. Rosalind is horrified at how Phebe is treating Silvius and bids him tell her she must love him, to be loved by Rosalind. Oliver, who has been hunting Orlando, enters and tells the tale of how his younger brother saved him from being slaughtered by a lioness, despite all the evil he has done. He explains that Orlando's injury prevented him from making it to the meeting with "Ganymede". Rosalind faints on hearing of the wound, though she tries (unsuccessfully) to convince Oliver she was playacting.

Enter Rosalind and Celia.

Rosalind.
How say you now? Is it not past two a' clock? And here much Orlando!

Celia.
I warrant you, with pure love and troubled brain, he hath ta'en his bow and arrows and is gone forth—to sleep. Look who comes here.

Enter Silvius.

Silvius.
My errand is to you, fair youth,
My gentle Phebe did bid me give you this.

Gives a letter.

I know not the contents, but as I guess
By the stern brow and waspish action
Which she did use as she was writing of it,
It bears an angry tenure. Pardon me,
I am but as a guiltless messenger.

Rosalind.
Patience herself would startle at this letter,
And play the swaggerer: bear this, bear all!
She says I am not fair, that I lack manners;
She calls me proud, and that she could not love me
Were man as rare as phoenix. 'Od's my will,
Her love is not the hare that I do hunt;
Why writes she so to me? Well, shepherd, well,
This is a letter of your own device.

Silvius.
No, I protest, I know not the contents,
Phebe did write it.

Rosalind.
                    Come, come, you are a fool,
And turn'd into the extremity of love.
I saw her hand, she has a leathern hand,
A freestone-colored hand. I verily did think
That her old gloves were on, but 'twas her hands;
She has a huswive's hand—but that's no matter.
I say she never did invent this letter,
This is a man's invention and his hand.

Silvius.
Sure it is hers.

Rosalind.
Why, 'tis a boisterous and a cruel style,
A style for challengers. Why, she defies me,
Like Turk to Christian. Women's gentle brain
Could not drop forth such giant-rude invention,
Such Ethiop words, blacker in their effect
Than in their countenance. Will you hear the letter?

Silvius.
So please you, for I never heard it yet;
Yet heard too much of Phebe's cruelty.

Rosalind.
She Phebes me. Mark how the tyrant writes.

Read.

"Art thou god to shepherd turn'd,
That a maiden's heart hath burn'd?"
Can a woman rail thus?

Silvius.
Call you this railing?

Rosalind.

Reads.

"Why, thy godhead laid apart,
Warr'st thou with a woman's heart?"
Did you ever hear such railing?
"Whiles the eye of man did woo me,
That could do no vengeance to me."
Meaning me a beast.
"If the scorn of your bright eyne
Have power to raise such love in mine,
Alack, in me what strange effect
Would they work in mild aspect?
Whiles you chid me, I did love;
How then might your prayers move?
He that brings this love to thee
Little knows this love in me;
And by him seal up thy mind,
Whether that thy youth and kind
Will the faithful offer take
Of me, and all that I can make,
Or else by him my love deny,
And then I'll study how to die."

Silvius.
Call you this chiding?

Celia.
Alas, poor shepherd!

Rosalind.
Do you pity him? No, he deserves no pity. Wilt thou love such a woman? What, to make thee an instrument, and play false strains upon thee? Not to be endur'd! Well, go your way to her (for I see love hath made thee a tame snake) and say this to her: that if she love me, I charge her to love thee; if she will not, I will never have her unless thou entreat for her. If you be a true lover, hence, and not a word; for here comes more company.

Exit Silvius
Enter Oliver.

Oliver.
Good morrow, fair ones. Pray you (if you know)
Where in the purlieus of this forest stands
A sheep-cote fenc'd about with olive-trees?

Celia.
West of this place, down in the neighbor bottom,
The rank of osiers by the murmuring stream
Left on your right hand brings you to the place.
But at this hour the house doth keep itself,
There's none within.

Oliver.
If that an eye may profit by a tongue,
Then should I know you by description—
Such garments and such years. "The boy is fair,
Of female favor, and bestows himself
Like a ripe sister; the woman low,
And browner than her brother." Are not you
The owner of the house I did inquire for?

Celia.
It is no boast, being ask'd, to say we are.

Oliver.
Orlando doth commend him to you both,
And to that youth he calls his Rosalind
He sends this bloody napkin. Are you he?

Rosalind.
I am. What must we understand by this?

Oliver.
Some of my shame, if you will know of me
What man I am, and how, and why, and where
This handkercher was stain'd.

Celia.
                    I pray you tell it.

Oliver.
When last the young Orlando parted from you
He left a promise to return again
Within an hour, and pacing through the forest,
Chewing the food of sweet and bitter fancy,
Lo what befell! He threw his eye aside,
And mark what object did present itself
Under an old oak, whose boughs were moss'd with age
And high top bald with dry antiquity:
A wretched ragged man, o'ergrown with hair,
Lay sleeping on his back; about his neck
A green and gilded snake had wreath'd itself,
Who with her head nimble in threats approach'd
The opening of his mouth; but suddenly
Seeing Orlando, it unlink'd itself,
And with indented glides did slip away
Into a bush, under which bush's shade
A lioness, with udders all drawn dry,
Lay couching, head on ground, with cat-like watch
When that the sleeping man should stir; for 'tis
The royal disposition of that beast
To prey on nothing that doth seem as dead.
This seen, Orlando did approach the man,
And found it was his brother, his elder brother.

Celia.
O, I have heard him speak of that same brother,
And he did render him the most unnatural
That liv'd amongst men.

Oliver.
                    And well he might so do,
For well I know he was unnatural.

Rosalind.
But to Orlando: did he leave him there,
Food to the suck'd and hungry lioness?

Oliver.
Twice did he turn his back, and purpos'd so;
But kindness, nobler ever than revenge,
And nature, stronger than his just occasion,
Made him give battle to the lioness,
Who quickly fell before him, in which hurtling
From miserable slumber I awaked.

Celia.
Are you his brother?

Rosalind.
                    Was't you he rescu'd?

Celia.
Was't you that did so oft contrive to kill him?

Oliver.
'Twas I; but 'tis not I. I do not shame
To tell you what I was, since my conversion
So sweetly tastes, being the thing I am.

Rosalind.
But for the bloody napkin?

Oliver.
                    By and by.
When from the first to last betwixt us two
Tears our recountments had most kindly bath'd,
As how I came into that desert place—
In brief, he led me to the gentle Duke,
Who gave me fresh array and entertainment,
Committing me unto my brother's love,
Who led me instantly unto his cave,
There stripp'd himself, and here upon his arm
The lioness had torn some flesh away,
Which all this while had bled; and now he fainted,
And cried in fainting upon Rosalind.
Brief, I recover'd him, bound up his wound,
And after some small space, being strong at heart,
He sent me hither, stranger as I am,
To tell this story, that you might excuse
His broken promise, and to give this napkin,
Dy'd in his blood, unto the shepherd youth
That he in sport doth call his Rosalind.

Rosalind faints.

Celia.
Why, how now, Ganymede, sweet Ganymede?

Oliver.
Many will swoon when they do look on blood.

Celia.
There is more in it. Cousin Ganymede!

Oliver.
Look, he recovers.

Rosalind.
I would I were at home.

Celia.
                    We'll lead you thither.
I pray you, will you take him by the arm?

Oliver.
Be of good cheer, youth. You a man?
You lack a man's heart.

Rosalind.
I do so, I confess it. Ah, sirrah, a body would think this was well counterfeited! I pray you tell your brother how well I counterfeited. Heigh-ho!

Oliver.
This was not counterfeit, there is too great testimony in your complexion that it was a passion of earnest.

Rosalind.
Counterfeit, I assure you.

Oliver.
Well then, take a good heart and counterfeit to be a man.

Rosalind.
So I do; but i' faith, I should have been a woman by right.

Celia.
Come, you look paler and paler. Pray you draw homewards. Good sir, go with us.

Oliver.
That will I, for I must bear answer back
How you excuse my brother, Rosalind.

Rosalind.
I shall devise something; but I pray you commend my counterfeiting to him. Will you go?

Exeunt.

Act 5

Scene 1

The Forest of Arden.

(Touchstone; Audrey; William; Corin)

Touchstone tells Audrey they will find a time to wed, despite the setback with Martext. William, a commoner in love with Audrey, is quickly driven off by Touchstone's nasty jesting at his expense.

Enter Clown (Touchstone) and Audrey.

Touchstone.
We shall find a time, Audrey, patience, gentle Audrey.

Audrey.
Faith, the priest was good enough, for all the old gentleman's saying.

Touchstone.
A most wicked Sir Oliver, Audrey, a most vile Martext. But, Audrey, there is a youth here in the forest lays claim to you.

Audrey.
Ay, I know who 'tis; he hath no interest in me in the world. Here comes the man you mean.

Enter William.

Touchstone.
It is meat and drink to me to see a clown. By my troth, we that have good wits have much to answer for; we shall be flouting; we cannot hold.

William.
Good ev'n, Audrey.

Audrey.
God ye good ev'n, William.

William.
And good ev'n to you, sir.

Touchstone.
Good ev'n, gentle friend. Cover thy head, cover thy head; nay, prithee be cover'd. How old are you, friend?

William.
Five and twenty, sir.

Touchstone.
A ripe age. Is thy name William?

William.
William, sir.

Touchstone.
A fair name. Wast born i' the forest here?

William.
Ay, sir, I thank God.

Touchstone.
"Thank God"—a good answer. Art rich?

William.
Faith, sir, so, so.

Touchstone.
"So, so" is good, very good, very excellent good; and yet it is not, it is but so, so. Art thou wise?

William.
Ay, sir, I have a pretty wit.

Touchstone.
Why, thou say'st well. I do now remember a saying, "The fool doth think he is wise, but the wise man knows himself to be a fool." The heathen philosopher, when he had a desire to eat a grape, would open his lips when he put it into his mouth, meaning thereby that grapes were made to eat and lips to open. You do love this maid?

William.
I do, sir.

Touchstone.
Give me your hand. Art thou learned?

William.
No, sir.

Touchstone.
Then learn this of me: to have, is to have. For it is a figure in rhetoric that drink, being pour'd out of a cup into a glass, by filling the one doth empty the other. For all your writers do consent that ipse is he: now, you are not ipse, for I am he.

William.
Which he, sir?

Touchstone.
He, sir, that must marry this woman. Therefore, you clown, abandon—which is in the vulgar leave—the society—which in the boorish is company—of this female—which in the common is woman; which together is, abandon the society of this female, or, clown, thou perishest; or to thy better understanding, diest; or (to wit) I kill thee, make thee away, translate thy life into death, thy liberty into bondage. I will deal in poison with thee, or in bastinado, or in steel; I will bandy with thee in faction; I will o'errun thee with policy; I will kill thee a hundred and fifty ways: therefore tremble and depart.

Audrey.
Do, good William.

William.
God rest you merry, sir.

Exit.
Enter Corin.

Act 5, Scene 2

Corin.
Our master and mistress seeks you. Come away, away!

Touchstone.
Trip, Audrey, trip, Audrey! I attend, I attend.

Exeunt.

Scene 2

Another part of the Forest of Arden.

(Orlando; Oliver; Rosalind; Silvius; Phebe)

Oliver and Celia have fallen in love at first sight and plan to marry on the morrow. Orlando's game with "Ganymede" is no longer enough to satisfy him and he is unhappy. He cheers up when "Ganymede" promises to produce Rosalind at the wedding the next day and marry the two of them off. Phebe and Silvius arrive, insisting on how they are in love with people who don't respond. Rosalind promises to fix everything at the wedding next day.

Enter Orlando and Oliver.

Orlando.
Is't possible that on so little acquaintance you should like her? That but seeing, you should love her? And loving, woo? And wooing, she should grant? And will you persever to enjoy her?

Oliver.
Neither call the giddiness of it in question, the poverty of her, the small acquaintance, my sudden wooing, nor her sudden consenting; but say with me, I love Aliena; say with her that she loves me; consent with both that we may enjoy each other. It shall be to your good; for my father's house and all the revenue that was old Sir Rowland's will I estate upon you, and here live and die a shepherd.

Enter Rosalind.

Orlando.
You have my consent. Let your wedding be tomorrow; thither will I invite the Duke and all 's contented followers. Go you and prepare Aliena; for look you, here comes my Rosalind.

Rosalind.
God save you, brother.

Oliver.
And you, fair sister.

Exit.

Rosalind.
O my dear Orlando, how it grieves me to see thee wear thy heart in a scarf!

Orlando.
It is my arm.

Rosalind.
I thought thy heart had been wounded with the claws of a lion.

Orlando.
Wounded it is, but with the eyes of a lady.

Rosalind.
Did your brother tell you how I counterfeited to sound when he show'd me your handkercher?

Orlando.
Ay, and greater wonders than that.

Rosalind.
O, I know where you are. Nay, 'tis true. There was never any thing so sudden but the fight of two rams, and Caesar's thrasonical brag of "I came, saw, and overcame." For your brother and my sister no sooner met but they look'd; no sooner look'd but they lov'd; no sooner lov'd but they sigh'd; no sooner sigh'd but they ask'd one another the reason; no sooner knew the reason but they sought the remedy: and in these degrees have they made a pair of stairs to marriage, which they will climb incontinent, or else be incontinent before marriage. They are in the very wrath of love, and they will together. Clubs cannot part them.

Orlando.
They shall be married tomorrow; and I will bid the Duke to the nuptial. But O, how bitter a thing it is to look into happiness through another man's eyes! By so much the more shall I tomorrow be at the height of heart-heaviness, by how much I shall think my brother happy in having what he wishes for.

Rosalind.
Why then tomorrow I cannot serve your turn for Rosalind?

Orlando.
I can live no longer by thinking.

Rosalind.
I will weary you then no longer with idle talking. Know of me then (for now I speak to some purpose) that I know you are a gentleman of good conceit. I speak not this that you should bear a good opinion of my knowledge, insomuch I say I know you are; neither do I labor for a greater esteem than may in some little measure draw a belief from you, to do yourself good, and not to grace me. Believe then, if you please, that I can do strange things. I have, since I was three year old, convers'd with a magician, most profound in his art, and yet not damnable. If you do love Rosalind so near the heart as your gesture cries it out, when your brother marries Aliena, shall you marry her. I know into what straits of fortune she is driven, and it is not impossible to me, if it appear not inconvenient to you, to set her before your eyes tomorrow, human as she is, and without any danger.

Orlando.
Speak'st thou in sober meanings?

Rosalind.
By my life I do, which I tender dearly, though I say I am a magician. Therefore put you in your best array, bid your friends; for if you will be married tomorrow, you shall; and to Rosalind, if you will.

Enter Silvius and Phebe.

Look, here comes a lover of mine and a lover of hers.

Phebe.
Youth, you have done me much ungentleness,
To show the letter that I writ to you.

Rosalind.
I care not if I have. It is my study
To seem despiteful and ungentle to you.
You are there followed by a faithful shepherd—
Look upon him, love him; he worships you.

Phebe.
Good shepherd, tell this youth what 'tis to love.

Silvius.
It is to be all made of sighs and tears,
And so am I for Phebe.

Phebe.
And I for Ganymede.

Orlando.
And I for Rosalind.

Rosalind.
And I for no woman.

Silvius.
It is to be all made of faith and service,
And so am I for Phebe.

Phebe.
And I for Ganymede.

Orlando.
And I for Rosalind.

Rosalind.
And I for no woman.

Silvius.
It is to be all made of fantasy,
All made of passion, and all made of wishes,
All adoration, duty, and observance,
All humbleness, all patience, and impatience,
All purity, all trial, all observance;
And so am I for Phebe.

Phebe.
And so am I for Ganymede.

Orlando.
And so am I for Rosalind.

Rosalind.
And so am I for no woman.

Phebe.
If this be so, why blame you me to love you?

Silvius.
If this be so, why blame you me to love you?

Orlando.
If this be so, why blame you me to love you?

Rosalind.
Why do you speak too, "Why blame you me to love you?"

Orlando.
To her that is not here, nor doth not hear.

Rosalind.
Pray you no more of this, 'tis like the howling of Irish wolves against the moon.

To Silvius.

I will help you if I can.

To Phebe.

I would love you if I could.—Tomorrow meet me all together.

To Phebe.

I will marry you, if ever I marry woman, and I'll be married tomorrow.

To Orlando.

I will satisfy you, if ever I satisfied man, and you shall be married tomorrow.

To Silvius.

I will content you, if what pleases you contents you, and you shall be married tomorrow.

To Orlando.

As you love Rosalind, meet.

To Silvius.

As you love Phebe, meet. And as I love no woman, I'll meet. So fare you well; I have left you commands.

Silvius.
I'll not fail, if I live.

Phebe.
Nor I.

Orlando.
Nor I.

Exeunt.

Scene 3

Another part of the Forest of Arden.

(Touchstone; Audrey; First Page; Second Page)

Touchstone has arranged to be married to Audrey the next day. He and two pages sing a pretty lyric.

Enter Clown (Touchstone) and Audrey.

Touchstone.
Tomorrow is the joyful day, Audrey, tomorrow will we be married.

Audrey.
I do desire it with all my heart; and I hope it is no dishonest desire to desire to be a woman of the world. Here come two of the banish'd Duke's pages.

Enter two Pages.

First Page.
Well met, honest gentleman.

Touchstone.
By my troth, well met. Come, sit, sit, and a song.

Second Page.
We are for you, sit i' th' middle.

First Page.
Shall we clap into't roundly, without hawking or spitting or saying we are hoarse, which are the only prologues to a bad voice?

Second Page.
I' faith, i' faith, and both in a tune, like two gypsies on a horse.

Song.

It was a lover and his lass,
With a hey, and a ho, and a hey nonino,
That o'er the green corn-field did pass,
In spring time, the only pretty ring time,
When birds do sing, hey ding a ding, ding,
Sweet lovers love the spring.
Between the acres of the rye,
With a hey, and a ho, and a hey nonino,
These pretty country folks would lie,
In spring time, etc.
This carol they began that hour,
With a hey, and a ho, and a hey nonino,
How that a life was but a flower,
In spring time, etc.
And therefore take the present time,
With a hey, and a ho, and a hey nonino,
For love is crowned with the prime,
In spring time, etc.

Touchstone.
Truly, young gentlemen, though there was no great matter in the ditty, yet the note was very untuneable.

First Page.
You are deceiv'd, sir, we kept time, we lost not our time.

Touchstone.
By my troth, yes; I count it but time lost to hear such a foolish song. God buy you, and God mend your voices! Come, Audrey.

Exeunt.

Scene 4

Another part of the Forest of Arden.

(Duke Senior; Amiens; Jaques; Orlando; Oliver; Celia; Rosalind; Silvius; Phebe; Touchstone; Audrey; Hymen; Jaques De Boys)

Rosalind repeats her promises to her father and the others. As she goes off, the others are distracted by Touchstone, who gives a virtuoso performance on the niceties of quarreling. Rosalind and Celia, out of their disguises, re-enter with Hymen, who properly sorts out the couples. Oliver and Orlando's middle brother enters and informs the assembled company that Duke Frederick has been converted by a holy man and has abdicated in favor of Duke Senior. All the exiles prepare to return home except Jaques, who intends to join Duke Frederick in his retreat to learn what he can from him. Unable to dissuade him, the others let him go and then dance together.

Enter Duke Senior, Amiens, Jaques, Orlando, Oliver, Celia.

Duke Senior.
Dost thou believe, Orlando, that the boy
Can do all this that he hath promised?

Orlando.
I sometimes do believe, and sometimes do not,
As those that fear they hope, and know they fear.

Enter Rosalind, Silvius, and Phebe.

Rosalind.
Patience once more, whiles our compact is urg'd:
You say, if I bring in your Rosalind,
You will bestow her on Orlando here?

Duke Senior.
That would I, had I kingdoms to give with her.

Rosalind.
And you say you will have her, when I bring her.

Orlando.
That would I, were I of all kingdoms king.

Rosalind.
You say you'll marry me, if I be willing?

Phebe.
That will I, should I die the hour after.

Rosalind.
But if you do refuse to marry me,
You'll give yourself to this most faithful shepherd?

Phebe.
So is the bargain.

Rosalind.
You say that you'll have Phebe, if she will?

Silvius.
Though to have her and death were both one thing.

Rosalind.
I have promis'd to make all this matter even:
Keep you your word, O Duke, to give your daughter;
You, yours, Orlando, to receive his daughter;
Keep you your word, Phebe, that you'll marry me,
Or else, refusing me, to wed this shepherd;
Keep your word, Silvius, that you'll marry her
If she refuse me; and from hence I go
To make these doubts all even.

Exeunt Rosalind and Celia.

Duke Senior.
I do remember in this shepherd boy
Some lively touches of my daughter's favor.

Orlando.
My lord, the first time that I ever saw him
Methought he was a brother to your daughter.
But, my good lord, this boy is forest-born,
And hath been tutor'd in the rudiments
Of many desperate studies by his uncle,
Whom he reports to be a great magician,
Obscured in the circle of this forest.

Enter Clown (Touchstone) and Audrey.

Jaques.
There is sure another flood toward, and these couples are coming to the ark. Here comes a pair of very strange beasts, which in all tongues are call'd fools.

Touchstone.
Salutation and greeting to you all!

Jaques.
Good my lord, bid him welcome. This is the motley-minded gentleman that I have so often met in the forest. He hath been a courtier, he swears.

Touchstone.
If any man doubt that, let him put me to my purgation. I have trod a measure, I have flatt'red a lady, I have been politic with my friend, smooth with mine enemy, I have undone three tailors, I have had four quarrels, and like to have fought one.

Jaques.
And how was that ta'en up?

Touchstone.
Faith, we met, and found the quarrel was upon the seventh cause.

Jaques.
How seventh cause? Good my lord, like this fellow.

Duke Senior.
I like him very well.

Touchstone.
God 'ild you, sir, I desire you of the like. I press in here, sir, amongst the rest of the country copulatives, to swear and to forswear, according as marriage binds and blood breaks. A poor virgin, sir, an ill-favor'd thing, sir, but mine own; a poor humor of mine, sir, to take that that no man else will. Rich honesty dwells like a miser, sir, in a poor house, as your pearl in your foul oyster.

Duke Senior.
By my faith, he is very swift and sententious.

Touchstone.
According to the fool's bolt, sir, and such dulcet diseases.

Jaques.
But for the seventh cause—how did you find the quarrel on the seventh cause?

Touchstone.
Upon a lie seven times remov'd (bear your body more seeming, Audrey), as thus, sir. I did dislike the cut of a certain courtier's beard. He sent me word, if I said his beard was not cut well, he was in the mind it was: this is call'd the Retort Courteous. If I sent him word again, it was not well cut, he would send me word he cut it to please himself: this is call'd the Quip Modest. If again, it was not well cut, he disabled my judgment: this is call'd the Reply Churlish. If again, it was not well cut, he would answer I spake not true: this is call'd the Reproof Valiant. If again, it was not well cut, he would say I lie: this is call'd the Countercheck Quarrelsome; and so to Lie Circumstantial and the Lie Direct.

Jaques.
And how oft did you say his beard was not well cut?

Touchstone.
I durst go no further than the Lie Circumstantial, nor he durst not give me the Lie Direct; and so we measur'd swords and parted.

Jaques.
Can you nominate in order now the degrees of the lie?

Touchstone.
O sir, we quarrel in print, by the book—as you have books for good manners. I will name you the degrees. The first, the Retort Courteous; the second, the Quip Modest; the third, the Reply Churlish; the fourth, the Reproof Valiant; the fift, the Countercheck Quarrelsome; the sixt, the Lie with Circumstance; the seventh, the Lie Direct. All these you may avoid but the Lie Direct; and you may avoid that too, with an If. I knew when seven justices could not take up a quarrel, but when the parties were met themselves, one of them thought but of an If, as, "If you said so, then I said so"; and they shook hands and swore brothers. Your If is the only peacemaker; much virtue in If.

Jaques.
Is not this a rare fellow, my lord? He's as good at any thing, and yet a fool.

Duke Senior.
He uses his folly like a stalking-horse, and under the presentation of that he shoots his wit.

Enter Hymen, Rosalind, and Celia. Still music.

Hymen.
Then is there mirth in heaven,
When earthly things made even
                      Atone together.
Good Duke, receive thy daughter,
Hymen from heaven brought her,
                      Yea, brought her hither,
That thou mightst join her hand with his
Whose heart within his bosom is.

Rosalind.

To Duke Senior.

To you I give myself, for I am yours.

To Orlando.

To you I give myself, for I am yours.

Duke Senior.
If there be truth in sight, you are my daughter.

Orlando.
If there be truth in sight, you are my Rosalind.

Phebe.
If sight and shape be true,
Why then my love adieu!

Rosalind.
I'll have no father, if you be not he;
I'll have no husband, if you be not he;
Nor ne'er wed woman, if you be not she.

Hymen.
Peace ho! I bar confusion,
'Tis I must make conclusion
                      Of these most strange events.
Here's eight that must take hands
To join in Hymen's bands,
                      If truth holds true contents.

To Orlando and Rosalind.

You and you no cross shall part;

To Oliver and Celia.

You and you are heart in heart;

To Phebe.

You to his love must accord,
Or have a woman to your lord;

To Touchstone and Audrey.

You and you are sure together,
As the winter to foul weather.—
Whiles a wedlock-hymn we sing,
Feed yourselves with questioning;
That reason wonder may diminish
How thus we met, and these things finish.

Song.

Wedding is great Juno's crown,
  O blessed bond of board and bed!
'Tis Hymen peoples every town,
  High wedlock then be honored.
Honor, high honor, and renown
To Hymen, god of every town!

Duke Senior.
O my dear niece, welcome thou art to me,
Even daughter, welcome, in no less degree.

Phebe.
I will not eat my word, now thou art mine,
Thy faith my fancy to thee doth combine.

Enter Second Brother (Jaques De Boys).

Jaques De Boys.
Let me have audience for a word or two.
I am the second son of old Sir Rowland,
That bring these tidings to this fair assembly.
Duke Frederick, hearing how that every day
Men of great worth resorted to this forest,
Address'd a mighty power, which were on foot
In his own conduct, purposely to take
His brother here, and put him to the sword;
And to the skirts of this wild wood he came;
Where, meeting with an old religious man,
After some question with him, was converted
Both from his enterprise and from the world,
His crown bequeathing to his banish'd brother,
And all their lands restor'd to them again
That were with him exil'd. This to be true,
I do engage my life.

Duke Senior.
Welcome, young man;
Thou offer'st fairly to thy brothers' wedding:
To one his lands withheld, and to the other
A land itself at large, a potent dukedom.
First, in this forest let us do those ends
That here were well begun and well begot;
And after, every of this happy number,

That have endur'd shrewd days and nights with us,
Shall share the good of our returned fortune,
According to the measure of their states.
Mean time, forget this new-fall'n dignity,
And fall into our rustic revelry.
Play, music, and you brides and bridegrooms all,
With measure heap'd in joy, to th' measures fall.

Jaques.
Sir, by your patience.—If I heard you rightly,
The Duke hath put on a religious life,
And thrown into neglect the pompous court?

Jaques De Boys.
He hath.

Jaques.
To him will I. Out of these convertites
There is much matter to be heard and learn'd.

To Duke Senior.

You to your former honor I bequeath,
Your patience and your virtue well deserves it;

To Orlando.

You to a love, that your true faith doth merit;

To Oliver.

You to your land, and love, and great allies;

To Silvius.

You to a long and well-deserved bed;

To Touchstone.

And you to wrangling, for thy loving voyage
Is but for two months victuall'd.—So to your pleasures,
I am for other than for dancing measures.

Duke Senior.
Stay, Jaques, stay.

Jaques.
To see no pastime I. What you would have
I'll stay to know at your abandon'd cave.

Exit.

Duke Senior.
Proceed, proceed. We'll begin these rites,
As we do trust they'll end, in true delights.

A dance.
Exeunt all but Rosalind.

Epilogue

(Rosalind)

Rosalind, breaking the fourth wall, comments on how unusual it is to see the epilogue spoken by a woman and, while lightly mocking them, expresses her hope that they enjoyed the play. (1 line)

Rosalind.
It is not the fashion to see the lady the epilogue; but it is no more unhandsome than to see the lord the prologue. If it be true that good wine needs no bush, 'tis true that a good play needs no epilogue. Yet to good wine they do use good bushes; and good plays prove the better by the help of good epilogues. What a case am I in then, that am neither a good epilogue, nor cannot insinuate with you in the behalf of a good play! I am not furnish'd like a beggar, therefore to beg will not become me. My way is to conjure you, and I'll begin with the women. I charge you, O women, for the love you bear to men, to like as much of this play as please you; and I charge you, O men, for the love you bear to women (as I perceive by your simp'ring, none of you hates them), that between you and the women the play may please. If I were a woman I would kiss as many of you as had beards that pleas'd me, complexions that lik'd me, and breaths that I defied not; and I am sure, as many as have good beards, or good faces, or sweet breaths, will for my kind offer, when I make curtsy, bid me farewell.

Exit.

Much Ado About Nothing

Act 1

Scene 1

Messina. Before Leonato's house.

(Leonato; Hero; Beatrice; Messenger; Don Pedro; Claudio; Benedick; Balthasar; Don John the Bastard)

Leonato, the governor of Messina, is informed that Don Pedro of Arragon and his troop will be arriving this evening, returning victorious from a battle in which they lost almost no one, and in which Count Claudio greatly distinguished himself. Leonato's niece Beatrice asks the Messenger about Benedick, mocking him greatly. It turns out that Benedick's best friend (this month) is Claudio. Don Pedro and his train arrive, including Claudio and Benedick, along with Don John, Don Pedro's half-brother who was fighting against him and lost the battle. Leonato invites them all to stay, and presents his daughter Hero to the Prince. Benedick's quick comments are answered by Beatrice, and the two engage in a battle of raillery that Benedick loses. The surly Don John accepts Leonato's welcome after Don Pedro announces that they shall stay a month. Left alone, Claudio reveals to Benedick that he has been taken by Hero's modesty and beauty. Benedick is appalled that yet another bachelor has been turned into a lover. Don Pedro returns for them and is informed of Claudio's love, and when Benedick insists that he will remain a stranger to love all his life, the other two gang up on him and joyfully imagine how much they will mock him if he ever does fall in love. Claudio asks Don Pedro for help in wooing Hero, and Don Pedro offers to woo her for him in disguise at the masked ball that night, to see how she takes the proposal, and to take care of the details with Leonato.

Enter Leonato, governor of Messina, Hero his daughter, and Beatrice his niece, with a Messenger.

Leonato.
I learn in this letter that Don Pedro of Arragon comes this night to Messina.

Messenger.
He is very near by this, he was not three leagues off when I left him.

Leonato.
How many gentlemen have you lost in this action?

Messenger.
But few of any sort, and none of name.

Leonato.
A victory is twice itself when the achiever brings home full numbers. I find here that Don Pedro hath bestow'd much honor on a young Florentine call'd Claudio.

Messenger.
Much deserv'd on his part, and equally rememb'red by Don Pedro. He hath borne himself beyond the promise of his age, doing in the figure of a lamb the feats of a lion. He hath indeed better bett'red expectation than you must expect of me to tell you how.

Leonato.
He hath an uncle here in Messina will be very much glad of it.

Messenger.
I have already deliver'd him letters, and there appears much joy in him, even so much that joy could not show itself modest enough without a badge of bitterness.

Leonato.
Did he break out into tears?

Messenger.
In great measure.

Leonato.
A kind overflow of kindness. There are no faces truer than those that are so wash'd. How much better is it to weep at joy than to joy at weeping!

Beatrice.
I pray you, is Signior Mountanto return'd from the wars or no?

Messenger.
I know none of that name, lady. There was none such in the army of any sort.

Leonato.
What is he that you ask for, niece?

Hero.
My cousin means Signior Benedick of Padua.

Messenger.
O, he's return'd, and as pleasant as ever he was.

Beatrice.
He set up his bills here in Messina, and challeng'd Cupid at the flight, and my uncle's fool, reading the challenge, subscrib'd for Cupid, and challeng'd him at the burbolt. I pray you, how many hath he kill'd and eaten in these wars? But how many hath he kill'd? For indeed I promis'd to eat all of his killing.

Leonato.
Faith, niece, you tax Signior Benedick too much, but he'll be meet with you, I doubt it not.

Messenger.
He hath done good service, lady, in these wars.

Beatrice.
You had musty victual, and he hath help to eat it. He is a very valiant trencherman, he hath an excellent stomach.

Messenger.
And a good soldier too, lady.

Beatrice.
And a good soldier to a lady, but what is he to a lord?

Messenger.
A lord to a lord, a man to a man, stuff'd with all honorable virtues.

Beatrice.
It is so indeed, he is no less than a stuff'd man. But for the stuffing—well, we are all mortal.

Leonato.
You must not, sir, mistake my niece. There is a kind of merry war betwixt Signior Benedick and her; they never meet but there's a skirmish of wit between them.

Beatrice.
Alas, he gets nothing by that. In our last conflict four of his five wits went halting off, and now is the whole man govern'd with one; so that if he have wit enough to keep himself warm, let him bear it for a difference between himself and his horse, for it is all the wealth that he hath left to be known a reasonable creature. Who is his companion now? He hath every month a new sworn brother.

Messenger.
Is't possible?

Beatrice.
Very easily possible. He wears his faith but as the fashion of his hat: it ever changes with the next block.

Messenger.
I see, lady, the gentleman is not in your books.

Beatrice.
No, and he were, I would burn my study. But I pray you, who is his companion? Is there no young squarer now that will make a voyage with him to the devil?

Messenger.
He is most in the company of the right noble Claudio.

Beatrice.
O Lord, he will hang upon him like a disease; he is sooner caught than the pestilence, and the taker runs presently mad. God help the noble Claudio! If he have caught the Benedick, it will cost him a thousand pound ere 'a be cur'd.

Messenger.
I will hold friends with you, lady.

Beatrice.
Do, good friend.

Leonato.
You will never run mad, niece.

Beatrice.
No, not till a hot January.

Messenger.
Don Pedro is approach'd.

Enter Don Pedro, Claudio, Benedick, Balthasar, and Don John the Bastard.

Don Pedro.
Good Signior Leonato, are you come to meet your trouble? The fashion of the world is to avoid cost, and you encounter it.

Leonato.
Never came trouble to my house in the likeness of your Grace, for trouble being gone, comfort should remain; but when you depart from me, sorrow abides and happiness takes his leave.

Don Pedro.
You embrace your charge too willingly. I think this is your daughter.

Leonato.
Her mother hath many times told me so.

Benedick.
Were you in doubt, sir, that you ask'd her?

Leonato.
Signior Benedick, no, for then were you a child.

Don Pedro.
You have it full, Benedick. We may guess by this what you are, being a man. Truly the lady fathers herself. Be happy, lady, for you are like an honorable father.

Benedick.
If Signior Leonato be her father, she would not have his head on her shoulders for all Messina, as like him as she is.

Beatrice.
I wonder that you will still be talking, Signior Benedick, nobody marks you.

Benedick.
What, my dear Lady Disdain! Are you yet living?

Beatrice.
Is it possible disdain should die while she hath such meet food to feed it as Signior Benedick? Courtesy itself must convert to disdain, if you come in her presence.

Benedick.
Then is courtesy a turncoat. But it is certain I am lov'd of all ladies, only you excepted; and I would I could find in my heart that I had not a hard heart, for truly I love none.

Beatrice.
A dear happiness to women, they would else have been troubled with a pernicious suitor. I thank God and my cold blood, I am of your humor for that: I had rather hear my dog bark at a crow than a man swear he loves me.

Benedick.
God keep your ladyship still in that mind! So some gentleman or other shall scape a predestinate scratch'd face.

Beatrice.
Scratching could not make it worse, and 'twere such a face as yours were.

Benedick.
Well, you are a rare parrot-teacher.

Beatrice.
A bird of my tongue is better than a beast of yours.

Benedick.
I would my horse had the speed of your tongue, and so good a continuer. But keep your way a' God's name, I have done.

Beatrice.
You always end with a jade's trick, I know you of old.

Don Pedro.
That is the sum of all: Leonato—Signior Claudio and Signior Benedick—my dear friend Leonato hath invited you all. I tell him we shall stay here at the least a month, and he heartily prays some occasion may detain us longer. I dare swear he is no hypocrite, but prays from his heart.

Leonato.
If you swear, my lord, you shall not be forsworn.

To Don John.

Let me bid you welcome, my lord, being reconcil'd to the Prince your brother: I owe you all duty.

Don John.
I thank you. I am not of many words, but I thank you.

Leonato.
Please it your Grace lead on?

Don Pedro.
Your hand, Leonato, we will go together.

Exeunt. Manent Benedick and Claudio.

Claudio.
Benedick, didst thou note the daughter of Signior Leonato?

Benedick.
I noted her not, but I look'd on her.

Claudio.
Is she not a modest young lady?

Benedick.
Do you question me, as an honest man should do, for my simple true judgment? Or would you have me speak after my custom, as being a profess'd tyrant to their sex?

Claudio.
No, I pray thee speak in sober judgment.

Benedick.
Why, i' faith, methinks she's too low for a high praise, too brown for a fair praise, and too little for a great praise; only this commendation I can afford her, that were she other than she is, she were unhandsome, and being no other but as she is, I do not like her.

Claudio.
Thou thinkest I am in sport. I pray thee tell me truly how thou lik'st her.

Benedick.
Would you buy her, that you inquire after her?

Claudio.
Can the world buy such a jewel?

Benedick.
Yea, and a case to put it into. But speak you this with a sad brow? Or do you play the flouting Jack, to tell us Cupid is a good hare-finder and Vulcan a rare carpenter? Come, in what key shall a man take you to go in the song?

Claudio.
In mine eye, she is the sweetest lady that ever I look'd on.

Benedick.
I can see yet without spectacles, and I see no such matter. There's her cousin, and she were not possess'd with a fury, exceeds her as much in beauty as the first of May doth the last of December. But I hope you have no intent to turn husband, have you?

Claudio.
I would scarce trust myself, though I had sworn the contrary, if Hero would be my wife.

Benedick.
Is't come to this? In faith, hath not the world one man but he will wear his cap with suspicion? Shall I never see a bachelor of threescore again? Go to, i' faith, and thou wilt needs thrust thy neck into a yoke, wear the print of it, and sigh away Sundays. Look, Don Pedro is return'd to seek you.

Enter Don Pedro.

Don Pedro.
What secret hath held you here, that you follow'd not to Leonato's?

Benedick.
I would your Grace would constrain me to tell.

Don Pedro.
I charge thee on thy allegiance.

Benedick.
You hear, Count Claudio, I can be secret as a dumb man; I would have you think so; but on my allegiance, mark you this, on my allegiance, he is in love. With who? Now that is your Grace's part. Mark how short his answer is: with Hero, Leonato's short daughter.

Claudio.
If this were so, so were it utt'red.

Benedick.
Like the old tale, my lord: "It is not so, nor 'twas not so, but indeed, God forbid it should be so."

Claudio.
If my passion change not shortly, God forbid it should be otherwise.

Don Pedro.
Amen, if you love her, for the lady is very well worthy.

Claudio.
You speak this to fetch me in, my lord.

Don Pedro.
By my troth, I speak my thought.

Claudio.
And in faith, my lord, I spoke mine.

Benedick.
And by my two faiths and troths, my lord, I spoke mine.

Claudio.
That I love her, I feel.

Don Pedro.
That she is worthy, I know.

Benedick.
That I neither feel how she should be lov'd, nor know how she should be worthy, is the opinion that fire cannot melt out of me; I will die in it at the stake.

Don Pedro.
Thou wast ever an obstinate heretic in the despite of beauty.

Claudio.
And never could maintain his part but in the force of his will.

Benedick.
That a woman conceiv'd me, I thank her; that she brought me up, I likewise give her most humble thanks; but that I will have a rechate winded in my forehead, or hang my bugle in an invisible baldrick, all women shall pardon me. Because I will not do them the wrong to mistrust any, I will do myself the right to trust none; and the fine is (for the which I may go the finer), I will live a bachelor.

Don Pedro.
I shall see thee, ere I die, look pale with love.

Benedick.
With anger, with sickness, or with hunger, my lord, not with love. Prove that ever I lose more blood with love than I will get again with drinking, pick out mine eyes with a ballad-maker's pen, and hang me up at the door of a brothel-house for the sign of blind Cupid.

Don Pedro.
Well, if ever thou dost fall from this faith, thou wilt prove a notable argument.

Benedick.
If I do, hang me in a bottle like a cat, and shoot at me, and he that hits me, let him be clapp'd on the shoulder, and call'd Adam.

Don Pedro.
Well, as time shall try:
"In time the savage bull doth bear the yoke."

Benedick.
The savage bull may, but if ever the sensible Benedick bear it, pluck off the bull's horns, and set them in my forehead, and let me be vildly painted, and in such great letters as they write "Here is good horse to hire," let them signify under my sign, "Here you may see Benedick the married man."

Claudio.
If this should ever happen, thou wouldst be horn-mad.

Don Pedro.
Nay, if Cupid have not spent all his quiver in Venice, thou wilt quake for this shortly.

Benedick.
I look for an earthquake too then.

Don Pedro.
Well, you will temporize with the hours. In the mean time, good Signior Benedick, repair to Leonato's, commend me to him, and tell him I will not fail him at supper, for indeed he hath made great preparation.

Benedick.
I have almost matter enough in me for such an embassage, and so I commit you—

Claudio.
To the tuition of God. From my house—if I had it—

Don Pedro.
The sixth of July. Your loving friend, Benedick.

Benedick.
Nay, mock not, mock not. The body of your discourse is sometime guarded with fragments, and the guards are but slightly basted on neither. Ere you flout old ends any further, examine your conscience, and so I leave you.

Exit.

Claudio.
My liege, your Highness now may do me good.

Don Pedro.
My love is thine to teach; teach it but how,
And thou shalt see how apt it is to learn
Any hard lesson that may do thee good.

Claudio.
Hath Leonato any son, my lord?

Don Pedro.
No child but Hero, she's his only heir.
Dost thou affect her, Claudio?

Claudio.
O my lord,
When you went onward on this ended action,
I look'd upon her with a soldier's eye,
That lik'd, but had a rougher task in hand
Than to drive liking to the name of love.
But now I am return'd, and that war-thoughts
Have left their places vacant, in their rooms
Come thronging soft and delicate desires,
All prompting me how fair young Hero is,
Saying I lik'd her ere I went to wars.

Don Pedro.
Thou wilt be like a lover presently,
And tire the hearer with a book of words.
If thou dost love fair Hero, cherish it,
And I will break with her, and with her father,
And thou shalt have her. Was't not to this end
That thou began'st to twist so fine a story?

Claudio.
How sweetly you do minister to love,
That know love's grief by his complexion!
But lest my liking might too sudden seem,
I would have salv'd it with a longer treatise.

Don Pedro.
What need the bridge much broader than the flood?
The fairest grant is the necessity.
Look what will serve is fit: 'tis once, thou lovest,
And I will fit thee with the remedy.
I know we shall have reveling tonight;
I will assume thy part in some disguise,
And tell fair Hero I am Claudio,
And in her bosom I'll unclasp my heart,
And take her hearing prisoner with the force
And strong encounter of my amorous tale;
Then after to her father will I break,
And the conclusion is, she shall be thine.
In practice let us put it presently.

Exeunt.

Scene 2

A room in Leonato's house.

(Leonato; Antonio)

Leonato's brother Antonio excitedly tells the governor that a servant overheard Don Pedro telling Claudio he was in love with Hero. Leonato goes to tell Hero of this, so that she will have an answer ready when Don Pedro speaks to her.

Enter Leonato and an old man Antonio, brother to Leonato, meeting.

Leonato.
How now, brother, where is my cousin, your son?
Hath he provided this music?

Antonio.
He is very busy about it. But, brother, I can tell you strange news that you yet dreamt not of.

Leonato.
Are they good?

Antonio.
As the event stamps them, but they have a good cover; they show well outward. The Prince and Count Claudio, walking in a thick-pleach'd alley in mine orchard,

were thus much overheard by a man of mine. The Prince discover'd to Claudio that he lov'd my niece your daughter, and meant to acknowledge it this night in a dance; and if he found her accordant, he meant to take the present time by the top, and instantly break with you of it.

Leonato.
Hath the fellow any wit that told you this?

Antonio.
A good sharp fellow. I will send for him, and question him yourself.

Leonato.
No, no, we will hold it as a dream till it appear itself; but I will acquaint my daughter withal, that she may be the better prepar'd for an answer, if peradventure this be true. Go you and tell her of it.

Several persons cross the stage.

Cousins, you know what you have to do. O, I cry you mercy, friend, go you with me, and I will use your skill. Good cousin, have a care this busy time.

Exeunt.

Scene 3

A hall in Leonato's house.

(Don John the Bastard; Conrade; Borachio)

Grumpy and ill-natured, Don John refuses to be cheered up by the fact that his brother has not punished him for rebelling. His henchman Conrade counsels patience, but Don John has no intention of being pleasant. His other henchman Borachio comes in, telling Don John that he overheard Don Pedro and Claudio discussing the wooing of Hero, and Don John immediately decides to seize the opportunity to cross the upstart. Both henchmen agree to help him.

Enter Don John the Bastard and Conrade, his companion.

Conrade.
What the good-year, my lord, why are you thus out of measure sad?

Don John.
There is no measure in the occasion that breeds, therefore the sadness is without limit.

Conrade.
You should hear reason.

Don John.
And when I have heard it, what blessing brings it?

Conrade.
If not a present remedy, at least a patient sufferance.

Don John.
I wonder that thou (being, as thou say'st thou art, born under Saturn) goest about to apply a moral medicine to a mortifying mischief. I cannot hide what I am: I must be sad when I have cause, and smile at no man's jests; eat when I have stomach, and wait for no man's leisure; sleep when I am drowsy, and tend on no man's business; laugh when I am merry, and claw no man in his humor.

Conrade.
Yea, but you must not make the full show of this till you may do it without controlment. You have of late stood out against your brother, and he hath ta'en you newly into his grace, where it is impossible you should take true root but by the fair weather that you make yourself. It is needful that you frame the season for your own harvest.

Don John.
I had rather be a canker in a hedge than a rose in his grace, and it better fits my blood to be disdain'd of all than to fashion a carriage to rob love from any. In this (though I cannot be said to be a flattering honest man) it must not be denied but I am a plain-dealing villain. I am trusted with a muzzle, and enfranchis'd with a clog, therefore I have decreed not to sing in my cage. If I had my mouth, I would bite; if I had my liberty, I would do my liking. In the mean time let me be that I am, and seek not to alter me.

Conrade.
Can you make no use of your discontent?

Don John.
I make all use of it, for I use it only. Who comes here?

Enter Borachio.

What news, Borachio?

Borachio.
I came yonder from a great supper. The Prince your brother is royally entertain'd by Leonato, and I can give you intelligence of an intended marriage.

Don John.
Will it serve for any model to build mischief on? What is he for a fool that betroths himself to unquietness?

Borachio.
Marry, it is your brother's right hand.

Don John.
Who, the most exquisite Claudio?

Borachio.
Even he.

Don John.
A proper squire! And who, and who? Which way looks he?

Borachio.
Marry, one Hero, the daughter and heir of Leonato.

Don John.
A very forward March-chick! How came you to this?

Borachio.
Being entertain'd for a perfumer, as I was smoking a musty room, comes me the Prince and Claudio, hand in hand in sad conference. I whipt me behind the arras, and there heard it agreed upon that the Prince should woo Hero for himself, and having obtain'd her, give her to Count Claudio.

Don John.
Come, come, let us thither, this may prove food to my displeasure. That young start-up hath all the glory of my overthrow. If I can cross him any way, I bless myself every way. You are both sure, and will assist me?

Conrade.
To the death, my lord.

Don John.
Let us to the great supper, their cheer is the greater that I am subdu'd. Would the cook were a' my mind! Shall we go prove what's to be done?

Borachio.
We'll wait upon your lordship.

Exeunt.

Act 2

Scene 1

A hall in Leonato's house.

(Leonato; Antonio; Hero; Beatrice; Margaret; Ursula; Kinsman; Prince Don Pedro; Claudio; Benedick; Don John; Borachio)

As they wait for the guests to arrive at the masked ball, Leonato, Antonio, Hero, and Beatrice discuss Don John and Benedick, Beatrice seizing the first opportunity to engage in yet more mocking of the latter, to the men's amusement. Hero is reminded to say yes if Don Pedro asks her to marry him. Don Pedro's masked party enters, and he quickly takes Hero aside, while Borachio attempts to dance with Margaret and Antonio tries to deny to Ursula that it is he behind the mask. Beatrice and Benedick, both masked, converse, and Beatrice badmouths him, knowing perfectly well who she's speaking to, though he does not realize that she knows. Don John sidles up to Claudio, pretending to mistake him for Benedick, and tells him that Don Pedro is actually wooing Hero on his own account. Claudio is quite convinced and decides to have nothing more to do with Hero, and is surly when Benedick tries to joke with him, soon leaving him. Don Pedro comes looking for Claudio, but is distracted by chatting with Benedick and egging him on to discourse on Beatrice. Claudio, Leonato, Beatrice and Hero come in, and Don Pedro reveals that he has obtained Hero for the Count. Claudio is overjoyed. Beatrice rejects the idea of a husband for herself. After she leaves, the four left behind decide that for their own amusement and to occupy the time until Claudio and Hero's wedding, they will try to make Beatrice and Benedick fall in love with each other.

Enter Leonato, Antonio his brother, Hero his daughter, and Beatrice his niece, Margaret, Ursula, and a Kinsman.

Leonato.
Was not Count John here at supper?

Antonio.
I saw him not.

Beatrice.
How tartly that gentleman looks! I never can see him but I am heart-burn'd an hour after.

Hero.
He is of a very melancholy disposition.

Beatrice.
He were an excellent man that were made just in the midway between him and Benedick: the one is too like an image and says nothing, and the other too like my lady's eldest son, evermore tattling.

Leonato.
Then half Signior Benedick's tongue in Count John's mouth, and half Count John's melancholy in Signior Benedick's face—

Beatrice.
With a good leg and a good foot, uncle, and money enough in his purse, such a man would win any woman in the world, if 'a could get her good will.

Leonato.
By my troth, niece, thou wilt never get thee a husband, if thou be so shrewd of thy tongue.

Antonio.
In faith, she's too curst.

Beatrice.
Too curst is more than curst. I shall lessen God's sending that way, for it is said, "God sends a curst cow short horns"—but to a cow too curst he sends none.

Leonato.
So, by being too curst, God will send you no horns.

Beatrice.
Just, if he send me no husband, for the which blessing I am at him upon my knees every morning and evening. Lord, I could not endure a husband with a beard on his face, I had rather lie in the woollen!

Leonato.
You may light on a husband that hath no beard.

Beatrice.
What should I do with him? Dress him in my apparel and make him my waiting-gentlewoman? He that hath a beard is more than a youth, and he that hath no beard is less than a man; and he that is more than a youth is not for me, and he that is less than a man, I am not for him; therefore I will even take sixpence in earnest of the berrord, and lead his apes into hell.

Leonato.
Well then, go you into hell.

Beatrice.
No, but to the gate, and there will the devil meet me like an old cuckold with horns on his head, and say, "Get you to heaven, Beatrice, get you to heaven, here's no place for you maids." So deliver I up my apes, and away to Saint Peter. For the heavens, he shows me where the bachelors sit, and there live we as merry as the day is long.

Antonio.

To Hero.

Well, niece, I trust you will be rul'd by your father.

Beatrice.
Yes, faith, it is my cousin's duty to make cur'sy and say, "Father, as it please you." But yet for all that, cousin, let him be a handsome fellow, or else make another cur'sy and say, "Father, as it please me."

Leonato.
Well, niece, I hope to see you one day fitted with a husband.

Beatrice.
Not till God make men of some other mettle than earth. Would it not grieve a woman to be overmaster'd with a piece of valiant dust? To make an account of her life to a clod of wayward marl? No, uncle, I'll none. Adam's sons are my brethren, and truly I hold it a sin to match in my kindred.

Leonato.
Daughter, remember what I told you. If the Prince do solicit you in that kind, you know your answer.

Beatrice.
The fault will be in the music, cousin, if you be not woo'd in good time. If the Prince be too important, tell him there is measure in every thing, and so dance out the answer. For hear me, Hero: wooing, wedding, and repenting, is as a Scotch jig, a measure, and a cinquepace; the first suit is hot and hasty, like a Scotch jig, and full as fantastical; the wedding, mannerly-modest, as a measure, full of state and ancientry; and then comes repentance, and with his bad legs falls into the cinquepace faster and faster, till he sink into his grave.

Leonato.
Cousin, you apprehend passing shrewdly.

Act 2, Scene 1

Beatrice.
I have a good eye, uncle, I can see a church by daylight.

Leonato.
The revelers are ent'ring, brother, make good room.

They put on their masks.
Enter Prince Don Pedro, Claudio, and Benedick, and Don John, and Borachio as maskers, with a Drum.

Don Pedro.
Lady, will you walk about with your friend?

Hero.
So you walk softly, and look sweetly, and say nothing, I am yours for the walk, and especially when I walk away.

Don Pedro.
With me in your company?

Hero.
I may say so when I please.

Don Pedro.
And when please you to say so?

Hero.
When I like your favor, for God defend the lute should be like the case!

Don Pedro.
My visor is Philemon's roof, within the house is Jove.

Hero.
Why then your visor should be thatch'd.

Don Pedro.
Speak low if you speak love.

They move aside.

Borachio.
Well, I would you did like me.

Margaret.
So would not I for your own sake, for I have many ill qualities.

Borachio.
Which is one?

Margaret.
I say my prayers aloud.

Borachio.
I love you the better; the hearers may cry amen.

Margaret.
God match me with a good dancer!

Borachio.
Amen.

Margaret.
And God keep him out of my sight when the dance is done! Answer, clerk.

Borachio.
No more words; the clerk is answer'd.

They move aside.

Ursula.
I know you well enough, you are Signior Antonio.

Antonio.
At a word, I am not.

Ursula.
I know you by the waggling of your head.

Antonio.
To tell you true, I counterfeit him.

Ursula.
You could never do him so ill-well, unless you were the very man. Here's his dry hand up and down. You are he, you are he.

Antonio.
At a word, I am not.

Ursula.
Come, come, do you think I do not know you by your excellent wit? Can virtue hide itself? Go to, mum, you are he. Graces will appear, and there's an end.

They move aside.

Beatrice.
Will you not tell me who told you so?

Benedick.
No, you shall pardon me.

Beatrice.
Nor will you not tell me who you are?

Benedick.
Not now.

Beatrice.
That I was disdainful, and that I had my good wit out of the "Hundred Merry Tales"—well, this was Signior Benedick that said so.

Benedick.
What's he?

Beatrice.
I am sure you know him well enough.

Benedick.
Not I, believe me.

Beatrice.
Did he never make you laugh?

Benedick.
I pray you, what is he?

Beatrice.
Why, he is the Prince's jester, a very dull fool; only his gift is in devising impossible slanders. None but libertines delight in him, and the commendation is not in his wit, but in his villainy, for he both pleases men and angers them, and then they laugh at him and beat him. I am sure he is in the fleet; I would he had boarded me.

Benedick.
When I know the gentleman, I'll tell him what you say.

Beatrice.
Do, do, he'll but break a comparison or two on me, which peradventure, not mark'd, or not laugh'd at, strikes him into melancholy, and then there's a partridge wing sav'd, for the fool will eat no supper that night.

Music for the dance begins.
We must follow the leaders.

Benedick.
In every good thing.

Beatrice.
Nay, if they lead to any ill, I will leave them at the next turning.

Dance.

Then exeunt all but Don John, Borachio, and Claudio.

Don John.
Sure my brother is amorous on Hero, and hath withdrawn her father to break with him about it. The ladies follow her, and but one visor remains.

Borachio.
And that is Claudio. I know him by his bearing.

Don John.
Are not you Signior Benedick?

Claudio.
You know me well, I am he.

Don John.
Signior, you are very near my brother in his love. He is enamor'd on Hero. I pray you dissuade him from her, she is no equal for his birth. You may do the part of an honest man in it.

Claudio.
How know you he loves her?

Don John.
I heard him swear his affection.

Borachio.
So did I too, and he swore he would marry her tonight.

Don John.
Come let us to the banquet.

Exeunt. Manet Claudio.

Claudio.
Thus answer I in name of Benedick,
But hear these ill news with the ears of Claudio.
'Tis certain so, the Prince woos for himself.
Friendship is constant in all other things
Save in the office and affairs of love;
Therefore all hearts in love use their own tongues.
Let every eye negotiate for itself,
And trust no agent; for beauty is a witch
Against whose charms faith melteth into blood.
This is an accident of hourly proof,
Which I mistrusted not. Farewell therefore Hero!

Enter Benedick.

Benedick.
Count Claudio?

Claudio.
Yea, the same.

Benedick.
Come, will you go with me?

Claudio.
Whither?

Benedick.
Even to the next willow, about your own business, County. What fashion will you wear the garland of? About your neck, like an usurer's chain? Or under your arm, like a lieutenant's scarf? You must wear it one way, for the Prince hath got your Hero.

Claudio.
I wish him joy of her.

Benedick.
Why, that's spoken like an honest drovier; so they sell bullocks. But did you think the Prince would have serv'd you thus?

Claudio.
I pray you leave me.

Benedick.
Ho, now you strike like the blind man. 'Twas the boy that stole your meat, and you'll beat the post.

Claudio.
If it will not be, I'll leave you.

Exit.

Benedick.
Alas, poor hurt fowl, now will he creep into sedges. But that my Lady Beatrice should know me, and not know me! The Prince's fool! Hah, it may be I go under that title because I am merry. Yea, but so I am apt to do myself wrong. I am not so reputed. It is the base (though bitter) disposition of Beatrice that puts the world into her person, and so gives me out. Well, I'll be reveng'd as I may.

Enter the Prince Don Pedro.

Don Pedro.
Now, signior, where's the Count? Did you see him?

Benedick.
Troth, my lord, I have play'd the part of Lady Fame. I found him here as melancholy as a lodge in a warren. I told him, and I think I told him true, that your Grace had got the good will of this young lady, and I off'red him my company to a willow-tree, either to make him a garland, as being forsaken, or to bind him up a rod, as being worthy to be whipt.

Don Pedro.
To be whipt? What's his fault?

Benedick.
The flat transgression of a schoolboy, who being over-joy'd with finding a bird's nest, shows it his companion, and he steals it.

Don Pedro.
Wilt thou make a trust a transgression? The transgression is in the stealer.

Benedick.
Yet it had not been amiss the rod had been made, and the garland too, for the garland he might have worn himself, and the rod he might have bestow'd on you, who (as I take it) have stol'n his bird's nest.

Don Pedro.
I will but teach them to sing, and restore them to the owner.

Benedick.
If their singing answer your saying, by my faith you say honestly.

Don Pedro.
The Lady Beatrice hath a quarrel to you. The gentleman that danc'd with her told her she is much wrong'd by you.

Benedick.
O, she misus'd me past the endurance of a block; an oak but with one green leaf on it would have answer'd her. My very visor began to assume life, and scold with her. She told me, not thinking I had been myself, that I was the Prince's jester, that I was duller than a great thaw, huddling jest upon jest with such impossible conveyance upon me that I stood like a man at a mark, with a whole army shooting at me. She speaks poniards, and every word stabs. If her breath were as terrible as her terminations, there were no living near her, she would infect to the north star. I would not marry her, though she were endow'd with all that

Adam had left him before he transgress'd. She would have made Hercules have turn'd spit, yea, and have cleft his club to make the fire too. Come, talk not of her; you shall find her the infernal Ate in good apparel. I would to God some scholar would conjure her, for certainly, while she is here, a man may live as quiet in hell as in a sanctuary, and people sin upon purpose, because they would go thither; so indeed all disquiet, horror, and perturbation follows her.

Enter Claudio and Beatrice, Leonato and Hero.

Don Pedro.
Look here she comes.

Benedick.
Will your Grace command me any service to the world's end? I will go on the slightest arrand now to the Antipodes that you can devise to send me on; I will fetch you a toothpicker now from the furthest inch of Asia, bring you the length of Prester John's foot, fetch you a hair off the great Cham's beard, do you any embassage to the Pigmies, rather than hold three words' conference with this harpy. You have no employment for me?

Don Pedro.
None, but to desire your good company.

Benedick.
O God, sir, here's a dish I love not, I cannot endure my Lady Tongue.

Exit.

Don Pedro.
Come, lady, come, you have lost the heart of Signior Benedick.

Beatrice.
Indeed, my lord, he lent it me awhile, and I gave him use for it, a double heart for his single one. Marry, once before he won it of me with false dice, therefore your Grace may well say I have lost it.

Don Pedro.
You have put him down, lady, you have put him down.

Beatrice.
So I would not he should do me, my lord, lest I should prove the mother of fools. I have brought Count Claudio, whom you sent me to seek.

Don Pedro.
Why, how now, Count, wherefore are you sad?

Claudio.
Not sad, my lord.

Don Pedro.
How then? Sick?

Claudio.
Neither, my lord.

Beatrice.
The Count is neither sad, nor sick, nor merry, nor well; but civil count, civil as an orange, and something of that jealous complexion.

Don Pedro.
I' faith, lady, I think your blazon to be true, though I'll be sworn, if he be so, his conceit is false. Here, Claudio, I have woo'd in thy name, and fair Hero is won. I have broke with her father, and his good will obtain'd. Name the day of marriage, and God give thee joy!

Leonato.
Count, take of me my daughter, and with her my fortunes. His Grace hath made the match, and all grace say amen to it.

Beatrice.
Speak, Count, 'tis your cue.

Claudio.
Silence is the perfectest herald of joy; I were but little happy, if I could say how much! Lady, as you are mine, I am yours. I give away myself for you, and dote upon the exchange.

Beatrice.
Speak, cousin, or (if you cannot) stop his mouth with a kiss, and let not him speak neither.

Don Pedro.
In faith, lady, you have a merry heart.

Beatrice.
Yea, my lord, I thank it—poor fool, it keeps on the windy side of care. My cousin tells him in his ear that he is in her heart.

Claudio.
And so she doth, cousin.

Beatrice.
Good Lord, for alliance! Thus goes every one to the world but I, and I am sunburnt. I may sit in a corner and cry "Heigh-ho for a husband!"

Don Pedro.
Lady Beatrice, I will get you one.

Beatrice.
I would rather have one of your father's getting. Hath your Grace ne'er a brother like you? Your father got excellent husbands, if a maid could come by them.

Don Pedro.
Will you have me, lady?

Beatrice.
No, my lord, unless I might have another for working-days. Your Grace is too costly to wear every day. But I beseech your Grace pardon me, I was born to speak all mirth and no matter.

Don Pedro.
Your silence most offends me, and to be merry best becomes you, for out a' question, you were born in a merry hour.

Beatrice.
No, sure, my lord, my mother cried, but then there was a star danc'd, and under that was I born. Cousins, God give you joy!

Leonato.
Niece, will you look to those things I told you of?

Beatrice.
I cry you mercy, uncle. By your Grace's pardon.

Exit Beatrice.

Don Pedro.
By my troth, a pleasant-spirited lady.

Leonato.
There's little of the melancholy element in her, my lord. She is never sad but when she sleeps, and not ever sad then; for I have heard my daughter say, she hath often dreamt of unhappiness, and wak'd herself with laughing.

Don Pedro.
She cannot endure to hear tell of a husband.

Leonato.
O, by no means, she mocks all her wooers out of suit.

Don Pedro.
She were an excellent wife for Benedick.

Leonato.
O Lord, my lord, if they were but a week married, they would talk themselves mad.

Don Pedro.
County Claudio, when mean you to go to church?

Claudio.
Tomorrow, my lord. Time goes on crutches till love have all his rites.

Leonato.
Not till Monday, my dear son, which is hence a just sevennight, and a time too brief too, to have all things answer my mind.

Don Pedro.
Come, you shake the head at so long a breathing, but I warrant thee, Claudio, the time shall not go dully by us. I will in the interim undertake one of Hercules' labors, which is, to bring Signior Benedick and the Lady Beatrice into a mountain of affection th' one with th' other. I would fain have it a match, and I doubt not but to fashion it, if you three will but minister such assistance as I shall give you direction.

Leonato.
My lord, I am for you, though it cost me ten nights' watchings.

Claudio.
And I, my lord.

Don Pedro.
And you too, gentle Hero?

Hero.
I will do any modest office, my lord, to help my cousin to a good husband.

Don Pedro.
And Benedick is not the unhopefullest husband that I know. Thus far can I praise him: he is of a noble strain, of approv'd valor, and confirm'd honesty. I will teach you how to humor your cousin, that she shall fall in love with Benedick, and I, with your two helps, will so practice on Benedick that, in despite of his quick wit and his queasy stomach, he shall fall in love with Beat-

rice. If we can do this, Cupid is no longer an archer; his glory shall be ours, for we are the only love-gods. Go in with me, and I will tell you my drift.

Exeunt.

Scene 2

Another room in Leonato's house.

(Don John; Borachio)

Don John detests Claudio so much that he is willing to try anything to hurt him. Borachio assures him that he has a surefire way to break up Claudio's wedding with Hero. Since Margaret is infatuated with him, he will arrange a meeting with her at midnight at Hero's window, where they will playact that Margaret is Hero. Don John will see to it that Don Pedro and Claudio see this, thus convincing them that Hero is unfaithful. Don John promises Borachio a large sum of money if he pulls it off.

Enter Don John and Borachio.

Don John.
It is so, the Count Claudio shall marry the daughter of Leonato.

Borachio.
Yea, my lord, but I can cross it.

Don John.
Any bar, any cross, any impediment will be med'cinable to me. I am sick in displeasure to him, and whatsoever comes athwart his affection ranges evenly with mine. How canst thou cross this marriage?

Borachio.
Not honestly, my lord, but so covertly that no dishonesty shall appear in me.

Don John.
Show me briefly how.

Borachio.
I think I told your lordship a year since, how much I am in the favor of Margaret, the waiting-gentlewoman to Hero.

Don John.
I remember.

Borachio.
I can, at any unseasonable instant of the night, appoint her to look out at her lady's chamber-window.

Don John.
What life is in that, to be the death of this marriage?

Borachio.
The poison of that lies in you to temper. Go you to the Prince your brother; spare not to tell him that he hath wrong'd his honor in marrying the renown'd Claudio—whose estimation do you mightily hold up—to a contaminated stale, such a one as Hero.

Don John.
What proof shall I make of that?

Borachio.
Proof enough to misuse the Prince, to vex Claudio, to undo Hero, and kill Leonato. Look you for any other issue?

Don John.
Only to despite them, I will endeavor any thing.

Borachio.
Go then, find me a meet hour to draw Don Pedro and the Count Claudio alone, tell them that you know that Hero loves me, intend a kind of zeal both to the Prince and Claudio—as in love of your brother's honor, who hath made this match, and his friend's reputation, who is thus like to be cozen'd with the semblance of a maid—that you have discover'd thus. They will scarcely believe this without trial. Offer them instances, which shall bear no less likelihood than to see me at her chamber-window, hear me call Margaret Hero, hear Margaret term me Claudio; and bring them to see this the very night, before the intended wedding—for in the mean time I will so fashion the matter that Hero shall be absent—and there shall appear such seeming truth of Hero's disloyalty, that jealousy shall be call'd assurance, and all the preparation overthrown.

Don John.
Grow this to what adverse issue it can, I will put it in practice. Be cunning in the working this, and thy fee is a thousand ducats.

Borachio.
Be you constant in the accusation, and my cunning shall not shame me.

Act 2, Scene 3

Don John.
I will presently go learn their day of marriage.

Exeunt.

Scene 3

Leonato's orchard.

(Benedick; Boy; Prince Don Pedro; Leonato; Claudio; Balthasar; Musicians; Beatrice)

Benedick grouses to himself about how love makes men become foolish. Seeing Don Pedro and Claudio approaching, he hides in the bushes. The two see him do so and put it to good use. Along with Leonato, they listen to a song sung by Balthazar and then they loudly discuss how Beatrice is deeply in love with Benedick, though she refuses to show it. Benedick is rather taken aback, but is convinced this is not a prank because Leonato joins in. They discuss and dismiss the idea of telling Benedick, saying that he would only mock her to death if he knew. Once they are certain Benedick has taken the bait, they leave, planning to have Hero do the same to Beatrice. Benedick reflects that after all, Beatrice is not such a bad party, and deciding that he is willing to put up with the mockery that will follow, determines to woo Beatrice. On this, she enters and shows absolutely no sign of being enamored, which Benedick manages to reinterpret as clearly showing her love.

Enter Benedick alone.

Benedick.
Boy!

Enter Boy.

Boy.
Signior?

Benedick.
In my chamber-window lies a book, bring it hither to me in the orchard.

Boy.
I am here already, sir.

Exit.

Benedick.
I know that, but I would have thee hence, and here again. I do much wonder that one man, seeing how much another man is a fool when he dedicates his behaviors to love, will, after he hath laugh'd at such shallow follies in others, become the argument of his own scorn by falling in love—and such a man is Claudio. I have known when there was no music with him but the drum and the fife, and now had he rather hear the tabor and the pipe; I have known when he would have walk'd ten mile afoot to see a good armor, and now will he lie ten nights awake carving the fashion of a new doublet; he was wont to speak plain and to the purpose (like an honest man and a soldier), and now is he turn'd orthography—his words are a very fantastical banquet, just so many strange dishes. May I be so converted and see with these eyes? I cannot tell; I think not. I will not be sworn but love may transform me to an oyster, but I'll take my oath on it, till he have made an oyster of me, he shall never make me such a fool. One woman is fair, yet I am well; another is wise, yet I am well; another virtuous, yet I am well; but till all graces be in one woman, one woman shall not come in my grace. Rich she shall be, that's certain; wise, or I'll none; virtuous, or I'll never cheapen her; fair, or I'll never look on her; mild, or come not near me; noble, or not I for an angel; of good discourse, an excellent musician, and her hair shall be of what color it please God. Hah! The Prince and Monsieur Love. I will hide me in the arbor.

Withdraws.
Enter Prince Don Pedro, Leonato, Claudio. Music within.

Don Pedro.
Come, shall we hear this music?

Claudio.
Yea, my good lord. How still the evening is,
As hush'd on purpose to grace harmony!

Don Pedro.
See you where Benedick hath hid himself?

Claudio.
O, very well, my lord. The music ended,
We'll fit the hid-fox with a pennyworth.

Enter Balthasar with Music.

Don Pedro.
Come, Balthasar, we'll hear that song again.

Balthasar.
O good my lord, tax not so bad a voice
To slander music any more than once.

Don Pedro.
It is the witness still of excellency
To put a strange face on his own perfection.
I pray thee sing, and let me woo no more.

Balthasar.
Because you talk of wooing, I will sing,
Since many a wooer doth commence his suit
To her he thinks not worthy, yet he woos,
Yet will he swear he loves.

Don Pedro.
                    Nay, pray thee come,
Or if thou wilt hold longer argument,
Do it in notes.

Balthasar.
                    Note this before my notes:
There's not a note of mine that's worth the noting.

Don Pedro.
Why, these are very crotchets that he speaks—
Note notes, forsooth, and nothing.

Air.

Benedick.
Now, divine air! Now is his soul ravish'd! Is it not strange that sheep's guts should hale souls out of men's bodies? Well, a horn for my money when all's done.

The Song

Balthasar.
Sigh no more, ladies, sigh no more,
Men were deceivers ever,
One foot in sea, and one on shore,
To one thing constant never.
Then sigh not so, but let them go,
And be you blithe and bonny,
Converting all your sounds of woe
Into hey nonny nonny.
Sing no more ditties, sing no more,
Of dumps so dull and heavy;
The fraud of men was ever so,
Since summer first was leavy.
Then sigh not so, etc.

Don Pedro.
By my troth, a good song.

Balthasar.
And an ill singer, my lord.

Don Pedro.
Ha, no, no, faith, thou sing'st well enough for a shift.

Benedick.
And he had been a dog that should have howl'd thus, they would have hang'd him, and I pray God his bad voice bode no mischief. I had as lief have heard the night-raven, come what plague could have come after it.

Don Pedro.
Yea, marry, dost thou hear, Balthasar? I pray thee get us some excellent music; for tomorrow night we would have it at the Lady Hero's chamber-window.

Balthasar.
The best I can, my lord.

Exit Balthasar.

Don Pedro.
Do so, farewell. Come hither, Leonato. What was it you told me of today, that your niece Beatrice was in love with Signior Benedick?

Claudio.

Aside.

O ay, stalk on, stalk on, the fowl sits.—I did never think that lady would have lov'd any man.

Leonato.
No, nor I neither, but most wonderful that she should so dote on Signior Benedick, whom she hath in all outward behaviors seem'd ever to abhor.

Benedick.
Is't possible? Sits the wind in that corner?

Leonato.
By my troth, my lord, I cannot tell what to think of it but that she loves him with an enrag'd affection; it is past the infinite of thought.

Don Pedro.
May be she doth but counterfeit.

Act 2, Scene 3

Claudio.
Faith, like enough.

Leonato.
O God! Counterfeit? There was never counterfeit of passion came so near the life of passion as she discovers it.

Don Pedro.
Why, what effects of passion shows she?

Claudio.

Aside.

Bait the hook well, this fish will bite.

Leonato.
What effects, my lord? She will sit you—you heard my daughter tell you how.

Claudio.
She did indeed.

Don Pedro.
How, how, I pray you? You amaze me, I would have thought her spirit had been invincible against all assaults of affection.

Leonato.
I would have sworn it had, my lord, especially against Benedick.

Benedick.
I should think this a gull, but that the white-bearded fellow speaks it. Knavery cannot sure hide himself in such reverence.

Claudio.

Aside.

He hath ta'en th' infection. Hold it up.

Don Pedro.
Hath she made her affection known to Benedick?

Leonato.
No, and swears she never will. That's her torment.

Claudio.
'Tis true indeed, so your daughter says. "Shall I," says she, "that have so oft encount'red him with scorn, write to him that I love him?"

Leonato.
This says she now when she is beginning to write to him, for she'll be up twenty times a night, and there will she sit in her smock till she have writ a sheet of paper. My daughter tells us all.

Claudio.
Now you talk of a sheet of paper, I remember a pretty jest your daughter told us of.

Leonato.
O, when she had writ it, and was reading it over, she found "Benedick" and "Beatrice" between the sheet?

Claudio.
That.

Leonato.
O, she tore the letter into a thousand half-pence; rail'd at herself, that she should be so immodest to write to one that she knew would flout her. "I measure him," says she, "by my own spirit, for I should flout him, if he writ to me, yea, though I love him, I should."

Claudio.
Then down upon her knees she falls, weeps, sobs, beats her heart, tears her hair, prays, curses: "O sweet Benedick! God give me patience!"

Leonato.
She doth indeed, my daughter says so; and the ecstasy hath so much overborne her that my daughter is sometime afeard she will do a desperate outrage to herself. It is very true.

Don Pedro.
It were good that Benedick knew of it by some other, if she will not discover it.

Claudio.
To what end? He would make but a sport of it, and torment the poor lady worse.

Don Pedro.
And he should, it were an alms to hang him. She's an excellent sweet lady, and (out of all suspicion) she is virtuous.

Claudio.
And she is exceeding wise.

Don Pedro.
In every thing but in loving Benedick.

Leonato.
O my lord, wisdom and blood combating in so tender a body, we have ten proofs to one that blood hath the victory. I am sorry for her, as I have just cause, being her uncle and her guardian.

Don Pedro.
I would she had bestow'd this dotage on me, I would have daff'd all other respects, and made her half myself. I pray you tell Benedick of it, and hear what 'a will say.

Leonato.
Were it good, think you?

Claudio.
Hero thinks surely she will die, for she says she will die if he love her not, and she will die ere she make her love known, and she will die if he woo her, rather than she will bate one breath of her accustom'd crossness.

Don Pedro.
She doth well. If she should make tender of her love, 'tis very possible he'll scorn it, for the man (as you know all) hath a contemptible spirit.

Claudio.
He is a very proper man.

Don Pedro.
He hath indeed a good outward happiness.

Claudio.
Before God, and in my mind, very wise.

Don Pedro.
He doth indeed show some sparks that are like wit.

Claudio.
And I take him to be valiant.

Don Pedro.
As Hector, I assure you, and in the managing of quarrels you may say he is wise, for either he avoids them with great discretion, or undertakes them with a most Christian-like fear.

Leonato.
If he do fear God, 'a must necessarily keep peace; if he break the peace, he ought to enter into a quarrel with fear and trembling.

Don Pedro.
And so will he do, for the man doth fear God, howsoever it seems not in him by some large jests he will make. Well, I am sorry for your niece. Shall we go seek Benedick, and tell him of her love?

Claudio.
Never tell him, my lord. Let her wear it out with good counsel.

Leonato.
Nay, that's impossible, she may wear her heart out first.

Don Pedro.
Well, we will hear further of it by your daughter, let it cool the while. I love Benedick well, and I could wish he would modestly examine himself, to see how much he is unworthy so good a lady.

Leonato.
My lord, will you walk? Dinner is ready.

Claudio.

Aside.

If he do not dote on her upon this, I will never trust my expectation.

Don Pedro.

Aside.

Let there be the same net spread for her, and that must your daughter and her gentlewomen carry. The sport will be, when they hold one an opinion of another's dotage, and no such matter; that's the scene that I would see, which will be merely a dumb show. Let us send her to call him in to dinner.

Exeunt Don Pedro, Claudio, and Leonato.

Benedick.

Coming forward.

This can be no trick: the conference was sadly borne; they have the truth of this from Hero; they seem to pity the lady. It seems her affections have their full bent. Love me? Why, it must be requited. I hear how I am censur'd; they say I will bear myself proudly, if I perceive the love come from her; they say too that she will rather die than give any sign of affection. I did never think to marry. I must not seem proud; happy are they that hear their detractions, and can put them to mending. They say the lady is fair; 'tis a truth, I can bear them witness; and virtuous; 'tis so, I cannot reprove it; and wise, but for loving me; by my troth, it is no addition to her wit, nor no great argument of her folly, for I will be horribly in love with her. I may chance have some odd quirks and remnants of wit broken on me, because I have rail'd so long against marriage; but doth not the appetite alter? A man loves the meat in his youth that he cannot endure in his age. Shall quips and sentences and these paper bullets of the brain awe a man from the career of his humor? No, the world must be peopled. When I said I would die a bachelor, I did not think I should live till I were married. Here comes Beatrice. By this day, she's a fair lady. I do spy some marks of love in her.

Enter Beatrice.

Beatrice.
Against my will I am sent to bid you come in to dinner.

Benedick.
Fair Beatrice, I thank you for your pains.

Beatrice.
I took no more pains for those thanks than you take pains to thank me. If it had been painful, I would not have come.

Benedick.
You take pleasure then in the message?

Beatrice.
Yea, just so much as you may take upon a knive's point, and choke a daw withal. You have no stomach, signior, fare you well.

Exit.

Benedick.
Ha! "Against my will I am sent to bid you come in to dinner"—there's a double meaning in that. "I took no more pains for those thanks than you took pains to thank me"—that's as much as to say, "Any pains that I take for you is as easy as thanks." If I do not take pity of her, I am a villain; if I do not love her, I am a Jew. I will go get her picture.

Exit.

Act 3
Scene 1

Leonato's garden.

(Hero; Margaret; Ursula; Beatrice)

Hero sends Margaret to fetch Beatrice and tell her to hide and eavesdrop on them in the orchard. When Beatrice sneaks in, Hero and Ursula spot her, and begin discussing Benedick and how deeply he is in love with Beatrice, as well as how the way she treats him is shameful. Once convinced that Beatrice has been caught, they leave, and Beatrice decides that if they're right, she will agree to marry Benedick.

Enter Hero and two gentlewomen, Margaret and Ursula.

Hero.
Good Margaret, run thee to the parlor,
There shalt thou find my cousin Beatrice
Proposing with the Prince and Claudio.
Whisper her ear, and tell her I and Ursley
Walk in the orchard, and our whole discourse
Is all of her. Say that thou overheardst us,
And bid her steal into the pleached bower,
Where honeysuckles, ripened by the sun,
Forbid the sun to enter, like favorites
Made proud by princes, that advance their pride
Against that power that bred it. There will she hide her,
To listen our propose. This is thy office;
Bear thee well in it, and leave us alone.

Margaret.
I'll make her come, I warrant you, presently.

Exit.

Hero.
Now, Ursula, when Beatrice doth come,
As we do trace this alley up and down,
Our talk must only be of Benedick.
When I do name him, let it be thy part
To praise him more than ever man did merit.
My talk to thee must be how Benedick
Is sick in love with Beatrice. Of this matter
Is little Cupid's crafty arrow made,
That only wounds by hearsay.

Enter Beatrice behind.

                        Now begin,
For look where Beatrice like a lapwing runs
Close by the ground, to hear our conference.

Ursula.
The pleasant'st angling is to see the fish
Cut with her golden oars the silver stream,
And greedily devour the treacherous bait;
So angle we for Beatrice, who even now
Is couched in the woodbine coverture.
Fear you not my part of the dialogue.

Hero.
Then go we near her, that her ear lose nothing
Of the false sweet bait that we lay for it.

They advance to the bower.

No, truly, Ursula, she is too disdainful,
I know her spirits are as coy and wild
As haggards of the rock.

Ursula.
                    But are you sure
That Benedick loves Beatrice so entirely?

Hero.
So says the Prince and my new-trothed lord.

Ursula.
And did they bid you tell her of it, madam?

Hero.
They did entreat me to acquaint her of it,
But I persuaded them, if they lov'd Benedick,
To wish him wrestle with affection,
And never to let Beatrice know of it.

Ursula.
Why did you so? Doth not the gentleman
Deserve as full as fortunate a bed
As ever Beatrice shall couch upon?

Hero.
O god of love! I know he doth deserve
As much as may be yielded to a man;
But nature never fram'd a woman's heart
Of prouder stuff than that of Beatrice.
Disdain and scorn ride sparkling in her eyes,
Misprising what they look on, and her wit
Values itself so highly that to her
All matter else seems weak. She cannot love,
Nor take no shape nor project of affection,
She is so self-endeared.

Ursula.
                    Sure I think so,
And therefore certainly it were not good
She knew his love, lest she'll make sport at it.

Hero.
Why, you speak truth. I never yet saw man,
How wise, how noble, young, how rarely featur'd,
But she would spell him backward. If fair-fac'd,
She would swear the gentleman should be her sister;
If black, why, Nature, drawing of an antic,
Made a foul blot; if tall, a lance ill-headed;
If low, an agot very vildly cut;
If speaking, why, a vane blown with all winds;
If silent, why, a block moved with none.
So turns she every man the wrong side out,
And never gives to truth and virtue that
Which simpleness and merit purchaseth.

Ursula.
Sure, sure, such carping is not commendable.

Hero.
No, not to be so odd, and from all fashions,
As Beatrice is, cannot be commendable.
But who dare tell her so? If I should speak,
She would mock me into air; O, she would laugh me
Out of myself, press me to death with wit.
Therefore let Benedick, like cover'd fire,
Consume away in sighs, waste inwardly.
It were a better death than die with mocks,
Which is as bad as die with tickling.

Ursula.
Yet tell her of it, hear what she will say.

Hero.
No, rather I will go to Benedick,
And counsel him to fight against his passion,
And truly I'll devise some honest slanders
To stain my cousin with. One doth not know
How much an ill word may empoison liking.

Ursula.
O, do not do your cousin such a wrong.
She cannot be so much without true judgment—
Having so swift and excellent a wit
As she is priz'd to have—as to refuse
So rare a gentleman as Signior Benedick.

Act 3, Scene 2

Hero.
He is the only man of Italy,
Always excepted my dear Claudio.

Ursula.
I pray you be not angry with me, madam,
Speaking my fancy: Signior Benedick,
For shape, for bearing, argument, and valor,
Goes foremost in report through Italy.

Hero.
Indeed he hath an excellent good name.

Ursula.
His excellence did earn it, ere he had it.
When are you married, madam?

Hero.
Why, every day tomorrow. Come go in,
I'll show thee some attires, and have thy counsel
Which is the best to furnish me tomorrow.

Ursula.

Aside.

She's limed, I warrant you. We have caught her, madam.

Hero.

Aside.

If it prove so, then loving goes by haps:
Some Cupid kills with arrows, some with traps.

Exeunt Hero and Ursula.

Beatrice.

Coming forward.

What fire is in mine ears? Can this be true?
Stand I condemn'd for pride and scorn so much?
Contempt, farewell, and maiden pride, adieu!
No glory lives behind the back of such.
And, Benedick, love on, I will requite thee,
Taming my wild heart to thy loving hand.
If thou dost love, my kindness shall incite thee
To bind our loves up in a holy band;
For others say thou dost deserve, and I
Believe it better than reportingly.

Exit.

Scene 2

A room in Leonato's house.

(Prince Don Pedro; Claudio; Benedick; Leonato; Don John the Bastard)

Don Pedro and Claudio make fun of Benedick for showing signs of being in love, especially for having shaved off his beard. Benedick takes Leonato aside, and Don Pedro and Claudio are convinced it is to ask for Beatrice's hand. Don John joins them, and tells them he has proof that Hero is unfaithful. He convinces them to watch outside her window that night, and both swear that if Don John's allegations are proved, they will publicly disgrace Hero in the church.

Enter Prince Don Pedro, Claudio, Benedick, and Leonato.

Don Pedro.
I do but stay till your marriage be consummate, and then go I toward Arragon.

Claudio.
I'll bring you thither, my lord, if you'll vouchsafe me.

Don Pedro.
Nay, that would be as great a soil in the new gloss of your marriage as to show a child his new coat and forbid him to wear it. I will only be bold with Benedick for his company, for from the crown of his head to the sole of his foot, he is all mirth. He hath twice or thrice cut Cupid's bow-string, and the little hangman dare not shoot at him. He hath a heart as sound as a bell, and his tongue is the clapper, for what his heart thinks, his tongue speaks.

Benedick.
Gallants, I am not as I have been.

Leonato.
So say I, methinks you are sadder.

Claudio.
I hope he be in love.

Don Pedro.
Hang him, truant, there's no true drop of blood in him to be truly touch'd with love. If he be sad, he wants money.

Benedick.
I have the toothache.

Don Pedro.
Draw it.

Benedick.
Hang it!

Claudio.
You must hang it first, and draw it afterwards.

Don Pedro.
What? Sigh for the toothache?

Leonato.
Where is but a humor or a worm.

Benedick.
Well, every one can master a grief but he that has it.

Claudio.
Yet say I, he is in love.

Don Pedro.
There is no appearance of fancy in him, unless it be a fancy that he hath to strange disguises—as to be a Dutchman today, a Frenchman tomorrow, or in the shape of two countries at once, as a German from the waist downward, all slops, and a Spaniard from the hip upward, no doublet. Unless he have a fancy to this foolery, as it appears he hath, he is no fool for fancy, as you would have it appear he is.

Claudio.
If he be not in love with some woman, there is no believing old signs. 'A brushes his hat a' mornings; what should that bode?

Don Pedro.
Hath any man seen him at the barber's?

Claudio.
No, but the barber's man hath been seen with him, and the old ornament of his cheek hath already stuff'd tennis-balls.

Leonato.
Indeed he looks younger than he did, by the loss of a beard.

Don Pedro.
Nay, 'a rubs himself with civet. Can you smell him out by that?

Claudio.
That's as much as to say, the sweet youth's in love.

Don Pedro.
The greatest note of it is his melancholy.

Claudio.
And when was he wont to wash his face?

Don Pedro.
Yea, or to paint himself? For the which I hear what they say of him.

Claudio.
Nay, but his jesting spirit, which is now crept into a lute-string, and now govern'd by stops.

Don Pedro.
Indeed that tells a heavy tale for him. Conclude, conclude, he is in love.

Claudio.
Nay, but I know who loves him.

Don Pedro.
That would I know too. I warrant one that knows him not.

Claudio.
Yes, and his ill conditions, and in despite of all, dies for him.

Don Pedro.
She shall be buried with her face upwards.

Benedick.
Yet is this no charm for the toothache. Old signior, walk aside with me, I have studied eight or nine wise words to speak to you, which these hobby-horses must not hear.

Exeunt Benedick and Leonato.

Don Pedro.
For my life, to break with him about Beatrice.

Claudio.
'Tis even so. Hero and Margaret have by this play'd their parts with Beatrice, and then the two bears will not bite one another when they meet.

Enter Don John the Bastard.

Don John.
My lord and brother, God save you!

Don Pedro.
Good den, brother.

Don John.
If your leisure serv'd, I would speak with you.

Don Pedro.
In private?

Don John.
If it please you, yet Count Claudio may hear, for what I would speak of concerns him.

Don Pedro.
What's the matter?

Don John.

To Claudio

Means your lordship to be married tomorrow?

Don Pedro.
You know he does.

Don John.
I know not that, when he knows what I know.

Claudio.
If there be any impediment, I pray you discover it.

Don John.
You may think I love you not; let that appear hereafter, and aim better at me by that I now will manifest. For my brother, I think he holds you well, and in dearness of heart hath help to effect your ensuing marriage—surely suit ill spent and labor ill bestow'd.

Don Pedro.
Why, what's the matter?

Don John.
I came hither to tell you, and circumstances short'ned (for she has been too long a-talking of), the lady is disloyal.

Claudio.
Who, Hero?

Don John.
Even she—Leonato's Hero, your Hero, every man's Hero.

Claudio.
Disloyal?

Don John.
The word is too good to paint out her wickedness. I could say she were worse; think you of a worse title, and I will fit her to it. Wonder not till further warrant. Go but with me tonight, you shall see her chamber-window ent'red, even the night before her wedding-day. If you love her then, tomorrow wed her; but it would better fit your honor to change your mind.

Claudio.
May this be so?

Don Pedro.
I will not think it.

Don John.
If you dare not trust that you see, confess not that you know. If you will follow me, I will show you enough, and when you have seen more, and heard more, proceed accordingly.

Claudio.
If I see any thing tonight why I should not marry her, tomorrow in the congregation, where I should wed, there will I shame her.

Don Pedro.
And as I woo'd for thee to obtain her, I will join with thee to disgrace her.

Don John.
I will disparage her no farther till you are my witnesses. Bear it coldly but till midnight, and let the issue show itself.

Don Pedro.
O day untowardly turn'd!

Claudio.
O mischief strangely thwarting!

Don John.
O plague right well prevented! So will you say when you have seen the sequel.

Exeunt.

Scene 3

Messina. A street.

(Dogberry; Verges; First Watchman; Second Watchman; Borachio; Conrade)

Dogberry and Verges, the captains of the Watch, organize their Watchmen for the night, though Dogberry's instructions leave rather a lot to be desired. Left to their own devices, the Watchmen decide to sit on a bench until it's time to go home. They overhear Borachio tell Conrade of the success of his plot, and how Claudio and Don Pedro are now convinced that Hero is unfaithful. Borachio has been well paid by Don John. The Watchmen arrest the two for evil plotting.

Enter Dogberry and his compartner Verges with the Watch.

Dogberry.
Are you good men and true?

Verges.
Yea, or else it were pity but they should suffer salvation, body and soul.

Dogberry.
Nay, that were a punishment too good for them, if they should have any allegiance in them, being chosen for the Prince's watch.

Verges.
Well, give them their charge, neighbor Dogberry.

Dogberry.
First, who think you the most desartless man to be constable?

First Watchman.
Hugh Oatcake, sir, or George Seacole, for they can write and read.

Dogberry.
Come hither, neighbor Seacole. God hath blest you with a good name. To be a well-favor'd man is the gift of fortune, but to write and read comes by nature.

Second Watchman.
Both which, Master Constable—

Dogberry.
You have: I knew it would be your answer. Well, for your favor, sir, why, give God thanks, and make no boast of it, and for your writing and reading, let that appear when there is no need of such vanity. You are thought here to be the most senseless and fit man for the constable of the watch; therefore bear you the lantern. This is your charge: you shall comprehend all vagrom men; you are to bid any man stand, in the Prince's name.

Second Watchman.
How if 'a will not stand?

Dogberry.
Why then take no note of him, but let him go, and presently call the rest of the watch together, and thank God you are rid of a knave.

Verges.
If he will not stand when he is bidden, he is none of the Prince's subjects.

Dogberry.
True, and they are to meddle with none but the Prince's subjects. You shall also make no noise in the streets; for, for the watch to babble and to talk, is most tolerable, and not to be endur'd.

Second Watchman.
We will rather sleep than talk, we know what belongs to a watch.

Dogberry.
Why, you speak like an ancient and most quiet watchman, for I cannot see how sleeping should offend; only have a care that your bills be not stol'n. Well, you are to call at all the alehouses, and bid those that are drunk get them to bed.

Second Watchman.
How if they will not?

Dogberry.
Why then let them alone till they are sober. If they make you not then the better answer, you may say they are not the men you took them for.

Second Watchman.
Well, sir.

Dogberry.
If you meet a thief, you may suspect him, by virtue of your office, to be no true man; and for such kind of men, the less you meddle or make with them, why, the more is for your honesty.

Second Watchman.
If we know him to be a thief, shall we not lay hands on him?

Dogberry.
Truly by your office you may, but I think they that touch pitch will be defil'd. The most peaceable way for

Act 3, Scene 3

you, if you do take a thief, is to let him show himself what he is, and steal out of your company.

Verges.
You have been always call'd a merciful man, partner.

Dogberry.
Truly, I would not hang a dog by my will, much more a man who hath any honesty in him.

Verges.
If you hear a child cry in the night, you must call to the nurse and bid her still it.

Second Watchman.
How if the nurse be asleep and will not hear us?

Dogberry.
Why then depart in peace, and let the child wake her with crying, for the ewe that will not hear her lamb when it baes will never answer a calf when he bleats.

Verges.
'Tis very true.

Dogberry.
This is the end of the charge: you, constable, are to present the Prince's own person. If you meet the Prince in the night, you may stay him.

Verges.
Nay, by'r lady, that I think 'a cannot.

Dogberry.
Five shillings to one on't, with any man that knows the statutes, he may stay him; marry, not without the Prince be willing, for indeed the watch ought to offend no man, and it is an offense to stay a man against his will.

Verges.
By'r lady, I think it be so.

Dogberry.
Ha, ah ha! Well, masters, good night. And there be any matter of weight chances, call up me. Keep your fellows' counsels and your own, and good night. Come, neighbor.

Second Watchman.
Well, masters, we hear our charge. Let us go sit here upon the church-bench till two, and then all to bed.

Dogberry.
One word more, honest neighbors. I pray you watch about Signior Leonato's door, for the wedding being there tomorrow, there is a great coil tonight. Adieu! Be vigitant, I beseech you.

Exeunt Dogberry and Verges.
Enter Borachio and Conrade.

Borachio.
What, Conrade!

Second Watchman.

Aside.

Peace, stir not.

Borachio.
Conrade, I say!

Conrade.
Here, man, I am at thy elbow.

Borachio.
Mass, and my elbow itch'd; I thought there would a scab follow.

Conrade.
I will owe thee an answer for that, and now forward with thy tale.

Borachio.
Stand thee close then under this penthouse, for it drizzles rain, and I will, like a true drunkard, utter all to thee.

Second Watchman.

Aside.

Some treason, masters, yet stand close.

Borachio.
Therefore know I have earn'd of Don John a thousand ducats.

Conrade.
Is it possible that any villainy should be so dear?

Borachio.
Thou shouldst rather ask if it were possible any villainy should be so rich; for when rich villains have need of poor ones, poor ones may make what price they will.

Conrade.
I wonder at it.

Borachio.
That shows thou art unconfirm'd. Thou knowest that the fashion of a doublet, or a hat, or a cloak, is nothing to a man.

Conrade.
Yes, it is apparel.

Borachio.
I mean the fashion.

Conrade.
Yes, the fashion is the fashion.

Borachio.
Tush, I may as well say the fool's the fool. But seest thou not what a deformed thief this fashion is?

Second Watchman.

Aside.

I know that Deformed; 'a has been a vile thief this seven year; 'a goes up and down like a gentleman. I remember his name.

Borachio.
Didst thou not hear somebody?

Conrade.
No, 'twas the vane on the house.

Borachio.
Seest thou not, I say, what a deformed thief this fashion is, how giddily 'a turns about all the hot-bloods between fourteen and five-and-thirty, sometimes fashioning them like Pharaoh's soldiers in the reechy painting, sometime like god Bel's priests in the old church-window, sometime like the shaven Hercules in the smirch'd worm-eaten tapestry, where his codpiece seems as massy as his club?

Conrade.
All this I see, and I see that the fashion wears out more apparel than the man. But art not thou thyself giddy with the fashion too, that thou hast shifted out of thy tale into telling me of the fashion?

Borachio.
Not so neither, but know that I have tonight woo'd Margaret, the Lady Hero's gentlewoman, by the name of Hero. She leans me out at her mistress' chamber-window, bids me a thousand times good night—I tell this tale vildly, I should first tell thee how the Prince, Claudio, and my master, planted and plac'd and possess'd by my master Don John, saw afar off in the orchard this amiable encounter.

Conrade.
And thought they Margaret was Hero?

Borachio.
Two of them did, the Prince and Claudio, but the devil my master knew she was Margaret; and partly by his oaths, which first possess'd them, partly by the dark night, which did deceive them, but chiefly by my villainy, which did confirm any slander that Don John had made, away went Claudio enrag'd; swore he would meet her as he was appointed next morning at the temple, and there, before the whole congregation, shame her with what he saw o'ernight, and send her home again without a husband.

Second Watchman.
We charge you, in the Prince's name, stand!

First Watchman.
Call up the right Master Constable. We have here recover'd the most dangerous piece of lechery that ever was known in the commonwealth.

Second Watchman.
And one Deformed is one of them; I know him, 'a wears a lock.

Conrade.
Masters, masters—

Second Watchman.
You'll be made bring Deformed forth, I warrant you.

Conrade.
Masters—

Second Watchman.
Never speak, we charge you; let us obey you to go with us.

Borachio.
We are like to prove a goodly commodity, being taken up of these men's bills.

Conrade.
A commodity in question, I warrant you. Come, we'll obey you.

Scene 4

Hero's apartment.

(Hero; Margaret; Ursula; Beatrice)

Hero prepares for her wedding with Ursula and Margaret's help, the latter disagreeing with her over what she should wear. Saucy Margaret teases the bride, and makes great mock of Beatrice once she arrives. Beatrice is showing all the signs of being in love, and Margaret takes every opportunity for lewd comments she can get. She suggests that Benedick is ripe for marriage himself, despite everything. Ursula announces that the procession is ready to go to the church.

Enter Hero and Margaret and Ursula.

Hero.
Good Ursula, wake my cousin Beatrice, and desire her to rise.

Ursula.
I will, lady.

Hero.
And bid her come hither.

Ursula.
Well.

Exit.

Margaret.
Troth, I think your other rebato were better.

Hero.
No, pray thee, good Meg, I'll wear this.

Margaret.
By my troth 's not so good, and I warrant your cousin will say so.

Hero.
My cousin's a fool, and thou art another. I'll wear none but this.

Margaret.
I like the new tire within excellently, if the hair were a thought browner; and your gown's a most rare fashion, i' faith. I saw the Duchess of Milan's gown that they praise so.

Hero.
O, that exceeds, they say.

Margaret.
By my troth 's but a night-gown in respect of yours: cloth a' gold and cuts, and lac'd with silver, set with pearls, down sleeves, side sleeves, and skirts, round underborne with a bluish tinsel; but for a fine, quaint, graceful, and excellent fashion, yours is worth ten on't.

Hero.
God give me joy to wear it, for my heart is exceeding heavy.

Margaret.
'Twill be heavier soon by the weight of a man.

Hero.
Fie upon thee, art not asham'd?

Margaret.
Of what, lady? Of speaking honorably? Is not marriage honorable in a beggar? Is not your lord honorable without marriage? I think you would have me say, "saving your reverence, a husband." And bad thinking do not wrest true speaking, I'll offend nobody. Is there any harm in "the heavier for a husband"? None, I think, and it be the right husband and the right wife; otherwise 'tis light, and not heavy. Ask my Lady Beatrice else, here she comes.

Enter Beatrice.

Hero.
Good morrow, coz.

Beatrice.
Good morrow, sweet Hero.

Hero.
Why, how now? Do you speak in the sick tune?

Beatrice.
I am out of all other tune, methinks.

Margaret.
Clap 's into "Light a' love"; that goes without a burden. Do you sing it, and I'll dance it.

Beatrice.
Ye light a' love with your heels! Then if your husband have stables enough, you'll see he shall lack no barns.

Margaret.
O illegitimate construction! I scorn that with my heels.

Beatrice.
'Tis almost five a' clock, cousin, 'tis time you were ready. By my troth, I am exceeding ill. Heigh-ho!

Margaret.
For a hawk, a horse, or a husband?

Beatrice.
For the letter that begins them all, H.

Margaret.
Well, and you be not turn'd Turk, there's no more sailing by the star.

Beatrice.
What means the fool, trow?

Margaret.
Nothing I, but God send every one their heart's desire!

Hero.
These gloves the Count sent me, they are an excellent perfume.

Beatrice.
I am stuff'd, cousin, I cannot smell.

Margaret.
A maid, and stuff'd! There's goodly catching of cold.

Beatrice.
O, God help me, God help me, how long have you profess'd apprehension?

Margaret.
Ever since you left it. Doth not my wit become me rarely?

Beatrice.
It is not seen enough, you should wear it in your cap. By my troth, I am sick.

Margaret.
Get you some of this distill'd carduus benedictus, and lay it to your heart; it is the only thing for a qualm.

Hero.
There thou prick'st her with a thistle.

Beatrice.
Benedictus! Why benedictus? You have some moral in this benedictus.

Margaret.
Moral? No, by my troth I have no moral meaning, I meant plain holy-thistle. You may think perchance that I think you are in love. Nay, by'r lady, I am not such a fool to think what I list, nor I list not to think what I can, nor indeed I cannot think, if I would think my heart out of thinking, that you are in love, or that you will be in love, or that you can be in love. Yet Benedick was such another, and now is he become a man. He swore he would never marry, and yet now in despite of his heart he eats his meat without grudging; and how you may be converted I know not, but methinks you look with your eyes as other women do.

Beatrice.
What pace is this that thy tongue keeps?

Margaret.
Not a false gallop.

Enter Ursula.

Ursula.
Madam, withdraw, the Prince, the Count, Signior Benedick, Don John, and all the gallants of the town are come to fetch you to church.

Hero.
Help to dress me, good coz, good Meg, good Ursula.

Exeunt.

Scene 5
Another room in Leonato's house.

(*Leonato; Constable Dogberry; Headborough Verges; Messenger*)

Dogberry and Verges attempt to tell Leonato that they have some important information for him, but the longwinded Dogberry, continually interrupting Verges, so bores Leonato that the latter has to run to church. Needing to get to the wedding, Leonato tells the constables to examine their prisoners themselves, and leaves.

Enter Leonato and the Constable Dogberry and the Headborough Verges.

Act 3, Scene 5

Leonato.
What would you with me, honest neighbor?

Dogberry.
Marry, sir, I would have some confidence with you that decerns you nearly.

Leonato.
Brief, I pray you, for you see it is a busy time with me.

Dogberry.
Marry, this it is, sir.

Verges.
Yes, in truth it is, sir.

Leonato.
What is it, my good friends?

Dogberry.
Goodman Verges, sir, speaks a little off the matter; an old man, sir, and his wits are not so blunt as, God help, I would desire they were, but in faith, honest as the skin between his brows.

Verges.
Yes, I thank God I am as honest as any man living, that is an old man, and no honester than I.

Dogberry.
Comparisons are odorous—palabras, neighbor Verges.

Leonato.
Neighbors, you are tedious.

Dogberry.
It pleases your worship to say so, but we are the poor Duke's officers; but truly, for mine own part, if I were as tedious as a king, I could find in my heart to bestow it all of your worship.

Leonato.
All thy tediousness on me, ah?

Dogberry.
Yea, and 'twere a thousand pound more than 'tis, for I hear as good exclamation on your worship as of any man in the city, and though I be but a poor man, I am glad to hear it.

Verges.
And so am I.

Leonato.
I would fain know what you have to say.

Verges.
Marry, sir, our watch tonight, excepting your worship's presence, ha' ta'en a couple of as arrant knaves as any in Messina.

Dogberry.
A good old man, sir, he will be talking; as they say, "When the age is in, the wit is out." God help us, it is a world to see! Well said, i' faith, neighbor Verges. Well, God's a good man; and two men ride of a horse, one must ride behind. An honest soul, i' faith, sir, by my troth he is, as ever broke bread; but God is to be worshipp'd; all men are not alike, alas, good neighbor!

Leonato.
Indeed, neighbor, he comes too short of you.

Dogberry.
Gifts that God gives.

Leonato.
I must leave you.

Dogberry.
One word, sir. Our watch, sir, have indeed comprehended two aspicious persons, and we would have them this morning examin'd before your worship.

Leonato.
Take their examination yourself, and bring it me. I am now in great haste, as it may appear unto you.

Dogberry.
It shall be suffigance.

Leonato.
Drink some wine ere you go; fare you well.

Enter a Messenger.

Messenger.
My lord, they stay for you to give your daughter to her husband.

Leonato.
I'll wait upon them, I am ready.

Exeunt Leonato and Messenger.

Dogberry.
Go, good partner, go, get you to Francis Seacole, bid him bring his pen and inkhorn to the jail. We are now to examination these men.

Verges.
And we must do it wisely.

Dogberry.
We will spare for no wit, I warrant you. Here's that shall drive some of them to a non-come; only get the learned writer to set down our excommunication, and meet me at the jail.

Exeunt.

Act 4

Scene 1

Messina. Inside a church.

(Prince Don Pedro; Don John the Bastard; Leonato; Friar Francis; Claudio; Benedick; Hero; Beatrice; Attendants)

The gathered assembly meets before Friar Francis, who begins the marriage ceremony. Claudio asks Hero whether she knows any reason they should not be married and she insists that she does not. Claudio then rejects her, accusing her of immorality; the confused Leonato attempts to defend her, and shocked Hero protests her innocence, but neither Claudio nor Don Pedro will have any of it, both swearing that they saw her the night before at her window, talking with Borachio. Claudio's insults, supported by Don Pedro and Don John, are so severe that Hero faints. The three accusers leave Leonato and his friends alone, Benedick remaining behind as well. Beside himself with grief and thinking himself dishonored, Leonato bemoans the day and wishes that Hero were dead. Benedick attempts to find some evidence to clear Hero, but Beatrice cannot help, as she did not sleep in Hero's room as customary the previous night. Friar Francis, however, is convinced of Hero's innocence. Restored, Hero still insists on her innocence, having no idea what she's being accused of. Benedick suspects Don John of being at the root of all this trouble, but Leonato is too confused to have an opinion, swearing vengeance on anyone who may have caused this. The Friar suggests that they announce that Hero died of grief and hide her away, giving time to find out what has happened and making Claudio pity her, while offering a way to sneak her off to a nunnery if she turns out to be guilty. Leonato and the Friar lead Hero away. Benedick attempts to console the tearful Beatrice. They slowly admit to each other that they are in love, Benedick finally offering to do anything for her as proof — at which she tells him to kill Claudio. Benedick refuses, and Beatrice's rage bursts forth, as she wishes she were a man so that she could fight Claudio herself. Despite his friendship for the Count, Benedick promises to challenge Claudio to a duel.

Enter Prince Don Pedro, Don John the Bastard, Leonato, Friar Francis, Claudio, Benedick, Hero, and Beatrice with Attendants.

Leonato.
Come, Friar Francis, be brief—only to the plain form of marriage, and you shall recount their particular duties afterwards.

Friar Francis.
You come hither, my lord, to marry this lady.

Claudio.
No.

Leonato.
To be married to her. Friar, you come to marry her.

Friar Francis.
Lady, you come hither to be married to this count.

Hero.
I do.

Friar Francis.
If either of you know any inward impediment why you should not be conjoin'd, I charge you on your souls to utter it.

Claudio.
Know you any, Hero?

Hero.
None, my lord.

Friar Francis.
Know you any, Count?

Leonato.
I dare make his answer, none.

Claudio.
O, what men dare do! What men may do! What men daily do, not knowing what they do!

Benedick.
How now! Interjections? Why then, some be of laughing, as, ah, ha, he!

Claudio.
Stand thee by, friar. Father, by your leave,
Will you with free and unconstrained soul
Give me this maid, your daughter?

Leonato.
As freely, son, as God did give her me.

Claudio.
And what have I to give you back whose worth
May counterpoise this rich and precious gift?

Don Pedro.
Nothing, unless you render her again.

Claudio.
Sweet Prince, you learn me noble thankfulness.
There, Leonato, take her back again.
Give not this rotten orange to your friend,
She's but the sign and semblance of her honor.
Behold how like a maid she blushes here!
O, what authority and show of truth
Can cunning sin cover itself withal!
Comes not that blood as modest evidence
To witness simple virtue? Would you not swear,
All you that see her, that she were a maid,
By these exterior shows? But she is none:
She knows the heat of a luxurious bed;
Her blush is guiltiness, not modesty.

Leonato.
What do you mean, my lord?

Claudio.
                    Not to be married,
Not to knit my soul to an approved wanton.

Leonato.
Dear my lord, if you, in your own proof,
Have vanquish'd the resistance of her youth,
And made defeat of her virginity—

Claudio.
I know what you would say. If I have known her,
You will say, she did embrace me as a husband,
And so extenuate the 'forehand sin.
No, Leonato,
I never tempted her with word too large,
But as a brother to his sister, show'd
Bashful sincerity and comely love.

Hero.
And seem'd I ever otherwise to you?

Claudio.
Out on thee seeming! I will write against it:
You seem to me as Dian in her orb,
As chaste as is the bud ere it be blown;
But you are more intemperate in your blood
Than Venus, or those pamp'red animals
That rage in savage sensuality.

Hero.
Is my lord well, that he doth speak so wide?

Leonato.
Sweet Prince, why speak not you?

Don Pedro.
                    What should I speak?
I stand dishonor'd, that have gone about
To link my dear friend to a common stale.

Leonato.
Are these things spoken, or do I but dream?

Don John.
Sir, they are spoken, and these things are true.

Benedick.
This looks not like a nuptial.

Hero.
                    "True"! O God!

Claudio.
Leonato, stand I here?
Is this the Prince? Is this the Prince's brother?
Is this face Hero's? Are our eyes our own?

Leonato.
All this is so, but what of this, my lord?

Claudio.
Let me but move one question to your daughter,
And by that fatherly and kindly power
That you have in her, bid her answer truly.

Leonato.
I charge thee do so, as thou art my child.

Hero.
O God defend me, how am I beset!
What kind of catechizing call you this?

Claudio.
To make you answer truly to your name.

Hero.
Is it not Hero? Who can blot that name
With any just reproach?

Claudio.
                     Marry, that can Hero,
Hero itself can blot out Hero's virtue.
What man was he talk'd with you yesternight
Out at your window betwixt twelve and one?
Now if you are a maid, answer to this.

Hero.
I talk'd with no man at that hour, my lord.

Don Pedro.
Why then are you no maiden. Leonato,
I am sorry you must hear. Upon mine honor,
Myself, my brother, and this grieved count
Did see her, hear her, at that hour last night
Talk with a ruffian at her chamber-window,
Who hath indeed, most like a liberal villain,
Confess'd the vile encounters they have had
A thousand times in secret.

Don John.
Fie, fie, they are not to be named, my lord,
Not to be spoke of;
There is not chastity enough in language
Without offense to utter them. Thus, pretty lady,
I am sorry for thy much misgovernment.

Claudio.
O Hero! What a Hero hadst thou been,
If half thy outward graces had been placed
About thy thoughts and counsels of thy heart!
But fare thee well, most foul, most fair! Farewell,
Thou pure impiety and impious purity!
For thee I'll lock up all the gates of love,
And on my eyelids shall conjecture hang,
To turn all beauty into thoughts of harm,
And never shall it more be gracious.

Leonato.
Hath no man's dagger here a point for me?

Hero swoons.

Beatrice.
Why, how now, cousin, wherefore sink you down?

Don John.
Come, let us go. These things, come thus to light,
Smother her spirits up.

Exeunt Don Pedro, Don John, and Claudio.

Benedick.
How doth the lady?

Beatrice.
                  Dead, I think. Help, uncle!
Hero, why, Hero! Uncle! Signior Benedick! Friar!

Leonato.
O Fate! Take not away thy heavy hand,
Death is the fairest cover for her shame
That may be wish'd for.

Beatrice.
                  How now, cousin Hero?

Friar Francis.
Have comfort, lady.

Leonato.
Dost thou look up?

Friar Francis.
                Yea, wherefore should she not?

Leonato.
Wherefore? Why, doth not every earthly thing
Cry shame upon her? Could she here deny
The story that is printed in her blood?
Do not live, Hero, do not ope thine eyes;
For did I think thou wouldst not quickly die,
Thought I thy spirits were stronger than thy shames,
Myself would, on the rearward of reproaches,
Strike at thy life. Griev'd I, I had but one?
Chid I for that at frugal nature's frame?
O, one too much by thee! Why had I one?
Why ever wast thou lovely in my eyes?
Why had I not with charitable hand
Took up a beggar's issue at my gates,
Who smirched thus and mir'd with infamy,
I might have said, "No part of it is mine;
This shame derives itself from unknown loins"?
But mine, and mine I lov'd, and mine I prais'd,
And mine that I was proud on, mine so much
That I myself was to myself not mine,

Valuing of her—why, she, O she is fall'n
Into a pit of ink, that the wide sea
Hath drops too few to wash her clean again,
And salt too little which may season give
To her foul tainted flesh!

Benedick.
            Sir, sir, be patient.
For my part I am so attir'd in wonder,
I know not what to say.

Beatrice.
O, on my soul, my cousin is belied!

Benedick.
Lady, were you her bedfellow last night?

Beatrice.
No, truly, not, although until last night,
I have this twelvemonth been her bedfellow.

Leonato.
Confirm'd, confirm'd! O, that is stronger made
Which was before barr'd up with ribs of iron!
Would the two princes lie, and Claudio lie,
Who lov'd her so, that speaking of her foulness,
Wash'd it with tears? Hence from her, let her die.

Friar Francis.
Hear me a little,
For I have only been silent so long,
And given way unto this course of fortune,
By noting of the lady. I have mark'd
A thousand blushing apparitions
To start into her face, a thousand innocent shames
In angel whiteness beat away those blushes,
And in her eye there hath appear'd a fire
To burn the errors that these princes hold
Against her maiden truth. Call me a fool,
Trust not my reading, nor my observations,
Which with experimental seal doth warrant
The tenure of my book; trust not my age,
My reverence, calling, nor divinity,
If this sweet lady lie not guiltless here
Under some biting error.

Leonato.
            Friar, it cannot be.
Thou seest that all the grace that she hath left
Is that she will not add to her damnation
A sin of perjury; she not denies it.
Why seek'st thou then to cover with excuse
That which appears in proper nakedness?

Friar Francis.
Lady, what man is he you are accus'd of?

Hero.
They know that do accuse me, I know none.
If I know more of any man alive
Than that which maiden modesty doth warrant,
Let all my sins lack mercy! O my father,
Prove you that any man with me convers'd
At hours unmeet, or that I yesternight
Maintain'd the change of words with any creature,
Refuse me, hate me, torture me to death!

Friar Francis.
There is some strange misprision in the princes.

Benedick.
Two of them have the very bent of honor,
And if their wisdoms be misled in this,
The practice of it lives in John the Bastard,
Whose spirits toil in frame of villainies.

Leonato.
I know not. If they speak but truth of her,
These hands shall tear her; if they wrong her honor,
The proudest of them shall well hear of it.
Time hath not yet so dried this blood of mine,
Nor age so eat up my invention,
Nor fortune made such havoc of my means,
Nor my bad life reft me so much of friends,
But they shall find, awak'd in such a kind,
Both strength of limb, and policy of mind,
Ability in means, and choice of friends,
To quit me of them throughly.

Friar Francis.
            Pause awhile,
And let my counsel sway you in this case.
Your daughter here the princes left for dead,
Let her awhile be secretly kept in,
And publish it that she is dead indeed.
Maintain a mourning ostentation,
And on your family's old monument
Hang mournful epitaphs, and do all rites
That appertain unto a burial.

Leonato.
What shall become of this? What will this do?

Friar Francis.
Marry, this well carried shall on her behalf
Change slander to remorse; that is some good.
But not for that dream I on this strange course,
But on this travail look for greater birth:
She dying, as it must be so maintain'd,
Upon the instant that she was accus'd,
Shall be lamented, pitied, and excus'd
Of every hearer; for it so falls out
That what we have we prize not to the worth
Whiles we enjoy it, but being lack'd and lost,
Why then we rack the value; then we find
The virtue that possession would not show us
Whiles it was ours. So will it fare with Claudio:
When he shall hear she died upon his words,
Th' idea of her life shall sweetly creep
Into his study of imagination,
And every lovely organ of her life
Shall come apparell'd in more precious habit,
More moving, delicate, and full of life,
Into the eye and prospect of his soul,
Than when she liv'd indeed. Then shall he mourn,
If ever love had interest in his liver,
And wish he had not so accused her;
No, though he thought his accusation true.
Let this be so, and doubt not but success
Will fashion the event in better shape
Than I can lay it down in likelihood.
But if all aim but this be levell'd false,
The supposition of the lady's death
Will quench the wonder of her infamy.
And if it sort not well, you may conceal her,
As best befits her wounded reputation,
In some reclusive and religious life,
Out of all eyes, tongues, minds, and injuries.

Benedick.
Signior Leonato, let the friar advise you,
And though you know my inwardness and love
Is very much unto the Prince and Claudio,
Yet, by mine honor, I will deal in this
As secretly and justly as your soul
Should with your body.

Leonato.
                              Being that I flow in grief,
The smallest twine may lead me.

Friar Francis.
'Tis well consented; presently away,
For to strange sores strangely they strain the cure.
Come, lady, die to live; this wedding-day
Perhaps is but prolong'd, have patience and endure.

Exit with all but Benedick and Beatrice.

Benedick.
Lady Beatrice, have you wept all this while?

Beatrice.
Yea, and I will weep a while longer.

Benedick.
I will not desire that.

Beatrice.
You have no reason, I do it freely.

Benedick.
Surely I do believe your fair cousin is wrong'd.

Beatrice.
Ah, how much might the man deserve of me that would right her!

Benedick.
Is there any way to show such friendship?

Beatrice.
A very even way, but no such friend.

Benedick.
May a man do it?

Beatrice.
It is a man's office, but not yours.

Benedick.
I do love nothing in the world so well as you—is not that strange?

Beatrice.
As strange as the thing I know not. It were as possible for me to say I lov'd nothing so well as you, but believe me not; and yet I lie not: I confess nothing, nor I deny nothing. I am sorry for my cousin.

Benedick.
By my sword, Beatrice, thou lovest me.

Beatrice.
Do not swear and eat it.

Benedick.
I will swear by it that you love me, and I will make him eat it that says I love not you.

Beatrice.
Will you not eat your word?

Benedick.
With no sauce that can be devis'd to it. I protest I love thee.

Beatrice.
Why then God forgive me!

Benedick.
What offense, sweet Beatrice?

Beatrice.
You have stay'd me in a happy hour, I was about to protest I lov'd you.

Benedick.
And do it with all thy heart.

Beatrice.
I love you with so much of my heart that none is left to protest.

Benedick.
Come, bid me do any thing for thee.

Beatrice.
Kill Claudio.

Benedick.
Ha, not for the wide world.

Beatrice.
You kill me to deny it. Farewell.

Benedick.
Tarry, sweet Beatrice.

Beatrice.
I am gone, though I am here; there is no love in you. Nay, I pray you let me go.

Benedick.
Beatrice—

Beatrice.
In faith, I will go.

Benedick.
We'll be friends first.

Beatrice.
You dare easier be friends with me than fight with mine enemy.

Benedick.
Is Claudio thine enemy?

Beatrice.
Is 'a not approv'd in the height a villain, that hath slander'd, scorn'd, dishonor'd my kinswoman? O that I were a man! What, bear her in hand until they come to take hands, and then with public accusation, uncover'd slander, unmitigated rancor—O God, that I were a man! I would eat his heart in the market-place.

Benedick.
Hear me, Beatrice—

Beatrice.
Talk with a man out at a window! A proper saying!

Benedick.
Nay, but, Beatrice—

Beatrice.
Sweet Hero, she is wrong'd, she is sland'red, she is undone.

Benedick.
Beat—

Beatrice.
Princes and counties! Surely a princely testimony, a goodly count, Count Comfect, a sweet gallant surely! O that I were a man for his sake! Or that I had any friend would be a man for my sake! But manhood is melted into cur'sies, valor into compliment, and men are only turn'd into tongue, and trim ones too. He is now as valiant as Hercules that only tells a lie, and swears it. I cannot be a man with wishing, therefore I will die a woman with grieving.

Benedick.
Tarry, good Beatrice. By this hand, I love thee.

Beatrice.
Use it for my love some other way than swearing by it.

Benedick.
Think you in your soul the Count Claudio hath wrong'd Hero?

Beatrice.
Yea, as sure as I have a thought or a soul.

Benedick.
Enough, I am engag'd, I will challenge him. I will kiss your hand, and so I leave you. By this hand, Claudio shall render me a dear account. As you hear of me, so think of me. Go comfort your cousin. I must say she is dead; and so farewell.

Exeunt.

Scene 2

Messina. A prison.

(Dogberry; Verges; Town Clerk Sexton; First Watchman; Second Watchman; Conrade; Borachio)

Dogberry, Verges and the Watch bring Borachio and Conrade before the Sexton to interrogate them. Despite Dogberry's inability to go about the interrogation properly, the story finally comes out, and the Sexton, who has heard of what happened at the church and thus knows that what was overheard is true, sends the prisoners to Leonato. Don John, it turns out, has fled.

Enter the Constables Dogberry and Verges, and the Town Clerk Sexton in gowns, and the Watch with Conrade and Borachio.

Dogberry.
Is our whole dissembly appear'd?

Verges.
O, a stool and a cushion for the sexton.

Sexton.
Which be the malefactors?

Dogberry.
Marry, that am I and my partner.

Verges.
Nay, that's certain, we have the exhibition to examine.

Sexton.
But which are the offenders that are to be examin'd? Let them come before Master Constable.

Dogberry.
Yea, marry, let them come before me. What is your name, friend?

Borachio.
Borachio.

Dogberry.
Pray write down Borachio. Yours, sirrah?

Conrade.
I am a gentleman, sir, and my name is Conrade.

Dogberry.
Write down Master Gentleman Conrade. Masters, do you serve God?

Both Conrade and Borachio.
Yea, sir, we hope.

Dogberry.
Write down, that they hope they serve God; and write God first, for God defend but God should go before such villains! Masters, it is prov'd already that you are little better than false knaves, and it will go near to be thought so shortly. How answer you for yourselves?

Conrade.
Marry, sir, we say we are none.

Dogberry.
A marvelous witty fellow, I assure you, but I will go about with him. Come you hither, sirrah; a word in your ear, sir. I say to you, it is thought you are false knaves.

Borachio.
Sir, I say to you, we are none.

Dogberry.
Well, stand aside. 'Fore God, they are both in a tale. Have you writ down, that they are none?

Sexton.
Master Constable, you go not the way to examine; you must call forth the watch that are their accusers.

Dogberry.
Yea, marry, that's the eftest way; let the watch come forth. Masters, I charge you in the Prince's name accuse these men.

First Watchman.
This man said, sir, that Don John, the Prince's brother, was a villain.

Dogberry.
Write down Prince John a villain. Why, this is flat perjury, to call a prince's brother villain.

Borachio.
Master Constable—

Dogberry.
Pray thee, fellow, peace. I do not like thy look, I promise thee.

Sexton.
What heard you him say else?

Second Watchman.
Marry, that he had receiv'd a thousand ducats of Don John for accusing the Lady Hero wrongfully.

Dogberry.
Flat burglary as ever was committed.

Verges.
Yea, by mass, that it is.

Sexton.
What else, fellow?

First Watchman.
And that Count Claudio did mean, upon his words, to disgrace Hero before the whole assembly, and not marry her.

Dogberry.
O villain! Thou wilt be condemn'd into everlasting redemption for this.

Sexton.
What else?

Both First and Second Watchmen.
This is all.

Sexton.
And this is more, masters, than you can deny. Prince John is this morning secretly stol'n away. Hero was in this manner accus'd, in this very manner refus'd, and upon the grief of this suddenly died. Master Constable, let these men be bound, and brought to Leonato's. I will go before and show him their examination.

Exit.

Dogberry.
Come let them be opinion'd.

Verges.
Let them be in the hands—

Conrade.
Off, Coxcomb!

Dogberry.
God's my life, where's the sexton? Let him write down the Prince's officer coxcomb. Come, bind them. Thou naughty varlet!

Conrade.
Away, you are an ass, you are an ass.

Dogberry.
Dost thou not suspect my place? Dost thou not suspect my years? O that he were here to write me down as ass! But, masters, remember that I am an ass; though it be not written down, yet forget not that I am an ass. No, thou villain, thou art full of piety, as shall be prov'd upon thee by good witness. I am a wise fellow, and which is more, an officer, and which is more, a householder, and which is more, as pretty a piece of flesh as any is in Messina, and one that knows the law, go to, and a rich fellow enough, go to, and a fellow that hath had losses, and one that hath two gowns, and every thing handsome about him. Bring him away. O that I had been writ down an ass!

Exeunt.

Act 5

Scene 1

Before Leonato's house.

(Leonato; Antonio; Prince Don Pedro; Claudio; Benedick; Dogberry; Verges; First Watchman; Second Watchman; Conrade; Borachio; Sexton)

Antonio tries to comfort the grief-stricken Leonato, but with little effect. When they cross paths with Don Pedro and Claudio, however, Antonio soon reveals that he is not as calm as he seems. Both brothers rail at the Prince and the Count, challenging them to fight, but the younger men refuse to duel with old men. Neither of them shows any remorse for Hero's death, insisting on the truth of their accusations. Leonato and Antonio leave in a rage, and Don Pedro and Claudio try to cheer themselves up by conversing with Benedick, who now arrives. They joke about the old men, but Benedick does not laugh, instead taking Claudio aside and challenging him. Don Pedro mocks him about Beatrice, but Benedick does not rise to the bait, rather resigning from his service to the Prince. Don Pedro and Claudio realize that he is serious. As he leaves, they joke that he is simply henpecked, but then Dogberry and the Watch arrives, and the two men discover that they were in the wrong. Realizing that this is why Don John has fled, Don Pedro is stricken with remorse, while Claudio feels deeply in love with Hero once again. Leonato enters to hear Borachio admit his villainy to his face, and confronts Don Pedro and Claudio, who offer to do anything he asks to be forgiven, though insisting their actions were only wrong because their information was false. Leonato orders them to sign an epitaph to Hero's grave, and to marry Antonio's daughter. Claudio agrees. Leonato wishes to confront Margaret over her part in the plot, but Borachio insists that she is innocent and did not know what he was up to.

Enter Leonato and his brother Antonio.

Antonio.
If you go on thus, you will kill yourself,
And 'tis not wisdom thus to second grief
Against yourself.

Leonato.
                  I pray thee cease thy counsel,
Which falls into mine ears as profitless
As water in a sieve. Give not me counsel,
Nor let no comforter delight mine ear
But such a one whose wrongs do suit with mine.
Bring me a father that so lov'd his child,
Whose joy of her is overwhelm'd like mine,
And bid him speak of patience;
Measure his woe the length and breadth of mine,
And let it answer every strain for strain,
As thus for thus, and such a grief for such,
In every lineament, branch, shape, and form;
If such a one will smile and stroke his beard,
And, sorrow wag, cry "hem!" when he should groan,
Patch grief with proverbs, make misfortune drunk
With candle-wasters, bring him yet to me,
And I of him will gather patience.
But there is no such man, for, brother, men
Can counsel and speak comfort to that grief
Which they themselves not feel, but tasting it,
Their counsel turns to passion, which before
Would give preceptial med'cine to rage,
Fetter strong madness in a silken thread,
Charm ache with air, and agony with words.
No, no, 'tis all men's office to speak patience
To those that wring under the load of sorrow,
But no man's virtue nor sufficiency
To be so moral when he shall endure
The like himself. Therefore give me no counsel,
My griefs cry louder than advertisement.

Antonio.
Therein do men from children nothing differ.

Leonato.
I pray thee peace. I will be flesh and blood,
For there was never yet philosopher
That could endure the toothache patiently,
However they have writ the style of gods,
And made a push at chance and sufferance.

Antonio.
Yet bend not all the harm upon yourself;
Make those that do offend you suffer too.

Leonato.
There thou speak'st reason; nay, I will do so.
My soul doth tell me Hero is belied,
And that shall Claudio know; so shall the Prince,
And all of them that thus dishonor her.

Enter Prince Don Pedro and Claudio.

Antonio.
Here comes the Prince and Claudio hastily.

Don Pedro.
Good den, good den.

Claudio.
                  Good day to both of you.

Leonato.
Hear you, my lords—

Don Pedro.
                We have some haste, Leonato.

Leonato.
Some haste, my lord! Well, fare you well, my lord.
Are you so hasty now? Well, all is one.

Don Pedro.
Nay, do not quarrel with us, good old man.

Antonio.
If he could right himself with quarreling,
Some of us would lie low.

Claudio.
                Who wrongs him?

Leonato.
Marry, thou dost wrong me, thou dissembler, thou—
Nay, never lay thy hand upon thy sword,
I fear thee not.

Claudio.
                    Marry, beshrew my hand,
If it should give your age such cause of fear.
In faith, my hand meant nothing to my sword.

Leonato.
Tush, tush, man, never fleer and jest at me;
I speak not like a dotard nor a fool,
As under privilege of age to brag
What I have done being young, or what would do
Were I not old. Know, Claudio, to thy head,
Thou hast so wrong'd mine innocent child and me
That I am forc'd to lay my reverence by,
And with grey hairs and bruise of many days,
Do challenge thee to trial of a man.
I say thou hast belied mine innocent child!
Thy slander hath gone through and through her heart,
And she lies buried with her ancestors—
O, in a tomb where never scandal slept,
Save this of hers, fram'd by thy villainy!

Claudio.
My villainy?

Leonato.
                    Thine, Claudio, thine, I say.

Don Pedro.
You say not right, old man.

Leonato.
                    My lord, my lord,
I'll prove it on his body, if he dare,
Despite his nice fence and his active practice,
His May of youth and bloom of lustihood.

Claudio.
Away, I will not have to do with you.

Leonato.
Canst thou so daff me? Thou hast kill'd my child.
If thou kill'st me, boy, thou shalt kill a man.

Antonio.
He shall kill two of us, and men indeed;
But that's no matter, let him kill one first.
Win me and wear me, let him answer me.
Come follow me, boy; come, sir boy, come follow me.
Sir boy, I'll whip you from your foining fence,
Nay, as I am a gentleman, I will.

Leonato.
Brother—

Antonio.
Content yourself. God knows I lov'd my niece,
And she is dead, slander'd to death by villains,
That dare as well answer a man indeed
As I dare take a serpent by the tongue.
Boys, apes, braggarts, Jacks, milksops!

Leonato.
Brother Anthony—

Antonio.
Hold you content. What, man! I know them, yea,
And what they weigh, even to the utmost scruple—
Scambling, outfacing, fashion-monging boys,
That lie and cog and flout, deprave and slander,
Go anticly, and show outward hideousness,
And speak off half a dozen dang'rous words,
How they might hurt their enemies—if they durst—
And this is all.

Leonato.
But, brother Anthony—

Antonio.
                    Come, 'tis no matter;
Do not you meddle, let me deal in this.

Don Pedro.
Gentlemen both, we will not wake your patience.
My heart is sorry for your daughter's death;
But on my honor she was charg'd with nothing
But what was true, and very full of proof.

Leonato.
My lord, my lord—

Don Pedro.
I will not hear you.

Leonato.
No? Come, brother, away! I will be heard.

Antonio.
And shall, or some of us will smart for it.

Exeunt ambo Leonato and Antonio.
Enter Benedick.

Don Pedro.
See, see, here comes the man we went to seek.

Claudio.
Now, signior, what news?

Benedick.
Good day, my lord.

Don Pedro.
Welcome, signior, you are almost come to part almost a fray.

Claudio.
We had lik'd to have had our two noses snapp'd off with two old men without teeth.

Don Pedro.
Leonato and his brother. What think'st thou? Had we fought, I doubt we should have been too young for them.

Benedick.
In a false quarrel there is no true valor. I came to seek you both.

Claudio.
We have been up and down to seek thee, for we are high-proof melancholy, and would fain have it beaten away. Wilt thou use thy wit?

Benedick.
It is in my scabbard, shall I draw it?

Don Pedro.
Dost thou wear thy wit by thy side?

Claudio.
Never any did so, though very many have been beside their wit. I will bid thee draw, as we do the minstrels, draw to pleasure us.

Don Pedro.
As I am an honest man, he looks pale. Art thou sick, or angry?

Claudio.
What, courage, man! What though care kill'd a cat, thou hast mettle enough in thee to kill care.

Benedick.
Sir, I shall meet your wit in the career, and you charge it against me. I pray you choose another subject.

Claudio.
Nay then give him another staff, this last was broke cross.

Don Pedro.
By this light, he changes more and more. I think he be angry indeed.

Claudio.
If he be, he knows how to turn his girdle.

Benedick.
Shall I speak a word in your ear?

Claudio.
God bless me from a challenge!

Benedick.

Aside to Claudio

You are a villain. I jest not; I will make it good how you dare, with what you dare, and when you dare. Do me right; or I will protest your cowardice. You have kill'd a sweet lady, and her death shall fall heavy on you. Let me hear from you.

Claudio.
Well, I will meet you, so I may have good cheer.

Don Pedro.
What, a feast, a feast?

Claudio.
I' faith, I thank him, he hath bid me to a calve's-head and a capon, the which if I do not carve most curiously, say my knife's naught. Shall I not find a woodcock too?

Benedick.
Sir, your wit ambles well, it goes easily.

Don Pedro.
I'll tell thee how Beatrice prais'd thy wit the other day. I said thou hadst a fine wit. "True," said she, "a fine little one." "No," said I, "a great wit." "Right," says she, "a great gross one." "Nay," said I, "a good wit." "Just," said she, "it hurts nobody." "Nay," said I, "the gentleman is wise." "Certain," said she, "a wise gentleman." "Nay," said I, "he hath the tongues." "That I believe," said she, "for he swore a thing to me on Monday night, which he forswore on Tuesday morning. There's a double tongue, there's two tongues." Thus did she an hour together trans-shape thy particular virtues, yet at last

she concluded with a sigh, thou wast the proper'st man in Italy.

Claudio.
For the which she wept heartily and said she car'd not.

Don Pedro.
Yea, that she did, but yet for all that, and if she did not hate him deadly, she would love him dearly. The old man's daughter told us all.

Claudio.
All, all, and, moreover, God saw him when he was hid in the garden.

Don Pedro.
But when shall we set the savage bull's horns on the sensible Benedick's head?

Claudio.
Yea, and text underneath, "Here dwells Benedick the married man"?

Benedick.
Fare you well, boy, you know my mind. I will leave you now to your gossip-like humor. You break jests as braggarts do their blades, which, God be thank'd, hurt not. My lord, for your many courtesies I thank you. I must discontinue your company. Your brother the bastard is fled from Messina. You have among you kill'd a sweet and innocent lady. For my Lord Lackbeard there, he and I shall meet, and till then peace be with him.

Exit.

Don Pedro.
He is in earnest.

Claudio.
In most profound earnest, and I'll warrant you, for the love of Beatrice.

Don Pedro.
And hath challeng'd thee?

Claudio.
Most sincerely.

Don Pedro.
What a pretty thing man is when he goes in his doublet and hose and leaves off his wit!

Enter Constables Dogberry and Verges, and the Watch with Conrade and Borachio.

Claudio.
He is then a giant to an ape, but then is an ape a doctor to such a man.

Don Pedro.
But soft you, let me be. Pluck up, my heart, and be sad. Did he not say my brother was fled?

Dogberry.
Come you, sir. If justice cannot tame you, she shall ne'er weigh more reasons in her balance. Nay, and you be a cursing hypocrite once, you must be look'd to.

Don Pedro.
How now? Two of my brother's men bound? Borachio one!

Claudio.
Hearken after their offense, my lord.

Don Pedro.
Officers, what offense have these men done?

Dogberry.
Marry, sir, they have committed false report; moreover they have spoken untruths; secondarily, they are slanders; sixth and lastly, they have belied a lady; thirdly, they have verified unjust things; and to conclude, they are lying knaves.

Don Pedro.
First, I ask thee what they have done; thirdly, I ask thee what's their offense; sixth and lastly, why they are committed; and to conclude, what you lay to their charge.

Claudio.
Rightly reason'd, and in his own division, and by my troth there's one meaning well suited.

Don Pedro.
Who have you offended, masters, that you are thus bound to your answer? This learned constable is too cunning to be understood. What's your offense?

Borachio.
Sweet Prince, let me go no farther to mine answer: do you hear me, and let this count kill me. I have deceiv'd even your very eyes. What your wisdoms could not discover, these shallow fools have brought to light, who in the night overheard me confessing to this man

how Don John your brother incens'd me to slander the Lady Hero, how you were brought into the orchard, and saw me court Margaret in Hero's garments, how you disgrac'd her when you should marry her. My villainy they have upon record, which I had rather seal with my death than repeat over to my shame. The lady is dead upon mine and my master's false accusation; and briefly, I desire nothing but the reward of a villain.

Don Pedro.
Runs not this speech like iron through your blood?

Claudio.
I have drunk poison whiles he utter'd it.

Don Pedro.
But did my brother set thee on to this?

Borachio.
Yea, and paid me richly for the practice of it.

Don Pedro.
He is compos'd and fram'd of treachery,
And fled he is upon this villainy.

Claudio.
Sweet Hero, now thy image doth appear
In the rare semblance that I lov'd it first.

Dogberry.
Come, bring away the plaintiffs. By this time our sexton hath reform'd Signior Leonato of the matter; and, masters, do not forget to specify, when time and place shall serve, that I am an ass.

Verges.
Here, here comes Master Signior Leonato, and the sexton too.

Enter Leonato, his brother Antonio, and the Sexton.

Leonato.
Which is the villain? Let me see his eyes,
That when I note another man like him
I may avoid him. Which of these is he?

Borachio.
If you would know your wronger, look on me.

Leonato.
Art thou the slave that with thy breath hast kill'd
Mine innocent child?

Borachio.
          Yea, even I alone.

Leonato.
No, not so, villain, thou beliest thyself.
Here stand a pair of honorable men,
A third is fled, that had a hand in it.
I thank you, princes, for my daughter's death;
Record it with your high and worthy deeds.
'Twas bravely done, if you bethink you of it.

Claudio.
I know not how to pray your patience,
Yet I must speak. Choose your revenge yourself,
Impose me to what penance your invention
Can lay upon my sin; yet sinn'd I not,
But in mistaking.

Don Pedro.
          By my soul, nor I,
And yet, to satisfy this good old man,
I would bend under any heavy weight
That he'll enjoin me to.

Leonato.
I cannot bid you bid my daughter live—
That were impossible—but I pray you both,
Possess the people in Messina here
How innocent she died, and if your love
Can labor aught in sad invention,
Hang her an epitaph upon her tomb,
And sing it to her bones, sing it tonight.
Tomorrow morning come you to my house,
And since you could not be my son-in-law,
Be yet my nephew. My brother hath a daughter,
Almost the copy of my child that's dead,
And she alone is heir to both of us.
Give her the right you should have giv'n her cousin,
And so dies my revenge.

Claudio.
          O noble sir!
Your overkindness doth wring tears from me.
I do embrace your offer, and dispose
For henceforth of poor Claudio.

Leonato.
Tomorrow then I will expect your coming,
Tonight I take my leave. This naughty man
Shall face to face be brought to Margaret,
Who I believe was pack'd in all this wrong,
Hir'd to it by your brother.

Borachio.
           No, by my soul she was not,
Nor knew not what she did when she spoke to me,
But always hath been just and virtuous
In any thing that I do know by her.

Dogberry.
Moreover, sir, which indeed is not under white and black, this plaintiff here, the offender, did call me ass. I beseech you let it be rememb'red in his punishment. And also, the watch heard them talk of one Deformed. They say he wears a key in his ear and a lock hanging by it, and borrows money in God's name, the which he hath us'd so long and never paid that now men grow hard-hearted and will lend nothing for God's sake. Pray you examine him upon that point.

Leonato.
I thank thee for thy care and honest pains.

Dogberry.
Your worship speaks like a most thankful and reverent youth, and I praise God for you.

Leonato.
There's for thy pains.

Dogberry.
God save the foundation!

Leonato.
Go, I discharge thee of thy prisoner, and I thank thee.

Dogberry.
I leave an arrant knave with your worship, which I beseech your worship to correct yourself, for the example of others. God keep your worship! I wish your worship well. God restore you to health! I humbly give you leave to depart, and if a merry meeting may be wish'd, God prohibit it! Come, neighbor.

Exeunt Dogberry and Verges.

Leonato.
Until tomorrow morning, lords, farewell.

Antonio.
Farewell, my lords, we look for you tomorrow.

Don Pedro.
We will not fail.

Claudio.
           Tonight I'll mourn with Hero.

Leonato.

To the Watch.

Bring you these fellows on.—We'll talk with Margaret,
How her acquaintance grew with this lewd fellow.

Exeunt severally.

Scene 2

Leonato's garden.

(Benedick; Margaret; Beatrice; Ursula)

Benedick and Margaret jest together; she leaves to call Beatrice for him. While waiting for her, Benedick reflects on his utter inability to write poetry. Beatrice arrives, and though they immediately start sparring, he manages to inform her of Claudio's acceptance of his challenge. Both insist that they are in love against their will. Ursula suddenly bursts in with the news that Hero's innocence has been proved, and they rush to find out more.

Enter Benedick and Margaret, meeting.

Benedick.
Pray thee, sweet Mistress Margaret, deserve well at my hands by helping me to the speech of Beatrice.

Margaret.
Will you then write me a sonnet in praise of my beauty?

Benedick.
In so high a style, Margaret, that no man living shall come over it, for in most comely truth thou deservest it.

Margaret.
To have no man come over me? Why, shall I always keep below stairs?

Benedick.
Thy wit is as quick as the greyhound's mouth, it catches.

Margaret.
And yours as blunt as the fencer's foils, which hit, but hurt not.

Benedick.
A most manly wit, Margaret, it will not hurt a woman. And so I pray thee call Beatrice; I give thee the bucklers.

Margaret.
Give us the swords, we have bucklers of our own.

Benedick.
If you use them, Margaret, you must put in the pikes with a vice, and they are dangerous weapons for maids.

Margaret.
Well, I will call Beatrice to you, who I think hath legs.

Exit Margaret.

Benedick.
And therefore will come.

Sings.

"The god of love,
That sits above,
And knows me, and knows me,
How pitiful I deserve"—

I mean in singing; but in loving, Leander the good swimmer, Troilus the first employer of pandars, and a whole bookful of these quondam carpet-mongers, whose names yet run smoothly in the even road of a blank verse, why, they were never so truly turn'd over and over as my poor self in love. Marry, I cannot show it in rhyme; I have tried. I can find out no rhyme to "lady" but "baby," an innocent rhyme; for "scorn," "horn," a hard rhyme; for "school," "fool," a babbling rhyme: very ominous endings. No, I was not born under a rhyming planet, nor I cannot woo in festival terms.

Enter Beatrice.

Sweet Beatrice, wouldst thou come when I call'd thee?

Beatrice.
Yea, signior, and depart when you bid me.

Benedick.
O, stay but till then!

Beatrice.
"Then" is spoken; fare you well now. And yet ere I go, let me go with that I came, which is, with knowing what hath pass'd between you and Claudio.

Benedick.
Only foul words—and thereupon I will kiss thee.

Beatrice.
Foul words is but foul wind, and foul wind is but foul breath, and foul breath is noisome; therefore I will depart unkiss'd.

Benedick.
Thou hast frighted the word out of his right sense, so forcible is thy wit. But I must tell thee plainly, Claudio undergoes my challenge, and either I must shortly hear from him, or I will subscribe him a coward. And I pray thee now tell me, for which of my bad parts didst thou first fall in love with me?

Beatrice.
For them all together, which maintain'd so politic a state of evil that they will not admit any good part to intermingle with them. But for which of my good parts did you first suffer love for me?

Benedick.
Suffer love! A good epithite! I do suffer love indeed, for I love thee against my will.

Beatrice.
In spite of your heart, I think. Alas, poor heart, if you spite it for my sake, I will spite it for yours, for I will never love that which my friend hates.

Benedick.
Thou and I are too wise to woo peaceably.

Beatrice.
It appears not in this confession; there's not one wise man among twenty that will praise himself.

Benedick.
An old, an old instance, Beatrice, that liv'd in the time of good neighbors. If a man do not erect in this age his own tomb ere he dies, he shall live no longer in monument than the bell rings and the widow weeps.

Beatrice.
And how long is that, think you?

Benedick.
Question: why, an hour in clamor and a quarter in rheum; therefore is it most expedient for the wise, if Don Worm (his conscience) find no impediment to the contrary, to be the trumpet of his own virtues, as I am to myself. So much for praising myself, who I my-

self will bear witness is praiseworthy. And now tell me, how doth your cousin?

Beatrice.
Very ill.

Benedick.
And how do you?

Beatrice.
Very ill too.

Benedick.
Serve God, love me, and mend. There will I leave you too, for here comes one in haste.

Enter Ursula.

Ursula.
Madam, you must come to your uncle, yonder's old coil at home. It is prov'd my Lady Hero hath been falsely accus'd, the Prince and Claudio mightily abus'd, and Don John is the author of all, who is fled and gone. Will you come presently?

Beatrice.
Will you go hear this news, signior?

Benedick.
I will live in thy heart, die in thy lap, and be buried in thy eyes; and moreover I will go with thee to thy uncle's.

Exeunt.

Scene 3

Messina. Inside a church.

(Claudio; Prince Don Pedro; Lord; Balthasar)

Before the tomb of Leonato's family, Claudio reads out his epitaph for Hero, and vows to perform the rite once a year. With Don Pedro, he goes to prepare for the wedding in the morning.

Enter Claudio, Prince Don Pedro, and three or four with tapers, including Balthasar.

Claudio.
Is this the monument of Leonato?

Lord.
It is, my lord.

Claudio.
Reading out of a scroll.
Epitaph

"Done to death by slanderous tongues
Was the Hero that here lies.
Death, in guerdon of her wrongs,
Gives her fame which never dies.
So the life that died with shame
Lives in death with glorious fame."
Hang thou there upon the tomb,

Hangs up the scroll.

Praising her when I am dumb.
Now, music, sound, and sing your solemn hymn.

Balthasar.
Song.

Pardon, goddess of the night,
Those that slew thy virgin knight,
For the which, with songs of woe,
Round about her tomb they go.
Midnight, assist our moan,
Help us to sigh and groan,
Heavily, heavily.
Graves, yawn and yield your dead,
Till death be uttered,
Heavily, heavily.

Claudio.
Now, unto thy bones good night!
Yearly will I do this rite.

Don Pedro.
Good morrow, masters, put your torches out.
The wolves have preyed, and look, the gentle day,
Before the wheels of Phoebus, round about
Dapples the drowsy east with spots of grey.
Thanks to you all, and leave us. Fare you well.

Claudio.
Good morrow, masters—each his several way.

Don Pedro.
Come let us hence, and put on other weeds,
And then to Leonato's we will go.

Claudio.
And Hymen now with luckier issue speed's
Than this for whom we rend'red up this woe.

Exeunt.

Scene 4

A room in Leonato's house.

(Leonato; Benedick; Beatrice; Margaret; Ursula; Antonio; Friar Francis; Hero; Prince Don Pedro; Claudio; Messenger)

Friar Francis, Leonato, Antonio and Benedick reflect on what has been learned, excusing the Prince and Claudio; Benedick is glad that he will no longer have to fight Claudio. They send the ladies away with instructions to return masked when they are called for. Benedick asks Leonato for Beatrice's hand. Don Pedro and Claudio arrive in good spirits. Claudio reaffirms his willingness to marry whichever lady is given to him, and the masked ladies enter. Before he is allowed to see her face, Claudio takes Hero by the hand and swears to marry her — and then he discovers that she is the still-living Hero. Friar Francis offers to explain everything once the marriage is over, but before they can make their way to the church, Benedick publicly asks Beatrice whether she loves him. She denies it as much as he denies loving her, while they work out that they have been set up. They decide to marry nevertheless, and Don Pedro mocks Benedick for marrying, despite all his promises, but Benedick will not rise to the bait and instead urges the Prince to marry as well. Benedick insists that they dance before getting married, though Leonato thinks it more proper to wait till after. News comes that Don John has been captured, but Benedick tells people to forget about him until the next day, and they all begin to dance.

Enter Leonato, Benedick, Beatrice, Margaret, Ursula, old man Antonio, Friar Francis, Hero.

Friar Francis.
Did I not tell you she was innocent?

Leonato.
So are the Prince and Claudio, who accus'd her
Upon the error that you heard debated.
But Margaret was in some fault for this,
Although against her will, as it appears
In the true course of all the question.

Antonio.
Well, I am glad that all things sorts so well.

Benedick.
And so am I, being else by faith enforc'd
To call young Claudio to a reckoning for it.

Leonato.
Well, daughter, and you gentlewomen all,
Withdraw into a chamber by yourselves,
And when I send for you, come hither masked.
The Prince and Claudio promis'd by this hour
To visit me. You know your office, brother:
You must be father to your brother's daughter,
And give her to young Claudio.

Exeunt Ladies.

Antonio.
Which I will do with confirm'd countenance.

Benedick.
Friar, I must entreat your pains, I think.

Friar Francis.
To do what, signior?

Benedick.
To bind me, or undo me—one of them.
Signior Leonato, truth it is, good signior,
Your niece regards me with an eye of favor.

Leonato.
That eye my daughter lent her, 'tis most true.

Benedick.
And I do with an eye of love requite her.

Leonato.
The sight whereof I think you had from me,
From Claudio, and the Prince. But what's your will?

Benedick.
Your answer, sir, is enigmatical,
But for my will, my will is your good will
May stand with ours, this day to be conjoin'd
In the state of honorable marriage,
In which, good friar, I shall desire your help.

Leonato.
My heart is with your liking.

Friar Francis.
              And my help.
Here comes the Prince and Claudio.

Enter Prince Don Pedro and Claudio and two or three other.

Act 5, Scene 4

Don Pedro.
Good morrow to this fair assembly.

Leonato.
Good morrow, Prince; good morrow, Claudio;
We here attend you. Are you yet determined
Today to marry with my brother's daughter?

Claudio.
I'll hold my mind were she an Ethiope.

Leonato.
Call her forth, brother, here's the friar ready.

Exit Antonio.

Don Pedro.
Good morrow, Benedick. Why, what's the matter,
That you have such a February face,
So full of frost, of storm, and cloudiness?

Claudio.
I think he thinks upon the savage bull.
Tush, fear not, man, we'll tip thy horns with gold,
And all Europa shall rejoice at thee,
As once Europa did at lusty Jove,
When he would play the noble beast in love.

Benedick.
Bull Jove, sir, had an amiable low,
And some such strange bull leapt your father's cow,
And got a calf in that same noble feat
Much like to you, for you have just his bleat.

Enter Brother Antonio, Hero, Beatrice, Margaret, Ursula, the ladies masked.

Claudio.
For this I owe you: here comes other reck'nings.
Which is the lady I must seize upon?

Antonio.
This same is she, and I do give you her.

Claudio.
Why then she's mine. Sweet, let me see your face.

Leonato.
No, that you shall not till you take her hand,
Before this friar, and swear to marry her.

Claudio.
Give me your hand before this holy friar—
I am your husband if you like of me.

Hero.

Unmasking.

And when I liv'd, I was your other wife,
And when you lov'd, you were my other husband.

Claudio.
Another Hero!

Hero.
                    Nothing certainer:
One Hero died defil'd, but I do live,
And surely as I live, I am a maid.

Don Pedro.
The former Hero! Hero that is dead!

Leonato.
She died, my lord, but whiles her slander liv'd.

Friar Francis.
All this amazement can I qualify,
When after that the holy rites are ended,
I'll tell you largely of fair Hero's death.
Mean time let wonder seem familiar,
And to the chapel let us presently.

Benedick.
Soft and fair, friar. Which is Beatrice?

Beatrice.

Unmasking.

I answer to that name. What is your will?

Benedick.
Do not you love me?

Beatrice.
                    Why, no, no more than reason.

Benedick.
Why then your uncle and the Prince and Claudio
Have been deceived. They swore you did.

Beatrice.
Do not you love me?

Benedick.
                    Troth, no, no more than reason.

Beatrice.
Why then my cousin, Margaret, and Ursula
Are much deceiv'd, for they did swear you did.

Benedick.
They swore that you were almost sick for me.

Beatrice.
They swore that you were well-nigh dead for me.

Benedick.
'Tis no such matter. Then you do not love me?

Beatrice.
No, truly, but in friendly recompense.

Leonato.
Come, cousin, I am sure you love the gentleman.

Claudio.
And I'll be sworn upon't that he loves her,
For here's a paper written in his hand,
A halting sonnet of his own pure brain,
Fashion'd to Beatrice.

Hero.
                    And here's another
Writ in my cousin's hand, stol'n from her pocket,
Containing her affection unto Benedick.

Benedick.
A miracle! Here's our own hands against our hearts. Come, I will have thee, but by this light, I take thee for pity.

Beatrice.
I would not deny you, but by this good day, I yield upon great persuasion, and partly to save your life, for I was told you were in a consumption.

Benedick.
Peace, I will stop your mouth.

Kissing her.

Don Pedro.
How dost thou, Benedick the married man?

Benedick.
I'll tell thee what, Prince: a college of wit-crackers cannot flout me out of my humor. Dost thou think I care for a satire or an epigram? No, if a man will be beaten with brains, 'a shall wear nothing handsome about him. In brief, since I do purpose to marry, I will think nothing to any purpose that the world can say against it, and therefore never flout at me for what I have said against it; for man is a giddy thing, and this is my conclusion. For thy part, Claudio, I did think to have beaten thee, but in that thou art like to be my kinsman, live unbruis'd, and love my cousin.

Claudio.
I had well hop'd thou wouldst have denied Beatrice, that I might have cudgell'd thee out of thy single life, to make thee a double-dealer, which out of question thou wilt be, if my cousin do not look exceeding narrowly to thee.

Benedick.
Come, come, we are friends. Let's have a dance ere we are married, that we may lighten our own hearts and our wives' heels.

Leonato.
We'll have dancing afterward.

Benedick.
First, of my word; therefore play, music. Prince, thou art sad, get thee a wife, get thee a wife. There is no staff more reverent than one tipp'd with horn.

Enter Messenger.

Messenger.
My lord, your brother John is ta'en in flight,
And brought with armed men back to Messina.

Benedick.
Think not on him till tomorrow. I'll devise thee brave punishments for him. Strike up, pipers.

Dance.
Exeunt.

The Tempest

Act 1

Scene 1

On a ship at sea.

(Ship-Master; Boatswain; Mariners; Alonso; Sebastian; Antonio; Ferdinand; Gonzalo)

The Captain and the Boatswain of a ship attempt to keep it from sinking in the midst of a raging storm. Their aristocrat passengers curse at them and remind them that they have the King of Naples on board, but the Boatswain points out to them that the waves don't care. The ship breaks and goes down.

A tempestuous noise of thunder and lightning heard. Enter a Ship-Master and a Boatswain.

Master of a Ship.
Boatswain!

Boatswain.
Here, master; what cheer?

Master of a Ship.
Good; speak to th' mariners. Fall to't, yarely, or we run ourselves aground. Bestir, bestir.

*Exit.
Enter Mariners.*

Boatswain.
Heigh, my hearts! Cheerly, cheerly, my hearts! Yare, yare! Take in the topsail. Tend to th' master's whistle.—Blow till thou burst thy wind, if room enough!

Enter Alonso, Sebastian, Antonio, Ferdinand, Gonzalo, and others.

Alonso.
Good boatswain, have care. Where's the master? Play the men.

Boatswain.
I pray now keep below.

Antonio.
Where is the master, bos'n?

Boatswain.
Do you not hear him? You mar our labor. Keep your cabins; you do assist the storm.

Gonzalo.
Nay, good, be patient.

Boatswain.
When the sea is. Hence! What cares these roarers for the name of king? To cabin! Silence! Trouble us not.

Gonzalo.
Good, yet remember whom thou hast aboard.

Boatswain.
None that I more love than myself. You are a councillor; if you can command these elements to silence, and work the peace of the present, we will not hand a rope more. Use your authority. If you cannot, give thanks you have liv'd so long, and make yourself ready in your cabin for the mischance of the hour, if it so hap.—Cheerly, good hearts!—Out of our way, I say.

Exit.

Gonzalo.
I have great comfort from this fellow. Methinks he hath no drowning mark upon him, his complexion is perfect gallows. Stand fast, good Fate, to his hanging, make the rope of his destiny our cable, for our own

doth little advantage. If he be not born to be hang'd, our case is miserable.

Exeunt.
Enter Boatswain.

Boatswain.
Down with the topmast! Yare! Lower, lower! Bring her to try with main-course.

A cry within.

A plague upon this howling! They are louder than the weather, or our office.

Enter Sebastian, Antonio, and Gonzalo.

Yet again? What do you here? Shall we give o'er and drown? Have you a mind to sink?

Sebastian.
A pox o' your throat, you bawling, blasphemous, incharitable dog!

Boatswain.
Work you then.

Antonio.
Hang, cur! Hang, you whoreson, insolent noisemaker! We are less afraid to be drown'd than thou art.

Gonzalo.
I'll warrant him for drowning, though the ship were no stronger than a nutshell, and as leaky as an unstanch'd wench.

Boatswain.
Lay her a-hold, a-hold! Set her two courses off to sea again! Lay her off.

Enter Mariners wet.

Mariners.
All lost! To prayers, to prayers! All lost!

Exeunt.

Boatswain.
What, must our mouths be cold?

Gonzalo.
The King and Prince at prayers, let's assist them, For our case is as theirs.

Sebastian.
I am out of patience.

Antonio.
We are merely cheated of our lives by drunkards. This wide-chopp'd rascal—would thou mightst lie drowning
The washing of ten tides!

Gonzalo.
He'll be hang'd yet,
Though every drop of water swear against it,
And gape at wid'st to glut him.

A confused noise within:

"Mercy on us!"—
"We split, we split!"—"Farewell, my wife and children!"—
"Farewell, brother!"—"We split, we split, we split!"

Exit Boatswain.

Antonio.
Let's all sink wi' th' King.

Sebastian.
Lee's take leave of him.

Exit with Antonio.

Gonzalo.
Now would I give a thousand furlongs of sea for an acre of barren ground, long heath, brown furze, any thing. The wills above be done! But I would fain die a dry death.

Exit.

Scene 2

The island. Before Prospero's cell.

(Prospero; Miranda; Ariel; Caliban; Ferdinand)

Miranda begs her father to calm the storm if he caused it, having seen the ship sink. She is sure that all aboard have drowned. Prospero reassures her that this was all only an illusion, and that in fact everyone is safe and the ship is undamaged. Putting aside his magic robes, he decides that it is time to tell Miranda the truth about himself and her. Once upon a time, he was the Duke of Milan, but he wasn't very good at his job, as he spent most of the time in his library. His brother Antonio

Act 1, Scene 2

slowly took over the government and finally, with the help of the King of Naples, took the Dukedom for himself, putting Prospero and Miranda out to sea in a tiny, rotting boat, which luckily brought them to this island. They did have some food and some books, given to them by a kindly gentleman, Gonzalo, who is on board the ship along with those who stole his throne, and so Prospero raised the storm to force them to land on the island as well. Having explained all this, Prospero sends Miranda to sleep so he can talk with his spirit servant Ariel. Ariel describes how he obeyed his orders, caused a good storm, and has placed the various people safely in different parts of the island. He then asks for his freedom. Prospero reminds Ariel that he saved him from the imprisonment that the old witch Sycorax had placed him in, and that Ariel owes him service. He threatens to torture the spirit just as much as Sycorax did if he doesn't obey. He sends Ariel off with orders to make himself invisible. Miranda wakes, and Prospero announces that they shall visit Caliban, Sycorax's son, who is Prospero's slave. Miranda is unwilling, as she does not enjoy Caliban's company, but Prospero insists. Caliban enters cursing Prospero and all the work he has to do, and claiming that he is the rightful ruler of the island, since he was there before Prospero. He reminds Prospero of how well they treated each other when first he arrived on the island, and how much they taught each other; Prospero reminds Caliban that he tried to rape Miranda. Miranda too upbraids Caliban for how he treated her, even though she taught him how to speak. Prospero orders him to go work, threatening to give him cramps and aches if he refuses. Caliban unwillingly submits. The invisible Ariel lures Ferdinand, the King's son, by his singing. Confused by the music, Ferdinand is certain his father has drowned and Ariel sings another song that appears to confirm this. Prospero shows Ferdinand to Miranda and she is amazed: she has never seen a young man before and she rather likes what she sees. Ferdinand too is taken by Miranda, thinking her a goddess, and after checking that she's a virgin, he announces himself as King of Naples (which he would be were his father dead) and begins wooing her. Prospero, however, who is not opposed to the idea of the two of them getting together, thinks they're moving a bit fast, and decides to play the stern, tyrannical father. He calls Ferdinand a traitor and announces that he will chain him up. Ferdinand seeks to fight, but Prospero makes his sword so heavy that he drops it. Miranda reassures the young man that her father's usually much nicer while Prospero whispers new commands to Ariel.

Enter Prospero and Miranda.

Miranda.
If by your art, my dearest father, you have
Put the wild waters in this roar, allay them.
The sky it seems would pour down stinking pitch,
But that the sea, mounting to th' welkin's cheek,
Dashes the fire out. O! I have suffered
With those that I saw suffer. A brave vessel
(Who had, no doubt, some noble creature in her)
Dash'd all to pieces! O, the cry did knock
Against my very heart. Poor souls, they perish'd.
Had I been any God of power, I would
Have sunk the sea within the earth or ere
It should the good ship so have swallow'd, and
The fraughting souls within her.

Prospero.
                    Be collected,
No more amazement. Tell your piteous heart
There's no harm done.

Miranda.
                    O woe the day!

Prospero.
                    No harm:
I have done nothing, but in care of thee
(Of thee my dear one, thee my daughter), who
Art ignorant of what thou art, nought knowing
Of whence I am, nor that I am more better
Than Prospero, master of a full poor cell,
And thy no greater father.

Miranda.
                    More to know
Did never meddle with my thoughts.

Prospero.
                    'Tis time
I should inform thee farther. Lend thy hand,
And pluck my magic garment from me. So,

Lays down his mantle.

Lie there, my art. Wipe thou thine eyes, have comfort.
The direful spectacle of the wrack, which touch'd
The very virtue of compassion in thee,
I have with such provision in mine art
So safely ordered that there is no soul—
No, not so much perdition as an hair
Betid to any creature in the vessel
Which thou heardst cry, which thou saw'st sink. Sit down,
For thou must now know farther.

Miranda.
                          You have often
Begun to tell me what I am, but stopp'd
And left me to a bootless inquisition,
Concluding, "Stay: not yet."

Prospero.
                        The hour's now come,
The very minute bids thee ope thine ear.
Obey, and be attentive. Canst thou remember
A time before we came unto this cell?
I do not think thou canst, for then thou wast not
Out three years old.

Miranda.
                      Certainly, sir, I can.

Prospero.
By what? By any other house, or person?
Of any thing the image, tell me, that
Hath kept with thy remembrance.

Miranda.
                        'Tis far off;
And rather like a dream than an assurance
That my remembrance warrants. Had I not
Four, or five, women once that tended me?

Prospero.
Thou hadst; and more, Miranda. But how is it
That this lives in thy mind? What seest thou else
In the dark backward and abysm of time?
If thou rememb'rest aught ere thou cam'st here,
How thou cam'st here thou mayst.

Miranda.
                      But that I do not.

Prospero.
Twelve year since, Miranda, twelve year since,
Thy father was the Duke of Milan and
A prince of power.

Miranda.
                    Sir, are not you my father?

Prospero.
Thy mother was a piece of virtue, and
She said thou wast my daughter; and thy father
Was Duke of Milan, and his only heir
And princess no worse issued.

Miranda.
                    O the heavens,
What foul play had we, that we came from thence?
Or blessed was't we did?

Prospero.
                    Both, both, my girl.
By foul play (as thou say'st) were we heav'd thence,
But blessedly help hither.

Miranda.
                    O, my heart bleeds
To think o' th' teen that I have turn'd you to,
Which is from my remembrance! Please you, farther.

Prospero.
My brother and thy uncle, call'd Antonio—
I pray thee mark me—that a brother should
Be so perfidious!—he whom next thyself
Of all the world I lov'd, and to him put
The manage of my state, as at that time
Through all the signories it was the first,
And Prospero the prime duke, being so reputed
In dignity, and for the liberal arts
Without a parallel; those being all my study,
The government I cast upon my brother,
And to my state grew stranger, being transported
And rapt in secret studies. Thy false uncle—
Dost thou attend me?

Miranda.
                  Sir, most heedfully.

Prospero.
Being once perfected how to grant suits,
How to deny them, who t' advance, and who
To trash for overtopping, new created
The creatures that were mine, I say, or chang'd 'em,
Or else new form'd 'em; having both the key
Of officer and office, set all hearts i' th' state
To what tune pleas'd his ear, that now he was
The ivy which had hid my princely trunk,
And suck'd my verdure out on't. Thou attend'st not!

Miranda.
O, good sir, I do.

Prospero.
                    I pray thee mark me.
I, thus neglecting worldly ends, all dedicated
To closeness and the bettering of my mind
With that which, but by being so retir'd,
O'er-priz'd all popular rate, in my false brother

Awak'd an evil nature, and my trust,
Like a good parent, did beget of him
A falsehood in its contrary, as great
As my trust was, which had indeed no limit,
A confidence sans bound. He being thus lorded,
Not only with what my revenue yielded,
But what my power might else exact—like one
Who having into truth, by telling of it,
Made such a sinner of his memory
To credit his own lie—he did believe
He was indeed the Duke, out o' th' substitution,
And executing th' outward face of royalty
With all prerogative. Hence his ambition growing—
Dost thou hear?

Miranda.
              Your tale, sir, would cure deafness.

Prospero.
To have no screen between this part he play'd
And him he play'd it for, he needs will be
Absolute Milan—me (poor man) my library
Was dukedom large enough: of temporal royalties
He thinks me now incapable; confederates
(So dry he was for sway) wi' th' King of Naples
To give him annual tribute, do him homage,
Subject his coronet to his crown, and bend
The dukedom yet unbow'd (alas, poor Milan!)
To most ignoble stooping.

Miranda.
                    O the heavens!

Prospero.
Mark his condition, and th' event, then tell me
If this might be a brother.

Miranda.
                          I should sin
To think but nobly of my grandmother.
Good wombs have borne bad sons.

Prospero.
                      Now the condition.
This King of Naples, being an enemy
To me inveterate, hearkens my brother's suit,
Which was, that he in lieu o' th' premises,
Of homage, and I know not how much tribute,
Should presently extirpate me and mine
Out of the dukedom, and confer fair Milan
With all the honors on my brother; whereon,
A treacherous army levied, one midnight
Fated to th' purpose, did Antonio open
The gates of Milan, and i' th' dead of darkness
The ministers for th' purpose hurried thence
Me and thy crying self.

Miranda.
                Alack, for pity!
I, not rememb'ring how I cried out then,
Will cry it o'er again. It is a hint
That wrings mine eyes to't.

Prospero.
              Hear a little further,
And then I'll bring thee to the present business
Which now's upon 's; without the which this story
Were most impertinent.

Miranda.
                Wherefore did they not
That hour destroy us?

Prospero.
              Well demanded, wench;
My tale provokes that question. Dear, they durst not,
So dear the love my people bore me; nor set
A mark so bloody on the business; but
With colors fairer painted their foul ends.
In few, they hurried us aboard a bark,
Bore us some leagues to sea, where they prepared
A rotten carcass of a butt, not rigg'd,
Nor tackle, sail, nor mast, the very rats
Instinctively have quit it. There they hoist us,
To cry to th' sea, that roar'd to us; to sigh
To th' winds, whose pity, sighing back again,
Did us but loving wrong.

Miranda.
                Alack, what trouble
Was I then to you!

Prospero.
              O, a cherubin
Thou wast that did preserve me. Thou didst smile,
Infused with a fortitude from heaven,
When I have deck'd the sea with drops full salt,
Under my burden groan'd, which rais'd in me
An undergoing stomach, to bear up
Against what should ensue.

Miranda.
              How came we ashore?

Prospero.
By Providence divine.
Some food we had, and some fresh water, that
A noble Neapolitan, Gonzalo,
Out of his charity, who being then appointed
Master of this design, did give us, with
Rich garments, linens, stuffs, and necessaries,
Which since have steaded much; so of his gentleness,
Knowing I lov'd my books, he furnish'd me
From mine own library with volumes that
I prize above my dukedom.

Miranda.
                              Would I might
But ever see that man!

Prospero.
                              Now I arise.

Puts on his robe.

Sit still, and hear the last of our sea-sorrow:
Here in this island we arriv'd, and here
Have I, thy schoolmaster, made thee more profit
Than other princess' can, that have more time
For vainer hours, and tutors not so careful.

Miranda.
Heavens thank you for't! And now I pray you, sir,
For still 'tis beating in my mind, your reason
For raising this sea-storm?

Prospero.
                    Know thus far forth:
By accident most strange, bountiful Fortune
(Now my dear lady) hath mine enemies
Brought to this shore; and by my prescience
I find my zenith doth depend upon
A most auspicious star, whose influence
If now I court not, but omit, my fortunes
Will ever after droop. Here cease more questions.
Thou art inclin'd to sleep; 'tis a good dullness,
And give it way. I know thou canst not choose.

Miranda sleeps.

Come away, servant, come; I am ready now,
Approach, my Ariel. Come.

Enter Ariel.

Ariel.
All hail, great master, grave sir, hail! I come
To answer thy best pleasure; be't to fly,
To swim, to dive into the fire, to ride
On the curl'd clouds. To thy strong bidding, task
Ariel, and all his quality.

Prospero.
                    Hast thou, spirit,
Perform'd to point the tempest that I bade thee?

Ariel.
To every article.
I boarded the King's ship; now on the beak,
Now in the waist, the deck, in every cabin,
I flam'd amazement. Sometime I'ld divide,
And burn in many places; on the topmast,
The yards and boresprit, would I flame distinctly,
Then meet and join. Jove's lightning, the precursors
O' th' dreadful thunder-claps, more momentary
And sight-outrunning were not; the fire and cracks
Of sulfurous roaring the most mighty Neptune
Seem to besiege, and make his bold waves tremble,
Yea, his dread trident shake.

Prospero.
                    My brave spirit!
Who was so firm, so constant, that this coil
Would not infect his reason?

Ariel.
                    Not a soul
But felt a fever of the mad, and play'd
Some tricks of desperation. All but mariners
Plung'd in the foaming brine, and quit the vessel;
Then all afire with me, the King's son, Ferdinand,
With hair up-staring (then like reeds, not hair),
Was the first man that leapt; cried, "Hell is empty,
And all the devils are here."

Prospero.
                    Why, that's my spirit!
But was not this nigh shore?

Ariel.
                    Close by, my master.

Prospero.
But are they, Ariel, safe?

Ariel.
                Not a hair perish'd;
On their sustaining garments not a blemish,
But fresher than before; and as thou badst me,
In troops I have dispers'd them 'bout the isle.
The King's son have I landed by himself,
Whom I left cooling of the air with sighs,
In an odd angle of the isle, and sitting,
His arms in this sad knot.

Prospero.
                Of the King's ship,
The mariners, say how thou hast dispos'd,
And all the rest o' th' fleet.

Ariel.
                Safely in harbor
Is the King's ship, in the deep nook, where once
Thou call'dst me up at midnight to fetch dew
From the still-vex'd Bermoothes, there she's hid;
The mariners all under hatches stowed,
Who, with a charm join'd to their suff'red labor,
I have left asleep; and for the rest o' th' fleet
(Which I dispers'd), they all have met again,
And are upon the Mediterranean float
Bound sadly home for Naples,
Supposing that they saw the King's ship wrack'd,
And his great person perish.

Prospero.
                Ariel, thy charge
Exactly is perform'd; but there's more work.
What is the time o' th' day?

Ariel.
                Past the mid season.

Prospero.
At least two glasses. The time 'twixt six and now
Must by us both be spent most preciously.

Ariel.
Is there more toil? Since thou dost give me pains,
Let me remember thee what thou hast promis'd,
Which is not yet perform'd me.

Prospero.
                How now? Moody?
What is't thou canst demand?

Ariel.
                My liberty.

Prospero.
Before the time be out? No more!

Ariel.
                I prithee,
Remember I have done thee worthy service,
Told thee no lies, made thee no mistakings, serv'd
Without or grudge or grumblings. Thou did promise
To bate me a full year.

Prospero.
                Dost thou forget
From what a torment I did free thee?

Ariel.
                No.

Prospero.
Thou dost; and think'st it much to tread the ooze
Of the salt deep,
To run upon the sharp wind of the north,
To do me business in the veins o' th' earth
When it is bak'd with frost.

Ariel.
                I do not, sir.

Prospero.
Thou liest, malignant thing! Hast thou forgot
The foul witch Sycorax, who with age and envy
Was grown into a hoop? Hast thou forgot her?

Ariel.
No, sir.

Prospero.
                Thou hast. Where was she born? Speak.
Tell me.

Ariel.
Sir, in Argier.

Prospero.
                O, was she so? I must
Once in a month recount what thou hast been,
Which thou forget'st. This damn'd witch Sycorax,
For mischiefs manifold, and sorceries terrible
To enter human hearing, from Argier
Thou know'st was banish'd; for one thing she did
They would not take her life. Is not this true?

Ariel.
Ay, sir.

Prospero.
This blue-ey'd hag was hither brought with child,
And here was left by th' sailors. Thou, my slave,
As thou report'st thyself, was then her servant,
And for thou wast a spirit too delicate
To act her earthy and abhorr'd commands,
Refusing her grand hests, she did confine thee,
By help of her more potent ministers,
And in her most unmitigable rage,
Into a cloven pine, within which rift
Imprison'd, thou didst painfully remain
A dozen years; within which space she died,
And left thee there, where thou didst vent thy groans
As fast as mill-wheels strike. Then was this island
(Save for the son that she did litter here,
A freckled whelp, hag-born) not honor'd with
A human shape.

Ariel.
     Yes—Caliban her son.

Prospero.
Dull thing, I say so; he, that Caliban
Whom now I keep in service. Thou best know'st
What torment I did find thee in; thy groans
Did make wolves howl, and penetrate the breasts
Of ever-angry bears. It was a torment
To lay upon the damn'd, which Sycorax
Could not again undo. It was mine art,
When I arriv'd and heard thee, that made gape
The pine, and let thee out.

Ariel.
     I thank thee, master.

Prospero.
If thou more murmur'st, I will rend an oak
And peg thee in his knotty entrails till
Thou hast howl'd away twelve winters.

Ariel.
     Pardon, master,
I will be correspondent to command
And do my spriting gently.

Prospero.
     Do so; and after two days
I will discharge thee.

Ariel.
     That's my noble master!
What shall I do? Say what? What shall I do?

Prospero.
Go make thyself like a nymph o' th' sea; be subject
To no sight but thine and mine, invisible
To every eyeball else. Go take this shape
And hither come in't. Go. Hence with diligence!

Exit Ariel.

Awake, dear heart, awake! Thou hast slept well,
Awake!

Miranda.
The strangeness of your story put
Heaviness in me.

Prospero.
     Shake it off. Come on,
We'll visit Caliban my slave, who never
Yields us kind answer.

Miranda.
     'Tis a villain, sir,
I do not love to look on.

Prospero.
     But as 'tis,
We cannot miss him. He does make our fire,
Fetch in our wood, and serves in offices
That profit us. What ho! Slave! Caliban!
Thou earth, thou! Speak.

Caliban.

Within.
     There's wood enough within.

Prospero.
Come forth, I say, there's other business for thee.
Come, thou tortoise, when?

Enter Ariel like a water-nymph.

Fine apparition! My quaint Ariel,
Hark in thine ear.

Ariel.
     My lord, it shall be done.

Exit.

Prospero.
Thou poisonous slave, got by the devil himself
Upon thy wicked dam, come forth!

Enter Caliban.

Caliban.
As wicked dew as e'er my mother brush'd
With raven's feather from unwholesome fen
Drop on you both! A south-west blow on ye,
And blister you all o'er!

Prospero.
For this, be sure, tonight thou shalt have cramps,
Side-stitches, that shall pen thy breath up; urchins
Shall, for that vast of night that they may work,
All exercise on thee; thou shalt be pinch'd
As thick as honeycomb, each pinch more stinging
Than bees that made 'em.

Caliban.
     I must eat my dinner.
This island's mine by Sycorax my mother,
Which thou tak'st from me. When thou cam'st first,
Thou strok'st me and made much of me, wouldst give me
Water with berries in't, and teach me how
To name the bigger light, and how the less,
That burn by day and night; and then I lov'd thee
And show'd thee all the qualities o' th' isle,
The fresh springs, brine-pits, barren place and fertile.
Curs'd be I that did so! All the charms
Of Sycorax, toads, beetles, bats, light on you!
For I am all the subjects that you have,
Which first was mine own king; and here you sty me
In this hard rock, whiles you do keep from me
The rest o' th' island.

Prospero.
     Thou most lying slave,
Whom stripes may move, not kindness! I have us'd thee
(Filth as thou art) with human care, and lodg'd thee
In mine own cell, till thou didst seek to violate
The honor of my child.

Caliban.
O ho, O ho, would't had been done!
Thou didst prevent me; I had peopled else
This isle with Calibans.

Miranda.
     Abhorred slave,
Which any print of goodness wilt not take,
Being capable of all ill! I pitied thee,
Took pains to make thee speak, taught thee each hour
One thing or other. When thou didst not, savage,
Know thine own meaning, but wouldst gabble like
A thing most brutish, I endow'd thy purposes
With words that made them known. But thy vild race
(Though thou didst learn) had that in't which good natures
Could not abide to be with; therefore wast thou
Deservedly confin'd into this rock,
Who hadst deserv'd more than a prison.

Caliban.
You taught me language, and my profit on't
Is, I know how to curse. The red-plague rid you
For learning me your language!

Prospero.
     Hag-seed, hence!
Fetch us in fuel, and be quick, thou'rt best,
To answer other business. Shrug'st thou, malice?
If thou neglect'st, or dost unwillingly
What I command, I'll rack thee with old cramps,
Fill all thy bones with aches, make thee roar
That beasts shall tremble at thy din.

Caliban.
     No, pray thee.

Aside.

I must obey. His art is of such pow'r,
It would control my dam's god, Setebos,
And make a vassal of him.

Prospero.
     So, slave, hence!

Exit Caliban.
Enter Ferdinand; and Ariel, invisible, playing and singing.
Ariel's Song

Ariel.
Come unto these yellow sands,
And then take hands:
Curtsied when you have, and kiss'd,
The wild waves whist:
Foot it featly here and there,
And, sweet sprites, the burden bear.
Hark, hark!

Burden, dispersedly, within.

Bow-wow.
The watch-dogs bark!

Burden, dispersedly, within.

Bow-wow.
Hark, hark, I hear
The strain of strutting chanticleer:

Cry within.

Cock-a-diddle-dow.

Ferdinand.
Where should this music be? I' th' air, or th' earth?
It sounds no more; and sure it waits upon
Some god o' th' island. Sitting on a bank,
Weeping again the King my father's wrack,
This music crept by me upon the waters,
Allaying both their fury and my passion
With its sweet air; thence I have follow'd it,
Or it hath drawn me rather. But 'tis gone.
No, it begins again.

Ariel's Song

Ariel.
Full fathom five thy father lies,
Of his bones are coral made:
Those are pearls that were his eyes:
Nothing of him that doth fade,
But doth suffer a sea-change
Into something rich and strange.
Sea-nymphs hourly ring his knell:

Burden within.

Ding-dong.
Hark now I hear them—ding-dong bell.

Ferdinand.
The ditty does remember my drown'd father.
This is no mortal business, nor no sound
That the earth owes. I hear it now above me.

Prospero.
The fringed curtains of thine eye advance,
And say what thou seest yond.

Miranda.
                    What, is't a spirit?
Lord, how it looks about! Believe me, sir,
It carries a brave form. But 'tis a spirit.

Prospero.
No, wench, it eats, and sleeps, and hath such senses
As we have—such. This gallant which thou seest
Was in the wrack; and but he's something stain'd
With grief (that's beauty's canker), thou mightst call him
A goodly person. He hath lost his fellows,
And strays about to find 'em.

Miranda.
                    I might call him
A thing divine, for nothing natural
I ever saw so noble.

Prospero.

Aside.
                    It goes on, I see,
As my soul prompts it. Spirit, fine spirit, I'll free thee
Within two days for this.

Ferdinand.
                    Most sure, the goddess
On whom these airs attend! Vouchsafe my pray'r
May know if you remain upon this island,
And that you will some good instruction give
How I may bear me here. My prime request,
Which I do last pronounce, is (O you wonder!)
If you be maid, or no?

Miranda.
                    No wonder, sir,
But certainly a maid.

Ferdinand.
                    My language? Heavens!
I am the best of them that speak this speech,
Were I but where 'tis spoken.

Prospero.
                  How? The best?
What wert thou, if the King of Naples heard thee?

Ferdinand.
A single thing, as I am now, that wonders
To hear thee speak of Naples. He does hear me,
And that he does I weep. Myself am Naples,
Who with mine eyes (never since at ebb) beheld
The King my father wrack'd.

Miranda.
                  Alack, for mercy!

Ferdinand.
Yes, faith, and all his lords, the Duke of Milan
And his brave son being twain.

Act 1, Scene 2

Prospero.

Aside.

                      The Duke of Milan
And his more braver daughter could control thee,
If now 'twere fit to do't. At the first sight
They have chang'd eyes. Delicate Ariel,
I'll set thee free for this.—A word, good sir,
I fear you have done yourself some wrong; a word.

Miranda.

Why speaks my father so ungently? This
Is the third man that e'er I saw; the first
That e'er I sigh'd for. Pity move my father
To be inclin'd my way!

Ferdinand.

                    O, if a virgin,
And your affection not gone forth, I'll make you
The Queen of Naples.

Prospero.

                Soft, sir, one word more.

Aside.

They are both in either's pow'rs; but this swift business
I must uneasy make, lest too light winning
Make the prize light.—One word more: I charge thee
That thou attend me. Thou dost here usurp
The name thou ow'st not, and hast put thyself
Upon this island as a spy, to win it
From me, the lord on't.

Ferdinand.

                No, as I am a man.

Miranda.

There's nothing ill can dwell in such a temple.
If the ill spirit have so fair a house,
Good things will strive to dwell with't.

Prospero.

              Follow me.—
Speak not you for him; he's a traitor.—Come,
I'll manacle thy neck and feet together.
Sea-water shalt thou drink; thy food shall be
The fresh-brook mussels, wither'd roots, and husks
Wherein the acorn cradled. Follow.

Ferdinand.

              No,
I will resist such entertainment till
Mine enemy has more pow'r.

He draws, and is charmed from moving.

Miranda.

              O dear father,
Make not too rash a trial of him, for
He's gentle, and not fearful.

Prospero.

              What, I say,
My foot my tutor? Put thy sword up, traitor,
Who mak'st a show but dar'st not strike, thy conscience
Is so possess'd with guilt. Come, from thy ward,
For I can here disarm thee with this stick,
And make thy weapon drop.

Miranda.

              Beseech you, father.

Prospero.

Hence! Hang not on my garments.

Miranda.

              Sir, have pity,
I'll be his surety.

Prospero.

              Silence! One word more
Shall make me chide thee, if not hate thee. What,
An advocate for an impostor? Hush!
Thou think'st there is no more such shapes as he,
Having seen but him and Caliban. Foolish wench,
To th' most of men this is a Caliban,
And they to him are angels.

Miranda.

              My affections
Are then most humble; I have no ambition
To see a goodlier man.

Prospero.

To Ferdinand.

Come on, obey:
Thy nerves are in their infancy again
And have no vigor in them.

Ferdinand.
                            So they are.
My spirits, as in a dream, are all bound up.
My father's loss, the weakness which I feel,
The wrack of all my friends, nor this man's threats
To whom I am subdu'd, are but light to me,
Might I but through my prison once a day
Behold this maid. All corners else o' th' earth
Let liberty make use of; space enough
Have I in such a prison.

Prospero.

Aside.
                               It works.

To Ferdinand.
                            Come on.—
Thou hast done well, fine Ariel!

To Ferdinand.
                            Follow me.

To Ariel.
Hark what thou else shalt do me.

Miranda.
                        Be of comfort,
My father's of a better nature, sir,
Than he appears by speech. This is unwonted
Which now came from him.

Prospero.
                      Thou shalt be as free
As mountain winds; but then exactly do
All points of my command.

Ariel.
                        To th' syllable.

Prospero.

To Ferdinand.
Come, follow.

To Miranda.
                    Speak not for him.

Exeunt.

Act 2

Scene 1

Another part of the island.

(Alonso; Sebastian; Antonio; Gonzalo; Adrian; Francisco; Ariel)

Alonso, Sebastian, Antonio, Gonzalo, and other shipwrecked lords wander on the island. Gonzalo insists they're much better off than they think. Sebastian and Antonio have no patience with the optimistic old man, and Alonso is convinced that his son Ferdinand is dead, though the others tell him the boy may have lived. Gonzalo shares his slightly vague utopian vision of what live on the island could be, which Antonio and Sebastian mock viciously to one another. Ariel comes in playing music that sends them almost all asleep, except Antonio and Sebastian, who stay awake to theoretically guard the King. Antonio, Prospero's brother, suggests to Sebastian that they now have an excellent opportunity to kill Alonso, thereby making Sebastian King of Naples, since they are certain Ferdinand is dead. Sebastian has some doubts, but Antonio points out how well usurping the throne of Milan worked for him. Just as they are about to commit the crime, Ariel comes and wakes Gonzalo, sent by Prospero who has magically seen what was about to happen. The traitors explain their drawn swords by claiming they heard wild beasts about. Alonso decides they shall continue to search for Sebastian.

Enter Alonso, Sebastian, Antonio, Gonzalo, Adrian, Francisco, and others.

Gonzalo.
Beseech you, sir, be merry; you have cause
(So have we all) of joy; for our escape
Is much beyond our loss. Our hint of woe
Is common: every day some sailor's wife,
The masters of some merchant, and the merchant
Have just our theme of woe; but for the miracle
(I mean our preservation), few in millions
Can speak like us. Then wisely, good sir, weigh
Our sorrow with our comfort.

Alonso.
                        Prithee peace.

Sebastian.
He receives comfort like cold porridge.

Antonio.
The visitor will not give him o'er so.

Sebastian.
Look, he's winding up the watch of his wit, by and by it will strike.

Gonzalo.
Sir—

Sebastian.
One. Tell.

Gonzalo.
When every grief is entertain'd that's offer'd, Comes to th' entertainer—

Sebastian.
A dollar.

Gonzalo.
Dolor comes to him indeed, you have spoken truer than you purpos'd.

Sebastian.
You have taken it wiselier than I meant you should.

Gonzalo.
Therefore, my lord—

Antonio.
Fie, what a spendthrift is he of his tongue!

Alonso.
I prithee spare.

Gonzalo.
Well, I have done. But yet—

Sebastian.
He will be talking.

Antonio.
Which, of he or Adrian, for a good wager, first begins to crow?

Sebastian.
The old cock.

Antonio.
The cock'rel.

Sebastian.
Done. The wager?

Antonio.
A laughter.

Sebastian.
A match!

Adrian.
Though this island seem to be desert—

Sebastian.
Ha, ha, ha!

Antonio.
So: you're paid!

Adrian.
Uninhabitable, and almost inaccessible—

Sebastian.
Yet—

Adrian.
Yet—

Antonio.
He could not miss't.

Adrian.
It must needs be of subtle, tender, and delicate temperance.

Antonio.
Temperance was a delicate wench.

Sebastian.
Ay, and a subtle, as he most learnedly deliver'd.

Adrian.
The air breathes upon us here most sweetly.

Sebastian.
As if it had lungs, and rotten ones.

Antonio.
Or, as 'twere perfum'd by a fen.

Gonzalo.
Here is every thing advantageous to life.

Antonio.
True, save means to live.

Sebastian.
Of that there's none, or little.

Gonzalo.
How lush and lusty the grass looks! How green!

Antonio.
The ground indeed is tawny.

Sebastian.
With an eye of green in't.

Antonio.
He misses not much.

Sebastian.
No; he doth but mistake the truth totally.

Gonzalo.
But the rarity of it is—which is indeed almost beyond credit—

Sebastian.
As many vouch'd rarities are.

Gonzalo.
That our garments, being (as they were) drench'd in the sea, hold notwithstanding their freshness and glosses, being rather new dy'd than stain'd with salt water.

Antonio.
If but one of his pockets could speak, would it not say he lies?

Sebastian.
Ay, or very falsely pocket up his report.

Gonzalo.
Methinks our garments are now as fresh as when we put them on first in Afric, at the marriage of the King's fair daughter Claribel to the King of Tunis.

Sebastian.
'Twas a sweet marriage, and we prosper well in our return.

Adrian.
Tunis was never grac'd before with such a paragon to their queen.

Gonzalo.
Not since widow Dido's time.

Antonio.
Widow? A pox o' that! How came that widow in? Widow Dido!

Sebastian.
What if he had said "widower Aeneas" too? Good Lord, how you take it!

Adrian.
"Widow Dido," said you? You make me study of that. She was of Carthage, not of Tunis.

Gonzalo.
This Tunis, sir, was Carthage.

Adrian.
Carthage?

Gonzalo.
I assure you, Carthage.

Antonio.
His word is more than the miraculous harp.

Sebastian.
He hath rais'd the wall, and houses too.

Antonio.
What impossible matter will he make easy next?

Sebastian.
I think he will carry this island home in his pocket, and give it his son for an apple.

Antonio.
And sowing the kernels of it in the sea, bring forth more islands.

Gonzalo.
Ay.

Antonio.
Why, in good time.

Gonzalo.
Sir, we were talking that our garments seem now as fresh as when we were at Tunis at the marriage of your daughter, who is now queen.

Antonio.
And the rarest that e'er came there.

Sebastian.
Bate, I beseech you, widow Dido.

Antonio.
O, widow Dido? Ay, widow Dido.

Gonzalo.
Is not, sir, my doublet as fresh as the first day I wore it? I mean, in a sort.

Antonio.
That 'sort' was well fish'd for.

Gonzalo.
When I wore it at your daughter's marriage?

Alonso.
You cram these words into mine ears against
The stomach of my sense. Would I had never
Married my daughter there! For coming thence,
My son is lost and (in my rate) she too,
Who is so far from Italy removed
I ne'er again shall see her. O thou mine heir
Of Naples and of Milan, what strange fish
Hath made his meal on thee?

Francisco.
                Sir, he may live.
I saw him beat the surges under him,
And ride upon their backs. He trod the water,
Whose enmity he flung aside, and breasted
The surge most swoll'n that met him. His bold head
'Bove the contentious waves he kept, and oared
Himself with his good arms in lusty stroke
To th' shore, that o'er his wave-worn basis bowed,
As stooping to relieve him. I not doubt
He came alive to land.

Alonso.
              No, no, he's gone.

Sebastian.
Sir, you may thank yourself for this great loss,
That would not bless our Europe with your daughter,
But rather loose her to an African,
Where she, at least, is banish'd from your eye,
Who hath cause to wet the grief on't.

Alonso.
              Prithee peace.

Sebastian.
You were kneel'd to, and importun'd otherwise
By all of us, and the fair soul herself
Weigh'd between loathness and obedience, at
Which end o' th' beam should bow. We have lost your son,
I fear forever. Milan and Naples have
More widows in them of this business' making
Than we bring men to comfort them.
The fault's your own.

Alonso.
            So is the dear'st o' th' loss.

Gonzalo.
My Lord Sebastian,
The truth you speak doth lack some gentleness,
And time to speak it in. You rub the sore,
When you should bring the plaster.

Sebastian.
            Very well.

Antonio.
And most chirurgeonly.

Gonzalo.
It is foul weather in us all, good sir,
When you are cloudy.

Sebastian.
            Fowl weather?

Antonio.
            Very foul.

Gonzalo.
Had I plantation of this isle, my lord—

Antonio.
He'd sow't with nettle-seed.

Sebastian.
            Or docks, or mallows.

Gonzalo.
And were the king on't, what would I do?

Sebastian.
Scape being drunk, for want of wine.

Gonzalo.
I' th' commonwealth I would, by contraries,
Execute all things; for no kind of traffic
Would I admit; no name of magistrate;
Letters should not be known; riches, poverty,
And use of service, none; contract, succession,
Bourn, bound of land, tilth, vineyard, none;
No use of metal, corn, or wine, or oil;
No occupation, all men idle, all;
And women too, but innocent and pure;
No sovereignty—

Sebastian.
                Yet he would be king on't.

Antonio.
The latter end of his commonwealth forgets the beginning.

Gonzalo.
All things in common nature should produce
Without sweat or endeavor: treason, felony,
Sword, pike, knife, gun, or need of any engine,
Would I not have; but nature should bring forth,
Of it own kind, all foison, all abundance,
To feed my innocent people.

Sebastian.
No marrying 'mong his subjects?

Antonio.
None, man, all idle—whores and knaves.

Gonzalo.
I would with such perfection govern, sir,
T' excel the golden age.

Sebastian.
                'save his Majesty!

Antonio.
Long live Gonzalo!

Gonzalo.
              And—do you mark me, sir?

Alonso.
Prithee no more; thou dost talk nothing to me.

Gonzalo.
I do well believe your Highness, and did it to minister occasion to these gentlemen, who are of such sensible and nimble lungs that they always use to laugh at nothing.

Antonio.
'Twas you we laugh'd at.

Gonzalo.
Who, in this kind of merry fooling, am nothing to you; so you may continue, and laugh at nothing still.

Antonio.
What a blow was there given!

Sebastian.
And it had not fall'n flat-long.

Gonzalo.
You are gentlemen of brave mettle; you would lift the moon out of her sphere, if she would continue in it five weeks without changing.

Enter Ariel invisible, playing solemn music.

Sebastian.
We would so, and then go a-batfowling.

Antonio.
Nay, good my lord, be not angry.

Gonzalo.
No, I warrant you, I will not adventure my discretion so weakly. Will you laugh me asleep, for I am very heavy?

Antonio.
Go sleep, and hear us.

All sleep except Alonso, Sebastian, and Antonio.

Alonso.
What, all so soon asleep! I wish mine eyes
Would, with themselves, shut up my thoughts. I find
They are inclin'd to do so.

Sebastian.
                Please you, sir,
Do not omit the heavy offer of it.
It seldom visits sorrow; when it doth,
It is a comforter.

Antonio.
                We two, my lord,
Will guard your person while you take your rest,
And watch your safety.

Alonso.
                Thank you. Wondrous heavy.

Alonso sleeps.
Exit Ariel.

Sebastian.
What a strange drowsiness possesses them!

Antonio.
It is the quality o' th' climate.

Sebastian.
                      Why
Doth it not then our eyelids sink? I find not
Myself dispos'd to sleep.

Antonio.
                      Nor I, my spirits are nimble.
They fell together all, as by consent;
They dropp'd, as by a thunder-stroke. What might,
Worthy Sebastian, O, what might—? No more—
And yet methinks I see it in thy face,
What thou shouldst be. Th' occasion speaks thee, and
My strong imagination sees a crown
Dropping upon thy head.

Sebastian.
                      What? Art thou waking?

Antonio.
Do you not hear me speak?

Sebastian.
                      I do, and surely
It is a sleepy language, and thou speak'st
Out of thy sleep. What is it thou didst say?
This is a strange repose, to be asleep
With eyes wide open—standing, speaking, moving—
And yet so fast asleep.

Antonio.
                      Noble Sebastian,
Thou let'st thy fortune sleep—die, rather; wink'st
Whiles thou art waking.

Sebastian.
                      Thou dost snore distinctly,
There's meaning in thy snores.

Antonio.
I am more serious than my custom; you
Must be so too, if heed me; which to do,
Trebles thee o'er.

Sebastian.
                      Well; I am standing water.

Antonio.
I'll teach you how to flow.

Sebastian.
                      Do so. To ebb
Hereditary sloth instructs me.

Antonio.
                      O!
If you but knew how you the purpose cherish
Whiles thus you mock it! How, in stripping it,
You more invest it! Ebbing men, indeed,
Most often, do so near the bottom run
By their own fear or sloth.

Sebastian.
                      Prithee say on.
The setting of thine eye and cheek proclaim
A matter from thee; and a birth, indeed,
Which throes thee much to yield.

Antonio.
                      Thus, sir:
Although this lord of weak remembrance, this
Who shall be of as little memory
When he is earth'd, hath here almost persuaded
(For he's a spirit of persuasion, only
Professes to persuade) the King his son's alive,
'Tis as impossible that he's undrown'd,
As he that sleeps here swims.

Sebastian.
                      I have no hope
That he's undrown'd.

Antonio.
                      O, out of that no hope
What great hope have you! No hope, that way, is
Another way so high a hope that even
Ambition cannot pierce a wink beyond,
But doubt discovery there. Will you grant with me
That Ferdinand is drown'd?

Sebastian.
                      He's gone.

Antonio.
                      Then tell me,
Who's the next heir of Naples?

Sebastian.
                      Claribel.

Antonio.
She that is Queen of Tunis; she that dwells
Ten leagues beyond man's life; she that from Naples
Can have no note, unless the sun were post—
The Man i' th' Moon's too slow—till new-born chins
Be rough and razorable; she that from whom
We all were sea-swallow'd, though some cast again

(And by that destiny) to perform an act
Whereof what's past is prologue, what to come
In yours and my discharge.

Sebastian.
                    What stuff is this? How say you?
'Tis true, my brother's daughter's Queen of Tunis,
So is she heir of Naples; 'twixt which regions
There is some space.

Antonio.
                    A space whose ev'ry cubit
Seems to cry out, "How shall that Claribel
Measure us back to Naples? Keep in Tunis,
And let Sebastian wake." Say this were death
That now hath seiz'd them, why, they were no worse
Than now they are. There be that can rule Naples
As well as he that sleeps; lords that can prate
As amply and unnecessarily
As this Gonzalo; I myself could make
A chough of as deep chat. O that you bore
The mind that I do! What a sleep were this
For your advancement! Do you understand me?

Sebastian.
Methinks I do.

Antonio.
                    And how does your content
Tender your own good fortune?

Sebastian.
                    I remember
You did supplant your brother Prospero.

Antonio.
                              True.
And look how well my garments sit upon me,
Much feater than before. My brother's servants
Were then my fellows, now they are my men.

Sebastian.
But, for your conscience?

Antonio.
Ay, sir; where lies that? If 'twere a kibe,
'Twould put me to my slipper; but I feel not
This deity in my bosom. Twenty consciences,
That stand 'twixt me and Milan, candied be they,
And melt ere they molest! Here lies your brother,
No better than the earth he lies upon,
If he were that which now he's like—that's dead,
Whom I with this obedient steel, three inches of it,
Can lay to bed forever; whiles you, doing thus,
To the perpetual wink for aye might put
This ancient morsel, this Sir Prudence, who
Should not upbraid our course. For all the rest,
They'll take suggestion as a cat laps milk;
They'll tell the clock to any business that
We say befits the hour.

Sebastian.
                    Thy case, dear friend,
Shall be my president: as thou got'st Milan,
I'll come by Naples. Draw thy sword. One stroke
Shall free thee from the tribute which thou payest,
And I the King shall love thee.

Antonio.
                    Draw together;
And when I rear my hand, do you the like,
To fall it on Gonzalo.

Sebastian.
                    O, but one word.

They talk apart.
Enter Ariel, invisible, with music and song.

Ariel.
My master through his art foresees the danger
That you, his friend, are in, and sends me forth
(For else his project dies) to keep them living.

Sings in Gonzalo's ear.

While you here do snoring lie,
Open-ey'd conspiracy
His time doth take.
If of life you keep a care,
Shake off slumber, and beware.
Awake, awake!

Antonio.
Then let us both be sudden.

Gonzalo.

Waking.
                    Now, good angels
Preserve the King!

Wakes Alonso.

Alonso.
Why, how now, ho! Awake? Why are you drawn?
Wherefore this ghastly looking?

Gonzalo.
                    What's the matter?

Sebastian.
Whiles we stood here securing your repose,
Even now, we heard a hollow burst of bellowing
Like bulls, or rather lions. Did't not wake you?
It struck mine ear most terribly.

Alonso.
                    I heard nothing.

Antonio.
O, 'twas a din to fright a monster's ear,
To make an earthquake; sure it was the roar
Of a whole herd of lions.

Alonso.
                    Heard you this, Gonzalo?

Gonzalo.
Upon mine honor, sir, I heard a humming
(And that a strange one too) which did awake me.
I shak'd you, sir, and cried. As mine eyes open'd,
I saw their weapons drawn. There was a noise,
That's verily. 'Tis best we stand upon our guard,
Or that we quit this place. Let's draw our weapons.

Alonso.
Lead off this ground, and let's make further search
For my poor son.

Gonzalo.
                    Heavens keep him from these beasts!
For he is sure i' th' island.

Alonso.
                    Lead away.

Ariel.
Prospero my lord shall know what I have done.
So, King, go safely on to seek thy son.

Exeunt.

Scene 2

Another part of the island.

(Caliban; Trinculo; Stephano)

Caliban is carrying a pile of wood to Prospero's cell, cursing the magician as he does so for forcing him to work by having spirits around him at all times ready to pinch him if he slacks off. He sees Trinculo, Alonso's jester, approaching, and thinking that this is a new spirit come to torment him, hides himself. Trinculo finds Caliban lying flat on the ground and thinks he's found a dead native; as thunder rolls, he hides under Caliban's coat. Stephano, Alonso's butler, comes in, drunk and drinking. Seeing the four legs coming out from under the coat on the ground, Stephano thinks he's found a monster, which he pokes and prods until Caliban protests. Stephano gives him some of his drink, and Trinculo emerges when he realizes who's there. Caliban finds the alcohol heavenly, decides the two fools must be gods, and offers to worship them. They make him drink more and more as he promises to do more and more for them, and they think they've well-landed. Caliban announces his freedom from Prospero in a drunken song.

Enter Caliban with a burden of wood.
A noise of thunder heard.

Caliban.
All the infections that the sun sucks up
From bogs, fens, flats, on Prosper fall, and make him
By inch-meal a disease! His spirits hear me,
And yet I needs must curse. But they'll nor pinch,
Fright me with urchin-shows, pitch me i' th' mire,
Nor lead me, like a fire-brand, in the dark
Out of my way, unless he bid 'em; but
For every trifle are they set upon me,
Sometime like apes that mow and chatter at me,
And after bite me; then like hedgehogs which
Lie tumbling in my barefoot way, and mount
Their pricks at my footfall; sometime am I
All wound with adders, who with cloven tongues
Do hiss me into madness.

Enter Trinculo.

Lo, now lo,
Here comes a spirit of his, and to torment me
For bringing wood in slowly. I'll fall flat,
Perchance he will not mind me.

Trinculo.
Here's neither bush nor shrub to bear off any weather at all. And another storm brewing, I hear it sing i' th' wind. Yond same black cloud, yond huge one, looks like a foul bumbard that would shed his liquor. If it should thunder as it did before, I know not where to

hide my head. Yond same cloud cannot choose but fall by pailfuls. What have we here? A man or a fish? Dead or alive? A fish, he smells like a fish; a very ancient and fish-like smell; a kind of, not-of-the-newest poor-John. A strange fish! Were I in England now (as once I was) and had but this fish painted, not a holiday fool there but would give a piece of silver. There would this monster make a man; any strange beast there makes a man. When they will not give a doit to relieve a lame beggar, they will lay out ten to see a dead Indian. Legg'd like a man; and his fins like arms! Warm, o' my troth! I do now let loose my opinion, hold it no longer: this is no fish, but an islander, that hath lately suffer'd by a thunderbolt.

Thunder.

Alas, the storm is come again! My best way is to creep under his gaberdine; there is no other shelter hereabout. Misery acquaints a man with strange bedfellows; I will here shroud till the dregs of the storm be past.

Enter Stephano, singing, a bottle in his hand.

Stephano.
"I shall no more to sea, to sea,
Here shall I die ashore—"
This is a very scurvy tune to sing at a man's funeral. Well, here's my comfort.

Drinks.
Sings.

"The master, the swabber, the boatswain, and I,
The gunner and his mate,
Lov'd Mall, Meg, and Marian, and Margery,
But none of us car'd for Kate;
For she had a tongue with a tang,
Would cry to a sailor, 'Go hang!'
She lov'd not the savor of tar nor of pitch,
Yet a tailor might scratch her where e'er she did itch.
Then to sea, boys, and let her go hang!"
This is a scurvy tune too; but here's my comfort.

Drinks.

Caliban.
Do not torment me! O!

Stephano.
What's the matter? Have we devils here? Do you put tricks upon 's with salvages and men of Inde? Ha? I have not scap'd drowning to be afeard now of your four legs; for it hath been said, "As proper a man as ever went on four legs cannot make him give ground"; and it shall be said so again while Stephano breathes at' nostrils.

Caliban.
The spirit torments me! O!

Stephano.
This is some monster of the isle with four legs, who hath got (as I take it) an ague. Where the devil should he learn our language? I will give him some relief, if it be but for that. If I can recover him, and keep him tame, and get to Naples with him, he's a present for any emperor that ever trod on neat's-leather.

Caliban.
Do not torment me, prithee. I'll bring my wood home faster.

Stephano.
He's in his fit now, and does not talk after the wisest. He shall taste of my bottle; if he have never drunk wine afore, it will go near to remove his fit. If I can recover him, and keep him tame, I will not take too much for him; he shall pay for him that hath him, and that soundly.

Caliban.
Thou dost me yet but little hurt; thou wilt anon, I know it by thy trembling. Now Prosper works upon thee.

Stephano.
Come on your ways. Open your mouth; here is that which will give language to you, cat. Open your mouth; this will shake your shaking, I can tell you, and that soundly. You cannot tell who's your friend. Open your chaps again.

Caliban drinks.

Trinculo.
I should know that voice; it should be—but he is drown'd; and these are devils. O, defend me!

Act 2, Scene 2

Stephano.
Four legs and two voices; a most delicate monster! His forward voice now is to speak well of his friend; his backward voice is to utter foul speeches and to detract. If all the wine in my bottle will recover him, I will help his ague. Come.

Caliban drinks again.

Amen! I will pour some in thy other mouth.

Trinculo.
Stephano!

Stephano.
Doth thy other mouth call me? Mercy, mercy! This is a devil, and no monster. I will leave him, I have no long spoon.

Trinculo.
Stephano! If thou beest Stephano, touch me, and speak to me; for I am Trinculo—be not afeard—thy good friend Trinculo.

Stephano.
If thou beest Trinculo, come forth. I'll pull thee by the lesser legs. If any be Trinculo's legs, these are they. Thou art very Trinculo indeed! How cam'st thou to be the siege of this moon-calf? Can he vent Trinculos?

Trinculo.
I took him to be kill'd with a thunder-stroke. But art thou not drown'd, Stephano? I hope now thou art not drown'd. Is the storm overblown? I hid me under the dead moon-calf's gaberdine for fear of the storm. And art thou living, Stephano? O Stephano, two Neapolitans scap'd!

Stephano.
Prithee do not turn me about, my stomach is not constant.

Caliban.

Aside.

These be fine things, and if they be not sprites.
That's a brave god, and bears celestial liquor.
I will kneel to him.

Stephano.
How didst thou scape? How cam'st thou hither? Swear by this bottle how thou cam'st hither—I escap'd upon a butt of sack which the sailors heav'd o'erboard—by this bottle, which I made of the bark of a tree with mine own hands since I was cast ashore.

Caliban.
I'll swear upon that bottle to be thy true subject, for the liquor is not earthly.

Stephano.
Here; swear then how thou escap'dst.

Trinculo.
Swom ashore, man, like a duck. I can swim like a duck, I'll be sworn.

Stephano.
Here, kiss the book.

Passing the bottle.

Though thou canst swim like a duck, thou art made like a goose.

Trinculo.
O Stephano, hast any more of this?

Stephano.
The whole butt, man. My cellar is in a rock by th' seaside, where my wine is hid. How now, moon-calf? How does thine ague?

Caliban.
Hast thou not dropp'd from heaven?

Stephano.
Out o' th' moon, I do assure thee. I was the Man i' th' Moon, when time was.

Caliban.
I have seen thee in her, and I do adore thee.
My mistress show'd me thee, and thy dog, and thy bush.

Stephano.
Come, swear to that; kiss the book. I will furnish it anon with new contents. Swear.

Caliban drinks.

Trinculo.
By this good light, this is a very shallow monster! I afeard of him? A very weak monster! The Man i' th' Moon? A most poor credulous monster! Well drawn, monster, in good sooth!

Caliban.
I'll show thee every fertile inch o' th' island;
And I will kiss thy foot. I prithee be my god.

Trinculo.
By this light, a most perfidious and drunken monster!
When 's god's asleep, he'll rob his bottle.

Caliban.
I'll kiss thy foot. I'll swear myself thy subject.

Stephano.
Come on then; down, and swear.

Trinculo.
I shall laugh myself to death at this puppy-headed monster. A most scurvy monster! I could find in my heart to beat him—

Stephano.
Come, kiss.

Trinculo.
But that the poor monster's in drink. An abominable monster!

Caliban.
I'll show thee the best springs; I'll pluck thee berries;
I'll fish for thee, and get thee wood enough.
A plague upon the tyrant that I serve!
I'll bear him no more sticks, but follow thee,
Thou wondrous man.

Trinculo.
A most ridiculous monster, to make a wonder of a poor drunkard!

Caliban.
I prithee let me bring thee where crabs grow;
And I with my long nails will dig thee pig-nuts,
Show thee a jay's nest, and instruct thee how
To snare the nimble marmazet. I'll bring thee
To clust'ring filberts, and sometimes I'll get thee
Young scamels from the rock. Wilt thou go with me?

Stephano.
I prithee now lead the way without any more talking. Trinculo, the King and all our company else being drown'd, we will inherit here. Here! Bear my bottle. Fellow Trinculo, we'll fill him by and by again.

Caliban.

Sings drunkenly.

Farewell, master; farewell, farewell!

Trinculo.
A howling monster; a drunken monster!

Caliban.
No more dams I'll make for fish,
Nor fetch in firing
At requiring,
Nor scrape trenchering, nor wash dish.
'Ban, 'Ban, Ca-Caliban
Has a new master, get a new man.
Freedom, high-day! High-day, freedom! Freedom, high-day, freedom!

Stephano.
O brave monster! Lead the way.

Exeunt.

Act 3

Scene 1

Before Prospero's cell.

(Ferdinand; Miranda; Prospero)

Ferdinand is stacking wood at Prospero's orders, though since Miranda is nearby and clearly pities him he does not mind the labor much. Miranda comes in and tries to comfort or help him, unaware that Prospero is watching them. He refuses to let her help, but they chat, Miranda giving away her name despite Prospero's admonitions. They soon admit that they are head over heels in love with each other, which delights the unseen Prospero.

Enter Ferdinand bearing a log.

Ferdinand.
There be some sports are painful, and their labor
Delight in them sets off; some kinds of baseness
Are nobly undergone; and most poor matters
Point to rich ends. This my mean task
Would be as heavy to me as odious, but
The mistress which I serve quickens what's dead,
And makes my labors pleasures. O, she is
Ten times more gentle than her father's crabbed;
And he's compos'd of harshness. I must remove
Some thousands of these logs, and pile them up,

Upon a sore injunction. My sweet mistress
Weeps when she sees me work, and says such baseness
Had never like executor. I forget;
But these sweet thoughts do even refresh my labors,
Most busil'est when I do it.

Enter Miranda, and Prospero at a distance, unseen.

Miranda.
      Alas, now pray you
Work not so hard. I would the lightning had
Burnt up those logs that you are enjoin'd to pile!
Pray set it down, and rest you. When this burns,
'Twill weep for having wearied you. My father
Is hard at study; pray now rest yourself,
He's safe for these three hours.

Ferdinand.
      O most dear mistress,
The sun will set before I shall discharge
What I must strive to do.

Miranda.
      If you'll sit down,
I'll bear your logs the while. Pray give me that,
I'll carry it to the pile.

Ferdinand.
      No, precious creature,
I had rather crack my sinews, break my back,
Than you should such dishonor undergo,
While I sit lazy by.

Miranda.
      It would become me
As well as it does you; and I should do it
With much more ease, for my good will is to it,
And yours it is against.

Prospero.

Aside.
      Poor worm, thou art infected!
This visitation shows it.

Miranda.
      You look wearily.

Ferdinand.
No, noble mistress, 'tis fresh morning with me
When you are by at night. I do beseech you—
Chiefly that I might set it in my prayers—
What is your name?

Miranda.
      Miranda.—O my father,
I have broke your hest to say so.

Ferdinand.
      Admir'd Miranda,
Indeed the top of admiration! Worth
What's dearest to the world! Full many a lady
I have ey'd with best regard, and many a time
Th' harmony of their tongues hath into bondage
Brought my too diligent ear. For several virtues
Have I lik'd several women, never any
With so full soul but some defect in her
Did quarrel with the noblest grace she ow'd,
And put it to the foil. But you, O you,
So perfect and so peerless, are created
Of every creature's best!

Miranda.
      I do not know
One of my sex; no woman's face remember,
Save, from my glass, mine own; nor have I seen
More that I may call men than you, good friend,
And my dear father. How features are abroad
I am skilless of; but by my modesty
(The jewel in my dower), I would not wish
Any companion in the world but you;
Nor can imagination form a shape,
Besides yourself, to like of. But I prattle
Something too wildly, and my father's precepts
I therein do forget.

Ferdinand.
      I am, in my condition,
A prince, Miranda; I do think, a king
(I would, not so!), and would no more endure
This wooden slavery than to suffer
The flesh-fly blow my mouth. Hear my soul speak:
The very instant that I saw you, did
My heart fly to your service, there resides,
To make me slave to it, and for your sake
Am I this patient log-man.

Miranda.
      Do you love me?

Ferdinand.
O heaven, O earth, bear witness to this sound,
And crown what I profess with kind event
If I speak true! If hollowly, invert

What best is boded me to mischief! I,
Beyond all limit of what else i' th' world,
Do love, prize, honor you.

Miranda.

                        I am a fool
To weep at what I am glad of.

Prospero.

Aside.

                     Fair encounter
Of two most rare affections! Heavens rain grace
On that which breeds between 'em!

Ferdinand.

                    Wherefore weep you?

Miranda.
At mine unworthiness, that dare not offer
What I desire to give; and much less take
What I shall die to want. But this is trifling,
And all the more it seeks to hide itself,
The bigger bulk it shows. Hence, bashful cunning,
And prompt me, plain and holy innocence!
I am your wife, if you will marry me;
If not, I'll die your maid. To be your fellow
You may deny me, but I'll be your servant,
Whether you will or no.

Ferdinand.

                 My mistress, dearest,
And I thus humble ever.

Miranda.

                 My husband then?

Ferdinand.
Ay, with a heart as willing
As bondage e'er of freedom. Here's my hand.

Miranda.
And mine, with my heart in't. And now farewell
Till half an hour hence.

Ferdinand.

               A thousand, thousand!

Exeunt Ferdinand and Miranda severally.

Prospero.
So glad of this as they I cannot be,
Who are surpris'd withal; but my rejoicing
At nothing can be more. I'll to my book,
For yet ere supper-time must I perform
Much business appertaining.

Exit.

Scene 2

Another part of the island.

(Caliban; Stephano; Trinculo; Ariel)

Trinculo mocks Caliban, who has no taste for him but worships Stephano. As Ariel comes in, invisible, Caliban begins to tell his new friends of how Prospero is a tyrant. Ariel says he is lying, and makes it sound as though Trinculo were speaking. When he denies it, Stephano beats him. Caliban encourages Stephano in his plot to become master of the island by telling him that they could kill Prospero during his afternoon nap, so long as they burn his books first, since they are the source of his power. The mutineers begin to sing and Ariel plays along; Trinculo and Stephano are terrified, but Caliban tells them that there are always noises on the island, some of which are so beautiful he thinks he's dreaming when he hears them. Caliban leads the other two on as Ariel flies off to warn Prospero.

Enter Caliban, Stephano, and Trinculo.

Stephano.
Tell not me. When the butt is out, we will drink water—not a drop before; therefore bear up and board 'em. Servant-monster, drink to me.

Trinculo.
Servant-monster? The folly of this island! They say there's but five upon this isle: we are three of them; if th' other two be brain'd like us, the state totters.

Stephano.
Drink, servant-monster, when I bid thee. Thy eyes are almost set in thy head.

Trinculo.
Where should they be set else? He were a brave monster indeed if they were set in his tail.

Stephano.
My man-monster hath drown'd his tongue in sack. For my part, the sea cannot drown me; I swam, ere I could recover the shore, five and thirty leagues off and on. By this light, thou shalt be my lieutenant, monster, or my standard.

Act 3, Scene 2

Trinculo.
Your lieutenant if you list, he's no standard.

Stephano.
We'll not run, Monsieur Monster.

Trinculo.
Nor go neither; but you'll lie like dogs, and yet say nothing neither.

Stephano.
Moon-calf, speak once in thy life, if thou beest a good moon-calf.

Caliban.
How does thy honor? Let me lick thy shoe. I'll not serve him, he is not valiant.

Trinculo.
Thou liest, most ignorant monster, I am in case to justle a constable. Why, thou debosh'd fish thou, was there ever man a coward that hath drunk so much sack as I today? Wilt thou tell a monstrous lie, being but half a fish and half a monster?

Caliban.
Lo, how he mocks me! Wilt thou let him, my lord?

Trinculo.
"Lord," quoth he? That a monster should be such a natural!

Caliban.
Lo, lo again. Bite him to death, I prithee.

Stephano.
Trinculo, keep a good tongue in your head. If you prove a mutineer—the next tree! The poor monster's my subject, and he shall not suffer indignity.

Caliban.
I thank my noble lord. Wilt thou be pleas'd to hearken once again to the suit I made to thee?

Stephano.
Marry, will I; kneel, and repeat it. I will stand, and so shall Trinculo.

Enter Ariel, invisible.

Caliban.
As I told thee before, I am subject to a tyrant,
A sorcerer, that by his cunning hath
Cheated me of the island.

Ariel.
Thou liest.

Caliban.
 Thou liest, thou jesting monkey thou!
I would my valiant master would destroy thee.
I do not lie.

Stephano.
Trinculo, if you trouble him any more in 's tale, by this hand, I will supplant some of your teeth.

Trinculo.
Why, I said nothing.

Stephano.
Mum then, and no more.—Proceed.

Caliban.
I say by sorcery he got this isle;
From me he got it. If thy greatness will
Revenge it on him—for I know thou dar'st,
But this thing dare not—

Stephano.
That's most certain.

Caliban.
Thou shalt be lord of it, and I'll serve thee.

Stephano.
How now shall this be compass'd? Canst thou bring me to the party?

Caliban.
Yea, yea, my lord. I'll yield him thee asleep,
Where thou mayst knock a nail into his head.

Ariel.
Thou liest, thou canst not.

Caliban.
What a pied ninny's this! Thou scurvy patch!
I do beseech thy greatness, give him blows,
And take his bottle from him. When that's gone,
He shall drink nought but brine, for I'll not show him
Where the quick freshes are.

Stephano.
Trinculo, run into no further danger; interrupt the monster one word further, and by this hand, I'll turn my mercy out o' doors, and make a stock-fish of thee.

Trinculo.
Why, what did I? I did nothing. I'll go farther off.

Stephano.
Didst thou not say he lied?

Ariel.
Thou liest.

Stephano.
Do I so? Take thou that.

Beats Trinculo.

As you like this, give me the lie another time.

Trinculo.
I did not give the lie. Out o' your wits, and hearing too? A pox o' your bottle! This can sack and drinking do. A murrain on your monster, and the devil take your fingers!

Caliban.
Ha, ha, ha!

Stephano.
Now forward with your tale.—Prithee stand further off.

Caliban.
Beat him enough. After a little time
I'll beat him too.

Stephano.
    Stand farther.—Come, proceed.

Caliban.
Why, as I told thee, 'tis a custom with him
I' th' afternoon to sleep. There thou mayst brain him,
Having first seiz'd his books; or with a log
Batter his skull, or paunch him with a stake,
Or cut his wezand with thy knife. Remember
First to possess his books; for without them
He's but a sot, as I am; nor hath not
One spirit to command: they all do hate him
As rootedly as I. Burn but his books.
He has brave utensils (for so he calls them)
Which when he has a house, he'll deck withal.
And that most deeply to consider is
The beauty of his daughter. He himself
Calls her a nonpareil. I never saw a woman
But only Sycorax my dam and she;
But she as far surpasseth Sycorax
As great'st does least.

Stephano.
    Is it so brave a lass?

Caliban.
Ay, lord, she will become thy bed, I warrant,
And bring thee forth brave brood.

Stephano.
Monster, I will kill this man. His daughter and I will be king and queen—'save our Graces! And Trinculo and thyself shall be viceroys. Dost thou like the plot, Trinculo?

Trinculo.
Excellent.

Stephano.
Give me thy hand. I am sorry I beat thee; but while thou liv'st keep a good tongue in thy head.

Caliban.
Within this half hour will he be asleep.
Wilt thou destroy him then?

Stephano.
    Ay, on mine honor.

Ariel.
This will I tell my master.

Caliban.
Thou mak'st me merry; I am full of pleasure,
Let us be jocund. Will you troll the catch
You taught me but while-ere?

Stephano.
At thy request, monster, I will do reason, any reason. Come on, Trinculo, let us sing.

Sings.

"Flout 'em and scout 'em,
And scout 'em and flout 'em!
Thought is free."

Caliban.
That's not the tune.

Ariel plays the tune on a tabor and pipe.

Stephano.
What is this same?

Trinculo.
This is the tune of our catch, play'd by the picture of Nobody.

Stephano.
If thou beest a man, show thyself in thy likeness. If thou beest a devil, take't as thou list.

Trinculo.
O, forgive me my sins!

Stephano.
He that dies pays all debts. I defy thee. Mercy upon us!

Caliban.
Art thou afeard?

Stephano.
No, monster, not I.

Caliban.
Be not afeard, the isle is full of noises,
Sounds, and sweet airs, that give delight and hurt not.
Sometimes a thousand twangling instruments
Will hum about mine ears; and sometime voices,
That if I then had wak'd after long sleep,
Will make me sleep again, and then in dreaming,
The clouds methought would open, and show riches
Ready to drop upon me, that when I wak'd
I cried to dream again.

Stephano.
This will prove a brave kingdom to me, where I shall have my music for nothing.

Caliban.
When Prospero is destroy'd.

Stephano.
That shall be by and by. I remember the story.

Trinculo.
The sound is going away. Let's follow it, and after do our work.

Stephano.
Lead, monster, we'll follow. I would I could see this taborer; he lays it on.

Trinculo.
Wilt come? I'll follow Stephano.

Exeunt.

Scene 3

Another part of the island.

(Alonso; Sebastian; Antonio; Gonzalo; Adrian; Francisco; Prospero; Shapes; Ariel)

Gonzalo is too weary to carry on walking, and Alonso is losing hope of finding Ferdinand. Antonio and Sebastian plan to kill them that night. Suddenly they hear music and spirits bring in a marvelous banquet, dancing for them. Unaware that Prospero is looking on, invisible, the noblemen approach to eat, but as they reach the table thunder rolls and Ariel appears in the shape of a harpy. The feast vanishes and Ariel castigates them for deposing Prospero. He vanishes, and the spirits dance mockingly for the lords. The three guilty men are distracted, Antonio and Sebastian rushing out with drawn swords to fight whatever fiends they meet while Alonso, keenly feeling his guilt and now certain that Ferdinand is dead, goes to drown himself. Gonzalo sends the other men after the three to stop them from doing anything foolish.

Enter Alonso, Sebastian, Antonio, Gonzalo, Adrian, Francisco, etc.

Gonzalo.
By'r lakin, I can go no further, sir,
My old bones aches. Here's a maze trod indeed
Through forth-rights and meanders! By your patience,
I needs must rest me.

Alonso.
                    Old lord, I cannot blame thee,
Who am myself attach'd with weariness
To th' dulling of my spirits. Sit down, and rest.
Even here I will put off my hope, and keep it
No longer for my flatterer. He is drown'd
Whom thus we stray to find, and the sea mocks
Our frustrate search on land. Well, let him go.

Antonio.

Aside to Sebastian

I am right glad that he's so out of hope.
Do not for one repulse forgo the purpose
That you resolv'd t' effect.

Sebastian.

Aside to Antonio

                    The next advantage

Will we take throughly.

Antonio.

Aside to Sebastian

      Let it be tonight,
For now they are oppress'd with travail, they
Will not, nor cannot, use such vigilance
As when they are fresh.

Sebastian.

Aside to Antonio

      I say tonight. No more.

Solemn and strange music.
Prospero on the top, invisible.

Alonso.
What harmony is this? My good friends, hark!

Gonzalo.
Marvelous sweet music!

Enter several strange Shapes, bringing in a banquet; and dance about it with gentle actions of salutations; and inviting the King, etc., to eat, they depart.

Alonso.
Give us kind keepers, heavens! What were these?

Sebastian.
A living drollery. Now I will believe
That there are unicorns; that in Arabia
There is one tree, the phoenix' throne, one phoenix
At this hour reigning there.

Antonio.
      I'll believe both;
And what does else want credit, come to me,
And I'll be sworn 'tis true. Travelers ne'er did lie,
Though fools at home condemn 'em.

Gonzalo.
      If in Naples
I should report this now, would they believe me?
If I should say I saw such islanders
(For, certes, these are people of the island),
Who though they are of monstrous shape, yet note
Their manners are more gentle, kind, than of
Our human generation you shall find
Many, nay, almost any.

Prospero.

Aside.

      Honest lord,
Thou hast said well; for some of you there present
Are worse than devils.

Alonso.
      I cannot too much muse
Such shapes, such gesture, and such sound expressing
(Although they want the use of tongue) a kind
Of excellent dumb discourse.

Prospero.

Aside.

      Praise in departing.

Francisco.
They vanish'd strangely.

Sebastian.
      No matter, since
They have left their viands behind; for we have stomachs.
Will't please you taste of what is here?

Alonso.
      Not I.

Gonzalo.
Faith, sir, you need not fear. When we were boys,
Who would believe that there were mountaineers,
Dew-lapp'd, like bulls, whose throats had hanging at 'em
Wallets of flesh? Or that there were such men
Whose heads stood in their breasts? Which now we find
Each putter-out of five for one will bring us
Good warrant of.

Alonso.
      I will stand to, and feed,
Although my last, no matter, since I feel
The best is past. Brother, my lord the Duke,
Stand to, and do as we.

Thunder and lightning.
Enter Ariel, like a harpy, claps his wings upon the table, and with a quaint device the banquet vanishes.

Ariel.
You are three men of sin, whom Destiny,
That hath to instrument this lower world
And what is in't, the never-surfeited sea
Hath caus'd to belch up you; and on this island
Where man doth not inhabit—you 'mongst men
Being most unfit to live. I have made you mad;
And even with such-like valor men hang and drown
Their proper selves.

Alonso, Sebastian, etc. draw their swords.

                  You fools! I and my fellows
Are ministers of Fate. The elements,
Of whom your swords are temper'd, may as well
Wound the loud winds, or with bemock'd-at stabs
Kill the still-closing waters, as diminish
One dowle that's in my plume. My fellow ministers
Are like invulnerable. If you could hurt,
Your swords are now too massy for your strengths,
And will not be uplifted. But remember
(For that's my business to you) that you three
From Milan did supplant good Prospero,
Expos'd unto the sea (which hath requit it)
Him, and his innocent child; for which foul deed
The pow'rs, delaying (not forgetting), have
Incens'd the seas and shores—yea, all the creatures,
Against your peace. Thee of thy son, Alonso,
They have bereft; and do pronounce by me
Ling'ring perdition (worse than any death
Can be at once) shall step by step attend
You and your ways, whose wraths to guard you from—
Which here, in this most desolate isle, else falls
Upon your heads—is nothing but heart's sorrow,
And a clear life ensuing.

He vanishes in thunder; then, to soft music, enter the Shapes again, and dance, with mocks and mows, and carrying out the table.

Prospero.
Bravely the figure of this harpy hast thou
Perform'd, my Ariel; a grace it had, devouring.
Of my instruction hast thou nothing bated
In what thou hadst to say; so with good life,
And observation strange, my meaner ministers
Their several kinds have done. My high charms work,
And these, mine enemies, are all knit up
In their distractions. They now are in my pow'r;
And in these fits I leave them, while I visit
Young Ferdinand, whom they suppose is drown'd,
And his and mine lov'd darling.

Exit above.

Gonzalo.
I' th' name of something holy, sir, why stand you
In this strange stare?

Alonso.
                  O, it is monstrous! Monstrous!
Methought the billows spoke, and told me of it;
The winds did sing it to me, and the thunder,
That deep and dreadful organ-pipe, pronounc'd
The name of Prosper; it did base my trespass.
Therefore my son i' th' ooze is bedded; and
I'll seek him deeper than e'er plummet sounded,
And with him there lie mudded.

Exit.

Sebastian.
                  But one fiend at a time,
I'll fight their legions o'er.

Antonio.
                  I'll be thy second.

Exeunt Sebastian and Antonio.

Gonzalo.
All three of them are desperate: their great guilt
(Like poison given to work a great time after)
Now gins to bite the spirits. I do beseech you
(That are of suppler joints) follow them swiftly,
And hinder them from what this ecstasy
May now provoke them to.

Adrian.
                  Follow, I pray you.

Exeunt omnes.

Act 4

Scene 1

Before Prospero's cell.

(Prospero; Ferdinand; Miranda; Ariel; Iris; Juno; Ceres; Nymphs; Reapers; Caliban; Stephano; Trinculo)

Prospero hands Miranda over to Ferdinand, telling the young man that he was only testing him, though he warns him to wait until they are married before getting up to anything. To celebrate, he gives them a show: spirits in the shape of Iris, Ceres, and Juno appear and bless the betrothed couple. Halfway through, Prospero suddenly remembers that Caliban and others are on their way to murder him, and the show breaks off. Commenting on the insubstantiality of the world, Prospero sends the two youngsters off for a nap while he prepares to deal with his other problems. Ariel has led the three drunkards through a terrible path, leaving them scratched, bruised, and muddy. Prospero has the spirit hang up his prettiest clothes on a laundry line. The three arrive, and Trinculo and Stephano are distracted by the clothes. Despite Caliban's urging that they get on with killing people, the other two spend the time dressing up until Prospero and Ariel set a pack of spirits looking like dogs on them, and they are chased out to be tormented further. Now Prospero has all of his enemies at his mercy; he promises Ariel that the spirit shall soon be free.

Enter Prospero, Ferdinand, and Miranda.

Prospero.
If I have too austerely punish'd you,
Your compensation makes amends, for I
Have given you here a third of mine own life,
Or that for which I live; who once again
I tender to thy hand. All thy vexations
Were but my trials of thy love, and thou
Hast strangely stood the test. Here, afore heaven,
I ratify this my rich gift. O Ferdinand,
Do not smile at me that I boast her off,
For thou shalt find she will outstrip all praise
And make it halt behind her.

Ferdinand.
                    I do believe it
Against an oracle.

Prospero.
Then, as my gift, and thine own acquisition
Worthily purchas'd, take my daughter. But
If thou dost break her virgin-knot before
All sanctimonious ceremonies may
With full and holy rite be minist'red,
No sweet aspersion shall the heavens let fall
To make this contract grow; but barren hate,
Sour-ey'd disdain, and discord shall bestrew
The union of your bed with weeds so loathly
That you shall hate it both. Therefore take heed,
As Hymen's lamps shall light you.

Ferdinand.
                    As I hope
For quiet days, fair issue, and long life,
With such love as 'tis now, the murkiest den,
The most opportune place, the strong'st suggestion
Our worser genius can, shall never melt
Mine honor into lust, to take away
The edge of that day's celebration,
When I shall think or Phoebus' steeds are founder'd
Or Night kept chain'd below.

Prospero.
                    Fairly spoke.
Sit then and talk with her, she is thine own.
What, Ariel! My industrious servant, Ariel!

Enter Ariel.

Ariel.
What would my potent master? Here I am.

Prospero.
Thou and thy meaner fellows your last service
Did worthily perform; and I must use you
In such another trick. Go bring the rabble
(o'er whom I give thee pow'r) here to this place.
Incite them to quick motion, for I must
Bestow upon the eyes of this young couple
Some vanity of mine art. It is my promise,
And they expect it from me.

Ariel.
                    Presently?

Prospero.
Ay, with a twink.

Ariel.
Before you can say "come" and "go,"
And breathe twice, and cry "so, so,"
Each one, tripping on his toe,
Will be here with mop and mow.
Do you love me, master? No?

Prospero.
Dearly, my delicate Ariel. Do not approach
Till thou dost hear me call.

Ariel.
                    Well; I conceive.

Exit.

Prospero.
Look thou be true; do not give dalliance
Too much the rein. The strongest oaths are straw
To th' fire i' th' blood. Be more abstenious,
Or else good night your vow!

Ferdinand.
                    I warrant you, sir,
The white cold virgin snow upon my heart
Abates the ardor of my liver.

Prospero.
                        Well.
Now come, my Ariel, bring a corollary,
Rather than want a spirit. Appear, and pertly!
No tongue! All eyes! Be silent.

Soft music.
Enter Iris.

Iris.
Ceres, most bounteous lady, thy rich leas
Of wheat, rye, barley, fetches, oats, and pease;
Thy turfy mountains, where live nibbling sheep,
And flat meads thatch'd with stover, them to keep;
Thy banks with pioned and twilled brims,
Which spungy April at thy hest betrims,
To make cold nymphs chaste crowns; and thy broom-groves,
Whose shadow the dismissed bachelor loves,
Being lass-lorn; thy pole-clipt vineyard,
And thy sea-marge, sterile and rocky-hard,
Where thou thyself dost air—the Queen o' th' sky,
Whose wat'ry arch and messenger am I,
Bids thee leave these, and with her sovereign Grace,
Here on this grass-plot, in this very place,
To come and sport. Her peacocks fly amain.

Juno descends slowly in her car.

Approach, rich Ceres, her to entertain.

Enter Ceres.

Ceres.
Hail, many-colored messenger, that ne'er
Dost disobey the wife of Jupiter;
Who with thy saffron wings upon my flow'rs
Diffusest honey-drops, refreshing show'rs,
And with each end of thy blue bow dost crown
My bosky acres and my unshrubb'd down,
Rich scarf to my proud earth—why hath thy Queen
Summon'd me hither, to this short-grass'd green?

Iris.
A contract of true love to celebrate,
And some donation freely to estate
On the bless'd lovers.

Ceres.
                  Tell me, heavenly bow,
If Venus or her son, as thou dost know,
Do now attend the Queen? Since they did plot
The means that dusky Dis my daughter got,
Her and her blind boy's scandall'd company
I have forsworn.

Iris.
            Of her society
Be not afraid. I met her Deity
Cutting the clouds towards Paphos; and her son
Dove-drawn with her. Here thought they to have done
Some wanton charm upon this man and maid,
Whose vows are, that no bed-right shall be paid
Till Hymen's torch be lighted; but in vain,
Mars's hot minion is return'd again;
Her waspish-headed son has broke his arrows,
Swears he will shoot no more, but play with sparrows,
And be a boy right out.

Juno alights.

Ceres.
                  Highest Queen of state,
Great Juno, comes, I know her by her gait.

Juno.
How does my bounteous sister? Go with me
To bless this twain, that they may prosperous be,
And honor'd in their issue.

They sing.

Juno.
Honor, riches, marriage-blessing,
Long continuance, and increasing,
Hourly joys be still upon you!
Juno sings her blessings on you.

Ceres.
Earth's increase, foison plenty,
Barns and garners never empty;
Vines with clust'ring bunches growing,
Plants with goodly burden bowing;
Spring come to you at the farthest
In the very end of harvest!
Scarcity and want shall shun you,
Ceres' blessing so is on you.

Ferdinand.
This is a most majestic vision, and
Harmonious charmingly. May I be bold
To think these spirits?

Prospero.
                    Spirits, which by mine art
I have from their confines call'd to enact
My present fancies.

Ferdinand.
                    Let me live here ever;
So rare a wond'red father and a wise
Makes this place Paradise.

Juno and Ceres whisper, and send Iris on employment.

Prospero.
                    Sweet now, silence!
Juno and Ceres whisper seriously;
There's something else to do. Hush and be mute,
Or else our spell is marr'd.

Iris.
You nymphs, call'd Naiades, of the windring brooks,
With your sedg'd crowns and ever-harmless looks,
Leave your crisp channels, and on this green land
Answer your summons; Juno does command.
Come, temperate nymphs, and help to celebrate
A contract of true love; be not too late.

Enter certain Nymphs.

You sunburn'd sicklemen, of August weary,
Come hither from the furrow and be merry.
Make holiday; your rye-straw hats put on,
And these fresh nymphs encounter every one
In country footing.

Enter certain Reapers, properly habited: they join with the Nymphs in a graceful dance, towards the end whereof Prospero starts suddenly, and speaks; after which, to a strange, hollow, and confused noise, they heavily vanish.

Prospero.

Aside.

I had forgot that foul conspiracy
Of the beast Caliban and his confederates
Against my life. The minute of their plot
Is almost come.

To the Spirits.
                    Well done, avoid; no more.

Ferdinand.
This is strange. Your father's in some passion
That works him strongly.

Miranda.
                    Never till this day
Saw I him touch'd with anger, so distemper'd.

Prospero.
You do look, my son, in a mov'd sort,
As if you were dismay'd; be cheerful, sir.
Our revels now are ended. These our actors
(As I foretold you) were all spirits, and
Are melted into air, into thin air,
And like the baseless fabric of this vision,
The cloud-capp'd tow'rs, the gorgeous palaces,
The solemn temples, the great globe itself,
Yea, all which it inherit, shall dissolve,
And like this insubstantial pageant faded
Leave not a rack behind. We are such stuff
As dreams are made on; and our little life
Is rounded with a sleep. Sir, I am vex'd;
Bear with my weakness, my old brain is troubled.
Be not disturb'd with my infirmity.
If you be pleas'd, retire into my cell,
And there repose. A turn or two I'll walk
To still my beating mind.

Both Ferdinand and Miranda.
                    We wish your peace.

Prospero.

To Ariel.

Come with a thought.

To Ferdinand and Miranda.
                    I thank thee.

Exeunt Ferdinand and Miranda.

                    Ariel! Come.

Enter Ariel.

Ariel.
Thy thoughts I cleave to. What's thy pleasure?

Prospero.
                              Spirit,
We must prepare to meet with Caliban.

Ariel.
Ay, my commander. When I presented Ceres,
I thought to have told thee of it, but I fear'd
Lest I might anger thee.

Prospero.
Say again, where didst thou leave these varlots?

Ariel.
I told you, sir, they were red-hot with drinking,
So full of valor that they smote the air
For breathing in their faces; beat the ground
For kissing of their feet; yet always bending
Towards their project. Then I beat my tabor,
At which like unback'd colts they prick'd their ears,
Advanc'd their eyelids, lifted up their noses
As they smelt music. So I charm'd their ears
That calf-like they my lowing follow'd through
Tooth'd briers, sharp furzes, pricking goss, and thorns,
Which ent'red their frail shins. At last I left them
I' th' filthy-mantled pool beyond your cell,
There dancing up to th' chins, that the foul lake
O'erstunk their feet.

Prospero.
                    This was well done, my bird.
Thy shape invisible retain thou still.
The trumpery in my house, go bring it hither,
For stale to catch these thieves.

Ariel.
                    I go, I go.

Exit.

Prospero.
A devil, a born devil, on whose nature
Nurture can never stick; on whom my pains,
Humanely taken, all, all lost, quite lost;
And as with age his body uglier grows,
So his mind cankers. I will plague them all,
Even to roaring.

Enter Ariel, loaden with glistering apparel, etc.

Come, hang them on this line.

Prospero and Ariel remain, invisible.
Enter Caliban, Stephano, and Trinculo, all wet.

Caliban.
Pray you tread softly, that the blind mole may not
Hear a foot fall; we now are near his cell.

Stephano.
Monster, your fairy, which you say is a harmless fairy,
has done little better than play'd the Jack with us.

Trinculo.
Monster, I do smell all horse-piss, at which my nose is
in great indignation.

Stephano.
So is mine. Do you hear, monster? If I should take a
displeasure against you, look you—

Trinculo.
Thou wert but a lost monster.

Caliban.
Good my lord, give me thy favor still.
Be patient, for the prize I'll bring thee to
Shall hoodwink this mischance; therefore speak softly,
All's hush'd as midnight yet.

Trinculo.
Ay, but to lose our bottles in the pool—

Stephano.
There is not only disgrace and dishonor in that, monster, but an infinite loss.

Trinculo.
That's more to me than my wetting; yet this is your
harmless fairy, monster!

Stephano.
I will fetch off my bottle, though I be o'er ears for my
labor.

Caliban.
Prithee, my king, be quiet. Seest thou here,
This is the mouth o' th' cell. No noise, and enter.
Do that good mischief which may make this island

Thine own forever, and I, thy Caliban,
For aye thy foot-licker.

Stephano.
Give me thy hand. I do begin to have bloody thoughts.

Trinculo.
O King Stephano! O peer! O worthy Stephano! Look what a wardrobe here is for thee!

Caliban.
Let it alone, thou fool, it is but trash.

Trinculo.
O, ho, monster! We know what belongs to a frippery. O King Stephano!

Stephano.
Put off that gown, Trinculo. By this hand, I'll have that gown.

Trinculo.
Thy Grace shall have it.

Caliban.
The dropsy drown this fool! What do you mean
To dote thus on such luggage? Let't alone
And do the murder first. If he awake,
From toe to crown he'll fill our skins with pinches,
Make us strange stuff.

Stephano.
Be you quiet, monster. Mistress line, is not this my jerkin? Now is the jerkin under the line. Now, jerkin, you are like to lose your hair, and prove a bald jerkin.

Trinculo.
Do, do; we steal by line and level, and't like your Grace.

Stephano.
I thank thee for that jest; here's a garment for't. Wit shall not go unrewarded while I am king of this country. 'Steal by line and level' is an excellent pass of pate; there's another garment for't.

Trinculo.
Monster, come put some lime upon your fingers, and away with the rest.

Caliban.
I will have none on't. We shall lose our time,
And all be turn'd to barnacles, or to apes
With foreheads villainous low.

Stephano.
Monster, lay-to your fingers. Help to bear this away where my hogshead of wine is, or I'll turn you out of my kingdom. Go to, carry this.

Trinculo.
And this.

Stephano.
Ay, and this.

A noise of hunters heard. Enter diverse Spirits in shape of dogs and hounds, hunting them about; Prospero and Ariel setting them on.

Prospero.
Hey, Mountain, hey!

Ariel.
Silver! There it goes, Silver!

Prospero.
Fury, Fury! There, Tyrant, there! Hark, hark!

Caliban, Stephano, and Trinculo are driven out.

Go, charge my goblins that they grind their joints
With dry convulsions, shorten up their sinews
With aged cramps, and more pinch-spotted make them
Than pard or cat o' mountain.

Ariel.
        Hark, they roar!

Prospero.
Let them be hunted soundly. At this hour
Lies at my mercy all mine enemies.
Shortly shall all my labors end, and thou
Shalt have the air at freedom. For a little
Follow, and do me service.

Exeunt.

Act 5

Scene 1

Before Prospero's cell.

(Prospero; Ariel; Alonso; Gonzalo; Sebastian; Antonio; Adrian; Francisco; Ferdinand; Miranda; Master of a Ship; Boatswain; Caliban; Stephano; Trinculo)

Prospero learns where exactly everyone is. Ariel describes the pain the lords are in, as well as their followers, particularly Gonzalo. The spirit comments that were he a human he would have pity on them. Prospero decides to forgive them, and sends Ariel to release them. To the various spirits he has commanded, Prospero swears to give up his magic. The noblemen are brought in and stand charmed in a circle. Prospero goes to dress himself in his old clothes as Duke of Milan. He reveals himself to them all, welcoming them, and Alonso, amazed, immediately gives up his claim to Milan. Prospero welcomes everybody, quietly warning Antonio and Sebastian that he knows about their treachery and could reveal it. Alonso tells Prospero that he is mourning his son, and Prospero comments that he himself has lost his daughter; Alonso laments and wishes that both were alive and married together. Prospero invites them into his cell and reveals Ferdinand and Miranda, alive and playing chess. Ferdinand is thrilled to see his father alive, while Miranda is exhilarated to discover the variety of human beings. Alonso agrees that they should marry while Gonzalo weeps for joy. Ariel brings in the ship's crew, who are not only well but can confirm that the ship is in perfect shape. Prospero promises again that he will free Ariel, whom he sends to bring in Caliban and the others. They arrive, looking ridiculous. Prospero hands Stephano and Trinculo over to Alonso, while acknowledging that Caliban is his responsibility. Caliban, sober now, realizes what a fool he has been to follow the drunkards. Prospero invites everyone into his cell to tell them the story of his life and of these last few hours. Then he promises Ariel that, once the spirit has given them a good breeze to sail them towards the royal fleet, he shall be free.

Enter Prospero in his magic robes, and Ariel.

Prospero.
Now does my project gather to a head:
My charms crack not; my spirits obey; and Time
Goes upright with his carriage. How's the day?

Ariel.
On the sixth hour, at which time, my lord,
You said our work should cease.

Prospero.
                I did say so,
When first I rais'd the tempest. Say, my spirit,
How fares the King and 's followers?

Ariel.
                Confin'd together
In the same fashion as you gave in charge,
Just as you left them; all prisoners, sir,
In the line-grove which weather-fends your cell;
They cannot budge till your release. The King,
His brother, and yours, abide all three distracted,
And the remainder mourning over them,
Brimful of sorrow and dismay; but chiefly
Him that you term'd, sir, "the good old Lord Gonzalo,"
His tears runs down his beard like winter's drops
From eaves of reeds. Your charm so strongly works 'em
That if you now beheld them, your affections
Would become tender.

Prospero.
              Dost thou think so, spirit?

Ariel.
Mine would, sir, were I human.

Prospero.
              And mine shall.
Hast thou, which art but air, a touch, a feeling
Of their afflictions, and shall not myself,
One of their kind, that relish all as sharply
Passion as they, be kindlier mov'd than thou art?
Though with their high wrongs I am struck to th' quick,
Yet, with my nobler reason, 'gainst my fury
Do I take part. The rarer action is
In virtue than in vengeance. They being penitent,
The sole drift of my purpose doth extend
Not a frown further. Go, release them, Ariel.
My charms I'll break, their senses I'll restore,
And they shall be themselves.

Ariel.
              I'll fetch them, sir.

Exit.
Prospero traces a magic circle with his staff.

Prospero.
Ye elves of hills, brooks, standing lakes, and groves,
And ye that on the sands with printless foot
Do chase the ebbing Neptune, and do fly him
When he comes back; you demi-puppets that
By moonshine do the green sour ringlets make,
Whereof the ewe not bites; and you whose pastime
Is to make midnight mushrumps, that rejoice

To hear the solemn curfew: by whose aid
(Weak masters though ye be) I have bedimm'd
The noontide sun, call'd forth the mutinous winds,
And 'twixt the green sea and the azur'd vault
Set roaring war; to the dread rattling thunder
Have I given fire, and rifted Jove's stout oak
With his own bolt; the strong-bas'd promontory
Have I made shake, and by the spurs pluck'd up
The pine and cedar. Graves at my command
Have wak'd their sleepers, op'd, and let 'em forth
By my so potent art. But this rough magic
I here abjure; and when I have requir'd
Some heavenly music (which even now I do)
To work mine end upon their senses that
This airy charm is for, I'll break my staff,
Bury it certain fathoms in the earth,
And deeper than did ever plummet sound
I'll drown my book.

Solemn music.
Here enters Ariel before; then Alonso, with a frantic gesture, attended by Gonzalo; Sebastian and Antonio in like manner, attended by Adrian and Francisco. They all enter the circle which Prospero had made, and there stand charm'd; which Prospero observing, speaks.

A solemn air, and the best comforter
To an unsettled fancy, cure thy brains,
Now useless, boil'd within thy skull! There stand,
For you are spell-stopp'd.
Holy Gonzalo, honorable man,
Mine eyes, ev'n sociable to the show of thine,
Fall fellowly drops. The charm dissolves apace,
And as the morning steals upon the night,
Melting the darkness, so their rising senses
Begin to chase the ignorant fumes that mantle
Their clearer reason. O good Gonzalo,
My true preserver, and a loyal sir
To him thou follow'st! I will pay thy graces
Home both in word and deed. Most cruelly
Didst thou, Alonso, use me and my daughter;
Thy brother was a furtherer in the act.
Thou art pinch'd for't now, Sebastian. Flesh and blood,
You, brother mine, that entertain'd ambition,
Expell'd remorse and nature, whom, with Sebastian
(Whose inward pinches therefore are most strong),
Would here have kill'd your king, I do forgive thee,
Unnatural though thou art.—Their understanding
Begins to swell, and the approaching tide
Will shortly fill the reasonable shores
That now lie foul and muddy. Not one of them
That yet looks on me, or would know me! Ariel,
Fetch me the hat and rapier in my cell.

Exit Ariel, and returns immediately.

I will discase me, and myself present
As I was sometime Milan. Quickly, spirit,
Thou shalt ere long be free.

Ariel sings and helps to attire him.

Ariel.
Where the bee sucks, there suck I,
In a cowslip's bell I lie;
There I couch when owls do cry.
On the bat's back I do fly
After summer merrily.
Merrily, merrily shall I live now,
Under the blossom that hangs on the bough.

Prospero.
Why, that's my dainty Ariel! I shall miss thee,
But yet thou shalt have freedom. So, so, so.
To the King's ship, invisible as thou art;
There shalt thou find the mariners asleep
Under the hatches. The master and the boatswain
Being awake, enforce them to this place;
And presently, I prithee.

Ariel.
I drink the air before me, and return
Or ere your pulse twice beat.

Exit.

Gonzalo.
All torment, trouble, wonder, and amazement
Inhabits here. Some heavenly power guide us
Out of this fearful country!

Prospero.
                Behold, sir King,
The wronged Duke of Milan, Prospero.
For more assurance that a living prince
Does now speak to thee, I embrace thy body,
And to thee and thy company I bid
A hearty welcome.

Alonso.
                Whe'er thou beest he or no,
Or some enchanted trifle to abuse me
(As late I have been), I not know. Thy pulse

Act 5, Scene 1

Beats as of flesh and blood; and since I saw thee,
Th' affliction of my mind amends, with which
I fear a madness held me. This must crave
(And if this be at all) a most strange story.
Thy dukedom I resign, and do entreat
Thou pardon me my wrongs. But how should Prospero
Be living, and be here?

Prospero.

To Gonzalo.

      First, noble friend,
Let me embrace thine age, whose honor cannot
Be measur'd or confin'd.

Gonzalo.

      Whether this be,
Or be not, I'll not swear.

Prospero.

     You do yet taste
Some subtleties o' th' isle, that will not let you
Believe things certain. Welcome, my friends all!

Aside to Sebastian and Antonio.

But you, my brace of lords, were I so minded,
I here could pluck his Highness' frown upon you
And justify you traitors. At this time
I will tell no tales.

Sebastian.

Aside.

     The devil speaks in him.

Prospero.

      No.
For you, most wicked sir, whom to call brother
Would even infect my mouth, I do forgive
Thy rankest fault—all of them; and require
My dukedom of thee, which perforce, I know
Thou must restore.

Alonso.

     If thou beest Prospero,
Give us particulars of thy preservation,
How thou hast met us here, whom three hours since
Were wrack'd upon this shore; where I have lost
(How sharp the point of this remembrance is!)
My dear son Ferdinand.

Prospero.

     I am woe for't, sir.

Alonso.
Irreparable is the loss, and patience
Says, it is past her cure.

Prospero.

     I rather think
You have not sought her help, of whose soft grace
For the like loss I have her sovereign aid,
And rest myself content.

Alonso.

     You the like loss?

Prospero.
As great to me as late, and supportable
To make the dear loss, have I means much weaker
Than you may call to comfort you; for I
Have lost my daughter.

Alonso.

     A daughter?
O heavens, that they were living both in Naples,
The King and Queen there! That they were, I wish
Myself were mudded in that oozy bed
Where my son lies. When did you lose your daughter?

Prospero.
In this last tempest. I perceive these lords
At this encounter do so much admire
That they devour their reason, and scarce think
Their eyes do offices of truth, their words
Are natural breath; but howsoev'r you have
Been justled from your senses, know for certain
That I am Prospero, and that very duke
Which was thrust forth of Milan, who most strangely
Upon this shore (where you were wrack'd) was landed,
To be the lord on't. No more yet of this,
For 'tis a chronicle of day by day,
Not a relation for a breakfast, nor
Befitting this first meeting. Welcome, sir;
This cell's my court. Here have I few attendants,
And subjects none abroad. Pray you look in.
My dukedom since you have given me again,
I will requite you with as good a thing,
At least bring forth a wonder, to content ye
As much as me my dukedom.

Here Prospero discovers Ferdinand and Miranda playing at chess.

Miranda.
Sweet lord, you play me false.

Ferdinand.
                    No, my dearest love,
I would not for the world.

Miranda.
Yes, for a score of kingdoms you should wrangle,
And I would call it fair play.

Alonso.
                        If this prove
A vision of the island, one dear son
Shall I twice lose.

Sebastian.
                      A most high miracle!

Ferdinand.
Though the seas threaten, they are merciful;
I have curs'd them without cause.

Kneels.

Alonso.
                Now all the blessings
Of a glad father compass thee about!
Arise, and say how thou cam'st here.

Miranda.
                      O wonder!
How many goodly creatures are there here!
How beauteous mankind is! O brave new world
That has such people in't!

Prospero.
                  'Tis new to thee.

Alonso.
What is this maid with whom thou wast at play?
Your eld'st acquaintance cannot be three hours.
Is she the goddess that hath sever'd us,
And brought us thus together?

Ferdinand.
                    Sir, she is mortal;
But by immortal Providence she's mine.
I chose her when I could not ask my father
For his advice, nor thought I had one. She
Is daughter to this famous Duke of Milan,
Of whom so often I have heard renown,
But never saw before; of whom I have
Receiv'd a second life; and second father
This lady makes him to me.

Alonso.
                        I am hers.
But O, how oddly will it sound that I
Must ask my child forgiveness!

Prospero.
                    There, sir, stop.
Let us not burden our remembrances with
A heaviness that's gone.

Gonzalo.
                  I have inly wept,
Or should have spoke ere this. Look down, you gods,
And on this couple drop a blessed crown!
For it is you that have chalk'd forth the way
Which brought us hither.

Alonso.
                  I say amen, Gonzalo!

Gonzalo.
Was Milan thrust from Milan, that his issue
Should become kings of Naples? O, rejoice
Beyond a common joy, and set it down
With gold on lasting pillars: in one voyage
Did Claribel her husband find at Tunis,
And Ferdinand, her brother, found a wife
Where he himself was lost; Prospero, his dukedom
In a poor isle; and all of us, ourselves,
When no man was his own.

Alonso.

To Ferdinand and Miranda.
                  Give me your hands.
Let grief and sorrow still embrace his heart
That doth not wish you joy!

Gonzalo.
                Be it so, amen!

Enter Ariel, with the Master and Boatswain amazedly following.

O, look, sir, look, sir, here is more of us.
I prophesied, if a gallows were on land,
This fellow could not drown. Now, blasphemy,
That swear'st grace o'erboard, not an oath on shore?
Hast thou no mouth by land? What is the news?

Boatswain.
The best news is, that we have safely found
Our king and company; the next, our ship—
Which, but three glasses since, we gave out split—
Is tight and yare, and bravely rigg'd as when
We first put out to sea.

Ariel.

Aside to Prospero

                Sir, all this service
Have I done since I went.

Prospero.

Aside to Ariel

                    My tricksy spirit!

Alonso.
These are not natural events, they strengthen
From strange to stranger. Say, how came you hither?

Boatswain.
If I did think, sir, I were well awake,
I'd strive to tell you. We were dead of sleep,
And (how we know not) all clapp'd under hatches,
Where, but even now, with strange and several noises
Of roaring, shrieking, howling, jingling chains,
And more diversity of sounds, all horrible,
We were awak'd; straightway, at liberty;
Where we, in all our trim, freshly beheld
Our royal, good, and gallant ship; our master
Cap'ring to eye her. On a trice, so please you,
Even in a dream, were we divided from them,
And were brought moping hither.

Ariel.

Aside to Prospero

                    Was't well done?

Prospero.

Aside to Ariel

Bravely, my diligence. Thou shalt be free.

Alonso.
This is as strange a maze as e'er men trod,
And there is in this business more than nature
Was ever conduct of. Some oracle
Must rectify our knowledge.

Prospero.
                    Sir, my liege,
Do not infest your mind with beating on
The strangeness of this business. At pick'd leisure,
Which shall be shortly, single I'll resolve you
(Which to you shall seem probable) of every
These happen'd accidents; till when, be cheerful
And think of each thing well.

Aside to Ariel.

                Come hither, spirit.
Set Caliban and his companions free;
Untie the spell.

Exit Ariel.

              How fares my gracious sir?
There are yet missing of your company
Some few odd lads that you remember not.

Enter Ariel, driving in Caliban, Stephano, and Trinculo in their stol'n apparel.

Stephano.
Every man shift for all the rest, and let no man take care for himself; for all is but fortune. Coraggio, bully-monster, coraggio!

Trinculo.
If these be true spies which I wear in my head, here's a goodly sight.

Caliban.
O Setebos, these be brave spirits indeed!
How fine my master is! I am afraid
He will chastise me.

Sebastian.
                Ha, ha!
What things are these, my Lord Antonio?
Will money buy 'em?

Antonio.
              Very like; one of them
Is a plain fish, and no doubt marketable.

Prospero.
Mark but the badges of these men, my lords,
Then say if they be true. This misshapen knave—
His mother was a witch, and one so strong
That could control the moon, make flows and ebbs,
And deal in her command without her power.
These three have robb'd me, and this demi-devil

(For he's a bastard one) had plotted with them
To take my life. Two of these fellows you
Must know and own, this thing of darkness I
Acknowledge mine.

Caliban.
                  I shall be pinch'd to death.

Alonso.
Is not this Stephano, my drunken butler?

Sebastian.
He is drunk now. Where had he wine?

Alonso.
And Trinculo is reeling ripe. Where should they
Find this grand liquor that hath gilded 'em?
How cam'st thou in this pickle?

Trinculo.
I have been in such a pickle since I saw you last that
I fear me will never out of my bones. I shall not fear
fly-blowing.

Sebastian.
Why, how now, Stephano?

Stephano.
O, touch me not, I am not Stephano, but a cramp.

Prospero.
You'd be king o' the isle, sirrah?

Stephano.
I should have been a sore one then.

Alonso.
This is a strange thing as e'er I look'd on.

Pointing to Caliban.

Prospero.
He is as disproportion'd in his manners
As in his shape. Go, sirrah, to my cell;
Take with you your companions. As you look
To have my pardon, trim it handsomely.

Caliban.
Ay, that I will; and I'll be wise hereafter,
And seek for grace. What a thrice-double ass
Was I to take this drunkard for a god,
And worship this dull fool!

Prospero.
          Go to, away!

Alonso.
Hence, and bestow your luggage where you found it.

Sebastian.
Or stole it, rather.

Exeunt Caliban, Stephano, and Trinculo.

Prospero.
Sir, I invite your Highness and your train
To my poor cell, where you shall take your rest
For this one night; which, part of it, I'll waste
With such discourse as, I not doubt, shall make it
Go quick away—the story of my life,
And the particular accidents gone by
Since I came to this isle. And in the morn
I'll bring you to your ship, and so to Naples,
Where I have hope to see the nuptial
Of these our dear-belov'd solemnized,
And thence retire me to my Milan, where
Every third thought shall be my grave.

Alonso.
                I long
To hear the story of your life, which must
Take the ear strangely.

Prospero.
                I'll deliver all,
And promise you calm seas, auspicious gales,
And sail so expeditious, that shall catch
Your royal fleet far off.

Aside to Ariel.
                My Ariel, chick,
That is thy charge. Then to the elements
Be free, and fare thou well!—Please you draw near.

Exeunt omnes.

Epilogue

(Prospero)

Prospero, bereft of his magic, asks the audience's help to send him home.

Prospero.
Now my charms are all o'erthrown,
And what strength I have's mine own,

Epilogue

Which is most faint. Now 'tis true,
I must be here confin'd by you,
Or sent to Naples. Let me not,
Since I have my dukedom got,
And pardon'd the deceiver, dwell
In this bare island by your spell,
But release me from my bands
With the help of your good hands.
Gentle breath of yours my sails
Must fill, or else my project fails,
Which was to please. Now I want
Spirits to enforce, art to enchant,
And my ending is despair,
Unless I be reliev'd by prayer,
Which pierces so, that it assaults
Mercy itself, and frees all faults.
As you from crimes would pardon'd be,
Let your indulgence set me free.

Exit.

The Comedy of Errors

Act 1

Scene 1

A hall in Duke Solinus's Palace.

(Duke of Ephesus; Egeon; Jailer; Officers; Attendants)

Egeon, a merchant of Syracuse, has been condemned to death by the Duke of Ephesus for daring to appear in Ephesus. Egeon tells the story of how he was separated from his wife and one of their twin sons by a storm at sea. When the son who remained with him reached the age of 18, he became inquisitive and asked to be able to try and find his bother. For five years, they searched in vain. Affected by the tale, the Duke gives Egeon a day's reprieve from execution to try to raise a 1000 marks to pay a fine rather than being killed.

Enter the Duke of Ephesus with Egeon the merchant of Syracuse, Jailer with Officers, and other Attendants.

Egeon.
Proceed, Solinus, to procure my fall,
And by the doom of death end woes and all.

Solinus, Duke of Ephesus.
Merchant of Syracuse, plead no more.
I am not partial to infringe our laws;
The enmity and discord which of late
Sprung from the rancorous outrage of your Duke
To merchants, our well-dealing countrymen,
Who, wanting guilders to redeem their lives,
Have seal'd his rigorous statutes with their bloods,
Excludes all pity from our threat'ning looks:
For since the mortal and intestine jars
'Twixt thy seditious countrymen and us,
It hath in solemn synods been decreed,
Both by the Syracusians and ourselves,
To admit no traffic to our adverse towns:
Nay more, if any born at Ephesus be seen
At any Syracusian marts and fairs;
Again, if any Syracusian born
Come to the bay of Ephesus, he dies,
His goods confiscate to the Duke's dispose,
Unless a thousand marks be levied
To quit the penalty and to ransom him.
Thy substance, valued at the highest rate,
Cannot amount unto a hundred marks,
Therefore by law thou art condemn'd to die.

Egeon.
Yet this my comfort, when your words are done,
My woes end likewise with the evening sun.

Solinus, Duke of Ephesus.
Well, Syracusian; say in brief the cause
Why thou departedst from thy native home,
And for what cause thou cam'st to Ephesus.

Egeon.
A heavier task could not have been impos'd
Than I to speak my griefs unspeakable:
Yet that the world may witness that my end
Was wrought by nature, not by vile offense,
I'll utter what my sorrow gives me leave.
In Syracuse was I born, and wed
Unto a woman, happy but for me,
And by me, had not our hap been bad:
With her I liv'd in joy; our wealth increas'd
By prosperous voyages I often made
To Epidamium, till my factor's death,
And the great care of goods at random left,
Drew me from kind embracements of my spouse;

From whom my absence was not six months old
Before herself (almost at fainting under
The pleasing punishment that women bear)
Had made provision for her following me,
And soon, and safe, arrived where I was.
There had she not been long but she became
A joyful mother of two goodly sons:
And, which was strange, the one so like the other
As could not be distinguish'd but by names.
That very hour, and in the self-same inn,
A mean woman was delivered
Of such a burden male, twins both alike.
Those, for their parents were exceeding poor,
I bought, and brought up to attend my sons.
My wife, not meanly proud of two such boys,
Made daily motions for our home return:
Unwilling I agreed. Alas! Too soon
We came aboard.
A league from Epidamium had we sail'd
Before the always-wind-obeying deep
Gave any tragic instance of our harm:
But longer did we not retain much hope;
For what obscured light the heavens did grant
Did but convey unto our fearful minds
A doubtful warrant of immediate death,
Which though myself would gladly have embrac'd,
Yet the incessant weepings of my wife,
Weeping before for what she saw must come,
And piteous plainings of the pretty babes,
That mourn'd for fashion, ignorant what to fear,
Forc'd me to seek delays for them and me.
And this it was (for other means was none):
The sailors sought for safety by our boat,
And left the ship, then sinking-ripe, to us.
My wife, more careful for the latter-born,
Had fast'ned him unto a small spare mast,
Such as sea-faring men provide for storms;
To him one of the other twins was bound,
Whilst I had been like heedful of the other.
The children thus dispos'd, my wife and I,
Fixing our eyes on whom our care was fix'd,
Fast'ned ourselves at either end the mast,
And floating straight, obedient to the stream,
Was carried towards Corinth, as we thought.
At length the sun, gazing upon the earth,
Dispers'd those vapors that offended us,
And by the benefit of his wished light
The seas wax'd calm, and we discovered
Two ships from far, making amain to us,
Of Corinth that, of Epidaurus this.
But ere they came—O, let me say no more!
Gather the sequel by that went before.

Solinus, Duke of Ephesus.
Nay, forward, old man, do not break off so,
For we may pity, though not pardon thee.

Egeon.
O, had the gods done so, I had not now
Worthily term'd them merciless to us!
For ere the ships could meet by twice five leagues,
We were encount'red by a mighty rock,
Which being violently borne upon,
Our helpful ship was splitted in the midst;
So that, in this unjust divorce of us,
Fortune had left to both of us alike
What to delight in, what to sorrow for.
Her part, poor soul! Seeming as burdened
With lesser weight, but not with lesser woe,
Was carried with more speed before the wind,
And in our sight they three were taken up
By fishermen of Corinth, as we thought.
At length, another ship had seiz'd on us,
And knowing whom it was their hap to save,
Gave healthful welcome to their shipwrack'd guests,
And would have reft the fishers of their prey,
Had not their bark been very slow of sail;
And therefore homeward did they bend their course.
Thus have you heard me sever'd from my bliss,
That by misfortunes was my life prolong'd,
To tell sad stories of my own mishaps.

Solinus, Duke of Ephesus.
And for the sake of them thou sorrowest for,
Do me the favor to dilate at full
What have befall'n of them and thee till now.

Egeon.
My youngest boy, and yet my eldest care,
At eighteen years became inquisitive
After his brother; and importun'd me
That his attendant—so his case was like,
Reft of his brother, but retain'd his name—
Might bear him company in the quest of him:
Whom whilst I labored of a love to see,
I hazarded the loss of whom I lov'd.
Five summers have I spent in farthest Greece,
Roaming clean through the bounds of Asia,
And coasting homeward, came to Ephesus;
Hopeless to find, yet loath to leave unsought
Or that, or any place that harbors men.

But here must end the story of my life,
And happy were I in my timely death,
Could all my travels warrant me they live.

Solinus, Duke of Ephesus.
Hapless Egeon, whom the fates have mark'd
To bear the extremity of dire mishap!
Now trust me, were it not against our laws,
Against my crown, my oath, my dignity,
Which princes, would they, may not disannul,
My soul should sue as advocate for thee:
But though thou art adjudged to the death,
And passed sentence may not be recall'd
But to our honor's great disparagement,
Yet will I favor thee in what I can;
Therefore, merchant, I'll limit thee this day
To seek thy health by beneficial help.
Try all the friends thou hast in Ephesus;
Beg thou, or borrow, to make up the sum,
And live: if no, then thou art doom'd to die.
Jailer, take him to thy custody.

Jailer.
I will, my lord.

Egeon.
Hopeless and helpless doth Egeon wend,
But to procrastinate his lifeless end.

Exeunt.

Scene 2

The mart.

(Antipholus Erotes of Syracuse; First Merchant; Dromio of Syracuse; Dromio of Ephesus)

Antipholus of Syracuse is warned by a merchant not to divulge his nationality for fear of being executed. He sends his servant, Dromio of Syracuse, to his inn with 1000 marks. He invites the merchant to dine with him, but having other engagements the merchant instead promises to meet him at five. Dromio of Ephesus comes in, sent by Adriana to search for his master Antipholus of Ephesus, who is late to dinner. Antipholus of Syracuse asks about his money, but Dromio of Ephesus has no idea what he's talking about. Antipholus of Syracuse, thinking that Dromio is trying to be funny, beats him for persisting in the jest.

Enter Antipholus Erotes of Syracuse, First Merchant, and Dromio of Syracuse.

First Merchant.
Therefore give out you are of Epidamium,
Lest that your goods too soon be confiscate:
This very day a Syracusian merchant
Is apprehended for arrival here;
And not being able to buy out his life,
According to the statute of the town,
Dies ere the weary sun set in the west.
There is your money that I had to keep.

Antipholus of Syracuse.
Go bear it to the Centaur, where we host,
And stay there, Dromio, till I come to thee.
Within this hour it will be dinner-time;
Till that, I'll view the manners of the town,
Peruse the traders, gaze upon the buildings,
And then return and sleep within mine inn,
For with long travel I am stiff and weary.
Get thee away.

Dromio of Syracuse.
Many a man would take you at your word,
And go indeed, having so good a mean.

Exit Dromio.

Antipholus of Syracuse.
A trusty villain, sir, that very oft,
When I am dull with care and melancholy,
Lightens my humor with his merry jests.
What, will you walk with me about the town,
And then go to my inn and dine with me?

First Merchant.
I am invited, sir, to certain merchants,
Of whom I hope to make much benefit;
I crave your pardon. Soon at five a' clock,
Please you, I'll meet with you upon the mart,
And afterward consort you till bed-time:
My present business calls me from you now.

Antipholus of Syracuse.
Farewell till then. I will go lose myself,
And wander up and down to view the city.

First Merchant.
Sir, I commend you to your own content.

Exit.

Antipholus of Syracuse.
He that commends me to mine own content,
Commends me to the thing I cannot get:
I to the world am like a drop of water,
That in the ocean seeks another drop,
Who, falling there to find his fellow forth
(Unseen, inquisitive), confounds himself.
So I, to find a mother and a brother,
In quest of them (unhappy), ah, lose myself.

Enter Dromio of Ephesus.

Here comes the almanac of my true date.
What now? How chance thou art return'd so soon?

Dromio of Ephesus.
Return'd so soon! Rather approach'd too late:
The capon burns, the pig falls from the spit;
The clock hath strucken twelve upon the bell:
My mistress made it one upon my cheek:
She is so hot, because the meat is cold:
The meat is cold, because you come not home:
You come not home, because you have no stomach:
You have no stomach, having broke your fast:
But we that know what 'tis to fast and pray,
Are penitent for your default today.

Antipholus of Syracuse.
Stop in your wind, sir; tell me this, I pray:
Where have you left the money that I gave you?

Dromio of Ephesus.
O—sixpence that I had a' We'n'sday last
To pay the saddler for my mistress' crupper?
The saddler had it, sir, I kept it not.

Antipholus of Syracuse.
I am not in a sportive humor now:
Tell me, and dally not, where is the money?
We being strangers here, how dar'st thou trust
So great a charge from thine own custody?

Dromio of Ephesus.
I pray you jest, sir, as you sit at dinner.
I from my mistress come to you in post:
If I return, I shall be post indeed,
For she will score your fault upon my pate:
Methinks your maw, like mine, should be your clock,
And strike you home without a messenger.

Antipholus of Syracuse.
Come, Dromio, come, these jests are out of season,
Reserve them till a merrier hour than this:
Where is the gold I gave in charge to thee?

Dromio of Ephesus.
To me, sir? Why, you gave no gold to me.

Antipholus of Syracuse.
Come on, sir knave, have done your foolishness,
And tell me how thou hast dispos'd thy charge.

Dromio of Ephesus.
My charge was but to fetch you from the mart
Home to your house, the Phoenix, sir, to dinner;
My mistress and her sister stays for you.

Antipholus of Syracuse.
Now, as I am a Christian, answer me,
In what safe place you have bestow'd my money;
Or I shall break that merry sconce of yours
That stands on tricks when I am undispos'd:
Where is the thousand marks thou hadst of me?

Dromio of Ephesus.
I have some marks of yours upon my pate;
Some of my mistress' marks upon my shoulders;
But not a thousand marks between you both.
If I should pay your worship those again,
Perchance you will not bear them patiently.

Antipholus of Syracuse.
Thy mistress' marks? What mistress, slave, hast thou?

Dromio of Ephesus.
Your worship's wife, my mistress at the Phoenix;
She that doth fast till you come home to dinner;
And prays that you will hie you home to dinner.

Antipholus of Syracuse.
What, wilt thou flout me thus unto my face,
Being forbid? There, take you that, sir knave.

Strikes Dromio.

Dromio of Ephesus.
What mean you, sir? For God sake hold your hands!
Nay, and you will not, sir, I'll take my heels.

Exit Dromio of Ephesus.

Antipholus of Syracuse.
Upon my life, by some device or other
The villain is o'erraught of all my money.
They say this town is full of cozenage:
As nimble jugglers that deceive the eye,
Dark-working sorcerers that change the mind,
Soul-killing witches that deform the body,
Disguised cheaters, prating mountebanks,
And many such-like liberties of sin:
If it prove so, I will be gone the sooner.
I'll to the Centaur to go seek this slave;
I greatly fear my money is not safe.

Exit.

Act 2

Scene 1

The house of Antipholus of Ephesus.

(Adriana; Luciana; Dromio of Ephesus)

Adriana, while impatiently awaiting her husband, talks to her sister, Luciana, about men's mastery over women. Dromio of Ephesus arrives and tells her how oddly her husband has been behaving, but is sent back to fetch him regardless. Adriana fears that her beauty is fading and that her husband is therefore turning elsewhere.

Enter Adriana, wife to Antipholus Sereptus of Ephesus, with Luciana, her sister.

Adriana.
Neither my husband nor the slave return'd,
That in such haste I sent to seek his master?
Sure, Luciana, it is two a' clock.

Luciana.
Perhaps some merchant hath invited him,
And from the mart he's somewhere gone to dinner.
Good sister, let us dine, and never fret;
A man is master of his liberty:
Time is their master, and when they see time,
They'll go or come; if so, be patient, sister.

Adriana.
Why should their liberty than ours be more?

Luciana.
Because their business still lies out a' door.

Adriana.
Look when I serve him so, he takes it ill.

Luciana.
O, know he is the bridle of your will.

Adriana.
There's none but asses will be bridled so.

Luciana.
Why, headstrong liberty is lash'd with woe:
There's nothing situate under heaven's eye
But hath his bound in earth, in sea, in sky.
The beasts, the fishes, and the winged fowls
Are their males' subjects and at their controls:
Man, more divine, the master of all these,
Lord of the wide world and wild wat'ry seas,
Indu'd with intellectual sense and souls,
Of more pre-eminence than fish and fowls,
Are masters to their females, and their lords:
Then let your will attend on their accords.

Adriana.
This servitude makes you to keep unwed.

Luciana.
Not this, but troubles of the marriage-bed.

Adriana.
But, were you wedded, you would bear some sway.

Luciana.
Ere I learn love, I'll practice to obey.

Adriana.
How if your husband start some other where?

Luciana.
Till he come home again, I would forbear.

Adriana.
Patience unmov'd! No marvel though she pause—
They can be meek that have no other cause:
A wretched soul, bruis'd with adversity,
We bid be quiet when we hear it cry;
But were we burd'ned with like weight of pain,
As much, or more, we should ourselves complain:
So thou, that hast no unkind mate to grieve thee,
With urging helpless patience would relieve me;
But if thou live to see like right bereft,
This fool-begg'd patience in thee will be left.

Luciana.
Well, I will marry one day, but to try.
Here comes your man, now is your husband nigh.

Enter Dromio of Ephesus.

Adriana.
Say, is your tardy master now at hand?

Dromio of Ephesus.
Nay, he's at two hands with me, and that my two ears can witness.

Adriana.
Say, didst thou speak with him? Know'st thou his mind?

Dromio of Ephesus.
Ay, ay, he told his mind upon mine ear. Beshrew his hand, I scarce could understand it.

Luciana.
Spake he so doubtfully, thou couldst not feel his meaning?

Dromio of Ephesus.
Nay, he struck so plainly, I could too well feel his blows; and withal so doubtfully, that I could scarce understand them.

Adriana.
But say, I prithee, is he coming home?
It seems he hath great care to please his wife.

Dromio of Ephesus.
Why, mistress, sure my master is horn-mad.

Adriana.
Horn-mad, thou villain!

Dromio of Ephesus.
              I mean not cuckold-mad—
But sure he is stark mad:
When I desir'd him to come home to dinner,
He ask'd me for a thousand marks in gold:
"'Tis dinner-time," quoth I: "My gold!" quoth he.
"Your meat doth burn," quoth I: "My gold!" quoth he.
"Will you come?" quoth I: "My gold!" quoth he;
"Where is the thousand marks I gave thee, villain?"
"The pig," quoth I, "is burn'd": "My gold!" quoth he.
"My mistress, sir," quoth I: "Hang up thy mistress!
I know not thy mistress, out on thy mistress!"

Luciana.
Quoth who?

Dromio of Ephesus.
Quoth my master.
"I know," quoth he, "no house, no wife, no mistress."
So that my arrant, due unto my tongue,
I thank him, I bare home upon my shoulders:
For, in conclusion, he did beat me there.

Adriana.
Go back again, thou slave, and fetch him home.

Dromio of Ephesus.
Go back again, and be new beaten home?
For God's sake send some other messenger.

Adriana.
Back, slave, or I will break thy pate across.

Dromio of Ephesus.
And he will bless that cross with other beating:
Between you I shall have a holy head.

Adriana.
Hence, prating peasant! Fetch thy master home.

Dromio of Ephesus.
Am I so round with you, as you with me,
That like a football you do spurn me thus?
You spurn me hence, and he will spurn me hither:
If I last in this service, you must case me in leather.

Exit.

Luciana.
Fie, how impatience low'reth in your face!

Adriana.
His company must do his minions grace,
Whilst I at home starve for a merry look:
Hath homely age th' alluring beauty took
From my poor cheek? Then he hath wasted it.
Are my discourses dull? Barren my wit?
If voluble and sharp discourse be marr'd,
Unkindness blunts it more than marble hard.
Do their gay vestments his affections bait?
That's not my fault, he's master of my state.
What ruins are in me that can be found,
By him not ruin'd? Then is he the ground
Of my defeatures. My decayed fair
A sunny look of his would soon repair.
But, too unruly deer, he breaks the pale,

And feeds from home; poor I am but his stale.

Luciana.
Self-harming jealousy—fie, beat it hence!

Adriana.
Unfeeling fools can with such wrongs dispense:
I know his eye doth homage otherwhere,
Or else what lets it but he would be here?
Sister, you know he promis'd me a chain;
Would that alone a' love he would detain,
So he would keep fair quarter with his bed!
I see the jewel best enamelled
Will lose his beauty; yet the gold bides still
That others touch and, often touching, will
Where gold; and no man that hath a name
By falsehood and corruption doth it shame.
Since that my beauty cannot please his eye,
I'll weep what's left away, and weeping die.

Luciana.
How many fond fools serve mad jealousy?

Exeunt.

Scene 2

A public place.

(*Antipholus Erotes of Syracuse; Dromio of Syracuse; Adriana; Luciana*)

Antipholus of Syracuse has discovered that Dromio of Syracuse did in fact deposit his money. The servant is confused at his master's claims of his playing a bad joke and does not understand what he has done to deserve a beating. Adriana and Luciana enter and mistake the two for husband and servant. The Syracusian Antipholus and Dromio are amazed at what is said to them. Adriana says she sent for Antipholus by Dromio (of Ephesus) and Dromio (of Syracuse) denies he ever spoke with the woman. Antipholus feels sure, because of what Dromio of Syracuse said to him, that he must have spoken to her. Dazed to be addressed lovingly by this unknown woman, Antipholus of Ephesus allows himself to be taken home by Adriana, who gives Dromio of Syracuse orders to see that nobody disturbs them while they dine together. The fact that these ladies they have never met know their names leaves Antipholus and Dromio wondering what witchcraft is at work.

Enter Antipholus Erotes of Syracuse.

Antipholus of Syracuse.
The gold I gave to Dromio is laid up
Safe at the Centaur, and the heedful slave
Is wand'red forth, in care to seek me out.
By computation and mine host's report,
I could not speak with Dromio since at first
I sent him from the mart! See, here he comes.

Enter Dromio of Syracuse.

How now, sir, is your merry humor alter'd?
As you love strokes, so jest with me again.
You know no Centaur? You receiv'd no gold?
Your mistress sent to have me home to dinner?
My house was at the Phoenix? Wast thou mad,
That thus so madly thou didst answer me?

Dromio of Syracuse.
What answer, sir? When spake I such a word?

Antipholus of Syracuse.
Even now, even here, not half an hour since.

Dromio of Syracuse.
I did not see you since you sent me hence
Home to the Centaur with the gold you gave me.

Antipholus of Syracuse.
Villain, thou didst deny the gold's receipt,
And toldst me of a mistress, and a dinner,
For which I hope thou feltst I was displeas'd.

Dromio of Syracuse.
I am glad to see you in this merry vein.
What means this jest? I pray you, master, tell me.

Antipholus of Syracuse.
Yea, dost thou jeer and flout me in the teeth?
Think'st thou I jest? Hold, take thou that, and that.

Beats Dromio.

Dromio of Syracuse.
Hold, sir, for God's sake! Now your jest is earnest,
Upon what bargain do you give it me?

Antipholus of Syracuse.
Because that I familiarly sometimes
Do use you for my fool, and chat with you,
Your sauciness will jest upon my love,
And make a common of my serious hours.
When the sun shines, let foolish gnats make sport,
But creep in crannies, when he hides his beams:
If you will jest with me, know my aspect,

Act 2, Scene 2

And fashion your demeanor to my looks,
Or I will beat this method in your sconce.

Dromio of Syracuse.
Sconce call you it? So you would leave battering, I had rather have it a head. And you use these blows long, I must get a sconce for my head, and ensconce it too, or else I shall seek my wit in my shoulders. But I pray, sir, why am I beaten?

Antipholus of Syracuse.
Dost thou not know?

Dromio of Syracuse.
Nothing, sir, but that I am beaten.

Antipholus of Syracuse.
Shall I tell you why?

Dromio of Syracuse.
Ay, sir, and wherefore; for they say, every why hath a wherefore.

Antipholus of Syracuse.
Why first—for flouting me, and then wherefore—
For urging it the second time to me.

Dromio of Syracuse.
Was there ever any man thus beaten out of season,
When in the why and the wherefore is neither rhyme nor reason?
Well, sir, I thank you.

Antipholus of Syracuse.
Thank me, sir, for what?

Dromio of Syracuse.
Marry, sir, for this something that you gave me for nothing.

Antipholus of Syracuse.
I'll make you amends next, to give you nothing for something. But say, sir, is it dinner-time?

Dromio of Syracuse.
No, sir, I think the meat wants that I have.

Antipholus of Syracuse.
In good time, sir: what's that?

Dromio of Syracuse.
Basting.

Antipholus of Syracuse.
Well, sir, then 'twill be dry.

Dromio of Syracuse.
If it be, sir, I pray you eat none of it.

Antipholus of Syracuse.
Your reason?

Dromio of Syracuse.
Lest it make you choleric, and purchase me another dry basting.

Antipholus of Syracuse.
Well, sir, learn to jest in good time—there's a time for all things.

Dromio of Syracuse.
I durst have denied that before you were so choleric.

Antipholus of Syracuse.
By what rule, sir?

Dromio of Syracuse.
Marry, sir, by a rule as plain as the plain bald pate of Father Time himself.

Antipholus of Syracuse.
Let's hear it.

Dromio of Syracuse.
There's no time for a man to recover his hair that grows bald by nature.

Antipholus of Syracuse.
May he not do it by fine and recovery?

Dromio of Syracuse.
Yes, to pay a fine for a periwig, and recover the lost hair of another man.

Antipholus of Syracuse.
Why is Time such a niggard of hair, being (as it is) so plentiful an excrement?

Dromio of Syracuse.
Because it is a blessing that he bestows on beasts, and what he hath scanted men in hair he hath given them in wit.

Antipholus of Syracuse.
Why, but there's many a man hath more hair than wit.

Dromio of Syracuse.
Not a man of those but he hath the wit to lose his hair.

Antipholus of Syracuse.
Why, thou didst conclude hairy men plain dealers without wit.

Dromio of Syracuse.
The plainer dealer, the sooner lost; yet he loseth it in a kind of jollity.

Antipholus of Syracuse.
For what reason?

Dromio of Syracuse.
For two—and sound ones too.

Antipholus of Syracuse.
Nay, not sound, I pray you.

Dromio of Syracuse.
Sure ones then.

Antipholus of Syracuse.
Nay, not sure, in a thing falsing.

Dromio of Syracuse.
Certain ones then.

Antipholus of Syracuse.
Name them.

Dromio of Syracuse.
The one, to save the money that he spends in tiring; the other, that at dinner they should not drop in his porridge.

Antipholus of Syracuse.
You would all this time have prov'd there is no time for all things.

Dromio of Syracuse.
Marry, and did, sir: namely, e'en no time to recover hair lost by nature.

Antipholus of Syracuse.
But your reason was not substantial, why there is no time to recover.

Dromio of Syracuse.
Thus I mend it: Time himself is bald, and therefore, to the world's end, will have bald followers.

Antipholus of Syracuse.
I knew 'twould be a bald conclusion. But soft, who wafts us yonder?

Enter Adriana and Luciana.

Adriana.
Ay, ay, Antipholus, look strange and frown,
Some other mistress hath thy sweet aspects:
I am not Adriana, nor thy wife.
The time was once, when thou unurg'd wouldst vow
That never words were music to thine ear,
That never object pleasing in thine eye,
That never touch well welcome to thy hand,
That never meat sweet-savor'd in thy taste,
Unless I spake, or look'd, or touch'd, or carv'd to thee.
How comes it now, my husband, O, how comes it,
That thou art then estranged from thyself?
Thyself I call it, being strange to me,
That, undividable incorporate,
Am better than thy dear self's better part.
Ah, do not tear away thyself from me;
For know, my love, as easy mayst thou fall
A drop of water in the breaking gulf,
And take unmingled thence that drop again,
Without addition or diminishing,
As take from me thyself and not me too.
How dearly would it touch thee to the quick,
Shouldst thou but hear I were licentious,
And that this body, consecrate to thee,
By ruffian lust should be contaminate?
Wouldst thou not spit at me, and spurn at me,
And hurl the name of husband in my face,
And tear the stain'd skin off my harlot brow,
And from my false hand cut the wedding-ring,
And break it with a deep-divorcing vow?
I know thou canst, and therefore see thou do it.
I am possess'd with an adulterate blot;
My blood is mingled with the crime of lust:
For if we two be one, and thou play false,
I do digest the poison of thy flesh,
Being strumpeted by thy contagion.
Keep then fair league and truce with thy true bed,
I live dis-stain'd, thou undishonored.

Antipholus of Syracuse.
Plead you to me, fair dame? I know you not:
In Ephesus I am but two hours old,
As strange unto your town as to your talk,
Who, every word by all my wit being scann'd,
Wants wit in all one word to understand.

Luciana.
Fie, brother, how the world is chang'd with you:
When were you wont to use my sister thus?
She sent for you by Dromio home to dinner.

Antipholus of Syracuse.
By Dromio?

Dromio of Syracuse.
By me?

Adriana.
By thee, and this thou didst return from him,
That he did buffet thee, and in his blows
Denied my house for his, me for his wife.

Antipholus of Syracuse.
Did you converse, sir, with this gentlewoman?
What is the course and drift of your compact?

Dromio of Syracuse.
I, sir? I never saw her till this time.

Antipholus of Syracuse.
Villain, thou liest, for even her very words
Didst thou deliver to me on the mart.

Dromio of Syracuse.
I never spake with her in all my life.

Antipholus of Syracuse.
How can she thus then call us by our names,
Unless it be by inspiration?

Adriana.
How ill agrees it with your gravity
To counterfeit thus grossly with your slave,
Abetting him to thwart me in my mood!
Be it my wrong you are from me exempt,
But wrong not that wrong with a more contempt.
Come, I will fasten on this sleeve of thine:
Thou art an elm, my husband, I a vine,
Whose weakness, married to thy stronger state,
Makes me with thy strength to communicate:
If aught possess thee from me, it is dross,
Usurping ivy, brier, or idle moss,
Who, all for want of pruning, with intrusion
Infect thy sap, and live on thy confusion.

Antipholus of Syracuse.
To me she speaks, she moves me for her theme:
What, was I married to her in my dream?
Or sleep I now and think I hear all this?
What error drives our eyes and ears amiss?
Until I know this sure uncertainty,
I'll entertain the offer'd fallacy.

Luciana.
Dromio, go bid the servants spread for dinner.

Dromio of Syracuse.
O for my beads! I cross me for a sinner.
This is the fairy land. O spite of spites!
We talk with goblins, owls, and sprites;
If we obey them not, this will ensue:
they'll suck our breath, or pinch us black and blue.

Luciana.
Why prat'st thou to thyself, and answer'st not?
Dromio, thou drumble, thou snail, thou slug, thou sot!

Dromio of Syracuse.
I am transformed, master, am not I?

Antipholus of Syracuse.
I think thou art in mind, and so am I.

Dromio of Syracuse.
Nay, master, both in mind and in my shape.

Antipholus of Syracuse.
Thou hast thine own form.

Dromio of Syracuse.
                    No, I am an ape.

Luciana.
If thou art chang'd to aught, 'tis to an ass.

Dromio of Syracuse.
'Tis true she rides me and I long for grass.
'Tis so, I am an ass, else it could never be
But I should know her as well as she knows me.

Adriana.
Come, come, no longer will I be a fool,
To put the finger in the eye and weep,
Whilst man and master laughs my woes to scorn.
Come, sir, to dinner. Dromio, keep the gate.
Husband, I'll dine above with you today,
And shrive you of a thousand idle pranks.
Sirrah, if any ask you for your master,
Say he dines forth, and let no creature enter.
Come, sister. Dromio, play the porter well.

Antipholus of Syracuse.
Am I in earth, in heaven, or in hell?
Sleeping or waking, mad or well-advis'd?
Known unto these, and to myself disguis'd?
I'll say as they say, and persever so,

And in this mist at all adventures go.

Dromio of Syracuse.
Master, shall I be porter at the gate?

Adriana.
Ay, and let none enter, lest I break your pate.

Luciana.
Come, come, Antipholus, we dine too late.

Exeunt.

Act 3

Scene 1

Before the house of Antipholus of Ephesus.

(Antipholus of Ephesus; Dromio of Ephesus; Angelo; Balthazar; Luce; Adriana; Dromio of Syracuse)

Antipholus of Ephesus invites the merchant Balthazar and Angelo the goldsmith to dine with him, asking them to support his excuse for being late. Antipholus calls Dromio of Ephesus drunk for trying to tell him that he raved about 1000 marks and denied his wife. When Antipholus of Ephesus knocks at the door of his house, Dromio of Syracuse, keeping the door within, refuses to let him enter. Luce the servant also refuses to let them in, as does Adriana, who insults Antipholus of Ephesus when he calls her his wife. Dromio of Ephesus is surprised that the keeper of the door is called Dromio and thinks he has usurped his name as well as his job. When Antipholus of Ephesus plans to break the door down, Balthazar advises him not to but simply to dine elsewhere. Out of spite Antipholus decides they should eat at a Courtezan's, and plans to give her a chain intended for his wife.

Enter Antipholus of Ephesus, his man Dromio of Ephesus, Angelo the goldsmith, and Balthazar the merchant.

Antipholus of Ephesus.
Good Signior Angelo, you must excuse us all,
My wife is shrewish when I keep not hours:
Say that I linger'd with you at your shop
To see the making of her carcanet,
And that tomorrow you will bring it home.
But here's a villain that would face me down
He met me on the mart, and that I beat him,
And charg'd him with a thousand marks in gold,
And that I did deny my wife and house.
Thou drunkard, thou, what didst thou mean by this?

Dromio of Ephesus.
Say what you will, sir, but I know what I know:
That you beat me at the mart, I have your hand to show;
If the skin were parchment, and the blows you gave were ink,
Your own handwriting would tell you what I think.

Antipholus of Ephesus.
I think thou art an ass.

Dromio of Ephesus.
     Marry, so it doth appear
By the wrongs I suffer, and the blows I bear.
I should kick, being kick'd, and being at that pass,
You would keep from my heels, and beware of an ass.

Antipholus of Ephesus.
Y' are sad, Signior Balthazar, pray God our cheer
May answer my good will and your good welcome here.

Balthazar.
I hold your dainties cheap, sir, and your welcome dear.

Antipholus of Ephesus.
O, Signior Balthazar, either at flesh or fish,
A table full of welcome makes scarce one dainty dish.

Balthazar.
Good meat, sir, is common; that every churl affords.

Antipholus of Ephesus.
And welcome more common, for that's nothing but words.

Balthazar.
Small cheer and great welcome makes a merry feast.

Antipholus of Ephesus.
Ay, to a niggardly host and more sparing guest:
But though my cates be mean, take them in good part;
Better cheer may you have, but not with better heart.
But soft, my door is lock'd; go bid them let us in.

Dromio of Ephesus.
Maud, Bridget, Marian, Cic'ly, Gillian, Ginn!

Act 3, Scene 1

Dromio of Syracuse.

Within.

Mome, malt-horse, capon, cox-comb, idiot, patch!
Either get thee from the door, or sit down at the hatch;
Dost thou conjure for wenches, that thou call'st for such store,
When one is one too many? Go get thee from the door.

Dromio of Ephesus.
What patch is made our porter? My master stays in the street.

Dromio of Syracuse.

Within.

Let him walk from whence he came, lest he catch cold on 's feet.

Antipholus of Ephesus.
Who talks within there? Ho, open the door!

Dromio of Syracuse.

Within.

Right, sir, I'll tell you when, and you'll tell me wherefore.

Antipholus of Ephesus.
Wherefore? For my dinner: I have not din'd today.

Dromio of Syracuse.

Within.

Nor today here you must not, come again when you may.

Antipholus of Ephesus.
What art thou that keep'st me out from the house I owe?

Dromio of Syracuse.

Within.

The porter for this time, sir, and my name is Dromio.

Dromio of Ephesus.
O villain, thou hast stol'n both mine office and my name:
The one ne'er got me credit, the other mickle blame.
If thou hadst been Dromio today in my place,
Thou wouldst have chang'd thy face for a name, or thy name for an ass.

Enter Luce within.

Luce.

Within.

What a coil is there, Dromio?
Who are those at the gate?

Dromio of Ephesus.
Let my master in, Luce.

Luce.

Within.

          Faith, no, he comes too late,
And so tell your master.

Dromio of Ephesus.
          O Lord, I must laugh!
Have at you with a proverb—Shall I set in my staff?

Luce.

Within.

Have at you with another, that's—When? Can you tell?

Dromio of Syracuse.

Within.

If thy name be called Luce—Luce, thou hast answer'd him well.

Antipholus of Ephesus.
Do you hear, you minion? You'll let us in, I hope?

Luce.

Within.

I thought to have ask'd you.

Dromio of Syracuse.

Within.

          And you said no.

Dromio of Ephesus.
So come help: well struck! There was blow for blow.

Antipholus of Ephesus.
Thou baggage, let me in.

Luce.

Within.

            Can you tell for whose sake?

Dromio of Ephesus.
Master, knock the door hard.

Luce.

Within.

            Let him knock till it ache.

Antipholus of Ephesus.
You'll cry for this, minion, if I beat the door down.

Luce.

Within.

What needs all that, and a pair of stocks in the town?

Enter Adriana within.

Adriana.

Within.

Who is that at the door that keeps all this noise?

Dromio of Syracuse.

Within.

By my troth, your town is troubled with unruly boys.

Antipholus of Ephesus.
Are you there, wife? You might have come before.

Adriana.

Within.

Your wife, sir knave? Go get you from the door.

Dromio of Ephesus.
If you went in pain, master, this knave would go sore.

Angelo.
Here is neither cheer, sir, nor welcome: we would fain have either.

Balthazar.
In debating which was best, we shall part with neither.

Dromio of Ephesus.
They stand at the door, master, bid them welcome hither.

Antipholus of Ephesus.
There is something in the wind, that we cannot get in.

Dromio of Ephesus.
You would say so, master, if your garments were thin.
Your cake here is warm within: you stand here in the cold.
It would make a man mad as a buck to be so bought and sold.

Antipholus of Ephesus.
Go fetch me something: I'll break ope the gate.

Dromio of Syracuse.

Within.

Break any breaking here, and I'll break your knave's pate.

Dromio of Ephesus.
A man may break a word with you, sir, and words are but wind:
Ay, and break it in your face, so he break it not behind.

Dromio of Syracuse.

Within.

It seems thou want'st breaking, out upon thee, hind!

Dromio of Ephesus.
Here's too much "out upon thee!"; I pray thee let me in.

Dromio of Syracuse.

Within.

Ay, when fowls have no feathers, and fish have no fin.

Antipholus of Ephesus.
Well, I'll break in: go borrow me a crow.

Dromio of Ephesus.
A crow without feather? Master, mean you so?
For a fish without a fin, there's a fowl without a feather:
If a crow help us in, sirrah, we'll pluck a crow together.

Antipholus of Ephesus.
Go, get thee gone, fetch me an iron crow.

Act 3, Scene 2

Balthazar.
Have patience, sir, O, let it not be so!
Herein you war against your reputation,
And draw within the compass of suspect
Th' unviolated honor of your wife.
Once this—your long experience of her wisdom,
Her sober virtue, years, and modesty,
Plead on her part some cause to you unknown;
And doubt not, sir, but she will well excuse
Why at this time the doors are made against you.
Be rul'd by me, depart in patience,
And let us to the Tiger all to dinner;
And about evening come yourself alone
To know the reason of this strange restraint.
If by strong hand you offer to break in
Now in the stirring passage of the day,
A vulgar comment will be made of it;
And that supposed by the common rout
Against your yet ungalled estimation,
That may with foul intrusion enter in,
And dwell upon your grave when you are dead;
For slander lives upon succession,
Forever hous'd where it gets possession.

Antipholus of Ephesus.
You have prevail'd. I will depart in quiet,
And in despite of mirth mean to be merry.
I know a wench of excellent discourse,
Pretty and witty; wild, and yet, too, gentle;
There will we dine. This woman that I mean,
My wife (but, I protest, without desert)
Hath oftentimes upbraided me withal:
To her will we to dinner.

To Angelo.

Get you home
And fetch the chain; by this I know 'tis made.
Bring it, I pray you, to the Porpentine,
For there's the house. That chain will I bestow
(Be it for nothing but to spite my wife)
Upon mine hostess there. Good sir, make haste.
Since mine own doors refuse to entertain me,
I'll knock elsewhere, to see if they'll disdain me.

Angelo.
I'll meet you at that place some hour hence.

Antipholus of Ephesus.
Do so. This jest shall cost me some expense.

Exeunt.

Scene 2

Before the house of Antipholus of Ephesus.

(Luciana; Antipholus of Syracuse; Dromio of Syracuse; Angelo)

Luciana tells Antipholus of Syracuse he should at least pretend he loves his wife, but he protests he has no wife and makes love to her instead. Dromio of Syracuse reports that a fat kitchen wench claimed him as her own and told him of marks on his arms and shoulders, which made him fear she was a witch. Antipholus gives orders for Dromio to pack and plan to leave as soon as possible. Angelo the goldsmith, finding Antipholus of Syracuse in the street, gives him the chain, which Antipholus protests he has not ordered, but the goldsmith says he has ordered it 20 times. Angelo says he will come for the money when they meet at supper, though Antipholus remarks he had better take it at once. Antipholus thinks it an odd place where people give strangers chains of gold on the street.

Enter Luciana with Antipholus of Syracuse.

Luciana.
And may it be that you have quite forgot
A husband's office? Shall, Antipholus,
Even in the spring of love, thy love-springs rot?
Shall love, in building, grow so ruinous?
If you did wed my sister for her wealth,
Then for her wealth's sake use her with more kindness:
Or if you like elsewhere, do it by stealth,
Muffle your false love with some show of blindness:
Let not my sister read it in your eye;
Be not thy tongue thy own shame's orator:
Look sweet, speak fair, become disloyalty;
Apparel vice like virtue's harbinger;
Bear a fair presence, though your heart be tainted;
Teach sin the carriage of a holy saint;
Be secret-false: what need she be acquainted?
What simple thief brags of his own attaint?
'Tis double wrong, to truant with your bed,
And let her read it in thy looks at board:
Shame hath a bastard fame, well managed;
Ill deeds is doubled with an evil word.
Alas, poor women, make us but believe
(Being compact of credit) that you love us;
Though others have the arm, show us the sleeve:
We in your motion turn, and you may move us.
Then, gentle brother, get you in again;
Comfort my sister, cheer her, call her wife:

'Tis holy sport to be a little vain,
When the sweet breath of flattery conquers strife.

Antipholus of Syracuse.
Sweet mistress—what your name is else, I know not,
Nor by what wonder you do hit of mine—
Less in your knowledge and your grace you show not
Than our earth's wonder, more than earth divine.
Teach me, dear creature, how to think and speak:
Lay open to my earthy gross conceit,
Smoth'red in errors, feeble, shallow, weak,
The folded meaning of your words' deceit.
Against my soul's pure truth why labor you,
To make it wander in an unknown field?
Are you a god? Would you create me new?
Transform me then, and to your pow'r I'll yield.
But if that I am I, then well I know
Your weeping sister is no wife of mine,
Nor to her bed no homage do I owe:
Far more, far more, to you do I decline.
O, train me not, sweet mermaid, with thy note,
To drown me in thy sister's flood of tears.
Sing, siren, for thyself, and I will dote;
Spread o'er the silver waves thy golden hairs,
And as a bed I'll take them, and there lie,
And in that glorious supposition think
He gains by death that hath such means to die:
Let Love, being light, be drowned if she sink!

Luciana.
What, are you mad, that you do reason so?

Antipholus of Syracuse.
Not mad, but mated—how, I do not know.

Luciana.
It is a fault that springeth from your eye.

Antipholus of Syracuse.
For gazing on your beams, fair sun, being by.

Luciana.
Gaze when you should, and that will clear your sight.

Antipholus of Syracuse.
As good to wink, sweet love, as look on night.

Luciana.
Why call you me love? Call my sister so.

Antipholus of Syracuse.
Thy sister's sister.

Luciana.
That's my sister.

Antipholus of Syracuse.
No;
It is thyself, mine own self's better part:
Mine eye's clear eye, my dear heart's dearer heart,
My food, my fortune, and my sweet hope's aim,
My sole earth's heaven, and my heaven's claim.

Luciana.
All this my sister is, or else should be.

Antipholus of Syracuse.
Call thyself sister, sweet, for I am thee:
Thee will I love and with thee lead my life;
Thou hast no husband yet, nor I no wife.
Give me thy hand.

Luciana.
O soft, sir, hold you still;
I'll fetch my sister to get her good will.

Exit.
Enter Dromio of Syracuse.

Antipholus of Syracuse.
Why, how now, Dromio, where run'st thou so fast?

Dromio of Syracuse.
Do you know me, sir? Am I Dromio? Am I your man? Am I myself?

Antipholus of Syracuse.
Thou art Dromio, thou art my man, thou art thyself.

Dromio of Syracuse.
I am an ass, I am a woman's man, and besides myself.

Antipholus of Syracuse.
What woman's man, and how besides thyself?

Dromio of Syracuse.
Marry, sir, besides myself, I am due to a woman: one that claims me, one that haunts me, one that will have me.

Antipholus of Syracuse.
What claim lays she to thee?

Dromio of Syracuse.
Marry, sir, such claim as you would lay to your horse, and she would have me as a beast; not that, I being a beast, she would have me, but that she, being a very beastly creature, lays claim to me.

Antipholus of Syracuse.
What is she?

Dromio of Syracuse.
A very reverent body: ay, such a one as a man may not speak of without he say "Sir-reverence." I have but lean luck in the match, and yet is she a wondrous fat marriage.

Antipholus of Syracuse.
How dost thou mean a fat marriage?

Dromio of Syracuse.
Marry, sir, she's the kitchen wench and all grease, and I know not what use to put her to but to make a lamp of her and run from her by her own light. I warrant, her rags and the tallow in them will burn a Poland winter: if she lives till doomsday, she'll burn a week longer than the whole world.

Antipholus of Syracuse.
What complexion is she of?

Dromio of Syracuse.
Swart, like my shoe, but her face nothing like so clean kept: for why? She sweats, a man may go over shoes in the grime of it.

Antipholus of Syracuse.
That's a fault that water will mend.

Dromio of Syracuse.
No, sir, 'tis in grain, Noah's flood could not do it.

Antipholus of Syracuse.
What's her name?

Dromio of Syracuse.
Nell, sir; but her name and three quarters, that's an ell and three quarters, will not measure her from hip to hip.

Antipholus of Syracuse.
Then she bears some breadth?

Dromio of Syracuse.
No longer from head to foot than from hip to hip: she is spherical, like a globe; I could find out countries in her.

Antipholus of Syracuse.
In what part of her body stands Ireland?

Dromio of Syracuse.
Marry, sir, in her buttocks, I found it out by the bogs.

Antipholus of Syracuse.
Where Scotland?

Dromio of Syracuse.
I found it by the barrenness, hard in the palm of the hand.

Antipholus of Syracuse.
Where France?

Dromio of Syracuse.
In her forehead, arm'd and reverted, making war against her heir.

Antipholus of Syracuse.
Where England?

Dromio of Syracuse.
I look'd for the chalky cliffs, but I could find no whiteness in them. But I guess, it stood in her chin, by the salt rheum that ran between France and it.

Antipholus of Syracuse.
Where Spain?

Dromio of Syracuse.
Faith, I saw it not; but I felt it hot in her breath.

Antipholus of Syracuse.
Where America, the Indies?

Dromio of Syracuse.
O, sir, upon her nose, all o'er embellish'd with rubies, carbuncles, sapphires, declining their rich aspect to the hot breath of Spain, who sent whole armadoes of carrects to be ballast at her nose.

Antipholus of Syracuse.
Where stood Belgia, the Netherlands?

Dromio of Syracuse.
O, sir, I did not look so low. To conclude, this drudge or diviner laid claim to me, call'd me Dromio, swore I was assur'd to her, told me what privy marks I had about me, as the mark of my shoulder, the mole in my neck, the great wart on my left arm, that I, amaz'd, ran from her as a witch.
And I think, if my breast had not been made of faith, and my heart of steel,
She had transform'd me to a curtal dog, and made me turn i' th' wheel.

Antipholus of Syracuse.
Go hie thee presently, post to the road,
And if the wind blow any way from shore,
I will not harbor in this town tonight.
If any bark put forth, come to the mart,
Where I will walk till thou return to me.
If every one knows us, and we know none,
'Tis time, I think, to trudge, pack, and be gone.

Dromio of Syracuse.
As from a bear a man would run for life,
So fly I from her that would be my wife.

Exit.

Antipholus of Syracuse.
There's none but witches do inhabit here,
And therefore 'tis high time that I were hence.
She that doth call me husband, even my soul
Doth for a wife abhor. But her fair sister,
Possess'd with such a gentle sovereign grace,
Of such enchanting presence and discourse,
Hath almost made me traitor to myself;
But lest myself be guilty to self-wrong,
I'll stop mine ears against the mermaid's song.

Enter Angelo with the chain.

Angelo.
Master Antipholus—

Antipholus of Syracuse.
                    Ay, that's my name.

Angelo.
I know it well, sir. Lo here's the chain.
I thought to have ta'en you at the Porpentine;
The chain unfinish'd made me stay thus long.

Antipholus of Syracuse.
What is your will that I shall do with this?

Angelo.
What please yourself, sir; I have made it for you.

Antipholus of Syracuse.
Made it for me, sir! I bespoke it not.

Angelo.
Not once, nor twice, but twenty times you have.
Go home with it, and please your wife withal,
And soon at supper-time I'll visit you,
And then receive my money for the chain.

Antipholus of Syracuse.
I pray you, sir, receive the money now,
For fear you ne'er see chain nor money more.

Angelo.
You are a merry man, sir, fare you well.

Exit.

Antipholus of Syracuse.
What I should think of this, I cannot tell:
But this I think, there's no man is so vain
That would refuse so fair an offer'd chain.
I see a man here needs not live by shifts,
When in the streets he meets such golden gifts.
I'll to the mart and there for Dromio stay:
If any ship put out, then straight away.

Exit.

Act 4

Scene 1

A public place.

(Second Merchant; Angelo; Officer; Antipholus of Ephesus; Dromio of Ephesus; Dromio of Syracuse)

The Second Merchant asks Angelo for the money the goldsmith owes him. Angelo explains that he himself is waiting for a payment from Antipholus of Ephesus and will be able to pay at five o'clock. Antipholus and Dromio of Ephesus come from the Courtezan's, and Antipholus sends Dromio to find a rope for whipping the servants back at his house. Antipholus chides Angelo for not bringing the chain he promised to give the Courtezan. Angelo thinks Antipholus is joking and asks for his money. Antipholus tells him to get it from his wife, as he hasn't the sum with him, and to take the chain to her. Angelo asks for the chain, which Antipholus says he hasn't got, and the two get into an argument about who has it. The Second Merchant orders Angelo to be arrested and Angelo orders Antipholus of Ephesus to be arrested, both being very angry at this disgrace. Dromio of Syracuse comes to say he has found the ship and has loaded their goods aboard. Antipholus accuses him of being drunk since he sent the other Dromio for rope's end and tells him to go to Adriana to bail him out. Angelo and Antipholus are taken away, Dromio wonderingly obeys.

Enter Second Merchant, Angelo the goldsmith, and an Officer.

Act 4, Scene 1

Second Merchant.
You know since Pentecost the sum is due,
And since I have not much importun'd you,
Nor now I had not, but that I am bound
To Persia, and want guilders for my voyage:
Therefore make present satisfaction,
Or I'll attach you by this officer.

Angelo.
Even just the sum that I do owe to you
Is growing to me by Antipholus,
And in the instant that I met with you
He had of me a chain. At five a'clock
I shall receive the money for the same:
Pleaseth you walk with me down to his house,
I will discharge my bond, and thank you too.

Enter Antipholus of Ephesus, Dromio of Ephesus from the Courtezan's.

Officer.
That labor may you save; see where he comes.

Antipholus of Ephesus.
While I go to the goldsmith's house, go thou
And buy a rope's end; that will I bestow
Among my wife and her confederates,
For locking me out of my doors by day.
But soft, I see the goldsmith. Get thee gone,
Buy thou a rope, and bring it home to me.

Dromio of Ephesus.
I buy a thousand pound a year! I buy a rope!

Exit Dromio.

Antipholus of Ephesus.
A man is well help up that trusts to you:
I promised your presence and the chain,
But neither chain nor goldsmith came to me:
Belike you thought our love would last too long
If it were chain'd together, and therefore came not.

Angelo.
Saving your merry humor, here's the note
How much your chain weighs to the utmost carat,
The fineness of the gold, and chargeful fashion,
Which doth amount to three odd ducats more
Than I stand debted to this gentleman.
I pray you see him presently discharg'd,
For he is bound to sea, and stays but for it.

Antipholus of Ephesus.
I am not furnish'd with the present money:
Besides, I have some business in the town.
Good signior, take the stranger to my house,
And with you take the chain, and bid my wife
Disburse the sum on the receipt thereof.
Perchance I will be there as soon as you.

Angelo.
Then you will bring the chain to her yourself?

Antipholus of Ephesus.
No, bear it with you, lest I come not time enough.

Angelo.
Well, sir, I will. Have you the chain about you?

Antipholus of Ephesus.
And if I have not, sir, I hope you have:
Or else you may return without your money.

Angelo.
Nay, come, I pray you, sir, give me the chain:
Both wind and tide stays for this gentleman,
And I, to blame, have held him here too long.

Antipholus of Ephesus.
Good Lord! You use this dalliance to excuse
Your breach of promise to the Porpentine:
I should have chid you for not bringing it,
But like a shrew you first begin to brawl.

Second Merchant.
The hour steals on, I pray you, sir, dispatch.

Angelo.
You hear how he importunes me—the chain!

Antipholus of Ephesus.
Why, give it to my wife, and fetch your money.

Angelo.
Come, come, you know I gave it you even now.
Either send the chain, or send me by some token.

Antipholus of Ephesus.
Fie, now you run this humor out of breath.
Come, where's the chain? I pray you let me see it.

Second Merchant.
My business cannot brook this dalliance.
Good sir, say whe'r you'll answer me or no:
If not, I'll leave him to the officer.

Antipholus of Ephesus.
I answer you? What should I answer you?

Angelo.
The money that you owe me for the chain.

Antipholus of Ephesus.
I owe you none, till I receive the chain.

Angelo.
You know I gave it you half an hour since.

Antipholus of Ephesus.
You gave me none, you wrong me much to say so.

Angelo.
You wrong me more, sir, in denying it.
Consider how it stands upon my credit.

Second Merchant.
Well, officer, arrest him at my suit.

Officer.
I do, and charge you in the Duke's name to obey me.

Angelo.
This touches me in reputation.
Either consent to pay this sum for me
Or I attach you by this officer.

Antipholus of Ephesus.
Consent to pay thee that I never had!
Arrest me, foolish fellow, if thou dar'st.

Angelo.
Here is thy fee, arrest him, officer.
I would not spare my brother in this case,
If he should scorn me so apparently.

Officer.
I do arrest you, sir: you hear the suit.

Antipholus of Ephesus.
I do obey thee, till I give thee bail.
But, sirrah, you shall buy this sport as dear
As all the metal in your shop will answer.

Angelo.
Sir, sir, I shall have law in Ephesus,
To your notorious shame, I doubt it not.

Enter Dromio of Syracuse from the bay.

Dromio of Syracuse.
Master, there's a bark of Epidamium
That stays but till her owner comes aboard,
And then, sir, she bears away. Our fraughtage, sir,
I have convey'd aboard, and I have bought
The oil, the balsamum, and aqua-vitae.
The ship is in her trim, the merry wind
Blows fair from land: they stay for nought at all
But for their owner, master, and yourself.

Antipholus of Ephesus.
How now? A madman? Why, thou peevish sheep,
What ship of Epidamium stays for me?

Dromio of Syracuse.
A ship you sent me to, to hire waftage.

Antipholus of Ephesus.
Thou drunken slave, I sent thee for a rope,
And told thee to what purpose and what end.

Dromio of Syracuse.
You sent me for a rope's end as soon:
You sent me to the bay, sir, for a bark.

Antipholus of Ephesus.
I will debate this matter at more leisure,
And teach your ears to list me with more heed.
To Adriana, villain, hie thee straight:
Give her this key, and tell her, in the desk
That's cover'd o'er with Turkish tapestry
There is a purse of ducats; let her send it.
Tell her I am arrested in the street,
And that shall bail me. Hie thee, slave, be gone!
On, officer, to prison till it come.

Exeunt all but Dromio of Syracuse.

Dromio of Syracuse.
To Adriana! That is where we din'd,
Where Dowsabel did claim me for her husband:
She is too big, I hope, for me to compass.
Thither I must, although against my will,
For servants must their masters' minds fulfill.

Exit.

Scene 2

A room in the house of Antipholus of Ephesus.

(Adriana; Luciana; Dromio of Syracuse)

Act 4, Scene 2

Luciana tells Adriana of Antipholus of Syracuse's protestation of love to her and Adriana rails against him, though acknowledging she loves him in her heart. Dromio of Syracuse comes in for gold and though Adriana is surprised her husband is in debt, she gives him the money to bring to Antipholus.

Enter Adriana and Luciana.

Adriana.
Ah, Luciana, did he tempt thee so?
Mightst thou perceive austerely in his eye
That he did plead in earnest? Yea or no?
Look'd he or red or pale, or sad or merrily?
What observation mad'st thou in this case
Of his heart's meteors tilting in his face?

Luciana.
First he denied you had in him no right.

Adriana.
He meant he did me none: the more my spite.

Luciana.
Then swore he that he was a stranger here.

Adriana.
And true he swore, though yet forsworn he were.

Luciana.
Then pleaded I for you.

Adriana.
                And what said he?

Luciana.
That love I begg'd for you, he begg'd of me.

Adriana.
With what persuasion did he tempt thy love?

Luciana.
With words that in an honest suit might move.
First he did praise my beauty, then my speech.

Adriana.
Didst speak him fair?

Luciana.
              Have patience, I beseech.

Adriana.
I cannot, nor I will not, hold me still,
My tongue, though not my heart, shall have his will.
He is deformed, crooked, old, and sere,
Ill-fac'd, worse bodied, shapeless every where;
Vicious, ungentle, foolish, blunt, unkind,
Stigmatical in making, worse in mind.

Luciana.
Who would be jealous then of such a one?
No evil lost is wail'd when it is gone.

Adriana.
Ah, but I think him better than I say,
And yet would herein others' eyes were worse:
Far from her nest the lapwing cries away;
My heart prays for him, though my tongue do curse.

Enter Dromio of Syracuse.

Dromio of Syracuse.
Here, go: the desk, the purse! Sweat now, make haste!

Luciana.
How hast thou lost thy breath?

Dromio of Syracuse.
              By running fast.

Adriana.
Where is thy master, Dromio? Is he well?

Dromio of Syracuse.
No, he's in Tartar limbo, worse than hell:
A devil in an everlasting garment hath him;
One whose hard heart is button'd up with steel;
A fiend, a fairy, pitiless and rough;
A wolf, nay worse, a fellow all in buff;
A back-friend, a shoulder-clapper, one that countermands
The passages of alleys, creeks, and narrow lands;
A hound that runs counter, and yet draws dry-foot well;
One that before the judgment carries poor souls to hell.

Adriana.
Why, man, what is the matter?

Dromio of Syracuse.
I do not know the matter, he is 'rested on the case.

Adriana.
What, is he arrested? Tell me at whose suit.

Dromio of Syracuse.
I know not at whose suit he is arrested well;
But 'a's in a suit of buff which 'rested him, that can I tell.
Will you send him, mistress, redemption, the money in his desk?

Adriana.
Go fetch it, sister.

Exit Luciana.

                    This I wonder at,
That he unknown to me should be in debt.
Tell me, was he arrested on a band?

Dromio of Syracuse.
Not on a band but on a stronger thing:
A chain, a chain! Do you not hear it ring?

Adriana.
What, the chain?

Dromio of Syracuse.
No, no, the bell, 'tis time that I were gone:
It was two ere I left him, and now the clock strikes one.

Adriana.
The hours come back! That did I never hear.

Dromio of Syracuse.
O yes, if any hour meet a sergeant, 'a turns back for very fear.

Adriana.
As if Time were in debt! How fondly dost thou reason!

Dromio of Syracuse.
Time is a very bankrupt and owes more than he's worth to season.
Nay, he's a thief too: have you not heard men say,
That Time comes stealing on by night and day?
If 'a be in debt and theft, and a sergeant in the way,
Hath he not reason to turn back an hour in a day?

Enter Luciana.

Adriana.
Go, Dromio, there's the money, bear it straight,
And bring thy master home immediately.
Come, sister, I am press'd down with conceit—
Conceit, my comfort and my injury.

Exeunt.

Scene 3

A public place.

(Antipholus of Syracuse; Dromio of Syracuse; Courtezan)

Antipholus of Syracuse, having been in the market place, is surprised to be greeted by all. Dromio of Syracuse enters with the money to bail him out, but Antipholus knows nothing of any arrest. He asks about his ship and Dromio answers saying he told him a short time before. The Courtezan enters, sees the chain, and asks for it in exchange for the ring she gave Antipholus of Ephesus, according to their bargain. Antipholus of Syracuse thinks she is a witch, and will have nothing to do with her. Cheated out of her ring, she thinks Antipholus of Syracuse is crazy and goes to tell the wife of Antipholus of Ephesus she was cheated by him.

Enter Antipholus of Syracuse.

Antipholus of Syracuse.
There's not a man I meet but doth salute me
As if I were their well-acquainted friend,
And every one doth call me by my name:
Some tender money to me, some invite me;
Some other give me thanks for kindnesses;
Some offer me commodities to buy.
Even now a tailor call'd me in his shop,
And show'd me silks that he had bought for me,
And therewithal took measure of my body.
Sure these are but imaginary wiles,
And Lapland sorcerers inhabit here.

Enter Dromio of Syracuse.

Dromio of Syracuse.
Master, here's the gold you sent me for. What, have you got the picture of old Adam new apparell'd?

Antipholus of Syracuse.
What gold is this? What Adam dost thou mean?

Dromio of Syracuse.
Not that Adam that kept the Paradise, but that Adam that keeps the prison; he that goes in the calve's-skin that was kill'd for the Prodigal; he that came behind you, sir, like an evil angel, and bid you forsake your liberty.

Antipholus of Syracuse.
I understand thee not.

Dromio of Syracuse.
No? Why, 'tis a plain case: he that went like a base-viol in a case of leather; the man, sir, that when gentlemen are tir'd, gives them a sob and 'rests them; he, sir, that takes pity on decay'd men and gives them suits of durance; he that sets up his rest to do more exploits with his mace than a morris-pike.

Antipholus of Syracuse.
What, thou mean'st an officer?

Dromio of Syracuse.
Ay, sir, the sergeant of the band: he that brings any man to answer it that breaks his band; one that thinks a man always going to bed and says, "God give you good rest!"

Antipholus of Syracuse.
Well, sir, there rest in your foolery. Is there any ships puts forth tonight? May we be gone?

Dromio of Syracuse.
Why, sir, I brought you word an hour since that the bark Expedition put forth tonight, and then were you hind'red by the sergeant to tarry for the hoy Delay. Here are the angels that you sent for to deliver you.

Antipholus of Syracuse.
The fellow is distract, and so am I,
And here we wander in illusions:
Some blessed power deliver us from hence!

Enter a Courtezan.

Courtezan.
Well met, well met, Master Antipholus.
I see, sir, you have found the goldsmith now.
Is that the chain you promis'd me today?

Antipholus of Syracuse.
Satan, avoid, I charge thee tempt me not.

Dromio of Syracuse.
Master, is this Mistress Satan?

Antipholus of Syracuse.
It is the devil.

Dromio of Syracuse.
Nay, she is worse, she is the devil's dam, and here she comes in the habit of a light wench; and thereof comes that the wenches say, "God damn me," that's as much to say, "God make me a light wench." It is written, they appear to men like angels of light, light is an effect of fire, and fire will burn: ergo, light wenches will burn. Come not near her.

Courtezan.
Your man and you are marvelous merry, sir.
Will you go with me? We'll mend our dinner here.

Dromio of Syracuse.
Master, if you do, expect spoon-meat, or bespeak a long spoon.

Antipholus of Syracuse.
Why, Dromio?

Dromio of Syracuse.
Marry, he must have a long spoon that must eat with the devil.

Antipholus of Syracuse.
Avoid then, fiend, what tell'st thou me of supping?
Thou art, as you are all, a sorceress:
I conjure thee to leave me and be gone.

Courtezan.
Give me the ring of mine you had at dinner,
Or, for my diamond, the chain you promis'd,
And I'll be gone, sir, and not trouble you.

Dromio of Syracuse.
Some devils ask but the parings of one's nail,
A rush, a hair, a drop of blood, a pin,
A nut, a cherry-stone;
But she, more covetous, would have a chain.
Master, be wise, and if you give it her,
The devil will shake her chain, and fright us with it.

Courtezan.
I pray you, sir, my ring, or else the chain;
I hope you do not mean to cheat me so?

Antipholus of Syracuse.
Avaunt, thou witch! Come, Dromio, let us go.

Dromio of Syracuse.
"Fly pride," says the peacock: mistress, that you know.

Exit with Antipholus of Syracuse.

Courtezan.
Now out of doubt Antipholus is mad,
Else would he never so demean himself.
A ring he hath of mine worth forty ducats,
And for the same he promis'd me a chain:
Both one and other he denies me now.

The reason that I gather he is mad,
Besides this present instance of his rage,
Is a mad tale he told today at dinner,
Of his own doors being shut against his entrance.
Belike his wife, acquainted with his fits,
On purpose shut the doors against his way.
My way is now to hie home to his house,
And tell his wife that, being lunatic,
He rush'd into my house, and took perforce
My ring away. This course I fittest choose,
For forty ducats is too much to lose.

Exit.

Scene 4

A street.

(Antipholus of Ephesus; Officer; Dromio of Ephesus; Adriana; Luciana; Courtezan; Pinch; Antipholus of Syracuse; Dromio of Syracuse; Officers)

Dromio of Ephesus, carrying a rope, meets Antipholus of Ephesus with the officers; then delivers the rope and receives a beating for not bringing money, while he denies he was sent for any. Adriana, Luciana, the Courtezan, and Pinch the schoolmaster enter, and Pinch attempts to exorcise Antipholus, receiving a beating for his pains. Antipholus, seconded by Dromio, tells a story of being shut out of his house at dinner, though Adriana says he dined with her. Adriana, seconded by Luciana, tells how she gave the money to Dromio (of Syracuse) but Dromio of Ephesus denies ever having got it. Master and servant are tied up as madmen. Antipholus accuses Adriana of having Pinch with her when she shut him out. Antipholus and Dromio are taken away, after Adriana promises to discharge the debt. Inquiring of the officer, Adriana finds that the money was for the chain, which the Courtezan claims was promised her in exchange for her ring. Antipholus and Dromio of Syracuse enter with drawn swords and the others flee, thinking they are loose again and out to kill them. Antipholus and Dromio are glad that witches fear swords, but Antipholus says he will not stay any longer in town; however Dromio feels, except for the fat woman claiming him, he would be willing to stay and turn witch himself.

Enter Antipholus of Ephesus with the Officer.

Antipholus of Ephesus.
Fear me not, man, I will not break away;
I'll give thee, ere I leave thee, so much money,
To warrant thee, as I am 'rested for.
My wife is in a wayward mood today,
And will not lightly trust the messenger,
That I should be attach'd in Ephesus;
I tell you, 'twill sound harshly in her ears.

Enter Dromio of Ephesus with a rope's end.

Here comes my man: I think he brings the money.
How now, sir? Have you that I sent you for?

Dromio of Ephesus.
Here's that, I warrant you, will pay them all.

Antipholus of Ephesus.
But where's the money?

Dromio of Ephesus.
Why, sir, I gave the money for the rope.

Antipholus of Ephesus.
Five hundred ducats, villain, for a rope?

Dromio of Ephesus.
I'll serve you, sir, five hundred at the rate.

Antipholus of Ephesus.
To what end did I bid thee hie thee home?

Dromio of Ephesus.
To a rope's end, sir, and to that end am I return'd.

Antipholus of Ephesus.
And to that end, sir, I will welcome you.

Beats Dromio.

Officer.
Good sir, be patient.

Dromio of Ephesus.
Nay, 'tis for me to be patient: I am in adversity.

Officer.
Good now, hold thy tongue.

Dromio of Ephesus.
Nay, rather persuade him to hold his hands.

Antipholus of Ephesus.
Thou whoreson, senseless villain!

Dromio of Ephesus.
I would I were senseless, sir, that I might not feel your blows.

Antipholus of Ephesus.
Thou art sensible in nothing but blows, and so is an ass.

Dromio of Ephesus.
I am an ass indeed; you may prove it by my long ears. I have serv'd him from the hour of my nativity to this instant, and have nothing at his hands for my service but blows. When I am cold, he heats me with beating; when I am warm, he cools me with beating. I am wak'd with it when I sleep, rais'd with it when I sit, driven out of doors with it when I go from home, welcom'd home with it when I return; nay, I bear it on my shoulders, as a beggar wont her brat; and I think when he hath lam'd me, I shall beg with it from door to door.

Enter Adriana, Luciana, Courtezan, and a schoolmaster call'd Pinch.

Antipholus of Ephesus.
Come go along, my wife is coming yonder.

Dromio of Ephesus.
Mistress, respice finem, respect your end, or rather, the prophecy like the parrot, "beware the rope's end."

Antipholus of Ephesus.
Wilt thou still talk?

Beats Dromio.

Courtezan.
How say you now? Is not your husband mad?

Adriana.
His incivility confirms no less.
Good Doctor Pinch, you are a conjurer,
Establish him in his true sense again,
And I will please you what you will demand.

Luciana.
Alas, how fiery, and how sharp, he looks!

Courtezan.
Mark, how he trembles in his ecstasy!

Doctor Pinch.
Give me your hand, and let me feel your pulse.

Antipholus of Ephesus.
There is my hand, and let it feel your ear.

Strikes Pinch.

Doctor Pinch.
I charge thee, Satan, hous'd within this man,
To yield possession to my holy prayers,
And to thy state of darkness hie thee straight:
I conjure thee by all the saints in heaven!

Antipholus of Ephesus.
Peace, doting wizard, peace! I am not mad.

Adriana.
O that thou wert not, poor distressed soul!

Antipholus of Ephesus.
You minion, you, are these your customers?
Did this companion with the saffron face
Revel and feast it at my house today,
Whilst upon me the guilty doors were shut,
And I denied to enter in my house?

Adriana.
O husband, God doth know you din'd at home,
Where would you had remain'd until this time,
Free from these slanders and this open shame.

Antipholus of Ephesus.
Din'd at home? Thou villain, what sayest thou?

Dromio of Ephesus.
Sir, sooth to say, you did not dine at home.

Antipholus of Ephesus.
Were not my doors lock'd up, and I shut out?

Dromio of Ephesus.
Perdie, your doors were lock'd, and you shut out.

Antipholus of Ephesus.
And did not she herself revile me there?

Dromio of Ephesus.
Sans fable, she herself revil'd you there.

Antipholus of Ephesus.
Did not her kitchen maid rail, taunt, and scorn me?

Dromio of Ephesus.
Certes she did, the kitchen vestal scorn'd you.

Antipholus of Ephesus.
And did not I in rage depart from thence?

Dromio of Ephesus.
In verity you did, my bones bears witness,
That since have felt the vigor of his rage.

Adriana.
Is't good to soothe him in these contraries?

Doctor Pinch.
It is no shame; the fellow finds his vein,
And yielding to him, humors well his frenzy.

Antipholus of Ephesus.
Thou hast suborn'd the goldsmith to arrest me.

Adriana.
Alas, I sent you money to redeem you,
By Dromio here, who came in haste for it.

Dromio of Ephesus.
Money by me? Heart and good will you might,
But surely, master, not a rag of money.

Antipholus of Ephesus.
Went'st not thou to her for a purse of ducats?

Adriana.
He came to me, and I deliver'd it.

Luciana.
And I am witness with her that she did.

Dromio of Ephesus.
God and the rope-maker bear me witness
That I was sent for nothing but a rope!

Doctor Pinch.
Mistress, both man and master is possess'd:
I know it by their pale and deadly looks.
They must be bound and laid in some dark room.

Antipholus of Ephesus.
Say wherefore didst thou lock me forth today?
And why dost thou deny the bag of gold?

Adriana.
I did not, gentle husband, lock thee forth.

Dromio of Ephesus.
And, gentle master, I receiv'd no gold;
But I confess, sir, that we were lock'd out.

Adriana.
Dissembling villain, thou speak'st false in both.

Antipholus of Ephesus.
Dissembling harlot, thou art false in all,
And art confederate with a damned pack
To make a loathsome abject scorn of me;
But with these nails I'll pluck out these false eyes
That would behold in me this shameful sport.

Enter three or four, and offer to bind him; he strives.

Adriana.
O, bind him, bind him, let him not come near me.

Doctor Pinch.
More company! The fiend is strong within him.

Luciana.
Ay me, poor man, how pale and wan he looks!

Antipholus of Ephesus.
What, will you murder me? Thou jailer, thou,
I am thy prisoner. Wilt thou suffer them
To make a rescue?

Officer.
              Masters, let him go:
He is my prisoner, and you shall not have him.

Doctor Pinch.
Go bind this man, for he is frantic too.

They offer to bind Dromio of Ephesus.

Adriana.
What wilt thou do, thou peevish officer?
Hast thou delight to see a wretched man
Do outrage and displeasure to himself?

Officer.
He is my prisoner; if I let him go,
The debt he owes will be requir'd of me.

Adriana.
I will discharge thee ere I go from thee:
Bear me forthwith unto his creditor,
And knowing how the debt grows, I will pay it.
Good Master Doctor, see him safe convey'd
Home to my house. O most unhappy day!

Antipholus of Ephesus.
O most unhappy strumpet!

Dromio of Ephesus.
Master, I am here ent'red in bond for you.

Antipholus of Ephesus.
Out on thee, villain, wherefore dost thou mad me?

Dromio of Ephesus.
Will you be bound for nothing? Be mad, good master,
Cry "The devil!"

Luciana.
God help, poor souls, how idlely do they talk!

Adriana.
Go bear him hence. Sister, go you with me.

Exeunt Manent Officer, Adriana, Luciana, Courtezan.

Say now, whose suit is he arrested at?

Officer.
One Angelo, a goldsmith. Do you know him?

Adriana.
I know the man; what is the sum he owes?

Officer.
Two hundred ducats.

Adriana.
        Say, how grows it due?

Officer.
Due for a chain your husband had of him.

Adriana.
He did bespeak a chain for me, but had it not.

Courtezan.
When as your husband all in rage today
Came to my house, and took away my ring—
The ring I saw upon his finger now—
Straight after did I meet him with a chain.

Adriana.
It may be so, but I did never see it.
Come, jailer, bring me where the goldsmith is,
I long to know the truth hereof at large.

Enter Antipholus of Syracuse, with his rapier drawn, and Dromio of Syracuse.

Luciana.
God for thy mercy! They are loose again.

Adriana.
And come with naked swords: let's call more help
To have them bound again.

Officer.
        Away, they'll kill us.

Exeunt omnes but Antipholus of Syracuse and Dromio of Syracuse as fast as may be, frighted.

Antipholus of Syracuse.
I see these witches are afraid of swords.

Dromio of Syracuse.
She that would be your wife now ran from you.

Antipholus of Syracuse.
Come to the Centaur, fetch our stuff from thence;
I long that we were safe and sound aboard.

Dromio of Syracuse.
Faith, stay here this night, they will surely do us no harm. You saw they speak us fair, give us gold: methinks they are such a gentle nation that, but for the mountain of mad flesh that claims marriage of me, I could find in my heart to stay here still, and turn witch.

Antipholus of Syracuse.
I will not stay tonight for all the town:
Therefore away, to get our stuff aboard.

Exeunt.

Act 5

Scene 1

A street before an abbey.

(Second Merchant; Angelo; Antipholus of Syracuse; Dromio of Syracuse; Adriana; Luciana; Courtezan; Lady Abbess; Duke of Ephesus; Egeon; Headsman; Officers; Messenger; Antipholus of Ephesus; Dromio of Ephesus)

The Second Merchant and Angelo, meeting Antipholus and Dromio of Syracuse, fight over the chain. Adriana, Luciana, the Courtezan, and others come, and Antipholus and Dromio take refuge in the priory, from whence the Lady Abbess refuses to deliver them. The Duke and Egeon enter, prepared for Egeon's execution. A messenger brings tidings of the escape of Antipholus and Dromio of Ephesus, who have beaten up the

servants and burnt Pinch's beard. Antipholus and
Dromio of Ephesus enter seeking justice against
Adriana. The Duke tries to unravel the mystery of the
conflicting testimonies. Egeon is denied by Antipholus
and Dromio of Ephesus. The Abbess enters with the
other Antipholus and Dromio, and all is explained. It
turns out that the Abbess is Egeon's long-lost wife. The
Duke pardons Egeon and all ends well.

Enter the Second Merchant and Angelo the goldsmith.

Angelo.
I am sorry, sir, that I have hind'red you,
But I protest he had the chain of me,
Though most dishonestly he doth deny it.

Second Merchant.
How is the man esteem'd here in the city?

Angelo.
Of very reverent reputation, sir,
Of credit infinite, highly belov'd,
Second to none that lives here in the city:
His word might bear my wealth at any time.

Second Merchant.
Speak softly, yonder, as I think, he walks.

*Enter Antipholus of Syracuse and Dromio of Syracuse
again.*

Angelo.
'Tis so; and that self chain about his neck,
Which he forswore most monstrously to have.
Good sir, draw near to me, I'll speak to him.
Signior Antipholus, I wonder much
That you would put me to this shame and trouble,
And, not without some scandal to yourself,
With circumstance and oaths so to deny
This chain which now you wear so openly.
Beside the charge, the shame, imprisonment,
You have done wrong to this my honest friend,
Who, but for staying on our controversy,
Had hoisted sail and put to sea today.
This chain you had of me, can you deny it?

Antipholus of Syracuse.
I think I had, I never did deny it.

Second Merchant.
Yes, that you did, sir, and forswore it too.

Antipholus of Syracuse.
Who heard me to deny it or forswear it?

Second Merchant.
These ears of mine thou know'st did hear thee;
Fie on thee, wretch, 'tis pity that thou liv'st
To walk where any honest men resort.

Antipholus of Syracuse.
Thou art a villain to impeach me thus:
I'll prove mine honor and mine honesty
Against thee presently, if thou dar'st stand.

Second Merchant.
I dare, and do defy thee for a villain.

They draw.
Enter Adriana, Luciana, Courtezan, and others.

Adriana.
Hold, hurt him not for God sake! He is mad.
Some get within him, take his sword away:
Bind Dromio too, and bear them to my house.

Dromio of Syracuse.
Run, master, run, for God's sake take a house!
This is some priory, in, or we are spoil'd.

*Exeunt Antipholus of Syracuse and Dromio of Syracuse
to the priory.*
Enter Lady Abbess Aemilia.

Aemilia.
Be quiet, people. Wherefore throng you hither?

Adriana.
To fetch my poor distracted husband hence.
Let us come in, that we may bind him fast,
And bear him home for his recovery.

Angelo.
I knew he was not in his perfect wits.

Second Merchant.
I am sorry now that I did draw on him.

Aemilia.
How long hath this possession held the man?

Adriana.
This week he hath been heavy, sour, sad,
And much different from the man he was;
But till this afternoon his passion
Ne'er brake into extremity of rage.

Aemilia.
Hath he not lost much wealth by wrack of sea?
Buried some dear friend? Hath not else his eye
Stray'd his affection in unlawful love—
A sin prevailing much in youthful men,
Who give their eyes the liberty of gazing?
Which of these sorrows is he subject to?

Adriana.
To none of these, except it be the last,
Namely, some love that drew him oft from home.

Aemilia.
You should for that have reprehended him.

Adriana.
Why, so I did.

Aemilia.
              Ay, but not rough enough.

Adriana.
As roughly as my modesty would let me.

Aemilia.
Haply, in private.

Adriana.
                  And in assemblies too.

Aemilia.
Ay, but not enough.

Adriana.
It was the copy of our conference:
In bed he slept not for my urging it;
At board he fed not for my urging it;
Alone, it was the subject of my theme;
In company I often glanced it;
Still did I tell him it was vild and bad.

Aemilia.
And thereof came it that the man was mad.
The venom clamors of a jealous woman
Poisons more deadly than a mad dog's tooth.
It seems his sleeps were hind'red by thy railing,
And thereof comes it that his head is light.
Thou say'st his meat was sauc'd with thy upbraidings:
Unquiet meals make ill digestions,
Thereof the raging fire of fever bred,
And what's a fever but a fit of madness?
Thou say'st his sports were hind'red by thy brawls:
Sweet recreation barr'd, what doth ensue
But moody and dull melancholy,
Kinsman to grim and comfortless despair,
And at her heels a huge infectious troop
Of pale distemperatures and foes to life?
In food, in sport, and life-preserving rest
To be disturb'd, would mad or man or beast:
The consequence is then, thy jealous fits
Hath scar'd thy husband from the use of wits.

Luciana.
She never reprehended him but mildly,
When he demean'd himself rough, rude, and wildly.
Why bear you these rebukes, and answer not?

Adriana.
She did betray me to my own reproof.
Good people, enter and lay hold on him.

Aemilia.
No, not a creature enters in my house.

Adriana.
Then let your servants bring my husband forth.

Aemilia.
Neither. He took this place for sanctuary,
And it shall privilege him from your hands
Till I have brought him to his wits again,
Or lose my labor in assaying it.

Adriana.
I will attend my husband, be his nurse,
Diet his sickness, for it is my office,
And will have no attorney but myself,
And therefore let me have him home with me.

Aemilia.
Be patient, for I will not let him stir
Till I have us'd the approved means I have,
With wholesome syrups, drugs, and holy prayers,
To make of him a formal man again:
It is a branch and parcel of mine oath,
A charitable duty of my order,
Therefore depart, and leave him here with me.

Adriana.
I will not hence, and leave my husband here;
And ill it doth beseem your holiness
To separate the husband and the wife.

Aemilia.
Be quiet and depart, thou shalt not have him.

Exit.

Luciana.
Complain unto the Duke of this indignity.

Adriana.
Come go: I will fall prostrate at his feet,
And never rise until my tears and prayers
Have won his Grace to come in person hither,
And take perforce my husband from the abbess.

Second Merchant.
By this I think the dial points at five.
Anon I'm sure the Duke himself in person
Comes this way to the melancholy vale,
The place of death and sorry execution,
Behind the ditches of the abbey here.

Angelo.
Upon what cause?

Second Merchant.
To see a reverent Syracusian merchant,
Who put unluckily into this bay
Against the laws and statutes of this town,
Beheaded publicly for his offense.

Angelo.
See where they come, we will behold his death.

Luciana.
Kneel to the Duke before he pass the abbey.

Enter the Duke of Ephesus attended and Egeon the merchant of Syracuse, bare-head, with the Headsman and other Officers.

Solinus, Duke of Ephesus.
Yet once again proclaim it publicly,
If any friend will pay the sum for him,
He shall not die, so much we tender him.

Adriana.
Justice, most sacred Duke, against the abbess!

Solinus, Duke of Ephesus.
She is a virtuous and a reverend lady,
It cannot be that she hath done thee wrong.

Adriana.
May it please your Grace, Antipholus my husband,
Who I made lord of me and all I had,
At your important letters—this ill day
A most outrageous fit of madness took him,
That desp'rately he hurried through the street—
With him his bondman, all as mad as he—
Doing displeasure to the citizens
By rushing in their houses, bearing thence
Rings, jewels, any thing his rage did like.
Once did I get him bound, and sent him home,
Whilst to take order for the wrongs I went,
That here and there his fury had committed.
Anon, I wot not by what strong escape,
He broke from those that had the guard of him,
And with his mad attendant and himself,
Each one with ireful passion, with drawn swords,
Met us again, and madly bent on us
Chas'd us away; till raising of more aid,
We came again to bind them. Then they fled
Into this abbey, whither we pursu'd them,
And here the abbess shuts the gates on us,
And will not suffer us to fetch him out,
Nor send him forth, that we may bear him hence.
Therefore, most gracious Duke, with thy command
Let him be brought forth, and borne hence for help.

Solinus, Duke of Ephesus.
Long since thy husband serv'd me in my wars,
And I to thee engag'd a prince's word,
When thou didst make him master of thy bed,
To do him all the grace and good I could.
Go some of you, knock at the abbey-gate,
And bid the Lady Abbess come to me:
I will determine this before I stir.

Enter a Messenger.

Messenger.
O mistress, mistress, shift and save yourself!
My master and his man are both broke loose,
Beaten the maids a-row, and bound the doctor,
Whose beard they have sing'd off with brands of fire,
And ever as it blaz'd, they threw on him
Great pails of puddled mire to quench the hair;
My master preaches patience to him, and the while
His man with scissors nicks him like a fool;
And sure (unless you send some present help)
Between them they will kill the conjurer.

Adriana.
Peace, fool, thy master and his man are here,
And that is false thou dost report to us.

Messenger.
Mistress, upon my life, I tell you true;
I have not breath'd almost since I did see it.
He cries for you, and vows, if he can take you,

To scorch your face, and to disfigure you.

Cry within.

Hark, hark, I hear him, mistress; fly, be gone!

Solinus, Duke of Ephesus.
Come stand by me, fear nothing. Guard with halberds!

Adriana.
Ay me, it is my husband! Witness you,
That he is borne about invisible:
Even now we hous'd him in the abbey here,
And now he's there, past thought of human reason.

Enter Antipholus of Ephesus and Dromio of Ephesus.

Antipholus of Ephesus.
Justice, most gracious Duke, O, grant me justice,
Even for the service that long since I did thee,
When I bestrid thee in the wars, and took
Deep scars to save thy life; even for the blood
That then I lost for thee, now grant me justice.

Egeon.
Unless the fear of death doth make me dote,
I see my son Antipholus and Dromio.

Antipholus of Ephesus.
Justice, sweet prince, against that woman there!
She whom thou gav'st to me to be my wife;
That hath abused and dishonored me,
Even in the strength and height of injury:
Beyond imagination is the wrong
That she this day hath shameless thrown on me.

Solinus, Duke of Ephesus.
Discover how, and thou shalt find me just.

Antipholus of Ephesus.
This day, great Duke, she shut the doors upon me,
While she with harlots feasted in my house.

Solinus, Duke of Ephesus.
A grievous fault! Say, woman, didst thou so?

Adriana.
No, my good lord. Myself, he, and my sister
Today did dine together: so befall my soul
As this is false he burdens me withal!

Luciana.
Ne'er may I look on day, nor sleep on night,
But she tells to your Highness simple truth!

Angelo.
O perjur'd woman! They are both forsworn:
In this the madman justly chargeth them.

Antipholus of Ephesus.
My liege, I am advised what I say,
Neither disturbed with the effect of wine,
Nor heady-rash, provok'd with raging ire,
Albeit my wrongs might make one wiser mad.
This woman lock'd me out this day from dinner;
That goldsmith there, were he not pack'd with her,
Could witness it, for he was with me then,
Who parted with me to go fetch a chain,
Promising to bring it to the Porpentine,
Where Balthazar and I did dine together.
Our dinner done, and he not coming thither,
I went to seek him. In the street I met him,
And in his company that gentleman.
There did this perjur'd goldsmith swear me down
That I this day of him receiv'd the chain,
Which, God he knows, I saw not; for the which
He did arrest me with an officer.
I did obey, and sent my peasant home
For certain ducats; he with none return'd.
Then fairly I bespoke the officer
To go in person with me to my house.
By th' way we met
My wife, her sister, and a rabble more
Of vild confederates. Along with them
They brought one Pinch, a hungry lean-fac'd villain,
A mere anatomy, a mountebank,
A threadbare juggler and a fortune-teller,
A needy, hollow-ey'd, sharp-looking wretch,
A living dead man. This pernicious slave,
Forsooth, took on him as a conjurer,
And gazing in mine eyes, feeling my pulse,
And with no face, as 'twere, outfacing me,
Cries out, I was possess'd. Then all together
They fell upon me, bound me, bore me thence,
And in a dark and dankish vault at home
There left me and my man, both bound together,
Till gnawing with my teeth my bonds in sunder,
I gain'd my freedom; and immediately
Ran hither to your Grace, whom I beseech
To give me ample satisfaction
For these deep shames and great indignities.

Angelo.
My lord, in truth, thus far I witness with him:
That he din'd not at home, but was lock'd out.

Solinus, Duke of Ephesus.
But had he such a chain of thee, or no?

Angelo.
He had, my lord, and when he ran in here,
These people saw the chain about his neck.

Second Merchant.
Besides, I will be sworn these ears of mine
Heard you confess you had the chain of him,
After you first forswore it on the mart,
And thereupon I drew my sword on you;
And then you fled into this abbey here,
From whence I think you are come by miracle.

Antipholus of Ephesus.
I never came within these abbey walls,
Nor ever didst thou draw thy sword on me;
I never saw the chain, so help me heaven;
And this is false you burden me withal.

Solinus, Duke of Ephesus.
Why, what an intricate impeach is this!
I think you all have drunk of Circe's cup.
If here you hous'd him, here he would have been;
If he were mad, he would not plead so coldly.
You say he din'd at home; the goldsmith here
Denies that saying. Sirrah, what say you?

Dromio of Ephesus.
Sir, he din'd with her there, at the Porpentine.

Courtezan.
He did, and from my finger snatch'd that ring.

Antipholus of Ephesus.
'Tis true, my liege, this ring I had of her.

Solinus, Duke of Ephesus.
Saw'st thou him enter at the abbey here?

Courtezan.
As sure, my liege, as I do see your Grace.

Solinus, Duke of Ephesus.
Why, this is strange. Go call the abbess hither.
I think you are all mated, or stark mad.

Exit one to the abbess.

Egeon.
Most mighty Duke, vouchsafe me speak a word:
Haply I see a friend will save my life,
And pay the sum that may deliver me.

Solinus, Duke of Ephesus.
Speak freely, Syracusian, what thou wilt.

Egeon.
Is not your name, sir, call'd Antipholus?
And is not that your bondman, Dromio?

Dromio of Ephesus.
Within this hour I was his bondman, sir,
But he, I thank him, gnaw'd in two my cords:
Now am I Dromio, and his man, unbound.

Egeon.
I am sure you both of you remember me.

Dromio of Ephesus.
Ourselves we do remember, sir, by you;
For lately we were bound as you are now.
You are not Pinch's patient, are you, sir?

Egeon.
Why look you strange on me? You know me well.

Antipholus of Ephesus.
I never saw you in my life till now.

Egeon.
O! Grief hath chang'd me since you saw me last,
And careful hours with time's deformed hand
Have written strange defeatures in my face:
But tell me yet, dost thou not know my voice?

Antipholus of Ephesus.
Neither.

Egeon.
Dromio, nor thou?

Dromio of Ephesus.
                  No, trust me, sir, nor I.

Egeon.
I am sure thou dost!

Dromio of Ephesus.
Ay, sir, but I am sure I do not—and whatsoever a man
denies, you are now bound to believe him.

Egeon.
Not know my voice! O time's extremity,
Hast thou so crack'd and splitted my poor tongue
In seven short years, that here my only son
Knows not my feeble key of untun'd cares?
Though now this grained face of mine be hid
In sap-consuming winter's drizzled snow,
And all the conduits of my blood froze up,
Yet hath my night of life some memory,
My wasting lamps some fading glimmer left,
My dull deaf ears a little use to hear:
All these old witnesses—I cannot err—
Tell me thou art my son Antipholus.

Antipholus of Ephesus.
I never saw my father in my life.

Egeon.
But seven years since, in Syracuse, boy,
Thou know'st we parted, but perhaps, my son,
Thou sham'st to acknowledge me in misery.

Antipholus of Ephesus.
The Duke, and all that know me in the city,
Can witness with me that it is not so.
I ne'er saw Syracuse in my life.

Solinus, Duke of Ephesus.
I tell thee, Syracusian, twenty years
Have I been patron to Antipholus,
During which time he ne'er saw Syracuse:
I see thy age and dangers make thee dote.

Enter the abbess with Antipholus of Syracuse and Dromio of Syracuse.

Aemilia.
Most mighty Duke, behold a man much wrong'd.

All gather to see them.

Adriana.
I see two husbands, or mine eyes deceive me.

Solinus, Duke of Ephesus.
One of these men is genius to the other:
And so of these, which is the natural man,
And which the spirit? Who deciphers them?

Dromio of Syracuse.
I, sir, am Dromio, command him away.

Dromio of Ephesus.
I, sir, am Dromio, pray let me stay.

Antipholus of Syracuse.
Egeon art thou not? Or else his ghost?

Dromio of Syracuse.
O my old master, who hath bound him here?

Aemilia.
Whoever bound him, I will loose his bonds,
And gain a husband by his liberty.
Speak, old Egeon, if thou be'st the man
That hadst a wife once call'd Aemilia,
That bore thee at a burden two fair sons.
O, if thou be'st the same Egeon, speak,
And speak unto the same Aemilia!

Egeon.
If I dream not, thou art Aemilia.
If thou art she, tell me, where is that son
That floated with thee on the fatal raft?

Aemilia.
By men of Epidamium he and I,
And the twin Dromio, all were taken up;
But by and by rude fishermen of Corinth
By force took Dromio and my son from them,
And me they left with those of Epidamium.
What then became of them I cannot tell;
I to this fortune that you see me in.

Solinus, Duke of Ephesus.
Why, here begins his morning story right:
These two Antipholus', these two so like,
And these two Dromios, one in semblance—
Besides her urging of her wrack at sea—
These are the parents to these children,
Which accidentally are met together.
Antipholus, thou cam'st from Corinth first?

Antipholus of Syracuse.
No, sir, not I, I came from Syracuse.

Solinus, Duke of Ephesus.
Stay, stand apart, I know not which is which.

Antipholus of Ephesus.
I came from Corinth, my most gracious lord—

Dromio of Ephesus.
And I with him.

Antipholus of Ephesus.
Brought to this town by that most famous warrior,
Duke Menaphon, your most renowned uncle.

Adriana.
Which of you two did dine with me today?

Antipholus of Syracuse.
I, gentle mistress.

Adriana.
                And are not you my husband?

Antipholus of Ephesus.
No, I say nay to that.

Antipholus of Syracuse.
And so do I, yet did she call me so;
And this fair gentlewoman, her sister here,
Did call me brother.

To Luciana.
                What I told you then
I hope I shall have leisure to make good,
If this be not a dream I see and hear.

Angelo.
That is the chain, sir, which you had of me.

Antipholus of Syracuse.
I think it be, sir, I deny it not.

Antipholus of Ephesus.
And you, sir, for this chain arrested me.

Angelo.
I think I did, sir, I deny it not.

Adriana.
I sent you money, sir, to be your bail,
By Dromio, but I think he brought it not.

Dromio of Ephesus.
No, none by me.

Antipholus of Syracuse.
This purse of ducats I receiv'd from you,
And Dromio my man did bring them me.
I see we still did meet each other's man,
And I was ta'en for him, and he for me,
And thereupon these errors are arose.

Antipholus of Ephesus.
These ducats pawn I for my father here.

Solinus, Duke of Ephesus.
It shall not need, thy father hath his life.

Courtezan.
Sir, I must have that diamond from you.

Antipholus of Ephesus.
There take it, and much thanks for my good cheer.

Aemilia.
Renowned Duke, vouchsafe to take the pains
To go with us into the abbey here,
And hear at large discoursed all our fortunes;
And all that are assembled in this place
That by this sympathized one day's error
Have suffer'd wrong, go keep us company,
And we shall make full satisfaction.
Thirty-three years have I but gone in travail
Of you, my sons, and till this present hour
My heavy burden ne'er delivered.
The Duke, my husband, and my children both,
And you the calendars of their nativity,
Go to a gossips' feast, and go with me—
After so long grief, such nativity!

Solinus, Duke of Ephesus.
With all my heart, I'll gossip at this feast.

Exeunt omnes. Manent the two Dromios and two brothers.

Dromio of Syracuse.
Master, shall I fetch your stuff from shipboard?

Antipholus of Ephesus.
Dromio, what stuff of mine hast thou embark'd?

Dromio of Syracuse.
Your goods that lay at host, sir, in the Centaur.

Antipholus of Syracuse.
He speaks to me. I am your master, Dromio.
Come go with us, we'll look to that anon.
Embrace thy brother there, rejoice with him.

Exit with Antipholus of Ephesus.

Dromio of Syracuse.
There is a fat friend at your master's house,
That kitchen'd me for you today at dinner:
She now shall be my sister, not my wife.

Dromio of Ephesus.
Methinks you are my glass, and not my brother:
I see by you I am a sweet-fac'd youth.
Will you walk in to see their gossiping?

Dromio of Syracuse.
Not I, sir, you are my elder.

Dromio of Ephesus.
That's a question; how shall we try it?

Dromio of Syracuse.
We'll draw cuts for the senior, till then, lead thou first.

Dromio of Ephesus.
Nay then thus:
We came into the world like brother and brother;
And now let's go hand in hand, not one before another.

Exeunt.

Julius Caesar

Act 1

Scene 1

Rome. A street.

(Flavius; Murellus; Commoners)

Rome is filled with celebrating commoners taking a day off work to go see Caesar's triumphant return from the civil wars. The tribunes Flavius and Murellus reproach them and order them to get back to work, accusing them of hypocrisy for celebrating the man who destroyed Pompey, their former idol. Flavius suggests they go about tearing down the decorations set up for Caesar's return. Murellus, more cautious, is uncertain whether they have the right too, as it is a religious feast day, but Flavius insists that the odds of Caesar growing too proud is great enough to take the risk.

Enter Flavius, Murellus, and certain Commoners over the stage.

Flavius.
Hence! Home, you idle creatures, get you home!
Is this a holiday? What, know you not,
Being mechanical, you ought not walk
Upon a laboring day without the sign
Of your profession? Speak, what trade art thou?

Carpenter.
Why, sir, a carpenter.

Murellus.
Where is thy leather apron and thy rule?
What dost thou with thy best apparel on?
You, sir, what trade are you?

Cobbler.
Truly, sir, in respect of a fine workman, I am but, as you would say, a cobbler.

Murellus.
But what trade art thou? Answer me directly.

Cobbler.
A trade, sir, that I hope I may use with a safe conscience, which is indeed, sir, a mender of bad soles.

Flavius.
What trade, thou knave? Thou naughty knave, what trade?

Cobbler.
Nay, I beseech you, sir, be not out with me; yet if you be out, sir, I can mend you.

Murellus.
What mean'st thou by that? Mend me, thou saucy fellow?

Cobbler.
Why, sir, cobble you.

Flavius.
Thou art a cobbler, art thou?

Cobbler.
Truly, sir, all that I live by is with the awl: I meddle with no tradesman's matters, nor women's matters; but withal I am indeed, sir, a surgeon to old shoes; when they are in great danger, I recover them. As proper men as ever trod upon neat's-leather have gone upon my handiwork.

Flavius.
But wherefore art not in thy shop today?
Why dost thou lead these men about the streets?

Cobbler.
Truly, sir, to wear out their shoes, to get myself into more work. But indeed, sir, we make holiday to see Caesar, and to rejoice in his triumph.

Murellus.
Wherefore rejoice? What conquest brings he home?
What tributaries follow him to Rome,
To grace in captive bonds his chariot-wheels?
You blocks, you stones, you worse than senseless things!
O you hard hearts, you cruel men of Rome,
Knew you not Pompey? Many a time and oft
Have you climb'd up to walls and battlements,
To tow'rs and windows, yea, to chimney-tops,
Your infants in your arms, and there have sate
The livelong day, with patient expectation,
To see great Pompey pass the streets of Rome;
And when you saw his chariot but appear,
Have you not made an universal shout,
That Tiber trembled underneath her banks
To hear the replication of your sounds
Made in her concave shores?
And do you now put on your best attire?
And do you now cull out a holiday?
And do you now strew flowers in his way,
That comes in triumph over Pompey's blood?
Be gone!
Run to your houses, fall upon your knees,
Pray to the gods to intermit the plague
That needs must light on this ingratitude.

Flavius.
Go, go, good countrymen, and for this fault
Assemble all the poor men of your sort;
Draw them to Tiber banks, and weep your tears
Into the channel, till the lowest stream
Do kiss the most exalted shores of all.

Exeunt all the Commoners.

See whe'er their basest metal be not mov'd;
They vanish tongue-tied in their guiltiness.
Go you down that way towards the Capitol,
This way will I. Disrobe the images,
If you do find them deck'd with ceremonies.

Murellus.
May we do so?
You know it is the feast of Lupercal.

Flavius.
It is no matter, let no images
Be hung with Caesar's trophies, I'll about,
And drive away the vulgar from the streets;
So do you too, where you perceive them thick.
These growing feathers pluck'd from Caesar's wing
Will make him fly an ordinary pitch,
Who else would soar above the view of men,
And keep us all in servile tearfulness.

Exeunt.

Scene 2

Rome. A public place.

(*Caesar; Antony; Calphurnia; Portia; Decius; Cicero; Brutus; Cassius; Casca; Citizens; Soothsayer; Murellus; Flavius*)

Caesar and his suite enter. Antony is dressed running the Lupercal race. Caesar reminds him to touch Calphurnia as he runs, as this may cure her barrenness. A Soothsayer cries out and warns Caesar to beware the Ides of March, but the great man pays him no heed. Cassius talks to Brutus when the latter chooses not to view the races. He has noticed that Brutus is not happy of late. Cassius reminds him that his ancestor freed Rome from the tyranny of the monarchy. Brutus, who loves Caesar, nevertheless fears that the mob might acclaim him king, which he could not stand; Cassius, on the other hand, is sharply envious of Caesar's elevation, pointing out that he is only a man, in many ways a weak man, but is being turned into a god by the people. Caesar leaves the forum and admits to Antony that he is weary of Cassius. Casca tells Cassius and Brutus how Caesar was offered a crown but, to the people's delight, rejected it, though it seemed clear he hoped they would encourage him to take it, and fell down in a fit. They arrange to meet again the next day; Casca mentions that Flavius and Murellus have been arrested. Cassius sees that he will have to do more to make Brutus take action, and plans to send him letters written in various hands urging him to take down Caesar.

Enter Caesar, Antony for the course, Calphurnia, Portia, Decius, Cicero, Brutus, Cassius, Casca, Citizens, and a Soothsayer; after them Murellus and Flavius.

Julius Caesar.
Calphurnia!

Casca.
                Peace ho, Caesar speaks.

Julius Caesar.
                       Calphurnia!

Calphurnia.
Here, my lord.

Julius Caesar.
Stand you directly in Antonio's way
When he doth run his course. Antonio!

Mark Antony.
Caesar, my lord?

Julius Caesar.
Forget not in your speed, Antonio,
To touch Calphurnia; for our elders say,
The barren, touched in this holy chase,
Shake off their sterile curse.

Mark Antony.
                I shall remember:
When Caesar says, "Do this," it is perform'd.

Julius Caesar.
Set on, and leave no ceremony out.

Flourish.

Soothsayer.
Caesar!

Julius Caesar.
Ha? Who calls?

Casca.
Bid every noise be still; peace yet again!

Julius Caesar.
Who is it in the press that calls on me?
I hear a tongue shriller than all the music
Cry "Caesar!" Speak, Caesar is turn'd to hear.

Soothsayer.
Beware the ides of March.

Julius Caesar.
                What man is that?

Marcus Brutus.
A soothsayer bids you beware the Ides of March.

Julius Caesar.
Set him before me, let me see his face.

Cassius.
Fellow, come from the throng, look upon Caesar.

Julius Caesar.
What say'st thou to me now? Speak once again.

Soothsayer.
Beware the Ides of March.

Julius Caesar.
He is a dreamer, let us leave him. Pass.

Sennet.
Exeunt. Manent Brutus and Cassius.

Cassius.
Will you go see the order of the course?

Marcus Brutus.
Not I.

Cassius.
I pray you do.

Marcus Brutus.
I am not gamesome; I do lack some part
Of that quick spirit that is in Antony.
Let me not hinder, Cassius, your desires;
I'll leave you.

Cassius.
Brutus, I do observe you now of late;
I have not from your eyes that gentleness
And show of love as I was wont to have.
You bear too stubborn and too strange a hand
Over your friend that loves you.

Marcus Brutus.
                Cassius,
Be not deceiv'd. If I have veil'd my look,
I turn the trouble of my countenance
Merely upon myself. Vexed I am
Of late with passions of some difference,
Conceptions only proper to myself,
Which give some soil, perhaps, to my behaviors;
But let not therefore my good friends be griev'd
(Among which number, Cassius, be you one),
Nor construe any further my neglect,

Than that poor Brutus, with himself at war,
Forgets the shows of love to other men.

Cassius.
Then, Brutus, I have much mistook your passion,
By means whereof this breast of mine hath buried
Thoughts of great value, worthy cogitations.
Tell me, good Brutus, can you see your face?

Marcus Brutus.
No, Cassius; for the eye sees not itself
But by reflection, by some other things.

Cassius.
'Tis just,
And it is very much lamented, Brutus,
That you have no such mirrors as will turn
Your hidden worthiness into your eye,
That you might see your shadow. I have heard
Where many of the best respect in Rome
(Except immortal Caesar), speaking of Brutus
And groaning underneath this age's yoke,
Have wish'd that noble Brutus had his eyes.

Marcus Brutus.
Into what dangers would you lead me, Cassius,
That you would have me seek into myself
For that which is not in me?

Cassius.
Therefore, good Brutus, be prepar'd to hear;
And since you know you cannot see yourself
So well as by reflection, I, your glass,
Will modestly discover to yourself
That of yourself which you yet know not of.
And be not jealous on me, gentle Brutus:
Were I a common laughter, or did use
To stale with ordinary oaths my love
To every new protester; if you know
That I do fawn on men and hug them hard,
And after scandal them; or if you know
That I profess myself in banqueting
To all the rout, then hold me dangerous.

Flourish and shout.

Marcus Brutus.
What means this shouting? I do fear the people
Choose Caesar for their king.

Cassius.
            Ay, do you fear it?
Then must I think you would not have it so.

Marcus Brutus.
I would not, Cassius, yet I love him well.
But wherefore do you hold me here so long?
What is it that you would impart to me?
If it be aught toward the general good,
Set honor in one eye and death i' th' other,
And I will look on both indifferently;
For let the gods so speed me as I love
The name of honor more than I fear death.

Cassius.
I know that virtue to be in you, Brutus,
As well as I do know your outward favor.
Well, honor is the subject of my story:
I cannot tell what you and other men
Think of this life; but, for my single self,
I had as lief not be as live to be
In awe of such a thing as I myself.
I was born free as Caesar, so were you;
We both have fed as well, and we can both
Endure the winter's cold as well as he;
For once, upon a raw and gusty day,
The troubled Tiber chafing with her shores,
Caesar said to me, "Dar'st thou, Cassius, now
Leap in with me into this angry flood,
And swim to yonder point?" Upon the word,
Accoutred as I was, I plunged in,
And bade him follow; so indeed he did.
The torrent roar'd, and we did buffet it
With lusty sinews, throwing it aside
And stemming it with hearts of controversy;
But ere we could arrive the point propos'd,
Caesar cried, "Help me, Cassius, or I sink!"
I, as Aeneas, our great ancestor,
Did from the flames of Troy upon his shoulder
The old Anchises bear, so from the waves of Tiber
Did I the tired Caesar. And this man
Is now become a god, and Cassius is
A wretched creature, and must bend his body
If Caesar carelessly but nod on him.
He had a fever when he was in Spain,
And when the fit was on him, I did mark
How he did shake—'tis true, this god did shake;
His coward lips did from their color fly,
And that same eye whose bend doth awe the world
Did lose his lustre, I did hear him groan;
Ay, and that tongue of his that bade the Romans

Mark him, and write his speeches in their books,
Alas, it cried, "Give me some drink, Titinius,"
As a sick girl. Ye gods, it doth amaze me
A man of such a feeble temper should
So get the start of the majestic world
And bear the palm alone.

Shout. Flourish.

Marcus Brutus.
Another general shout!
I do believe that these applauses are
For some new honors that are heap'd on Caesar.

Cassius.
Why, man, he doth bestride the narrow world
Like a Colossus, and we petty men
Walk under his huge legs, and peep about
To find ourselves dishonorable graves.
Men at some time are masters of their fates;
The fault, dear Brutus, is not in our stars,
But in ourselves, that we are underlings.
Brutus and Caesar: what should be in that "Caesar"?
Why should that name be sounded more than yours?
Write them together, yours is as fair a name;
Sound them, it doth become the mouth as well;
Weigh them, it is as heavy; conjure with 'em,
"Brutus" will start a spirit as soon as "Caesar."
Now in the names of all the gods at once,
Upon what meat doth this our Caesar feed
That he is grown so great? Age, thou art sham'd!
Rome, thou hast lost the breed of noble bloods!
When went there by an age since the great flood
But it was fam'd with more than with one man?
When could they say, till now, that talk'd of Rome,
That her wide walks encompass'd but one man?
Now is it Rome indeed and room enough,
When there is in it but one only man.
O! You and I have heard our fathers say
There was a Brutus once that would have brook'd
Th' eternal devil to keep his state in Rome
As easily as a king.

Marcus Brutus.
That you do love me, I am nothing jealous;
What you would work me to, I have some aim.
How I have thought of this, and of these times,
I shall recount hereafter. For this present,
I would not (so with love I might entreat you)
Be any further mov'd. What you have said
I will consider; what you have to say
I will with patience hear, and find a time
Both meet to hear and answer such high things.
Till then, my noble friend, chew upon this:
Brutus had rather be a villager
Than to repute himself a son of Rome
Under these hard conditions as this time
Is like to lay upon us.

Cassius.
I am glad that my weak words
Have struck but thus much show of fire from Brutus.

Enter Caesar and his Train.

Marcus Brutus.
The games are done, and Caesar is returning.

Cassius.
As they pass by, pluck Casca by the sleeve,
And he will (after his sour fashion) tell you
What hath proceeded worthy note today.

Marcus Brutus.
I will do so. But look you, Cassius,
The angry spot doth glow on Caesar's brow,
And all the rest look like a chidden train:
Calphurnia's cheek is pale, and Cicero
Looks with such ferret and such fiery eyes
As we have seen him in the Capitol,
Being cross'd in conference by some senators.

Cassius.
Casca will tell us what the matter is.

Julius Caesar.
Antonio!

Mark Antony.
Caesar?

Julius Caesar.
Let me have men about me that are fat,
Sleek-headed men and such as sleep a-nights.
Yond Cassius has a lean and hungry look,
He thinks too much; such men are dangerous.

Mark Antony.
Fear him not, Caesar, he's not dangerous,
He is a noble Roman, and well given.

Julius Caesar.
Would he were fatter! But I fear him not.
Yet if my name were liable to fear,
I do not know the man I should avoid
So soon as that spare Cassius. He reads much,
He is a great observer, and he looks
Quite through the deeds of men. He loves no plays,
As thou dost, Antony; he hears no music;
Seldom he smiles, and smiles in such a sort
As if he mock'd himself, and scorn'd his spirit
That could be mov'd to smile at any thing.
Such men as he be never at heart's ease
Whiles they behold a greater than themselves,
And therefore are they very dangerous.
I rather tell thee what is to be fear'd
Than what I fear; for always I am Caesar.
Come on my right hand, for this ear is deaf,
And tell me truly what thou think'st of him.

Sennet. Exeunt Caesar and his Train. Casca stays.

Casca.
You pull'd me by the cloak, would you speak with me?

Marcus Brutus.
Ay, Casca, tell us what hath chanc'd today
That Caesar looks so sad.

Casca.
Why, you were with him, were you not?

Marcus Brutus.
I should not then ask Casca what had chanc'd.

Casca.
Why, there was a crown offer'd him; and being offer'd him, he put it by with the back of his hand thus, and then the people fell a-shouting.

Marcus Brutus.
What was the second noise for?

Casca.
Why, for that too.

Cassius.
They shouted thrice; what was the last cry for?

Casca.
Why, for that too.

Marcus Brutus.
Was the crown offer'd him thrice?

Casca.
Ay, marry, was't, and he put it by thrice, every time gentler than other; and at every putting-by mine honest neighbors shouted.

Cassius.
Who offer'd him the crown?

Casca.
Why, Antony.

Marcus Brutus.
Tell us the manner of it, gentle Casca.

Casca.
I can as well be hang'd as tell the manner of it: it was mere foolery, I did not mark it. I saw Mark Antony offer him a crown—yet 'twas not a crown neither, 'twas one of these coronets—and as I told you, he put it by once; but for all that, to my thinking, he would fain have had it. Then he offer'd it to him again; then he put it by again; but, to my thinking, he was very loath to lay his fingers off it. And then he offer'd it the third time; he put it the third time by; and still as he refus'd it, the rabblement howted, and clapp'd their chopp'd hands, and threw up their sweaty night-caps, and utter'd such a deal of stinking breath because Caesar refus'd the crown, that it had, almost, chok'd Caesar, for he swounded, and fell down at it; and for mine own part, I durst not laugh, for fear of opening my lips and receiving the bad air.

Cassius.
But soft I pray you; what, did Caesar swound?

Casca.
He fell down in the market-place, and foam'd at mouth, and was speechless.

Marcus Brutus.
'Tis very like, he hath the falling sickness.

Cassius.
No, Caesar hath it not; but you, and I,
And honest Casca, we have the falling sickness.

Casca.
I know not what you mean by that, but I am sure Caesar fell down. If the tag-rag people did not clap him and hiss him, according as he pleas'd and displeas'd them, as they use to do the players in the theatre, I am no true man.

Marcus Brutus.
What said he when he came unto himself?

Casca.
Marry, before he fell down, when he perceiv'd the common herd was glad he refus'd the crown, he pluck'd me ope his doublet, and offer'd them his throat to cut. And I had been a man of any occupation, if I would not have taken him at a word, I would I might go to hell among the rogues. And so he fell. When he came to himself again, he said, if he had done or said any thing amiss, he desir'd their worships to think it was his infirmity. Three or four wenches, where I stood, cried, "Alas, good soul!" and forgave him with all their hearts. But there's no heed to be taken of them; if Caesar had stabb'd their mothers, they would have done no less.

Marcus Brutus.
And after that, he came thus sad away?

Casca.
Ay.

Cassius.
Did Cicero say any thing?

Casca.
Ay, he spoke Greek.

Cassius.
To what effect?

Casca.
Nay, and I tell you that, I'll ne'er look you i' th' face again. But those that understood him smil'd at one another, and shook their heads; but, for mine own part, it was Greek to me. I could tell you more news too. Murellus and Flavius, for pulling scarfs off Caesar's images, are put to silence. Fare you well. There was more foolery yet, if I could remember it.

Cassius.
Will you sup with me tonight, Casca?

Casca.
No, I am promis'd forth.

Cassius.
Will you dine with me tomorrow?

Casca.
Ay, if I be alive, and your mind hold, and your dinner worth the eating.

Cassius.
Good, I will expect you.

Casca.
Do so. Farewell both.

Exit.

Marcus Brutus.
What a blunt fellow is this grown to be!
He was quick mettle when he went to school.

Cassius.
So is he now in execution
Of any bold or noble enterprise,
However he puts on this tardy form.
This rudeness is a sauce to his good wit,
Which gives men stomach to digest his words
With better appetite.

Marcus Brutus.
And so it is. For this time I will leave you;
Tomorrow, if you please to speak with me,
I will come home to you; or, if you will,
Come home to me, and I will wait for you.

Cassius.
I will do so; till then, think of the world.

Exit Brutus.

Well, Brutus, thou art noble; yet I see
Thy honorable mettle may be wrought
From that it is dispos'd; therefore it is meet
That noble minds keep ever with their likes;
For who so firm that cannot be seduc'd?
Caesar doth bear me hard, but he loves Brutus.
If I were Brutus now and he were Cassius,
He should not humor me. I will this night,
In several hands, in at his windows throw,
As if they came from several citizens,
Writings, all tending to the great opinion
That Rome holds of his name; wherein obscurely
Caesar's ambition shall be glanced at.
And after this let Caesar seat him sure,
For we will shake him, or worse days endure.

Exit.

Scene 3

Rome. A street.

(Casca; Cicero; Cassius; Cinna)

Cicero and Casca meet in the middle of a tremendous storm. The cynical Casca has been brought to the edge of terror, and tells Cicero of the various strange omens that have occurred that night. Casca and Cassius meet, and the undaunted Cassius uses the storm as an image to incite Casca against Caesar. The senate has decided to name Caesar king the next day. Other conspirators join them; Cassius gives them letters for Brutus and they plan to meet at his house the next day to convince him to participate in the plot.

Thunder and lightning.
Enter from opposite sides Casca with his sword drawn and Cicero.

Cicero.
Good even, Casca; brought you Caesar home?
Why are you breathless, and why stare you so?

Casca.
Are not you mov'd, when all the sway of earth
Shakes like a thing unfirm? O Cicero,
I have seen tempests when the scolding winds
Have riv'd the knotty oaks, and I have seen
Th' ambitious ocean swell, and rage, and foam,
To be exalted with the threat'ning clouds;
But never till tonight, never till now,
Did I go through a tempest dropping fire.
Either there is a civil strife in heaven,
Or else the world, too saucy with the gods,
Incenses them to send destruction.

Cicero.
Why, saw you any thing more wonderful?

Casca.
A common slave—you know him well by sight—
Held up his left hand, which did flame and burn
Like twenty torches join'd; and yet his hand,
Not sensible of fire, remain'd unscorch'd.
Besides—I ha' not since put up my sword—
Against the Capitol I met a lion,
Who glaz'd upon me, and went surly by,
Without annoying me. And there were drawn
Upon a heap a hundred ghastly women,
Transformed with their fear, who swore they saw
Men, all in fire, walk up and down the streets.
And yesterday the bird of night did sit
Even at noon-day upon the market-place,
Howting and shrieking. When these prodigies
Do so conjointly meet, let not men say,
"These are their reasons, they are natural";
For I believe they are portentous things
Unto the climate that they point upon.

Cicero.
Indeed, it is a strange-disposed time;
But men may construe things after their fashion,
Clean from the purpose of the things themselves.
Comes Caesar to the Capitol tomorrow?

Casca.
He doth; for he did bid Antonio
Send word to you he would be there tomorrow.

Cicero.
Good night then, Casca; this disturbed sky
Is not to walk in.

Casca.
                    Farewell, Cicero.

Exit Cicero.
Enter Cassius.

Cassius.
Who's there?

Casca.
                    A Roman.

Cassius.
                    Casca, by your voice.

Casca.
Your ear is good. Cassius, what night is this!

Cassius.
A very pleasing night to honest men.

Casca.
Who ever knew the heavens menace so?

Cassius.
Those that have known the earth so full of faults.
For my part, I have walk'd about the streets,
Submitting me unto the perilous night;
And thus unbraced, Casca, as you see,
Have bar'd my bosom to the thunder-stone;
And when the cross blue lightning seem'd to open
The breast of heaven, I did present myself

Even in the aim and very flash of it.

Casca.
But wherefore did you so much tempt the heavens?
It is the part of men to fear and tremble
When the most mighty gods by tokens send
Such dreadful heralds to astonish us.

Cassius.
You are dull, Casca; and those sparks of life
That should be in a Roman you do want,
Or else you use not. You look pale, and gaze,
And put on fear, and cast yourself in wonder,
To see the strange impatience of the heavens;
But if you would consider the true cause
Why all these fires, why all these gliding ghosts,
Why birds and beasts from quality and kind,
Why old men, fools, and children calculate,
Why all these things change from their ordinance,
Their natures, and preformed faculties,
To monstrous quality—why, you shall find
That heaven hath infus'd them with these spirits,
To make them instruments of fear and warning
Unto some monstrous state.
Now could I, Casca, name to thee a man
Most like this dreadful night,
That thunders, lightens, opens graves, and roars
As doth the lion in the Capitol—
A man no mightier than thyself, or me,
In personal action, yet prodigious grown,
And fearful, as these strange eruptions are.

Casca.
'Tis Caesar that you mean; is it not, Cassius?

Cassius.
Let it be who it is; for Romans now
Have thews and limbs like to their ancestors;
But woe the while, our fathers' minds are dead,
And we are govern'd with our mothers' spirits;
Our yoke and sufferance show us womanish.

Casca.
Indeed, they say, the senators tomorrow
Mean to establish Caesar as a king;
And he shall wear his crown by sea and land,
In every place, save here in Italy.

Cassius.
I know where I will wear this dagger then;
Cassius from bondage will deliver Cassius.
Therein, ye gods, you make the weak most strong;
Therein, ye gods, you tyrants do defeat;
Nor stony tower, nor walls of beaten brass,
Nor airless dungeon, nor strong links of iron,
Can be retentive to the strength of spirit;
But life, being weary of these worldly bars,
Never lacks power to dismiss itself.
If I know this, know all the world besides,
That part of tyranny that I do bear
I can shake off at pleasure.

Thunder still.

Casca.
               So can I;
So every bondman in his own hand bears
The power to cancel his captivity.

Cassius.
And why should Caesar be a tyrant then?
Poor man, I know he would not be a wolf,
But that he sees the Romans are but sheep;
He were no lion, were not Romans hinds.
Those that with haste will make a mighty fire
Begin it with weak straws. What trash is Rome?
What rubbish and what offal? When it serves
For the base matter to illuminate
So vile a thing as Caesar! But, O grief,
Where hast thou led me? I, perhaps, speak this
Before a willing bondman; then I know
My answer must be made. But I am arm'd,
And dangers are to me indifferent.

Casca.
You speak to Casca, and to such a man
That is no fleering tell-tale. Hold, my hand.
Be factious for redress of all these griefs,
And I will set this foot of mine as far
As who goes farthest.

Cassius.
              There's a bargain made.
Now know you, Casca, I have mov'd already
Some certain of the noblest-minded Romans
To undergo with me an enterprise
Of honorable-dangerous consequence;
And I do know, by this they stay for me
In Pompey's Porch; for now, this fearful night,
There is no stir or walking in the streets;
And the complexion of the element
In favor's like the work we have in hand,
Most bloody, fiery, and most terrible.

Enter Cinna.

Casca.
Stand close a while, for here comes one in haste.

Cassius.
'Tis Cinna, I do know him by his gait,
He is a friend. Cinna, where haste you so?

Cinna.
To find out you. Who's that? Metellus Cimber?

Cassius.
No, it is Casca, one incorporate
To our attempts. Am I not stay'd for, Cinna?

Cinna.
I am glad on't. What a fearful night is this!
There's two or three of us have seen strange sights.

Cassius.
Am I not stay'd for? Tell me.

Cinna.
                    Yes, you are.
O Cassius, if you could
But win the noble Brutus to our party—

Cassius.
Be you content. Good Cinna, take this paper,
And look you lay it in the praetor's chair,
Where Brutus may but find it; and throw this
In at his window; set this up with wax
Upon old Brutus' statue. All this done,
Repair to Pompey's Porch, where you shall find us.
Is Decius Brutus and Trebonius there?

Cinna.
All but Metellus Cimber, and he's gone
To seek you at your house. Well, I will hie,
And so bestow these papers as you bade me.

Cassius.
That done, repair to Pompey's theatre.

Exit Cinna.

Come, Casca, you and I will yet, ere day,
See Brutus at his house. Three parts of him
Is ours already, and the man entire
Upon the next encounter yields him ours.

Casca.
O, he sits high in all the people's hearts;
And that which would appear offense in us,
His countenance, like richest alchymy,
Will change to virtue and to worthiness.

Cassius.
Him and his worth, and our great need of him,
You have right well conceited. Let us go,
For it is after midnight, and ere day
We will awake him and be sure of him.

Exeunt.

Act 2

Scene 1

Rome. Brutus's orchard.

(Brutus; Lucius; Cassius; Casca; Decius; Cinna; Metellus; Trebonius; Portia; Caius Ligarius)

Sleepless, Brutus considers that he has no good reason to be rid of Caesar other than the likelihood that he will do something tyrannous, though he never has yet, and the only way to be rid of him is to kill him. His servant Lucius brings him yet another anonymous letter found in an odd place, again inciting Brutus to rise up against Caesar. He resolves that he will. The other conspirators arrive and agree that they are all there for the same purpose. Many of them want to add Cicero to their number, but Brutus refuses, arguing that he will insist on leading. Brutus also insists that they kill only Caesar, so that they will not appear to be carrying out a bloodthirsty coup, but rather a necessary surgery. Cassius in the end agrees, but still thinks Antony should be killed as well. Decius Brutus promises to make sure that Caesar goes to the Capitol that day. The conspirators leave, waiting to meet again at the time of the assassination. Brutus's wife Portia, who has been worried by her husband's concerned looks and insomnia, asks him what the matter is; he promises to tell her later. Caius Ligarius, with a handkerchief hiding his face, comes to assure Brutus that he will join the conspiracy.

Enter Brutus in his orchard.

Marcus Brutus.
What, Lucius, ho!
I cannot by the progress of the stars
Give guess how near to day. Lucius, I say!

I would it were my fault to sleep so soundly.
When, Lucius, when? Awake, I say! What, Lucius!

Enter Lucius.

Lucius.
Call'd you, my lord?

Marcus Brutus.
Get me a taper in my study, Lucius.
When it is lighted, come and call me here.

Lucius.
I will, my lord.

Exit.

Marcus Brutus.
It must be by his death; and for my part,
I know no personal cause to spurn at him,
But for the general. He would be crown'd:
How that might change his nature, there's the question.
It is the bright day that brings forth the adder,
And that craves wary walking. Crown him that,
And then I grant we put a sting in him
That at his will he may do danger with.
Th' abuse of greatness is when it disjoins
Remorse from power; and to speak truth of Caesar,
I have not known when his affections sway'd
More than his reason. But 'tis a common proof
That lowliness is young ambition's ladder,
Whereto the climber-upward turns his face;
But when he once attains the upmost round,
He then unto the ladder turns his back,
Looks in the clouds, scorning the base degrees
By which he did ascend. So Caesar may;
Then lest he may, prevent. And since the quarrel
Will bear no color for the thing he is,
Fashion it thus: that what he is, augmented,
Would run to these and these extremities;
And therefore think him as a serpent's egg,
Which, hatch'd, would as his kind grow mischievous,
And kill him in the shell.

Enter Lucius.

Lucius.
The taper burneth in your closet, sir.
Searching the window for a flint, I found
This paper, thus seal'd up, and I am sure
It did not lie there when I went to bed.

Gives him the letter.

Marcus Brutus.
Get you to bed again, it is not day.
Is not tomorrow, boy, the ides of March?

Lucius.
I know not, sir.

Marcus Brutus.
Look in the calendar, and bring me word.

Lucius.
I will, sir.

Exit.

Marcus Brutus.
The exhalations whizzing in the air
Give so much light that I may read by them.

Opens the letter and reads.

"Brutus, thou sleep'st; awake, and see thyself!
Shall Rome, etc. Speak, strike, redress!"
"Brutus, thou sleep'st; awake!"
Such instigations have been often dropp'd
Where I have took them up.
"Shall Rome, etc." Thus must I piece it out:
Shall Rome stand under one man's awe? What, Rome?
My ancestors did from the streets of Rome
The Tarquin drive when he was call'd a king.
"Speak, strike, redress!" Am I entreated
To speak and strike? O Rome, I make thee promise,
If the redress will follow, thou receivest
Thy full petition at the hand of Brutus!

Enter Lucius.

Lucius.
Sir, March is wasted fifteen days.

Knock within.

Marcus Brutus.
'Tis good. Go to the gate, somebody knocks.

Exit Lucius.

Since Cassius first did whet me against Caesar,
I have not slept.
Between the acting of a dreadful thing

And the first motion, all the interim is
Like a phantasma or a hideous dream.
The Genius and the mortal instruments
Are then in council; and the state of a man,
Like to a little kingdom, suffers then
The nature of an insurrection.

Enter Lucius.

Lucius.
Sir, 'tis your brother Cassius at the door,
Who doth desire to see you.

Marcus Brutus.
                Is he alone?

Lucius.
No, sir, there are more with him.

Marcus Brutus.
                Do you know them?

Lucius.
No, sir, their hats are pluck'd about their ears,
And half their faces buried in their cloaks,
That by no means I may discover them
By any mark of favor.

Marcus Brutus.
                Let 'em enter.

Exit Lucius.

They are the faction. O Conspiracy,
Sham'st thou to show thy dang'rous brow by night,
When evils are most free? O then, by day
Where wilt thou find a cavern dark enough
To mask thy monstrous visage? Seek none, Conspiracy!
Hide it in smiles and affability;
For if thou path, thy native semblance on,
Not Erebus itself were dim enough
To hide thee from prevention.

Enter the conspirators, Cassius, Casca, Decius, Cinna, Metellus, and Trebonius.

Cassius.
I think we are too bold upon your rest.
Good morrow, Brutus, do we trouble you?

Marcus Brutus.
I have been up this hour, awake all night.
Know I these men that come along with you?

Cassius.
Yes, every man of them; and no man here
But honors you; and every one doth wish
You had but that opinion of yourself
Which every noble Roman bears of you.
This is Trebonius.

Marcus Brutus.
                He is welcome hither.

Cassius.
This, Decius Brutus.

Marcus Brutus.
                He is welcome too.

Cassius.
This, Casca; this, Cinna; and this, Metellus Cimber.

Marcus Brutus.
They are all welcome.
What watchful cares do interpose themselves
Betwixt your eyes and night?

Cassius.
Shall I entreat a word?

They whisper.

Decius Brutus.
Here lies the east; doth not the day break here?

Casca.
No.

Cinna.
O, pardon, sir, it doth; and yon grey lines
That fret the clouds are messengers of day.

Casca.
You shall confess that you are both deceiv'd.
Here, as I point my sword, the sun arises,
Which is a great way growing on the south,
Weighing the youthful season of the year.
Some two months hence, up higher toward the north
He first presents his fire, and the high east
Stands, as the Capitol, directly here.

Marcus Brutus.
Give me your hands all over, one by one.

Cassius.
And let us swear our resolution.

Marcus Brutus.
No, not an oath! If not the face of men,
The sufferance of our souls, the time's abuse—
If these be motives weak, break off betimes,
And every man hence to his idle bed;
So let high-sighted tyranny range on,
Till each man drop by lottery. But if these
(As I am sure they do) bear fire enough
To kindle cowards, and to steel with valor
The melting spirits of women, then, countrymen,
What need we any spur but our own cause
To prick us to redress? What other bond
Than secret Romans, that have spoke the word
And will not palter? And what other oath
Than honesty to honesty engag'd
That this shall be, or we will fall for it?
Swear priests and cowards, and men cautelous,
Old feeble carrions, and such suffering souls
That welcome wrongs; unto bad causes swear
Such creatures as men doubt; but do not stain
The even virtue of our enterprise,
Nor th' insuppressive mettle of our spirits,
To think that or our cause or our performance
Did need an oath; when every drop of blood
That every Roman bears, and nobly bears,
Is guilty of a several bastardy,
If he do break the smallest particle
Of any promise that hath pass'd from him.

Cassius.
But what of Cicero? Shall we sound him?
I think he will stand very strong with us.

Casca.
Let us not leave him out.

Cinna.
               No, by no means.

Metellus Cimber.
O, let us have him, for his silver hairs
Will purchase us a good opinion,
And buy men's voices to commend our deeds.
It shall be said his judgment rul'd our hands;
Our youths and wildness shall no whit appear,
But all be buried in his gravity.

Marcus Brutus.
O, name him not; let us not break with him,
For he will never follow any thing
That other men begin.

Cassius.
               Then leave him out.

Casca.
Indeed he is not fit.

Decius Brutus.
Shall no man else be touch'd but only Caesar?

Cassius.
Decius, well urg'd. I think it is not meet,
Mark Antony, so well belov'd of Caesar,
Should outlive Caesar. We shall find of him
A shrewd contriver; and you know, his means,
If he improve them, may well stretch so far
As to annoy us all; which to prevent,
Let Antony and Caesar fall together.

Marcus Brutus.
Our course will seem too bloody, Caius Cassius,
To cut the head off and then hack the limbs—
Like wrath in death and envy afterwards;
For Antony is but a limb of Caesar.
Let's be sacrificers, but not butchers, Caius.
We all stand up against the spirit of Caesar,
And in the spirit of men there is no blood;
O that we then could come by Caesar's spirit,
And not dismember Caesar! But, alas,
Caesar must bleed for it! And, gentle friends,
Let's kill him boldly, but not wrathfully;
Let's carve him as a dish fit for the gods,
Not hew him as a carcass fit for hounds;
And let our hearts, as subtle masters do,
Stir up their servants to an act of rage,
And after seem to chide 'em. This shall make
Our purpose necessary, and not envious;
Which so appearing to the common eyes,
We shall be call'd purgers, not murderers,
And for Mark Antony, think not of him;
For he can do no more than Caesar's arm
When Caesar's head is off.

Cassius.
               Yet I fear him,
For in the ingrafted love he bears to Caesar—

Marcus Brutus.
Alas, good Cassius, do not think of him.
If he love Caesar, all that he can do
Is to himself—take thought and die for Caesar;
And that were much he should, for he is given
To sports, to wildness, and much company.

Trebonius.
There is no fear in him; let him not die,
For he will live, and laugh at this hereafter.

Clock strikes.

Marcus Brutus.
Peace, count the clock.

Cassius.
              The clock hath stricken three.

Trebonius.
'Tis time to part.

Cassius.
              But it is doubtful yet
Whether Caesar will come forth today or no;
For he is superstitious grown of late,
Quite from the main opinion he held once
Of fantasy, of dreams, and ceremonies.
It may be these apparent prodigies,
The unaccustom'd terror of this night,
And the persuasion of his augurers
May hold him from the Capitol today.

Decius Brutus.
Never fear that. If he be so resolv'd,
I can o'ersway him; for he loves to hear
That unicorns may be betray'd with trees,
And bears with glasses, elephants with holes,
Lions with toils, and men with flatterers;
But when I tell him he hates flatterers
He says he does, being then most flattered.
Let me work;
For I can give his humor the true bent,
And I will bring him to the Capitol.

Cassius.
Nay, we will all of us be there to fetch him.

Marcus Brutus.
By the eight hour; is that the uttermost?

Cinna.
Be that the uttermost, and fail not then.

Metellus Cimber.
Caius Ligarius doth bear Caesar hard,
Who rated him for speaking well of Pompey;
I wonder none of you have thought of him.

Marcus Brutus.
Now, good Metellus, go along by him.
He loves me well, and I have given him reasons;
Send him but hither, and I'll fashion him.

Cassius.
The morning comes upon's. We'll leave you, Brutus,
And, friends, disperse yourselves; but all remember
What you have said, and show yourselves true Romans.

Marcus Brutus.
Good gentlemen, look fresh and merrily;
Let not our looks put on our purposes,
But bear it as our Roman actors do,
With untir'd spirits and formal constancy.
And so good morrow to you every one.

Exeunt. Manet Brutus.

Boy! Lucius! Fast asleep? It is no matter,
Enjoy the honey-heavy dew of slumber.
Thou hast no figures nor no fantasies,
Which busy care draws in the brains of men;
Therefore thou sleep'st so sound.

Enter Portia.

Portia.
              Brutus, my lord!

Marcus Brutus.
Portia! What mean you? Wherefore rise you now?
It is not for your health thus to commit
Your weak condition to the raw cold morning.

Portia.
Nor for yours neither. Y' have ungently, Brutus,
Stole from my bed; and yesternight at supper
You suddenly arose and walk'd about,
Musing and sighing, with your arms across;
And when I ask'd you what the matter was,
You star'd upon me with ungentle looks.
I urg'd you further; then you scratch'd your head,
And too impatiently stamp'd with your foot.

Yet I insisted, yet you answer'd not,
But with an angry wafter of your hand
Gave sign for me to leave you. So I did,
Fearing to strengthen that impatience
Which seem'd too much enkindled; and withal
Hoping it was but an effect of humor,
Which sometime hath his hour with every man.
It will not let you eat, nor talk, nor sleep;
And could it work so much upon your shape
As it hath much prevail'd on your condition,
I should not know you Brutus. Dear my lord,
Make me acquainted with your cause of grief.

Marcus Brutus.
I am not well in health, and that is all.

Portia.
Brutus is wise, and were he not in health,
He would embrace the means to come by it.

Marcus Brutus.
Why, so I do. Good Portia, go to bed.

Portia.
Is Brutus sick? And is it physical
To walk unbraced and suck up the humors
Of the dank morning? What, is Brutus sick?
And will he steal out of his wholesome bed
To dare the vile contagion of the night,
And tempt the rheumy and unpurged air
To add unto his sickness? No, my Brutus,
You have some sick offense within your mind,
Which, by the right and virtue of my place,
I ought to know of; and upon my knees
I charm you, by my once commended beauty,
By all your vows of love, and that great vow
Which did incorporate and make us one,
That you unfold to me, yourself, your half,
Why you are heavy, and what men tonight
Have had resort to you; for here have been
Some six or seven, who did hide their faces
Even from darkness.

Marcus Brutus.
                Kneel not, gentle Portia.

Portia.
I should not need, if you were gentle Brutus.
Within the bond of marriage, tell me, Brutus,
Is it excepted I should know no secrets
That appertain to you? Am I yourself
But, as it were, in sort or limitation.

To keep with you at meals, comfort your bed,
And talk to you sometimes? Dwell I but in the suburbs
Of your good pleasure? If it be no more,
Portia is Brutus' harlot, not his wife.

Marcus Brutus.
You are my true and honorable wife,
As dear to me as are the ruddy drops
That visit my sad heart.

Portia.
If this were true, then should I know this secret.
I grant I am a woman; but withal
A woman that Lord Brutus took to wife.
I grant I am a woman; but withal
A woman well reputed, Cato's daughter.
Think you I am no stronger than my sex,
Being so father'd and so husbanded?
Tell me your counsels, I will not disclose 'em.
I have made strong proof of my constancy,
Giving myself a voluntary wound
Here, in the thigh; can I bear that with patience,
And not my husband's secrets?

Marcus Brutus.
                O ye gods!
Render me worthy of this noble wife!

Knock.

Hark, hark, one knocks! Portia, go in a while,
And by and by thy bosom shall partake
The secrets of my heart.
All my engagements I will construe to thee,
All the charactery of my sad brows.
Leave me with haste.

Exit Portia.

                Lucius, who's that knocks?

Enter Lucius and Caius Ligarius.

Lucius.
Here is a sick man that would speak with you.

Marcus Brutus.
Caius Ligarius, that Metellus spake of.
Boy, stand aside.

Exit Lucius.

Caius Ligarius, how?

Act 2, Scene 2

Caius Ligarius.
Vouchsafe good morrow from a feeble tongue.

Marcus Brutus.
O, what a time have you chose out, brave Caius,
To wear a kerchief! Would you were not sick!

Caius Ligarius.
I am not sick, if Brutus have in hand
Any exploit worthy the name of honor.

Marcus Brutus.
Such an exploit have I in hand, Ligarius,
Had you a healthful ear to hear of it.

Caius Ligarius.
By all the gods that Romans bow before,
I here discard my sickness! Soul of Rome!
Brave son, deriv'd from honorable loins!
Thou, like an exorcist, hast conjur'd up
My mortified spirit. Now bid me run,
And I will strive with things impossible,
Yea, get the better of them. What's to do?

Marcus Brutus.
A piece of work that will make sick men whole.

Caius Ligarius.
But are not some whole that we must make sick?

Marcus Brutus.
That must we also. What it is, my Caius,
I shall unfold to thee, as we are going,
To whom it must be done.

Caius Ligarius.
Set on your foot,
And with a heart new-fir'd I follow you,
To do I know not what; but it sufficeth
That Brutus leads me on.

Thunder.

Marcus Brutus.
      Follow me then.

Exeunt.

Scene 2

Rome. Caesar's house.

(*Julius Caesar; Caesar's Servant; Calphurnia; Decius; Brutus; Ligarius; Metellus; Casca; Trebonius; Cinna; Publius; Mark Antony*)

Caesar's sleep has been disturbed by the storm and his wife Calphurnia's bad dreams. He calls for the priests to make sacrifices to see what sort of a day it will be. Calphurnia begs him not to go to the Capitol, terrified by the omen ridden dreams she has had. The priests report back that they are unable to read anything in the entrails today, and recommend that he stay home. He agrees to do so. Decius Brutus arrives and convinces him to go, first reinterpreting Calphurnia's dream to give it a happy meaning, and secondly implying that Caesar will be a coward to stay.

Thunder and lightning.
Enter Julius Caesar in his night-gown.

Julius Caesar.
Nor heaven nor earth have been at peace tonight.
Thrice hath Calphurnia in her sleep cried out,
"Help, ho! They murder Caesar!" Who's within?

Enter a Servant.

Caesar's Servant.
My lord?

Julius Caesar.
Go bid the priests do present sacrifice,
And bring me their opinions of success.

Caesar's Servant.
I will, my lord.

Exit.
Enter Calphurnia.

Calphurnia.
What mean you, Caesar? Think you to walk forth?
You shall not stir out of your house today.

Julius Caesar.
Caesar shall forth; the things that threaten'd me
Ne'er look'd but on my back; when they shall see
The face of Caesar, they are vanished.

Calphurnia.
Caesar, I never stood on ceremonies,
Yet now they fright me. There is one within,
Besides the things that we have heard and seen,
Recounts most horrid sights seen by the watch.
A lioness hath whelped in the streets,

And graves have yawn'd and yielded up their dead;
Fierce fiery warriors fight upon the clouds
In ranks and squadrons and right form of war,
Which drizzled blood upon the Capitol;
The noise of battle hurtled in the air;
Horses did neigh, and dying men did groan,
And ghosts did shriek and squeal about the streets.
O Caesar, these things are beyond all use,
And I do fear them.

Julius Caesar.
                        What can be avoided
Whose end is purpos'd by the mighty gods?
Yet Caesar shall go forth; for these predictions
Are to the world in general as to Caesar.

Calphurnia.
When beggars die there are no comets seen;
The heavens themselves blaze forth the death of princes.

Julius Caesar.
Cowards die many times before their deaths,
The valiant never taste of death but once.
Of all the wonders that I yet have heard,
It seems to me most strange that men should fear,
Seeing that death, a necessary end,
Will come when it will come.

Enter a Servant.
                        What say the augurers?

Caesar's Servant.
They would not have you to stir forth today.
Plucking the entrails of an offering forth,
They could not find a heart within the beast.

Julius Caesar.
The gods do this in shame of cowardice;
Caesar should be a beast without a heart
If he should stay at home today for fear.
No, Caesar shall not; Danger knows full well
That Caesar is more dangerous than he.
We are two lions litter'd in one day,
And I the elder and more terrible;
And Caesar shall go forth.

Calphurnia.
                      Alas, my lord,
Your wisdom is consum'd in confidence.
Do not go forth today; call it my fear
That keeps you in the house, and not your own.
We'll send Mark Antony to the Senate-house,
And he shall say you are not well today.
Let me, upon my knee, prevail in this.

Julius Caesar.
Mark Antony shall say I am not well,
And for thy humor I will stay at home.

Enter Decius.

Here's Decius Brutus, he shall tell them so.

Decius Brutus.
Caesar, all hail! Good morrow, worthy Caesar,
I come to fetch you to the Senate-house.

Julius Caesar.
And you are come in very happy time
To bear my greeting to the senators,
And tell them that I will not come today.
Cannot, is false; and that I dare not, falser:
I will not come today. Tell them so, Decius.

Calphurnia.
Say he is sick.

Julius Caesar.
                  Shall Caesar send a lie?
Have I in conquest stretch'd mine arm so far,
To be afeard to tell greybeards the truth?
Decius, go tell them Caesar will not come.

Decius Brutus.
Most mighty Caesar, let me know some cause,
Lest I be laugh'd at when I tell them so.

Julius Caesar.
The cause is in my will, I will not come:
That is enough to satisfy the Senate.
But for your private satisfaction,
Because I love you, I will let you know.
Calphurnia here, my wife, stays me at home:
She dreamt tonight she saw my statuë,
Which, like a fountain with an hundred spouts,
Did run pure blood; and many lusty Romans
Came smiling and did bathe their hands in it.
And these does she apply for warnings and portents
And evils imminent, and on her knee
Hath begg'd that I will stay at home today.

Decius Brutus.
This dream is all amiss interpreted,
It was a vision fair and fortunate.
Your statue spouting blood in many pipes,

In which so many smiling Romans bath'd,
Signifies that from you great Rome shall suck
Reviving blood, and that great men shall press
For tinctures, stains, relics, and cognizance.
This by Calphurnia's dream is signified.

Julius Caesar.
And this way have you well expounded it.

Decius Brutus.
I have, when you have heard what I can say;
And know it now: the Senate have concluded
To give this day a crown to mighty Caesar.
If you shall send them word you will not come,
Their minds may change. Besides, it were a mock
Apt to be render'd, for some one to say,
"Break up the Senate till another time,
When Caesar's wife shall meet with better dreams."
If Caesar hide himself, shall they not whisper,
"Lo Caesar is afraid"?
Pardon me, Caesar, for my dear dear love
To your proceeding bids me tell you this;
And reason to my love is liable.

Julius Caesar.
How foolish do your fears seem now, Calphurnia!
I am ashamed I did yield to them.
Give me my robe, for I will go.

Enter Brutus, Ligarius, Metellus, Casca, Trebonius, Cinna, and Publius.

And look where Publius is come to fetch me.

Publius.
Good morrow, Caesar.

Julius Caesar.
              Welcome, Publius.
What, Brutus, are you stirr'd so early too?
Good morrow, Casca. Caius Ligarius,
Caesar was ne'er so much your enemy
As that same ague which hath made you lean.
What is't a' clock?

Marcus Brutus.
              Caesar, 'tis strucken eight.

Julius Caesar.
I thank you for your pains and courtesy.

Enter Antony.

See, Antony, that revels long a-nights,
Is notwithstanding up. Good morrow, Antony.

Mark Antony.
So to most noble Caesar.

Julius Caesar.
Bid them prepare within;
I am to blame to be thus waited for.
Now, Cinna; now, Metellus; what, Trebonius:
I have an hour's talk in store for you;
Remember that you call on me today;
Be near me, that I may remember you.

Trebonius.
Caesar, I will;

Aside.

And so near will I be,
That your best friends shall wish I had been further.

Julius Caesar.
Good friends, go in, and taste some wine with me,
And we, like friends, will straightway go together.

Marcus Brutus.

Aside.

That every like is not the same, O Caesar,
The heart of Brutus earns to think upon!

Exeunt.

Scene 3

Rome. A street near the capitol.

(Artemidorus)

Artemidorus rereads a letter he hopes to deliver to Caesar that warns him against the conspirators.

Enter Artemidorus reading a paper.

Artemidorus of Cnidos.
"Caesar, beware of Brutus; take heed of Cassius; come not near Casca; have an eye to Cinna; trust not Trebonius; mark well Metellus Cimber; Decius Brutus loves thee not; thou hast wrong'd Caius Ligarius. There is but one mind in all these men, and it is bent against Caesar. If thou beest not immortal, look about you; security gives way to conspiracy. The mighty gods defend thee! Thy lover, Artemidorus."
Here will I stand till Caesar pass along,
And as a suitor will I give him this.
My heart laments that virtue cannot live

Out of the teeth of emulation.
If thou read this, O Caesar, thou mayest live;
If not, the Fates with traitors do contrive.

Exit.

Scene 4

Rome. A street before the house of Brutus.

(Portia; Lucius; Soothsayer)

The nervous Portia sends Lucius to see what is happening at the Capitol. She sees the Soothsayer take place to speak to Caesar again and is terrified that he may know something.

Enter Portia and Lucius.

Portia.
I prithee, boy, run to the Senate-house;
Stay not to answer me, but get thee gone.
Why dost thou stay?

Lucius.
              To know my errand, madam.

Portia.
I would have had thee there and here again
Ere I can tell thee what thou shouldst do there.—
O constancy, be strong upon my side,
Set a huge mountain 'tween my heart and tongue!
I have a man's mind, but a woman's might.
How hard it is for women to keep counsel!—
Art thou here yet?

Lucius.
              Madam, what should I do?
Run to the Capitol, and nothing else?
And so return to you, and nothing else?

Portia.
Yes, bring me word, boy, if thy lord look well,
For he went sickly forth; and take good note
What Caesar doth, what suitors press to him.
Hark, boy, what noise is that?

Lucius.
I hear none, madam.

Portia.
              Prithee listen well;
I heard a bustling rumor, like a fray,
And the wind brings it from the Capitol.

Lucius.
Sooth, madam, I hear nothing.

Enter the Soothsayer.

Portia.
Come hither, fellow; which way hast thou been?

Soothsayer.
At mine own house, good lady.

Portia.
What is't a' clock?

Soothsayer.
              About the ninth hour, lady.

Portia.
Is Caesar yet gone to the Capitol?

Soothsayer.
Madam, not yet; I go to take my stand,
To see him pass on to the Capitol.

Portia.
Thou hast some suit to Caesar, hast thou not?

Soothsayer.
That I have, lady, if it will please Caesar
To be so good to Caesar as to hear me:
I shall beseech him to befriend himself.

Portia.
Why, know'st thou any harm's intended towards him?

Soothsayer.
None that I know will be, much that I fear may chance.
Good morrow to you. Here the street is narrow;
The throng that follows Caesar at the heels,
Of senators, of praetors, common suitors,
Will crowd a feeble man almost to death.
I'll get me to a place more void, and there
Speak to great Caesar as he comes along.

Exit.

Portia.
I must go in. Ay me! How weak a thing
The heart of woman is! O Brutus,
The heavens speed thee in thine enterprise!
Sure the boy heard me.—Brutus hath a suit
That Caesar will not grant.—O, I grow faint.—

Run, Lucius, and commend me to my lord,
Say I am merry. Come to me again,
And bring me word what he doth say to thee.

Exeunt severally.

Act 3

Scene 1

Rome. Before the capitol; the Senate sitting above.

(Caesar; Brutus; Cassius; Casca; Decius; Metellus; Trebonius; Cinna; Antony; Lepidus; Artemidorus; Publius; Popilius; Soothsayer; Antony's Messenger; Octavius's Attendant)

Caesar points out to the Soothsayer that it is the Ides of March, but the Soothsayer reminds him that they are not yet over. Artemidorus attempts to give his letter to Caesar, but the latter insists that since it concerns him, he will deal with it last. The conspirators slowly surround Caesar, and at an opportune moment stab him to death. The bystanders flee in terror. Caesar's last thought is horror at the realization that Brutus is one of the conspirators. The conspirators bathe their hands in Caesar's blood, hoping to make it a holy act. A Messenger from Antony asks to be allowed to approach in safety, promising to pledge allegiance to Brutus if he can give a good reason for Caesar's death. Cassius is uncertain, but Brutus is sure he will be able to win Antony over. Antony enters and shakes hands with the conspirators, agreeing to wait until they have calmed the commoners down before anything else happens. Antony cannot keep himself from praising Caesar a bit too much for present company. He asks permission to deliver Caesar's funeral oration; Brutus agrees, since he plans to explain the murder first and thus imagines that all will be safe. Cassius grows ever more worried. Left alone with the corpse, Antony speaks to Caesar, begging his pardon for being so gentle but promising revenge. He sends a message to Caesar's nephew Octavius, who is outside Rome, warning him not to enter yet, as it is not safe. He carries Caesar's corpse to the Forum.

Flourish. Enter Caesar, Brutus, Cassius, Casca, Decius, Metellus, Trebonius, Cinna, Antony, Lepidus, Artemidorus, Publius, Popilius, and the Soothsayer.

Julius Caesar.
The Ides of March are come.

Soothsayer.
Ay, Caesar, but not gone.

Artemidorus of Cnidos.
Hail, Caesar! Read this schedule.

Decius Brutus.
Trebonius doth desire you to o'er-read
(At your best leisure) this his humble suit.

Artemidorus of Cnidos.
O Caesar, read mine first; for mine's a suit
That touches Caesar nearer. Read it, great Caesar.

Julius Caesar.
What touches us ourself shall be last serv'd.

Artemidorus of Cnidos.
Delay not, Caesar, read it instantly.

Julius Caesar.
What, is the fellow mad?

Publius.
      Sirrah, give place.

Cassius.
What, urge you your petitions in the street?
Come to the Capitol.

Caesar enters the Capitol, the rest following.

Popilius Lena.
I wish your enterprise today may thrive.

Cassius.
What enterprise, Popilius?

Popilius Lena.
      Fare you well.

Leaves him and joins Caesar.

Marcus Brutus.
What said Popilius Lena?

Cassius.
He wish'd today our enterprise might thrive.
I fear our purpose is discovered.

Marcus Brutus.
Look how he makes to Caesar; mark him.

Cassius.
Casca, be sudden, for we fear prevention.
Brutus, what shall be done? If this be known,
Cassius or Caesar never shall turn back,
For I will slay myself.

Marcus Brutus.
      Cassius, be constant;
Popilius Lena speaks not of our purposes,
For look he smiles, and Caesar doth not change.

Cassius.
Trebonius knows his time; for look you, Brutus,
He draws Mark Antony out of the way.

Exeunt Antony and Trebonius.

Decius Brutus.
Where is Metellus Cimber? Let him go
And presently prefer his suit to Caesar.

Marcus Brutus.
He is address'd; press near and second him.

Cinna.
Casca, you are the first that rears your hand.

Julius Caesar.
Are we all ready? What is now amiss
That Caesar and his Senate must redress?

Metellus Cimber.
Most high, most mighty, and most puissant Caesar,
Metellus Cimber throws before thy seat
An humble heart.

Kneeling.

Julius Caesar.
      I must prevent thee, Cimber.
These couchings and these lowly courtesies
Might fire the blood of ordinary men,
And turn preordinance and first decree
Into the law of children. Be not fond
To think that Caesar bears such rebel blood
That will be thaw'd from the true quality
With that which melteth fools—I mean sweet words,
Low-crooked curtsies, and base spaniel fawning.
Thy brother by decree is banished;
If thou dost bend, and pray, and fawn for him,
I spurn thee like a cur out of my way.
Know, Caesar doth not wrong, nor without cause
Will he be satisfied.

Metellus Cimber.
Is there no voice more worthy than my own,
To sound more sweetly in great Caesar's ear
For the repealing of my banish'd brother?

Marcus Brutus.
I kiss thy hand, but not in flattery, Caesar;
Desiring thee that Publius Cimber may
Have an immediate freedom of repeal.

Julius Caesar.
What, Brutus?

Cassius.
      Pardon, Caesar! Caesar, pardon!
As low as to thy foot doth Cassius fall,
To beg enfranchisement for Publius Cimber.

Julius Caesar.
I could be well mov'd, if I were as you;
If I could pray to move, prayers would move me;
But I am constant as the northern star,
Of whose true-fix'd and resting quality
There is no fellow in the firmament.
The skies are painted with unnumb'red sparks,
They are all fire, and every one doth shine;
But there's but one in all doth hold his place.
So in the world: 'tis furnish'd well with men,
And men are flesh and blood, and apprehensive;
Yet in the number I do know but one
That unassailable holds on his rank,
Unshak'd of motion; and that I am he,
Let me a little show it, even in this—
That I was constant Cimber should be banish'd,
And constant do remain to keep him so.

Cinna.
O Caesar—

Julius Caesar.
      Hence! Wilt thou lift up Olympus?

Decius Brutus.
Great Caesar—

Julius Caesar.
      Doth not Brutus bootless kneel?

Casca.
Speak hands for me!

They stab Caesar.

Act 3, Scene 1

Julius Caesar.
Et tu, Brute?—Then fall Caesar!

Dies.

Cinna.
Liberty! Freedom! Tyranny is dead!
Run hence, proclaim, cry it about the streets.

Cassius.
Some to the common pulpits, and cry out,
"Liberty, freedom, and enfranchisement!"

Marcus Brutus.
People and senators, be not affrighted;
Fly not, stand still; ambition's debt is paid.

Casca.
Go to the pulpit, Brutus.

Decius Brutus.
      And Cassius too.

Marcus Brutus.
Where's Publius?

Cinna.
Here, quite confounded with this mutiny.

Metellus Cimber.
Stand fast together, lest some friend of Caesar's
Should chance—

Marcus Brutus.
Talk not of standing. Publius, good cheer,
There is no harm intended to your person,
Nor to no Roman else. So tell them, Publius.

Cassius.
And leave us, Publius, lest that the people,
Rushing on us, should do your age some mischief.

Marcus Brutus.
Do so, and let no man abide this deed,
But we the doers.

Exeunt all but the Conspirators.
Enter Trebonius.

Cassius.
Where is Antony?

Trebonius.
      Fled to his house amaz'd.
Men, wives, and children stare, cry out, and run,
As it were doomsday.

Marcus Brutus.
      Fates, we will know your pleasures.
That we shall die, we know, 'tis but the time,
And drawing days out, that men stand upon.

Casca.
Why, he that cuts off twenty years of life
Cuts off so many years of fearing death.

Marcus Brutus.
Grant that, and then is death a benefit;
So are we Caesar's friends, that have abridg'd
His time of fearing death. Stoop, Romans, stoop,
And let us bathe our hands in Caesar's blood
Up to the elbows, and besmear our swords;
Then walk we forth, even to the market-place,
And waving our red weapons o'er our heads,
Let's all cry, "Peace, freedom, and liberty!"

Cassius.
Stoop then, and wash. How many ages hence
Shall this our lofty scene be acted over
In states unborn and accents yet unknown!

Marcus Brutus.
How many times shall Caesar bleed in sport,
That now on Pompey's basis lies along
No worthier than the dust!

Cassius.
      So oft as that shall be,
So often shall the knot of us be call'd
The men that gave their country liberty.

Decius Brutus.
What, shall we forth?

Cassius.
      Ay, every man away.
Brutus shall lead, and we will grace his heels
With the most boldest and best hearts of Rome.

Enter a Servant.

Marcus Brutus.
Soft, who comes here? A friend of Antony's.

Caesar's Servant.
Thus, Brutus, did my master bid me kneel;
Thus did Mark Antony bid me fall down;
And being prostrate, thus he bade me say:
Brutus is noble, wise, valiant, and honest;
Caesar was mighty, bold, royal, and loving.
Say, I love Brutus, and I honor him;
Say, I fear'd Caesar, honor'd him, and lov'd him.
If Brutus will vouchsafe that Antony
May safely come to him, and be resolv'd
How Caesar hath deserv'd to lie in death,
Mark Antony shall not love Caesar dead
So well as Brutus living; but will follow
The fortunes and affairs of noble Brutus
Thorough the hazards of this untrod state
With all true faith. So says my master Antony.

Marcus Brutus.
Thy master is a wise and valiant Roman,
I never thought him worse.
Tell him, so please him come unto this place,
He shall be satisfied; and, by my honor,
Depart untouch'd.

Caesar's Servant.
                      I'll fetch him presently.

Exit Servant.

Marcus Brutus.
I know that we shall have him well to friend.

Cassius.
I wish we may; but yet have I a mind
That fears him much; and my misgiving still
Falls shrewdly to the purpose.

Enter Antony.

Marcus Brutus.
But here comes Antony. Welcome, Mark Antony!

Mark Antony.
O mighty Caesar! Dost thou lie so low?
Are all thy conquests, glories, triumphs, spoils,
Shrunk to this little measure? Fare thee well!
I know not, gentlemen, what you intend,
Who else must be let blood, who else is rank;
If I myself, there is no hour so fit
As Caesar's death's hour, nor no instrument
Of half that worth as those your swords, made rich
With the most noble blood of all this world.
I do beseech ye, if you bear me hard,
Now, whilst your purpled hands do reek and smoke,
Fulfill your pleasure. Live a thousand years,
I shall not find myself so apt to die;
No place will please me so, no mean of death,
As here by Caesar, and by you cut off,
The choice and master spirits of this age.

Marcus Brutus.
O Antony! Beg not your death of us.
Though now we must appear bloody and cruel,
As by our hands and this our present act
You see we do, yet see you but our hands,
And this the bleeding business they have done.
Our hearts you see not, they are pitiful;
And pity to the general wrong of Rome—
As fire drives out fire, so pity pity—
Hath done this deed on Caesar. For your part,
To you our swords have leaden points, Mark Antony;
Our arms in strength of malice, and our hearts
Of brothers' temper, do receive you in
With all kind love, good thoughts, and reverence.

Cassius.
Your voice shall be as strong as any man's
In the disposing of new dignities.

Marcus Brutus.
Only be patient till we have appeas'd
The multitude, beside themselves with fear,
And then we will deliver you the cause
Why I, that did love Caesar when I struck him,
Have thus proceeded.

Mark Antony.
                    I doubt not of your wisdom.
Let each man render me his bloody hand.
First, Marcus Brutus, will I shake with you;
Next, Caius Cassius, do I take your hand;
Now, Decius Brutus, yours; now yours, Metellus;
Yours, Cinna; and, my valiant Casca, yours;
Though last, not least in love, yours, good Trebonius.
Gentlemen all—alas, what shall I say?
My credit now stands on such slippery ground
That one of two bad ways you must conceit me,
Either a coward or a flatterer.
That I did love thee, Caesar, O, 'tis true;
If then thy spirit look upon us now,
Shall it not grieve thee dearer than thy death,
To see thy Antony making his peace,
Shaking the bloody fingers of thy foes,

Most noble! In the presence of thy corse?
Had I as many eyes as thou hast wounds,
Weeping as fast as they stream forth thy blood,
It would become me better than to close
In terms of friendship with thine enemies.
Pardon me, Julius! Here wast thou bay'd, brave hart,
Here didst thou fall, and here thy hunters stand,
Sign'd in thy spoil, and crimson'd in thy lethe.
O world! Thou wast the forest to this hart,
And this indeed, O world, the heart of thee.
How like a deer, strucken by many princes,
Dost thou here lie!

Cassius.
Mark Antony—

Mark Antony.
                    Pardon me, Caius Cassius!
The enemies of Caesar shall say this:
Then, in a friend, it is cold modesty.

Cassius.
I blame you not for praising Caesar so,
But what compact mean you to have with us?
Will you be prick'd in number of our friends,
Or shall we on, and not depend on you?

Mark Antony.
Therefore I took your hands, but was indeed
Sway'd from the point, by looking down on Caesar.
Friends am I with you all, and love you all,
Upon this hope, that you shall give me reasons
Why, and wherein, Caesar was dangerous.

Marcus Brutus.
Or else were this a savage spectacle.
Our reasons are so full of good regard
That were you, Antony, the son of Caesar,
You should be satisfied.

Mark Antony.
                    That's all I seek,
And am, moreover, suitor that I may
Produce his body to the market-place,
And in the pulpit, as becomes a friend,
Speak in the order of his funeral.

Marcus Brutus.
You shall, Mark Antony.

Cassius.
            Brutus, a word with you.

Aside to Brutus.

You know not what you do. Do not consent
That Antony speak in his funeral.
Know you how much the people may be mov'd
By that which he will utter?

Marcus Brutus.
                    By your pardon—
I will myself into the pulpit first,
And show the reason of our Caesar's death.
What Antony shall speak, I will protest
He speaks by leave and by permission;
And that we are contented Caesar shall
Have all true rites and lawful ceremonies.
It shall advantage more than do us wrong.

Cassius.
I know not what may fall, I like it not.

Marcus Brutus.
Mark Antony, here take you Caesar's body.
You shall not in your funeral speech blame us,
But speak all good you can devise of Caesar,
And say you do't by our permission;
Else shall you not have any hand at all
About his funeral. And you shall speak
In the same pulpit whereto I am going,
After my speech is ended.

Mark Antony.
                    Be it so;
I do desire no more.

Marcus Brutus.
Prepare the body then, and follow us.

Exeunt. Manet Antony.

Mark Antony.
O, pardon me, thou bleeding piece of earth,
That I am meek and gentle with these butchers!
Thou art the ruins of the noblest man
That ever lived in the tide of times.
Woe to the hand that shed this costly blood!
Over thy wounds now do I prophesy
(Which like dumb mouths do ope their ruby lips
To beg the voice and utterance of my tongue)
A curse shall light upon the limbs of men;
Domestic fury and fierce civil strife

Shall cumber all the parts of Italy;
Blood and destruction shall be so in use,
And dreadful objects so familiar,
That mothers shall but smile when they behold
Their infants quartered with the hands of war;
All pity chok'd with custom of fell deeds;
And Caesar's spirit, ranging for revenge,
With Ate by his side come hot from hell,
Shall in these confines with a monarch's voice
Cry "Havoc!" and let slip the dogs of war,
That this foul deed shall smell above the earth
With carrion men, groaning for burial.

Enter Octavius's Attendant.

You serve Octavius Caesar, do you not?

Octavio's Attendant.
I do, Mark Antony.

Mark Antony.
Caesar did write for him to come to Rome.

Octavio's Attendant.
He did receive his letters, and is coming,
And bid me say to you by word of mouth—
O Caesar!—

Seeing the body.

Mark Antony.
Thy heart is big; get thee apart and weep.
Passion, I see, is catching, for mine eyes,
Seeing those beads of sorrow stand in thine,
Began to water. Is thy master coming?

Octavio's Attendant.
He lies tonight within seven leagues of Rome.

Mark Antony.
Post back with speed, and tell him what hath chanc'd.
Here is a mourning Rome, a dangerous Rome,
No Rome of safety for Octavius yet;
Hie hence, and tell him so. Yet stay awhile,
Thou shalt not back till I have borne this corse
Into the market-place. There shall I try,
In my oration, how the people take
The cruel issue of these bloody men,
According to the which thou shalt discourse
To young Octavius of the state of things.
Lend me your hand.

Exeunt with Caesar's body.

Scene 2

The Forum.

(Brutus; Cassius; First Plebeian; Second Plebeian; Third Plebeian; Fourth Plebeian; Fifth Plebeian; Plebeians; Mark Antony; Caesar; Octavius's Attendant)

In precise, legalistic prose, Brutus explains to the mob why he killed Caesar, explaining that he did it for the sake of freedom and equality, and that he loves Rome more than he did Caesar. The mob approves. Then Antony comes to give Caesar's funeral speech, a perfectly-tuned, fiery, rabble-rousing piece that undoes all that Brutus has accomplished and whips the mob into a rage, sending them rioting to kill all the conspirators they can find. By this point Brutus and Cassius have fled from Rome; Antony goes to meet Octavius and Lepidus.

Enter Brutus and Cassius with the Plebeians.

All Plebeians.
We will be satisfied! Let us be satisfied!

Marcus Brutus.
Then follow me, and give me audience, friends.
Cassius, go you into the other street,
And part the numbers.
Those that will hear me speak, let 'em stay here;
Those that will follow Cassius, go with him;
And public reasons shall be rendered
Of Caesar's death.

First Plebeian.
                    I will hear Brutus speak.

Second Plebeian.
I will hear Cassius, and compare their reasons,
When severally we hear them rendered.

Exit Cassius with Second Plebeian and some of the Plebeians.
Brutus goes into the pulpit.

Third Plebeian.
The noble Brutus is ascended; silence!

Marcus Brutus.
Be patient till the last.
Romans, countrymen, and lovers, hear me for my cause, and be silent, that you may hear. Believe me for mine honor, and have respect to mine honor, that you may believe. Censure me in your wisdom, and awake

your senses, that you may the better judge. If there be any in this assembly, any dear friend of Caesar's, to him I say, that Brutus' love to Caesar was no less than his. If then that friend demand why Brutus rose against Caesar, this is my answer: Not that I lov'd Caesar less, but that I lov'd Rome more. Had you rather Caesar were living, and die all slaves, than that Caesar were dead, to live all freemen? As Caesar lov'd me, I weep for him; as he was fortunate, I rejoice at it; as he was valiant, I honor him; but, as he was ambitious, I slew him. There is tears for his love; joy for his fortune; honor for his valor; and death for his ambition. Who is here so base that would be a bondman? If any, speak, for him have I offended. Who is here so rude that would not be a Roman? If any, speak, for him have I offended. Who is here so vile that will not love his country? If any, speak, for him have I offended. I pause for a reply.

All Plebeians.
None, Brutus, none.

Marcus Brutus.
Then none have I offended. I have done no more to Caesar than you shall do to Brutus. The question of his death is enroll'd in the Capitol: his glory not extenuated, wherein he was worthy; nor his offenses enforc'd, for which he suffer'd death.

Enter Mark Antony and others with Caesar's body.

Here comes his body, mourn'd by Mark Antony, who, though he had no hand in his death, shall receive the benefit of his dying, a place in the commonwealth, as which of you shall not? With this I depart, that, as I slew my best lover for the good of Rome, I have the same dagger for myself, when it shall please my country to need my death.

All Plebeians.
Live, Brutus, live, live!

First Plebeian.
Bring him with triumph home unto his house.

Third Plebeian.
Give him a statue with his ancestors.

Fourth Plebeian.
Let him be Caesar.

Fifth Plebeian.
    Caesar's better parts
Shall be crown'd in Brutus.

First Plebeian.
    We'll bring him to his house
With shouts and clamors.

Marcus Brutus.
    My countrymen—

Third Plebeian.
Peace, silence! Brutus speaks.

First Plebeian.
    Peace ho!

Marcus Brutus.
Good countrymen, let me depart alone,
And, for my sake, stay here with Antony.
Do grace to Caesar's corpse, and grace his speech
Tending to Caesar's glories, which Mark Antony
(By our permission) is allow'd to make.
I do entreat you, not a man depart,
Save I alone, till Antony have spoke.

Exit.

First Plebeian.
Stay ho, and let us hear Mark Antony.

Fourth Plebeian.
Let him go up into the public chair,
We'll hear him. Noble Antony, go up.

Mark Antony.
For Brutus' sake, I am beholding to you.

Goes into the pulpit.

Fifth Plebeian.
What does he say of Brutus?

Fourth Plebeian.
    He says, for Brutus' sake
He finds himself beholding to us all.

Fifth Plebeian.
'Twere best he speak no harm of Brutus here!

First Plebeian.
This Caesar was a tyrant.

Fourth Plebeian.
                       Nay, that's certain:
We are blest that Rome is rid of him.

Third Plebeian.
Peace, let us hear what Antony can say.

Mark Antony.
You gentle Romans—

All Plebeians.
                   Peace ho, let us hear him.

Mark Antony.
Friends, Romans, countrymen, lend me your ears!
I come to bury Caesar, not to praise him.
The evil that men do lives after them,
The good is oft interred with their bones;
So let it be with Caesar. The noble Brutus
Hath told you Caesar was ambitious;
If it were so, it was a grievous fault,
And grievously hath Caesar answer'd it.
Here, under leave of Brutus and the rest
(For Brutus is an honorable man,
So are they all, all honorable men),
Come I to speak in Caesar's funeral.
He was my friend, faithful and just to me;
But Brutus says he was ambitious,
And Brutus is an honorable man.
He hath brought many captives home to Rome,
Whose ransoms did the general coffers fill;
Did this in Caesar seem ambitious?
When that the poor have cried, Caesar hath wept;
Ambition should be made of sterner stuff:
Yet Brutus says he was ambitious,
And Brutus is an honorable man.
You all did see that on the Lupercal
I thrice presented him a kingly crown,
Which he did thrice refuse. Was this ambition?
Yet Brutus says he was ambitious,
And sure he is an honorable man.
I speak not to disprove what Brutus spoke,
But here I am to speak what I do know.
You all did love him once, not without cause;
What cause withholds you then to mourn for him?
O judgment! Thou art fled to brutish beasts,
And men have lost their reason. Bear with me,
My heart is in the coffin there with Caesar,
And I must pause till it come back to me.

First Plebeian.
Methinks there is much reason in his sayings.

Third Plebeian.
If thou consider rightly of the matter,
Caesar has had great wrong.

Fourth Plebeian.
                     Has he, masters?
I fear there will a worse come in his place.

Fifth Plebeian.
Mark'd ye his words? He would not take the crown,
Therefore 'tis certain he was not ambitious.

First Plebeian.
If it be found so, some will dear abide it.

Third Plebeian.
Poor soul, his eyes are red as fire with weeping.

Fourth Plebeian.
There's not a nobler man in Rome than Antony.

Fifth Plebeian.
Now mark him, he begins again to speak.

Mark Antony.
But yesterday the word of Caesar might
Have stood against the world; now lies he there,
And none so poor to do him reverence.
O masters! If I were dispos'd to stir
Your hearts and minds to mutiny and rage,
I should do Brutus wrong, and Cassius wrong,
Who (you all know) are honorable men.
I will not do them wrong; I rather choose
To wrong the dead, to wrong myself and you,
Than I will wrong such honorable men.
But here's a parchment with the seal of Caesar,
I found it in his closet, 'tis his will.
Let but the commons hear this testament—
Which, pardon me, I do not mean to read—
And they would go and kiss dead Caesar's wounds,
And dip their napkins in his sacred blood;
Yea, beg a hair of him for memory,
And dying, mention it within their wills,
Bequeathing it as a rich legacy
Unto their issue.

Fifth Plebeian.
We'll hear the will. Read it, Mark Antony.

All Plebeians.
The will, the will! We will hear Caesar's will.

Mark Antony.
Have patience, gentle friends, I must not read it.
It is not meet you know how Caesar lov'd you:
You are not wood, you are not stones, but men;
And, being men, hearing the will of Caesar,
It will inflame you, it will make you mad.
'Tis good you know not that you are his heirs,
For if you should, O, what would come of it?

Fifth Plebeian.
Read the will, we'll hear it, Antony.
You shall read us the will, Caesar's will.

Mark Antony.
Will you be patient? Will you stay awhile?
I have o'ershot myself to tell you of it.
I fear I wrong the honorable men
Whose daggers have stabb'd Caesar; I do fear it.

Fifth Plebeian.
They were traitors; honorable men!

All Plebeians.
The will! The testament!

Third Plebeian.
They were villains, murderers. The will, read the will!

Mark Antony.
You will compel me then to read the will?
Then make a ring about the corpse of Caesar,
And let me show you him that made the will.
Shall I descend? And will you give me leave?

All Plebeians.
Come down.

Third Plebeian.
Descend.

Fourth Plebeian.
You shall have leave.

Antony comes down from the pulpit.

Fifth Plebeian.
A ring, stand round.

First Plebeian.
Stand from the hearse, stand from the body.

Third Plebeian.
Room for Antony, most noble Antony.

Mark Antony.
Nay, press not so upon me, stand far off.

All Plebeians.
Stand back; room, bear back!

Mark Antony.
If you have tears, prepare to shed them now.
You all do know this mantle. I remember
The first time ever Caesar put it on;
'Twas on a summer's evening, in his tent,
That day he overcame the Nervii.
Look, in this place ran Cassius' dagger through;
See what a rent the envious Casca made;
Through this the well-beloved Brutus stabb'd,
And as he pluck'd his cursed steel away,
Mark how the blood of Caesar followed it,
As rushing out of doors to be resolv'd
If Brutus so unkindly knock'd or no;
For Brutus, as you know, was Caesar's angel.
Judge, O you gods, how dearly Caesar lov'd him!
This was the most unkindest cut of all;
For when the noble Caesar saw him stab,
Ingratitude, more strong than traitors' arms,
Quite vanquish'd him. Then burst his mighty heart,
And in his mantle muffling up his face,
Even at the base of Pompey's statue
(Which all the while ran blood) great Caesar fell.
O, what a fall was there, my countrymen!
Then I, and you, and all of us fell down,
Whilst bloody treason flourish'd over us.
O now you weep, and I perceive you feel
The dint of pity. These are gracious drops.
Kind souls, what weep you when you but behold
Our Caesar's vesture wounded? Look you here,

Lifting Caesar's mantle.

Here is himself, marr'd as you see with traitors.

First Plebeian.
O piteous spectacle!

Third Plebeian.
O noble Caesar!

Fourth Plebeian.
O woeful day!

Fifth Plebeian.
O traitors, villains!

First Plebeian.
O most bloody sight!

Third Plebeian.
We will be reveng'd!

All Plebeians.
Revenge! About! Seek! Burn! Fire! Kill! Slay! Let not a traitor live!

Mark Antony.
Stay, countrymen.

First Plebeian.
Peace there, hear the noble Antony.

Third Plebeian.
We'll hear him, we'll follow him, we'll die with him.

Mark Antony.
Good friends, sweet friends, let me not stir you up
To such a sudden flood of mutiny.
They that have done this deed are honorable.
What private griefs they have, alas, I know not,
That made them do it. They are wise and honorable,
And will no doubt with reasons answer you.
I come not, friends, to steal away your hearts.
I am no orator, as Brutus is;
But (as you know me all) a plain blunt man
That love my friend, and that they know full well
That gave me public leave to speak of him.
For I have neither wit, nor words, nor worth,
Action, nor utterance, nor the power of speech
To stir men's blood; I only speak right on.
I tell you that which you yourselves do know,
Show you sweet Caesar's wounds, poor, poor, dumb mouths,
And bid them speak for me. But were I Brutus,
And Brutus Antony, there were an Antony
Would ruffle up your spirits, and put a tongue
In every wound of Caesar, that should move
The stones of Rome to rise and mutiny.

All Plebeians.
We'll mutiny.

First Plebeian.
          We'll burn the house of Brutus.

Fourth Plebeian.
Away then, come, seek the conspirators.

Mark Antony.
Yet hear me, countrymen, yet hear me speak.

All Plebeians.
Peace ho, hear Antony, most noble Antony!

Mark Antony.
Why, friends, you go to do you know not what.
Wherein hath Caesar thus deserv'd your loves?
Alas you know not! I must tell you then:
You have forgot the will I told you of.

All Plebeians.
Most true. The will! Let's stay and hear the will.

Mark Antony.
Here is the will, and under Caesar's seal:
To every Roman citizen he gives,
To every several man, seventy-five drachmaes.

Third Plebeian.
Most noble Caesar! We'll revenge his death.

Fourth Plebeian.
O royal Caesar!

Mark Antony.
Hear me with patience.

All Plebeians.
Peace ho!

Mark Antony.
Moreover, he hath left you all his walks,
His private arbors and new-planted orchards,
On this side Tiber; he hath left them you,
And to your heirs for ever-common pleasures,
To walk abroad and recreate yourselves.
Here was a Caesar! When comes such another?

First Plebeian.
Never, never! Come, away, away!
We'll burn his body in the holy place,
And with the brands fire the traitors' houses.
Take up the body.

Third Plebeian.
Go fetch fire.

Fourth Plebeian.
Pluck down benches.

Fifth Plebeian.
Pluck down forms, windows, any thing.

Exeunt Plebeians with the body.

Mark Antony.
Now let it work. Mischief, thou art afoot,
Take thou what course thou wilt!

Enter Octavius's Servant.

How now, fellow?

Octavius's Attendant.
Sir, Octavius is already come to Rome.

Mark Antony.
Where is he?

Octavius's Attendant.
He and Lepidus are at Caesar's house.

Mark Antony.
And thither will I straight to visit him;
He comes upon a wish. Fortune is merry,
And in this mood will give us any thing.

Octavius's Attendant.
I heard him say, Brutus and Cassius
Are rid like madmen through the gates of Rome.

Mark Antony.
Belike they had some notice of the people,
How I had mov'd them. Bring me to Octavius.

Exeunt.

Scene 3

Rome. A street.

(Cinna, a Poet; Plebeians)

The poet Cinna is torn to pieces by the inflamed mob for the misfortune of having the same name as one of the conspirators.

Enter Cinna the poet, and after him the Plebeians.

Cinna, a Poet.
I dreamt tonight that I did feast with Caesar,
And things unluckily charge my fantasy.
I have no will to wander forth of doors,
Yet something leads me forth.

First Plebeian.
What is your name?

Second Plebeian.
Whither are you going?

Third Plebeian.
Where do you dwell?

Fourth Plebeian.
Are you a married man or a bachelor?

Second Plebeian.
Answer every man directly.

First Plebeian.
Ay, and briefly.

Fourth Plebeian.
Ay, and wisely.

Third Plebeian.
Ay, and truly, you were best.

Cinna, a Poet.
What is my name? Whither am I going? Where do I dwell? Am I a married man or a bachelor? Then to answer every man directly and briefly, wisely and truly: wisely, I say, I am a bachelor.

Second Plebeian.
That's as much as to say, they are fools that marry. You'll bear me a bang for that, I fear. Proceed directly.

Cinna, a Poet.
Directly, I am going to Caesar's funeral.

First Plebeian.
As a friend or an enemy?

Cinna, a Poet.
As a friend.

Second Plebeian.
That matter is answer'd directly.

Fourth Plebeian.
For your dwelling—briefly.

Cinna, a Poet.
Briefly, I dwell by the Capitol.

Third Plebeian.
Your name, sir, truly.

Cinna, a Poet.
Truly, my name is Cinna.

First Plebeian.
Tear him to pieces, he's a conspirator.

Cinna, a Poet.
I am Cinna the poet, I am Cinna the poet.

Fourth Plebeian.
Tear him for his bad verses, tear him for his bad verses.

Cinna, a Poet.
I am not Cinna the conspirator.

Fourth Plebeian.
It is no matter, his name's Cinna. Pluck but his name out of his heart, and turn him going.

Third Plebeian.
Tear him, tear him! Come, brands ho, fire-brands! To Brutus', to Cassius'; burn all! Some to Decius' house, and some to Casca's; some to Ligarius'. Away, go!

Exeunt all the Plebeians dragging off Cinna.

Act 4

Scene 1

A house in Rome.

(Antony; Octavius; Lepidus)

Antony, Octavius, and Lepidus, now the rulers of Rome, make up execution lists, trading family members who shall die. After Lepidus leaves, Antony admits that he scorns the man, but that he is useful enough. Octavius and Antony agree to join forces and consider how to deal with the army that Brutus and Cassius are raising.

Enter Antony, Octavius, and Lepidus.

Mark Antony.
These many then shall die, their names are prick'd.

Octavius Caesar.
Your brother too must die; consent you, Lepidus?

M. Aemilius Lepidus.
I do consent—

Octavius Caesar.
            Prick him down, Antony.

M. Aemilius Lepidus.
Upon condition Publius shall not live,
Who is your sister's son, Mark Antony.

Mark Antony.
He shall not live; look, with a spot I damn him.
But, Lepidus, go you to Caesar's house;
Fetch the will hither, and we shall determine
How to cut off some charge in legacies.

M. Aemilius Lepidus.
What? Shall I find you here?

Octavius Caesar.
Or here or at the Capitol.

Exit Lepidus.

Mark Antony.
This is a slight unmeritable man,
Meet to be sent on errands; is it fit,
The threefold world divided, he should stand
One of the three to share it?

Octavius Caesar.
            So you thought him,
And took his voice who should be prick'd to die
In our black sentence and proscription.

Mark Antony.
Octavius, I have seen more days than you,
And though we lay these honors on this man
To ease ourselves of diverse sland'rous loads,
He shall but bear them as the ass bears gold,
To groan and sweat under the business,
Either led or driven, as we point the way;
And having brought our treasure where we will,
Then take we down his load, and turn him off
(Like to the empty ass) to shake his ears
And graze in commons.

Octavius Caesar.
            You may do your will;
But he's a tried and valiant soldier.

Mark Antony.
So is my horse, Octavius, and for that
I do appoint him store of provender.
It is a creature that I teach to fight,
To wind, to stop, to run directly on,
His corporal motion govern'd by my spirit;
And in some taste is Lepidus but so:
He must be taught, and train'd, and bid go forth;

Act 4, Scene 2

A barren-spirited fellow; one that feeds
On objects, arts, and imitations,
Which, out of use and stal'd by other men,
Begin his fashion. Do not talk of him
But as a property. And now, Octavius,
Listen great things. Brutus and Cassius
Are levying powers; we must straight make head;
Therefore let our alliance be combin'd,
Our best friends made, our means stretch'd,
And let us presently go sit in council,
How covert matters may be best disclos'd,
And open perils surest answered.

Octavius Caesar.
Let us do so; for we are at the stake,
And bay'd about with many enemies,
And some that smile have in their hearts, I fear,
Millions of mischiefs.

Exeunt.

Scene 2

A camp near Sardis. Before Brutus's tent.

(Brutus; Lucilius; Lucius; Titinius; Pindarus; Cassius; First Soldier; Second Soldier; Third Soldier)

Cassius and Brutus meet. Neither of them is pleased with the other, but Brutus insists they not let his be seen publicly.

Drum. Enter Brutus, Lucilius, Lucius, and the army. Titinius and Pindarus meet them.

Marcus Brutus.
Stand ho!

Lucilius.
Give the word ho! And stand.

Marcus Brutus.
What now, Lucilius, is Cassius near?

Lucilius.
He is at hand, and Pindarus is come
To do you salutation from his master.

Marcus Brutus.
He greets me well. Your master, Pindarus,
In his own change, or by ill officers,
Hath given me some worthy cause to wish
Things done undone; but if he be at hand
I shall be satisfied.

Pindarus.
               I do not doubt
But that my noble master will appear
Such as he is, full of regard and honor.

Marcus Brutus.
He is not doubted. A word, Lucilius,
How he receiv'd you; let me be resolv'd.

Lucilius.
With courtesy and with respect enough,
But not with such familiar instances,
Nor with such free and friendly conference,
As he hath us'd of old.

Marcus Brutus.
               Thou hast describ'd
A hot friend cooling. Ever note, Lucilius,
When love begins to sicken and decay
It useth an enforced ceremony.
There are no tricks in plain and simple faith;
But hollow men, like horses hot at hand,
Make gallant show and promise of their mettle;

Low march within.

But when they should endure the bloody spur,
They fall their crests, and like deceitful jades
Sink in the trial. Comes his army on?

Lucilius.
They mean this night in Sardis to be quarter'd.
The greater part, the horse in general,
Are come with Cassius.

Enter Cassius and his powers.

Marcus Brutus.
Hark, he is arriv'd.
March gently on to meet him.

Cassius.
Stand ho!

Marcus Brutus.
Stand ho! Speak the word along.

First Soldier.
Stand!

Second Soldier.
Stand!

Third Soldier.
Stand!

Cassius.
Most noble brother, you have done me wrong.

Marcus Brutus.
Judge me, you gods! Wrong I mine enemies?
And if not so, how should I wrong a brother?

Cassius.
Brutus, this sober form of yours hides wrongs,
And when you do them—

Marcus Brutus.
                Cassius, be content,
Speak your griefs softly; I do know you well.
Before the eyes of both our armies here
(Which should perceive nothing but love from us)
Let us not wrangle. Bid them move away;
Then in my tent, Cassius, enlarge your griefs,
And I will give you audience.

Cassius.
                Pindarus,
Bid our commanders lead their charges off
A little from this ground.

Marcus Brutus.
Lucius, do you the like, and let no man
Come to our tent till we have done our conference.
Let Lucilius and Titinius guard our door.

Exeunt. Manent Brutus and Cassius, who withdraw into Brutus' tent, while Lucilius and Titinius mount guard without.

Scene 3

Inside Brutus's tent.

(Brutus; Cassius; Poet; Lucilius; Titinius; Lucius; Messala; Varrus; Claudio; Ghost of Caesar)

Cassius reproves Brutus for paying no attention to his letters begging for mercy on a friend; Brutus accuses him of taking bribes. Brutus cannot abide this, as it ruins the image of the conspirators as noble, ethical men, which he thinks their strongest point. The two quarrel bitterly, Cassius pointing out that he is the more experienced soldier. In the end, they are reconciled. Brutus tells Cassius that Portia has committed suicide, and that his grief is only one of the cares pressing on him and making him short-tempered. They hear that the triumvirate has put to death possibly as many as a hundred senators. Other news informs them that the enemy is gathering at Philippi; Cassius would rather not fight there, but Brutus insists. Brutus has Lucius play him some music, but the servant is exhausted and falls asleep. The Ghost of Caesar appears, naming itself as Brutus's evil spirit, and tells him that they will meet again at Philippi. Brutus seeks to see whether anybody else saw the ghost, but no one has.

The scene continues inside Brutus' tent while Lucilius and Titinius mount guard without.

Cassius.
That you have wrong'd me doth appear in this:
You have condemn'd and noted Lucius Pella
For taking bribes here of the Sardians;
Wherein my letters, praying on his side,
Because I knew the man, was slighted off.

Marcus Brutus.
You wrong'd yourself to write in such a case.

Cassius.
In such a time as this it is not meet
That every nice offense should bear his comment.

Marcus Brutus.
Let me tell you, Cassius, you yourself
Are much condemn'd to have an itching palm,
To sell and mart your offices for gold
To undeservers.

Cassius.
                I, an itching palm?
You know that you are Brutus that speaks this,
Or, by the gods, this speech were else your last.

Marcus Brutus.
The name of Cassius honors this corruption,
And chastisement doth therefore hide his head.

Cassius.
Chastisement?

Marcus Brutus.
Remember March, the ides of March remember:
Did not great Julius bleed for justice' sake?
What villain touch'd his body, that did stab
And not for justice? What? Shall one of us,
That struck the foremost man of all this world
But for supporting robbers, shall we now
Contaminate our fingers with base bribes?
And sell the mighty space of our large honors

For so much trash as may be grasped thus?
I had rather be a dog, and bay the moon,
Than such a Roman.

Cassius.
                    Brutus, bait not me,
I'll not endure it. You forget yourself
To hedge me in. I am a soldier, I,
Older in practice, abler than yourself
To make conditions.

Marcus Brutus.
              Go to; you are not, Cassius.

Cassius.
I am.

Marcus Brutus.
I say you are not.

Cassius.
Urge me no more, I shall forget myself;
Have mind upon your health; tempt me no farther.

Marcus Brutus.
Away, slight man!

Cassius.
Is't possible?

Marcus Brutus.
                 Hear me, for I will speak.
Must I give way and room to your rash choler?
Shall I be frighted when a madman stares?

Cassius.
O ye gods, ye gods, must I endure all this?

Marcus Brutus.
All this? Ay, more. Fret till your proud heart break;
Go show your slaves how choleric you are,
And make your bondmen tremble. Must I bouge?
Must I observe you? Must I stand and crouch
Under your testy humor? By the gods,
You shall digest the venom of your spleen
Though it do split you; for, from this day forth,
I'll use you for my mirth, yea, for my laughter,
When you are waspish.

Cassius.
                Is it come to this?

Marcus Brutus.
You say you are a better soldier:
Let it appear so; make your vaunting true,
And it shall please me well. For mine own part,
I shall be glad to learn of noble men.

Cassius.
You wrong me every way; you wrong me, Brutus:
I said an elder soldier, not a better.
Did I say "better"?

Marcus Brutus.
            If you did, I care not.

Cassius.
When Caesar liv'd, he durst not thus have mov'd me.

Marcus Brutus.
Peace, peace, you durst not so have tempted him.

Cassius.
I durst not?

Marcus Brutus.
No.

Cassius.
What? Durst not tempt him?

Marcus Brutus.
              For your life you durst not.

Cassius.
Do not presume too much upon my love,
I may do that I shall be sorry for.

Marcus Brutus.
You have done that you should be sorry for.
There is no terror, Cassius, in your threats;
For I am arm'd so strong in honesty
That they pass by me as the idle wind,
Which I respect not. I did send to you
For certain sums of gold, which you denied me;
For I can raise no money by vile means.
By heaven, I had rather coin my heart
And drop my blood for drachmaes than to wring
From the hard hands of peasants their vile trash
By any indirection. I did send
To you for gold to pay my legions,
Which you denied me. Was that done like Cassius?
Should I have answer'd Caius Cassius so?
When Marcus Brutus grows so covetous
To lock such rascal counters from his friends,
Be ready, gods, with all your thunderbolts,

Dash him to pieces!

Cassius.
                I denied you not.

Marcus Brutus.
You did.

Cassius.
I did not. He was but a fool that brought
My answer back. Brutus hath riv'd my heart.
A friend should bear his friend's infirmities;
But Brutus makes mine greater than they are.

Marcus Brutus.
I do not, till you practice them on me.

Cassius.
You love me not.

Marcus Brutus.
               I do not like your faults.

Cassius.
A friendly eye could never see such faults.

Marcus Brutus.
A flatterer's would not, though they do appear
As huge as high Olympus.

Cassius.
Come, Antony, and young Octavius, come,
Revenge yourselves alone on Cassius,
For Cassius is a-weary of the world;
Hated by one he loves, brav'd by his brother,
Check'd like a bondman, all his faults observ'd,
Set in a note-book, learn'd, and conn'd by rote,
To cast into my teeth. O, I could weep
My spirit from mine eyes! There is my dagger,
And here my naked breast; within, a heart
Dearer than Pluto's mine, richer than gold:
If that thou be'st a Roman, take it forth.
I, that denied thee gold, will give my heart:
Strike as thou didst at Caesar; for I know,
When thou didst hate him worst, thou lovedst him better
Than ever thou lovedst Cassius.

Marcus Brutus.
                  Sheathe your dagger.
Be angry when you will, it shall have scope;
Do what you will, dishonor shall be humor.
O Cassius, you are yoked with a lamb
That carries anger as the flint bears fire,
Who, much enforced, shows a hasty spark,
And straight is cold again.

Cassius.
                Hath Cassius liv'd
To be but mirth and laughter to his Brutus,
When grief and blood ill-temper'd vexeth him?

Marcus Brutus.
When I spoke that, I was ill-temper'd too.

Cassius.
Do you confess so much? Give me your hand.

Marcus Brutus.
And my heart too.

Cassius.
               O Brutus!

Marcus Brutus.
               What's the matter?

Cassius.
Have not you love enough to bear with me,
When that rash humor which my mother gave me
Makes me forgetful?

Marcus Brutus.
             Yes, Cassius, and from henceforth,
When you are over-earnest with your Brutus,
He'll think your mother chides, and leave you so.

Enter a Poet to Lucilius and Titinius as they stand on guard.

A Poet.
Let me go in to see the generals.
There is some grudge between 'em; 'tis not meet
They be alone.

Lucilius.
You shall not come to them.

A Poet.
Nothing but death shall stay me.

Brutus and Cassius step out of the tent.

Cassius.
How now? What's the matter?

A Poet.
For shame, you generals! What do you mean?
Love, and be friends, as two such men should be,
For I have seen more years, I'm sure, than ye.

Cassius.
Ha, ha! How vildly doth this cynic rhyme!

Marcus Brutus.
Get you hence, sirrah; saucy fellow, hence!

Cassius.
Bear with him, Brutus, 'tis his fashion.

Marcus Brutus.
I'll know his humor, when he knows his time.
What should the wars do with these jigging fools?
Companion, hence!

Cassius.
            Away, away, be gone!

Exit Poet.

Marcus Brutus.
Lucilius and Titinius, bid the commanders
Prepare to lodge their companies tonight.

Cassius.
And come yourselves, and bring Messala with you
Immediately to us.

Exeunt Lucilius and Titinius.

Marcus Brutus.
To Lucius within.
            Lucius, a bowl of wine!

Brutus and Cassius return into the tent.

Cassius.
I did not think you could have been so angry.

Marcus Brutus.
O Cassius, I am sick of many griefs.

Cassius.
Of your philosophy you make no use,
If you give place to accidental evils.

Marcus Brutus.
No man bears sorrow better. Portia is dead.

Cassius.
Ha? Portia?

Marcus Brutus.
She is dead.

Cassius.
How scap'd I killing when I cross'd you so?
O insupportable and touching loss!
Upon what sickness?

Marcus Brutus.
            Impatient of my absence,
And grief that young Octavius with Mark Antony
Have made themselves so strong—for with her death
That tidings came. With this she fell distract,
And (her attendants absent) swallow'd fire.

Cassius.
And died so?

Marcus Brutus.
            Even so.

Cassius.
            O ye immortal gods!

Enter Boy Lucius with wine and tapers.

Marcus Brutus.
Speak no more of her. Give me a bowl of wine.
In this I bury all unkindness, Cassius.

Drinks.

Cassius.
My heart is thirsty for that noble pledge.
Fill, Lucius, till the wine o'erswell the cup;
I cannot drink too much of Brutus' love.

Drinks.
Exit Lucius.
Enter Titinius and Messala.

Marcus Brutus.
Come in, Titinius. Welcome, good Messala.
Now sit we close about this taper here,
And call in question our necessities.

Cassius.
Portia, art thou gone?

Marcus Brutus.
                      No more, I pray you.
Messala, I have here received letters
That young Octavius and Mark Antony
Come down upon us with a mighty power,
Bending their expedition toward Philippi.

Messala.
Myself have letters of the self-same tenure.

Marcus Brutus.
With what addition?

Messala.
That by proscription and bills of outlawry
Octavius, Antony, and Lepidus
Have put to death an hundred senators.

Marcus Brutus.
Therein our letters do not well agree;
Mine speak of seventy senators that died
By their proscriptions, Cicero being one.

Cassius.
Cicero one?

Messala.
                    Cicero is dead,
And by that order of proscription.
Had you your letters from your wife, my lord?

Marcus Brutus.
No, Messala.

Messala.
Nor nothing in your letters writ of her?

Marcus Brutus.
Nothing, Messala.

Messala.
              That, methinks, is strange.

Marcus Brutus.
Why ask you? Hear you aught of her in yours?

Messala.
No, my lord.

Marcus Brutus.
Now as you are a Roman tell me true.

Messala.
Then like a Roman bear the truth I tell:
For certain she is dead, and by strange manner.

Marcus Brutus.
Why, farewell, Portia. We must die, Messala.
With meditating that she must die once,
I have the patience to endure it now.

Messala.
Even so great men great losses should endure.

Cassius.
I have as much of this in art as you,
But yet my nature could not bear it so.

Marcus Brutus.
Well, to our work alive. What do you think
Of marching to Philippi presently?

Cassius.
I do not think it good.

Marcus Brutus.
              Your reason?

Cassius.
                This it is:
'Tis better that the enemy seek us;
So shall he waste his means, weary his soldiers,
Doing himself offense, whilst we, lying still,
Are full of rest, defense, and nimbleness.

Marcus Brutus.
Good reasons must of force give place to better:
The people 'twixt Philippi and this ground
Do stand but in a forc'd affection,
For they have grudg'd us contribution.
The enemy, marching along by them,
By them shall make a fuller number up,
Come on refresh'd, new-added, and encourag'd;
From which advantage shall we cut him off
If at Philippi we do face him there,
These people at our back.

Cassius.
              Hear me, good brother.

Marcus Brutus.
Under your pardon. You must note beside
That we have tried the utmost of our friends,
Our legions are brimful, our cause is ripe:
The enemy increaseth every day;
We, at the height, are ready to decline.
There is a tide in the affairs of men,
Which taken at the flood, leads on to fortune;
Omitted, all the voyage of their life

Act 4, Scene 3

Is bound in shallows and in miseries.
On such a full sea are we now afloat,
And we must take the current when it serves,
Or lose our ventures.

Cassius.
                    Then with your will go on;
We'll along ourselves, and meet them at Philippi.

Marcus Brutus.
The deep of night is crept upon our talk,
And nature must obey necessity,
Which we will niggard with a little rest.
There is no more to say?

Cassius.
                    No more. Good night.
Early tomorrow will we rise, and hence.

Marcus Brutus.
Lucius!

Enter Lucius.

                    My gown.

Exit Lucius.

                    Farewell, good Messala.
Good night, Titinius. Noble, noble Cassius,
Good night, and good repose.

Cassius.
                    O my dear brother!
This was an ill beginning of the night.
Never come such division 'tween our souls!
Let it not, Brutus.

Enter Lucius with the gown.

Marcus Brutus.
                    Every thing is well.

Cassius.
Good night, my lord.

Marcus Brutus.
                    Good night, good brother.

Both Titinius and Messala.
Good night, Lord Brutus.

Marcus Brutus.
                    Farewell every one.

Exeunt all but Brutus and Lucius.

Give me the gown. Where is thy instrument?

Lucius.
Here in the tent.

Marcus Brutus.
                    What, thou speak'st drowsily?
Poor knave, I blame thee not, thou art o'erwatch'd.
Call Claudio and some other of my men,
I'll have them sleep on cushions in my tent.

Lucius.
Varrus and Claudio!

Enter Varrus and Claudio.

Varrus.
Calls my lord?

Marcus Brutus.
I pray you, sirs, lie in my tent and sleep;
It may be I shall raise you by and by
On business to my brother Cassius.

Varrus.
So please you, we will stand and watch your pleasure.

Marcus Brutus.
I will not have it so. Lie down, good sirs,
It may be I shall otherwise bethink me.

Varrus and Claudio lie down.

Look, Lucius, here's the book I sought for so;
I put it in the pocket of my gown.

Lucius.
I was sure your lordship did not give it me.

Marcus Brutus.
Bear with me, good boy, I am much forgetful.
Canst thou hold up thy heavy eyes awhile,
And touch thy instrument a strain or two?

Lucius.
Ay, my lord, an't please you.

Marcus Brutus.
                    It does, my boy.
I trouble thee too much, but thou art willing.

Lucius.
It is my duty, sir.

Marcus Brutus.
I should not urge thy duty past thy might;
I know young bloods look for a time of rest.

Lucius.
I have slept, my lord, already.

Marcus Brutus.
It was well done, and thou shalt sleep again;
I will not hold thee long. If I do live,
I will be good to thee.

Music, and a song.

This is a sleepy tune. O murd'rous slumber!
Layest thou thy leaden mace upon my boy,
That plays thee music? Gentle knave, good night;
I will not do thee so much wrong to wake thee.
If thou dost nod, thou break'st thy instrument,
I'll take it from thee; and, good boy, good night.
Let me see, let me see; is not the leaf turn'd down
Where I left reading? Here it is, I think.

Enter the Ghost of Caesar.

How ill this taper burns! Ha! Who comes here?
I think it is the weakness of mine eyes
That shapes this monstrous apparition.
It comes upon me. Art thou any thing?
Art thou some god, some angel, or some devil,
That mak'st my blood cold, and my hair to stare?
Speak to me what thou art.

Ghost of Julius Caesar.
Thy evil spirit, Brutus.

Marcus Brutus.
                      Why com'st thou?

Ghost of Julius Caesar.
To tell thee thou shalt see me at Philippi.

Marcus Brutus.
Well; then I shall see thee again?

Ghost of Julius Caesar.
Ay, at Philippi.

Marcus Brutus.
Why, I will see thee at Philippi then.

Exit Ghost.

Now I have taken heart thou vanishest.
Ill spirit, I would hold more talk with thee.
Boy, Lucius! Varrus! Claudio! Sirs, awake!
Claudio!

Lucius.
The strings, my lord, are false.

Marcus Brutus.
He thinks he still is at his instrument.
Lucius, awake!

Lucius.
My lord?

Marcus Brutus.
Didst thou dream, Lucius, that thou so criedst out?

Lucius.
My lord, I do not know that I did cry.

Marcus Brutus.
Yes, that thou didst. Didst thou see any thing?

Lucius.
Nothing, my lord.

Marcus Brutus.
Sleep again, Lucius. Sirrah Claudio!

To Varrus.

Fellow thou, awake!

Varrus.
My lord?

Claudio.
My lord?

Marcus Brutus.
Why did you so cry out, sirs, in your sleep?

Both Claudio and Varrus.
Did we, my lord?

Marcus Brutus.
                    Ay. Saw you any thing?

Varrus.
No, my lord, I saw nothing.

Claudio.
                  Nor I, my lord.

Marcus Brutus.
Go and commend me to my brother Cassius;
Bid him set on his pow'rs betimes before,
And we will follow.

Act 5

Scene 1

The plains of Philippi.

(Octavius; Antony; Messenger; Brutus; Cassius; Lucilius; Titinius; Messala)

Octavius and Antony are not the best of partners for a battle, having deeply divergent opinions on matters. Octavius simply refuses to do as Antony asks and calmly takes the part of the battle that he chooses. Cassius, Brutus, and their armies enter and the leaders taunt each other. The cynical Cassius is starting to believe in ill omens and is worried about the outcome of the battle. Brutus and Cassius say farewell to each other, well aware that if they lose, they will never see one another again. They discuss whether, if beaten, they will kill themselves.

Enter Octavius, Antony, and their army.

Octavius Caesar.
Now, Antony, our hopes are answered.
You said the enemy would not come down,
But keep the hills and upper regions.
It proves not so: their battles are at hand;
They mean to warn us at Philippi here,
Answering before we do demand of them.

Mark Antony.
Tut, I am in their bosoms, and I know
Wherefore they do it. They could be content
To visit other places, and come down
With fearful bravery, thinking by this face
To fasten in our thoughts that they have courage;
But 'tis not so.

Enter a Messenger.

Messenger.
                    Prepare you, generals.
The enemy comes on in gallant show;
Their bloody sign of battle is hung out,
And something to be done immediately.

Mark Antony.
Octavius, lead your battle softly on
Upon the left hand of the even field.

Octavius Caesar.
Upon the right hand I, keep thou the left.

Mark Antony.
Why do you cross me in this exigent?

Octavius Caesar.
I do not cross you; but I will do so.

March.
Drum. Enter Brutus, Cassius, and their army; Lucilius, Titinius, Messala, and others.

Marcus Brutus.
They stand, and would have parley.

Cassius.
Stand fast, Titinius; we must out and talk.

Octavius Caesar.
Mark Antony, shall we give sign of battle?

Mark Antony.
No, Caesar, we will answer on their charge.
Make forth, the generals would have some words.

Octavius Caesar.
Stir not until the signal.

Marcus Brutus.
Words before blows; is it so, countrymen?

Octavius Caesar.
Not that we love words better, as you do.

Marcus Brutus.
Good words are better than bad strokes, Octavius.

Mark Antony.
In your bad strokes, Brutus, you give good words;
Witness the hole you made in Caesar's heart,
Crying, "Long live! Hail, Caesar!"

Cassius.
                    Antony,
The posture of your blows are yet unknown;
But for your words, they rob the Hybla bees,
And leave them honeyless.

Mark Antony.
                    Not stingless too?

Marcus Brutus.
O yes, and soundless too;
For you have stol'n their buzzing, Antony,
And very wisely threat before you sting.

Mark Antony.
Villains! You did not so, when your vile daggers
Hack'd one another in the sides of Caesar.
You show'd your teeth like apes, and fawn'd like hounds,
And bow'd like bondmen, kissing Caesar's feet;
Whilst damned Casca, like a cur, behind
Struck Caesar on the neck. O you flatterers!

Cassius.
Flatterers? Now, Brutus, thank yourself;
This tongue had not offended so today,
If Cassius might have rul'd.

Octavius Caesar.
Come, come, the cause. If arguing make us sweat,
The proof of it will turn to redder drops.
Look,
I draw a sword against conspirators;
When think you that the sword goes up again?
Never, till Caesar's three and thirty wounds
Be well aveng'd; or till another Caesar
Have added slaughter to the sword of traitors.

Marcus Brutus.
Caesar, thou canst not die by traitors' hands,
Unless thou bring'st them with thee.

Octavius Caesar.
                        So I hope;
I was not born to die on Brutus' sword.

Marcus Brutus.
O, if thou wert the noblest of thy strain,
Young man, thou couldst not die more honorable.

Cassius.
A peevish schoolboy, worthless of such honor,
Join'd with a masker and a reveller!

Mark Antony.
Old Cassius still!

Octavius Caesar.
                        Come, Antony; away!
Defiance, traitors, hurl we in your teeth.
If you dare fight today, come to the field;
If not, when you have stomachs.

Exeunt Octavius, Antony, and army.

Cassius.
Why now blow wind, swell billow, and swim bark!
The storm is up, and all is on the hazard.

Marcus Brutus.
Ho, Lucilius, hark, a word with you.

Lucilius and then Messala stand forth.

Lucilius.
My lord.

Brutus and Lucilius converse apart.

Cassius.
Messala!

Messala.
                What says my general?

Cassius.
                Messala,
This is my birthday; as this very day
Was Cassius born. Give me thy hand, Messala.
Be thou my witness that against my will
(As Pompey was) am I compell'd to set
Upon one battle all our liberties.
You know that I held Epicurus strong,
And his opinion; now I change my mind,
And partly credit things that do presage.
Coming from Sardis, on our former ensign
Two mighty eagles fell, and there they perch'd,
Gorging and feeding from our soldiers' hands,
Who to Philippi here consorted us.
This morning are they fled away and gone,
And in their steads do ravens, crows, and kites
Fly o'er our heads, and downward look on us
As we were sickly prey. Their shadows seem
A canopy most fatal, under which
Our army lies, ready to give up the ghost.

Messala.
Believe not so.

Cassius.
                I but believe it partly,
For I am fresh of spirit, and resolv'd
To meet all perils very constantly.

Marcus Brutus.
Even so, Lucilius.

Cassius.
                    Now, most noble Brutus,
The gods today stand friendly, that we may,
Lovers in peace, lead on our days to age!
But since the affairs of men rests still incertain,
Let's reason with the worst that may befall.
If we do lose this battle, then is this
The very last time we shall speak together:
What are you then determined to do?

Marcus Brutus.
Even by the rule of that philosophy
By which I did blame Cato for the death
Which he did give himself—I know not how,
But I do find it cowardly and vile,
For fear of what might fall, so to prevent
The time of life—arming myself with patience
To stay the providence of some high powers
That govern us below.

Cassius.
                    Then, if we lose this battle,
You are contented to be led in triumph
Thorough the streets of Rome?

Marcus Brutus.
No, Cassius, no. Think not, thou Roman,
That ever Brutus will go bound to Rome;
He bears too great a mind. But this same day
Must end that work the ides of March begun.
And whether we shall meet again I know not;
Therefore our everlasting farewell take:
For ever, and forever, farewell, Cassius!
If we do meet again, why, we shall smile;
If not, why then this parting was well made.

Cassius.
For ever, and forever, farewell, Brutus!
If we do meet again, we'll smile indeed;
If not, 'tis true this parting was well made.

Marcus Brutus.
Why then lead on. O that a man might know
The end of this day's business ere it come!
But it sufficeth that the day will end,
And then the end is known. Come ho, away!

Exeunt.

Scene 2

The plains of Philippi. The battlefield.

(Brutus; Messala)

Brutus commands an attack on Octavius's army, certain that one strong push against them is all that's needed.

Alarum. Enter Brutus and Messala.

Marcus Brutus.
Ride, ride, Messala, ride, and give these bills
Unto the legions on the other side.

Loud alarum.

Let them set on at once; for I perceive
But cold demeanor in Octavio's wing,
And sudden push gives them the overthrow.
Ride, ride, Messala, let them all come down.

Exeunt.

Scene 3

The plains of Philippi. Another part of the battlefield.

(Cassius; Titinius; Pindarus; Messala; Brutus; Cato; Strato; Volumnius; Lucilius)

Cassius grows convinced that the battle is going against him. Convinced that he is about to be captured by the opposing forces, he frees his slave Pindarus on condition that the man stab him, which he does. It turns out that Brutus has beaten Octavius, as Antony beat Cassius. Yet it turns out that Cassius was in no danger at all. Brutus weeps, but rallies his troops for another fight.

Alarums. Enter Cassius and Titinius.

Cassius.
O, look, Titinius, look, the villains fly!
Myself have to mine own turn'd enemy.
This ensign here of mine was turning back;
I slew the coward, and did take it from him.

Titinius.
O Cassius, Brutus gave the word too early,
Who, having some advantage on Octavius,
Took it too eagerly. His soldiers fell to spoil,
Whilst we by Antony are all enclos'd.

Enter Pindarus.

Pindarus.
Fly further off, my lord, fly further off;
Mark Antony is in your tents, my lord;
Fly therefore, noble Cassius, fly far off.

Cassius.
This hill is far enough. Look, look, Titinius,
Are those my tents where I perceive the fire?

Titinius.
They are, my lord.

Cassius.
                Titinius, if thou lovest me,
Mount thou my horse, and hide thy spurs in him
Till he have brought thee up to yonder troops
And here again, that I may rest assur'd
Whether yond troops are friend or enemy.

Titinius.
I will be here again, even with a thought.

Exit.

Cassius.
Go, Pindarus, get higher on that hill;
My sight was ever thick; regard Titinius,
And tell me what thou not'st about the field.

Pindarus goes up.

This day I breathed first: time is come round,
And where I did begin, there shall I end;
My life is run his compass. Sirrah, what news?

Pindarus.

Above.

O my lord!

Cassius.
What news?

Pindarus.
Titinius is enclosed round about
With horsemen, that make to him on the spur,
Yet he spurs on. Now they are almost on him.
Now, Titinius! Now some light. O, he lights too.
He's ta'en.

Shout.

And hark, they shout for joy.

Cassius.
Come down, behold no more.
O, coward that I am, to live so long,
To see my best friend ta'en before my face!

Pindarus descends.

Come hither, sirrah.
In Parthia did I take thee prisoner,
And then I swore thee, saving of thy life,
That whatsoever I did bid thee do,
Thou shouldst attempt it. Come now, keep thine oath;
Now be a freeman, and with this good sword,
That ran through Caesar's bowels, search this bosom.
Stand not to answer; here, take thou the hilts,
And when my face is cover'd, as 'tis now,
Guide thou the sword.

Pindarus stabs him.

Caesar, thou art reveng'd,
Even with the sword that kill'd thee.

Dies.

Pindarus.
So, I am free; yet would not so have been,
Durst I have done my will. O Cassius,
Far from this country Pindarus shall run,
Where never Roman shall take note of him.

Exit.
Enter Titinius and Messala.

Messala.
It is but change, Titinius; for Octavius
Is overthrown by noble Brutus' power,
As Cassius' legions are by Antony.

Titinius.
These tidings will well comfort Cassius.

Messala.
Where did you leave him?

Titinius.
                All disconsolate,
With Pindarus his bondman, on this hill.

Messala.
Is not that he that lies upon the ground?

Titinius.
He lies not like the living. O my heart!

Messala.
Is not that he?

Titinius.
　　　　　　　No, this was he, Messala,
But Cassius is no more. O setting sun,
As in thy red rays thou dost sink tonight,
So in his red blood Cassius' day is set!
The sun of Rome is set. Our day is gone,
Clouds, dews, and dangers come; our deeds are done!
Mistrust of my success hath done this deed.

Messala.
Mistrust of good success hath done this deed.
O hateful error, melancholy's child,
Why dost thou show to the apt thoughts of men
The things that are not? O error, soon conceiv'd,
Thou never com'st unto a happy birth,
But kill'st the mother that engend'red thee!

Titinius.
What, Pindarus? Where art thou, Pindarus?

Messala.
Seek him, Titinius, whilst I go to meet
The noble Brutus, thrusting this report
Into his ears; I may say "thrusting" it;
For piercing steel, and darts envenomed,
Shall be as welcome to the ears of Brutus
As tidings of this sight.

Titinius.
　　　　　　　Hie you, Messala,
And I will seek for Pindarus the while.

Exit Messala.

Why didst thou send me forth, brave Cassius?
Did I not meet thy friends? And did not they
Put on my brows this wreath of victory,
And bid me give it thee? Didst thou not hear their shouts?
Alas, thou hast misconstrued every thing.
But hold thee, take this garland on thy brow;
Thy Brutus bid me give it thee, and I
Will do his bidding. Brutus, come apace,
And see how I regarded Caius Cassius.
By your leave, gods!—this is a Roman's part.
Come, Cassius' sword, and find Titinius' heart.

Dies.

Alarum. Enter Brutus, Messala, young Cato, Strato, Volumnius, and Lucilius.

Marcus Brutus.
Where, where, Messala, doth his body lie?

Messala.
Lo yonder, and Titinius mourning it.

Marcus Brutus.
Titinius' face is upward.

Young Cato.
　　　　　　　He is slain.

Marcus Brutus.
O Julius Caesar, thou art mighty yet!
Thy spirit walks abroad, and turns our swords
In our own proper entrails.

Low alarums.

Young Cato.
　　　　　　　Brave Titinius!
Look whe'er he have not crown'd dead Cassius!

Marcus Brutus.
Are yet two Romans living such as these?
The last of all the Romans, fare thee well!
It is impossible that ever Rome
Should breed thy fellow. Friends, I owe more tears
To this dead man than you shall see me pay.
I shall find time, Cassius; I shall find time.
Come therefore, and to Thasos send his body;
His funerals shall not be in our camp,
Lest it discomfort us. Lucilius, come,
And come, young Cato, let us to the field,
Labio and Flavio set our battles on.
'Tis three a' clock, and, Romans, yet ere night
We shall try fortune in a second fight.

Exeunt.

Scene 4

The plains of Philippi. Another part of the battlefield.

(Brutus; Messala; Cato; Lucilius; Flavius; First Soldier of Antony's; Second Soldier of Antony's; Antony)

Brutus tries to keep his soldiers' spirits up even as it becomes clear they are defeated. Lucilius pretends to be Brutus in the hopes of giving him time to flee. Antony gives orders that the real Brutus be found.

Alarum. Enter Brutus, Messala, young Cato, Lucilius, and Flavius.

Marcus Brutus.
Yet, countrymen! O yet, hold up your heads!

Exit.

Young Cato.
What bastard doth not? Who will go with me?
I will proclaim my name about the field.
I am the son of Marcus Cato, ho!
A foe to tyrants, and my country's friend.
I am the son of Marcus Cato, ho!

Enter Antony's Soldiers and fight.

Lucilius.
And I am Brutus, Marcus Brutus, I,
Brutus, my country's friend; know me for Brutus!

Young Cato is slain.

O young and noble Cato, art thou down?
Why, now thou diest as bravely as Titinius,
And mayst be honor'd, being Cato's son.

First Soldier of Antony's.
Yield, or thou diest.

Lucilius.
                 Only I yield to die;
There is so much that thou wilt kill me straight:
Kill Brutus, and be honor'd in his death.

First Soldier of Antony's.
We must not. A noble prisoner!

Enter Antony.

Second Soldier of Antony's.
Room ho! Tell Antony, Brutus is ta'en.

First Soldier of Antony's.
I'll tell the news. Here comes the general.
Brutus is ta'en, Brutus is ta'en, my lord!

Mark Antony.
Where is he?

Lucilius.
Safe, Antony, Brutus is safe enough.
I dare assure thee that no enemy
Shall ever take alive the noble Brutus;
The gods defend him from so great a shame!
When you do find him, or alive or dead,
He will be found like Brutus, like himself.

Mark Antony.
This is not Brutus, friend, but, I assure you,
A prize no less in worth. Keep this man safe,
Give him all kindness; I had rather have
Such men my friends than enemies. Go on,
And see whe'er Brutus be alive or dead,
And bring us word unto Octavius' tent
How every thing is chanc'd.

Exeunt.

Scene 5

The plains of Philippi. Another part of the battlefield.

(*Brutus; Dardanius; Clitus; Strato; Volumnius; Antony; Octavius; Messala; Lucilius*)

The defeated Brutus begs one of his last few followers to kill him, but they all refuse. Having seen Caesar's Ghost again, Brutus knows that it is time for him to die. Finally, Strato agrees to hold the sword so that Brutus can run on it. As he dies, Brutus insists he is much more willing to kill himself than he was to kill Caesar. Antony and Octavius pay their respects to Brutus's body, acknowledging that he alone of all the conspirators committed his crime because he thought it was the right thing to do, not out of personal spite.

Enter Brutus, Dardanius, Clitus, Strato, and Volumnius.

Marcus Brutus.
Come, poor remains of friends, rest on this rock.

Clitus.
Statilius show'd the torchlight, but, my lord,
He came not back. He is or ta'en or slain.

Marcus Brutus.
Sit thee down, Clitus; slaying is the word,
It is a deed in fashion. Hark thee, Clitus.

Whispering.

Clitus.
What, I, my lord? No, not for all the world.

Marcus Brutus.
Peace then, no words.

Clitus.
                    I'll rather kill myself.

Marcus Brutus.
Hark thee, Dardanius.

Whispering.

Dardanius.
                    Shall I do such a deed?

Clitus.
O Dardanius!

Dardanius.
O Clitus!

Clitus.
What ill request did Brutus make to thee?

Dardanius.
To kill him, Clitus. Look, he meditates.

Clitus.
Now is that noble vessel full of grief,
That it runs over even at his eyes.

Marcus Brutus.
Come hither, good Volumnius; list a word.

Volumnius.
What says my lord?

Marcus Brutus.
                Why, this, Volumnius:
The ghost of Caesar hath appear'd to me
Two several times by night; at Sardis once,
And this last night, here in Philippi fields.
I know my hour is come.

Volumnius.
                Not so, my lord.

Marcus Brutus.
Nay, I am sure it is, Volumnius.
Thou seest the world, Volumnius, how it goes;
Our enemies have beat us to the pit.

Low alarums.

It is more worthy to leap in ourselves
Than tarry till they push us. Good Volumnius,
Thou know'st that we two went to school together;
Even for that our love of old, I prithee
Hold thou my sword—hilts, whilest I run on it.

Volumnius.
That's not an office for a friend, my lord.

Alarum still.

Clitus.
Fly, fly, my lord, there is no tarrying here.

Marcus Brutus.
Farewell to you, and you, and you, Volumnius.
Strato, thou hast been all this while asleep;
Farewell to thee too, Strato. Countrymen,
My heart doth joy that yet in all my life
I found no man but he was true to me.
I shall have glory by this losing day
More than Octavius and Mark Antony
By this vile conquest shall attain unto.
So fare you well at once, for Brutus' tongue
Hath almost ended his live's history.
Night hangs upon mine eyes, my bones would rest,
That have but labor'd to attain this hour.

Alarum. Cry within, "Fly, fly, fly!"

Clitus.
Fly, my lord, fly.

Marcus Brutus.
                Hence! I will follow.

Exeunt Clitus, Dardanius, and Volumnius.

I prithee, Strato, stay thou by thy lord.
Thou art a fellow of a good respect;
Thy life hath had some smatch of honor in it.
Hold then my sword, and turn away thy face,
While I do run upon it. Wilt thou, Strato?

Strato.
Give me your hand first. Fare you well, my lord.

Marcus Brutus.
Farewell, good Strato.

Runs on his sword.

Caesar, now be still,
I kill'd not thee with half so good a will.

Dies.
Alarum. Retreat. Enter Antony, Octavius, Messala, Lucilius, and the army.

Octavius Caesar.
What man is that?

Messala.
My master's man. Strato, where is thy master?

Strato.
Free from the bondage you are in, Messala;
The conquerors can but make a fire of him;
For Brutus only overcame himself,
And no man else hath honor by his death.

Lucilius.
So Brutus should be found. I thank thee, Brutus,
That thou hast prov'd Lucilius' saying true.

Octavius Caesar.
All that serv'd Brutus, I will entertain them.
Fellow, wilt thou bestow thy time with me?

Strato.
Ay, if Messala will prefer me to you.

Octavius Caesar.
Do so, good Messala.

Messala.
How died my master, Strato?

Strato.
I held the sword, and he did run on it.

Messala.
Octavius, then take him to follow thee,
That did the latest service to my master.

Mark Antony.
This was the noblest Roman of them all:
All the conspirators, save only he,
Did that they did in envy of great Caesar;
He, only in a general honest thought
And common good to all, made one of them.
His life was gentle, and the elements
So mix'd in him that Nature might stand up
And say to all the world, "This was a man!"

Octavius Caesar.
According to his virtue let us use him,
With all respect and rites of burial.
Within my tent his bones tonight shall lie,
Most like a soldier, ordered honorably.
So call the field to rest, and let's away,
To part the glories of this happy day.

Exeunt omnes.

The Taming of the Shrew

Act 1

Scene 1

Before an alehouse on a heath.

(Christopher Sly; First Servingman; Second Servingman; Third Servingman; Page (Bartholomew); Hostess; Lord; First Huntsman; Second Huntsman; First Player; Second Player)

The drunken, penniless Christopher Sly is ejected from a tavern, though he protests that he is of respectable birth. He passes out. A Lord out hunting comes across him, and decides to amuse himself by dressing Sly up like a lord, to find out whether it would be possible to convince him that his life as a beggar was only a dream. His Servants pick Sly up and bear him away. A troop of traveling actors pass by and the Lord decides to add them to his joke/experiment. He orders his page Bartholomew to dress up as a woman and pretend to be Sly's wife. The Lord then goes to make sure that none of his Servants will laugh and give away the trick.

Enter beggar, Christopher Sly, and Hostess.

Christopher Sly.
I'll pheeze you, in faith.

Hostess.
A pair of stocks, you rogue!

Christopher Sly.
Y' are a baggage, the Slys are no rogues. Look in the chronicles; we came in with Richard Conqueror. Therefore paucas pallabris, let the world slide. Sessa!

Hostess.
You will not pay for the glasses you have burst?

Christopher Sly.
No, not a denier. Go by, Saint Jeronimy! Go to thy cold bed, and warm thee.

Hostess.
I know my remedy; I must go fetch the thirdborough.

Exit.

Christopher Sly.
Third, or fourth, or fifth borough, I'll answer him by law. I'll not budge an inch, boy; let him come, and kindly.

Falls asleep.
Wind horns. Enter a Lord from hunting, with his Train.

Lord.
Huntsman, I charge thee, tender well my hounds
(Brach Merriman, the poor cur, is emboss'd),
And couple Clowder with the deep-mouth'd brach.
Saw'st thou not, boy, how Silver made it good
At the hedge-corner, in the coldest fault?
I would not lose the dog for twenty pound.

First Huntsman.
Why, Belman is as good as he, my lord;
He cried upon it at the merest loss,
And twice today pick'd out the dullest scent.
Trust me, I take him for the better dog.

Lord.
Thou art a fool; if Echo were as fleet,
I would esteem him worth a dozen such.
But sup them well, and look unto them all,
Tomorrow I intend to hunt again.

First Huntsman.
I will, my lord.

Lord.
What's here? One dead, or drunk? See, doth he breathe?

Second Huntsman.
He breathes, my lord. Were he not warm'd with ale,
This were a bed but cold to sleep so soundly.

Lord.
O monstrous beast, how like a swine he lies!
Grim death, how foul and loathsome is thine image!
Sirs, I will practice on this drunken man.
What think you, if he were convey'd to bed,
Wrapp'd in sweet clothes, rings put upon his fingers,
A most delicious banquet by his bed,
And brave attendants near him when he wakes,
Would not the beggar then forget himself?

First Huntsman.
Believe me, lord, I think he cannot choose.

Second Huntsman.
It would seem strange unto him when he wak'd.

Lord.
Even as a flatt'ring dream or worthless fancy.
Then take him up, and manage well the jest.
Carry him gently to my fairest chamber,
And hang it round with all my wanton pictures.
Balm his foul head in warm distilled waters,
And burn sweet wood to make the lodging sweet.
Procure me music ready when he wakes,
To make a dulcet and a heavenly sound;
And if he chance to speak, be ready straight,
And with a low submissive reverence
Say, "What is it your honor will command?"
Let one attend him with a silver basin
Full of rose-water and bestrew'd with flowers,
Another bear the ewer, the third a diaper,
And say, "Will't please your lordship cool your hands?"
Some one be ready with a costly suit,
And ask him what apparel he will wear;
Another tell him of his hounds and horse,
And that his lady mourns at his disease.
Persuade him that he hath been lunatic,
And when he says he is, say that he dreams,
For he is nothing but a mighty lord.
This do, and do it kindly, gentle sirs;
It will be pastime passing excellent,
If it be husbanded with modesty.

First Huntsman.
My lord, I warrant you we will play our part
As he shall think by our true diligence
He is no less than what we say he is.

Lord.
Take him up gently and to bed with him,
And each one to his office when he wakes.

Some bear out Sly.
Sound trumpets.

Sirrah, go see what trumpet 'tis that sounds.

Exit Servingman.

Belike some noble gentleman that means
(Traveling some journey) to repose him here.

Enter Servingman.

How now? Who is it?

First Servingman.
An't please your honor, players
That offer service to your lordship.

Enter Players.

Lord.
Bid them come near. Now, fellows, you are welcome.

All Players.
We thank your honor.

Lord.
Do you intend to stay with me tonight?

Second Player.
So please your lordship to accept our duty.

Lord.
With all my heart. This fellow I remember
Since once he play'd a farmer's eldest son.
'Twas where you woo'd the gentlewoman so well.
I have forgot your name; but sure that part
Was aptly fitted and naturally perform'd.

First Player.
I think 'twas Soto that your honor means.

Lord.
'Tis very true; thou didst it excellent.
Well, you are come to me in happy time,
The rather for I have some sport in hand,
Wherein your cunning can assist me much.
There is a lord will hear you play tonight;
But I am doubtful of your modesties,
Lest, over-eyeing of his odd behavior
(For yet his honor never heard a play),
You break into some merry passion,
And so offend him; for I tell you, sirs,
If you should smile, he grows impatient.

First Player.
Fear not, my lord, we can contain ourselves,
Were he the veriest antic in the world.

Lord.
Go, sirrah, take them to the buttery,
And give them friendly welcome every one.
Let them want nothing that my house affords.

Exit one with the Players.

Sirrah, go you to Barthol'mew my page,
And see him dress'd in all suits like a lady;
That done, conduct him to the drunkard's chamber,
And call him madam, do him obeisance.
Tell him from me, as he will win my love,
He bear himself with honorable action,
Such as he hath observ'd in noble ladies
Unto their lords, by them accomplished;
Such duty to the drunkard let him do,
With soft low tongue and lowly courtesy,
And say, "What is't your honor will command,
Wherein your lady, and your humble wife,
May show her duty and make known her love?"
And then with kind embracements, tempting kisses,
And with declining head into his bosom,
Bid him shed tears, as being overjoyed
To see her noble lord restor'd to health,
Who for this seven years hath esteemed him
No better than a poor and loathsome beggar.
And if the boy have not a woman's gift
To rain a shower of commanded tears,
An onion will do well for such a shift,
Which in a napkin (being close convey'd)
Shall in despite enforce a watery eye.
See this dispatch'd with all the haste thou canst;
Anon I'll give thee more instructions.

Exit First Servingman.

I know the boy will well usurp the grace,
Voice, gait, and action of a gentlewoman.
I long to hear him call the drunkard husband,
And how my men will stay themselves from laughter
When they do homage to this simple peasant.
I'll in to counsel them; haply my presence
May well abate the over-merry spleen,
Which otherwise would grow into extremes.

Exeunt.

Act 2

Scene 1

Before an alehouse on a heath.

(Christopher Sly; First Servingman; Second Servingman; Third Servingman; Page (Bartholomew); Hostess; Lord; First Huntsman; Second Huntsman; First Player; Second Player)

The drunken, penniless Christopher Sly is ejected from a tavern, though he protests that he is of respectable birth. He passes out. A Lord out hunting comes across him, and decides to amuse himself by dressing Sly up like a lord, to find out whether it would be possible to convince him that his life as a beggar was only a dream. His Servants pick Sly up and bear him away. A troop of traveling actors pass by and the Lord decides to add them to his joke/experiment. He orders his page Bartholomew to dress up as a woman and pretend to be Sly's wife. The Lord then goes to make sure that none of his Servants will laugh and give away the trick.

Enter beggar, Christopher Sly, and Hostess.

Christopher Sly.
I'll pheeze you, in faith.

Hostess.
A pair of stocks, you rogue!

Christopher Sly.
Y' are a baggage, the Slys are no rogues. Look in the chronicles; we came in with Richard Conqueror. Therefore paucas pallabris, let the world slide. Sessa!

Hostess.
You will not pay for the glasses you have burst?

Christopher Sly.
No, not a denier. Go by, Saint Jeronimy! Go to thy cold bed, and warm thee.

Hostess.
I know my remedy; I must go fetch the thirdborough.

Exit.

Christopher Sly.
Third, or fourth, or fifth borough, I'll answer him by law. I'll not budge an inch, boy; let him come, and kindly.

Falls asleep.
Wind horns. Enter a Lord from hunting, with his Train.

Lord.
Huntsman, I charge thee, tender well my hounds
(Brach Merriman, the poor cur, is emboss'd),
And couple Clowder with the deep-mouth'd brach.
Saw'st thou not, boy, how Silver made it good
At the hedge-corner, in the coldest fault?
I would not lose the dog for twenty pound.

First Huntsman.
Why, Belman is as good as he, my lord;
He cried upon it at the merest loss,
And twice today pick'd out the dullest scent.
Trust me, I take him for the better dog.

Lord.
Thou art a fool; if Echo were as fleet,
I would esteem him worth a dozen such.
But sup them well, and look unto them all,
Tomorrow I intend to hunt again.

First Huntsman.
I will, my lord.

Lord.
What's here? One dead, or drunk? See, doth he breathe?

Second Huntsman.
He breathes, my lord. Were he not warm'd with ale,
This were a bed but cold to sleep so soundly.

Lord.
O monstrous beast, how like a swine he lies!
Grim death, how foul and loathsome is thine image!
Sirs, I will practice on this drunken man.
What think you, if he were convey'd to bed,
Wrapp'd in sweet clothes, rings put upon his fingers,
A most delicious banquet by his bed,
And brave attendants near him when he wakes,
Would not the beggar then forget himself?

First Huntsman.
Believe me, lord, I think he cannot choose.

Second Huntsman.
It would seem strange unto him when he wak'd.

Lord.
Even as a flatt'ring dream or worthless fancy.
Then take him up, and manage well the jest.
Carry him gently to my fairest chamber,
And hang it round with all my wanton pictures.
Balm his foul head in warm distilled waters,
And burn sweet wood to make the lodging sweet.
Procure me music ready when he wakes,
To make a dulcet and a heavenly sound;
And if he chance to speak, be ready straight,
And with a low submissive reverence
Say, "What is it your honor will command?"
Let one attend him with a silver basin
Full of rose-water and bestrew'd with flowers,
Another bear the ewer, the third a diaper,
And say, "Will't please your lordship cool your hands?"
Some one be ready with a costly suit,
And ask him what apparel he will wear;
Another tell him of his hounds and horse,
And that his lady mourns at his disease.
Persuade him that he hath been lunatic,
And when he says he is, say that he dreams,
For he is nothing but a mighty lord.
This do, and do it kindly, gentle sirs;
It will be pastime passing excellent,
If it be husbanded with modesty.

First Huntsman.
My lord, I warrant you we will play our part
As he shall think by our true diligence
He is no less than what we say he is.

Lord.
Take him up gently and to bed with him,
And each one to his office when he wakes.

Some bear out Sly.
Sound trumpets.

Sirrah, go see what trumpet 'tis that sounds.

Exit Servingman.

Belike some noble gentleman that means
(Traveling some journey) to repose him here.

Enter Servingman.

How now? Who is it?

First Servingman.
An't please your honor, players
That offer service to your lordship.

Enter Players.

Lord.
Bid them come near. Now, fellows, you are welcome.

All Players.
We thank your honor.

Lord.
Do you intend to stay with me tonight?

Second Player.
So please your lordship to accept our duty.

Lord.
With all my heart. This fellow I remember
Since once he play'd a farmer's eldest son.
'Twas where you woo'd the gentlewoman so well.
I have forgot your name; but sure that part
Was aptly fitted and naturally perform'd.

First Player.
I think 'twas Soto that your honor means.

Lord.
'Tis very true; thou didst it excellent.
Well, you are come to me in happy time,
The rather for I have some sport in hand,
Wherein your cunning can assist me much.
There is a lord will hear you play tonight;
But I am doubtful of your modesties,
Lest, over-eyeing of his odd behavior
(For yet his honor never heard a play),
You break into some merry passion,
And so offend him; for I tell you, sirs,
If you should smile, he grows impatient.

First Player.
Fear not, my lord, we can contain ourselves,
Were he the veriest antic in the world.

Lord.
Go, sirrah, take them to the buttery,
And give them friendly welcome every one.
Let them want nothing that my house affords.

Exit one with the Players.

Sirrah, go you to Barthol'mew my page,
And see him dress'd in all suits like a lady;
That done, conduct him to the drunkard's chamber,
And call him madam, do him obeisance.
Tell him from me, as he will win my love,
He bear himself with honorable action,
Such as he hath observ'd in noble ladies
Unto their lords, by them accomplished;
Such duty to the drunkard let him do,
With soft low tongue and lowly courtesy,
And say, "What is't your honor will command,
Wherein your lady, and your humble wife,
May show her duty and make known her love?"
And then with kind embracements, tempting kisses,
And with declining head into his bosom,
Bid him shed tears, as being overjoyed
To see her noble lord restor'd to health,
Who for this seven years hath esteemed him
No better than a poor and loathsome beggar.
And if the boy have not a woman's gift
To rain a shower of commanded tears,
An onion will do well for such a shift,
Which in a napkin (being close convey'd)
Shall in despite enforce a watery eye.
See this dispatch'd with all the haste thou canst;
Anon I'll give thee more instructions.

Exit First Servingman.

I know the boy will well usurp the grace,
Voice, gait, and action of a gentlewoman.
I long to hear him call the drunkard husband,
And how my men will stay themselves from laughter
When they do homage to this simple peasant.
I'll in to counsel them; haply my presence
May well abate the over-merry spleen,
Which otherwise would grow into extremes.

Exeunt.

Act 3

Scene 1

Padua. A public square.

(Lucentio; Tranio; Baptista; Katherina; Bianca; Gremio; Hortensio; Biondello; First Servingman; Sly; Page (Bartholomew))

Lucentio has come to Padua to study, though his servant Tranio wants to be sure that they don't forget the pleasurable side of life. They see Baptista pass by, being harassed by Gremio and Hortensio; both are wooing Baptista's younger daughter, Bianca, but Baptista refuses to let her be wed until he has married off her elder sister Katherina. Neither suitor is delighted at that particular idea, and the bad-tempered Katherina soon shows why as she wildly curses both suitors. The docile and obedient Bianca goes in at her father's request, though as she speaks she enthralls Lucentio. Baptista announces his intention that his daughters should be well-educated, and asks Gremio and Hortensio to send him any good teachers they know. He goes in and Katherina follows. The two rivals for Bianca agree that since they can't even be proper rivals until Katherina is married, they should join forces to effect that happy event. They depart. Lucentio is still in a love daze, and Tranio has much to do to snap him out of it and point out the problem that Bianca has been hidden from all suitors until Katherina is married. Lucentio decides that he will become one of Bianca's schoolmasters as an opportunity to get to know her, while Tranio will pretend to be Lucentio. They exchange clothes. Lucentio adds another instruction to Tranio: that he become one of Bianca's official wooers himself. (Sly, watching all this, is bored, sleepy, and paying little attention; though he claims to be enjoying the play, he wishes it were over.)

Enter Lucentio and his man Tranio.

Lucentio.
Tranio, since for the great desire I had
To see fair Padua, nursery of arts,
I am arriv'd for fruitful Lombardy,
The pleasant garden of great Italy,
And by my father's love and leave am arm'd
With his good will and thy good company,
My trusty servant, well approv'd in all,
Here let us breathe, and haply institute
A course of learning and ingenious studies.
Pisa, renowned for grave citizens,
Gave me my being and my father first,
A merchant of great traffic through the world,
Vincentio, come of the Bentivolii;
Vincentio's son, brought up in Florence,
It shall become to serve all hopes conceiv'd,
To deck his fortune with his virtuous deeds.
And therefore, Tranio, for the time I study,
Virtue and that part of philosophy
Will I apply that treats of happiness
By virtue specially to be achiev'd.
Tell me thy mind, for I have Pisa left
And am to Padua come, as he that leaves
A shallow plash to plunge him in the deep,
And with satiety seeks to quench his thirst.

Tranio.
Mi perdonato, gentle master mine;
I am, in all affected as yourself,
Glad that you thus continue your resolve
To suck the sweets of sweet philosophy.
Only, good master, while we do admire
This virtue and this moral discipline,
Let's be no Stoics nor no stocks, I pray,
Or so devote to Aristotle's checks
As Ovid be an outcast quite abjur'd.
Balk logic with acquaintance that you have,
And practice rhetoric in your common talk,
Music and poesy use to quicken you,
The mathematics, and the metaphysics,
Fall to them as you find your stomach serves you:
No profit grows where is no pleasure ta'en.
In brief, sir, study what you most affect.

Lucentio.
Gramercies, Tranio, well dost thou advise.
If, Biondello, thou wert come ashore,
We could at once put us in readiness,
And take a lodging fit to entertain
Such friends as time in Padua shall beget.
But stay a while, what company is this?

Tranio.
Master, some show to welcome us to town.

Enter Baptista with his two daughters, Katherina and Bianca, Gremio, a pantaloon, Hortensio, suitor to Bianca. Lucentio, Tranio stand by.

Baptista.
Gentlemen, importune me no farther,
For how I firmly am resolv'd you know:
That is, not to bestow my youngest daughter
Before I have a husband for the elder.
If either of you both love Katherina,
Because I know you well, and love you well,
Leave shall you have to court her at your pleasure.

Gremio.
To cart her rather; she's too rough for me.
There, there, Hortensio, will you any wife?

Act 3, Scene 1

Katherina.

To Baptista.

I pray you, sir, is it your will
To make a stale of me amongst these mates?

Hortensio.
Mates, maid, how mean you that? No mates for you,
Unless you were of gentler, milder mould.

Katherina.
I' faith, sir, you shall never need to fear.
Iwis it is not half way to her heart;
But if it were, doubt not her care should be
To comb your noddle with a three-legg'd stool,
And paint your face, and use you like a fool.

Hortensio.
From all such devils, good Lord deliver us!

Gremio.
And me too, good Lord!

Tranio.
Husht, master, here's some good pastime toward;
That wench is stark mad or wonderful froward.

Lucentio.
But in the other's silence do I see
Maid's mild behavior and sobriety.
Peace, Tranio!

Tranio.
Well said, master, mum, and gaze your fill.

Baptista.
Gentlemen, that I may soon make good
What I have said, Bianca, get you in,
And let it not displease thee, good Bianca,
For I will love thee ne'er the less, my girl.

Katherina.
A pretty peat! It is best
Put finger in the eye, and she knew why.

Bianca.
Sister, content you in my discontent.
Sir, to your pleasure humbly I subscribe;
My books and instruments shall be my company,
On them to look and practice by myself.

Lucentio.
Hark, Tranio, thou mayst hear Minerva speak.

Hortensio.
Signior Baptista, will you be so strange?
Sorry am I that our good will effects
Bianca's grief.

Gremio.
Why will you mew her up,
Signior Baptista, for this fiend of hell,
And make her bear the penance of her tongue?

Baptista.
Gentlemen, content ye; I am resolv'd.
Go in, Bianca.

Exit Bianca.

And for I know she taketh most delight
In music, instruments, and poetry,
Schoolmasters will I keep within my house,
Fit to instruct her youth. If you, Hortensio,
Or, Signior Gremio, you, know any such,
Prefer them hither; for to cunning men
I will be very kind, and liberal
To mine own children in good bringing-up,
And so farewell. Katherina, you may stay,
For I have more to commune with Bianca.

Exit.

Katherina.
Why, and I trust I may go too, may I not? What, shall I be appointed hours, as though, belike, I knew not what to take and what to leave? Ha!

Exit.

Gremio.
You may go to the devil's dam; your gifts are so good, here's none will hold you. Their love is not so great, Hortensio, but we may blow our nails together, and fast it fairly out. Our cake's dough on both sides. Farewell; yet for the love I bear my sweet Bianca, if I can by any means light on a fit man to teach her that wherein she delights, I will wish him to her father.

Hortensio.
So will I, Signior Gremio. But a word, I pray. Though the nature of our quarrel yet never brook'd parle, know now upon advice, it toucheth us both, that we may yet again have access to our fair mistress, and be happy rivals in Bianca's love, to labor and effect one thing specially.

Gremio.
What's that, I pray?

Hortensio.
Marry, sir, to get a husband for her sister.

Gremio.
A husband! A devil.

Hortensio.
I say, a husband.

Gremio.
I say, a devil. Think'st thou, Hortensio, though her father be very rich, any man is so very a fool to be married to hell?

Hortensio.
Tush, Gremio; though it pass your patience and mine to endure her loud alarums, why, man, there be good fellows in the world, and a man could light on them, would take her with all faults, and money enough.

Gremio.
I cannot tell; but I had as lief take her dowry with this condition: to be whipt at the high cross every morning.

Hortensio.
Faith, as you say, there's small choice in rotten apples. But come, since this bar in law makes us friends, it shall be so far forth friendly maintain'd till by helping Baptista's eldest daughter to a husband we set his youngest free for a husband, and then have to't afresh. Sweet Bianca, happy man be his dole! He that runs fastest gets the ring. How say you, Signior Gremio?

Gremio.
I am agreed, and would I had given him the best horse in Padua to begin his wooing that would thoroughly woo her, wed her, and bed her, and rid the house of her! Come on.

Exeunt ambo Gremio and Hortensio. Manent Tranio and Lucentio.

Tranio.
I pray, sir, tell me, is it possible
That love should of a sudden take such hold?

Lucentio.
O Tranio, till I found it to be true,
I never thought it possible or likely.
But see, while idly I stood looking on,
I found the effect of love in idleness,
And now in plainness do confess to thee,
That art to me as secret and as dear
As Anna to the Queen of Carthage was:
Tranio, I burn, I pine, I perish, Tranio,
If I achieve not this young modest girl.
Counsel me, Tranio, for I know thou canst;
Assist me, Tranio, for I know thou wilt.

Tranio.
Master, it is no time to chide you now,
Affection is not rated from the heart.
If love have touch'd you, nought remains but so,
"Redime te captum quam queas minimo."

Lucentio.
Gramercies, lad. Go forward, this contents;
The rest will comfort, for thy counsel's sound.

Tranio.
Master, you look'd so longly on the maid,
Perhaps you mark'd not what's the pith of all.

Lucentio.
O yes, I saw sweet beauty in her face,
Such as the daughter of Agenor had,
That made great Jove to humble him to her hand,
When with his knees he kiss'd the Cretan strond.

Tranio.
Saw you no more? Mark'd you not how her sister
Began to scold, and raise up such a storm
That mortal ears might hardly endure the din?

Lucentio.
Tranio, I saw her coral lips to move,
And with her breath she did perfume the air.
Sacred and sweet was all I saw in her.

Tranio.
Nay, then 'tis time to stir him from his trance.
I pray, awake, sir; if you love the maid,
Bend thoughts and wits to achieve her. Thus it stands:
Her elder sister is so curst and shrewd
That till the father rid his hands of her,
Master, your love must live a maid at home,
And therefore has he closely mew'd her up,
Because she will not be annoy'd with suitors.

Lucentio.
Ah, Tranio, what a cruel father's he?
But art thou not advis'd, he took some care
To get her cunning schoolmasters to instruct her?

Tranio.
Ay, marry, am I, sir; and now 'tis plotted.

Lucentio.
I have it, Tranio.

Tranio.
                Master, for my hand,
Both our inventions meet and jump in one.

Lucentio.
Tell me thine first.

Tranio.
                You will be schoolmaster,
And undertake the teaching of the maid:
That's your device.

Lucentio.
                It is; may it be done?

Tranio.
Not possible; for who shall bear your part,
And be in Padua here Vincentio's son,
Keep house and ply his book, welcome his friends,
Visit his countrymen, and banquet them?

Lucentio.
Basta, content thee; for I have it full.
We have not yet been seen in any house,
Nor can we be distinguish'd by our faces
For man or master. Then it follows thus:
Thou shalt be master, Tranio, in my stead;
Keep house and port and servants, as I should.
I will some other be, some Florentine,
Some Neapolitan, or meaner man of Pisa.
'Tis hatch'd, and shall be so. Tranio, at once
Uncase thee; take my color'd hat and cloak.
When Biondello comes, he waits on thee,
But I will charm him first to keep his tongue.

Tranio.
So had you need.
In brief, sir, sith it your pleasure is,
And I am tied to be obedient—
For so your father charg'd me at our parting;
"Be serviceable to my son," quoth he,
Although I think 'twas in another sense—
I am content to be Lucentio,
Because so well I love Lucentio.

Lucentio.
Tranio, be so, because Lucentio loves,
And let me be a slave, t' achieve that maid
Whose sudden sight hath thrall'd my wounded eye.

Enter Biondello.

Here comes the rogue. Sirrah, where have you been?

Biondello.
Where have I been? Nay, how now, where are you?
Master, has my fellow Tranio stol'n your clothes? Or
you stol'n his? Or both? Pray what's the news?

Lucentio.
Sirrah, come hither, 'tis no time to jest,
And therefore frame your manners to the time.
Your fellow Tranio here, to save my life,
Puts my apparel and my count'nance on,
And I for my escape have put on his;
For in a quarrel since I came ashore
I kill'd a man, and fear I was descried.
Wait you on him, I charge you, as becomes,
While I make way from hence to save my life.
You understand me?

Biondello.
                Ay, sir!—

Aside.
                Ne'er a whit.

Lucentio.
And not a jot of Tranio in your mouth,
Tranio is chang'd into Lucentio.

Biondello.
The better for him, would I were so too!

Tranio.
So could I, faith, boy, to have the next wish after,
That Lucentio indeed had Baptista's youngest daughter.
But, sirrah, not for my sake, but your master's, I advise
You use your manners discreetly in all kind of companies.
When I am alone, why then I am Tranio;
But in all places else your master Lucentio.

Lucentio.
Tranio, let's go.
One thing more rests, that thyself execute—
To make one among these wooers. If thou ask me why,
Sufficeth my reasons are both good and weighty.

Exeunt.
The Presenters above speaks.

First Servingman.
My lord, you nod, you do not mind the play.

Christopher Sly.
Yes, by Saint Anne, do I. A good matter, surely; comes there any more of it?

Page (Bartholomew).
My lord, 'tis but begun.

Christopher Sly.
'Tis a very excellent piece of work, madam lady; would 'twere done!

They sit and mark.

Scene 2

Padua. Before Hortensio's house.

(Petruchio; Grumio; Hortensio; Gremio; Lucentio; Tranio; Biondello)

Petruchio has come to visit his good friend Hortensio, accompanied by his servant Grumio, who misunderstands him constantly and is beaten for it. Hortensio greets them and tries to make things up between them. Finally Petruchio explains matters: his father is dead, and he is seeking a wife. A rich wife, that is, and nothing else matters. Hortensio, delighted, sees an opportunity to get Katherina off the scene, though he warns Petruchio how ill-tempered the lady is. Learning Baptista's name, Petruchio remarks that his father was a friend, and boldly determines to go woo the lady at once. Hortensio holds him back, explaining his love for Bianca, and asks Petruchio to introduce him (in disguise) to Baptista as a music teacher for Bianca. Gremio comes in with Lucentio disguised as a teacher; he has hired the young man on condition that Lucentio press his suit to Bianca. Hortensio tells Gremio that he has found Katherina a husband, and Gremio is delighted, if skeptical about Petruchio's willingness once he meets her. Tranio enters dressed up as Lucentio, and boldly announces himself as yet another suitor for Bianca, despite Gremio and Hortensio's protests. He proposes that despite their rivalry, Bianca's suitors should be friends, and invites them to drink with him that afternoon, leaving Lucentio a clear field.

Enter Petruchio and his man Grumio.

Petruchio.
Verona, for a while I take my leave
To see my friends in Padua, but of all
My best beloved and approved friend,
Hortensio; and I trow this is his house.
Here, sirrah Grumio, knock, I say.

Grumio.
Knock, sir? Whom should I knock? Is there any man has rebus'd your worship?

Petruchio.
Villain, I say, knock me here soundly.

Grumio.
Knock you here, sir? Why, sir, what am I, sir, that I should knock you here, sir?

Petruchio.
Villain, I say, knock me at this gate,
And rap me well, or I'll knock your knave's pate.

Grumio.
My master is grown quarrelsome. I should knock you first,
And then I know after who comes by the worst.

Petruchio.
Will it not be?
Faith, sirrah, and you'll not knock, I'll ring it.
I'll try how you can sol, fa, and sing it.

He wrings him by the ears.

Grumio.
Help, masters, help, my master is mad.

Petruchio.
Now knock when I bid you, sirrah villain!

Enter Hortensio.

Hortensio.
How now, what's the matter? My old friend Grumio! And my good friend Petruchio! How do you all at Verona?

Act 3, Scene 2

Petruchio.
Signior Hortensio, come you to part the fray? Con tutto il cuore, ben trovato, may I say.

Hortensio.
Alla nostra casa ben venuto, molto honorato signor mio Petruchio.
Rise, Grumio, rise, we will compound this quarrel.

Grumio.
Nay, 'tis no matter, sir, what he 'leges in Latin. If this be not a lawful cause for me to leave his service, look you, sir. He bid me knock him and rap him soundly, sir. Well, was it fit for a servant to use his master so, being perhaps (for aught I see) two and thirty, a peep out?
Whom would to God I had well knock'd at first,
Then had not Grumio come by the worst.

Petruchio.
A senseless villain! Good Hortensio,
I bade the rascal knock upon your gate,
And could not get him for my heart to do it.

Grumio.
Knock at the gate? O heavens! Spake you not these words plain, "Sirrah, knock me here; rap me here; knock me well, and knock me soundly"? And come you now with "knocking at the gate"?

Petruchio.
Sirrah, be gone, or talk not, I advise you.

Hortensio.
Petruchio, patience, I am Grumio's pledge.
Why, this' a heavy chance 'twixt him and you,
Your ancient, trusty, pleasant servant Grumio.
And tell me now, sweet friend, what happy gale
Blows you to Padua here from old Verona?

Petruchio.
Such wind as scatters young men through the world
To seek their fortunes farther than at home,
Where small experience grows. But in a few,
Signior Hortensio, thus it stands with me:
Antonio, my father, is deceas'd,
And I have thrust myself into this maze,
Happily to wive and thrive as best I may.
Crowns in my purse I have, and goods at home,
And so am come abroad to see the world.

Hortensio.
Petruchio, shall I then come roundly to thee,
And wish thee to a shrewd ill-favor'd wife?
Thou'dst thank me but a little for my counsel;
And yet I'll promise thee she shall be rich,
And very rich. But th' art too much my friend,
And I'll not wish thee to her.

Petruchio.
Signior Hortensio, 'twixt such friends as we
Few words suffice; and therefore, if thou know
One rich enough to be Petruchio's wife
(As wealth is burden of my wooing dance),
Be she as foul as was Florentius' love,
As old as Sibyl, and as curst and shrewd
As Socrates' Xantippe, or a worse,
She moves me not, or not removes at least
Affection's edge in me. Whe'er she is as rough
As are the swelling Adriatic seas,
I come to wive it wealthily in Padua;
If wealthily, then happily in Padua.

Grumio.
Nay, look you, sir, he tells you flatly what his mind is. Why, give him gold enough, and marry him to a puppet or an aglet-baby, or an old trot with ne'er a tooth in her head, though she have as many diseases as two and fifty horses. Why, nothing comes amiss, so money comes withal.

Hortensio.
Petruchio, since we are stepp'd thus far in,
I will continue that I broach'd in jest.
I can, Petruchio, help thee to a wife
With wealth enough, and young and beauteous,
Brought up as best becomes a gentlewoman.
Her only fault, and that is faults enough,
Is that she is intolerable curst
And shrewd and froward, so beyond all measure,
That were my state far worser than it is,
I would not wed her for a mine of gold.

Petruchio.
Hortensio, peace! Thou know'st not gold's effect.
Tell me her father's name, and 'tis enough;
For I will board her, though she chide as loud
As thunder when the clouds in autumn crack.

Hortensio.
Her father is Baptista Minola,
An affable and courteous gentleman.
Her name is Katherina Minola,

Renown'd in Padua for her scolding tongue.

Petruchio.
I know her father, though I know not her,
And he knew my deceased father well.
I will not sleep, Hortensio, till I see her,
And therefore let me be thus bold with you
To give you over at this first encounter,
Unless you will accompany me thither.

Grumio.
I pray you, sir, let him go while the humor lasts. A' my word, and she knew him as well as I do, she would think scolding would do little good upon him. She may perhaps call him half a score knaves or so. Why, that's nothing; and he begin once, he'll rail in his rope-tricks. I'll tell you what, sir, and she stand him but a little, he will throw a figure in her face, and so disfigure her with it, that she shall have no more eyes to see withal than a cat. You know him not, sir.

Hortensio.
Tarry, Petruchio, I must go with thee,
For in Baptista's keep my treasure is.
He hath the jewel of my life in hold,
His youngest daughter, beautiful Bianca,
And her withholds from me and other more,
Suitors to her and rivals in my love;
Supposing it a thing impossible,
For those defects I have before rehears'd,
That ever Katherina will be woo'd.
Therefore this order hath Baptista ta'en,
That none shall have access unto Bianca
Till Katherine the curst have got a husband.

Grumio.
Katherine the curst!
A title for a maid of all titles the worst.

Hortensio.
Now shall my friend Petruchio do me grace,
And offer me disguis'd in sober robes
To old Baptista as a schoolmaster
Well seen in music, to instruct Bianca,
That so I may by this device at least
Have leave and leisure to make love to her,
And unsuspected court her by herself.

Enter Gremio, and Lucentio disguised as Cambio, a schoolmaster.

Grumio.
Here's no knavery! See, to beguile the old folks, how the young folks lay their heads together! Master, master, look about you! Who goes there? Ha!

Hortensio.
Peace, Grumio, it is the rival of my love. Petruchio, stand by a while.

Grumio.
A proper stripling, and an amorous!

They stand aside.

Gremio.
O, very well, I have perus'd the note.
Hark you, sir, I'll have them very fairly bound—
All books of love, see that at any hand—
And see you read no other lectures to her.
You understand me. Over and beside
Signior Baptista's liberality,
I'll mend it with a largess. Take your paper too,
And let me have them very well perfum'd;
For she is sweeter than perfume itself
To whom they go to. What will you read to her?

Lucentio (as Cambio).
What e'er I read to her, I'll plead for you
As for my patron, stand you so assur'd,
As firmly as yourself were still in place,
Yea, and perhaps with more successful words
Than you—unless you were a scholar, sir.

Gremio.
O this learning, what a thing it is!

Grumio.
O this woodcock, what an ass it is!

Petruchio.
Peace, sirrah!

Hortensio.
Grumio, mum!

Coming forward.
      God save you, Signior Gremio.

Gremio.
And you are well met, Signior Hortensio.
Trow you whither I am going? To Baptista Minola.
I promis'd to inquire carefully
About a schoolmaster for the fair Bianca,

And by good fortune I have lighted well
On this young man; for learning and behavior
Fit for her turn, well read in poetry
And other books, good ones, I warrant ye.

Hortensio.
'Tis well; and I have met a gentleman
Hath promis'd me to help me to another,
A fine musician to instruct our mistress;
So shall I no whit be behind in duty
To fair Bianca, so beloved of me.

Gremio.
Beloved of me, and that my deeds shall prove.

Grumio.
And that his bags shall prove.

Hortensio.
Gremio, 'tis now no time to vent our love;
Listen to me, and if you speak me fair,
I'll tell you news indifferent good for either,
Here is a gentleman whom by chance I met,
Upon agreement from us to his liking,
Will undertake to woo curst Katherine,
Yea, and to marry her, if her dowry please.

Gremio.
So said, so done, is well.
Hortensio, have you told him all her faults?

Petruchio.
I know she is an irksome brawling scold.
If that be all, masters, I hear no harm.

Gremio.
No, say'st me so, friend? What countryman?

Petruchio.
Born in Verona, old Antonio's son.
My father dead, my fortune lives for me,
And I do hope good days and long to see.

Gremio.
O sir, such a life, with such a wife, were strange;
But if you have a stomach, to't a' God's name;
You shall have me assisting you in all.
But will you woo this wild-cat?

Petruchio.
                    Will I live?

Grumio.
Will he woo her? Ay—or I'll hang her.

Petruchio.
Why came I hither but to that intent?
Think you a little din can daunt mine ears?
Have I not in my time heard lions roar?
Have I not heard the sea, puff'd up with winds,
Rage like an angry boar chafed with sweat?
Have I not heard great ordnance in the field,
And heaven's artillery thunder in the skies?
Have I not in a pitched battle heard
Loud 'larums, neighing steeds, and trumpets' clang?
And do you tell me of a woman's tongue,
That gives not half so great a blow to hear
As will a chestnut in a farmer's fire?
Tush, tush, fear boys with bugs.

Grumio.
                    For he fears none.

Gremio.
Hortensio, hark.
This gentleman is happily arriv'd,
My mind presumes, for his own good and ours.

Hortensio.
I promis'd we would be contributors,
And bear his charge of wooing, whatsoe'er.

Gremio.
And so we will, provided that he win her.

Grumio.
I would I were as sure of a good dinner.

Enter Tranio brave, as Lucentio, and Biondello.

Tranio (as Lucentio).
Gentlemen, God save you. If I may be bold,
Tell me, I beseech you, which is the readiest way
To the house of Signior Baptista Minola?

Biondello.
He that has the two fair daughters? Is't he you mean?

Tranio (as Lucentio).
Even he, Biondello.

Gremio.
Hark you, sir, you mean not her to—

Tranio (as Lucentio).
Perhaps him and her, sir; what have you to do?

Petruchio.
Not her that chides, sir, at any hand, I pray.

Tranio (as Lucentio).
I love no chiders, sir. Biondello, let's away.

Lucentio.

Aside.

Well begun, Tranio.

Hortensio.
              Sir, a word ere you go.
Are you a suitor to the maid you talk of, yea or no?

Tranio (as Lucentio).
And if I be, sir, is it any offense?

Gremio.
No; if without more words you will get you hence.

Tranio (as Lucentio).
Why, sir, I pray, are not the streets as free
For me as for you?

Gremio.
              But so is not she.

Tranio (as Lucentio).
For what reason, I beseech you?

Gremio.
              For this reason, if you'll know,
That she's the choice love of Signior Gremio.

Hortensio.
That she's the chosen of Signior Hortensio.

Tranio (as Lucentio).
Softly, my masters! If you be gentlemen,
Do me this right: hear me with patience.
Baptista is a noble gentleman,
To whom my father is not all unknown,
And were his daughter fairer than she is,
She may more suitors have, and me for one.
Fair Leda's daughter had a thousand wooers,
Then well one more may fair Bianca have;
And so she shall. Lucentio shall make one,
Though Paris came in hope to speed alone.

Gremio.
What, this gentleman will out-talk us all.

Lucentio (as Cambio).
Sir, give him head, I know he'll prove a jade.

Petruchio.
Hortensio, to what end are all these words?

Hortensio.
Sir, let me be so bold as ask you,
Did you yet ever see Baptista's daughter?

Tranio (as Lucentio).
No, sir, but hear I do that he hath two:
The one as famous for a scolding tongue,
As is the other for beauteous modesty.

Petruchio.
Sir, sir, the first's for me, let her go by.

Gremio.
Yea, leave that labor to great Hercules,
And let it be more than Alcides' twelve.

Petruchio.
Sir, understand you this of me, in sooth:
The youngest daughter, whom you hearken for,
Her father keeps from all access of suitors,
And will not promise her to any man,
Until the elder sister first be wed.
The younger then is free, and not before.

Tranio (as Lucentio).
If it be so, sir, that you are the man
Must stead us all, and me amongst the rest;
And if you break the ice, and do this feat,
Achieve the elder, set the younger free
For our access—whose hap shall be to have her
Will not so graceless be to be ingrate.

Hortensio.
Sir, you say well, and well you do conceive,
And since you do profess to be a suitor,
You must, as we do, gratify this gentleman,
To whom we all rest generally beholding.

Tranio (as Lucentio).
Sir, I shall not be slack; in sign whereof,
Please ye we may contrive this afternoon,
And quaff carouses to our mistress' health,
And do as adversaries do in law,
Strive mightily, but eat and drink as friends.

Both Grumio and Biondello.
O excellent motion! Fellows, let's be gone.

Hortensio.
The motion's good indeed, and be it so,
Petruchio, I shall be your ben venuto.

Exeunt.

Act 4

Scene 1

Padua. A room in Baptista Minola's house.

(Katherina; Bianca; Baptista; Gremio; Lucentio; Petruchio; Hortensio; Tranio; Biondello; Baptista's Servant)

Katherina has tied up her sister Bianca and fiercely interrogates her about her suitors. Bianca promises to do anything her sister wants. Baptista enters just as Katherina slaps the younger girl, and is grieved. Katherina protests against his favoritism, but Baptista feels only self pity. Gremio and Petruchio come in, accompanied by the disguised Lucentio and Hortensio, and Petruchio bluntly announces his intention of wooing Katherina while presenting Hortensio as a musician. Baptista is as skeptical as everyone else, but welcomes Petruchio for his father's sake, as well as agreeing to employ Lucentio (under the name of Cambio). Tranio introduces himself as Lucentio, explaining that he has come to woo Bianca, and Baptista accepts the gifts of books and a lute that he has brought given Lucentio's father's reputation. He sends the tutors off to his daughters. Petruchio gets down to business, asking what dowry he'll receive. As it is sufficient, he is quite happy to continue, blithely informing Baptista that he'll have no trouble wooing Katherina. Hortensio comes in, having been beaten up by Katherina for trying to teach her. Petruchio finds this promising, and asks Baptista to send Katherina in. The lady arrives, and Petruchio begins to woo her by the name of Kate. As she rants and rails at him, he refuses to do anything but compliment her and inform her that he intends to marry her. When she strikes him, he merely warns her not to again, lest he retaliate in kind. Their ability to match wits is quite evident as she insults him and he simply takes it for granted that they will marry. When Baptista and company return to hear her cursing, Petruchio insists she's only putting on a show and that they're very happy with each other. Announcing they'll marry on Sunday, he takes off to Venice to arrange matters. Gremio and Tranio immediately begin harping on Bianca; they begin outdoing each other in monetary offers. In the end Baptista decides Tranio/Lucentio's offer is the best, and promises him Bianca so long as his father can confirm the offer made. Tranio realizes he'll need to come up with a father.

Enter Katherina and Bianca.

Bianca.
Good sister, wrong me not, nor wrong yourself,
To make a bondmaid and a slave of me—
That I disdain; but for these other gawds,
Unbind my hands, I'll pull them off myself,
Yea, all my raiment, to my petticoat,
Or what you will command me will I do,
So well I know my duty to my elders.

Katherina.
Of all thy suitors here I charge thee tell
Whom thou lov'st best; see thou dissemble not.

Bianca.
Believe me, sister, of all the men alive
I never yet beheld that special face
Which I could fancy more than any other.

Katherina.
Minion, thou liest. Is't not Hortensio?

Bianca.
If you affect him, sister, here I swear
I'll plead for you myself, but you shall have him.

Katherina.
O then belike you fancy riches more:
You will have Gremio to keep you fair.

Bianca.
Is it for him you do envy me so?
Nay then you jest, and now I well perceive
You have but jested with me all this while.
I prithee, sister Kate, untie my hands.

Katherina.
If that be jest, then all the rest was so.

Strikes her.
Enter Baptista.

Baptista.
Why, how now, dame, whence grows this insolence?
Bianca, stand aside. Poor girl, she weeps.
Go ply thy needle, meddle not with her.

For shame, thou hilding of a devilish spirit,
Why dost thou wrong her that did ne'er wrong thee?
When did she cross thee with a bitter word?

Katherina.
Her silence flouts me, and I'll be reveng'd.

Flies after Bianca.

Baptista.
What, in my sight? Bianca, get thee in.

Exit Bianca.

Katherina.
What, will you not suffer me? Nay, now I see
She is your treasure, she must have a husband;
I must dance barefoot on her wedding-day,
And for your love to her lead apes in hell.
Talk not to me, I will go sit and weep,
Till I can find occasion of revenge.

Exit.

Baptista.
Was ever gentleman thus griev'd as I?
But who comes here?

Enter Gremio, Lucentio in the habit of a mean man, Petruchio with Hortensio as a musician, and Tranio as Lucentio with his boy Biondello bearing a lute and books.

Gremio.
Good morrow, neighbor Baptista.

Baptista.
Good morrow, neighbor Gremio. God save you, gentlemen!

Petruchio.
And you, good sir! Pray have you not a daughter
Call'd Katherina, fair and virtuous?

Baptista.
I have a daughter, sir, call'd Katherina.

Gremio.
You are too blunt, go to it orderly.

Petruchio.
You wrong me, Signior Gremio, give me leave.
I am a gentleman of Verona, sir,
That hearing of her beauty and her wit,
Her affability and bashful modesty,
Her wondrous qualities and mild behavior,
Am bold to show myself a forward guest
Within your house, to make mine eye the witness
Of that report which I so oft have heard.
And for an entrance to my entertainment,
I do present you with a man of mine,

Presenting Hortensio.

Cunning in music and the mathematics,
To instruct her fully in those sciences,
Whereof I know she is not ignorant.
Accept of him, or else you do me wrong.
His name is Litio, born in Mantua.

Baptista.
Y' are welcome, sir, and he, for your good sake.
But for my daughter Katherine, this I know,
She is not for your turn, the more my grief.

Petruchio.
I see you do not mean to part with her,
Or else you like not of my company.

Baptista.
Mistake me not, I speak but as I find.
Whence are you, sir? What may I call your name?

Petruchio.
Petruchio is my name, Antonio's son,
A man well known throughout all Italy.

Baptista.
I know him well; you are welcome for his sake.

Gremio.
Saving your tale, Petruchio, I pray
Let us that are poor petitioners speak too.
Backare! You are marvelous forward.

Petruchio.
O, pardon me, Signior Gremio, I would fain be doing.

Gremio.
I doubt it not, sir; but you will curse your wooing.
Neighbor, this is a gift very grateful, I am sure of it.
To express the like kindness, myself, that have been
more kindly beholding to you than any, freely give
unto you this young scholar,

Presenting Lucentio.

that hath been long studying at Rheims, as cunning in Greek, Latin, and other languages, as the other in music and mathematics. His name is Cambio; pray accept his service.

Baptista.
A thousand thanks, Signior Gremio. Welcome, good Cambio.

To Tranio.

But, gentle sir, methinks you walk like a stranger. May I be so bold to know the cause of your coming?

Tranio (as Lucentio).
Pardon me, sir, the boldness is mine own,
That being a stranger in this city here,
Do make myself a suitor to your daughter,
Unto Bianca, fair and virtuous.
Nor is your firm resolve unknown to me,
In the preferment of the eldest sister.
This liberty is all that I request,
That upon knowledge of my parentage,
I may have welcome 'mongst the rest that woo,
And free access and favor as the rest;
And toward the education of your daughters,
I here bestow a simple instrument,
And this small packet of Greek and Latin books.
If you accept them, then their worth is great.

Baptista.
Lucentio is your name, of whence, I pray?

Tranio (as Lucentio).
Of Pisa, sir, son to Vincentio.

Baptista.
A mighty man of Pisa; by report
I know him well. You are very welcome, sir.
Take you the lute, and you the set of books.
You shall go see your pupils presently.
Holla, within!

Enter Baptista's Servant.

Sirrah, lead these gentlemen
To my daughters, and tell them both,
These are their tutors. Bid them use them well.

Exit Baptista's Servant with Lucentio and Hortensio, Biondello following.

We will go walk a little in the orchard,
And then to dinner. You are passing welcome,
And so I pray you all to think yourselves.

Petruchio.
Signior Baptista, my business asketh haste,
And every day I cannot come to woo.
You knew my father well, and in him me,
Left solely heir to all his lands and goods,
Which I have bettered rather than decreas'd.
Then tell me, if I get your daughter's love,
What dowry shall I have with her to wife?

Baptista.
After my death, the one half of my lands,
And in possession twenty thousand crowns.

Petruchio.
And for that dowry, I'll assure her of
Her widowhood, be it that she survive me,
In all my lands and leases whatsoever.
Let specialties be therefore drawn between us,
That covenants may be kept on either hand.

Baptista.
Ay, when the special thing is well obtain'd,
That is, her love; for that is all in all.

Petruchio.
Why, that is nothing; for I tell you, father,
I am as peremptory as she proud-minded;
And where two raging fires meet together,
They do consume the thing that feeds their fury.
Though little fire grows great with little wind,
Yet extreme gusts will blow out fire and all;
So I to her, and so she yields to me,
For I am rough, and woo not like a babe.

Baptista.
Well mayst thou woo, and happy be thy speed!
But be thou arm'd for some unhappy words.

Petruchio.
Ay, to the proof, as mountains are for winds,
That shake not, though they blow perpetually.

Enter Hortensio as Litio with his head broke.

Baptista.
How now, my friend, why dost thou look so pale?

Hortensio (as Litio).
For fear, I promise you, if I look pale.

Baptista.
What, will my daughter prove a good musician?

Hortensio (as Litio).
I think she'll sooner prove a soldier,
Iron may hold with her, but never lutes.

Baptista.
Why then thou canst not break her to the lute?

Hortensio (as Litio).
Why no, for she hath broke the lute to me.
I did but tell her she mistook her frets,
And bow'd her hand to teach her fingering;
When, with a most impatient devilish spirit,
"Frets, call you these?" quoth she, "I'll fume with them."
And with that word she struck me on the head,
And through the instrument my pate made way,
And there I stood amazed for a while,
As on a pillory, looking through the lute,
While she did call me rascal fiddler
And twangling Jack, with twenty such vild terms,
As had she studied to misuse me so.

Petruchio.
Now by the world, it is a lusty wench!
I love her ten times more than e'er I did.
O, how I long to have some chat with her!

Baptista.
Well, go with me and be not so discomfited.
Proceed in practice with my younger daughter;
She's apt to learn, and thankful for good turns.
Signior Petruchio, will you go with us,
Or shall I send my daughter Kate to you?

Petruchio.
I pray you do. I'll attend her here,

Exit Baptista with Gremio, Tranio, and Hortensio. Manet Petruchio.

And woo her with some spirit when she comes.
Say that she rail, why then I'll tell her plain
She sings as sweetly as a nightingale;
Say that she frown, I'll say she looks as clear
As morning roses newly wash'd with dew;
Say she be mute, and will not speak a word,
Then I'll commend her volubility,
And say she uttereth piercing eloquence;
If she do bid me pack, I'll give her thanks,
As though she bid me stay by her a week;
If she deny to wed, I'll crave the day
When I shall ask the banes, and when be married.
But here she comes, and now, Petruchio, speak.

Enter Katherina.

Good morrow, Kate, for that's your name, I hear.

Katherina.
Well have you heard, but something hard of hearing:
They call me Katherine that do talk of me.

Petruchio.
You lie, in faith, for you are call'd plain Kate,
And bonny Kate, and sometimes Kate the curst;
But Kate, the prettiest Kate in Christendom,
Kate of Kate-Hall, my super-dainty Kate,
For dainties are all Kates, and therefore, Kate,
Take this of me, Kate of my consolation—
Hearing thy mildness prais'd in every town,
Thy virtues spoke of, and thy beauty sounded,
Yet not so deeply as to thee belongs,
Myself am mov'd to woo thee for my wife.

Katherina.
Mov'd! In good time! Let him that mov'd you hither
Remove you hence. I knew you at the first
You were a moveable.

Petruchio.
        Why, what's a moveable?

Katherina.
A join'd-stool.

Petruchio.
        Thou hast hit it; come sit on me.

Katherina.
Asses are made to bear, and so are you.

Petruchio.
Women are made to bear, and so are you.

Katherina.
No such jade as you, if me you mean.

Petruchio.
Alas, good Kate, I will not burden thee,
For knowing thee to be but young and light.

Katherina.
Too light for such a swain as you to catch,
And yet as heavy as my weight should be.

Petruchio.
Should be! Should—buzz!

Katherina.
              Well ta'en, and like a buzzard.

Petruchio.
O slow-wing'd turtle, shall a buzzard take thee?

Katherina.
Ay, for a turtle, as he takes a buzzard.

Petruchio.
Come, come, you wasp, i' faith you are too angry.

Katherina.
If I be waspish, best beware my sting.

Petruchio.
My remedy is then to pluck it out.

Katherina.
Ay, if the fool could find it where it lies.

Petruchio.
Who knows not where a wasp does wear his sting?
In his tail.

Katherina.
In his tongue.

Petruchio.
Whose tongue?

Katherina.
Yours, if you talk of tales, and so farewell.

Petruchio.
What, with my tongue in your tail? Nay, come again,
Good Kate; I am a gentleman—

Katherina.
              That I'll try.

She strikes him.

Petruchio.
I swear I'll cuff you, if you strike again.

Katherina.
So may you lose your arms.
If you strike me, you are no gentleman,
And if no gentleman, why then no arms.

Petruchio.
A herald, Kate? O, put me in thy books!

Katherina.
What is your crest? A coxcomb?

Petruchio.
A combless cock, so Kate will be my hen.

Katherina.
No cock of mine, you crow too like a craven.

Petruchio.
Nay, come, Kate, come; you must not look so sour.

Katherina.
It is my fashion when I see a crab.

Petruchio.
Why, here's no crab, and therefore look not sour.

Katherina.
There is, there is.

Petruchio.
Then show it me.

Katherina.
Had I a glass, I would.

Petruchio.
What, you mean my face?

Katherina.
Well aim'd of such a young one.

Petruchio.
Now, by Saint George, I am too young for you.

Katherina.
Yet you are wither'd.

Petruchio.
'Tis with cares.

Katherina.
I care not.

Petruchio.
Nay, hear you, Kate. In sooth you scape not so.

Katherina.
I chafe you if I tarry. Let me go.

Petruchio.
No, not a whit, I find you passing gentle:
'Twas told me you were rough and coy and sullen,
And now I find report a very liar;
For thou art pleasant, gamesome, passing courteous,
But slow in speech, yet sweet as spring-time flowers.
Thou canst not frown, thou canst not look askaunce,
Nor bite the lip, as angry wenches will,
Nor hast thou pleasure to be cross in talk;
But thou with mildness entertain'st thy wooers,
With gentle conference, soft, and affable.
Why does the world report that Kate doth limp?
O sland'rous world! Kate like the hazel-twig
Is straight and slender, and as brown in hue
As hazel-nuts, and sweeter than the kernels.
O, let me see thee walk. Thou dost not halt.

Katherina.
Go, fool, and whom thou keep'st command.

Petruchio.
Did ever Dian so become a grove
As Kate this chamber with her princely gait?
O, be thou Dian, and let her be Kate,
And then let Kate be chaste, and Dian sportful!

Katherina.
Where did you study all this goodly speech?

Petruchio.
It is extempore, from my mother-wit.

Katherina.
A witty mother! Witless else her son.

Petruchio.
Am I not wise?

Katherina.
Yes, keep you warm.

Petruchio.
Marry, so I mean, sweet Katherine, in thy bed;
And therefore setting all this chat aside,
Thus in plain terms: your father hath consented
That you shall be my wife; your dowry 'greed on;
And will you, nill you, I will marry you.
Now, Kate, I am a husband for your turn,
For by this light whereby I see thy beauty,
Thy beauty that doth make me like thee well,
Thou must be married to no man but me;
For I am he am born to tame you, Kate,
And bring you from a wild Kate to a Kate
Conformable as other household Kates.

Enter Baptista, Gremio, Tranio as Lucentio.

Here comes your father. Never make denial;
I must and will have Katherine to my wife.

Baptista.
Now, Signior Petruchio, how speed you with my daughter?

Petruchio.
How but well, sir? How but well?
It were impossible I should speed amiss.

Baptista.
Why, how now, daughter Katherine, in your dumps?

Katherina.
Call you me daughter? Now I promise you
You have show'd a tender fatherly regard,
To wish me wed to one half lunatic,
A madcap ruffian and a swearing Jack,
That thinks with oaths to face the matter out.

Petruchio.
Father, 'tis thus: yourself and all the world,
That talk'd of her, have talk'd amiss of her.
If she be curst, it is for policy,
For she's not froward, but modest as the dove;
She is not hot, but temperate as the morn;
For patience she will prove a second Grissel,
And Roman Lucrece for her chastity;
And to conclude, we have 'greed so well together
That upon Sunday is the wedding-day.

Katherina.
I'll see thee hang'd on Sunday first.

Gremio.
Hark, Petruchio, she says she'll see thee hang'd first.

Tranio (as Lucentio).
Is this your speeding? Nay then good night our part!

Petruchio.
Be patient, gentlemen, I choose her for myself.
If she and I be pleas'd, what's that to you?
'Tis bargain'd 'twixt us twain, being alone,
That she shall still be curst in company.
I tell you 'tis incredible to believe
How much she loves me. O, the kindest Kate,
She hung about my neck, and kiss on kiss
She vied so fast, protesting oath on oath,

That in a twink she won me to her love.
O, you are novices! 'tis a world to see
How tame, when men and women are alone,
A meacock wretch can make the curstest shrew.
Give me thy hand, Kate, I will unto Venice
To buy apparel 'gainst the wedding-day.
Provide the feast, father, and bid the guests,
I will be sure my Katherine shall be fine.

Baptista.
I know not what to say, but give me your hands.
God send you joy, Petruchio, 'tis a match.

Both Gremio and Tranio.
Amen, say we. We will be witnesses.

Petruchio.
Father, and wife, and gentlemen, adieu.
I will to Venice, Sunday comes apace.
We will have rings and things, and fine array;
And kiss me, Kate, we will be married a' Sunday.

Exeunt Petruchio and Katherine severally.

Gremio.
Was ever match clapp'd up so suddenly?

Baptista.
Faith, gentlemen, now I play a merchant's part,
And venture madly on a desperate mart.

Tranio (as Lucentio).
'Twas a commodity lay fretting by you;
'Twill bring you gain, or perish on the seas.

Baptista.
The gain I seek is, quiet in the match.

Gremio.
No doubt but he hath got a quiet catch.
But now, Baptista, to your younger daughter;
Now is the day we long have looked for.
I am your neighbor, and was suitor first.

Tranio (as Lucentio).
And I am one that love Bianca more
Than words can witness, or your thoughts can guess.

Gremio.
Youngling, thou canst not love so dear as I.

Tranio (as Lucentio).
Greybeard, thy love doth freeze.

Gremio.
                But thine doth fry.
Skipper, stand back, 'tis age that nourisheth.

Tranio (as Lucentio).
But youth in ladies' eyes that flourisheth.

Baptista.
Content you, gentlemen, I will compound this strife.
'Tis deeds must win the prize, and he of both
That can assure my daughter greatest dower
Shall have my Bianca's love.
Say, Signior Gremio, what can you assure her?

Gremio.
First, as you know, my house within the city
Is richly furnished with plate and gold,
Basins and ewers to lave her dainty hands;
My hangings all of Tyrian tapestry;
In ivory coffers I have stuff'd my crowns;
In cypress chests my arras counterpoints,
Costly apparel, tents, and canopies,
Fine linen, Turkey cushions boss'd with pearl,
Valance of Venice gold in needle-work;
Pewter and brass, and all things that belongs
To house or house-keeping. Then at my farm
I have a hundred milch-kine to the pail,
Six score fat oxen standing in my stalls,
And all things answerable to this portion.
Myself am struck in years, I must confess,
And if I die tomorrow, this is hers,
If whilst I live she will be only mine.

Tranio (as Lucentio).
That "only" came well in. Sir, list to me:
I am my father's heir and only son.
If I may have your daughter to my wife,
I'll leave her houses three or four as good,
Within rich Pisa walls, as any one
Old Signior Gremio has in Padua,
Besides two thousand ducats by the year
Of fruitful land, all which shall be her jointer.
What, have I pinch'd you, Signior Gremio?

Gremio.
Two thousand ducats by the year of land!

Aside.

My land amounts not to so much in all.—
That she shall have, besides an argosy
That now is lying in Marsellis road.
What, have I chok'd you with an argosy?

Tranio (as Lucentio).
Gremio, 'tis known my father hath no less
Than three great argosies, besides two galliasses
And twelve tight galleys. These I will assure her,
And twice as much, what e'er thou off'rest next.

Gremio.
Nay, I have off'red all, I have no more,
And she can have no more than all I have;
If you like me, she shall have me and mine.

Tranio (as Lucentio).
Why then the maid is mine from all the world,
By your firm promise; Gremio is outvied.

Baptista.
I must confess your offer is the best,
And let your father make her the assurance,
She is your own, else you must pardon me;
If you should die before him, where's her dower?

Tranio (as Lucentio).
That's but a cavil; he is old, I young.

Gremio.
And may not young men die as well as old?

Baptista.
Well, gentlemen,
I am thus resolv'd: on Sunday next you know
My daughter Katherine is to be married.
Now on the Sunday following shall Bianca
Be bride to you, if you make this assurance;
If not, to Signior Gremio.
And so I take my leave, and thank you both.

Exit.

Gremio.
Adieu, good neighbor. Now I fear thee not.
Sirrah, young gamester, your father were a fool
To give thee all, and in his waning age
Set foot under thy table. Tut, a toy!
An old Italian fox is not so kind, my boy.

Exit.

Tranio.
A vengeance on your crafty withered hide!
Yet I have fac'd it with a card of ten.
'Tis in my head to do my master good.
I see no reason but suppos'd Lucentio
Must get a father, call'd suppos'd Vincentio;
And that's a wonder. Fathers commonly
Do get their children; but in this case of wooing,
A child shall get a sire, if I fail not of my cunning.

Exit.

Act 5

Scene 1

Padua. Baptista's house.

(Lucentio; Hortensio; Bianca; Baptista's Messenger)

Hortensio and Lucentio quarrel over whose turn it is to teach Bianca, but she settles the matter by announcing that she's old enough to set her own schedule. She tells Hortensio to go tune his lute while she studies her Latin with Lucentio, who woos her in between sentences as she repeatedly makes Hortensio go away. Lucentio realizes that Hortensio has interest in Bianca, but when the disguised music teacher hands her a love note, she is not impressed. Hortensio is worried that Lucentio may be in love.

Enter Lucentio as Cambio, Hortensio as Litio, and Bianca.

Lucentio (as Cambio).
Fiddler, forbear, you grow too forward, sir.
Have you so soon forgot the entertainment
Her sister Katherine welcom'd you withal?

Hortensio (as Litio).
But, wrangling pedant, this is
The patroness of heavenly harmony.
Then give me leave to have prerogative,
And when in music we have spent an hour,
Your lecture shall have leisure for as much.

Lucentio (as Cambio).
Preposterous ass, that never read so far
To know the cause why music was ordain'd!
Was it not to refresh the mind of man
After his studies or his usual pain?
Then give me leave to read philosophy,
And while I pause, serve in your harmony.

Hortensio (as Litio).
Sirrah, I will not bear these braves of thine.

Bianca.
Why, gentlemen, you do me double wrong
To strive for that which resteth in my choice.

I am no breeching scholar in the schools,
I'll not be tied to hours, nor 'pointed times,
But learn my lessons as I please myself.
And to cut off all strife, here sit we down:
Take you your instrument, play you the whiles,
His lecture will be done ere you have tun'd.

Hortensio (as Litio).
You'll leave his lecture when I am in tune?

Lucentio (as Cambio).
That will be never, tune your instrument.

Bianca.
Where left we last?

Lucentio (as Cambio).
Here, madam:
"Hic ibat Simois; hic est Sigeia tellus;
Hic steterat Priami regia celsa senis."

Bianca.
Construe them.

Lucentio (as Cambio).
"Hic ibat," as I told you before, "Simois," I am Lucentio, "hic est," son unto Vincentio of Pisa, "Sigeia tellus," disguis'd thus to get your love, "Hic steterat," and that Lucentio that comes a-wooing, "Priami," is my man Tranio, "regia," bearing my port, "celsa senis," that we might beguile the old pantaloon.

Hortensio (as Litio).
Madam, my instrument's in tune.

Bianca.
Let's hear. O fie, the treble jars.

Lucentio (as Cambio).
Spit in the hole, man, and tune again.

Bianca.
Now let me see if I can construe it: "Hic ibat Simois," I know you not, "hic est Sigeia tellus," I trust you not, "Hic steterat Priami," take heed he hear us not, "regia," presume not, "celsa senis," despair not.

Hortensio (as Litio).
Madam, 'tis now in tune.

Lucentio (as Cambio).
　　　　　　　All but the base.

Hortensio (as Litio).
The base is right, 'tis the base knave that jars.

Aside.

How fiery and forward our pedant is!
Now, for my life, the knave doth court my love:
Pedascule, I'll watch you better yet.

Bianca.
In time I may believe, yet I mistrust.

Lucentio (as Cambio).
Mistrust it not, for sure Aeacides
Was Ajax, call'd so from his grandfather.

Bianca.
I must believe my master, else, I promise you,
I should be arguing still upon that doubt.
But let it rest. Now, Litio, to you:
Good master, take it not unkindly, pray,
That I have been thus pleasant with you both.

Hortensio (as Litio).

To Lucentio.

You may go walk, and give me leave a while;
My lessons make no music in three parts.

Lucentio (as Cambio).
Are you so formal, sir? Well, I must wait,

Aside.

And watch withal, for but I be deceiv'd,
Our fine musician groweth amorous.

Hortensio (as Litio).
Madam, before you touch the instrument,
To learn the order of my fingering,
I must begin with rudiments of art,
To teach you gamut in a briefer sort,
More pleasant, pithy, and effectual,
Than hath been taught by any of my trade;
And there it is in writing, fairly drawn.

Bianca.
Why, I am past my gamut long ago.

Hortensio (as Litio).
Yet read the gamut of Hortensio.

Bianca.

Reads.

"Gamut I am, the ground of all accord:
A re, to plead Hortensio's passion;
B mi, Bianca, take him for thy lord,
C fa ut, that loves with all affection.
D sol re, one cliff, two notes have I,
E la mi, show pity, or I die."
Call you this gamut? Tut, I like it not.
Old fashions please me best; I am not so nice
To change true rules for odd inventions.

Enter Baptista's Messenger.

Baptista's Messenger.
Mistress, your father prays you leave your books,
And help to dress your sister's chamber up.
You know tomorrow is the wedding-day.

Bianca.
Farewell, sweet masters both, I must be gone.

Exeunt Bianca and Baptista's Messenger.

Lucentio (as Cambio).
Faith, mistress, then I have no cause to stay.

Exit.

Hortensio.
But I have cause to pry into this pedant.
Methinks he looks as though he were in love;
Yet if thy thoughts, Bianca, be so humble
To cast thy wand'ring eyes on every stale,
Seize thee that list. If once I find thee ranging,
Hortensio will be quit with thee by changing.

Exit.

Scene 2

Padua. Before Baptista's house.

(Baptista; Gremio; Tranio; Katherina; Bianca; Lucentio; Attendants; Biondello; Petruchio; Grumio; Hortensio)

On Kate and Petruchio's wedding say, Petruchio still hasn't shown up. Katherina is deeply shamed by the fact that not only is she to be wed but her groom might leave her standing at the altar. Even her father is sympathetic. The servant Biondello arrives with the news that Petruchio is on his way, but dressed like a penniless madman. He arrives and despite everyone's protests marches into church dressed as he is, pointing out that Katherina is not marrying his clothes. Tranio informs Lucentio that they need to quickly find him a father. Gremio comes out of the church and reports that Petruchio went through the marriage ceremony like a brute, swearing, hitting the priest, calling for wine, and otherwise making Katherina seem downright docile. The wedding party comes out, and Petruchio tells them to go and have the wedding feast without him. Refusing to stay, he insists that Katherina follow him away; when she protests, he carries her off. People can't help but laugh and admit they're a well-matched couple, and they all go in to the feast, Baptista letting Tranio and Bianca take the places of honor.

Enter Baptista, Gremio, Tranio as Lucentio, Katherine, Bianca, Lucentio as Cambio, and others, attendants.

Baptista.

To Tranio.

Signior Lucentio, this is the 'pointed day,
That Katherine and Petruchio should be married,
And yet we hear not of our son-in-law.
What will be said? What mockery will it be,
To want the bridegroom when the priest attends
To speak the ceremonial rites of marriage?
What says Lucentio to this shame of ours?

Katherina.
No shame but mine. I must forsooth be forc'd
To give my hand oppos'd against my heart
Unto a mad-brain rudesby full of spleen,
Who woo'd in haste, and means to wed at leisure.
I told you, I, he was a frantic fool,
Hiding his bitter jests in blunt behavior;
And to be noted for a merry man,
He'll woo a thousand, 'point the day of marriage,
Make friends, invite, and proclaim the banes,
Yet never means to wed where he hath woo'd.
Now must the world point at poor Katherine,
And say, "Lo, there is mad Petruchio's wife,
If it would please him come and marry her!"

Tranio (as Lucentio).
Patience, good Katherine, and Baptista too.
Upon my life, Petruchio means but well,
Whatever fortune stays him from his word.
Though he be blunt, I know him passing wise;
Though he be merry, yet withal he's honest.

Katherina.
Would Katherine had never seen him though!

Exit weeping followed by Bianca and others.

Baptista.
Go, girl, I cannot blame thee now to weep,
For such an injury would vex a very saint,
Much more a shrew of thy impatient humor.

Enter Biondello.

Biondello.
Master, master, news, old news, and such news as you never heard of!

Baptista.
Is it new and old too? How may that be?

Biondello.
Why, is it not news to hear of Petruchio's coming?

Baptista.
Is he come?

Biondello.
Why, no, sir.

Baptista.
What then?

Biondello.
He is coming.

Baptista.
When will he be here?

Biondello.
When he stands where I am, and sees you there.

Tranio.
But say, what to thine old news?

Biondello.
Why, Petruchio is coming in a new hat and an old jerkin; a pair of old breeches thrice turn'd; a pair of boots that have been candle-cases, one buckled, another lac'd; an old rusty sword ta'en out of the town armory, with a broken hilt, and chapeless; with two broken points; his horse hipp'd, with an old mothy saddle and stirrups of no kindred; besides, possess'd with the glanders and like to mose in the chine, troubled with the lampass, infected with the fashions, full of windgalls, sped with spavins, ray'd with the yellows, past cure of the fives, stark spoil'd with the staggers, begnawn with the bots, sway'd in the back, and shoulder-shotten, near-legg'd before, and with a half-cheek'd bit and a head-stall of sheep's leather, which being restrain'd to keep him from stumbling, hath been often burst, and now repair'd with knots; one girth six times piec'd, and a woman's crupper of velure, which hath two letters for her name fairly set down in studs, and here and there piec'd with packthread.

Baptista.
Who comes with him?

Biondello.
O, sir, his lackey, for all the world caparison'd like the horse; with a linen stock on one leg, and a kersey boothose on the other, gart'red with a red and blue list; an old hat, and the humor of forty fancies prick'd in't for a feather: a monster, a very monster in apparel, and not like a Christian footboy or a gentleman's lackey.

Tranio (as Lucentio).
'Tis some odd humor pricks him to this fashion;
Yet oftentimes he goes but mean apparell'd.

Baptista.
I am glad he's come, howsoe'er he comes.

Biondello.
Why, sir, he comes not.

Baptista.
Didst thou not say he comes?

Biondello.
Who? That Petruchio came?

Baptista.
Ay, that Petruchio came.

Biondello.
No, sir, I say his horse comes, with him on his back.

Baptista.
Why, that's all one.

Biondello.
Nay, by Saint Jamy,
I hold you a penny,
A horse and a man
Is more than one,
And yet not many.

Enter Petruchio and Grumio.

Petruchio.
Come, where be these gallants? Who's at home?

Baptista.
You are welcome, sir.

Petruchio.
And yet I come not well.

Baptista.
And yet you halt not.

Tranio (as Lucentio).
Not so well apparell'd
As I wish you were.

Petruchio.
Were it better I should rush in thus:

Pretends great excitement.

But where is Kate? Where is my lovely bride?
How does my father?—Gentles, methinks you frown,
And wherefore gaze this goodly company,
As if they saw some wondrous monument,
Some comet or unusual prodigy?

Baptista.
Why, sir, you know this is your wedding-day.
First were we sad, fearing you would not come,
Now sadder, that you come so unprovided.
Fie, doff this habit, shame to your estate,
An eye-sore to our solemn festival!

Tranio (as Lucentio).
And tell us what occasion of import
Hath all so long detain'd you from your wife,
And sent you hither so unlike yourself?

Petruchio.
Tedious it were to tell, and harsh to hear—
Sufficeth I am come to keep my word,
Though in some part enforced to digress,
Which at more leisure I will so excuse
As you shall well be satisfied with all.
But where is Kate? I stay too long from her.
The morning wears, 'tis time we were at church.

Tranio (as Lucentio).
See not your bride in these unreverent robes,
Go to my chamber, put on clothes of mine.

Petruchio.
Not I, believe me, thus I'll visit her.

Baptista.
But thus, I trust, you will not marry her.

Petruchio.
Good sooth, even thus; therefore ha' done with words;
To me she's married, not unto my clothes.
Could I repair what she will wear in me,
As I can change these poor accoutrements,
'Twere well for Kate, and better for myself.
But what a fool am I to chat with you,
When I should bid good morrow to my bride,
And seal the title with a lovely kiss!

Exit with Grumio.

Tranio (as Lucentio).
He hath some meaning in his mad attire.
We will persuade him, be it possible,
To put on better ere he go to church.

Baptista.
I'll after him, and see the event of this.

Exit with Gremio and Attendants.

Tranio (as Lucentio).
But, sir, love concerneth us to add
Her father's liking, which to bring to pass,
As before imparted to your worship,
I am to get a man—what e'er he be,
It skills not much, we'll fit him to our turn—
And he shall be Vincentio of Pisa,
And make assurance here in Padua
Of greater sums than I have promised.
So shall you quietly enjoy your hope,
And marry sweet Bianca with consent.

Lucentio (as Cambio).
Were it not that my fellow schoolmaster
Doth watch Bianca's steps so narrowly,
'Twere good methinks to steal our marriage,
Which once perform'd, let all the world say no,
I'll keep mine own, despite of all the world.

Tranio (as Lucentio).
That by degrees we mean to look into,
And watch our vantage in this business.
We'll overreach the greybeard, Gremio,
The narrow-prying father, Minola,

The quaint musician, amorous Litio,
All for my master's sake, Lucentio.

Enter Gremio.

Signior Gremio, came you from the church?

Gremio.
As willingly as e'er I came from school.

Tranio (as Lucentio).
And is the bride and bridegroom coming home?

Gremio.
A bridegroom, say you? 'Tis a groom indeed,
A grumbling groom, and that the girl shall find.

Tranio (as Lucentio).
Curster than she? Why, 'tis impossible.

Gremio.
Why, he's a devil, a devil, a very fiend.

Tranio (as Lucentio).
Why, she's a devil, a devil, the devil's dam.

Gremio.
Tut, she's a lamb, a dove, a fool to him!
I'll tell you, Sir Lucentio: when the priest
Should ask if Katherine should be his wife,
"Ay, by gogs-wouns," quoth he, and swore so loud,
That all amaz'd the priest let fall the book,
And as he stoop'd again to take it up,
This mad-brain'd bridegroom took him such a cuff
That down fell priest and book, and book and priest.
"Now take them up," quoth he, "if any list."

Tranio (as Lucentio).
What said the wench when he rose again?

Gremio.
Trembled and shook; for why, he stamp'd and swore
As if the vicar meant to cozen him.
But after many ceremonies done,
He calls for wine. "A health!" quoth he, as if
He had been aboard, carousing to his mates
After a storm, quaff'd off the muscadel,
And threw the sops all in the sexton's face,
Having no other reason
But that his beard grew thin and hungerly,
And seem'd to ask him sops as he was drinking.
This done, he took the bride about the neck,
And kiss'd her lips with such a clamorous smack
That at the parting all the church did echo.

And I seeing this, came thence for very shame,
And after me I know the rout is coming.
Such a mad marriage never was before.
Hark, hark, I hear the minstrels play.

Music plays.
Enter Petruchio, Kate, Bianca, Hortensio as Litio, Baptista, Grumio, and Train.

Petruchio.
Gentlemen and friends, I thank you for your pains.
I know you think to dine with me today,
And have prepared great store of wedding cheer,
But so it is, my haste doth call me hence,
And therefore here I mean to take my leave.

Baptista.
Is't possible you will away tonight?

Petruchio.
I must away today, before night come.
Make it no wonder; if you knew my business,
You would entreat me rather go than stay.
And, honest company, I thank you all
That have beheld me give away myself
To this most patient, sweet, and virtuous wife.
Dine with my father, drink a health to me,
For I must hence, and farewell to you all.

Tranio (as Lucentio).
Let us entreat you stay till after dinner.

Petruchio.
It may not be.

Gremio.
      Let me entreat you.

Petruchio.
It cannot be.

Katherina.
      Let me entreat you.

Petruchio.
I am content.

Katherina.
Are you content to stay?

Petruchio.
I am content you shall entreat me stay,
But yet not stay, entreat me how you can.

Katherina.
Now if you love me stay.

Petruchio.
                Grumio, my horse.

Grumio.
Ay, sir, they be ready; the oats have eaten the horses.

Katherina.
Nay then,
Do what thou canst, I will not go today,
No, nor tomorrow—not till I please myself.
The door is open, sir, there lies your way;
You may be jogging whiles your boots are green.
For me, I'll not be gone till I please myself.
'Tis like you'll prove a jolly surly groom,
That take it on you at the first so roundly.

Petruchio.
O Kate, content thee, prithee be not angry.

Katherina.
I will be angry; what hast thou to do?
Father, be quiet, he shall stay my leisure.

Gremio.
Ay, marry, sir, now it begins to work.

Katherina.
Gentlemen, forward to the bridal dinner.
I see a woman may be made a fool,
If she had not a spirit to resist.

Petruchio.
They shall go forward, Kate, at thy command.
Obey the bride, you that attend on her.
Go to the feast, revel and domineer,
Carouse full measure to her maidenhead,
Be mad and merry, or go hang yourselves;
But for my bonny Kate, she must with me.
Nay, look not big, nor stamp, nor stare, nor fret,
I will be master of what is mine own.
She is my goods, my chattels, she is my house,
My household stuff, my field, my barn,
My horse, my ox, my ass, my any thing;
And here she stands, touch her whoever dare,
I'll bring mine action on the proudest he
That stops my way in Padua. Grumio,
Draw forth thy weapon, we are beset with thieves;
Rescue thy mistress if thou be a man
Fear not, sweet wench, they shall not touch thee, Kate!
I'll buckler thee against a million.

Exeunt Petruchio, Katherina, and Grumio.

Baptista.
Nay, let them go, a couple of quiet ones.

Gremio.
Went they not quickly, I should die with laughing.

Tranio (as Lucentio).
Of all mad matches never was the like.

Lucentio (as Cambio).
Mistress, what's your opinion of your sister?

Bianca.
That being mad herself, she's madly mated.

Gremio.
I warrant him, Petruchio is Kated.

Baptista.
Neighbors and friends, though bride and bridegroom wants
For to supply the places at the table,
You know there wants no junkets at the feast.
Lucentio, you shall supply the bridegroom's place,
And let Bianca take her sister's room.

Tranio (as Lucentio).
Shall sweet Bianca practice how to bride it?

Baptista.
She shall, Lucentio. Come, gentlemen, let's go.

Exeunt.

Act 6

Scene 1

Petruchio's country house.

(Grumio; Curtis; Joseph; Nathaniel; Peter; Philip; Nicholas; Petruchio; Katherina)

Freezing cold, Grumio arrives at Petruchio's house to prepare it for his master's arrival with Kate. He tells the other servants how Kate fell off her horse into the mud and Petruchio didn't help her up. Petruchio arrives, bullying the servants, and throwing the supper they bring him back in their faces. Insisting the food was terrible, he refuses to let Kate have anything to eat. He takes her to the bedroom and lectures her before coming

Act 6, Scene 1

out and making further plans to keep her from sleep that night. He is taming her with the same techniques used to train falcons.

Enter Grumio.

Grumio.
Fie, fie on all tir'd jades, on all mad masters, and all foul ways! Was ever man so beaten? Was ever man so ray'd? Was ever man so weary? I am sent before to make a fire, and they are coming after to warm them. Now were not I a little pot and soon hot, my very lips might freeze to my teeth, my tongue to the roof of my mouth, my heart in my belly, ere I should come by a fire to thaw me. But I with blowing the fire shall warm myself; for considering the weather, a taller man than I will take cold. Holla, ho, Curtis!

Enter Curtis.

Curtis.
Who is that calls so coldly?

Grumio.
A piece of ice. If thou doubt it, thou mayst slide from my shoulder to my heel with no greater a run but my head and my neck. A fire, good Curtis.

Curtis.
Is my master and his wife coming, Grumio?

Grumio.
O ay, Curtis, ay, and therefore fire, fire; cast on no water.

Curtis.
Is she so hot a shrew as she's reported?

Grumio.
She was, good Curtis, before this frost; but thou know'st winter tames man, woman, and beast; for it hath tam'd my old master and my new mistress and myself, fellow Curtis.

Curtis.
Away, you three-inch fool! I am no beast.

Grumio.
Am I but three inches? Why, thy horn is a foot, and so long am I at the least. But wilt thou make a fire, or shall I complain on thee to our mistress, whose hand (she being now at hand) thou shalt soon feel, to thy cold comfort, for being slow in thy hot office?

Curtis.
I prithee, good Grumio, tell me, how goes the world?

Grumio.
A cold world, Curtis, in every office but thine, and therefore fire. Do thy duty and have thy duty, for my master and mistress are almost frozen to death.

Curtis.
There's fire ready, and therefore, good Grumio, the news.

Grumio.
Why, "Jack, boy! Ho, boy!" and as much news as wilt thou.

Curtis.
Come, you are so full of cony-catching!

Grumio.
Why, therefore fire, for I have caught extreme cold. Where's the cook? Is supper ready, the house trimm'd, rushes strew'd, cobwebs swept, the servingmen in their new fustian, their white stockings, and every officer his wedding garment on? Be the Jacks fair within, the Gills fair without, the carpets laid, and every thing in order?

Curtis.
All ready; and therefore I pray thee, news.

Grumio.
First, know my horse is tir'd, my master and mistress fall'n out.

Curtis.
How?

Grumio.
Out of their saddles into the dirt, and thereby hangs a tale.

Curtis.
Let's ha't, good Grumio.

Grumio.
Lend thine ear.

Curtis.
Here.

Grumio.
There.

Strikes him.

Curtis.
This 'tis to feel a tale, not to hear a tale.

Grumio.
And therefore 'tis call'd a sensible tale; and this cuff was but to knock at your ear, and beseech list'ning. Now I begin: Imprimis, we came down a foul hill, my master riding behind my mistress—

Curtis.
Both of one horse?

Grumio.
What's that to thee?

Curtis.
Why, a horse.

Grumio.
Tell thou the tale. But hadst thou not cross'd me, thou shouldst have heard how her horse fell, and she under her horse; thou shouldst have heard in how miry a place, how she was bemoil'd, how he left her with the horse upon her, how he beat me because her horse stumbled, how she waded through the dirt to pluck him off me; how he swore, how she pray'd that never pray'd before; how I cried, how the horses ran away, how her bridle was burst; how I lost my crupper, with many things of worthy memory, which now shall die in oblivion, and thou return unexperienc'd to thy grave.

Curtis.
By this reck'ning he is more shrew than she.

Grumio.
Ay, and that thou and the proudest of you all shall find when he comes home. But what talk I of this? Call forth Nathaniel, Joseph, Nicholas, Philip, Walter, Sugarsop, and the rest; let their heads be slickly comb'd, their blue coats brush'd, and their garters of an indifferent knit; let them curtsy with their left legs, and not presume to touch a hair of my master's horse-tail till they kiss their hands. Are they all ready?

Curtis.
They are.

Grumio.
Call them forth.

Curtis.
Do you hear, ho? You must meet my master to countenance my mistress.

Grumio.
Why, she hath a face of her own.

Curtis.
Who knows not that?

Grumio.
Thou, it seems, that calls for company to countenance her.

Curtis.
I call them forth to credit her.

Enter four or five Servingmen.

Grumio.
Why, she comes to borrow nothing of them.

Nathaniel.
Welcome home, Grumio!

Philip.
How now, Grumio?

Joseph.
What, Grumio!

Nicholas.
Fellow Grumio!

Nathaniel.
How now, old lad?

Grumio.
Welcome, you; how now, you; what, you; fellow, you—and thus much for greeting. Now, my spruce companions, is all ready, and all things neat?

Nathaniel.
All things is ready. How near is our master?

Grumio.
E'en at hand, alighted by this; and therefore be not—Cock's passion, silence! I hear my master.

Enter Petruchio and Kate.

Petruchio.
Where be these knaves? What, no man at door
To hold my stirrup, nor to take my horse?
Where is Nathaniel, Gregory, Philip?

Act 6, Scene 1

All Servants.
Here, here, sir, here, sir.

Petruchio.
Here, sir! Here, sir! Here, sir! Here, sir!
You loggerheaded and unpolish'd grooms!
What? No attendance? No regard? No duty?
Where is the foolish knave I sent before?

Grumio.
Here, sir, as foolish as I was before.

Petruchio.
You peasant swain, you whoreson malt-horse drudge!
Did I not bid thee meet me in the park,
And bring along these rascal knaves with thee?

Grumio.
Nathaniel's coat, sir, was not fully made,
And Gabr'el's pumps were all unpink'd i' th' heel;
There was no link to color Peter's hat,
And Walter's dagger was not come from sheathing;
There were none fine but Adam, Rafe, and Gregory;
The rest were ragged, old, and beggarly,
Yet, as they are, here are they come to meet you.

Petruchio.
Go, rascals, go, and fetch my supper in.

Exeunt Servants.
Sings.

"Where is the life that late I led?
Where are those"—
Sit down, Kate, and welcome. Soud, soud, soud, soud!

Enter Servants with supper.

Why, when, I say? Nay, good sweet Kate, be merry.
Off with my boots, you rogues! You villains, when?

Sings.

"It was the friar of orders grey,
As he forth walked on his way"—
Out, you rogue, you pluck my foot awry.
Take that, and mend the plucking off the other.

Strikes him.

Be merry, Kate. Some water here; what ho!

Enter one with water.

Where's my spaniel Troilus? Sirrah, get you hence,
And bid my cousin Ferdinand come hither;
One, Kate, that you must kiss, and be acquainted with.
Where are my slippers? Shall I have some water?
Come, Kate, and wash, and welcome heartily.
You whoreson villain, will you let it fall?

Strikes him.

Katherina.
Patience, I pray you, 'twas a fault unwilling.

Petruchio.
A whoreson, beetle-headed, flap-ear'd knave!
Come, Kate, sit down, I know you have a stomach.
Will you give thanks, sweet Kate, or else shall I?
What's this? Mutton?

Joseph.
                    Ay.

Petruchio.
                    Who brought it?

Peter.
                    I.

Petruchio.
'Tis burnt, and so is all the meat.
What dogs are these? Where is the rascal cook?
How durst you, villains, bring it from the dresser
And serve it thus to me that love it not?
There, take it to you, trenchers, cups, and all.

He throws down the table and meat and all, and beats them.

You heedless joltheads and unmanner'd slaves!
What, do you grumble? I'll be with you straight.

Exeunt Servants.

Katherina.
I pray you, husband, be not so disquiet.
The meat was well, if you were so contented.

Petruchio.
I tell thee, Kate, 'twas burnt and dried away,
And I expressly am forbid to touch it;
For it engenders choler, planteth anger,
And better 'twere that both of us did fast,
Since of ourselves, ourselves are choleric,
Than feed it with such overroasted flesh.
Be patient, tomorrow't shall be mended,
And for this night we'll fast for company.

Come, I will bring thee to thy bridal chamber.

Exeunt.
Enter Servants severally.

Nathaniel.
Peter, didst ever see the like?

Peter.
He kills her in her own humor.

Enter Curtis, a servant.

Grumio.
Where is he?

Curtis.
In her chamber, making a sermon of continency to her,
And rails, and swears, and rates, that she, poor soul,
Knows not which way to stand, to look, to speak,
And sits as one new risen from a dream.
Away, away, for he is coming hither.

Exeunt.
Enter Petruchio.

Petruchio.
Thus have I politicly begun my reign,
And 'tis my hope to end successfully.
My falcon now is sharp and passing empty,
And till she stoop, she must not be full-gorg'd,
For then she never looks upon her lure.
Another way I have to man my haggard,
To make her come, and know her keeper's call,
That is, to watch her, as we watch these kites
That bate and beat and will not be obedient.
She eat no meat today, nor none shall eat;
Last night she slept not, nor tonight she shall not;
As with the meat, some undeserved fault
I'll find about the making of the bed,
And here I'll fling the pillow, there the bolster,
This way the coverlet, another way the sheets.
Ay, and amid this hurly I intend
That all is done in reverend care of her,
And in conclusion, she shall watch all night,
And if she chance to nod I'll rail and brawl,
And with the clamor keep her still awake.
This is a way to kill a wife with kindness,
And thus I'll curb her mad and headstrong humor.
He that knows better how to tame a shrew,
Now let him speak; 'tis charity to shew.

Exit.

Scene 2

Padua. Before Baptista's house.

(Tranio; Hortensio; Bianca; Lucentio; Biondello; Pedant)

Tranio and Hortensio see Lucentio and Bianca canoodling, and Tranio immediately makes an oath to no longer woo her, as does Hortensio, who swears he'll go marry a widow who's in love with him instead. Hortensio leaves and Tranio informs the lovers that he has rid them of the man. Biondello announces that he has finally found them an old man to play the part of Lucentio's father. Tranio tells the schoolmaster who comes in that there is war between Padua and his city, and tells him to disguise himself and pretend to be Vincentio to save himself. He agrees with gratitude, and Tranio trains him to play the part.

Enter Tranio as Lucentio and Hortensio as Litio.

Tranio (as Lucentio).
Is't possible, friend Litio, that Mistress Bianca
Doth fancy any other but Lucentio?
I tell you, sir, she bears me fair in hand.

Hortensio (as Litio).
Sir, to satisfy you in what I have said,
Stand by and mark the manner of his teaching.

They stand aside.
Enter Bianca and Lucentio as Cambio.

Lucentio (as Cambio).
Now, mistress, profit you in what you read?

Bianca.
What, master, read you? First resolve me that.

Lucentio (as Cambio).
I read that I profess, the Art to Love.

Bianca.
And may you prove, sir, master of your art!

Lucentio (as Cambio).
While you, sweet dear, prove mistress of my heart!

They retire.

Hortensio (as Litio).
Quick proceeders, marry! Now tell me, I pray,
You that durst swear that your mistress Bianca
Lov'd none in the world so well as Lucentio.

Tranio (as Lucentio).
O despiteful love, unconstant womankind!
I tell thee, Litio, this is wonderful.

Hortensio (as Litio).
Mistake no more, I am not Litio,
Nor a musician, as I seem to be,
But one that scorn to live in this disguise
For such a one as leaves a gentleman,
And makes a god of such a cullion.
Know, sir, that I am call'd Hortensio.

Tranio (as Lucentio).
Signior Hortensio, I have often heard
Of your entire affection to Bianca,
And since mine eyes are witness of her lightness,
I will with you, if you be so contented,
Forswear Bianca and her love forever.

Hortensio (as Litio).
See how they kiss and court! Signior Lucentio,
Here is my hand, and here I firmly vow
Never to woo her more, but do forswear her
As one unworthy all the former favors
That I have fondly flatter'd her withal.

Tranio (as Lucentio).
And here I take the like unfeigned oath,
Never to marry with her though she would entreat.
Fie on her, see how beastly she doth court him!

Hortensio.
Would all the world but he had quite forsworn!
For me, that I may surely keep mine oath,
I will be married to a wealthy widow,
Ere three days pass, which hath as long lov'd me
As I have lov'd this proud disdainful haggard.
And so farewell, Signior Lucentio.
Kindness in women, not their beauteous looks,
Shall win my love, and so I take my leave,
In resolution as I swore before.

Exit.

Tranio (as Lucentio).
Mistress Bianca, bless you with such grace
As 'longeth to a lover's blessed case!
Nay, I have ta'en you napping, gentle love,
And have forsworn you with Hortensio.

Bianca.
Tranio, you jest, but have you both forsworn me?

Tranio (as Lucentio).
Mistress, we have.

Lucentio (as Cambio).
              Then we are rid of Litio.

Tranio (as Lucentio).
I' faith, he'll have a lusty widow now,
That shall be woo'd and wedded in a day.

Bianca.
God give him joy!

Tranio (as Lucentio).
Ay, and he'll tame her.

Bianca.
              He says so, Tranio?

Tranio (as Lucentio).
Faith, he is gone unto the taming-school.

Bianca.
The taming-school! What, is there such a place?

Tranio (as Lucentio).
Ay, mistress, and Petruchio is the master,
That teacheth tricks eleven and twenty long,
To tame a shrew and charm her chattering tongue.

Enter Biondello.

Biondello.
O master, master, I have watch'd so long
That I am dog-weary, but at last I spied
An ancient angel coming down the hill,
Will serve the turn.

Tranio (as Lucentio).
What is he, Biondello?

Biondello.
Master, a marcantant, or a pedant,
I know not what, but formal in apparel,
In gait and countenance surely like a father.

Lucentio (as Cambio).
And what of him, Tranio?

Tranio (as Lucentio).
If he be credulous, and trust my tale,
I'll make him glad to seem Vincentio,
And give assurance to Baptista Minola,
As if he were the right Vincentio.
Take in your love, and then let me alone.

Exeunt Lucentio and Bianca.
Enter a Pedant.

Pedant.
God save you, sir!

Tranio (as Lucentio).
              And you, sir! You are welcome.
Travel you far on, or are you at the farthest?

Pedant.
Sir, at the farthest for a week or two,
But then up farther, and as far as Rome,
And so to Tripoli, if God lend me life.

Tranio (as Lucentio).
What countryman, I pray?

Pedant.
                   Of Mantua.

Tranio (as Lucentio).
Of Mantua, sir? Marry, God forbid!
And come to Padua, careless of your life?

Pedant.
My life, sir? How, I pray? For that goes hard.

Tranio (as Lucentio).
'Tis death for any one in Mantua
To come to Padua. Know you not the cause?
Your ships are stay'd at Venice, and the Duke,
For private quarrel 'twixt your Duke and him,
Hath publish'd and proclaim'd it openly.
'Tis marvel, but that you are but newly come,
You might have heard it else proclaim'd about.

Pedant.
Alas, sir, it is worse for me than so,
For I have bills for money by exchange
From Florence, and must here deliver them.

Tranio (as Lucentio).
Well, sir, to do you courtesy,
This will I do, and this I will advise you.
First, tell me, have you ever been at Pisa?

Pedant.
Ay, sir, in Pisa have I often been,
Pisa renowned for grave citizens.

Tranio (as Lucentio).
Among them know you one Vincentio?

Pedant.
I know him not, but I have heard of him;
A merchant of incomparable wealth.

Tranio (as Lucentio).
He is my father, sir, and sooth to say,
In count'nance somewhat doth resemble you.

Biondello.

Aside.

As much as an apple doth an oyster, and all one.

Tranio (as Lucentio).
To save your life in this extremity,
This favor will I do you for his sake;
And think it not the worst of all your fortunes
That you are like to Sir Vincentio.
His name and credit shall you undertake,
And in my house you shall be friendly lodg'd.
Look that you take upon you as you should;
You understand me, sir? So shall you stay
Till you have done your business in the city.
If this be court'sy, sir, accept of it.

Pedant.
O sir, I do, and will repute you ever
The patron of my life and liberty.

Tranio (as Lucentio).
Then go with me to make the matter good.
This by the way I let you understand:
My father is here look'd for every day,
To pass assurance of a dow'r in marriage
'Twixt me and one Baptista's daughter here.
In all these circumstances I'll instruct you;
Go with me to clothe you as becomes you.

Exeunt.

Scene 3

A room in Petruchio's house.

(Katherina; Grumio; Petruchio; Hortensio; Tailor; Haberdasher)

Katherina begs Grumio to give her some food, but he finds something wrong with everything he could offer. As she beats him, Petruchio comes in with Hortensio, who has come to learn from him how to make a woman obedient. He whispers to Hortensio to eat all the food up before Katherina can have any while he distracts her by promising to have beautiful new clothes made for her. Katherina likes the clothes proposed to hear by the tailors a great deal, but Petruchio insists they are vile and throws both Tailor and clothes out — telling Hortensio on the side to make sure the Tailor gets paid all the same. He tells Kate that they'll have to go visit her father dressed as they are. He also insists that it's seven o'clock despite Katherina's insistence that it's actually two.

Enter Katherina and Grumio.

Grumio.
No, no, forsooth I dare not for my life.

Katherina.
The more my wrong, the more his spite appears.
What, did he marry me to famish me?
Beggars that come unto my father's door
Upon entreaty have a present alms,
If not, elsewhere they meet with charity;
But I, who never knew how to entreat,
Nor never needed that I should entreat,
Am starv'd for meat, giddy for lack of sleep,
With oaths kept waking, and with brawling fed;
And that which spites me more than all these wants,
He does it under name of perfect love;
As who should say, if I should sleep or eat,
'Twere deadly sickness, or else present death.
I prithee go, and get me some repast;
I care not what, so it be wholesome food.

Grumio.
What say you to a neat's foot?

Katherina.
'Tis passing good, I prithee let me have it.

Grumio.
I fear it is too choleric a meat.
How say you to a fat tripe finely broil'd?

Katherina.
I like it well, good Grumio, fetch it me.

Grumio.
I cannot tell, I fear 'tis choleric.
What say you to a piece of beef and mustard?

Katherina.
A dish that I do love to feed upon.

Grumio.
Ay, but the mustard is too hot a little.

Katherina.
Why then the beef, and let the mustard rest.

Grumio.
Nay then I will not, you shall have the mustard,
Or else you get no beef of Grumio.

Katherina.
Then both or one, or any thing thou wilt.

Grumio.
Why then the mustard without the beef.

Katherina.
Go get thee gone, thou false deluding slave,

Beats him.

That feed'st me with the very name of meat.
Sorrow on thee and all the pack of you
That triumph thus upon my misery!
Go get thee gone, I say.

Enter Petruchio and Hortensio with meat.

Petruchio.
How fares my Kate? What, sweeting, all amort?

Hortensio.
Mistress, what cheer?

Katherina.
                    Faith, as cold as can be.

Petruchio.
Pluck up thy spirits, look cheerfully upon me.
Here, love, thou seest how diligent I am
To dress thy meat myself, and bring it thee.
I am sure, sweet Kate, this kindness merits thanks.
What, not a word? Nay then, thou lov'st it not;
And all my pains is sorted to no proof.
Here, take away this dish.

Katherina.
                    I pray you let it stand.

Petruchio.
The poorest service is repaid with thanks,
And so shall mine before you touch the meat.

Katherina.
I thank you, sir.

Hortensio.
Signior Petruchio, fie, you are to blame.
Come, Mistress Kate, I'll bear you company.

Petruchio.

Aside.

Eat it up all, Hortensio, if thou lovest me.—
Much good do it unto thy gentle heart!
Kate, eat apace. And now, my honey love,
Will we return unto thy father's house,
And revel it as bravely as the best,
With silken coats and caps, and golden rings,
With ruffs and cuffs, and fardingales, and things,
With scarfs and fans, and double change of brav'ry,
With amber bracelets, beads, and all this knav'ry.
What, hast thou din'd? The tailor stays thy leisure,
To deck thy body with his ruffling treasure.

Enter Tailor.

Come, tailor, let us see these ornaments;
Lay forth the gown.

Enter Haberdasher.
                    What news with you, sir?

Haberdasher.
Here is the cap your worship did bespeak.

Petruchio.
Why, this was moulded on a porringer—
A velvet dish. Fie, fie, 'tis lewd and filthy.
Why, 'tis a cockle or a walnut-shell,
A knack, a toy, a trick, a baby's cap.
Away with it! Come let me have a bigger.

Katherina.
I'll have no bigger, this doth fit the time,
And gentlewomen wear such caps as these.

Petruchio.
When you are gentle, you shall have one too,
And not till then.

Hortensio.

Aside.

That will not be in haste.

Katherina.
Why, sir, I trust I may have leave to speak,
And speak I will. I am no child, no babe;
Your betters have endur'd me say my mind,
And if you cannot, best you stop your ears.
My tongue will tell the anger of my heart,
Or else my heart concealing it will break,
And rather than it shall, I will be free,
Even to the uttermost, as I please, in words.

Petruchio.
Why, thou say'st true, it is a paltry cap,
A custard-coffin, a bauble, a silken pie.
I love thee well in that thou lik'st it not.

Katherina.
Love me, or love me not, I like the cap,
And it I will have, or I will have none.

Exit Haberdasher.

Petruchio.
Thy gown? Why, ay. Come, tailor, let us see't.
O mercy, God, what masquing stuff is here?
What's this? A sleeve? 'Tis like a demi-cannon.
What, up and down carv'd like an apple-tart?
Here's snip and nip and cut and slish and slash,
Like to a censer in a barber's shop.
Why, what a' devil's name, tailor, call'st thou this?

Hortensio.

Aside.

I see she's like to have neither cap nor gown.

Tailor.
You bid me make it orderly and well,
According to the fashion and the time.

Petruchio.
Marry, and did; but if you be rememb'red,
I did not bid you mar it to the time.
Go hop me over every kennel home,
For you shall hop without my custom, sir.

I'll none of it; hence, make your best of it.

Katherina.
I never saw a better fashion'd gown,
More quaint, more pleasing, nor more commendable.
Belike you mean to make a puppet of me.

Petruchio.
Why, true, he means to make a puppet of thee.

Tailor.
She says your worship means to make a puppet of her.

Petruchio.
O monstrous arrogance! Thou liest, thou thread, thou thimble,
Thou yard, three-quarters, half-yard, quarter, nail!
Thou flea, thou nit, thou winter-cricket thou!
Brav'd in mine own house with a skein of thread?
Away, thou rag, thou quantity, thou remnant,
Or I shall so bemete thee with thy yard
As thou shalt think on prating whilst thou liv'st!
I tell thee, I, that thou hast marr'd her gown.

Tailor.
Your worship is deceiv'd, the gown is made
Just as my master had direction.
Grumio gave order how it should be done.

Grumio.
I gave him no order, I gave him the stuff.

Tailor.
But how did you desire it should be made?

Grumio.
Marry, sir, with needle and thread.

Tailor.
But did you not request to have it cut?

Grumio.
Thou hast fac'd many things.

Tailor.
I have.

Grumio.
Face not me; thou hast brav'd many men, brave not me; I will neither be fac'd nor brav'd. I say unto thee, I bid thy master cut out the gown, but I did not bid him cut it to pieces. Ergo, thou liest.

Tailor.
Why, here is the note of the fashion to testify.

Petruchio.
Read it.

Grumio.
The note lies in 's throat if he say I said so.

Tailor.
Reads.
"Imprimis, a loose-bodied gown"—

Grumio.
Master, if ever I said loose-bodied gown, sew me in the skirts of it, and beat me to death with a bottom of brown thread. I said a gown.

Petruchio.
Proceed.

Tailor.
Reads.
"With a small compass'd cape"—

Grumio.
I confess the cape.

Tailor.
Reads.
"With a trunk sleeve"—

Grumio.
I confess two sleeves.

Tailor.
Reads.
"The sleeves curiously cut."

Petruchio.
Ay, there's the villainy.

Grumio.
Error i' th' bill, sir, error i' th' bill! I commanded the sleeves should be cut out, and sew'd up again, and that I'll prove upon thee, though thy little finger be arm'd in a thimble.

Tailor.
This is true that I say; and I had thee in place where, thou shouldst know it.

Grumio.
I am for thee straight. Take thou the bill, give me thy mete-yard, and spare not me.

Hortensio.
God-a-mercy, Grumio, then he shall have no odds.

Petruchio.
Well, sir, in brief, the gown is not for me.

Grumio.
You are i' th' right, sir, 'tis for my mistress.

Petruchio.
Go take it up unto thy master's use.

Grumio.
Villain, not for thy life! Take up my mistress' gown for thy master's use!

Petruchio.
Why, sir, what's your conceit in that?

Grumio.
O, sir, the conceit is deeper than you think for:
Take up my mistress' gown to his master's use!
O fie, fie, fie!

Petruchio.

Aside.

Hortensio, say thou wilt see the tailor paid.—
Go take it hence, be gone, and say no more.

Hortensio.
Tailor, I'll pay thee for thy gown tomorrow,
Take no unkindness of his hasty words
Away, I say, commend me to thy master.

Exit Tailor.

Petruchio.
Well, come, my Kate, we will unto your father's
Even in these honest mean habiliments;
Our purses shall be proud, our garments poor,
For 'tis the mind that makes the body rich;
And as the sun breaks through the darkest clouds,
So honor peereth in the meanest habit.
What, is the jay more precious than the lark,
Because his feathers are more beautiful?
Or is the adder better than the eel,
Because his painted skin contents the eye?
O no, good Kate; neither art thou the worse
For this poor furniture and mean array.
If thou accountedst it shame, lay it on me,
And therefore frolic, we will hence forthwith,
To feast and sport us at thy father's house.
Go call my men, and let us straight to him,
And bring our horses unto Long-lane end;
There will we mount, and thither walk on foot.
Let's see, I think 'tis now some seven a' clock,
And well we may come there by dinner-time.

Katherina.
I dare assure you, sir, 'tis almost two,
And 'twill be supper-time ere you come there.

Petruchio.
It shall be seven ere I go to horse.
Look what I speak, or do, or think to do,
You are still crossing it. Sirs, let't alone,
I will not go today, and ere I do,
It shall be what a' clock I say it is.

Hortensio.

Aside.

Why, so this gallant will command the sun.

Exeunt.

Scene 4

Padua. Before Baptista's house.

(Tranio; Pedant; Biondello; Baptista; Lucentio; Peter)

Tranio and the schoolmaster, dressed up as Vincentio, arrive at Baptista's house. The schoolmaster assures Baptista that he will allow "his son" to marry. With Baptista indoors, busy chatting with the supposed Vincentio, Lucentio has the opportunity he needs to secretly marry Bianca, which he goes off to suggest to her.

Enter Tranio as Lucentio, and the Pedant dress'd like Vincentio, booted and bare-headed.

Tranio (as Lucentio).
Sir, this is the house, please it you that I call?

Act 6, Scene 4

Pedant.
Ay, what else? And but I be deceived,
Signior Baptista may remember me
Near twenty years ago in Genoa,
Where we were lodgers at the Pegasus.

Tranio (as Lucentio).
'Tis well, and hold your own in any case
With such austerity as 'longeth to a father.

Enter Biondello.

Pedant.
I warrant you. But, sir, here comes your boy;
'Twere good he were school'd.

Tranio (as Lucentio).
Fear you not him. Sirrah Biondello,
Now do your duty throughly, I advise you.
Imagine 'twere the right Vincentio.

Biondello.
Tut, fear not me.

Tranio (as Lucentio).
But hast thou done thy errand to Baptista?

Biondello.
I told him that your father was at Venice,
And that you look'd for him this day in Padua.

Tranio (as Lucentio).
Th' art a tall fellow; hold thee that to drink.
Here comes Baptista; set your countenance, sir.

Enter Baptista and Lucentio as Cambio.

Signior Baptista, you are happily met.

To the Pedant.

Sir, this is the gentleman I told you of.
I pray you stand good father to me now,
Give me Bianca for my patrimony.

Pedant (as as Vincentio).
Soft, son!
Sir, by your leave, having come to Padua
To gather in some debts, my son Lucentio
Made me acquainted with a weighty cause
Of love between your daughter and himself;
And for the good report I hear of you,
And for the love he beareth to your daughter,
And she to him, to stay him not too long,
I am content, in a good father's care,
To have him match'd; and if you please to like
No worse than I, upon some agreement
Me shall you find ready and willing
With one consent to have her so bestowed;
For curious I cannot be with you,
Signior Baptista, of whom I hear so well.

Baptista.
Sir, pardon me in what I have to say—
Your plainness and your shortness please me well.
Right true it is, your son Lucentio here
Doth love my daughter, and she loveth him,
Or both dissemble deeply their affections;
And therefore if you say no more than this,
That like a father you will deal with him,
And pass my daughter a sufficient dower,
The match is made, and all is done:
Your son shall have my daughter with consent.

Tranio (as Lucentio).
I thank you, sir. Where then do you know best
We be affied and such assurance ta'en
As shall with either part's agreement stand?

Baptista.
Not in my house, Lucentio, for you know
Pitchers have ears, and I have many servants;
Besides, old Gremio is heark'ning still,
And happily we might be interrupted.

Tranio (as Lucentio).
Then at my lodging, and it like you.
There doth my father lie; and there this night
We'll pass the business privately and well.
Send for your daughter by your servant here;
My boy shall fetch the scrivener presently.
The worst is this, that at so slender warning,
You are like to have a thin and slender pittance.

Baptista.
It likes me well. Cambio, hie you home,
And bid Bianca make her ready straight;
And if you will, tell what hath happened:
Lucentio's father is arriv'd in Padua,
And how she's like to be Lucentio's wife.

Exit Lucentio.

Biondello.
I pray the gods she may with all my heart!

Tranio (as Lucentio).
Dally not with the gods, but get thee gone.

Exit Biondello.
Enter Peter, a servant, who whispers to Tranio.

Signior Baptista, shall I lead the way?
Welcome! One mess is like to be your cheer.
Come, sir, we will better it in Pisa.

Baptista.
I follow you.

Exeunt.
Enter Lucentio as Cambio and Biondello.

Biondello.
Cambio!

Lucentio (as Cambio).
What say'st thou, Biondello?

Biondello.
You saw my master wink and laugh upon you?

Lucentio (as Cambio).
Biondello, what of that?

Biondello.
Faith, nothing; but h'as left me here behind to expound the meaning or moral of his signs and tokens.

Lucentio (as Cambio).
I pray thee moralize them.

Biondello.
Then thus: Baptista is safe, talking with the deceiving father of a deceitful son.

Lucentio (as Cambio).
And what of him?

Biondello.
His daughter is to be brought by you to the supper.

Lucentio (as Cambio).
And then?

Biondello.
The old priest of Saint Luke's church is at your command at all hours.

Lucentio (as Cambio).
And what of all this?

Biondello.
I cannot tell, except they are busied about a counterfeit assurance. Take you assurance of her, cum privilegio ad imprimendum solum; to th' church take the priest, clerk, and some sufficient honest witnesses.
If this be not that you look for, I have no more to say,
But bid Bianca farewell forever and a day.

Lucentio (as Cambio).
Hear'st thou, Biondello?

Biondello.
I cannot tarry. I knew a wench married in an afternoon as she went to the garden for parsley to stuff a rabbit, and so may you, sir. And so adieu, sir; my master hath appointed me to go to Saint Luke's to bid the priest be ready to come against you come with your appendix.

Exit.

Lucentio.
I may and will, if she be so contented.
She will be pleas'd, then wherefore should I doubt?
Hap what hap may, I'll roundly go about her;
It shall go hard if Cambio go without her.

Exit.

Scene 5

A public road.

(Petruchio; Kate; Hortensio; Servants; Vincentio)

Petruchio, Katherina, and Hortensio make their way towards Padua. Petruchio insists that the sun is actually the moon, and so that they won't have to stand there all day Katherina agrees with him and says that she'll claim anything is whatever Petruchio says it is. Hortensio congratulates Petruchio on having tamed her. Lucentio's father Vincentio meets up with them as he goes to visit his son in Padua, and Petruchio tests Katherina by having her pretend that the old man is a young woman. Kate does so, much to Vincentio's confusion. Learning who he is, Petruchio delightedly informs him that Lucentio will soon be his brother-in-law. Vincentio wonders where Petruchio can be trusted, but Hortensio assures him it's true. Hortensio goes off to find the widow and marry her.

Enter Petruchio, Kate, Hortensio, and Servants.

Petruchio.
Come on a' God's name, once more toward our father's.
Good Lord, how bright and goodly shines the moon!

Katherina.
The moon! The sun—it is not moonlight now.

Petruchio.
I say it is the moon that shines so bright.

Katherina.
I know it is the sun that shines so bright.

Petruchio.
Now by my mother's son, and that's myself,
It shall be moon, or star, or what I list,
Or ere I journey to your father's house.—
Go on, and fetch our horses back again.—
Evermore cross'd and cross'd, nothing but cross'd!

Hortensio.
Say as he says, or we shall never go.

Katherina.
Forward, I pray, since we have come so far,
And be it moon, or sun, or what you please;
And if you please to call it a rush-candle,
Henceforth I vow it shall be so for me.

Petruchio.
I say it is the moon.

Katherina.
             I know it is the moon.

Petruchio.
Nay then you lie; it is the blessed sun.

Katherina.
Then God be blest, it is the blessed sun,
But sun it is not, when you say it is not;
And the moon changes even as your mind.
What you will have it nam'd, even that it is,
And so it shall be so for Katherine.

Hortensio.
Petruchio, go thy ways, the field is won.

Petruchio.
Well, forward, forward, thus the bowl should run,
And not unluckily against the bias.
But soft, company is coming here.

Enter Vincentio.

To Vincentio.
Good morrow, gentle mistress, where away?
Tell me, sweet Kate, and tell me truly too,
Hast thou beheld a fresher gentlewoman?
Such war of white and red within her cheeks!
What stars do spangle heaven with such beauty,
As those two eyes become that heavenly face?
Fair lovely maid, once more good day to thee.
Sweet Kate, embrace her for her beauty's sake.

Hortensio.
'A will make the man mad, to make a woman of him.

Katherina.
Young budding virgin, fair, and fresh, and sweet,
Whither away, or where is thy abode?
Happy the parents of so fair a child!
Happier the man whom favorable stars
Allots thee for his lovely bedfellow!

Petruchio.
Why, how now, Kate, I hope thou art not mad.
This is a man, old, wrinkled, faded, withered,
And not a maiden, as thou say'st he is.

Katherina.
Pardon, old father, my mistaking eyes,
That have been so bedazzled with the sun,
That every thing I look on seemeth green;
Now I perceive thou are a reverend father.
Pardon, I pray thee, for my mad mistaking.

Petruchio.
Do, good old grandsire, and withal make known
Which way thou travelest—if along with us,
We shall be joyful of thy company.

Lord.
Fair sir, and you my merry mistress,
That with your strange encounter much amaz'd me,
My name is call'd Vincentio, my dwelling Pisa,
And bound I am to Padua, there to visit
A son of mine, which long I have not seen.

Petruchio.
What is his name?

Lord.
             Lucentio, gentle sir.

Petruchio.
Happily met, the happier for thy son.
And now by law, as well as reverend age,
I may entitle thee my loving father.
The sister to my wife, this gentlewoman,
Thy son by this hath married. Wonder not,
Nor be not grieved; she is of good esteem,
Her dowry wealthy, and of worthy birth;
Beside, so qualified as may beseem
The spouse of any noble gentleman.
Let me embrace with old Vincentio,
And wander we to see thy honest son,
Who will of thy arrival be full joyous.

Lord.
But is this true, or is it else your pleasure,
Like pleasant travelers, to break a jest
Upon the company you overtake?

Hortensio.
I do assure thee, father, so it is.

Petruchio.
Come go along and see the truth hereof,
For our first merriment hath made thee jealous.

Exeunt all but Hortensio.

Hortensio.
Well, Petruchio, this has put me in heart.
Have to my widow! And if she be froward,
Then hast thou taught Hortensio to be untoward.

Exit.

Act 7

Scene 1

Padua. Before Lucentio's house.

(Biondello; Lucentio; Bianca; Gremio; Petruchio; Kate; Vincentio; Grumio; Attendants; Pedant; Servants; Baptista; Tranio; Officer)

Bianca and Lucentio sneak off to the church to get married. Petruchio, Kate, Vincentio, and Gremio arrive. Vincentio tries to be let in, but the schoolmaster refuses him from the window, insisting that he himself is Lucentio's father. Biondello enters and keeps up the charade despite Vincentio's rage. Tranio enters in his expensive clothes, and Vincentio is horrified to see a servant so dressed, presuming that his son and the servant have been spending all their money. Vincentio insists that he is in fact a servant, but Tranio denies it and continues to insist that he is Lucentio, leaving Vincentio to believe that Tranio has murdered his master and taken his place. Pretending to think Vincentio mad, Tranio calls for an Officer to arrest him. Gremio believes Vincentio to be who he says he is, but cannot swear to it. All is cleared up when Lucentio and Bianca come in. Lucentio begs his father's pardon as he explains what has happened; Baptista is angry he has married his daughter without permission, but Vincentio promises to make a good deal for her while swearing he'll be revenged on Tranio. They go in to work out all the details of what has occurred. Before going in, Petruchio asks Kate for a kiss, and though she is ashamed to do so in the public street, she acquiesces.

Enter Biondello, Lucentio, and Bianca; Gremio is out before.

Biondello.
Softly and swiftly, sir, for the priest is ready.

Lucentio.
I fly, Biondello; but they may chance to need thee at home, therefore leave us.

Biondello.
Nay, faith, I'll see the church a' your back, and then come back to my master's as soon as I can.

Exeunt Lucentio, Bianca, and Biondello.

Gremio.
I marvel Cambio comes not all this while.

Enter Petruchio, Kate, Vincentio, Grumio, with Attendants.

Petruchio.
Sir, here's the door, this is Lucentio's house.
My father's bears more toward the market-place;
Thither must I, and here I leave you, sir.

Vincentio.
You shall not choose but drink before you go.
I think I shall command your welcome here;
And by all likelihood some cheer is toward.

Knock.

Act 7, Scene 1

Gremio.
They're busy within, you were best knock louder.

Pedant looks out of the window.

Pedant (as as Vincentio).
What's he that knocks as he would beat down the gate?

Vincentio.
Is Signior Lucentio within, sir?

Pedant (as as Vincentio).
He's within, sir, but not to be spoken withal.

Vincentio.
What if a man bring him a hundred pound or two, to make merry withal?

Pedant (as as Vincentio).
Keep your hundred pounds to yourself, he shall need none so long as I live.

Petruchio.
Nay, I told you your son was well belov'd in Padua. Do you hear, sir?—to leave frivolous circumstances, I pray you tell Signior Lucentio that his father is come from Pisa, and is here at the door to speak with him.

Pedant (as as Vincentio).
Thou liest, his father is come from Padua and here looking out at the window.

Vincentio.
Art thou his father?

Pedant (as as Vincentio).
Ay, sir, so his mother says, if I may believe her.

Petruchio.
To Vincentio.
Why, how now, gentleman? Why, this is flat knavery, to take upon you another man's name.

Pedant (as as Vincentio).
Lay hands on the villain. I believe 'a means to cozen somebody in this city under my countenance.

Enter Biondello.

Biondello.
I have seen them in the church together, God send 'em good shipping! But who is here? Mine old master Vincentio! Now we are undone and brought to nothing.

Vincentio.
Seeing Biondello.
Come hither, crack-hemp.

Biondello.
I hope I may choose, sir.

Vincentio.
Come hither, you rogue. What, have you forgot me?

Biondello.
Forgot you? No, sir. I could not forget you, for I never saw you before in all my life.

Vincentio.
What, you notorious villain, didst thou never see thy master's father, Vincentio?

Biondello.
What, my old worshipful old master? Yes, marry, sir—see where he looks out of the window.

Vincentio.
Is't so indeed?

He beats Biondello.

Biondello.
Help, help, help! Here's a madman will murder me.

Exit.

Pedant (as as Vincentio).
Help, son! Help, Signior Baptista!

Exit above.

Petruchio.
Prithee, Kate, let's stand aside and see the end of this controversy.

They retire.
Enter Pedant below with Servants, Baptista, Tranio as Lucentio.

Tranio.
Sir, what are you that offer to beat my servant?

Vincentio.
What am I, sir? Nay, what are you, sir? O immortal gods! O fine villain! A silken doublet, a velvet hose, a scarlet cloak, and a copatain hat! O, I am undone, I am undone! While I play the good husband at home, my son and my servant spend all at the university.

Tranio.
How now, what's the matter?

Baptista.
What, is the man lunatic?

Tranio.
Sir, you seem a sober ancient gentleman by your habit; but your words show you a madman. Why, sir, what 'cerns it you if I wear pearl and gold? I thank my good father, I am able to maintain it.

Vincentio.
Thy father! O villain, he is a sailmaker in Bergamo.

Baptista.
You mistake, sir, you mistake, sir. Pray what do you think is his name?

Vincentio.
His name! As if I knew not his name! I have brought him up ever since he was three years old, and his name is Tranio.

Pedant (as as Vincentio).
Away, away, mad ass, his name is Lucentio, and he is mine only son, and heir to the lands of me, Signior Vincentio.

Vincentio.
Lucentio! O, he hath murd'red his master! Lay hold on him, I charge you, in the Duke's name. O, my son, my son! Tell me, thou villain, where is my son Lucentio?

Tranio (as Lucentio).
Call forth an officer.

Exit Servant, who returns with an Officer.

Carry this mad knave to the jail. Father Baptista, I charge you see that he be forthcoming.

Vincentio.
Carry me to the jail?

Gremio.
Stay, officer, he shall not go to prison.

Baptista.
Talk not, Signior Gremio; I say he shall go to prison.

Gremio.
Take heed, Signior Baptista, lest you be cony-catch'd in this business. I dare swear this is the right Vincentio.

Pedant.
Swear if thou dar'st.

Gremio.
Nay, I dare not swear it.

Tranio.
Then thou wert best say that I am not Lucentio.

Gremio.
Yes, I know thee to be Signior Lucentio.

Baptista.
Away with the dotard, to the jail with him!

Enter Biondello, Lucentio, and Bianca.

Vincentio.
Thus strangers may be hal'd and abus'd. O monstrous villain!

Biondello.
O, we are spoil'd and—yonder he is. Deny him, forswear him, or else we are all undone.

Exeunt Biondello, Tranio, and Pedant as fast as may be.

Lucentio.
Pardon, sweet father.

Kneel.

Lord.
                    Lives my sweet son?

Bianca.
Pardon, dear father.

Baptista.
                    How hast thou offended?
Where is Lucentio?

Lucentio.
                    Here's Lucentio,
Right son to the right Vincentio,
That have by marriage made thy daughter mine,

Act 7, Scene 2

While counterfeit supposes blear'd thine eyne.

Gremio.
Here's packing, with a witness, to deceive us all!

Vincentio.
Where is that damned villain Tranio,
That fac'd and braved me in this matter so?

Baptista.
Why, tell me, is not this my Cambio?

Bianca.
Cambio is chang'd into Lucentio.

Lucentio.
Love wrought these miracles. Bianca's love
Made me exchange my state with Tranio,
While he did bear my countenance in the town,
And happily I have arrived at the last
Unto the wished haven of my bliss.
What Tranio did, myself enforc'd him to;
Then pardon him, sweet father, for my sake.

Vincentio.
I'll slit the villain's nose, that would have sent me to the jail.

Baptista.
But do you hear, sir? Have you married my daughter without asking my good will?

Vincentio.
Fear not, Baptista, we will content you, go to; but I will in to be reveng'd for this villainy.

Exit.

Baptista.
And I, to sound the depth of this knavery.

Exit.

Lucentio.
Look not pale, Bianca, thy father will not frown.

Exeunt Lucentio and Bianca.

Gremio.
My cake is dough, but I'll in among the rest,
Out of hope of all but my share of the feast.

Exit.

Katherina.
Husband, let's follow, to see the end of this ado.

Petruchio.
First kiss me, Kate, and we will.

Katherina.
What, in the midst of the street?

Petruchio.
What, art thou asham'd of me?

Katherina.
No, sir, God forbid, but asham'd to kiss.

Petruchio.
Why then let's home again. Come, sirrah, let's away.

Katherina.
Nay, I will give thee a kiss; now pray thee, love, stay.

Petruchio.
Is not this well? Come, my sweet Kate:
Better once than never, for never too late.

Exeunt.

Scene 2

Padua. Lucentio's house.

(Baptista; Vincentio; Gremio; Pedant; Lucentio; Bianca; Petruchio; Katherina; Hortensio; Tranio; Biondello; Grumio; Widow; Servingmen)

Everybody shows up for the celebratory feast of Lucentio's wedding, including Hortensio and the Widow he has married. Tranio is back in his place with the servants. The Widow insults Katherina for a shrew, and Hortensio and Petruchio make bets on who will win the battle of wits. Bianca leads the two away and the men begin discussing their wives. Baptista tells Petruchio that of the three newlyweds, he doubtless has the most obedient, but Petruchio denies this. He suggests that each of the three send a message calling their wives back, and they put bets on who will respond best. To everyone's amazement except Petruchio's, Bianca and the Widow refuse to come, as they are busy talking; Katherina, however, comes immediately. Petruchio sends her to fetch the other two. When they arrive, he orders Kate to trample on her hat, which she does, and the other two scorn her for it. Petruchio tells Kate to tell the others what their duty is, and she extols complete obedience to one's husband. Hortensio and

Lucentio are amazed at what Petruchio has managed to accomplish.

Enter Baptista, Vincentio, Gremio, the Pedant, Lucentio, and Bianca; Petruchio, Katherina, Hortensio, Tranio, Biondello, Grumio, and Widow: the servingmen with Tranio bringing in a banquet.

Lucentio.
At last, though long, our jarring notes agree,
And time it is, when raging war is done,
To smile at scapes and perils overblown.
My fair Bianca, bid my father welcome,
While I with self-same kindness welcome thine.
Brother Petruchio, sister Katherina,
And thou, Hortensio, with thy loving widow,
Feast with the best, and welcome to my house.
My banquet is to close our stomachs up
After our great good cheer. Pray you sit down,
For now we sit to chat as well as eat.

Petruchio.
Nothing but sit and sit, and eat and eat!

Baptista.
Padua affords this kindness, son Petruchio.

Petruchio.
Padua affords nothing but what is kind.

Hortensio.
For both our sakes, I would that word were true.

Petruchio.
Now, for my life, Hortensio fears his widow.

Widow.
Then never trust me if I be afeard.

Petruchio.
You are very sensible, and yet you miss my sense:
I mean Hortensio is afeard of you.

Widow.
He that is giddy thinks the world turns round.

Petruchio.
Roundly replied.

Katherina.
                    Mistress, how mean you that?

Widow.
Thus I conceive by him.

Petruchio.
Conceives by me! How likes Hortensio that?

Hortensio.
My widow says, thus she conceives her tale.

Petruchio.
Very well mended. Kiss him for that, good widow.

Katherina.
"He that is giddy thinks the world turns round":
I pray you tell me what you meant by that.

Widow.
Your husband, being troubled with a shrew,
Measures my husband's sorrow by his woe:
And now you know my meaning.

Katherina.
A very mean meaning.

Widow.
                    Right, I mean you.

Katherina.
And I am mean indeed, respecting you.

Petruchio.
To her, Kate!

Hortensio.
To her, widow!

Petruchio.
A hundred marks, my Kate does put her down.

Hortensio.
That's my office.

Petruchio.
Spoke like an officer. Ha' to thee, lad!

Drinks to Hortensio.

Baptista.
How likes Gremio these quick-witted folks?

Gremio.
Believe me, sir, they butt together well.

Bianca.
Head, and butt! An hasty-witted body
Would say your head and butt were head and horn.

Vincentio.
Ay, mistress bride, hath that awakened you?

Bianca.
Ay, but not frighted me, therefore I'll sleep again.

Petruchio.
Nay, that you shall not, since you have begun;
Have at you for a bitter jest or two!

Bianca.
Am I your bird? I mean to shift my bush,
And then pursue me as you draw your bow.
You are welcome all.

Exit Bianca with Katherina and Widow.

Petruchio.
She hath prevented me. Here, Signior Tranio,
This bird you aim'd at, though you hit her not;
Therefore a health to all that shot and miss'd.

Tranio.
O, sir, Lucentio slipp'd me like his greyhound,
Which runs himself, and catches for his master.

Petruchio.
A good swift simile, but something currish.

Tranio.
'Tis well, sir, that you hunted for yourself;
'Tis thought your deer does hold you at a bay.

Baptista.
O, O, Petruchio, Tranio hits you now.

Lucentio.
I thank thee for that gird, good Tranio.

Hortensio.
Confess, confess, hath he not hit you here?

Petruchio.
'A has a little gall'd me, I confess;
And as the jest did glance away from me,
'Tis ten to one it maim'd you two outright.

Baptista.
Now in good sadness, son Petruchio,
I think thou hast the veriest shrew of all.

Petruchio.
Well, I say no; and therefore for assurance
Let's each one send unto his wife,
And he whose wife is most obedient,
To come at first when he doth send for her,
Shall win the wager which we will propose.

Hortensio.
Content. What's the wager?

Lucentio.
                    Twenty crowns.

Petruchio.
Twenty crowns!
I'll venture so much of my hawk or hound,
But twenty times so much upon my wife.

Lucentio.
A hundred then.

Hortensio.
                    Content.

Petruchio.
                    A match! 'Tis done.

Hortensio.
Who shall begin?

Lucentio.
                    That will I.
Go, Biondello, bid your mistress come to me.

Biondello.
I go.

Exit.

Baptista.
Son, I'll be your half, Bianca comes.

Lucentio.
I'll have no halves; I'll bear it all myself.

Enter Biondello.

How now, what news?

Biondello.
            Sir, my mistress sends you word
That she is busy, and she cannot come.

Petruchio.
How? She is busy, and she cannot come!
Is that an answer?

Gremio.
                Ay, and a kind one too.
Pray God, sir, your wife send you not a worse.

Petruchio.
I hope better.

Hortensio.
Sirrah Biondello, go and entreat my wife
To come to me forthwith.

Exit Biondello.

Petruchio.
                    O ho, entreat her!
Nay then she must needs come.

Hortensio.
                I am afraid, sir,
Do what you can, yours will not be entreated.

Enter Biondello.

Now, where's my wife?

Biondello.
She says you have some goodly jest in hand.
She will not come; she bids you come to her.

Petruchio.
Worse and worse; she will not come! O vile,
Intolerable, not to be endur'd!
Sirrah Grumio, go to your mistress,
Say I command her come to me.

Exit Grumio.

Hortensio.
I know her answer.

Petruchio.
               What?

Hortensio.
                  She will not.

Petruchio.
The fouler fortune mine, and there an end.

Enter Katherina.

Baptista.
Now, by my holidam, here comes Katherina!

Katherina.
What is your will, sir, that you send for me?

Petruchio.
Where is your sister, and Hortensio's wife?

Katherina.
They sit conferring by the parlor fire.

Petruchio.
Go fetch them hither. If they deny to come,
Swinge me them soundly forth unto their husbands.
Away, I say, and bring them hither straight.

Exit Katherina.

Lucentio.
Here is a wonder, if you talk of a wonder.

Hortensio.
And so it is; I wonder what it bodes.

Petruchio.
Marry, peace it bodes, and love, and quiet life,
An awe full rule, and right supremacy;
And to be short, what not, that's sweet and happy.

Baptista.
Now fair befall thee, good Petruchio!
The wager thou hast won, and I will add
Unto their losses twenty thousand crowns,
Another dowry to another daughter,
For she is chang'd, as she had never been.

Petruchio.
Nay, I will win my wager better yet,
And show more sign of her obedience,
Her new-built virtue and obedience.

Enter Kate, Bianca, and Widow.

See where she comes, and brings your froward wives
As prisoners to her womanly persuasion.
Katherine, that cap of yours becomes you not;
Off with that bauble, throw it under-foot.

Katherina throws down her cap.

Widow.
Lord, let me never have a cause to sigh,
Till I be brought to such a silly pass!

Bianca.
Fie, what a foolish duty call you this?

Lucentio.
I would your duty were as foolish too.
The wisdom of your duty, fair Bianca,
Hath cost me a hundred crowns since supper-time.

Bianca.
The more fool you for laying on my duty.

Petruchio.
Katherine, I charge thee tell these headstrong women
What duty they do owe their lords and husbands.

Widow.
Come, come, you're mocking; we will have no telling.

Petruchio.
Come on, I say, and first begin with her.

Widow.
She shall not.

Petruchio.
I say she shall, and first begin with her.

Katherina.
Fie, fie, unknit that threat'ning unkind brow,
And dart not scornful glances from those eyes,
To wound thy lord, thy king, thy governor.
It blots thy beauty, as frosts do bite the meads,
Confounds thy fame, as whirlwinds shake fair buds,
And in no sense is meet or amiable.
A woman mov'd is like a fountain troubled,
Muddy, ill-seeming, thick, bereft of beauty,
And while it is so, none so dry or thirsty
Will deign to sip, or touch one drop of it.
Thy husband is thy lord, thy life, thy keeper,
Thy head, thy sovereign; one that cares for thee,
And for thy maintenance; commits his body
To painful labor, both by sea and land;
To watch the night in storms, the day in cold,
Whilst thou li'st warm at home, secure and safe;
And craves no other tribute at thy hands
But love, fair looks, and true obedience—
Too little payment for so great a debt.
Such duty as the subject owes the prince,
Even such a woman oweth to her husband;
And when she is froward, peevish, sullen, sour,
And not obedient to his honest will,
What is she but a foul contending rebel,
And graceless traitor to her loving lord?
I am asham'd that women are so simple
To offer war where they should kneel for peace,
Or seek for rule, supremacy, and sway,
When they are bound to serve, love, and obey.
Why are our bodies soft, and weak, and smooth,
Unapt to toil and trouble in the world,
But that our soft conditions, and our hearts,
Should well agree with our external parts?
Come, come, you froward and unable worms!
My mind hath been as big as one of yours,
My heart as great, my reason haply more,
To bandy word for word and frown for frown;
But now I see our lances are but straws,
Our strength as weak, our weakness past compare,
That seeming to be most which we indeed least are.
Then vail your stomachs, for it is no boot,
And place your hands below your husband's foot;
In token of which duty, if he please,
My hand is ready, may it do him ease.

Petruchio.
Why, there's a wench! Come on, and kiss me, Kate.

Lucentio.
Well, go thy ways, old lad, for thou shalt ha't.

Vincentio.
'Tis a good hearing when children are toward.

Lucentio.
But a harsh hearing when women are froward.

Petruchio.
Come, Kate, we'll to bed.
We three are married, but you two are sped.

To Lucentio.

'Twas I won the wager, though you hit the white,
And being a winner, God give you good night!

Exit Petruchio with Katherina.

Hortensio.
Now go thy ways, thou hast tam'd a curst shrew.

Lucentio.
'Tis a wonder, by your leave, she will be tam'd so.

Exeunt.

Othello

Act 1

Scene 1

Venice. A street.

(Roderigo; Iago; Brabantio; Servants)

Iago tells Roderigo why he hates Othello: he sought to be his lieutenant, but the foreigner Michael Cassio was preferred. Roderigo is distraught that Desdemona, whom he loves, has run off with the Moor Othello and married him; with Iago, he rouses Desdemona's father Brabantio, who at first simply accuses Roderigo of making mischief, but soon has to admit that his daughter is missing. Not wishing to be recognized, Iago leaves, while Brabantio rouses his servants and forms a search party to hunt down Othello.

Enter Roderigo and Iago.

Roderigo.
Tush, never tell me! I take it much unkindly
That thou, Iago, who hast had my purse
As if the strings were thine, shouldst know of this.

Iago.
'Sblood, but you'll not hear me.
If ever I did dream of such a matter,
Abhor me.

Roderigo.
Thou toldst me thou didst hold him in thy hate.

Iago.
Despise me
If I do not. Three great ones of the city,
In personal suit to make me his lieutenant,
Off-capp'd to him; and, by the faith of man,
I know my price, I am worth no worse a place.
But he (as loving his own pride and purposes)
Evades them with a bombast circumstance
Horribly stuff'd with epithites of war,
And in conclusion,
Nonsuits my mediators; for, "Certes," says he,
"I have already chose my officer."
And what was he?
Forsooth, a great arithmetician,
One Michael Cassio, a Florentine
(A fellow almost damn'd in a fair wife),
That never set a squadron in the field,
Nor the division of a battle knows
More than a spinster—unless the bookish theoric,
Wherein the toged consuls can propose
As masterly as he. Mere prattle, without practice,
Is all his soldiership. But he, sir, had th' election;
And I, of whom his eyes had seen the proof
At Rhodes, at Cyprus, and on other grounds
Christen'd and heathen, must be belee'd and calm'd
By debitor and creditor—this counter—caster,
He (in good time!) must his lieutenant be,
And I (God bless the mark!) his Moorship's ancient.

Roderigo.
By heaven, I rather would have been his hangman.

Iago.
Why, there's no remedy. 'Tis the curse of service;
Preferment goes by letter and affection,
And not by old gradation, where each second
Stood heir to th' first. Now, sir, be judge yourself
Whether I in any just term am affin'd
To love the Moor.

Roderigo.
              I would not follow him then.

Iago.
O, sir, content you;
I follow him to serve my turn upon him.
We cannot all be masters, nor all masters
Cannot be truly follow'd. You shall mark
Many a duteous and knee-crooking knave
That (doting on his own obsequious bondage)
Wears out his time, much like his master's ass,
For nought but provender, and when he's old, cashier'd.
Whip me such honest knaves. Others there are
Who, trimm'd in forms and visages of duty,
Keep yet their hearts attending on themselves,
And throwing but shows of service on their lords,
Do well thrive by them; and when they have lin'd their coats,
Do themselves homage. These fellows have some soul,
And such a one do I profess myself. For, sir,
It is as sure as you are Roderigo,
Were I the Moor, I would not be Iago.
In following him, I follow but myself;
Heaven is my judge, not I for love and duty,
But seeming so, for my peculiar end;
For when my outward action doth demonstrate
The native act and figure of my heart
In complement extern, 'tis not long after
But I will wear my heart upon my sleeve
For daws to peck at: I am not what I am.

Roderigo.
What a full fortune does the thick-lips owe
If he can carry't thus!

Iago.
              Call up her father.
Rouse him, make after him, poison his delight,
Proclaim him in the streets; incense her kinsmen,
And though he in a fertile climate dwell,
Plague him with flies. Though that his joy be joy,
Yet throw such changes of vexation on't,
As it may lose some color.

Roderigo.
Here is her father's house, I'll call aloud.

Iago.
Do, with like timorous accent and dire yell
As when, by night and negligence, the fire
Is spied in populous cities.

Roderigo.
What ho! Brabantio, Signior Brabantio, ho!

Iago.
Awake! What ho, Brabantio! Thieves, thieves!
Look to your house, your daughter, and your bags!
Thieves, thieves!

Enter Brabantio above at a window.

Brabantio.
What is the reason of this terrible summons?
What is the matter there?

Roderigo.
Signior, is all your family within?

Iago.
Are your doors lock'd?

Brabantio.
              Why? Wherefore ask you this?

Iago.
'Zounds, sir, y' are robb'd! For shame, put on your gown;
Your heart is burst, you have lost half your soul;
Even now, now, very now, an old black ram
Is tupping your white ewe. Arise, arise!
Awake the snorting citizens with the bell,
Or else the devil will make a grandsire of you.
Arise, I say!

Brabantio.
              What, have you lost your wits?

Roderigo.
Most reverend signior, do you know my voice?

Brabantio.
Not I; what are you?

Roderigo.
My name is Roderigo.

Brabantio.
              The worser welcome;
I have charg'd thee not to haunt about my doors.
In honest plainness thou hast heard me say
My daughter is not for thee; and now, in madness
(Being full of supper and distemp'ring draughts),
Upon malicious bravery dost thou come
To start my quiet.

Roderigo.
Sir, sir, sir—

Brabantio.
                But thou must needs be sure
My spirits and my place have in their power
To make this bitter to thee.

Roderigo.
                Patience, good sir.

Brabantio.
What tell'st thou me of robbing? This is Venice;
My house is not a grange.

Roderigo.
                Most grave Brabantio,
In simple and pure soul I come to you.

Iago.
'Zounds, sir, you are one of those that will not serve
God, if the devil bid you. Because we come to do you
service, and you think we are ruffians, you'll have
your daughter cover'd with a Barbary horse, you'll
have your nephews neigh to you; you'll have coursers
for cousins, and gennets for germans.

Brabantio.
What profane wretch art thou?

Iago.
I am one, sir, that comes to tell you your daughter and
the Moor are now making the beast with two backs.

Brabantio.
Thou art a villain.

Iago.
                You are a senator.

Brabantio.
This thou shalt answer; I know thee, Roderigo.

Roderigo.
Sir, I will answer any thing. But I beseech you,
If't be your pleasure and most wise consent
(As partly I find it is) that your fair daughter,
At this odd-even and dull watch o' th' night,
Transported with no worse nor better guard
But with a knave of common hire, a gundolier,
To the gross clasps of a lascivious Moor—
If this be known to you, and your allowance,
We then have done you bold and saucy wrongs;
But if you know not this, my manners tell me
We have your wrong rebuke. Do not believe
That, from the sense of all civility,
I thus would play and trifle with your reverence.
Your daughter (if you have not given her leave),
I say again, hath made a gross revolt,
Tying her duty, beauty, wit, and fortunes
In an extravagant and wheeling stranger
Of here and every where. Straight satisfy yourself.
If she be in her chamber or your house,
Let loose on me the justice of the state
For thus deluding you.

Brabantio.
                Strike on the tinder, ho!
Give me a taper! Call up all my people!
This accident is not unlike my dream,
Belief of it oppresses me already.
Light, I say, light!

Exit above.

Iago.
                Farewell; for I must leave you.
It seems not meet, nor wholesome to my place,
To be produced (as, if I stay, I shall)
Against the Moor; for I do know the state
(How ever this may gall him with some check)
Cannot with safety cast him, for he's embark'd
With such loud reason to the Cyprus wars
(Which even now stands in act) that, for their souls,
Another of his fathom they have none
To lead their business; in which regard,
Though I do hate him as I do hell-pains,
Yet, for necessity of present life,
I must show out a flag and sign of love,
Which is indeed but sign. That you shall surely find him,
Lead to the Sagittary the raised search;
And there will I be with him. So farewell.

Exit.
Enter below Brabantio in his night-gown with Servants and torches.

Brabantio.
It is too true an evil; gone she is;
And what's to come of my despised time
Is nought but bitterness. Now, Roderigo,
Where didst thou see her?—O unhappy girl!—
With the Moor, say'st thou?—Who would be a father!—

How didst thou know 'twas she?—O, she deceives me
Past thought!—What said she to you?—Get more tapers;
Raise all my kindred.—Are they married, think you?

Roderigo.
Truly, I think they are.

Brabantio.
O heaven! How got she out? O treason of the blood!
Fathers, from hence trust not your daughters' minds
By what you see them act. Is there not charms
By which the property of youth and maidhood
May be abus'd? Have you not read, Roderigo,
Of some such thing?

Roderigo.
         Yes, sir, I have indeed.

Brabantio.
Call up my brother.—O would you had had her!—
Some one way, some another.—Do you know
Where we may apprehend her and the Moor?

Roderigo.
I think I can discover him, if you please
To get good guard and go along with me.

Brabantio.
Pray you lead on. At every house I'll call
(I may command at most).—Get weapons, ho!
And raise some special officers of night.—
On, good Roderigo, I will deserve your pains.

Exeunt.

Scene 2

Venice. Another street.

(Othello; Iago; Attendants; Cassio; Officers; Brabantio; Roderigo)

Iago asks Othello whether he is properly married, warning that he is at risk from Brabantio and needs everything to be as legal as possible. Othello points out that he has done Venice enough service to outweigh Brabantio's weighty position. He insists he will not hide from Brabantio's men, but the group who arrives looking for him turns out to be headed by Cassio, who has been sent to fetch Othello to a council of war. Brabantio arrives with his men, and both parties draw swords; Iago makes sure to take on Roderigo so that no one will guess at their friendship. Othello refuses to fight, and points out that he has just been summoned to the Duke. Hearing that the Council is in session, Brabantio decides to make his case directly to the Senate.

Enter Othello, Iago, Attendants with torches.

Iago.
Though in the trade of war I have slain men,
Yet do I hold it very stuff o' th' conscience
To do no contriv'd murder. I lack iniquity
Sometime to do me service. Nine or ten times
I had thought t' have yerk'd him here under the ribs.

Othello.
'Tis better as it is.

Iago.
         Nay, but he prated,
And spoke such scurvy and provoking terms
Against your honor,
That with the little godliness I have
I did full hard forbear him. But I pray you, sir,
Are you fast married? Be assur'd of this,
That the magnifico is much belov'd,
And hath in his effect a voice potential
As double as the Duke's. He will divorce you,
Or put upon you what restraint or grievance
The law (with all his might to enforce it on)
Will give him cable.

Othello.
         Let him do his spite;
My services which I have done the signiory
Shall out—tongue his complaints. 'Tis yet to know—
Which, when I know that boasting is an honor,
I shall provulgate—I fetch my life and being
From men of royal siege, and my demerits
May speak, unbonneted, to as proud a fortune
As this that I have reach'd; for know, Iago,
But that I love the gentle Desdemona,
I would not my unhoused free condition
Put into circumscription and confine
For the sea's worth. But look, what lights come yond?

Enter Cassio with Officers and torches.

Iago.
Those are the raised father and his friends.
You were best go in.

Othello.
                 Not I; I must be found.
My parts, my title, and my perfect soul
Shall manifest me rightly. Is it they?

Iago.
By Janus, I think no.

Othello.
The servants of the Duke? And my lieutenant?
The goodness of the night upon you, friends!
What is the news?

Cassio.
             The Duke does greet you, general,
And he requires your haste-post-haste appearance,
Even on the instant.

Othello.
             What is the matter, think you?

Cassio.
Something from Cyprus, as I may divine;
It is a business of some heat. The galleys
Have sent a dozen sequent messengers
This very night at one another's heels;
And many of the consuls, rais'd and met,
Are at the Duke's already. You have been hotly call'd for;
When, being not at your lodging to be found,
The Senate hath sent about three several quests
To search you out.

Othello.
            'Tis well I am found by you.
I will but spend a word here in the house,
And go with you.

Exit.

Cassio.
          Ancient, what makes he here?

Iago.
Faith, he tonight hath boarded a land carrack.
If it prove lawful prize, he's made forever.

Cassio.
I do not understand.

Iago.
            He's married.

Cassio.
            To who?

Enter Othello.

Iago.
Marry, to—Come, captain, will you go?

Othello.
            Have with you.

Cassio.
Here comes another troop to seek for you.

Enter Brabantio, Roderigo, with Officers with torches and weapons.

Iago.
It is Brabantio. General, be advis'd,
He comes to bad intent.

Othello.
            Holla, stand there!

Roderigo.
Signior, it is the Moor.

Brabantio.
           Down with him, thief!

They draw on both sides.

Iago.
You, Roderigo! Come, sir, I am for you.

Othello.
Keep up your bright swords, for the dew will rust them.
Good signior, you shall more command with years
Than with your weapons.

Brabantio.
O thou foul thief, where hast thou stow'd my daughter?
Damn'd as thou art, thou hast enchanted her,
For I'll refer me to all things of sense,
If she in chains of magic were not bound,
Whether a maid so tender, fair, and happy,
So opposite to marriage that she shunn'd
The wealthy curled darlings of our nation,
Would ever have, t' incur a general mock,
Run from her guardage to the sooty bosom
Of such a thing as thou—to fear, not to delight!
Judge me the world, if 'tis not gross in sense,

That thou hast practic'd on her with foul charms,
Abus'd her delicate youth with drugs or minerals
That weakens motion. I'll have't disputed on,
'Tis probable, and palpable to thinking.
I therefore apprehend and do attach thee
For an abuser of the world, a practicer
Of arts inhibited and out of warrant.
Lay hold upon him, if he do resist
Subdue him at his peril.

Othello.
                        Hold your hands,
Both you of my inclining, and the rest.
Were it my cue to fight, I should have known it
Without a prompter. Whither will you that I go
To answer this your charge?

Brabantio.
                        To prison, till fit time
Of law and course of direct session
Call thee to answer.

Othello.
                        What if I do obey?
How may the Duke be therewith satisfied,
Whose messengers are here about my side,
Upon some present business of the state,
To bring me to him?

Officer.
                        'Tis true, most worthy signior;
The Duke's in council, and your noble self
I am sure is sent for.

Brabantio.
                        How? The Duke in council?
In this time of the night? Bring him away;
Mine's not an idle cause. The Duke himself,
Or any of my brothers of the state,
Cannot but feel this wrong as 'twere their own;
For if such actions may have passage free,
Bond-slaves and pagans shall our statesmen be.

Exeunt.

Scene 3

Venice. A council chamber.

(Duke; First Senator; Second Senator; Officers; Sailor; First Messenger; Brabantio; Othello; Cassio; Iago; Roderigo; Desdemona; Attendants)

The Duke and the Senators look over the conflicting reports they are receiving about a Turkish fleet that seems to be aiming either for Rhodes or for Cyprus. They soon work out that the attack on Rhodes was merely a feint and that Cyprus is the true target. Brabantio and Othello arrive; the Duke is glad to see Othello, who will lead the Venetian forces against the Turks, but Brabantio interrupts and insists on having his case against the Moor heard. He insists that Desdemona has been bewitched, and the Duke promises immediate vengeance until he hears that the accused is Othello. Things then get a bit more complicated, and Othello is asked to tell his version of what has happened. He admits to marrying Desdemona, but insists the only magic he used was telling stories of his life. Desdemona, sent for, confirms this, and explains that she now owes her obedience to her husband more than to her father. Brabantio unwillingly gives in, and begs that the subject be changed and that they get to affairs of state. Othello is commanded to leave at once for Cyprus; when the men discuss where Desdemona should stay while he is away, the lady speaks up and asks permission to follow her newlywed husband to Cyprus. Brabantio tells Othello not to trust Desdemona, since if she is capable of betraying her father, she could do the same to her husband. Othello denies this. He entrusts Desdemona to Iago. Left alone with Roderigo, Iago bullies the young man out of his depressed insistence that he wishes to drown himself. Instead, Iago encourages him to disguise himself and follow them all to Cyprus, claiming that Desdemona will never put up with a black man for long, and that therefore Roderigo will have a chance at her when she gets bored with the novelty. Roderigo is convinced and goes to sell his lands for cash. Iago is delighted, since he tends to pillage Roderigo's purse. He reflects on how he hates Othello, and believes that he has been cuckolded by the Moor. Hoping to destroy him if at all possible, Iago considers his options, and begins to see the outlines of a plan.

Enter Duke and Senators set at a table, with lights and Officers.

Duke of Venice.
There's no composition in these news
That gives them credit.

First Senator.
                        Indeed, they are disproportioned;
My letters say a hundred and seven galleys.

Duke of Venice.
And mine, a hundred forty.

Second Senator.
                And mine, two hundred!
But though they jump not on a just accompt
(As in these cases where the aim reports,
'Tis oft with difference), yet do they all confirm
A Turkish fleet, and bearing up to Cyprus.

Duke of Venice.
Nay, it is possible enough to judgment.
I do not so secure me in the error
But the main article I do approve
In fearful sense.

Sailor.

Within.
                What ho, what ho, what ho!

Enter Sailor.

Officer.
A messenger from the galleys.

Duke of Venice.
            Now? What's the business?

Sailor.
The Turkish preparation makes for Rhodes,
So was I bid report here to the state
By Signior Angelo.

Exit Sailor.

Duke of Venice.
How say you by this change?

First Senator.
                This cannot be
By no assay of reason; 'tis a pageant
To keep us in false gaze. When we consider
Th' importancy of Cyprus to the Turk,
And let ourselves again but understand
That, as it more concerns the Turk than Rhodes,
So may he with more facile question bear it,
For that it stands not in such warlike brace,
But altogether lacks th' abilities
That Rhodes is dress'd in—if we make thought of this,
We must not think the Turk is so unskillful
To leave that latest which concerns him first,
Neglecting an attempt of ease and gain
To wake and wage a danger profitless.

Duke of Venice.
Nay, in all confidence, he's not for Rhodes.

Officer.
Here is more news.

Enter the First Messenger.

First Messenger.
The Ottomites, reverend and gracious,
Steering with due course toward the isle of Rhodes,
Have there injointed them with an after fleet.

First Senator.
Ay, so I thought. How many, as you guess?

First Messenger.
Of thirty sail; and now they do restem
Their backward course, bearing with frank appearance
Their purposes toward Cyprus. Signior Montano,
Your trusty and most valiant servitor,
With his free duty recommends you thus,
And prays you to believe him.

Exit First Messenger.

Duke of Venice.
'Tis certain then for Cyprus.
Marcus Luccicos, is not he in town?

First Senator.
He's now in Florence.

Duke of Venice.
Write from us to him, post-post-haste. Dispatch!

First Senator.
Here comes Brabantio and the valiant Moor.

Enter Brabantio, Othello, Cassio, Iago, Roderigo, and Officers.

Duke of Venice.
Valiant Othello, we must straight employ you
Against the general enemy Ottoman.

To Brabantio.

I did not see you; welcome, gentle signior,
We lack'd your counsel and your help tonight.

Brabantio.
So did I yours. Good your Grace, pardon me:
Neither my place, nor aught I heard of business,
Hath rais'd me from my bed, nor doth the general care
Take hold on me; for my particular grief
Is of so flood-gate and o'erbearing nature
That it engluts and swallows other sorrows,
And it is still itself.

Duke of Venice.
     Why? What's the matter?

Brabantio.
My daughter! O, my daughter!

All.
     Dead?

Brabantio.
     Ay, to me:
She is abus'd, stol'n from me, and corrupted
By spells and medicines bought of mountebanks;
For nature so prepost'rously to err
(Being not deficient, blind, or lame of sense)
Sans witchcraft could not.

Duke of Venice.
Who e'er he be that in this foul proceeding
Hath thus beguil'd your daughter of herself,
And you of her, the bloody book of law
You shall yourself read in the bitter letter
After your own sense; yea, though our proper son
Stood in your action.

Brabantio.
     Humbly I thank your Grace.
Here is the man—this Moor, whom now, it seems,
Your special mandate for the state affairs
Hath hither brought.

All.
     We are very sorry for't.

Duke of Venice.

To Othello.

What, in your own part, can you say to this?

Brabantio.
Nothing, but this is so.

Othello.
Most potent, grave, and reverend signiors,
My very noble and approv'd good masters:
That I have ta'en away this old man's daughter,
It is most true; true I have married her;
The very head and front of my offending
Hath this extent, no more. Rude am I in my speech,
And little bless'd with the soft phrase of peace;
For since these arms of mine had seven years' pith,
Till now some nine moons wasted, they have us'd
Their dearest action in the tented field;
And little of this great world can I speak
More than pertains to feats of broils and battle,
And therefore little shall I grace my cause
In speaking for myself. Yet (by your gracious patience)
I will a round unvarnish'd tale deliver
Of my whole course of love—what drugs, what charms,
What conjuration, and what mighty magic
(For such proceeding I am charg'd withal)
I won his daughter.

Brabantio.
     A maiden, never bold;
Of spirit so still and quiet that her motion
Blush'd at herself; and she, in spite of nature,
Of years, of country, credit, every thing,
To fall in love with what she fear'd to look on!
It is a judgment main'd, and most imperfect,
That will confess perfection so could err
Against all rules of nature, and must be driven
To find out practices of cunning hell
Why this should be. I therefore vouch again
That with some mixtures pow'rful o'er the blood,
Or with some dram (conjur'd to this effect)
He wrought upon her.

Duke of Venice.
     To vouch this is no proof,
Without more wider and more overt test
Than these thin habits and poor likelihoods
Of modern seeming do prefer against him.

First Senator.
But, Othello, speak.
Did you by indirect and forced courses
Subdue and poison this young maid's affections?
Or came it by request, and such fair question
As soul to soul affordeth?

Othello.
                            I do beseech you,
Send for the lady to the Sagittary,
And let her speak of me before her father.
If you do find me foul in her report,
The trust, the office I do hold of you,
Not only take away, but let your sentence
Even fall upon my life.

Duke of Venice.
                        Fetch Desdemona hither.

Exeunt two or three.

Othello.
Ancient, conduct them; you best know the place.

Exit Iago.

And, till she come, as truly as to heaven
I do confess the vices of my blood,
So justly to your grave ears I'll present
How I did thrive in this fair lady's love,
And she in mine.

Duke of Venice.
Say it, Othello.

Othello.
Her father lov'd me, oft invited me;
Still question'd me the story of my life
From year to year—the battles, sieges, fortunes,
That I have pass'd.
I ran it through, even from my boyish days
To th' very moment that he bade me tell it;
Wherein I spoke of most disastrous chances:
Of moving accidents by flood and field,
Of hair-breadth scapes i' th' imminent deadly breach,
Of being taken by the insolent foe
And sold to slavery, of my redemption thence
And portance in my travel's history;
Wherein of antres vast and deserts idle,
Rough quarries, rocks, and hills whose heads touch heaven,
It was my hint to speak—such was my process—
And of the Cannibals that each other eat,
The Anthropophagi, and men whose heads
Do grow beneath their shoulders. These things to hear
Would Desdemona seriously incline;
But still the house affairs would draw her thence,
Which ever as she could with haste dispatch,
She'ld come again, and with a greedy ear
Devour up my discourse. Which I observing,
Took once a pliant hour, and found good means
To draw from her a prayer of earnest heart
That I would all my pilgrimage dilate,
Whereof by parcels she had something heard,
But not intentively. I did consent,
And often did beguile her of her tears,
When I did speak of some distressful stroke
That my youth suffer'd. My story being done,
She gave me for my pains a world of sighs;
She swore, in faith 'twas strange, 'twas passing strange;
'Twas pitiful, 'twas wondrous pitiful.
She wish'd she had not heard it, yet she wish'd
That heaven had made her such a man. She thank'd me,
And bade me, if I had a friend that lov'd her,
I should but teach him how to tell my story,
And that would woo her. Upon this hint I spake:
She lov'd me for the dangers I had pass'd,
And I lov'd her that she did pity them.
This only is the witchcraft I have us'd.
Here comes the lady; let her witness it.

Enter Desdemona, Iago, Attendants.

Duke of Venice.
I think this tale would win my daughter too.
Good Brabantio,
Take up this mangled matter at the best;
Men do their broken weapons rather use
Than their bare hands.

Brabantio.
                        I pray you hear her speak.
If she confess that she was half the wooer,
Destruction on my head if my bad blame
Light on the man! Come hither, gentle mistress.
Do you perceive in all this noble company
Where most you owe obedience?

Desdemona.
                          My noble father,
I do perceive here a divided duty:
To you I am bound for life and education;
My life and education both do learn me
How to respect you; you are the lord of duty;
I am hitherto your daughter. But here's my husband;
And so much duty as my mother show'd
To you, preferring you before her father,

Act 1, Scene 3

So much I challenge that I may profess
Due to the Moor, my lord.

Brabantio.
                God be with you! I have done.
Please it your Grace, on to the state affairs.
I had rather to adopt a child than get it.
Come hither, Moor:
I here do give thee that with all my heart
Which but thou hast already, with all my heart
I would keep from thee. For your sake, jewel,
I am glad at soul I have no other child,
For thy escape would teach me tyranny,
To hang clogs on them. I have done, my lord.

Duke of Venice.
Let me speak like yourself, and lay a sentence,
Which as a grise or step, may help these lovers
Into your favor.
When remedies are past, the griefs are ended
By seeing the worst, which late on hopes depended.
To mourn a mischief that is past and gone
Is the next way to draw new mischief on.
What cannot be preserv'd when Fortune takes,
Patience her injury a mock'ry makes.
The robb'd that smiles steals something from the thief;
He robs himself that spends a bootless grief.

Brabantio.
So let the Turk of Cyprus us beguile,
We lose it not, so long as we can smile.
He bears the sentence well that nothing bears
But the free comfort which from thence he hears;
But he bears both the sentence and the sorrow
That, to pay grief, must of poor patience borrow.
These sentences, to sugar or to gall,
Being strong on both sides, are equivocal.
But words are words; I never yet did hear
That the bruis'd heart was pierced through the ear.
I humbly beseech you proceed to th' affairs of state.

Duke of Venice.
The Turk with a most mighty preparation makes for Cyprus. Othello, the fortitude of the place is best known to you; and though we have there a substitute of most allow'd sufficiency, yet opinion, a sovereign mistress of effects, throws a more safer voice on you. You must therefore be content to slubber the gloss of your new fortunes with this more stubborn and boist'rous expedition.

Othello.
The tyrant custom, most grave senators,
Hath made the flinty and steel couch of war
My thrice-driven bed of down. I do agnize
A natural and prompt alacrity
I find in hardness; and do undertake
This present wars against the Ottomites.
Most humbly therefore bending to your state,
I crave fit disposition for my wife,
Due reference of place and exhibition,
With such accommodation and besort
As levels with her breeding.

Duke of Venice.
                If you please,
Be't at her father's.

Brabantio.
                I will not have it so.

Othello.
Nor I.

Desdemona.
                Nor I; I would not there reside,
To put my father in impatient thoughts
By being in his eye. Most gracious Duke,
To my unfolding lend your prosperous ear,
And let me find a charter in your voice
T' assist my simpleness.

Duke of Venice.
What would you, Desdemona?

Desdemona.
That I did love the Moor to live with him,
My downright violence, and storm of fortunes,
May trumpet to the world. My heart's subdu'd
Even to the very quality of my lord.
I saw Othello's visage in his mind,
And to his honors and his valiant parts
Did I my soul and fortunes consecrate.
So that, dear lords, if I be left behind,
A moth of peace, and he go to the war,
The rites for why I love him are bereft me,
And I a heavy interim shall support
By his dear absence. Let me go with him.

Othello.
Let her have your voice.
Vouch with me, heaven, I therefore beg it not
To please the palate of my appetite,
Nor to comply with heat (the young affects

In me defunct) and proper satisfaction;
But to be free and bounteous to her mind.
And heaven defend your good souls, that you think
I will your serious and great business scant
For she is with me. No, when light-wing'd toys
Of feather'd Cupid seel with wanton dullness
My speculative and offic'd instruments,
That my disports corrupt and taint my business,
Let housewives make a skillet of my helm,
And all indign and base adversities
Make head against my estimation!

Duke of Venice.
Be it as you shall privately determine,
Either for her stay or going; th' affair cries haste,
And speed must answer it.

First Senator. You must away tonight.

Desdemona.
Tonight, my lord?

Duke of Venice. This night.

Othello. With all my heart.

Duke of Venice.
At nine i' th' morning here we'll meet again.
Othello, leave some officer behind,
And he shall our commission bring to you;
And such things else of quality and respect
As doth import you.

Othello. So please your Grace, my ancient;
A man he is of honesty and trust.
To his conveyance I assign my wife,
With what else needful your good Grace shall think
To be sent after me.

Duke of Venice. Let it be so.
Good night to every one.

To Brabantio.

And, noble signior,
If virtue no delighted beauty lack,
Your son-in-law is far more fair than black.

First Senator.
Adieu, brave Moor, use Desdemona well.

Brabantio.
Look to her, Moor, if thou hast eyes to see;
She has deceiv'd her father, and may thee.

Exeunt Duke, Senators, Officers, etc.

Othello.
My life upon her faith! Honest Iago,
My Desdemona must I leave to thee.
I prithee let thy wife attend on her,
And bring them after in the best advantage.
Come, Desdemona, I have but an hour
Of love, of wordly matter and direction,
To spend with thee. We must obey the time.

Exit with Desdemona.

Roderigo.
Iago—

Iago.
What say'st thou, noble heart?

Roderigo.
What will I do, think'st thou?

Iago.
Why, go to bed and sleep.

Roderigo.
I will incontinently drown myself.

Iago.
If thou dost, I shall never love thee after. Why, thou silly gentleman?

Roderigo.
It is silliness to live, when to live is torment; and then have we a prescription to die, when death is our physician.

Iago.
O villainous! I have look'd upon the world for four times seven years, and since I could distinguish betwixt a benefit and an injury, I never found man that knew how to love himself. Ere I would say I would drown myself for the love of a guinea hen, I would change my humanity with a baboon.

Roderigo.
What should I do? I confess it is my shame to be so fond, but it is not in my virtue to amend it.

Iago.
Virtue? A fig! 'Tis in ourselves that we are thus or thus. Our bodies are our gardens, to the which our wills are gardeners; so that if we will plant nettles or sow lettuce, set hyssop and weed up tine, supply it with one gender of herbs or distract it with many, either to have it sterile with idleness or manur'd with industry—why, the power and corrigible authority of this lies in our wills. If the beam of our lives had not one scale of reason to poise another of sensuality, the blood and baseness of our natures would conduct us to most prepost'rous conclusions. But we have reason to cool our raging motions, our carnal stings, our unbitted lusts; whereof I take this that you call love to be a sect or scion.

Roderigo.
It cannot be.

Iago.
It is merely a lust of the blood and a permission of the will. Come, be a man! Drown thyself? Drown cats and blind puppies! I have profess'd me thy friend, and I confess me knit to thy deserving with cables of perdurable toughness. I could never better stead thee than now. Put money in thy purse; follow thou the wars; defeat thy favor with an usurp'd beard. I say put money in thy purse. It cannot be long that Desdemona should continue her love to the Moor—put money in thy purse—nor he his to her. It was a violent commencement in her, and thou shalt see an answerable sequestration—put but money in thy purse. These Moors are changeable in their wills—fill thy purse with money. The food that to him now is as luscious as locusts, shall be to him shortly as acerb as the coloquintida. She must change for youth; when she is sated with his body, she will find the error of her choice. She must have change, she must; therefore put money in thy purse. If thou wilt needs damn thyself, do it a more delicate way than drowning. Make all the money thou canst. If sanctimony and a frail vow betwixt an erring barbarian and a super-subtle Venetian be not too hard for my wits and all the tribe of hell, thou shalt enjoy her; therefore make money. A pox of drowning thyself, it is clean out of the way. Seek thou rather to be hang'd in compassing thy joy than to be drown'd and go without her.

Roderigo.
Wilt thou be fast to my hopes, if I depend on the issue?

Iago.
Thou art sure of me—go make money. I have told thee often, and I retell thee again and again, I hate the Moor. My cause is hearted; thine hath no less reason. Let us be conjunctive in our revenge against him. If thou canst cuckold him, thou dost thyself a pleasure, me a sport. There are many events in the womb of time which will be deliver'd. Traverse, go, provide thy money. We will have more of this tomorrow. Adieu.

Roderigo.
Where shall we meet i' th' morning?

Iago.
At my lodging.

Roderigo.
I'll be with thee betimes.

Iago.
Go to, farewell. Do you hear, Roderigo?

Roderigo.
What say you?

Iago.
No more of drowning, do you hear?

Roderigo.
I am chang'd.

Iago.
Go to, farewell. Put money enough in your purse.

Roderigo.
I'll sell all my land.

Exit.

Iago.
Thus do I ever make my fool my purse;
For I mine own gain'd knowledge should profane
If I would time expend with such a snipe
But for my sport and profit. I hate the Moor,
And it is thought abroad that 'twixt my sheets
H'as done my office. I know not if't be true,
But I, for mere suspicion in that kind,
Will do as if for surety. He holds me well,
The better shall my purpose work on him.
Cassio's a proper man. Let me see now:
To get his place and to plume up my will

In double knavery—How? How?—Let's see—
After some time, to abuse Othello's ear
That he is too familiar with his wife.
He hath a person and a smooth dispose
To be suspected—fram'd to make women false.
The Moor is of a free and open nature,
That thinks men honest that but seem to be so,
And will as tenderly be led by th' nose
As asses are.
I have't. It is engend'red. Hell and night
Must bring this monstrous birth to the world's light.

Exit.

Act 2

Scene 1

A sea port in Cyprus.

(Montano; First Gentleman; SecondGentleman; Third Gentleman; Cassio; Second Messenger; Desdemona; Iago; Roderigo; Emilia; Attendants; Othello)

A storm rages at sea and the governor of Cyprus, Montano, cannot see which ships are being wrecked and which are not. News arrives that the Turkish fleet has been destroyed. Cassio arrives to inform the Cypriots that Othello is approaching, so long as he has not been lost in the storm. The next ship to arrive bears Iago and his wife Emilia, who is attending on Desdemona. Desdemona is worried about Othello, and passes the time by asking Iago to give his opinion on women. Finally, Othello safely arrives. He greets everyone, and gives his instructions. Iago is left to unload the ship, but before he goes on his errand he convinces Roderigo that Desdemona is in love with the smooth, courtly Cassio. Roderigo finds this hard to believe, but Iago is insistent, and urges Roderigo to find a way to quarrel with Cassio that night, so that the latter's lack of discipline will cause him to be dismissed, leaving Iago in his place. Roderigo agrees to the scheme. Iago's plan is still incomplete, but he is slowly working it out, as he thinks on how he may begin to mislead Othello. He reveals that he is afraid that Cassio may have cuckolded him as well, and his aim to get into Desdemona's bed in revenge on Othello.

Enter Montano and two Gentlemen.

Montano.
What from the cape can you discern at sea?

First Gentleman.
Nothing at all, it is a high-wrought flood.
I cannot, 'twixt the heaven and the main,
Descry a sail.

Montano.
Methinks the wind hath spoke aloud at land,
A fuller blast ne'er shook our battlements.
If it hath ruffian'd so upon the sea,
What ribs of oak, when mountains melt on them,
Can hold the mortise? What shall we hear of this?

Second Gentleman.
A segregation of the Turkish fleet:
For do but stand upon the foaming shore,
The chidden billow seems to pelt the clouds,
The wind-shak'd surge, with high and monstrous mane,
Seems to cast water on the burning Bear,
And quench the guards of th' ever-fixed Pole;
I never did like molestation view
On the enchafed flood.

Montano.
                    If that the Turkish fleet
Be not enshelter'd and embay'd, they are drown'd;
It is impossible to bear it out.

Enter a Third Gentleman.

Third Gentleman.
News, lads! Our wars are done.
The desperate tempest hath so bang'd the Turks,
That their designment halts. A noble ship of Venice
Hath seen a grievous wrack and sufferance
On most part of their fleet.

Montano.
How? Is this true?

Third Gentleman.
                    The ship is here put in,
A Veronesa; Michael Cassio,
Lieutenant to the warlike Moor Othello,
Is come on shore; the Moor himself at sea,
And is in full commission here for Cyprus.

Montano.
I am glad on't; 'tis a worthy governor.

Act 2, Scene 1

Third Gentleman.
But this same Cassio, though he speak of comfort
Touching the Turkish loss, yet he looks sadly,
And prays the Moor be safe; for they were parted
With foul and violent tempest.

Montano.
                        Pray heaven he be;
For I have serv'd him, and the man commands
Like a full soldier. Let's to the sea-side, ho!
As well to see the vessel that's come in
As to throw out our eyes for brave Othello,
Even till we make the main and th' aerial blue
An indistinct regard.

Third Gentleman.
                        Come, let's do so;
For every minute is expectancy
Of more arrivance.

Enter Cassio.

Cassio.
Thanks you, the valiant of this warlike isle,
That so approve the Moor! O, let the heavens
Give him defense against the elements,
For I have lost him on a dangerous sea.

Montano.
Is he well shipp'd?

Cassio.
His bark is stoutly timber'd, and his pilot
Of very expert and approv'd allowance;
Therefore my hopes (not surfeited to death)
Stand in bold cure.

Within,
            "A sail, a sail, a sail!"

Enter the Second Messenger.

Cassio.
What noise?

Second Messenger.
The town is empty; on the brow o' th' sea
Stand ranks of people, and they cry, "A sail!"

Cassio.
My hopes do shape him for the governor.

A shot.

Second Gentleman.
They do discharge their shot of courtesy;
Our friends at least.

Cassio.
                        I pray you, sir, go forth,
And give us truth who 'tis that is arriv'd.

Second Gentleman.
I shall.

Exit.

Montano.
But, good lieutenant, is your general wiv'd?

Cassio.
Most fortunately: he hath achiev'd a maid
That paragons description and wild fame;
One that excels the quirks of blazoning pens,
And in th' essential vesture of creation
Does tire the ingener.

Enter Second Gentleman.

            How now? Who has put in?

Second Gentleman.
'Tis one Iago, ancient to the general.

Cassio.
H'as had most favorable and happy speed:
Tempests themselves, high seas, and howling winds,
The gutter'd rocks and congregated sands,
Traitors ensteep'd to enclog the guiltless keel,
As having sense of beauty, do omit
Their mortal natures, letting go safely by
The divine Desdemona.

Montano.
                        What is she?

Cassio.
She that I spake of, our great captain's captain,
Left in the conduct of the bold Iago,
Whose footing here anticipates our thoughts
A se'nnight's speed. Great Jove, Othello guard,
And swell his sail with thine own pow'rful breath,
That he may bless this bay with his tall ship,
Make love's quick pants in Desdemona's arms,
Give renew'd fire to our extincted spirits,
And bring all Cyprus comfort!

Enter Desdemona, Iago, Roderigo, and Emilia, with Attendants.

                     O, behold,
The riches of the ship is come on shore!
You men of Cyprus, let her have your knees.
Hail to thee, lady! And the grace of heaven,
Before, behind thee, and on every hand,
Enwheel thee round!

Desdemona.
                I thank you, valiant Cassio.
What tidings can you tell me of my lord?

Cassio.
He is not yet arriv'd, nor know I aught
But that he's well and will be shortly here.

Desdemona.
O, but I fear—How lost you company?

Cassio.
The great contention of the sea and skies
Parted our fellowship.

Within,
              "A sail, a sail!"

A shot.
              But hark! A sail.

Second Gentleman.
They give their greeting to the citadel.
This likewise is a friend.

Cassio.
              See for the news.

Exit Second Gentleman.

Good ancient, you are welcome.

To Emilia.
              Welcome, mistress.
Let it not gall your patience, good Iago,
That I extend my manners; 'tis my breeding
That gives me this bold show of courtesy.

Kissing her.

Iago.
Sir, would she give you so much of her lips
As of her tongue she oft bestows on me,
You would have enough.

Desdemona.
              Alas! She has no speech.

Iago.
In faith, too much;
I find it still, when I have list to sleep.
Marry, before your ladyship, I grant,
She puts her tongue a little in her heart,
And chides with thinking.

Emilia.
You have little cause to say so.

Iago.
Come on, come on; you are pictures out a' doors,
Bells in your parlors, wild-cats in your kitchens,
Saints in your injuries, devils being offended,
Players in your huswifery, and huswives in your beds.

Desdemona.
O, fie upon thee, slanderer!

Iago.
Nay, it is true, or else I am a Turk:
You rise to play, and go to bed to work.

Emilia.
You shall not write my praise.

Iago.
              No, let me not.

Desdemona.
What wouldst write of me, if thou shouldst praise me?

Iago.
O gentle lady, do not put me to't,
For I am nothing if not critical.

Desdemona.
Come on, assay.—There's one gone to the harbor?

Iago.
Ay, madam.

Desdemona.
I am not merry; but I do beguile
The thing I am by seeming otherwise.—
Come, how wouldst thou praise me?

Iago.
I am about it, but indeed my invention
Comes from my pate as birdlime does from frieze,
It plucks out brains and all. But my Muse labors,

And thus she is deliver'd:
If she be fair and wise, fairness and wit,
The one's for use, the other useth it.

Desdemona.
Well prais'd! How if she be black and witty?

Iago.
If she be black, and thereto have a wit,
She'll find a white that shall her blackness hit.

Desdemona.
Worse and worse.

Emilia.
How if fair and foolish?

Iago.
She never yet was foolish that was fair,
For even her folly help'd her to an heir.

Desdemona.
These are old fond paradoxes to make fools laugh i' th' alehouse. What miserable praise hast thou for her that's foul and foolish?

Iago.
There's none so foul and foolish thereunto,
But does foul pranks which fair and wise ones do.

Desdemona.
O heavy ignorance! Thou praisest the worst best. But what praise couldst thou bestow on a deserving woman indeed—one that in the authority of her merit, did justly put on the vouch of very malice itself?

Iago.
She that was ever fair, and never proud,
Had tongue at will, and yet was never loud,
Never lack'd gold, and yet went never gay,
Fled from her wish, and yet said, "Now I may";
She that being ang'red, her revenge being nigh,
Bade her wrong stay, and her displeasure fly;
She that in wisdom never was so frail
To change the cod's head for the salmon's tail;
She that could think, and nev'r disclose her mind,
See suitors following, and not look behind:
She was a wight (if ever such wight were)—

Desdemona.
To do what?

Iago.
To suckle fools and chronicle small beer.

Desdemona.
O most lame and impotent conclusion! Do not learn of him, Emilia, though he be thy husband. How say you, Cassio? Is he not a most profane and liberal counsellor?

Cassio.
He speaks home, madam. You may relish him more in the soldier than in the scholar.

Iago.

Aside.

He takes her by the palm; ay, well said, whisper. With as little a web as this will I ensnare as great a fly as Cassio. Ay, smile upon her, do; I will gyve thee in thine own courtship. You say true, 'tis so indeed. If such tricks as these strip you out of your lieutenantry, it had been better you had not kiss'd your three fingers so oft, which now again you are most apt to play the sir in. Very good; well kiss'd! An excellent courtesy! 'Tis so indeed. Yet again, your fingers to your lips? Would they were clyster-pipes for your sake!

Trumpets within.

—The Moor! I know his trumpet.

Cassio.
'Tis truly so.

Desdemona.
Let's meet him and receive him.

Cassio.
Lo, where he comes!

Enter Othello and Attendants.

Othello.
O my fair warrior!

Desdemona.
          My dear Othello!

Othello.
It gives me wonder great as my content
To see you here before me. O my soul's joy!
If after every tempest come such calms,
May the winds blow till they have waken'd death!
And let the laboring bark climb hills of seas

Olympus-high, and duck again as low
As hell's from heaven! If it were now to die,
'Twere now to be most happy; for I fear
My soul hath her content so absolute
That not another comfort like to this
Succeeds in unknown fate.

Desdemona.
                The heavens forbid
But that our loves and comforts should increase
Even as our days do grow!

Othello.
                Amen to that, sweet powers!
I cannot speak enough of this content,
It stops me here; it is too much of joy.
And this, and this, the greatest discords be

They kiss.

That e'er our hearts shall make!

Iago.

Aside.
                O, you are well tun'd now!
But I'll set down the pegs that make this music,
As honest as I am.

Othello.
                Come; let us to the castle.
News, friends: our wars are done; the Turks are drown'd.
How does my old acquaintance of this isle?
Honey, you shall be well desir'd in Cyprus,
I have found great love amongst them. O my sweet,
I prattle out of fashion, and I dote
In mine own comforts. I prithee, good Iago,
Go to the bay and disembark my coffers.
Bring thou the master to the citadel;
He is a good one, and his worthiness
Does challenge much respect. Come, Desdemona,
Once more, well met at Cyprus.

Exeunt Othello and Desdemona with all but Iago and Roderigo.

Iago.

To an Attendant, as he is going out.

Do thou meet me presently at the harbor.—Come hither. If thou be'st valiant (as they say base men being in love have then a nobility in their natures more than is native to them), list me. The lieutenant tonight watches on the court of guard. First, I must tell thee this: Desdemona is directly in love with him.

Roderigo.
With him? Why, 'tis not possible.

Iago.
Lay thy finger thus; and let thy soul be instructed. Mark me with what violence she first lov'd the Moor, but for bragging and telling her fantastical lies. To love him still for prating—let not thy discreet heart think it. Her eye must be fed; and what delight shall she have to look on the devil? When the blood is made dull with the act of sport, there should be, again to inflame it and to give satiety a fresh appetite, loveliness in favor, sympathy in years, manners, and beauties—all which the Moor is defective in. Now for want of these requir'd conveniences, her delicate tenderness will find itself abus'd, begin to heave the gorge, disrelish and abhor the Moor; very nature will instruct her in it and compel her to some second choice. Now, sir, this granted (as it is a most pregnant and unforc'd position), who stands so eminent in the degree of this fortune as Cassio does? A knave very voluble; no further conscionable than in putting on the mere form of civil and humane seeming, for the better compass of his salt and most hidden loose affection? Why, none, why, none—a slipper and subtle knave, a finder-out of occasion; that has an eye can stamp and counterfeit advantages, though true advantage never present itself; a devilish knave. Besides, the knave is handsome, young, and hath all those requisites in him that folly and green minds look after; a pestilent complete knave, and the woman hath found him already.

Roderigo.
I cannot believe that in her, she's full of most bless'd condition.

Iago.
Bless'd fig's-end! The wine she drinks is made of grapes. If she had been bless'd, she would never have lov'd the Moor. Bless'd pudding! Didst thou not see her paddle with the palm of his hand? Didst not mark that?

Roderigo.
Yes, that I did; but that was but courtesy.

Iago.
Lechery, by this hand; an index and obscure prologue to the history of lust and foul thoughts. They met so near with their lips that their breaths embrac'd together. Villainous thoughts, Roderigo! When these mutualities so marshal the way, hard at hand comes the master and main exercise, th' incorporate conclusion. Pish! But, sir, be you rul'd by me. I have brought you from Venice. Watch you tonight; for the command, I'll lay't upon you. Cassio knows you not. I'll not be far from you. Do you find some occasion to anger Cassio, either by speaking too loud, or tainting his discipline, or from what other course you please, which the time shall more favorably minister.

Roderigo.
Well.

Iago.
Sir, he's rash and very sudden in choler, and happily may strike at you—provoke him that he may; for even out of that will I cause these of Cyprus to mutiny, whose qualification shall come into no true taste again but by the displanting of Cassio. So shall you have a shorter journey to your desires by the means I shall then have to prefer them; and the impediment most profitably remov'd, without the which there were no expectation of our prosperity.

Roderigo.
I will do this, if you can bring it to any opportunity.

Iago.
I warrant thee. Meet me by and by at the citadel. I must fetch his necessaries ashore. Farewell.

Roderigo.
Adieu.

Exit.

Iago.
That Cassio loves her, I do well believe't;
That she loves him, 'tis apt and of great credit.
The Moor (howbeit that I endure him not)
Is of a constant, loving, noble nature,
And I dare think he'll prove to Desdemona
A most dear husband. Now I do love her too,
Not out of absolute lust (though peradventure
I stand accomptant for as great a sin),
But partly led to diet my revenge,
For that I do suspect the lusty Moor
Hath leap'd into my seat; the thought whereof
Doth (like a poisonous mineral) gnaw my inwards;
And nothing can or shall content my soul
Till I am even'd with him, wife for wife;
Or failing so, yet that I put the Moor
At least into a jealousy so strong
That judgment cannot cure. Which thing to do,
If this poor trash of Venice, whom I trace
For his quick hunting, stand the putting on,
I'll have our Michael Cassio on the hip,
Abuse him to the Moor in the rank garb
(For I fear Cassio with my night-cap too),
Make the Moor thank me, love me, and reward me,
For making him egregiously an ass,
And practicing upon his peace and quiet
Even to madness. 'Tis here; but yet confus'd,
Knavery's plain face is never seen till us'd.

Exit.

Scene 2

Cyprus. A street.

(Herald)

A Herald reads out Othello's proclamation that in thanks for the victory over the Turks the night should be one of reveling. (1 line)

Enter Othello's Herald with a proclamation; people following.

Herald.
It is Othello's pleasure, our noble and valiant general, that upon certain tidings now arriv'd, importing the mere perdition of the Turkish fleet, every man put himself into triumph; some to dance, some to make bonfires, each man to what sport and revels his addiction leads him; for besides these beneficial news, it is the celebration of his nuptial. So much was his pleasure should be proclaim'd. All offices are open, and there is full liberty of feasting from this present hour of five till the bell have told eleven. Heaven bless the isle of Cyprus and our noble general Othello!

Exeunt.

Scene 3

Cyprus. A castle hall.

(Othello; Desdemona; Cassio; Attendants; Iago; Montano; Gentlemen; Servants; Roderigo)

Othello gives the command of the night watch to Cassio before retiring with Desdemona to consummate their marriage. Iago makes some bluff comments about Desdemona to Cassio, who replies in courtly terms, and insists that the lieutenant drink with him and some other friends. Cassio tries to beg off, pleading that he has no head for wine, but Iago convinces him. Cassio is soon blind drunk, though he insists that he is not. Iago insinuates that he gets this way very often to Montano, who is shocked that Othello should give him such a responsible position. Roderigo begins a quarrel with Cassio, and Iago manages to manipulate this into a general brawl, setting off the alarm bell. Montano and Cassio begin to duel, and Cassio gravely wounds the older man. Othello enters and angrily commands everyone to behave themselves, then asks Iago to explain what happened. Iago pretends he can't quite work out how the fight began, but subtly points to Cassio as the one at fault; Cassio can only mumble a request for pardon rather than explain anything. Seeing how badly Montano is wounded, Othello immediately strips Cassio of his rank of lieutenant, despite his friendship for the other man. Desdemona comes to see what the matter is; Othello quiets her and leads her home while putting Iago in charge of calming the town. As he slowly sobers up, Cassio bemoans the loss of his reputation, but Iago insists this is only a small setback and encourages him to ask Desdemona to intercede for him with Othello. Left alone, Iago congratulates himself for giving such genuinely good advice to Cassio, since he will turn it to his own advantage by convincing Othello that Desdemona is pleading for Cassio out of desire for him. Roderigo appears to complain that he is almost out of money, has been beaten up, and does not see anything going well for himself, but Iago reassures him, explaining that things take time and sending him off. Iago decides to have his wife plead to Desdemona on Cassio's behalf as well, and to make Othello see Cassio talking to Desdemona.

Enter Othello, Desdemona, Cassio, and Attendants.

Othello.
Good Michael, look you to the guard tonight.
Let's teach ourselves that honorable stop,
Not to outsport discretion.

Cassio.
Iago hath direction what to do;
But notwithstanding with my personal eye
Will I look to't.

Othello.
　　　　　　Iago is most honest.
Michael, good night. Tomorrow with your earliest
Let me have speech with you.

To Desdemona.

　　　　　　Come, my dear love,
The purchase made, the fruits are to ensue;
That profit's yet to come 'tween me and you.—
Good night.

Exit with Desdemona and Attendants.
Enter Iago.

Cassio.
Welcome, Iago; we must to the watch.

Iago.
Not this hour, lieutenant; 'tis not yet ten o' th' clock. Our general cast us thus early for the love of his Desdemona; who let us not therefore blame. He hath not yet made wanton the night with her; and she is sport for Jove.

Cassio.
She's a most exquisite lady.

Iago.
And I'll warrant her, full of game.

Cassio.
Indeed she's a most fresh and delicate creature.

Iago.
What an eye she has! Methinks it sounds a parley to provocation.

Cassio.
An inviting eye; and yet methinks right modest.

Iago.
And when she speaks, is it not an alarum to love?

Cassio.
She is indeed perfection.

Iago.
Well—happiness to their sheets! Come, lieutenant, I have a stoup of wine, and here without are a brace of Cyprus gallants that would fain have a measure to the health of black Othello.

Cassio.
Not tonight, good Iago, I have very poor and unhappy brains for drinking. I could well wish courtesy would invent some other custom of entertainment.

Iago.
O, they are our friends—but one cup, I'll drink for you.

Cassio.
I have drunk but one cup tonight—and that was craftily qualified too—and behold what innovation it makes here. I am infortunate in the infirmity, and dare not task my weakness with any more.

Iago.
What, man? 'Tis a night of revels, the gallants desire it.

Cassio.
Where are they?

Iago.
Here, at the door; I pray you call them in.

Cassio.
I'll do't, but it dislikes me.

Exit.

Iago.
If I can fasten but one cup upon him,
With that which he hath drunk tonight already,
He'll be as full of quarrel and offense
As my young mistress' dog. Now, my sick fool Roderigo,
Whom love hath turn'd almost the wrong side out,
To Desdemona hath tonight carous'd
Potations pottle-deep; and he's to watch.
Three else of Cyprus, noble swelling spirits
That hold their honors in a wary distance,
The very elements of this warlike isle,
Have I tonight fluster'd with flowing cups,
And they watch too. Now 'mongst this flock of drunkards
Am I to put our Cassio in some action
That may offend the isle. But here they come.

Enter Cassio, Montano, and Gentlemen; Servants follow with wine.

If consequence do but approve my dream,
My boat sails freely, both with wind and stream.

Cassio.
'Fore God, they have given me a rouse already.

Montano.
Good faith, a little one; not past a pint, as I am a soldier.

Iago.
Some wine ho!

Sings.

"And let me the canakin clink, clink;
And let me the canakin clink.
A soldier's a man;
O, man's life's but a span;
Why then let a soldier drink."
Some wine, boys!

Cassio.
'Fore God, an excellent song.

Iago.
I learn'd it in England, where indeed they are most potent in potting; your Dane, your German, and your swag-bellied Hollander—Drink ho!—are nothing to your English.

Cassio.
Is your Englishman so exquisite in his drinking?

Iago.
Why, he drinks you, with facility, your Dane dead drunk; he sweats not to overthrow your Almain; he gives your Hollander a vomit ere the next pottle can be fill'd.

Cassio.
To the health of our general!

Montano.
I am for it, lieutenant; and I'll do you justice.

Iago.
O sweet England!

Sings.

"King Stephen was and—a worthy peer,
His breeches cost him but a crown;
He held them sixpence all too dear,
With that he call'd the tailor lown;
He was a wight of high renown,
And thou art but of low degree.
'Tis pride that pulls the country down,

Then take thy auld cloak about thee."
Some wine ho!

Cassio.
'Fore God, this is a more exquisite song than the other.

Iago.
Will you hear't again?

Cassio.
No; for I hold him to be unworthy of his place that does those things. Well, God's above all; and there be souls must be sav'd, and there be souls must not be sav'd.

Iago.
It's true, good lieutenant.

Cassio.
For mine own part—no offense to the general, nor any man of quality—I hope to be sav'd.

Iago.
And so do I too, lieutenant.

Cassio.
Ay; but by your leave, not before me; the lieutenant is to be sav'd before the ancient. Let's have no more of this; let's to our affairs.—God forgive us our sins!—Gentlemen, let's look to our business. Do not think, gentlemen, I am drunk: this is my ancient, this is my right hand, and this is my left hand. I am not drunk now; I can stand well enough, and I speak well enough.

All.
Excellent well.

Cassio.
Why, very well then; you must not think then that I am drunk.

Exit.

Montano.
To th' platform, masters, come, let's set the watch.

The Gentlemen follow Cassio off.

Iago.
You see this fellow that is gone before:
He's a soldier fit to stand by Caesar
And give direction; and do but see his vice,
'Tis to his virtue a just equinox,
The one as long as th' other. 'Tis pity of him.
I fear the trust Othello puts him in,
On some odd time of his infirmity,
Will shake this island.

Montano.
                    But is he often thus?

Iago.
'Tis evermore the prologue to his sleep.
He'll watch the horologe a double set
If drink rock not his cradle.

Montano.
                    It were well
The general were put in mind of it.
Perhaps he sees it not, or his good nature
Prizes the virtue that appears in Cassio,
And looks not on his evils. Is not this true?

Enter Roderigo.

Iago.

Aside to him.

How now, Roderigo?
I pray you, after the lieutenant, go.

Exit Roderigo.

Montano.
And 'tis great pity that the noble Moor
Should hazard such a place as his own second
With one of an ingraft infirmity;
It were an honest action to say
So to the Moor.

Iago.
                    Not I, for this fair island.
I do love Cassio well; and would do much
To cure him of this evil.

Cry within:

"Help! Help!"
                    But hark, what noise?

Enter Cassio pursuing Roderigo.

Cassio.
'Zounds, you rogue! You rascal!

Act 2, Scene 3

Montano.
What's the matter, lieutenant?

Cassio.
A knave teach me my duty? I'll beat the knave into a twiggen bottle.

Roderigo.
Beat me?

Cassio.
Dost thou prate, rogue?

Striking Roderigo.

Montano.
Nay, good lieutenant; I pray you, sir, hold your hand.

Staying him.

Cassio.
Let me go, sir, or I'll knock you o'er the mazzard.

Montano.
Come, come—you're drunk.

Cassio.
Drunk?

They fight.

Iago.

Aside to Roderigo.

Away, I say; go out and cry a mutiny.

Exit Roderigo.

Nay, good lieutenant—God's will, gentlemen—
Help ho!—lieutenant—sir—Montano—sir—
Help, masters!—Here's a goodly watch indeed!

A bell rung.

Who's that which rings the bell? Diablo, ho!
The town will rise. God's will, lieutenant, hold!
You'll be asham'd forever.

Enter Othello and Gentlemen with weapons.

Othello.
What is the matter here?

Montano.
　　　　　　'Zounds, I bleed still,
I am hurt to th' death. He dies.

Assailing Cassio again.

Othello.
　　　　　　Hold, for your lives!

Iago.
Hold ho! Lieutenant—sir—Montano—gentlemen—
Have you forgot all place of sense and duty?
Hold! The general speaks to you; hold, for shame!

Othello.
Why, how now ho? From whence ariseth this?
Are we turn'd Turks, and to ourselves do that
Which heaven hath forbid the Ottomites?
For Christian shame, put by this barbarous brawl.
He that stirs next to carve for his own rage
Holds his soul light; he dies upon his motion.
Silence that dreadful bell, it frights the isle
From her propriety. What is the matter, masters?
Honest Iago, that looks dead with grieving,
Speak: who began this? On thy love, I charge thee!

Iago.
I do not know. Friends all, but now, even now;
In quarter, and in terms like bride and groom
Devesting them for bed; and then, but now
(As if some planet had unwitted men),
Swords out, and tilting one at other's breast,
In opposition bloody. I cannot speak
Any beginning to this peevish odds;
And would in action glorious I had lost
Those legs that brought me to a part of it.

Othello.
How comes it, Michael, you are thus forgot?

Cassio.
I pray you pardon me, I cannot speak.

Othello.
Worthy Montano, you were wont to be civil;
The gravity and stillness of your youth
The world hath noted, and your name is great
In mouths of wisest censure. What's the matter
That you unlace your reputation thus,
And spend your rich opinion for the name
Of a night-brawler? Give me answer to it.

Montano.
Worthy Othello, I am hurt to danger.
Your officer, Iago, can inform you—
While I spare speech, which something now offends me—
Of all that I do know, nor know I aught
By me that's said or done amiss this night,
Unless self-charity be sometimes a vice,
And to defend ourselves it be a sin
When violence assails us.

Othello.
                    Now by heaven,
My blood begins my safer guides to rule,
And passion, having my best judgment collied,
Assays to lead the way. 'Zounds, if I stir,
Or do but lift this arm, the best of you
Shall sink in my rebuke. Give me to know
How this foul rout began; who set it on;
And he that is approv'd in this offense,
Though he had twinn'd with me, both at a birth,
Shall lose me. What, in a town of war,
Yet wild, the people's hearts brimful of fear,
To manage private and domestic quarrel?
In night, and on the court and guard of safety?
'Tis monstrous. Iago, who began't?

Montano.
If partially affin'd, or leagu'd in office,
Thou dost deliver more or less than truth,
Thou art no soldier.

Iago.
                Touch me not so near;
I had rather have this tongue cut from my mouth
Than it should do offense to Michael Cassio;
Yet I persuade myself, to speak the truth
Shall nothing wrong him. Thus it is, general:
Montano and myself being in speech,
There comes a fellow crying out for help,
And Cassio following him with determin'd sword
To execute upon him. Sir, this gentleman
Steps in to Cassio and entreats his pause;
Myself the crying fellow did pursue,
Lest by his clamor (as it so fell out)
The town might fall in fright. He, swift of foot,
Outran my purpose; and I return'd the rather
For that I heard the clink and fall of swords,
And Cassio high in oath; which till tonight
I ne'er might say before. When I came back
(For this was brief), I found them close together
At blow and thrust, even as again they were
When you yourself did part them.
More of this matter cannot I report.
But men are men; the best sometimes forget.
Though Cassio did some little wrong to him,
As men in rage strike those that wish them best,
Yet surely Cassio, I believe, receiv'd
From him that fled some strange indignity
Which patience could not pass.

Othello.
                    I know, Iago,
Thy honesty and love doth mince this matter,
Making it light to Cassio. Cassio, I love thee,
But never more be officer of mine.

Enter Desdemona attended.

Look if my gentle love be not rais'd up!
I'll make thee an example.

Desdemona.
What is the matter, dear?

Othello.
                All's well now, sweeting;
Come away to bed.

To Montano.
                Sir, for your hurts,
Myself will be your surgeon.—Lead him off.

Some lead Montano off.

Iago, look with care about the town,
And silence those whom this vild brawl distracted.
Come, Desdemona, 'tis the soldiers' life
To have their balmy slumbers wak'd with strife.

Exit with Desdemona, Gentlemen, and Attendants.

Iago.
What, are you hurt, lieutenant?

Cassio.
Ay, past all surgery.

Iago.
Marry, God forbid!

Cassio.
Reputation, reputation, reputation! O, I have lost my reputation! I have lost the immortal part of myself,

and what remains is bestial. My reputation, Iago, my reputation!

Iago.
As I am an honest man, I had thought you had receiv'd some bodily wound; there is more sense in that than in reputation. Reputation is an idle and most false imposition; oft got without merit, and lost without deserving. You have lost no reputation at all, unless you repute yourself such a loser. What, man, there are more ways to recover the general again. You are but now cast in his mood, a punishment more in policy than in malice, even so as one would beat his offenseless dog to affright an imperious lion. Sue to him again, and he's yours.

Cassio.
I will rather sue to be despis'd than to deceive so good a commander with so slight, so drunken, and so indiscreet an officer. Drunk? And speak parrot? And squabble? Swagger? Swear? And discourse fustian with one's own shadow? O thou invisible spirit of wine, if thou hast no name to be known by, let us call thee devil!

Iago.
What was he that you follow'd with your sword? What had he done to you?

Cassio.
I know not.

Iago.
Is't possible?

Cassio.
I remember a mass of things, but nothing distinctly; a quarrel, but nothing wherefore. O God, that men should put an enemy in their mouths to steal away their brains! That we should, with joy, pleasance, revel, and applause, transform ourselves into beasts!

Iago.
Why, but you are now well enough. How came you thus recover'd?

Cassio.
It hath pleas'd the devil drunkenness to give place to the devil wrath: one unperfectness shows me another, to make me frankly despise myself.

Iago.
Come, you are too severe a moraler. As the time, the place, and the condition of this country stands, I could heartily wish this had not befall'n; but since it is as it is, mend it for your own good.

Cassio.
I will ask him for my place again, he shall tell me I am a drunkard! Had I as many mouths as Hydra, such an answer would stop them all. To be now a sensible man, by and by a fool, and presently a beast! O strange! Every inordinate cup is unbless'd, and the ingredient is a devil.

Iago.
Come, come; good wine is a good familiar creature, if it be well us'd; exclaim no more against it. And, good lieutenant, I think you think I love you.

Cassio.
I have well approv'd it, sir. I drunk!

Iago.
You, or any man living, may be drunk at a time, man. I'll tell you what you shall do. Our general's wife is now the general—I may say so in this respect, for that he hath devoted and given up himself to the contemplation, mark, and denotement of her parts and graces. Confess yourself freely to her; importune her help to put you in your place again. She is of so free, so kind, so apt, so bless'd a disposition, she holds it a vice in her goodness not to do more than she is requested. This broken joint between you and her husband entreat her to splinter; and my fortunes against any lay worth naming, this crack of your love shall grow stronger than it was before.

Cassio.
You advise me well.

Iago.
I protest, in the sincerity of love and honest kindness.

Cassio.
I think it freely; and betimes in the morning I will beseech the virtuous Desdemona to undertake for me. I am desperate of my fortunes if they check me here.

Iago.
You are in the right. Good night, lieutenant, I must to the watch.

Cassio.
Good night, honest Iago.

Exit Cassio.

Iago.
And what's he then that says I play the villain,
When this advice is free I give, and honest,
Probal to thinking, and indeed the course
To win the Moor again? For 'tis most easy
Th' inclining Desdemona to subdue
In any honest suit; she's fram'd as fruitful
As the free elements. And then for her
To win the Moor, were't to renounce his baptism,
All seals and symbols of redeemed sin,
His soul is so enfetter'd to her love,
That she may make, unmake, do what she list,
Even as her appetite shall play the god
With his weak function. How am I then a villain,
To counsel Cassio to this parallel course,
Directly to his good? Divinity of hell!
When devils will the blackest sins put on,
They do suggest at first with heavenly shows,
As I do now; for whiles this honest fool
Plies Desdemona to repair his fortune,
And she for him pleads strongly to the Moor,
I'll pour this pestilence into his ear—
That she repeals him for her body's lust,
And by how much she strives to do him good,
She shall undo her credit with the Moor.
So will I turn her virtue into pitch,
And out of her own goodness make the net
That shall enmesh them all.

Enter Roderigo.

How now, Roderigo?

Roderigo.
I do follow here in the chase, not like a hound that hunts, but one that fills up the cry. My money is almost spent; I have been tonight exceedingly well cudgell'd; and I think the issue will be, I shall have so much experience for my pains; and so, with no money at all and a little more wit, return again to Venice.

Iago.
How poor are they that have not patience!
What wound did ever heal but by degrees?
Thou know'st we work by wit, and not by witchcraft,
And wit depends on dilatory time.
Does't not go well? Cassio hath beaten thee,
And thou by that small hurt hast cashier'd Cassio.
Though other things grow fair against the sun,
Yet fruits that blossom first will first be ripe.
Content thyself a while. By the mass, 'tis morning;
Pleasure and action make the hours seem short.
Retire thee, go where thou art billeted.
Away, I say, thou shalt know more hereafter.
Nay, get thee gone.

Exit Roderigo.

Two things are to be done:
My wife must move for Cassio to her mistress—
I'll set her on—
Myself a while to draw the Moor apart,
And bring him jump when he may Cassio find
Soliciting his wife. Ay, that's the way;
Dull not device by coldness and delay.

Exit.

Act 3

Scene 1

Cyprus. Before the castle.

(Cassio; 1. MUS.; Musicians; Clown; Iago; Emilia)

Cassio pays some musicians to serenade Othello, but a Clown arrives to tell them that the general is in no mood for music, and pays them to stop. Cassio asks him to fetch Emilia. Iago, passing by, says he will send Emilia in himself, and promises to occupy Othello so that Cassio can speak to Desdemona uninterrupted. Emilia comes in to tell Cassio that Desdemona has already spoken for him, but that Othello is arguing that it would harm his reputation to restore Cassio. Nevertheless, she agrees to get him some time with Desdemona.

Enter Cassio with Musicians.

Cassio.
Masters, play here, I will content your pains;
Something that's brief; and bid "Good morrow, general."

They play, and enter the Clown.

Clown.
Why, masters, have your instruments been in Naples, that they speak i' th' nose thus?

First Musician.
How, sir? How?

Clown.
Are these, I pray you, wind instruments?

First Musician.
Ay, marry, are they, sir.

Clown.
O, thereby hangs a tail.

First Musician.
Whereby hangs a tale, sir?

Clown.
Marry, sir, by many a wind instrument that I know. But, masters, here's money for you; and the general so likes your music, that he desires you for love's sake to make no more noise with it.

First Musician.
Well, sir, we will not.

Clown.
If you have any music that may not be heard, to't again; but (as they say) to hear music the general does not greatly care.

First Musician.
We have none such, sir.

Clown.
Then put up your pipes in your bag, for I'll away. Go, vanish into air, away!

Exeunt Musicians.

Cassio.
Dost thou hear, mine honest friend?

Clown.
No, I hear not your honest friend; I hear you.

Cassio.
Prithee keep up thy quillets. There's a poor piece of gold for thee. If the gentlewoman that attends the general's wife be stirring, tell her there's one Cassio entreats her a little favor of speech. Wilt thou do this?

Clown.
She is stirring, sir. If she will stir hither, I shall seem to notify unto her.

Cassio.
Do, good my friend.

Exit Clown.
Enter Iago.

                In happy time, Iago.

Iago.
You have not been a-bed then?

Cassio.
Why, no; the day had broke
Before we parted. I have made bold, Iago,
To send in to your wife. My suit to her
Is that she will to virtuous Desdemona
Procure me some access.

Iago.
        I'll send her to you presently;
And I'll devise a mean to draw the Moor
Out of the way, that your converse and business
May be more free.

Cassio.
I humbly thank you for't.

Exit Iago.

I never knew a Florentine more kind and honest.

Enter Emilia.

Emilia.
Good morrow, good lieutenant. I am sorry
For your displeasure; but all will sure be well.
The general and his wife are talking of it,
And she speaks for you stoutly. The Moor replies
That he you hurt is of great fame in Cyprus,
And great affinity; and that in wholesome wisdom
He might not but refuse you. But he protests he loves you,
And needs no other suitor but his likings
To take the safest occasion by the front
To bring you in again.

Cassio.
        Yet I beseech you,
If you think fit, or that it may be done,
Give me advantage of some brief discourse
With Desdemon alone.

Emilia.
                              Pray you come in.
I will bestow you where you shall have time
To speak your bosom freely.

Cassio.
                            I am much bound to you.

Exeunt.

Scene 2

Cyprus. A room in the castle.

(Othello; Iago; Gentlemen)

Othello gives Iago letters to send off to Venice and leaves to examine the forts of Cyprus.

Enter Othello, Iago, and Gentlemen.

Othello.
These letters give, Iago, to the pilot,
And by him do my duties to the Senate.
That done, I will be walking on the works;
Repair there to me.

Iago.
                       Well, my good lord, I'll do't.

Othello.
This fortification, gentlemen, shall we see't?

All Gentlemen.
We'll wait upon your lordship.

Exeunt.

Scene 3

Cyprus. The garden of the castle.

(Desdemona; Cassio; Emilia; Othello; Iago)

Desdemona assures Cassio she will do all she can for him. Cassio leaves when he sees Othello and Iago approach, as he is too embarrassed to stay and hear Desdemona argue for him. Seeing Cassio leave, Iago mutters that he does not like this, but refuses to explain what he means to Othello; he insists that it cannot have been Cassio near Desdemona, since Cassio has no reason to look so guilty. Desdemona comes and pesters Othello about Cassio, and the general finally promises to see Cassio when she pleases after she insists she'll give him no peace until he does so. She leaves after this fervent pleading and Iago makes the most of the opportunity. Appearing to be reticent, he slowly expresses his worries that Cassio and Desdemona may be too familiar with each other. Othello forces him to explain what he means, and though Iago repeats that this may only be his imagination, and warns the general against jealousy, he brings Othello to believe that Desdemona and Cassio may be having an affair. So sure is Othello of Iago's honesty that he credits his insinuations, though the sight of Desdemona leads him to doubt his own thoughts. Desdemona returns to find her husband in a very different temper from when she last saw him; when he complains of a pain on his forehead (his cuckold's horns), she offers to bind it with her handkerchief, but he dismisses it as too small. The handkerchief falls to the floor, and Emilia picks it up, happy to have found it, since Iago has often asked her to steal it for him. She gives it to Iago, though he refuses to tell her what he plans to do with it. To himself he plans to lose the handkerchief in Cassio's room, to become a physical proof to Othello. The general returns, distracted, unable to take his mind off his suspicions. Convincing himself, he bids farewell to his happiness, and rages at Iago, telling him to provide genuine proof of his allegations. Iago asks what sort of proof he can provide, pointing out that direct evidence would be hard to come by. He claims, however, that he recently heard Cassio speak in his sleep as if to Desdemona, and Othello takes this as proof. What's more, says Iago, he recently saw Cassio wipe his face with the handkerchief that was Othello's first gift to his wife. Othello swears to kill them both, and Iago vows to help him. Othello officially makes Iago his lieutenant.

Enter Desdemona, Cassio, and Emilia.

Desdemona.
Be thou assur'd, good Cassio, I will do
All my abilities in thy behalf.

Emilia.
Good madam, do. I warrant it grieves my husband
As if the cause were his.

Desdemona.
O, that's an honest fellow. Do not doubt, Cassio,
But I will have my lord and you again
As friendly as you were.

Cassio.
                      Bounteous madam,
What ever shall become of Michael Cassio,
He's never any thing but your true servant.

Desdemona.
I know't; I thank you. You do love my lord;
You have known him long, and be you well assur'd
He shall in strangeness stand no farther off
Than in a politic distance.

Cassio.
                    Ay, but, lady,
That policy may either last so long,
Or feed upon such nice and waterish diet,
Or breed itself so out of circumstances,
That I being absent and my place supplied,
My general will forget my love and service.

Desdemona.
Do not doubt that; before Emilia here,
I give thee warrant of thy place. Assure thee,
If I do vow a friendship, I'll perform it
To the last article. My lord shall never rest,
I'll watch him tame, and talk him out of patience;
His bed shall seem a school, his board a shrift,
I'll intermingle every thing he does
With Cassio's suit. Therefore be merry, Cassio,
For thy solicitor shall rather die
Than give thy cause away.

Enter Othello and Iago.

Emilia.
Madam, here comes my lord.

Cassio.
Madam, I'll take my leave.

Desdemona.
Why, stay, and hear me speak.

Cassio.
Madam, not now; I am very ill at ease,
Unfit for mine own purposes.

Desdemona.
Well, do your discretion.

Exit Cassio.

Iago.
Hah? I like not that.

Othello.
                    What dost thou say?

Iago.
Nothing, my lord; or if—I know not what.

Othello.
Was not that Cassio parted from my wife?

Iago.
Cassio, my lord? No, sure, I cannot think it,
That he would steal away so guilty-like,
Seeing your coming.

Othello.
                    I do believe 'twas he.

Desdemona.
How now, my lord?
I have been talking with a suitor here,
A man that languishes in your displeasure.

Othello.
Who is't you mean?

Desdemona.
Why, your lieutenant, Cassio. Good my lord,
If I have any grace or power to move you,
His present reconciliation take;
For if he be not one that truly loves you,
That errs in ignorance and not in cunning,
I have no judgment in an honest face.
I prithee call him back.

Othello.
                    Went he hence now?

Desdemona.
Yes, faith; so humbled
That he hath left part of his grief with me
To suffer with him. Good love, call him back.

Othello.
Not now, sweet Desdemon, some other time.

Desdemona.
But shall't be shortly?

Othello.
                    The sooner, sweet, for you.

Desdemona.
Shall't be tonight at supper?

Othello.
                    No, not tonight.

Desdemona.
Tomorrow dinner then?

Othello.
                    I shall not dine at home;
I meet the captains at the citadel.

Desdemona.
Why then tomorrow night, or Tuesday morn;
On Tuesday noon, or night; on We'n'sday morn.
I prithee name the time, but let it not
Exceed three days. In faith, he's penitent;
And yet his trespass, in our common reason
(Save that they say the wars must make example
Out of her best), is not almost a fault
T' incur a private check. When shall he come?
Tell me, Othello. I wonder in my soul
What you would ask me that I should deny,
Or stand so mamm'ring on. What? Michael Cassio,
That came a-wooing with you, and so many a time,
When I have spoke of you dispraisingly,
Hath ta'en your part—to have so much to do
To bring him in! By'r lady, I could do much—

Othello.
Prithee no more; let him come when he will;
I will deny thee nothing.

Desdemona.
                    Why, this is not a boon;
'Tis as I should entreat you wear your gloves,
Or feed on nourishing dishes, or keep you warm,
Or sue to you to do a peculiar profit
To your own person. Nay, when I have a suit
Wherein I mean to touch your love indeed,
It shall be full of poise and difficult weight,
And fearful to be granted.

Othello.
                    I will deny thee nothing;
Whereon, I do beseech thee, grant me this,
To leave me but a little to myself.

Desdemona.
Shall I deny you? No. Farewell, my lord.

Othello.
Farewell, my Desdemona, I'll come to thee straight.

Desdemona.
Emilia, come.—Be as your fancies teach you;
What e'er you be, I am obedient.

Exit with Emilia.

Othello.
Excellent wretch! Perdition catch my soul
But I do love thee! And when I love thee not,
Chaos is come again.

Iago.
My noble lord—

Othello.
                    What dost thou say, Iago?

Iago.
Did Michael Cassio, when you woo'd my lady,
Know of your love?

Othello.
He did, from first to last. Why dost thou ask?

Iago.
But for a satisfaction of my thought,
No further harm.

Othello.
                    Why of thy thought, Iago?

Iago.
I did not think he had been acquainted with her.

Othello.
O yes, and went between us very oft.

Iago.
Indeed!

Othello.
Indeed? Ay, indeed. Discern'st thou aught in that?
Is he not honest?

Iago.
                    Honest, my lord?

Othello.
Honest? Ay, honest.

Iago.
                    My lord, for aught I know.

Othello.
What dost thou think?

Iago.
                    Think, my lord?

Othello.
Think, my lord? By heaven, thou echo'st me,
As if there were some monster in thy thought
Too hideous to be shown. Thou dost mean something.
I heard thee say even now, thou lik'st not that,
When Cassio left my wife. What didst not like?
And when I told thee he was of my counsel
In my whole course of wooing, thou criedst, "Indeed!"
And didst contract and purse thy brow together,
As if thou then hadst shut up in thy brain
Some horrible conceit. If thou dost love me,
Show me thy thought.

Iago.
My lord, you know I love you.

Othello.
              I think thou dost;
And for I know thou'rt full of love and honesty,
And weigh'st thy words before thou giv'st them breath,
Therefore these stops of thine fright me the more;
For such things in a false disloyal knave
Are tricks of custom; but in a man that's just
They're close dilations, working from the heart,
That passion cannot rule.

Iago.
              For Michael Cassio,
I dare be sworn I think that he is honest.

Othello.
I think so too.

Iago.
              Men should be what they seem,
Or those that be not, would they might seem none!

Othello.
Certain, men should be what they seem.

Iago.
Why then I think Cassio's an honest man.

Othello.
Nay, yet there's more in this.
I prithee speak to me as to thy thinkings,
As thou dost ruminate, and give thy worst of thoughts
The worst of words.

Iago.
              Good my lord, pardon me:
Though I am bound to every act of duty,
I am not bound to that all slaves are free to.
Utter my thoughts? Why, say they are vild and false,
As where's that palace whereinto foul things
Sometimes intrude not? Who has that breast so pure
But some uncleanly apprehensions
Keep leets and law-days and in sessions sit
With meditations lawful?

Othello.
Thou dost conspire against thy friend, Iago,
If thou but think'st him wrong'd, and mak'st his ear
A stranger to thy thoughts.

Iago.
              I do beseech you,
Though I perchance am vicious in my guess
(As I confess it is my nature's plague
To spy into abuses, and oft my jealousy
Shapes faults that are not), that your wisdom then,
From one that so imperfectly conjects,
Would take no notice, nor build yourself a trouble
Out of his scattering and unsure observance.
It were not for your quiet nor your good,
Nor for my manhood, honesty, and wisdom,
To let you know my thoughts.

Othello.
'Zounds, what dost thou mean?

Iago.
Good name in man and woman, dear my lord,
Is the immediate jewel of their souls.
Who steals my purse steals trash; 'tis something, nothing;
'Twas mine, 'tis his, and has been slave to thousands;
But he that filches from me my good name
Robs me of that which not enriches him,
And makes me poor indeed.

Othello.
By heaven, I'll know thy thoughts.

Iago.
You cannot, if my heart were in your hand,
Nor shall not, whilst 'tis in my custody.

Othello.
Ha?

Iago.
                O, beware, my lord, of jealousy!
It is the green-ey'd monster which doth mock
The meat it feeds on. That cuckold lives in bliss
Who, certain of his fate, loves not his wronger;
But O, what damned minutes tells he o'er
Who dotes, yet doubts; suspects, yet strongly loves!

Othello.
O misery!

Iago.
Poor and content is rich, and rich enough,
But riches fineless is as poor as winter
To him that ever fears he shall be poor.
Good God, the souls of all my tribe defend
From jealousy!

Othello.
                Why? Why is this?
Think'st thou I'd make a life of jealousy?
To follow still the changes of the moon
With fresh suspicions? No! To be once in doubt
Is once to be resolv'd. Exchange me for a goat,
When I shall turn the business of my soul
To such exsufflicate and blown surmises,
Matching thy inference. 'Tis not to make me jealous
To say my wife is fair, feeds well, loves company,
Is free of speech, sings, plays, and dances well;
Where virtue is, these are more virtuous.
Nor from mine own weak merits will I draw
The smallest fear or doubt of her revolt,
For she had eyes, and chose me. No, Iago,
I'll see before I doubt; when I doubt, prove;
And on the proof, there is no more but this—
Away at once with love or jealousy!

Iago.
I am glad of this, for now I shall have reason
To show the love and duty that I bear you
With franker spirit; therefore (as I am bound)
Receive it from me. I speak not yet of proof.
Look to your wife, observe her well with Cassio,
Wear your eyes thus, not jealous nor secure.
I would not have your free and noble nature,
Out of self-bounty, be abus'd; look to't.
I know our country disposition well:
In Venice they do let God see the pranks
They dare not show their husbands; their best conscience
Is not to leave't undone, but keep't unknown.

Othello.
Dost thou say so?

Iago.
She did deceive her father, marrying you,
And when she seem'd to shake and fear your looks,
She lov'd them most.

Othello.
                And so she did.

Iago.
                Why, go to then.
She that so young could give out such a seeming
To seel her father's eyes up, close as oak,
He thought 'twas witchcraft—but I am much to blame;
I humbly do beseech you of your pardon
For too much loving you.

Othello.
                I am bound to thee forever.

Iago.
I see this hath a little dash'd your spirits.

Othello.
Not a jot, not a jot.

Iago.
                I' faith, I fear it has.
I hope you will consider what is spoke
Comes from my love. But I do see y' are mov'd.
I am to pray you not to strain my speech
To grosser issues nor to larger reach
Than to suspicion.

Othello.
I will not.

Iago.
                Should you do so, my lord,
My speech should fall into such vild success
Which my thoughts aim'd not. Cassio's my worthy friend—
My lord, I see y' are mov'd.

Othello.
                No, not much mov'd:
I do not think but Desdemona's honest.

Iago.
Long live she so! And long live you to think so!

Othello.
And yet how nature erring from itself—

Iago.
Ay, there's the point; as (to be bold with you)
Not to affect many proposed matches
Of her own clime, complexion, and degree,
Whereto we see in all things nature tends—
Foh, one may smell in such, a will most rank,
Foul disproportions, thoughts unnatural.
But (pardon me) I do not in position
Distinctly speak of her, though I may fear
Her will, recoiling to her better judgment,
May fall to match you with her country forms,
And happily repent.

Othello.
     Farewell, farewell!
If more thou dost perceive, let me know more;
Set on thy wife to observe. Leave me, Iago.

Iago.

Going.

My lord, I take my leave.

Othello.
Why did I marry? This honest creature, doubtless,
Sees and knows more, much more, than he unfolds.

Iago.

Returning.

My lord, I would I might entreat your honor
To scan this thing no farther; leave it to time.
Although 'tis fit that Cassio have his place—
For sure he fills it up with great ability—
Yet if you please to hold him off awhile,
You shall by that perceive him and his means.
Note if your lady strain his entertainment
With any strong or vehement importunity;
Much will be seen in that. In the mean time,
Let me be thought too busy in my fears
(As worthy cause I have to fear I am)
And hold her free, I do beseech your honor.

Othello.
Fear not my government.

Iago.
I once more take my leave.

Exit.

Othello.
This fellow's of exceeding honesty,
And knows all qualities, with a learned spirit,
Of human dealings. If I do prove her haggard,
Though that her jesses were my dear heart-strings,
I'd whistle her off, and let her down the wind
To prey at fortune. Haply, for I am black,
And have not those soft parts of conversation
That chamberers have, or for I am declin'd
Into the vale of years (yet that's not much),
She's gone. I am abus'd, and my relief
Must be to loathe her. O curse of marriage!
That we can call these delicate creatures ours,
And not their appetites! I had rather be a toad
And live upon the vapor of a dungeon
Than keep a corner in the thing I love
For others' uses. Yet 'tis the plague of great ones,
Prerogativ'd are they less than the base;
'Tis destiny unshunnable, like death.
Even then this forked plague is fated to us
When we do quicken. Look where she comes:

Enter Desdemona and Emilia.

If she be false, O then heaven mocks itself!
I'll not believe't.

Desdemona.
     How now, my dear Othello?
Your dinner, and the generous islanders
By you invited, do attend your presence.

Othello.
I am to blame.

Desdemona.
     Why do you speak so faintly?
Are you not well?

Othello.
I have a pain upon my forehead, here.

Desdemona.
Faith, that's with watching, 'twill away again.
Let me but bind it hard, within this hour
It will be well.

Othello.
                    Your napkin is too little;

He puts the handkerchief from him, and it drops.

Let it alone. Come, I'll go in with you.

Desdemona.
I am very sorry that you are not well.

Exit with Othello.

Emilia.
I am glad I have found this napkin;
This was her first remembrance from the Moor.
My wayward husband hath a hundred times
Woo'd me to steal it; but she so loves the token
(For he conjur'd her she should ever keep it)
That she reserves it evermore about her
To kiss and talk to. I'll have the work ta'en out,
And give't Iago. What he will do with it
Heaven knows, not I;
I nothing but to please his fantasy.

Enter Iago.

Iago.
How now? What do you here alone?

Emilia.
Do not you chide; I have a thing for you.

Iago.
You have a thing for me? It is a common thing—

Emilia.
Hah?

Iago.
To have a foolish wife.

Emilia.
O, is that all? What will you give me now
For that same handkerchief?

Iago.
                    What handkerchief?

Emilia.
What handkerchief?
Why, that the Moor first gave to Desdemona,
That which so often you did bid me steal.

Iago.
Hast stol'n it from her?

Emilia.
No, faith; she let it drop by negligence,
And to th' advantage, I, being here, took't up.
Look, here 'tis.

Iago.
                    A good wench, give it me.

Emilia.
What will you do with't, that you have been so earnest
To have me filch it?

Iago.

Snatching it.
                    Why, what is that to you?

Emilia.
If it be not for some purpose of import,
Give't me again. Poor lady, she'll run mad
When she shall lack it.

Iago.
Be not acknown on't; I have use for it.
Go, leave me.

Exit Emilia.

I will in Cassio's lodging lose this napkin,
And let him find it. Trifles light as air
Are to the jealous confirmations strong
As proofs of holy writ; this may do something.
The Moor already changes with my poison:
Dangerous conceits are in their natures poisons,
Which at the first are scarce found to distaste,
But with a little act upon the blood
Burn like the mines of sulphur.

Enter Othello.
                    I did say so.
Look where he comes! Not poppy, nor mandragora,
Nor all the drowsy syrups of the world
Shall ever medicine thee to that sweet sleep
Which thou ow'dst yesterday.

Othello.
                    Ha, ha, false to me?

Iago.
Why, how now, general? No more of that.

Othello.
Avaunt, be gone! Thou hast set me on the rack.
I swear 'tis better to be much abus'd
Than but to know't a little.

Iago.
                How now, my lord?

Othello.
What sense had I in her stol'n hours of lust?
I saw't not, thought it not; it harm'd not me.
I slept the next night well, fed well, was free and merry;
I found not Cassio's kisses on her lips.
He that is robb'd, not wanting what is stol'n,
Let him not know't, and he's not robb'd at all.

Iago.
I am sorry to hear this.

Othello.
I had been happy, if the general camp,
Pioners and all, had tasted her sweet body,
So I had nothing known. O now, forever
Farewell the tranquil mind! Farewell content!
Farewell the plumed troops and the big wars
That makes ambition virtue! O, farewell!
Farewell the neighing steed and the shrill trump,
The spirit-stirring drum, th' ear-piercing fife,
The royal banner, and all quality,
Pride, pomp, and circumstance of glorious war!
And O you mortal engines, whose rude throats
Th' immortal Jove's dread clamors counterfeit,
Farewell! Othello's occupation's gone.

Iago.
Is't possible, my lord?

Othello.
Villain, be sure thou prove my love a whore;

Taking him by the throat.

Be sure of it. Give me the ocular proof,
Or by the worth of mine eternal soul,
Thou hadst been better have been born a dog
Than answer my wak'd wrath!

Iago.
                Is't come to this?

Othello.
Make me to see't; or (at the least) so prove it
That the probation bear no hinge nor loop
To hang a doubt on; or woe upon thy life!

Iago.
My noble lord—

Othello.
If thou dost slander her and torture me,
Never pray more; abandon all remorse;
On horror's head horrors accumulate;
Do deeds to make heaven weep, all earth amaz'd;
For nothing canst thou to damnation add
Greater than that.

Iago.
                O grace! O heaven forgive me!
Are you a man? Have you a soul? Or sense?
God buy you; take mine office. O wretched fool,
That lov'st to make thine honesty a vice!
O monstrous world! Take note, take note, O world,
To be direct and honest is not safe.
I thank you for this profit, and from hence
I'll love no friend, sith love breeds such offense.

Othello.
Nay, stay. Thou shouldst be honest.

Iago.
I should be wise—for honesty's a fool
And loses that it works for.

Othello.
                By the world,
I think my wife be honest, and think she is not;
I think that thou art just, and think thou art not.
I'll have some proof. Her name, that was as fresh
As Dian's visage, is now begrim'd and black
As mine own face. If there be cords, or knives,
Poison, or fire, or suffocating streams,
I'll not endure it. Would I were satisfied!

Iago.
I see, sir, you are eaten up with passion;
I do repent me that I put it to you.
You would be satisfied?

Othello.
                Would? Nay, and I will.

Iago.
And may; but how? How satisfied, my lord?
Would you, the supervisor, grossly gape on?
Behold her topp'd?

Othello.
                Death and damnation! O!

Iago.
It were a tedious difficulty, I think,
To bring them to that prospect; damn them then,
If ever mortal eyes do see them bolster
More than their own. What then? How then?
What shall I say? Where's satisfaction?
It is impossible you should see this,
Were they as prime as goats, as hot as monkeys,
As salt as wolves in pride, and fools as gross
As ignorance made drunk. But yet, I say,
If imputation and strong circumstances
Which lead directly to the door of truth
Will give you satisfaction, you might have't.

Othello.
Give me a living reason she's disloyal.

Iago.
I do not like the office;
But sith I am ent'red in this cause so far
(Prick'd to't by foolish honesty and love),
I will go on. I lay with Cassio lately,
And being troubled with a raging tooth,
I could not sleep.
There are a kind of men, so loose of soul,
That in their sleeps will mutter their affairs;
One of this kind is Cassio.
In sleep I heard him say, "Sweet Desdemona,
Let us be wary, let us hide our loves";
And then, sir, would he gripe and wring my hand;
Cry, "O sweet creature!" then kiss me hard,
As if he pluck'd up kisses by the roots
That grew upon my lips; then laid his leg
Over my thigh, and sigh'd, and kiss'd, and then
Cried, "Cursed fate that gave thee to the Moor!"

Othello.
O monstrous! Monstrous!

Iago.
                Nay, this was but his dream.

Othello.
But this denoted a foregone conclusion.

Iago.
'Tis a shrewd doubt, though it be but a dream,
And this may help to thicken other proofs
That do demonstrate thinly.

Othello.
                I'll tear her all to pieces.

Iago.
Nay, yet be wise; yet we see nothing done;
She may be honest yet. Tell me but this,
Have you not sometimes seen a handkerchief
Spotted with strawberries in your wive's hand?

Othello.
I gave her such a one; 'twas my first gift.

Iago.
I know not that; but such a handkerchief
(I am sure it was your wive's) did I today
See Cassio wipe his beard with.

Othello.
                If it be that—

Iago.
If it be that, or any that was hers,
It speaks against her with the other proofs.

Othello.
O that the slave had forty thousand lives!
One is too poor, too weak for my revenge.
Now do I see 'tis true. Look here, Iago,
All my fond love thus do I blow to heaven.
'Tis gone.
Arise, black vengeance, from the hollow hell!
Yield up, O love, thy crown and hearted throne
To tyrannous hate! Swell, bosom, with thy fraught,
For 'tis of aspics' tongues!

Iago.
                Yet be content.

Othello.
O blood, blood, blood!

Iago.
Patience, I say; your mind perhaps may change.

Othello.
Never, Iago. Like to the Pontic Sea,
Whose icy current and compulsive course
Nev'r feels retiring ebb, but keeps due on
To the Propontic and the Hellespont,

Even so my bloody thoughts, with violent pace,
Shall nev'r look back, nev'r ebb to humble love,
Till that a capable and wide revenge
Swallow them up.

He kneels.

Now by yond marble heaven,
In the due reverence of a sacred vow
I here engage my words.

Iago.
                         Do not rise yet.

Iago kneels.

Witness, you ever-burning lights above,
You elements that clip us round about,
Witness that here Iago doth give up
The execution of his wit, hands, heart,
To wrong'd Othello's service! Let him command,
And to obey shall be in me remorse,
What bloody business ever.

They rise.

Othello.
                    I greet thy love,
Not with vain thanks, but with acceptance bounteous,
And will upon the instant put thee to't:
Within these three days let me hear thee say
That Cassio's not alive.

Iago.
My friend is dead; 'tis done at your request.
But let her live.

Othello.
Damn her, lewd minx! O, damn her, damn her!
Come go with me apart, I will withdraw
To furnish me with some swift means of death
For the fair devil. Now art thou my lieutenant.

Iago.
I am your own forever.

Exeunt.

Scene 4

Cyprus. Before the castle.

(Desdemona; Emilia; Clown; Othello; Iago; Cassio; Bianca)

Desdemona sends the Clown to fetch Cassio. She is worried about having lost her handkerchief, but Emilia does not tell her what she knows where it has gone. Still, Desdemona insists that Othello is not the jealous type, and states her determination to nag him until he restores Cassio to his position as lieutenant. Othello comes in, and when Desdemona asks him about Cassio, he claims to have a cold and asks to borrow her handkerchief. Desdemona says she doesn't have it on her, and he tells her off for it, saying that it is a magical handkerchief, the loss of which will make him hate her. Desdemona is horrified at the thought, and Othello accuses her of losing it; she says that she simply left it at home. She tries to get him off his obsession with the handkerchief by bringing up Cassio again, but this merely enrages him until he stalks away. Desdemona is hurt, while Emilia expresses her low opinion of men. Cassio and Iago appear, Cassio asking Desdemona again for her help, but she has to explain that Othello is not himself. Iago pretends concern and goes off to find out what the matter is. Desdemona chides herself for bothering Othello when clearly some matter of state is occupying his thoughts, though Emilia is skeptical. The ladies leave. Cassio meets his lady friend Bianca, who is angry with him for leaving her alone for so long; he asks her to take out the embroidery of the handkerchief he found in his room, and she accuses him of having a new lover. He tells her to be quiet and asks her to leave him alone, not wanting Othello to see him with a woman in case it hurts his suit. He promises to see her soon.

Enter Desdemona, Emilia, and Clown.

Desdemona.
Do you know, sirrah, where Lieutenant Cassio lies?

Clown.
I dare not say he lies any where.

Desdemona.
Why, man?

Clown.
He's a soldier, and for me to say a soldier lies, 'tis stabbing.

Desdemona.
Go to! Where lodges he?

Clown.
To tell you where he lodges, is to tell you where I lie.

Desdemona.
Can any thing be made of this?

Clown.
I know not where he lodges, and for me to devise a lodging and say he lies here, or he lies there, were to lie in mine own throat.

Desdemona.
Can you inquire him out, and be edified by report?

Clown.
I will catechize the world for him, that is, make questions, and by them answer.

Desdemona.
Seek him, bid him come hither. Tell him I have mov'd my lord on his behalf, and hope all will be well.

Clown.
To do this is within the compass of man's wit, and therefore I will attempt the doing it.

Exit Clown.

Desdemona.
Where should I lose the handkerchief, Emilia?

Emilia.
I know not, madam.

Desdemona.
Believe me, I had rather have lost my purse
Full of crusadoes; and but my noble Moor
Is true of mind, and made of no such baseness
As jealous creatures are, it were enough
To put him to ill thinking.

Emilia.
                    Is he not jealous?

Desdemona.
Who, he? I think the sun where he was born
Drew all such humors from him.

Emilia.
                    Look where he comes.

Enter Othello.

Desdemona.
I will not leave him now till Cassio
Be call'd to him.—How is't with you, my lord?

Othello.
Well, my good lady.

Aside.
                    O, hardness to dissemble!—
How do you, Desdemona?

Desdemona.
                    Well, my good lord.

Othello.
Give me your hand. This hand is moist, my lady.

Desdemona.
It yet hath felt no age nor known no sorrow.

Othello.
This argues fruitfulness and liberal heart;
Hot, hot, and moist. This hand of yours requires
A sequester from liberty: fasting and prayer,
Much castigation, exercise devout,
For here's a young and sweating devil here
That commonly rebels. 'Tis a good hand,
A frank one.

Desdemona.
                    You may, indeed, say so;
For 'twas that hand that gave away my heart.

Othello.
A liberal hand. The hearts of old gave hands;
But our new heraldry is hands, not hearts.

Desdemona.
I cannot speak of this. Come now, your promise.

Othello.
What promise, chuck?

Desdemona.
I have sent to bid Cassio come speak with you.

Othello.
I have a salt and sorry rheum offends me;
Lend me thy handkerchief.

Desdemona.
                    Here, my lord.

Othello.
That which I gave you.

Desdemona.
                    I have it not about me.

Act 3, Scene 4

Othello.
Not?

Desdemona.
                No, faith, my lord.

Othello.
That's a fault. That handkerchief
Did an Egyptian to my mother give;
She was a charmer, and could almost read
The thoughts of people. She told her, while she kept it,
'Twould make her amiable, and subdue my father
Entirely to her love; but if she lost it,
Or made a gift of it, my father's eye
Should hold her loathed, and his spirits should hunt
After new fancies. She, dying, gave it me,
And bid me, when my fate would have me wiv'd,
To give it her. I did so; and take heed on't,
Make it a darling like your precious eye.
To lose't or give't away were such perdition
As nothing else could match.

Desdemona.
                Is't possible?

Othello.
'Tis true; there's magic in the web of it.
A sibyl, that had numb'red in the world
The sun to course two hundred compasses,
In her prophetic fury sew'd the work;
The worms were hallowed that did breed the silk,
And it was dy'd in mummy which the skillful
Conserv'd of maidens' hearts.

Desdemona.
                I' faith! Is't true?

Othello.
Most veritable, therefore look to't well.

Desdemona.
Then would to God that I had never seen't!

Othello.
Ha? Wherefore?

Desdemona.
Why do you speak so startingly and rash?

Othello.
Is't lost? Is't gone? Speak, is't out o' th' way?

Desdemona.
Heaven bless us!

Othello.
Say you?

Desdemona.
It is not lost; but what and if it were?

Othello.
How?

Desdemona.
I say, it is not lost.

Othello.
                Fetch't, let me see't.

Desdemona.
Why, so I can, sir, but I will not now.
This is a trick to put me from my suit.
Pray you let Cassio be receiv'd again.

Othello.
Fetch me the handkerchief, my mind misgives.

Desdemona.
Come, come;
You'll never meet a more sufficient man.

Othello.
The handkerchief!

Desdemona.
                I pray talk me of Cassio.

Othello.
The handkerchief!

Desdemona.
                A man that all his time
Hath founded his good fortunes on your love,
Shar'd dangers with you—

Othello.
The handkerchief!

Desdemona.
I' faith, you are to blame.

Othello.
'Zounds!

Exit Othello.

Emilia.
Is not this man jealous?

Desdemona.
I nev'r saw this before.
Sure, there's some wonder in this handkerchief;
I am most unhappy in the loss of it.

Emilia.
'Tis not a year or two shows us a man:
They are all but stomachs, and we all but food;
They eat us hungerly, and when they are full
They belch us.

Enter Iago and Cassio.

Look you, Cassio and my husband!

Iago.
There is no other way: 'tis she must do't;
And lo the happiness! Go, and importune her.

Desdemona.
How now, good Cassio, what's the news with you?

Cassio.
Madam, my former suit. I do beseech you
That by your virtuous means I may again
Exist, and be a member of his love
Whom I, with all the office of my heart,
Entirely honor. I would not be delay'd.
If my offense be of such mortal kind
That nor my service past, nor present sorrows,
Nor purpos'd merit in futurity,
Can ransom me into his love again,
But to know so must be my benefit;
So shall I clothe me in a forc'd content,
And shut myself up in some other course,
To fortune's alms.

Desdemona.
Alas, thrice-gentle Cassio,
My advocation is not now in tune.
My lord is not my lord; nor should I know him
Were he in favor as in humor alter'd.
So help me every spirit sanctified,
As I have spoken for you all my best,
And stood within the blank of his displeasure
For my free speech! You must awhile be patient.
What I can do, I will; and more I will
Than for myself I dare. Let that suffice you.

Iago.
Is my lord angry?

Emilia.
He went hence but now;
And certainly in strange unquietness.

Iago.
Can he be angry? I have seen the cannon
When it hath blown his ranks into the air,
And like the devil from his very arm
Puff'd his own brother—and is he angry?
Something of moment then. I will go meet him.
There's matter in't indeed, if he be angry.

Desdemona.
I prithee do so.

Exit Iago.

Something sure of state,
Either from Venice, or some unhatch'd practice
Made demonstrable here in Cyprus to him,
Hath puddled his clear spirit; and in such cases
Men's natures wrangle with inferior things,
Though great ones are their object. 'Tis even so;
For let our finger ache, and it endues
Our other healthful members even to a sense
Of pain. Nay, we must think men are not gods,
Nor of them look for such observancy
As fits the bridal. Beshrew me much, Emilia,
I was (unhandsome warrior as I am)
Arraigning his unkindness with my soul;
But now I find I had suborn'd the witness,
And he's indicted falsely.

Emilia.
Pray heaven it be state matters, as you think,
And no conception nor no jealous toy
Concerning you.

Desdemona.
Alas the day, I never gave him cause.

Emilia.
But jealous souls will not be answer'd so;
They are not ever jealous for the cause,
But jealous for they're jealous. It is a monster
Begot upon itself, born on itself.

Desdemona.
Heaven keep the monster from Othello's mind!

Emilia.
Lady, amen.

Desdemona.
I will go seek him. Cassio, walk hereabout;
If I do find him fit, I'll move your suit
And seek to effect it to my uttermost.

Cassio.
I humbly thank your ladyship.

Exeunt Desdemona and Emilia.
Enter Bianca.

Bianca.
'Save you, friend Cassio!

Cassio.
                What make you from home?
How is't with you, my most fair Bianca?
I'faith, sweet love, I was coming to your house.

Bianca.
And I was going to your lodging, Cassio.
What? Keep a week away? Seven days and nights?
Eightscore eight hours? And lovers' absent hours,
More tedious than the dial eightscore times?
O weary reck'ning!

Cassio.
                Pardon me, Bianca.
I have this while with leaden thoughts been press'd,
But I shall in a more continuate time
Strike off this score of absence. Sweet Bianca,

Giving her Desdemona's handkerchief.

Take me this work out.

Bianca.
                O Cassio, whence came this?
This is some token from a newer friend;
To the felt absence now I feel a cause.
Is't come to this? Well, well.

Cassio.
                Go to, woman!
Throw your vild guesses in the devil's teeth,
From whence you have them. You are jealous now
That this is from some mistress, some remembrance;
No, by my faith, Bianca.

Bianca.
                Why, whose is it?

Cassio.
I know not, neither; I found it in my chamber.
I like the work well; ere it be demanded
(As like enough it will) I would have it copied.
Take it, and do't, and leave me for this time.

Bianca.
Leave you? Wherefore?

Cassio.
I do attend here on the general,
And think it no addition, nor my wish,
To have him see me woman'd.

Bianca.
                Why, I pray you?

Cassio.
Not that I love you not.

Bianca.
                But that you do not love me.
I pray you bring me on the way a little,
And say if I shall see you soon at night.

Cassio.
'Tis but a little way that I can bring you,
For I attend here; but I'll see you soon.

Bianca.
'Tis very good; I must be circumstanc'd.

Exeunt omnes.

Act 4

Scene 1

Cyprus. Before the castle.

(Othello; Iago; Cassio; Bianca; Lodovico; Desdemona; Attendants)

Iago continues to torment Othello, dropping suggestions into his ear while arguing that they are not great transgressions, which just works Othello up even more. He finally pushes Othello so far that the general becomes incoherent and finally falls down into a trance. Cassio enters and is concerned, but Iago tells him it's merely an epileptic fit and asks him to leave. Reviving Othello, he proposes to have a chat with Cassio about Desdemona, letting Othello overhear. Othello agrees. What Iago actually does is talk to Cassio about Bianca, walking about so that Othello can only hear portions of the discussion. Cassio's laughter as he mocks Bianca enrages Othello; even worse, Bianca herself arrives to rant at Cassio about the handkerchief, and Othello sees that Cassio has given that precious keepsake to a prostitute. Cassio runs after Bianca; Othello is now determined to kill both Cassio and Desdemona. Iago offers to take care of Cassio, recommending that Othello strangle Desdemona in her bed. Desdemona's cousin Lodovico arrives from Venice with letters from the Senate that call Othello home and name Cassio the new governor of Cyprus. As Desdemona explains the situation to Lodovico, Othello hears her praises of Cassio and gets so worked up that he strikes out at her, to Lodovico's amazement. When the Venetian protests and asks him to apologize to her, he merely sneers at her sarcastically, orders her to go home, and leaves himself. Lodovico worries for his wits, and Iago implies that what he saw is by no means the worst.

Enter Othello and Iago.

Iago.
Will you think so?

Othello.
                        Think so, Iago?

Iago.
                        What,
To kiss in private?

Othello.
                        An unauthoriz'd kiss!

Iago.
Or to be naked with her friend in bed
An hour, or more, not meaning any harm?

Othello.
Naked in bed, Iago, and not mean harm?
It is hypocrisy against the devil.
They that mean virtuously, and yet do so,
The devil their virtue tempts, and they tempt heaven.

Iago.
If they do nothing, 'tis a venial slip;
But if I give my wife a handkerchief—

Othello.
What then?

Iago.
Why then 'tis hers, my lord, and being hers,
She may, I think, bestow't on any man.

Othello.
She is protectress of her honor too;
May she give that?

Iago.
Her honor is an essence that's not seen;
They have it very oft that have it not.
But for the handkerchief—

Othello.
By heaven, I would most gladly have forgot it.
Thou saidst (O, it comes o'er my memory,
As doth the raven o'er the infectious house,
Boding to all) he had my handkerchief.

Iago.
Ay; what of that?

Othello.
                        That's not so good now.

Iago.
                        What
If I had said I had seen him do you wrong?
Or heard him say—as knaves be such abroad,
Who having by their own importunate suit,
Or voluntary dotage of some mistress,
Convinced or supplied them, cannot choose
But they must blab—

Othello.
                        Hath he said any thing?

Iago.
He hath, my lord, but be you well assur'd,
No more than he'll unswear.

Othello.
                        What hath he said?

Iago.
Faith, that he did—I know not what he did.

Othello.
What? What?

Iago.
Lie—

Othello.
                        With her?

Iago.
                        With her? On her; what you will.

Othello.
Lie with her? Lie on her? We say lie on her, when they belie her. Lie with her! 'Zounds, that's fulsome! Handkerchief—confessions—handkerchief! To confess, and be hang'd for his labor—first to be hang'd, and then to confess. I tremble at it. Nature would not invest herself in such shadowing passion without some instruction. It is not words that shakes me thus. Pish! Noses, ears, and lips. Is't possible? Confess? Handkerchief? O devil!

Falls in a trance.

Iago.
Work on,
My medicine, work! Thus credulous fools are caught,
And many worthy and chaste dames even thus
(All guiltless) meet reproach.—What ho! My lord!
My lord, I say! Othello!

Enter Cassio.

How now, Cassio?

Cassio.
What's the matter?

Iago.
My lord is fall'n into an epilepsy.
This is his second fit; he had one yesterday.

Cassio.
Rub him about the temples.

Iago.
No, forbear,
The lethargy must have his quiet course;
If not, he foams at mouth, and by and by
Breaks out to savage madness. Look, he stirs.
Do you withdraw yourself a little while,
He will recover straight. When he is gone,
I would on great occasion speak with you.

Exit Cassio.

How is it, general? Have you not hurt your head?

Othello.
Dost thou mock me?

Iago.
I mock you not, by heaven.
Would you would bear your fortune like a man!

Othello.
A horned man's a monster and a beast.

Iago.
There's many a beast then in a populous city,
And many a civil monster.

Othello.
Did he confess it?

Iago.
Good sir, be a man;
Think every bearded fellow that's but yok'd
May draw with you. There's millions now alive
That nightly lie in those unproper beds
Which they dare swear peculiar; your case is better.
O, 'tis the spite of hell, the fiend's arch-mock,
To lip a wanton in a secure couch,
And to suppose her chaste! No, let me know,
And knowing what I am, I know what she shall be.

Othello.
O, thou art wise; 'tis certain.

Iago.
Stand you a while apart,
Confine yourself but in a patient list.
Whilst you were here o'erwhelmed with your grief
(A passion most unsuiting such a man),
Cassio came hither. I shifted him away,
And laid good 'scuses upon your ecstasy;
Bade him anon return and here speak with me,
The which he promis'd. Do but encave yourself,
And mark the fleers, the gibes, and notable scorns
That dwell in every region of his face,
For I will make him tell the tale anew:
Where, how, how oft, how long ago, and when
He hath, and is again to cope your wife.
I say, but mark his gesture. Marry, patience,
Or I shall say y' are all in all in spleen,
And nothing of a man.

Othello.
Dost thou hear, Iago,
I will be found most cunning in my patience;
But (dost thou hear) most bloody.

Iago.
That's not amiss,
But yet keep time in all. Will you withdraw?

Othello withdraws.

Now will I question Cassio of Bianca,

A huswife that by selling her desires
Buys herself bread and clothes. It is a creature
That dotes on Cassio (as 'tis the strumpet's plague
To beguile many and be beguil'd by one);
He, when he hears of her, cannot restrain
From the excess of laughter. Here he comes.

Enter Cassio.

As he shall smile, Othello shall go mad;
And his unbookish jealousy must construe
Poor Cassio's smiles, gestures, and light behaviors
Quite in the wrong. How do you now, lieutenant?

Cassio.
The worser that you give me the addition
Whose want even kills me.

Iago.
Ply Desdemona well, and you are sure on't.

Speaking lower.

Now, if this suit lay in Bianca's pow'r,
How quickly should you speed!

Cassio.
     Alas, poor caitiff!

Othello.
Look how he laughs already!

Iago.
I never knew woman love man so.

Cassio.
Alas, poor rogue, I think, i' faith, she loves me.

Othello.
Now he denies it faintly, and laughs it out.

Iago.
Do you hear, Cassio?

Othello.
     Now he importunes him
To tell it o'er. Go to, well said, well said.

Iago.
She gives it out that you shall marry her.
Do you intend it?

Cassio.
Ha, ha, ha!

Othello.
Do you triumph, Roman? Do you triumph?

Cassio.
I marry her! What? A customer! Prithee bear some charity to my wit, do not think it so unwholesome. Ha, ha, ha!

Othello.
So, so, so, so; they laugh that wins.

Iago.
Faith, the cry goes that you marry her.

Cassio.
Prithee say true.

Iago.
I am a very villain else.

Othello.
Have you scor'd me? Well.

Cassio.
This is the monkey's own giving out. She is persuaded I will marry her, out of her own love and flattery, not out of my promise.

Othello.
Iago beckons me; now he begins the story.

Cassio.
She was here even now; she haunts me in every place. I was the other day talking on the sea-bank with certain Venetians, and thither comes the bauble, and by this hand, falls me thus about my neck—

Othello.
Crying, "O dear Cassio!" as it were; his gesture imports it.

Cassio.
So hangs, and lolls, and weeps upon me; so hales and pulls me. Ha, ha, ha!

Othello.
Now he tells how she pluck'd him to my chamber. O, I see that nose of yours, but not that dog I shall throw it to.

Cassio.
Well, I must leave her company.

Iago.
Before me! Look where she comes.

Enter Bianca.

Cassio.
'Tis such another fitchew! Marry, a perfum'd one!—What do you mean by this haunting of me?

Bianca.
Let the devil and his dam haunt you! What did you mean by that same handkerchief you gave me even now? I was a fine fool to take it. I must take out the work? A likely piece of work, that you should find it in your chamber, and know not who left it there! This is some minx's token, and I must take out the work? There, give it your hobby-horse. Wheresoever you had it, I'll take out no work on't.

Cassio.
How now, my sweet Bianca? How now? How now?

Othello.
By heaven, that should be my handkerchief!

Bianca.
An' you'll come to supper tonight, you may; an' you will not, come when you are next prepar'd for.

Exit.

Iago.
After her, after her.

Cassio.
Faith, I must, she'll rail in the streets else.

Iago.
Will you sup there?

Cassio.
Faith, I intend so.

Iago.
Well, I may chance to see you; for I would very fain speak with you.

Cassio.
Prithee come; will you?

Iago.
Go to; say no more.

Exit Cassio.

Othello.

Advancing.
How shall I murder him, Iago?

Iago.
Did you perceive how he laugh'd at his vice?

Othello.
O Iago!

Iago.
And did you see the handkerchief?

Othello.
Was that mine?

Iago.
Yours, by this hand. And to see how he prizes the foolish woman your wife! She gave it him, and he hath giv'n it his whore.

Othello.
I would have him nine years a-killing. A fine woman! A fair woman! A sweet woman!

Iago.
Nay, you must forget that.

Othello.
Ay, let her rot, and perish, and be damn'd tonight, for she shall not live. No, my heart is turn'd to stone; I strike it, and it hurts my hand. O, the world hath not a sweeter creature! She might lie by an emperor's side and command him tasks.

Iago.
Nay, that's not your way.

Othello.
Hang her, I do but say what she is. So delicate with her needle! An admirable musician! O, she will sing the savageness out of a bear. Of so high and plenteous wit and invention!

Iago.
She's the worse for all this.

Othello.
O, a thousand, a thousand times. And then of so gentle a condition!

Iago.
Ay, too gentle.

Othello.
Nay, that's certain. But yet the pity of it, Iago! O Iago, the pity of it, Iago!

Iago.
If you are so fond over her iniquity, give her patent to offend, for if it touch not you, it comes near nobody.

Othello.
I will chop her into messes. Cuckold me!

Iago.
O, 'tis foul in her.

Othello.
With mine officer!

Iago.
That's fouler.

Othello.
Get me some poison, Iago, this night. I'll not expostulate with her, lest her body and beauty unprovide my mind again. This night, Iago.

Iago.
Do it not with poison; strangle her in her bed, even the bed she hath contaminated.

Othello.
Good, good; the justice of it pleases; very good.

Iago.
And for Cassio, let me be his undertaker. You shall hear more by midnight.

Othello.
Excellent good.

A trumpet.

What trumpet is that same?

Iago.
I warrant, something from Venice.

Enter Lodovico, Desdemona, and Attendants.

              'Tis Lodovico—
This comes from the Duke. See, your wife's with him.

Lodovico.
God save you, worthy general!

Othello.
              With all my heart, sir.

Lodovico.
The Duke and the senators of Venice greet you.

Gives him a letter.

Othello.
I kiss the instrument of their pleasures.

Opens the letter and reads.

Desdemona.
And what's the news, good cousin Lodovico?

Iago.
I am very glad to see you, signior;
Welcome to Cyprus.

Lodovico.
I thank you. How does Lieutenant Cassio?

Iago.
Lives, sir.

Desdemona.
Cousin, there's fall'n between him and my lord
An unkind breach; but you shall make all well.

Othello.
Are you sure of that?

Desdemona.
My lord?

Othello.

Reads.

"This fail you not to do, as you will—"

Lodovico.
He did not call; he's busy in the paper.
Is there division 'twixt my lord and Cassio?

Desdemona.
A most unhappy one. I would do much
T' atone them, for the love I bear to Cassio.

Othello.
Fire and brimstone!

Desdemona.
              My lord?

Othello.
              Are you wise?

Desdemona.
What, is he angry?

Lodovico.
May be th' letter mov'd him;
For as I think, they do command him home,
Deputing Cassio in his government.

Desdemona.
By my troth, I am glad on't.

Othello.
Indeed?

Desdemona.
My lord?

Othello.
I am glad to see you mad.

Desdemona.
Why, sweet Othello?

Othello.

Striking her.
Devil!

Desdemona.
I have not deserv'd this.

Lodovico.
My lord, this would not be believ'd in Venice,
Though I should swear I saw't. 'Tis very much,
Make her amends; she weeps.

Othello.
O devil, devil!
If that the earth could teem with woman's tears,
Each drop she falls would prove a crocodile.
Out of my sight!

Desdemona.
I will not stay to offend you.

Going.

Lodovico.
Truly, an obedient lady:
I do beseech your lordship call her back.

Othello.
Mistress!

Desdemona.
My lord?

Othello.
What would you with her, sir?

Lodovico.
Who, I, my lord?

Othello.
Ay, you did wish that I would make her turn.
Sir, she can turn, and turn; and yet go on
And turn again; and she can weep, sir, weep;
And she's obedient, as you say, obedient;
Very obedient—Proceed you in your tears.—
Concerning this, sir—O well-painted passion!—
I am commanded home.—Get you away;
I'll send for you anon.—Sir, I obey the mandate,
And will return to Venice.—Hence, avaunt!

Exit Desdemona.

Cassio shall have my place. And, sir, tonight
I do entreat that we may sup together.
You are welcome, sir, to Cyprus.—Goats and monkeys!

Exit.

Lodovico.
Is this the noble Moor whom our full Senate
Call all in all sufficient? Is this the nature
Whom passion could not shake? Whose solid virtue
The shot of accident nor dart of chance
Could neither graze nor pierce?

Iago.
He is much chang'd.

Lodovico.
Are his wits safe? Is he not light of brain?

Iago.
He's that he is; I may not breathe my censure
What he might be. If what he might he is not,
I would to heaven he were!

Lodovico.
What? Strike his wife?

Iago.
Faith, that was not so well; yet would I knew
That stroke would prove the worst!

Lodovico.
                      Is it his use?
Or did the letters work upon his blood,
And new-create this fault?

Iago.
                      Alas, alas!
It is not honesty in me to speak
What I have seen and known. You shall observe him,
And his own courses will denote him so
That I may save my speech. Do but go after,
And mark how he continues.

Lodovico.
I am sorry that I am deceiv'd in him.

Exeunt.

Scene 2

Cyprus. A room in the castle.

(Othello; Emilia; Desdemona; Roderigo; Iago)

Othello questions Emilia, who swears that there is nothing between Desdemona and Cassio, but Othello refuses to believe her. He has Desdemona come in, and interrogates her, though Desdemona cannot see what it is he suspects her of. In the end he accuses her bluntly, and she protests her innocence with great dignity. He insults her callously, sneers at Emilia and leaves. Grieving, Desdemona asks Emilia to put her wedding sheets on the bed that night, and to call Iago to her. Iago comes in, feigning concern, and tries to console Desdemona while Emilia rails against whatever villain convinced Othello his wife was false. Iago tells Desdemona that it is only the cares of state that have disturbed Othello, and that things will get better. Desdemona and Emilia leave for the dinner for the Venetians. Roderigo comes to find Iago, reproaching him for not advancing his suit to Desdemona; he threatens to speak to Desdemona himself. This Iago cannot permit, for Roderigo has sent rich jewels to Desdemona that he, Iago, has taken for himself. Iago tells Roderigo that Cassio is to replace Othello on Cyprus, and that Othello is being sent farther away yet, and that therefore the only way to make sure Othello and Desdemona stay would be to kill Cassio so that he is not capable of taking on his new role. He offers to show Roderigo where the best place to lie in wait for Cassio would be; Roderigo needs more convincing, however.

Enter Othello and Emilia.

Othello.
You have seen nothing then?

Emilia.
Nor ever heard—nor ever did suspect.

Othello.
Yes, you have seen Cassio and she together.

Emilia.
But then I saw no harm, and then I heard
Each syllable that breath made up between them.

Othello.
What? Did they never whisper?

Emilia.
                      Never, my lord.

Othello.
Nor send you out o' th' way?

Emilia.
Never.

Othello.
To fetch her fan, her gloves, her mask, nor nothing?

Emilia.
Never, my lord.

Othello.
That's strange.

Emilia.
I durst, my lord, to wager she is honest;
Lay down my soul at stake. If you think other,
Remove your thought; it doth abuse your bosom.
If any wretch have put this in your head,
Let heaven requite it with the serpent's curse!
For if she be not honest, chaste, and true,
There's no man happy; the purest of their wives
Is foul as slander.

Othello.
                      Bid her come hither; go.

Exit Emilia.

She says enough; yet she's a simple bawd
That cannot say as much. This is a subtile whore,
A closet lock and key of villainous secrets;
And yet she'll kneel and pray; I have seen her do't.

Enter Desdemona and Emilia.

Desdemona.
My lord, what is your will?

Othello.
     Pray you, chuck, come hither.

Desdemona.
What is your pleasure?

Othello.
      Let me see your eyes;
Look in my face.

Desdemona.
     What horrible fancy's this?

Othello.

To Emilia.

Some of your function, mistress;
Leave procreants alone, and shut the door;
Cough, or cry "hem," if anybody come.
Your mystery, your mystery; nay, dispatch.

Exit Emilia.

Desdemona.
Upon my knee, what doth your speech import?
I understand a fury in your words,
But not the words.

Othello.
Why? What art thou?

Desdemona.
    Your wife, my lord; your true
And loyal wife.

Othello.
     Come swear it, damn thyself,
Lest being like one of heaven, the devils themselves
Should fear to seize thee; therefore be double damn'd:
Swear thou art honest.

Desdemona.
     Heaven doth truly know it.

Othello.
Heaven truly knows that thou art false as hell.

Desdemona.
To whom, my lord? With whom? How am I false?

Othello.
Ah, Desdemon! Away, away, away!

Desdemona.
Alas the heavy day! Why do you weep?
Am I the motive of these tears, my lord?
If haply you my father do suspect
An instrument of this your calling back,
Lay not your blame on me. If you have lost him,
Why, I have lost him too.

Othello.
     Had it pleas'd heaven
To try me with affliction, had they rain'd
All kind of sores and shames on my bare head,
Steep'd me in poverty to the very lips,
Given to captivity me and my utmost hopes,
I should have found in some place of my soul
A drop of patience; but, alas, to make me
The fixed figure for the time of scorn
To point his slow unmoving finger at!
Yet could I bear that too, well, very well;
But there, where I have garner'd up my heart,
Where either I must live or bear no life;
The fountain from the which my current runs
Or else dries up: to be discarded thence!
Or keep it as a cistern for foul toads
To knot and gender in! Turn thy complexion there,
Patience, thou young and rose-lipp'd cherubin—
Ay, here look grim as hell!

Desdemona.
I hope my noble lord esteems me honest.

Othello.
O ay, as summer flies are in the shambles,
That quicken even with blowing. O thou weed!
Who art so lovely fair and smell'st so sweet
That the sense aches at thee, would thou hadst never been born!

Desdemona.
Alas, what ignorant sin have I committed?

Othello.
Was this fair paper, this most goodly book,
Made to write "whore" upon? What committed?
Committed? O thou public commoner,
I should make very forges of my cheeks,
That would to cinders burn up modesty,
Did I but speak thy deeds. What committed?
Heaven stops the nose at it, and the moon winks;

The bawdy wind, that kisses all it meets,
Is hush'd within the hollow mine of earth
And will not hear't. What committed?
Impudent strumpet!

Desdemona.
                By heaven, you do me wrong.

Othello.
Are not you a strumpet?

Desdemona.
                No, as I am a Christian.
If to preserve this vessel for my lord
From any other foul unlawful touch
Be not to be a strumpet, I am none.

Othello.
What, not a whore?

Desdemona.
              No, as I shall be sav'd.

Othello.
Is't possible?

Desdemona.
O, heaven forgive us!

Othello.
              I cry you mercy then.
I took you for that cunning whore of Venice
That married with Othello.—

Raising his voice.

              You, mistress,

Enter Emilia.

That have the office opposite to Saint Peter,
And keeps the gate of hell! You, you! Ay, you!
We have done our course; there's money for your pains.
I pray you turn the key and keep our counsel.

Exit.

Emilia.
Alas, what does this gentleman conceive?
How do you, madam? How do you, my good lady?

Desdemona.
Faith, half asleep.

Emilia.
Good madam, what's the matter with my lord?

Desdemona.
With who?

Emilia.
Why, with my lord, madam.

Desdemona.
Who is thy lord?

Emilia.
              He that is yours, sweet lady.

Desdemona.
I have none. Do not talk to me, Emilia;
I cannot weep, nor answers have I none
But what should go by water. Prithee tonight
Lay on my bed my wedding-sheets—remember;
And call thy husband hither.

Emilia.
              Here's a change indeed!

Exit.

Desdemona.
'Tis meet I should be us'd so, very meet.
How have I been behav'd, that he might stick
The small'st opinion on my least misuse?

Enter Iago and Emilia.

Iago.
What is your pleasure, madam? How is't with you?

Desdemona.
I cannot tell. Those that do teach young babes
Do it with gentle means and easy tasks.
He might have chid me so; for in good faith
I am a child to chiding.

Iago.
              What is the matter, lady?

Emilia.
Alas, Iago, my lord hath so bewhor'd her,
Thrown such despite and heavy terms upon her,
That true hearts cannot bear it.

Desdemona.
Am I that name, Iago?

Iago.
                What name, fair lady?

Desdemona.
Such as she said my lord did say I was.

Emilia.
He call'd her whore. A beggar in his drink
Could not have laid such terms upon his callet.

Iago.
Why did he so?

Desdemona.
I do not know; I am sure I am none such.

Iago.
Do not weep, do not weep. Alas the day!

Emilia.
Hath she forsook so many noble matches?
Her father? And her country? And her friends?
To be call'd whore? Would it not make one weep?

Desdemona.
It is my wretched fortune.

Iago.
                Beshrew him for't!
How comes this trick upon him?

Desdemona.
                Nay, heaven doth know.

Emilia.
I will be hang'd if some eternal villain,
Some busy and insinuating rogue,
Some cogging, cozening slave, to get some office,
Have not devis'd this slander. I will be hang'd else.

Iago.
Fie, there is no such man; it is impossible.

Desdemona.
If any such there be, heaven pardon him!

Emilia.
A halter pardon him! And hell gnaw his bones!
Why should he call her whore? Who keeps her company?
What place? What time? What form? What likelihood?
The Moor's abus'd by some most villainous knave,
Some base notorious knave, some scurvy fellow.
O heaven, that such companions thou'dst unfold,
And put in every honest hand a whip
To lash the rascals naked through the world
Even from the east to th' west!

Iago.
                Speak within door.

Emilia.
O fie upon them! Some such squire he was
That turn'd your wit the seamy side without,
And made you to suspect me with the Moor.

Iago.
You are a fool; go to.

Desdemona.
                Alas, Iago,
What shall I do to win my lord again?
Good friend, go to him; for by this light of heaven,
I know not how I lost him. Here I kneel:
If e'er my will did trespass 'gainst his love,
Either in discourse of thought or actual deed,
Or that mine eyes, mine ears, or any sense
Delighted them in any other form;
Or that I do not yet, and ever did,
And ever will (though he do shake me off
To beggarly divorcement) love him dearly,
Comfort forswear me! Unkindness may do much,
And his unkindness may defeat my life,
But never taint my love. I cannot say "whore."
It does abhor me now I speak the word;
To do the act that might the addition earn,
Not the world's mass of vanity could make me.

Iago.
I pray you be content; 'tis but his humor.
The business of the state does him offense,
And he does chide with you.

Desdemona.
If 'twere no other—

Iago.
                It is but so, I warrant.

Trumpets within.

Hark how these instruments summon to supper!
The messengers of Venice stays the meat.
Go in, and weep not; all things shall be well.

Exeunt Desdemona and Emilia.
Enter Roderigo.

How now, Roderigo?

Roderigo.
I do not find that thou deal'st justly with me.

Iago.
What in the contrary?

Roderigo.
Every day thou daff'st me with some device, Iago, and rather, as it seems to me now, keep'st from me all conveniency than suppliest me with the least advantage of hope. I will indeed no longer endure it; nor am I yet persuaded to put up in peace what already I have foolishly suff'red.

Iago.
Will you hear me, Roderigo?

Roderigo.
Faith, I have heard too much; for your words and performances are no kin together.

Iago.
You charge me most unjustly.

Roderigo.
With nought but truth. I have wasted myself out of my means. The jewels you have had from me to deliver Desdemona would half have corrupted a votarist. You have told me she hath receiv'd them and return'd me expectations and comforts of sudden respect and acquaintance, but I find none.

Iago.
Well, go to; very well.

Roderigo.
Very well! Go to! I cannot go to, man, nor 'tis not very well. By this hand, I think it is scurvy, and begin to find myself fopp'd in it.

Iago.
Very well.

Roderigo.
I tell you 'tis not very well. I will make myself known to Desdemona. If she will return me my jewels, I will give over my suit and repent my unlawful solicitation; if not, assure yourself I will seek satisfaction of you.

Iago.
You have said now.

Roderigo.
Ay; and said nothing but what I protest intendment of doing.

Iago.
Why, now I see there's mettle in thee, and even from this instant do build on thee a better opinion than ever before. Give me thy hand, Roderigo. Thou hast taken against me a most just exception; but yet I protest I have dealt most directly in thy affair.

Roderigo.
It hath not appear'd.

Iago.
I grant indeed it hath not appear'd; and your suspicion is not without wit and judgment. But, Roderigo, if thou hast that in thee indeed, which I have greater reason to believe now than ever (I mean purpose, courage, and valor), this night show it. If thou the next night following enjoy not Desdemona, take me from this world with treachery and devise engines for my life.

Roderigo.
Well; what is it? Is it within reason and compass?

Iago.
Sir, there is especial commission come from Venice to depute Cassio in Othello's place.

Roderigo.
Is that true? Why then Othello and Desdemona return again to Venice.

Iago.
O no; he goes into Mauritania and taketh away with him the fair Desdemona, unless his abode be ling'red here by some accident; wherein none can be so determinate as the removing of Cassio.

Roderigo.
How do you mean, removing him?

Iago.
Why, by making him uncapable of Othello's place: knocking out his brains.

Roderigo.
And that you would have me to do?

Iago.
Ay; if you dare do yourself a profit and a right. He sups tonight with a harlotry, and thither will I go to him—he knows not yet of his honorable fortune. If you will watch his going thence (which I will fashion to fall out between twelve and one), you may take him at your pleasure. I will be near to second your attempt, and he shall fall between us. Come, stand not amaz'd at it, but go along with me; I will show you such a necessity in his death that you shall think yourself bound to put it on him. It is now high supper-time, and the night grows to waste. About it.

Roderigo.
I will hear further reason for this.

Iago.
And you shall be satisfied.

Exeunt.

Scene 3

Cyprus. Another room in the castle.

(Othello; Lodovico; Desdemona; Emilia; Attendants)

After dinner, Othello leads Lodovico and his attendants to their lodgings, ordering Desdemona to go to bed and dismiss Emilia. Emilia is concerned. Desdemona remembers a maid in her parents' house who died of love, and sings a sad song that the maid had. She innocently asks Emilia if there actually are women who cheat on their husbands, and Emilia assures her that there are; when Desdemona says she would never do such a thing, Emilia replies that she might if the stakes were high enough. Emilia argues that the men are to blame if women do commit adultery, since the men do so themselves. Desdemona is shocked.

Enter Othello, Lodovico, Desdemona, Emilia, and Attendants.

Lodovico.
I do beseech you, sir, trouble yourself no further.

Othello.
O, pardon me; 'twill do me good to walk.

Lodovico.
Madam, good night; I humbly thank your ladyship.

Desdemona.
Your honor is most welcome.

Othello.
                    Will you walk, sir?
O, Desdemona!

Desdemona.
My lord?

Othello.
Get you to bed on th' instant, I will be return'd forthwith. Dismiss your attendant there. Look't be done.

Desdemona.
I will, my lord.

Exeunt Othello, Lodovico, and Attendants.

Emilia.
How goes it now? He looks gentler than he did.

Desdemona.
He says he will return incontinent,
And hath commanded me to go to bed,
And bid me to dismiss you.

Emilia.
                    Dismiss me?

Desdemona.
It was his bidding; therefore, good Emilia,
Give me my nightly wearing, and adieu.
We must not now displease him.

Emilia.
I would you had never seen him!

Desdemona.
So would not I. My love doth so approve him,
That even his stubbornness, his checks, his frowns—
Prithee unpin me—have grace and favor in them.

Emilia.
I have laid those sheets you bade me on the bed.

Desdemona.
All's one. Good faith, how foolish are our minds!
If I do die before thee, prithee shroud me
In one of these same sheets.

Emilia.
                    Come, come; you talk.

Desdemona.
My mother had a maid call'd Barbary;
She was in love, and he she lov'd prov'd mad,
And did forsake her. She had a song of "Willow,"

An old thing 'twas, but it express'd her fortune,
And she died singing it. That song tonight
Will not go from my mind; I have much to do
But to go hang my head all at one side
And sing it like poor Barbary. Prithee dispatch.

Emilia.
Shall I go fetch your night-gown?

Desdemona.
                No, unpin me here.
This Lodovico is a proper man.

Emilia.
A very handsome man.

Desdemona.
He speaks well.

Emilia.
I know a lady in Venice would have walk'd barefoot to Palestine for a touch of his nether lip.

Desdemona.

Singing.

"The poor soul sat sighing by a sycamore tree,
Sing all a green willow;
Her hand on her bosom, her head on her knee,
Sing willow, willow, willow.
The fresh streams ran by her, and murmur'd her moans,
Sing willow, willow, willow;
Her salt tears fell from her, and soft'ned the stones,
Sing willow"—
Lay by these—

Singing.

"— willow, willow"—
Prithee hie thee; he'll come anon—

Singing.

"Sing all a green willow must be my garland.
Let nobody blame him, his scorn I approve"—
Nay, that's not next. Hark, who is't that knocks?

Emilia.
It's the wind.

Desdemona.

Singing.

"I call'd my love false love; but what said he then?
Sing willow, willow, willow;
If I court more women, you'll couch with more men."—
So get thee gone, good night. Mine eyes do itch;
Doth that bode weeping?

Emilia.
                'Tis neither here nor there.

Desdemona.
I have heard it said so. O, these men, these men!
Dost thou in conscience think—tell me, Emilia—
That there be women do abuse their husbands
In such gross kind?

Emilia.
                There be some such, no question.

Desdemona.
Wouldst thou do such a deed for all the world?

Emilia.
Why, would not you?

Desdemona.
                No, by this heavenly light!

Emilia.
Nor I neither by this heavenly light;
I might do't as well i' th' dark.

Desdemona.
Wouldst thou do such a deed for all the world?

Emilia.
The world's a huge thing; it is a great price
For a small vice.

Desdemona.
Good troth, I think thou wouldst not.

Emilia.
By my troth, I think I should, and undo't when I had done't. Marry, I would not do such a thing for a joint-ring, nor for measures of lawn, nor for gowns, petticoats, nor caps, nor any petty exhibition; but, for all the whole world—'ud's pity, who would not make her husband a cuckold to make him a monarch? I should venture purgatory for't.

Desdemona.
Beshrew me, if I would do such a wrong
For the whole world.

Emilia.
Why, the wrong is but a wrong i' th' world; and having the world for your labor, 'tis a wrong in your own world, and you might quickly make it right.

Desdemona.
I do not think there is any such woman.

Emilia.
Yes, a dozen; and as many to th' vantage as would
store the world they play'd for.
But I do think it is their husbands' faults
If wives do fall. Say that they slack their duties,
And pour our treasures into foreign laps;
Or else break out in peevish jealousies,
Throwing restraint upon us; or say they strike us,
Or scant our former having in despite:
Why, we have galls; and though we have some grace,
Yet have we some revenge. Let husbands know
Their wives have sense like them; they see, and smell,
And have their palates both for sweet and sour,
As husbands have. What is it that they do
When they change us for others? Is it sport?
I think it is. And doth affection breed it?
I think it doth. Is't frailty that thus errs?
It is so too. And have not we affections,
Desires for sport, and frailty, as men have?
Then let them use us well; else let them know,
The ills we do, their ills instruct us so.

Desdemona.
Good night, good night. God me such uses send,
Not to pick bad from bad, but by bad mend.

Exeunt.

Act 5

Scene 1

Cyprus. A street.

(*Iago; Roderigo; Cassio; Othello; Lodovico; Gratiano; Bianca; Emilia*)

Iago places Roderigo at the right spot to kill Cassio; which one of the two dies does not much matter to Iago, who needs to be rid of both of them. When Cassio appears, Roderigo misses him; Cassio fights back and wounds Roderigo, while Iago stabs Cassio in the leg from behind. Othello hears Cassio's cries and is delighted, thinking he is dead. Lodovico and Gratiano arrive at the scene, wondering what has happened; Iago appears as if just woken, and in the dark stabs Roderigo to death. The confusion is great, and when Bianca arrives, Iago manages to pin the blame on her and orders her arrested on suspicion of having arranged the crime. He binds up Cassio's wounds and sends him to a doctor. Emilia arrives to find out what all the noise is about, and Iago sends her to tell Othello and Desdemona what has happened. He realizes that things may or may not go well for him tonight.

Enter Iago and Roderigo.

Iago.
Here, stand behind this bulk, straight will he come.
Wear thy good rapier bare, and put it home.
Quick, quick, fear nothing; I'll be at thy elbow.
It makes us, or it mars us, think on that,
And fix most firm thy resolution.

Roderigo.
Be near at hand, I may miscarry in't.

Iago.
Here, at thy hand; be bold, and take thy stand.

Retires.

Roderigo.
I have no great devotion to the deed,
And yet he hath given me satisfying reasons.
'Tis but a man gone. Forth my sword; he dies.

Iago.
I have rubb'd this young quat almost to the sense,
And he grows angry. Now, whether he kill Cassio,
Or Cassio him, or each do kill the other,
Every way makes my gain. Live Roderigo,
He calls me to a restitution large
Of gold and jewels that I bobb'd from him
As gifts to Desdemona;
It must not be. If Cassio do remain,
He hath a daily beauty in his life
That makes me ugly; and besides, the Moor
May unfold me to him; there stand I in much peril.
No, he must die. Be't so. I hear him coming.

Enter Cassio.

Roderigo.
I know his gait, 'tis he.—Villain, thou diest!

Makes a pass at Cassio.

Cassio.
That thrust had been mine enemy indeed,
But that my coat is better than thou know'st.
I will make proof of thine.

Draws, and wounds Roderigo.

Roderigo.
                    O, I am slain.

Iago from behind wounds Cassio in the leg, and exit.

Cassio.
I am maim'd forever. Help ho! Murder, murder!

Falls.
Enter Othello.

Othello.
The voice of Cassio! Iago keeps his word.

Roderigo.
O, villain that I am!

Othello.
                    It is even so.

Cassio.
O, help ho! Light! A surgeon!

Othello.
'Tis he!—O brave Iago, honest and just,
That hast such noble sense of thy friend's wrong!
Thou teachest me. Minion, your dear lies dead,
And your unblest fate hies. Strumpet, I come.
Forth of my heart those charms, thine eyes, are blotted;
Thy bed, lust-stain'd, shall with lust's blood be spotted.

Exit Othello.
Enter Lodovico and Gratiano.

Cassio.
What ho! No watch? No passage? Murder, murder!

Gratiano.
'Tis some mischance, the voice is very direful.

Cassio.
O, help!

Lodovico.
Hark!

Roderigo.
O wretched villin!

Lodovico.
Two or three groan. 'Tis heavy night;
These may be counterfeits; let's think't unsafe
To come in to the cry without more help.

Roderigo.
Nobody come? Then shall I bleed to death.

Enter Iago with a light.

Lodovico.
Hark!

Gratiano.
Here's one comes in his shirt, with light and weapons.

Iago.
Who's there? Whose noise is this that cries on murder?

Lodovico.
We do not know.

Iago.
                    Did not you hear a cry?

Cassio.
Here, here! For heaven sake help me!

Iago.
                    What's the matter?

Gratiano.
This is Othello's ancient, as I take it.

Lodovico.
The same indeed, a very valiant fellow.

Iago.
What are you here that cry so grievously?

Cassio.
Iago? O, I am spoil'd, undone by villains!
Give me some help.

Iago.
O me, lieutenant! What villains have done this?

Cassio.
I think that one of them is hereabout,
And cannot make away.

Iago.
              O treacherous villains!

To Lodovico and Gratiano.

What are you there?
Come in, and give some help.

Roderigo.
O, help me there!

Cassio.
That's one of them.

Iago.
            O murd'rous slave! O villain!

Stabs Roderigo.

Roderigo.
O damn'd Iago! O inhuman dog!

Iago.
Kill men i' th' dark?—Where be these bloody thieves?—
How silent is this town!—Ho, murder, murder!—
What may you be? Are you of good or evil?

Lodovico.
As you shall prove us, praise us.

Iago.
Signior Lodovico?

Lodovico.
He, sir.

Iago.
I cry you mercy. Here's Cassio hurt by villains.

Gratiano.
Cassio?

Iago.
How is't, brother?

Cassio.
My leg is cut in two.

Iago.
         Marry, heaven forbid!
Light, gentlemen! I'll bind it with my shirt.

Enter Bianca.

Bianca.
What is the matter ho? Who is't that cried?

Iago.
Who is't that cried?

Bianca.
O my dear Cassio, my sweet Cassio!
O Cassio, Cassio, Cassio!

Iago.
O notable strumpet! Cassio, may you suspect
Who they should be that have thus mangled you?

Cassio.
No.

Gratiano.
I am sorry to find you thus; I have been to seek you.

Iago.
Lend me a garter. So.—O for a chair
To bear him easily hence!

Bianca.
Alas, he faints! O Cassio, Cassio, Cassio!

Iago.
Gentlemen all, I do suspect this trash
To be a party in this injury.—
Patience awhile, good Cassio.—Come, come;
Lend me a light. Know we this face or no?
Alas, my friend and my dear countryman
Roderigo! No—yes, sure—O heaven, Roderigo!

Gratiano.
What, of Venice?

Iago.
Even he, sir; did you know him?

Gratiano.
              Know him? Ay.

Iago.
Signior Gratiano? I cry your gentle pardon;
These bloody accidents must excuse my manners
That so neglected you.

Gratiano.
                    I am glad to see you.

Iago.
How do you, Cassio? O, a chair, a chair!

Gratiano.
Roderigo!

Iago.
He, he, 'tis he.

A chair brought in.

                    O, that's well said: the chair.
Some good man bear him carefully from hence,
I'll fetch the general's surgeon.

To Bianca.

For you, mistress,
Save you your labor.—He that lies slain here, Cassio,
Was my dear friend. What malice was between you?

Cassio.
None in the world; nor do I know the man.

Iago.

To Bianca.

What? Look you pale?—O, bear him out o' th' air.

Cassio and Roderigo are borne off.

Stay you, good gentlemen.—Look you pale, mistress?—
Do you perceive the gastness of her eye?—
Nay, an' you stare, we shall hear more anon.—
Behold her well; I pray you look upon her.
Do you see, gentlemen? Nay, guiltiness will speak,
Though tongues were out of use.

Enter Emilia.

Emilia.
Alas, what is the matter? What is the matter, husband?

Iago.
Cassio hath here been set on in the dark
By Roderigo and fellows that are scap'd.
He's almost slain, and Roderigo quite dead.

Emilia.
Alas, good gentleman! Alas, good Cassio!

Iago.
This is the fruits of whoring. Prithee, Emilia,
Go know of Cassio where he supp'd tonight.

To Bianca.

What, do you shake at that?

Bianca.
He supp'd at my house, but I therefore shake not.

Iago.
O, did he so? I charge you go with me.

Emilia.
O fie upon thee, strumpet!

Bianca.
I am no strumpet, but of life as honest
As you that thus abuse me.

Emilia.
                As I? Fough, fie upon thee!

Iago.
Kind gentlemen, let's go see poor Cassio dress'd.
Come, mistress, you must tell 's another tale.
Emilia, run you to the citadel,
And tell my lord and lady what hath happ'd.—
Will you go on afore?

Aside.

                    This is the night
That either makes me, or foredoes me quite.

Exeunt.

Scene 2

A bedchamber in the castle.

(*Othello; Desdemona; Emilia; Montano; Gratiano; Iago; Lodovico; Cassio; Officers*)

Othello enters the bedchamber where Desdemona lies sleeping, considering how it is necessary that she die. He kisses her, almost convincing himself not to kill her, but he steels himself to the task. His kisses wake her. He orders her to pray, informing her that she is about to die. She begs for mercy, denying all of his accusations, but he refuses to listen and smothers her. Emilia knocks at the door, calling for Othello. Thinking that she has come to tell him of Cassio's death, he is uncertain what to do, reluctant to let her in lest she try to speak to Desdemona. In the end he lets her in, and she blurts out her news. At that moment Desdemona calls out, and Emilia runs to her and tries to unsuccessfully revive her. Desdemona insists that nobody did anything to her and dies. Othello calls her a liar and tells Emilia that he killed her. He tells Emilia why, and she is horrified and does not want to believe him when he says that Iago was the one who accused Desdemona. Despite Othello's threats, she opens the door and yells out for help. Montano, Gratiano and Iago enter, and Emilia begs her husband to deny what Othello has said, but he cannot. He orders her to be quiet and go home, but she refuses, and when Othello brings out the proof of the handkerchief, she tells him that it was she who stole the handkerchief and gave it to Iago. Iago denies it, but Othello sees the truth and rushes at him; Iago stabs Emilia and runs out. The others chase after him, leaving Othello and Emilia with Desdemona's body. He finds a spare sword in the room and arms himself with it, but does nothing as the extent of what he has done crushes him. Lodovico enters with the injured Cassio and the captured Iago. The story is unraveled, but Iago refuses to give any explanation for what he has done. Lodovico informs Othello that he must come with them to Venice, but Othello begs him to wait a moment; he explains what he has done in the state's service, and thinking of one last example, he stabs himself. Dying, he drags himself to the bed to kiss Desdemona one last time as he dies. Lodovico plans to return to Venice, begging Cassio to make Iago suffer before he dies.

Enter Othello with a light and Desdemona in her bed asleep.

Othello.
It is the cause, it is the cause, my soul;
Let me not name it to you, you chaste stars,
It is the cause. Yet I'll not shed her blood,
Nor scar that whiter skin of hers than snow,
And smooth as monumental alabaster.
Yet she must die, else she'll betray more men.
Put out the light, and then put out the light:
If I quench thee, thou flaming minister,
I can again thy former light restore,
Should I repent me; but once put out thy light,
Thou cunning'st pattern of excelling nature,
I know not where is that Promethean heat
That can thy light relume. When I have pluck'd thy rose,
I cannot give it vital growth again,
It needs must wither. I'll smell thee on the tree.

Kisses her.

O balmy breath, that dost almost persuade
Justice to break her sword! One more, one more.
Be thus when thou art dead, and I will kill thee
And love thee after. One more, and that's the last.
So sweet was ne'er so fatal. I must weep,
But they are cruel tears. This sorrow's heavenly,
It strikes where it doth love. She wakes.

Desdemona.
Who's there? Othello?

Othello.
                    Ay, Desdemona.

Desdemona.
Will you come to bed, my lord?

Othello.
Have you pray'd tonight, Desdemon?

Desdemona.
                    Ay, my lord.

Othello.
If you bethink yourself of any crime
Unreconcil'd as yet to heaven and grace,
Solicit for it straight.

Desdemona.
Alack, my lord, what may you mean by that?

Othello.
Well, do it, and be brief, I will walk by.
I would not kill thy unprepared spirit,
No, heaven forefend! I would not kill thy soul.

Desdemona.
Talk you of killing?

Othello.
                    Ay, I do.

Desdemona.
                    Then heaven
Have mercy on me!

Othello.
                    Amen, with all my heart!

Desdemona.
If you say so, I hope you will not kill me.

Othello.
Humh!

Desdemona.
And yet I fear you; for you're fatal then
When your eyes roll so. Why I should fear I know not,
Since guiltiness I know not; but yet I feel I fear.

Othello.
Think on thy sins.

Desdemona.
                    They are loves I bear to you.

Othello.
Ay, and for that thou di'st.

Desdemona.
That death's unnatural that kills for loving.
Alas, why gnaw you so your nether lip?
Some bloody passion shakes your very frame.
These are portents; but yet I hope, I hope,
They do not point on me.

Othello.
                    Peace, and be still!

Desdemona.
I will so. What's the matter?

Othello.
That handkerchief which I so lov'd, and gave thee,
Thou gav'st to Cassio.

Desdemona.
               No, by my life and soul!
Send for the man, and ask him.

Othello.
                 Sweet soul, take heed,
Take heed of perjury, thou art on thy death-bed.

Desdemona.
Ay, but not yet to die.

Othello.
                    Yes, presently:
Therefore confess thee freely of thy sin;
For to deny each article with oath
Cannot remove nor choke the strong conception
That I do groan withal. Thou art to die.

Desdemona.
Then Lord have mercy on me!

Othello.
                    I say, amen.

Desdemona.
And have you mercy too! I never did
Offend you in my life; never lov'd Cassio
But with such general warranty of heaven
As I might love. I never gave him token.

Othello.
By heaven, I saw my handkerchief in 's hand.
O perjur'd woman, thou dost stone my heart,
And mak'st me call what I intend to do
A murder, which I thought a sacrifice.
I saw the handkerchief.

Desdemona.
                    He found it then;
I never gave it him. Send for him hither;
Let him confess a truth.

Othello.
                    He hath confess'd.

Desdemona.
What, my lord?

Othello.
That he hath us'd thee.

Desdemona.
                  How? Unlawfully?

Othello.
                      Ay.

Desdemona.
He will not say so.

Othello.
                  No—his mouth is stopp'd;
Honest Iago hath ta'en order for't.

Desdemona.
O, my fear interprets. What, is he dead?

Othello.
Had all his hairs been lives, my great revenge
Had stomach for them all.

Desdemona.
Alas, he is betray'd and I undone!

Othello.
Out, strumpet! Weep'st thou for him to my face?

Desdemona.
O, banish me, my lord, but kill me not!

Othello.
Down, strumpet!

Desdemona.
Kill me tomorrow, let me live tonight!

Othello.
Nay, an' you strive—

Desdemona.
But half an hour!

Othello.
            Being done, there is no pause.

Desdemona.
But while I say one prayer!

Othello.
            It is too late.

Smothers her.

Desdemona.
O Lord, Lord, Lord!

Emilia.

At the door, within.

My lord, my lord!
What ho! My lord, my lord!

Othello.
What noise is this? Not dead? Not yet quite dead?
I that am cruel am yet merciful,
I would not have thee linger in thy pain.
So, so.

Emilia.

Within.
            What ho! My lord, my lord!

Othello.
            Who's there?

Emilia.

Within.
O, good my lord, I would speak a word with you!

Othello.
Yes.—'Tis Emilia.—By and by.—She's dead.
'Tis like she comes to speak of Cassio's death;
The noise was high. Hah, no more moving?
Still as the grave. Shall she come in? Were't good?
I think she stirs again. No. What's best to do?
If she come in, she'll sure speak to my wife.
My wife, my wife! What wife? I have no wife.
O insupportable! O heavy hour!
Methinks it should be now a huge eclipse
Of sun and moon, and that th' affrighted globe
Did yawn at alteration.

Emilia.

Within.
            I do beseech you
That I may speak with you. O, good my lord!

Othello.
I had forgot thee. O, come in, Emilia.—
Soft, by and by, let me the curtains draw.—
Where art thou?

Unlocks the door.
Enter Emilia.
            What's the matter with thee now?

Emilia.
O, my good lord, yonder's foul murders done!

Othello.
What? Now?

Emilia.
But now, my lord.

Othello.
It is the very error of the moon,
She comes more nearer earth than she was wont,
And makes men mad.

Emilia.
Cassio, my lord, hath kill'd a young Venetian
Call'd Roderigo.

Othello.
            Roderigo kill'd?
And Cassio kill'd?

Emilia.
            No, Cassio is not kill'd.

Othello.
Not Cassio kill'd? Then murder's out of tune,
And sweet revenge grows harsh.

Desdemona.
O, falsely, falsely murder'd!

Emilia.
                O Lord, what cry is that?

Othello.
That? What?

Emilia.
Out, and alas, that was my lady's voice.
Help, help, ho, help! O lady, speak again!
Sweet Desdemona, O sweet mistress, speak!

Desdemona.
A guiltless death I die.

Emilia.
O, who hath done this deed?

Desdemona.
Nobody; I myself. Farewell!
Commend me to my kind lord. O, farewell!

Dies.

Othello.
Why, how should she be murd'red?

Emilia.
                Alas! Who knows?

Othello.
You heard her say herself, it was not I.

Emilia.
She said so; I must needs report the truth.

Othello.
She's like a liar gone to burning hell:
'Twas I that kill'd her.

Emilia.
                O, the more angel she,
And you the blacker devil!

Othello.
She turn'd to folly, and she was a whore.

Emilia.
Thou dost belie her, and thou art a devil.

Othello.
She was false as water.

Emilia.
                Thou art rash as fire to say
That she was false. O, she was heavenly true!

Othello.
Cassio did top her; ask thy husband else.
O, I were damn'd beneath all depth in hell
But that I did proceed upon just grounds
To this extremity. Thy husband knew it all.

Emilia.
My husband?

Othello.
Thy husband.

Emilia.
That she was false to wedlock?

Othello.
Ay, with Cassio. Nay, had she been true,
If heaven would make me such another world
Of one entire and perfect chrysolite,
I'd not have sold her for it.

Emilia.
                My husband?

Othello.
Ay, 'twas he that told me on her first.
An honest man he is, and hates the slime
That sticks on filthy deeds.

Emilia.
                My husband?

Othello.
What needs this iterance, woman? I say thy husband.

Emilia.
O mistress, villainy hath made mocks with love!
My husband say she was false?

Othello.
                He, woman:
I say thy husband; dost understand the word?
My friend, thy husband, honest, honest Iago.

Emilia.
If he say so, may his pernicious soul
Rot half a grain a day! He lies to th' heart.
She was too fond of her most filthy bargain.

Othello.
Hah?

Emilia.
Do thy worst!
This deed of thine is no more worthy heaven
Than thou wast worthy her.

Othello.
     Peace, you were best.

Emilia.
Thou hast not half that pow'r to do me harm
As I have to be hurt. O gull, O dolt,
As ignorant as dirt! Thou hast done a deed—
I care not for thy sword, I'll make thee known,
Though I lost twenty lives. Help, help, ho, help!
The Moor hath kill'd my mistress! Murder, murder!

Enter Montano, Gratiano, and Iago, with others.

Montano.
What is the matter? How now, general?

Emilia.
O, are you come, Iago? You have done well,
That men must lay their murders on your neck.

Gratiano.
What is the matter?

Emilia.
Disprove this villain, if thou be'st a man.
He says thou toldst him that his wife was false.
I know thou didst not; thou'rt not such a villain.
Speak, for my heart is full.

Iago.
I told him what I thought, and told no more
Than what he found himself was apt and true.

Emilia.
But did you ever tell him she was false?

Iago.
I did.

Emilia.
You told a lie, an odious, damned lie;
Upon my soul, a lie, a wicked lie.
She false with Cassio? Did you say with Cassio?

Iago.
With Cassio, mistress. Go to, charm your tongue.

Emilia.
I will not charm my tongue; I am bound to speak.
My mistress here lies murdered in her bed—

All.
O heavens forefend!

Emilia.
And your reports have set the murder on.

Othello.
Nay, stare not, masters, it is true indeed.

Gratiano.
'Tis a strange truth.

Montano.
O monstrous act!

Emilia.
     Villainy, villainy, villainy!
I think upon't, I think—I smell't—O villainy!
I thought so then—I'll kill myself for grief—
O villainy! Villainy!

Iago.
What, are you mad? I charge you get you home.

Emilia.
Good gentlemen, let me have leave to speak.
'Tis proper I obey him; but not now.
Perchance, Iago, I will ne'er go home.

Othello.
O, O, O!

Othello falls on the bed.

Emilia.
     Nay, lay thee down and roar;
For thou hast kill'd the sweetest innocent
That e'er did lift up eye.

Othello.

Rising.

     O, she was foul!
I scarce did know you, uncle; there lies your niece,
Whose breath, indeed, these hands have newly stopp'd.
I know this act shows horrible and grim.

Gratiano.
Poor Desdemon! I am glad thy father's dead.
Thy match was mortal to him, and pure grief
Shore his old thread in twain. Did he live now,
This sight would make him do a desperate turn,
Yea, curse his better angel from his side,
And fall to reprobance.

Othello.
'Tis pitiful; but yet Iago knows
That she with Cassio hath the act of shame
A thousand times committed. Cassio confess'd it,
And she did gratify his amorous works
With that recognizance and pledge of love
Which I first gave her. I saw it in his hand;
It was a handkerchief, an antique token
My father gave my mother.

Emilia.
O God! O heavenly God!

Iago.
'Zounds, hold your peace.

Emilia.
          'Twill out, 'twill out! I peace?
No, I will speak as liberal as the north:
Let heaven and men and devils, let them all,
All, all, cry shame against me, yet I'll speak.

Iago.
Be wise, and get you home.

Emilia.
          I will not.

Iago offers to stab Emilia.

Gratiano.
          Fie,
Your sword upon a woman?

Emilia.
O thou dull Moor, that handkerchief thou speak'st of
I found by fortune, and did give my husband;
For often, with a solemn earnestness
(More than indeed belong'd to such a trifle),
He begg'd of me to steal't.

Iago.
          Villainous whore!

Emilia.
She give it Cassio? No, alas, I found it,
And I did give't my husband.

Iago.
          Filth, thou liest!

Emilia.
By heaven, I do not, I do not, gentlemen.
O murd'rous coxcomb, what should such a fool
Do with so good a wife?

Othello.
          Are there no stones in heaven
But what serves for the thunder?—Precious villain!

*The Moor runs at Iago; Montano disarms Othello.
Iago kills his wife.*

Gratiano.
The woman falls; sure he hath kill'd his wife.

Emilia.
Ay, ay! O, lay me by my mistress' side.

Exit Iago.

Gratiano.
He's gone, but his wife's kill'd.

Montano.
'Tis a notorious villain. Take you this weapon
Which I have here recover'd from the Moor.
Come guard the door without; let him not pass,
But kill him rather. I'll after that same villain,
For 'tis a damned slave.

Exit with all but Othello and Emilia.

Othello.
          I am not valiant neither,
But every puny whipster gets my sword.
But why should honor outlive honesty?
Let it go all.

Emilia.
          What did thy song bode, lady?
Hark, canst thou hear me? I will play the swan,
And die in music.

Sings.

Willow, willow, willow.
Moor, she was chaste; she lov'd thee, cruel Moor;

Act 5, Scene 2

So come my soul to bliss, as I speak true;
So speaking as I think, alas, I die.

Dies.

Othello.
I have another weapon in this chamber;
It was a sword of Spain, the ice-brook's temper—
O, here it is. Uncle, I must come forth.

Gratiano.

Within.

If thou attempt it, it will cost thee dear:
Thou hast no weapon, and perforce must suffer.

Othello.
Look in upon me then and speak with me,
Or naked as I am I will assault thee.

Enter Gratiano.

Gratiano.
What is the matter?

Othello.
                    Behold, I have a weapon;
A better never did itself sustain
Upon a soldier's thigh. I have seen the day
That with this little arm, and this good sword,
I have made my way through more impediments
Than twenty times your stop. But (O vain boast!)
Who can control his fate? 'Tis not so now.
Be not afraid though you do see me weapon'd;
Here is my journey's end, here is my butt
And very sea-mark of my utmost sail.
Do you go back dismay'd? 'Tis a lost fear;
Man but a rush against Othello's breast,
And he retires. Where should Othello go?
Now—how dost thou look now? O ill-starr'd wench,
Pale as thy smock! When we shall meet at compt,
This look of thine will hurl my soul from heaven,
And fiends will snatch at it. Cold, cold, my girl?
Even like thy chastity. O cursed, cursed slave!
Whip me, ye devils,
From the possession of this heavenly sight!
Blow me about in winds! Roast me in sulphur!
Wash me in steep-down gulfs of liquid fire!
O Desdemon! Dead, Desdemon! Dead!
O, O!

Enter Lodovico, Cassio in a chair, Montano, and Iago guarded, with Officers.

Lodovico.
Where is this rash and most unfortunate man?

Othello.
That's he that was Othello; here I am.

Lodovico.
Where is that viper? Bring the villain forth.

Othello.
I look down towards his feet; but that's a fable.
If that thou be'st a devil, I cannot kill thee.

Wounds Iago.

Lodovico.
Wrench his sword from him.

Iago.
                    I bleed, sir, but not kill'd.

Othello.
I am not sorry neither, I'ld have thee live;
For in my sense, 'tis happiness to die.

Lodovico.
O thou Othello, that was once so good,
Fall'n in the practice of a damned slave,
What shall be said to thee?

Othello.
                    Why, any thing:
An honorable murderer, if you will;
For nought I did in hate, but all in honor.

Lodovico.
This wretch hath part confess'd his villainy.
Did you and he consent in Cassio's death?

Othello.
Ay.

Cassio.
Dear general, I never gave you cause.

Othello.
I do believe it, and I ask your pardon.
Will you, I pray, demand that demi-devil
Why he hath thus ensnar'd my soul and body?

Iago.
Demand me nothing; what you know, you know:
From this time forth I never will speak word.

Lodovico.
What? Not to pray?

Gratiano.
                Torments will ope your lips.

Othello.
Well, thou dost best.

Lodovico.
Sir, you shall understand what hath befall'n,
Which, as I think, you know not. Here is a letter
Found in the pocket of the slain Roderigo,
And here another. The one of them imports
The death of Cassio to be undertook
By Roderigo.

Othello.
O villain!

Cassio.
              Most heathenish and most gross!

Lodovico.
Now here's another discontented paper,
Found in his pocket too; and this it seems
Roderigo meant t' have sent this damned villain;
But that, belike, Iago in the nick
Came in and satisfied him.

Othello.
              O thou pernicious caitiff!—
How came you, Cassio, by that handkerchief
That was my wive's?

Cassio.
              I found it in my chamber:
And he himself confess'd it but even now,
That there he dropp'd it for a special purpose
Which wrought to his desire.

Othello.
              O fool, fool, fool!

Cassio.
There is besides, in Roderigo's letter,
How he upbraids Iago, that he made him
Brave me upon the watch, whereon it came
That I was cast; and even but now he spake
(After long seeming dead) Iago hurt him,
Iago set him on.

Lodovico.
You must forsake this room and go with us.
Your power and your command is taken off,
And Cassio rules in Cyprus. For this slave,
If there be any cunning cruelty
That can torment him much, and hold him long,
It shall be his. You shall close prisoner rest,
Till that the nature of your fault be known
To the Venetian state. Come, bring away.

Othello.
Soft you; a word or two before you go.
I have done the state some service, and they know't—
No more of that. I pray you, in your letters,
When you shall these unlucky deeds relate,
Speak of me as I am; nothing extenuate,
Nor set down aught in malice. Then must you speak
Of one that lov'd not wisely but too well;
Of one not easily jealous, but being wrought,
Perplexed in the extreme; of one whose hand
(Like the base Indian) threw a pearl away
Richer than all his tribe; of one whose subdu'd eyes,
Albeit unused to the melting mood,
Drops tears as fast as the Arabian trees
Their medicinable gum. Set you down this;
And say besides, that in Aleppo once,
Where a malignant and a turban'd Turk
Beat a Venetian and traduc'd the state,
I took by th' throat the circumcised dog,
And smote him—thus.

He stabs himself.

Lodovico.
O bloody period!

Gratiano.
              All that is spoke is marr'd.

Othello.
I kiss'd thee ere I kill'd thee. No way but this,
Killing myself, to die upon a kiss.

Falls on the bed and dies.

Cassio.
This did I fear, but thought he had no weapon;
For he was great of heart.

Lodovico.

To Iago.

                O Spartan dog,
More fell than anguish, hunger, or the sea!
Look on the tragic loading of this bed;
This is thy work. The object poisons sight,
Let it be hid. Gratiano, keep the house,
And seize upon the fortunes of the Moor,
For they succeed on you. To you, Lord Governor,
Remains the censure of this hellish villain,
The time, the place, the torture, O, enforce it!
Myself will straight aboard, and to the state
This heavy act with heavy heart relate.

Exeunt.

King Lear

Act 1

Scene 1

King Lear's palace.

(Kent; Gloucester; Edmund; King Lear; Cornwall; Albany; Goneril; Regan; Cordelia; Attendants; Gloucester; France; Burgundy)

The Earls of Kent and Gloucester discuss the King's project to divide the kingdom, remarking that it is impossible to tell which of his two sons-in-law he intends to treat best. Gloucester introduces his bastard son Edmund to Kent, making raunchy comments about him as he does so. Lear and his retinue enter. The King calls for the Duke of Burgundy and the King of France to be brought in, and while they are waiting explains that he is dividing his kingdom between his three daughters while he takes his retirement. To decide which daughter gets which portion, he asks them to tell him how much they love him. Goneril, the wife of the Duke of Albany, and Regan, the wife of the Duke of Cornwall, both speak flatteringly and are given their shares; but Cordelia, the youngest, unmarried, is unwilling to be a hypocrite and refuses to say anything. Pressed further, she makes a lukewarm declaration that enrages Lear. He disinherits her on the spot and splits the last third of the country between the elder daughters. Kent intervenes, attempting to calm Lear down, but the furious King exiles him for his pains. He informs the court that while he is giving up all political power to the two Dukes his sons-in-law, he will keep a hundred knights to serve him and go between their houses month by month, at their charge. Burgundy and France enter and are informed that Cordelia will no longer bring any dowry with her; Burgundy immediately abandons his suit, but the King of France chooses to marry her. Lear lets him take her without offering any blessing. Cordelia bids her sisters farewell. Left alone, Goneril and Regan discuss their father and his wayward temper, and agree to be on guard against him.

Enter Kent, Gloucester, and Edmund.

Earl of Kent.
I thought the King had more affected the Duke of Albany than Cornwall.

Earl of Gloucester.
It did always seem so to us; but now in the division of the kingdom, it appears not which of the Dukes he values most, for equalities are so weigh'd, that curiosity in neither can make choice of either's moi'ty.

Earl of Kent.
Is not this your son, my lord?

Earl of Gloucester.
His breeding, sir, hath been at my charge. I have so often blush'd to acknowledge him, that now I am braz'd to't.

Earl of Kent.
I cannot conceive you.

Earl of Gloucester.
Sir, this young fellow's mother could; whereupon she grew round-womb'd, and had indeed, sir, a son for her cradle ere she had a husband for her bed. Do you smell a fault?

Earl of Kent.
I cannot wish the fault undone, the issue of it being so proper.

Earl of Gloucester.
But I have a son, sir, by order of law, some year elder than this, who yet is no dearer in my account. Though this knave came something saucily to the world before he was sent for, yet was his mother fair, there was good sport at his making, and the whoreson must be acknowledg'd. Do you know this noble gentleman, Edmund?

Edmund.
No, my lord.

Earl of Gloucester.
My Lord of Kent. Remember him hereafter as my honorable friend.

Edmund.
My services to your lordship.

Earl of Kent.
I must love you, and sue to know you better.

Edmund.
Sir, I shall study deserving.

Earl of Gloucester.
He hath been out nine years, and away he shall again.

Sound a sennet.

The King is coming.

Enter one bearing a coronet, then King Lear, Cornwall, Albany, Goneril, Regan, Cordelia, and Attendants.

Lear, King of Britain.
Attend the lords of France and Burgundy, Gloucester.

Earl of Gloucester.
I shall, my lord.

Exit with Edmund.

Lear, King of Britain.
Mean time we shall express our darker purpose.
Give me the map there. Know that we have divided
In three our kingdom; and 'tis our fast intent
To shake all cares and business from our age,
Conferring them on younger strengths, while we
Unburden'd crawl toward death. Our son of Cornwall,
And you, our no less loving son of Albany,
We have this hour a constant will to publish
Our daughters' several dowers, that future strife
May be prevented now. The princes, France and Burgundy,
Great rivals in our youngest daughter's love,
Long in our court have made their amorous sojourn,
And here are to be answer'd. Tell me, my daughters
(Since now we will divest us both of rule,
Interest of territory, cares of state),
Which of you shall we say doth love us most,
That we our largest bounty may extend
Where nature doth with merit challenge? Goneril,
Our eldest-born, speak first.

Goneril.
Sir, I love you more than words can wield the matter,
Dearer than eyesight, space, and liberty,
Beyond what can be valued, rich or rare,
No less than life, with grace, health, beauty, honor;
As much as child e'er lov'd, or father found;
A love that makes breath poor, and speech unable:
Beyond all manner of so much I love you.

Cordelia.

Aside.

What shall Cordelia speak? Love, and be silent.

Lear, King of Britain.
Of all these bounds, even from this line to this,
With shadowy forests and with champains rich'd,
With plenteous rivers and wide-skirted meads,
We make thee lady. To thine and Albany's issue
Be this perpetual. What says our second daughter,
Our dearest Regan, wife of Cornwall? Speak.

Regan.
I am made of that self metal as my sister,
And prize me at her worth. In my true heart
I find she names my very deed of love;
Only she comes too short, that I profess
Myself an enemy to all other joys
Which the most precious square of sense possesses,
And find I am alone felicitate
In your dear Highness' love.

Cordelia.

Aside.

          Then poor Cordelia!
And yet not so, since I am sure my love's
More ponderous than my tongue.

Lear, King of Britain.
To thee and thine hereditary ever
Remain this ample third of our fair kingdom,
No less in space, validity, and pleasure,
Than that conferr'd on Goneril.—Now, our joy,
Although our last and least, to whose young love
The vines of France and milk of Burgundy
Strive to be interess'd, what can you say to draw
A third more opulent than your sisters'? Speak.

Cordelia.
Nothing, my lord.

Lear, King of Britain.
Nothing?

Cordelia.
Nothing.

Lear, King of Britain.
Nothing will come of nothing, speak again.

Cordelia.
Unhappy that I am, I cannot heave
My heart into my mouth. I love your Majesty
According to my bond, no more nor less.

Lear, King of Britain.
How, how, Cordelia? Mend your speech a little,
Lest you may mar your fortunes.

Cordelia.
                    Good my lord,
You have begot me, bred me, lov'd me: I
Return those duties back as are right fit,
Obey you, love you, and most honor you.
Why have my sisters husbands, if they say
They love you all? Happily, when I shall wed,
That lord whose hand must take my plight shall carry
Half my love with him, half my care and duty.
Sure I shall never marry like my sisters,
To love my father all.

Lear, King of Britain.
But goes thy heart with this?

Cordelia.
                    Ay, my good lord.

Lear, King of Britain.
So young, and so untender?

Cordelia.
So young, my lord, and true.

Lear, King of Britain.
Let it be so: thy truth then be thy dow'r!
For by the sacred radiance of the sun,
The mysteries of Hecat and the night;
By all the operation of the orbs,
From whom we do exist and cease to be;
Here I disclaim all my paternal care,
Propinquity and property of blood,
And as a stranger to my heart and me
Hold thee from this forever. The barbarous Scythian,
Or he that makes his generation messes
To gorge his appetite, shall to my bosom
Be as well neighbor'd, pitied, and reliev'd,
As thou my sometime daughter.

Earl of Kent.
                    Good my liege—

Lear, King of Britain.
Peace, Kent!
Come not between the dragon and his wrath;
I lov'd her most, and thought to set my rest
On her kind nursery.

To Cordelia.
                    Hence, and avoid my sight!—
So be my grave my peace, as here I give
Her father's heart from her. Call France. Who stirs?
Call Burgundy. Cornwall and Albany,
With my two daughters' dow'rs digest the third;
Let pride, which she calls plainness, marry her.
I do invest you jointly with my power,
Pre-eminence, and all the large effects
That troop with majesty. Ourself, by monthly course,
With reservation of an hundred knights
By you to be sustain'd, shall our abode
Make with you by due turn. Only we shall retain
The name, and all th' addition to a king;
The sway, revenue, execution of the rest,
Beloved sons, be yours, which to confirm,
This coronet part between you.

Earl of Kent.
                    Royal Lear,
Whom I have ever honor'd as my king,
Lov'd as my father, as my master follow'd,
As my great patron thought on in my prayers—

Lear, King of Britain.
The bow is bent and drawn, make from the shaft.

Earl of Kent.
Let it fall rather, though the fork invade
The region of my heart; be Kent unmannerly
When Lear is mad. What wouldest thou do, old man?
Think'st thou that duty shall have dread to speak
When power to flattery bows? To plainness honor's bound,
When majesty falls to folly. Reserve thy state,
And in thy best consideration check
This hideous rashness. Answer my life my judgment,
Thy youngest daughter does not love thee least,
Nor are those empty-hearted whose low sounds
Reverb no hollowness.

Lear, King of Britain.
     Kent, on thy life, no more.

Earl of Kent.
My life I never held but as a pawn
To wage against thine enemies, ne'er fear'd to lose it,
Thy safety being motive.

Lear, King of Britain.
      Out of my sight!

Earl of Kent.
See better, Lear, and let me still remain
The true blank of thine eye.

Lear, King of Britain.
Now, by Apollo—

Earl of Kent.
     Now, by Apollo, King,
Thou swear'st thy gods in vain.

Lear, King of Britain.
      O vassal! Miscreant!

Starts to draw his sword.

Both Albany and Cornwall.
Dear sir, forbear.

Earl of Kent.
Kill thy physician, and the fee bestow
Upon the foul disease. Revoke thy gift,
Or whilst I can vent clamor from my throat,
I'll tell thee thou dost evil.

Lear, King of Britain.
     Hear me, recreant,
On thine allegiance, hear me!
That thou hast sought to make us break our vow—
Which we durst never yet—and with strain'd pride
To come betwixt our sentence and our power,
Which nor our nature nor our place can bear,
Our potency made good, take thy reward.
Five days we do allot thee, for provision
To shield thee from disasters of the world,
And on the sixth to turn thy hated back
Upon our kingdom. If, on the tenth day following,
Thy banish'd trunk be found in our dominions,
The moment is thy death. Away! By Jupiter,
This shall not be revok'd.

Earl of Kent.
Fare thee well, King; sith thus thou wilt appear,
Freedom lives hence, and banishment is here.

To Cordelia.

The gods to their dear shelter take thee, maid,
That justly think'st and hast most rightly said!

To Regan and Goneril.

And your large speeches may your deeds approve,
That good effects may spring from words of love.
Thus Kent, O princes, bids you all adieu,
He'll shape his old course in a country new.

Exit.
Flourish. Enter Gloucester with France and Burgundy, Attendants.

Earl of Gloucester.
Here's France and Burgundy, my noble lord.

Lear, King of Britain.
My Lord of Burgundy,
We first address toward you, who with this king
Hath rivall'd for our daughter. What, in the least,
Will you require in present dower with her,
Or cease your quest of love?

Duke of Burgundy.
     Most royal Majesty,
I crave no more than hath your Highness offer'd,
Nor will you tender less.

Lear, King of Britain.
                      Right noble Burgundy,
When she was dear to us, we did hold her so,
But now her price is fallen. Sir, there she stands:
If aught within that little seeming substance,
Or all of it, with our displeasure piec'd,
And nothing more, may fitly like your Grace,
She's there, and she is yours.

Duke of Burgundy.
                      I know no answer.

Lear, King of Britain.
Will you, with those infirmities she owes,
Unfriended, new adopted to our hate,
Dow'r'd with our curse, and stranger'd with our oath,
Take her, or leave her?

Duke of Burgundy.
                      Pardon me, royal sir,
Election makes not up in such conditions.

Lear, King of Britain.
Then leave her, sir, for by the pow'r that made me,
I tell you all her wealth.

To France.
                      For you, great King,
I would not from your love make such a stray
To match you where I hate; therefore beseech you
T' avert your liking a more worthier way
Than on a wretch whom Nature is asham'd
Almost t' acknowledge hers.

King of France.
                      This is most strange,
That she, whom even but now was your best object,
The argument of your praise, balm of your age,
The best, the dearest, should in this trice of time
Commit a thing so monstrous, to dismantle
So many folds of favor. Sure her offense
Must be of such unnatural degree
That monsters it, or your fore-vouch'd affection
Fall into taint; which to believe of her
Must be a faith that reason without miracle
Should never plant in me.

Cordelia.
                      I yet beseech your Majesty—
If for I want that glib and oily art
To speak and purpose not, since what I well intend,
I'll do't before I speak—that you make known
It is no vicious blot, murder, or foulness,
No unchaste action, or dishonored step,
That hath depriv'd me of your grace and favor,
But even for want of that for which I am richer—
A still-soliciting eye, and such a tongue
That I am glad I have not, though not to have it
Hath lost me in your liking.

Lear, King of Britain.
                      Better thou
Hadst not been born than not t' have pleas'd me better.

King of France.
Is it but this—a tardiness in nature
Which often leaves the history unspoke
That it intends to do? My Lord of Burgundy,
What say you to the lady? Love's not love
When it is mingled with regards that stands
Aloof from th' entire point. Will you have her?
She is herself a dowry.

Duke of Burgundy.
                      Royal King,
Give but that portion which yourself propos'd,
And here I take Cordelia by the hand,
Duchess of Burgundy.

Lear, King of Britain.
Nothing. I have sworn, I am firm.

Duke of Burgundy.
I am sorry then you have so lost a father
That you must lose a husband.

Cordelia.
                      Peace be with Burgundy!
Since that respects of fortune are his love,
I shall not be his wife.

King of France.
Fairest Cordelia, that art most rich being poor,
Most choice forsaken, and most lov'd despis'd,
Thee and thy virtues here I seize upon,
Be it lawful I take up what's cast away.
Gods, gods! 'Tis strange that from their cold'st neglect
My love should kindle to inflam'd respect.
Thy dow'rless daughter, King, thrown to my chance,
Is queen of us, of ours, and our fair France.
Not all the dukes of wat'rish Burgundy
Can buy this unpriz'd precious maid of me.
Bid them farewell, Cordelia, though unkind,
Thou losest here, a better where to find.

Lear, King of Britain.
Thou hast her, France, let her be thine, for we
Have no such daughter, nor shall ever see
That face of hers again.

To Cordelia.

      Therefore be gone,
Without our grace, our love, our benison.—
Come, noble Burgundy.

Flourish. Exeunt all but France, Goneril, Regan, and Cordelia.

King of France.
Bid farewell to your sisters.

Cordelia.
The jewels of our father, with wash'd eyes
Cordelia leaves you. I know you what you are,
And like a sister am most loath to call
Your faults as they are named. Love well our father;
To your professed bosoms I commit him,
But yet, alas, stood I within his grace,
I would prefer him to a better place.
So farewell to you both.

Regan.
Prescribe not us our duty.

Goneril.
     Let your study
Be to content your lord, who hath receiv'd you
At fortune's alms. You have obedience scanted,
And well are worth the want that you have wanted.

Cordelia.
Time shall unfold what plighted cunning hides,
Who covers faults, at last with shame derides.
Well may you prosper!

King of France.
     Come, my fair Cordelia.

Exeunt France and Cordelia.

Goneril.
Sister, it is not little I have to say of what most nearly appertains to us both. I think our father will hence tonight.

Regan.
That's most certain, and with you; next month with us.

Goneril.
You see how full of changes his age is; the observation we have made of it hath not been little. He always lov'd our sister most, and with what poor judgment he hath now cast her off appears too grossly.

Regan.
'Tis the infirmity of his age, yet he hath ever but slenderly known himself.

Goneril.
The best and soundest of his time hath been but rash; then must we look from his age to receive not alone the imperfections of long-ingraff'd condition, but therewithal the unruly waywardness that infirm and choleric years bring with them.

Regan.
Such unconstant starts are we like to have from him as this of Kent's banishment.

Goneril.
There is further compliment of leave-taking between France and him. Pray you let us hit together; if our father carry authority with such disposition as he bears, this last surrender of his will but offend us.

Regan.
We shall further think of it.

Goneril.
We must do something, and i' th' heat.

Exeunt.

Scene 2

The Earl of Gloucester's castle.

(Edmund the Bastard; Gloucester; Edgar)

Edmund the Bastard inveighs against the discrimination society imposes on illegitimate children. He plans to trick his way into gaining his legitimate brother Edgar's lands. Gloucester is distracted by all the upheaval, and comes across Edmund as he reads a letter supposedly sent to him by Edgar. Gloucester insists on reading the forgery, in which Edgar ostensibly tries to gain Edmund's support for murdering their father. Gloucester swallows this hook and sinker, and asks Edmund to look into the matter. Edmund gloats as the old man leaves. Edgar appears, and Edmund warns him that Gloucester is displeased with him, and encourages him to stay away from their father and lock himself in Edmund's room. Edmund laughs at how easily he can manipulate his family.

Enter Edmund the Bastard with a letter.

Edmund.
Thou, Nature, art my goddess, to thy law
My services are bound. Wherefore should I
Stand in the plague of custom, and permit
The curiosity of nations to deprive me,
For that I am some twelve or fourteen moonshines
Lag of a brother? Why bastard? Wherefore base?
When my dimensions are as well-compact,
My mind as generous, and my shape as true,
As honest madam's issue? Why brand they us
With base? With baseness? Bastardy? Base, base?
Who, in the lusty stealth of nature, take
More composition, and fierce quality,
Than doth within a dull, stale, tired bed
Go to th' creating a whole tribe of fops,
Got 'tween asleep and wake? Well then,
Legitimate Edgar, I must have your land.
Our father's love is to the bastard Edmund
As to th' legitimate. Fine word, "legitimate"!
Well, my legitimate, if this letter speed
And my invention thrive, Edmund the base
Shall top th' legitimate. I grow, I prosper:
Now, gods, stand up for bastards!

Enter Gloucester.

Earl of Gloucester.
Kent banish'd thus? And France in choler parted?
And the King gone tonight? Prescrib'd his pow'r,
Confin'd to exhibition? All this done
Upon the gad? Edmund, how now? What news?

Edmund.
So please your lordship, none.

Putting up the letter.

Earl of Gloucester.
Why so earnestly seek you to put up that letter?

Edmund.
I know no news, my lord.

Earl of Gloucester.
What paper were you reading?

Edmund.
Nothing, my lord.

Earl of Gloucester.
No? What needed then that terrible dispatch of it into your pocket? The quality of nothing hath not such need to hide itself. Let's see. Come, if it be nothing, I shall not need spectacles.

Edmund.
I beseech you, sir, pardon me. It is a letter from my brother that I have not all o'er-read; and for so much as I have perus'd, I find it not fit for your o'erlooking.

Earl of Gloucester.
Give me the letter, sir.

Edmund.
I shall offend either to detain or give it: the contents, as in part I understand them, are to blame.

Earl of Gloucester.
Let's see, let's see.

Edmund.
I hope, for my brother's justification, he wrote this but as an essay or taste of my virtue.

Earl of Gloucester.

Reads.

"This policy and reverence of age makes the world bitter to the best of our times; keeps our fortunes from us till our oldness cannot relish them. I begin to find an idle and fond bondage in the oppression of aged tyranny, who sways, not as it hath power, but as it is suffer'd. Come to me, that of this I may speak more. If our father would sleep till I wak'd him, you should enjoy half his revenue forever, and live the belov'd of your brother. Edgar."
Hum? Conspiracy?
"Sleep till I wake him, you should enjoy half his revenue."
My son Edgar! Had he a hand to write this? A heart and brain to breed it in?—When came you to this? Who brought it?

Edmund.
It was not brought me, my lord; there's the cunning of it. I found it thrown in at the casement of my closet.

Earl of Gloucester.
You know the character to be your brother's?

Edmund.
If the matter were good, my lord, I durst swear it were his; but in respect of that, I would fain think it were not.

Earl of Gloucester.
It is his.

Edmund.
It is his hand, my lord; but I hope his heart is not in the contents.

Earl of Gloucester.
Has he never before sounded you in this business?

Edmund.
Never, my lord. But I have heard him oft maintain it to be fit that, sons at perfect age and fathers declin'd, the father should be as ward to the son, and the son manage his revenue.

Earl of Gloucester.
O villain, villain! His very opinion in the letter. Abhorred villain! Unnatural, detested, brutish villain! Worse than brutish! Go, sirrah, seek him; I'll apprehend him. Abominable villain! Where is he?

Edmund.
I do not well know, my lord. If it shall please you to suspend your indignation against my brother till you can derive from him better testimony of his intent, you should run a certain course; where, if you violently proceed against him, mistaking his purpose, it would make a great gap in your own honor and shake in pieces the heart of his obedience. I dare pawn down my life for him that he hath writ this to feel my affection to your honor, and to no other pretense of danger.

Earl of Gloucester.
Think you so?

Edmund.
If your honor judge it meet, I will place you where you shall hear us confer of this, and by an auricular assurance have your satisfaction, and that without any further delay than this very evening.

Earl of Gloucester.
He cannot be such a monster—

Edmund.
Nor is not, sure.

Earl of Gloucester.
To his father, that so tenderly and entirely loves him. Heaven and earth! Edmund, seek him out; wind me into him, I pray you. Frame the business after your own wisdom. I would unstate myself to be in a due resolution.

Edmund.
I will seek him, sir, presently; convey the business as I shall find means, and acquaint you withal.

Earl of Gloucester.
These late eclipses in the sun and moon portend no good to us. Though the wisdom of nature can reason it thus and thus, yet nature finds itself scourg'd by the sequent effects. Love cools, friendship falls off, brothers divide: in cities, mutinies; in countries, discord; in palaces, treason; and the bond crack'd 'twixt son and father. This villain of mine comes under the prediction; there's son against father: the King falls from bias of nature; there's father against child. We have seen the best of our time. Machinations, hollowness, treachery, and all ruinous disorders follow us disquietly to our graves. Find out this villain, Edmund, it shall lose thee nothing, do it carefully. And the noble and true-hearted Kent banish'd! His offense, honesty! 'Tis strange.

Exit.

Edmund.
This is the excellent foppery of the world, that when we are sick in fortune—often the surfeits of our own behavior—we make guilty of our disasters the sun, the moon, and stars, as if we were villains on necessity, fools by heavenly compulsion, knaves, thieves, and treachers by spherical predominance; drunkards, liars, and adulterers by an enforc'd obedience of planetary influence; and all that we are evil in, by a divine thrusting on. An admirable evasion of whoremaster man, to lay his goatish disposition on the charge of a star! My father compounded with my mother under the Dragon's tail, and my nativity was under Ursa Major, so that it follows, I am rough and lecherous. Fut, I should have been that I am, had the maidenl'est star in the firmament twinkled on my bastardizing. Edgar—

Enter Edgar.

Pat! He comes like the catastrophe of the old comedy. My cue is villainous melancholy, with a sigh like Tom o' Bedlam.—O, these eclipses do portend these divisions! Fa, sol, la, mi.

Humming these notes.

Edgar.
How now, brother Edmund, what serious contemplation are you in?

Edmund.
I am thinking, brother, of a prediction I read this other day, what should follow these eclipses.

Edgar.
Do you busy yourself with that?

Edmund.
I promise you, the effects he writes of succeed unhappily, as of unnaturalness between the child and the parent, death, dearth, dissolutions of ancient amities, divisions in state, menaces and maledictions against king and nobles, needless diffidences, banishment of friends, dissipation of cohorts, nuptial breaches, and I know not what.

Edgar.
How long have you been a sectary astronomical?

Edmund.
Come, come, when saw you my father last?

Edgar.
The night gone by.

Edmund.
Spake you with him?

Edgar.
Ay, two hours together.

Edmund.
Parted you in good terms? Found you no displeasure in him by word nor countenance?

Edgar.
None at all.

Edmund.
Bethink yourself wherein you may have offended him; and at my entreaty forbear his presence until some little time hath qualified the heat of his displeasure, which at this instant so rageth in him, that with the mischief of your person it would scarcely allay.

Edgar.
Some villain hath done me wrong.

Edmund.
That's my fear. I pray you have a continent forbearance till the speed of his rage goes slower; and as I say, retire with me to my lodging, from whence I will fitly bring you to hear my lord speak. Pray ye go, there's my key. If you do stir abroad, go arm'd.

Edgar.
Arm'd, brother?

Edmund.
Brother, I advise you to the best; I am no honest man if there be any good meaning toward you. I have told you what I have seen and heard; but faintly, nothing like the image and horror of it. Pray you away.

Edgar.
Shall I hear from you anon?

Edmund.
I do serve you in this business.

Exit Edgar.

A credulous father and a brother noble,
Whose nature is so far from doing harms
That he suspects none; on whose foolish honesty
My practices ride easy. I see the business.
Let me, if not by birth, have lands by wit:
All with me's meet that I can fashion fit.

Exit.

Scene 3

The Duke of Albany's palace.

(Goneril; Oswald)

Goneril is sick and tired of hosting her father and his hundred knights, who are growing more and more rowdy. She orders her servants to stop treating them so well, in the hopes that this will drive them away, and decides that she will refuse to see her father when he returns from the hunt. She writes to Regan so that the latter will know how things stand.

Enter Goneril and Steward Oswald.

Goneril.
Did my father strike my gentleman for chiding of his Fool?

Oswald.
Ay, madam.

Goneril.
By day and night he wrongs me, every hour
He flashes into one gross crime or other
That sets us all at odds. I'll not endure it.
His knights grow riotous, and himself upbraids us
On every trifle. When he returns from hunting,
I will not speak with him; say I am sick.
If you come slack of former services,
You shall do well; the fault of it I'll answer.

Horns within.

Oswald.
He's coming, madam, I hear him.

Goneril.
Put on what weary negligence you please,
You and your fellows; I'd have it come to question.
If he distaste it, let him to my sister,
Whose mind and mine I know in that are one,
Not to be overrul'd. Idle old man,
That still would manage those authorities
That he hath given away! Now by my life
Old fools are babes again, and must be us'd
With checks as flatteries, when they are seen abus'd.
Remember what I have said.

Oswald.
               Well, madam.

Goneril.
And let his knights have colder looks among you;
What grows of it, no matter. Advise your fellows so.
I would breed from hence occasions, and I shall,
That I may speak. I'll write straight to my sister
To hold my very course. Prepare for dinner.

Exeunt.

Scene 4

A hall in the Duke of Albany's palace.

(Kent; Lear; Knights; Attendants; Oswald; Fool; Goneril; Albany)

Kent has shaved off his beard and disguised himself as a commoner. He asks Lear to let him serve, pretending not to know who the King is. Lear accepts. Oswald, Goneril's steward, pays no attention to Lear as he passes through, and one of Lear's men points out that the other servants are being haughty as well. Oswald, called back, refuses to acknowledge Lear as anything more than his mistress' father, and Kent beats him up. While waiting to speak to Goneril, Lear trades barbs with his Fool, who reproves him for giving away his land and hence his power. Goneril enters, and rebukes Lear for the wildness and insolence of his followers. Lear is affronted, unable to believe that he is being treated with so little respect, and behaves as though Goneril were not his daughter. She requires that he dismiss some of his followers, and in a rage he immediately decides to leave for Regan's. Albany, entering, is shocked to find Lear raving, as he has no idea what on earth is going on. Lear lays a powerful curse on Goneril, begging the gods to make her sterile, and leaves. Albany is uncertain which way to turn, but Goneril tells him to be quiet. She sends Oswald to Regan's to inform her of what has occurred and what Lear has said.

Enter Kent disguised as Caius.

Earl of Kent.
If but as well I other accents borrow,
That can my speech defuse, my good intent
May carry through itself to that full issue
For which I raz'd my likeness. Now, banish'd Kent,
If thou canst serve where thou dost stand condemn'd,
So may it come, thy master, whom thou lov'st,
Shall find thee full of labors.

Horns within. Enter Lear, Knights, and Attendants from hunting.

Lear, King of Britain.
Let me not stay a jot for dinner, go get it ready.

Exit an Attendant.

How now, what art thou?

Earl of Kent.
A man, sir.

Lear, King of Britain.
What dost thou profess? What wouldst thou with us?

Earl of Kent.
I do profess to be no less than I seem, to serve him truly that will put me in trust, to love him that is honest, to converse with him that is wise and says little, to fear judgment, to fight when I cannot choose, and to eat no fish.

Lear, King of Britain.
What art thou?

Earl of Kent.
A very honest-hearted fellow, and as poor as the King.

Lear, King of Britain.
If thou be'st as poor for a subject as he's for a king, th' art poor enough. What wouldst thou?

Earl of Kent.
Service.

Lear, King of Britain.
Who wouldst thou serve?

Earl of Kent.
You.

Lear, King of Britain.
Dost thou know me, fellow?

Earl of Kent.
No, sir, but you have that in your countenance which I would fain call master.

Lear, King of Britain.
What's that?

Earl of Kent.
Authority.

Lear, King of Britain.
What services canst do?

Earl of Kent.
I can keep honest counsel, ride, run, mar a curious tale in telling it, and deliver a plain message bluntly. That which ordinary men are fit for, I am qualified in, and the best of me is diligence.

Lear, King of Britain.
How old art thou?

Earl of Kent.
Not so young, sir, to love a woman for singing, nor so old to dote on her for any thing. I have years on my back forty-eight.

Lear, King of Britain.
Follow me, thou shalt serve me. If I like thee no worse after dinner, I will not part from thee yet. Dinner, ho, dinner! Where's my knave? My Fool? Go you and call my Fool hither.

Exit an Attendant.
Enter Steward Oswald.

You, you, sirrah, where's my daughter?

Oswald.
So please you—

Exit.

Lear, King of Britain.
What says the fellow there? Call the clotpole back.

Exit a Knight.

Where's my Fool? Ho! I think the world's asleep.

Enter Knight.

How now? Where's that mongrel?

Knight.
He says, my lord, your daughter is not well.

Lear, King of Britain.
Why came not the slave back to me when I call'd him?

Knight.
Sir, he answer'd me in the roundest manner, he would not.

Lear, King of Britain.
He would not?

Knight.
My lord, I know not what the matter is, but to my judgment your Highness is not entertain'd with that ceremonious affection as you were wont. There's a great abatement of kindness appears as well in the general dependents as in the Duke himself also, and your daughter.

Lear, King of Britain.
Ha? Say'st thou so?

Knight.
I beseech you pardon me, my lord, if I be mistaken, for my duty cannot be silent when I think your Highness wrong'd.

Act 1, Scene 4

Lear, King of Britain.
Thou but rememb'rest me of mine own conception. I have perceiv'd a most faint neglect of late, which I have rather blam'd as mine own jealous curiosity than as a very pretense and purpose of unkindness. I will look further into't. But where's my Fool? I have not seen him this two days.

Knight.
Since my young lady's going into France, sir, the Fool hath much pin'd away.

Lear, King of Britain.
No more of that, I have noted it well. Go you and tell my daughter I would speak with her.

Exit an Attendant.

Go you call hither my Fool.

Exit another Attendant.
Enter Steward Oswald.

O, you, sir, you, come you hither, sir. Who am I, sir?

Oswald.
My lady's father.

Lear, King of Britain.
"My lady's father"? My lord's knave! You whoreson dog, you slave, you cur!

Oswald.
I am none of these, my lord, I beseech your pardon.

Lear, King of Britain.
Do you bandy looks with me, you rascal?

Striking him.

Oswald.
I'll not be strucken, my lord.

Earl of Kent.
Nor tripp'd neither, you base football player.

Tripping up his heels.

Lear, King of Britain.
I thank thee, fellow. Thou serv'st me, and I'll love thee.

Earl of Kent.
Come, sir, arise, away! I'll teach you differences. Away, away! If you will measure your lubber's length again, tarry; but away! Go to, have you wisdom? So.

Pushes Oswald out.

Lear, King of Britain.
Now, my friendly knave, I thank thee, there's earnest of thy service.

Giving Kent money.
Enter Fool.

Fool.
Let me hire him too, here's my coxcomb.

Offering Kent his cap.

Lear, King of Britain.
How now, my pretty knave, how dost thou?

Fool.
Sirrah, you were best take my coxcomb.

Earl of Kent.
Why, Fool?

Fool.
Why? For taking one's part that's out of favor. Nay, and thou canst not smile as the wind sits, thou'lt catch cold shortly. There, take my coxcomb. Why, this fellow has banish'd two on 's daughters, and did the third a blessing against his will; if thou follow him, thou must needs wear my coxcomb.—How now, nuncle? Would I had two coxcombs and two daughters!

Lear, King of Britain.
Why, my boy?

Fool.
If I gave them all my living, I'ld keep my coxcombs myself. There's mine, beg another of thy daughters.

Lear, King of Britain.
Take heed, sirrah—the whip.

Fool.
Truth's a dog must to kennel, he must be whipt out, when the Lady Brach may stand by th' fire and stink.

Lear, King of Britain.
A pestilent gall to me!

Fool.
Sirrah, I'll teach thee a speech.

Lear, King of Britain.
Do.

Fool.
Mark it, nuncle:
Have more than thou showest,
Speak less than thou knowest,
Lend less than thou owest,
Ride more than thou goest,
Learn more than thou trowest,
Set less than thou throwest;
Leave thy drink and thy whore,
And keep in a' door,
And thou shalt have more
Than two tens to a score.

Earl of Kent.
This is nothing, Fool.

Fool.
Then 'tis like the breath of an unfee'd lawyer, you gave me nothing for't. Can you make no use of nothing, nuncle?

Lear, King of Britain.
Why, no, boy, nothing can be made out of nothing.

Fool.
To Kent.

Prithee tell him, so much the rent of his land comes to. He will not believe a fool.

Lear, King of Britain.
A bitter fool!

Fool.
Dost thou know the difference, my boy, between a bitter fool and a sweet one?

Lear, King of Britain.
No, lad, teach me.

Fool.
That lord that counsell'd thee
          To give away thy land,
Come place him here by me,
          Do thou for him stand.
The sweet and bitter fool
          Will presently appear:
The one in motley here,
          The other found out there.

Lear, King of Britain.
Dost thou call me fool, boy?

Fool.
All thy other titles thou hast given away, that thou wast born with.

Earl of Kent.
This is not altogether fool, my lord.

Fool.
No, faith, lords and great men will not let me; if I had a monopoly out, they would have part an't. And ladies too, they will not let me have all the fool to myself, they'll be snatching. Nuncle, give me an egg, and I'll give thee two crowns.

Lear, King of Britain.
What two crowns shall they be?

Fool.
Why, after I have cut the egg i' th' middle and eat up the meat, the two crowns of the egg. When thou clovest thy crown i' th' middle and gav'st away both parts, thou bor'st thine ass on thy back o'er the dirt. Thou hadst little wit in thy bald crown when thou gav'st thy golden one away. If I speak like myself in this, let him be whipt that first finds it so.

Sings.

"Fools had ne'er less grace in a year,
For wise men are grown foppish,
And know not how their wits to wear,
Their manners are so apish."

Lear, King of Britain.
When were you wont to be so full of songs, sirrah?

Fool.
I have us'd it, nuncle, e'er since thou mad'st thy daughters thy mothers, for when thou gav'st them the rod, and put'st down thine own breeches,

Sings.

"Then they for sudden joy did weep,
And I for sorrow sung,
That such a king should play bo-peep,
And go the fools among."
Prithee, nuncle, keep a schoolmaster that can teach thy Fool to lie—I would fain learn to lie.

Lear, King of Britain.
And you lie, sirrah, we'll have you whipt.

Fool.
I marvel what kin thou and thy daughters are. They'll have me whipt for speaking true; thou'lt have me whipt for lying; and sometimes I am whipt for holding my peace. I had rather be any kind o' thing than a Fool, and yet I would not be thee, nuncle: thou hast par'd thy wit o' both sides, and left nothing i' th' middle. Here comes one o' the parings.

Enter Goneril.

Lear, King of Britain.
How now, daughter? What makes that frontlet on?
You are too much of late i' th' frown.

Fool.
Thou wast a pretty fellow when thou hadst no need to care for her frowning, now thou art an O without a figure. I am better than thou art now, I am a Fool, thou art nothing.

To Goneril.

Yes, forsooth, I will hold my tongue; so your face bids me, though you say nothing.
      Mum, mum:
  He that keeps nor crust nor crumb,
  Weary of all, shall want some.

Pointing to Lear.

     That's a sheal'd peascod.

Goneril.
Not only, sir, this your all-licens'd Fool,
But other of your insolent retinue
Do hourly carp and quarrel, breaking forth
In rank and not-to-be-endur'd riots. Sir,
I had thought, by making this well known unto you,
To have found a safe redress, but now grow fearful,
By what yourself too late have spoke and done,
That you protect this course and put it on
By your allowance; which if you should, the fault
Would not scape censure, nor the redresses sleep,
Which, in the tender of a wholesome weal,
Might in their working do you that offense,
Which else were shame, that then necessity
Will call discreet proceeding.

Fool.
     For you know, nuncle,
"*The hedge-sparrow fed the cuckoo so long,*
That it had it head bit off by it young."
So out went the candle, and we were left darkling.

Lear, King of Britain.
Are you our daughter?

Goneril.
I would you would make use of your good wisdom
(Whereof I know you are fraught) and put away
These dispositions which of late transport you
From what you rightly are.

Fool.
May not an ass know when the cart draws the horse?

Sings.

"Whoop, Jug! I love thee."

Lear, King of Britain.
Does any here know me? This is not Lear.
Does Lear walk thus? Speak thus? Where are his eyes?
Either his notion weakens, his discernings
Are lethargied—Ha! Waking? 'Tis not so.
Who is it that can tell me who I am?

Fool.
Lear's shadow.

Lear, King of Britain.
I would learn that, for by the marks of sovereignty,
Knowledge, and reason, I should be false persuaded
I had daughters.

Fool.
Which they will make an obedient father.

Lear, King of Britain.
Your name, fair gentlewoman?

Goneril.
This admiration, sir, is much o' th' savor
Of other your new pranks. I do beseech you
To understand my purposes aright,
As you are old and reverend, should be wise.
Here do you keep a hundred knights and squires,
Men so disorder'd, so debosh'd and bold,
That this our court, infected with their manners,
Shows like a riotous inn. Epicurism and lust
Makes it more like a tavern or a brothel
Than a grac'd palace. The shame itself doth speak

For instant remedy. Be then desir'd
By her, that else will take the thing she begs,
A little to disquantity your train,
And the remainders that shall still depend,
To be such men as may besort your age,
Which know themselves and you.

Lear, King of Britain.
                    Darkness and devils!
Saddle my horses; call my train together!
Degenerate bastard, I'll not trouble thee;
Yet have I left a daughter.

Goneril.
You strike my people,
And your disorder'd rabble make servants of their betters.

Enter Albany.

Lear, King of Britain.
Woe, that too late repents!—O, sir, are you come?
Is it your will? Speak, sir.—Prepare my horses.—
Ingratitude! Thou marble-hearted fiend,
More hideous when thou show'st thee in a child
Than the sea-monster.

Duke of Albany.
                Pray, sir, be patient.

Lear, King of Britain.

To Goneril.

Detested kite, thou liest.
My train are men of choice and rarest parts,
That all particulars of duty know,
And in the most exact regard support
The worships of their name. O most small fault,
How ugly didst thou in Cordelia show!
Which, like an engine, wrench'd my frame of nature
From the fix'd place; drew from my heart all love,
And added to the gall. O Lear, Lear, Lear!
Beat at this gate, that let thy folly in

Striking his head.

And thy dear judgment out! Go, go, my people.

Exeunt Knights and Kent.

Duke of Albany.
My lord, I am guiltless as I am ignorant
Of what hath moved you.

Lear, King of Britain.
                    It may be so, my lord.
Hear, Nature, hear, dear goddess, hear!
Suspend thy purpose, if thou didst intend
To make this creature fruitful.
Into her womb convey sterility,
Dry up in her the organs of increase,
And from her derogate body never spring
A babe to honor her! If she must teem,
Create her child of spleen, that it may live
And be a thwart disnatur'd torment to her.
Let it stamp wrinkles in her brow of youth,
With cadent tears fret channels in her cheeks,
Turn all her mother's pains and benefits
To laughter and contempt, that she may feel
How sharper than a serpent's tooth it is
To have a thankless child!—Away, away!

Exit.

Duke of Albany.
Now, gods that we adore, whereof comes this?

Goneril.
Never afflict yourself to know more of it,
But let his disposition have that scope
As dotage gives it.

Enter Lear.

Lear, King of Britain.
What, fifty of my followers at a clap?
Within a fortnight?

Duke of Albany.
                What's the matter, sir?

Lear, King of Britain.
I'll tell thee.

To Goneril.

Life and death! I am asham'd
That thou hast power to shake my manhood thus,
That these hot tears, which break from me perforce,
Should make thee worth them. Blasts and fogs upon thee!
Th' untented woundings of a father's curse
Pierce every sense about thee! Old fond eyes,

Beweep this cause again, I'll pluck ye out,
And cast you, with the waters that you loose,
To temper clay. Yea, is't come to this?
Ha? Let it be so: I have another daughter,
Who I am sure is kind and comfortable.
When she shall hear this of thee, with her nails
She'll flea thy wolvish visage. Thou shalt find
That I'll resume the shape which thou dost think
I have cast off forever.

Exit.

Goneril.
                    Do you mark that?

Duke of Albany.
I cannot be so partial, Goneril,
To the great love I bear you—

Goneril.
Pray you, content.—What, Oswald, ho!

To the Fool.

You, sir, more knave than fool, after your master.

Fool.
Nuncle Lear, nuncle Lear, tarry, take the Fool with
thee.
A fox, when one has caught her,
And such a daughter,
Should sure to the slaughter,
If my cap would buy a halter,
So the Fool follows after.

Exit.

Goneril.
This man hath had good counsel—a hundred knights!
'Tis politic and safe to let him keep
At point a hundred knights; yes, that on every dream,
Each buzz, each fancy, each complaint, dislike,
He may enguard his dotage with their pow'rs,
And hold our lives in mercy.—Oswald, I say!

Duke of Albany.
Well, you may fear too far.

Goneril.
                Safer than trust too far.
Let me still take away the harms I fear,
Not fear still to be taken. I know his heart.
What he hath utter'd I have writ my sister;

If she sustain him and his hundred knights,
When I have show'd th' unfitness—

Enter Steward Oswald.

                How now, Oswald?
What, have you writ that letter to my sister?

Oswald.
Ay, madam.

Goneril.
Take you some company, and away to horse.
Inform her full of my particular fear,
And thereto add such reasons of your own
As may compact it more. Get you gone,
And hasten your return.

Exit Oswald.

                No, no, my lord,
This milky gentleness and course of yours
Though I condemn not, yet, under pardon,
You are much more attax'd for want of wisdom
Than prais'd for harmful mildness.

Duke of Albany.
How far your eyes may pierce I cannot tell:
Striving to better, oft we mar what's well.

Goneril.
Nay then—

Duke of Albany.
Well, well, th' event.

Exeunt.

Scene 5

Court before the palace.

(Lear; Kent; Fool; First Gentleman)

Lear sends Kent with letters to Gloucester. The fool wisely reproaches Lear for having become old before he became wise. Lear, fearing madness, begs the heavens to keep him in his right wits.

Enter Lear, Kent disguised as Caius, and Fool.

Lear, King of Britain.
Go you before to Gloucester with these letters. Acquaint my daughter no further with any thing you know than comes from her demand out of the letter.

If your diligence be not speedy, I shall be there afore you.

Earl of Kent.
I will not sleep, my lord, till I have deliver'd your letter.

Exit.

Fool.
If a man's brains were in 's heels, were't not in danger of kibes?

Lear, King of Britain.
Ay, boy.

Fool.
Then I prithee be merry, thy wit shall not go slipshod.

Lear, King of Britain.
Ha, ha, ha!

Fool.
Shalt see thy other daughter will use thee kindly, for though she's as like this as a crab's like an apple, yet I can tell what I can tell.

Lear, King of Britain.
What canst tell, boy?

Fool.
She will taste as like this as a crab does to a crab. Thou canst tell why one's nose stands i' th' middle on 's face?

Lear, King of Britain.
No.

Fool.
Why, to keep one's eyes of either side 's nose, that what a man cannot smell out, he may spy into.

Lear, King of Britain.
I did her wrong.

Fool.
Canst tell how an oyster makes his shell?

Lear, King of Britain.
No.

Fool.
Nor I neither; but I can tell why a snail has a house.

Lear, King of Britain.
Why?

Fool.
Why, to put 's head in, not to give it away to his daughters, and leave his horns without a case.

Lear, King of Britain.
I will forget my nature. So kind a father! Be my horses ready?

Fool.
Thy asses are gone about 'em. The reason why the seven stars are no more than seven is a pretty reason.

Lear, King of Britain.
Because they are not eight.

Fool.
Yes indeed, thou wouldst make a good Fool.

Lear, King of Britain.
To take't again perforce! Monster ingratitude!

Fool.
If thou wert my Fool, nuncle, I'd have thee beaten for being old before thy time.

Lear, King of Britain.
How's that?

Fool.
Thou shouldst not have been old till thou hadst been wise.

Lear, King of Britain.
O, let me not be mad, not mad, sweet heaven!
Keep me in temper, I would not be mad!

Enter First Gentleman.

How now, are the horses ready?

First Gentleman.
Ready, my lord.

Lear, King of Britain.
Come, boy.

Exeunt Lear and First Gentleman.

Fool.
She that's a maid now, and laughs at my departure,
Shall not be a maid long, unless things be cut shorter.

Exit.

Act 2

Scene 1

The Earl of Gloucester's castle.

(Edmund; Curan; Edgar; Gloucester; Servants; Cornwall; Regan; Attendants)

Edmund finds out that Regan and her husband Cornwall will be visiting his father, and that there are rumors that Cornwall and the Duke of Albany are arming against each other. Seizing the opportunity presented by the Duke's visit, Edmund convinces Edgar to flee, warning him that it is rumored that he has spoken against the Duke and that is the reason why Cornwall is on his way. They stage a fight and Edgar runs off. Edmund wounds himself and pretends to his father that his brother is the cause; he claims that he was fighting Edgar to stop him from killing Gloucester. Gloucester announces he will ask Cornwall to condemn Edgar to death. Cornwall, approving of young Edmund's apparent valor and loyalty, takes him to his service. Regan explains that she prefers to deal with her father at Gloucester's rather that at her own house, given what she has heard from her sister.

Enter Bastard Edmund and Curan severally.

Edmund.
'Save thee, Curan.

Curan.
And you, sir. I have been with your father, and given him notice that the Duke of Cornwall and Regan his duchess will be here with him this night.

Edmund.
How comes that?

Curan.
Nay, I know not. You have heard of the news abroad, I mean the whisper'd ones, for they are yet but ear-bussing arguments?

Edmund.
Not I. Pray you, what are they?

Curan.
Have you heard of no likely wars toward, 'twixt the Dukes of Cornwall and Albany?

Edmund.
Not a word.

Curan.
You may do then in time. Fare you well, sir.

Exit.

Edmund.
The Duke be here tonight? The better! Best!
This weaves itself perforce into my business.
My father hath set guard to take my brother,
And I have one thing, of a queasy question,
Which I must act. Briefness and fortune, work!
Brother, a word! Descend. Brother, I say!

Enter Edgar.

My father watches: O sir, fly this place,
Intelligence is given where you are hid;
You have now the good advantage of the night.
Have you not spoken 'gainst the Duke of Cornwall?
He's coming hither, now i' th' night, i' th' haste,
And Regan with him. Have you nothing said
Upon his party 'gainst the Duke of Albany?
Advise yourself.

Edgar.
I am sure on't, not a word.

Edmund.
I hear my father coming. Pardon me:
In cunning I must draw my sword upon you.
Draw, seem to defend yourself; now quit you well.—
Yield! Come before my father. Light ho, here!—
Fly, brother.—Torches, torches!—So farewell.

Exit Edgar.

Some blood drawn on me would beget opinion

Wounds his arm.

Of my more fierce endeavor. I have seen drunkards
Do more than this in sport.—Father, father!
Stop, stop! No help?

Enter Gloucester, and Servants with torches.

Earl of Gloucester.
Now, Edmund, where's the villain?

Edmund.
Here stood he in the dark, his sharp sword out,
Mumbling of wicked charms, conjuring the moon
To stand 's auspicious mistress.

Earl of Gloucester.
                But where is he?

Edmund.
Look, sir, I bleed.

Earl of Gloucester.
                     Where is the villain, Edmund?

Edmund.
Fled this way, sir, when by no means he could—

Earl of Gloucester.
Pursue him, ho! Go after.

Exeunt some Servants.
                  By no means what?

Edmund.
Persuade me to the murder of your lordship,
But that I told him, the revengive gods
'Gainst parricides did all the thunder bend,
Spoke, with how manifold and strong a bond
The child was bound to th' father; sir, in fine,
Seeing how loathly opposite I stood
To his unnatural purpose, in fell motion
With his prepared sword he charges home
My unprovided body, latch'd mine arm;
And when he saw my best alarum'd spirits,
Bold in the quarrel's right, rous'd to th' encounter,
Or whether gasted by the noise I made,
Full suddenly he fled.

Earl of Gloucester.
                    Let him fly far.
Not in this land shall he remain uncaught;
And found—dispatch. The noble Duke my master,
My worthy arch and patron, comes tonight.
By his authority I will proclaim it,
That he which finds him shall deserve our thanks,
Bringing the murderous coward to the stake;
He that conceals him, death.

Edmund.
When I dissuaded him from his intent,
And found him pight to do it, with curst speech
I threaten'd to discover him; he replied,
"Thou unpossessing bastard, dost thou think,
If I would stand against thee, would the reposal
Of any trust, virtue, or worth in thee
Make thy words faith'd? No. What I should deny
(As this I would, ay, though thou didst produce
My very character), I'ld turn it all
To thy suggestion, plot, and damned practice;
And thou must make a dullard of the world
If they not thought the profits of my death
Were very pregnant and potential spirits
To make thee seek it."

Earl of Gloucester.
                  O strange and fast'ned villain!
Would he deny his letter, said he? I never got him.

Tucket within.

Hark, the Duke's trumpets! I know not why he comes.
All ports I'll bar, the villain shall not scape;
The Duke must grant me that. Besides, his picture
I will send far and near, that all the kingdom
May have due note of him, and of my land,
Loyal and natural boy, I'll work the means
To make thee capable.

Enter Cornwall, Regan, and Attendants.

Duke of Cornwall.
How now, my noble friend? Since I came hither
(Which I can call but now) I have heard strange news.

Regan.
If it be true, all vengeance comes too short
Which can pursue th' offender. How dost, my lord?

Earl of Gloucester.
O madam, my old heart is crack'd, it's crack'd!

Regan.
What, did my father's godson seek your life?
He whom my father nam'd, your Edgar?

Earl of Gloucester.
O lady, lady, shame would have it hid!

Regan.
Was he not companion with the riotous knights
That tended upon my father?

Earl of Gloucester.
I know not, madam. 'Tis too bad, too bad.

Edmund.
Yes, madam, he was of that consort.

Regan.
No marvel then, though he were ill affected:
'Tis they have put him on the old man's death,
To have th' expense and waste of his revenues.
I have this present evening from my sister

Been well inform'd of them, and with such cautions,
That if they come to sojourn at my house,
I'll not be there.

Duke of Cornwall.
　　　　　　　Nor I, assure thee, Regan.
Edmund, I hear that you have shown your father
A child-like office.

Edmund.
　　　　　　　It was my duty, sir.

Earl of Gloucester.
He did bewray his practice, and receiv'd
This hurt you see, striving to apprehend him.

Duke of Cornwall.
Is he pursued?

Earl of Gloucester.
　　　　　　　Ay, my good lord.

Duke of Cornwall.
If he be taken, he shall never more
Be fear'd of doing harm. Make your own purpose,
How in my strength you please. For you, Edmund,
Whose virtue and obedience doth this instant
So much commend itself, you shall be ours.
Natures of such deep trust we shall much need;
You we first seize on.

Edmund.
　　　　　　　I shall serve you, sir,
Truly, however else.

Earl of Gloucester.
　　　　　　　For him I thank your Grace.

Duke of Cornwall.
You know not why we came to visit you?

Regan.
Thus out of season, threading dark-ey'd night:
Occasions, noble Gloucester, of some prize,
Wherein we must have use of your advice.
Our father he hath writ, so hath our sister,
Of differences, which I best thought it fit
To answer from our home; the several messengers
From hence attend dispatch. Our good old friend,
Lay comforts to your bosom, and bestow
Your needful counsel to our businesses,
Which craves the instant use.

Earl of Gloucester.
　　　　　　　I serve you, madam.
Your Graces are right welcome.

Flourish. Exeunt.

Scene 2

Before Gloucester's castle.

(Kent; Oswald; Edmund; Cornwall; Regan; Gloucester; Servants)

Oswald arrives; not recognizing Kent, he takes him for one of Gloucester's servants and asks where he can put his horse. Kent roundly insults him, and the two come to blows. Edmund attempts to stop the quarrel, but Kent turns on him. Gloucester and Cornwall appear and demand to know the cause for the fight. Kent refuses to do much more than insult Oswald, trying Cornwall's patience until the Duke explodes and sentences Kent to the stocks. Gloucester disapproves of stocking the King's messenger, but Cornwall is obdurate, and takes it on his own head. Gloucester apologizes to Kent, who tells him not to worry. Left alone, Kent rereads a letter he has received from Cordelia, whom he has informed of his disguise.

Enter Kent disguised as Caius and Steward Oswald severally.

Oswald.
Good dawning to thee, friend. Art of this house?

Earl of Kent.
Ay.

Oswald.
Where may we set our horses?

Earl of Kent.
I' th' mire.

Oswald.
Prithee, if thou lov'st me, tell me.

Earl of Kent.
I love thee not.

Oswald.
Why then I care not for thee.

Earl of Kent.
If I had thee in Lipsbury pinfold, I would make thee care for me.

Oswald.
Why dost thou use me thus? I know thee not.

Earl of Kent.
Fellow, I know thee.

Oswald.
What dost thou know me for?

Earl of Kent.
A knave, a rascal, an eater of broken meats; a base, proud, shallow, beggarly, three-suited, hundred-pound, filthy worsted-stocking knave; a lily-liver'd, action-taking, whoreson, glass-gazing, superserviceable, finical rogue; one-trunk-inheriting slave; one that wouldst be a bawd in way of good service, and art nothing but the composition of a knave, beggar, coward, pandar, and the son and heir of a mongrel bitch; one whom I will beat into clamorous whining, if thou deni'st the least syllable of thy addition.

Oswald.
Why, what a monstrous fellow art thou, thus to rail on one that is neither known of thee nor knows thee?

Earl of Kent.
What a brazen-fac'd varlet art thou, to deny thou knowest me? Is it two days since I tripp'd up thy heels, and beat thee before the King? Draw, you rogue, for though it be night, yet the moon shines;

Drawing his sword.

I'll make a sop o' th' moonshine of you, you whoreson cullionly barber-monger, draw!

Oswald.
Away, I have nothing to do with thee.

Earl of Kent.
Draw, you rascal! You come with letters against the King, and take Vanity the puppet's part against the royalty of her father. Draw, you rogue, or I'll so carbonado your shanks! Draw, you rascal! Come your ways.

Oswald.
Help ho! Murder, help!

Earl of Kent.
Strike, you slave! Stand, rogue, stand, you neat slave! Strike!

Beating him.

Oswald.
Help ho! Murder, murder!

Enter Bastard Edmund, with his rapier drawn.

Edmund.
How now, what's the matter? Part!

Earl of Kent.
With you, goodman boy, and you please! Come, I'll flesh ye, come on, young master.

Enter Cornwall, Regan, Gloucester, Servants.

Earl of Gloucester.
Weapons? Arms? What's the matter here?

Duke of Cornwall.
Keep peace, upon your lives!
He dies that strikes again. What is the matter?

Regan.
The messengers from our sister and the King.

Duke of Cornwall.
What is your difference? Speak.

Oswald.
I am scarce in breath, my lord.

Earl of Kent.
No marvel, you have so bestirr'd your valor. You cowardly rascal, Nature disclaims in thee: a tailor made thee.

Duke of Cornwall.
Thou art a strange fellow. A tailor make a man?

Earl of Kent.
A tailor, sir; a stone-cutter or a painter could not have made him so ill, though they had been but two years o' th' trade.

Duke of Cornwall.
Speak yet, how grew your quarrel?

Oswald.
This ancient ruffian, sir, whose life I have spar'd at suit of his grey beard—

Earl of Kent.
Thou whoreson zed, thou unnecessary letter! My lord, if you'll give me leave, I will tread this unbolted villain into mortar, and daub the wall of a jakes with him. Spare my grey beard, you wagtail?

Duke of Cornwall.
Peace, sirrah!
You beastly knave, know you no reverence?

Earl of Kent.
Yes, sir, but anger hath a privilege.

Duke of Cornwall.
Why art thou angry?

Earl of Kent.
That such a slave as this should wear a sword,
Who wears no honesty. Such smiling rogues as these,
Like rats, oft bite the holy cords a-twain
Which are t' intrinse t' unloose; smooth every passion
That in the natures of their lords rebel,
Being oil to fire, snow to the colder moods;
Renege, affirm, and turn their halcyon beaks
With every gale and vary of their masters,
Knowing nought (like dogs) but following.
A plague upon your epileptic visage!
Smile you my speeches, as I were a fool?
Goose, and I had you upon Sarum plain,
I'ld drive ye cackling home to Camelot.

Duke of Cornwall.
What, art thou mad, old fellow?

Earl of Gloucester.
How fell you out? Say that.

Earl of Kent.
No contraries hold more antipathy
Than I and such a knave.

Duke of Cornwall.
Why dost thou call him knave? What is his fault?

Earl of Kent.
His countenance likes me not.

Duke of Cornwall.
No more, perchance, does mine, nor his, nor hers.

Earl of Kent.
Sir, 'tis my occupation to be plain:
I have seen better faces in my time
Than stands on any shoulder that I see
Before me at this instant.

Duke of Cornwall.
                    This is some fellow
Who, having been prais'd for bluntness, doth affect
A saucy roughness, and constrains the garb
Quite from his nature. He cannot flatter, he,
An honest mind and plain, he must speak truth!
And they will take't, so; if not, he's plain.
These kind of knaves I know, which in this plainness
Harbor more craft and more corrupter ends
Than twenty silly-ducking observants
That stretch their duties nicely.

Earl of Kent.
Sir, in good faith, in sincere verity,
Under th' allowance of your great aspect,
Whose influence, like the wreath of radiant fire
On flick'ring Phoebus' front—

Duke of Cornwall.
                    What mean'st by this?

Earl of Kent.
To go out of my dialect, which you discommend so
much. I know, sir, I am no flatterer. He that beguil'd
you in a plain accent was a plain knave, which for my
part I will not be, though I should win your displeasure to entreat me to't.

Duke of Cornwall.
What was th' offense you gave him?

Oswald.
I never gave him any.
It pleas'd the King his master very late
To strike at me upon his misconstruction,
When he, compact, and flattering his displeasure,
Tripp'd me behind; being down, insulted, rail'd,
And put upon him such a deal of man
That worthied him, got praises of the King
For him attempting who was self-subdued,
And in the fleshment of this dread exploit,
Drew on me here again.

Earl of Kent.
                    None of these rogues and cowards
But Ajax is their fool.

Duke of Cornwall.
                    Fetch forth the stocks!
You stubborn ancient knave, you reverent braggart,
We'll teach you.

Earl of Kent.
                    Sir, I am too old to learn.
Call not your stocks for me, I serve the King,
On whose employment I was sent to you.
You shall do small respects, show too bold malice

Against the grace and person of my master,
Stocking his messenger.

Duke of Cornwall.
Fetch forth the stocks! As I have life and honor,
There shall he sit till noon.

Regan.
Till noon? Till night, my lord, and all night too.

Earl of Kent.
Why, madam, if I were your father's dog,
You should not use me so.

Regan.
              Sir, being his knave, I will.

Duke of Cornwall.
This is a fellow of the self-same color
Our sister speaks of. Come, bring away the stocks!

Stocks brought out.

Earl of Gloucester.
Let me beseech your Grace not to do so.
His fault is much, and the good King his master
Will check him for't. Your purpos'd low correction
Is such as basest and contemned'st wretches
For pilf'rings and most common trespasses
Are punish'd with. The King must take it ill
That he, so slightly valued in his messenger,
Should have him thus restrained.

Duke of Cornwall.
              I'll answer that.

Regan.
My sister may receive it much more worse
To have her gentleman abus'd, assaulted,
For following her affairs. Put in his legs.

Kent is put in the stocks.

Come, my good lord, away.

Exit with all but Gloucester and Kent.

Earl of Gloucester.
I am sorry for thee, friend, 'tis the Duke's pleasure,
Whose disposition, all the world well knows,
Will not be rubb'd nor stopp'd. I'll entreat for thee.

Earl of Kent.
Pray do not, sir. I have watch'd and travel'd hard:
Some time I shall sleep out, the rest I'll whistle.
A good man's fortune may grow out at heels.
Give you good morrow!

Earl of Gloucester.
The Duke's to blame in this, 'twill be ill taken.

Exit.

Earl of Kent.
Good King, that must approve the common saw,
Thou out of heaven's benediction com'st
To the warm sun!
Approach, thou beacon to this under globe,
That by thy comfortable beams I may
Peruse this letter. Nothing almost sees miracles
But misery. I know 'tis from Cordelia,
Who hath most fortunately been inform'd
Of my obscured course;

Reads.

"—and shall find time
From this enormous state—seeking to give
Losses their remedies."—
All weary and o'erwatch'd,
Take vantage, heavy eyes, not to behold
This shameful lodging.
Fortune, good night; smile once more, turn thy wheel.

Sleeps.

Scene 3

A wood.

(Edgar)

Edgar, tracked throughout the kingdom, decides to disguise himself as a mad, filthy beggar in hopes of escaping.

Enter Edgar.

Edgar.
I heard myself proclaim'd,
And by the happy hollow of a tree
Escap'd the hunt. No port is free, no place
That guard and most unusual vigilance
Does not attend my taking. Whiles I may scape
I will preserve myself, and am bethought

To take the basest and most poorest shape
That ever penury, in contempt of man,
Brought near to beast. My face I'll grime with filth,
Blanket my loins, elf all my hairs in knots,
And with presented nakedness outface
The winds and persecutions of the sky.
The country gives me proof and president
Of Bedlam beggars, who, with roaring voices,
Strike in their numb'd and mortified arms
Pins, wooden pricks, nails, sprigs of rosemary;
And with this horrible object, from low farms,
Poor pelting villages, sheep-cotes, and mills,
Sometimes with lunatic bans, sometime with prayers,
Enforce their charity. Poor Turlygod! Poor Tom!
That's something yet: Edgar I nothing am.

Exit.

Scene 4

Before Gloucester's castle.

(Lear; Fool; First Gentleman; Kent; Gloucester; Cornwall; Regan; Servants; Oswald; Goneril)

Lear and his retinue arrive at Gloucester's. The King finds it odd that Regan and Cornwall decided to leave their castle just as they heard of his approach, and that Kent has not returned. Kent salutes him from the stocks, and Lear is incensed at the insult, though he at first refuses to believe that Regan and Cornwall are responsible. Lear feels himself on the verge of losing control. Kent and the Fool banter as the King asks to see his daughter and son-in-law, but the latter two refuse, as they are exceedingly tired. Lear tries desperately to keep control of his increasingly demented temper. When Regan and Cornwall finally appear, Lear appeals to his daughter, weeping over Goneril's bad treatment of him, but is shocked when Regan refuses to share his opinion. He attempts to reassure himself that she will never treat him the way Goneril did, but at that moment Goneril herself arrives, and the two sisters band together. Regan refuses to take Lear in, making the eminently reasonable point that she is not prepared to receive him; Goneril refuses to take him back unless he dismisses fifty of his knights. Between them they whittle down the number of knights he should be allowed, until they refuse to take any followers with him. His powerlessness brought home to him, Lear tries desperately not to weep. He stalks off with the Fool, despite the coming storm. Gloucester is worried about him, but the two sisters and Cornwall prevent him from helping the King. Cornwall coldly orders that the doors be barred against the storm, trapping Lear outside.

Enter Lear, Fool, and First Gentleman. Kent, disguised as Caius, in the stocks.

Lear, King of Britain.
'Tis strange that they should so depart from home,
And not send back my messenger.

First Gentleman.
                    As I learn'd,
The night before there was no purpose in them
Of this remove.

Earl of Kent.
                    Hail to thee, noble master!

Lear, King of Britain.
Ha?
Mak'st thou this shame thy pastime?

Earl of Kent.
                    No, my lord.

Fool.
Hah, ha, he wears cruel garters. Horses are tied by the heads, dogs and bears by th' neck, monkeys by th' loins, and men by th' legs. When a man's overlusty at legs, then he wears wooden nether-stocks.

Lear, King of Britain.
What's he that hath so much thy place mistook
To set thee here?

Earl of Kent.
                    It is both he and she,
Your son and daughter.

Lear, King of Britain.
No.

Earl of Kent.
Yes.

Lear, King of Britain.
No, I say.

Earl of Kent.
I say yea.

Lear, King of Britain.
No, no, they would not.

Earl of Kent.
Yes, they have.

Lear, King of Britain.
By Jupiter, I swear no.

Earl of Kent.
By Juno, I swear ay.

Lear, King of Britain.
                They durst not do't;
They could not, would not do't. 'Tis worse than murder
To do upon respect such violent outrage.
Resolve me with all modest haste which way
Thou mightst deserve, or they impose, this usage,
Coming from us.

Earl of Kent.
               My lord, when at their home
I did commend your Highness' letters to them,
Ere I was risen from the place that showed
My duty kneeling, came there a reeking post,
Stew'd in his haste, half breathless, panting forth
From Goneril his mistress salutations;
Deliver'd letters, spite of intermission,
Which presently they read; on those contents
They summon'd up their meiny, straight took horse,
Commanded me to follow, and attend
The leisure of their answer, gave me cold looks:
And meeting here the other messenger,
Whose welcome I perceiv'd had poison'd mine—
Being the very fellow which of late
Display'd so saucily against your Highness—
Having more man than wit about me, drew.
He rais'd the house with loud and coward cries.
Your son and daughter found this trespass worth
The shame which here it suffers.

Fool.
Winter's not gone yet, if the wild geese fly that way.
Fathers that wear rags
                Do make their children blind,
But fathers that bear bags
                Shall see their children kind.
Fortune, that arrant whore,
                Ne'er turns the key to th' poor.
But for all this, thou shalt have as many dolors for thy daughters as thou canst tell in a year.

Lear, King of Britain.
O how this mother swells up toward my heart!
Hysterica passio, down, thou climbing sorrow,
Thy element's below.—Where is this daughter?

Earl of Kent.
With the Earl, sir, here within.

Lear, King of Britain.
                       Follow me not,
Stay here.

Exit.

First Gentleman.
Made you no more offense but what you speak of?

Earl of Kent.
None.
How chance the King comes with so small a number?

Fool.
And thou hadst been set i' th' stocks for that question, thou'dst well deserv'd it.

Earl of Kent.
Why, Fool?

Fool.
We'll set thee to school to an ant, to teach thee there's no laboring i' th' winter. All that follow their noses are led by their eyes but blind men, and there's not a nose among twenty but can smell him that's stinking. Let go thy hold when a great wheel runs down a hill, lest it break thy neck with following; but the great one that goes upward, let him draw thee after. When a wise man gives thee better counsel, give me mine again, I would have none but knaves follow it, since a fool gives it.
That sir which serves and seeks for gain,
And follows but for form,
Will pack when it begins to rain,
And leave thee in the storm.
But I will tarry, the Fool will stay,
And let the wise man fly.
The knave turns fool that runs away,
The Fool no knave, perdie.

Earl of Kent.
Where learn'd you this, Fool?

Fool.
Not i' th' stocks, fool.

Enter Lear and Gloucester.

Lear, King of Britain.
Deny to speak with me? They are sick? They are weary?
They have travel'd all the night? Mere fetches,
The images of revolt and flying off.
Fetch me a better answer.

Earl of Gloucester.
                    My dear lord,
You know the fiery quality of the Duke,
How unremovable and fix'd he is
In his own course.

Lear, King of Britain.
Vengeance! Plague! Death! Confusion!
Fiery? What quality? Why, Gloucester, Gloucester,
I'd speak with the Duke of Cornwall and his wife.

Earl of Gloucester.
Well, my good lord, I have inform'd them so.

Lear, King of Britain.
'Inform'd them?' Dost thou understand me, man?

Earl of Gloucester.
Ay, my good lord.

Lear, King of Britain.
The King would speak with Cornwall, the dear father
Would with his daughter speak, commands, tends service.
Are they inform'd of this? My breath and blood!
'Fiery?' The fiery Duke? Tell the hot Duke that—
No, but not yet, may be he is not well:
Infirmity doth still neglect all office
Whereto our health is bound; we are not ourselves
When nature, being oppress'd, commands the mind
To suffer with the body. I'll forbear,
And am fallen out with my more headier will,
To take the indispos'd and sickly fit
For the sound man.

Looking on Kent.

                    Death on my state! Wherefore
Should he sit here? This act persuades me
That this remotion of the Duke and her
Is practice only. Give me my servant forth.
Go tell the Duke, and 's wife, I'd speak with them—
Now, presently. Bid them come forth and hear me,
Or at their chamber-door I'll beat the drum
Till it cry sleep to death.

Earl of Gloucester.
I would have all well betwixt you.

Exit.

Lear, King of Britain.
O me, my heart! My rising heart! But down!

Fool.
Cry to it, nuncle, as the cockney did to the eels when she put 'em i' th' paste alive; she knapp'd 'em o' th' coxcombs with a stick, and cried, "Down, wantons, down!" 'Twas her brother that, in pure kindness to his horse, butter'd his hay.

Enter Cornwall, Regan, Gloucester, Servants.

Lear, King of Britain.
Good morrow to you both.

Duke of Cornwall.
                    Hail to your Grace!

Kent here set at liberty.

Regan.
I am glad to see your Highness.

Lear, King of Britain.
Regan, I think you are; I know what reason
I have to think so. If thou shouldst not be glad,
I would divorce me from thy mother's tomb,
Sepulchring an adult'ress.

To Kent.

                    O, are you free?
Some other time for that.

Exit Kent.

                    Beloved Regan,
Thy sister's naught. O Regan, she hath tied
Sharp-tooth'd unkindness, like a vulture, here.

Points to his heart.

I can scarce speak to thee; thou'lt not believe
With how deprav'd a quality—O Regan!

Regan.
I pray you, sir, take patience. I have hope
You less know how to value her desert
Than she to scant her duty.

Lear, King of Britain.
                     Say? How is that?

Regan.
I cannot think my sister in the least
Would fail her obligation. If, sir, perchance
She have restrain'd the riots of your followers,
'Tis on such ground and to such wholesome end
As clears her from all blame.

Lear, King of Britain.
My curses on her!

Regan.
                 O sir, you are old,
Nature in you stands on the very verge
Of his confine. You should be rul'd and led
By some discretion that discerns your state
Better than you yourself. Therefore I pray you
That to our sister you do make return.
Say you have wrong'd her.

Lear, King of Britain.
                  Ask her forgiveness?
Do you but mark how this becomes the house!
"Dear daughter, I confess that I am old;

Kneeling.

Age is unnecessary. On my knees I beg
That you'll vouchsafe me raiment, bed, and food."

Regan.
Good sir, no more; these are unsightly tricks.
Return you to my sister.

Lear, King of Britain.

Rising.

                   Never, Regan:
She hath abated me of half my train;
Look'd black upon me, struck me with her tongue,
Most serpent-like, upon the very heart.
All the stor'd vengeances of heaven fall
On her ingrateful top! Strike her young bones,
You taking airs, with lameness!

Duke of Cornwall.
                Fie, sir, fie!

Lear, King of Britain.
You nimble lightnings, dart your blinding flames
Into her scornful eyes! Infect her beauty,
You fen-suck'd fogs, drawn by the pow'rful sun,
To fall and blister!

Regan.
             O the blest gods! So
Will you wish on me, when the rash mood is on.

Lear, King of Britain.
No, Regan, thou shalt never have my curse.
Thy tender-hefted nature shall not give
Thee o'er to harshness. Her eyes are fierce, but thine
Do comfort, and not burn. 'Tis not in thee
To grudge my pleasures, to cut off my train,
To bandy hasty words, to scant my sizes,
And in conclusion to oppose the bolt
Against my coming in. Thou better know'st
The offices of nature, bond of childhood,
Effects of courtesy, dues of gratitude:
Thy half o' th' kingdom hast thou not forgot,
Wherein I thee endow'd.

Regan.
           Good sir, to th' purpose.

Lear, King of Britain.
Who put my man i' th' stocks?

Tucket within.
Enter Steward Oswald.

Duke of Cornwall.
             What trumpet's that?

Regan.
I know't, my sister's. This approves her letter,
That she would soon be here.

To Oswald.
              Is your lady come?

Lear, King of Britain.
This is a slave whose easy-borrowed pride
Dwells in the fickle grace of her he follows.
Out, varlet, from my sight!

Act 2, Scene 4

Duke of Cornwall.
⠀⠀⠀⠀⠀⠀⠀⠀⠀What means your Grace?

Enter Goneril.

Lear, King of Britain.
Who stock'd my servant? Regan, I have good hope
Thou didst not know on't. Who comes here? O heavens!
If you do love old men, if your sweet sway
Allow obedience, if you yourselves are old,
Make it your cause; send down, and take my part.

To Goneril.

Art not asham'd to look upon this beard?
O Regan, will you take her by the hand?

Goneril.
Why not by th' hand, sir? How have I offended?
All's not offense that indiscretion finds
And dotage terms so.

Lear, King of Britain.
⠀⠀⠀⠀⠀⠀⠀⠀⠀O sides, you are too tough!
Will you yet hold? How came my man i' th' stocks?

Duke of Cornwall.
I set him there, sir; but his own disorders
Deserv'd much less advancement.

Lear, King of Britain.
⠀⠀⠀⠀⠀⠀⠀⠀⠀You? Did you?

Regan.
I pray you, father, being weak, seem so.
If till the expiration of your month
You will return and sojourn with my sister,
Dismissing half your train, come then to me.
I am now from home, and out of that provision
Which shall be needful for your entertainment.

Lear, King of Britain.
Return to her? And fifty men dismiss'd?
No, rather I abjure all roofs, and choose
To wage against the enmity o' th' air,
To be a comrade with the wolf and owl—
Necessity's sharp pinch. Return with her?
Why, the hot-blooded France, that dowerless took
Our youngest born, I could as well be brought
To knee his throne, and squire-like, pension beg
To keep base life afoot. Return with her?
Persuade me rather to be slave and sumpter
To this detested groom.

Pointing at Oswald.

Goneril.
⠀⠀⠀⠀⠀⠀⠀⠀⠀At your choice, sir.

Lear, King of Britain.
I prithee, daughter, do not make me mad.
I will not trouble thee, my child; farewell:
We'll no more meet, no more see one another.
But yet thou art my flesh, my blood, my daughter—
Or rather a disease that's in my flesh,
Which I must needs call mine. Thou art a bile,
A plague-sore, or embossed carbuncle,
In my corrupted blood. But I'll not chide thee,
Let shame come when it will, I do not call it.
I do not bid the thunder-bearer shoot,
Nor tell tales of thee to high-judging Jove.
Mend when thou canst, be better at thy leisure,
I can be patient, I can stay with Regan,
I and my hundred knights.

Regan.
⠀⠀⠀⠀⠀⠀⠀⠀⠀Not altogether so,
I look'd not for you yet, nor am provided
For your fit welcome. Give ear, sir, to my sister,
For those that mingle reason with your passion
Must be content to think you old, and so—
But she knows what she does.

Lear, King of Britain.
⠀⠀⠀⠀⠀⠀⠀⠀⠀Is this well spoken?

Regan.
I dare avouch it, sir. What, fifty followers?
Is it not well? What should you need of more?
Yea, or so many? Sith that both charge and danger
Speak 'gainst so great a number? How in one house
Should many people under two commands
Hold amity? 'Tis hard, almost impossible.

Goneril.
Why might not you, my lord, receive attendance
From those that she calls servants or from mine?

Regan.
Why not, my lord? If then they chanc'd to slack ye,
We could control them. If you will come to me
(For now I spy a danger), I entreat you
To bring but five and twenty; to no more
Will I give place or notice.

Lear, King of Britain.
I gave you all—

Regan.
                And in good time you gave it.

Lear, King of Britain.
Made you my guardians, my depositaries,
But kept a reservation to be followed
With such a number. What, must I come to you
With five and twenty? Regan, said you so?

Regan.
And speak't again, my lord, no more with me.

Lear, King of Britain.
Those wicked creatures yet do look well-favor'd
When others are more wicked; not being the worst
Stands in some rank of praise.

To Goneril.
                I'll go with thee,
Thy fifty yet doth double five and twenty,
And thou art twice her love.

Goneril.
                Hear me, my lord:
What need you five and twenty? Ten? Or five?
To follow in a house where twice so many
Have a command to tend you?

Regan.
                What need one?

Lear, King of Britain.
O, reason not the need! Our basest beggars
Are in the poorest thing superfluous.
Allow not nature more than nature needs,
Man's life is cheap as beast's. Thou art a lady;
If only to go warm were gorgeous,
Why, nature needs not what thou gorgeous wear'st,
Which scarcely keeps thee warm. But for true need—
You heavens, give me that patience, patience I need!
You see me here, you gods, a poor old man,
As full of grief as age, wretched in both.
If it be you that stirs these daughters' hearts
Against their father, fool me not so much
To bear it tamely; touch me with noble anger,
And let not women's weapons, water-drops,
Stain my man's cheeks! No, you unnatural hags,
I will have such revenges on you both
That all the world shall—I will do such things—
What they are yet I know not, but they shall be
The terrors of the earth! You think I'll weep:
No, I'll not weep.
I have full cause of weeping, but this heart

Storm and tempest.

Shall break into a hundred thousand flaws
Or ere I'll weep. O Fool, I shall go mad!

Exeunt Lear, Gloucester, First Gentleman, and Fool.

Duke of Cornwall.
Let us withdraw, 'twill be a storm.

Regan.
This house is little, the old man and 's people
Cannot be well bestow'd.

Goneril.
'Tis his own blame hath put himself from rest,
And must needs taste his folly.

Regan.
For his particular, I'll receive him gladly,
But not one follower.

Goneril.
                So am I purpos'd.
Where is my Lord of Gloucester?

Duke of Cornwall.
Followed the old man forth.

Enter Gloucester.
                He is return'd.

Earl of Gloucester.
The King is in high rage.

Duke of Cornwall.
                Whither is he going?

Earl of Gloucester.
He calls to horse, but will I know not whither.

Duke of Cornwall.
'Tis best to give him way, he leads himself.

Goneril.
My lord, entreat him by no means to stay.

Earl of Gloucester.
Alack, the night comes on, and the bleak winds
Do sorely ruffle; for many miles about
There's scarce a bush.

Regan.
> O sir, to willful men,
The injuries that they themselves procure
Must be their schoolmasters. Shut up your doors.
He is attended with a desperate train,
And what they may incense him to, being apt
To have his ear abus'd, wisdom bids fear.

Duke of Cornwall.
Shut up your doors, my lord, 'tis a wild night,
My Regan counsels well. Come out o' th' storm.

Exeunt.

Act 3

Scene 1

A heath.

(Kent; First Gentleman)

Kent meets a gentleman of the king's court, who informs him of Lear's wild, grief-stricken ravings, and that the King is accompanied now only by the Fool. Kent in turn tells him that the French have set foot on Britain's shores, and asks him to go to Dover to tell Cordelia just how Lear has been treated.

Storm still. Enter Kent disguised as Caius and First Gentleman severally.

Earl of Kent.
Who's there, besides foul weather?

First Gentleman.
One minded like the weather, most unquietly.

Earl of Kent.
I know you. Where's the King?

First Gentleman.
Contending with the fretful elements;
Bids the wind blow the earth into the sea,
Or swell the curled waters 'bove the main,
That things might change or cease, tears his white hair,
Which the impetuous blasts with eyeless rage
Catch in their fury, and make nothing of,
Strives in his little world of man to outscorn
The to-and-fro-conflicting wind and rain.
This night, wherein the cub-drawn bear would couch,
The lion and the belly-pinched wolf
Keep their fur dry, unbonneted he runs,
And bids what will take all.

Earl of Kent.
> But who is with him?

First Gentleman.
None but the Fool, who labors to outjest
His heart-struck injuries.

Earl of Kent.
> Sir, I do know you,
And dare upon the warrant of my note
Commend a dear thing to you. There is division
(Although as yet the face of it is cover'd
With mutual cunning) 'twixt Albany and Cornwall;
Who have—as who have not, that their great stars
Thron'd and set high?—servants, who seem no less,
Which are to France the spies and speculations
Intelligent of our state. What hath been seen,
Either in snuffs and packings of the Dukes,
Or the hard rein which both of them hath borne
Against the old kind King; or something deeper,
Whereof (perchance) these are but furnishings—
But true it is, from France there comes a power
Into this scattered kingdom, who already
Wise in our negligence, have secret feet
In some of our best ports, and are at point
To show their open banner. Now to you:
If on my credit you dare build so far
To make your speed to Dover, you shall find
Some that will thank you, making just report
Of how unnatural and bemadding sorrow
The King hath cause to plain.
I am a gentleman of blood and breeding,
And from some knowledge and assurance, offer
This office to you.

First Gentleman.
I will talk further with you.

Earl of Kent.
> No, do not.
For confirmation that I am much more
Than my out-wall, open this purse and take
What it contains. If you shall see Cordelia
(As fear not but you shall), show her this ring,
And she will tell you who that fellow is
That yet you do not know. Fie on this storm!
I will go seek the King.

First Gentleman.
Give me your hand. Have you no more to say?

Earl of Kent.
Few words, but to effect, more than all yet:
That when we have found the King—in which your pain
That way, I'll this—he that first lights on him
Holla the other.

Exeunt severally.

Scene 2

Another part of the heath.

(Lear; Fool; Kent)

Lear rages against the storm, comparing it favorably to his daughters, since he never did anything for the storm. The Fool begs him to take shelter. Kent finds them, and is horrified to see that Lear has lost his grip on reality. He convinces Lear to go into a hovel, and for the first time Lear shows a trace of kindness for another human being, asking the Fool how he is. Lear and the fool are roaming about. Lear is defying the hurricane. Kent finds the odd pair and urges Lear to seek shelter. They go into a nearby hovel.

Storm still. Enter Lear and Fool.

Lear, King of Britain.
Blow, winds, and crack your cheeks! Rage, blow!
You cataracts and hurricanoes, spout
Till you have drench'd our steeples, drown'd the cocks!
You sulph'rous and thought-executing fires,
Vaunt-couriers of oak-cleaving thunderbolts,
Singe my white head! And thou, all-shaking thunder,
Strike flat the thick rotundity o' th' world!
Crack nature's moulds, all germains spill at once
That makes ingrateful man!

Fool.
O nuncle, court holy-water in a dry house is better than this rain-water out o' door. Good nuncle, in, ask thy daughters blessing. Here's a night pities neither wise men nor fools.

Lear, King of Britain.
Rumble thy bellyful! Spit, fire! Spout, rain!
Nor rain, wind, thunder, fire are my daughters.
I tax not you, you elements, with unkindness;
I never gave you kingdom, call'd you children;
You owe me no subscription. Then let fall
Your horrible pleasure. Here I stand your slave,
A poor, infirm, weak, and despis'd old man;
But yet I call you servile ministers,
That will with two pernicious daughters join
Your high-engender'd battles 'gainst a head
So old and white as this. O, ho! 'Tis foul.

Fool.
He that has a house to put 's head in has a good head-piece.
   The codpiece that will house
            Before the head has any,
   The head and he shall louse:
            So beggars marry many.
   The man that makes his toe
            What he his heart should make,
   Shall of a corn cry woe,
            And turn his sleep to wake.
For there was never yet fair woman but she made mouths in a glass.

Enter Kent disguised as Caius.

Lear, King of Britain.
No, I will be the pattern of all patience, I will say nothing.

Earl of Kent.
Who's there?

Fool.
Marry, here's grace and a codpiece—that's a wise man and a fool.

Earl of Kent.
Alas, sir, are you here? Things that love night
Love not such nights as these. The wrathful skies
Gallow the very wanderers of the dark,
And make them keep their caves. Since I was man,
Such sheets of fire, such bursts of horrid thunder,
Such groans of roaring wind and rain, I never
Remember to have heard. Man's nature cannot carry
Th' affliction nor the fear.

Lear, King of Britain.
                    Let the great gods,
That keep this dreadful pudder o'er our heads,
Find out their enemies now. Tremble, thou wretch
That hast within thee undivulged crimes
Unwhipt of justice! Hide thee, thou bloody hand;

Thou perjur'd, and thou simular of virtue
That art incestuous! Caitiff, to pieces shake,
That under covert and convenient seeming
Has practic'd on man's life! Close pent-up guilts,
Rive your concealing continents, and cry
These dreadful summoners grace. I am a man
More sinn'd against than sinning.

Earl of Kent.
                    Alack, bare-headed?
Gracious my lord, hard by here is a hovel,
Some friendship will it lend you 'gainst the tempest.
Repose you there, while I to this hard house
(More harder than the stones whereof 'tis rais'd,
Which even but now, demanding after you,
Denied me to come in) return, and force
Their scanted courtesy.

Lear, King of Britain.
                    My wits begin to turn.
Come on, my boy. How dost, my boy? Art cold?
I am cold myself. Where is this straw, my fellow?
The art of our necessities is strange
And can make vild things precious. Come, your hovel.
Poor Fool and knave, I have one part in my heart
That's sorry yet for thee.

Fool.

Sings.

"He that has and a little tiny wit—
With heigh-ho, the wind and the rain—
Must make content with his fortunes fit,
Though the rain it raineth every day."

Lear, King of Britain.
True, boy. Come bring us to this hovel.

Exit with Kent.

Fool.
This is a brave night to cool a courtezan. I'll speak a prophecy ere I go:
When priests are more in word than matter;
When brewers mar their malt with water;
When nobles are their tailors' tutors;
No heretics burn'd, but wenches' suitors;
Then shall the realm of Albion
Come to great confusion.
When every case in law is right;
No squire in debt, nor no poor knight;
When slanders do not live in tongues;
Nor cutpurses come not to throngs;
When usurers tell their gold i' th' field,
And bawds and whores do churches build;
Then comes the time, who lives to see't,
That going shall be us'd with feet.
This prophecy Merlin shall make, for I live before his time.

Exit.

Scene 3

Gloucester's castle.

(Gloucester; Edmund)

Gloucester bemoans to Edmund that Cornwall and Regan took away his command over his own house for speaking pityingly of Lear, whom they strictly forbid him to help. He tells Edmund that there are rumors of a rift between Cornwall and Albany, as well as that the French have landed. Gloucester also mysteriously says that Lear will be revenged, as a letter he has hidden away proves. Edmund immediately resolves to tell Cornwall this.

Enter Gloucester and Edmund with lights.

Earl of Gloucester.
Alack, alack, Edmund, I like not this unnatural dealing. When I desir'd their leave that I might pity him, they took from me the use of mine own house, charg'd me on pain of perpetual displeasure neither to speak of him, entreat for him, or any way sustain him.

Edmund.
Most savage and unnatural!

Earl of Gloucester.
Go to; say you nothing. There is division between the Dukes, and a worse matter than that. I have receiv'd a letter this night—'tis dangerous to be spoken; I have lock'd the letter in my closet. These injuries the King now bears will be reveng'd home; there is part of a power already footed: we must incline to the King. I will look him and privily relieve him. Go you and maintain talk with the Duke, that my charity be not of him perceiv'd. If he ask for me, I am ill and gone to bed. If I die for't (as no less is threat'ned me), the King my old master must be reliev'd. There is strange things toward, Edmund, pray you be careful.

Exit.

Edmund.
This courtesy, forbid thee, shall the Duke
Instantly know, and of that letter too.
This seems a fair deserving, and must draw me
That which my father loses: no less than all.
The younger rises when the old doth fall.

Exit.

Scene 4

The heath. Before a hovel.

(Lear; Kent; Fool; Edgar; Gloucester)

Kent has a hard time persuading Lear to enter the hovel, as the King is too busy ruminating on his wrongs. In the end he insists that the Fool go first, while he takes pity on the homeless of the world. Edgar, disguised as the mad Poor Tom, suddenly emerges from the hovel, almost naked and gabbling nonsense. Lear insists that Poor Tom could only have been brought so low by his daughters' mistreatment. Looking at the beggar, it occurs to him that this is all man is, and to match him Lear tears off his clothes. Gloucester enters, and Edgar pretends to think him a devil; the old man fails to recognize his son, just as Lear did not recognize his godson. Gloucester begs Lear to follow him somewhere warm, despite Regan's prohibition. Lear agrees to go, but insists that Poor Tom accompany him.

Enter Lear, Kent disguised as Caius, and Fool.

Earl of Kent.
Here is the place, my lord; good my lord, enter,
The tyranny of the open night's too rough
For nature to endure.

Storm still.

Lear, King of Britain.
                Let me alone.

Earl of Kent.
Good my lord, enter here.

Lear, King of Britain.
                Wilt break my heart?

Earl of Kent.
I had rather break mine own. Good my lord, enter.

Lear, King of Britain.
Thou think'st 'tis much that this contentious storm
Invades us to the skin; so 'tis to thee;
But where the greater malady is fix'd,
The lesser is scarce felt. Thou'dst shun a bear,
But if thy flight lay toward the roaring sea,
Thou'dst meet the bear i' th' mouth. When the mind's free,
The body's delicate; this tempest in my mind
Doth from my senses take all feeling else,
Save what beats there—filial ingratitude!
Is it not as this mouth should tear this hand
For lifting food to't? But I will punish home.
No, I will weep no more. In such a night
To shut me out? Pour on, I will endure.
In such a night as this? O Regan, Goneril!
Your old kind father, whose frank heart gave all—
O, that way madness lies, let me shun that!
No more of that.

Earl of Kent.
                Good my lord, enter here.

Lear, King of Britain.
Prithee go in thyself, seek thine own ease.
This tempest will not give me leave to ponder
On things would hurt me more. But I'll go in.

To the Fool.

In, boy, go first.—You houseless poverty—
Nay, get thee in; I'll pray, and then I'll sleep.

Exit Fool.

Poor naked wretches, wheresoe'er you are,
That bide the pelting of this pitiless storm,
How shall your houseless heads and unfed sides,
Your loop'd and window'd raggedness, defend you
From seasons such as these? O, I have ta'en
Too little care of this! Take physic, pomp,
Expose thyself to feel what wretches feel,
That thou mayst shake the superflux to them,
And show the heavens more just.

Edgar.

Within.

Fathom and half, fathom and half! Poor Tom!

Enter Fool from the hovel.

Fool.
Come not in here, nuncle, here's a spirit. Help me, help me!

Earl of Kent.
Give me thy hand. Who's there?

Fool.
A spirit, a spirit! He says his name's poor Tom.

Earl of Kent.
What art thou that dost grumble there i' th' straw? Come forth.

Enter Edgar disguised as a madman.

Edgar.
Away, the foul fiend follows me! Through the sharp hawthorn blow the cold winds. Humh, go to thy bed and warm thee.

Lear, King of Britain.
Didst thou give all to thy daughters? And art thou come to this?

Edgar.
Who gives any thing to poor Tom? Whom the foul fiend hath led through fire and through flame, through ford and whirlpool, o'er bog and quagmire; that hath laid knives under his pillow, and halters in his pew, set ratsbane by his porridge, made him proud of heart, to ride on a bay trotting-horse over four-inch'd bridges, to course his own shadow for a traitor. Bless thy five wits! Tom's a-cold—O do de, do de, do de. Bless thee from whirlwinds, star-blasting, and taking! Do poor Tom some charity, whom the foul fiend vexes. There could I have him now—and there—and there again—and there.

Storm still.

Lear, King of Britain.
Has his daughters brought him to this pass? Couldst thou save nothing? Wouldst thou give 'em all?

Fool.
Nay, he reserv'd a blanket, else we had been all sham'd.

Lear, King of Britain.
Now all the plagues that in the pendulous air Hang fated o'er men's faults light on thy daughters!

Earl of Kent.
He hath no daughters, sir.

Lear, King of Britain.
Death, traitor! Nothing could have subdu'd nature
To such a lowness but his unkind daughters.
Is it the fashion, that discarded fathers
Should have thus little mercy on their flesh?
Judicious punishment! 'Twas this flesh begot
Those pelican daughters.

Edgar.
Pillicock sat on Pillicock-Hill, alow! Alow, loo, loo!

Fool.
This cold night will turn us all to fools and madmen.

Edgar.
Take heed o' th' foul fiend. Obey thy parents, keep thy word's justice, swear not, commit not with man's sworn spouse, set not thy sweet heart on proud array. Tom's a-cold.

Lear, King of Britain.
What hast thou been?

Edgar.
A servingman! Proud in heart and mind; that curl'd my hair; wore gloves in my cap; serv'd the lust of my mistress' heart, and did the act of darkness with her; swore as many oaths as I spake words, and broke them in the sweet face of heaven: one that slept in the contriving of lust, and wak'd to do it. Wine lov'd I deeply, dice dearly; and in woman out-paramour'd the Turk. False of heart, light of ear, bloody of hand; hog in sloth, fox in stealth, wolf in greediness, dog in madness, lion in prey. Let not the creaking of shoes nor the rustling of silks betray thy poor heart to woman. Keep thy foot out of brothels, thy hand out of plackets, thy pen from lenders' books, and defy the foul fiend. Still through the hawthorn blows the cold wind: says suum, mun, nonny. Dolphin my boy, boy, sessa! Let him trot by.

Storm still.

Lear, King of Britain.
Thou wert better in a grave than to answer with thy uncover'd body this extremity of the skies. Is man no more than this? Consider him well. Thou ow'st the worm no silk, the beast no hide, the sheep no wool, the cat no perfume. Ha? Here's three on 's are sophis-

ticated. Thou art the thing itself: unaccommodated man is no more but such a poor, bare, fork'd animal as thou art. Off, off, you lendings! Come, unbutton here.

Tearing off his clothes.

Fool.
Prithee, nuncle, be contented, 'tis a naughty night to swim in. Now a little fire in a wild field were like an old lecher's heart, a small spark, all the rest on 's body cold.

Enter Gloucester with a torch.

Look, here comes a walking fire.

Edgar.
This is the foul fiend Flibbertigibbet; he begins at curfew, and walks till the first cock; he gives the web and the pin, squinies the eye, and makes the hare-lip; mildews the white wheat, and hurts the poor creature of earth.
Swithold footed thrice the 'old,
He met the night-mare and her nine-fold;
         Bid her alight,
         And her troth plight,
And aroint thee, witch, aroint thee!

Earl of Kent.
How fares your Grace?

Lear, King of Britain.
What's he?

Earl of Kent.
Who's there? What is't you seek?

Earl of Gloucester.
What are you there? Your names?

Edgar.
Poor Tom, that eats the swimming frog, the toad, the tadpole, the wall-newt, and the water; that in the fury of his heart, when the foul fiend rages, eats cow-dung for sallets; swallows the old rat and the ditch-dog; drinks the green mantle of the standing pool; who is whipt from tithing to tithing, and stock-punish'd and imprison'd; who hath had three suits to his back, six shirts to his body—
        Horse to ride, and weapon to wear;
        But mice and rats, and such small deer,
        Have been Tom's food for seven long year.
Beware my follower. Peace, Smulkin, peace, thou fiend!

Earl of Gloucester.
What, hath your Grace no better company?

Edgar.
The prince of darkness is a gentleman. Modo he's call'd, and Mahu.

Earl of Gloucester.
Our flesh and blood, my lord, is grown so vild
That it doth hate what gets it.

Edgar.
Poor Tom's a-cold.

Earl of Gloucester.
Go in with me; my duty cannot suffer
T' obey in all your daughters' hard commands.
Though their injunction be to bar my doors,
And let this tyrannous night take hold upon you,
Yet have I ventured to come seek you out,
And bring you where both fire and food is ready.

Lear, King of Britain.
First let me talk with this philosopher.
What is the cause of thunder?

Earl of Kent.
Good my lord, take his offer, go into th' house.

Lear, King of Britain.
I'll talk a word with this same learned Theban.
What is your study?

Edgar.
How to prevent the fiend, and to kill vermin.

Lear, King of Britain.
Let me ask you one word in private.

Earl of Kent.
Importune him once more to go, my lord,
His wits begin t' unsettle.

Earl of Gloucester.
        Canst thou blame him?

Storm still.

His daughters seek his death. Ah, that good Kent!
He said it would be thus, poor banish'd man.
Thou sayest the King grows mad, I'll tell thee, friend,
I am almost mad myself. I had a son,
Now outlaw'd from my blood; he sought my life,
But lately, very late. I lov'd him, friend,
No father his son dearer; true to tell thee,

The grief hath craz'd my wits. What a night's this!
I do beseech your Grace—

Lear, King of Britain.
O, cry you mercy, sir.
Noble philosopher, your company.

Edgar.
Tom's a-cold.

Earl of Gloucester.
In, fellow, there, into th' hovel; keep thee warm.

Lear, King of Britain.
Come, let's in all.

Earl of Kent.
This way, my lord.

Lear, King of Britain.
With him;
I will keep still with my philosopher.

Earl of Kent.
Good my lord, soothe him; let him take the fellow.

Earl of Gloucester.
Take him you on.

Earl of Kent.
Sirrah, come on; go along with us.

Lear, King of Britain.
Come, good Athenian.

Earl of Gloucester.
No words, no words, hush.

Edgar.
Child Rowland to the dark tower came,
His word was still, "Fie, foh, and fum,
I smell the blood of a British man."

Exeunt.

Scene 5

Gloucester's castle.

(Cornwall; Edmund)

Edmund has shown Cornwall his father's secret letter, and Cornwall is infuriated, swearing to be revenged on the old man. Edmund hypocritically laments the fight he had to hold between loyalty to his father and to his country. Cornwall names him Duke of Gloucester in his father's stead.

Enter Cornwall and Edmund.

Duke of Cornwall.
I will have my revenge ere I depart his house.

Edmund.
How, my lord, I may be censur'd, that nature thus gives way to loyalty, something fears me to think of.

Duke of Cornwall.
I now perceive, it was not altogether your brother's evil disposition made him seek his death; but a provoking merit, set a-work by a reprovable badness in himself.

Edmund.
How malicious is my fortune, that I must repent to be just! This is the letter which he spoke of, which approves him an intelligent party to the advantages of France. O heavens! That this treason were not; or not I the detector!

Duke of Cornwall.
Go with me to the Duchess.

Edmund.
If the matter of this paper be certain, you have mighty business in hand.

Duke of Cornwall.
True or false, it hath made thee Earl of Gloucester. Seek out where thy father is, that he may be ready for our apprehension.

Edmund.
Aside.

If I find him comforting the King, it will stuff his suspicion more fully.—I will persever in my course of loyalty, though the conflict be sore between that and my blood.

Duke of Cornwall.
I will lay trust upon thee; and thou shalt find a dearer father in my love.

Exeunt.

Scene 6

A chamber in a farmhouse adjoining the castle.

(Kent; Gloucester; Lear; Edgar; Fool)

Gloucester brings Lear and his bedraggled retinue to a small farmhouse adjoining his castle, promising to return soon with things to make it more comfortable. Lear appoints Kent, the Fool, and Edgar as judges and proceeds to hold a trial of his daughters for their ingratitude. Moved, Edgar finds it harder and harder to keep up his role. Kent tries to persuade Lear to sleep. Gloucester returns in a hurry, having overheard a plot against Lear's life; he urges Kent to take the King towards Dover.

Enter Kent disguised as Caius and Gloucester.

Earl of Gloucester.
Here is better than the open air, take it thankfully. I will piece out the comfort with what addition I can. I will not be long from you.

Earl of Kent.
All the pow'r of his wits have given way to his impatience. The gods reward your kindness!

Exit Gloucester.
Enter Lear, Edgar, and Fool.

Edgar.
Frateretto calls me, and tells me Nero is an angler in the lake of darkness. Pray, innocent, and beware the foul fiend.

Fool.
Prithee, nuncle, tell me whether a madman be a gentleman or a yeoman?

Lear, King of Britain.
A king, a king!

Fool.
No, he's a yeoman that has a gentleman to his son; for he's a mad yeoman that sees his son a gentleman before him.

Lear, King of Britain.
To have a thousand with red burning spits
Come hizzing in upon 'em—

Edgar.
The foul fiend bites my back.

Fool.
He's mad that trusts in the tameness of a wolf, a horse's health, a boy's love, or a whore's oath.

Lear, King of Britain.
It shall be done, I will arraign them straight.

To Edgar.

Come sit thou here, most learned justicer;

To the Fool.

Thou, sapient sir, sit here. Now, you she-foxes—

Edgar.
Look where he stands and glares! Want'st thou eyes at trial, madam?

Sings.

"Come o'er the bourn, Bessy, to me"—

Fool.

Sings.

Her boat hath a leak,
And she must not speak
Why she dares not come over to thee.

Edgar.
The foul fiend haunts poor Tom in the voice of a nightingale. Hoppedance cries in Tom's belly for two white herring. Croak not, black angel, I have no food for thee.

Earl of Kent.
How do you, sir? Stand you not so amaz'd.
Will you lie down and rest upon the cushions?

Lear, King of Britain.
I'll see their trial first, bring in their evidence.

To Edgar.

Thou robed man of justice, take thy place,

To the Fool.

And thou, his yoke-fellow of equity,
Bench by his side.

To Kent.

You are o' th' commission,
Sit you too.

Edgar.
        Let us deal justly.

Sings.

Sleepest or wakest thou, jolly shepherd?

Thy sheep be in the corn,
And for one blast of thy minikin mouth,
Thy sheep shall take no harm.
Purr the cat is grey.

Lear, King of Britain.
Arraign her first, 'tis Goneril. I here take my oath before this honorable assembly, she kick'd the poor king her father.

Fool.
Come hither, mistress. Is your name Goneril?

Lear, King of Britain.
She cannot deny it.

Fool.
Cry you mercy, I took you for a join-stool.

Lear, King of Britain.
And here's another, whose warp'd looks proclaim
What store her heart is made an. Stop her there!
Arms, arms, sword, fire! Corruption in the place!
False justicer, why hast thou let her scape?

Edgar.
Bless thy five wits!

Earl of Kent.
O pity! Sir, where is the patience now
That you so oft have boasted to retain?

Edgar.

Aside.

My tears begin to take his part so much,
They mar my counterfeiting.

Lear, King of Britain.
The little dogs and all,
Trey, Blanch, and Sweetheart, see, they bark at me.

Edgar.
Tom will throw his head at them. Avaunt, you curs!
Be thy mouth or black or white,
Tooth that poisons if it bite;
Mastiff, greyhound, mongrel grim,
Hound or spaniel, brach or lym,
Or bobtail tike or trundle-tail,
Tom will make him weep and wail,
For with throwing thus my head,
Dogs leapt the hatch, and all are fled.
Do de, de, de. Sessa! Come, march to wakes and fairs and market towns. Poor Tom, thy horn is dry.

Lear, King of Britain.
Then let them anatomize Regan; see what breeds about her heart. Is there any cause in nature that make these hard hearts?

To Edgar.

You, sir, I entertain for one of my hundred; only I do not like the fashion of your garments. You will say they are Persian, but let them be chang'd.

Earl of Kent.
Now, good my lord, lie here and rest awhile.

Lear, King of Britain.
Make no noise, make no noise, draw the curtains. So, so; we'll go to supper i' th' morning.

Fool.
And I'll go to bed at noon.

Enter Gloucester.

Earl of Gloucester.
Come hither, friend; where is the King my master?

Earl of Kent.
Here, sir, but trouble him not—his wits are gone.

Earl of Gloucester.
Good friend, I prithee take him in thy arms;
I have o'erheard a plot of death upon him.
There is a litter ready, lay him in't,
And drive toward Dover, friend, where thou shalt meet
Both welcome and protection. Take up thy master;
If thou shouldst dally half an hour, his life,
With thine and all that offer to defend him,
Stand in assured loss. Take up, take up,
And follow me, that will to some provision
Give thee quick conduct.

Earl of Kent.
          Oppressed nature sleeps.
This rest might yet have balm'd thy broken sinews,
Which, if convenience will not allow,
Stand in hard cure.

To the Fool.

Come help to bear thy master;
Thou must not stay behind.

Earl of Gloucester.
                    Come, come, away.

Exeunt all but Edgar.

Edgar.
When we our betters see bearing our woes,
We scarcely think our miseries our foes.
Who alone suffers, suffers most i' th' mind,
Leaving free things and happy shows behind,
But then the mind much sufferance doth o'erskip,
When grief hath mates, and bearing fellowship.
How light and portable my pain seems now,
When that which makes me bend makes the King bow:
He childed as I fathered! Tom, away!
Mark the high noises, and thyself bewray
When false opinion, whose wrong thoughts defile thee,
In thy just proof repeals and reconciles thee.
What will hap more tonight, safe scape the King!
Lurk, lurk.

Exit.

Scene 7

Gloucester's castle.

(Cornwall; Regan; Goneril; Edmund; First Servant; Second Servant; Third Servant; Oswald; Gloucester)

Cornwall sends Goneril to warn Albany that the French army has landed, and tells Edmund to accompany her, to avoid his seeing what, exactly, is going to be done to Gloucester, whom servants have gone to seek. The sisters want him immediately punished. Oswald informs them that the King has been sent towards Dover. Gloucester is brought in, and Regan and Cornwall have him tied to a chair. They interrogate him about his links to France, pulling out the letter that Edmund told them about. Gloucester admits that he has communicated with them, but insists his correspondent was a neutral party. They do not believe him. Asked why he sent the King to Dover despite orders to the contrary, he finally bursts out how he wanted to protect Lear from his daughters. Cornwall puts out one of Gloucester's eyes, and is about to do the other when his servant insist that he stop. Cornwall fights the servant, who wounds him, and Regan stabs the servant from behind. Despite his wound, Cornwall pulls out Gloucester's other eye, and when he calls on Edmund for help, Regan informs him that it was Edmund who betrayed him. Just blinded, Gloucester sees the truth about his sons. The wounded Cornwall realizes that his wound is both serious and ill-timed. He orders that Gloucester be turned out. The servants decide to ask the madman to guide Gloucester. One of them dresses Gloucester's wounded eyes.

Enter Cornwall, Regan, Goneril, Bastard Edmund, and Servants.

Duke of Cornwall.

To Goneril.

Post speedily to my lord your husband, show him this letter. The army of France is landed.—Seek out the traitor Gloucester.

Exeunt some of the Servants.

Regan.
Hang him instantly.

Goneril.
Pluck out his eyes.

Duke of Cornwall.
Leave him to my displeasure. Edmund, keep you our sister company; the revenges we are bound to take upon your traitorous father are not fit for your beholding. Advise the Duke, where you are going, to a most festinate preparation; we are bound to the like. Our posts shall be swift and intelligent betwixt us. Farewell, dear sister, farewell, my Lord of Gloucester.

Enter Steward Oswald.

How now? Where's the King?

Oswald.
My Lord of Gloucester hath convey'd him hence.
Some five or six and thirty of his knights,
Hot questrists after him, met him at gate,
Who, with some other of the lord's dependents,
Are gone with him toward Dover, where they boast
To have well-armed friends.

Duke of Cornwall.
                    Get horses for your mistress.

Goneril.
Farewell, sweet lord, and sister.

Act 3, Scene 7

Duke of Cornwall.
Edmund, farewell.

Exeunt Goneril, Edmund, and Oswald.

Go seek the traitor Gloucester,
Pinion him like a thief, bring him before us.

Exeunt other Servants.

Though well we may not pass upon his life
Without the form of justice, yet our power
Shall do a court'sy to our wrath, which men
May blame, but not control.

Enter Gloucester, brought in by two or three Servants.

Who's there? The traitor?

Regan.
Ingrateful fox, 'tis he.

Duke of Cornwall.
Bind fast his corky arms.

Earl of Gloucester.
What means your Graces? Good my friends, consider
You are my guests. Do me no foul play, friends.

Duke of Cornwall.
Bind him, I say.

Servants bind him.

Regan.
Hard, hard. O filthy traitor!

Earl of Gloucester.
Unmerciful lady as you are, I'm none.

Duke of Cornwall.
To this chair bind him. Villain, thou shalt find—

Regan plucks his beard.

Earl of Gloucester.
By the kind gods, 'tis most ignobly done
To pluck me by the beard.

Regan.
So white, and such a traitor?

Earl of Gloucester.
Naughty lady,
These hairs which thou dost ravish from my chin
Will quicken and accuse thee. I am your host,
With robber's hands my hospitable favors
You should not ruffle thus. What will you do?

Duke of Cornwall.
Come, sir, what letters had you late from France?

Regan.
Be simple-answer'd, for we know the truth.

Duke of Cornwall.
And what confederacy have you with the traitors
Late footed in the kingdom?

Regan.
To whose hands you have sent the lunatic King—
Speak.

Earl of Gloucester.
I have a letter guessingly set down,
Which came from one that's of a neutral heart,
And not from one oppos'd.

Duke of Cornwall.
Cunning.

Regan.
And false.

Duke of Cornwall.
Where hast thou sent the King?

Earl of Gloucester.
To Dover.

Regan.
Wherefore to Dover? Wast thou not charg'd at peril—

Duke of Cornwall.
Wherefore to Dover? Let him answer that.

Earl of Gloucester.
I am tied to th' stake, and I must stand the course.

Regan.
Wherefore to Dover?

Earl of Gloucester.
Because I would not see thy cruel nails
Pluck out his poor old eyes, nor thy fierce sister
In his anointed flesh rash boarish fangs.
The sea, with such a storm as his bare head
In hell-black night endur'd, would have buoy'd up
And quench'd the stelled fires;
Yet, poor old heart, he help the heavens to rain.
If wolves had at thy gate howl'd that dearn time,
Thou shouldst have said, "Good porter, turn the key."

All cruels else subscribe; but I shall see
The winged vengeance overtake such children.

Duke of Cornwall.
See't shalt thou never. Fellows, hold the chair,
Upon these eyes of thine I'll set my foot.

Earl of Gloucester.
He that will think to live till he be old,
Give me some help! O cruel! O you gods!

Regan.
One side will mock another; th' other too.

Duke of Cornwall.
If you see vengeance—

First Servant.
     Hold your hand, my lord!
I have serv'd you ever since I was a child;
But better service have I never done you
Than now to bid you hold.

Regan.
     How now, you dog?

First Servant.
If you did wear a beard upon your chin,
I'ld shake it on this quarrel. What do you mean?

Duke of Cornwall.
My villain!

Draw and fight.

First Servant.
Nay then come on, and take the chance of anger.

Cornwall is wounded.

Regan.
Give me thy sword. A peasant stand up thus?

She takes a sword and runs at him behind; kills him.

First Servant.
O, I am slain! My lord, you have one eye left
To see some mischief on him. O!

He dies.

Duke of Cornwall.
Lest it see more, prevent it. Out, vild jelly!
Where is thy lustre now?

Earl of Gloucester.
All dark and comfortless! Where's my son Edmund?
Edmund, enkindle all the sparks of nature,
To quit this horrid act.

Regan.
     Out, treacherous villain!
Thou call'st on him that hates thee. It was he
That made the overture of thy treasons to us,
Who is too good to pity thee.

Earl of Gloucester.
O my follies! Then Edgar was abus'd.
Kind gods, forgive me that, and prosper him!

Regan.
Go thrust him out at gates, and let him smell
His way to Dover.

Exit one with Gloucester.

     How is't, my lord? How look you?

Duke of Cornwall.
I have receiv'd a hurt; follow me, lady.—
Turn out that eyeless villain; throw this slave
Upon the dunghill. Regan, I bleed apace,
Untimely comes this hurt. Give me your arm.

Exit, led by Regan.

Second Servant.
I'll never care what wickedness I do,
If this man come to good.

Third Servant.
     If she live long,
And in the end meet the old course of death,
Women will all turn monsters.

Second Servant.
Let's follow the old Earl, and get the Bedlam
To lead him where he would; his roguish madness
Allows itself to any thing.

Third Servant.
Go thou. I'll fetch some flax and whites of eggs
To apply to his bleeding face. Now heaven help him!

Exeunt severally.

Act 4

Scene 1

A heath.

(Edgar; Gloucester; Old Man)

Edgar meets his blinded father, led by an old tenant of his whom he pushes away, and realizes that things can always get worse. Gloucester has reached a rare depth of despair and utterly lost faith that there is any good in the universe; Edgar overhears him and realizes that his father now knows he was tricked. The old man asks Edgar to lead Gloucester, and he agrees, though uncertain how long he will be able to keep up his pretense of being Poor Tom. Gloucester asks to be led to a high cliff near Dover.

Enter Edgar.

Edgar.
Yet better thus, and known to be contemn'd,
Than still contemn'd and flatter'd. To be worst,
The lowest and most dejected thing of fortune,
Stands still in esperance, lives not in fear.
The lamentable change is from the best,
The worst returns to laughter. Welcome then,
Thou unsubstantial air that I embrace:
The wretch that thou hast blown unto the worst
Owes nothing to thy blasts.

Enter Gloucester led by an Old Man.

                    But who comes here?
My father, parti-ey'd? World, world, O world!
But that thy strange mutations make us hate thee,
Life would not yield to age.

Old Man.
                O my good lord,
I have been your tenant, and your father's tenant,
These fourscore years.

Earl of Gloucester.
Away, get thee away! Good friend, be gone,
Thy comforts can do me no good at all;
Thee they may hurt.

Old Man.
              You cannot see your way.

Earl of Gloucester.
I have no way, and therefore want no eyes;
I stumbled when I saw. Full oft 'tis seen,
Our means secure us, and our mere defects
Prove our commodities. O dear son Edgar,
The food of thy abused father's wrath!
Might I but live to see thee in my touch,
I'd say I had eyes again.

Old Man.
              How now? Who's there?

Edgar.

Aside.

O gods! Who is't can say, "I am at the worst"?
I am worse than e'er I was.

Old Man.
              'Tis poor mad Tom.

Edgar.

Aside.

And worse I may be yet: the worst is not
So long as we can say, "This is the worst."

Old Man.
Fellow, where goest?

Earl of Gloucester.
              Is it a beggar-man?

Old Man.
Madman and beggar too.

Earl of Gloucester.
He has some reason, else he could not beg.
I' th' last night's storm I such a fellow saw,
Which made me think a man a worm. My son
Came then into my mind, and yet my mind
Was then scarce friends with him. I have heard more since.
As flies to wanton boys are we to th' gods,
They kill us for their sport.

Edgar.

Aside.

              How should this be?
Bad is the trade that must play fool to sorrow,
Ang'ring itself and others.—Bless thee, master!

Earl of Gloucester.
Is that the naked fellow?

Old Man.
                    Ay, my lord.

Earl of Gloucester.
Then prithee get thee away. If for my sake
Thou wilt o'ertake us hence a mile or twain
I' th' way toward Dover, do it for ancient love,
And bring some covering for this naked soul,
Which I'll entreat to lead me.

Old Man.
                    Alack, sir, he is mad.

Earl of Gloucester.
'Tis the time's plague, when madmen lead the blind.
Do as I bid thee, or rather do thy pleasure;
Above the rest, be gone.

Old Man.
I'll bring him the best 'parel that I have,
Come on't what will.

Exit.

Earl of Gloucester.
Sirrah, naked fellow—

Edgar.
Poor Tom's a-cold.

Aside.
                    I cannot daub it further.

Earl of Gloucester.
Come hither, fellow.

Edgar.

Aside.

And yet I must.—Bless thy sweet eyes, they bleed.

Earl of Gloucester.
Know'st thou the way to Dover?

Edgar.
Both stile and gate, horse-way and foot-path. Poor Tom hath been scar'd out of his good wits. Bless thee, good man's son, from the foul fiend! Five fiends have been in poor Tom at once: of lust, as Obidicut; Hobbididence, prince of dumbness; Mahu, of stealing; Modo, of murder; Flibbertigibbet, of mopping and mowing, who since possesses chambermaids and waiting-women. So, bless thee, master!

Earl of Gloucester.
Here, take this purse, thou whom the heav'ns' plagues
Have humbled to all strokes. That I am wretched
Makes thee the happier; heavens, deal so still!
Let the superfluous and lust-dieted man,
That slaves your ordinance, that will not see
Because he does not feel, feel your pow'r quickly;
So distribution should undo excess,
And each man have enough. Dost thou know Dover?

Edgar.
Ay, master.

Earl of Gloucester.
There is a cliff, whose high and bending head
Looks fearfully in the confined deep.
Bring me but to the very brim of it,
And I'll repair the misery thou dost bear
With something rich about me. From that place
I shall no leading need.

Edgar.
                    Give me thy arm;
Poor Tom shall lead thee.

Exeunt.

Scene 2
Before the Duke of Albany's palace.

(Goneril; Edmund; Oswald; Albany; First Messenger)

Oswald informs Goneril that her husband's reaction to the news of recent events is not at all what might have been expected. Goneril blames it on his weakness, and sends Edmund back to Cornwall to lead his armies. Goneril is quite taken with Edmund, considering him much more of a man than her husband. Albany, entering, reveals the extent to which he despises his wife for her treatment of Lear. Goneril reviles him as a wimp. Albany swears he'd kill her were she not a woman. At this point, news comes that Cornwall has died of his wounds. Goneril worries that Regan may gain Edmund's love, being widowed and thus able to marry him. Albany swears he will revenge Gloucester's eyes.

Enter Goneril, Bastard Edmund.

Goneril.
Welcome, my lord. I marvel our mild husband
Not met us on the way.

Enter Oswald, the Steward.

Now, where's your master?

Oswald.
Madam, within, but never man so chang'd.
I told him of the army that was landed;
He smil'd at it. I told him you were coming;
His answer was, "The worse." Of Gloucester's treachery,
And of the loyal service of his son,
When I inform'd him, then he call'd me sot,
And told me I had turn'd the wrong side out.
What most he should dislike seems pleasant to him;
What like, offensive.

Goneril.

To Edmund.

              Then shall you go no further.
It is the cowish terror of his spirit
That dares not undertake; he'll not feel wrongs
Which tie him to an answer. Our wishes on the way
May prove effects. Back, Edmund, to my brother,
Hasten his musters and conduct his pow'rs.
I must change names at home, and give the distaff
Into my husband's hands. This trusty servant
Shall pass between us. Ere long you are like to hear
(If you dare venture in your own behalf)
A mistress's command. Wear this; spare speech.
Decline your head: this kiss, if it durst speak,
Would stretch thy spirits up into the air.
Conceive, and fare thee well.

Edmund.
Yours in the ranks of death.

Exit.

Goneril.
              My most dear Gloucester!
O, the difference of man and man!
To thee a woman's services are due,
A fool usurps my bed.

Oswald.
              Madam, here comes my lord.

Exit.
Enter Albany.

Goneril.
I have been worth the whistling.

Duke of Albany.
              O Goneril,
You are not worth the dust which the rude wind
Blows in your face. I fear your disposition;
That nature which contemns it origin
Cannot be bordered certain in itself.
She that herself will sliver and disbranch
From her material sap, perforce must wither,
And come to deadly use.

Goneril.
No more, the text is foolish.

Duke of Albany.
Wisdom and goodness to the vild seem vild,
Filths savor but themselves. What have you done?
Tigers, not daughters, what have you perform'd?
A father, and a gracious aged man,
Whose reverence even the head-lugg'd bear would lick,
Most barbarous, most degenerate, have you madded.
Could my good brother suffer you to do it?
A man, a prince, by him so benefited!
If that the heavens do not their visible spirits
Send quickly down to tame these vild offenses,
It will come,
Humanity must perforce prey on itself,
Like monsters of the deep.

Goneril.
              Milk-liver'd man,
That bear'st a cheek for blows, a head for wrongs,
Who hast not in thy brows an eye discerning
Thine honor from thy suffering, that not know'st
Fools do those villains pity who are punish'd
Ere they have done their mischief, where's thy drum?
France spreads his banners in our noiseless land,
With plumed helm thy state begins to threat,
Whilst thou, a moral fool, sits still and cries,
"Alack, why does he so?"

Duke of Albany.
              See thyself, devil!
Proper deformity shows not in the fiend
So horrid as in woman.

Goneril.
              O vain fool!

Duke of Albany.
Thou changed and self-cover'd thing, for shame
Bemonster not thy feature. Were't my fitness
To let these hands obey my blood,
They are apt enough to dislocate and tear
Thy flesh and bones. Howe'er thou art a fiend,
A woman's shape doth shield thee.

Goneril.
Marry, your manhood mew!

Enter First Messenger.

Duke of Albany.
What news?

First Messenger.
O my good lord, the Duke of Cornwall's dead,
Slain by his servant, going to put out
The other eye of Gloucester.

Duke of Albany.
                    Gloucester's eyes?

First Messenger.
A servant that he bred, thrill'd with remorse,
Oppos'd against the act, bending his sword
To his great master, who, thereat enraged,
Flew on him, and amongst them fell'd him dead,
But not without that harmful stroke which since
Hath pluck'd him after.

Duke of Albany.
                    This shows you are above,
You justicers, that these our nether crimes
So speedily can venge! But, O poor Gloucester,
Lost he his other eye?

First Messenger.
                    Both, both, my lord.
This letter, madam, craves a speedy answer;
'Tis from your sister.

Goneril.

Aside.
                    One way I like this well,
But being widow, and my Gloucester with her,
May all the building in my fancy pluck
Upon my hateful life. Another way,
The news is not so tart.—I'll read, and answer.

Exit.

Duke of Albany.
Where was his son when they did take his eyes?

First Messenger.
Come with my lady hither.

Duke of Albany.
                    He is not here.

First Messenger.
No, my good lord, I met him back again.

Duke of Albany.
Knows he the wickedness?

First Messenger.
Ay, my good lord; 'twas he inform'd against him,
And quit the house on purpose that their punishment
Might have the freer course.

Duke of Albany.
                    Gloucester, I live
To thank thee for the love thou show'dst the King,
And to revenge thine eyes. Come hither, friend,
Tell me what more thou know'st.

Exeunt.

Scene 3

The French camp near Dover.

(Kent; First Gentleman)

Kent meets the Gentlemen he sent with news to Dover, from whom learns that troubles at home have forced the King of France to leave his army and return to his country, leaving Cordelia and a marshal in charge. The Gentleman tells Kent of Cordelia's grief as she heard how her sisters treated their father. Kent tells him that Lear refuses to see his daughter, so ashamed is he of how he treated her.

Enter Kent and First Gentleman.

Earl of Kent.
Why the King of France is so suddenly gone back, know you no reason?

First Gentleman.
Something he left imperfect in the state, which since his coming forth is thought of, which imports to the kingdom so much fear and danger that his personal return was most requir'd and necessary.

Earl of Kent.
Who hath he left behind him general?

First Gentleman.
The Marshal of France, Monsieur La Fer.

Earl of Kent.
Did your letters pierce the Queen to any demonstration of grief?

First Gentleman.
Ay, sir, she took them, read them in my presence,
And now and then an ample tear trill'd down
Her delicate cheek. It seem'd she was a queen
Over her passion, who, most rebel-like,
Sought to be king o'er her.

Earl of Kent.
                O then it mov'd her.

First Gentleman.
Not to a rage, patience and sorrow strove
Who should express her goodliest. You have seen
Sunshine and rain at once; her smiles and tears
Were like a better way: those happy smilets
That play'd on her ripe lip seem'd not to know
What guests were in her eyes, which, parted thence,
As pearls from diamonds dropp'd. In brief,
Sorrow would be a rarity most beloved,
If all could so become it.

Earl of Kent.
                Made she no verbal question?

First Gentleman.
Faith, once or twice she heav'd the name of "father"
Pantingly forth, as if it press'd her heart;
Cried, "Sisters, sisters! Shame of ladies, sisters!
Kent! Father! Sisters! What, i' th' storm? I' th' night?
Let pity not be believ'd!" There she shook
The holy water from her heavenly eyes,
And, clamor-moistened, then away she started
To deal with grief alone.

Earl of Kent.
                It is the stars,
The stars above us, govern our conditions,
Else one self mate and make could not beget
Such different issues. You spoke not with her since?

First Gentleman.
No.

Earl of Kent.
Was this before the King return'd?

First Gentleman.
                No, since.

Earl of Kent.
Well, sir, the poor distressed Lear's i' th' town,
Who sometime, in his better tune, remembers
What we are come about, and by no means
Will yield to see his daughter.

First Gentleman.
                Why, good sir?

Earl of Kent.
A sovereign shame so elbows him: his own unkindness,
That stripp'd her from his benediction, turn'd her
To foreign casualties, gave her dear rights
To his dog-hearted daughters—these things sting
His mind so venomously, that burning shame
Detains him from Cordelia.

First Gentleman.
                Alack, poor gentleman!

Earl of Kent.
Of Albany's and Cornwall's powers you heard not?

First Gentleman.
'Tis so, they are afoot.

Earl of Kent.
Well, sir, I'll bring you to our master Lear,
And leave you to attend him. Some dear cause
Will in concealment wrap me up awhile;
When I am known aright, you shall not grieve
Lending me this acquaintance. I pray you go
Along with me.

Exeunt.

Scene 4

The French camp near Dover. A tent.

(*Cordelia; Doctor; Soldiers; Officer; French Messenger*)

Cordelia asks a doctor whether he can cure Lear's madness; the doctor assures her that all Lear needs is proper rest. She sends out men to seek for him, just as she learns that the British forces are near at hand.

Enter, with Drum and Colors, Cordelia, Doctor, and Soldiers.

Cordelia.
Alack, 'tis he! Why, he was met even now
As mad as the vex'd sea, singing aloud,
Crown'd with rank fumitor and furrow-weeds,
With hardocks, hemlock, nettles, cuckoo-flow'rs,
Darnel, and all the idle weeds that grow
In our sustaining corn. A century send forth;
Search every acre in the high-grown field,
And bring him to our eye.

Exit an Officer.

                    What can man's wisdom
In the restoring his bereaved sense?
He that helps him take all my outward worth.

Doctor.
There is means, madam.
Our foster-nurse of nature is repose,
The which he lacks; that to provoke in him
Are many simples operative, whose power
Will close the eye of anguish.

Cordelia.
                    All blest secrets,
All you unpublish'd virtues of the earth,
Spring with my tears; be aidant and remediate
In the good man's distress! Seek, seek for him,
Lest his ungovern'd rage dissolve the life
That wants the means to lead it.

Enter French Messenger.

French Messenger.
                    News, madam!
The British pow'rs are marching hitherward.

Cordelia.
'Tis known before; our preparation stands
In expectation of them. O dear father,
It is thy business that I go about;
Therefore great France
My mourning and importun'd tears hath pitied.
No blown ambition doth our arms incite,
But love, dear love, and our ag'd father's right.
Soon may I hear and see him!

Exeunt.

Scene 5

Gloucester's Castle.

(Regan; Oswald)

Regan talks to Oswald about recent events. She is disturbed that Gloucester was not killed, and concerned about why Goneril would be writing to Edmund, with whom she is in love and whom she believes she has arranged to marry. She tells Oswald that whoever kills Gloucester will benefit from the deed. Oswald is excited at the prospect.

Enter Regan and Steward Oswald.

Regan.
But are my brother's pow'rs set forth?

Oswald.
                    Ay, madam.

Regan.
Himself in person there?

Oswald.
                    Madam, with much ado;
Your sister is the better soldier.

Regan.
Lord Edmund spake not with your lord at home?

Oswald.
No, madam.

Regan.
What might import my sister's letter to him?

Oswald.
I know not, lady.

Regan.
Faith, he is posted hence on serious matter.
It was great ignorance, Gloucester's eyes being out,
To let him live; where he arrives he moves
All hearts against us. Edmund, I think, is gone,
In pity of his misery, to dispatch
His nighted life; moreover to descry
The strength o' th' enemy.

Oswald.
I must needs after him, madam, with my letter.

Regan.
Our troops set forth tomorrow, stay with us;
The ways are dangerous.

Oswald.
                    I may not, madam;
My lady charg'd my duty in this business.

Regan.
Why should she write to Edmund? Might not you
Transport her purposes by word? Belike
Some things—I know not what. I'll love thee much—
Let me unseal the letter.

Oswald.
                  Madam, I had rather—

Regan.
I know your lady does not love her husband,
I am sure of that; and at her late being here
She gave strange eliads and most speaking looks
To noble Edmund. I know you are of her bosom.

Oswald.
I, madam?

Regan.
I speak in understanding: y' are; I know't.
Therefore I do advise you take this note:
My lord is dead; Edmund and I have talk'd,
And more convenient is he for my hand
Than for your lady's. You may gather more.
If you do find him, pray you give him this;
And when your mistress hears thus much from you,
I pray desire her call her wisdom to her.
So fare you well.
If you do chance to hear of that blind traitor,
Preferment falls on him that cuts him off.

Oswald.
Would I could meet him, madam! I should show
What party I do follow.

Regan.
                Fare thee well.

Exeunt.

Scene 6

Fields near Dover.

(Gloucester; Edgar; Lear; First Gentleman; Attendants; Oswald)

Edgar leads Gloucester to a field, pretending it is the high cliff the old man asked for. Gloucester notices that Edgar is speaking better than he did, and that the ground does not feel steep at all, but Edgar convinces him he is wrong. Hoping to commit suicide, Gloucester jumps, thinking he has leapt off the cliff. Changing his voice, Edgar pretends to find him, and convinces him that the madman leading him was actually the devil—hoping thereby to stop his father from trying to kill himself again. Lear, madly dressed with wild flowers, comes in, talking madly; Gloucester recognizes his voice and tries to kiss the King's hand. Finally, Lear admits that he recognizes the blind man. Gentlemen seeking Lear finally find him, but the King runs away. Edgar gets news of the coming battle from one of the gentlemen. Oswald enters, recognizing Gloucester, and attempts to kill him. Edgar kills him instead. As he lies dying, Oswald asks the 'peasant' to take the letters he is carrying to Edmund. Edgar opens them, and find a love letter from Goneril, plotting to kill Albany. Disgusted, he leads Gloucester off, hoping to find a friend to lodge him with until the battle is done.

Enter Gloucester and Edgar dressed like a peasant.

Earl of Gloucester.
When shall I come to th' top of that same hill?

Edgar.
You do climb up it now. Look how we labor.

Earl of Gloucester.
Methinks the ground is even.

Edgar.
                  Horrible steep.
Hark, do you hear the sea?

Earl of Gloucester.
                  No, truly.

Edgar.
Why then your other senses grow imperfect
By your eyes' anguish.

Earl of Gloucester.
                  So may it be indeed.
Methinks thy voice is alter'd, and thou speak'st
In better phrase and matter than thou didst.

Edgar.
Y' are much deceiv'd. In nothing am I chang'd
But in my garments.

Earl of Gloucester.
                  Methinks y' are better spoken.

Edgar.
Come on, sir, here's the place; stand still. How fearful
And dizzy 'tis, to cast one's eyes so low!
The crows and choughs that wing the midway air
Show scarce so gross as beetles. Half way down
Hangs one that gathers sampire, dreadful trade!
Methinks he seems no bigger than his head.
The fishermen that walk upon the beach
Appear like mice; and yond tall anchoring bark,
Diminish'd to her cock; her cock, a buoy
Almost too small for sight. The murmuring surge,
That on th' unnumb'red idle pebble chafes,
Cannot be heard so high. I'll look no more,
Lest my brain turn, and the deficient sight
Topple down headlong.

Earl of Gloucester.
                    Set me where you stand.

Edgar.
Give me your hand. You are now within a foot
Of th' extreme verge. For all beneath the moon
Would I not leap upright.

Earl of Gloucester.
                         Let go my hand.
Here, friend, 's another purse; in it a jewel
Well worth a poor man's taking. Fairies and gods
Prosper it with thee! Go thou further off:
Bid me farewell, and let me hear thee going.

Edgar.
Now fare ye well, good sir.

Earl of Gloucester.
With all my heart.

Edgar.

Aside.

Why I do trifle thus with his despair
Is done to cure it.

Earl of Gloucester.
                    O you mighty gods!

He kneels.

This world I do renounce, and in your sights
Shake patiently my great affliction off.
If I could bear it longer, and not fall
To quarrel with your great opposeless wills,
My snuff and loathed part of nature should
Burn itself out. If Edgar live, O bless him!
Now, fellow, fare thee well.

He falls.

Edgar.
                    Gone, sir; farewell!
And yet I know not how conceit may rob
The treasury of life, when life itself
Yields to the theft. Had he been where he thought,
By this had thought been past. Alive or dead?—
Ho, you, sir! Friend! Hear you, sir! Speak!—
Thus might he pass indeed; yet he revives.—
What are you, sir?

Earl of Gloucester.
                    Away, and let me die.

Edgar.
Hadst thou been aught but goss'mer, feathers, air
(So many fathom down precipitating),
Thou'dst shiver'd like an egg: but thou dost breathe,
Hast heavy substance, bleed'st not, speak'st, art sound.
Ten masts at each make not the altitude
Which thou hast perpendicularly fell.
Thy life's a miracle. Speak yet again.

Earl of Gloucester.
But have I fall'n, or no?

Edgar.
From the dread summit of this chalky bourn.
Look up a-height, the shrill-gorg'd lark so far
Cannot be seen or heard. Do but look up.

Earl of Gloucester.
Alack, I have no eyes.
Is wretchedness depriv'd that benefit,
To end itself by death? 'Twas yet some comfort,
When misery could beguile the tyrant's rage,
And frustrate his proud will.

Edgar.
                         Give me your arm.
Up—so. How is't? Feel you your legs? You stand.

Earl of Gloucester.
Too well, too well.

Edgar.
                    This is above all strangeness.
Upon the crown o' th' cliff, what thing was that
Which parted from you?

Earl of Gloucester.
                A poor unfortunate beggar.

Edgar.
As I stood here below, methought his eyes
Were two full moons; he had a thousand noses,
Horns welk'd and waved like the enridged sea.
It was some fiend; therefore, thou happy father,
Think that the clearest gods, who make them honors
Of men's impossibilities, have preserved thee.

Earl of Gloucester.
I do remember now. Henceforth I'll bear
Affliction till it do cry out itself
"Enough, enough," and die. That thing you speak of,
I took it for a man; often 'twould say,
"The fiend, the fiend!"—he led me to that place.

Edgar.
Bear free and patient thoughts.

Enter Lear mad, crowned with weeds and flowers.
                But who comes here?
The safer sense will ne'er accommodate
His master thus.

Lear, King of Britain.
No, they cannot touch me for coining, I am the King himself.

Edgar.
O thou side—piercing sight!

Lear, King of Britain.
Nature's above art in that respect. There's your press-money. That fellow handles his bow like a crow-keeper; draw me a clothier's yard. Look, look, a mouse! Peace, peace, this piece of toasted cheese will do't. There's my gauntlet, I'll prove it on a giant. Bring up the brown bills. O, well flown, bird! I' th' clout, i' th' clout—hewgh! Give the word.

Edgar.
Sweet marjorum.

Lear, King of Britain.
Pass.

Earl of Gloucester.
I know that voice.

Lear, King of Britain.
Ha! Goneril with a white beard? They flatter'd me like a dog, and told me I had the white hairs in my beard ere the black ones were there. To say "ay" and "no" to every thing that I said! "Ay," and "no" too, was no good divinity. When the rain came to wet me once, and the wind to make me chatter, when the thunder would not peace at my bidding, there I found 'em, there I smelt 'em out. Go to, they are not men o' their words: they told me I was every thing. 'Tis a lie, I am not ague-proof.

Earl of Gloucester.
The trick of that voice I do well remember;
Is't not the King?

Lear, King of Britain.
                Ay, every inch a king!
When I do stare, see how the subject quakes.
I pardon that man's life. What was thy cause?
Adultery?
Thou shalt not die. Die for adultery? No,
The wren goes to't, and the small gilded fly
Does lecher in my sight.
Let copulation thrive; for Gloucester's bastard son
Was kinder to his father than my daughters
Got 'tween the lawful sheets.
To't, luxury, pell-mell, for I lack soldiers.
Behold yond simp'ring dame,
Whose face between her forks presages snow;
That minces virtue, and does shake the head
To hear of pleasure's name—
The fitchew nor the soiled horse goes to't
With a more riotous appetite.
Down from the waist they are Centaurs,
Though women all above;
But to the girdle do the gods inherit,
Beneath is all the fiends': there's hell, there's darkness,
There is the sulfurous pit, burning, scalding,
Stench, consumption. Fie, fie, fie! Pah, pah!
Give me an ounce of civet; good apothecary,
Sweeten my imagination. There's money for thee.

Earl of Gloucester.
O, let me kiss that hand!

Lear, King of Britain.
Let me wipe it first, it smells of mortality.

Earl of Gloucester.
O ruin'd piece of nature! This great world
Shall so wear out to nought. Dost thou know me?

Lear, King of Britain.
I remember thine eyes well enough. Dost thou squiny at me? No, do thy worst, blind Cupid, I'll not love. Read thou this challenge; mark but the penning of it.

Earl of Gloucester.
Were all thy letters suns, I could not see.

Edgar.

Aside.

I would not take this from report; it is,
And my heart breaks at it.

Lear, King of Britain.
Read.

Earl of Gloucester.
What, with the case of eyes?

Lear, King of Britain.
O ho, are you there with me? No eyes in your head, nor no money in your purse? Your eyes are in a heavy case, your purse in a light, yet you see how this world goes.

Earl of Gloucester.
I see it feelingly.

Lear, King of Britain.
What, art mad? A man may see how this world goes with no eyes. Look with thine ears; see how yond justice rails upon yond simple thief. Hark in thine ear: change places, and handy-dandy, which is the justice, which is the thief? Thou hast seen a farmer's dog bark at a beggar?

Earl of Gloucester.
Ay, sir.

Lear, King of Britain.
And the creature run from the cur? There thou mightst behold the great image of authority: a dog's obey'd in office.
Thou rascal beadle, hold thy bloody hand!
Why dost thou lash that whore? Strip thy own back,
Thou hotly lusts to use her in that kind
For which thou whip'st her. The usurer hangs the cozener.
Thorough tatter'd clothes small vices do appear;
Robes and furr'd gowns hide all. Plate sin with gold,
And the strong lance of justice hurtless breaks;
Arm it in rags, a pigmy's straw does pierce it.
None does offend, none, I say none, I'll able 'em.
Take that of me, my friend, who have the power
To seal th' accuser's lips. Get thee glass eyes,
And like a scurvy politician, seem
To see the things thou dost not. Now, now, now, now.
Pull off my boots; harder, harder-so.

Edgar.

Aside.

O, matter and impertinency mix'd,
Reason in madness!

Lear, King of Britain.
If thou wilt weep my fortunes, take my eyes.
I know thee well enough, thy name is Gloucester.
Thou must be patient; we came crying hither.
Thou know'st, the first time that we smell the air
We wawl and cry. I will preach to thee. Mark.

Lear takes off his crown of weeds and flowers.

Earl of Gloucester.
Alack, alack the day!

Lear, King of Britain.
When we are born, we cry that we are come
To this great stage of fools.—This' a good block.
It were a delicate stratagem, to shoe
A troop of horse with felt. I'll put't in proof,
And when I have stol'n upon these son-in-laws,
Then kill, kill, kill, kill, kill, kill!

Enter First Gentleman with Attendants.

First Gentleman.
O, here he is: lay hand upon him.—Sir,
Your most dear daughter—

Lear, King of Britain.
No rescue? What, a prisoner? I am even
The natural fool of fortune. Use me well,
You shall have ransom. Let me have surgeons,
I am cut to th' brains.

First Gentleman.
               You shall have any thing.

Act 4, Scene 6

Lear, King of Britain.
No seconds? All myself?
Why, this would make a man a man of salt
To use his eyes for garden water-pots,
Ay, and laying autumn's dust.

First Gentleman.
     Good sir—

Lear, King of Britain.
I will die bravely, like a smug bridegroom. What?
I will be jovial. Come, come, I am a king,
Masters, know you that?

First Gentleman.
You are a royal one, and we obey you.

Lear, King of Britain.
Then there's life in't. Come, and you get it, you shall
get it by running. Sa, sa, sa, sa.

Exit running; Attendants follow.

First Gentleman.
A sight most pitiful in the meanest wretch,
Past speaking of in a king! Thou hast one daughter
Who redeems nature from the general curse
Which twain have brought her to.

Edgar.
Hail, gentle sir.

First Gentleman.
     Sir, speed you: what's your will?

Edgar.
Do you hear aught, sir, of a battle toward?

First Gentleman.
Most sure and vulgar; every one hears that,
Which can distinguish sound.

Edgar.
     But by your favor,
How near's the other army?

First Gentleman.
Near and on speedy foot; the main descry
Stands on the hourly thought.

Edgar.
     I thank you, sir, that's all.

First Gentleman.
Though that the Queen on special cause is here,
Her army is mov'd on.

Edgar.
     I thank you, sir.

Exit First Gentleman.

Earl of Gloucester.
You ever—gentle gods, take my breath from me,
Let not my worser spirit tempt me again
To die before you please!

Edgar.
     Well pray you, father.

Earl of Gloucester.
Now, good sir, what are you?

Edgar.
A most poor man, made tame to fortune's blows,
Who, by the art of known and feeling sorrows,
Am pregnant to good pity. Give me your hand,
I'll lead you to some biding.

Earl of Gloucester.
     Hearty thanks;
The bounty and the benison of heaven
To boot, and boot!

Enter Steward Oswald.

Oswald.
A proclaim'd prize! Most happy!
That eyeless head of thine was first fram'd flesh
To raise my fortunes. Thou old unhappy traitor,
Briefly thyself remember; the sword is out
That must destroy thee.

Earl of Gloucester.
     Now let thy friendly hand
Put strength enough to't.

Edgar interposes.

Oswald.
     Wherefore, bold peasant,
Durst thou support a publish'd traitor? Hence,
Lest that th' infection of his fortune take
Like hold on thee. Let go his arm.

Edgar.
Chill not let go, zir, without vurther cagion.

Oswald.
Let go, slave, or thou di'st!

Edgar.
Good gentleman, go your gait, and let poor voke pass. And chud ha' bin zwagger'd out of my life, 'twould not ha' bin zo long as 'tis by a vortnight. Nay, come not near th' old man; keep out, che vor' ye, or I'ce try whither your costard or my ballow be the harder. Chill be plain with you.

Oswald.
Out, dunghill!

They fight.

Edgar.
Chill pick your teeth, zir. Come, no matter vor your foins.

Oswald.
Slave, thou hast slain me. Villain, take my purse:
If ever thou wilt thrive, bury my body,
And give the letters which thou find'st about me
To Edmund Earl of Gloucester; seek him out
Upon the English party. O untimely death!
Death!

He dies.

Edgar.
I know thee well; a serviceable villain,
As duteous to the vices of thy mistress
As badness would desire.

Earl of Gloucester.
                What, is he dead?

Edgar.
Sit you down, father; rest you.
Let's see these pockets; the letters that he speaks of
May be my friends. He's dead; I am only sorry
He had no other deathsman. Let us see.
Leave, gentle wax, and, manners, blame us not:
To know our enemies' minds, we rip their hearts,
Their papers is more lawful.

Reads the letter.

"Let our reciprocal vows be rememb'red. You have many opportunities to cut him off; if your will want not, time and place will be fruitfully offer'd. There is nothing done, if he return the conqueror; then am I the prisoner, and his bed my jail; from the loath'd warmth whereof deliver me, and supply the place for your labor. Your (wife, so I would say) affectionate servant, Goneril."
O indistinguish'd space of woman's will!:
A plot upon her virtuous husband's life,
And the exchange my brother! Here, in the sands,
Thee I'll rake up, the post unsanctified
Of murderous lechers; and in the mature time
With this ungracious paper strike the sight
Of the death-practic'd Duke. For him 'tis well
That of thy death and business I can tell.

Earl of Gloucester.
The King is mad; how stiff is my vild sense
That I stand up, and have ingenious feeling
Of my huge sorrows! Better I were distract,
So should my thoughts be sever'd from my griefs,
And woes by wrong imaginations lose
The knowledge of themselves.

Drum afar off.

Edgar.
                Give me your hand;
Far off methinks I hear the beaten drum.
Come, father, I'll bestow you with a friend.

Exeunt.

Scene 7

The French camp near Dover. A tent.

(Cordelia; Kent; Doctor; Lear; Servants; First Gentleman)

Kent and Cordelia meet, and he asks permission to remain disguised for the time being. The doctor tells Cordelia that it is time to wake Lear up, which they do by playing music. Cordelia kisses him awake, and the doctor insists that she be the first to speak to him. Lear at first refuses to believe that it is she, terrified that he is still mad and merely dreaming of her. Gentle and humble now, he goes to walk with her outside. Kent learns what the rumors of the day are.

Enter Cordelia, Kent still dressed as Caius, and Doctor.

Cordelia.
O thou good Kent, how shall I live and work
To match thy goodness? My life will be too short,

And every measure fail me.

Earl of Kent.
To be acknowledg'd, madam, is o'erpaid.
All my reports go with the modest truth,
Nor more nor clipt, but so.

Cordelia.
                    Be better suited,
These weeds are memories of those worser hours;
I prithee put them off.

Earl of Kent.
                    Pardon, dear madam,
Yet to be known shortens my made intent.
My boon I make it, that you know me not
Till time and I think meet.

Cordelia.
Then be't so, my good lord.

To the Doctor.

How does the King?

Doctor.
                    Madam, sleeps still.

Cordelia.
                    O you kind gods!
Cure this great breach in his abused nature,
Th' untun'd and jarring senses, O, wind up
Of this child-changed father!

Doctor.
                    So please your Majesty
That we may wake the King? He hath slept long.

Cordelia.
Be govern'd by your knowledge, and proceed
I' th' sway of your own will. Is he array'd?

First Gentleman.
Ay, madam; in the heaviness of sleep
We put fresh garments on him.

Doctor.
Be by, good madam, when we do awake him,
I doubt not of his temperance.

Cordelia.
                    Very well.

Enter Lear in a chair carried by Servants. First Gentleman in attendance. Soft music.

Doctor.
Please you draw near.—Louder the music there!

Cordelia.
O my dear father, restoration hang
Thy medicine on my lips, and let this kiss
Repair those violent harms that my two sisters
Have in thy reverence made.

Earl of Kent.
Kind and dear princess!

Cordelia.
Had you not been their father, these white flakes
Did challenge pity of them. Was this a face
To be oppos'd against the warring winds?
To stand against the deep dread-bolted thunder?
In the most terrible and nimble stroke
Of quick cross lightning? To watch—poor perdu!—
With this thin helm? Mine enemy's dog,
Though he had bit me, should have stood that night
Against my fire, and wast thou fain, poor father,
To hovel thee with swine and rogues forlorn
In short and musty straw? Alack, alack,
'Tis wonder that thy life and wits at once
Had not concluded all. He wakes, speak to him.

Doctor.
Madam, do you, 'tis fittest.

Cordelia.
How does my royal lord? How fares your Majesty?

Lear, King of Britain.
You do me wrong to take me out o' th' grave:
Thou art a soul in bliss, but I am bound
Upon a wheel of fire, that mine own tears
Do scald like molten lead.

Cordelia.
                    Sir, do you know me?

Lear, King of Britain.
You are a spirit, I know; when did you die?

Cordelia.
Still, still, far wide!

Doctor.
He's scarce awake, let him alone a while.

Lear, King of Britain.
Where have I been? Where am I? Fair daylight?
I am mightily abus'd; I should ev'n die with pity
To see another thus. I know not what to say.
I will not swear these are my hands. Let's see,
I feel this pin prick. Would I were assur'd
Of my condition!

Cordelia.
                O, look upon me, sir,
And hold your hand in benediction o'er me.
No, sir, you must not kneel.

Lear, King of Britain.
                Pray do not mock me.
I am a very foolish fond old man,
Fourscore and upward, not an hour more nor less;
And to deal plainly,
I fear I am not in my perfect mind.
Methinks I should know you, and know this man,
Yet I am doubtful: for I am mainly ignorant
What place this is, and all the skill I have
Remembers not these garments; nor I know not
Where I did lodge last night. Do not laugh at me,
For (as I am a man) I think this lady
To be my child Cordelia.

Cordelia.
                And so I am; I am.

Lear, King of Britain.
Be your tears wet? Yes, faith. I pray weep not.
If you have poison for me, I will drink it.
I know you do not love me, for your sisters
Have (as I do remember) done me wrong:
You have some cause, they have not.

Cordelia.
                No cause, no cause.

Lear, King of Britain.
Am I in France?

Earl of Kent.
                In your own kingdom, sir.

Lear, King of Britain.
Do not abuse me.

Doctor.
Be comforted, good madam, the great rage,
You see, is kill'd in him, and yet it is danger
To make him even o'er the time he has lost.
Desire him to go in, trouble him no more
Till further settling.

Cordelia.
Will't please your Highness walk?

Lear, King of Britain.
                You must bear with me.
Pray you now forget, and forgive; I am old and foolish.

Exeunt. Manent Kent and First Gentleman.

First Gentleman.
Holds it true, sir, that the Duke of Cornwall was so slain?

Earl of Kent.
Most certain, sir.

First Gentleman.
Who is conductor of his people?

Earl of Kent.
As 'tis said, the bastard son of Gloucester.

First Gentleman.
They say Edgar, his banish'd son, is with the Earl of Kent in Germany.

Earl of Kent.
Report is changeable. 'Tis time to look about, the powers of the kingdom approach apace.

First Gentleman.
The arbiterment is like to be bloody. Fare you well, sir.

Exit.

Earl of Kent.
My point and period will be throughly wrought,
Or well or ill, as this day's battle's fought.

Exit.

Act 5

Scene 1

The British camp near Dover.

(Edmund; Regan; First Gentleman; Second Gentleman; Albany; Goneril; Soldiers; Edgar)

Edmund sends to find out whether Albany has changed his mind yet again about how to go about the battle. Jealous, Regan asks Edmund to assure her that he does not love Goneril, which he does. Albany insists that he is only fighting because the opposing army is French, not against Lear. Edmund and Albany arrange a later meeting to discuss combining their forces. Regan insists that Goneril not follow, to keep her away from Edmund. Edgar, disguised, enters and gives Albany the love letter he found, promising the Duke that a champion will vouch for its truth if he asks for one. Edmund urges Albany to go to the battle, which is about to begin. Alone, he reflects on how he has won the love of both sisters, and cannot decide between them, though they both have their uses. He is determined to make sure that Albany's plan to be merciful to Cordelia and Lear fails.

Enter, with Drum and Colors, Edmund, Regan, Gentlemen, and Soldiers.

Edmund.
Know of the Duke if his last purpose hold,
Or whether since he is advis'd by aught
To change the course. He's full of alteration
And self-reproving—bring his constant pleasure.

To Second Gentleman, who goes out.

Regan.
Our sister's man is certainly miscarried.

Edmund.
'Tis to be doubted, madam.

Regan.
                    Now, sweet lord,
You know the goodness I intend upon you:
Tell me but truly, but then speak the truth,
Do you not love my sister?

Edmund.
                    In honor'd love.

Regan.
But have you never found my brother's way
To the forfended place?

Edmund.
                    That thought abuses you.

Regan.
I am doubtful that you have been conjunct
And bosom'd with her—as far as we call hers.

Edmund.
No, by mine honor, madam.

Regan.
I never shall endure her. Dear my lord,
Be not familiar with her.

Edmund.
                    Fear me not.
She and the Duke her husband!

Enter, with Drum and Colors, Albany, Goneril, Soldiers.

Goneril.

Aside.

I had rather lose the battle than that sister
Should loosen him and me.

Duke of Albany.
Our very loving sister, well bemet.
Sir, this I heard: the King is come to his daughter,
With others whom the rigor of our state
Forc'd to cry out. Where I could not be honest,
I never yet was valiant. For this business,
It touches us as France invades our land,
Not bolds the King, with others whom, I fear,
Most just and heavy causes make oppose.

Edmund.
Sir, you speak nobly.

Regan.
                    Why is this reason'd?

Goneril.
Combine together 'gainst the enemy;
For these domestic and particular broils
Are not the question here.

Duke of Albany.
                    Let's then determine
With th' ancient of war on our proceeding.

Edmund.
I shall attend you presently at your tent.

Regan.
Sister, you'll go with us?

Goneril.
No.

Regan.
'Tis most convenient, pray go with us.

Goneril.

Aside.

O ho, I know the riddle.—I will go.

Exeunt both the armies.
As they are going out, enter Edgar disguised. Albany remains.

Edgar.
If e'er your Grace had speech with man so poor,
Hear me one word.

Duke of Albany.
                I'll overtake you.—Speak.

Edgar.
Before you fight the battle, ope this letter.
If you have victory, let the trumpet sound
For him that brought it. Wretched though I seem,
I can produce a champion that will prove
What is avouch'd there. If you miscarry,
Your business of the world hath so an end,
And machination ceases. Fortune love you!

Duke of Albany.
Stay till I have read the letter.

Edgar.
                I was forbid it.
When time shall serve, let but the herald cry,
And I'll appear again.

Duke of Albany.
Why, fare thee well, I will o'erlook thy paper.

Exit Edgar.
Enter Edmund.

Edmund.
The enemy's in view, draw up your powers.
Here is the guess of their true strength and forces,
By diligent discovery, but your haste
Is now urg'd on you.

Duke of Albany.
                We will greet the time.

Exit.

Edmund.
To both these sisters have I sworn my love;
Each jealous of the other, as the stung
Are of the adder. Which of them shall I take?
Both? One? Or neither? Neither can be enjoy'd
If both remain alive: to take the widow
Exasperates, makes mad her sister Goneril,
And hardly shall I carry out my side,
Her husband being alive. Now then, we'll use
His countenance for the battle, which being done,
Let her who would be rid of him devise
His speedy taking off. As for the mercy
Which he intends to Lear and to Cordelia,
The battle done, and they within our power,
Shall never see his pardon; for my state
Stands on me to defend, not to debate.

Exit.

Scene 2

The battlefield between the two camps.

(Powers of France; Cordelia; Lear; Edgar; Gloucester)

Edgar sits Gloucester against a tree out of harm's way to wait for the battle to be over. Soon after, he rushes back in: the French have lost, and they are all in danger. Edgar leads Gloucester away.

Alarum within. Enter, with Drum and Colors, the Powers of France over the stage, Cordelia with her Father in her hand, and exeunt.
Enter Edgar and Gloucester.

Edgar.
Here, father, take the shadow of this tree
For your good host; pray that the right may thrive.
If ever I return to you again,
I'll bring you comfort.

Earl of Gloucester.
                Grace go with you, sir!

Exit Edgar.
Alarum and retreat within.
Enter Edgar.

Edgar.
Away, old man, give me thy hand, away!
King Lear hath lost, he and his daughter ta'en.
Give me thy hand; come on.

Earl of Gloucester.
No further, sir, a man may rot even here.

Edgar.
What, in ill thoughts again? Men must endure
Their going hence even as their coming hither,
Ripeness is all. Come on.

Earl of Gloucester.
                And that's true too.

Exeunt.

Scene 3

The British camp near Dover.

(Edmund; Lear; Cordelia; Soldiers; First Captain; Second Captain; Albany; Goneril; Regan; Herald; Edgar; Second Gentleman; Kent; Second Messenger)

Edmund's forces have captured Lear and Cordelia, and he sends them off to jail. Lear consoles his daughter with the fact that they will be together. Edmund bribes a captain to follow them and make an end of them. Albany enters, asking for the captives, and Edmund explains that he will produce them the next day. Albany puts him in his place, reminding him that he is not one of the rulers of the land. Regan immediately insists that he might as well be, as she intends to marry him. Goneril challenges her on this, and the quarrel escalates until Regan calls on Edmund to use his army to attack Albany's. Albany arrests Edmund for treason and challenges him. Regan is taken ill and has to leave, which is hardly surprising as Goneril has poisoned her. Edgar, masked, appears to take up the challenge against Edmund. They fight, and Edgar bests his half-brother. When Goneril tries to protest on a technicality, Albany proves to her that he has her love letter, and advises her to stay quiet. Goneril, reminding Albany that she is Lear's heir, not him, leaves. Edgar identifies himself, and tells of how Gloucester died when he told his father who he was. A messenger rushes in: Goneril has stabbed herself. Albany orders the bodies of the two sisters brought in, while Kent appears, looking for Lear. Suddenly remembering the existence of the old king, Albany asks Edmund where he sent them. Edmund, in his dying moments, tries to do some good and advises them to run, admitting that Lear and Cordelia are to be executed on his orders. But it is too late: Lear enters, holding the hanged Cordelia in his arms. He tries desperately to find some sign that Cordelia is still alive, but in vain. He recognizes Kent, but refuses to listen to his friend's story of also being his servant 'Caius'. Albany announces his intent to give supreme power back to Lear, but the old King dies. Albany asks Kent and Edgar to rule, but Kent intends to follow his master.

Enter in conquest, with Drum and Colors, Edmund, Lear and Cordelia as prisoners, Soldiers, Captain.

Edmund.
Some officers take them away. Good guard,
Until their greater pleasures first be known
That are to censure them.

Cordelia.
            We are not the first
Who with best meaning have incurr'd the worst.
For thee, oppressed king, I am cast down,
Myself could else out-frown false Fortune's frown.
Shall we not see these daughters and these sisters?

Lear, King of Britain.
No, no, no, no! Come let's away to prison:
We two alone will sing like birds i' th' cage;
When thou dost ask me blessing, I'll kneel down
And ask of thee forgiveness. So we'll live,
And pray, and sing, and tell old tales, and laugh
At gilded butterflies, and hear poor rogues
Talk of court news; and we'll talk with them too—
Who loses and who wins; who's in, who's out—
And take upon 's the mystery of things
As if we were God's spies; and we'll wear out,
In a wall'd prison, packs and sects of great ones,
That ebb and flow by th' moon.

Edmund.
            Take them away.

Lear, King of Britain.
Upon such sacrifices, my Cordelia,
The gods themselves throw incense. Have I caught thee?
He that parts us shall bring a brand from heaven,
And fire us hence like foxes. Wipe thine eyes;
The good-years shall devour them, flesh and fell,
Ere they shall make us weep! We'll see 'em starv'd first.
Come.

Exit with Cordelia, guarded.

Edmund.
                    Come hither, captain; hark.
Take thou this note

Giving a paper.

                    go follow them to prison.
One step I have advanc'd thee; if thou dost
As this instructs thee, thou dost make thy way
To noble fortunes. Know thou this, that men
Are as the time is: to be tender-minded
Does not become a sword. Thy great employment
Will not bear question; either say thou'lt do't,
Or thrive by other means.

First Captain.
                    I'll do't, my lord.

Edmund.
About it, and write happy when th' hast done.
Mark, I say instantly, and carry it so
As I have set it down.

First Captain.
I cannot draw a cart, nor eat dried oats,
If it be man's work, I'll do't.

Exit First Captain.
Flourish. Enter Albany, Goneril, Regan, another Captain, Soldiers.

Duke of Albany.
Sir, you have show'd today your valiant strain,
And fortune led you well. You have the captives
Who were the opposites of this day's strife;
I do require them of you, so to use them
As we shall find their merits and our safety
May equally determine.

Edmund.
                    Sir, I thought it fit
To send the old and miserable King
To some retention and appointed guard,
Whose age had charms in it, whose title more,
To pluck the common bosom on his side,
And turn our impress'd lances in our eyes
Which do command them. With him I sent the Queen,
My reason all the same, and they are ready
Tomorrow, or at further space, t' appear
Where you shall hold your session. At this time
We sweat and bleed: the friend hath lost his friend,
And the best quarrels, in the heat, are curs'd
By those that feel their sharpness.
The question of Cordelia and her father
Requires a fitter place.

Duke of Albany.
                    Sir, by your patience,
I hold you but a subject of this war,
Not as a brother.

Regan.
                    That's as we list to grace him.
Methinks our pleasure might have been demanded
Ere you had spoke so far. He led our powers,
Bore the commission of my place and person,
The which immediacy may well stand up,
And call itself your brother.

Goneril.
                    Not so hot.
In his own grace he doth exalt himself,
More than in your addition.

Regan.
                    In my rights,
By me invested, he compeers the best.

Goneril.
That were the most, if he should husband you.

Regan.
Jesters do oft prove prophets.

Goneril.
                    Holla, holla!
That eye that told you so look'd but a-squint.

Regan.
Lady, I am not well, else I should answer
From a full-flowing stomach. General,
Take thou my soldiers, prisoners, patrimony;
Dispose of them, of me; the walls is thine.
Witness the world, that I create thee here
My lord and master.

Goneril.
                    Mean you to enjoy him?

Duke of Albany.
The let-alone lies not in your good will.

Edmund.
Nor in thine, lord.

Duke of Albany.
                    Half-blooded fellow, yes.

Regan.

To Edmund.

Let the drum strike, and prove my title thine.

Duke of Albany.
Stay yet, hear reason. Edmund, I arrest thee
On capital treason, and in thy attaint,
This gilded serpent

Pointing to Goneril.
                    For your claim, fair sister,
I bar it in the interest of my wife;
'Tis she is sub-contracted to this lord,
And I, her husband, contradict your banes.
If you will marry, make your loves to me,
My lady is bespoke.

Goneril.
                    An enterlude!

Duke of Albany.
Thou art armed, Gloucester, let the trumpet sound.
If none appear to prove upon thy person
Thy heinous, manifest, and many treasons,
There is my pledge

Throwing down a glove.
                    I'll make it on thy heart,
Ere I taste bread, thou art in nothing less
Than I have here proclaim'd thee.

Regan.
                    Sick, O, sick!

Goneril.

Aside.

If not, I'll ne'er trust medicine.

Edmund.
There's my exchange.

Throwing down a glove.
                    What in the world he is
That names me traitor, villain-like he lies.
Call by the trumpet; he that dares approach:
On him, on you—who not?—I will maintain
My truth and honor firmly.

Duke of Albany.
A herald, ho!

Edmund.
                    A herald, ho, a herald!

Duke of Albany.
Trust to thy single virtue, for thy soldiers,
All levied in my name, have in my name
Took their discharge.

Regan.
                    My sickness grows upon me.

Duke of Albany.
She is not well, convey her to my tent.

Exit Regan, led.
Enter a Herald.

Come hither, herald. Let the trumpet sound,
And read out this.

Second Captain.
Sound, trumpet!

A trumpet sounds.

Herald.

Reads.

"If any man of quality or degree within the lists of the army will maintain upon Edmund, supposed Earl of Gloucester, that he is a manifold traitor, let him appear by the third sound of the trumpet. He is bold in his defense."

Edmund.
Sound!

First trumpet.

Herald.
Again!

Second trumpet.

Herald.
Again!

Third trumpet.
Trumpet answers within.
Enter Edgar at the third sound, armed, a Trumpet before him.

Duke of Albany.
Ask him his purposes, why he appears
Upon this call o' th' trumpet.

Herald.
                      What are you?
Your name, your quality? And why you answer
This present summons?

Edgar.
                 Know, my name is lost,
By treason's tooth bare-gnawn and canker-bit,
Yet am I noble as the adversary
I come to cope.

Duke of Albany.
                 Which is that adversary?

Edgar.
What's he that speaks for Edmund Earl of Gloucester?

Edmund.
Himself; what say'st thou to him?

Edgar.
                 Draw thy sword,
That if my speech offend a noble heart,
Thy arm may do thee justice; here is mine:
Behold, it is my privilege,
The privilege of mine honors,
My oath, and my profession. I protest,
Maugre thy strength, place, youth, and eminence,
Despite thy victor-sword and fire-new fortune,
Thy valor, and thy heart, thou art a traitor;
False to thy gods, thy brother, and thy father,
Conspirant 'gainst this high illustrious prince,
And from th' extremest upward of thy head
To the descent and dust below thy foot,
A most toad-spotted traitor. Say thou "No,"
This sword, this arm, and my best spirits are bent
To prove upon thy heart, whereto I speak,
Thou liest.

Edmund.
           In wisdom I should ask thy name,
But since thy outside looks so fair and warlike,
And that thy tongue some say of breeding breathes,
What safe and nicely I might well delay
By rule of knighthood, I disdain and spurn.
Back do I toss these treasons to thy head,
With the hell-hated lie o'erwhelm thy heart,
Which for they yet glance by, and scarcely bruise,
This sword of mine shall give them instant way
Where they shall rest forever. Trumpets, speak!

Alarums. They fight. Edmund falls.

Duke of Albany.
Save him, save him!

Goneril.
            This is practice, Gloucester.
By th' law of war thou wast not bound to answer
An unknown opposite. Thou art not vanquish'd,
But cozen'd and beguil'd.

Duke of Albany.
            Shut your mouth, dame,
Or with this paper shall I stopple it. Hold, sir.—
Thou worse than any name, read thine own evil.
No tearing, lady, I perceive you know it.

Goneril.
Say if I do, the laws are mine, not thine;
Who can arraign me for't?

Duke of Albany.
            Most monstrous! O!
Know'st thou this paper?

Goneril.
            Ask me not what I know.

Exit.

Duke of Albany.
Go after her; she's desperate, govern her.

Edmund.
What you have charg'd me with, that have I done,
And more, much more, the time will bring it out.
'Tis past, and so am I. But what art thou
That hast this fortune on me? If thou'rt noble,
I do forgive thee.

Edgar.
            Let's exchange charity.
I am no less in blood than thou art, Edmund;
If more, the more th' hast wrong'd me.
My name is Edgar, and thy father's son.
The gods are just, and of our pleasant vices
Make instruments to plague us:
The dark and vicious place where thee he got
Cost him his eyes.

Edmund.
                    th' hast spoken right, 'tis true.
The wheel is come full circle, I am here.

Duke of Albany.
Methought thy very gait did prophesy
A royal nobleness. I must embrace thee.
Let sorrow split my heart, if ever I
Did hate thee or thy father.

Edgar.
                  Worthy prince, I know't.

Duke of Albany.
Where have you hid yourself?
How have you known the miseries of your father?

Edgar.
By nursing them, my lord. List a brief tale,
And when 'tis told, O that my heart would burst!
The bloody proclamation to escape,
That follow'd me so near (O, our lives' sweetness!
That we the pain of death would hourly die
Rather than die at once!), taught me to shift
Into a madman's rags, t' assume a semblance
That very dogs disdain'd; and in this habit
Met I my father with his bleeding rings,
Their precious stones new lost; became his guide,
Led him, begg'd for him, sav'd him from despair;
Never (O fault!) reveal'd myself unto him,
Until some half hour past, when I was arm'd.
Not sure, though hoping, of this good success,
I ask'd his blessing, and from first to last
Told him our pilgrimage. But his flaw'd heart
(Alack, too weak the conflict to support!)
'Twixt two extremes of passion, joy and grief,
Burst smilingly.

Edmund.
                  This speech of yours hath mov'd me,
And shall perchance do good: but speak you on,
You look as you had something more to say.

Duke of Albany.
If there be more, more woeful, hold it in,
For I am almost ready to dissolve,
Hearing of this.

Edgar.
                This would have seem'd a period
To such as love not sorrow, but another,
To amplify too much, would make much more,
And top extremity. Whilst I
Was big in clamor, came there in a man,
Who, having seen me in my worst estate,
Shunn'd my abhorr'd society, but then finding
Who 'twas that so endur'd, with his strong arms
He fastened on my neck and bellowed out
As he'd burst heaven, threw him on my father,
Told the most piteous tale of Lear and him
That ever ear received, which in recounting,
His grief grew puissant and the strings of life
Began to crack. Twice then the trumpets sounded,
And there I left him tranc'd.

Duke of Albany.
                But who was this?

Edgar.
Kent, sir, the banish'd Kent, who in disguise
Followed his enemy king, and did him service
Improper for a slave.

Enter Second Gentleman with a bloody knife.

Second Gentleman.
Help, help! O, help!

Edgar.
                What kind of help?

Duke of Albany.
              Speak, man.

Edgar.
What means this bloody knife?

Second Gentleman.
                'Tis hot, it smokes,
It came even from the heart of—O, she's dead!

Duke of Albany.
Who dead? Speak, man.

Second Gentleman.
Your lady, sir, your lady; and her sister
By her is poison'd; she confesses it.

Edmund.
I was contracted to them both; all three
Now marry in an instant.

Edgar.
                Here comes Kent.

Enter Kent.

Duke of Albany.
Produce the bodies, be they alive or dead.

Exit Second Gentleman.

This judgment of the heavens, that makes us tremble,
Touches us not with pity.—O, is this he?
The time will not allow the compliment
Which very manners urges.

Earl of Kent.
                    I am come
To bid my king and master aye good night.
Is he not here?

Duke of Albany.
                    Great thing of us forgot!
Speak, Edmund, where's the King? And where's
Cordelia?

Goneril and Regan's bodies brought out.

Seest thou this object, Kent?

Earl of Kent.
Alack, why thus?

Edmund.
                    Yet Edmund was belov'd!
The one the other poison'd for my sake,
And after slew herself.

Duke of Albany.
Even so. Cover their faces.

Edmund.
I pant for life. Some good I mean to do,
Despite of mine own nature. Quickly send
(Be brief in it) to th' castle, for my writ
Is on the life of Lear and on Cordelia.
Nay, send in time.

Duke of Albany.
                    Run, run, O, run!

Edgar.
To who, my lord? Who has the office? Send
Thy token of reprieve.

Edmund.
Well thought on. Take my sword. The captain—
Give it the captain.

Duke of Albany.
                    Haste thee, for thy life.

Exit Edgar.

Edmund.
He hath commission from thy wife and me
To hang Cordelia in the prison, and
To lay the blame upon her own despair,
That she fordid herself.

Duke of Albany.
The gods defend her! Bear him hence awhile.

Edmund is borne off.
Enter Lear with Cordelia in his arms, Edgar and Second Gentleman following.

Lear, King of Britain.
Howl, howl, howl! O, you are men of stones!
Had I your tongues and eyes, I'd use them so
That heaven's vault should crack. She's gone forever!
I know when one is dead, and when one lives;
She's dead as earth. Lend me a looking-glass,
If that her breath will mist or stain the stone,
Why then she lives.

Earl of Kent.
                    Is this the promis'd end?

Edgar.
Or image of that horror?

Duke of Albany.
                    Fall, and cease!

Lear, King of Britain.
This feather stirs, she lives! If it be so,
It is a chance which does redeem all sorrows
That ever I have felt.

Earl of Kent.
Kneeling.
                    O my good master!

Lear, King of Britain.
Prithee away.

Edgar.
                    'Tis noble Kent, your friend.

Lear, King of Britain.
A plague upon you, murderers, traitors all!
I might have sav'd her, now she's gone forever!
Cordelia, Cordelia, stay a little. Ha!
What is't thou say'st? Her voice was ever soft,
Gentle, and low, an excellent thing in woman.
I kill'd the slave that was a-hanging thee.

Second Gentleman.
'Tis true, my lords, he did.

Lear, King of Britain.
                     Did I not, fellow?
I have seen the day, with my good biting falchion
I would have made them skip. I am old now,
And these same crosses spoil me. Who are you?
Mine eyes are not o' th' best; I'll tell you straight.

Earl of Kent.
If Fortune brag of two she lov'd and hated,
One of them we behold.

Lear, King of Britain.
This is a dull sight. Are you not Kent?

Earl of Kent.
                     The same:
Your servant Kent. Where is your servant Caius?

Lear, King of Britain.
He's a good fellow, I can tell you that;
He'll strike, and quickly too. He's dead and rotten.

Earl of Kent.
No, my good lord, I am the very man—

Lear, King of Britain.
I'll see that straight.

Earl of Kent.
That from your first of difference and decay,
Have follow'd your sad steps—

Lear, King of Britain.
                     You are welcome hither.

Earl of Kent.
Nor no man else. All's cheerless, dark, and deadly.
Your eldest daughters have foredone themselves,
And desperately are dead.

Lear, King of Britain.
                     Ay, so I think.

Duke of Albany.
He knows not what he says, and vain is it
That we present us to him.

Edgar.
                     Very bootless.

Enter Second Messenger.

Second Messenger.
Edmund is dead, my lord.

Duke of Albany.
                     That's but a trifle here.
You lords and noble friends, know our intent.
What comfort to this great decay may come
Shall be applied. For us, we will resign,
During the life of this old majesty,
To him our absolute power.

To Edgar and Kent.
                     You, to your rights,
With boot, and such addition as your honors
Have more than merited. All friends shall taste
The wages of their virtue, and all foes
The cup of their deservings. O, see, see!

Lear, King of Britain.
And my poor fool is hang'd! No, no, no life!
Why should a dog, a horse, a rat, have life,
And thou no breath at all? Thou'lt come no more,
Never, never, never, never, never.
Pray you undo this button. Thank you, sir.
Do you see this? Look on her! Look her lips,
Look there, look there!

He dies.

Edgar.
                     He faints. My lord, my lord!

Earl of Kent.
Break, heart, I prithee break!

Edgar.
                     Look up, my lord.

Earl of Kent.
Vex not his ghost. O, let him pass, he hates him
That would upon the rack of this tough world
Stretch him out longer.

Edgar.
     He is gone indeed.

Earl of Kent.
The wonder is he hath endur'd so long,
He but usurp'd his life.

Duke of Albany.
Bear them from hence. Our present business
Is general woe.

To Kent and Edgar.
     Friends of my soul, you twain
Rule in this realm, and the gor'd state sustain.

Earl of Kent.
I have a journey, sir, shortly to go:
My master calls me, I must not say no.

Edgar.
The weight of this sad time we must obey,
Speak what we feel, not what we ought to say:
The oldest hath borne most; we that are young
Shall never see so much, nor live so long.

Exeunt with a dead march.

The Winter's Tale

Act 1

Scene 1

Sicilia. An antechamber in Leontes' palace.

(Camillo; Archidamus)

Camillo, Lord of Sicily, and Archidamus, Lord of Bohemia, exchange compliments on the royal treatment accorded the Bohemian visit. Archidamus claims that Bohemia will be unable to match such treatment when the King of Sicily, Leontes, returns the visit. Camillo remarks on the strong, long-lasting friendship between the two kings, who were brought up together, and on the promising Prince of Sicily, Mamillius.

Enter Camillo and Archidamus.

Archidamus.
If you shall chance, Camillo, to visit Bohemia on the like occasion whereon my services are now on foot, you shall see (as I have said) great difference betwixt our Bohemia and your Sicilia.

Camillo.
I think, this coming summer, the King of Sicilia means to pay Bohemia the visitation which he justly owes him.

Archidamus.
Wherein our entertainment shall shame us: we will be justified in our loves; for indeed—

Camillo.
Beseech you—

Archidamus.
Verily, I speak it in the freedom of my knowledge: we cannot with such magnificence—in so rare—I know not what to say—We will give you sleepy drinks, that your senses (unintelligent of our insufficiency) may, though they cannot praise us, as little accuse us.

Camillo.
You pay a great deal too dear for what's given freely.

Archidamus.
Believe me, I speak as my understanding instructs me, and as mine honesty puts it to utterance.

Camillo.
Sicilia cannot show himself overkind to Bohemia. They were train'd together in their childhoods; and there rooted betwixt them then such an affection, which cannot choose but branch now. Since their more mature dignities and royal necessities made separation of their society, their encounters (though not personal) hath been royally attorney'd with interchange of gifts, letters, loving embassies, that they have seem'd to be together, though absent; shook hands, as over a vast; and embrac'd as it were from the ends of oppos'd winds. The heavens continue their loves!

Archidamus.
I think there is not in the world either malice or matter to alter it. You have an unspeakable comfort of your young prince Mamillius: it is a gentleman of the greatest promise that ever came into my note.

Camillo.
I very well agree with you in the hopes of him; it is a gallant child; one that, indeed, physics the subject,

makes old hearts fresh. They that went on crutches ere he was born desire yet their life to see him a man.

Archidamus.
Would they else be content to die?

Camillo.
Yes; if there were no other excuse why they should desire to live.

Archidamus.
If the King had no son, they would desire to live on crutches till he had one.

Exeunt.

Scene 2

Sicilia. A room of state in Leontes' palace.

(Leontes; Hermione; Mamillius; Polixenes; Camillo; Attendants)

Leontes urges his friend Polixenes of Bohemia to stay longer, but Polixenes insists that he must return the next day, having already been absent from his kingdom for nine months. Leontes urges his pregnant wife Hermione to help convince Polixenes to stay, and she finally bullies him into extending his visit by a week. They engage in light-hearted conversation, Polixenes talking about his childhood with Leontes. Seeing them so friendly, Leontes becomes suspicious, thinking they are far too close. He tries to distract himself by talking to Mamillius, but his fears are too strong and he becomes convinced that he is being cuckolded. He covers up his fears when Polixenes and Hermione notice his discomfort, and he and his best friend discuss their children. Polixenes and Hermione go for a walk in the garden, and Leontes is even more convinced by how quickly they leave him. As he tells Mamillius to go play, his diseased imaginings grow more and more stronger until he is fully convinced that his wife is cheating on him with his best friend. He begins to sound out Camillo's opinion in the matter, twisting things to find his evidence, to Camillo's distress and horror. Camillo defends the Queen's honor, but Leontes is too far gone in his conviction, and demands that Camillo poison Polixenes. Camillo agrees on condition that Leontes swear to be kind to Hermione afterwards. The King insists he will not cast any slurs on her reputation. Camillo is torn between duty to his King and duty to himself. When Polixenes enters, sensing a coldness in his treatment, Camillo is soon brought to admit what has happened. He urges the Bohemian King to flee, and asks to come along. Polixenes agrees, and they leave.

Enter Leontes, Hermione, Mamillius, Polixenes, Camillo, and Attendants.

Polixenes, King of Bohemia.
Nine changes of the wat'ry star hath been
The shepherd's note since we have left our throne
Without a burden. Time as long again
Would be fill'd up, my brother, with our thanks,
And yet we should, for perpetuity,
Go hence in debt. And therefore, like a cipher
(Yet standing in rich place), I multiply
With one "We thank you" many thousands more
That go before it.

Leontes, King of Sicilia.
                    Stay your thanks a while,
And pay them when you part.

Polixenes, King of Bohemia.
                    Sir, that's tomorrow.
I am question'd by my fears of what may chance
Or breed upon our absence, that may blow
No sneaping winds at home, to make us say,
"This is put forth too truly." Besides, I have stay'd
To tire your royalty.

Leontes, King of Sicilia.
                    We are tougher, brother,
Than you can put us to't.

Polixenes, King of Bohemia.
                    No longer stay.

Leontes, King of Sicilia.
One sev'nnight longer.

Polixenes, King of Bohemia.
                    Very sooth, tomorrow.

Leontes, King of Sicilia.
We'll part the time between 's then; and in that
I'll no gainsaying.

Polixenes, King of Bohemia.
                    Press me not, beseech you, so.
There is no tongue that moves, none, none i' th' world,
So soon as yours could win me. So it should now,
Were there necessity in your request, although
'Twere needful I denied it. My affairs
Do even drag me homeward; which to hinder
Were (in your love) a whip to me; my stay,
To you a charge and trouble. To save both,
Farewell, our brother.

Leontes, King of Sicilia.
>Tongue-tied our queen? Speak you.

Hermione.
I had thought, sir, to have held my peace until
You had drawn oaths from him not to stay. You, sir,
Charge him too coldly. Tell him you are sure
All in Bohemia's well; this satisfaction
The by-gone day proclaim'd. Say this to him,
He's beat from his best ward.

Leontes, King of Sicilia.
>Well said, Hermione.

Hermione.
To tell he longs to see his son were strong;
But let him say so then, and let him go;
But let him swear so, and he shall not stay,
We'll thwack him hence with distaffs.
Yet of your royal presence I'll adventure
The borrow of a week. When at Bohemia
You take my lord, I'll give him my commission
To let him there a month behind the gest
Prefix'd for 's parting; yet, good deed, Leontes,
I love thee not a jar o' th' clock behind
What lady she her lord. You'll stay?

Polixenes, King of Bohemia.
>No, madam.

Hermione.
Nay, but you will?

Polixenes, King of Bohemia.
>I may not, verily.

Hermione.
Verily?
You put me off with limber vows; but I,
Though you would seek t' unsphere the stars with oaths,
Should yet say, "Sir, no going." Verily,
You shall not go; a lady's "verily" is
As potent as a lord's. Will you go yet?
Force me to keep you as a prisoner,
Not like a guest: so you shall pay your fees
When you depart, and save your thanks. How say you?
My prisoner? Or my guest? By your dread "verily,"
One of them you shall be.

Polixenes, King of Bohemia.
>Your guest then, madam.
To be your prisoner should import offending,
Which is for me less easy to commit
Than you to punish.

Hermione.
>Not your jailer then,
But your kind hostess. Come, I'll question you
Of my lord's tricks and yours when you were boys.
You were pretty lordings then?

Polixenes, King of Bohemia.
>We were, fair queen,
Two lads that thought there was no more behind
But such a day tomorrow as today,
And to be boy eternal.

Hermione.
>Was not my lord
The verier wag o' th' two?

Polixenes, King of Bohemia.
We were as twinn'd lambs that did frisk i' th' sun,
And bleat the one at th' other. What we chang'd
Was innocence for innocence; we knew not
The doctrine of ill-doing, nor dream'd
That any did. Had we pursu'd that life,
And our weak spirits ne'er been higher rear'd
With stronger blood, we should have answer'd heaven
Boldly, "Not guilty"; the imposition clear'd,
Hereditary ours.

Hermione.
>By this we gather
You have tripp'd since.

Polixenes, King of Bohemia.
>O my most sacred lady,
Temptations have since then been born to 's: for
In those unfledg'd days was my wife a girl;
Your precious self had then not cross'd the eyes
Of my young playfellow.

Hermione.
>Grace to boot!
Of this make no conclusion, lest you say
Your queen and I are devils. Yet go on,
Th' offenses we have made you do we'll answer,
If you first sinn'd with us, and that with us
You did continue fault, and that you slipp'd not
With any but with us.

Leontes, King of Sicilia.
                      Is he won yet?

Hermione.
He'll stay, my lord.

Leontes, King of Sicilia.
                      At my request he would not.
Hermione, my dearest, thou never spok'st
To better purpose.

Hermione.
                    Never?

Leontes, King of Sicilia.
                    Never, but once.

Hermione.
What? Have I twice said well? When was't before?
I prithee tell me; cram 's with praise, and make 's
As fat as tame things. One good deed dying tongueless
Slaughters a thousand waiting upon that.
Our praises are our wages. You may ride 's
With one soft kiss a thousand furlongs ere
With spur we heat an acre. But to th' goal:
My last good deed was to entreat his stay;
What was my first? It has an elder sister,
Or I mistake you. O, would her name were Grace!
But once before I spoke to th' purpose? When?
Nay, let me have't; I long.

Leontes, King of Sicilia.
                      Why, that was when
Three crabbed months had sour'd themselves to death,
Ere I could make thee open thy white hand,
And clap thyself my love; then didst thou utter,
"I am yours forever."

Hermione.
                    'Tis Grace indeed.
Why, lo you now! I have spoke to th' purpose twice:
The one forever earn'd a royal husband;
Th' other for some while a friend.

Gives her hand to Polixenes.

Leontes, King of Sicilia.

Aside.
                    Too hot, too hot!
To mingle friendship far is mingling bloods.
I have tremor cordis on me; my heart dances,
But not for joy; not joy. This entertainment
May a free face put on, derive a liberty
From heartiness, from bounty, fertile bosom,
And well become the agent; 't may—I grant.
But to be paddling palms and pinching fingers,
As now they are, and making practic'd smiles,
As in a looking-glass; and then to sigh, as 'twere
The mort o' th' deer—O, that is entertainment
My bosom likes not, nor my brows! Mamillius,
Art thou my boy?

Mamillius.
                  Ay, my good lord.

Leontes, King of Sicilia.
                  I' fecks!
Why, that's my bawcock. What? Hast smutch'd thy nose?
They say it is a copy out of mine. Come, captain,
We must be neat; not neat, but cleanly, captain:
And yet the steer, the heckfer, and the calf
Are all call'd neat.—Still virginalling
Upon his palm?—How now, you wanton calf,
Art thou my calf?

Mamillius.
                Yes, if you will, my lord.

Leontes, King of Sicilia.
Thou want'st a rough pash and the shoots that I have,
To be full like me; yet they say we are
Almost as like as eggs; women say so—
That will say any thing. But were they false
As o'er-dy'd blacks, as wind, as waters, false
As dice are to be wish'd by one that fixes
No bourn 'twixt his and mine, yet were it true
To say this boy were like me. Come, sir page,
Look on me with your welkin eye. Sweet villain!
Most dear'st! My collop! Can thy dam?—may't be?—
Affection! Thy intention stabs the center.
Thou dost make possible things not so held,
Communicat'st with dreams (how can this be?),
With what's unreal thou co-active art,
And fellow'st nothing. Then 'tis very credent
Thou mayst co-join with something, and thou dost
(And that beyond commission), and I find it
(And that to the infection of my brains
And hard'ning of my brows).

Polixenes, King of Bohemia.
                  What means Sicilia?

Hermione.
He something seems unsettled.

Polixenes, King of Bohemia.
                    How? My lord?

Leontes, King of Sicilia.
What cheer? How is't with you, best brother?

Hermione.
                    You look
As if you held a brow of much distraction.
Are you mov'd, my lord?

Leontes, King of Sicilia.
                    No, in good earnest.
How sometimes nature will betray its folly!
Its tenderness! And make itself a pastime
To harder bosoms! Looking on the lines
Of my boy's face, methoughts I did recoil
Twenty-three years, and saw myself unbreech'd
In my green velvet coat, my dagger muzzled,
Lest it should bite its master, and so prove
(As ornament oft does) too dangerous.
How like (methought) I then was to this kernel,
This squash, this gentleman. Mine honest friend,
Will you take eggs for money?

Mamillius.
No, my lord, I'll fight.

Leontes, King of Sicilia.
You will? Why, happy man be 's dole! My brother,
Are you so fond of your young prince as we
Do seem to be of ours?

Polixenes, King of Bohemia.
                    If at home, sir,
He's all my exercise, my mirth, my matter;
Now my sworn friend, and then mine enemy;
My parasite, my soldier, statesman, all.
He makes a July's day short as December,
And with his varying childness cures in me
Thoughts that would thick my blood.

Leontes, King of Sicilia.
                    So stands this squire
Offic'd with me. We two will walk, my lord,
And leave you to your graver steps. Hermione,
How thou lov'st us, show in our brother's welcome;
Let what is dear in Sicily be cheap.
Next to thyself and my young rover, he's
Apparent to my heart.

Hermione.
                    If you would seek us,
We are yours i' th' garden. Shall 's attend you there?

Leontes, King of Sicilia.
To your own bents dispose you; you'll be found,
Be you beneath the sky.

Aside.
                    I am angling now,
Though you perceive me not how I give line.
Go to, go to!
How she holds up the neb! The bill to him!
And arms her with the boldness of a wife
To her allowing husband!

Exeunt Polixenes, Hermione, and Attendants.
                    Gone already!
Inch-thick, knee-deep, o'er head and ears a fork'd one!
Go play, boy, play. Thy mother plays, and I
Play too, but so disgrac'd a part, whose issue
Will hiss me to my grave: contempt and clamor
Will be my knell. Go play, boy, play. There have been
(Or I am much deceiv'd) cuckolds ere now,
And many a man there is (even at this present,
Now, while I speak this) holds his wife by th' arm,
That little thinks she has been sluic'd in 's absence,
And his pond fish'd by his next neighbor—by
Sir Smile, his neighbor. Nay, there's comfort in't,
Whiles other men have gates, and those gates open'd,
As mine, against their will. Should all despair
That have revolted wives, the tenth of mankind
Would hang themselves. Physic for't there's none.
It is a bawdy planet, that will strike
Where 'tis predominant; and 'tis pow'rful—think it—
From east, west, north, and south. Be it concluded,
No barricado for a belly. Know't,
It will let in and out the enemy,
With bag and baggage. Many thousand on 's
Have the disease, and feel't not. How now, boy?

Mamillius.
I am like you, they say.

Leontes, King of Sicilia.
                    Why, that's some comfort.
What? Camillo there?

Camillo.
Ay, my good lord.

Leontes, King of Sicilia.
Go play, Mamillius, thou'rt an honest man.

Exit Mamillius.

Camillo, this great sir will yet stay longer.

Camillo.
You had much ado to make his anchor hold,
When you cast out, it still came home.

Leontes, King of Sicilia.
      Didst note it?

Camillo.
He would not stay at your petitions, made
His business more material.

Leontes, King of Sicilia.
      Didst perceive it?

Aside.

They're here with me already, whisp'ring, rounding:
"Sicilia is a so-forth." 'Tis far gone,
When I shall gust it last.—How came't, Camillo,
That he did stay?

Camillo.
    At the good Queen's entreaty.

Leontes, King of Sicilia.
At the Queen's be't; "good" should be pertinent,
But so it is, it is not. Was this taken
By any understanding pate but thine?
For thy conceit is soaking, will draw in
More than the common blocks. Not noted, is't,
But of the finer natures? By some severals
Of head-piece extraordinary? Lower messes
Perchance are to this business purblind? Say.

Camillo.
Business, my lord? I think most understand
Bohemia stays here longer.

Leontes, King of Sicilia.
      Ha?

Camillo.
     Stays here longer.

Leontes, King of Sicilia.
Ay, but why?

Camillo.
To satisfy your Highness and the entreaties
Of our most gracious mistress.

Leontes, King of Sicilia.
    Satisfy?
Th' entreaties of your mistress? Satisfy?
Let that suffice. I have trusted thee, Camillo,
With all the nearest things to my heart, as well
My chamber-councils, wherein, priest-like, thou
Hast cleans'd my bosom: I from thee departed
Thy penitent reform'd. But we have been
Deceiv'd in thy integrity, deceiv'd
In that which seems so.

Camillo.
    Be it forbid, my lord!

Leontes, King of Sicilia.
To bide upon't: thou art not honest; or
If thou inclin'st that way, thou art a coward,
Which hoxes honesty behind, restraining
From course requir'd; or else thou must be counted
A servant grafted in my serious trust
And therein negligent; or else a fool,
That seest a game play'd home, the rich stake drawn,
And tak'st it all for jest.

Camillo.
    My gracious lord,
I may be negligent, foolish, and fearful:
In every one of these no man is free
But that his negligence, his folly, fear,
Among the infinite doings of the world,
Sometime puts forth. In your affairs, my lord,
If ever I were willful-negligent,
It was my folly; if industriously
I play'd the fool, it was my negligence,
Not weighing well the end; if ever fearful
To do a thing, where I the issue doubted,
Whereof the execution did cry out
Against the non-performance, 'twas a fear
Which oft infects the wisest: these, my lord,
Are such allow'd infirmities that honesty
Is never free of. But beseech your Grace
Be plainer with me, let me know my trespass
By its own visage. If I then deny it,
'Tis none of mine.

Leontes, King of Sicilia.
                    Ha' not you seen, Camillo
(But that's past doubt; you have, or your eye-glass
Is thicker than a cuckold's horn), or heard
(For to a vision so apparent rumor
Cannot be mute), or thought (for cogitation
Resides not in that man that does not think)
My wife is slippery? If thou wilt confess,
Or else be impudently negative,
To have nor eyes nor ears nor thought, then say
My wife's a hobby-horse, deserves a name
As rank as any flax-wench that puts to
Before her troth-plight: say't and justify't.

Camillo.
I would not be a stander-by to hear
My sovereign mistress clouded so, without
My present vengeance taken. 'Shrew my heart,
You never spoke what did become you less
Than this; which to reiterate were sin
As deep as that, though true.

Leontes, King of Sicilia.
                    Is whispering nothing?
Is leaning cheek to cheek? Is meeting noses?
Kissing with inside lip? Stopping the career
Of laughter with a sigh (a note infallible
Of breaking honesty)? Horsing foot on foot?
Skulking in corners? Wishing clocks more swift?
Hours, minutes? Noon, midnight? And all eyes
Blind with the pin and web but theirs, theirs only,
That would unseen be wicked? Is this nothing?
Why then the world and all that's in't is nothing,
The covering sky is nothing, Bohemia nothing,
My wife is nothing, nor nothing have these nothings,
If this be nothing.

Camillo.
                    Good my lord, be cur'd
Of this diseas'd opinion, and betimes,
For 'tis most dangerous.

Leontes, King of Sicilia.
                    Say it be, 'tis true.

Camillo.
No, no, my lord.

Leontes, King of Sicilia.
                    It is: you lie, you lie!
I say thou liest, Camillo, and I hate thee,
Pronounce thee a gross lout, a mindless slave,
Or else a hovering temporizer, that
Canst with thine eyes at once see good and evil,
Inclining to them both. Were my wive's liver
Infected as her life, she would not live
The running of one glass.

Camillo.
                    Who does infect her?

Leontes, King of Sicilia.
Why, he that wears her like her medal hanging
About his neck, Bohemia—who, if I
Had servants true about me, that bare eyes
To see alike mine honor as their profits
(Their own particular thrifts), they would do that
Which should undo more doing; ay, and thou,
His cupbearer—whom I from meaner form
Have bench'd and rear'd to worship, who mayst see
Plainly as heaven sees earth and earth sees heaven,
How I am gall'd—mightst bespice a cup,
To give mine enemy a lasting wink;
Which draught to me were cordial.

Camillo.
                    Sir, my lord,
I could do this, and that with no rash potion,
But with a ling'ring dram that should not work
Maliciously, like poison; but I cannot
Believe this crack to be in my dread mistress
(So sovereignly being honorable).
I have lov'd thee—

Leontes, King of Sicilia.
                    Make that thy question, and go rot!
Dost think I am so muddy, so unsettled,
To appoint myself in this vexation, sully
The purity and whiteness of my sheets
(Which to preserve is sleep, which being spotted
Is goads, thorns, nettles, tails of wasps),
Give scandal to the blood o' th' Prince my son
(Who I do think is mine and love as mine),
Without ripe moving to't? Would I do this?
Could man so blench?

Camillo.
                    I must believe you, sir.
I do, and will fetch off Bohemia for't;
Provided that, when he's remov'd, your Highness
Will take again your queen as yours at first,
Even for your son's sake, and thereby for sealing
The injury of tongues in courts and kingdoms
Known and allied to yours.

Leontes, King of Sicilia.
                      Thou dost advise me
Even so as I mine own course have set down.
I'll give no blemish to her honor, none.

Camillo.
My lord,
Go then; and with a countenance as clear
As friendship wears at feasts, keep with Bohemia
And with your queen. I am his cupbearer:
If from me he have wholesome beverage,
Account me not your servant.

Leontes, King of Sicilia.
                      This is all:
Do't, and thou hast the one half of my heart;
Do't not, thou split'st thine own.

Camillo.
                      I'll do't, my lord.

Leontes, King of Sicilia.
I will seem friendly, as thou hast advis'd me.

Exit.

Camillo.
O miserable lady! But for me,
What case stand I in? I must be the poisoner
Of good Polixenes, and my ground to do't
Is the obedience to a master; one
Who, in rebellion with himself, will have
All that are his so too. To do this deed,
Promotion follows. If I could find example
Of thousands that had struck anointed kings
And flourish'd after, I'd not do't; but since
Nor brass nor stone nor parchment bears not one,
Let villainy itself forswear't. I must
Forsake the court. To do't, or no, is certain
To me a break-neck. Happy star reign now!
Here comes Bohemia.

Enter Polixenes.

Polixenes, King of Bohemia.
                    This is strange; methinks
My favor here begins to warp. Not speak?
Good day, Camillo.

Camillo.
                      Hail, most royal sir!

Polixenes, King of Bohemia.
What is the news i' th' court?

Camillo.
                      None rare, my lord.

Polixenes, King of Bohemia.
The King hath on him such a countenance
As he had lost some province and a region
Lov'd as he loves himself. Even now I met him
With customary compliment, when he,
Wafting his eyes to th' contrary and falling
A lip of much contempt, speeds from me, and
So leaves me to consider what is breeding
That changes thus his manners.

Camillo.
I dare not know, my lord.

Polixenes, King of Bohemia.
How, dare not? Do not? Do you know, and dare not?
Be intelligent to me, 'tis thereabouts:
For to yourself, what you do know, you must,
And cannot say you dare not. Good Camillo,
Your chang'd complexions are to me a mirror
Which shows me mine chang'd too; for I must be
A party in this alteration, finding
Myself thus alter'd with't.

Camillo.
                      There is a sickness
Which puts some of us in distemper, but
I cannot name the disease, and it is caught
Of you that yet are well.

Polixenes, King of Bohemia.
                      How caught of me?
Make me not sighted like the basilisk.
I have look'd on thousands, who have sped the better
By my regard, but kill'd none so. Camillo,
As you are certainly a gentleman, thereto
Clerk-like experienc'd, which no less adorns
Our gentry than our parents' noble names,
In whose success we are gentle, I beseech you,
If you know aught which does behove my knowledge
Thereof to be inform'd, imprison't not
In ignorant concealment.

Camillo.
                      I may not answer.

Polixenes, King of Bohemia.
A sickness caught of me, and yet I well?
I must be answer'd. Dost thou hear, Camillo,
I conjure thee, by all the parts of man
Which honor does acknowledge, whereof the least
Is not this suit of mine, that thou declare
What incidency thou dost guess of harm
Is creeping toward me; how far off, how near,
Which way to be prevented, if to be;
If not, how best to bear it.

Camillo.
                       Sir, I will tell you,
Since I am charg'd in honor and by him
That I think honorable. Therefore mark my counsel,
Which must be ev'n as swiftly followed as
I mean to utter it; or both yourself and me
Cry lost, and so good night!

Polixenes, King of Bohemia.
                       On, good Camillo.

Camillo.
I am appointed him to murder you.

Polixenes, King of Bohemia.
By whom, Camillo?

Camillo.
                       By the King.

Polixenes, King of Bohemia.
                       For what?

Camillo.
He thinks, nay, with all confidence he swears,
As he had seen't or been an instrument
To vice you to't, that you have touch'd his queen
Forbiddenly.

Polixenes, King of Bohemia.
                       O then, my best blood turn
To an infected jelly, and my name
Be yok'd with his that did betray the Best!
Turn then my freshest reputation to
A savor that may strike the dullest nostril
Where I arrive, and my approach be shunn'd,
Nay, hated too, worse than the great'st infection
That e'er was heard or read!

Camillo.
                       Swear his thought over
By each particular star in heaven, and
By all their influences, you may as well
Forbid the sea for to obey the moon
As or by oath remove or counsel shake
The fabric of his folly, whose foundation
Is pil'd upon his faith, and will continue
The standing of his body.

Polixenes, King of Bohemia.
                       How should this grow?

Camillo.
I know not; but I am sure 'tis safer to
Avoid what's grown than question how 'tis born.
If therefore you dare trust my honesty,
That lies enclosed in this trunk which you
Shall bear along impawn'd, away tonight!
Your followers I will whisper to the business,
And will by twos and threes at several posterns
Clear them o' th' city. For myself, I'll put
My fortunes to your service, which are here
By this discovery lost. Be not uncertain,
For by the honor of my parents, I
Have utt'red truth; which if you seek to prove,
I dare not stand by; nor shall you be safer
Than one condemn'd by the King's own mouth—thereon
His execution sworn.

Polixenes, King of Bohemia.
                       I do believe thee:
I saw his heart in 's face. Give me thy hand,
Be pilot to me, and thy places shall
Still neighbor mine. My ships are ready, and
My people did expect my hence departure
Two days ago. This jealousy
Is for a precious creature: as she's rare,
Must it be great; and as his person's mighty,
Must it be violent; and as he does conceive
He is dishonor'd by a man which ever
Profess'd to him, why, his revenges must
In that be made more bitter. Fear o'ershades me.
Good expedition be my friend, and comfort
The gracious queen, part of his theme, but nothing
Of his ill-ta'en suspicion! Come, Camillo,
I will respect thee as a father, if
Thou bear'st my life off. Hence! Let us avoid.

Camillo.
It is in mine authority to command
The keys of all the posterns. Please your Highness
To take the urgent hour. Come, sir, away.

Exeunt.

Act 2

Scene 1

Sicilia. A room in Leontes' palace.

(Queen Hermione; Mamillius; First Lady; Second Lady; Leontes; Antigonus; Lords)

Mamillius is playing in the company of his mother and her Ladies, whom he is quickly outgrowing. Hermione tries to calm him down by asking him to tell her a tale; just as he's about to tell a horror story, Leontes bursts in with the Lords of his court and orders Hermione's arrest for adultery. He has Mamillius carried off to avoid his being infected by her mother. He accuses her of treason, of Camillo being her accomplice, his evidence being that Camillo has fled with Polixenes. Leontes's Lords, led by Antigonus, beg him to show her mercy as she is escorted out with her Ladies, but he insists that he has all the proof he needs to condemn her. To prove he is no tyrant, Leontes points out that he has sent emissaries to the oracle at Delphi to question Apollo about the truth of the case. He himself is quite convinced, but he is sure that the oracle will convert the skeptics of his court. Antigonus comments that they are likely to become the laughingstock of the world.

Enter Hermione, Mamillius, Ladies.

Hermione.
Take the boy to you; he so troubles me,
'Tis past enduring.

First Lady.
                    Come, my gracious lord,
Shall I be your playfellow?

Mamillius.
                    No, I'll none of you.

First Lady.
Why, my sweet lord?

Mamillius.
You'll kiss me hard and speak to me as if
I were a baby still.—I love you better.

Second Lady.
And why so, my lord?

Mamillius.
                    Not for because
Your brows are blacker, yet black brows they say
Become some women best, so that there be not
Too much hair there, but in a semicircle,
Or a half-moon made with a pen.

Second Lady.
                    Who taught' this?

Mamillius.
I learn'd it out of women's faces. Pray now
What color are your eyebrows?

First Lady.
                    Blue, my lord.

Mamillius.
Nay, that's a mock. I have seen a lady's nose
That has been blue, but not her eyebrows.

First Lady.
                    Hark ye,
The Queen your mother rounds apace: we shall
Present our services to a fine new prince
One of these days, and then you'ld wanton with us,
If we would have you.

Second Lady.
                    She is spread of late
Into a goodly bulk. Good time encounter her!

Hermione.
What wisdom stirs amongst you? Come, sir, now
I am for you again. Pray you sit by us,
And tell 's a tale.

Mamillius.
                    Merry, or sad, shall't be?

Hermione.
As merry as you will.

Mamillius.
A sad tale's best for winter. I have one
Of sprites and goblins.

Hermione.
                    Let's have that, good sir.
Come on, sit down, come on, and do your best
To fright me with your sprites; you're pow'rful at it.

Mamillius.
There was a man—

Hermione.
                    Nay, come sit down; then on.

Mamillius.
Dwelt by a churchyard. I will tell it softly,
Yond crickets shall not hear it.

Hermione.
                    Come on then,
And give't me in mine ear.

Enter Leontes, Antigonus, Lords, and others.

Leontes, King of Sicilia.
Was he met there? His train? Camillo with him?

First Lord.
Behind the tuft of pines I met them; never
Saw I men scour so on their way. I ey'd them
Even to their ships.

Leontes, King of Sicilia.
                    How blest am I
In my just censure! In my true opinion!
Alack, for lesser knowledge! How accurs'd
In being so blest! There may be in the cup
A spider steep'd, and one may drink; depart,
And yet partake no venom (for his knowledge
Is not infected), but if one present
Th' abhorr'd ingredient to his eye, make known
How he hath drunk, he cracks his gorge, his sides,
With violent hefts. I have drunk, and seen the spider.
Camillo was his help in this, his pandar.
There is a plot against my life, my crown;
All's true that is mistrusted. That false villain
Whom I employ'd was pre-employ'd by him:
He has discover'd my design, and I
Remain a pinch'd thing; yea, a very trick
For them to play at will. How came the posterns
So easily open?

First Lord.
                    By his great authority,
Which often hath no less prevail'd than so
On your command.

Leontes, King of Sicilia.
                    I know't too well.
Give me the boy. I am glad you did not nurse him.
Though he does bear some signs of me, yet you
Have too much blood in him.

Hermione.
                    What is this? Sport?

Leontes, King of Sicilia.
Bear the boy hence, he shall not come about her.
Away with him! And let her sport herself
With that she's big with, for 'tis Polixenes
Has made thee swell thus.

Hermione.
                    But I'd say he had not;
And I'll be sworn you would believe my saying,
Howe'er you lean to th' nayward.

Leontes, King of Sicilia.
                    You, my lords,
Look on her, mark her well; be but about
To say she is a goodly lady, and
The justice of your hearts will thereto add
'Tis pity she's not honest—honorable.
Praise her but for this her without-door form
(Which on my faith deserves high speech) and straight
The shrug, the hum or ha (these petty brands
That calumny doth use—O, I am out—
That mercy does, for calumny will sear
Virtue itself), these shrugs, these hums and ha's,
When you have said she's goodly, come between
Ere you can say she's honest: but be't known
(From him that has most cause to grieve it should be)
She's an adult'ress.

Hermione.
                    Should a villain say so,
The most replenish'd villain in the world,
He were as much more villain: you, my lord,
Do but mistake.

Leontes, King of Sicilia.
                    You have mistook, my lady,
Polixenes for Leontes. O thou thing!
Which I'll not call a creature of thy place,
Lest barbarism (making me the precedent)
Should a like language use to all degrees,
And mannerly distinguishment leave out
Betwixt the prince and beggar. I have said
She's an adult'ress, I have said with whom:
More—she's a traitor, and Camillo is
A federary with her, and one that knows
What she should shame to know herself,
But with her most vild principal—that she's
A bed-swerver, even as bad as those
That vulgars give bold'st titles; ay, and privy
To this their late escape.

Hermione.
>No, by my life,

Privy to none of this. How will this grieve you,
When you shall come to clearer knowledge, that
You thus have publish'd me! Gentle my lord,
You scarce can right me throughly, then, to say
You did mistake.

Leontes, King of Sicilia.
>No; if I mistake

In those foundations which I build upon,
The center is not big enough to bear
A schoolboy's top. Away with her, to prison!
He who shall speak for her is afar off guilty
But that he speaks.

Hermione.
>There's some ill planet reigns;

I must be patient, till the heavens look
With an aspect more favorable. Good my lords,
I am not prone to weeping, as our sex
Commonly are, the want of which vain dew
Perchance shall dry your pities; but I have
That honorable grief lodg'd here which burns
Worse than tears drown. Beseech you all, my lords,
With thoughts so qualified as your charities
Shall best instruct you, measure me; and so
The King's will be perform'd!

Leontes, King of Sicilia.
>Shall I be heard?

Hermione.
Who is't that goes with me? Beseech your Highness
My women may be with me, for you see
My plight requires it. Do not weep, good fools,
There is no cause. When you shall know your mistress
Has deserv'd prison, then abound in tears
As I come out; this action I now go on
Is for my better grace. Adieu, my lord,
I never wish'd to see you sorry, now
I trust I shall. My women, come, you have leave.

Leontes, King of Sicilia.
Go, do our bidding; hence!

Exit Queen guarded, with Ladies.

First Lord.
Beseech your Highness call the Queen again.

Antigonus.
Be certain what you do, sir, lest your justice
Prove violence, in the which three great ones suffer,
Yourself, your queen, your son.

First Lord.
>For her, my lord,

I dare my life lay down—and will do't, sir,
Please you t' accept it—that the Queen is spotless
I' th'eyes of heaven and to you—I mean,
In this which you accuse her.

Antigonus.
>If it prove

She's otherwise, I'll keep my stables where
I lodge my wife; I'll go in couples with her;
Than when I feel and see her no farther trust her;
For every inch of woman in the world,
Ay, every dram of woman's flesh is false,
If she be.

Leontes, King of Sicilia.
>Hold your peaces.

First Lord.
>Good my lord—

Antigonus.
It is for you we speak, not for ourselves.
You are abus'd, and by some putter-on
That will be damn'd for't. Would I knew the villain,
I would land-damn him. Be she honor-flaw'd,
I have three daughters: the eldest is eleven;
The second and the third, nine, and some five;
If this prove true, they'll pay for't. By mine honor,
I'll geld 'em all; fourteen they shall not see
To bring false generations. They are co-heirs,
And I had rather glib myself than they
Should not produce fair issue.

Leontes, King of Sicilia.
>Cease, no more.

You smell this business with a sense as cold
As is a dead man's nose; but I do see't, and feel't,
As you feel doing thus

Grasps his arm.
>—and see withal

The instruments that feel.

Antigonus.
                        If it be so,
We need no grave to bury honesty,
There's not a grain of it the face to sweeten
Of the whole dungy earth.

Leontes, King of Sicilia.
                        What? Lack I credit?

First Lord.
I had rather you did lack than I, my lord,
Upon this ground; and more it would content me
To have her honor true than your suspicion,
Be blam'd for't how you might.

Leontes, King of Sicilia.
                        Why, what need we
Commune with you of this, but rather follow
Our forceful instigation? Our prerogative
Calls not your counsels, but our natural goodness
Imparts this; which if you—or stupefied
Or seeming so in skill—cannot, or will not,
Relish a truth like us, inform yourselves
We need no more of your advice. The matter,
The loss, the gain, the ord'ring on't, is all
Properly ours.

Antigonus.
                        And I wish, my liege,
You had only in your silent judgment tried it,
Without more overture.

Leontes, King of Sicilia.
                        How could that be?
Either thou art most ignorant by age,
Or thou wert born a fool. Camillo's flight,
Added to their familiarity
(Which was as gross as ever touch'd conjecture,
That lack'd sight only, nought for approbation
But only seeing, all other circumstances
Made up to th' deed), doth push on this proceeding.
Yet, for a greater confirmation
(For in an act of this importance 'twere
Most piteous to be wild), I have dispatch'd in post
To sacred Delphos, to Apollo's temple,
Cleomines and Dion, whom you know
Of stuff'd sufficiency. Now, from the oracle
They will bring all, whose spiritual counsel had,
Shall stop or spur me. Have I done well?

First Lord.
Well done, my lord.

Leontes, King of Sicilia.
Though I am satisfied, and need no more
Than what I know, yet shall the oracle
Give rest to th' minds of others—such as he,

Points at Antigonus.

Whose ignorant credulity will not
Come up to th' truth. So have we thought it good
From our free person she should be confin'd,
Lest that the treachery of the two fled hence
Be left her to perform. Come follow us,
We are to speak in public; for this business
Will raise us all.

Antigonus.

Aside.
                        To laughter, as I take it,
If the good truth were known.

Exeunt.

Scene 2

Sicilia. The outer room of a prison.

(Paulina; Gentleman Attendant; Attendants; Jailer; Emilia)

Paulina attempts to visit Hermione in prison, but the Jailer refuses to let her, citing his orders. He agrees to let Hermione's lady-in-waiting Emilia come out instead. Emilia informs Paulina that the Queen has prematurely given birth to a healthy daughter. Certain that the sight of the baby will soften Leontes's heart, Paulina suggests she should take the baby to the King and plead for Hermione's pardon. The Jailer is uncertain whether he has any authority to let the baby leave the jail, but Paulina convinces him that he can legally do so.

Enter Paulina, a Gentleman, and Attendants.

Paulina.
The keeper of the prison, call to him;
Let him have knowledge who I am.

Exit Gentleman.
                        Good lady,
No court in Europe is too good for thee,
What dost thou then in prison?

Enter Gentleman with the Jailer.

                    Now, good sir,
You know me, do you not?

Jailer.
                         For a worthy lady,
And one who much I honor.

Paulina.
                         Pray you then,
Conduct me to the Queen.

Jailer.
                         I may not, madam:
To the contrary I have express commandment.

Paulina.
Here's ado, to lock up honesty
And honor from th' access of gentle visitors.
Is't lawful, pray you, to see her women?
Any of them? Emilia?

Jailer.
                         So please you, madam,
To put apart these your attendants, I
Shall bring Emilia forth.

Paulina.
                         I pray now call her.—
Withdraw yourselves.

Exeunt Gentleman and Attendants.

Jailer.
                         And, madam, I must
Be present at your conference.

Paulina.
Well; be't so; prithee.

Exit Jailer.

Here's such ado to make no stain a stain
As passes coloring.

Enter Jailer with Emilia.

                         Dear gentlewoman,
How fares our gracious lady?

Emilia.
As well as one so great and so forlorn
May hold together. On her frights and griefs
(Which never tender lady hath borne greater)
She is, something before her time, deliver'd.

Paulina.
A boy?

Emilia.
                         A daughter, and a goodly babe,
Lusty and like to live. The Queen receives
Much comfort in't; says, "My poor prisoner,
I am innocent as you."

Paulina.
                         I dare be sworn.
These dangerous, unsafe lunes i' th' King, beshrew them!
He must be told on't, and he shall. The office
Becomes a woman best. I'll take't upon me.
If I prove honey-mouth'd, let my tongue blister;
And never to my red-look'd anger be
The trumpet any more. Pray you, Emilia,
Commend my best obedience to the Queen.
If she dares trust me with her little babe,
I'll show't the King, and undertake to be
Her advocate to th' loud'st. We do not know
How he may soften at the sight o' th' child:
The silence often of pure innocence
Persuades when speaking fails.

Emilia.
                         Most worthy madam,
Your honor and your goodness is so evident
That your free undertaking cannot miss
A thriving issue. There is no lady living
So meet for this great errand. Please your ladyship
To visit the next room, I'll presently
Acquaint the Queen of your most noble offer,
Who but today hammered of this design,
But durst not tempt a minister of honor,
Lest she should be denied.

Paulina.
                         Tell her, Emilia,
I'll use that tongue I have. If wit flow from't
As boldness from my bosom, let't not be doubted
I shall do good.

Emilia.
                         Now be you blest for it!
I'll to the Queen.—Please you, come something nearer.

Jailer.
Madam, if't please the Queen to send the babe,
I know not what I shall incur to pass it,
Having no warrant.

Paulina.
                You need not fear it, sir.
This child was prisoner to the womb, and is
By law and process of great Nature thence
Freed and enfranchis'd, not a party to
The anger of the King, nor guilty of
(If any be) the trespass of the Queen.

Jailer.
I do believe it.

Paulina.
Do not you fear. Upon mine honor, I
Will stand betwixt you and danger.

Exeunt.

Scene 3

Sicilia. A room in Leontes' palace.

(Leontes; Servants; Paulina; Child; Antigonus; Lords)

Sleepless, Leontes worries about Mamillius, who has fallen ill. The King supposes that it the knowledge of his mother's dishonor that has made him sick. Restless, trying to take his mind off the image of Polixenes and Camillo laughing at him, he asks to be left alone, but Paulina forces her way in, despite the best efforts of her husband Antigonus and the other Lords. Leontes tells Antigonus to control his wife and sneers at him as a henpecked old fool when he says he cannot. Carrying the newborn baby, Paulina courageously asserts Hermione's complete innocence to Leontes and presents the child to him. He rejects it as being Polixenes's bastard and begins to rave against Hermione, the child, and Paulina, threatening to have her burnt as a witch. She calls him a tyrant to his face. Leontes orders Antigonus to take the baby and burn it, accusing him of encouraging Paulina, but he protests that he did not, which the other Lords confirm. When Antigonus promises he would do anything to prefer the baby's being killed, Leontes orders him to take it and abandon it in some desert place. Unwilling though he is, Antigonus swears to do so and leaves with the baby as Leontes reaffirms his unwillingness to raise someone else's child. News comes that Dion and Cleomines have returned from Delphi with the oracle's answer; Leontes orders that a public trial of Hermione be arranged.

Enter Leontes; Servants keeping the door.

Leontes, King of Sicilia.
Nor night, nor day, no rest. It is but weakness
To bear the matter thus—mere weakness. If
The cause were not in being—part o' th' cause,
She th' adult'ress; for the harlot king
Is quite beyond mine arm, out of the blank
And level of my brain, plot-proof; but she
I can hook to me—say that she were gone,
Given to the fire, a moi'ty of my rest
Might come to me again. Who's there?

First Servant.

Advancing.
                My lord?

Leontes, King of Sicilia.
How does the boy?

First Servant.
                He took good rest tonight;
'Tis hop'd his sickness is discharg'd.

Leontes, King of Sicilia.
To see his nobleness,
Conceiving the dishonor of his mother!
He straight declin'd, droop'd, took it deeply,
Fasten'd and fix'd the shame on't in himself,
Threw off his spirit, his appetite, his sleep,
And downright languish'd. Leave me solely; go,
See how he fares.

Exit First Servant.

                Fie, fie, no thought of him;
The very thought of my revenges that way
Recoil upon me: in himself too mighty,
And in his parties, his alliance. Let him be,
Until a time may serve. For present vengeance,
Take it on her. Camillo and Polixenes
Laugh at me; make their pastime at my sorrow:
They should not laugh if I could reach them, nor
Shall she, within my pow'r.

Enter Paulina with a child; Antigonus and Lords endeavoring to hold her back.

First Lord.
                You must not enter.

Paulina.
Nay, rather, good my lords, be second to me.
Fear you his tyrannous passion more, alas,
Than the Queen's life? A gracious innocent soul,
More free than he is jealous.

Antigonus.
                         That's enough.

Second Servant.
Madam—he hath not slept tonight, commanded
None should come at him.

Paulina.
                         Not so hot, good sir,
I come to bring him sleep. 'Tis such as you,
That creep like shadows by him, and do sigh
At each his needless heavings, such as you
Nourish the cause of his awaking. I
Do come with words as medicinal as true,
Honest as either, to purge him of that humor
That presses him from sleep.

Leontes, King of Sicilia.
                         What noise there, ho?

Paulina.
No noise, my lord, but needful conference
About some gossips for your Highness.

Leontes, King of Sicilia.
                         How?
Away with that audacious lady! Antigonus,
I charg'd thee that she should not come about me:
I knew she would.

Antigonus.
                         I told her so, my lord,
On your displeasure's peril and on mine,
She should not visit you.

Leontes, King of Sicilia.
                         What? Canst not rule her?

Paulina.
From all dishonesty he can. In this,
Unless he take the course that you have done—
Commit me for committing honor—trust it,
He shall not rule me.

Antigonus.
                         La you now, you hear!
When she will take the rein I let her run,

Aside.

But she'll not stumble.

Paulina.
                         Good my liege, I come—
And I beseech you hear me, who professes
Myself your loyal servant, your physician,
Your most obedient counsellor; yet that dares
Less appear so, in comforting your evils,
Than such as most seem yours—I say, I come
From your good queen.

Leontes, King of Sicilia.
Good queen?

Paulina.
Good queen, my lord, good queen, I say good queen,
And would by combat make her good, so were I
A man, the worst about you.

Leontes, King of Sicilia.
                         Force her hence.

Paulina.
Let him that makes but trifles of his eyes
First hand me. On mine own accord I'll off,
But first I'll do my errand. The good queen
(For she is good) hath brought you forth a daughter—
Here 'tis—commends it to your blessing.

Laying down the child.

Leontes, King of Sicilia.
                         Out!
A mankind witch! Hence with her, out o' door!
A most intelligencing bawd!

Paulina.
                         Not so.
I am as ignorant in that, as you
In so entit'ling me; and no less honest
Than you are mad; which is enough, I'll warrant
(As this world goes), to pass for honest.

Leontes, King of Sicilia.
                         Traitors!
Will you not push her out?

To Antigonus.

                         Give her the bastard,
Thou dotard, thou art woman-tir'd; unroosted
By thy Dame Partlet here. Take up the bastard,
Take't up, I say; give't to thy crone.

Paulina.
                          For ever
Unvenerable be thy hands, if thou
Tak'st up the Princess by that forced baseness
Which he has put upon't!

Leontes, King of Sicilia.
                          He dreads his wife.

Paulina.
So I would you did; then 'twere past all doubt
You'd call your children yours.

Leontes, King of Sicilia.
                          A nest of traitors!

Antigonus.
I am none, by this good light.

Paulina.
                          Nor I, nor any
But one that's here—and that's himself; for he
The sacred honor of himself, his queen's,
His hopeful son's, his babe's, betrays to slander,
Whose sting is sharper than the sword's, and will not
(For as the case now stands, it is a curse
He cannot be compell'd to't) once remove
The root of his opinion, which is rotten
As ever oak or stone was sound.

Leontes, King of Sicilia.
                          A callat
Of boundless tongue, who late hath beat her husband,
And now baits me! This brat is none of mine,
It is the issue of Polixenes.
Hence with it, and together with the dam
Commit them to the fire!

Paulina.
                          It is yours:
And might we lay th' old proverb to your charge,
So like you, 'tis the worse. Behold, my lords,
Although the print be little, the whole matter
And copy of the father—eye, nose, lip,
The trick of 's frown, his forehead, nay, the valley,
The pretty dimples of his chin and cheek, his smiles,
The very mould and frame of hand, nail, finger.
And thou, good goddess Nature, which hast made it
So like to him that got it, if thou hast
The ordering of the mind too, 'mongst all colors
No yellow in't, lest she suspect, as he does,
Her children not her husband's!

Leontes, King of Sicilia.
                          A gross hag!
And, lozel, thou art worthy to be hang'd,
That wilt not stay her tongue.

Antigonus.
                          Hang all the husbands
That cannot do that feat, you'll leave yourself
Hardly one subject.

Leontes, King of Sicilia.
                          Once more, take her hence.

Paulina.
A most unworthy and unnatural lord
Can do no more.

Leontes, King of Sicilia.
                          I'll ha' thee burnt.

Paulina.
                          I care not:
It is an heretic that makes the fire,
Not she which burns in't. I'll not call you tyrant;
But this most cruel usage of your queen
(Not able to produce more accusation
Than your own weak-hing'd fancy) something savors
Of tyranny, and will ignoble make you,
Yea, scandalous to the world.

Leontes, King of Sicilia.
                          On your allegiance,
Out of the chamber with her! Were I a tyrant,
Where were her life? She durst not call me so,
If she did know me one. Away with her!

Paulina.
I pray you do not push me, I'll be gone.
Look to your babe, my lord, 'tis yours. Jove send her
A better guiding spirit! What needs these hands?
You, that are thus so tender o'er his follies,
Will never do him good, not one of you.
So, so. Farewell, we are gone.

Exit.

Leontes, King of Sicilia.
Thou, traitor, hast set on thy wife to this.
My child? Away with't! Even thou, that hast
A heart so tender o'er it, take it hence,
And see it instantly consum'd with fire.
Even thou, and none but thou. Take it up straight.
Within this hour bring me word 'tis done

(And by good testimony), or I'll seize thy life,
With what thou else call'st thine. If thou refuse
And wilt encounter with my wrath, say so;
The bastard brains with these my proper hands
Shall I dash out. Go, take it to the fire,
For thou set'st on thy wife.

Antigonus.
       I did not, sir.
These lords, my noble fellows, if they please,
Can clear me in't.

All Lords.
      We can. My royal liege,
He is not guilty of her coming hither.

Leontes, King of Sicilia.
You're liars all.

First Lord.
Beseech your Highness, give us better credit.
We have always truly serv'd you, and beseech'
So to esteem of us; and on our knees we beg
(As recompense of our dear services
Past and to come) that you do change this purpose,
Which being so horrible, so bloody, must
Lead on to some foul issue. We all kneel.

Leontes, King of Sicilia.
I am a feather for each wind that blows.
Shall I live on to see this bastard kneel
And call me father? Better burn it now
Than curse it then. But be it; let it live.
It shall not neither.

To Antigonus.
     You, sir, come you hither:
You that have been so tenderly officious
With Lady Margery, your midwife there,
To save this bastard's life—for 'tis a bastard,
So sure as this beard's grey—what will you adventure
To save this brat's life?

Antigonus.
      Any thing, my lord,
That my ability may undergo
And nobleness impose; at least thus much:
I'll pawn the little blood which I have left
To save the innocent—any thing possible.

Leontes, King of Sicilia.
It shall be possible. Swear by this sword
Thou wilt perform my bidding.

Antigonus.
     I will, my lord.

Leontes, King of Sicilia.
Mark and perform it—seest thou? For the fail
Of any point in't shall not only be
Death to thyself but to thy lewd-tongu'd wife,
Whom for this time we pardon. We enjoin thee,
As thou art liegeman to us, that thou carry
This female bastard hence, and that thou bear it
To some remote and desert place quite out
Of our dominions, and that there thou leave it
(Without more mercy) to it own protection,
And favor of the climate. As by strange fortune
It came to us, I do in justice charge thee,
On thy soul's peril, and thy body's torture,
That thou commend it strangely to some place
Where chance may nurse or end it. Take it up.

Antigonus.
I swear to do this—though a present death
Had been more merciful. Come on, poor babe.
Some powerful spirit instruct the kites and ravens
To be thy nurses! Wolves and bears, they say,
Casting their savageness aside, have done
Like offices of pity. Sir, be prosperous
In more than this deed does require! And blessing
Against this cruelty fight on thy side,
Poor thing, condemn'd to loss!

Exit with the child.

Leontes, King of Sicilia.
     No! I'll not rear
Another's issue.

Enter Third Servant.

Third Servant.
     Please' your Highness, posts
From those you sent to th' oracle are come
An hour since. Cleomines and Dion,
Being well arriv'd from Delphos, are both landed,
Hasting to th' court.

First Lord.
                So please you, sir, their speed
Hath been beyond accompt.

Leontes, King of Sicilia.
                     Twenty-three days
They have been absent. 'Tis good speed; foretells
The great Apollo suddenly will have
The truth of this appear. Prepare you, lords,
Summon a session, that we may arraign
Our most disloyal lady; for as she hath
Been publicly accus'd, so shall she have
A just and open trial. While she lives
My heart will be a burden to me. Leave me,
And think upon my bidding.

Exeunt.

Act 3

Scene 1

Sicilia. A sea port.

(Cleomines; Dion)

Cleomines and Dion, stopping for fresh horses on their return from the oracle, comment on the awe inspiring spectacle of the temple at Delphi. They hope that the sealed answer they are bearing will prove to Hermione's advantage.

Enter Cleomines and Dion.

Cleomines.
The climate's delicate, the air most sweet,
Fertile the isle, the temple much surpassing
The common praise it bears.

Dion.
                I shall report,
For most it caught me, the celestial habits
(Methinks I so should term them) and the reverence
Of the grave wearers. O, the sacrifice!
How ceremonious, solemn, and unearthly
It was i' th' off'ring!

Cleomines.
              But of all, the burst
And the ear-deaf'ning voice o' th' oracle,
Kin to Jove's thunder, so surpris'd my sense,
That I was nothing.

Dion.
            If th' event o' th' journey
Prove as successful to the Queen (O be't so!)
As it hath been to us rare, pleasant, speedy,
The time is worth the use on't.

Cleomines.
                Great Apollo
Turn all to th' best! These proclamations,
So forcing faults upon Hermione,
I little like.

Dion.
              The violent carriage of it
Will clear or end the business. When the oracle
(Thus by Apollo's great divine seal'd up)
Shall the contents discover, something rare
Even then will rush to knowledge. Go; fresh horses!
And gracious be the issue!

Exeunt.

Scene 2

Sicilia. A court of justice.

(Leontes; Lords; Hermione; Paulina; Ladies; Officers; Cleomines; Dion; Servant)

Leontes opens Hermione's trial, announcing that he has made it a public one so that he shall not be accused of tyranny or of injustice — though he is at once judge, jury and accuser. Hermione is brought into the court and her indictment read out, accusing her of adultery and planning to kill Leontes. She denies it all and protests at the treatment meted out at her, particularly being dragged to court while still recovering from giving birth. She challenges all of Leontes's delusions, but he clings to them. Seeing there will be no mercy from him, she puts her case in the hands of the oracle of Apollo. Dion and Cleomines bring in the scroll from Delphi, swearing that they have not opened or altered it in any way. The oracle is read out: it declares Hermione innocent, Polixenes blameless, Camillo faithful, Leontes a tyrant, and the baby his child. It also announces that Leontes shall live without an heir unless that which has been lost is found. Leontes denies the truth of the oracle and orders the trial to proceed, at which point a messenger Servant announces that Mamillius has died. Hermione faints and is carried out, while Leontes, realizing this is Apollo's vengeance for sacrilege, swears he will make amends for what he has done. But Paulina comes in to announce that Hermione has died and unleashes a tirade aimed at the King, listing all his crimes. Leontes does not protest, and in the end she begs the King's pardon, but he acknowledges that she has only spoken the truth. Leontes swears to mourn daily at the tombs of his wife and child for the rest of his life.

Enter Leontes, Lords, Officers.

Leontes, King of Sicilia.
This sessions (to our great grief we pronounce)
Even pushes 'gainst our heart—the party tried,
The daughter of a king, our wife, and one
Of us too much belov'd. Let us be clear'd
Of being tyrannous, since we so openly
Proceed in justice, which shall have due course,
Even to the guilt or the purgation.
Produce the prisoner.

Officer.
It is his Highness' pleasure that the Queen
Appear in person here in court.

Enter Hermione (as to her trial), Paulina, and Ladies attending.

      Silence!

Leontes, King of Sicilia.
Read the indictment.

Officer.

Reads.

"Hermione, queen to the worthy Leontes, King of Sicilia, thou art here accused and arraigned of high treason, in committing adultery with Polixenes, King of Bohemia, and conspiring with Camillo to take away the life of our sovereign lord the King, thy royal husband: the pretense whereof being by circumstances partly laid open, thou, Hermione, contrary to the faith and allegiance of a true subject, didst counsel and aid them, for their better safety, to fly away by night."

Hermione.
Since what I am to say must be but that
Which contradicts my accusation, and
The testimony on my part no other
But what comes from myself, it shall scarce boot me
To say "Not guilty." Mine integrity,
Being counted falsehood, shall (as I express it)
Be so receiv'd. But thus, if pow'rs divine
Behold our human actions (as they do),
I doubt not then but innocence shall make
False accusation blush, and tyranny
Tremble at patience. You, my lord, best know
(Who least will seem to do so) my past life
Hath been as continent, as chaste, as true,
As I am now unhappy; which is more
Than history can pattern, though devis'd
And play'd to take spectators. For behold me,
A fellow of the royal bed, which owe
A moi'ty of the throne, a great king's daughter,
The mother to a hopeful prince, here standing
To prate and talk for life and honor 'fore
Who please to come and hear. For life, I prize it
As I weigh grief, which I would spare; for honor,
'Tis a derivative from me to mine,
And only that I stand for. I appeal
To your own conscience, sir, before Polixenes
Came to your court, how I was in your grace,
How merited to be so; since he came,
With what encounter so uncurrent I
Have strain'd t' appear thus; if one jot beyond
The bound of honor, or in act or will
That way inclining, hard'ned be the hearts
Of all that hear me, and my near'st of kin
Cry fie upon my grave!

Leontes, King of Sicilia.
      I ne'er heard yet
That any of these bolder vices wanted
Less impudence to gainsay what they did
Than to perform it first.

Hermione.
      That's true enough,
Though 'tis a saying, sir, not due to me.

Leontes, King of Sicilia.
You will not own it.

Hermione.
      More than mistress of
Which comes to me in name of fault, I must not
At all acknowledge. For Polixenes
(With whom I am accus'd), I do confess
I lov'd him as in honor he requir'd;
With such a kind of love as might become
A lady like me; with a love even such,
So, and no other, as yourself commanded;
Which not to have done I think had been in me
Both disobedience and ingratitude
To you and toward your friend, whose love had spoke,
Even since it could speak, from an infant, freely,
That it was yours. Now for conspiracy,

I know not how it tastes, though it be dish'd
For me to try how. All I know of it
Is that Camillo was an honest man;
And why he left your court, the gods themselves
(Wotting no more than I) are ignorant.

Leontes, King of Sicilia.
You knew of his departure, as you know
What you have underta'en to do in 's absence.

Hermione.
Sir,
You speak a language that I understand not.
My life stands in the level of your dreams,
Which I'll lay down.

Leontes, King of Sicilia.
                    Your actions are my dreams.
You had a bastard by Polixenes,
And I but dream'd it. As you were past all shame
(Those of your fact are so), so past all truth;
Which to deny concerns more than avails; for as
Thy brat hath been cast out, like to itself,
No father owning it (which is indeed
More criminal in thee than it), so thou
Shall feel our justice; in whose easiest passage
Look for no less than death.

Hermione.
                    Sir, spare your threats.
The bug which you would fright me with, I seek.
To me can life be no commodity;
The crown and comfort of my life, your favor,
I do give lost, for I do feel it gone,
But know not how it went. My second joy
And first-fruits of my body, from his presence
I am barr'd, like one infectious. My third comfort
(Starr'd most unluckily) is from my breast
(The innocent milk in it most innocent mouth)
Hal'd out to murder; myself on every post
Proclaim'd a strumpet; with immodest hatred
The child-bed privilege denied, which 'longs
To women of all fashion; lastly, hurried
Here to this place, i' th' open air, before
I have got strength of limit. Now, my liege,
Tell me what blessings I have here alive,
That I should fear to die? Therefore proceed.
But yet hear this—mistake me not; no life
(I prize it not a straw), but for mine honor,
Which I would free—if I shall be condemn'd
Upon surmises (all proofs sleeping else
But what your jealousies awake), I tell you
'Tis rigor and not law. Your honors all,
I do refer me to the oracle:
Apollo be my judge!

First Lord.
                    This your request
Is altogether just; therefore bring forth,
And in Apollo's name, his oracle.

Exeunt certain Officers.

Hermione.
The Emperor of Russia was my father.
O that he were alive, and here beholding
His daughter's trial! That he did but see
The flatness of my misery, yet with eyes
Of pity, not revenge!

Enter Officers with Cleomines, Dion.

Officer.
You here shall swear upon this sword of justice,
That you, Cleomines and Dion, have
Been both at Delphos, and from thence have brought
This seal'd-up oracle, by the hand deliver'd
Of great Apollo's priest; and that since then
You have not dar'd to break the holy seal
Nor read the secrets in't.

Both Cleomines and Dion.
                    All this we swear.

Leontes, King of Sicilia.
Break up the seals, and read.

Officer.

Reads.

"Hermione is chaste, Polixenes blameless, Camillo a true subject, Leontes a jealous tyrant, his innocent babe truly begotten, and the King shall live without an heir, if that which is lost be not found."

All Lords.
Now blessed be the great Apollo!

Hermione.
                    Praised!

Leontes, King of Sicilia.
Hast thou read truth?

Officer.
                    Ay, my lord, even so
As it is here set down.

Leontes, King of Sicilia.
There is no truth at all i' th' oracle.
The sessions shall proceed; this is mere falsehood.

Enter First Servant.

First Servant.
My lord the King! The King!

Leontes, King of Sicilia.
                    What is the business?

First Servant.
O sir, I shall be hated to report it!
The Prince your son, with mere conceit and fear
Of the Queen's speed, is gone.

Leontes, King of Sicilia.
                    How? Gone?

First Servant.
                    Is dead.

Leontes, King of Sicilia.
Apollo's angry, and the heavens themselves
Do strike at my injustice.

Hermione swoons.

                    How now there?

Paulina.
This news is mortal to the Queen. Look down
And see what death is doing.

Leontes, King of Sicilia.
                    Take her hence;
Her heart is but o'ercharg'd; she will recover.
I have too much believ'd mine own suspicion.
Beseech you tenderly apply to her
Some remedies for life.

Exeunt Paulina and Ladies with Hermione.

                    Apollo, pardon
My great profaneness 'gainst thine oracle!
I'll reconcile me to Polixenes,
New woo my queen, recall the good Camillo,
Whom I proclaim a man of truth, of mercy;
For being transported by my jealousies
To bloody thoughts, and to revenge, I chose
Camillo for the minister to poison
My friend Polixenes; which had been done,
But that the good mind of Camillo tardied
My swift command, though I with death and with
Reward did threaten and encourage him,
Not doing it and being done. He (most humane
And fill'd with honor) to my kingly guest
Unclasp'd my practice, quit his fortunes here
(Which you knew great), and to the hazard of
All incertainties himself commended,
No richer than his honor. How he glisters
Through my rust! And how his piety
Does my deeds make the blacker!

Enter Paulina.

Paulina.
                    Woe the while!
O, cut my lace, lest my heart, cracking it,
Break too!

First Lord.
                    What fit is this, good lady?

Paulina.
What studied torments, tyrant, hast for me?
What wheels? Racks? Fires? What flaying? Boiling
In leads or oils? What old or newer torture
Must I receive, whose every word deserves
To taste of thy most worst? Thy tyranny,
Together working with thy jealousies
(Fancies too weak for boys, too green and idle
For girls of nine), O, think what they have done,
And then run mad indeed—stark mad! For all
Thy by-gone fooleries were but spices of it.
That thou betrayedst Polixenes, 'twas nothing—
That did but show thee, of a fool, inconstant,
And damnable ingrateful; nor was't much
Thou wouldst have poison'd good Camillo's honor,
To have him kill a king—poor trespasses,
More monstrous standing by; whereof I reckon
The casting forth to crows thy baby-daughter
To be or none or little—though a devil
Would have shed water out of fire ere done't;
Nor is't directly laid to thee, the death
Of the young Prince, whose honorable thoughts
(Thoughts high for one so tender) cleft the heart
That could conceive a gross and foolish sire
Blemish'd his gracious dam; this is not, no,
Laid to thy answer: but the last—O lords,
When I have said, cry "Woe!"—the Queen, the Queen,

The sweet'st, dear'st creature's dead, and vengeance for't
Not dropp'd down yet.

First Lord.
                      The higher pow'rs forbid!

Paulina.
I say she's dead; I'll swear't. If word nor oath
Prevail not, go and see. If you can bring
Tincture or lustre in her lip, her eye,
Heat outwardly or breath within, I'll serve you
As I would do the gods. But, O thou tyrant!
Do not repent these things, for they are heavier
Than all thy woes can stir; therefore betake thee
To nothing but despair. A thousand knees,
Ten thousand years together, naked, fasting,
Upon a barren mountain, and still winter
In storm perpetual, could not move the gods
To look that way thou wert.

Leontes, King of Sicilia.
                      Go on, go on;
Thou canst not speak too much, I have deserv'd
All tongues to talk their bitt'rest.

First Lord.
                      Say no more.
Howe'er the business goes, you have made fault
I' th' boldness of your speech.

Paulina.
                      I am sorry for't.
All faults I make, when I shall come to know them,
I do repent. Alas, I have show'd too much
The rashness of a woman; he is touch'd
To th' noble heart. What's gone and what's past help
Should be past grief. Do not receive affliction
At my petition; I beseech you, rather
Let me be punish'd, that have minded you
Of what you should forget. Now, good my liege,
Sir, royal sir, forgive a foolish woman.
The love I bore your queen—lo, fool again!—
I'll speak of her no more, nor of your children;
I'll not remember you of my own lord,
Who is lost too. Take your patience to you,
And I'll say nothing.

Leontes, King of Sicilia.
                      Thou didst speak but well
When most the truth; which I receive much better
Than to be pitied of thee. Prithee bring me
To the dead bodies of my queen and son.
One grave shall be for both; upon them shall
The causes of their death appear (unto
Our shame perpetual). Once a day I'll visit
The chapel where they lie, and tears shed there
Shall be my recreation. So long as nature
Will bear up with this exercise, so long
I daily vow to use it. Come, and lead me
To these sorrows.

Exeunt.

Scene 3

Bohemia. A desert country near the sea.

(Antigonus; Mariner; Bear; Old Shepherd; Clown)

Antigonus lands on the sea coast of Bohemia with the baby. He is warned by the Mariner who brought him there that a storm is coming and that the area is known for being inhabited by beasts of prey. Setting the baby down, Antigonus tells it how he had a vision of Hermione that told him to bring the child to Bohemia and to name it Perdita, and also that because he agreed to do this task he wold never see his wife again. He lays Perdita down with a scroll and a bundle beside her and prepares to leave as the storm begins. He is chased off by a bear. A Old Shepherd enters, complaining about hot-headed youth, and finds Perdita, whom he presumes to be the child of some waiting-woman who was forced to hide it. His son the Clown enters and recounts how he saw a ship be wrecked by the storm and Antigonus being eaten alive by the bear. Discovering the gold that Antigonus left with Perdita, they decide to keep both child and gold. The Clown goes off to see if the bear's done with Antigonus yet, and whether there's anything left to bury.

Enter Antigonus and a Mariner with the babe.

Antigonus.
Thou art perfect then, our ship hath touch'd upon
The deserts of Bohemia?

Mariner.
                      Ay, my lord, and fear
We have landed in ill time: the skies look grimly,
And threaten present blusters. In my conscience,
The heavens with that we have in hand are angry,
And frown upon 's.

Antigonus.
Their sacred wills be done! Go get aboard;

Look to thy bark, I'll not be long before
I call upon thee.

Mariner.
Make your best haste, and go not
Too far i' th' land; 'tis like to be loud weather.
Besides, this place is famous for the creatures
Of prey that keep upon't.

Antigonus.
      Go thou away,
I'll follow instantly.

Mariner.
       I am glad at heart
To be so rid o' th' business.

Exit.

Antigonus.
      Come, poor babe.
I have heard (but not believ'd) the spirits o' th' dead
May walk again. If such thing be, thy mother
Appear'd to me last night; for ne'er was dream
So like a waking. To me comes a creature,
Sometimes her head on one side, some another—
I never saw a vessel of like sorrow,
So fill'd, and so becoming; in pure white robes,
Like very sanctity, she did approach
My cabin where I lay; thrice bow'd before me,
And (gasping to begin some speech) her eyes
Became two spouts; the fury spent, anon
Did this break from her: "Good Antigonus,
Since fate (against thy better disposition)
Hath made thy person for the thrower-out
Of my poor babe, according to thine oath,
Places remote enough are in Bohemia,
There weep and leave it crying; and for the babe
Is counted lost forever, Perdita
I prithee call't. For this ungentle business,
Put on thee by my lord, thou ne'er shalt see
Thy wife Paulina more." And so, with shrieks,
She melted into air. Affrighted much,
I did in time collect myself and thought
This was so, and no slumber. Dreams are toys,
Yet for this once, yea, superstitiously,
I will be squar'd by this. I do believe
Hermione hath suffer'd death, and that
Apollo would (this being indeed the issue
Of King Polixenes) it should here be laid,
Either for life or death, upon the earth
Of its right father. Blossom, speed thee well!

Laying down the child, with a scroll.

There lie, and there thy character; there these,

Placing a bundle beside it.

Which may, if Fortune please, both breed thee, pretty,
And still rest thine.

Thunder.
      The storm begins. Poor wretch,
That for thy mother's fault art thus expos'd
To loss, and what may follow! Weep I cannot,
But my heart bleeds; and most accurs'd am I
To be by oath enjoin'd to this. Farewell!
The day frowns more and more; thou'rt like to have
A lullaby too rough. I never saw
The heavens so dim by day. A savage clamor!
Well may I get aboard! This is the chase;
I am gone forever.

Exit pursued by a bear.
Enter Shepherd.

Old Shepherd.
I would there were no age between ten and three-and-twenty, or that youth would sleep out the rest; for there is nothing in the between but getting wenches with child, wronging the ancientry, stealing, fighting—

Horns.

Hark you now! Would any but these boil'd-brains of nineteen and two-and-twenty hunt this weather? They have scar'd away two of my best sheep, which I fear the wolf will sooner find than the master. If any where I have them, 'tis by the sea-side, browsing of ivy. Good luck, and't be thy will! What have we here? Mercy on 's, a barne? A very pretty barne! A boy, or a child, I wonder? A pretty one, a very pretty one: sure some scape. Though I am not bookish, yet I can read waiting-gentlewoman in the scape. This has been some stair-work, some trunk-work, some behind-door-work. They were warmer that got this than the poor thing is here. I'll take it up for pity, yet I'll tarry till my son come; he hallow'd but even now. Whoa-ho-hoa!

Enter Clown.

Clown.
Hilloa, loa!

Old Shepherd.
What? Art so near? If thou'lt see a thing to talk on when thou art dead and rotten, come hither. What ail'st thou, man?

Clown.
I have seen two such sights, by sea and by land! But I am not to say it is a sea, for it is now the sky, betwixt the firmament and it you cannot thrust a bodkin's point.

Old Shepherd.
Why, boy, how is it?

Clown.
I would you did but see how it chafes, how it rages, how it takes up the shore! But that's not to the point. O, the most piteous cry of the poor souls! Sometimes to see 'em, and not to see 'em; now the ship boring the moon with her mainmast, and anon swallow'd with yeast and froth, as you'ld thrust a cork into a hogshead. And then for the land-service, to see how the bear tore out his shoulder-bone, how he cried to me for help, and said his name was Antigonus, a nobleman. But to make an end of the ship, to see how the sea flap-dragon'd it; but, first, how the poor souls roar'd, and the sea mock'd them; and how the poor gentleman roar'd, and the bear mock'd him, both roaring louder than the sea or weather.

Old Shepherd.
Name of mercy, when was this, boy?

Clown.
Now, now; I have not wink'd since I saw these sights. The men are not yet cold under water, nor the bear half din'd on the gentleman. He's at it now.

Old Shepherd.
Would I had been by, to have help'd the old man!

Clown.
I would you had been by the ship side, to have help'd her; there your charity would have lack'd footing.

Old Shepherd.
Heavy matters, heavy matters! But look thee here, boy. Now bless thyself: thou met'st with things dying, I with things new-born. Here's a sight for thee; look thee, a bearing-cloth for a squire's child! Look thee here, take up, take up, boy; open't. So, let's see—it was told me I should be rich by the fairies. This is some changeling; open't; what's within, boy?

Clown.
You're a made old man; if the sins of your youth are forgiven you, you're well to live. Gold, all gold!

Old Shepherd.
This is fairy gold, boy, and 'twill prove so. Up with't, keep it close. Home, home, the next way. We are lucky, boy, and to be so still requires nothing but secrecy. Let my sheep go. Come, good boy, the next way home.

Clown.
Go you the next way with your findings; I'll go see if the bear be gone from the gentleman and how much he hath eaten. They are never curst but when they are hungry. If there be any of him left, I'll bury it.

Old Shepherd.
That's a good deed. If thou mayest discern by that which is left of him what he is, fetch me to th' sight of him.

Clown.
Marry, will I; and you shall help to put him i' th' ground.

Old Shepherd.
'Tis a lucky day, boy, and we'll do good deeds on't.

Exeunt.

Act 4

Scene 1

(Time)

The Chorus, Time itself, tells us of the passing of sixteen years, how Leontes has shut himself up in his palace while Perdita grew up in the Shepherd's care, and how the girl has fallen in love with Florizel, Polixenes's son, who loves her in return.

Enter Time, the Chorus.

Time, as Chorus.
I, that please some, try all, both joy and terror
Of good and bad, that makes and unfolds error,
Now take upon me, in the name of Time,
To use my wings. Impute it not a crime
To me, or my swift passage, that I slide

O'er sixteen years and leave the growth untried
Of that wide gap, since it is in my pow'r
To o'erthrow law, and in one self-born hour
To plant and o'erwhelm custom. Let me pass
The same I am, ere ancient'st order was,
Or what is now receiv'd. I witness to
The times that brought them in; so shall I do
To th' freshest things now reigning, and make stale
The glistering of this present, as my tale
Now seems to it. Your patience this allowing,
I turn my glass, and give my scene such growing
As you had slept between. Leontes leaving—
Th' effects of his fond jealousies so grieving
That he shuts up himself—imagine me,
Gentle spectators, that I now may be
In fair Bohemia, and remember well,
I mentioned a son o' th' King's, which Florizel
I now name to you; and with speed so pace
To speak of Perdita, now grown in grace
Equal with wond'ring. What of her ensues
I list not prophesy; but let Time's news
Be known when 'tis brought forth. A shepherd's daughter,
And what to her adheres, which follows after,
Is th' argument of Time. Of this allow,
If ever you have spent time worse ere now;
If never, yet that Time himself doth say,
He wishes earnestly you never may.

Exit.

Scene 2

Bohemia. A room in the palace of Polixenes.

(Polixenes; Camillo)

Camillo seeks Polixenes's permission to return to Sicilia, but Polixenes orders him to stay, as he still needs his services — and, also, does not want to hear about Sicilia. He asks Camillo whether he knows where Florizel is, but all Camillo knows is that he has often been absent of late. Polixenes has found out that the Prince has been spending a lot of time at the house of a poor shepherd who sixteen years ago became extremely rich, without anyone knowing how. Camillo knows of this shepherd, and also of his daughter. Polixenes fears that the girl is what is drawing Florizel. They decide to disguise themselves to spy on Florizel.

Enter Polixenes and Camillo.

Polixenes, King of Bohemia.
I pray thee, good Camillo, be no more importunate. 'Tis a sickness denying thee any thing; a death to grant this.

Camillo.
It is fifteen years since I saw my country; though I have for the most part been air'd abroad, I desire to lay my bones there. Besides, the penitent King, my master, hath sent for me, to whose feeling sorrows I might be some allay (or I o'erween to think so), which is another spur to my departure.

Polixenes, King of Bohemia.
As thou lov'st me, Camillo, wipe not out the rest of thy services by leaving me now. The need I have of thee, thine own goodness hath made. Better not to have had thee than thus to want thee. Thou, having made me businesses which none without thee can sufficiently manage, must either stay to execute them thyself, or take away with thee the very services thou hast done; which if I have not enough consider'd (as too much I cannot), to be more thankful to thee shall be my study, and my profit therein the heaping friendships. Of that fatal country Sicilia, prithee speak no more, whose very naming punishes me with the remembrance of that penitent (as thou call'st him) and reconcil'd king, my brother, whose loss of his most precious queen and children are even now to be afresh lamented. Say to me, when saw'st thou the Prince Florizel, my son? Kings are no less unhappy, their issue not being gracious, than they are in losing them when they have approv'd their virtues.

Camillo.
Sir, it is three days since I saw the Prince. What his happier affairs may be, are to me unknown; but I have (missingly) noted, he is of late much retir'd from court, and is less frequent to his princely exercises than formerly he hath appear'd.

Polixenes, King of Bohemia.
I have consider'd so much, Camillo, and with some care, so far that I have eyes under my service which look upon his removedness; from whom I have this intelligence, that he is seldom from the house of a most homely shepherd, a man, they say, that from very nothing, and beyond the imagination of his neighbors, is grown into an unspeakable estate.

Camillo.
I have heard, sir, of such a man, who hath a daughter of most rare note. The report of her is extended more than can be thought to begin from such a cottage.

Polixenes, King of Bohemia.
That's likewise part of my intelligence; but (I fear) the angle that plucks our son thither. Thou shalt accompany us to the place, where we will (not appearing what we are) have some question with the shepherd; from whose simplicity I think it not uneasy to get the cause of my son's resort thither. Prithee be my present partner in this business, and lay aside the thoughts of Sicilia.

Camillo.
I willingly obey your command.

Polixenes, King of Bohemia.
My best Camillo! We must disguise ourselves.

Exeunt.

Scene 3

Bohemia. A road near the shepherd's cottage.

(Autolycus; Clown)

Autolycus, pickpocket, conman, and rogue, sings to himself as he wanders along. He has recently been dismissed from Florizel's service, but he has no fears for his future. The Clown comes alone, having been sent by his sister Perdita to fetch supplies for the sheep-shearing festival that she is hosting. Autolycus immediately pretends to have been beaten and robbed, naming his aggressor as one Autolycus. As the Clown helps him up Autolycus picks his pocket before refusing his offer of money. As the Clown goes off to market, Autolycus promises himself to go to the sheep-shearing, as there will be many opportunities for theft there.

Enter Autolycus singing.

Autolycus.
When daffodils begin to peer,
With heigh, the doxy over the dale!
Why, then comes in the sweet o' the year,
For the red blood reigns in the winter's pale.
The white sheet bleaching on the hedge,
With hey, the sweet birds, O how they sing!
Doth set my pugging tooth an edge,
For a quart of ale is a dish for a king.
The lark, that tirra-lyra chaunts,
With heigh, with heigh, the thrush and the jay!
Are summer songs for me and my aunts,
While we lie tumbling in the hay.
I have serv'd Prince Florizel, and in my time wore three-pile, but now I am out of service.
But shall I go mourn for that, my dear?
The pale moon shines by night;
And when I wander here and there,
I then do most go right.
If tinkers may have leave to live,
And bear the sow-skin bouget,
Then my account I well may give,
And in the stocks avouch it.
My traffic is sheets; when the kite builds, look to lesser linen. My father nam'd me Autolycus, who being, as I am, litter'd under Mercury, was likewise a snapper-up of unconsider'd trifles. With die and drab I purchas'd this caparison, and my revenue is the silly cheat. Gallows and knock are too powerful on the highway. Beating and hanging are terrors to me. For the life to come, I sleep out the thought of it. A prize, a prize!

Enter Clown.

Clown.
Let me see: every 'leven wether tods, every tod yields pound and odd shilling; fifteen hundred shorn, what comes the wool to?

Autolycus.

Aside.

If the springe hold, the cock's mine.

Clown.
I cannot do't without compters. Let me see: what am I to buy for our sheep-shearing feast? Three pound of sugar, five pound of currants, rice—what will this sister of mine do with rice? But my father hath made her mistress of the feast, and she lays it on. She hath made me four and twenty nosegays for the shearers (three-man song-men all, and very good ones), but they are most of them means and bases; but one Puritan amongst them, and he sings psalms to horn-pipes. I must have saffron to color the warden pies; mace; dates, none—that's out of my note; nut-megs, seven; a race or two of ginger, but that I may beg; four pounds of prunes, and as many of raisins o' th' sun.

Autolycus.
O that ever I was born!

Groveling on the ground.

Clown.
I' th' name of me—

Autolycus.
O, help me, help me! Pluck but off these rags; and then, death, death!

Clown.
Alack, poor soul, thou hast need of more rags to lay on thee, rather than have these off.

Autolycus.
O sir, the loathsomeness of them offend me more than the stripes I have receiv'd, which are mighty ones and millions.

Clown.
Alas, poor man, a million of beating may come to a great matter.

Autolycus.
I am robb'd, sir, and beaten; my money and apparel ta'en from me, and these detestable things put upon me.

Clown.
What, by a horseman, or a footman?

Autolycus.
A footman, sweet sir, a footman.

Clown.
Indeed, he should be a footman by the garments he has left with thee. If this be a horseman's coat, it hath seen very hot service. Lend me thy hand, I'll help thee. Come, lend me thy hand.

Autolycus.
O good sir, tenderly, O!

Clown.
Alas, poor soul!

Autolycus.
O good sir, softly, good sir! I fear, sir, my shoulder-blade is out.

Clown.
How now? Canst stand?

Autolycus.
Softly, dear sir;

Picking his pocket

good sir, softly. You ha' done me a charitable office.

Clown.
Dost lack any money? I have a little money for thee.

Autolycus.
No, good sweet sir; no, I beseech you, sir. I have a kinsman not past three quarters of a mile hence, unto whom I was going. I shall there have money, or any thing I want, Offer me no money, I pray you, that kills my heart.

Clown.
What manner of fellow was he that robb'd you?

Autolycus.
A fellow, sir, that I have known to go about with troll-my-dames. I knew him once a servant of the Prince. I cannot tell, good sir, for which of his virtues it was, but he was certainly whipt out of the court.

Clown.
His vices, you would say; there's no virtue whipt out of the court. They cherish it to make it stay there; and yet it will no more but abide.

Autolycus.
Vices, I would say, sir. I know this man well; he hath been since an ape-bearer, then a process-server, a bailiff, then he compass'd a motion of the Prodigal Son, and married a tinker's wife within a mile where my land and living lies; and, having flown over many knavish professions, he settled only in rogue. Some call him Autolycus.

Clown.
Out upon him! Prig, for my life, prig! He haunts wakes, fairs, and bear-baitings.

Autolycus.
Very true, sir; he, sir, he. That's the rogue that put me into this apparel.

Clown.
Not a more cowardly rogue in all Bohemia. If you had but look'd big, and spit at him, he'd have run.

Act 4, Scene 4

Autolycus.
I must confess to you, sir, I am no fighter. I am false of heart that way, and that he knew, I warrant him.

Clown.
How do you now?

Autolycus.
Sweet sir, much better than I was: I can stand and walk. I will even take my leave of you, and pace softly towards my kinsman's.

Clown.
Shall I bring thee on the way?

Autolycus.
No, good-fac'd sir, no, sweet sir.

Clown.
Then fare thee well, I must go buy spices for our sheep-shearing.

Exit.

Autolycus.
Prosper you, sweet sir! Your purse is not hot enough to purchase your spice. I'll be with you at your sheep-shearing too. If I make not this cheat bring out another, and the shearers prove sheep, let me be unroll'd, and my name put in the book of virtue!

Song.

Jog on, jog on, the foot-path way,
And merrily hent the stile-a;
A merry heart goes all the day,
Your sad tires in a mile-a.

Exit.

Scene 4

Bohemia. A shepherd's cottage.

(Florizel; Perdita; Clown; Polixenes; Camillo; Mopsa; Dorcas; Servants; Old Shepherd; Servant of the Old Shepherd; Shepherds and Shepherdesses; Autolycus; Satyrs)

Florizel, dressed in rustic clothing, and Perdita, who is dressed up as Queen of the Feast, meet and talk of their love. The modest girl is worried that Polixenes will find out about them, but Florizel reassures her that even if that happened, he would stay with her. The Old Shepherd comes in with Polixenes and Camillo in disguise as an old bearded men, and bids Perdita to stop mooning about with her swain and go about her duties as mistress of the feast. She greets the guests, offering them flowers, and argues with Polixenes over cross-breeding flowers: he approves of the practice, while she thinks that diluting the family line is wrong. As he witnesses his son and Perdita coo over one another, Polixenes is forced to admit that the girl seems much more noble than she ought to be. As the Shepherds and Shepherdesses all dance, Polixenes asks the Old Shepherd about his daughter's suitor; the Shepherd tells him that he is named Doricles and he is hopeful the two shall marry. A servant announces a peddler, who is finally brought in and turns out to be Autolycus in disguise. The Clown, who is beset by two women who both claim he promised to take them to the feast, is in trouble with both because he had all his money stolen and cannot keep his promise to purchase them trinkets. As the Shepherds go off to see Autolycus's wares, some others come in to dance a masque of savages, though the Shepherd fears he may be boring Polixenes and Camillo. After the dance, Polixenes decides that it's time to find out what Florizel's intentions are, and begins to interrogate him. Florizel swears his true affection, and officially asks Perdita to marry him. She agrees, to the Old Shepherd's delight. Polixenes, however, asks Florizel whether he doesn't think that his father ought to know about this. Florizel denies it and Polixenes reveals himself, to the shock of the guests and of the Old Shepherd. Threatening Florizel with disinheritance if he ever goes near Perdita again, the King swears to Perdita that he will have her tortured to death if she tries to get the Prince back. After he leaves, Perdita reflects that she almost told the King that they are both human beings, but held back. She urges Florizel to go, reminding him that she predicted this would happen for a long time. The Shepherd, realizing that Perdita knew very well who "Doricles" was, castigates them both for having brought such shame on him. Florizel resolves to flee with Perdita. Camillo, seeing an opportunity, suggests that they go to Sicilia and appear before Leontes as ambassadors from Polixenes. He promises to give them all the help they need. Autolycus re-enters, chuckling over how while selling his trinkets he could see who had the most money and proceeded to pick their pockets. Camillo bribes him to exchange clothes with Florizel, and he is more than willing. The lovers leave for their ship, while Camillo goes off to tell Polixenes, knowing that the King will chase after his son and bring Camillo along, and therefore Camillo will at last be able to see Sicilia again. Autolycus sees what is going on. The Old Shepherd and his enter on their way to tell the King how they found Perdita on the seashore, and that she is not therefore really a member of their family. They are carrying all the things they found with *her. Autolycus, now dressed up as a rich man, pretends to be a nobleman and offers to be their advocate at the court, spinning tales of how Polixenes has threatened to have them tortured. They offer a good deal of money for his service, and he accepts it, and his actual intention is to get in well with his former master Florizel by bringing the Shepherd and the Clown to him.*

Enter Florizel, Perdita.

Florizel.
These your unusual weeds to each part of you
Does give a life; no shepherdess, but Flora
Peering in April's front. This your sheep-shearing
Is as a meeting of the petty gods,
And you the queen on't.

Perdita.
                    Sir, my gracious lord,
To chide at your extremes it not becomes me.
O, pardon, that I name them! Your high self,
The gracious mark o' th' land, you have obscur'd
With a swain's wearing, and me, poor lowly maid,
Most goddess-like prank'd up. But that our feasts
In every mess have folly, and the feeders
Digest 't with a custom, I should blush
To see you so attir'd—swoon, I think,
To show myself a glass.

Florizel.
                    I bless the time
When my good falcon made her flight across
Thy father's ground.

Perdita.
                    Now Jove afford you cause!
To me the difference forges dread; your greatness
Hath not been us'd to fear. Even now I tremble
To think your father, by some accident,
Should pass this way as you did. O, the Fates!
How would he look to see his work, so noble,
Vildly bound up? What would he say? Or how
Should I, in these my borrowed flaunts, behold
The sternness of his presence?

Florizel.
                    Apprehend
Nothing but jollity. The gods themselves
(Humbling their deities to love) have taken
The shapes of beasts upon them. Jupiter
Became a bull and bellow'd; the green Neptune
A ram and bleated; and the fire-rob'd god,
Golden Apollo, a poor humble swain,
As I seem now. Their transformations
Were never for a piece of beauty rarer,
Nor in a way so chaste, since my desires
Run not before mine honor, nor my lusts
Burn hotter than my faith.

Perdita.
                    O but, sir,
Your resolution cannot hold when 'tis
Oppos'd (as it must be) by th' pow'r of the King.
One of these two must be necessities,
Which then will speak, that you must change this purpose,
Or I my life.

Florizel.
                    Thou dear'st Perdita,
With these forc'd thoughts I prithee darken not
The mirth o' th' feast. Or I'll be thine, my fair,
Or not my father's; for I cannot be
Mine own, nor any thing to any, if
I be not thine. To this I am most constant,
Though destiny say no. Be merry, gentle!
Strangle such thoughts as these with any thing
That you behold the while. Your guests are coming:
Lift up your countenance, as it were the day
Of celebration of that nuptial, which
We two have sworn shall come.

Perdita.
                    O Lady Fortune,
Stand you auspicious!

Florizel.
                    See, your guests approach,
Address yourself to entertain them sprightly,
And let's be red with mirth.

Enter Shepherd, Clown, Polixenes and Camillo disguised, Mopsa, Dorcas, Servants.

Old Shepherd.
Fie, daughter, when my old wife liv'd, upon
This day she was both pantler, butler, cook,
Both dame and servant; welcom'd all, serv'd all;
Would sing her song, and dance her turn; now here,
At upper end o' th' table, now i' th' middle;
On his shoulder, and his; her face o' fire
With labor, and the thing she took to quench it
She would to each one sip. You are retired,
As if you were a feasted one and not

The hostess of the meeting. Pray you bid
These unknown friends to 's welcome, for it is
A way to make us better friends, more known.
Come, quench your blushes, and present yourself
That which you are, mistress o' th' feast. Come on,
And bid us welcome to your sheep-shearing,
As your good flock shall prosper.

Perdita.

To Polixenes.

      Sir, welcome.
It is my father's will I should take on me
The hostess-ship o' th' day.

To Camillo.

       You're welcome, sir.
Give me those flow'rs there, Dorcas. Reverend sirs,
For you there's rosemary and rue; these keep
Seeming and savor all the winter long.
Grace and remembrance be to you both,
And welcome to our shearing!

Polixenes, King of Bohemia.
       Shepherdess
(A fair one are you!), well you fit our ages
With flow'rs of winter.

Perdita.
     Sir, the year growing ancient,
Not yet on summer's death, nor on the birth
Of trembling winter, the fairest flow'rs o' th' season
Are our carnations and streak'd gillyvors
(Which some call Nature's bastards). Of that kind
Our rustic garden's barren, and I care not
To get slips of them.

Polixenes, King of Bohemia.
      Wherefore, gentle maiden,
Do you neglect them?

Perdita.
      For I have heard it said,
There is an art which in their piedness shares
With great creating Nature.

Polixenes, King of Bohemia.
       Say there be;
Yet Nature is made better by no mean
But Nature makes that mean; so over that art
Which you say adds to Nature, is an art
That Nature makes. You see, sweet maid, we marry
A gentler scion to the wildest stock,
And make conceive a bark of baser kind
By bud of nobler race. This is an art
Which does mend Nature—change it rather; but
The art itself is Nature.

Perdita.
    So it is.

Polixenes, King of Bohemia.
Then make your garden rich in gillyvors,
And do not call them bastards.

Perdita.
     I'll not put
The dibble in earth to set one slip of them;
No more than were I painted I would wish
This youth should say 'twere well, and only therefore
Desire to breed by me. Here's flow'rs for you:
Hot lavender, mints, savory, marjoram,
The marigold, that goes to bed wi' th' sun,
And with him rises weeping. These are flow'rs
Of middle summer, and I think they are given
To men of middle age. Y' are very welcome.

Camillo.
I should leave grazing, were I of your flock,
And only live by gazing.

Perdita.
    Out, alas!
You'ld be so lean, that blasts of January
Would blow you through and through. Now, my fair'st friend,
I would I had some flow'rs o' th' spring that might
Become your time of day—and yours, and yours,
That wear upon your virgin branches yet
Your maidenheads growing. O Proserpina,
For the flow'rs now, that, frighted, thou let'st fall
From Dis's wagon! Daffodils,
That come before the swallow dares, and take
The winds of March with beauty; violets, dim,
But sweeter than the lids of Juno's eyes,
Or Cytherea's breath; pale primeroses,
That die unmarried, ere they can behold
Bright Phoebus in his strength (a malady
Most incident to maids); bold oxlips, and
The crown imperial; lilies of all kinds
(The flow'r-de-luce being one). O, these I lack,
To make you garlands of, and my sweet friend,
To strew him o'er and o'er!

Florizel.
                What? Like a corse?

Perdita.
No, like a bank, for love to lie and play on;
Not like a corse; or if—not to be buried,
But quick and in mine arms. Come, take your flow'rs.
Methinks I play as I have seen them do
In Whitsun pastorals. Sure this robe of mine
Does change my disposition.

Florizel.
                    What you do
Still betters what is done. When you speak, sweet,
I'ld have you do it ever; when you sing,
I'ld have you buy and sell so; so give alms;
Pray so; and for the ord'ring your affairs,
To sing them too. When you do dance, I wish you
A wave o' th' sea, that you might ever do
Nothing but that; move still, still so,
And own no other function. Each your doing
(So singular in each particular)
Crowns what you are doing in the present deeds,
That all your acts are queens.

Perdita.
                O Doricles,
Your praises are too large. But that your youth,
And the true blood which peeps fairly through't,
Do plainly give you out an unstain'd shepherd,
With wisdom I might fear, my Doricles,
You woo'd me the false way.

Florizel.
                I think you have
As little skill to fear as I have purpose
To put you to't. But come, our dance, I pray.
Your hand, my Perdita. So turtles pair
That never mean to part.

Perdita.
                I'll swear for 'em.

Polixenes, King of Bohemia.
This is the prettiest low-born lass that ever
Ran on the green-sord. Nothing she does, or seems,
But smacks of something greater than herself,
Too noble for this place.

Camillo.
                He tells her something
That makes her blood look on't. Good sooth, she is
The queen of curds and cream.

Clown.
                Come on. Strike up.

Dorcas.
Mopsa must be your mistress; marry, garlic,
To mend her kissing with!

Mopsa.
                Now in good time!

Clown.
Not a word, a word, we stand upon our manners.
Come, strike up.

Music.
Here a dance of Shepherds and Shepherdesses.

Polixenes, King of Bohemia.
Pray, good shepherd, what fair swain is this
Which dances with your daughter?

Old Shepherd.
They call him Doricles, and boasts himself
To have a worthy feeding; but I have it
Upon his own report, and I believe it.
He looks like sooth. He says he loves my daughter.
I think so too; for never gaz'd the moon
Upon the water as he'll stand and read
As 'twere my daughter's eyes; and to be plain,
I think there is not half a kiss to choose
Who loves another best.

Polixenes, King of Bohemia.
                She dances featly.

Old Shepherd.
So she does any thing, though I report it
That should be silent. If young Doricles
Do light upon her, she shall bring him that
Which he not dreams of.

Enter Servant of the Old Shepherd.

Servant of the Old Shepherd.
O master! If you did but hear the pedlar at the door, you would never dance again after a tabor and pipe; no, the bagpipe could not move you. He sings several tunes faster than you'll tell money; he utters them as he had eaten ballads and all men's ears grew to his tunes.

Clown.
He could never come better; he shall come in. I love a ballad but even too well, if it be doleful matter merrily set down, or a very pleasant thing indeed and sung lamentably.

Servant of the Old Shepherd.
He hath songs for man or woman, of all sizes; no milliner can so fit his customers with gloves. He has the prettiest love-songs for maids, so without bawdry, which is strange; with such delicate burdens of dildos and fadings, "jump her and thump her"; and where some stretch-mouth'd rascal would (as it were) mean mischief, and break a foul gap into the matter, he makes the maid to answer, "Whoop, do me no harm, good man"—puts him off, slights him, with "Whoop, do me no harm, good man."

Polixenes, King of Bohemia.
This is a brave fellow.

Clown.
Believe me, thou talkest of an admirable conceited fellow. Has he any unbraided wares?

Servant of the Old Shepherd.
He hath ribbons of all the colors i' th' rainbow; points more than all the lawyers in Bohemia can learnedly handle, though they come to him by th' gross; inkles, caddises, cambrics, lawns. Why, he sings 'em over as they were gods or goddesses: you would think a smock were a she-angel, he so chants to the sleeve-hand and the work about the square on't.

Clown.
Prithee bring him in, and let him approach singing.

Perdita.
Forewarn him that he use no scurrilous words in 's tunes.

Exit Servant of the Old Shepherd.

Clown.
You have of these pedlars, that have more in them than you'ld think, sister.

Perdita.
Ay, good brother, or go about to think.

Enter Autolycus singing.

Autolycus.
Lawn as white as driven snow,
Cypress black as e'er was crow,
Gloves as sweet as damask roses,
Masks for faces and for noses;
Bugle-bracelet, necklace amber,
Perfume for a lady's chamber;
Golden quoifs and stomachers
For my lads to give their dears;
Pins and poking-sticks of steel;
What maids lack from head to heel:
Come buy of me, come; come buy, come buy,
Buy, lads, or else your lasses cry:
Come buy.

Clown.
If I were not in love with Mopsa, thou shouldst take no money of me, but being enthrall'd as I am, it will also be the bondage of certain ribbons and gloves.

Mopsa.
I was promis'd them against the feast, but they come not too late now.

Dorcas.
He hath promis'd you more than that, or there be liars.

Mopsa.
He hath paid you all he promis'd you. May be he has paid you more, which will shame you to give him again.

Clown.
Is there no manners left among maids? Will they wear their plackets where they should bear their faces? Is there not milking-time? When you are going to bed? Or kiln-hole? To whistle off these secrets, but you must be tittle-tattling before all our guests? 'Tis well they are whisp'ring. Clamor your tongues, and not a word more.

Mopsa.
I have done. Come, you promis'd me a tawdry-lace and a pair of sweet gloves.

Clown.
Have I not told thee how I was cozen'd by the way, and lost all my money?

Autolycus.
And indeed, sir, there are cozeners abroad, therefore it behooves men to be wary.

Clown.
Fear not thou, man, thou shalt lose nothing here.

Autolycus.
I hope so, sir, for I have about me many parcels of charge.

Clown.
What hast here? Ballads?

Mopsa.
Pray now buy some. I love a ballet in print, a-life, for then we are sure they are true.

Autolycus.
Here's one to a very doleful tune, how a usurer's wife was brought to bed of twenty money-bags at a burden, and how she long'd to eat adders' heads, and toads carbonado'd.

Mopsa.
Is it true, think you?

Autolycus.
Very true, and but a month old.

Dorcas.
Bless me from marrying a usurer!

Autolycus.
Here's the midwife's name to't, one Mistress Tale-porter, and five or six honest wives that were present. Why should I carry lies abroad?

Mopsa.
Pray you now buy it.

Clown.
Come on, lay it by; and let's first see more ballads. We'll buy the other things anon.

Autolycus.
Here's another ballad, of a fish that appear'd upon the coast on We'n'sday the fourscore of April, forty thousand fathom above water, and sung this ballad against the hard hearts of maids. It was thought she was a woman, and was turn'd into a cold fish for she would not exchange flesh with one that lov'd her. The ballad is very pitiful, and as true.

Dorcas.
Is it true too, think you?

Autolycus.
Five justices' hands at it, and witnesses more than my pack will hold.

Clown.
Lay it by too. Another.

Autolycus.
This is a merry ballad, but a very pretty one.

Mopsa.
Let's have some merry ones.

Autolycus.
Why, this is a passing merry one and goes to the tune of "Two maids wooing a man." There's scarce a maid westward but she sings it. 'Tis in request, I can tell you.

Mopsa.
We can both sing it. If thou'lt bear a part, thou shalt hear; 'tis in three parts.

Dorcas.
We had the tune on't a month ago.

Autolycus.
I can bear my part, you must know 'tis my occupation. Have at it with you.

Song.

Autolycus.
Get you hence, for I must go
Where it fits not you to know.

Dorcas.
Whither?

Mopsa.
O, whither?

Dorcas.
Whither?

Mopsa.
It becomes thy oath full well,
Thou to me thy secrets tell.

Dorcas.
Me too; let me go thither.

Mopsa.
Or thou goest to th' grange, or mill.

Dorcas.
If to either, thou dost ill.

Autolycus.
Neither.

Dorcas.
What, neither?

Autolycus.
Neither.

Dorcas.
Thou hast sworn my love to be.

Mopsa.
Thou hast sworn it more to me:
Then whither goest? Say, whither?

Clown.
We'll have this song out anon by ourselves. My father and the gentlemen are in sad talk, and we'll not trouble them. Come bring away thy pack after me. Wenches, I'll buy for you both. Pedlar, let's have the first choice. Follow me, girls.

Exit with Dorcas and Mopsa.

Autolycus.
And you shall pay well for 'em.

Song.

Will you buy any tape,
Or lace for your cape,
My dainty duck, my dear-a?
Any silk, any thread,
Any toys for your head
Of the new'st and fin'st, fin'st wear-a?
Come to the pedlar,
Money's a meddler,
That doth utter all men's ware-a.

Exit.
Enter First Servant.

First Servant.
Master, there is three carters, three shepherds, three neat-herds, three swine-herds, that have made themselves all men of hair. They call themselves Saltiers, and they have a dance which the wenches say is a gallimaufry of gambols, because they are not in't; but they themselves are o' th' mind (if it be not too rough for some that know little but bowling) it will please plentifully.

Old Shepherd.
Away! We'll none on't. Here has been too much homely foolery already. I know, sir, we weary you.

Polixenes, King of Bohemia.
You weary those that refresh us. Pray let's see these four threes of herdsmen.

First Servant.
One three of them, by their own report, sir, hath danc'd before the King; and not the worst of the three but jumps twelve foot and a half by th' square.

Old Shepherd.
Leave your prating. Since these good men are pleas'd, let them come in; but quickly now.

First Servant.
Why, they stay at door, sir.

Exit.
Here a dance of twelve Satyrs.

Polixenes, King of Bohemia.
O, father, you'll know more of that hereafter.

To Camillo.

Is it not too far gone? 'Tis time to part them.
He's simple, and tells much.

To Florizel.

              How now, fair shepherd?
Your heart is full of something that does take
Your mind from feasting. Sooth, when I was young,
And handed love as you do, I was wont
To load my she with knacks. I would have ransack'd
The pedlar's silken treasury, and have pour'd it
To her acceptance; you have let him go,
And nothing marted with him. If your lass
Interpretation should abuse, and call this
Your lack of love or bounty, you were straited
For a reply, at least if you make a care
Of happy holding her.

Florizel.

              Old sir, I know
She prizes not such trifles as these are.
The gifts she looks from me are pack'd and lock'd
Up in my heart, which I have given already,

But not deliver'd. O, hear me breathe my life
Before this ancient sir, whom, it should seem,
Hath sometime lov'd! I take thy hand, this hand,
As soft as dove's down and as white as it,
Or Ethiopian's tooth, or the fann'd snow that's bolted
By th' northern blasts twice o'er.

Polixenes, King of Bohemia.
                          What follows this?
How prettily th' young swain seems to wash
The hand was fair before! I have put you out.
But to your protestation; let me hear
What you profess.

Florizel.
                Do, and be witness to't.

Polixenes, King of Bohemia.
And this my neighbor too?

Florizel.
                          And he, and more
Than he, and men—the earth, the heavens, and all:
That were I crown'd the most imperial monarch,
Thereof most worthy, were I the fairest youth
That ever made eye swerve, had force and knowledge
More than was ever man's, I would not prize them
Without her love; for her, employ them all,
Commend them and condemn them to her service,
Or to their own perdition.

Polixenes, King of Bohemia.
                        Fairly offer'd.

Camillo.
This shows a sound affection.

Old Shepherd.
                    But, my daughter,
Say you the like to him?

Perdita.
                    I cannot speak
So well, nothing so well; no, nor mean better.
By th' pattern of mine own thoughts I cut out
The purity of his.

Old Shepherd.
                  Take hands, a bargain!
And, friends unknown, you shall bear witness to't:
I give my daughter to him, and will make
Her portion equal his.

Florizel.
              O, that must be
I' th' virtue of your daughter. One being dead,
I shall have more than you can dream of yet,
Enough then for your wonder. But come on,
Contract us 'fore these witnesses.

Old Shepherd.
                Come, your hand;
And, daughter, yours.

Polixenes, King of Bohemia.
            Soft, swain, awhile, beseech you.
Have you a father?

Florizel.
            I have; but what of him?

Polixenes, King of Bohemia.
Knows he of this?

Florizel.
            He neither does, nor shall.

Polixenes, King of Bohemia.
Methinks a father
Is at the nuptial of his son a guest
That best becomes the table. Pray you once more,
Is not your father grown incapable
Of reasonable affairs? Is he not stupid
With age and alt'ring rheums? Can he speak? Hear?
Know man from man? Dispute his own estate?
Lies he not bed-rid? And again does nothing
But what he did being childish?

Florizel.
            No, good sir;
He has his health, and ampler strength indeed
Than most have of his age.

Polixenes, King of Bohemia.
              By my white beard,
You offer him, if this be so, a wrong
Something unfilial. Reason my son
Should choose himself a wife, but as good reason
The father (all whose joy is nothing else
But fair posterity) should hold some counsel
In such a business.

Florizel.
            I yield all this;
But for some other reasons, my grave sir,
Which 'tis not fit you know, I not acquaint
My father of this business.

Polixenes, King of Bohemia.
                      Let him know't.

Florizel.
He shall not.

Polixenes, King of Bohemia.
                      Prithee let him.

Florizel.
                      No, he must not.

Old Shepherd.
Let him, my son. He shall not need to grieve
At knowing of thy choice.

Florizel.
                      Come, come, he must not.
Mark our contract.

Polixenes, King of Bohemia.
                      Mark your divorce, young sir,

Discovering himself.

Whom son I dare not call. Thou art too base
To be acknowledg'd. Thou, a sceptre's heir,
That thus affects a sheep-hook! Thou, old traitor,
I am sorry that by hanging thee I can
But shorten thy life one week. And thou, fresh piece
Of excellent witchcraft, whom of force must know
The royal fool thou cop'st with—

Old Shepherd.
                      O, my heart!

Polixenes, King of Bohemia.
I'll have thy beauty scratch'd with briers and made
More homely than thy state. For thee, fond boy,
If I may ever know thou dost but sigh
That thou no more shalt see this knack (as never
I mean thou shalt), we'll bar thee from succession,
Not hold thee of our blood, no, not our kin,
Farre than Deucalion off. Mark thou my words.
Follow us to the court. Thou, churl, for this time,
Though full of our displeasure, yet we free thee
From the dead blow of it. And you, enchantment—
Worthy enough a herdsman, yea, him too,
That makes himself (but for our honor therein)
Unworthy thee—if ever, henceforth, thou
These rural latches to his entrance open,
Or hoop his body more with thy embraces,
I will devise a death as cruel for thee
As thou art tender to't.

Exit.

Perdita.
                      Even here undone!
I was not much afeard; for once or twice
I was about to speak, and tell him plainly
The self-same sun that shines upon his court
Hides not his visage from our cottage, but
Looks on alike. Will't please you, sir, be gone?
I told you what would come of this. Beseech you
Of your own state take care. This dream of mine
Being now awake, I'll queen it no inch farther,
But milk my ewes, and weep.

Camillo.
                      Why, how now, father?
Speak ere thou diest.

Old Shepherd.
                      I cannot speak, nor think,
Nor dare to know that which I know.

To Florizel.

                      O sir,
You have undone a man of fourscore three,
That thought to fill his grave in quiet; yea,
To die upon the bed my father died,
To lie close by his honest bones; but now
Some hangman must put on my shroud and lay me
Where no priest shovels in dust.

To Perdita.

                      O cursed wretch,
That knew'st this was the Prince, and wouldst adventure
To mingle faith with him!—Undone, undone!
If I might die within this hour, I have liv'd
To die when I desire.

Exit.

Florizel.
                      Why look you so upon me?
I am but sorry, not afeard; delay'd,
But nothing alt'red. What I was, I am:
More straining on for plucking back, not following
My leash unwillingly.

Camillo.
      Gracious my lord,
You know your father's temper. At this time
He will allow no speech (which I do guess
You do not purpose to him) and as hardly
Will he endure your sight as yet, I fear.
Then till the fury of his Highness settle
Come not before him.

Florizel.
       I not purpose it.
I think Camillo?

Camillo.
      Even he, my lord.

Perdita.
How often have I told you 'twould be thus!
How often said my dignity would last
But till 'twere known!

Florizel.
      It cannot fail, but by
The violation of my faith, and then
Let nature crush the sides o' th' earth together,
And mar the seeds within! Lift up thy looks.
From my succession wipe me, father, I
Am heir to my affection.

Camillo.
     Be advis'd.

Florizel.
I am—and by my fancy. If my reason
Will thereto be obedient, I have reason;
If not, my senses, better pleas'd with madness,
Do bid it welcome.

Camillo.
     This is desperate, sir.

Florizel.
So call it; but it does fulfill my vow;
I needs must think it honesty. Camillo,
Not for Bohemia, nor the pomp that may
Be thereat gleaned, for all the sun sees, or
The close earth wombs, or the profound seas hides
In unknown fathoms, will I break my oath
To this my fair belov'd. Therefore, I pray you,
As you have ever been my father's honor'd friend,
When he shall miss me (as, in faith, I mean not
To see him any more), cast your good counsels
Upon his passion. Let myself and Fortune
Tug for the time to come. This you may know,
And so deliver: I am put to sea
With her who here I cannot hold on shore;
And most opportune to her need I have
A vessel rides fast by, but not prepar'd
For this design. What course I mean to hold
Shall nothing benefit your knowledge, nor
Concern me the reporting.

Camillo.
      O my lord,
I would your spirit were easier for advice,
Or stronger for your need.

Florizel.
Hark, Perdita!

Drawing her aside.
To Camillo.

I'll hear you by and by.

Camillo.
      He's irremovable,
Resolv'd for flight. Now were I happy if
His going I could frame to serve my turn,
Save him from danger, do him love and honor,
Purchase the sight again of dear Sicilia
And that unhappy king, my master, whom
I so much thirst to see.

Florizel.
      Now, good Camillo,
I am so fraught with curious business that
I leave out ceremony.

Camillo.
      Sir, I think
You have heard of my poor services, i' th' love
That I have borne your father?

Florizel.
      Very nobly
Have you deserv'd. It is my father's music
To speak your deeds; not little of his care
To have them recompens'd as thought on.

Camillo.
     Well, my lord,
If you may please to think I love the King,
And through him what's nearest to him, which is
Your gracious self, embrace but my direction,
If your more ponderous and settled project
May suffer alteration. On mine honor,

I'll point you where you shall have such receiving
As shall become your Highness, where you may
Enjoy your mistress—from the whom, I see,
There's no disjunction to be made, but by
(As heavens forefend!) your ruin—marry her,
And with my best endeavors in your absence,
Your discontenting father strive to qualify,
And bring him up to liking.

Florizel.
      How, Camillo,
May this (almost a miracle) be done?
That I may call thee something more than man,
And after that trust to thee.

Camillo.
      Have you thought on
A place whereto you'll go?

Florizel.
      Not any yet:
But as th' unthought-on accident is guilty
To what we wildly do, so we profess
Ourselves to be the slaves of chance, and flies
Of every wind that blows.

Camillo.
      Then list to me.
This follows, if you will not change your purpose
But undergo this flight: make for Sicilia,
And there present yourself and your fair princess
(For so I see she must be) 'fore Leontes.
She shall be habited as it becomes
The partner of your bed. Methinks I see
Leontes opening his free arms, and weeping
His welcomes forth; asks thee there, son, forgiveness,
As 'twere i' th' father's person; kisses the hands
Of your fresh princess; o'er and o'er divides him
'Twixt his unkindness and his kindness: th' one
He chides to hell, and bids the other grow
Faster than thought or time.

Florizel.
      Worthy Camillo,
What color for my visitation shall I
Hold up before him?

Camillo.
      Sent by the King your father
To greet him and to give him comforts. Sir,
The manner of your bearing towards him, with
What you (as from your father) shall deliver,
Things known betwixt us three, I'll write you down,
The which shall point you forth at every sitting
What you must say; that he shall not perceive
But that you have your father's bosom there,
And speak his very heart.

Florizel.
      I am bound to you.
There is some sap in this.

Camillo.
      A course more promising
Than a wild dedication of yourselves
To unpath'd waters, undream'd shores, most certain
To miseries enough; no hope to help you,
But as you shake off one, to take another;
Nothing so certain as your anchors, who
Do their best office, if they can but stay you
Where you'll be loath to be. Besides you know,
Prosperity's the very bond of love,
Whose fresh complexion and whose heart together
Affliction alters.

Perdita.
      One of these is true:
I think affliction may subdue the check,
But not take in the mind.

Camillo.
      Yea? Say you so?
There shall not at your father's house these seven years
Be born another such.

Florizel.
      My good Camillo,
She's as forward of her breeding as
She is i' th' rear 'our birth.

Camillo.
      I cannot say 'tis pity
She lacks instructions, for she seems a mistress
To most that teach.

Perdita.
      Your pardon, sir; for this
I'll blush you thanks.

Florizel.
      My prettiest Perdita!
But O, the thorns we stand upon! Camillo,
Preserver of my father, now of me,
The medicine of our house, how shall we do?
We are not furnish'd like Bohemia's son,

Nor shall appear in Sicilia.

Camillo.
               My lord,
Fear none of this. I think you know my fortunes
Do all lie there. It shall be so my care
To have you royally appointed, as if
The scene you play were mine. For instance, sir,
That you may know you shall not want—one word.

They talk aside.
Enter Autolycus laughing.

Autolycus.
Ha, ha, what a fool Honesty is! And Trust, his sworn brother, a very simple gentleman! I have sold all my trompery; not a counterfeit stone, not a ribbon, glass, pomander, brooch, table-book, ballad, knife, tape, glove, shoe-tie, bracelet, horn-ring, to keep my pack from fasting. They throng who should buy first, as if my trinkets had been hallow'd and brought a benediction to the buyer; by which means I saw whose purse was best in picture, and what I saw, to my good use I rememb'red. My clown (who wants but something to be a reasonable man) grew so in love with the wenches' song, that he would not stir his pettitoes till he had both tune and words, which so drew the rest of the herd to me that all their other senses stuck in ears. You might have pinch'd a placket, it was senseless; 'twas nothing to geld a codpiece of a purse; I would have fil'd keys off that hung in chains. No hearing, no feeling, but my sir's song, and admiring the nothing of it. So that in this time of lethargy I pick'd and cut most of their festival purses; and had not the old man come in with a whoobub against his daughter and the King's son, and scar'd my choughs from the chaff, I had not left a purse alive in the whole army.

Camillo, Florizel, and Perdita come forward.

Camillo.
Nay, but my letters, by this means being there
So soon as you arrive, shall clear that doubt.

Florizel.
And those that you'll procure from King Leontes?

Camillo.
Shall satisfy your father.

Perdita.
               Happy be you!
All that you speak shows fair.

Camillo.
Who have we here?

Seeing Autolycus.
               We'll make an instrument of this; omit
Nothing may give us aid.

Autolycus.

Aside.

If they have overheard me now—why, hanging.

Camillo.
How now, good fellow? Why shak'st thou so?
Fear not, man, here's no harm intended to thee.

Autolycus.
I am a poor fellow, sir.

Camillo.
Why, be so still; here's nobody will steal that from thee. Yet for the outside of thy poverty we must make an exchange; therefore discase thee instantly (thou must think there's a necessity in't) and change garments with this gentleman. Though the pennyworth on his side be the worst, yet hold thee, there's some boot.

Giving money.

Autolycus.
I am a poor fellow, sir.

Aside.

I know ye well enough.

Camillo.
Nay, prithee dispatch. The gentleman is half flayed already.

Autolycus.
Are you in earnest, sir?

Aside.

I smell the trick on't.

Florizel.
Dispatch, I prithee.

Autolycus.
Indeed I have had earnest, but I cannot with conscience take it.

Camillo.
Unbuckle, unbuckle.

Florizel and Autolycus exchange garments.

Fortunate mistress (let my prophecy
Come home to ye!), you must retire yourself
Into some covert. Take your sweetheart's hat
And pluck it o'er your brows, muffle your face,
Dismantle you, and (as you can) disliken
The truth of your own seeming, that you may
(For I do fear eyes over) to shipboard
Get undescried.

Perdita.
                    I see the play so lies
That I must bear a part.

Camillo.
                    No remedy.
Have you done there?

Florizel.
                    Should I now meet my father,
He would not call me son.

Camillo.
                    Nay, you shall have no hat.

Giving it to Perdita.

Come, lady, come. Farewell, my friend.

Autolycus.
                    Adieu, sir.

Florizel.
O Perdita! What have we twain forgot?
Pray you a word.

Camillo.

Aside.

What I do next shall be to tell the King
Of this escape, and whither they are bound;
Wherein my hope is I shall so prevail
To force him after; in whose company
I shall re-view Sicilia, for whose sight
I have a woman's longing.

Florizel.
                    Fortune speed us!
Thus we set on, Camillo, to th' sea-side.

Camillo.
The swifter speed the better.

Exit with Florizel and Perdita.

Autolycus.
I understand the business, I hear it. To have an open ear, a quick eye, and a nimble hand, is necessary for a cutpurse; a good nose is requisite also, to smell out work for th' other senses. I see this is the time that the unjust man doth thrive. What an exchange had this been, without boot! What a boot is here, with this exchange! Sure the gods do this year connive at us, and we may do any thing extempore. The Prince himself is about a piece of iniquity: stealing away from his father with his clog at his heels. If I thought it were a piece of honesty to acquaint the King withal, I would not do't. I hold it the more knavery to conceal it; and therein am I constant to my profession.

Enter Clown and Shepherd.

Aside, aside, here is more matter for a hot brain. Every lane's end, every shop, church, session, hanging, yields a careful man work.

Clown.
See, see; what a man you are now! There is no other way but to tell the King she's a changeling, and none of your flesh and blood.

Old Shepherd.
Nay, but hear me.

Clown.
Nay—but hear me.

Old Shepherd.
Go to then.

Clown.
She being none of your flesh and blood, your flesh and blood has not offended the King, and so your flesh and blood is not to be punish'd by him. Show those things you found about her, those secret things, all but what she has with her. This being done, let the law go whistle; I warrant you.

Old Shepherd.
I will tell the King all, every word, yea, and his son's pranks too; who, I may say, is no honest man, neither to his father nor to me, to go about to make me the King's brother-in-law.

Clown.
Indeed brother-in-law was the farthest off you could have been to him, and then your blood had been the dearer by I know how much an ounce.

Autolycus.

Aside.

Very wisely, puppies!

Old Shepherd.
Well; let us to the King. There is that in this fardel will make him scratch his beard.

Autolycus.

Aside.

I know not what impediment this complaint may be to the flight of my master.

Clown.
Pray heartily he be at' palace.

Autolycus.

Aside.

Though I am not naturally honest, I am so sometimes by chance. Let me pocket up my pedlar's excrement.

Takes off his false beard.

How now, rustics, whither are you bound?

Old Shepherd.
To th' palace, and it like your worship.

Autolycus.
Your affairs there? What? With whom? The condition of that fardel? The place of your dwelling? Your names? Your ages? Of what having? Breeding? And any thing that is fitting to be known—discover.

Clown.
We are but plain fellows, sir.

Autolycus.
A lie; you are rough and hairy. Let me have no lying. It becomes none but tradesmen, and they often give us soldiers the lie, but we pay them for it with stamped coin, not stabbing steel, therefore they do not give us the lie.

Clown.
Your worship had like to have given us one, if you had not taken yourself with the manner.

Old Shepherd.
Are you a courtier, and't like you, sir?

Autolycus.
Whether it like me or no, I am a courtier. Seest thou not the air of the court in these enfoldings? Hath not my gait in it the measure of the court? Receives not thy nose court-odor from me? Reflect I not on thy baseness court-contempt? Think'st thou, for that I insinuate, that toze from thee thy business, I am therefore no courtier? I am courtier cap-a-pe, and one that will either push on or pluck back thy business there; whereupon I command thee to open thy affair.

Old Shepherd.
My business, sir, is to the King.

Autolycus.
What advocate hast thou to him?

Old Shepherd.
I know not, and't like you.

Clown.
Advocate's the court-word for a pheasant. Say you have none.

Old Shepherd.
None, sir; I have no pheasant cock, nor hen.

Autolycus.
How blessed are we that are not simple men!
Yet nature might have made me as these are,
Therefore I will not disdain.

Clown.
This cannot be but a great courtier.

Old Shepherd.
His garments are rich, but he wears them not handsomely.

Clown.
He seems to be the more noble in being fantastical. A great man, I'll warrant; I know by the picking on 's teeth.

Autolycus.
The fardel there? What's i' th' fardel? Wherefore that box?

Old Shepherd.
Sir, there lies such secrets in this fardel and box, which none must know but the King, and which he shall know within this hour, if I may come to th' speech of him.

Autolycus.
Age, thou hast lost thy labor.

Old Shepherd.
Why, sir?

Autolycus.
The King is not at the palace. He is gone aboard a new ship to purge melancholy and air himself; for if thou be'st capable of things serious, thou must know the King is full of grief.

Old Shepherd.
So 'tis said, sir—about his son, that should have married a shepherd's daughter.

Autolycus.
If that shepherd be not in hand-fast, let him fly. The curses he shall have, the tortures he shall feel, will break the back of man, the heart of monster.

Clown.
Think you so, sir?

Autolycus.
Not he alone shall suffer what wit can make heavy and vengeance bitter; but those that are germane to him (though remov'd fifty times) shall all come under the hangman; which though it be great pity, yet it is necessary. An old sheep-whistling rogue, a ram-tender, to offer to have his daughter come into grace! Some say he shall be ston'd; but that death is too soft for him, say I. Draw our throne into a sheep-cote!—all deaths are too few, the sharpest too easy.

Clown.
Has the old man e'er a son, sir, do you hear, and't like you, sir?

Autolycus.
He has a son, who shall be flay'd alive; then 'nointed over with honey, set on the head of a wasp's nest; then stand till he be three quarters and a dram dead; then recover'd again with aqua-vitae or some other hot infusion; then, raw as he is (and in the hottest day prognostication proclaims), shall he be set against a brick-wall, the sun looking with a southward eye upon him, where he is to behold him with flies blown to death. But what talk we of these traitorly rascals, whose miseries are to be smil'd at, their offenses being so capital? Tell me (for you seem to be honest plain men) what you have to the King. Being something gently consider'd, I'll bring you where he is aboard, tender your persons to his presence, whisper him in your behalfs; and if it be in man besides the King to effect your suits, here is man shall do it.

Clown.
He seems to be of great authority. Close with him, give him gold; and though authority be a stubborn bear, yet he is oft led by the nose with gold. Show the inside of your purse to the outside of his hand, and no more ado. Remember "ston'd," and "flay'd alive."

Old Shepherd.
And't please you, sir, to undertake the business for us, here is that gold I have. I'll make it as much more, and leave this young man in pawn till I bring it you.

Autolycus.
After I have done what I promis'd?

Old Shepherd.
Ay, sir.

Autolycus.
Well, give me the moi'ty. Are you a party in this business?

Clown.
In some sort, sir; but though my case be a pitiful one, I hope I shall not be flay'd out of it.

Autolycus.
O, that's the case of the shepherd's son. Hang him, he'll be made an example.

Clown.
Comfort, good comfort! We must to the King, and show our strange sights. He must know 'tis none of your daughter, nor my sister; we are gone else. Sir, I will give you as much as this old man does when the

business is perform'd, and remain (as he says) your pawn till it be brought you.

Autolycus.
I will trust you. Walk before toward the sea-side, go on the right hand, I will but look upon the hedge, and follow you.

Clown.
We are bless'd in this man, as I may say, even bless'd.

Old Shepherd.
Let's before, as he bids us. He was provided to do us good.

Exeunt Shepherd and Clown.

Autolycus.
If I had a mind to be honest, I see Fortune would not suffer me: she drops booties in my mouth. I am courted now with a double occasion: gold and a means to do the Prince my master good; which who knows how that may turn back to my advancement? I will bring these two moles, these blind ones, aboard him. If he think it fit to shore them again, and that the complaint they have to the King concerns him nothing, let him call me rogue for being so far officious, for I am proof against that title, and what shame else belongs to't. To him will I present them, there may be matter in it.

Exit.

Act 5

Scene 1

Sicilia. A room in the palace of Leontes.

(Leontes; Cleomines; Dion; Paulina; Servants; Florizel; Perdita; Lord)

The noblemen of Sicilia try to convince Leontes that he has does enough penance for his crimes, but Paulina encourages his continued feeling of guilt, taking every opportunity to mention his sins. The noblemen reproach her for it, questioning why she does not want the King to marry again and therefore provide them with an heir. Rejecting the idea that anyone could be worthy of replacing Hermione, and that the oracle forbids Leontes from marrying again, she makes the King swear not to marry again without her consent. A servant announces the arrival of Florizel and his bride, praising the latter almost to excess. Leontes welcomes them, recognizing Florizel's resemblance to Polixenes in his youth. He is quite taken with Perdita. Florizel claims that he was sent by his father and that Perdita is a Libyan princess he just married. Leontes extends his hospitality to them, but just at that moment, an incredulous Sicilian Lord reports that Polixenes himself has arrived in Sicilia and is demanding that his son be arrested, as his so-called "Libyan princess" is in fact merely a shepherd's daughter. Florizel realizes that Camillo has betrayed them, and the Lord confirms that Camillo is with Polixenes, and is presently interrogating the terrified Shepherd and his son, whom they found in Florizel's train. Leontes is disappointed in Florizel for his unfilial actions, but the Prince begs himself to intervene on their behalf with Polixenes. Leontes admits to finding Perdita rather attractive, a train of thought quickly nixed by Paulina, and agrees to go greet Polixenes and see what can be done.

Enter Leontes, Cleomines, Dion, Paulina, Servants.

Cleomines.
Sir, you have done enough, and have perform'd
A saint-like sorrow. No fault could you make
Which you have not redeem'd; indeed paid down
More penitence than done trespass. At the last
Do as the heavens have done, forget your evil,
With them, forgive yourself.

Leontes, King of Sicilia.
                    Whilest I remember
Her and her virtues, I cannot forget
My blemishes in them, and so still think of
The wrong I did myself; which was so much
That heirless it hath made my kingdom, and
Destroy'd the sweet'st companion that e'er man
Bred his hopes out of.

Paulina.
              True, too true, my lord.
If, one by one, you wedded all the world,
Or, from the all that are, took something good
To make a perfect woman, she you kill'd
Would be unparallel'd.

Leontes, King of Sicilia.
                I think so. Kill'd?
She I kill'd? I did so; but thou strik'st me
Sorely, to say I did. It is as bitter
Upon thy tongue as in my thought. Now, good now,
Say so but seldom.

Cleomines.
                    Not at all, good lady.
You might have spoken a thousand things that would
Have done the time more benefit, and grac'd
Your kindness better.

Paulina.
                    You are one of those
Would have him wed again.

Dion.
                    If you would not so,
You pity not the state, nor the remembrance
Of his most sovereign name; consider little
What dangers, by his Highness' fail of issue,
May drop upon his kingdom, and devour
Incertain lookers-on. What were more holy
Than to rejoice the former queen is well?
What holier than, for royalty's repair,
For present comfort, and for future good,
To bless the bed of majesty again
With a sweet fellow to't?

Paulina.
                    There is none worthy,
Respecting her that's gone. Besides, the gods
Will have fulfill'd their secret purposes;
For has not the divine Apollo said,
Is't not the tenor of his oracle,
That King Leontes shall not have an heir
Till his lost child be found? Which that it shall,
Is all as monstrous to our human reason
As my Antigonus to break his grave,
And come again to me; who, on my life,
Did perish with the infant. 'Tis your counsel
My lord should to the heavens be contrary,
Oppose against their wills.

To Leontes.
                    Care not for issue,
The crown will find an heir. Great Alexander
Left his to th' worthiest; so his successor
Was like to be the best.

Leontes, King of Sicilia.
                    Good Paulina,
Who hast the memory of Hermione,
I know, in honor, O, that ever I
Had squar'd me to thy counsel! Then, even now,
I might have look'd upon my queen's full eyes,
Have taken treasure from her lips—

Paulina.
                    And left them
More rich for what they yielded.

Leontes, King of Sicilia.
                    Thou speak'st truth:
No more such wives, therefore no wife. One worse,
And better us'd, would make her sainted spirit
Again possess her corpse, and on this stage
(Where we offenders now) appear soul-vex'd,
And begin, "Why to me—?"

Paulina.
                    Had she such power,
She had just cause.

Leontes, King of Sicilia.
                    She had, and would incense me
To murder her I married.

Paulina.
                    I should so:
Were I the ghost that walk'd, I'ld bid you mark
Her eye, and tell me for what dull part in't
You chose her; then I'ld shriek, that even your ears
Should rift to hear me, and the words that follow'd
Should be "Remember mine."

Leontes, King of Sicilia.
                    Stars, stars,
And all eyes else dead coals! Fear thou no wife;
I'll have no wife, Paulina.

Paulina.
                    Will you swear
Never to marry but by my free leave?

Leontes, King of Sicilia.
Never, Paulina, so be bless'd my spirit!

Paulina.
Then, good my lords, bear witness to his oath.

Cleomines.
You tempt him overmuch.

Paulina.
                    Unless another,
As like Hermione as is her picture,
Affront his eye.

Cleomines.
                    Good madam—

Paulina.
                        I have done.
Yet if my lord will marry—if you will, sir,
No remedy but you will—give me the office
To choose you a queen. She shall not be so young
As was your former, but she shall be such
As (walk'd your first queen's ghost) it should take joy
To see her in your arms.

Leontes, King of Sicilia.
                        My true Paulina,
We shall not marry till thou bid'st us.

Paulina.
                        That
Shall be when your first queen's again in breath;
Never till then.

Enter First Servant.

First Servant.
One that gives out himself Prince Florizel,
Son of Polixenes, with his princess (she
The fairest I have yet beheld), desires access
To your high presence.

Leontes, King of Sicilia.
                What with him? He comes not
Like to his father's greatness. His approach,
So out of circumstance and sudden, tells us
'Tis not a visitation fram'd, but forc'd
By need and accident. What train?

First Servant.
                            But few,
And those but mean.

Leontes, King of Sicilia.
                His princess, say you, with him?

First Servant.
Ay; the most peerless piece of earth, I think,
That e'er the sun shone bright on.

Paulina.
                            O Hermione,
As every present time doth boast itself
Above a better gone, so must thy grave
Give way to what's seen now! Sir, you yourself
Have said and writ so, but your writing now
Is colder than that theme, "She had not been,
Nor was not to be equall'd"—thus your verse
Flow'd with her beauty once. 'Tis shrewdly ebb'd,
To say you have seen a better.

First Servant.
                        Pardon, madam:
The one I have almost forgot—your pardon—
The other, when she has obtain'd your eye,
Will have your tongue too. This is a creature,
Would she begin a sect, might quench the zeal
Of all professors else, make proselytes
Of who she but bid follow.

Paulina.
                    How? Not women?

First Servant.
Women will love her, that she is a woman
More worth than any man; men, that she is
The rarest of all women.

Leontes, King of Sicilia.
                        Go, Cleomines;
Yourself, assisted with your honor'd friends,
Bring them to our embracement.

Exeunt Cleomines and others.
                        Still, 'tis strange
He thus should steal upon us.

Paulina.
                    Had our prince,
Jewel of children, seen this hour, he had pair'd
Well with this lord; there was not full a month
Between their births.

Leontes, King of Sicilia.
Prithee no more; cease. Thou know'st
He dies to me again when talk'd of. Sure
When I shall see this gentleman, thy speeches
Will bring me to consider that which may
Unfurnish me of reason. They are come.

Enter Florizel, Perdita, Cleomines, and others.

Your mother was most true to wedlock, Prince,
For she did print your royal father off,
Conceiving you. Were I but twenty-one,
Your father's image is so hit in you
(His very air) that I should call you brother,
As I did him, and speak of something wildly
By us perform'd before. Most dearly welcome!
And your fair princess—goddess! O! Alas,
I lost a couple, that 'twixt heaven and earth
Might thus have stood, begetting wonder, as

You, gracious couple, do; and then I lost
(All mine own folly) the society,
Amity too, of your brave father, whom
(Though bearing misery) I desire my life
Once more to look on him.

Florizel.
                              By his command
Have I here touch'd Sicilia, and from him
Give you all greetings that a king (at friend)
Can send his brother; and but infirmity
(Which waits upon worn times) hath something seiz'd
His wish'd ability, he had himself
The lands and waters 'twixt your throne and his
Measur'd to look upon you; whom he loves
(He bade me say so) more than all the sceptres,
And those that bear them, living.

Leontes, King of Sicilia.
                              O my brother,
Good gentleman! The wrongs I have done thee stir
Afresh within me, and these thy offices,
So rarely kind, are as interpreters
Of my behind-hand slackness.—Welcome hither,
As is the spring to th' earth. And hath he too
Expos'd this paragon to th' fearful usage
(At least ungentle) of the dreadful Neptune,
To greet a man not worth her pains, much less
Th' adventure of her person?

Florizel.
                              Good my lord,
She came from Libya.

Leontes, King of Sicilia.
                              Where the warlike Smalus,
That noble honor'd lord, is fear'd and lov'd?

Florizel.
Most royal sir, from thence; from him, whose daughter
His tears proclaim'd his, parting with her; thence
(A prosperous south-wind friendly) we have cross'd,
To execute the charge my father gave me
For visiting your Highness. My best train
I have from your Sicilian shores dismiss'd;
Who for Bohemia bend, to signify
Not only my success in Libya, sir,
But my arrival, and my wife's, in safety
Here, where we are.

Leontes, King of Sicilia.
                              The blessed gods
Purge all infection from our air whilest you
Do climate here! You have a holy father,
A graceful gentleman, against whose person
(So sacred as it is) I have done sin,
For which the heavens, taking angry note,
Have left me issueless; and your father's bless'd
(As he from heaven merits it) with you,
Worthy his goodness. What might I have been,
Might I a son and daughter now have look'd on,
Such goodly things as you?

Enter a Lord.

First Lord.
                              Most noble sir,
That which I shall report will bear no credit,
Were not the proof so nigh. Please you, great sir,
Bohemia greets you from himself by me;
Desires you to attach his son, who has
(His dignity and duty both cast off)
Fled from his father, from his hopes, and with
A shepherd's daughter.

Leontes, King of Sicilia.
                              Where's Bohemia? Speak.

First Lord.
Here, in your city; I now came from him.
I speak amazedly, and it becomes
My marvel and my message. To your court
Whiles he was hast'ning (in the chase, it seems,
Of this fair couple), meets he on the way
The father of this seeming lady, and
Her brother, having both their country quitted
With this young prince.

Florizel.
                              Camillo has betray'd me;
Whose honor and whose honesty till now
Endur'd all weathers.

First Lord.
                              Lay't so to his charge:
He's with the King your father.

Leontes, King of Sicilia.
                              Who? Camillo?

First Lord.
Camillo, sir; I spake with him; who now
Has these poor men in question. Never saw I
Wretches so quake: they kneel, they kiss the earth;
Forswear themselves as often as they speak.
Bohemia stops his ears, and threatens them
With diverse deaths in death.

Perdita.
                    O my poor father!
The heaven sets spies upon us, will not have
Our contract celebrated.

Leontes, King of Sicilia.
                    You are married?

Florizel.
We are not, sir, nor are we like to be.
The stars, I see, will kiss the valleys first;
The odds for high and low's alike.

Leontes, King of Sicilia.
                    My lord,
Is this the daughter of a king?

Florizel.
                    She is,
When once she is my wife.

Leontes, King of Sicilia.
That "once," I see, by your good father's speed,
Will come on very slowly. I am sorry,
Most sorry, you have broken from his liking,
Where you were tied in duty; and as sorry
Your choice is not so rich in worth as beauty,
That you might well enjoy her.

Florizel.
                    Dear, look up.
Though Fortune, visible an enemy,
Should chase us with my father, pow'r no jot
Hath she to change our loves. Beseech you, sir,
Remember since you ow'd no more to time
Than I do now. With thought of such affections,
Step forth mine advocate. At your request
My father will grant precious things as trifles.

Leontes, King of Sicilia.
Would he do so, I'd beg your precious mistress,
Which he counts but a trifle.

Paulina.
                    Sir, my liege,
Your eye hath too much youth in't. Not a month
'Fore your queen died, she was more worth such gazes
Than what you look on now.

Leontes, King of Sicilia.
                    I thought of her,
Even in these looks I made.

To Florizel.
                    But your petition
Is yet unanswer'd. I will to your father.
Your honor not o'erthrown by your desires,
I am friend to them and you. Upon which errand
I now go toward him; therefore follow me,
And mark what way I make. Come, good my lord.

Exeunt.

Scene 2

Sicilia. Before Leontes' palace.

(Autolycus; First Gentleman; Second Gentleman; Third Gentleman; Shepherd; Clown)

To Autolycus's questions, a First Gentleman replies that he cannot give the full details of what's going on, as he was sent out of the room, but he saw the package that the Shepherd brought along with him opened, and Leontes and Camillo's awestruck, mute response. A Second Gentleman enters with the news that Perdita has been proven to be Leontes's daughter and that the oracle is thus fulfilled. A Third Gentleman comes in, bringing with him the confirmation that all the pieces of the puzzle fit together. Leontes and Polixenes have been reunited, and all the details of the story worked out. Everyone is feeling very emotional, Perdita in particular weeping over the story of her mother's death, which Leontes honestly confessed to. Paulina has told the court that she owns a very lifelike statue of Hermione and invited the court to come and see it. The Gentlemen decide to join the crowd, remarking on how often Paulina has visited the small house it is kept in. Autolycus is a bit disturbed to have been the cause of all these discoveries, as causing so much happiness is not really his business, but he cannot help remarking that were he not known as a thief he would presently be amply rewarded. This is evidenced as the Shepherd and the Clown comes in, richly dressed as noblemen, having just been made noblemen by the Kings. The Clown is particularly delighted at being called a brother by Prince Florizel. He makes Autolycus promise to mend his ways, which Autolycus does. They go off to see the statue.

Enter Autolycus and a Gentleman.

Autolycus.
Beseech you, sir, were you present at this relation?

First Gentleman.
I was by at the opening of the fardel, heard the old shepherd deliver the manner how he found it; whereupon, after a little amazedness, we were all commanded out of the chamber; only this, methought, I heard the shepherd say, he found the child.

Autolycus.
I would most gladly know the issue of it.

First Gentleman.
I make a broken delivery of the business; but the changes I perceiv'd in the King and Camillo were very notes of admiration. They seem'd almost, with staring on one another, to tear the cases of their eyes. There was speech in their dumbness, language in their very gesture; they look'd as they had heard of a world ransom'd, or one destroy'd. A notable passion of wonder appear'd in them; but the wisest beholder, that knew no more but seeing, could not say if th' importance were joy or sorrow; but in the extremity of the one, it must needs be.

Enter another Gentleman.

Here comes a gentleman that haply knows more. The news, Rogero?

Second Gentleman.
Nothing but bonfires. The oracle is fulfill'd; the King's daughter is found. Such a deal of wonder is broken out within this hour that ballad-makers cannot be able to express it.

Enter another Gentleman.

Here comes the Lady Paulina's steward, he can deliver you more. How goes it now, sir? This news, which is call'd true, is so like an old tale, that the verity of it is in strong suspicion. Has the King found his heir?

Third Gentleman.
Most true, if ever truth were pregnant by circumstance. That which you hear you'll swear you see, there is such unity in the proofs. The mantle of Queen Hermione's; her jewel about the neck of it; the letters of Antigonus found with it, which they know to be his character; the majesty of the creature in resemblance of the mother; the affection of nobleness which nature shows above her breeding; and many other evidences proclaim her, with all certainty, to be the King's daughter. Did you see the meeting of the two kings?

Second Gentleman.
No.

Third Gentleman.
Then have you lost a sight which was to be seen, cannot be spoken of. There might you have beheld one joy crown another, so and in such manner that it seem'd sorrow wept to take leave of them, for their joy waded in tears. There was casting up of eyes, holding up of hands, with countenance of such distraction that they were to be known by garment, not by favor. Our king, being ready to leap out of himself for joy of his found daughter, as if that joy were now become a loss, cries, "O, thy mother, thy mother!"; then asks Bohemia forgiveness; then embraces his son-in-law; then again worries he his daughter with clipping her. Now he thanks the old shepherd, which stands by like a weather-bitten conduit of many kings' reigns. I never heard of such another encounter, which lames report to follow it, and undoes description to do it.

Second Gentleman.
What, pray you, became of Antigonus, that carried hence the child?

Third Gentleman.
Like an old tale still, which will have matter to rehearse, though credit be asleep and not an ear open: he was torn to pieces with a bear. This avouches the shepherd's son, who has not only his innocence (which seems much) to justify him, but a handkerchief and rings of his that Paulina knows.

First Gentleman.
What became of his bark and his followers?

Third Gentleman.
Wrack'd the same instant of their master's death, and in the view of the shepherd; so that all the instruments which aided to expose the child were even then lost when it was found. But O, the noble combat that 'twixt joy and sorrow was fought in Paulina! She had one eye declin'd for the loss of her husband, another elevated that the oracle was fulfill'd. She lifted the

Princess from the earth, and so locks her in embracing, as if she would pin her to her heart, that she might no more be in danger of losing.

First Gentleman.
The dignity of this act was worth the audience of kings and princes, for by such was it acted.

Third Gentleman.
One of the prettiest touches of all, and that which angled for mine eyes (caught the water though not the fish), was when, at the relation of the Queen's death (with the manner how she came to't bravely confess'd and lamented by the King), how attentiveness wounded his daughter, till (from one sign of dolor to another) she did (with an "Alas!"), I would fain say, bleed tears; for I am sure my heart wept blood. Who was most marble there chang'd color; some swounded, all sorrow'd. If all the world could have seen't, the woe had been universal.

First Gentleman.
Are they return'd to the court?

Third Gentleman.
No. The Princess hearing of her mother's statue, which is in the keeping of Paulina—a piece many years in doing and now newly perform'd by that rare Italian master, Julio Romano, who, had he himself eternity and could put breath into his work, would beguile Nature of her custom, so perfectly he is her ape. He so near to Hermione hath done Hermione that they say one would speak to her and stand in hope of answer. Thither with all greediness of affection are they gone, and there they intend to sup.

Second Gentleman.
I thought she had some great matter there in hand, for she hath privately twice or thrice a day, ever since the death of Hermione, visited that remov'd house. Shall we thither, and with our company piece the rejoicing?

First Gentleman.
Who would be thence that has the benefit of access? Every wink of an eye some new grace will be born. Our absence makes us unthrifty to our knowledge. Let's along.

Exeunt Gentlemen.

Autolycus.
Now, had I not the dash of my former life in me, would preferment drop on my head. I brought the old man and his son aboard the Prince; told him I heard them talk of a fardel, and I know not what; but he at that time, overfond of the shepherd's daughter (so he then took her to be), who began to be much sea-sick, and himself little better, extremity of weather continuing, this mystery remain'd undiscover'd. But 'tis all one to me; for had I been the finder-out of this secret, it would not have relish'd among my other discredits.

Enter Shepherd and Clown.

Here come those I have done good to against my will, and already appearing in the blossoms of their fortune.

Old Shepherd.
Come, boy, I am past more children, but thy sons and daughters will be all gentlemen born.

Clown.
You are well met, sir. You denied to fight with me this other day, because I was no gentleman born. See you these clothes? Say you see them not and think me still no gentleman born. You were best say these robes are not gentlemen born. Give me the lie, do; and try whether I am not now a gentleman born.

Autolycus.
I know you are now, sir, a gentleman born.

Clown.
Ay, and have been so any time these four hours.

Old Shepherd.
And so have I, boy.

Clown.
So you have. But I was a gentleman born before my father; for the King's son took me by the hand, and call'd me brother; and then the two kings call'd my father brother; and then the Prince, my brother, and the Princess, my sister, call'd my father father; and so we wept; and there was the first gentleman-like tears that ever we shed.

Old Shepherd.
We may live, son, to shed many more.

Clown.
Ay; or else 'twere hard luck, being in so preposterous estate as we are.

Autolycus.
I humbly beseech you, sir, to pardon me all the faults I have committed to your worship, and to give me your good report to the Prince my master.

Old Shepherd.
Prithee, son, do; for we must be gentle, now we are gentlemen.

Clown.
Thou wilt amend thy life?

Autolycus.
Ay, and it like your good worship.

Clown.
Give me thy hand: I will swear to the Prince thou art as honest a true fellow as any is in Bohemia.

Old Shepherd.
You may say it, but not swear it.

Clown.
Not swear it, now I am a gentleman? Let boors and franklins say it, I'll swear it.

Old Shepherd.
How if it be false, son?

Clown.
If it be ne'er so false, a true gentleman may swear it in the behalf of his friend; and I'll swear to the Prince thou art a tall fellow of thy hands, and that thou wilt not be drunk; but I know thou art no tall fellow of thy hands, and that thou wilt be drunk; but I'll swear it, and I would thou wouldst be a tall fellow of thy hands.

Autolycus.
I will prove so, sir, to my power.

Clown.
Ay, by any means prove a tall fellow. If I do not wonder how thou dar'st venture to be drunk, not being a tall fellow, trust me not. Hark, the kings and the princes, our kindred, are going to see the Queen's picture. Come, follow us; we'll be thy good masters.

Exeunt.

Scene 3

A chapel in Paulina's house.

(Leontes; Polixenes; Florizel; Perdita; Camillo; Paulina; Lords; Hermione)

Leontes thanks Paulina for having been a comfort to him, and Paulina greets him to her house. She reveals the statue of Hermione. All are awed and amazed by it, particularly the fact that the sculptor has even added sixteen years to her face to make her look as though she had aged along with them all. Leontes feels his shame yet more keenly and Perdita, struck by the statue's lifelikeness, kneels as if for her mother's blessing. Paulina prevents anyone from touching the statue, as it has only just been painted and might smear. Leontes is deeply moved, swearing that he can almost see the statue breathe. Paulina tells him that, if he has the strength to witness it, she can make the statue move. Leontes begs her to do so, promising not to think it caused by witchcraft. Paulina calls for music, and calls to the statue, telling her it is time. Hermione comes down from the plinth and takes Leontes's hand, who is amazed to find it warm. Hermione wordlessly embraces him, and when Perdita kneels at her feet, gives her mother's blessing. As she begins to ask questions about where Perdita has been, Paulina tells them that all things will be explained, but that she is leaving to grieve over Antigonus's death. Leontes tells her to stay, and to join in their joy by suggesting that she marry Camillo, who has been pining for her. All reconciled, they leave to discuss events further.

Enter Leontes, Polixenes, Florizel, Perdita, Camillo, Paulina, Lords, etc.

Leontes, King of Sicilia.
O grave and good Paulina, the great comfort
That I have had of thee!

Paulina.
                What, sovereign sir,
I did not well, I meant well. All my services
You have paid home; but that you have vouchsaf'd,
With your crown'd brother and these your contracted
Heirs of your kingdoms, my poor house to visit,
It is a surplus of your grace, which never
My life may last to answer.

Leontes, King of Sicilia.
                O Paulina,
We honor you with trouble; but we came
To see the statue of our queen. Your gallery

Have we pass'd through, not without much content
In many singularities; but we saw not
That which my daughter came to look upon,
The statue of her mother.

Paulina.
                        As she liv'd peerless,
So her dead likeness, I do well believe,
Excels what ever yet you look'd upon,
Or hand of man hath done; therefore I keep it
Lonely, apart. But here it is; prepare
To see the life as lively mock'd as ever
Still sleep mock'd death. Behold, and say 'tis well.

Paulina draws a curtain, and discovers Hermione standing like a statue.

I like your silence, it the more shows off
Your wonder; but yet speak. First, you, my liege;
Comes it not something near?

Leontes, King of Sicilia.
                        Her natural posture!
Chide me, dear stone, that I may say indeed
Thou art Hermione; or rather, thou art she
In thy not chiding; for she was as tender
As infancy and grace. But yet, Paulina,
Hermione was not so much wrinkled, nothing
So aged as this seems.

Polixenes, King of Bohemia.
                        O, not by much.

Paulina.
So much the more our carver's excellence,
Which lets go by some sixteen years, and makes her
As she liv'd now.

Leontes, King of Sicilia.
                        As now she might have done,
So much to my good comfort as it is
Now piercing to my soul. O, thus she stood,
Even with such life of majesty (warm life,
As now it coldly stands), when first I woo'd her!
I am asham'd; does not the stone rebuke me
For being more stone than it? O royal piece,
There's magic in thy majesty, which has
My evils conjur'd to remembrance, and
From thy admiring daughter took the spirits,
Standing like stone with thee.

Perdita.
                        And give me leave,
And do not say 'tis superstition, that
I kneel, and then implore her blessing. Lady,
Dear queen, that ended when I but began,
Give me that hand of yours to kiss.

Paulina.
                        O, patience!
The statue is but newly fix'd; the color's
Not dry.

Camillo.
My lord, your sorrow was too sore laid on,
Which sixteen winters cannot blow away,
So many summers dry. Scarce any joy
Did ever so long live; no sorrow
But kill'd itself much sooner.

Polixenes, King of Bohemia.
                        Dear my brother,
Let him that was the cause of this have pow'r
To take off so much grief from you as he
Will piece up in himself.

Paulina.
                        Indeed, my lord,
If I had thought the sight of my poor image
Would thus have wrought you (for the stone is mine),
I'ld not have show'd it.

Leontes, King of Sicilia.
                        Do not draw the curtain.

Paulina.
No longer shall you gaze on't, lest your fancy
May think anon it moves.

Leontes, King of Sicilia.
                        Let be, let be.
Would I were dead but that methinks already—
What was he that did make it? See, my lord,
Would you not deem it breath'd? And that those veins
Did verily bear blood?

Polixenes, King of Bohemia.
                        Masterly done!
The very life seems warm upon her lip.

Leontes, King of Sicilia.
The fixure of her eye has motion in't,
As we are mock'd with art.

Paulina.
                I'll draw the curtain.
My lord's almost so far transported that
He'll think anon it lives.

Leontes, King of Sicilia.
                    O sweet Paulina,
Make me to think so twenty years together!
No settled senses of the world can match
The pleasure of that madness. Let't alone.

Paulina.
I am sorry, sir, I have thus far stirr'd you; but
I could afflict you farther.

Leontes, King of Sicilia.
                  Do, Paulina;
For this affliction has a taste as sweet
As any cordial comfort. Still methinks
There is an air comes from her. What fine chisel
Could ever yet cut breath? Let no man mock me,
For I will kiss her.

Paulina.
                Good my lord, forbear.
The ruddiness upon her lip is wet;
You'll mar it if you kiss it; stain your own
With oily painting. Shall I draw the curtain?

Leontes, King of Sicilia.
No! Not these twenty years.

Perdita.
                So long could I
Stand by, a looker-on.

Paulina.
                Either forbear,
Quit presently the chapel, or resolve you
For more amazement. If you can behold it,
I'll make the statue move indeed, descend,
And take you by the hand; but then you'll think
(Which I protest against) I am assisted
By wicked powers.

Leontes, King of Sicilia.
                What you can make her do,
I am content to look on; what to speak,
I am content to hear; for 'tis as easy
To make her speak as move.

Paulina.
                It is requir'd
You do awake your faith. Then, all stand still.
On; those that think it is unlawful business
I am about, let them depart.

Leontes, King of Sicilia.
                Proceed;
No foot shall stir.

Paulina.
                Music! Awake her! Strike!

Music.

'Tis time; descend; be stone no more; approach;
Strike all that look upon with marvel. Come;
I'll fill your grave up. Stir; nay, come away;
Bequeath to death your numbness; for from him
Dear life redeems you. You perceive she stirs.

Hermione comes down.

Start not; her actions shall be holy, as
You hear my spell is lawful. Do not shun her
Until you see her die again, for then
You kill her double. Nay, present your hand.
When she was young, you woo'd her; now, in age,
Is she become the suitor?

Leontes, King of Sicilia.
                O, she's warm!
If this be magic, let it be an art
Lawful as eating.

Polixenes, King of Bohemia.
                She embraces him.

Camillo.
She hangs about his neck.
If she pertain to life let her speak too.

Polixenes, King of Bohemia.
Ay, and make it manifest where she has liv'd,
Or how stol'n from the dead.

Paulina.
                That she is living,
Were it but told you, should be hooted at
Like an old tale; but it appears she lives,
Though yet she speak not. Mark a little while.
Please you to interpose, fair madam, kneel,
And pray your mother's blessing. Turn, good lady,
Our Perdita is found.

Hermione.
      You gods, look down
And from your sacred vials pour your graces
Upon my daughter's head! Tell me, mine own,
Where hast thou been preserv'd? Where liv'd? How found
Thy father's court? For thou shalt hear that I,
Knowing by Paulina that the oracle
Gave hope thou wast in being, have preserv'd
Myself to see the issue.

Paulina.
      There's time enough for that;
Least they desire (upon this push) to trouble
Your joys with like relation. Go together,
You precious winners all; your exultation
Partake to every one. I, an old turtle,
Will wing me to some wither'd bough, and there
My mate (that's never to be found again)
Lament till I am lost.

Leontes, King of Sicilia.
      O, peace, Paulina!
Thou shouldst a husband take by my consent,
As I by thine a wife: this is a match,
And made between 's by vows. Thou hast found mine,
But how, is to be question'd; for I saw her
(As I thought) dead; and have (in vain) said many
A prayer upon her grave. I'll not seek far
(For him, I partly know his mind) to find thee
An honorable husband. Come, Camillo,
And take her by the hand, whose worth and honesty
Is richly noted; and here justified
By us, a pair of kings. Let's from this place.
What? Look upon my brother. Both your pardons,
That e'er I put between your holy looks
My ill suspicion. This' your son-in-law,
And son unto the King, whom heavens directing
Is troth-plight to your daughter. Good Paulina,
Lead us from hence, where we may leisurely
Each one demand, and answer to his part
Perform'd in this wide gap of time, since first
We were dissever'd. Hastily lead away.

Exeunt.

Richard III

Act 1

Scene 1

London. A street.

(Richard Duke of Gloucester; Clarence; Guard; Brakenbury; Lord Hastings)

Richard Duke of Gloucester reflects on how little peacetime suits him, since his physical aspects prevents him from the pursuits of love. To occupy his time, he has convinced his brother King Edward that their brother Clarence is dangerous. Clarence is brought in, being led to the Tower. Richard hypocritically blames the Queen and promises to give Clarence all the help he can. Clarence is taken away. Hastings, just released from jail, reports that the King is dangerously ill. Richard hopes his brother will die, but not before Clarence is done away with. He also plans to marry the Lady Anne, whose husband and father-in-law he both killed.

Enter Richard Duke of Gloucester solus.

Richard, Duke of Gloucester.
Now is the winter of our discontent
Made glorious summer by this son of York;
And all the clouds that low'r'd upon our house
In the deep bosom of the ocean buried.
Now are our brows bound with victorious wreaths,
Our bruised arms hung up for monuments,
Our stern alarums chang'd to merry meetings,
Our dreadful marches to delightful measures.
Grim-visag'd War hath smooth'd his wrinkled front;
And now, in stead of mounting barbed steeds
To fright the souls of fearful adversaries,
He capers nimbly in a lady's chamber
To the lascivious pleasing of a lute.
But I, that am not shap'd for sportive tricks,
Nor made to court an amorous looking-glass;
I, that am rudely stamp'd, and want love's majesty
To strut before a wanton ambling nymph;
I, that am curtail'd of this fair proportion,
Cheated of feature by dissembling nature,
Deform'd, unfinish'd, sent before my time
Into this breathing world, scarce half made up,
And that so lamely and unfashionable
That dogs bark at me as I halt by them—
Why, I, in this weak piping time of peace,
Have no delight to pass away the time,
Unless to see my shadow in the sun
And descant on mine own deformity.
And therefore, since I cannot prove a lover
To entertain these fair well-spoken days,
I am determined to prove a villain
And hate the idle pleasures of these days.
Plots have I laid, inductions dangerous,
By drunken prophecies, libels, and dreams,
To set my brother Clarence and the King
In deadly hate the one against the other;
And if King Edward be as true and just
As I am subtle, false, and treacherous,
This day should Clarence closely be mew'd up
About a prophecy, which says that G
Of Edward's heirs the murderer shall be.
Dive, thoughts, down to my soul, here Clarence comes!

Enter Clarence, guarded, and Brakenbury, Lieutenant of the Tower.

Brother, good day. What means this armed guard
That waits upon your Grace?

George, Duke of Clarence.
                              His Majesty,
Tend'ring my person's safety, hath appointed
This conduct to convey me to the Tower.

Richard, Duke of Gloucester.
Upon what cause?

George, Duke of Clarence.
                  Because my name is George.

Richard, Duke of Gloucester.
Alack, my lord, that fault is none of yours;
He should for that commit your godfathers.
O, belike his Majesty hath some intent
That you should be new christ'ned in the Tower.
But what's the matter, Clarence, may I know?

George, Duke of Clarence.
Yea, Richard, when I know; but I protest
As yet I do not. But, as I can learn,
He hearkens after prophecies and dreams,
And from the cross-row plucks the letter G,
And says a wizard told him that by G
His issue disinherited should be;
And for my name of George begins with G,
It follows in his thought that I am he.
These (as I learn) and such-like toys as these
Hath mov'd his Highness to commit me now.

Richard, Duke of Gloucester.
Why, this it is, when men are rul'd by women:
'Tis not the King that sends you to the Tower;
My Lady Grey his wife, Clarence, 'tis she
That tempers him to this extremity.
Was it not she, and that good man of worship,
Anthony Woodvile, her brother there,
That made him send Lord Hastings to the Tower,
From whence this present day he is delivered?
We are not safe, Clarence, we are not safe.

George, Duke of Clarence.
By heaven, I think there is no man is secure
But the Queen's kindred, and night-walking heralds
That trudge betwixt the King and Mistress Shore.
Heard you not what an humble suppliant
Lord Hastings was to her for his delivery?

Richard, Duke of Gloucester.
Humbly complaining to her deity
Got my Lord Chamberlain his liberty.
I'll tell you what, I think it is our way,
If we will keep in favor with the King,
To be her men and wear her livery.
The jealous o'erworn widow and herself,
Since that our brother dubb'd them gentlewomen,
Are mighty gossips in our monarchy.

Sir Robert Brakenbury.
I beseech your Graces both to pardon me:
His Majesty hath straitly given in charge
That no man shall have private conference
(Of what degree soever) with your brother.

Richard, Duke of Gloucester.
Even so? And please your worship, Brakenbury,
You may partake of any thing we say:
We speak no treason, man. We say the King
Is wise and virtuous, and his noble queen
Well struck in years, fair, and not jealous;
We say that Shore's wife hath a pretty foot,
A cherry lip, a bonny eye, a passing pleasing tongue;
And that the Queen's kindred are made gentlefolks.
How say you, sir? Can you deny all this?

Sir Robert Brakenbury.
With this, my lord, myself have nought to do.

Richard, Duke of Gloucester.
Naught to do with Mistress Shore? I tell thee, fellow,
He that doth naught with her (excepting one)
Were best to do it secretly alone.

Sir Robert Brakenbury.
What one, my lord?

Richard, Duke of Gloucester.
Her husband, knave. Wouldst thou betray me?

Sir Robert Brakenbury.
I do beseech your Grace to pardon me, and withal
Forbear your conference with the noble Duke.

George, Duke of Clarence.
We know thy charge, Brakenbury, and will obey.

Richard, Duke of Gloucester.
We are the Queen's abjects, and must obey.
Brother, farewell, I will unto the King,
And whatsoe'er you will employ me in,
Were it to call King Edward's widow sister,
I will perform it to enfranchise you.
Mean time, this deep disgrace in brotherhood
Touches me deeper than you can imagine.

George, Duke of Clarence.
I know it pleaseth neither of us well.

Richard, Duke of Gloucester.
Well, your imprisonment shall not be long,
I will deliver you, or else lie for you.
Mean time, have patience.

George, Duke of Clarence.
                I must perforce. Farewell.

Exit Clarence with Brakenbury and Guard.

Richard, Duke of Gloucester.
Go tread the path that thou shalt ne'er return:
Simple plain Clarence, I do love thee so
That I will shortly send thy soul to heaven,
If heaven will take the present at our hands.
But who comes here? The new-delivered Hastings?

Enter Lord Hastings.

Lord Hastings.
Good time of day unto my gracious lord!

Richard, Duke of Gloucester.
As much unto my good Lord Chamberlain!
Well are you welcome to the open air.
How hath your lordship brook'd imprisonment?

Lord Hastings.
With patience, noble lord, as prisoners must;
But I shall live, my lord, to give them thanks
That were the cause of my imprisonment.

Richard, Duke of Gloucester.
No doubt, no doubt, and so shall Clarence too,
For they that were your enemies are his,
And have prevail'd as much on him as you.

Lord Hastings.
More pity that the eagles should be mew'd,
Whiles kites and buzzards prey at liberty.

Richard, Duke of Gloucester.
What news abroad?

Lord Hastings.
No news so bad abroad as this at home:
The King is sickly, weak, and melancholy,
And his physicians fear him mightily.

Richard, Duke of Gloucester.
Now by Saint John, that news is bad indeed!
O, he hath kept an evil diet long,
And overmuch consum'd his royal person:
'Tis very grievous to be thought upon.
Where is he? In his bed?

Lord Hastings.
He is.

Richard, Duke of Gloucester.
Go you before, and I will follow you.

Exit Hastings.

He cannot live, I hope, and must not die
Till George be pack'd with post-horse up to heaven.
I'll in, to urge his hatred more to Clarence
With lies well steel'd with weighty arguments,
And if I fail not in my deep intent,
Clarence hath not another day to live:
Which done, God take King Edward to his mercy,
And leave the world for me to bustle in!
For then I'll marry Warwick's youngest daughter.
What though I kill'd her husband and her father?
The readiest way to make the wench amends
Is to become her husband and her father:
The which will I, not all so much for love
As for another secret close intent
By marrying her which I must reach unto.
But yet I run before my horse to market:
Clarence still breathes, Edward still lives and reigns;
When they are gone, then must I count my gains.

Exit.

Scene 2

London. Another street.

(Henry the Sixth; Halberds; Lady Anne; Tressel; Berkeley; Richard Duke of Gloucester; Gentleman)

Lady Anne follows the coffin of Henry VI to the grave, the only mourner. She bids the bearers set it down a while so that she can mourn properly. As she curses the King's murderer, Richard enters. He refuses to let the funeral proceed, insisting on speaking to Anne. Despite her grief and insults, he begins to woo her, insisting that he only committed his murders out of love for her. He manages to undermine every argument she makes and though she suspects him of hypocrisy, she cannot help being moved. She soon agrees to wear his ring. He lets her leave, and delightedly congratulates himself on his feat.

Enter the corpse of Henry the Sixth, with Halberds to guard it, Lady Anne being the mourner, attended by Tressel and Berkeley.

Lady Anne.
Set down, set down your honorable load,
If honor may be shrouded in a hearse,
Whilst I awhile obsequiously lament
Th' untimely fall of virtuous Lancaster.
Poor key-cold figure of a holy king,
Pale ashes of the house of Lancaster,
Thou bloodless remnant of that royal blood,
Be it lawful that I invocate thy ghost
To hear the lamentations of poor Anne,
Wife to thy Edward, to thy slaught'red son,
Stabb'd by the self-same hand that made these wounds!
Lo, in these windows that let forth thy life
I pour the helpless balm of my poor eyes.
O, cursed be the hand that made these holes!
Cursed the heart that had the heart to do it!
Cursed the blood that let this blood from hence!
More direful hap betide that hated wretch
That makes us wretched by the death of thee
Than I can wish to wolves—to spiders, toads,
Or any creeping venom'd thing that lives!
If ever he have child, abortive be it,
Prodigious, and untimely brought to light,
Whose ugly and unnatural aspect
May fright the hopeful mother at the view,
And that be heir to his unhappiness!
If ever he have wife, let her be made
More miserable by the life of him
Than I am made by my young lord and thee!
Come now towards Chertsey with your holy load,
Taken from Paul's to be interred there;
And still as you are weary of this weight,
Rest you, whiles I lament King Henry's corse.

Enter Richard Duke of Gloucester.

Richard, Duke of Gloucester.
Stay, you that bear the corse, and set it down.

Lady Anne.
What black magician conjures up this fiend
To stop devoted charitable deeds?

Richard, Duke of Gloucester.
Villains, set down the corse, or, by Saint Paul,
I'll make a corse of him that disobeys.

Gentleman.
My lord, stand back, and let the coffin pass.

Richard, Duke of Gloucester.
Unmanner'd dog, stand thou when I command.
Advance thy halberd higher than my breast,
Or by Saint Paul I'll strike thee to my foot,
And spurn upon thee, beggar, for thy boldness.

Lady Anne.
What do you tremble? Are you all afraid?
Alas, I blame you not, for you are mortal,
And mortal eyes cannot endure the devil.—
Avaunt, thou dreadful minister of hell!
Thou hadst but power over his mortal body,
His soul thou canst not have. Therefore be gone.

Richard, Duke of Gloucester.
Sweet saint, for charity, be not so curst.

Lady Anne.
Foul devil, for God's sake hence, and trouble us not,
For thou hast made the happy earth thy hell,
Fill'd it with cursing cries and deep exclaims.
If thou delight to view thy heinous deeds,
Behold this pattern of thy butcheries.
O gentlemen, see, see dead Henry's wounds
Open their congeal'd mouths and bleed afresh!
Blush, blush, thou lump of foul deformity;
For 'tis thy presence that exhales this blood
From cold and empty veins where no blood dwells.
Thy deeds inhuman and unnatural
Provokes this deluge most unnatural.
O God! Which this blood mad'st, revenge his death!
O earth! Which this blood drink'st, revenge his death!
Either heav'n with lightning strike the murd'rer dead;
Or earth gape open wide and eat him quick,
As thou dost swallow up this good king's blood,
Which his hell-govern'd arm hath butchered!

Richard, Duke of Gloucester.
Lady, you know no rules of charity,
Which renders good for bad, blessings for curses.

Lady Anne.
Villain, thou know'st nor law of God nor man:
No beast so fierce but knows some touch of pity.

Richard, Duke of Gloucester.
But I know none, and therefore am no beast.

Lady Anne.
O wonderful, when devils tell the troth!

Richard, Duke of Gloucester.
More wonderful, when angels are so angry.
Vouchsafe, divine perfection of a woman,
Of these supposed crimes, to give me leave
By circumstance but to acquit myself.

Lady Anne.
Vouchsafe, defus'd infection of a man,
Of these known evils, but to give me leave
By circumstance t' accuse thy cursed self.

Richard, Duke of Gloucester.
Fairer than tongue can name thee, let me have
Some patient leisure to excuse myself.

Lady Anne.
Fouler than heart can think thee, thou canst make
No excuse current but to hang thyself.

Richard, Duke of Gloucester.
By such despair I should accuse myself.

Lady Anne.
And by despairing shalt thou stand excused
For doing worthy vengeance on thyself,
That didst unworthy slaughter upon others.

Richard, Duke of Gloucester.
Say that I slew them not?

Lady Anne.
Then say they were not slain.
But dead they are, and, devilish slave, by thee.

Richard, Duke of Gloucester.
I did not kill your husband.

Lady Anne.
     Why then he is alive.

Richard, Duke of Gloucester.
Nay, he is dead, and slain by Edward's hands.

Lady Anne.
In thy foul throat thou li'st! Queen Margaret saw
Thy murd'rous falchion smoking in his blood;
The which thou once didst bend against her breast,
But that thy brothers beat aside the point.

Richard, Duke of Gloucester.
I was provoked by her sland'rous tongue,
That laid their guilt upon my guiltless shoulders.

Lady Anne.
Thou wast provoked by thy bloody mind,
That never dream'st on aught but butcheries.
Didst thou not kill this king?

Richard, Duke of Gloucester.
       I grant ye.

Lady Anne.
Dost grant me, hedgehog? Then God grant me too
Thou mayst be damned for that wicked deed!
O, he was gentle, mild, and virtuous!

Richard, Duke of Gloucester.
The better for the King of Heaven that hath him.

Lady Anne.
He is in heaven, where thou shalt never come.

Richard, Duke of Gloucester.
Let him thank me that help to send him thither;
For he was fitter for that place than earth.

Lady Anne.
And thou unfit for any place, but hell.

Richard, Duke of Gloucester.
Yes, one place else, if you will hear me name it.

Lady Anne.
Some dungeon.

Richard, Duke of Gloucester.
    Your bedchamber.

Lady Anne.
Ill rest betide the chamber where thou liest!

Richard, Duke of Gloucester.
So will it, madam, till I lie with you.

Lady Anne.
I hope so.

Richard, Duke of Gloucester.
I know so. But, gentle Lady Anne,
To leave this keen encounter of our wits
And fall something into a slower method:
Is not the causer of the timeless deaths
Of these Plantagenets, Henry and Edward,
As blameful as the executioner?

Lady Anne.
Thou wast the cause, and most accurs'd effect.

Richard, Duke of Gloucester.
Your beauty was the cause of that effect—
Your beauty, that did haunt me in my sleep
To undertake the death of all the world,
So I might live one hour in your sweet bosom.

Lady Anne.
If I thought that, I tell thee, homicide,
These nails should rent that beauty from my cheeks.

Richard, Duke of Gloucester.
These eyes could not endure that beauty's wrack;
You should not blemish it, if I stood by:
As all the world is cheered by the sun,
So I by that; it is my day, my life.

Lady Anne.
Black night o'ershade thy day, and death thy life!

Richard, Duke of Gloucester.
Curse not thyself, fair creature—thou art both.

Lady Anne.
I would I were, to be reveng'd on thee.

Richard, Duke of Gloucester.
It is a quarrel most unnatural,
To be reveng'd on him that loveth thee.

Lady Anne.
It is a quarrel just and reasonable,
To be reveng'd on him that kill'd my husband.

Richard, Duke of Gloucester.
He that bereft thee, lady, of thy husband,
Did it to help thee to a better husband.

Lady Anne.
His better doth not breathe upon the earth.

Richard, Duke of Gloucester.
He lives, that loves thee better than he could.

Lady Anne.
Name him.

Richard, Duke of Gloucester.
                    Plantagenet.

Lady Anne.
                    Why, that was he.

Richard, Duke of Gloucester.
The self-same name, but one of better nature.

Lady Anne.
Where is he?

Richard, Duke of Gloucester.
                    Here.

She spits at him.
                    Why dost thou spit at me?

Lady Anne.
Would it were mortal poison for thy sake!

Richard, Duke of Gloucester.
Never came poison from so sweet a place.

Lady Anne.
Never hung poison on a fouler toad.
Out of my sight, thou dost infect mine eyes!

Richard, Duke of Gloucester.
Thine eyes, sweet lady, have infected mine.

Lady Anne.
Would they were basilisks, to strike thee dead!

Richard, Duke of Gloucester.
I would they were, that I might die at once;
For now they kill me with a living death.
Those eyes of thine from mine have drawn salt tears,
Sham'd their aspects with store of childish drops:
These eyes, which never shed remorseful tear—
No, when my father York and Edward wept
To hear the piteous moan that Rutland made
When black-fac'd Clifford shook his sword at him;
Nor when thy warlike father, like a child,
Told the sad story of my father's death,
And twenty times made pause to sob and weep,
That all the standers-by had wet their cheeks
Like trees bedash'd with rain—in that sad time
My manly eyes did scorn an humble tear;
And what these sorrows could not thence exhale,
Thy beauty hath, and made them blind with weeping.
I never sued to friend nor enemy;
My tongue could never learn sweet smoothing word;
But now thy beauty is propos'd my fee,
My proud heart sues, and prompts my tongue to speak.

She looks scornfully at him.

Teach not thy lip such scorn; for it was made
For kissing, lady, not for such contempt.
If thy revengeful heart cannot forgive,

Lo here I lend thee this sharp-pointed sword,
Which if thou please to hide in this true breast,
And let the soul forth that adoreth thee,
I lay it naked to the deadly stroke,
And humbly beg the death upon my knee.

He lays his breast open: she offers at it with his sword.

Nay, do not pause: for I did kill King Henry—
But 'twas thy beauty that provoked me.
Nay, now dispatch: 'twas I that stabb'd young Edward
But 'twas thy heavenly face that set me on.

She falls the sword.

Take up the sword again, or take up me.

Lady Anne.
Arise, dissembler! Though I wish thy death,
I will not be thy executioner.

Richard, Duke of Gloucester.
Then bid me kill myself, and I will do it.

Lady Anne.
I have already.

Richard, Duke of Gloucester.
                       That was in thy rage.
Speak it again, and even with the word
This hand, which for thy love did kill thy love,
Shall for thy love kill a far truer love;
To both their deaths shalt thou be accessary.

Lady Anne.
I would I knew thy heart.

Richard, Duke of Gloucester.
'Tis figur'd in my tongue.

Lady Anne.
I fear me both are false.

Richard, Duke of Gloucester.
Then never was man true.

Lady Anne.
Well, well, put up your sword.

Richard, Duke of Gloucester.
Say then my peace is made.

Lady Anne.
That shalt thou know hereafter.

Richard, Duke of Gloucester.
But shall I live in hope?

Lady Anne.
All men, I hope, live so.

Richard, Duke of Gloucester.
Vouchsafe to wear this ring.

Lady Anne.
To take is not to give.

Gloucester slips the ring on her finger.

Richard, Duke of Gloucester.
Look how my ring encompasseth thy finger,
Even so thy breast encloseth my poor heart:
Wear both of them, for both of them are thine.
And if thy poor devoted servant may
But beg one favor at thy gracious hand,
Thou dost confirm his happiness forever.

Lady Anne.
What is it?

Richard, Duke of Gloucester.
That it may please you leave these sad designs
To him that hath most cause to be a mourner,
And presently repair to Crosby House;
Where (after I have solemnly interr'd
At Chertsey monast'ry this noble king,
And wet his grave with my repentant tears)
I will with all expedient duty see you.
For diverse unknown reasons, I beseech you,
Grant me this boon.

Lady Anne.
With all my heart, and much it joys me too,
To see you are become so penitent.
Tressel and Berkeley, go along with me.

Richard, Duke of Gloucester.
Bid me farewell.

Lady Anne.
                     'Tis more than you deserve;
But since you teach me how to flatter you,
Imagine I have said farewell already.

Exeunt two, Tressel and Berkeley, with Anne.

Richard, Duke of Gloucester.
Sirs, take up the corse.

Gentleman.
Towards Chertsey, noble lord?

Richard, Duke of Gloucester.
No; to White-Friars, there attend my coming.

Exit corpse with Halberds.

Was ever woman in this humor woo'd?
Was ever woman in this humor won?
I'll have her, but I will not keep her long.
What? I, that kill'd her husband and his father,
To take her in her heart's extremest hate,
With curses in her mouth, tears in her eyes,
The bleeding witness of my hatred by,
Having God, her conscience, and these bars against me,
And I no friends to back my suit at all
But the plain devil and dissembling looks?
And yet to win her! All the world to nothing!
Hah!
Hath she forgot already that brave prince,
Edward, her lord, whom I, some three months since,
Stabb'd in my angry mood at Tewksbury?
A sweeter and a lovelier gentleman,
Fram'd in the prodigality of nature—
Young, valiant, wise, and (no doubt) right royal—
The spacious world cannot again afford.
And will she yet abase her eyes on me,
That cropp'd the golden prime of this sweet prince
And made her widow to a woeful bed?
On me, whose all not equals Edward's moi'ty?
On me, that halts and am misshapen thus?
My dukedom to a beggarly denier,
I do mistake my person all this while!
Upon my life, she finds (although I cannot)
Myself to be a marv'lous proper man.
I'll be at charges for a looking-glass,
And entertain a score or two of tailors
To study fashions to adorn my body:
Since I am crept in favor with myself,
I will maintain it with some little cost.
But first I'll turn yon fellow in his grave,
And then return lamenting to my love.
Shine out, fair sun, till I have bought a glass,
That I may see my shadow as I pass.

Exit.

Scene 3

London. The palace.

(*Queen Mother Elizabeth; Lord Rivers; Marquess of Dorset; Lord Grey; Buckingham; Lord Stanley; Richard Duke of Gloucester; Lord Hastings; Queen Margaret; Catesby; Murderers*)

The Queen is desperately worried about the King's health, as in the event of his death Richard would be Regent, and he has no love for her or her family. Rivers and Grey try to reassure her. Buckingham announces that the King is better and is hoping to reconcile his brother and his wife. Richard and Hastings come in and begin to quarrel over who started their quarrel. Richard openly defies the Queen and her family, scorning them for their lower-class roots. Old Queen Margaret, Henry VI's widow, sneaks in and listens to them quarreling; finally she comes forward and curses them one by one for killing her husband and son, and stealing the throne. The others gang up on her and she leaves, calling for a bad end on them all, except Buckingham, who is innocent of either murder. Buckingham refuses to pay any attention to her warning against Richard. A message from the King requests everyone's presence, and they leave to go to him, except Richard, who gives two Murderers a warrant to kill Clarence at the Tower.

Enter the Queen Mother Elizabeth, Lord Rivers, Marquess of Dorset, and Lord Grey.

Earl Rivers.
Have patience, madam, there's no doubt his Majesty
Will soon recover his accustom'd health.

Lord Grey.
In that you brook it ill, it makes him worse;
Therefore for God's sake entertain good comfort,
And cheer his Grace with quick and merry eyes.

Queen Elizabeth.
If he were dead, what would betide on me?

Lord Grey.
No other harm but loss of such a lord.

Queen Elizabeth.
The loss of such a lord includes all harms.

Lord Grey.
The heavens have blest you with a goodly son
To be your comforter when he is gone.

Queen Elizabeth.
Ah! He is young; and his minority
Is put unto the trust of Richard Gloucester,
A man that loves not me, nor none of you.

Act 1, Scene 3

Earl Rivers.
Is it concluded he shall be Protector?

Queen Elizabeth.
It is determin'd, not concluded yet;
But so it must be, if the King miscarry.

Enter Buckingham and Lord Stanley, Earl of Derby.

Lord Grey.
Here come the lords of Buckingham and Derby.

Duke of Buckingham.
Good time of day unto your royal Grace!

Lord Stanley.
God make your Majesty joyful, as you have been!

Queen Elizabeth.
The Countess Richmond, good my Lord of Derby,
To your good prayer will scarcely say amen.
Yet, Derby, notwithstanding she's your wife
And loves not me, be you, good lord, assur'd
I hate not you for her proud arrogance.

Lord Stanley.
I do beseech you, either not believe
The envious slanders of her false accusers;
Or if she be accus'd on true report,
Bear with her weakness, which I think proceeds
From wayward sickness and no grounded malice.

Queen Elizabeth.
Saw you the King today, my Lord of Derby?

Lord Stanley.
But now the Duke of Buckingham and I
Are come from visiting his Majesty.

Queen Elizabeth.
What likelihood of his amendment, lords?

Duke of Buckingham.
Madam, good hope, his Grace speaks cheerfully.

Queen Elizabeth.
God grant him health! Did you confer with him?

Duke of Buckingham.
Ay, madam, he desires to make atonement
Between the Duke of Gloucester and your brothers,
And between them and my Lord Chamberlain,
And sent to warn them to his royal presence.

Queen Elizabeth.
Would all were well! But that will never be:
I fear our happiness is at the height.

Enter Richard Duke of Gloucester and Lord Hastings.

Richard, Duke of Gloucester.
They do me wrong, and I will not endure it!
Who is it that complains unto the King
That I, forsooth, am stern, and love them not?
By holy Paul, they love his Grace but lightly
That fill his ears with such dissentious rumors.
Because I cannot flatter and look fair,
Smile in men's faces, smooth, deceive, and cog,
Duck with French nods and apish courtesy,
I must be held a rancorous enemy.
Cannot a plain man live and think no harm,
But thus his simple truth must be abus'd
With silken, sly, insinuating Jacks?

Lord Grey.
To who in all this presence speaks your Grace?

Richard, Duke of Gloucester.
To thee, that hast nor honesty nor grace:
When have I injur'd thee? When done thee wrong?
Or thee? Or thee? Or any of your faction?
A plague upon you all! His royal Grace
(Whom God preserve better than you would wish!)
Cannot be quiet scarce a breathing while
But you must trouble him with lewd complaints.

Queen Elizabeth.
Brother of Gloucester, you mistake the matter:
The King, on his own royal disposition
(And not provok'd by any suitor else),
Aiming, belike, at your interior hatred,
That in your outward action shows itself
Against my children, brothers, and myself,
Makes him to send, that he may learn the ground.

Richard, Duke of Gloucester.
I cannot tell, the world is grown so bad
That wrens make prey where eagles dare not perch.
Since every Jack became a gentleman,
There's many a gentle person made a Jack.

Queen Elizabeth.
Come, come, we know your meaning, brother Gloucester;
You envy my advancement and my friends'.
God grant we never may have need of you!

Richard, Duke of Gloucester.
Mean time, God grants that I have need of you.
Our brother is imprison'd by your means,
Myself disgrac'd, and the nobility
Held in contempt, while great promotions
Are daily given to ennoble those
That scarce some two days since were worth a noble.

Queen Elizabeth.
By Him that rais'd me to this careful height
From that contented hap which I enjoy'd,
I never did incense his Majesty
Against the Duke of Clarence, but have been
An earnest advocate to plead for him.
My lord, you do me shameful injury
Falsely to draw me in these vile suspects.

Richard, Duke of Gloucester.
You may deny that you were not the mean
Of my Lord Hastings' late imprisonment.

Earl Rivers.
She may, my lord, for—

Richard, Duke of Gloucester.
She may, Lord Rivers! Why, who knows not so?
She may do more, sir, than denying that:
She may help you to many fair preferments,
And then deny her aiding hand therein
And lay those honors on your high desert.
What may she not, she may, ay, marry, may she.

Earl Rivers.
What, marry, may she?

Richard, Duke of Gloucester.
What, marry, may she? Marry with a king,
A bachelor, and a handsome stripling too:
Iwis your grandam had a worser match.

Queen Elizabeth.
My Lord of Gloucester, I have too long borne
Your blunt upbraidings and your bitter scoffs.
By heaven, I will acquaint his Majesty
Of those gross taunts that oft I have endur'd.
I had rather be a country servant maid
Than a great queen with this condition,
To be so baited, scorn'd, and stormed at.

Enter old Queen Margaret behind.

Small joy have I in being England's queen.

Queen Margaret.

Aside.

And less'ned be that small, God I beseech him!
Thy honor, state, and seat is due to me.

Richard, Duke of Gloucester.
What? Threat you me with telling of the King?
Tell him, and spare not. Look what I have said,
I will avouch't in presence of the King.
I dare adventure to be sent to th' Tow'r.
'Tis time to speak, my pains are quite forgot.

Queen Margaret.

Aside.

Out, devil! I do remember them too well:
Thou kill'dst my husband Henry in the Tower,
And Edward, my poor son, at Tewksbury.

Richard, Duke of Gloucester.
Ere you were queen, ay, or your husband king,
I was a pack-horse in his great affairs:
A weeder-out of his proud adversaries,
A liberal rewarder of his friends;
To royalize his blood I spent mine own.

Queen Margaret.

Aside.

Ay, and much better blood than his or thine.

Richard, Duke of Gloucester.
In all which time you and your husband Grey
Were factious for the house of Lancaster;
And, Rivers, so were you. Was not your husband
In Margaret's battle at Saint Albans slain?
Let me put in your minds, if you forget,
What you have been ere this, and what you are;
Withal, what I have been, and what I am.

Queen Margaret.

Aside.

A murd'rous villain, and so still thou art.

Richard, Duke of Gloucester.
Poor Clarence did forsake his father, Warwick,
Ay, and forswore himself—which Jesu pardon!—

Queen Margaret.

Aside.

Which God revenge!

Richard, Duke of Gloucester.
To fight on Edward's party for the crown,
And for his meed, poor lord, he is mewed up.
I would to God my heart were flint, like Edward's,
Or Edward's soft and pitiful, like mine:
I am too childish-foolish for this world.

Queen Margaret.

Aside.

Hie thee to hell for shame, and leave this world,
Thou cacodemon, there thy kingdom is.

Earl Rivers.
My Lord of Gloucester, in those busy days,
Which here you urge to prove us enemies,
We follow'd then our lord, our sovereign king.
So should we you, if you should be our king.

Richard, Duke of Gloucester.
If I should be? I had rather be a pedlar:
Far be it from my heart, the thought thereof!

Queen Elizabeth.
As little joy, my lord, as you suppose
You should enjoy, were you this country's king—
As little joy you may suppose in me
That I enjoy, being the queen thereof.

Queen Margaret.

Aside.

A little joy enjoys the queen thereof,
For I am she, and altogether joyless.
I can no longer hold me patient.

Comes forward.

Hear me, you wrangling pirates, that fall out
In sharing that which you have pill'd from me!
Which of you trembles not that looks on me?
If not, that I am queen, you bow like subjects,
Yet that, by you depos'd, you quake like rebels?
Ah, gentle villain, do not turn away!

Richard, Duke of Gloucester.
Foul wrinkled witch, what mak'st thou in my sight?

Queen Margaret.
But repetition of what thou hast marr'd,
That will I make before I let thee go.

Richard, Duke of Gloucester.
Wert thou not banished on pain of death?

Queen Margaret.
I was; but I do find more pain in banishment
Than death can yield me here by my abode.
A husband and a son thou ow'st to me—
And thou a kingdom—all of you allegiance.
This sorrow that I have, by right is yours,
And all the pleasures you usurp are mine.

Richard, Duke of Gloucester.
The curse my noble father laid on thee
When thou didst crown his warlike brows with paper,
And with thy scorns drew'st rivers from his eyes,
And then, to dry them, gav'st the Duke a clout
Steep'd in the faultless blood of pretty Rutland—
His curses then, from bitterness of soul
Denounc'd against thee, are all fall'n upon thee;
And God, not we, hath plagu'd thy bloody deed.

Queen Elizabeth.
So just is God, to right the innocent.

Lord Hastings.
O, 'twas the foulest deed to slay that babe,
And the most merciless, that e'er was heard of!

Earl Rivers.
Tyrants themselves wept when it was reported.

Marquess of Dorset.
No man but prophesied revenge for it.

Duke of Buckingham.
Northumberland, then present, wept to see it.

Queen Margaret.
What? Were you snarling all before I came,
Ready to catch each other by the throat,
And turn you all your hatred now on me?
Did York's dread curse prevail so much with heaven
That Henry's death, my lovely Edward's death,
Their kingdom's loss, my woeful banishment,
Should all but answer for that peevish brat?
Can curses pierce the clouds and enter heaven?
Why then give way, dull clouds, to my quick curses!
Though not by war, by surfeit die your king,
As ours by murder, to make him a king!

Edward thy son, that now is Prince of Wales,
For Edward our son, that was Prince of Wales,
Die in his youth by like untimely violence!
Thyself a queen, for me that was a queen,
Outlive thy glory like my wretched self!
Long mayst thou live to wail thy children's death,
And see another, as I see thee now,
Deck'd in thy rights as thou art stall'd in mine!
Long die thy happy days before thy death,
And after many length'ned hours of grief,
Die neither mother, wife, nor England's queen!
Rivers and Dorset, you were standers-by,
And so wast thou, Lord Hastings, when my son
Was stabb'd with bloody daggers: God, I pray him
That none of you may live his natural age,
But by some unlook'd accident cut off!

Richard, Duke of Gloucester.
Have done thy charm, thou hateful with'red hag.

Queen Margaret.
And leave out thee? Stay, dog, for thou shalt hear me.
If heaven have any grievous plague in store
Exceeding those that I can wish upon thee,
O, let them keep it till thy sins be ripe,
And then hurl down their indignation
On thee, the troubler of the poor world's peace!
The worm of conscience still begnaw thy soul!
Thy friends suspect for traitors while thou liv'st,
And take deep traitors for thy dearest friends!
No sleep close up that deadly eye of thine,
Unless it be while some tormenting dream
Affrights thee with a hell of ugly devils!
Thou elvish-mark'd, abortive, rooting hog!
Thou that wast seal'd in thy nativity
The slave of nature and the son of hell!
Thou slander of thy heavy mother's womb!
Thou loathed issue of thy father's loins!
Thou rag of honor! Thou detested—

Richard, Duke of Gloucester.
Margaret.

Queen Margaret.
                    Richard!

Richard, Duke of Gloucester.
                    Ha!

Queen Margaret.
                    I call thee not.

Richard, Duke of Gloucester.
I cry thee mercy then; for I did think
That thou hadst call'd me all these bitter names.

Queen Margaret.
Why, so I did, but look'd for no reply.
O, let me make the period to my curse!

Richard, Duke of Gloucester.
'Tis done by me, and ends in "Margaret."

Queen Elizabeth.
Thus have you breath'd your curse against yourself.

Queen Margaret.
Poor painted queen, vain flourish of my fortune!
Why strew'st thou sugar on that bottled spider
Whose deadly web ensnareth thee about?
Fool, fool, thou whet'st a knife to kill thyself.
The day will come that thou shalt wish for me
To help thee curse this poisonous bunch-back'd toad.

Lord Hastings.
False-boding woman, end thy frantic curse,
Lest to thy harm thou move our patience.

Queen Margaret.
Foul shame upon you, you have all mov'd mine.

Earl Rivers.
Were you well serv'd, you would be taught your duty.

Queen Margaret.
To serve me well, you all should do me duty,
Teach me to be your queen, and you my subjects:
O, serve me well, and teach yourselves that duty!

Marquess of Dorset.
Dispute not with her, she is lunatic.

Queen Margaret.
Peace, Master Marquess, you are malapert,
Your fire-new stamp of honor is scarce current.
O that your young nobility could judge
What 'twere to lose it and be miserable!
They that stand high have many blasts to shake them,
And if they fall, they dash themselves to pieces.

Richard, Duke of Gloucester.
Good counsel, marry! Learn it, learn it, Marquess.

Marquess of Dorset.
It touches you, my lord, as much as me.

Richard, Duke of Gloucester.
Ay, and much more; but I was born so high,
Our aery buildeth in the cedar's top
And dallies with the wind and scorns the sun.

Queen Margaret.
And turns the sun to shade—alas, alas!
Witness my son, now in the shade of death,
Whose bright out-shining beams thy cloudy wrath
Hath in eternal darkness folded up.
Your aery buildeth in our aery's nest:
O God that seest it, do not suffer it!
As it is won with blood, lost be it so!

Duke of Buckingham.
Peace, peace, for shame! If not, for charity.

Queen Margaret.
Urge neither charity nor shame to me.

Turning to the others.

Uncharitably with me have you dealt,
And shamefully my hopes, by you, are butcher'd.
My charity is outrage, life my shame,
And in that shame still live my sorrow's rage!

Duke of Buckingham.
Have done, have done.

Queen Margaret.
O princely Buckingham, I'll kiss thy hand
In sign of league and amity with thee.
Now fair befall thee and thy noble house!
Thy garments are not spotted with our blood;
Nor thou within the compass of my curse.

Duke of Buckingham.
Nor no one here; for curses never pass
The lips of those that breathe them in the air.

Queen Margaret.
I will not think but they ascend the sky,
And there awake God's gentle-sleeping peace.
O Buckingham, take heed of yonder dog!
Look when he fawns he bites; and when he bites,
His venom tooth will rankle to the death.
Have not to do with him, beware of him;
Sin, death, and hell have set their marks on him,
And all their ministers attend on him.

Richard, Duke of Gloucester.
What doth she say, my Lord of Buckingham?

Duke of Buckingham.
Nothing that I respect, my gracious lord.

Queen Margaret.
What, dost thou scorn me for my gentle counsel?
And soothe the devil that I warn thee from?
O but remember this another day,
When he shall split thy very heart with sorrow,
And say poor Margaret was a prophetess!
Live each of you the subjects to his hate,
And he to yours, and all of you to God's!

Exit.

Duke of Buckingham.
My hair doth stand an end to hear her curses.

Earl Rivers.
And so doth mine. I muse why she's at liberty.

Richard, Duke of Gloucester.
I cannot blame her; by God's holy Mother,
She hath had too much wrong, and I repent
My part thereof that I have done to her.

Queen Elizabeth.
I never did her any to my knowledge.

Richard, Duke of Gloucester.
Yet you have all the vantage of her wrong.
I was too hot to do somebody good
That is too cold in thinking of it now.
Marry, as for Clarence, he is well repaid;
He is frank'd up to fatting for his pains—
God pardon them that are the cause thereof!

Earl Rivers.
A virtuous and a Christian-like conclusion—
To pray for them that have done scathe to us.

Richard, Duke of Gloucester.
So do I ever—

Speaks to himself.

being well advis'd;
For had I curs'd now, I had curs'd myself.

Enter Catesby.

Sir William Catesby.
Madam, his Majesty doth call for you,
And for your Grace, and yours, my gracious lord.

Queen Elizabeth.
Catesby, I come. Lords, will you go with me?

Earl Rivers.
We wait upon your Grace.

Exeunt all but Gloucester.

Richard, Duke of Gloucester.
I do the wrong, and first begin to brawl.
The secret mischiefs that I set abroach
I lay unto the grievous charge of others.
Clarence, who I indeed have cast in darkness,
I do beweep to many simple gulls—
Namely, to Derby, Hastings, Buckingham—
And tell them 'tis the Queen and her allies
That stir the King against the Duke my brother.
Now they believe it, and withal whet me
To be reveng'd on Rivers, Dorset, Grey.
But then I sigh, and, with a piece of scripture,
Tell them that God bids us do good for evil:
And thus I clothe my naked villainy
With odd old ends stol'n forth of holy writ,
And seem a saint, when most I play the devil.

Enter two Murderers.

But soft, here come my executioners.
How now, my hardy, stout, resolved mates,
Are you now going to dispatch this thing?

First Murderer.
We are, my lord, and come to have the warrant,
That we may be admitted where he is.

Richard, Duke of Gloucester.
Well thought upon, I have it here about me.

Gives the warrant.

When you have done, repair to Crosby Place.
But, sirs, be sudden in the execution,
Withal obdurate, do not hear him plead;
For Clarence is well-spoken, and perhaps
May move your hearts to pity if you mark him.

First Murderer.
Tut, tut, my lord, we will not stand to prate;
Talkers are no good doers. Be assur'd;
We go to use our hands, and not our tongues.

Richard, Duke of Gloucester.
Your eyes drop millstones, when fools' eyes fall tears.
I like you, lads, about your business straight.
Go, go, dispatch.

First Murderer.
We will, my noble lord.

Exeunt.

Scene 4

London. The Tower.

(Clarence; Keeper; Brakenbury; Murderers)

Clarence tells his keeper of the terrible dream he had, in which he saw himself drown and accused after death of all the treasons he has committed. He keenly feels his guilt. The two Murderers enter, showing their warrant to Brakenbury, the commander of the Tower, who does not want to know why they have come. The two Murderers debate a little about going through with the deed, one of them being somewhat conscience-stricken at the idea, but remembering that they will be well paid, they decide to go through with it. They wake Clarence, who tries to reason with them, but they throw his guilt in his face, inform him that their warrant is from the King, and when he begs them to go to Richard for help, tell him that it is Richard who sent them to kill him. They stab him and drag his body to another room to drown him in a barrel of wine. One of the murderers repents, and tells the other that he will not accept the fee for killing Clarence.

Enter Clarence and Keeper.

Keeper in the Tower.
Why looks your Grace so heavily today?

George, Duke of Clarence.
O, I have pass'd a miserable night,
So full of fearful dreams, of ugly sights,
That, as I am a Christian faithful man,
I would not spend another such a night
Though 'twere to buy a world of happy days—
So full of dismal terror was the time.

Keeper in the Tower.
What was your dream, my lord? I pray you tell me.

George, Duke of Clarence.
Methoughts that I had broken from the Tower
And was embark'd to cross to Burgundy,

And in my company my brother Gloucester,
Who from my cabin tempted me to walk
Upon the hatches. Thence we look'd toward England,
And cited up a thousand heavy times,
During the wars of York and Lancaster,
That had befall'n us. As we pac'd along
Upon the giddy footing of the hatches,
Methought that Gloucester stumbled, and in falling
Struck me (that thought to stay him) overboard
Into the tumbling billows of the main.
O Lord, methought what pain it was to drown!
What dreadful noise of waters in my ears!
What sights of ugly death within my eyes!
Methoughts I saw a thousand fearful wracks;
A thousand men that fishes gnaw'd upon;
Wedges of gold, great anchors, heaps of pearl,
Inestimable stones, unvalued jewels,
All scatt'red in the bottom of the sea:
Some lay in dead men's skulls, and in the holes
Where eyes did once inhabit, there were crept
(As 'twere in scorn of eyes) reflecting gems,
That woo'd the slimy bottom of the deep,
And mock'd the dead bones that lay scatt'red by.

Keeper in the Tower.
Had you such leisure in the time of death
To gaze upon these secrets of the deep?

George, Duke of Clarence.
Methought I had, and often did I strive
To yield the ghost; but still the envious flood
Stopp'd in my soul, and would not let it forth
To find the empty, vast, and wand'ring air,
But smother'd it within my panting bulk,
Who almost burst to belch it in the sea.

Keeper in the Tower.
Awak'd you not in this sore agony?

George, Duke of Clarence.
No, no, my dream was lengthen'd after life.
O then began the tempest to my soul!
I pass'd (methought) the melancholy flood,
With that sour ferryman which poets write of,
Unto the kingdom of perpetual night.
The first that there did greet my stranger soul
Was my great father-in-law, renowned Warwick,
Who spake aloud, "What scourge for perjury
Can this dark monarchy afford false Clarence?"
And so he vanish'd. Then came wand'ring by
A shadow like an angel, with bright hair
Dabbled in blood, and he shriek'd out aloud,
"Clarence is come—false, fleeting, perjur'd Clarence,
That stabb'd me in the field by Tewksbury:
Seize on him, Furies, take him unto torment!"
With that (methoughts) a legion of foul fiends
Environ'd me, and howled in mine ears
Such hideous cries that with the very noise
I, trembling, wak'd, and for a season after
Could not believe but that I was in hell,
Such terrible impression made my dream.

Keeper in the Tower.
No marvel, lord, though it affrighted you;
I am afraid (methinks) to hear you tell it.

Keeper in the Tower.
Ah, Keeper, Keeper, I have done these things
(That now give evidence against my soul)
For Edward's sake, and see how he requites me!
O God! If my deep pray'rs cannot appease thee,
But thou wilt be aveng'd on my misdeeds,
Yet execute thy wrath in me alone!
O, spare my guiltless wife and my poor children!
Keeper, I prithee sit by me awhile.
My soul is heavy, and I fain would sleep.

Keeper in the Tower.
I will, my lord. God give your Grace good rest!

Clarence sleeps.
Enter Brakenbury, the Lieutenant.

Sir Robert Brakenbury.
Sorrow breaks seasons and reposing hours,
Makes the night morning and the noontide night:
Princes have but their titles for their glories,
An outward honor for an inward toil,
And for unfelt imaginations
They often feel a world of restless cares;
So that between their titles and low name
There's nothing differs but the outward fame.

Enter two Murderers.

First Murderer.
Ho, who's here?

Sir Robert Brakenbury.
What wouldst thou, fellow? And how cam'st thou hither?

First Murderer.
I would speak with Clarence, and I came hither on my legs.

Sir Robert Brakenbury.
What, so brief?

Second Murderer.
'Tis better, sir, than to be tedious. Let him see our commission, and talk no more.

Brakenbury reads it.

Sir Robert Brakenbury.
I am in this commanded to deliver
The noble Duke of Clarence to your hands.
I will not reason what is meant hereby,
Because I will be guiltless from the meaning.
There lies the Duke asleep, and there the keys.
I'll to the King and signify to him
That thus I have resign'd to you my charge.

First Murderer.
You may, sir, 'tis a point of wisdom. Fare you well.

Exit Brakenbury with Keeper.

Second Murderer.
What, shall I stab him as he sleeps?

First Murderer.
No, he'll say 'twas done cowardly when he wakes.

Second Murderer.
Why, he shall never wake until the great Judgment Day.

First Murderer.
Why, then he'll say we stabb'd him sleeping.

Second Murderer.
The urging of that word "judgment" hath bred a kind of remorse in me.

First Murderer.
What? Art thou afraid?

Second Murderer.
Not to kill him, having a warrant, but to be damn'd for killing him, from the which no warrant can defend me.

First Murderer.
I thought thou hadst been resolute.

Second Murderer.
So I am—to let him live.

First Murderer.
I'll back to the Duke of Gloucester and tell him so.

Second Murderer.
Nay, I prithee stay a little. I hope this passionate humor of mine will change. It was wont to hold me but while one tells twenty.

First Murderer.
How dost thou feel thyself now?

Second Murderer.
Faith, some certain dregs of conscience are yet within me.

First Murderer.
Remember our reward when the deed's done.

Second Murderer.
'Zounds, he dies! I had forgot the reward.

First Murderer.
Where's thy conscience now?

Second Murderer.
O, in the Duke of Gloucester's purse.

First Murderer.
When he opens his purse to give us our reward, thy conscience flies out.

Second Murderer.
'Tis no matter, let it go. There's few or none will entertain it.

First Murderer.
What if it come to thee again?

Second Murderer.
I'll not meddle with it, it makes a man a coward. A man cannot steal, but it accuseth him; a man cannot swear, but it checks him; a man cannot lie with his neighbor's wife, but it detects him. 'Tis a blushing shame-fac'd spirit that mutinies in a man's bosom. It fills a man full of obstacles. It made me once restore a purse of gold that (by chance) I found. It beggars any man that keeps it. It is turn'd out of towns and cities for a dangerous thing, and every man that means to

Act 1, Scene 4

live well endeavors to trust to himself and live without it.

First Murderer.
'Zounds, 'tis even now at my elbow, persuading me not to kill the Duke.

Second Murderer.
Take the devil in thy mind, and believe him not; he would insinuate with thee but to make thee sigh.

First Murderer.
I am strong-fram'd, he cannot prevail with me.

Second Murderer.
Spoke like a tall man that respects thy reputation. Come, shall we fall to work?

First Murderer.
Take him on the costard with the hilts of thy sword, and then throw him into the malmsey-butt in the next room.

Second Murderer.
O excellent device! And make a sop of him.

First Murderer.
Soft, he wakes.

Second Murderer.
Strike!

First Murderer.
No, we'll reason with him.

George, Duke of Clarence.
Where art thou, Keeper? Give me a cup of wine.

Second Murderer.
You shall have wine enough, my lord, anon.

George, Duke of Clarence.
In God's name, what art thou?

First Murderer.
A man, as you are.

George, Duke of Clarence.
But not, as I am, royal.

Second Murderer.
Nor you, as we are, loyal.

George, Duke of Clarence.
Thy voice is thunder, but thy looks are humble.

First Murderer.
My voice is now the King's, my looks mine own.

George, Duke of Clarence.
How darkly and how deadly dost thou speak!
Your eyes do menace me. Why look you pale?
Who sent you hither? Wherefore do you come?

Both First and Second Murderers.
To, to, to—

George, Duke of Clarence.
To murder me?

Both First and Second Murderers.
Ay, ay.

George, Duke of Clarence.
You scarcely have the hearts to tell me so,
And therefore cannot have the hearts to do it.
Wherein, my friends, have I offended you?

First Murderer.
Offended us you have not, but the King.

George, Duke of Clarence.
I shall be reconcil'd to him again.

Second Murderer.
Never, my lord, therefore prepare to die.

George, Duke of Clarence.
Are you drawn forth among a world of men
To slay the innocent? What is my offense?
Where is the evidence that doth accuse me?
What lawful quest have given their verdict up
Unto the frowning judge? Or who pronounc'd
The bitter sentence of poor Clarence' death?
Before I be convict by course of law,
To threaten me with death is most unlawful.
I charge you, as you hope to have redemption
By Christ's dear blood shed for our grievous sins,
That you depart, and lay no hands on me.
The deed you undertake is damnable.

First Murderer.
What we will do, we do upon command.

Second Murderer.
And he that hath commanded is our King.

George, Duke of Clarence.
Erroneous vassals, the great King of kings
Hath in the table of his law commanded
That thou shalt do no murder. Will you then
Spurn at his edict, and fulfill a man's?
Take heed; for he holds vengeance in his hand,
To hurl upon their heads that break his law.

Second Murderer.
And that same vengeance doth he hurl on thee
For false forswearing and for murder too.
Thou didst receive the sacrament to fight
In quarrel of the house of Lancaster.

First Murderer.
And like a traitor to the name of God
Didst break that vow, and with thy treacherous blade
Unrip'st the bowels of thy sov'reign's son.

Second Murderer.
Whom thou wast sworn to cherish and defend.

First Murderer.
How canst thou urge God's dreadful law to us,
When thou hast broke it in such dear degree?

George, Duke of Clarence.
Alas! For whose sake did I that ill deed?
For Edward, for my brother, for his sake.
He sends you not to murder me for this,
For in that sin he is as deep as I.
If God will be avenged for the deed,
O, know you yet he doth it publicly.
Take not the quarrel from his pow'rful arm;
He needs no indirect or lawless course
To cut off those that have offended him.

First Murderer.
Who made thee then a bloody minister,
When gallant-springing brave Plantagenet,
That princely novice, was struck dead by thee?

George, Duke of Clarence.
My brother's love, the devil, and my rage.

First Murderer.
Thy brother's love, our duty, and thy faults
Provoke us hither now to slaughter thee.

George, Duke of Clarence.
O, if you love my brother, hate not me!
I am his brother and I love him well.
If you are hir'd for meed, go back again,
And I will send you to my brother Gloucester,
Who shall reward you better for my life
Than Edward will for tidings of my death.

Second Murderer.
You are deceiv'd, your brother Gloucester hates you.

George, Duke of Clarence.
O no; he loves me and he holds me dear.
Go you to him from me.

First Murderer.
      Ay, so we will.

George, Duke of Clarence.
Tell him, when that our princely father York
Blest his three sons with his victorious arm,
And charg'd us from his soul to love each other,)
He little thought of this divided friendship.
Bid Gloucester think of this, and he will weep.

First Murderer.
Ay, millstones, as he lesson'd us to weep.

George, Duke of Clarence.
O, do not slander him, for he is kind.

First Murderer.
Right, as snow in harvest. Come, you deceive yourself,
'Tis he that sends us to destroy you here.

George, Duke of Clarence.
It cannot be, for he bewept my fortune,
And hugg'd me in his arms, and swore with sobs
That he would labor my delivery.

First Murderer.
Why, so he doth, when he delivers you
From this earth's thralldom to the joys of heaven.

Second Murderer.
Make peace with God, for you must die, my lord.

George, Duke of Clarence.
Have you that holy feeling in your souls
To counsel me to make my peace with God,
And are you yet to your own souls so blind
That you will war with God by murd'ring me?
O, sirs, consider, they that set you on
To do this deed will hate you for the deed.

Second Murderer.
What shall we do?

George, Duke of Clarence.
                Relent, and save your souls.
Which of you, if you were a prince's son,
Being pent from liberty, as I am now,
If two such murderers as yourselves came to you,
Would not entreat for life?

First Murderer.
Relent? No: 'tis cowardly and womanish.

George, Duke of Clarence.
Not to relent is beastly, savage, devilish.
My friend

To Second Murderer

                I spy some pity in thy looks.
O, if thine eye be not a flatterer,
Come thou on my side, and entreat for me,
As you would beg, were you in my distress.
A begging prince what beggar pities not?

Second Murderer.
Look behind you, my lord.

First Murderer.
Take that! And that!

Stabs him.

                If all this will not do,
I'll drown you in the malmsey-butt within.

Exit with the body.

Second Murderer.
A bloody deed, and desperately dispatch'd!
How fain, like Pilate, would I wash my hands
Of this most grievous murder!

Enter First Murderer.

First Murderer.
How now? What mean'st thou, that thou help'st me not?
By heavens, the Duke shall know how slack you have been!

Second Murderer.
I would he knew that I had sav'd his brother!
Take thou the fee and tell him what I say,
For I repent me that the Duke is slain.

Exit.

First Murderer.
So do not I. Go, coward as thou art.
Well, I'll go hide the body in some hole
Till that the Duke give order for his burial;
And when I have my meed, I will away,
For this will out, and then I must not stay.

Exit.

Act 2

Scene 1

London. The palace.

(*King Edward; Queen Elizabeth; Lord Marquess Dorset; Rivers; Hastings; Catesby; Buckingham; Grey; Ratcliffe; Gloucester; Stanley*)

King Edward is pleased as he manages to reconcile all the warring parties, who swear friendship. Richard pretends shock and horror when Clarence is mentioned, and reveals that he has been killed. The King mourns, horrified, and remembers all that was good about his brother. Richard lays the blame for the execution on the Queen's family.

Flourish. Enter the King Edward sick, the Queen Elizabeth, Lord Marquess Dorset, Rivers, Hastings, Catesby, Buckingham, Grey, and others.

King Edward the Fourth.
Why, so: now have I done a good day's work.
You peers, continue this united league.
I every day expect an embassage
From my Redeemer to redeem me hence;
And more in peace my soul shall part to heaven,
Since I have made my friends at peace on earth.
Hastings and Rivers, take each other's hand,
Dissemble not your hatred, swear your love.

Earl Rivers.
By heaven, my soul is purg'd from grudging hate,
And with my hand I seal my true heart's love.

Lord Hastings.
So thrive I, as I truly swear the like!

King Edward the Fourth.
Take heed you dally not before your king,
Lest He that is the supreme King of kings
Confound your hidden falsehood and award
Either of you to be the other's end.

Lord Hastings.
So prosper I, as I swear perfect love!

Earl Rivers.
And I, as I love Hastings with my heart!

King Edward the Fourth.
Madam, yourself is not exempt from this;
Nor you, son Dorset; Buckingham, nor you;
You have been factious one against the other.
Wife, love Lord Hastings, let him kiss your hand,
And what you do, do it unfeignedly.

Queen Elizabeth.
There, Hastings, I will never more remember
Our former hatred, so thrive I and mine!

King Edward the Fourth.
Dorset, embrace him; Hastings, love Lord Marquess.

Marquess of Dorset.
This interchange of love, I here protest,
Upon my part shall be inviolable.

Lord Hastings.
And so swear I.

They embrace.

King Edward the Fourth.
Now, princely Buckingham, seal thou this league
With thy embracements to my wive's allies,
And make me happy in your unity.

Duke of Buckingham.
When ever Buckingham doth turn his hate
Upon your Grace

To the Queen.

But with all duteous love
Doth cherish you and yours, God punish me
With hate in those where I expect most love!
When I have most need to employ a friend,
And most assured that he is a friend,
Deep, hollow, treacherous, and full of guile
Be he unto me! This do I beg of God,
When I am cold in love to you or yours.

They embrace.

King Edward the Fourth.
A pleasing cordial, princely Buckingham,
Is this thy vow unto my sickly heart.
There wanteth now our brother Gloucester here
To make the blessed period of this peace.

Duke of Buckingham.
And in good time,
Here comes Sir Richard Ratcliffe and the Duke.

Enter Ratcliffe and Gloucester.

Richard, Duke of Gloucester.
Good morrow to my sovereign king and queen,
And, princely peers, a happy time of day!

King Edward the Fourth.
Happy indeed, as we have spent the day.
Gloucester, we have done deeds of charity,
Made peace of enmity, fair love of hate,
Between these swelling wrong-incensed peers.

Richard, Duke of Gloucester.
A blessed labor, my most sovereign lord.
Among this princely heap, if any here
By false intelligence or wrong surmise
Hold me a foe—
If I unwittingly, or in my rage,
Have aught committed that is hardly borne
By any in this presence, I desire
To reconcile me to his friendly peace.
'Tis death to me to be at enmity;
I hate it, and desire all good men's love.
First, madam, I entreat true peace of you,
Which I will purchase with my duteous service;
Of you, my noble cousin Buckingham,
If ever any grudge were lodg'd between us;
Of you, and you, Lord Rivers, and of Dorset,
That all without desert have frown'd on me;
Dukes, earls, lords, gentlemen—indeed of all.
I do not know that Englishman alive
With whom my soul is any jot at odds
More than the infant that is born tonight.
I thank my God for my humility.

Queen Elizabeth.
A holy day shall this be kept hereafter.
I would to God all strifes were well compounded.
My sovereign lord, I do beseech your Highness
To take our brother Clarence to your grace.

Richard, Duke of Gloucester.
Why, madam, have I off'red love for this,
To be so flouted in this royal presence?
Who knows not that the gentle Duke is dead?

They all start.

You do him injury to scorn his corse.

King Edward the Fourth.
Who knows not he is dead? Who knows he is?

Queen Elizabeth.
All-seeing heaven, what a world is this!

Duke of Buckingham.
Look I so pale, Lord Dorset, as the rest?

Marquess of Dorset.
Ay, my good lord, and no man in the presence
But his red color hath forsook his cheeks.

King Edward the Fourth.
Is Clarence dead? The order was revers'd.

Richard, Duke of Gloucester.
But he, poor man, by your first order died,
And that a winged Mercury did bear;
Some tardy cripple bare the countermand,
That came too lag to see him buried.
God grant that some, less noble and less loyal,
Nearer in bloody thoughts, but not in blood,
Deserve not worse than wretched Clarence did,
And yet go current from suspicion!

Enter Stanley, Earl of Derby.

Lord Stanley.
A boon, my sovereign, for my service done!

Kneels.

King Edward the Fourth.
I prithee peace, my soul is full of sorrow.

Lord Stanley.
I will not rise, unless your Highness hear me.

King Edward the Fourth.
Then say at once what is it thou requests.

Lord Stanley.
The forfeit, sovereign, of my servant's life,
Who slew today a riotous gentleman
Lately attendant on the Duke of Norfolk.

King Edward the Fourth.
Have I a tongue to doom my brother's death,
And shall that tongue give pardon to a slave?
My brother kill'd no man, his fault was thought,
And yet his punishment was bitter death.
Who sued to me for him? Who (in my wrath)
Kneel'd at my feet and bid me be advis'd?
Who spoke of brotherhood? Who spoke of love?
Who told me how the poor soul did forsake
The mighty Warwick and did fight for me?
Who told me, in the field at Tewksbury,
When Oxford had me down, he rescued me,
And said, "Dear brother, live, and be a king"?
Who told me, when we both lay in the field
Frozen (almost) to death, how he did lap me
Even in his own garments, and did give himself
(All thin and naked) to the numb cold night?
All this from my remembrance brutish wrath
Sinfully pluck'd, and not a man of you
Had so much grace to put it in my mind.
But when your carters or your waiting vassals
Have done a drunken slaughter, and defac'd
The precious image of our dear Redeemer,
You straight are on your knees for pardon, pardon,
And I (unjustly too) must grant it you.

Stanley rises.

But for my brother not a man would speak,
Nor I (ungracious) speak unto myself
For him, poor soul. The proudest of you all
Have been beholding to him in his life;
Yet none of you would once beg for his life.
O God! I fear thy justice will take hold
On me and you, and mine and yours, for this.
Come, Hastings, help me to my closet. Ah, poor Clarence!

Exeunt some with King and Queen.

Richard, Duke of Gloucester.
This is the fruits of rashness! Mark'd you not
How that the guilty kindred of the Queen
Look'd pale when they did hear of Clarence' death?
O, they did urge it still unto the King!
God will revenge it. Come, lords, will you go

To comfort Edward with our company.

Duke of Buckingham.
We wait upon your Grace.

Exeunt.

Scene 2

London. The palace.

(Duchess of York; Edward Plantagenet; Margaret Plantagenet; Queen Elizabeth; Rivers; Dorset; Richard of Gloucester; Buckingham; Earl of Derby; Hastings; Ratcliffe)

Clarence's young children asks their grandmother the Duchess of York whether their father is dead; she insists that he is not. When Clarence's son mentions Richard's weeping when talking about Clarence, the Duchess comments that her son was almost certainly being hypocritical. She admits to loathing him. The Queen enters wailing, bearing the news of King Edward's death. Richard arrives, speaking consolingly; he asks for his mother's blessing, but she does not give a complete one. Buckingham suggests that the new King be fetched by a small number of people, to avoid worrying people that the civil wars might be starting up again. Richard and Buckingham agree to make sure they are among those going to fetch the King.

Enter the old Duchess of York with the two children of Clarence (Edward and Margaret Plantagenet).

Edward Plantagenet.
Good grandam, tell us, is our father dead?

Duchess of York.
No, boy.

Margaret Plantagenet.
Why do you weep so oft, and beat your breast,
And cry, "O Clarence, my unhappy son!"?

Edward Plantagenet.
Why do you look on us, and shake your head,
And call us orphans, wretches, castaways,
If that our noble father were alive?

Duchess of York.
My pretty cousins, you mistake me both:
I do lament the sickness of the King,
As loath to lose him, not your father's death;
It were lost sorrow to wail one that's lost.

Edward Plantagenet.
Then you conclude, my grandam, he is dead.
The King mine uncle is to blame for it.
God will revenge it, whom I will importune
With earnest prayers all to that effect.

Margaret Plantagenet.
And so will I.

Duchess of York.
Peace, children, peace, the King doth love you well.
Incapable and shallow innocents,
You cannot guess who caus'd your father's death.

Edward Plantagenet.
Grandam, we can; for my good uncle Gloucester
Told me the King, provok'd to it by the Queen,
Devis'd impeachments to imprison him;
And when my uncle told me so, he wept,
And pitied me, and kindly kiss'd my cheek;
Bade me rely on him as on my father,
And he would love me dearly as a child.

Duchess of York.
Ah! That deceit should steal such gentle shape,
And with a virtuous visor hide deep vice!
He is my son—ay, and therein my shame,
Yet from my dugs he drew not this deceit.

Edward Plantagenet.
Think you my uncle did dissemble, grandam?

Duchess of York.
Ay, boy.

Edward Plantagenet.
I cannot think it. Hark, what noise is this?

Enter the Queen Elizabeth with her hair about her ears; Rivers and Dorset after her.

Queen Elizabeth.
Ah! Who shall hinder me to wail and weep,
To chide my fortune, and torment myself?
I'll join with black despair against my soul,
And to myself become an enemy.

Duchess of York.
What means this scene of rude impatience?

Queen Elizabeth.
To make an act of tragic violence.
Edward, my lord, thy son, our king, is dead!
Why grow the branches when the root is gone?
Why wither not the leaves that want their sap?
If you will live, lament; if die, be brief,
That our swift-winged souls may catch the King's,
Or like obedient subjects follow him
To his new kingdom of ne'er-changing night.

Duchess of York.
Ah, so much interest have I in thy sorrow
As I had title in thy noble husband!
I have bewept a worthy husband's death,
And liv'd with looking on his images;
But now two mirrors of his princely semblance
Are crack'd in pieces by malignant death,
And I for comfort have but one false glass,
That grieves me when I see my shame in him.
Thou art a widow; yet thou art a mother,
And hast the comfort of thy children left;
But death hath snatch'd my husband from mine arms,
And pluck'd two crutches from my feeble hands,
Clarence and Edward. O, what cause have I
(Thine being but a moi'ty of my moan)
To overgo thy woes and drown thy cries!

Edward Plantagenet.
Ah, aunt! You wept not for our father's death;
How can we aid you with our kindred tears?

Margaret Plantagenet.
Our fatherless distress was left unmoan'd,
Your widow-dolor likewise be unwept!

Queen Elizabeth.
Give me no help in lamentation,
I am not barren to bring forth complaints.
All springs reduce their currents to mine eyes,
That I being govern'd by the watery moon,
May send forth plenteous tears to drown the world!
Ah for my husband, for my dear Lord Edward!

Children.
Ah for our father, for our dear Lord Clarence!

Duchess of York.
Alas for both, both mine, Edward and Clarence!

Queen Elizabeth.
What stay had I but Edward? And he's gone.

Children.
What stay had we but Clarence? And he's gone.

Duchess of York.
What stays had I but they? And they are gone.

Queen Elizabeth.
Was never widow had so dear a loss.

Children.
Were never orphans had so dear a loss.

Duchess of York.
Was never mother had so dear a loss.
Alas! I am the mother of these griefs:
Their woes are parcell'd, mine is general.
She for an Edward weeps, and so do I;
I for a Clarence weep, so doth not she;
These babes for Clarence weep, and so do I;
I for an Edward weep, so do not they.
Alas! You three on me, threefold distress'd,
Pour all your tears. I am your sorrow's nurse,
And I will pamper it with lamentation.

Marquess of Dorset.
Comfort, dear mother, God is much displeas'd
That you take with unthankfulness his doing.
In common worldly things 'tis call'd ungrateful
With dull unwillingness to repay a debt,
Which with a bounteous hand was kindly lent;
Much more to be thus opposite with heaven,
For it requires the royal debt it lent you.

Earl Rivers.
Madam, bethink you like a careful mother
Of the young Prince your son. Send straight for him,
Let him be crown'd, in him your comfort lives.
Drown desperate sorrow in dead Edward's grave,
And plant your joys in living Edward's throne.

Enter Richard of Gloucester, Buckingham, Stanley Earl of Derby, Hastings, and Ratcliffe.

Richard, Duke of Gloucester.
Sister, have comfort. All of us have cause
To wail the dimming of our shining star;
But none can help our harms by wailing them.
Madam, my mother, I do cry you mercy,
I did not see your Grace. Humbly on my knee
I crave your blessing.

Duchess of York.
God bless thee, and put meekness in thy breast,
Love, charity, obedience, and true duty!

Richard, Duke of Gloucester.
Amen!—

Aside.

                  And make me die a good old man!
That is the butt-end of a mother's blessing.
I marvel that her Grace did leave it out.

Duke of Buckingham.
You cloudy princes and heart-sorrowing peers
That bear this heavy mutual load of moan,
Now cheer each other in each other's love.
Though we have spent our harvest of this king,
We are to reap the harvest of his son.
The broken rancor of your high-swoll'n hates,
But lately splinter'd, knit, and join'd together,
Must gently be preserv'd, cherish'd, and kept.
Me seemeth good that, with some little train,
Forthwith from Ludlow the young Prince be fet
Hither to London, to be crown'd our king.

Earl Rivers.
Why with some little train, my Lord of Buckingham?

Duke of Buckingham.
Marry, my lord, lest by a multitude
The new-heal'd wound of malice should break out,
Which would be so much the more dangerous,
By how much the estate is green and yet ungovern'd.
Where every horse bears his commanding rein
And may direct his course as please himself,
As well the fear of harm, as harm apparent,
In my opinion, ought to be prevented.

Richard, Duke of Gloucester.
I hope the King made peace with all of us,
And the compact is firm and true in me.

Earl Rivers.
And so in me, and so (I think) in all.
Yet since it is but green, it should be put
To no apparent likelihood of breach,
Which haply by much company might be urg'd;
Therefore I say with noble Buckingham,
That it is meet so few should fetch the Prince.

Lord Hastings.
And so say I.

Richard, Duke of Gloucester.
Then be it so, and go we to determine
Who they shall be that straight shall post to Ludlow.
Madam, and you, my sister, will you go
To give your censures in this business?

Both Queen Elizabeth and Duchess of York.
With all our hearts.

Exeunt. Manent Buckingham and Richard.

Duke of Buckingham.
My lord, whoever journeys to the Prince,
For God sake let not us two stay at home;
For by the way, I'll sort occasion,
As index to the story we late talk'd of,
To part the Queen's proud kindred from the Prince.

Richard, Duke of Gloucester.
My other self, my counsel's consistory,
My oracle, my prophet, my dear cousin,
I, as a child, will go by thy direction.
Toward Ludlow then, for we'll not stay behind.

Exeunt.

Scene 3

London. A street.

(First Citizen; Second Citizen; Third Citizen)

Three Citizens express their fears of the events that are to follow the King's death.

Enter one Citizen at one door and another at the other.

First Citizen.
Good morrow, neighbor, whither away so fast?

Second Citizen.
I promise you, I scarcely know myself.
Hear you the news abroad?

First Citizen.
                Yes, that the King is dead.

Second Citizen.
Ill news, by'r lady—seldom comes the better.
I fear, I fear 'twill prove a giddy world.

Enter another Citizen.

Third Citizen.
Neighbors, God speed!

First Citizen.
              Give you good morrow, sir.

Third Citizen.
Doth the news hold of good King Edward's death?

Second Citizen.
Ay, sir, it is too true, God help the while!

Third Citizen.
Then, masters, look to see a troublous world.

First Citizen.
No, no, by God's good grace his son shall reign.

Third Citizen.
Woe to that land that's govern'd by a child!

Second Citizen.
In him there is a hope of government,
Which in his nonage, council under him,
And in his full and ripened years, himself,
No doubt shall then, and till then, govern well.

First Citizen.
So stood the state when Henry the Sixth
Was crown'd in Paris but at nine months old.

Third Citizen.
Stood the state so? No, no, good friends, God wot,
For then this land was famously enrich'd
With politic grave counsel; then the King
Had virtuous uncles to protect his Grace.

First Citizen.
Why, so hath this, both by his father and mother.

Third Citizen.
Better it were they all came by his father,
Or by his father there were none at all;
For emulation who shall now be nearest
Will touch us all too near, if God prevent not.
O, full of danger is the Duke of Gloucester,
And the Queen's sons and brothers haught and proud!
And were they to be rul'd, and not to rule,
This sickly land might solace as before.

First Citizen.
Come, come, we fear the worst; all will be well.

Third Citizen.
When clouds are seen, wise men put on their cloaks;
When great leaves fall, then winter is at hand;
When the sun sets, who doth not look for night?
Untimely storms makes men expect a dearth.
All may be well; but if God sort it so,
'Tis more than we deserve or I expect.

Second Citizen.
Truly, the hearts of men are full of fear.
You cannot reason (almost) with a man
That looks not heavily and full of dread.

Third Citizen.
Before the days of change, still is it so.
By a divine instinct men's minds mistrust
Ensuing danger; as by proof we see
The water swell before a boist'rous storm.
But leave it all to God. Whither away?

Second Citizen.
Marry, we were sent for to the justices.

Third Citizen.
And so was I. I'll bear you company.

Exeunt.

Scene 4

London. The palace.

(Archbishop of York; Duke of York; Queen Elizabeth; Duchess of York; Messenger to the Queen)

The Duchess of York, the Queen and the Archbishop of York discuss matters with the King's younger son, the Duke of York, in attendance. The boy comments on his uncle Richard, who shares his name. The Queen makes certain that some matters are not discussed in the boy's presence. News comes that Richard has arrested Rivers, Grey, and Vaughan and had them imprisoned. In fear, the Queen decides to take sanctuary with her son.

Enter Archbishop of York, the young Duke of York, the Queen Elizabeth, and the Duchess of York.

Thomas Rotherham, Archbishop of York.
Last night, I hear, they lay at Stony-Stratford,
And at Northampton they do rest tonight.
Tomorrow, or next day, they will be here.

Duchess of York.
I long with all my heart to see the Prince.

I hope he is much grown since last I saw him.

Queen Elizabeth.
But I hear no; they say my son of York
Has almost overta'en him in his growth.

Richard, Duke of York.
Ay, mother, but I would not have it so.

Duchess of York.
Why, my good cousin, it is good to grow.

Richard, Duke of York.
Grandam, one night as we did sit at supper,
My uncle Rivers talk'd how I did grow
More than my brother. "Ay," quoth my uncle Gloucester,
"Small herbs have grace, great weeds do grow apace."
And since, methinks I would not grow so fast,
Because sweet flow'rs are slow and weeds make haste.

Duchess of York.
Good faith, good faith, the saying did not hold
In him that did object the same to thee:
He was the wretched'st thing when he was young,
So long a-growing and so leisurely
That if his rule were true, he should be gracious.

Thomas Rotherham, Archbishop of York.
And so no doubt he is, my gracious madam.

Duchess of York.
I hope he is, but yet let mothers doubt.

Richard, Duke of York.
Now by my troth, if I had been rememb'red,
I could have given my uncle's Grace a flout,
To touch his growth nearer than he touch'd mine.

Duchess of York.
How, my young York? I prithee let me hear it.

Richard, Duke of York.
Marry (they say) my uncle grew so fast
That he could gnaw a crust at two hours old;
'Twas full two years ere I could get a tooth.
Grandam, this would have been a biting jest.

Duchess of York.
I prithee, pretty York, who told thee this?

Richard, Duke of York.
Grandam, his nurse.

Duchess of York.
His nurse? Why, she was dead ere thou wast born.

Richard, Duke of York.
If 'twere not she, I cannot tell who told me.

Queen Elizabeth.
A parlous boy! Go to, you are too shrewd.

Duchess of York.
Good madam, be not angry with the child.

Queen Elizabeth.
Pitchers have ears.

Enter Messenger to the Queen.

Thomas Rotherham, Archbishop of York.
Here comes a messenger. What news?

Messenger to the Queen.
Such news, my lord, as grieves me to report.

Queen Elizabeth.
How doth the Prince?

Messenger to the Queen.
     Well, madam, and in health.

Duchess of York.
What is thy news?

Messenger to the Queen.
Lord Rivers and Lord Grey are sent to Pomfret,
And with them Sir Thomas Vaughan, prisoners.

Duchess of York.
Who hath committed them?

Messenger to the Queen.
      The mighty dukes,
Gloucester and Buckingham.

Thomas Rotherham, Archbishop of York.
     For what offense?

Messenger to the Queen.
The sum of all I can I have disclos'd.
Why, or for what, the nobles were committed
Is all unknown to me, my gracious lord.

Queen Elizabeth.
Ay me! I see the ruin of my house:
The tiger now hath seiz'd the gentle hind;
Insulting tyranny begins to jut
Upon the innocent and aweless throne.

Welcome destruction, blood, and massacre!
I see (as in a map) the end of all.

Duchess of York.
Accursed and unquiet wrangling days,
How many of you have mine eyes beheld!
My husband lost his life to get the crown,
And often up and down my sons were toss'd
For me to joy and weep their gain and loss;
And being seated, and domestic broils
Clean overblown, themselves, the conquerors,
Make war upon themselves, brother to brother,
Blood to blood, self against self. O, preposterous
And frantic outrage, end thy damned spleen,
Or let me die, to look on death no more!

Queen Elizabeth.
Come, come, my boy, we will to sanctuary.
Madam, farewell.

Duchess of York.
             Stay, I will go with you.

Queen Elizabeth.
You have no cause.

Thomas Rotherham, Archbishop of York.

To the Queen.

My gracious lady, go,
And thither bear your treasure and your goods.
For my part, I'll resign unto your Grace
The seal I keep, and so betide to me
As well I tender you and all of yours!
Go, I'll conduct you to the sanctuary.

Exeunt.

Act 3

Scene 1

London. A street.

(Prince Edward; Duke of Gloucester; Duke of Buckingham; Cardinal Bourchier; Catesby; Lord Mayor; Lord Hastings; York)

Richard, Buckingham, and others escort the new King to London. The boy wishes his other uncles were with them, but Richard assures him that they were traitors. They expect to find the Queen and York waiting for them, but Lord Hastings informs them that they have taken sanctuary. They send Cardinal Bourchier to bring York, overcoming his scruples about infringing sanctuary. Richard suggests to the King that he should spend the time until his coronation at the Tower. York arrives, and trades jokes with Richard, though he goes too far when he refers to Richard's crooked back. Both children are suspicious of Richard, but they go to the Tower all the same, despite York's fear of ghosts. Buckingham and Richard send Catesby to find out whether Hastings would support Richard in taking the throne. Richard suggests chopping off Lord Hastings's head if he will not join them, and promises Buckingham the earldom of Herford once he is King.

The trumpets sound. Enter young Prince Edward, the Dukes of Gloucester and Buckingham, Lord Cardinal Bourchier, Catesby, with others.

Duke of Buckingham.
Welcome, sweet Prince, to London, to your chamber.

Richard, Duke of Gloucester.
Welcome, dear cousin, my thoughts' sovereign,
The weary way hath made you melancholy.

Edward, Prince of Wales.
No, uncle, but our crosses on the way
Have made it tedious, wearisome, and heavy.
I want more uncles here to welcome me.

Richard, Duke of Gloucester.
Sweet Prince, the untainted virtue of your years
Hath not yet div'd into the world's deceit;
Nor more can you distinguish of a man
Than of his outward show, which, God he knows,
Seldom or never jumpeth with the heart.
Those uncles which you want were dangerous;
Your Grace attended to their sug'red words,
But look'd not on the poison of their hearts.
God keep you from them, and from such false friends!

Edward, Prince of Wales.
God keep me from false friends!—but they were none.

Richard, Duke of Gloucester.
My lord, the Mayor of London comes to greet you.

Enter Lord Mayor and his Train.

Lord Mayor of London.
God bless your Grace with health and happy days!

Edward, Prince of Wales.
I thank you, good my lord, and thank you all.

Mayor and Train stand aside.

I thought my mother and my brother York
Would long ere this have met us on the way.
Fie, what a slug is Hastings, that he comes not
To tell us whether they will come or no!

Enter Lord Hastings.

Duke of Buckingham.
And in good time, here comes the sweating lord.

Edward, Prince of Wales.
Welcome, my lord. What, will our mother come?

Lord Hastings.
On what occasion, God he knows, not I,
The Queen your mother and your brother York
Have taken sanctuary. The tender Prince
Would fain have come with me to meet your Grace,
But by his mother was perforce withheld.

Duke of Buckingham.
Fie, what an indirect and peevish course
Is this of hers! Lord Cardinal, will your Grace
Persuade the Queen to send the Duke of York
Unto his princely brother presently?
If she deny, Lord Hastings, go with him,
And from her jealous arms pluck him perforce.

Cardinal Bourchier.
My Lord of Buckingham, if my weak oratory
Can from his mother win the Duke of York,
Anon expect him here; but if she be obdurate
To mild entreaties, God in heaven forbid
We should infringe the holy privilege
Of blessed sanctuary! Not for all this land
Would I be guilty of so deep a sin.

Duke of Buckingham.
You are too senseless-obstinate, my lord,
Too ceremonious and traditional.
Weigh it but with the grossness of this age,
You break not sanctuary in seizing him.
The benefit thereof is always granted
To those whose dealings have deserv'd the place
And those who have the wit to claim the place.
This prince hath neither claim'd it nor deserv'd it,
And therefore, in mine opinion, cannot have it.
Then taking him from thence that is not there,
You break no privilege nor charter there.
Oft have I heard of sanctuary men,
But sanctuary children never till now.

Cardinal Bourchier.
My lord, you shall overrule my mind for once.
Come on, Lord Hastings, will you go with me?

Lord Hastings.
I go, my lord.

Edward, Prince of Wales.
Good lords, make all the speedy haste you may.

Exeunt Cardinal and Lord Hastings.

Say, uncle Gloucester, if our brother come,
Where shall we sojourn till our coronation?

Richard, Duke of Gloucester.
Where it seems best unto your royal self.
If I may counsel you, some day or two
Your Highness shall repose you at the Tower;
Then where you please, and shall be thought most fit
For your best health and recreation.

Edward, Prince of Wales.
I do not like the Tower, of any place.
Did Julius Caesar build that place, my lord?

Duke of Buckingham.
He did, my gracious lord, begin that place,
Which, since, succeeding ages have re-edified.

Edward, Prince of Wales.
Is it upon record, or else reported
Successively from age to age, he built it?

Duke of Buckingham.
Upon record, my gracious lord.

Edward, Prince of Wales.
But say, my lord, it were not regist'red,
Methinks the truth should live from age to age,
As 'twere retail'd to all posterity,
Even to the general all-ending day.

Richard, Duke of Gloucester.

Aside.

So wise so young, they say do never live long.

Edward, Prince of Wales.
What say you, uncle?

Richard, Duke of Gloucester.
I say, without characters fame lives long.

Aside.

Thus, like the formal Vice, Iniquity,
I moralize two meanings in one word.

Edward, Prince of Wales.
That Julius Caesar was a famous man;
With what his valor did enrich his wit,
His wit set down to make his valor live.
Death makes no conquest of this conqueror,
For now he lives in fame though not in life.
I'll tell you what, my cousin Buckingham—

Duke of Buckingham.
What, my gracious lord?

Edward, Prince of Wales.
And if I live until I be a man,
I'll win our ancient right in France again,
Or die a soldier as I liv'd a king.

Richard, Duke of Gloucester.

Aside.

Short summers lightly have a forward spring.

Enter young York, Hastings, Cardinal Bourchier.

Duke of Buckingham.
Now in good time, here comes the Duke of York.

Edward, Prince of Wales.
Richard of York, how fares our loving brother?

Richard, Duke of York.
Well, my dread lord—so must I call you now.

Edward, Prince of Wales.
Ay, brother, to our grief, as it is yours.
Too late he died that might have kept that title,
Which by his death hath lost much majesty.

Richard, Duke of Gloucester.
How fares our cousin, noble Lord of York?

Richard, Duke of York.
I thank you, gentle uncle. O my lord,
You said that idle weeds are fast in growth:
The Prince my brother hath outgrown me far.

Richard, Duke of Gloucester.
He hath, my lord.

Richard, Duke of York.
And therefore is he idle?

Richard, Duke of Gloucester.
O my fair cousin, I must not say so.

Richard, Duke of York.
Then he is more beholding to you than I.

Richard, Duke of Gloucester.
He may command me as my sovereign,
But you have power in me as in a kinsman.

Richard, Duke of York.
I pray you, uncle, give me this dagger.

Richard, Duke of Gloucester.
My dagger, little cousin? With all my heart.

Edward, Prince of Wales.
A beggar, brother?

Richard, Duke of York.
Of my kind uncle, that I know will give,
And being but a toy, which is no grief to give.

Richard, Duke of Gloucester.
A greater gift than that I'll give my cousin.

Richard, Duke of York.
A greater gift? O, that's the sword to it.

Richard, Duke of Gloucester.
Ay, gentle cousin, were it light enough.

Richard, Duke of York.
O then I see you will part but with light gifts!
In weightier things you'll say a beggar nay.

Richard, Duke of Gloucester.
It is too heavy for your Grace to wear.

Richard, Duke of York.
I weigh it lightly, were it heavier.

Richard, Duke of Gloucester.
What, would you have my weapon, little lord?

Richard, Duke of York.
I would, that I might thank you as you call me.

Richard, Duke of Gloucester.
How?

Richard, Duke of York.
Little.

Edward, Prince of Wales.
My Lord of York will still be cross in talk.
Uncle, your Grace knows how to bear with him.

Richard, Duke of York.
You mean, to bear me, not to bear with me.
Uncle, my brother mocks both you and me:
Because that I am little, like an ape,
He thinks that you should bear me on your shoulders.

Duke of Buckingham.

Aside to Hastings

With what a sharp-provided wit he reasons!
To mitigate the scorn he gives his uncle,
He prettily and aptly taunts himself:
So cunning and so young is wonderful.

Richard, Duke of Gloucester.
My lord, will't please you pass along?
Myself and my good cousin Buckingham
Will to your mother, to entreat of her
To meet you at the Tower and welcome you.

Richard, Duke of York.
What, will you go unto the Tower, my lord?

Edward, Prince of Wales.
My Lord Protector needs will have it so.

Richard, Duke of York.
I shall not sleep in quiet at the Tower.

Richard, Duke of Gloucester.
Why, what should you fear?

Richard, Duke of York.
Marry, my uncle Clarence' angry ghost.
My grandam told me he was murd'red there.

Edward, Prince of Wales.
I fear no uncles dead.

Richard, Duke of Gloucester.
Nor none that live, I hope.

Edward, Prince of Wales.
And if they live, I hope I need not fear.
But come, my lord; with a heavy heart,
Thinking on them, go I unto the Tower.

A sennet. Exeunt Prince Edward, York, Hastings, Cardinal Bourchier, and others. Manent Richard, Buckingham, and Catesby.

Duke of Buckingham.
Think you, my lord, this little prating York
Was not incensed by his subtle mother
To taunt and scorn you thus opprobriously?

Richard, Duke of Gloucester.
No doubt, no doubt. O, 'tis a perilous boy,
Bold, quick, ingenious, forward, capable:
He is all the mother's, from the top to toe.

Duke of Buckingham.
Well, let them rest. Come hither, Catesby.
Thou art sworn as deeply to effect what we intend
As closely to conceal what we impart.
Thou know'st our reasons urg'd upon the way;
What think'st thou? Is it not an easy matter
To make William Lord Hastings of our mind
For the installment of this noble Duke
In the seat royal of this famous isle?

Sir William Catesby.
He for his father's sake so loves the Prince
That he will not be won to aught against him.

Duke of Buckingham.
What think'st thou then of Stanley? Will not he?

Sir William Catesby.
He will do all in all as Hastings doth.

Duke of Buckingham.
Well then, no more but this: go, gentle Catesby,
And as it were far off, sound thou Lord Hastings
How he doth stand affected to our purpose,
And summon him tomorrow to the Tower
To sit about the coronation.
If thou dost find him tractable to us,
Encourage him, and tell him all our reasons;
If he be leaden, icy, cold, unwilling,
Be thou so too, and so break off the talk,
And give us notice of his inclination;
For we tomorrow hold divided Councils,
Wherein thyself shalt highly be employ'd.

Richard, Duke of Gloucester.
Commend me to Lord William. Tell him, Catesby,
His ancient knot of dangerous adversaries
Tomorrow are let blood at Pomfret Castle,
And bid my lord, for joy of this good news,

Give Mistress Shore one gentle kiss the more.

Duke of Buckingham.
Good Catesby, go effect this business soundly.

Sir William Catesby.
My good lords both, with all the heed I can.

Richard, Duke of Gloucester.
Shall we hear from you, Catesby, ere we sleep?

Sir William Catesby.
You shall, my lord.

Richard, Duke of Gloucester.
At Crosby House, there shall you find us both.

Exit Catesby.

Duke of Buckingham.
Now, my lord, what shall we do if we perceive
Lord Hastings will not yield to our complots?

Richard, Duke of Gloucester.
Chop off his head! Something we will determine.
And look when I am king, claim thou of me
The earldom of Herford, and all the moveables
Whereof the King my brother was possess'd.

Duke of Buckingham.
I'll claim that promise at your Grace's hand.

Richard, Duke of Gloucester.
And look to have it yielded with all kindness.
Come, let us sup betimes, that afterwards
We may digest our complots in some form.

Exeunt.

Scene 2

Before Lord Hastings' house.

(Stanley Messenger; Lord Hastings; Catesby; Lord Stanley; Pursuivant; Sir John; Buckingham)

Lord Hastings receives a messenger from Lord Stanley, who has had a premonitory dream about Richard and urges Hastings to flee with him to the north. Hastings refuses to take a dream seriously. Catesby comes to sound Hastings out, informing him that the Queen's family is to be executed that day, but Hastings admits to being glad at that, he refuses to betray his deceased master and bypass his son's right to the throne for Richard. Stanley arrives, and warns Hastings against his self-sufficiency, but Hastings brushes off his fears.

Enter a Messenger to the door of Hastings.

Stanley Messenger.
My lord! My lord!

Lord Hastings.
Within.
Who knocks?

Stanley Messenger.
One from the Lord Stanley.

Lord Hastings.
Within.
What is't a' clock?

Stanley Messenger.
Upon the stroke of four.

Enter Lord Hastings.

Lord Hastings.
Cannot my Lord Stanley sleep these tedious nights?

Stanley Messenger.
So it appears by that I have to say:
First, he commends him to your noble self.

Lord Hastings.
What then?

Stanley Messenger.
Then certifies your lordship that this night
He dreamt the boar had rased off his helm.
Besides, he says there are two Councils kept;
And that may be determin'd at the one
Which may make you and him to rue at th' other.
Therefore he sends to know your lordship's pleasure,
If you will presently take horse with him,
And with all speed post with him toward the north,
To shun the danger that his soul divines.

Lord Hastings.
Go, fellow, go, return unto thy lord,
Bid him not fear the separated Council:
His honor and myself are at the one,
And at the other is my good friend Catesby;
Where nothing can proceed that toucheth us

Whereof I shall not have intelligence.
Tell him his fears are shallow, without instance;
And for his dreams, I wonder he's so simple
To trust the mock'ry of unquiet slumbers.
To fly the boar before the boar pursues
Were to incense the boar to follow us,
And make pursuit where he did mean no chase.
Go, bid thy master rise and come to me,
And we will both together to the Tower,
Where he shall see the boar will use us kindly.

Stanley Messenger.
I'll go, my lord, and tell him what you say.

Exit.
Enter Catesby.

Sir William Catesby.
Many good morrows to my noble lord!

Lord Hastings.
Good morrow, Catesby, you are early stirring.
What news, what news, in this our tott'ring state?

Sir William Catesby.
It is a reeling world indeed, my lord,
And I believe will never stand upright
Till Richard wear the garland of the realm.

Lord Hastings.
How? Wear the garland? Dost thou mean the crown?

Sir William Catesby.
Ay, my good lord.

Lord Hastings.
I'll have this crown of mine cut from my shoulders
Before I'll see the crown so foul misplac'd.
But canst thou guess that he doth aim at it?

Sir William Catesby.
Ay, on my life, and hopes to find you forward
Upon his party for the gain thereof;
And thereupon he sends you this good news,
That this same very day your enemies,
The kindred of the Queen, must die at Pomfret.

Lord Hastings.
Indeed I am no mourner for that news,
Because they have been still my adversaries;
But that I'll give my voice on Richard's side
To bar my master's heirs in true descent,
God knows I will not do it, to the death!

Sir William Catesby.
God keep your lordship in that gracious mind!

Lord Hastings.
But I shall laugh at this a twelvemonth hence,
That they which brought me in my master's hate,
I live to look upon their tragedy.
Well, Catesby, ere a fortnight make me older,
I'll send some packing that yet think not on't.

Sir William Catesby.
'Tis a vile thing to die, my gracious lord,
When men are unprepar'd and look not for it.

Lord Hastings.
O monstrous, monstrous! And so falls it out
With Rivers, Vaughan, Grey; and so 'twill do
With some men else, that think themselves as safe
As thou and I, who (as thou know'st) are dear
To princely Richard and to Buckingham.

Sir William Catesby.
The princes both make high account of you—

Aside.
For they account his head upon the bridge.

Lord Hastings.
I know they do, and I have well deserv'd it.

Enter Lord Stanley.

Come on, come on, where is your boar-spear, man?
Fear you the boar, and go so unprovided?

Lord Stanley.
My lord, good morrow, good morrow, Catesby.
You may jest on, but, by the holy rood,
I do not like these several Councils, I.

Lord Hastings.
My lord,
I hold my life as dear as you do yours,
And never in my days, I do protest,
Was it so precious to me as 'tis now.
Think you, but that I know our state secure,
I would be so triumphant as I am?

Lord Stanley.
The lords at Pomfret, when they rode from London,
Were jocund, and suppos'd their states were sure,
And they indeed had no cause to mistrust;
But yet you see how soon the day o'ercast.
This sudden stab of rancor I misdoubt;

Pray God, I say, I prove a needless coward!
What, shall we toward the Tower? The day is spent.

Lord Hastings.
Come, come, have with you. Wot you what, my lord?
Today the lords you talk'd of are beheaded.

Lord Stanley.
They, for their truth, might better wear their heads
Than some that have accus'd them wear their hats.
But come, my lord, let's away.

Enter a Pursuivant, also named Hastings.

Lord Hastings.
Go on before, I'll talk with this good fellow.

Exeunt Lord Stanley and Catesby.

How now, sirrah? How goes the world with thee?

Pursuivant.
The better that your lordship please to ask.

Lord Hastings.
I tell thee, man, 'tis better with me now
Than when thou met'st me last where now we meet.
Then was I going prisoner to the Tower,
By the suggestion of the Queen's allies;
But now I tell thee (keep it to thyself)
This day those enemies are put to death,
And I in better state than e'er I was.

Pursuivant.
God hold it, to your honor's good content!

Lord Hastings.
Gramercy, fellow. There, drink that for me.

Throws him his purse.

Pursuivant.
I thank your honor.

Exit Pursuivant.
Enter Sir John, a Priest.

Sir John.
Well met, my lord, I am glad to see your honor.

Lord Hastings.
I thank thee, good Sir John, with all my heart.
I am in your debt for your last exercise;
Come the next Sabbath, and I will content you.

He whispers in his ear.

Sir John.
I'll wait upon your lordship.

Enter Buckingham.

Duke of Buckingham.
What, talking with a priest, Lord Chamberlain?
Your friends at Pomfret, they do need the priest,
Your honor hath no shriving work in hand.

Lord Hastings.
Good faith, and when I met this holy man
The men you talk of came into my mind.
What, go you toward the Tower?

Duke of Buckingham.
I do, my lord, but long I cannot stay there.
I shall return before your lordship thence.

Lord Hastings.
Nay, like enough, for I stay dinner there.

Duke of Buckingham.

Aside.

And supper too, although thou know'st it not.—
Come, will you go?

Lord Hastings.
　　　　　　I'll wait upon your lordship.

Exeunt.

Scene 3

Pomfret Castle.

(Sir Richard Ratcliffe; Halberds; Rivers; Grey; Vaughan)

Ratcliff leads Rivers, Grey, and Vaughan to death. They recall Queen Margaret's curses, which have been fulfilled, and hope that the curses she heaped on Richard, Hastings, and Buckingham will also come true.

Enter Sir Richard Ratcliffe with Halberds, carrying the nobles Rivers, Grey, and Vaughan to death at Pomfret.

Sir Richard Ratcliffe.
Come, bring forth the prisoners.

Earl Rivers.
Sir Richard Ratcliffe, let me tell thee this:
Today shalt thou behold a subject die
For truth, for duty, and for loyalty.

Lord Grey.
God bless the Prince from all the pack of you!
A knot you are of damned blood-suckers.

Sir Thomas Vaughan.
You live that shall cry woe for this hereafter.

Sir Richard Ratcliffe.
Dispatch, the limit of your lives is out.

Earl Rivers.
O Pomfret, Pomfret! O thou bloody prison!
Fatal and ominous to noble peers!
Within the guilty closure of thy walls
Richard the Second here was hack'd to death;
And for more slander to thy dismal seat,
We give to thee our guiltless blood to drink.

Lord Grey.
Now Margaret's curse is fall'n upon our heads,
When she exclaim'd on Hastings, you, and I,
For standing by when Richard stabb'd her son.

Earl Rivers.
Then curs'd she Richard, then curs'd she Buckingham,
Then curs'd she Hastings. O, remember, God,
To hear her prayer for them, as now for us!
And for my sister and her princely sons,
Be satisfied, dear God, with our true blood,
Which, as thou know'st, unjustly must be spilt.

Sir Richard Ratcliffe.
Make haste, the hour of death is expiate.

Earl Rivers.
Come, Grey, come, Vaughan, let us here embrace.
Farewell, until we meet again in heaven.

Exeunt.

Scene 4

The Tower of London.

(Buckingham; Stanley; Hastings; Bishop of Ely; Norfolk; Ratcliffe; Lovel; Gloucester; Bishop of Ely)

The Lords meet in council to decide on a date for their new King's coronation. Hastings presumes to speak for Richard, who is late. Richard arrives and sends the Bishop of Ely to fetch him some strawberries. He asks the council what sentence should be passed on anyone caught conspiring against him and Hastings suggests that death would be appropriate. Richard immediately accuses him of conspiring, claiming that Hastings has withered his arm through witchcraft, and condemns him to immediate execution. Hastings reflects on his own foolish sense of security and on Margaret's curses. Ratcliffe and Lovel lead him to his death.

Enter Buckingham, Stanley, Earl of Derby, Hastings, Bishop of Ely, Norfolk, Ratcliffe, Lovel, with others, at a table.

Lord Hastings.
Now, noble peers, the cause why we are met
Is to determine of the coronation.
In God's name speak, when is the royal day?

Duke of Buckingham.
Is all things ready for the royal time?

Lord Stanley.
It is, and wants but nomination.

John Morton, Bishop of Ely.
Tomorrow then I judge a happy day.

Duke of Buckingham.
Who knows the Lord Protector's mind herein?
Who is most inward with the noble Duke?

John Morton, Bishop of Ely.
Your Grace, we think, should soonest know his mind.

Duke of Buckingham.
We know each other's faces; for our hearts,
He knows no more of mine than I of yours,
Or I of his, my lord, than you of mine.
Lord Hastings, you and he are near in love.

Lord Hastings.
I thank his Grace, I know he loves me well;
But for his purpose in the coronation,
I have not sounded him, nor he deliver'd
His gracious pleasure any way therein.
But you, my honorable lords, may name the time,
And in the Duke's behalf I'll give my voice,
Which I presume he'll take in gentle part.

Enter Gloucester.

Act 3, Scene 4

John Morton, Bishop of Ely.
In happy time, here comes the Duke himself.

Richard, Duke of Gloucester.
My noble lords and cousins all, good morrow.
I have been long a sleeper; but I trust
My absence doth neglect no great design,
Which by my presence might have been concluded.

Duke of Buckingham.
Had you not come upon your cue, my lord,
William Lord Hastings had pronounc'd your part,
I mean your voice for crowning of the King.

Richard, Duke of Gloucester.
Than my Lord Hastings no man might be bolder,
His lordship knows me well and loves me well.
My Lord of Ely, when I was last in Holborn,
I saw good strawberries in your garden there.
I do beseech you send for some of them.

John Morton, Bishop of Ely.
Marry, and will, my lord, with all my heart.

Exit Bishop.

Richard, Duke of Gloucester.
Cousin of Buckingham, a word with you.

Drawing him aside.

Catesby hath sounded Hastings in our business,
And finds the testy gentleman so hot
That he will lose his head ere give consent
His master's child, as worshipfully he terms it,
Shall lose the royalty of England's throne.

Duke of Buckingham.
Withdraw yourself a while, I'll go with you.

Exeunt Gloucester and Buckingham.

Lord Stanley.
We have not yet set down this day of triumph.
Tomorrow, in my judgment, is too sudden,
For I myself am not so well provided
As else I would be, were the day prolong'd.

Enter the Bishop of Ely.

John Morton, Bishop of Ely.
Where is my lord the Duke of Gloucester?
I have sent for these strawberries.

Lord Hastings.
His Grace looks cheerfully and smooth this morning;
There's some conceit or other likes him well,
When that he bids good morrow with such spirit.
I think there's never a man in Christendom
Can lesser hide his love or hate than he,
For by his face straight shall you know his heart.

Lord Stanley.
What of his heart perceive you in his face
By any livelihood he show'd today?

Lord Hastings.
Marry, that with no man here he is offended;
For were he, he had shown it in his looks.

Lord Stanley.
I pray God he be not, I say.

Enter Richard of Gloucester and Buckingham

Richard, Duke of Gloucester.
I pray you all, tell me what they deserve
That do conspire my death with devilish plots
Of damned witchcraft, and that have prevail'd
Upon my body with their hellish charms?

Lord Hastings.
The tender love I bear your Grace, my lord,
Makes me most forward in this princely presence
To doom th' offenders, whosoe'er they be:
I say, my lord, they have deserved death.

Richard, Duke of Gloucester.
Then be your eyes the witness of their evil.
Look how I am bewitch'd; behold, mine arm
Is like a blasted sapling, wither'd up;
And this is Edward's wife, that monstrous witch,
Consorted with that harlot, strumpet Shore,
That by their witchcraft thus have marked me.

Lord Hastings.
If they have done this deed, my noble lord—

Richard, Duke of Gloucester.
If? Thou protector of this damned strumpet,
Talk'st thou to me of "ifs"? Thou art a traitor.
Off with his head! Now by Saint Paul I swear
I will not dine until I see the same.
Lovel and Ratcliffe, look that it be done:
The rest that love me, rise, and follow me.

Exeunt. Manent Lovel and Ratcliffe with the Lord Hastings.

Lord Hastings.
Woe, woe for England, not a whit for me!
For I, too fond, might have prevented this.
Stanley did dream the boar did rase our helms,
And I did scorn it and disdain to fly.
Three times today my foot-cloth horse did scumble,
And started when he look'd upon the Tower,
As loath to bear me to the slaughter-house.
O now I need the priest that spake to me!
I now repent I told the pursuivant,
As too triumphing, how mine enemies
Today at Pomfret bloodily were butcher'd,
And I myself secure, in grace and favor.
O Margaret, Margaret, now thy heavy curse
Is lighted on poor Hastings' wretched head!

Sir Richard Ratcliffe.
Come, come, dispatch, the Duke would be at dinner,
Make a short shrift, he longs to see your head.

Lord Hastings.
O momentary grace of mortal men,
Which we more hunt for than the grace of God!
Who builds his hope in air of your good looks
Lives like a drunken sailor on a mast,
Ready with every nod to tumble down
Into the fatal bowels of the deep.

Lord Lovel.
Come, come, dispatch, 'tis bootless to exclaim.

Lord Hastings.
O bloody Richard! Miserable England!
I prophesy the fearfull'st time to thee
That ever wretched age hath look'd upon.
Come, lead me to the block; bear him my head.
They smile at me who shortly shall be dead.

Exeunt.

Scene 5

The Tower-walls.

(Richard of Gloucester; Buckingham; Mayor; Catesby; Lovel; Ratcliffe)

Richard and Buckingham have dressed themselves in poor quality armor, to suggest that they armed themselves in a hurry. Pretending to be in fear of a sudden attack by conspirators, they explain to the Mayor of London that Hastings was a traitor and had to be executed at once, without a trial. The Mayor agrees to go and explain this to the citizens of London. Richard sends Buckingham after the Mayor to start spreading rumors among the people to try and bring dead King Edward into disrepute, in the hopes of making them favor Richard's bid for the crown. Richard gives orders that Clarence's children be hidden away and Edward's kept away from all visitors.

Enter Richard of Gloucester and Buckingham in rotten armor, marvelous ill-favored.

Richard, Duke of Gloucester.
Come, cousin, canst thou quake and change thy color,
Murder thy breath in middle of a word,
And then again begin, and stop again,
As if thou were distraught and mad with terror?

Duke of Buckingham.
Tut, I can counterfeit the deep tragedian,
Speak and look back, and pry on every side,
Tremble and start at wagging of a straw;
Intending deep suspicion, ghastly looks
Are at my service, like enforced smiles;
And both are ready in their offices
At any time to grace my stratagems.
But what, is Catesby gone?

Richard, Duke of Gloucester.
He is, and see, he brings the Mayor along.

Enter the Mayor and Catesby.

Duke of Buckingham.
Lord Mayor—

Richard, Duke of Gloucester.
Look to the drawbridge there!

Duke of Buckingham.
Hark, a drum!

Richard, Duke of Gloucester.
Catesby, o'erlook the walls.

Duke of Buckingham.
Lord Mayor, the reason we have sent—

Richard, Duke of Gloucester.
Look back, defend thee, here are enemies!

Act 3, Scene 5

Duke of Buckingham.
God and our innocence defend and guard us!

Enter Lovel and Ratcliffe with Hastings' head.

Richard, Duke of Gloucester.
Be patient, they are friends—Ratcliffe and Lovel.

Lord Lovel.
Here is the head of that ignoble traitor,
The dangerous and unsuspected Hastings.

Richard, Duke of Gloucester.
So dear I lov'd the man that I must weep.
I took him for the plainest harmless creature
That breath'd upon the earth a Christian;
Made him my book, wherein my soul recorded
The history of all her secret thoughts.
So smooth he daub'd his vice with show of virtue
That, his apparent open guilt omitted—
I mean, his conversation with Shore's wife—
He liv'd from all attainder of suspects.

Duke of Buckingham.
Well, well, he was the covert'st shelt'red traitor
That ever liv'd. Look ye, my Lord Mayor,
Would you imagine, or almost believe,
Were't not that by great preservation
We live to tell it, that the subtile traitor
This day had plotted, in the Council-house,
To murder me and my good Lord of Gloucester?

Lord Mayor of London.
Had he done so?

Richard, Duke of Gloucester.
What? Think you we are Turks or infidels?
Or that we would, against the form of law,
Proceed thus rashly in the villain's death,
But that the extreme peril of the case,
The peace of England, and our persons' safety,
Enforc'd us to this execution?

Lord Mayor of London.
Now fair befall you! He deserv'd his death,
And your good Graces both have well proceeded,
To warn false traitors from the like attempts.

Duke of Buckingham.
I never look'd for better at his hands
After he once fell in with Mistress Shore.
Yet had we not determin'd he should die
Until your lordship came to see his end,
Which now the loving haste of these our friends,
Something against our meanings, have prevented;
Because, my lord, I would have had you heard
The traitor speak, and timorously confess
The manner and the purpose of his treasons,
That you might well have signified the same
Unto the citizens, who haply may
Misconster us in him and wail his death.

Lord Mayor of London.
But, my good lord, your Grace's words shall serve
As well as I had seen, and heard him speak;
And do not doubt, right noble princes both,
That I'll acquaint our duteous citizens
With all your just proceedings in this cause.

Richard, Duke of Gloucester.
And to that end we wish'd your lordship here,
T' avoid the censures of the carping world.

Duke of Buckingham.
Which since you come too late of our intent,
Yet witness what you hear we did intend.
And so, my good Lord Mayor, we bid farewell.

Exit Mayor.

Richard, Duke of Gloucester.
Go after, after, cousin Buckingham.
The Mayor towards Guildhall hies him in all post.
There, at your meet'st advantage of the time,
Infer the bastardy of Edward's children.
Tell them how Edward put to death a citizen
Only for saying he would make his son
Heir to the Crown—meaning indeed his house,
Which by the sign thereof was termed so.
Moreover, urge his hateful luxury
And bestial appetite in change of lust,
Which stretch'd unto their servants, daughters, wives,
Even where his raging eye or savage heart,
Without control, lusted to make a prey.
Nay, for a need, thus far come near my person:
Tell them, when that my mother went with child
Of that insatiate Edward, noble York,
My princely father, then had wars in France,
And by true computation of the time,
Found that the issue was not his begot;
Which well appeared in his lineaments,
Being nothing like the noble Duke my father.
Yet touch this sparingly, as 'twere far off,

Because, my lord, you know my mother lives.

Duke of Buckingham.
Doubt not, my lord, I'll play the orator
As if the golden fee for which I plead
Were for myself—and so, my lord, adieu.

Richard, Duke of Gloucester.
If you thrive well, bring them to Baynard's Castle,
Where you shall find me well accompanied
With reverend fathers and well-learned bishops.

Duke of Buckingham.
I go, and towards three or four a' clock
Look for the news that the Guildhall affords.

Exit Buckingham.

Richard, Duke of Gloucester.
Go, Lovel, with all speed to Doctor Shaw;

To Catesby.

Go thou to Friar Penker; bid them both
Meet me within this hour at Baynard's Castle.

Exeunt Lovel and Catesby.
To Ratcliffe.

Now will I go to take some privy order
To draw the brats of Clarence out of sight,
And to give order that no manner person
Have any time recourse unto the Princes.

Exeunt.

Scene 6

London. A street.

(Scrivener)

A Scrivener reflects on the hypocrisy of what is going on, having written out Hastings's indictment hours before he was arrested. He comments that it is perfectly obvious that a coup is going on, but that nobody has the courage to say so.

Enter a Scrivener with a paper in his hand.

Scrivener.
Here is the indictment of the good Lord Hastings,
Which in a set hand fairly is engross'd
That it may be today read o'er in Paul's.
And mark how well the sequel hangs together:
Eleven hours I have spent to write it over,
For yesternight by Catesby was it sent me;
The precedent was full as long a-doing,
And yet within these five hours Hastings liv'd,
Untainted, unexamin'd, free, at liberty.
Here's a good world the while! Who is so gross
That cannot see this palpable device?
Yet who's so bold but says he sees it not?
Bad is the world, and all will come to nought,
When such ill dealing must be seen in thought.

Exit.

Scene 7

Baynard's castle.

(Richard of Gloucester; Buckingham; Mayor; Aldermen; First Citizen; Second Citizen; Third Citizen; Catesby; Two Bishops)

Buckingham reports to Richard that the citizens are reluctant to proclaim him King. The Mayor and his aldermen come to visit Richard, who quickly hides. Buckingham assures the Mayor that Richard is studying religion with a pair of priests. Buckingham and Catesby play a hypocritical game, insisting that Richard is worried at seeing such a crowd coming for him. When Richard enters, accompanied by Two Bishops, Buckingham urges him to seize the crown, but Richard refuses. Buckingham threatens to dethrone the entire family, and stalks out with the Mayor and his men. Richard has them called back and, insisting that it is entirely against his will, accepts to become King. He agrees to be crowned the next day and goes back in with the Bishops.

Enter Richard of Gloucester and Buckingham at several doors.

Richard, Duke of Gloucester.
How now, how now, what say the citizens?

Duke of Buckingham.
Now, by the holy Mother of our Lord,
The citizens are mum, say not a word.

Richard, Duke of Gloucester.
Touch'd you the bastardy of Edward's children?

Duke of Buckingham.
I did, with his contract with Lady Lucy,
And his contract by deputy in France,
Th' unsatiate greediness of his desire,

And his enforcement of the city wives,
His tyranny for trifles, his own bastardy,
As being got, your father then in France,
And his resemblance, being not like the Duke.
Withal I did infer your lineaments,
Being the right idea of your father,
Both in your form and nobleness of mind;
Laid open all your victories in Scotland,
Your discipline in war, wisdom in peace,
Your bounty, virtue, fair humility;
Indeed, left nothing fitting for your purpose
Untouch'd or slightly handled in discourse.
And when mine oratory drew to an end,
I bid them that did love their country's good
Cry, "God save Richard, England's royal king!"

Richard, Duke of Gloucester.
And did they so?

Duke of Buckingham.
No, so God help me, they spake not a word,
But like dumb statues, or breathing stones,
Star'd each on other, and look'd deadly pale;
Which when I saw, I reprehended them,
And ask'd the Mayor what meant this willful silence.
His answer was, the people were not used
To be spoke to but by the Recorder.
Then he was urg'd to tell my tale again:
"Thus saith the Duke, thus hath the Duke inferr'd"—
But nothing spake in warrant from himself.
When he had done, some followers of mine own,
At lower end of the hall, hurl'd up their caps,
And some ten voices cried, "God save King Richard!"
And thus I took the vantage of those few:
"Thanks, gentle citizens and friends," quoth I,
"This general applause and cheerful shout
Argues your wisdoms and your love to Richard"—
And even here brake off, and came away.

Richard, Duke of Gloucester.
What tongueless blocks were they! Would they not speak?

Duke of Buckingham.
No, by my troth, my lord.

Richard, Duke of Gloucester.
Will not the Mayor then and his brethren come?

Duke of Buckingham.
The Mayor is here at hand. Intend some fear,
Be not you spoke with but by mighty suit;
And look you get a prayer-book in your hand,
And stand between two churchmen, good my lord—
For on that ground I'll make a holy descant—
And be not easily won to our requests:
Play the maid's part, still answer nay, and take it.

Richard, Duke of Gloucester.
I go; and if you plead as well for them
As I can say nay to thee for myself,
No doubt we bring it to a happy issue.

Duke of Buckingham.
Go, go up to the leads, the Lord Mayor knocks.

Exit Gloucester.
Enter the Mayor, Aldermen, and Citizens.

Welcome, my lord! I dance attendance here;
I think the Duke will not be spoke withal.

Enter Catesby.

Now, Catesby, what says your lord to my request?

Sir William Catesby.
He doth entreat your Grace, my noble lord,
To visit him tomorrow or next day.
He is within, with two right reverend fathers,
Divinely bent to meditation,
And in no worldly suits would he be mov'd,
To draw him from his holy exercise.

Duke of Buckingham.
Return, good Catesby, to the gracious Duke,
Tell him, myself, the Mayor and Aldermen,
In deep designs, in matter of great moment,
No less importing than our general good,
Are come to have some conference with his Grace.

Sir William Catesby.
I'll signify so much unto him straight.

Exit.

Duke of Buckingham.
Ah ha, my lord, this prince is not an Edward!
He is not lulling on a lewd love-bed,
But on his knees at meditation;
Not dallying with a brace of courtezans,
But meditating with two deep divines;
Not sleeping, to engross his idle body,

But praying, to enrich his watchful soul.
Happy were England, would this virtuous prince
Take on his Grace the sovereignty thereof,
But sure I fear we shall not win him to it.

Lord Mayor of London.
Marry, God defend his Grace should say us nay!

Duke of Buckingham.
I fear he will. Here Catesby comes again.

Enter Catesby.

Now, Catesby, what says his Grace?

Sir William Catesby.
My lord,
He wonders to what end you have assembled
Such troops of citizens to come to him,
His Grace not being warn'd thereof before:
He fears, my lord, you mean no good to him.

Duke of Buckingham.
Sorry I am my noble cousin should
Suspect me that I mean no good to him.
By heaven, we come to him in perfit love,
And so once more return and tell his Grace.

Exit Catesby.

When holy and devout religious men
Are at their beads, 'tis much to draw them thence,
So sweet is zealous contemplation.

Enter Richard of Gloucester aloft, between two Bishops. Catesby returns.

Lord Mayor of London.
See where his Grace stands, 'tween two clergymen!

Duke of Buckingham.
Two props of virtue for a Christian prince,
To stay him from the fall of vanity;
And see, a book of prayer in his hand—
True ornaments to know a holy man.
Famous Plantagenet, most gracious prince,
Lend favorable ear to our requests,
And pardon us the interruption
Of thy devotion and right Christian zeal.

Richard, Duke of Gloucester.
My lord, there needs no such apology.
I do beseech your Grace to pardon me,
Who, earnest in the service of my God,
Deferr'd the visitation of my friends.
But leaving this, what is your Grace's pleasure?

Duke of Buckingham.
Even that (I hope) which pleaseth God above
And all good men of this ungovern'd isle.

Richard, Duke of Gloucester.
I do suspect I have done some offense
That seems disgracious in the city's eye,
And that you come to reprehend my ignorance.

Duke of Buckingham.
You have, my lord. Would it might please your Grace,
On our entreaties, to amend your fault!

Richard, Duke of Gloucester.
Else wherefore breathe I in a Christian land?

Duke of Buckingham.
Know then, it is your fault that you resign
The supreme seat, the throne majestical,
The sceptred office of your ancestors,
Your state of fortune, and your due of birth,
The lineal glory of your royal house,
To the corruption of a blemish'd stock;
Whiles in the mildness of your sleepy thoughts,
Which here we waken to our country's good,
The noble isle doth want her proper limbs;
Her face defac'd with scars of infamy,
Her royal stock graft with ignoble plants,
And almost should'red in the swallowing gulf
Of dark forgetfulness and deep oblivion.
Which to recure, we heartily solicit
Your gracious self to take on you the charge
And kingly government of this your land:
Not as protector, steward, substitute,
Or lowly factor for another's gain;
But as successively, from blood to blood,
Your right of birth, your empery, your own.
For this, consorted with the citizens,
Your very worshipful and loving friends,
And by their vehement instigation,
In this just cause come I to move your Grace.

Richard, Duke of Gloucester.
I cannot tell if to depart in silence,
Or bitterly to speak in your reproof,
Best fitteth my degree or your condition.
If not to answer, you might haply think
Tongue-tied ambition, not replying, yielded
To bear the golden yoke of sovereignty,

Act 3, Scene 7

Which fondly you would here impose on me.
If to reprove you for this suit of yours,
So season'd with your faithful love to me,
Then on the other side, I check'd my friends.
Therefore—to speak, and to avoid the first,
And then, in speaking, not to incur the last—
Definitively thus I answer you:
Your love deserves my thanks, but my desert
Unmeritable shuns your high request.
First, if all obstacles were cut away,
And that my path were even to the crown,
As the ripe revenue and due of birth,
Yet so much is my poverty of spirit,
So mighty and so many my defects,
That I would rather hide me from my greatness—
Being a bark to brook no mighty sea—
Than in my greatness covet to be hid
And in the vapor of my glory smother'd.
But God be thank'd, there is no need of me,
And much I need to help you, were there need:
The royal tree hath left us royal fruit,
Which mellow'd by the stealing hours of time,
Will well become the seat of majesty,
And make (no doubt) us happy by his reign.
On him I lay that you would lay on me,
The right and fortune of his happy stars,
Which God defend that I should wring from him!

Duke of Buckingham.
My lord, this argues conscience in your Grace,
But the respects thereof are nice and trivial,
All circumstances well considered.
You say that Edward is your brother's son:
So say we too, but not by Edward's wife;
For first was he contract to Lady Lucy—
Your mother lives a witness to his vow—
And afterward by substitute betroth'd
To Bona, sister to the King of France.
These both put off, a poor petitioner,
A care-craz'd mother to a many sons,
A beauty-waning and distressed widow,
Even in the afternoon of her best days,
Made prize and purchase of his wanton eye,
Seduc'd the pitch and height of his degree
To base declension and loath'd bigamy.
By her, in his unlawful bed, he got
This Edward, whom our manners call the Prince.
More bitterly could I expostulate,
Save that for reverence to some alive,
I give a sparing limit to my tongue.

Then, good my lord, take to your royal self
This proffer'd benefit of dignity;
If not to bless us and the land withal,
Yet to draw forth your noble ancestry
From the corruption of abusing times
Unto a lineal true-derived course.

Lord Mayor of London.
Do, good my lord, your citizens entreat you.

Duke of Buckingham.
Refuse not, mighty lord, this proffer'd love.

Sir William Catesby.
O, make them joyful, grant their lawful suit!

Richard, Duke of Gloucester.
Alas, why would you heap this care on me?
I am unfit for state and majesty.
I do beseech you take it not amiss,
I cannot nor I will not yield to you.

Duke of Buckingham.
If you refuse it—as, in love and zeal,
Loath to depose the child, your brother's son;
As well we know your tenderness of heart
And gentle, kind, effeminate remorse,
Which we have noted in you to your kindred
And egally indeed to all estates—
Yet know, whe'er you accept our suit or no,
Your brother's son shall never reign our king,
But we will plant some other in the throne,
To the disgrace and downfall of your house;
And in this resolution here we leave you.
Come, citizens. 'Zounds, I'll entreat no more.

Richard, Duke of Gloucester.
O, do not swear, my Lord of Buckingham.

Exeunt Buckingham, Mayor, Aldermen, and Citizens.

Sir William Catesby.
Call him again, sweet prince, accept their suit.
If you deny them, all the land will rue it.

Richard, Duke of Gloucester.
Will you enforce me to a world of cares?
Call them again, I am not made of stones,
But penetrable to your kind entreaties,
Albeit against my conscience and my soul.

Enter Buckingham and the rest.

Cousin of Buckingham, and sage grave men,

Since you will buckle Fortune on my back,
To bear her burden whe'er I will or no,
I must have patience to endure the load;
But if black scandal or foul-fac'd reproach
Attend the sequel of your imposition,
Your mere enforcement shall acquittance me
From all the impure blots and stains thereof;
For God doth know, and you may partly see,
How far I am from the desire of this.

Lord Mayor of London.
God bless your Grace! We see it and will say it.

Richard, Duke of Gloucester.
In saying so you shall but say the truth.

Duke of Buckingham.
Then I salute you with this royal title—
Long live Richard, England's worthy king!

All.
Amen.

Duke of Buckingham.
Tomorrow may it please you to be crown'd?

Richard, Duke of Gloucester.
Even when you please, for you will have it so.

Duke of Buckingham.
Tomorrow then we will attend your Grace,
And so most joyfully we take our leave.

Richard, Duke of Gloucester.

To the Bishops.

Come, let us to our holy work again.—
Farewell, my cousin, farewell, gentle friends.

Exeunt.

Act 4

Scene 1

Outside the Tower.

(Queen Elizabeth; Duchess of York; Marquess Dorset; Duchess Anne of Gloucester; Lady Margaret Plantagenet; Lieutenant Brakenbury; Stanley)

The dowager Queen, accompanied by the Duchess of York and Lady Anne (who is now Richard's wife) tries to be let into the Tower to see her children, but Brakenbury is forced to refuse them access, by Richard's orders. Stanley arrives to summon Anne to her coronation as Queen. Stanley and the Queen urge Dorset to escape England and join Richmond on the Continent. Lady Anne feels that she has brought her own misery upon herself, and is fairly certain that Richard will kill her soon. The Duchess offers her best hopes for them own, but there is little of it.

Enter the Queen Elizabeth, the Duchess of York, and Marquess Dorset at one door; Anne Duchess of Gloucester leading Lady Margaret Plantagenet, Clarence's young daughter, at another door.

Duchess of York.
Who meets us here? My niece Plantagenet,
Led in the hand of her kind aunt of Gloucester?
Now, for my life, she's wand'ring to the Tower,
On pure heart's love, to greet the tender Prince.
Daughter, well met.

Lady Anne.
                    God give your Graces both
A happy and a joyful time of day!

Queen Elizabeth.
As much to you, good sister! Whither away?

Lady Anne.
No farther than the Tower, and as I guess,
Upon the like devotion as yourselves,
To gratulate the gentle Princes there.

Queen Elizabeth.
Kind sister, thanks, we'll enter all together.

Enter the Lieutenant Brakenbury.

And in good time, here the Lieutenant comes.
Master Lieutenant, pray you, by your leave,
How doth the Prince and my young son of York?

Sir Robert Brakenbury.
Right well, dear madam. By your patience,
I may not suffer you to visit them,
The King hath strictly charg'd the contrary.

Queen Elizabeth.
The King? Who's that?

Sir Robert Brakenbury.
                    I mean the Lord Protector.

Queen Elizabeth.
The Lord protect him from that kingly title!
Hath he set bounds between their love and me?
I am their mother, who shall bar me from them?

Duchess of York.
I am their father's mother, I will see them.

Lady Anne.
Their aunt I am in law, in love their mother;
Then bring me to their sights. I'll bear thy blame,
And take thy office from thee on my peril.

Sir Robert Brakenbury.
No, madam, no; I may not leave it so:
I am bound by oath, and therefore pardon me.

Exit Lieutenant.
Enter Stanley.

Lord Stanley.
Let me but meet you, ladies, an hour hence,
And I'll salute your Grace of York as mother
And reverend looker-on of two fair queens.

To Anne.

Come, madam, you must straight to Westminster,
There to be crowned Richard's royal queen.

Queen Elizabeth.
Ah, cut my lace asunder,
That my pent heart may have some scope to beat,
Or else I swoon with this dead-killing news!

Lady Anne.
Despiteful tidings, O unpleasing news!

Marquess of Dorset.
Be of good cheer. Mother, how fares your Grace?

Queen Elizabeth.
O Dorset, speak not to me, get thee gone!
Death and destruction dogs thee at thy heels;
Thy mother's name is ominous to children.
If thou wilt outstrip death, go cross the seas,
And live with Richmond, from the reach of hell.
Go hie thee, hie thee from this slaughter-house,
Lest thou increase the number of the dead,
And make me die the thrall of Margaret's curse,
Nor mother, wife, nor England's counted queen.

Lord Stanley.
Full of wise care is this your counsel, madam;
Take all the swift advantage of the hours.
You shall have letters from me to my son
In your behalf, to meet you on the way.
Be not ta'en tardy by unwise delay.

Duchess of York.
O ill-dispersing wind of misery!
O my accursed womb, the bed of death!
A cockatrice hast thou hatch'd to the world,
Whose unavoided eye is murderous.

Lord Stanley.
Come, madam, come, I in all haste was sent.

Lady Anne.
And I with all unwillingness will go.
O would to God that the inclusive verge
Of golden metal that must round my brow
Were red-hot steel, to sear me to the brains!
Anointed let me be with deadly venom,
And die ere men can say, "God save the Queen!"

Queen Elizabeth.
Go, go, poor soul, I envy not thy glory,
To feed my humor wish thyself no harm.

Lady Anne.
No! Why? When he that is my husband now
Came to me as I follow'd Henry's corse,
When scarce the blood was well wash'd from his hands
Which issued from my other angel husband,
And that dear saint which then I weeping follow'd—
O, when, I say, I look'd on Richard's face,
This was my wish: "Be thou," quoth I, "accurs'd
For making me, so young, so old a widow!
And when thou wed'st, let sorrow haunt thy bed;
And be thy wife—if any be so mad—
More miserable by the life of thee
Than thou hast made me by my dear lord's death!"
Lo, ere I can repeat this curse again,
Within so small a time, my woman's heart
Grossly grew captive to his honey words,
And prov'd the subject of mine own soul's curse,
Which hitherto hath held my eyes from rest;
For never yet one hour in his bed
Did I enjoy the golden dew of sleep,
But with his timorous dreams was still awak'd.
Besides, he hates me for my father Warwick,
And will, no doubt, shortly be rid of me.

Queen Elizabeth.
Poor heart, adieu, I pity thy complaining.

Lady Anne.
No more than with my soul I mourn for yours.

Marquess of Dorset.
Farewell, thou woeful welcomer of glory!

Lady Anne.
Adieu, poor soul, that tak'st thy leave of it!

Duchess of York.

To Dorset.

Go thou to Richmond, and good fortune guide thee!

To Anne.

Go thou to Richard, and good angels tend thee!

To Queen Elizabeth.

Go thou to sanctuary, and good thoughts possess thee!
I to my grave, where peace and rest lie with me!
Eighty odd years of sorrow have I seen,
And each hour's joy wrack'd with a week of teen.

Queen Elizabeth.
Stay, yet look back with me unto the Tower.
Pity, you ancient stones, those tender babes
Whom envy hath immur'd within your walls—
Rough cradle for such little pretty ones!
Rude ragged nurse, old sullen playfellow
For tender princes—use my babies well!
So foolish sorrows bids your stones farewell.

Exeunt.

Scene 2

London. The palace.

(*King Richard; Buckingham; Catesby; Ratcliffe; Lovel; Page; Stanley; Sir James Tyrrel*)

Richard, in the full panoply of kingship, ascends his throne and speaks to Buckingham alone, at first insinuating and then flat out telling him that he wishes the two princes in the Tower to be killed. Buckingham at first pretends not to understand, and then asks for time to think. Seeing that Buckingham is growing cautious, Richard resolves to no longer trust him, and sends a Page to find a man who will obey unquestioningly.

Stanley brings the news of Dorset's flight. Richard sends Catesby to spread the rumor that Anne is fatally ill, as he has decided that for the safety of his crown he will have to marry his brother's daughter. At the same time he intends to marry Clarence's daughter to some poor gentleman of low rank, leaving her no threat to him. He finds his agent for murdering the princes in Sir James Tyrrel, who unhesitatingly agrees to do the deed. Buckingham returns to ask for the earldom he was promised. Richard refuses, and Buckingham, both insulted at Richard's lack of gratitude and suddenly afraid of sharing Hastings's fate, decides to flee.

Sound a sennet. Enter Richard in pomp, crowned; Buckingham, Catesby, Ratcliffe, Lovel, a Page, and others.

King Richard III.
Stand all apart. Cousin of Buckingham—

Duke of Buckingham.
My gracious sovereign?

King Richard III.
Give me thy hand.

Here he ascendeth the throne. Sound.

Thus high, by thy advice
And thy assistance, is King Richard seated;
But shall we wear these glories for a day?
Or shall they last, and we rejoice in them?

Duke of Buckingham.
Still live they, and forever let them last!

King Richard III.
Ah, Buckingham, now do I play the touch,
To try if thou be current gold indeed.
Young Edward lives: think now what I would speak.

Duke of Buckingham.
Say on, my loving lord.

King Richard III.
Why, Buckingham, I say I would be king.

Duke of Buckingham.
Why, so you are, my thrice-renowned lord.

King Richard III.
Ha? Am I king? 'Tis so—but Edward lives.

Duke of Buckingham.
True, noble prince.

King Richard III.
                   O bitter consequence,
That Edward still should live true noble prince!
Cousin, thou wast not wont to be so dull.
Shall I be plain? I wish the bastards dead,
And I would have it suddenly perform'd.
What say'st thou now? Speak suddenly, be brief.

Duke of Buckingham.
Your Grace may do your pleasure.

King Richard III.
Tut, tut, thou art all ice, thy kindness freezes.
Say, have I thy consent that they shall die?

Duke of Buckingham.
Give me some little breath, some pause, dear lord,
Before I positively speak in this.
I will resolve you herein presently.

Exit Buckingham.

Sir William Catesby.

Aside to a stander-by.

The King is angry, see, he gnaws his lip.

King Richard III.
I will converse with iron-witted fools
And unrespective boys; none are for me
That look into me with considerate eyes.
High-reaching Buckingham grows circumspect.
Boy!

Page.
My lord?

King Richard III.
Know'st thou not any whom corrupting gold
Will tempt unto a close exploit of death?

Page.
I know a discontented gentleman
Whose humble means match not his haughty spirit.
Gold were as good as twenty orators,
And will, no doubt, tempt him to any thing.

King Richard III.
What is his name?

Page.
               His name, my lord, is Tyrrel.

King Richard III.
I partly know the man; go call him hither, boy.

Exit Page.

The deep-revolving witty Buckingham
No more shall be the neighbor to my counsels.
Hath he so long held out with me untir'd,
And stops he now for breath? Well, be it so.

Enter Stanley.

How now, Lord Stanley, what's the news?

Lord Stanley.
Know, my loving lord,
The Marquess Dorset, as I hear, is fled
To Richmond, in the parts where he abides.

Stands apart.

King Richard III.
Come hither, Catesby. Rumor it abroad
That Anne, my wife, is very grievous sick;
I will take order for her keeping close.
Inquire me out some mean poor gentleman,
Whom I will marry straight to Clarence' daughter;
The boy is foolish, and I fear not him.
Look how thou dream'st! I say again, give out
That Anne, my queen, is sick and like to die.
About it, for it stands me much upon
To stop all hopes whose growth may damage me.

Exit Catesby.

I must be married to my brother's daughter,
Or else my kingdom stands on brittle glass.
Murder her brothers and then marry her—
Uncertain way of gain! But I am in
So far in blood that sin will pluck on sin.
Tear-falling pity dwells not in this eye.

Enter Page with Sir James Tyrrel.

Is thy name Tyrrel?

Sir James Tyrrel.
James Tyrrel, and your most obedient subject.

King Richard III.
Art thou indeed?

Sir James Tyrrel.
               Prove me, my gracious lord.

King Richard III.
Dar'st thou resolve to kill a friend of mine?

Sir James Tyrrel.
Please you;
But I had rather kill two enemies.

King Richard III.
Why, there thou hast it; two deep enemies,
Foes to my rest and my sweet sleep's disturbers,
Are they that I would have thee deal upon:
Tyrrel, I mean those bastards in the Tower.

Sir James Tyrrel.
Let me have open means to come to them,
And soon I'll rid you from the fear of them.

King Richard III.
Thou sing'st sweet music. Hark, come hither, Tyrrel.
Go, by this token. Rise, and lend thine ear.

Whispers.

There is no more but so; say it is done,
And I will love thee and prefer thee for it.

Sir James Tyrrel.
I will dispatch it straight.

Exit.
Enter Buckingham.

Duke of Buckingham.
My lord, I have consider'd in my mind
The late request that you did sound me in.

King Richard III.
Well, let that rest. Dorset is fled to Richmond.

Duke of Buckingham.
I hear the news, my lord.

King Richard III.
Stanley, he is your wive's son: well, look unto it.

Duke of Buckingham.
My lord, I claim the gift, my due by promise,
For which your honor and your faith is pawn'd,
Th' earldom of Herford, and the moveables,
Which you have promised I shall possess.

King Richard III.
Stanley, look to your wife. If she convey
Letters to Richmond, you shall answer it.

Duke of Buckingham.
What says your Highness to my just request?

King Richard III.
I do remember me, Henry the Sixth
Did prophesy that Richmond should be king,
When Richmond was a little peevish boy.
A king—perhaps—perhaps—

Duke of Buckingham.
My lord—

King Richard III.
How chance the prophet could not at that time
Have told me, I being by, that I should kill him?

Duke of Buckingham.
My lord, your promise for the earldom—

King Richard III.
Richmond! When last I was at Exeter,
The mayor in courtesy show'd me the castle,
And call'd it Rouge-mount, at which name I started,
Because a bard of Ireland told me once
I should not live long after I saw Richmond.

Duke of Buckingham.
My lord—

King Richard III.
Ay, what's a' clock?

Duke of Buckingham.
I am thus bold to put your Grace in mind
Of what you promis'd me.

King Richard III.
                Well, but what's a' clock?

Duke of Buckingham.
Upon the stroke of ten.

King Richard III.
                Well, let it strike.

Duke of Buckingham.
Why let it strike?

King Richard III.
Because that like a Jack thou keep'st the stroke
Betwixt thy begging and my meditation.
I am not in the giving vein today.

Duke of Buckingham.
May it please you to resolve me in my suit.

King Richard III.
Thou troubles! Me, I am not in the vein.

Exit with all but Buckingham.

Duke of Buckingham.
And is it thus? Repays he my deep service
With such contempt? Made I him king for this?
O, let me think on Hastings, and be gone
To Brecknock while my fearful head is on!

Exit.

Scene 3

London. The palace.

(Tyrrel; King Richard; Ratcliffe)

The remorseful Tyrrel returns to tell Richard that the princes have been murdered. Richard is relieved, as all his plans for his safety are coming to fruition: Clarence's son is locked up, his daughter married to a man of low rank, and Anne is dead. To prevent Richmond from marrying his brother's daughter and thereby gaining a claim to the throne, Richard has resolved to marry her himself. Ratcliffe brings news that Buckingham has raised a rebellion.

Enter Tyrrel.

Sir James Tyrrel.
The tyrannous and bloody act is done,
The most arch deed of piteous massacre
That ever yet this land was guilty of.
Dighton and Forrest, who I did suborn
To do this piece of ruthless butchery,
Albeit they were flesh'd villains, bloody dogs,
Melted with tenderness and kind compassion,
Wept like two children in their deaths' sad story.
"O, thus," quoth Dighton, "lay the gentle babes."
"Thus, thus," quoth Forrest, "girdling one another
Within their alabaster innocent arms.
Their lips were four red roses on a stalk,
Which in their summer beauty kiss'd each other.
A book of prayers on their pillow lay,
Which once," quoth Forrest, "almost chang'd my mind;
But O! The devil"—there the villain stopp'd;
When Dighton thus told on, "We smothered
The most replenished sweet work of Nature
That from the prime creation e'er she framed."
Hence both are gone with conscience and remorse
They could not speak; and so I left them both,
To bear this tidings to the bloody King.

Enter King Richard.

And here he comes. All health, my sovereign lord!

King Richard III.
Kind Tyrrel, am I happy in thy news?

Sir James Tyrrel.
If to have done the thing you gave in charge
Beget your happiness, be happy then,
For it is done.

King Richard III.
                    But didst thou see them dead?

Sir James Tyrrel.
I did, my lord.

King Richard III.
                    And buried, gentle Tyrrel?

Sir James Tyrrel.
The chaplain of the Tower hath buried them,
But where (to say the truth) I do not know.

King Richard III.
Come to me, Tyrrel, soon, at after-supper,
When thou shalt tell the process of their death.
Mean time, but think how I may do thee good,
And be inheritor of thy desire.
Farewell till then.

Sir James Tyrrel.
                    I humbly take my leave.

Exit.

King Richard III.
The son of Clarence have I pent up close,
His daughter meanly have I match'd in marriage,
The sons of Edward sleep in Abraham's bosom,
And Anne my wife hath bid this world good night.
Now for I know the Britain Richmond aims
At young Elizabeth, my brother's daughter,
And by that knot looks proudly on the crown,
To her go I, a jolly thriving wooer.

Enter Ratcliffe.

Sir Richard Ratcliffe.
My lord—

King Richard III.
Good or bad news, that thou com'st in so bluntly?

Sir Richard Ratcliffe.
Bad news, my lord. Morton is fled to Richmond,
And Buckingham, back'd with the hardy Welshmen,
Is in the field, and still his power increaseth.

King Richard III.
Ely with Richmond troubles me more near
Than Buckingham and his rash-levied strength.
Come, I have learn'd that fearful commenting
Is leaden servitor to dull delay;
Delay leads impotent and snail-pac'd beggary.
Then fiery expedition be my wing,
Jove's Mercury, and herald for a king!
Go muster men. My counsel is my shield;
We must be brief when traitors brave the field.

Exeunt.

Scene 4

London. Before the palace.

(Queen Margaret; Duchess of York; Queen Elizabeth; King Richard; Ratcliffe; Catesby; Lord Stanley; First Messenger; Second Messenger; Third Messenger; Fourth Messenger)

Queen Margaret comes to witness the grief of her enemies. Queen Elizabeth and the Duchess of York come in, grieving over the death of their children/grandchildren. Margaret comes forth to remind them that they are not the only ones who have suffered. Together the women consider their woes and the need they have to curse. Margaret leaves for the final time. As Richard passes by with his army, his mother and sister-in-law accuse him of all his foul crimes, until he orders his drummers and trumpeters to drown them out. The Duchess of York gives him a mother's curse, swearing never to see him again. After she leaves, Richard begins to speak to the dowager Queen about her daughter. Thinking he means to have her killed, she pleads for the girl's life, but discovers that Richard wishes to marry her. She is horrified, but he argues with her just as he did with Anne; in the end, she appears to be won over. Richard is distracted as his various followers come in for news and instructions. Stanley brings news that Richmond has raised an army and is crossing over to England to claim the throne.

Stanley offers to muster men, but Richard distrusts him and orders him to leave his son behind as a hostage. News of rebellion arrives from all corners of the kingdom, but soon there is also news that Buckingham has been defeated and captured. Richmond, however, has landed with his army.

Enter old Queen Margaret.

Queen Margaret.
So now prosperity begins to mellow
And drop into the rotten mouth of death.
Here in these confines slyly have I lurk'd,
To watch the waning of mine enemies.
A dire induction am I witness to,
And will to France, hoping the consequence
Will prove as bitter, black, and tragical.
Withdraw thee, wretched Margaret; who comes here?

Retires.
Enter Duchess of York and Queen Elizabeth.

Queen Elizabeth.
Ah, my poor princes! Ah, my tender babes!
My unblown flow'rs, new-appearing sweets!
If yet your gentle souls fly in the air
And be not fix'd in doom perpetual,
Hover about me with your aery wings
And hear your mother's lamentation!

Queen Margaret.

Aside.

Hover about her; say that right for right
Hath dimm'd your infant morn to aged night.

Duchess of York.
So many miseries have craz'd my voice
That my woe-wearied tongue is still and mute.
Edward Plantagenet, why art thou dead?

Queen Margaret.

Aside.

Plantagenet doth quit Plantagenet,
Edward for Edward pays a dying debt.

Queen Elizabeth.
Wilt thou, O God, fly from such gentle lambs,
And throw them in the entrails of the wolf?
When didst thou sleep when such a deed was done?

Act 4, Scene 4

Queen Margaret.

Aside.

When holy Harry died, and my sweet son.

Duchess of York.
Dead life, blind sight, poor mortal-living ghost,
Woe's scene, world's shame, grave's due by life usurp'd,
Brief abstract and record of tedious days,
Rest thy unrest on England's lawful earth,

Sitting down.

Unlawfully made drunk with innocent blood!

Queen Elizabeth.
Ah, that thou wouldst as soon afford a grave
As thou canst yield a melancholy seat!
Then would I hide my bones, not rest them here.
Ah, who hath any cause to mourn but we?

Sitting down by her.

Queen Margaret.

Coming forward.

If ancient sorrow be most reverent,
Give mine the benefit of seniory,
And let my griefs frown on the upper hand.
If sorrow can admit society,

Sitting down with them.

Tell over your woes again by viewing mine:
I had an Edward, till a Richard kill'd him;
I had a Harry, till a Richard kill'd him:
Thou hadst an Edward, till a Richard kill'd him;
Thou hadst a Richard, till a Richard kill'd him.

Duchess of York.
I had a Richard too, and thou didst kill him;
I had a Rutland too, thou help'st to kill him.

Queen Margaret.
Thou hadst a Clarence too, and Richard kill'd him.
From forth the kennel of thy womb hath crept
A hell-hound that doth hunt us all to death:
That dog, that had his teeth before his eyes
To worry lambs and lap their gentle blood,
That foul defacer of God's handiwork,
That excellent grand tyrant of the earth
That reigns in galled eyes of weeping souls,
Thy womb let loose to chase us to our graves.
O upright, just, and true-disposing God,
How do I thank thee that this carnal cur
Preys on the issue of his mother's body,
And makes her pew-fellow with others' moan!

Duchess of York.
O Harry's wife, triumph not in my woes!
God witness with me, I have wept for thine.

Queen Margaret.
Bear with me; I am hungry for revenge,
And now I cloy me with beholding it.
Thy Edward he is dead, that kill'd my Edward;
Thy other Edward dead, to quit my Edward;
Young York he is but boot, because both they
Match'd not the high perfection of my loss.
Thy Clarence he is dead that stabb'd my Edward,
And the beholders of this frantic play,
Th' adulterate Hastings, Rivers, Vaughan, Grey,
Untimely smoth'red in their dusky graves.
Richard yet lives, hell's black intelligencer,
Only reserv'd their factor to buy souls
And send them thither; but at hand, at hand,
Ensues his piteous and unpitied end.
Earth gapes, hell burns, fiends roar, saints pray,
To have him suddenly convey'd from hence.
Cancel his bond of life, dear God, I pray,
That I may live and say, "The dog is dead."

Queen Elizabeth.
O, thou didst prophesy the time would come
That I should wish for thee to help me curse
That bottled spider, that foul bunch-back'd toad!

Queen Margaret.
I call'd thee then vain flourish of my fortune;
I call'd thee then poor shadow, painted queen,
The presentation of but what I was;
The flattering index of a direful pageant;
One heav'd a-high, to be hurl'd down below;
A mother only mock'd with two fair babes;
A dream of what thou wast, a garish flag
To be the aim of every dangerous shot;
A sign of dignity, a breath, a bubble;
A queen in jest, only to fill the scene.
Where is thy husband now? Where be thy brothers?
Where be thy two sons? Wherein dost thou joy?
Who sues, and kneels, and says, "God save the Queen"?
Where be the bending peers that flattered thee?

Where be the thronging troops that followed thee?
Decline all this, and see what now thou art:
For happy wife, a most distressed widow;
For joyful mother, one that wails the name;
For one being sued to, one that humbly sues;
For queen, a very caitiff crown'd with care;
For she that scorn'd at me, now scorn'd of me;
For she being feared of all, now fearing one;
For she commanding all, obey'd of none.
Thus hath the course of justice whirl'd about,
And left thee but a very prey to time,
Having no more but thought of what thou wast
To torture thee the more, being what thou art.
Thou didst usurp my place, and dost thou not
Usurp the just proportion of my sorrow?
Now thy proud neck bears half my burden'd yoke,
From which even here I slip my weary head,
And leave the burden of it all on thee.
Farewell, York's wife, and queen of sad mischance,
These English woes shall make me smile in France.

Queen Elizabeth.
O thou well skill'd in curses, stay awhile,
And teach me how to curse mine enemies!

Queen Margaret.
Forbear to sleep the nights, and fast the days;
Compare dead happiness with living woe;
Think that thy babes were sweeter than they were,
And he that slew them fouler than he is.
Bett'ring thy loss makes the bad causer worse;
Revolving this will teach thee how to curse.

Queen Elizabeth.
My words are dull, O, quicken them with thine!

Queen Margaret.
Thy woes will make them sharp and pierce like mine.

Exit Queen Margaret.

Duchess of York.
Why should calamity be full of words?

Queen Elizabeth.
Windy attorneys to their client's woes,
Aery succeeders of intestate joys,
Poor breathing orators of miseries,
Let them have scope! Though what they will impart
Help nothing else, yet do they ease the heart.

Duchess of York.
If so then, be not tongue-tied; go with me,
And in the breath of bitter words let's smother
My damned son that thy two sweet sons smother'd.
The trumpet sounds, be copious in exclaims.

Enter King Richard and his Train marching, with Drums and Trumpets.

King Richard III.
Who intercepts me in my expedition?

Duchess of York.
O, she that might have intercepted thee,
By strangling thee in her accursed womb,
From all the slaughters, wretch, that thou hast done!

Queen Elizabeth.
Hid'st thou that forehead with a golden crown
Where should be branded, if that right were right,
The slaughter of the prince that ow'd that crown,
And the dire death of my poor sons and brothers?
Tell me, thou villain-slave, where are my children?

Duchess of York.
Thou toad, thou toad, where is thy brother Clarence?
And little Ned Plantagenet, his son?

Queen Elizabeth.
Where is the gentle Rivers, Vaughan, Grey?

Duchess of York.
Where is kind Hastings?

King Richard III.
A flourish, trumpets! Strike alarum, drums!
Let not the heavens hear these tell-tale women
Rail on the Lord's anointed. Strike, I say!

Flourish. Alarums.

Either be patient and entreat me fair,
Or with the clamorous report of war
Thus will I drown your exclamations.

Duchess of York.
Art thou my son?

King Richard III.
Ay, I thank God, my father, and yourself.

Duchess of York.
Then patiently hear my impatience.

Act 4, Scene 4

King Richard III.
Madam, I have a touch of your condition,
That cannot brook the accent of reproof.

Duchess of York.
O, let me speak!

King Richard III.
     Do then, but I'll not hear.

Duchess of York.
I will be mild and gentle in my words.

King Richard III.
And brief, good mother, for I am in haste.

Duchess of York.
Art thou so hasty? I have stay'd for thee,
God knows, in torment and in agony.

King Richard III.
And came I not at last to comfort you?

Duchess of York.
No, by the holy rood, thou know'st it well,
Thou cam'st on earth to make the earth my hell.
A grievous burden was thy birth to me,
Tetchy and wayward was thy infancy;
Thy school-days frightful, desp'rate, wild, and furious,
Thy prime of manhood daring, bold, and venturous;
Thy age confirm'd, proud, subtle, sly, and bloody,
More mild, but yet more harmful—kind in hatred.
What comfortable hour canst thou name
That ever grac'd me with thy company?

King Richard III.
Faith, none, but Humphrey Hour, that call'd your Grace
To breakfast once, forth of my company.
If I be so disgracious in your eye,
Let me march on and not offend you, madam.
Strike up the drum.

Duchess of York.
     I prithee hear me speak.

King Richard III.
You speak too bitterly.

Duchess of York.
     Hear me a word;
For I shall never speak to thee again.

King Richard III.
So.

Duchess of York.
Either thou wilt die by God's just ordinance
Ere from this war thou turn a conqueror,
Or I with grief and extreme age shall perish
And never more behold thy face again.
Therefore take with thee my most grievous curse,
Which in the day of battle tire thee more
Than all the complete armor that thou wear'st!
My prayers on the adverse party fight,
And there the little souls of Edward's children
Whisper the spirits of thine enemies
And promise them success and victory.
Bloody thou art, bloody will be thy end;
Shame serves thy life and doth thy death attend.

Exit.

Queen Elizabeth.
Though far more cause, yet much less spirit to curse
Abides in me; I say amen to her.

King Richard III.
Stay, madam, I must talk a word with you.

Queen Elizabeth.
I have no more sons of the royal blood
For thee to slaughter. For my daughters, Richard,
They shall be praying nuns, not weeping queens;
And therefore level not to hit their lives.

King Richard III.
You have a daughter call'd Elizabeth,
Virtuous and fair, royal and gracious.

Queen Elizabeth.
And must she die for this? O, let her live!
And I'll corrupt her manners, stain her beauty,
Slander myself as false to Edward's bed,
Throw over her the veil of infamy.
So she may live unscarr'd of bleeding slaughter,
I will confess she was not Edward's daughter.

King Richard III.
Wrong not her birth, she is a royal princess.

Queen Elizabeth.
To save her life, I'll say she is not so.

King Richard III.
Her life is safest only in her birth.

Queen Elizabeth.
And only in that safety died her brothers.

King Richard III.
Lo at their birth good stars were opposite.

Queen Elizabeth.
No, to their lives ill friends were contrary.

King Richard III.
All unavoided is the doom of destiny.

Queen Elizabeth.
True—when avoided grace makes destiny:
My babes were destin'd to a fairer death,
If grace had blest thee with a fairer life.

King Richard III.
You speak as if that I had slain my cousins!

Queen Elizabeth.
Cousins indeed, and by their uncle cozen'd
Of comfort, kingdom, kindred, freedom, life.
Whose hand soever lanch'd their tender hearts,
Thy head (all indirectly) gave direction.
No doubt the murd'rous knife was dull and blunt
Till it was whetted on thy stone-hard heart
To revel in the entrails of my lambs.
But that still use of grief makes wild grief tame,
My tongue should to thy ears not name my boys
Till that my nails were anchor'd in thine eyes;
And I, in such a desp'rate bay of death,
Like a poor bark of sails and tackling reft,
Rush all to pieces on thy rocky bosom.

King Richard III.
Madam, so thrive I in my enterprise
And dangerous success of bloody wars,
As I intend more good to you and yours
Than ever you or yours by me were harm'd!

Queen Elizabeth.
What good is cover'd with the face of heaven,
To be discover'd, that can do me good?

King Richard III.
Th' advancement of your children, gentle lady.

Queen Elizabeth.
Up to some scaffold, there to lose their heads.

King Richard III.
Unto the dignity and height of fortune,
The high imperial type of this earth's glory.

Queen Elizabeth.
Flatter my sorrow with report of it;
Tell me, what state, what dignity, what honor,
Canst thou demise to any child of mine?

King Richard III.
Even all I have—ay, and myself and all—
Will I withal endow a child of thine;
So in the Lethe of thy angry soul
Thou drown the sad remembrance of those wrongs
Which thou supposest I have done to thee.

Queen Elizabeth.
Be brief, lest that the process of thy kindness
Last longer telling than thy kindness' date.

King Richard III.
Then know that from my soul I love thy daughter.

Queen Elizabeth.
My daughter's mother thinks it with her soul.

King Richard III.
What do you think?

Queen Elizabeth.
That thou dost love my daughter from thy soul;
So from thy soul's love didst thou love her brothers,
And from my heart's love I do thank thee for it.

King Richard III.
Be not so hasty to confound my meaning:
I mean that with my soul I love thy daughter,
And do intend to make her Queen of England.

Queen Elizabeth.
Well then, who dost thou mean shall be her king?

King Richard III.
Even he that makes her queen. Who should be else?

Queen Elizabeth.
What, thou?

King Richard III.
              Even so. How think you of it?

Queen Elizabeth.
How canst thou woo her?

King Richard III.
                That would I learn of you,
As one being best acquainted with her humor.

Queen Elizabeth.
And wilt thou learn of me?

King Richard III.
                Madam, with all my heart.

Queen Elizabeth.
Send to her by the man that slew her brothers
A pair of bleeding hearts; thereon engrave
"Edward" and "York"; then haply will she weep.
Therefore present to her—as sometimes Margaret
Did to thy father, steep'd in Rutland's blood—
A handkercher, which, say to her, did drain
The purple sap from her sweet brother's body,
And bid her wipe her weeping eyes withal.
If this inducement move her not to love,
Send her a letter of thy noble deeds:
Tell her thou mad'st away her uncle Clarence,
Her uncle Rivers, ay (and for her sake!),
Mad'st quick conveyance with her good aunt Anne.

King Richard III.
You mock me, madam, this is not the way
To win your daughter.

Queen Elizabeth.
                There is no other way,
Unless thou couldst put on some other shape
And not be Richard that hath done all this.

King Richard III.
Say that I did all this for love of her.

Queen Elizabeth.
Nay then indeed she cannot choose but hate thee,
Having bought love with such a bloody spoil.

King Richard III.
Look what is done cannot be now amended:
Men shall deal unadvisedly sometimes,
Which after-hours gives leisure to repent.
If I did take the kingdom from your sons,
To make amends I'll give it to your daughter;
If I have kill'd the issue of your womb,
To quicken your increase, I will beget
Mine issue of your blood upon your daughter.
A grandam's name is little less in love
Than is the doting title of a mother;
They are as children but one step below,
Even of your metal, of your very blood;
Of all one pain, save for a night of groans
Endur'd of her, for whom you bid like sorrow.
Your children were vexation to your youth,
But mine shall be a comfort to your age.
The loss you have is but a son being king,
And by that loss your daughter is made queen.
I cannot make you what amends I would,
Therefore accept such kindness as I can.
Dorset your son, that with a fearful soul
Leads discontented steps in foreign soil,
This fair alliance quickly shall call home
To high promotions and great dignity.
The King, that calls your beauteous daughter wife,
Familiarly shall call thy Dorset brother;
Again shall you be mother to a king;
And all the ruins of distressful times
Repair'd with double riches of content.
What? We have many goodly days to see:
The liquid drops of tears that you have shed
Shall come again, transform'd to orient pearl,
Advantaging their love with interest
Of ten times double gain of happiness.
Go then, my mother, to thy daughter go,
Make bold her bashful years with your experience;
Prepare her ears to hear a wooer's tale;
Put in her tender heart th' aspiring flame
Of golden sovereignty; acquaint the Princess
With the sweet silent hours of marriage joys;
And when this arm of mine hath chastised
The petty rebel, dull-brain'd Buckingham,
Bound with triumphant garlands will I come
And lead thy daughter to a conqueror's bed;
To whom I will retail my conquest won,
And she shall be sole victoress, Caesar's Caesar.

Queen Elizabeth.
What were I best to say? Her father's brother
Would be her lord? Or shall I say her uncle?
Or he that slew her brothers and her uncles?
Under what title shall I woo for thee,
That God, the law, my honor, and her love
Can make seem pleasing to her tender years?

King Richard III.
Infer fair England's peace by this alliance.

Queen Elizabeth.
Which she shall purchase with still-lasting war.

King Richard III.
Tell her the King, that may command, entreats.

Queen Elizabeth.
That at her hands which the King's King forbids.

King Richard III.
Say she shall be a high and mighty queen.

Queen Elizabeth.
To vail the title, as her mother doth.

King Richard III.
Say I will love her everlastingly.

Queen Elizabeth.
But how long shall that title "ever" last?

King Richard III.
Sweetly in force unto her fair live's end.

Queen Elizabeth.
But how long fairly shall her sweet life last?

King Richard III.
As long as heaven and nature lengthens it.

Queen Elizabeth.
As long as hell and Richard likes of it.

King Richard III.
Say I, her sovereign, am her subject low.

Queen Elizabeth.
But she, your subject, loathes such sovereignty.

King Richard III.
Be eloquent in my behalf to her.

Queen Elizabeth.
An honest tale speeds best being plainly told.

King Richard III.
Then plainly to her tell my loving tale.

Queen Elizabeth.
Plain and not honest is too harsh a style.

King Richard III.
Your reasons are too shallow and too quick.

Queen Elizabeth.
O no, my reasons are too deep and dead—
Too deep and dead, poor infants, in their graves.

King Richard III.
Harp not on that string, madam, that is past.

Queen Elizabeth.
Harp on it still shall I till heart-strings break.

King Richard III.
Now by my George, my Garter, and my crown—

Queen Elizabeth.
Profan'd, dishonor'd, and the third usurp'd.

King Richard III.
I swear—

Queen Elizabeth.
            By nothing, for this is no oath:
Thy George, profan'd, hath lost his lordly honor;
Thy Garter, blemish'd, pawn'd his knightly virtue;
Thy crown, usurp'd, disgrac'd his kingly glory.
If something thou wouldst swear to be believ'd,
Swear then by something that thou hast not wrong'd.

King Richard III.
Then by myself—

Queen Elizabeth.
            Thyself is self-misus'd.

King Richard III.
Now by the world—

Queen Elizabeth.
            'Tis full of thy foul wrongs.

King Richard III.
My father's death—

Queen Elizabeth.
            Thy life hath it dishonor'd.

King Richard III.
Why then, by God—

Queen Elizabeth.
            God's wrong is most of all:
If thou didst fear to break an oath with him,
The unity the King my husband made
Thou hadst not broken, nor my brothers died.
If thou hadst fear'd to break an oath by him,
Th' imperial metal, circling now thy head,
Had grac'd the tender temples of my child,
And both the Princes had been breathing here,
Which now, two tender bedfellows for dust,
Thy broken faith hath made the prey for worms.

What canst thou swear by now?

King Richard III.
                       The time to come.

Queen Elizabeth.
That thou hast wronged in the time o'erpast;
For I myself have many tears to wash
Hereafter time, for time past wrong'd by thee.
The children live whose fathers thou hast slaughter'd,
Ungovern'd youth, to wail it in their age;
The parents live whose children thou hast butcher'd,
Old barren plants, to wail it with their age.
Swear not by time to come, for that thou hast
Misus'd ere us'd, by times ill-us'd o'erpast.

King Richard III.
As I intend to prosper and repent,
So thrive I in my dangerous affairs
Of hostile arms! Myself myself confound!
Heaven and fortune bar me happy hours!
Day, yield me not thy light, nor, night, thy rest!
Be opposite all planets of good luck
To my proceeding, if with dear heart's love,
Immaculate devotion, holy thoughts,
I tender not thy beauteous princely daughter!
In her consists my happiness and thine;
Without her, follows to myself and thee,
Herself, the land, and many a Christian soul,
Death, desolation, ruin, and decay.
It cannot be avoided but by this;
It will not be avoided but by this.
Therefore, dear mother—I must call you so—
Be the attorney of my love to her.
Plead what I will be, not what I have been;
Not my deserts, but what I will deserve.
Urge the necessity and state of times,
And be not peevish-fond in great designs.

Queen Elizabeth.
Shall I be tempted of the devil thus?

King Richard III.
Ay, if the devil tempt you to do good.

Queen Elizabeth.
Shall I forget myself to be myself?

King Richard III.
Ay, if yourself's remembrance wrong yourself.

Queen Elizabeth.
Yet thou didst kill my children.

King Richard III.
But in your daughter's womb I bury them;
Where in that nest of spicery they will breed
Selves of themselves, to your recomforture.

Queen Elizabeth.
Shall I go win my daughter to thy will?

King Richard III.
And be a happy mother by the deed.

Queen Elizabeth.
I go. Write to me very shortly,
And you shall understand from me her mind.

King Richard III.
Bear her my true love's kiss; and so farewell.

Exit Queen Elizabeth.

Relenting fool, and shallow, changing woman!

Enter Ratcliffe, Catesby following.

How now? What news?

Sir Richard Ratcliffe.
Most mighty sovereign, on the western coast
Rideth a puissant navy; to our shores
Throng many doubtful hollow-hearted friends,
Unarm'd, and unresolv'd to beat them back.
'Tis thought that Richmond is their admiral;
And there they hull, expecting but the aid
Of Buckingham to welcome them ashore.

King Richard III.
Some light-foot friend post to the Duke of Norfolk;
Ratcliffe, thyself—or Catesby—where is he?

Sir William Catesby.
Here, my good lord.

King Richard III.
                       Catesby, fly to the Duke.

Sir William Catesby.
I will, my lord, with all convenient haste.

King Richard III.
Ratcliffe, come hither. Post to Salisbury;
When thou com'st thither—

To Catesby.

Dull unmindful villain,
Why stay'st thou here, and go'st not to the Duke?

Sir William Catesby.
First, mighty liege, tell me your Highness' pleasure,
What from your Grace I shall deliver to him.

King Richard III.
O, true, good Catesby. Bid him levy straight
The greatest strength and power that he can make,
And meet me suddenly at Salisbury.

Sir William Catesby.
I go.

Exit.

Sir Richard Ratcliffe.
What, may it please you, shall I do at Salisbury?

King Richard III.
Why, what wouldst thou do there before I go?

Sir Richard Ratcliffe.
Your Highness told me I should post before.

King Richard III.
My mind is chang'd.

Enter Lord Stanley.

Stanley, what news with you?

Lord Stanley.
None good, my liege, to please you with the hearing,
Nor none so bad but well may be reported.

King Richard III.
Hoy-day, a riddle! Neither good nor bad!
What need'st thou run so many miles about,
When thou mayest tell thy tale the nearest way?
Once more, what news?

Lord Stanley.
Richmond is on the seas.

King Richard III.
There let him sink, and be the seas on him!
White-liver'd runagate, what doth he there?

Lord Stanley.
I know not, mighty sovereign, but by guess.

King Richard III.
Well, as you guess?

Lord Stanley.
Stirr'd up by Dorset, Buckingham, and Morton,
He makes for England, here to claim the crown.

King Richard III.
Is the chair empty? Is the sword unsway'd?
Is the King dead? The empire unpossess'd?
What heir of York is there alive but we?
And who is England's king but great York's heir?
Then tell me, what makes he upon the seas?

Lord Stanley.
Unless for that, my liege, I cannot guess.

King Richard III.
Unless for that he comes to be your liege,
You cannot guess wherefore the Welshman comes.
Thou wilt revolt and fly to him, I fear.

Lord Stanley.
No, my good lord, therefore mistrust me not.

King Richard III.
Where is thy power then, to beat him back?
Where be thy tenants and thy followers?
Are they not now upon the western shore,
Safe-conducting the rebels from their ships?

Lord Stanley.
No, my good lord, my friends are in the north.

King Richard III.
Cold friends to me! What do they in the north,
When they should serve their sovereign in the west?

Lord Stanley.
They have not been commanded, mighty King.
Pleaseth your Majesty to give me leave,
I'll muster up my friends and meet your Grace
Where and what time your Majesty shall please.

King Richard III.
Ay, thou wouldst be gone to join with Richmond;
But I'll not trust thee.

Lord Stanley.
Most mighty sovereign,
You have no cause to hold my friendship doubtful.
I never was nor never will be false.

King Richard III.
Go then, and muster men; but leave behind
Your son, George Stanley. Look your heart be firm,
Or else his head's assurance is but frail.

Lord Stanley.
So deal with him as I prove true to you.

Exit Stanley.
Enter First Messenger.

First Messenger.
My gracious sovereign, now in Devonshire,
As I by friends am well advertised,
Sir Edward Courtney and the haughty prelate,
Bishop of Exeter, his elder brother,
With many more confederates, are in arms.

Enter another Messenger.

Second Messenger.
In Kent, my liege, the Guilfords are in arms,
And every hour more competitors
Flock to the rebels, and their power grows strong.

Enter another Messenger.

Third Messenger.
My lord, the army of great Buckingham—

King Richard III.
Out on you, owls! Nothing but songs of death?

He striketh him.

There, take thou that, till thou bring better news.

Third Messenger.
The news I have to tell your Majesty
Is that by sudden floods and fall of waters
Buckingham's army is dispers'd and scatter'd,
And he himself wand'red away alone,
No man knows whither.

King Richard III.
     I cry thee mercy;
There is my purse to cure that blow of thine.
Hath any well-advised friend proclaim'd
Reward to him that brings the traitor in?

Third Messenger.
Such proclamation hath been made, my lord.

Enter another Messenger.

Fourth Messenger.
Sir Thomas Lovel and Lord Marquess Dorset,
'Tis said, my liege, in Yorkshire are in arms.
But this good comfort bring I to your Highness:
The Britain navy is dispers'd by tempest.
Richmond in Dorsetshire sent out a boat
Unto the shore, to ask those on the banks
If they were his assistants, yea or no;
Who answer'd him, they came from Buckingham
Upon his party. He, mistrusting them,
Hois'd sail, and made his course again for Britain.

King Richard III.
March on, march on, since we are up in arms,
If not to fight with foreign enemies,
Yet to beat down these rebels here at home.

Enter Catesby.

Sir William Catesby.
My liege, the Duke of Buckingham is taken—
That is the best news. That the Earl of Richmond
Is with a mighty power landed at Milford
Is colder tidings, yet they must be told.

King Richard III.
Away towards Salisbury! While we reason here,
A royal battle might be won and lost.
Some one take order Buckingham be brought
To Salisbury, the rest march on with me.

Flourish. Exeunt.

Scene 5

Lord Stanley's house.

(Stanley; Sir Christopher Urswick)

Stanley sends a message to Richmond assuring him of his support, but explaining that his son is a hostage and that he cannot therefore do anything openly on Richmond's part as yet. He also lets him know that the Queen has agreed to let her daughter marry Richmond, despite her promise to Richard.

Enter Stanley the Earl of Derby, and Sir Christopher Urswick, a priest.

Lord Stanley.
Sir Christopher, tell Richmond this from me:
That in the sty of the most deadly boar
My son George Stanley is frank'd up in hold;

If I revolt, off goes young George's head;
The fear of that holds off my present aid.
So get thee gone; commend me to thy lord.
Withal say that the Queen hath heartily consented
He should espouse Elizabeth her daughter.
But tell me, where is princely Richmond now?

Christopher Urswick.
At Pembroke or at Ha'rford-West in Wales.

Lord Stanley.
What men of name resort to him?

Christopher Urswick.
Sir Walter Herbert, a renowned soldier,
Sir Gilbert Talbot, Sir William Stanley,
Oxford, redoubted Pembroke, Sir James Blunt,
And Rice ap Thomas, with a valiant crew,
And many other of great name and worth;
And towards London do they bend their power,
If by the way they be not fought withal.

Lord Stanley.
Well, hie thee to thy lord; I kiss his hand.
My letter will resolve him of my mind.
Farewell.

Exeunt.

Act 5

Scene 1

Salisbury. An open place.

(Buckingham; Halberds/Officers; Sheriff)

As he is led to his death, Buckingham learns that Richard will not speak to him. He reflects on his crimes and how he called this fate down upon himself in earlier days, and recalls Margaret's curse.

Enter Buckingham, with Halberds and the Sheriff, led to execution.

Duke of Buckingham.
Will not King Richard let me speak with him?

Sheriff of Wiltshire.
No, my good lord, therefore be patient.

Duke of Buckingham.
Hastings, and Edward's children, Grey and Rivers,
Holy King Henry and thy fair son Edward,
Vaughan, and all that have miscarried
By underhand corrupted foul injustice,
If that your moody discontented souls
Do through the clouds behold this present hour,
Even for revenge mock my destruction!
This is All-Souls' day, fellow, is it not?

Sheriff of Wiltshire.
It is, my lord.

Duke of Buckingham.
Why then All-Souls' day is my body's doomsday.
This is the day which, in King Edward's time,
I wish'd might fall on me when I was found
False to his children and his wive's allies;
This is the day wherein I wish'd to fall
By the false faith of him whom most I trusted;
This, this All-Souls' day to my fearful soul,
Is the determin'd respite of my wrongs.
That high All-Seer, which I dallied with,
Hath turn'd my feigned prayer on my head,
And given in earnest what I begg'd in jest.
Thus doth he force the swords of wicked men
To turn their own points in their masters' bosoms;
Thus Margaret's curse falls heavy on my neck:
"When he," quoth she, "shall split thy heart with sorrow,
Remember Margaret was a prophetess."
Come lead me, officers, to the block of shame;
Wrong hath but wrong, and blame the due of blame.

Exeunt Buckingham and Sheriff with Officers.

Scene 2

The camp near Tamworth.

(Richmond; Oxford; Sir James Blunt; Sir Walter Herbert)

Richmond receives Stanley's message and learns that Richard is nearby. He and his allies are reassured by the fact that Richard has no friends, only frightened servants.

Enter Richmond, Oxford, Sir James Blunt, Sir Walter Herbert, and others, with Drum and Colors.

Henry, Earl of Richmond.
Fellows in arms, and my most loving friends,
Bruis'd underneath the yoke of tyranny,
Thus far into the bowels of the land

Have we march'd on without impediment;
And here receive we from our father Stanley
Lines of fair comfort and encouragement.
The wretched, bloody, and usurping boar,
That spoil'd your summer fields and fruitful vines,
Swills your warm blood like wash and makes his trough
In your embowell'd bosoms—this foul swine
Is now even in the center of this isle,
Near to the town of Leicester, as we learn.
From Tamworth thither is but one day's march.
In God's name cheerly on, courageous friends,
To reap the harvest of perpetual peace
By this one bloody trial of sharp war.

Earl of Oxford.
Every man's conscience is a thousand men,
To fight against this guilty homicide.

Sir Walter Herbert.
I doubt not but his friends will turn to us.

Sir James Blunt.
He hath no friends but what are friends for fear,
Which in his dearest need will fly from him.

Henry, Earl of Richmond.
All for our vantage. Then in God's name march!
True hope is swift and flies with swallow's wings,
Kings it makes gods, and meaner creatures kings.

Exeunt omnes.

Scene 3

Bosworth Field.

(King Richard; Norfolk; Ratcliffe; Earl of Surrey; Soldiers; Richmond; Sir William Brandon; Oxford; Dorset; Blunt; Herbert; Catesby; Stanley; Ghost of Prince Edward; Ghost of King Henry VI; Ghost of Clarence; Ghost of Rivers; Ghost of Grey; Ghost of Vaughan; Ghosts of two young Princes; Ghost of Hastings; Ghost of Lady Anne; Ghost of Buckingham; First Lord to Richmond; Second Lord to Richmond; Attendants; Fifth Messenger)

Richmond and Richard set up their respective tents. Richard is reassured by the low number of rebels. Richmond aligns his forces. Richard checks on the location of his leaders and sends a message to Stanley, reminding him that his son is a hostage. Richard then goes to sleep, less certain than he lets on. Richmond and Stanley confer, the older man giving him advice.

Richmond prays before going to sleep. As both Richard and Richmond are asleep, the ghosts of all of Richard's victims appear, one by one: Henry VI's son, Henry VI himself, Clarence, Rivers, Grey, Vaughan, the Two Princes, Hastings, Lady Anne, Buckingham: all appear, and curse Richard, urging him to despair and die, before offering encouragement to Richmond. Richard wakes in a panic, thinking an assassin is near. He reflects on matters, realizing how alone he is, and beginning to feel the weight of his sins. He realizes that nobody, not even himself, can pity him. He prepares for battle with less confidence that he might have had. Richmond, meanwhile, wakes in high good spirits, having slept wonderfully well, and urges his soldiers to fight well, since their cause is just: the fight against tyranny. Norfolk tells Richard of a warning he received implying that Richard has been betrayed. Richard gives a speech to his soldiers, insulting the enemy as one easily defeated. Just as the battle is about to begin, he hears that Stanley has refused to join him. Needing to concentrate on the fight, he has no time to execute Stanley's son.

Enter at one door King Richard, in arms, with Norfolk, Ratcliffe, and the Earl of Surrey, with others.

King Richard III.
Here pitch our tent, even here in Bosworth field.
My Lord of Surrey, why look you so sad?

Earl of Surrey.
My heart is ten times lighter than my looks.

King Richard III.
My Lord of Norfolk—

Duke of Norfolk.
Here, most gracious liege.

King Richard III.
Norfolk, we must have knocks. Ha, must we not?

Duke of Norfolk.
We must both give and take, my loving lord.

King Richard III.
Up with my tent! Here will I lie tonight

Soldiers begin to set up the King's tent.

But where tomorrow? Well, all's one for that.
Who hath descried the number of the traitors?

Duke of Norfolk.
Six or seven thousand is their utmost power.

King Richard III.
Why, our battalia trebles that account;
Besides, the King's name is a tower of strength,
Which they upon the adverse faction want.
Up with the tent! Come, noble gentlemen,
Let us survey the vantage of the ground.
Call for some men of sound direction:
Let's lack no discipline, make no delay,
For, lords, tomorrow is a busy day.

Exeunt.
Enter at the other door Richmond, Sir William Brandon, Oxford, and Dorset, Blunt, Herbert, and others. Some of the soldiers pitch Richmond's tent.

Henry, Earl of Richmond.
The weary sun hath made a golden set,
And by the bright tract of his fiery car
Gives token of a goodly day tomorrow.
Sir William Brandon, you shall bear my standard.
Give me some ink and paper in my tent;
I'll draw the form and model of our battle,
Limit each leader to his several charge,
And part in just proportion our small power.
My Lord of Oxford—you, Sir William Brandon—
And you, Sir Walter Herbert—stay with me.
The Earl of Pembroke keeps his regiment;
Good Captain Blunt, bear my good-night to him,
And by the second hour in the morning
Desire the Earl to see me in my tent.
Yet one thing more, good captain, do for me—
Where is Lord Stanley quarter'd, do you know?

Sir James Blunt.
Unless I have mista'en his colors much
(Which well I am assur'd I have not done),
His regiment lies half a mile at least
South from the mighty power of the King.

Henry, Earl of Richmond.
If without peril it be possible,
Sweet Blunt, make some good means to speak with him,
And give him from me this most needful note.

Sir James Blunt.
Upon my life, my lord, I'll undertake it,
And so God give you quiet rest tonight!

Henry, Earl of Richmond.
Good night, good Captain Blunt.

Exit Blunt.
                  Come, gentlemen,
Let us consult upon tomorrow's business.
In to my tent, the dew is raw and cold.

They withdraw into the tent.
Enter to his tent King Richard, Ratcliffe, Norfolk, and Catesby.

King Richard III.
What is't a' clock?

Sir William Catesby.
                It's supper-time, my lord,
It's nine a' clock.

King Richard III.
                I will not sup tonight.
Give me some ink and paper.
What? Is my beaver easier than it was?
And all my armor laid into my tent?

Sir William Catesby.
It is, my liege, and all things are in readiness.

King Richard III.
Good Norfolk, hie thee to thy charge,
Use careful watch, choose trusty sentinels.

Duke of Norfolk.
I go, my lord.

King Richard III.
Stir with the lark tomorrow, gentle Norfolk.

Duke of Norfolk.
I warrant you, my lord.

Exit.

King Richard III.
Catesby!

Sir William Catesby.
My lord?

King Richard III.
            Send out a pursuivant-at-arms
To Stanley's regiment, bid him bring his power
Before sunrising, lest his son George fall
Into the blind cave of eternal night.

Act 5, Scene 3

Exit Catesby.

Fill me a bowl of wine. Give me a watch.
Saddle white Surrey for the field tomorrow.
Look that my staves be sound, and not too heavy.
Ratcliffe!

Sir Richard Ratcliffe.
My lord?

King Richard III.
Saw'st thou the melancholy Lord Northumberland?

Sir Richard Ratcliffe.
Thomas the Earl of Surrey and himself,
Much about cock-shut time, from troop to troop
Went through the army, cheering up the soldiers.

King Richard III.
So, I am satisfied. Give me a bowl of wine.
I have not that alacrity of spirit
Nor cheer of mind that I was wont to have.

Wine brought.

Set it down. Is ink and paper ready?

Sir Richard Ratcliffe.
It is, my lord.

King Richard III.
             Bid my guard watch; leave me.
Ratcliffe, about the mid of night come to my tent
And help to arm me. Leave me, I say.

Exit Ratcliffe. Richard sleeps.
Enter Stanley the Earl of Derby to Richmond in his tent,
Lords and others attending.

Lord Stanley.
Fortune and victory sit on thy helm!

Henry, Earl of Richmond.
All comfort that the dark night can afford
Be to thy person, noble father-in-law!
Tell me, how fares our loving mother?

Lord Stanley.
I, by attorney, bless thee from thy mother,
Who prays continually for Richmond's good.
So much for that. The silent hours steal on,
And flaky darkness breaks within the east.
In brief—for so the season bids us be—
Prepare thy battle early in the morning,
And put thy fortune to the arbitrement
Of bloody strokes and mortal-staring war.
I, as I may—that which I would I cannot—
With best advantage will deceive the time,
And aid thee in this doubtful shock of arms;
But on thy side I may not be too forward,
Lest being seen, thy brother, tender George,
Be executed in his father's sight.
Farewell! The leisure and the fearful time
Cuts off the ceremonious vows of love
And ample interchange of sweet discourse
Which so long sund'red friends should dwell upon.
God give us leisure for these rites of love!
Once more, adieu! Be valiant, and speed well!

Henry, Earl of Richmond.
Good lords, conduct him to his regiment.
I'll strive with troubled thoughts to take a nap,
Lest leaden slumber peize me down tomorrow,
When I should mount with wings of victory.
Once more, good night, kind lords and gentlemen.

Exeunt. Manet Richmond.

O Thou whose captain I account myself,
Look on my forces with a gracious eye;
Put in their hands thy bruising irons of wrath,
That they may crush down with a heavy fall
The usurping helmets of our adversaries;
Make us thy ministers of chastisement,
That we may praise thee in the victory!
To thee I do commend my watchful soul
Ere I let fall the windows of mine eyes:
Sleeping and waking, O, defend me still!

Sleeps.
Enter the Ghost of young Prince Edward of Lancaster,
son to Henry the Sixth, to Richard.

Ghost of Prince Edward of Lancaster.

To Richard.

Let me sit heavy on thy soul tomorrow!
Think how thou stab'st me in my prime of youth
At Tewksbury. Despair therefore and die!

To Richmond.

Be cheerful, Richmond, for the wronged souls
Of butchered princes fight in thy behalf.
King Henry's issue, Richmond, comforts thee.

Enter the Ghost of King Henry the Sixth.

Ghost of King Henry VI.

To Richard.

When I was mortal, my anointed body
By thee was punched full of deadly holes.
Think on the Tower and me. Despair and die!
Harry the Sixth bids thee despair and die.

To Richmond.

Virtuous and holy, be thou conqueror!
Harry, that prophesied thou shouldst be king,
Doth comfort thee in thy sleep. Live and flourish!

Enter the Ghost of Clarence.

Ghost of Clarence.

To Richard.

Let me sit heavy in thy soul tomorrow,
I that was wash'd to death with fulsome wine,
Poor Clarence, by thy guile betray'd to death!
Tomorrow in the battle think on me,
And fall thy edgeless sword. Despair and die!

To Richmond.

Thou offspring of the house of Lancaster,
The wronged heirs of York do pray for thee.
Good angels guard thy battle! Live and flourish!

Enter the Ghosts of Rivers, Grey, Vaughan.

Ghost of Earl Rivers.

To Richard.

Let me sit heavy in thy soul tomorrow,
Rivers, that died at Pomfret! Despair and die!

Ghost of Lord Grey.

To Richard.

Think upon Grey, and let thy soul despair!

Ghost of Sir Thomas Vaughan.

To Richard.

Think upon Vaughan, and with guilty fear
Let fall thy lance. Despair and die!

All Ghosts.

To Richmond.

Awake and think our wrongs in Richard's bosom
Will conquer him! Awake and win the day!

Enter the Ghosts of the two young Princes.

Ghosts of Princes.

To Richard.

Dream on thy cousins smothered in the Tower.
Let us be lead within thy bosom, Richard,
And weigh thee down to ruin, shame, and death!
Thy nephews' souls bid thee despair and die!

To Richmond.

Sleep, Richmond, sleep in peace and wake in joy.
Good angels guard thee from the boar's annoy!
Live and beget a happy race of kings!
Edward's unhappy sons do bid thee flourish.

Enter the Ghost of Hastings.

Ghost of Lord Hastings.

To Richard.

Bloody and guilty, guiltily awake,
And in a bloody battle end thy days!
Think on Lord Hastings. Despair and die!

To Richmond.

Quiet untroubled soul, awake, awake!
Arm, fight, and conquer for fair England's sake!

Enter the Ghost of Lady Anne, his wife.

Ghost of Lady Anne.

To Richard.

Richard, thy wife, that wretched Anne thy wife,
That never slept a quiet hour with thee,
Now fills thy sleep with perturbations.
Tomorrow in the battle think on me,
And fall thy edgeless sword. Despair and die!

To Richmond.

Thou quiet soul, sleep thou a quiet sleep,
Dream of success and happy victory!
Thy adversary's wife doth pray for thee.

Enter the Ghost of Buckingham.

Ghost of Duke of Buckingham.

To Richard.

The first was I that help'd thee to the crown;
The last was I that felt thy tyranny.
O, in the battle think on Buckingham,
And die in terror of thy guiltiness!
Dream on, dream on, of bloody deeds and death;
Fainting, despair; despairing, yield thy breath!

To Richmond.

I died for hope ere I could lend thee aid,
But cheer thy heart, and be thou not dismay'd.
God and good angels fight on Richmond's side,
And Richard falls in height of all his pride!

The Ghosts vanish. Richard starteth up out of a dream.

King Richard III.
Give me another horse! Bind up my wounds!
Have mercy, Jesu! Soft, I did but dream.
O coward conscience, how dost thou afflict me!
The lights burn blue. It is now dead midnight.
Cold fearful drops stand on my trembling flesh.
What do I fear? Myself? There's none else by.
Richard loves Richard, that is, I am I.
Is there a murderer here? No. Yes, I am.
Then fly. What, from myself? Great reason why—
Lest I revenge. What, myself upon myself?
Alack, I love myself. Wherefore? For any good
That I myself have done unto myself?
O no! Alas, I rather hate myself
For hateful deeds committed by myself.
I am a villain; yet I lie, I am not.
Fool, of thyself speak well; fool, do not flatter:
My conscience hath a thousand several tongues,
And every tongue brings in a several tale,
And every tale condemns me for a villain.
Perjury, perjury, in the highest degree;
Murder, stern murder, in the direst degree;
All several sins, all us'd in each degree,
Throng to the bar, crying all, "Guilty! Guilty!"
I shall despair; there is no creature loves me,
And if I die no soul will pity me.
And wherefore should they, since that I myself
Find in myself no pity to myself?
Methought the souls of all that I had murder'd
Came to my tent, and every one did threat
Tomorrow's vengeance on the head of Richard.

Enter Ratcliffe.

Sir Richard Ratcliffe.
My lord!

King Richard III.
'Zounds, who is there?

Sir Richard Ratcliffe.
Ratcliffe, my lord, 'tis I. The early village cock
Hath twice done salutation to the morn,
Your friends are up and buckle on their armor.

King Richard III.
O Ratcliffe, I have dream'd a fearful dream!
What think'st thou—will our friends prove all true?

Sir Richard Ratcliffe.
No doubt, my lord.

King Richard III.
      O Ratcliffe, I fear, I fear!

Sir Richard Ratcliffe.
Nay, good my lord, be not afraid of shadows.

King Richard III.
By the apostle Paul, shadows tonight
Have struck more terror to the soul of Richard
Than can the substance of ten thousand soldiers
Armed in proof and led by shallow Richmond.
'Tis not yet near day. Come, go with me,
Under our tents I'll play the ease-dropper,
To see if any mean to shrink from me.

Exeunt.
Enter the Lords to Richmond sitting in his tent.

First Lord to Richmond.
Good morrow, Richmond!

Henry, Earl of Richmond.
Cry mercy, lords and watchful gentlemen,
That you have ta'en a tardy sluggard here.

Second Lord to Richmond.
How have you slept, my lord?

Henry, Earl of Richmond.
The sweetest sleep and fairest-boding dreams
That ever ent'red in a drowsy head
Have I since your departure had, my lords.

Methought their souls whose bodies Richard murder'd
Came to my tent and cried on victory.
I promise you, my soul is very jocund
In the remembrance of so fair a dream.
How far into the morning is it, lords?

First Lord to Richmond.
Upon the stroke of four.

Henry, Earl of Richmond.
Why, then 'tis time to arm and give direction.

His oration to his Soldiers.

More than I have said, loving countrymen,
The leisure and enforcement of the time
Forbids to dwell upon, yet remember this:
God and our good cause fight upon our side;
The prayers of holy saints and wronged souls,
Like high-rear'd bulwarks, stand before our faces.
Richard except, those whom we fight against
Had rather have us win than him they follow:
For what is he they follow? Truly, gentlemen,
A bloody tyrant and a homicide;
One rais'd in blood, and one in blood established;
One that made means to come by what he hath,
And slaughtered those that were the means to help him;
A base foul stone, made precious by the foil
Of England's chair, where he is falsely set;
One that hath ever been God's enemy.
Then if you fight against God's enemy,
God will in justice ward you as his soldiers;
If you do sweat to put a tyrant down,
You sleep in peace, the tyrant being slain;
If you do fight against your country's foes,
Your country's fat shall pay your pains the hire;
If you do fight in safeguard of your wives,
Your wives shall welcome home the conquerors;
If you do free your children from the sword,
Your children's children quits it in your age.
Then in the name of God and all these rights,
Advance your standards, draw your willing swords.
For me, the ransom of my bold attempt
Shall be this cold corpse on the earth's cold face;
But if I thrive, the gain of my attempt
The least of you shall share his part thereof.
Sound drums and trumpets boldly and cheerfully.
God and Saint George! Richmond and victory!

Exeunt.

Enter King Richard, Ratcliffe, Attendants, and forces.

King Richard III.
What said Northumberland as touching Richmond?

Sir Richard Ratcliffe.
That he was never trained up in arms.

King Richard III.
He said the truth, and what said Surrey then?

Sir Richard Ratcliffe.
He smil'd and said, "The better for our purpose."

King Richard III.
He was in the right, and so indeed it is.

The clock striketh.

Tell the clock there. Give me a calendar.
Who saw the sun today?

Sir Richard Ratcliffe.
                    Not I, my lord.

King Richard III.
Then he disdains to shine, for by the book
He should have brav'd the east an hour ago.
A black day will it be to somebody.
Ratcliffe!

Sir Richard Ratcliffe.
My lord?

King Richard III.
                    The sun will not be seen today,
The sky doth frown and low'r upon our army.
I would these dewy tears were from the ground.
Not shine today? Why, what is that to me
More than to Richmond? For the self-same heaven
That frowns on me looks sadly upon him.

Enter Norfolk.

Duke of Norfolk.
Arm, arm, my lord, the foe vaunts in the field.

King Richard III.
Come, bustle, bustle! Caparison my horse!
Call up Lord Stanley, bid him bring his power.
I will lead forth my soldiers to the plain,
And thus my battle shall be ordered:
My foreward shall be drawn out all in length,
Consisting equally of horse and foot;
Our archers shall be placed in the midst;

Act 5, Scene 4

John Duke of Norfolk, Thomas Earl of Surrey,
Shall have the leading of this foot and horse.
They thus directed, we will follow
In the main battle, whose puissance on either side
Shall be well winged with our chiefest horse.
This, and Saint George to boot! What think'st thou,
Norfolk?

Duke of Norfolk.
A good direction, warlike sovereign.

He sheweth him a paper.

This found I on my tent this morning.

Reads.

"Jockey of Norfolk, be not so bold,
For Dickon thy master is bought and sold."

King Richard III.
A thing devised by the enemy.
Go, gentlemen, every man unto his charge.
Let not our babbling dreams affright our souls;
Conscience is but a word that cowards use,
Devis'd at first to keep the strong in awe:
Our strong arms be our conscience, swords our law!
March on, join bravely, let us to it pell-mell;
If not to heaven, then hand in hand to hell.

His oration to his Army.

What shall I say more than I have inferr'd?
Remember whom you are to cope withal:
A sort of vagabonds, rascals, and runaways,
A scum of Britains and base lackey peasants,
Whom their o'ercloyed country vomits forth
To desperate adventures and assur'd destruction.
You sleeping safe, they bring to you unrest;
You having lands, and blest with beauteous wives,
They would restrain the one, distain the other.
And who doth lead them but a paltry fellow,
Long kept in Britain at our mother's cost?
A milksop, one that never in his life
Felt so much cold as over shoes in snow?
Let's whip these stragglers o'er the seas again;
Lash hence these overweening rags of France,
These famish'd beggars weary of their lives,
Who (but for dreaming on this fond exploit)
For want of means, poor rats, had hang'd themselves.
If we be conquered, let men conquer us,
And not these bastard Britains, whom our fathers
Have in their own land beaten, bobb'd, and thump'd,

And in record left them the heirs of shame.
Shall these enjoy our lands? Lie with our wives?
Ravish our daughters?

Drum afar off.

      Hark, I hear their drum.
Fight, gentlemen of England! Fight, bold yeomen!
Draw, archers, draw your arrows to the head!
Spur your proud horses hard, and ride in blood;
Amaze the welkin with your broken staves!

Enter a Messenger.

What says Lord Stanley? Will he bring his power?

Fifth Messenger.
My lord, he doth deny to come.

King Richard III.
Off with his son George's head!

Duke of Norfolk.
My lord, the enemy is past the marsh,
After the battle let George Stanley die.

King Richard III.
A thousand hearts are great within my bosom.
Advance our standards, set upon our foes.
Our ancient word of courage, fair Saint George,
Inspire us with the spleen of fiery dragons!
Upon them! Victory sits on our helms.

Exeunt.

Scene 4

Another part of Bosworth Field.

(Norfolk; Catesby; King Richard)

Though the battle is going against him, Richard has been doing wonders on the field, searching for Richmond wherever he might be. He calls desperately for a horse, but insists he will not run away.

Alarum. Excursions. Enter Norfolk and forces fighting; to him Catesby.

Sir William Catesby.
Rescue, my Lord of Norfolk, rescue, rescue!
The King enacts more wonders than a man,
Daring an opposite to every danger.
His horse is slain, and all on foot he fights,
Seeking for Richmond in the throat of death.

Rescue, fair lord, or else the day is lost!

Alarums. Enter King Richard.

King Richard III.
A horse, a horse! My kingdom for a horse!

Sir William Catesby.
Withdraw, my lord, I'll help you to a horse.

King Richard III.
Slave, I have set my life upon a cast,
And I will stand the hazard of the die.
I think there be six Richmonds in the field;
Five have I slain today in stead of him.
A horse, a horse! My kingdom for a horse!

Exeunt.

Scene 5

Another part of Bosworth Field.

(King Richard; Richmond; Stanley; First Lord to Richmond; Second Lord to Richmond)

Richard and Richmond meet and fight, and Richmond kills his opponent. Stanley crowns him with the crown he has taken from Richard's head. Richmond promises the civil wars are now at an end, as he, the heir of Lancaster, will marry Edward IV's daughter, the heir of York.

Alarum. Enter King Richard and Richmond; they fight; Richard is slain.
Then, retreat being sounded, flourish, and enter Richmond, Stanley the Earl of Derby, bearing the crown, with other Lords, etc.

Henry, Earl of Richmond.
God and your arms be prais'd, victorious friends,
The day is ours, the bloody dog is dead.

Lord Stanley.
Courageous Richmond, well hast thou acquit thee.
Lo here this long-usurped royalty
From the dead temples of this bloody wretch
Have I pluck'd off to grace thy brows withal.
Wear it, enjoy it, and make much of it.

Henry, Earl of Richmond.
Great God of heaven, say amen to all!
But tell me, is young George Stanley living?

Lord Stanley.
He is, my lord, and safe in Leicester town,
Whither, if it please you, we may now withdraw us.

Henry, Earl of Richmond.
What men of name are slain on either side?

Lord Stanley.
John Duke of Norfolk, Walter Lord Ferrers,
Sir Robert Brakenbury, and Sir William Brandon.

Henry, Earl of Richmond.
Inter their bodies as become their births.
Proclaim a pardon to the soldiers fled
That in submission will return to us,
And then as we have ta'en the sacrament,
We will unite the White Rose and the Red.
Smile heaven upon this fair conjunction,
That long have frown'd upon their enmity!
What traitor hears me, and says not amen?
England hath long been mad and scarr'd herself:
The brother blindly shed the brother's blood,
The father rashly slaughter'd his own son,
The son, compell'd, been butcher to the sire.
All this divided York and Lancaster,
Divided in their dire division,
O now let Richmond and Elizabeth,
The true succeeders of each royal house,
By God's fair ordinance conjoin together!
And let their heirs (God, if thy will be so)
Enrich the time to come with smooth-fac'd peace,
With smiling plenty, and fair prosperous days!
Abate the edge of traitors, gracious Lord,
That would reduce these bloody days again,
And make poor England weep in streams of blood!
Let them not live to taste this land's increase
That would with treason wound this fair land's peace!
Now civil wounds are stopp'd, peace lives again;
That she may long live here, God say amen!

Exeunt.

The Merry Wives of Windsor

Act 1

Scene 1

Windsor. A street in front of Page's house.

(*Justice Shallow; Slender; Sir Hugh Evans; Page; Falstaff; Bardolph; Nym; Pistol; Anne Page; Mistress Ford; Mistress Margaret Page; Simple*)

Sir Robert Shallow, Justice of the Peace is raging against Falstaff to Sir Hugh Evans, his nephew Slender supporting him. Evans tries to calm him down, but to no avail. They also discuss Anne Page and what a good match she would be for Slender. Her father George Page comes in, and they exchange compliments. Falstaff and his followers arrive, and while they admit to poaching Shallow's deer, they deny other charges. Page invites them all to dinner to make them all friends again. Slender hangs back, feeling worried about eating at the same table as Anne when he has not prepared any compliments for her. Anne comes out to ask him in, and he makes a fool of himself, managing only to talk of fighting and bear-baiting. Page comes out and bullies him into joining them at dinner.

Enter Justice Shallow, Slender, Sir Hugh Evans.

Robert Shallow.
Sir Hugh, persuade me not; I will make a Star Chamber matter of it. If he were twenty Sir John Falstaffs, he shall not abuse Robert Shallow, esquire.

Abraham Slender.
In the county of Gloucester, Justice of Peace and Coram.

Robert Shallow.
Ay, cousin Slender, and Custa-lorum.

Abraham Slender.
Ay, and Rato-lorum too; and a gentleman born, Master Parson, who writes himself Armigero, in any bill, warrant, quittance, or obligation, Armigero.

Robert Shallow.
Ay, that I do, and have done any time these three hundred years.

Abraham Slender.
All his successors (gone before him) hath done't; and all his ancestors (that come after him) may. They may give the dozen white luces in their coat.

Robert Shallow.
It is an old coat.

Sir Hugh Evans.
The dozen white louses do become an old coat well; it agrees well, passant. It is a familiar beast to man, and signifies love.

Robert Shallow.
The luce is the fresh fish, the salt fish is an old coat.

Abraham Slender.
I may quarter, coz.

Robert Shallow.
You may, by marrying.

Sir Hugh Evans.
It is marring indeed, if he quarter it.

Robert Shallow.
Not a whit.

Sir Hugh Evans.
Yes, py'r lady. If he has a quarter of your coat, there is but three skirts for yourself, in my simple conjectures. But that is all one. If Sir John Falstaff have committed disparagements unto you, I am of the church, and will be glad to do my benevolence to make atonements and compromises between you.

Robert Shallow.
The Council shall hear it, it is a riot.

Sir Hugh Evans.
It is not meet the Council hear a riot; there is no fear of Got in a riot. The Council, look you, shall desire to hear the fear of Got, and not to hear a riot. Take your vizaments in that.

Robert Shallow.
Ha! O' my life, if I were young again, the sword should end it.

Sir Hugh Evans.
It is petter that friends is the sword, and end it; and there is also another device in my prain, which peradventure prings goot discretions with it: there is Anne Page, which is daughter to Master George Page, which is pretty virginity.

Abraham Slender.
Mistress Anne Page? She has brown hair, and speaks small like a woman.

Sir Hugh Evans.
It is that fery person for all the orld, as just as you will desire, and seven hundred pounds of moneys, and gold, and silver, is her grandsire upon his death's-bed (Got deliver to a joyful resurrections!) give, when she is able to overtake seventeen years old. It were a goot motion if we leave our pribbles and prabbles, and desire a marriage between Master Abraham and Mistress Anne Page.

Abraham Slender.
Did her grandsire leave her seven hundred pound?

Sir Hugh Evans.
Ay, and her father is make her a petter penny.

Abraham Slender.
I know the young gentlewoman, she has good gifts.

Sir Hugh Evans.
Seven hundred pounds, and possibilities, is goot gifts.

Robert Shallow.
Well, let us see honest Master Page. Is Falstaff there?

Sir Hugh Evans.
Shall I tell you a lie? I do despise a liar as I do despise one that is false, or as I despise one that is not true. The knight Sir John is there, and I beseech you be rul'd by your well-willers. I will peat the door for Master Page.

Knocks.

What ho! Got pless your house here!

George Page.

Within.

Who's there?

Enter Page.

Sir Hugh Evans.
Here is Got's plessing, and your friend, and Justice Shallow, and here young Master Slender, that peradventures shall tell you another tale, if matters grow to your likings.

George Page.
I am glad to see your worships well. I thank you for my venison, Master Shallow.

Robert Shallow.
Master Page, I am glad to see you. Much good do it your good heart! I wish'd your venison better, it was ill kill'd. How doth good Mistress Page?—and I thank you always with my heart, la! With my heart.

George Page.
Sir, I thank you.

Robert Shallow.
Sir, I thank you; by yea and no, I do.

George Page.
I am glad to see you, good Master Slender.

Abraham Slender.
How does your fallow greyhound, sir? I heard say he was outrun on Cotsall.

George Page.
It could not be judg'd, sir.

Abraham Slender.
You'll not confess, you'll not confess.

Robert Shallow.
That he will not. 'Tis your fault, 'tis your fault; 'tis a good dog.

George Page.
A cur, sir.

Robert Shallow.
Sir! He's a good dog, and a fair dog—can there be more said? He is good, and fair. Is Sir John Falstaff here?

George Page.
Sir, he is within; and I would I could do a good office between you.

Sir Hugh Evans.
It is spoke as a Christians ought to speak.

Robert Shallow.
He hath wrong'd me, Master Page.

George Page.
Sir, he doth in some sort confess it.

Robert Shallow.
If it be confess'd, it is not redress'd. Is not that so, Master Page? He hath wrong'd me, indeed he hath, at a word he hath. Believe me, Robert Shallow, esquire, saith he is wrong'd.

George Page.
Here comes Sir John.

Enter Sir John Falstaff, Bardolph, Nym, Pistol.

Sir John Falstaff.
Now, Master Shallow, you'll complain of me to the King?

Robert Shallow.
Knight, you have beaten my men, kill'd my deer, and broke open my lodge.

Sir John Falstaff.
But not kiss'd your keeper's daughter?

Robert Shallow.
Tut, a pin! This shall be answer'd.

Sir John Falstaff.
I will answer it straight: I have done all this. That is now answer'd.

Robert Shallow.
The Council shall know this.

Sir John Falstaff.
'Twere better for you if it were known in counsel. You'll be laugh'd at.

Sir Hugh Evans.
Pauca verba; Sir John, good worts.

Sir John Falstaff.
Good worts? Good cabbage. Slender, I broke your head; what matter have you against me?

Abraham Slender.
Marry, sir, I have matter in my head against you, and against your cony-catching rascals, Bardolph, Nym, and Pistol. They carried me to the tavern and made me drunk, and afterward pick'd my pocket.

Bardolph.
You Banbury cheese!

Abraham Slender.
Ay, it is no matter.

Pistol.
How now, Mephostophilus?

Abraham Slender.
Ay, it is no matter.

Nym.
Slice, I say! Pauca, pauca. Slice, that's my humor.

Abraham Slender.
Where's Simple, my man? Can you tell, cousin?

Sir Hugh Evans.
Peace, I pray you. Now let us understand. There is three umpires in this matter, as I understand: that is, Master Page (fidelicet Master Page) and there is myself (fidelicet myself) and the three party is (lastly and finally) mine host of the Garter.

George Page.
We three to hear it and end it between them.

Sir Hugh Evans.
Fery goot. I will make a prief of it in my note-book, and we will afterwards ork upon the cause with as great discreetly as we can.

Sir John Falstaff.
Pistol!

Pistol.
He hears with ears.

Sir Hugh Evans.
The tevil and his tam! What phrase is this? "He hears with ear"? Why, it is affectations.

Sir John Falstaff.
Pistol, did you pick Master Slender's purse?

Abraham Slender.
Ay, by these gloves, did he, or I would I might never come in mine own great chamber again else, of seven groats in mill-sixpences, and two Edward shovel-boards, that cost me two shilling and two pence a-piece of Yead Miller—by these gloves.

Sir John Falstaff.
Is this true, Pistol?

Sir Hugh Evans.
No, it is false, if it is a pick-purse.

Pistol.
Ha, thou mountain-foreigner! Sir John, and master mine,
I combat challenge of this latten bilbo.
Word of denial in thy labras here!
Word of denial! Froth and scum, thou liest!

Abraham Slender.
By these gloves, then 'twas he.

Nym.
Be avis'd, sir, and pass good humors. I will say "marry trap" with you, if you run the nuthook's humor on me—that is the very note of it.

Abraham Slender.
By this hat, then he in the red face had it; for though I cannot remember what I did when you made me drunk, yet I am not altogether an ass.

Sir John Falstaff.
What say you, Scarlet and John?

Bardolph.
Why, sir, for my part, I say the gentleman had drunk himself out of his five sentences.

Sir Hugh Evans.
It is his five senses. Fie, what the ignorance is!

Bardolph.
And being fap, sir, was (as they say) cashier'd; and so conclusions pass'd the careers.

Abraham Slender.
Ay, you spake in Latin then too: but 'tis no matter; I'll ne'er be drunk whilst I live again, but in honest, civil, godly company, for this trick. If I be drunk, I'll be drunk with those that have the fear of God, and not with drunken knaves.

Sir Hugh Evans.
So Got udge me, that is a virtuous mind.

Sir John Falstaff.
You hear all these matters denied, gentlemen; you hear it.

Enter Anne Page with wine, Mistress Ford, Mistress Page.

George Page.
Nay, daughter, carry the wine in, we'll drink within.

Exit Anne Page.

Abraham Slender.
O heaven! This is Mistress Anne Page.

George Page.
How now, Mistress Ford?

Sir John Falstaff.
Mistress Ford, by my troth, you are very well met. By your leave, good mistress.

Kisses her.

George Page.
Wife, bid these gentlemen welcome. Come, we have a hot venison pasty to dinner. Come, gentlemen, I hope we shall drink down all unkindness.

Exeunt all except Shallow, Slender, and Evans.

Abraham Slender.
I had rather than forty shillings I had my Book of Songs and Sonnets here.

Enter Simple.

How now, Simple, where have you been? I must wait on myself, must I? You have not the Book of Riddles about you, have you?

Peter Simple.
Book of Riddles? Why, did you not lend it to Alice Shortcake upon All-hallowmas last, a fortnight afore Michaelmas?

Robert Shallow.
Come, coz, come, coz, we stay for you. A word with you, coz; marry, this, coz: there is as 'twere a tender, a kind of tender, made afar off by Sir Hugh here. Do you understand me?

Abraham Slender.
Ay, sir, you shall find me reasonable. If it be so, I shall do that that is reason.

Robert Shallow.
Nay, but understand me.

Abraham Slender.
So I do, sir.

Sir Hugh Evans.
Give ear to his motions: Master Slender, I will description the matter to you, if you be capacity of it.

Abraham Slender.
Nay, I will do as my cousin Shallow says. I pray you pardon me; he's a Justice of Peace in his country, simple though I stand here.

Sir Hugh Evans.
But that is not the question: the question is concerning your marriage.

Robert Shallow.
Ay, there's the point, sir.

Sir Hugh Evans.
Marry, is it; the very point of it—to Mistress Anne Page.

Abraham Slender.
Why, if it be so, I will marry her upon any reasonable demands.

Sir Hugh Evans.
But can you affection the oman? Let us command to know that of your mouth, or of your lips; for diverse philosophers hold that the lips is parcel of the mouth. Therefore precisely, can you carry your good will to the maid?

Robert Shallow.
Cousin Abraham Slender, can you love her?

Abraham Slender.
I hope, sir, I will do as it shall become one that would do reason.

Sir Hugh Evans.
Nay, Got's lords and his ladies, you must speak possitable, if you can carry her your desires towards her.

Robert Shallow.
That you must. Will you, upon good dowry, marry her?

Abraham Slender.
I will do a greater thing than that, upon your request, cousin, in any reason.

Robert Shallow.
Nay, conceive me, conceive me, sweet coz; what I do is to pleasure you, coz. Can you love the maid?

Abraham Slender.
I will marry her, sir, at your request; but if there be no great love in the beginning, yet heaven may decrease it upon better acquaintance, when we are married and have more occasion to know one another. I hope, upon familiarity will grow more content. But if you say, "Marry her," I will marry her; that I am freely dissolv'd, and dissolutely.

Sir Hugh Evans.
It is a fery discretion answer, save the fall is in the ord "dissolutely." The ort is (according to our meaning) "resolutely." His meaning is good.

Robert Shallow.
Ay—I think my cousin meant well.

Abraham Slender.
Ay, or else I would I might be hang'd, la!

Robert Shallow.
Here comes fair Mistress Anne.

Enter Anne Page.

Would I were young for your sake, Mistress Anne!

Mistress Anne Page.
The dinner is on the table. My father desires your worships' company.

Robert Shallow.
I will wait on him, fair Mistress Anne.

Sir Hugh Evans.
'Od's plessed will! I will not be absence at the grace.

Exeunt Shallow and Evans.

Mistress Anne Page.
Will't please your worship to come in, sir?

Abraham Slender.
No, I thank you, forsooth, heartily; I am very well.

Mistress Anne Page.
The dinner attends you, sir.

Abraham Slender.
I am not a-hungry, I thank you, forsooth. Go, sirrah, for all you are my man, go wait upon my cousin Shallow.

Exit Simple.

A Justice of Peace sometime may be beholding to his friend for a man. I keep but three men and a boy yet, till my mother be dead. But what though? Yet I live like a poor gentleman born.

Mistress Anne Page.
I may not go in without your worship; they will not sit till you come.

Abraham Slender.
I' faith, I'll eat nothing. I thank you as much as though I did.

Mistress Anne Page.
I pray you, sir, walk in.

Abraham Slender.
I had rather walk here, I thank you. I bruis'd my shin th' other day with playing at sword and dagger with a master of fence (three veneys for a dish of stew'd prunes) and by my troth, I cannot abide the smell of hot meat since. Why do your dogs bark so? Be there bears i' th' town?

Mistress Anne Page.
I think there are, sir, I heard them talk'd of.

Abraham Slender.
I love the sport well, but I shall as soon quarrel at it as any man in England. You are afraid if you see the bear loose, are you not?

Mistress Anne Page.
Ay indeed, sir.

Abraham Slender.
That's meat and drink to me, now. I have seen Sackerson loose twenty times, and have taken him by the chain; but (I warrant you) the women have so cried and shriek'd at it, that it pass'd. But women, indeed, cannot abide 'em, they are very ill-favor'd rough things.

Enter Page.

George Page.
Come, gentle Master Slender, come; we stay for you.

Abraham Slender.
I'll eat nothing, I thank you, sir.

George Page.
By cock and pie, you shall not choose, sir! Come, come.

Abraham Slender.
Nay, pray you lead the way.

George Page.
Come on, sir.

Abraham Slender.
Mistress Anne, yourself shall go first.

Mistress Anne Page.
Not I, sir, pray you keep on.

Abraham Slender.
Truly I will not go first; truly la! I will not do you that wrong.

Mistress Anne Page.
I pray you, sir.

Abraham Slender.
I'll rather be unmannerly than troublesome. You do yourself wrong indeed la!

Exeunt.

Scene 2

Windsor. A street in front of Page's house.

(Evans; Simple)

Evans gives Slender's servant Simple a letter to give to Mistress Quickly, Dr. Caius's nurse and housekeeper, asking her to advance Slender's suit to her friend Anne Page.

Enter Evans and Simple from dinner.

Sir Hugh Evans.
Go your ways, and ask of Doctor Caius' house which is the way; and there dwells one Mistress Quickly, which is in the manner of his nurse—or his dry nurse—or his cook—or his laundry—his washer and his wringer.

Peter Simple.
Well, sir.

Sir Hugh Evans.
Nay, it is petter yet. Give her this letter; for it is a oman that altogether's acquaintance with Mistress Anne Page; and the letter is to desire and require her to solicit your master's desires to Mistress Anne Page. I pray you be gone. I will make an end of my dinner; there's pippins and cheese to come.

Exeunt.

Scene 3

A room in the Garter Inn.

(Falstaff; Host; Bardolph; Nym; Pistol; Robin)

Falstaff admits that he's running out of money and can't afford to keep all his followers on any longer. He dismisses Bardolph from his service and the Host takes him on as tapster. To make money, he sees no remedy but to engage in some fraud or other, and he tells Nym and Pistol how much Mistress Ford and Mistress Page admired him at dinner. Since they are in charge of their household finances, he decides to seduce them to get his hands on the money. He asks Nym and Pistol to carry a letter to each, but they refuse. He turns them off in anger, keeping only Robin the page, to whom he gives the letters. Nym and Pistol decide to revenge themselves on the fat knight by informing on him.

Enter Falstaff, Host, Bardolph, Nym, Pistol, Robin, Falstaff's page.

Sir John Falstaff.
Mine host of the Garter!

Host of the Garter Inn.
What says my bully-rook? Speak scholarly and wisely.

Sir John Falstaff.
Truly, mine host, I must turn away some of my followers.

Host of the Garter Inn.
Discard, bully Hercules, cashier; let them wag; trot, trot.

Sir John Falstaff.
I sit at ten pounds a week.

Host of the Garter Inn.
Thou'rt an emperor—Caesar, Keiser, and Pheazar. I will entertain Bardolph; he shall draw, he shall tap. Said I well, bully Hector?

Sir John Falstaff.
Do so, good mine host.

Host of the Garter Inn.
I have spoke; let him follow.

To Bardolph.

Let me see thee froth and lime. I am at a word; follow.

Exit.

Sir John Falstaff.
Bardolph, follow him. A tapster is a good trade. An old cloak makes a new jerkin; a wither'd servingman a fresh tapster. Go, adieu.

Bardolph.
It is a life that I have desir'd. I will thrive.

Pistol.
O base Hungarian wight! Wilt thou the spigot wield?

Exit Bardolph.

Nym.
He was gotten in drink. Is not the humor conceited?

Sir John Falstaff.
I am glad I am so acquit of this tinderbox; his thefts were too open; his filching was like an unskillful singer, he kept not time.

Nym.
The good humor is to steal at a minute's rest.

Pistol.
"Convey," the wise it call. "Steal"? Foh! A fico for the phrase!

Sir John Falstaff.
Well, sirs, I am almost out at heels.

Pistol.
Why then let kibes ensue.

Sir John Falstaff.
There is no remedy; I must cony-catch, I must shift.

Pistol.
Young ravens must have food.

Sir John Falstaff.
Which of you know Ford of this town?

Pistol.
I ken the wight; he is of substance good.

Sir John Falstaff.
My honest lads, I will tell you what I am about.

Pistol.
Two yards, and more.

Sir John Falstaff.
No quips now, Pistol! Indeed I am in the waist two yards about; but I am now about no waste; I am about thrift. Briefly—I do mean to make love to Ford's wife. I spy entertainment in her. She discourses, she carves, she gives the leer of invitation. I can construe the action of her familiar style, and the hardest voice of her behavior (to be English'd rightly) is, "I am Sir John Falstaff's."

Pistol.
He hath studied her well, and translated her will, out of honesty into English.

Nym.
The anchor is deep. Will that humor pass?

Sir John Falstaff.
Now, the report goes she has all the rule of her husband's purse. He hath a legion of angels.

Pistol.
As many devils entertain; and "To her, boy," say I.

Nym.
The humor rises; it is good. Humor me the angels.

Sir John Falstaff.
I have writ me here a letter to her; and here another to Page's wife, who even now gave me good eyes too, examin'd my parts with most judicious iliads; sometimes the beam of her view gilded my foot, sometimes my portly belly.

Pistol.
Then did the sun on dunghill shine.

Nym.
I thank thee for that humor.

Sir John Falstaff.
O, she did so course o'er my exteriors with such a greedy intention, that the appetite of her eye did seem to scorch me up like a burning-glass! Here's another letter to her. She bears the purse too; she is a region in Guiana, all gold and bounty. I will be cheaters to them both, and they shall be exchequers to me. They shall be my East and West Indies, and I will trade to them both. Go, bear thou this letter to Mistress Page; and thou this to Mistress Ford. We will thrive, lads, we will thrive.

Pistol.
Shall I Sir Pandarus of Troy become,
And by my side wear steel? Then Lucifer take all!

Nym.
I will run no base humor. Here, take the humor-letter; I will keep the havior of reputation.

Sir John Falstaff.

To Robin.

Hold, sirrah, bear you these letters tightly;
Sail like my pinnace to these golden shores.
Rogues, hence, avaunt, vanish like hailstones; go!
Trudge! Plod away i' th' hoof! Seek shelter, pack!
Falstaff will learn the humor of the age,
French thrift, you rogues—myself and skirted page.

Exeunt Falstaff and Robin.

Pistol.
Let vultures gripe thy guts! For gourd and fullam holds,
And high and low beguiles the rich and poor.
Tester I'll have in pouch when thou shalt lack,

Base Phrygian Turk!

Nym.
I have operations in my head which be humors of revenge.

Pistol.
Wilt thou revenge?

Nym.
By welkin and her star!

Pistol.
With wit or steel?

Nym.
With both the humors, I.
I will discuss the humor of this love to Page.

Pistol.
And I to Ford shall eke unfold
How Falstaff (varlet vile)
His dove will prove, his gold will hold,
And his soft couch defile.

Nym.
My humor shall not cool. I will incense Page to deal with poison; I will possess him with yallowness, for the revolt of mine is dangerous—that is my true humor.

Pistol.
Thou art the Mars of malcontents. I second thee; troop on.

Exeunt.

Scene 4

A room in Dr. Caius's house.

(Mistress Quickly; Simple; John Rugby; Doctor Caius; Fenton)

Simple delivers the letter to Mistress Quickly, who interrogates him to try and work out who exactly Slender is. Dr. Caius returns all of a sudden and Mistress Quickly, knowing that the doctor will be enraged if he finds some stranger in his house, hides Simple in the closet. Alas, the Doctor needs to find some herbs in the closet and discovers Simple there, who blurts out his errand. As Dr. Caius fancies himself in love with Anne Page himself, he writes out a challenge to Hugh Evans, believing that the parson was wooing on his own behalf. Mistress Quickly reassures the Doctor that he will obtain Anne's hand, though she knows perfectly well this is unlikely. Fenton comes in to ask Mistress Quickly how his own suit to Anne is going. She assures him it goes well, and he pays her, though she does not believe Anne actually loves him.

Enter Mistress Quickly, Simple.

Mistress Quickly.
What, John Rugby!

Enter John Rugby.

I pray thee go to the casement, and see if you can see my master, Master Doctor Caius, coming. If he do, i' faith, and find any body in the house, here will be an old abusing of God's patience and the King's English.

John Rugby.
I'll go watch.

Mistress Quickly.
Go, and we'll have a posset for't soon at night, in faith, at the latter end of a sea-coal fire.

Exit Rugby.

An honest, willing, kind fellow as ever servant shall come in house withal; and I warrant you, no tell-tale nor no breed-bate. His worst fault is, that he is given to prayer; he is something peevish that way; but nobody but has his fault—but let that pass. Peter Simple, you say your name is?

Peter Simple.
Ay, for fault of a better.

Mistress Quickly.
And Master Slender's your master?

Peter Simple.
Ay, forsooth.

Mistress Quickly.
Does he not wear a great round beard, like a glover's paring-knife?

Peter Simple.
No, forsooth; he hath but a little whey-face, with a little yellow beard, a Cain-color'd beard.

Mistress Quickly.
A softly-sprighted man, is he not?

Peter Simple.
Ay, forsooth; but he is as tall a man of his hands as any is between this and his head. He hath fought with a warrener.

Mistress Quickly.
How say you? O, I should remember him. Does he not hold up his head (as it were) and strut in his gait?

Peter Simple.
Yes indeed does he.

Mistress Quickly.
Well, heaven send Anne Page no worse fortune! Tell Master Parson Evans I will do what I can for your master. Anne is a good girl, and I wish—

Enter Rugby.

John Rugby.
Out alas! Here comes my master.

Mistress Quickly.
We shall all be shent. Run in here, good young man; go into this closet. He will not stay long.

Shuts Simple in the closet.

What, John Rugby! John! What, John, I say! Go, John, go inquire for my master; I doubt he be not well, that he comes not home.

Singing.

And down, down, adown-a, etc.

Enter Doctor Caius.

Doctor Caius.
Vat is you sing? I do not like des toys. Pray you go and vetch me in my closet une boîte en verd, a box, a green-a box. Do intend vat I speak? A green-a box.

Mistress Quickly.
Ay, forsooth, I'll fetch it you.

Aside.

I am glad he went not in himself; if he had found the young man, he would have been horn-mad.

Doctor Caius.
Fe, fe, fe, fe! Ma foi, il fait fort chaud. O, je m'en vois à la cour—la grande affaire.

Mistress Quickly.
Is it this, sir?

Doctor Caius.
Oui, mette le au mon pocket; dépêche, quickly. Vere is dat knave Rugby?

Mistress Quickly.
What, John Rugby! John!

John Rugby.
Here, sir!

Doctor Caius.
You are John Rugby, and you are Jack Rugby. Come, take-a your rapier, and come after my heel to the court.

John Rugby.
'Tis ready, sir, here in the porch.

Doctor Caius.
By my trot, I tarry too long. 'Od's me! Qu'ai-je oublié? Dere is some simples in my closet, dat I vill not for the varld I shall leave behind.

Mistress Quickly.
Ay me, he'll find the young man there, and be mad!

Doctor Caius.
O diable, diable! Vat is in my closet? Villainy! Laroon!

Pulling Simple out.

Rugby, my rapier!

Mistress Quickly.
Good master, be content.

Doctor Caius.
Wherefore shall I be content-a?

Mistress Quickly.
The young man is an honest man.

Doctor Caius.
What shall de honest man do in my closet? Dere is no honest man dat shall come in my closet.

Mistress Quickly.
I beseech you be not so phlegmatic. Hear the truth of it: he came of an errand to me from Parson Hugh.

Doctor Caius.
Vell?

Peter Simple.
Ay, forsooth; to desire her to—

Mistress Quickly.
Peace, I pray you.

Doctor Caius.
Peace-a your tongue.—Speak-a your tale.

Peter Simple.
To desire this honest gentlewoman, your maid, to speak a good word to Mistress Anne Page for my master in the way of marriage.

Mistress Quickly.
This is all indeed la! But I'll ne'er put my finger in the fire, and need not.

Doctor Caius.
Sir Hugh send-a you? Rugby, baillez me some paper. Tarry you a little-a while.

Writes.

Mistress Quickly.

Aside to Simple

I am glad he is so quiet. If he had been throughly mov'd, you should have heard him so loud and so melancholy. But notwithstanding, man, I'll do you your master what good I can; and the very yea and the no is, the French doctor, my master (I may call him my master, look you, for I keep his house; and I wash, wring, brew, bake, scour, dress meat and drink, make the beds, and do all myself)—

Peter Simple.

Aside to Quickly

'Tis a great charge to come under one body's hand.

Mistress Quickly.

Aside to Simple

Are you avis'd o' that? You shall find it a great charge; and to be up early and down late; but notwithstanding (to tell you in your ear, I would have no words of it) my master himself is in love with Mistress Anne Page; but notwithstanding that, I know Anne's mind—that's neither here nor there.

Doctor Caius.
You jack'nape, give-a this letter to Sir Hugh. By gar, it is a shallenge. I will cut his troat in de park; and I will teach a scurvy jack-a-nape priest to meddle or make— You may be gone; it is not good you tarry here. By gar, I will cut all his two stones; by gar, he shall not have a stone to throw at his dog.

Exit Simple.

Mistress Quickly.
Alas! He speaks but for his friend.

Doctor Caius.
It is no matter-a ver dat. Do not you tell-a me dat I shall have Anne Page for myself? By gar, I vill kill de Jack priest; and I have appointed mine host of de Jarteer to measure our weapon. By gar, I will myself have Anne Page.

Mistress Quickly.
Sir, the maid loves you, and all shall be well. We must give folks leave to prate; what the good-jer!

Doctor Caius.
Rugby, come to the court with me. By gar, if I have not Anne Page, I shall turn your head out of my door. Follow my heels, Rugby.

Exeunt Caius and Rugby.

Mistress Quickly.
You shall have Anne—fool's-head of your own. No, I know Anne's mind for that. Never a woman in Windsor knows more of Anne's mind than I do, nor can do more than I do with her, I thank heaven.

Fenton.

Within.

Who's within there, ho?

Mistress Quickly.
Who's there, I trow? Come near the house, I pray you.

Enter Fenton.

Fenton.
How now, good woman, how dost thou?

Mistress Quickly.
The better that it pleases your good worship to ask.

Fenton.
What news? How does pretty Mistress Anne?

Mistress Quickly.
In truth, sir, and she is pretty, and honest, and gentle, and one that is your friend; I can tell you that by the way, I praise heaven for it.

Fenton.
Shall I do any good, think'st thou? Shall I not lose my suit?

Mistress Quickly.
Troth, sir, all is in His hands above. But notwithstanding, Master Fenton, I'll be sworn on a book she loves you. Have not your worship a wart above your eye?

Fenton.
Yes, marry, have I, what of that?

Mistress Quickly.
Well, thereby hangs a tale. Good faith, it is such another Nan; but (I detest) an honest maid as ever broke bread. We had an hour's talk of that wart. I shall never laugh but in that maid's company! But, indeed, she is given too much to allicholy and musing; but for you—well—go to.

Fenton.
Well; I shall see her today. Hold, there's money for thee. Let me have thy voice in my behalf. If thou seest her before me, commend me.

Mistress Quickly.
Will I? I' faith, that we will; and I will tell your worship more of the wart the next time we have confidence, and of other wooers.

Fenton.
Well, farewell, I am in great haste now.

Mistress Quickly.
Farewell to your worship.

Exit Fenton.

Truly, an honest gentleman; but Anne loves him not; for I know Anne's mind as well as another does. Out upon't! What have I forgot?

Exit.

Act 2

Scene 1

Windsor. A street in front of Page's house.

(Mistress Margaret Page; Mistress Ford; Ford; Pistol; Page; Nym; Mistress Quickly; Host; Shallow)

Mistress Page rereads Falstaff's letter, outraged at the man's presumption. Her friend Mistress Ford arrives, having herself received such a letter and, comparing them, they realize they are exactly the same with the exception of their names. The two plan to revenge themselves on him and go in to discuss how. Ford arrives home, accompanied by Pistol, who is warning him of Falstaff's designs on his wife. Nym in the meantime informs Page of the same. Ford believes Pistol while Page is skeptical of Nym. The two wives decide to use Mistress Quickly as their messenger to Falstaff. Page and Ford discuss the accusations brought against Falstaff; Page points out that the informers are servants Falstaff has sacked, but Ford is still suspicious. The Host arrives in a jolly mood to tell Ford and Page about the upcoming duel between the Welsh parson and the French doctor. Ford, wanting to find out what Falstaff is up to, bribes the Host to introduce him to the knight under the pseudonym "Brook".

Enter Mistress Page, reading of a letter.

Mistress Margaret Page.
What, have I scap'd love-letters in the holiday-time of my beauty, and am I now a subject for them? Let me see.

Reads.

"Ask me no reason why I love you, for though Love use Reason for his precisian, he admits him not for his counsellor. You are not young, no more am I; go to then, there's sympathy. You are merry, so am I; ha, ha! Then there's more sympathy. You love sack, and so do I; would you desire better sympathy? Let it suffice thee, Mistress Page—at the least if the love of a soldier can suffice—that I love thee. I will not say, pity me—'tis not a soldier-like phrase—but I say, love me. By me,
Thine own true knight,
By day or night,
Or any kind of light,
With all his might
For thee to fight,
John Falstaff."

What a Herod of Jewry is this! O wicked, wicked world! One that is well-nigh worn to pieces with age to show himself a young gallant! What an unweigh'd behavior hath this Flemish drunkard pick'd (with the devil's name!) out of my conversation, that he dares in this manner assay me? Why, he hath not been thrice in my company! What should I say to him? I was then frugal of my mirth. Heaven forgive me! Why, I'll exhibit a bill in the parliament for the putting down of men. How shall I be reveng'd on him? For reveng'd I will be! As sure as his guts are made of puddings.

Enter Mistress Ford.

Mistress Alice Ford.
Mistress Page, trust me, I was going to your house.

Mistress Margaret Page.
And trust me, I was coming to you. You look very ill.

Mistress Alice Ford.
Nay, I'll ne'er believe that; I have to show to the contrary.

Mistress Margaret Page.
Faith, but you do, in my mind.

Mistress Alice Ford.
Well—I do then; yet I say I could show you to the contrary. O Mistress Page, give me some counsel!

Mistress Margaret Page.
What's the matter, woman?

Mistress Alice Ford.
O woman—if it were not for one trifling respect, I could come to such honor!

Mistress Margaret Page.
Hang the trifle, woman, take the honor. What is it? Dispense with trifles. What is it?

Mistress Alice Ford.
If I would but go to hell for an eternal moment or so, I could be knighted.

Mistress Margaret Page.
What? Thou liest! Sir Alice Ford! These knights will hack, and so thou shouldst not alter the article of thy gentry.

Mistress Alice Ford.
We burn daylight. Here, read, read; perceive how I might be knighted. I shall think the worse of fat men, as long as I have an eye to make difference of men's liking: and yet he would not swear; prais'd women's modesty; and gave such orderly and well-behav'd reproof to all uncomeliness, that I would have sworn his disposition would have gone to the truth of his words; but they do no more adhere and keep place together than the hundred Psalms to the tune of "Greensleeves." What tempest, I trow, threw this whale (with so many tuns of oil in his belly) ashore at Windsor? How shall I be reveng'd on him? I think the best way were to entertain him with hope, till the wicked fire of lust have melted him in his own grease. Did you ever hear the like?

Mistress Margaret Page.
Letter for letter; but that the name of Page and Ford differs! To thy great comfort in this mystery of ill opinions, here's the twin-brother of thy letter; but let thine inherit first, for I protest mine never shall. I warrant he hath a thousand of these letters, writ with blank space for different names (sure, more!); and these are of the second edition. He will print them, out of doubt; for he cares not what he puts into the press, when he would put us two. I had rather be a giantess, and lie under Mount Pelion. Well—I will find you twenty lascivious turtles ere one chaste man.

Mistress Alice Ford.
Why, this is the very same: the very hand; the very words. What doth he think of us?

Mistress Margaret Page.
Nay, I know not; it makes me almost ready to wrangle with mine own honesty. I'll entertain myself like one that I am not acquainted withal; for sure unless he know some strain in me that I know not myself, he would never have boarded me in this fury.

Mistress Alice Ford.
"Boarding," call you it? I'll be sure to keep him above deck.

Mistress Margaret Page.
So will I; if he come under my hatches, I'll never to sea again. Let's be reveng'd on him: let's appoint him a meeting, give him a show of comfort in his suit, and lead him on with a fine-baited delay, till he hath pawn'd his horses to mine host of the Garter.

Mistress Alice Ford.
Nay, I will consent to act any villainy against him, that may not sully the chariness of our honesty. O that my husband saw this letter! It would give eternal food to his jealousy.

Mistress Margaret Page.
Why, look where he comes; and my good man too. He's as far from jealousy as I am from giving him cause, and that (I hope) is an unmeasurable distance.

Mistress Alice Ford.
You are the happier woman.

Mistress Margaret Page.
Let's consult together against this greasy knight. Come hither.

They retire.
Enter Ford with Pistol; Page with Nym.

Francis Ford.
Well, I hope it be not so.

Pistol.
Hope is a curtal dog in some affairs. Sir John affects thy wife.

Francis Ford.
Why, sir, my wife is not young.

Pistol.
He woos both high and low, both rich and poor,
Both young and old, one with another, Ford.
He loves the gallimaufry, Ford. Perpend.

Francis Ford.
Love my wife?

Pistol.
With liver burning hot. Prevent; or go thou
Like Sir Actaeon he, with Ringwood at thy heels—
O, odious is the name!

Francis Ford.
What name, sir?

Pistol.
The horn, I say. Farewell.
Take heed, have open eye, for thieves do foot by night.
Take heed, ere summer comes or cuckoo-birds do sing.
Away, Sir Corporal Nym!
Believe it, Page, he speaks sense.

Exit.

Francis Ford.

Aside.

I will be patient; I will find out this.

Nym.

To Page.

And this is true; I like not the humor of lying. He hath wrong'd me in some humors. I should have borne the humor'd letter to her; but I have a sword, and it shall bite upon my necessity. He loves your wife: there's the short and the long. My name is Corporal Nym; I speak, and I avouch; 'tis true; my name is Nym, and Falstaff loves your wife. Adieu. I love not the humor of bread and cheese and there's the humor of it. Adieu.

Exit.

George Page.
"The humor of it," quoth 'a! Here's a fellow frights English out of his wits.

Francis Ford.
I will seek out Falstaff.

George Page.
I never heard such a drawling, affecting rogue.

Francis Ford.
If I do find it—well.

George Page.
I will not believe such a Cataian, though the priest o' th' town commended him for a true man.

Francis Ford.
'Twas a good sensible fellow—well.

Mrs. Page and Mrs. Ford come forward.

George Page.
How now, Meg?

Mistress Margaret Page.
Whither go you, George, hark you?

Mistress Alice Ford.
How now, sweet Frank, why art thou melancholy?

Francis Ford.
I melancholy? I am not melancholy. Get you home; go.

Mistress Alice Ford.
Faith, thou hast some crotchets in thy head now. Will you go, Mistress Page?

Mistress Margaret Page.
Have with you. You'll come to dinner, George?

Aside to Mrs. Ford.

Look who comes yonder. She shall be our messenger to this paltry knight.

Mistress Alice Ford.

Aside to Mrs. Page

Trust me, I thought on her. She'll fit it.

Enter Mistress Quickly.

Mistress Margaret Page.
You are come to see my daughter Anne?

Mistress Quickly.
Ay, forsooth; and I pray, how does good Mistress Anne?

Mistress Margaret Page.
Go in with us and see. We have an hour's talk with you.

Exeunt Mrs. Page, Mrs. Ford, and Mrs. Quickly.

George Page.
How now, Master Ford?

Francis Ford.
You heard what this knave told me, did you not?

George Page.
Yes, and you heard what the other told me?

Francis Ford.
Do you think there is truth in them?

George Page.
Hang 'em, slaves! I do not think the knight would offer it; but these that accuse him in his intent towards our wives are a yoke of his discarded men—very rogues, now they be out of service.

Francis Ford.
Were they his men?

George Page.
Marry, were they.

Francis Ford.
I like it never the better for that. Does he lie at the Garter?

George Page.
Ay, marry, does he. If he should intend this voyage toward my wife, I would turn her loose to him; and what he gets more of her than sharp words, let it lie on my head.

Francis Ford.
I do not misdoubt my wife; but I would be loath to turn them together. A man may be too confident. I would have nothing lie on my head. I cannot be thus satisfied.

Enter Host.

George Page.
Look where my ranting host of the Garter comes. There is either liquor in his pate, or money in his purse, when he looks so merrily. How now, mine host?

Host of the Garter Inn.
How now, bully-rook? Thou'rt a gentleman. Cavaleiro Justice, I say!

Enter Shallow.

Robert Shallow.
I follow, mine host, I follow. Good even and twenty, good Master Page! Master Page, will you go with us? We have sport in hand.

Host of the Garter Inn.
Tell him, Cavaleiro Justice; tell him, bully-rook.

Robert Shallow.
Sir, there is a fray to be fought between Sir Hugh the Welsh priest and Caius the French doctor.

Francis Ford.
Good mine host o' th' Garter, a word with you.

Host of the Garter Inn.
What say'st thou, my bully-rook?

Ford and the Host talk.

Robert Shallow.

To Page.

Will you go with us to behold it? My merry host hath had the measuring of their weapons, and, I think, hath appointed them contrary places; for, believe me, I hear the parson is no jester. Hark, I will tell you what our sport shall be.

They converse apart.

Host of the Garter Inn.
Hast thou no suit against my knight, my guest-cavalier?

Francis Ford.
None, I protest; but I'll give you a pottle of burnt sack to give me recourse to him and tell him my name is Brook—only for a jest.

Host of the Garter Inn.
My hand, bully; thou shalt have egress and regress—said I well?—and thy name shall be Brook. It is a merry knight. Will you go, An-heires?

Robert Shallow.
Have with you, mine host.

George Page.
I have heard the Frenchman hath good skill in his rapier.

Robert Shallow.
Tut, sir; I could have told you more. In these times you stand on distance: your passes, stoccadoes, and I know not what. 'Tis the heart, Master Page, 'tis here, 'tis here. I have seen the time, with my long sword I would have made you four tall fellows skip like rats.

Host of the Garter Inn.
Here, boys, here, here! Shall we wag?

George Page.
Have with you. I had rather hear them scold than fight.

Exeunt Host, Shallow, and Page.

Francis Ford.
Though Page be a secure fool, and stands so firmly on his wife's frailty, yet I cannot put off my opinion so easily. She was in his company at Page's house; and what they made there, I know not. Well, I will look further into't, and I have a disguise to sound Falstaff. If I find her honest, I lose not my labor; if she be otherwise, 'tis labor well bestow'd.

Exit.

Scene 2

A room in the Garter Inn.

(*Falstaff; Pistol; Robin; Mistress Quickly; Bardolph; Ford*)

Pistol begs Falstaff for some money, but Falstaff absolutely refuses. Mistress Quickly arrives with a message for Falstaff, though it takes her forever to get around to it. She tells him that both Mistress Ford and Mistress Page were quite taken with their letters. Mistress Ford has sent word that her husband will be absent between ten and eleven the next day, while Mistress Page's message is that she hopes to find a time when her husband won't be around. She asks that he send her Robin, which he does. Bardolph arrives to introduce "Brook". He is of course Ford in disguise; he explains to Falstaff that he has been wooing Mistress Ford without success, and offers Falstaff a great deal of money if he will help. Falstaff agrees, revealing his own rendezvous with Mistress Ford in the process. Left alone, Ford is horrified to discover that his wife is setting up meetings with other men. He decides he will interrupt their rendezvous.

Enter Falstaff, Pistol.

Pistol.
I will retort the sum in equipage.

Sir John Falstaff.
I will not lend thee a penny.

Pistol.
Why then the world's mine oyster,
Which I with sword will open.

Sir John Falstaff.
Not a penny. I have been content, sir, you should lay my countenance to pawn. I have grated upon my good friends for three reprieves for you and your coach-fellow Nym; or else you had look'd through the grate,

like a geminy of baboons. I am damn'd in hell for swearing to gentlemen my friends, you were good soldiers and tall fellows; and when Mistress Bridget lost the handle of her fan, I took't upon mine honor thou hadst it not.

Pistol.
Didst not thou share? Hadst thou not fifteen pence?

Sir John Falstaff.
Reason, you rogue, reason; think'st thou I'll endanger my soul gratis? At a word, hang no more about me, I am no gibbet for you. Go—a short knife and a throng!—to your manor of Pickt-hatch! Go. You'll not bear a letter for me, you rogue? You stand upon your honor! Why, thou unconfinable baseness, it is as much as I can do to keep the terms of my honor precise. I, I, I myself sometimes, leaving the fear of God on the left hand, and hiding mine honor in my necessity, am fain to shuffle, to hedge, and to lurch; and yet you, rogue, will ensconce your rags, your cat-a-mountain looks, your red-lattice phrases, and your bold-beating oaths, under the shelter of your honor! You will not do it? You!

Pistol.
I do relent. What would thou more of man?

Enter Robin.

Robin.
Sir, here's a woman would speak with you.

Sir John Falstaff.
Let her approach.

Enter Mistress Quickly.

Mistress Quickly.
Give your worship good morrow.

Sir John Falstaff.
Good morrow, goodwife.

Mistress Quickly.
Not so, and't please your worship.

Sir John Falstaff.
Good maid then.

Mistress Quickly.
I'll be sworn,
As my mother was the first hour I was born.

Sir John Falstaff.
I do believe the swearer. What with me?

Mistress Quickly.
Shall I vouchsafe your worship a word or two?

Sir John Falstaff.
Two thousand, fair woman, and I'll vouchsafe thee the hearing.

Mistress Quickly.
There is one Mistress Ford, sir—I pray come a little nearer this ways. I myself dwell with Master Doctor Caius—

Sir John Falstaff.
Well, on. Mistress Ford, you say—

Mistress Quickly.
Your worship says very true. I pray your worship come a little nearer this ways.

Sir John Falstaff.
I warrant thee, nobody hears—mine own people, mine own people.

Mistress Quickly.
Are they so? God bless them and make them his servants!

Sir John Falstaff.
Well; Mistress Ford, what of her?

Mistress Quickly.
Why, sir, she's a good creature. Lord, Lord, your worship's a wanton! Well—heaven forgive you, and all of us, I pray—

Sir John Falstaff.
Mistress Ford; come, Mistress Ford—

Mistress Quickly.
Marry, this is the short and the long of it: you have brought her into such a canaries as 'tis wonderful. The best courtier of them all (when the court lay at Windsor) could never have brought her to such a canary; yet there has been knights, and lords, and gentlemen, with their coaches; I warrant you, coach after coach, letter after letter, gift after gift; smelling so sweetly, all musk, and so rushling, I warrant you, in silk and gold, and in such alligant terms, and in such wine and sugar of the best, and the fairest, that would have won any woman's heart; and I warrant you, they could never get an eye-wink of her. I had my-

self twenty angels given me this morning, but I defy all angels (in any such sort, as they say) but in the way of honesty; and I warrant you, they could never get her so much as sip on a cup with the proudest of them all, and yet there has been earls, nay (which is more) pensioners, but I warrant you all is one with her.

Sir John Falstaff.
But what says she to me? Be brief, my good she-Mercury.

Mistress Quickly.
Marry, she hath receiv'd your letter—for the which she thanks you a thousand times—and she gives you to notify that her husband will be absence from his house between ten and eleven.

Sir John Falstaff.
Ten and eleven?

Mistress Quickly.
Ay, forsooth; and then you may come and see the picture, she says, that you wot of. Master Ford her husband will be from home. Alas, the sweet woman leads an ill life with him. He's a very jealousy man. She leads a very frampold life with him, good heart.

Sir John Falstaff.
Ten and eleven. Woman, commend me to her, I will not fail her.

Mistress Quickly.
Why, you say well. But I have another messenger to your worship. Mistress Page hath her hearty commendations to you too; and let me tell you in your ear, she's as fartuous a civil modest wife, and one (I tell you) that will not miss you morning nor evening prayer, as any is in Windsor, whoe'er be the other; and she bade me tell your worship that her husband is seldom from home, but she hopes there will come a time. I never knew a woman so dote upon a man; surely I think you have charms, la; yes, in truth.

Sir John Falstaff.
Not I, I assure thee. Setting the attraction of my good parts aside, I have no other charms.

Mistress Quickly.
Blessing on your heart for't!

Sir John Falstaff.
But I pray thee tell me this: has Ford's wife and Page's wife acquainted each other how they love me?

Mistress Quickly.
That were a jest indeed! They have not so little grace, I hope. That were a trick indeed! But Mistress Page would desire you to send her your little page, of all loves. Her husband has a marvelous infection to the little page; and truly Master Page is an honest man. Never a wife in Windsor leads a better life than she does: do what she will, say what she will, take all, pay all, go to bed when she list, rise when she list, all is as she will; and truly she deserves it, for if there be a kind woman in Windsor, she is one. You must send her your page, no remedy.

Sir John Falstaff.
Why, I will.

Mistress Quickly.
Nay, but do so then, and look you, he may come and go between you both; and in any case have a nay-word, that you may know one another's mind, and the boy never need to understand any thing; for 'tis not good that children should know any wickedness. Old folks, you know, have discretion, as they say, and know the world.

Sir John Falstaff.
Fare thee well, commend me to them both. There's my purse, I am yet thy debtor. Boy, go along with this woman.

Exeunt Mrs. Quickly and Robin.

This news distracts me!

Pistol.

Aside.

This punk is one of Cupid's carriers.
Clap on more sails, pursue; up with your fights;
Give fire! She is my prize, or ocean whelm them all!

Exit.

Sir John Falstaff.
Say'st thou so, old Jack? Go thy ways. I'll make more of thy old body than I have done. Will they yet look after thee? Wilt thou, after the expense of so much money, be now a gainer? Good body, I thank thee. Let them say 'tis grossly done, so it be fairly done, no matter.

Enter Bardolph.

Bardolph.
Sir John, there's one Master Brook below would fain speak with you, and be acquainted with you; and hath sent your worship a morning's draught of sack.

Sir John Falstaff.
Brook is his name?

Bardolph.
Ay, sir.

Sir John Falstaff.
Call him in.

Exit Bardolph.

Such Brooks are welcome to me, that o'erflows such liquor. Ah, ha! Mistress Ford and Mistress Page, have I encompass'd you? Go to, via!

Enter Bardolph with Ford disguised like Brook.

Francis Ford.
God save you, sir!

Sir John Falstaff.
And you, sir! Would you speak with me?

Francis Ford.
I make bold, to press with so little preparation upon you.

Sir John Falstaff.
You're welcome. What's your will? Give us leave, drawer.

Exit Bardolph.

Francis Ford.
Sir, I am a gentleman that have spent much. My name is Brook.

Sir John Falstaff.
Good Master Brook, I desire more acquaintance of you.

Francis Ford.
Good Sir John, I sue for yours—not to charge you, for I must let you understand I think myself in better plight for a lender than you are; the which hath something embold'ned me to this unseason'd intrusion; for they say, if money go before, all ways do lie open.

Sir John Falstaff.
Money is a good soldier, sir, and will on.

Francis Ford.
Troth, and I have a bag of money here troubles me. If you will help to bear it, Sir John, take all, or half, for easing me of the carriage.

Sir John Falstaff.
Sir, I know not how I may deserve to be your porter.

Francis Ford.
I will tell you, sir, if you will give me the hearing.

Sir John Falstaff.
Speak, good Master Brook, I shall be glad to be your servant.

Francis Ford.
Sir, I hear you are a scholar (I will be brief with you), and you have been a man long known to me, though I had never so good means as desire to make myself acquainted with you. I shall discover a thing to you, wherein I must very much lay open mine own imperfection; but, good Sir John, as you have one eye upon my follies, as you hear them unfolded, turn another into the register of your own, that I may pass with a reproof the easier, sith you yourself know how easy it is to be such an offender.

Sir John Falstaff.
Very well, sir, proceed.

Francis Ford.
There is a gentlewoman in this town, her husband's name is Ford.

Sir John Falstaff.
Well, sir.

Francis Ford.
I have long lov'd her, and I protest to you, bestow'd much on her; follow'd her with a doting observance; engross'd opportunities to meet her; fee'd every slight occasion that could but niggardly give me sight of her; not only bought many presents to give her, but have given largely to many to know what she would have given; briefly, I have pursu'd her as love hath pursu'd me, which hath been on the wing of all occasions. But whatsoever I have merited, either in my mind or in my means, meed I am sure I have receiv'd none, unless experience be a jewel—that I have purchas'd at an infinite rate, and that hath taught me to say this:

"Love like a shadow flies when substance love pursues,
Pursuing that that flies, and flying what pursues."

Sir John Falstaff.
Have you receiv'd no promise of satisfaction at her hands?

Francis Ford.
Never.

Sir John Falstaff.
Have you importun'd her to such a purpose?

Francis Ford.
Never.

Sir John Falstaff.
Of what quality was your love then?

Francis Ford.
Like a fair house built on another man's ground, so that I have lost my edifice by mistaking the place where I erected it.

Sir John Falstaff.
To what purpose have you unfolded this to me?

Francis Ford.
When I have told you that, I have told you all. Some say that, though she appear honest to me, yet in other places she enlargeth her mirth so far that there is shrewd construction made of her. Now, Sir John, here is the heart of my purpose: you are a gentleman of excellent breeding, admirable discourse, of great admittance, authentic in your place and person, generally allow'd for your many war-like, court-like, and learned preparations.

Sir John Falstaff.
O sir!

Francis Ford.
Believe it, for you know it. There is money, spend it, spend it; spend more; spend all I have; only give me so much of your time in exchange of it, as to lay an amiable siege to the honesty of this Ford's wife. Use your art of wooing; win her to consent to you; if any man may, you may as soon as any.

Sir John Falstaff.
Would it apply well to the vehemency of your affection, that I should win what you would enjoy? Methinks you prescribe to yourself very preposterously.

Francis Ford.
O, understand my drift. She dwells so securely on the excellency of her honor, that the folly of my soul dares not present itself; she is too bright to be look'd against. Now, could I come to her with any detection in my hand, my desires had instance and argument to commend themselves. I could drive her then from the ward of her purity, her reputation, her marriage vow, and a thousand other her defenses, which now are too too strongly embattled against me. What say you to't, Sir John?

Sir John Falstaff.
Master Brook, I will first make bold with your money; next, give me your hand; and last, as I am a gentleman, you shall, and you will, enjoy Ford's wife.

Francis Ford.
O good sir!

Sir John Falstaff.
I say you shall.

Francis Ford.
Want no money, Sir John, you shall want none.

Sir John Falstaff.
Want no Mistress Ford, Master Brook, you shall want none. I shall be with her (I may tell you) by her own appointment; even as you came in to me, her assistant or go-between parted from me. I say I shall be with her between ten and eleven; for at that time the jealous rascally knave her husband will be forth. Come you to me at night, you shall know how I speed.

Francis Ford.
I am blest in your acquaintance. Do you know Ford, sir?

Sir John Falstaff.
Hang him, poor cuckoldly knave, I know him not. Yet I wrong him to call him poor. They say the jealous wittolly knave hath masses of money, for the which his wife seems to me well-favor'd. I will use her as the key of the cuckoldly rogue's coffer, and there's my harvest-home.

Francis Ford.
I would you knew Ford, sir, that you might avoid him if you saw him.

Sir John Falstaff.
Hang him, mechanical salt-butter rogue! I will stare him out of his wits; I will awe him with my cudgel; it shall hang like a meteor o'er the cuckold's horns. Master Brook, thou shalt know I will predominate over the peasant, and thou shalt lie with his wife. Come to me soon at night. Ford's a knave, and I will aggravate his style; thou, Master Brook, shalt know him for knave, and cuckold. Come to me soon at night.

Exit.

Francis Ford.
What a damn'd Epicurean rascal is this! My heart is ready to crack with impatience. Who says this is improvident jealousy? My wife hath sent to him, the hour is fix'd, the match is made. Would any man have thought this? See the hell of having a false woman! My bed shall be abus'd, my coffers ransack'd, my reputation gnawn at, and I shall not only receive this villainous wrong, but stand under the adoption of abominable terms, and by him that does me this wrong. Terms! Names! Amaimon sounds well; Lucifer, well; Barbason, well; yet they are devils' additions, the names of fiends; but Cuckold! Wittol!—Cuckold! The devil himself hath not such a name. Page is an ass, a secure ass; he will trust his wife, he will not be jealous. I will rather trust a Fleming with my butter, Parson Hugh the Welshman with my cheese, an Irishman with my aqua-vitae bottle, or a thief to walk my ambling gelding, than my wife with herself. Then she plots, then she ruminates, then she devises; and what they think in their hearts they may effect, they will break their hearts but they will effect. God be prais'd for my jealousy! Eleven o' clock the hour. I will prevent this, detect my wife, be reveng'd on Falstaff, and laugh at Page. I will about it; better three hours too soon than a minute too late. Fie, fie, fie! Cuckold, cuckold, cuckold!

Exit.

Scene 3

A field near Windsor.

(Caius; Rugby; Page; Shallow; Slender; Host)

Dr. Caius awaits Sir Hugh for their duel, swearing that he will kill the Welshman. The Host arrives with Page, Shallow, and Slender and persuades the doctor to go to Frogmore, saying that Anne Page is there, while in fact it is where Sir Hugh is.

Enter Caius, Rugby.

Doctor Caius.
Jack Rugby!

John Rugby.
Sir?

Doctor Caius.
Vat is the clock, Jack?

John Rugby.
'Tis past the hour, sir, that Sir Hugh promis'd to meet.

Doctor Caius.
By gar, he has save his soul, dat he is no come; he has pray his Pible well, dat he is no come. By gar, Jack Rugby, he is dead already, if he be come.

John Rugby.
He is wise, sir; he knew your worship would kill him if he came.

Doctor Caius.
By gar, de herring is no dead so as I vill kill him. Take your rapier, Jack, I vill tell you how I vill kill him.

John Rugby.
Alas, sir, I cannot fence.

Doctor Caius.
Villainy, take your rapier.

John Rugby.
Forbear; here's company.

Enter Page, Shallow, Slender, Host.

Host of the Garter Inn.
God bless thee, bully-doctor!

Robert Shallow.
God save you, Master Doctor Caius!

George Page.
Now, good Master Doctor!

Abraham Slender.
Give you good morrow, sir.

Doctor Caius.
Vat be all you, one, two, tree, four, come for?

Host of the Garter Inn.
To see thee fight, to see thee foin, to see thee traverse, to see thee here, to see thee there, to see thee pass thy puncto, thy stock, thy reverse, thy distance, thy montant. Is he dead, my Ethiopian? Is he dead, my Francisco? Ha, bully? What says my Aesculapius? My Galien? My heart of elder? Ha? Is he dead, bully-stale? Is he dead?

Doctor Caius.
By gar, he is de coward Jack priest of de vorld; he is not show his face.

Host of the Garter Inn.
Thou art a Castalion-King-Urinal! Hector of Greece, my boy!

Doctor Caius.
I pray you bear witness that me have stay six or seven, two, tree hours for him, and he is no come.

Robert Shallow.
He is the wiser man, Master Doctor: he is a curer of souls, and you a curer of bodies. If you should fight, you go against the hair of your professions. Is it not true, Master Page?

George Page.
Master Shallow, you have yourself been a great fighter, though now a man of peace.

Robert Shallow.
Bodykins, Master Page, though I now be old and of the peace, if I see a sword out, my finger itches to make one. Though we are justices and doctors and churchmen, Master Page, we have some salt of our youth in us, we are the sons of women, Master Page.

George Page.
'Tis true, Master Shallow.

Robert Shallow.
It will be found so, Master Page. Master Doctor Caius, I am come to fetch you home. I am sworn of the peace. You have show'd yourself a wise physician, and Sir Hugh hath shown himself a wise and patient churchman. You must go with me, Master Doctor.

Host of the Garter Inn.
Pardon, guest-justice. A word, Mounseur Mock-water.

Doctor Caius.
Mock-vater? Vat is dat?

Host of the Garter Inn.
Mock-water, in our English tongue, is valor, bully.

Doctor Caius.
By gar, then I have as much mock-vater as de Englishman. Scurvy Jack-dog priest! By gar, me vill cut his ears.

Host of the Garter Inn.
He will clapper-claw thee tightly, bully.

Doctor Caius.
Clapper-de-claw? Vat is dat?

Host of the Garter Inn.
That is, he will make thee amends.

Doctor Caius.
By gar, me do look he shall clapper-de-claw me, for, by gar, me vill have it.

Host of the Garter Inn.
And I will provoke him to't, or let him wag.

Doctor Caius.
Me tank you for dat.

Host of the Garter Inn.
And moreover, bully—but first, Master Guest, and Master Page, and eke Cavaleiro Slender, go you through the town to Frogmore.

Aside to them.

George Page.
Sir Hugh is there, is he?

Host of the Garter Inn.
He is there. See what humor he is in; and I will bring the doctor about by the fields. Will it do well?

Robert Shallow.
We will do it.

All Page, Shallow and Slender.
Adieu, good Master Doctor.

Exeunt all but the Host, Caius, and Rugby.

Doctor Caius.
By gar, me vill kill de priest, for he speak for a jack-an-ape to Anne Page.

Host of the Garter Inn.
Let him die; but first sheathe thy impatience, throw cold water on thy choler. Go about the fields with me through Frogmore, I will bring thee where Mistress Anne Page is, at a farm-house a-feasting; and thou shalt woo her. Cried game? Said I well?

Doctor Caius.
By gar, me dank you vor dat. By gar, I love you; and I shall procure-a you de good guest: de earl, de knight, de lords, de gentlemen, my patients.

Host of the Garter Inn.
For the which I will be thy adversary toward Anne Page. Said I well?

Doctor Caius.
By gar, 'tis good; vell said.

Host of the Garter Inn.
Let us wag then.

Doctor Caius.
Come at my heels, Jack Rugby.

Exeunt.

Act 3

Scene 1

A field near Frogmore.

(Evans; Simple; Page; Shallow; Slender; Host; Caius; Rugby)

Sir Hugh is waiting for Dr. Caius, singing to himself to try and keep his courage up. Shallow, Slender, and Page come in and tell Evans that they are hoping to reconcile him with the doctor. The Host brings Caius in, and while they exchange threats, he admits that he has tricked them, arranging that they wouldn't meet so he could make them avoid the duel. Caius and Evans plot revenge.

Enter Evans, Simple.

Sir Hugh Evans.
I pray you now, good Master Slender's servingman, and friend Simple by your name, which way have you look'd for Master Caius, that calls himself Doctor of Physic?

Peter Simple.
Marry, sir, the pittie-ward, the park-ward—every way; Old Windsor way, and every way but the town way.

Sir Hugh Evans.
I most fehemently desire you you will also look that way.

Peter Simple.
I will, sir.

Exit.

Sir Hugh Evans.
Jeshu pless my soul! How full of chollors I am and trempling of mind! I shall be glad if he have deceiv'd me. How melancholies I am! I will knog his urinals about his knave's costard when I have good opportunities for the ork. Pless my soul!

Sings.

"To shallow rivers, to whose falls
Melodious birds sings madrigals;
There will we make our peds of roses,
And a thousand fragrant posies.
To shallow—"
Mercy on me! I have a great dispositions to cry.

Sings.

"Melodious birds sing madrigals—
When as I sat in Pabylon—
And a thousand vagram posies.
To shallow, etc."

Enter Simple.

Peter Simple.
Yonder he is coming, this way, Sir Hugh.

Sir Hugh Evans.
He's welcome.

Sings.

"To shallow rivers, to whose falls—"
Heaven prosper the right! What weapons is he?

Peter Simple.
No weapons, sir. There comes my master, Master Shallow, and another gentleman—from Frogmore, over the stile, this way.

Sir Hugh Evans.
Pray you give me my gown, or else keep it in your arms.

Reads in a book.
Enter Page, Shallow, Slender.

Robert Shallow.
How now, Master Parson? Good morrow, good Sir Hugh. Keep a gamester from the dice, and a good student from his book, and it is wonderful.

Abraham Slender.

Aside.

Ah, sweet Anne Page!

George Page.
God save you, good Sir Hugh!

Sir Hugh Evans.
God pless you from his mercy sake, all of you!

Robert Shallow.
What? The sword and the word? Do you study them both, Master Parson?

George Page.
And youthful still, in your doublet and hose, this raw rheumatic day?

Sir Hugh Evans.
There is reasons and causes for it.

George Page.
We are come to you to do a good office, Master Parson.

Sir Hugh Evans.
Fery well; what is it?

George Page.
Yonder is a most reverend gentleman, who, belike having receiv'd wrong by some person, is at most odds with his own gravity and patience that ever you saw.

Robert Shallow.
I have liv'd fourscore years and upward; I never heard a man of his place, gravity, and learning, so wide of his own respect.

Sir Hugh Evans.
What is he?

George Page.
I think you know him: Master Doctor Caius, the renown'd French physician.

Sir Hugh Evans.
Got's will, and his passion of my heart! I had as lief you would tell me of a mess of porridge.

George Page.
Why?

Sir Hugh Evans.
He has no more knowledge in Hibocrates and Galen—and he is a knave besides, a cowardly knave as you would desires to be acquainted withal.

George Page.
I warrant you, he's the man should fight with him.

Abraham Slender.

Aside.

O sweet Anne Page!

Enter Host, Caius, Rugby.

Robert Shallow.
It appears so by his weapons. Keep them asunder; here comes Doctor Caius.

Evans and Caius offer to fight.

George Page.
Nay, good Master Parson, keep in your weapon.

Robert Shallow.
So do you, good Master Doctor.

Host of the Garter Inn.
Disarm them, and let them question. Let them keep their limbs whole and hack our English.

Doctor Caius.
I pray you let-a me speak a word with your ear. Vherefore vill you not meet-a me?

Sir Hugh Evans.

Aside to Caius

Pray you use your patience in good time.

Doctor Caius.
By gar, you are de coward, de Jack dog, John ape.

Sir Hugh Evans.

Aside to Caius

Pray you let us not be laughing-stocks to other men's humors. I desire you in friendship, and I will one way or other make you amends.

Aloud.

I will knog your urinals about your knave's cogscomb for missing your meetings and appointments.

Doctor Caius.
Diable! Jack Rugby—mine host de Jarteer—have I not stay for him to kill him? Have I not, at de place I did appoint?

Sir Hugh Evans.
As I am a Christians-soul, now look you; this is the place appointed. I'll be judgment by mine host of the Garter.

Host of the Garter Inn.
Peace, I say, Gallia and Gaul, French and Welsh, soul-curer and body-curer!

Doctor Caius.
Ay, dat is very good, excellant.

Host of the Garter Inn.
Peace, I say! Hear mine host of the Garter. Am I politic? Am I subtle? Am I a Machiavel? Shall I lose my doctor? No, he gives me the potions and the motions. Shall I lose my parson? My priest? My Sir Hugh? No, he gives me the proverbs and the no-verbs. Give me thy hand, terrestial; so. Give me thy hand, celestial; so. Boys of art, I have deceiv'd you both; I have directed you to wrong places. Your hearts are mighty, your skins are whole, and let burnt sack be the issue. Come, lay their swords to pawn. Follow me, lads of peace; follow, follow, follow.

Exit.

Robert Shallow.
Afore God, a mad host. Follow, gentlemen, follow.

Abraham Slender.

Aside.

O sweet Anne Page!

Exeunt Shallow, Slender, and Page.

Doctor Caius.
Ha, do I perceive dat? Have you make-a de sot of us, ha, ha?

Sir Hugh Evans.
This is well! He has made us his vlouting-stog. I desire you that we may be friends; and let us knog our prains together to be revenge on this same scall, scurvy, cogging companion, the host of the Garter.

Doctor Caius.
By gar, with all my heart. He promise to bring me where is Anne Page; by gar, he deceive me too.

Sir Hugh Evans.
Well, I will smite his noddles. Pray you follow.

Exeunt.

Scene 2

Windsor. A street.

(*Mistress Margaret Page; Robin; Ford; Page; Shallow; Slender; Host; Evans; Caius; Rugby*)

Mistress Page and Robin meet Ford as they go to visit his wife. Hearing that Robin used to be Falstaff's servant, Ford is horrified, convinced that Page is a fool who cannot see how his wife is betraying him. When the crowd coming back from the failed duel comes up the street, Ford, hoping to catch his wife in the act and prove Page wrong, insists that they follow him to his house. He only manages to convince Evans, Caius, and Page, as Slender and the others are going to help him woo Anne.

Enter Mistress Page, Robin.

Mistress Margaret Page.
Nay, keep your way, little gallant; you were wont to be a follower, but now you are a leader. Whether had you rather lead mine eyes, or eye your master's heels?

Robin.
I had rather, forsooth, go before you like a man than follow him like a dwarf.

Mistress Margaret Page.
O, you are a flattering boy, now I see you'll be a courtier.

Enter Ford.

Francis Ford.
Well met, Mistress Page. Whither go you?

Mistress Margaret Page.
Truly, sir, to see your wife. Is she at home?

Francis Ford.
Ay, and as idle as she may hang together, for want of company. I think if your husbands were dead, you two would marry.

Mistress Margaret Page.
Be sure of that—two other husbands.

Francis Ford.
Where had you this pretty weathercock?

Mistress Margaret Page.
I cannot tell what the dickens his name is my husband had him of. What do you call your knight's name, sirrah?

Robin.
Sir John Falstaff.

Francis Ford.
Sir John Falstaff!

Mistress Margaret Page.
He, he—I can never hit on 's name. There is such a league between my goodman and he! Is your wife at home indeed?

Francis Ford.
Indeed she is.

Mistress Margaret Page.
By your leave, sir. I am sick till I see her.

Exeunt Mrs. Page and Robin.

Francis Ford.
Has Page any brains? Hath he any eyes? Hath he any thinking? Sure they sleep, he hath no use of them. Why, this boy will carry a letter twenty mile, as easy as a cannon will shoot point-blank twelve score. He pieces out his wive's inclination; he gives her folly motion and advantage; and now she's going to my wife, and Falstaff's boy with her. A man may hear this show'r sing in the wind. And Falstaff's boy with her! Good plots, they are laid, and our revolted wives share damnation together. Well, I will take him, then torture my wife, pluck the borrow'd veil of modesty from the so-seeming Mistress Page, divulge Page himself for a secure and willful Actaeon; and to these violent proceedings all my neighbors shall cry aim.

Clock heard.

The clock gives me my cue, and my assurance bids me search—there I shall find Falstaff. I shall be rather prais'd for this than mock'd; for it is as positive as the earth is firm that Falstaff is there. I will go.

Enter Page, Shallow, Slender, Host, Evans, Caius, Rugby.

Page, Shallow, Slender, Host, Evans, Caius, Rugby.
Well met, Master Ford.

Francis Ford.
Trust me, a good knot. I have good cheer at home, and I pray you all go with me.

Robert Shallow.
I must excuse myself, Master Ford.

Abraham Slender.
And so must I, sir. We have appointed to dine with Mistress Anne, and I would not break with her for more money than I'll speak of.

Robert Shallow.
We have linger'd about a match between Anne Page and my cousin Slender, and this day we shall have our answer.

Abraham Slender.
I hope I have your good will, father Page.

George Page.
You have, Master Slender, I stand wholly for you; but my wife, Master Doctor, is for you altogether.

Doctor Caius.
Ay, be-gar, and de maid is love-a me. My nursh-a Quickly tell me so mush.

Host of the Garter Inn.
What say you to young Master Fenton? He capers, he dances, he has eyes of youth; he writes verses, he speaks holiday, he smells April and May—he will carry't, he will carry't—'tis in his buttons—he will carry't.

George Page.
Not by my consent, I promise you. The gentleman is of no having. He kept company with the wild Prince and Poins; he is of too high a region, he knows too much. No, he shall not knit a knot in his fortunes with the finger of my substance. If he take her, let him take her simply. The wealth I have waits on my consent, and my consent goes not that way.

Francis Ford.
I beseech you heartily, some of you go home with me to dinner. Besides your cheer, you shall have sport; I will show you a monster. Master Doctor, you shall go, so shall you, Master Page, and you, Sir Hugh.

Robert Shallow.
Well, fare you well. We shall have the freer wooing at Master Page's.

Exeunt Shallow and Slender.

Doctor Caius.
Go home, John Rugby, I come anon.

Exit Rugby.

Host of the Garter Inn.
Farewell, my hearts. I will to my honest knight Falstaff, and drink canary with him.

Exit.

Francis Ford.
Aside.
I think I shall drink in pipe-wine first with him; I'll make him dance.—Will you go, gentles?

Page, Evans, and Caius.
Have with you to see this monster.

Exeunt.

Scene 3

A room in Ford's house.

(Mistress Ford; Mistress Margaret Page; First Servant; Second Servant; Robin; Falstaff; Ford; Page; Caius; Evans)

Mistress Ford and Mistress Page instruct the servants to take out the laundry basket when they are told to, without any pausing, and to dump the contents in the ditch. Mistress Page hides as Falstaff comes in. He begins to woo Mistress Ford; at the right moment, Robin rushes in to announce Mistress Page. Not wanting her to discover that he is two-timing her, Falstaff hides behind a tapestry while Mistress Page, in a flurry, announces that Ford and others are coming. Mistress Ford admits to having a man in the house, and Mistress Page suggests that he sneak out in the laundry basket. In a panic, Falstaff appears and consents, while Mistress Page scolds him for dissembling. He is carried out by the servants just as Ford frantically bursts in and searches the house. The two wives reproach him for his suspicions. Shocked at the extent of his jealousy, Mistress Ford decides to cure her husband of it while she and Mistress Page plan more tricks on Falstaff. Ford invites his friends to dinner all the same and they accept, though Page suggests that they will mock him the next morning. Caius and Evans remind each other not to forget the Host.

Enter Mistress Ford, Mistress Page.

Mistress Alice Ford.
What, John! What, Robert!

Mistress Margaret Page.
Quickly, quickly! Is the buck-basket—

Mistress Alice Ford.
I warrant. What, Robin, I say!

Enter Servants with a great buck-basket.

Mistress Margaret Page.
Come, come, come.

Mistress Alice Ford.
Here, set it down.

Mistress Margaret Page.
Give your men the charge, we must be brief.

Mistress Alice Ford.
Marry, as I told you before, John and Robert, be ready here hard by in the brew-house, and when I suddenly call you, come forth, and (without any pause or staggering) take this basket on your shoulders. That done, trudge with it in all haste, and carry it among the whitsters in Datchet-mead, and there empty it in the muddy ditch close by the Thames side.

Mistress Margaret Page.
You will do it?

Mistress Alice Ford.
I ha' told them over and over, they lack no direction. Be gone, and come when you are call'd.

Exeunt Servants.

Mistress Margaret Page.
Here comes little Robin.

Enter Robin.

Mistress Alice Ford.
How now, my eyas-musket, what news with you?

Robin.
My master, Sir John, is come in at your back door, Mistress Ford, and requests your company.

Mistress Margaret Page.
You little Jack-a-Lent, have you been true to us?

Robin.
Ay, I'll be sworn. My master knows not of your being here, and hath threat'ned to put me into everlasting liberty if I tell you of it; for he swears he'll turn me away.

Mistress Margaret Page.
Thou'rt a good boy. This secrecy of thine shall be a tailor to thee, and shall make thee a new doublet and hose. I'll go hide me.

Mistress Alice Ford.
Do so. Go tell thy master I am alone.

Exit Robin.

Mistress Page, remember you your cue.

Mistress Margaret Page.
I warrant thee, if I do not act it, hiss me.

Exit.

Mistress Alice Ford.
Go to then. We'll use this unwholesome humidity, this gross wat'ry pumpion. We'll teach him to know turtles from jays.

Enter Falstaff.

Sir John Falstaff.
"Have I caught thee, my heavenly jewel?" Why, now let me die, for I have liv'd long enough. This is the period of my ambition. O this blessed hour!

Mistress Alice Ford.
O sweet Sir John!

Sir John Falstaff.
Mistress Ford, I cannot cog, I cannot prate, Mistress Ford. Now shall I sin in my wish: I would thy husband were dead. I'll speak it before the best lord, I would make thee my lady.

Mistress Alice Ford.
I your lady, Sir John? Alas, I should be a pitiful lady!

Sir John Falstaff.
Let the court of France show me such another. I see how thine eye would emulate the diamond. Thou hast the right arch'd beauty of the brow that becomes the ship-tire, the tire-valiant, or any tire of Venetian admittance.

Mistress Alice Ford.
A plain kerchief, Sir John. My brows become nothing else, nor that well neither.

Sir John Falstaff.
By the Lord, thou art a tyrant to say so. Thou wouldst make an absolute courtier, and the firm fixture of thy foot would give an excellent motion to thy gait in a semicircled farthingale. I see what thou wert, if Fortune thy foe were not, Nature thy friend. Come, thou canst not hide it.

Mistress Alice Ford.
Believe me, there's no such thing in me.

Sir John Falstaff.
What made me love thee? Let that persuade thee there's something extraordinary in thee. Come, I cannot cog and say thou art this and that, like a many of these lisping hawthorn buds, that come like women in men's apparel, and smell like Bucklersbury in simple time—I cannot; but I love thee, none but thee; and thou deserv'st it.

Mistress Alice Ford.
Do not betray me, sir. I fear you love Mistress Page.

Sir John Falstaff.
Thou mightst as well say I love to walk by the Counter-gate, which is as hateful to me as the reek of a lime-kill.

Mistress Alice Ford.
Well, heaven knows how I love you, and you shall one day find it.

Sir John Falstaff.
Keep in that mind, I'll deserve it.

Mistress Alice Ford.
Nay, I must tell you, so you do; or else I could not be in that mind.

Enter Robin.

Robin.
Mistress Ford, Mistress Ford! Here's Mistress Page at the door, sweating, and blowing, and looking wildly, and would needs speak with you presently.

Sir John Falstaff.
She shall not see me, I will ensconce me behind the arras.

Mistress Alice Ford.
Pray you do so, she's a very tattling woman.

Falstaff stands behind the arras.
Enter Mistress Page.

What's the matter? How now?

Mistress Margaret Page.
O Mistress Ford, what have you done? You're sham'd, y' are overthrown, y' are undone forever!

Mistress Alice Ford.
What's the matter, good Mistress Page?

Mistress Margaret Page.
O well-a-day, Mistress Ford, having an honest man to your husband, to give him such cause of suspicion!

Mistress Alice Ford.
What cause of suspicion?

Mistress Margaret Page.
What cause of suspicion? Out upon you! How am I mistook in you!

Mistress Alice Ford.
Why, alas, what's the matter?

Mistress Margaret Page.
Your husband's coming hither, woman, with all the officers in Windsor, to search for a gentleman that he says is here now in the house; by your consent to take an ill advantage of his absence. You are undone.

Mistress Alice Ford.
'Tis not so, I hope.

Mistress Margaret Page.
Pray heaven it be not so, that you have such a man here; but 'tis most certain your husband's coming, with half Windsor at his heels, to search for such a one. I come before to tell you. If you know yourself clear, why, I am glad of it; but if you have a friend here, convey, convey him out. Be not amaz'd, call all your senses to you, defend your reputation, or bid farewell to your good life forever.

Mistress Alice Ford.
What shall I do? There is a gentleman, my dear friend; and I fear not mine own shame so much as his peril. I had rather than a thousand pound he were out of the house.

Mistress Margaret Page.
For shame, never stand "you had rather" and "you had rather." Your husband's here at hand, bethink you of some conveyance. In the house you cannot hide him. O, how have you deceiv'd me! Look, here is a basket; if he be of any reasonable stature, he may creep in here, and throw foul linen upon him, as if it were going to bucking; or—it is whiting-time—send him by your two men to Datchet-mead.

Mistress Alice Ford.
He's too big to go in there. What shall I do?

Sir John Falstaff.

Starting from his concealment.

Let me see't, let me see't, O, let me see't! I'll in, I'll in. Follow your friend's counsel. I'll in.

Mistress Margaret Page.
What, Sir John Falstaff?

Aside.

Are these your letters, knight?

Sir John Falstaff.

To Mrs. Page.

I love thee. Help me away.—Let me creep in here. I'll never—

Goes into the basket; they put clothes over him.

Mistress Margaret Page.
Help to cover your master, boy. Call your men, Mistress Ford. You dissembling knight!

Mistress Alice Ford.
What, John! Robert! John!

Exit Robin.
Enter Servants.

Go take up these clothes here quickly. Where's the cowl-staff? Look how you drumble! Carry them to the laundress in Datchet-mead; quickly, come.

Enter Ford, Page, Caius, Evans.

Francis Ford.
Pray you come near. If I suspect without cause, why then make sport at me, then let me be your jest, I deserve it. How now? Whither bear you this?

First Servant.
To the laundress, forsooth.

Mistress Alice Ford.
Why, what have you to do whither they bear it? You were best meddle with buck-washing.

Francis Ford.
Buck! I would I could wash myself of the buck! Buck, buck, buck! Ay, buck! I warrant you, buck, and of the season too, it shall appear.

Exeunt Servants with the basket.

Gentlemen, I have dream'd tonight; I'll tell you my dream. Here, here, here be my keys. Ascend my chambers, search, seek, find out. I'll warrant we'll unkennel the fox. Let me stop this way first.

Locking the door.

So, now uncape.

George Page.
Good Master Ford, be contented. You wrong yourself too much.

Francis Ford.
True, Master Page. Up, gentlemen, you shall see sport anon. Follow me, gentlemen.

Exit.

Sir Hugh Evans.
This is fery fantastical humors and jealousies.

Doctor Caius.
By gar, 'tis no the fashion of France; it is not jealous in France.

George Page.
Nay, follow him, gentlemen, see the issue of his search.

Exeunt Page, Caius, and Evans.

Mistress Margaret Page.
Is there not a double excellency in this?

Mistress Alice Ford.
I know not which pleases me better, that my husband is deceiv'd, or Sir John.

Mistress Margaret Page.
What a taking was he in when your husband ask'd who was in the basket!

Mistress Alice Ford.
I am half afraid he will have need of washing, so throwing him into the water will do him a benefit.

Mistress Margaret Page.
Hang him, dishonest rascal! I would all of the same strain were in the same distress.

Mistress Alice Ford.
I think my husband hath some special suspicion of Falstaff's being here, for I never saw him so gross in his jealousy till now.

Mistress Margaret Page.
I will lay a plot to try that, and we will yet have more tricks with Falstaff. His dissolute disease will scarce obey this medicine.

Mistress Alice Ford.
Shall we send that foolish carrion, Mistress Quickly, to him, and excuse his throwing into the water, and give him another hope, to betray him to another punishment?

Mistress Margaret Page.
We will do it. Let him be sent for tomorrow, eight a' clock, to have amends.

Enter Ford, Page, Caius, and Evans.

Francis Ford.
I cannot find him. May be the knave bragg'd of that he could not compass.

Mistress Margaret Page.

Aside to Mrs. Ford

Heard you that?

Mistress Alice Ford.
You use me well, Master Ford, do you?

Francis Ford.
Ay, I do so.

Mistress Alice Ford.
Heaven make you better than your thoughts!

Francis Ford.
Amen!

Mistress Margaret Page.
You do yourself mighty wrong, Master Ford.

Francis Ford.
Ay, ay; I must bear it.

Sir Hugh Evans.
If there be any pody in the house, and in the chambers, and in the coffers, and in the presses, heaven forgive my sins at the day of judgment!

Doctor Caius.
Be-gar, nor I too; there is no-bodies.

George Page.
Fie, fie, Master Ford, are you not asham'd? What spirit, what devil suggests this imagination? I would not ha' your distemper in this kind for the wealth of Windsor Castle.

Francis Ford.
'Tis my fault, Master Page. I suffer for it.

Sir Hugh Evans.
You suffer for a pad conscience. Your wife is as honest a omans as I will desires among five thousand, and five hundred too.

Doctor Caius.
By gar, I see 'tis an honest woman.

Francis Ford.
Well, I promis'd you a dinner. Come, come, walk in the park. I pray you pardon me; I will hereafter make known to you why I have done this. Come, wife, come, Mistress Page, I pray you pardon me; pray heartly pardon me.

George Page.
Let's go in, gentlemen, but (trust me) we'll mock him. I do invite you tomorrow morning to my house to breakfast; after, we'll a-birding together. I have a fine hawk for the bush. Shall it be so?

Francis Ford.
Any thing.

Sir Hugh Evans.
If there is one, I shall make two in the company.

Doctor Caius.
If there be one or two, I shall make-a the turd.

Francis Ford.
Pray you go, Master Page.

Exit with Page.

Sir Hugh Evans.
I pray you now remembrance tomorrow on the lousy knave, mine host.

Doctor Caius.
Dat is good, by gar; with all my heart!

Sir Hugh Evans.
A lousy knave, to have his gibes and his mockeries!

Exeunt.

Scene 4

A room in Page's house.

(Fenton; Anne Page; Shallow; Slender; Mistress Quickly; Page; Mistress Margaret Page)

Fenton tells Anne how unlikely it is that her father will ever approve of him, but she asks him to keep trying. Anne sees Slender approaching, and comments on how her father approves of him only because he's rich. Slender attempts to woo her, but greatly needs his uncle Shallow's help. He admits he is only running after her because her father and his uncle insist on it. Page comes out to invite them all in and tells Fenton to leave Anne alone. Fenton pleads with Mistress Page, while Anne asks her to spare her from marrying Slender, but Mistress Page intends Dr. Caius to be Anne's husband. Mistress Quickly assures Fenton that Anne likes him thanks to her. By now, she is a go-between for all three suitors, not to mention the messenger between the two wives and Falstaff.

Enter Fenton, Anne Page.

Fenton.
I see I cannot get thy father's love,
Therefore no more turn me to him, sweet Nan.

Mistress Anne Page.
Alas, how then?

Fenton.
            Why, thou must be thyself.
He doth object I am too great of birth,
And that my state being gall'd with my expense,
I seek to heal it only by his wealth.
Besides these, other bars he lays before me,
My riots past, my wild societies,
And tells me 'tis a thing impossible
I should love thee but as a property.

Mistress Anne Page.
May be he tells you true.

Fenton.
No, heaven so speed me in my time to come!
Albeit I will confess thy father's wealth
Was the first motive that I woo'd thee, Anne;
Yet wooing thee, I found thee of more value
Than stamps in gold, or sums in sealed bags;
And 'tis the very riches of thyself
That now I aim at.

Mistress Anne Page.
            Gentle Master Fenton,
Yet seek my father's love, still seek it, sir.
If opportunity and humblest suit
Cannot attain it, why then hark you hither!

They converse apart.
Enter Shallow, Slender, Mistress Quickly.

Robert Shallow.
Break their talk, Mistress Quickly, my kinsman shall speak for himself.

Abraham Slender.
I'll make a shaft or a bolt on't. 'Slid, 'tis but venturing.

Robert Shallow.
Be not dismay'd.

Abraham Slender.
No, she shall not dismay me. I care not for that, but that I am afeard.

Mistress Quickly.
Hark ye, Master Slender would speak a word with you.

Mistress Anne Page.
I come to him.

Aside.
            This is my father's choice.
O, what a world of vild ill-favor'd faults
Looks handsome in three hundred pounds a year!

Mistress Quickly.
And how does good Master Fenton? Pray you a word with you.

Robert Shallow.
She's coming; to her, coz. O boy, thou hadst a father!

Abraham Slender.
I had a father, Mistress Anne, my uncle can tell you good jests of him. Pray you, uncle, tell Mistress Anne the jest how my father stole two geese out of a pen, good uncle.

Robert Shallow.
Mistress Anne, my cousin loves you.

Abraham Slender.
Ay, that I do—as well as I love any woman in Gloucestershire.

Robert Shallow.
He will maintain you like a gentlewoman.

Abraham Slender.
Ay, that I will, come cut and long-tail, under the degree of a squire.

Robert Shallow.
He will make you a hundred and fifty pounds jointure.

Mistress Anne Page.
Good Master Shallow, let him woo for himself.

Robert Shallow.
Marry, I thank you for it; I thank you for that good comfort. She calls you, coz. I'll leave you.

Mistress Anne Page.
Now, Master Slender—

Abraham Slender.
Now, good Mistress Anne—

Mistress Anne Page.
What is your will?

Abraham Slender.
My will? 'Od's heartlings, that's a pretty jest indeed! I ne'er made my will yet, I thank heaven. I am not such a sickly creature, I give heaven praise.

Mistress Anne Page.
I mean, Master Slender, what would you with me?

Abraham Slender.
Truly, for mine own part, I would little or nothing with you. Your father and my uncle hath made motions. If it be my luck, so; if not, happy man be his dole! They can tell you how things go better than I can. You may ask your father, here he comes.

Enter Page, Mistress Page.

George Page.
Now, Master Slender. Love him, daughter Anne.
Why, how now? What does Master Fenton here?
You wrong me, sir, thus still to haunt my house.
I told you, sir, my daughter is dispos'd of.

Fenton.
Nay, Master Page, be not impatient.

Mistress Margaret Page.
Good Master Fenton, come not to my child.

George Page.
She is no match for you.

Fenton.
Sir, will you hear me?

George Page.
          No, good Master Fenton.
Come, Master Shallow; come, son Slender, in.
Knowing my mind, you wrong me, Master Fenton.

Exeunt Page, Shallow, and Slender.

Mistress Quickly.
Speak to Mistress Page.

Fenton.
Good Mistress Page, for that I love your daughter
In such a righteous fashion as I do,
Perforce, against all checks, rebukes, and manners,
I must advance the colors of my love,
And not retire. Let me have your good will.

Mistress Anne Page.
Good mother, do not marry me to yond fool.

Mistress Margaret Page.
I mean it not, I seek you a better husband.

Mistress Quickly.
That's my master, Master Doctor.

Mistress Anne Page.
Alas, I had rather be set quick i' th' earth,
And bowl'd to death with turnips!

Mistress Margaret Page.
Come, trouble not yourself. Good Master Fenton,
I will not be your friend nor enemy.
My daughter will I question how she loves you,
And as I find her, so am I affected.
Till then farewell, sir; she must needs go in,
Her father will be angry.

Fenton.
Farewell, gentle mistress; farewell, Nan.

Exeunt Mrs. Page and Anne.

Mistress Quickly.
This is my doing now. "Nay," said I, "will you cast away your child on a fool, and a physician? Look on Master Fenton." This is my doing.

Fenton.
I thank thee; and I pray thee, once tonight
Give my sweet Nan this ring. There's for thy pains.

Mistress Quickly.
Now heaven send thee good fortune!

Exit Fenton.

A kind heart he hath. A woman would run through fire and water for such a kind heart. But yet I would my master had Mistress Anne; or I would Master Slender had her; or, in sooth, I would Master Fenton had her. I will do what I can for them all three, for so I have promis'd, and I'll be as good as my word, but speciously for Master Fenton. Well, I must of another errand to Sir John Falstaff from my two mistresses. What a beast am I to slack it!

Exit.

Scene 5

A room in the Garter Inn.

(Falstaff; Bardolph; Mistress Quickly; Ford)

Falstaff returns to the Inn after crawling out of the mud, roaring for sack. Mistress Quickly comes in with a message from Mistress Ford, apologizing for the "accidental" dunking in the river, and telling him that Ford will be absent the next morning. Falstaff agrees to go visit her again. Just as he wonders where "Brook" has got to, Ford enters in his disguise, asking how things are going. Falstaff tells the whole adventure, revealing how he was snuck out of the house and that he has another rendezvous planned. Ford is incensed at having been fooled, and swears that he will catch Falstaff the next time.

Enter Falstaff.

Sir John Falstaff.
Bardolph, I say!

Enter Bardolph.

Bardolph.
Here, sir.

Sir John Falstaff.
Go fetch me a quart of sack, put a toast in't.

Exit Bardolph.

Have I liv'd to be carried in a basket like a barrow of butcher's offal? And to be thrown in the Thames? Well, and I be serv'd such another trick, I'll have my brains ta'en out and butter'd, and give them to a dog for a new-year's gift. The rogues slighted me into the river with as little remorse as they would have drown'd a blind bitch's puppies, fifteen i' th' litter; and you may know by my size that I have a kind of alacrity in sinking; and the bottom were as deep as hell, I should down. I had been drown'd, but that the shore was shelvy and shallow—a death that I abhor; for the water swells a man; and what a thing should I have been when I had been swell'd! I should have been a mountain of mummy.

Enter Bardolph with sack.

Bardolph.
Here's Mistress Quickly, sir, to speak with you.

Sir John Falstaff.
Come, let me pour in some sack to the Thames water; for my belly's as cold as if I had swallow'd snowballs for pills to cool the reins. Call her in.

Bardolph.
Come in, woman!

Enter Mistress Quickly.

Mistress Quickly.
By your leave; I cry you mercy! Give your worship good morrow.

Sir John Falstaff.
Take away these chalices. Go, brew me a pottle of sack finely.

Bardolph.
With eggs, sir?

Sir John Falstaff.
Simple of itself; I'll no pullet-sperm in my brewage.

Exit Bardolph.

How now?

Mistress Quickly.
Marry, sir, I come to your worship from Mistress Ford.

Act 3, Scene 5

Sir John Falstaff.
Mistress Ford? I have had ford enough. I was thrown into the ford; I have my belly full of ford.

Mistress Quickly.
Alas the day! Good heart, that was not her fault. She does so take on with her men; they mistook their erection.

Sir John Falstaff.
So did I mine, to build upon a foolish woman's promise.

Mistress Quickly.
Well, she laments, sir, for it, that it would yearn your heart to see it. Her husband goes this morning a-birding; she desires you once more to come to her, between eight and nine. I must carry her word quickly. She'll make you amends, I warrant you.

Sir John Falstaff.
Well, I will visit her, tell her so. And bid her think what a man is: let her consider his frailty, and then judge of my merit.

Mistress Quickly.
I will tell her.

Sir John Falstaff.
Do so. Between nine and ten, say'st thou?

Mistress Quickly.
Eight and nine, sir.

Sir John Falstaff.
Well, be gone; I will not miss her.

Mistress Quickly.
Peace be with you, sir.

Exit.

Sir John Falstaff.
I marvel I hear not of Master Brook; he sent me word to stay within. I like his money well. O, here he comes.

Enter Ford disguised.

Francis Ford.
Bless you, sir!

Sir John Falstaff.
Now, Master Brook, you come to know what hath pass'd between me and Ford's wife?

Francis Ford.
That indeed, Sir John, is my business.

Sir John Falstaff.
Master Brook, I will not lie to you. I was at her house the hour she appointed me.

Francis Ford.
And sped you, sir?

Sir John Falstaff.
Very ill-favoredly, Master Brook.

Francis Ford.
How so, sir? Did she change her determination?

Sir John Falstaff.
No, Master Brook, but the peaking cornuto her husband, Master Brook, dwelling in a continual 'larum of jealousy, comes me in the instant of our encounter, after we had embrac'd, kiss'd, protested, and, as it were, spoke the prologue of our comedy; and at his heels a rabble of his companions, thither provok'd and instigated by his distemper, and, forsooth, to search his house for his wive's love.

Francis Ford.
What? While you were there?

Sir John Falstaff.
While I was there.

Francis Ford.
And did he search for you, and could not find you?

Sir John Falstaff.
You shall hear. As good luck would have it, comes in one Mistress Page; gives intelligence of Ford's approach; and in her invention, and Ford's wive's distraction, they convey'd me into a buck-basket.

Francis Ford.
A buck-basket?

Sir John Falstaff.
By the Lord, a buck-basket! Ramm'd me in with foul shirts and smocks, socks, foul stockings, greasy napkins, that, Master Brook, there was the rankest compound of villainous smell that ever offended nostril.

Francis Ford.
And how long lay you there?

Sir John Falstaff.
Nay, you shall hear, Master Brook, what I have suffer'd to bring this woman to evil for your good. Being thus cramm'd in the basket, a couple of Ford's knaves, his hinds, were call'd forth by their mistress to carry me in the name of foul clothes to Datchet-lane. They took me on their shoulders; met the jealous knave their master in the door, who ask'd them once or twice what they had in their basket. I quak'd for fear, lest the lunatic knave would have search'd it; but fate (ordaining he should be a cuckold) held his hand. Well, on went he for a search, and away went I for foul clothes. But mark the sequel, Master Brook. I suffer'd the pangs of three several deaths: first, an intolerable fright, to be detected with a jealous rotten bell-wether; next, to be compass'd like a good bilbo in the circumference of a peck, hilt to point, heel to head; and then to be stopp'd in like a strong distillation with stinking clothes that fretted in their own grease. Think of that—a man of my kidney. Think of that—that am as subject to heat as butter; a man of continual dissolution and thaw. It was a miracle to scape suffocation. And in the height of this bath (when I was more than half stew'd in grease, like a Dutch dish) to be thrown into the Thames, and cool'd, glowing-hot, in that surge, like a horse-shoe; think of that—hissing-hot—think of that, Master Brook.

Francis Ford.
In good sadness, sir, I am sorry that for my sake you have suffer'd all this. My suit then is desperate; you'll undertake her no more?

Sir John Falstaff.
Master Brook, I will be thrown into Etna, as I have been into Thames, ere I will leave her thus. Her husband is this morning gone a-birding. I have receiv'd from her another embassy of meeting. 'Twixt eight and nine is the hour, Master Brook.

Francis Ford.
'Tis past eight already, sir.

Sir John Falstaff.
Is it? I will then address me to my appointment. Come to me at your convenient leisure, and you shall know how I speed; and the conclusion shall be crown'd with your enjoying her. Adieu. You shall have her, Master Brook. Master Brook, you shall cuckold Ford.

Exit.

Francis Ford.
Hum! Ha? Is this a vision? Is this a dream? Do I sleep? Master Ford, awake! Awake, Master Ford! There's a hole made in your best coat, Master Ford. This 'tis to be married! This 'tis to have linen and buck-baskets! Well, I will proclaim myself what I am. I will now take the lecher; he is at my house. He cannot scape me; 'tis impossible he should; he cannot creep into a halfpenny purse, nor into a pepper-box. But lest the devil that guides him should aid him, I will search impossible places. Though what I am I cannot avoid, yet to be what I would not shall not make me tame. If I have horns to make one mad, let the proverb go with me: I'll be horn-mad.

Exit.

Act 4
Scene 1

Windsor. A street.

(Mistress Margaret Page; Mistress Quickly; William; Evans)

Mistress Page is leading her son William to school when she meets Evans (who is also the schoolmaster), who announces that there is no school today. Mistress Page asks him to put William through his paces, as Page claims the boy isn't learning anything. Evans takes the boy through his Latin; Mistress Quickly, however, doesn't speak the language and thinks it's all a mass of dirty words. She is offended that a child is being taught such rude things.

Enter Mistress Page, Mistress Quickly, William.

Mistress Margaret Page.
Is he at Master Ford's already, think'st thou?

Mistress Quickly.
Sure he is by this—or will be presently. But truly he is very courageous mad about his throwing into the water. Mistress Ford desires you to come suddenly.

Mistress Margaret Page.
I'll be with her by and by; I'll but bring my young man here to school.

Enter Evans.

Look where his master comes; 'tis a playing-day, I see. How now, Sir Hugh, no school today?

Sir Hugh Evans.
No; Master Slender is let the boys leave to play.

Mistress Quickly.
Blessing of his heart!

Mistress Margaret Page.
Sir Hugh, my husband says my son profits nothing in the world at his book. I pray you ask him some questions in his accidence.

Sir Hugh Evans.
Come hither, William; hold up your head; come.

Mistress Margaret Page.
Come on, sirrah; hold up your head. Answer your master, be not afraid.

Sir Hugh Evans.
William, how many numbers is in nouns?

William Page.
Two.

Mistress Quickly.
Truly, I thought there had been one number more, because they say, "'Od's nouns."

Sir Hugh Evans.
Peace your tattlings! What is "fair," William?

William Page.
Pulcher.

Mistress Quickly.
Poulcats? There are fairer things than poulcats sure.

Sir Hugh Evans.
You are a very simplicity oman; I pray you peace. What is lapis, William?

William Page.
A stone.

Sir Hugh Evans.
And what is 'a stone,' William?

William Page.
A pebble.

Sir Hugh Evans.
No; it is lapis. I pray you remember in your prain.

William Page.
Lapis.

Sir Hugh Evans.
That is a good William. What is he, William, that does lend articles?

William Page.
Articles are borrow'd of the pronoun, and be thus declin'd, Singulariter, nominativo, hic, haec, hoc.

Sir Hugh Evans.
Nominativo, hig, hag, hog; pray you mark; genitivo, hujus. Well, what is your accusative case?

William Page.
Accusativo, hinc.

Sir Hugh Evans.
I pray you have your remembrance, child. Accusativo, hung, hang, hog.

Mistress Quickly.
"Hang-hog" is Latin for bacon, I warrant you.

Sir Hugh Evans.
Leave your prabbles, oman. What is the focative case, William?

William Page.
O—vocativo, O.

Sir Hugh Evans.
Remember, William, focative is caret.

Mistress Quickly.
And that's a good root.

Sir Hugh Evans.
Oman, forbear.

Mistress Margaret Page.
Peace!

Sir Hugh Evans.
What is your genitive case plural, William?

William Page.
Genitive case?

Sir Hugh Evans.
Ay.

William Page.
Genitivo, horum, harum, horum.

Mistress Quickly.
Vengeance of Jinny's case! Fie on her! Never name her, child, if she be a whore.

Sir Hugh Evans.
For shame, oman.

Mistress Quickly.
You do ill to teach the child such words. He teaches him to "hic" and to "hac," which they'll do fast enough of themselves, and to call "horum,"—fie upon you!

Sir Hugh Evans.
Oman, art thou lunatics? Hast thou no understandings for thy cases and the numbers of the genders? Thou art as foolish Christian creatures as I would desires.

Mistress Margaret Page.
Prithee hold thy peace.

Sir Hugh Evans.
Show me now, William, some declensions of your pronouns.

William Page.
Forsooth, I have forgot.

Sir Hugh Evans.
It is qui, quae, quod: if you forget your qui's, your quae's, and your quod's, you must be preeches. Go your ways and play, go.

Mistress Margaret Page.
He is a better scholar than I thought he was.

Sir Hugh Evans.
He is a good sprag memory. Farewell, Mistress Page.

Mistress Margaret Page.
Adieu, good Sir Hugh.

Exit Evans.

Get you home, boy. Come, we stay too long.

Exeunt.

Scene 2

A room in Ford's house.

(*Falstaff; Mistress Ford; Mistress Margaret Page; First Servant; Second Servant; Ford; Page; Caius; Evans; Shallow*)

Falstaff meets with Mistress Ford again, when Mistress Page arrives to announce that Ford and others are again on their way. Falstaff refuses to go in the basket again, and the only solution they can find is for him to dress up as a woman and pretend to be the fat woman of Brainford, the aunt of Ford's maid, whom Ford loathes as a witch. As he disguises himself, Mistress Page warns Mistress Ford that Ford knows about the laundry basket, so she gets her servants to carry it out again. Ford forces them to put it down and searches through it. By this stage his friends are convinced he's lost his wits. When Falstaff comes downstairs in his disguise, Ford is furious that the old witch has come to his house, which he has forbidden, and has "her" beaten out of doors. Sir Hugh is convinced she must be a witch indeed, given the beard she has. The wives laugh and decide the time has come to tell their husbands everything, hoping to find a new trick to play on Falstaff with their help.

Enter Falstaff, Mistress Ford.

Sir John Falstaff.
Mistress Ford, your sorrow hath eaten up my sufferance. I see you are obsequious in your love, and I profess requital to a hair's breadth, not only, Mistress Ford, in the simple office of love, but in all the accoutrement, complement, and ceremony of it. But are you sure of your husband now?

Mistress Alice Ford.
He's a-birding, sweet Sir John.

Mistress Margaret Page.

Within.

What ho, gossip Ford! What ho!

Mistress Alice Ford.
Step into th' chamber, Sir John.

Exit Falstaff.
Enter Mistress Page.

Mistress Margaret Page.
How now, sweet heart, who's at home besides yourself?

Mistress Alice Ford.
Why, none but mine own people.

Mistress Margaret Page.
Indeed?

Mistress Alice Ford.
No, certainly.

Aside to her.

Speak louder.

Mistress Margaret Page.
Truly, I am so glad you have nobody here.

Mistress Alice Ford.
Why?

Mistress Margaret Page.
Why, woman, your husband is in his old lines again. He so takes on yonder with my husband; so rails against all married mankind; so curses all Eve's daughters, of what complexion soever; and so buffets himself on the forehead, crying, "Peer out, peer out!", that any madness I ever yet beheld seem'd but tameness, civility, and patience to this his distemper he is in now. I am glad the fat knight is not here.

Mistress Alice Ford.
Why, does he talk of him?

Mistress Margaret Page.
Of none but him, and swears he was carried out, the last time he search'd for him, in a basket; protests to my husband he is now here, and hath drawn him and the rest of their company from their sport, to make another experiment of his suspicion. But I am glad the knight is not here. Now he shall see his own foolery.

Mistress Alice Ford.
How near is he, Mistress Page?

Mistress Margaret Page.
Hard by, at street end; he will be here anon.

Mistress Alice Ford.
I am undone! The knight is here.

Mistress Margaret Page.
Why then you are utterly sham'd, and he's but a dead man. What a woman are you? Away with him, away with him! Better shame than murder.

Mistress Alice Ford.
Which way should he go? How should I bestow him? Shall I put him into the basket again?

Enter Falstaff.

Sir John Falstaff.
No, I'll come no more i' th' basket. May I not go out ere he come?

Mistress Margaret Page.
Alas! Three of Master Ford's brothers watch the door with pistols, that none shall issue out; otherwise you might slip away ere he came. But what make you here?

Sir John Falstaff.
What shall I do? I'll creep up into the chimney.

Mistress Alice Ford.
There they always use to discharge their birding-pieces. Creep into the kill-hole.

Sir John Falstaff.
Where is it?

Mistress Alice Ford.
He will seek there, on my word. Neither press, coffer, chest, trunk, well, vault, but he hath an abstract for the remembrance of such places, and goes to them by his note. There is no hiding you in the house.

Sir John Falstaff.
I'll go out then.

Mistress Margaret Page.
If you go out in your own semblance, you die, Sir John—unless you go out disguis'd.

Mistress Alice Ford.
How might we disguise him?

Mistress Margaret Page.
Alas the day, I know not! There is no woman's gown big enough for him; otherwise he might put on a hat, a muffler, and a kerchief, and so escape.

Sir John Falstaff.
Good hearts, devise something; any extremity rather than a mischief.

Mistress Alice Ford.
My maid's aunt, the fat woman of Brainford, has a gown above.

Mistress Margaret Page.
On my word, it will serve him; she's as big as he is. And there's her thrumm'd hat and her muffler too. Run up, Sir John.

Mistress Alice Ford.
Go, go, sweet Sir John. Mistress Page and I will look some linen for your head.

Mistress Margaret Page.
Quick, quick! We'll come dress you straight. Put on the gown the while.

Exit Falstaff.

Mistress Alice Ford.
I would my husband would meet him in this shape. He cannot abide the old woman of Brainford. He swears she's a witch, forbade her my house, and hath threat'ned to beat her.

Mistress Margaret Page.
Heaven guide him to thy husband's cudgel; and the devil guide his cudgel afterwards!

Mistress Alice Ford.
But is my husband coming?

Mistress Margaret Page.
Ay, in good sadness, is he, and talks of the basket too, howsoever he hath had intelligence.

Mistress Alice Ford.
We'll try that; for I'll appoint my men to carry the basket again, to meet him at the door with it, as they did last time.

Mistress Margaret Page.
Nay, but he'll be here presently. Let's go dress him like the witch of Brainford.

Mistress Alice Ford.
I'll first direct my men what they shall do with the basket. Go up, I'll bring linen for him straight.

Exit.

Mistress Margaret Page.
Hang him, dishonest varlet! We cannot misuse him enough.
We'll leave a proof, by that which we will do,
Wives may be merry, and yet honest too:
We do not act that often jest and laugh;
'Tis old, but true: still swine eats all the draff.

Exit.
Enter Mistress Ford with two Servants.

Mistress Alice Ford.
Go, sirs, take the basket again on your shoulders. Your master is hard at door. If he bid you set it down, obey him. Quickly, dispatch.

Exit.

First Servant.
Come, come, take it up.

Second Servant.
Pray heaven it be not full of knight again.

First Servant.
I hope not, I had lief as bear so much lead.

Enter Ford, Page, Caius, Evans, Shallow.

Francis Ford.
Ay, but if it prove true, Master Page, have you any way then to unfool me again? Set down the basket, villain! Somebody call my wife. Youth in a basket! O you panderly rascals, there's a knot, a ging, a pack, a conspiracy against me. Now shall the devil be sham'd. What, wife, I say! Come, come forth! Behold what honest clothes you send forth to bleaching!

George Page.
Why, this passes, Master Ford. You are not to go loose any longer, you must be pinion'd.

Sir Hugh Evans.
Why, this is lunatics! This is mad as a mad dog!

Robert Shallow.
Indeed, Master Ford, this is not well indeed.

Francis Ford.
So say I too, sir.

Enter Mistress Ford.

Come hither, Mistress Ford, Mistress Ford, the honest woman, the modest wife, the virtuous creature, that hath the jealous fool to her husband! I suspect without cause, mistress, do I?

Mistress Alice Ford.
Heaven be my witness you do, and if you suspect me in any dishonesty.

Francis Ford.
Well said, brazen-face! Hold it out. Come forth, sirrah!

Pulling clothes out of the basket.

George Page.
This passes!

Mistress Alice Ford.
Are you not asham'd? Let the clothes alone.

Francis Ford.
I shall find you anon.

Sir Hugh Evans.
'Tis unreasonable! Will you take up your wive's clothes? Come away.

Francis Ford.
Empty the basket, I say!

Mistress Alice Ford.
Why, man, why?

Francis Ford.
Master Page, as I am a man, there was one convey'd out of my house yesterday in this basket. Why may not he be there again? In my house I am sure he is. My intelligence is true, my jealousy is reasonable. Pluck me out all the linen.

Mistress Alice Ford.
If you find a man there, he shall die a flea's death.

George Page.
Here's no man.

Robert Shallow.
By my fidelity, this is not well, Master Ford; this wrongs you.

Sir Hugh Evans.
Master Ford, you must pray, and not follow the imaginations of your own heart. This is jealousies.

Francis Ford.
Well, he's not here I seek for.

George Page.
No, nor no where else but in your brain.

Francis Ford.
Help to search my house this one time. If I find not what I seek, show no color for my extremity; let me forever be your table-sport. Let them say of me, "As jealous as Ford, that search'd a hollow walnut for his wive's leman." Satisfy me once more, once more search with me.

Mistress Alice Ford.
What ho, Mistress Page! Come you and the old woman down; my husband will come into the chamber.

Francis Ford.
Old woman? What old woman's that?

Mistress Alice Ford.
Why, it is my maid's aunt of Brainford.

Francis Ford.
A witch, a quean, an old cozening quean! Have I not forbid her my house? She comes of errands, does she? We are simple men, we do not know what's brought to pass under the profession of fortune-telling. She works by charms, by spells, by th' figure, and such daub'ry as this is, beyond our element; we know nothing. Come down, you witch, you hag you, come down, I say!

Mistress Alice Ford.
Nay, good, sweet husband! Good gentlemen, let him not strike the old woman.

Enter Falstaff disguised like an old woman, and Mistress Page with him.

Mistress Margaret Page.
Come, Mother Prat, come give me your hand.

Francis Ford.
I'll prat her. Out of my door, you witch, you rag, you baggage, you poulcat, you runnion! Out, out! I'll conjure you, I'll fortune-tell you!

Ford beats him, and he runs away.

Mistress Margaret Page.
Are you not asham'd? I think you have kill'd the poor woman.

Mistress Alice Ford.
Nay, he will do it.—'Tis a goodly credit for you.

Francis Ford.
Hang her, witch!

Sir Hugh Evans.
By yea and no, I think the oman is a witch indeed. I like not when a oman has a great peard. I spy a great peard under his muffler.

Francis Ford.
Will you follow, gentlemen? I beseech you follow; see but the issue of my jealousy. If I cry out thus upon no trail, never trust me when I open again.

George Page.
Let's obey his humor a little further. Come, gentlemen.

Exeunt Ford, Page, Shallow, Caius, and Evans.

Mistress Margaret Page.
Trust me, he beat him most pitifully.

Mistress Alice Ford.
Nay, by th' mass, that he did not; he beat him most unpitifully, methought.

Mistress Margaret Page.
I'll have the cudgel hallow'd and hung o'er the altar; it hath done meritorious service.

Mistress Alice Ford.
What think you? May we, with the warrant of womanhood and the witness of a good conscience, pursue him with any further revenge?

Mistress Margaret Page.
The spirit of wantonness is sure scar'd out of him. If the devil have him not in fee-simple, with fine and recovery, he will never, I think, in the way of waste, attempt us again.

Mistress Alice Ford.
Shall we tell our husbands how we have serv'd him?

Mistress Margaret Page.
Yes, by all means; if it be but to scrape the figures out of your husband's brains. If they can find in their hearts the poor unvirtuous fat knight shall be any further afflicted, we two will still be the ministers.

Mistress Alice Ford.
I'll warrant they'll have him publicly sham'd, and methinks there would be no period to the jest, should he not be publicly sham'd.

Mistress Margaret Page.
Come, to the forge with it, then shape it. I would not have things cool.

Exeunt.

Scene 3

A room in the Garter Inn.

(Host; Bardolph)

Bardolph tells the Host that his German guests, who have taken over the whole inn, want to use three of his horses. They have promised that a Duke will be visiting the next day. The Host agrees, planning to overcharge them.

Enter Host and Bardolph.

Bardolph.
Sir, the Germans desire to have three of your horses. The Duke himself will be tomorrow at court, and they are going to meet him.

Host of the Garter Inn.
What duke should that be comes so secretly? I hear not of him in the court. Let me speak with the gentlemen; they speak English?

Bardolph.
Ay, sir; I'll call them to you.

Host of the Garter Inn.
They shall have my horses, but I'll make them pay; I'll sauce them. They have had my house a week at command. I have turn'd away my other guests; they must come off. I'll sauce them, come.

Exeunt.

Scene 4

A room in Ford's house.

(Page; Ford; Mistress Margaret Page; Mistress Ford; Evans)

The wives have told the story to the men, who are delighted at the tale. Ford promises he will never be suspicious of his wife again. They plot together to prank Falstaff one more time, by getting him to disguise himself as Herne the Hunter, a creature from folklore with deer horns on his head who is said to haunt the

Act 4, Scene 4

park at midnight. Then the rest of them, dressed as fairies, will attack him; when the truth is known, he'll be a laughing stock. Evans promises to train his schoolchildren so they can be extra fairies. They intend to dress Anne as Queen of the Fairies, and Page plans to have Slender steal her away and marry her; Mistress Page, however, intends to have Caius do the same.

Enter Page, Ford, Mistress Page, Mistress Ford, and Evans.

Sir Hugh Evans.
'Tis one of the best discretions of a oman as ever I did look upon.

George Page.
And did he send you both these letters at an instant?

Mistress Margaret Page.
Within a quarter of an hour.

Francis Ford.
Pardon me, wife, henceforth do what thou wilt.
I rather will suspect the sun with cold
Than thee with wantonness. Now doth thy honor stand,
In him that was of late an heretic,
As firm as faith.

George Page.
          'Tis well, 'tis well, no more.
Be not as extreme in submission as in offense;
But let our plot go forward. Let our wives
Yet once again (to make us public sport)
Appoint a meeting with this old fat fellow,
Where we may take him, and disgrace him for it.

Francis Ford.
There is no better way than that they spoke of.

George Page.
How? To send him word they'll meet him in the park at midnight? Fie, fie, he'll never come.

Sir Hugh Evans.
You say he has been thrown in the rivers, and has been grievously peaten as an old oman. Methinks there should be terrors in him that he should not come; methinks his flesh is punish'd, he shall have no desires.

George Page.
So think I too.

Mistress Alice Ford.
Devise but how you'll use him when he comes,
And let us two devise to bring him thither.

Mistress Margaret Page.
There is an old tale goes, that Herne the Hunter
(Sometime a keeper here in Windsor forest)
Doth all the winter-time, at still midnight,
Walk round about an oak, with great ragg'd horns,
And there he blasts the tree, and takes the cattle,
And makes milch-kine yield blood, and shakes a chain
In a most hideous and dreadful manner.
You have heard of such a spirit, and well you know
The superstitious idle-headed eld
Receiv'd and did deliver to our age
This tale of Herne the Hunter for a truth.

George Page.
Why, yet there want not many that do fear
In deep of night to walk by this Herne's oak.
But what of this?

Mistress Alice Ford.
          Marry, this is our device:
That Falstaff at that oak shall meet with us,
Disguis'd like Herne, with huge horns on his head.

George Page.
Well, let it not be doubted but he'll come,
And in this shape when you have brought him thither,
What shall be done with him? What is your plot?

Mistress Margaret Page.
That likewise have we thought upon, and thus:
Nan Page (my daughter) and my little son,
And three or four more of their growth, we'll dress
Like urchins, ouphes, and fairies, green and white,
With rounds of waxen tapers on their heads,
And rattles in their hands. Upon a sudden,
As Falstaff, she, and I are newly met,
Let them from forth a sawpit rush at once
With some diffused song. Upon their sight,
We two in great amazedness will fly;
Then let them all encircle him about,
And fairy-like to pinch the unclean knight;
And ask him why, that hour of fairy revel,
In their so sacred paths he dares to tread
In shape profane.

Mistress Alice Ford.
    And till he tell the truth,
Let the supposed fairies pinch him sound,
And burn him with their tapers.

Mistress Margaret Page.
    The truth being known,
We'll all present ourselves; dis-horn the spirit,
And mock him home to Windsor.

Francis Ford.
    The children must
Be practic'd well to this, or they'll nev'r do't.

Sir Hugh Evans.
I will teach the children their behaviors; and I will be like a jack-an-apes also, to burn the knight with my taber.

Francis Ford.
That will be excellent. I'll go buy them vizards.

Mistress Margaret Page.
My Nan shall be the queen of all the fairies,
Finely attired in a robe of white.

George Page.
That silk will I go buy.

Aside.

And in that time
Shall Master Slender steal my Nan away,
And marry her at Eton.—Go, send to Falstaff straight.

Francis Ford.
Nay, I'll to him again in name of Brook;
He'll tell me all his purpose. Sure he'll come.

Mistress Margaret Page.
Fear not you that. Go get us properties
And tricking for our fairies.

Sir Hugh Evans.
Let us about it. It is admirable pleasures and fery honest knaveries.

Exeunt Page, Ford, and Evans.

Mistress Margaret Page.
Go, Mistress Ford,
Send Quickly to Sir John, to know his mind.

Exit Mrs. Ford.

I'll to the doctor, he hath my good will,
And none but he, to marry with Nan Page.
That Slender (though well landed) is an idiot;
And he my husband best of all affects.
The doctor is well money'd, and his friends
Potent at court. He, none but he, shall have her,
Though twenty thousand worthier come to crave her.

Exit.

Scene 5

A room in the Garter Inn.

(Host; Simple; Falstaff; Bardolph; Evans; Caius; Mistress Quickly)

Simple comes to speak to Falstaff about a chain that Nym cheated Slender out of. The Host doesn't think Falstaff is there, since he only saw an old fat woman go up, but Falstaff emerges from his room to answer Simple's questions. Bardolph arrives to warn the Host that the Germans have stolen the horses. The Host doesn't want to believe him until Evans arrives to warn him about a gang of German conmen, and Caius shows up to tell him that there is no German Duke at the court. The Host rushes out to try and track the thieves down. Mistress Quickly brings Falstaff the letter asking him to go to the park that night.

Enter Host, Simple.

Host of the Garter Inn.
What wouldst thou have, boor? What, thick-skin? Speak, breathe, discuss; brief, short, quick, snap.

Peter Simple.
Marry, sir, I come to speak with Sir John Falstaff from Master Slender.

Host of the Garter Inn.
There's his chamber, his house, his castle, his standing-bed and truckle-bed; 'tis painted about with the story of the Prodigal, fresh and new. Go, knock and call; he'll speak like an Anthropophaginian unto thee. Knock, I say.

Peter Simple.
There's an old woman, a fat woman, gone up into his chamber. I'll be so bold as stay, sir, till she come down. I come to speak with her indeed.

Act 4, Scene 5

Host of the Garter Inn.
Ha? A fat woman? The knight may be robb'd. I'll call. Bully-knight! Bully Sir John! Speak from thy lungs military. Art thou there? It is thine host, thine Ephesian, calls.

Sir John Falstaff.

Above.

How now, mine host?

Host of the Garter Inn.
Here's a Bohemian-Tartar tarries the coming down of thy fat woman. Let her descend, bully, let her descend; my chambers are honorable. Fie, privacy? Fie!

Enter Falstaff.

Sir John Falstaff.
There was, mine host, an old fat woman even now with me, but she's gone.

Peter Simple.
Pray you, sir, was't not the wise woman of Brainford?

Sir John Falstaff.
Ay, marry, was it, mussel-shell, what would you with her?

Peter Simple.
My master, sir, my Master Slender, sent to her, seeing her go thorough the streets, to know, sir, whether one Nym, sir, that beguil'd him of a chain, had the chain or no.

Sir John Falstaff.
I spake with the old woman about it.

Peter Simple.
And what says she, I pray, sir?

Sir John Falstaff.
Marry, she says that the very same man that beguil'd Master Slender of his chain cozen'd him of it.

Peter Simple.
I would I could have spoken with the woman herself. I had other things to have spoken with her too from him.

Sir John Falstaff.
What are they? Let us know.

Host of the Garter Inn.
Ay; come; quick.

Peter Simple.
I may not conceal them, sir.

Host of the Garter Inn.
Conceal them, or thou diest.

Peter Simple.
Why, sir, they were nothing but about Mistress Anne Page, to know if it were my master's fortune to have her or no.

Sir John Falstaff.
'Tis, 'tis his fortune.

Peter Simple.
What, sir?

Sir John Falstaff.
To have her, or no. Go; say the woman told me so.

Peter Simple.
May I be bold to say so, sir?

Sir John Falstaff.
Ay, sir; like who more bold?

Peter Simple.
I thank your worship. I shall make my master glad with these tidings.

Exit.

Host of the Garter Inn.
Thou art clerkly, thou art clerkly, Sir John. Was there a wise woman with thee?

Sir John Falstaff.
Ay, that there was, mine host, one that hath taught me more wit than ever I learn'd before in my life; and I paid nothing for it neither, but was paid for my learning.

Enter Bardolph.

Bardolph.
Out alas, sir, cozenage! Mere cozenage.

Host of the Garter Inn.
Where be my horses? Speak well of them, varletto.

Bardolph.
Run away with the cozeners; for so soon as I came beyond Eton, they threw me off from behind one of them, in a slough of mire; and set spurs and away, like three German devils, three Doctor Faustuses.

Host of the Garter Inn.
They are gone but to meet the Duke, villain, do not say they be fled. Germans are honest men.

Enter Evans.

Sir Hugh Evans.
Where is mine host?

Host of the Garter Inn.
What is the matter, sir?

Sir Hugh Evans.
Have a care of your entertainments. There is a friend of mine come to town, tells me there is three cozen-germans that has cozen'd all the hosts of Readins, of Maidenhead, of Colebrook, of horses and money. I tell you for good will, look you. You are wise and full of gibes and vlouting-stocks, and 'tis not convenient you should be cozen'd. Fare you well.

Exit.
Enter Caius.

Doctor Caius.
Vere is mine host de Jarteer?

Host of the Garter Inn.
Here, Master Doctor, in perplexity and doubtful dilemma.

Doctor Caius.
I cannot tell vat is dat; but it is tell-a me dat you make grand preparation for a duke de Jamany. By my trot, dere is no duke that the court is know to come. I tell you for good will; adieu.

Exit.

Host of the Garter Inn.
Hue and cry, villain, go! Assist me, knight, I am undone! Fly, run, hue and cry, villain! I am undone!

Exeunt Host and Bardolph.

Sir John Falstaff.
I would all the world might be cozen'd, for I have been cozen'd and beaten too. If it should come to the ear of the court, how I have been transform'd, and how my transformation hath been wash'd and cudgell'd, they would melt me out of my fat drop by drop, and liquor fishermen's boots with me. I warrant they would whip me with their fine wits till I were as crestfall'n as a dried pear. I never prosper'd since I forswore myself at primero. Well, if my wind were but long enough to say my prayers, I would repent.

Enter Mistress Quickly.

Now? Whence come you?

Mistress Quickly.
From the two parties, forsooth.

Sir John Falstaff.
The devil take one party and his dam the other! And so they shall be both bestow'd. I have suffer'd more for their sakes—more than the villainous inconstancy of man's disposition is able to bear.

Mistress Quickly.
And have not they suffer'd? Yes, I warrant; speciously one of them. Mistress Ford, good heart, is beaten black and blue, that you cannot see a white spot about her.

Sir John Falstaff.
What tellest thou me of black and blue? I was beaten myself into all the colors of the rainbow; and I was like to be apprehended for the witch of Brainford. But that my admirable dexterity of wit, my counterfeiting the action of an old woman, deliver'd me, the knave constable had set me i' th' stocks, i' th' common stocks, for a witch.

Mistress Quickly.
Sir—let me speak with you in your chamber. You shall hear how things go, and, I warrant, to your content. Here is a letter will say somewhat. Good hearts, what ado here is to bring you together! Sure, one of you does not serve heaven well, that you are so cross'd.

Sir John Falstaff.
Come up into my chamber.

Exeunt.

Scene 6

Another room in the Garter Inn.

(Fenton; Host)

Fenton offers to pay the Host even more than he lost when his horses were stolen as long as he will have a priest ready between twelve and one. He and Anne have decided that she will slip away with him instead of either Slender or Caius. The Host agrees.

Enter Fenton, Host.

Host of the Garter Inn.
Master Fenton, talk not to me, my mind is heavy; I will give over all.

Fenton.
Yet hear me speak. Assist me in my purpose,
And (as I am a gentleman) I'll give thee
A hundred pound in gold more than your loss.

Host of the Garter Inn.
I will hear you, Master Fenton, and I will (at the least) keep your counsel.

Fenton.
From time to time I have acquainted you
With the dear love I bear to fair Anne Page,
Who mutually hath answer'd my affection
(So far forth as herself might be her chooser)
Even to my wish. I have a letter from her
Of such contents as you will wonder at;
The mirth whereof so larded with my matter,
That neither, singly, can be manifested
Without the show of both. Fat Falstaff
Hath a great scene; the image of the jest
I'll show you here at large. Hark, good mine host:
Tonight at Herne's oak, just 'twixt twelve and one,
Must my sweet Nan present the Fairy Queen;
The purpose why, is here; in which disguise,
While other jests are something rank on foot,
Her father hath commanded her to slip
Away with Slender, and with him at Eton
Immediately to marry. She hath consented.
Now, sir,
Her mother (even strong against that match
And firm for Doctor Caius) hath appointed
That he shall likewise shuffle her away,
While other sports are tasking of their minds,
And at the dean'ry, where a priest attends,
Straight marry her. To this her mother's plot
She (seemingly obedient) likewise hath
Made promise to the doctor. Now, thus it rests:
Her father means she shall be all in white;
And in that habit, when Slender sees his time
To take her by the hand and bid her go,
She shall go with him. Her mother hath intended
(The better to denote her to the doctor,
For they must all be mask'd and vizarded)
That quaint in green she shall be loose enrob'd,
With ribands pendant, flaring 'bout her head;
And when the doctor spies his vantage ripe,
To pinch her by the hand, and on that token,
The maid hath given consent to go with him.

Host of the Garter Inn.
Which means she to deceive, father or mother?

Fenton.
Both, my good host, to go along with me.
And here it rests, that you'll procure the vicar
To stay for me at church, 'twixt twelve and one,
And in the lawful name of marrying,
To give our hearts united ceremony.

Host of the Garter Inn.
Well, husband your device; I'll to the vicar.
Bring you the maid, you shall not lack a priest.

Fenton.
So shall I evermore be bound to thee;
Besides, I'll make a present recompense.

Exeunt.

Act 5
Scene 1

A room in the Garter Inn.

(Falstaff; Mistress Quickly; Ford)

Falstaff sends Mistress Quickly off to find the bits of costume he'll need. Ford comes in disguised as Brook, and Falstaff tells him he'll be in the park at midnight.

Enter Falstaff, Mistress Quickly.

Sir John Falstaff.
Prithee no more prattling. Go, I'll hold. This is the third time; I hope good luck lies in odd numbers. Away, go. They say there is divinity in odd numbers, either in nativity, chance, or death. Away!

Mistress Quickly.
I'll provide you a chain, and I'll do what I can to get you a pair of horns.

Sir John Falstaff.
Away, I say, time wears, hold up your head and mince.

Exit Mrs. Quickly.
Enter Ford disguised.

How now, Master Brook? Master Brook, the matter will be known tonight, or never. Be you in the park about midnight, at Herne's oak, and you shall see wonders.

Francis Ford.
Went you not to her yesterday, sir, as you told me you had appointed?

Sir John Falstaff.
I went to her, Master Brook, as you see, like a poor old man, but I came from her, Master Brook, like a poor old woman. That same knave Ford, her husband, hath the finest mad devil of jealousy in him, Master Brook, that ever govern'd frenzy. I will tell you—he beat me grievously, in the shape of a woman; for in the shape of man, Master Brook, I fear not Goliath with a weaver's beam, because I know also life is a shuttle. I am in haste, go along with me, I'll tell you all, Master Brook. Since I pluck'd geese, play'd truant, and whipt top, I knew not what 'twas to be beaten till lately. Follow me, I'll tell you strange things of this knave Ford, on whom tonight I will be reveng'd, and I will deliver his wife into your hand. Follow. Strange things in hand, Master Brook! Follow.

Exeunt.

Scene 2

Windsor Park.

(Page; Shallow; Slender)

Page, Shallow, and Slender hide themselves in the park ditch, double-checking that Slender knows how he'll recognize Anne, who will be dressed in white.

Enter Page, Shallow, Slender.

George Page.
Come, come; we'll couch i' th' castle-ditch till we see the light of our fairies. Remember, son Slender, my daughter.

Abraham Slender.
Ay, forsooth, I have spoke with her, and we have a nay-word how to know one another. I come to her in white, and cry "mum"; she cries "budget"; and by that we know one another.

Robert Shallow.
That's good too; but what needs either your "mum" or her "budget"? The white will decipher her well enough. It hath struck ten a' clock.

George Page.
The night is dark, light and spirits will become it well. Heaven prosper our sport! No man means evil but the devil, and we shall know him by his horns. Let's away; follow me.

Exeunt.

Scene 3

A street leading to the Windsor Park.

(Mistress Margaret Page; Mistress Ford; Caius)

Mistress Page reminds Dr. Caius that Anne will be dressed in green that night, so that he may recognize her and make off with her. She and Mistress Ford make their way to the oak, having checked that everybody in is place.

Enter Mistress Page, Mistress Ford, Caius.

Mistress Margaret Page.
Master Doctor, my daughter is in green. When you see your time, take her by the hand, away with her to the deanery, and dispatch it quickly. Go before into the park; we two must go together.

Doctor Caius.
I know vat I have to do. Adieu.

Mistress Margaret Page.
Fare you well, sir.

Exit Caius.

My husband will not rejoice so much at the abuse of Falstaff as he will chafe at the doctor's marrying my daughter. But 'tis no matter; better a little chiding than a great deal of heart-break.

Mistress Alice Ford.
Where is Nan now, and her troop of fairies, and the Welsh devil Hugh?

Mistress Margaret Page.
They are all couch'd in a pit hard by Herne's oak, with obscur'd lights; which, at the very instant of Falstaff's and our meeting, they will at once display to the night.

Mistress Alice Ford.
That cannot choose but amaze him.

Mistress Margaret Page.
If he be not amaz'd, he will be mock'd; if he be amaz'd, he will every way be mock'd.

Mistress Alice Ford.
We'll betray him finely.

Mistress Margaret Page.
Against such lewdsters, and their lechery,
Those that betray them do no treachery.

Mistress Alice Ford.
The hour draws on. To the oak, to the oak!

Exeunt.

Scene 4
Windsor Park.

(Evans; Children of Windsor; Boy; Postmaster's Boy)

Hugh Evans, dressed as a satyr, marshals his procession of schoolchildren disguised as fairies, reminding them of their role. (1 line)

Enter Evans like a satyr and others as fairies.

Sir Hugh Evans.
Trib, trib, fairies; come, and remember your parts. Be pold, I pray you. Follow me into the pit, and when I give the watch-ords, do as I pid you. Come, come, trib, trib.

Exeunt.

Scene 5
Another part of Windsor Park.

(Falstaff; Mistress Margaret Page; Mistress Ford; Evans; Pistol; Mistress Quickly; Doctor Caius; Slender; Fenton; Page; Ford; Children of Windsor; Boy; Postmaster's Boy; Anne Page)

The disguised Falstaff compares himself to Jupiter and all the transformations he made in the name of love. Both Mistress Ford and Mistress Page arrive, and he urges them to divide him up when they suddenly hear a sound of horns. The women fly in pretended fear. Falstaff is confused, and then terrified as he suddenly finds himself surrounded by fairies. When they find him, they begin to pinch him and burn him with their candles while preaching against lechery. During this, Caius exits with a fairy dressed in green and Slender with a fairy dressed in white, while Fenton and Anne sneak off together. The horns sound again and the "fairies" run off. Falstaff finds himself faced with the two wives and their husbands, who mock him. Falstaff claims he realized that those weren't actual fairies. They point out all his flaws to him, which in the end he can't help but take good-naturedly. Page invites him to come have a drink and laugh at his wife, since he's managed to play a trick on her himself — getting Anne married to Slender. But Slender comes in protesting that he's just been almost married to a boy. Mistress Page explains that it's her fault and that she set this up so that Anne could marry Caius, but Caius enters to complain that he has been married to a boy. There is momentary confusion, until Fenton and Anne enter together, and beg forgiveness. Since they are married, her parents make the best of it. Mistress Page suggests that they all go home and have a good laugh over the events of the past few days, Sir John included.

Enter Falstaff with a buck's head upon him.

Sir John Falstaff.
The Windsor bell hath struck twelve; the minute draws on. Now the hot-bloodied gods assist me! Remember, Jove, thou wast a bull for thy Europa, love set on thy horns. O powerful love, that in some respects makes a beast a man; in some other, a man a beast. You were also, Jupiter, a swan for the love of Leda. O omnipotent love, how near the god drew to the complexion of a goose! A fault done first in the form of a beast (O Jove, a beastly fault!) and then another fault in the semblance of a fowl—think on't, Jove, a foul fault! When gods have hot backs, what shall poor men do? For me, I am here a Windsor stag, and the fattest, I think, i' th' forest. Send me a cool rut-time, Jove, or who can blame me to piss my tallow? Who comes here? My doe?

Enter Mistress Page, Mistress Ford.

Mistress Alice Ford.
Sir John? Art thou there, my deer? My male deer?

Sir John Falstaff.
My doe with the black scut? Let the sky rain potatoes; let it thunder to the tune of "Green-sleeves," hail kissing-comfits, and snow eringoes; let there come a tempest of provocation, I will shelter me here.

Embracing her.

Mistress Alice Ford.
Mistress Page is come with me, sweet heart.

Sir John Falstaff.
Divide me like a brib'd-buck, each a haunch. I will keep my sides to myself, my shoulders for the fellow of this walk—and my horns I bequeath your husbands. Am I a woodman, ha? Speak I like Herne the hunter? Why, now is Cupid a child of conscience, he makes restitution. As I am a true spirit, welcome!

There is a noise of horns.

Mistress Margaret Page.
Alas, what noise?

Mistress Alice Ford.
Heaven forgive our sins!

Sir John Falstaff.
What should this be?

Both Mistress Ford and Mistress Page.
Away, away!

The two women run away.

Sir John Falstaff.
I think the devil will not have me damn'd, lest the oil that's in me should set hell on fire; he would never else cross me thus.

Enter Evans like a satyr, Anne Page and Boys dressed like fairies, Pistol as Hobgoblin, Mistress Quickly like the Queen of Fairies.
They sing a song about him and afterward speak.

Mistress Quickly.
Fairies, black, grey, green, and white,
You moonshine revelers, and shades of night,
You orphan heirs of fixed destiny,
Attend your office and your quality.
Crier Hobgoblin, make the fairy Oyes.

Pistol.
Elves, list your names; silence, you aery toys!
Cricket, to Windsor chimneys shalt thou leap;
Where fires thou find'st unrak'd and hearths unswept,
There pinch the maids as blue as bilberry;
Our radiant Queen hates sluts and sluttery.

Sir John Falstaff.
They are fairies, he that speaks to them shall die.
I'll wink and couch; no man their works must eye.

Lies down upon his face.

Sir Hugh Evans.
Where's Bede? Go you, and where you find a maid
That ere she sleep has thrice her prayers said,
Raise up the organs of her fantasy,
Sleep she as sound as careless infancy;
But those as sleep and think not on their sins,
Pinch them, arms, legs, backs, shoulders, sides, and shins.

Mistress Quickly.
About, about;
Search Windsor Castle, elves, within and out.
Strew good luck, ouphes, on every sacred room,
That it may stand till the perpetual doom
In state as wholesome as in state 'tis fit,
Worthy the owner, and the owner it.
The several chairs of order look you scour
With juice of balm and every precious flow'r;
Each fair installment, coat, and sev'ral crest,
With loyal blazon, evermore be blest!
And nightly, meadow-fairies, look you sing,
Like to the Garter's compass, in a ring.
Th' expressure that it bears, green let it be,
More fertile-fresh than all the field to see;
And "Honi soit qui mal y pense" write
In em'rald tuffs, flow'rs purple, blue, and white,
Like sapphire, pearl, and rich embroidery,
Buckled below fair knighthood's bending knee:
Fairies use flow'rs for their charactery.
Away, disperse! But till 'tis one a' clock,

Our dance of custom, round about the oak
Of Herne the hunter, let us not forget.

Sir Hugh Evans.
Pray you lock hand in hand; yourselves in order set;
And twenty glow-worms shall our lanterns be,
To guide our measure round about the tree.
But stay, I smell a man of middle-earth.

Sir John Falstaff.
Heavens defend me from that Welsh fairy, lest he transform me to a piece of cheese!

Pistol.
Vild worm, thou wast o'erlook'd even in thy birth.

Mistress Quickly.
With trial-fire touch me his finger-end.
If he be chaste, the flame will back descend
And turn him to no pain; but if he start,
It is the flesh of a corrupted heart.

Pistol.
A trial, come.

Sir Hugh Evans.
Come, will this wood take fire?

They put the tapers to his fingers, and he starts.

Sir John Falstaff.
O, O, O!

Mistress Quickly.
Corrupt, corrupt, and tainted in desire!
About him, fairies, sing a scornful rhyme,
And as you trip, still pinch him to your time.

The Song

Fie on sinful fantasy!
Fie on lust and luxury!
Lust is but a bloody fire,
Kindled with unchaste desire,
Fed in heart, whose flames aspire,
As thoughts do blow them, higher and higher.
Pinch him, fairies, mutually!
Pinch him for his villainy!
Pinch him, and burn him, and turn him about,
Till candles, and starlight, and moonshine be out.

Here they pinch him and sing about him. And the Doctor Caius comes one way, and steals away a boy in green; and Slender another way; he takes a boy in white; and Fenton steals Mistress Anne Page. And a noise of hunting is made within; and all the fairies run away. Falstaff pulls off his buck's head, and rises up.
Enter Page, Ford, Mistress Page, and Mistress Ford.

George Page.
Nay, do not fly, I think we have watch'd you now.
Will none but Herne the hunter serve your turn?

Mistress Margaret Page.
I pray you come, hold up the jest no higher.
Now, good Sir John, how like you Windsor wives?
See you these, husband? Do not these fair yokes
Become the forest better than the town?

Francis Ford.
Now, sir, who's a cuckold now? Master Brook, Falstaff's a knave, a cuckoldly knave; here are his horns, Master Brook; and, Master Brook, he hath enjoy'd nothing of Ford's but his buck-basket his cudgel, and twenty pounds of money, which must be paid to Master Brook. His horses are arrested for it, Master Brook.

Mistress Alice Ford.
Sir John, we have had ill luck; we could never meet. I will never take you for my love again, but I will always count you my deer.

Sir John Falstaff.
I do begin to perceive that I am made an ass.

Francis Ford.
Ay, and an ox too; both the proofs are extant.

Sir John Falstaff.
And these are not fairies? I was three or four times in the thought they were not fairies, and yet the guiltiness of my mind, the sudden surprise of my powers, drove the grossness of the foppery into a receiv'd belief, in despite of the teeth of all rhyme and reason, that they were fairies. See now how wit may be made a Jack-a-Lent, when 'tis upon ill employment!

Sir Hugh Evans.
Sir John Falstaff, serve Got, and leave your desires, and fairies will not pinse you.

Francis Ford.
Well said, fairy Hugh.

Sir Hugh Evans.
And leave you your jealousies too, I pray you.

Francis Ford.
I will never mistrust my wife again, till thou art able to woo her in good English.

Sir John Falstaff.
Have I laid my brain in the sun and dried it, that it wants matter to prevent so gross o'erreaching as this? Am I ridden with a Welsh goat too? Shall I have a coxcomb of frieze? 'Tis time I were chok'd with a piece of toasted cheese.

Sir Hugh Evans.
Seese is not good to give putter; your belly is all putter.

Sir John Falstaff.
"Seese" and "putter"! Have I liv'd to stand at the taunt of one that makes fritters of English? This is enough to be the decay of lust and late-walking through the realm.

Mistress Margaret Page.
Why, Sir John, do you think, though we would have thrust virtue out of our hearts by the head and shoulders, and have given ourselves without scruple to hell, that ever the devil could have made you our delight?

Francis Ford.
What, a hodge-pudding? A bag of flax?

Mistress Margaret Page.
A puff'd man?

George Page.
Old, cold, wither'd, and of intolerable entrails?

Francis Ford.
And one that is as slanderous as Satan?

George Page.
And as poor as Job?

Francis Ford.
And as wicked as his wife?

Sir Hugh Evans.
And given to fornications, and to taverns, and sack, and wine, and metheglins, and to drinkings and swearings and starings, pribbles and prabbles?

Sir John Falstaff.
Well, I am your theme. You have the start of me, I am dejected. I am not able to answer the Welsh flannel; ignorance itself is a plummet o'er me. Use me as you will.

Francis Ford.
Marry, sir, we'll bring you to Windsor, to one Master Brook that you have cozen'd of money, to whom you should have been a pander. Over and above that you have suffer'd, I think to repay that money will be a biting affliction.

George Page.
Yet be cheerful, knight. Thou shalt eat a posset tonight at my house, where I will desire thee to laugh at my wife, that now laughs at thee. Tell her Master Slender hath married her daughter.

Mistress Margaret Page.

Aside.

Doctors doubt that. If Anne Page be my daughter, she is, by this, Doctor Caius' wife.

Enter Slender.

Abraham Slender.
Whoa ho, ho! Father Page!

George Page.
Son? How now? How now, son? Have you dispatch'd?

Abraham Slender.
Dispatch'd? I'll make the best in Gloucestershire know on't. Would I were hang'd la, else!

George Page.
Of what, son?

Abraham Slender.
I came yonder at Eton to marry Mistress Anne Page, and she's a great lubberly boy. If it had not been i' th' church, I would have swing'd him, or he should have swing'd me. If I did not think it had been Anne Page, would I might never stir!—and 'tis a postmaster's boy.

George Page.
Upon my life then, you took the wrong.

Abraham Slender.
When need you tell me that? I think so, when I took a boy for a girl. If I had been married to him (for all he was in woman's apparel) I would not have had him.

George Page.
Why, this is your own folly. Did not I tell you how you should know my daughter by her garments?

Abraham Slender.
I went to her in white and cried "mum," and she cried "budget," as Anne and I had appointed, and yet it was not Anne, but a postmaster's boy.

Mistress Margaret Page.
Good George, be not angry. I knew of your purpose; turn'd my daughter into green; and indeed she is now with the Doctor at the dean'ry, and there married.

Enter Caius.

Doctor Caius.
Vere is Mistress Page? By gar, I am cozen'd. I ha' married oon garsoon, a boy; oon pesant, by gar. A boy! It is not Anne Page. By gar, I am cozen'd.

Mistress Margaret Page.
Why? Did you take her in green?

Doctor Caius.
Ay, be-gar, and 'tis a boy. Be-gar, I'll raise all Windsor.

Exit.

Francis Ford.
This is strange. Who hath got the right Anne?

George Page.
My heart misgives me. Here comes Master Fenton.

Enter Fenton and Anne Page.

How now, Master Fenton?

Mistress Anne Page.
Pardon, good father! Good my mother, pardon!

George Page.
Now, mistress, how chance you went not with Master Slender?

Mistress Margaret Page.
Why went you not with Master Doctor, maid?

Fenton.
You do amaze her. Hear the truth of it.
You would have married her most shamefully,
Where there was no proportion held in love.
The truth is, she and I (long since contracted)
Are now so sure that nothing can dissolve us.
Th' offense is holy that she hath committed,
And this deceit loses the name of craft,
Of disobedience, or unduteous title,
Since therein she doth evitate and shun
A thousand irreligious cursed hours
Which forced marriage would have brought upon her.

Francis Ford.
Stand not amaz'd; here is no remedy.
In love, the heavens themselves do guide the state;
Money buys lands, and wives are sold by fate.

Sir John Falstaff.
I am glad, though you have ta'en a special stand to strike at me, that your arrow hath glanc'd.

George Page.
Well, what remedy? Fenton, heaven give thee joy!
What cannot be eschew'd must be embrac'd.

Sir John Falstaff.
When night-dogs run, all sorts of deer are chas'd.

Mistress Margaret Page.
Well, I will muse no further. Master Fenton,
Heaven give you many, many merry days!
Good husband, let us every one go home,
And laugh this sport o'er by a country fire—
Sir John and all.

Francis Ford.
            Let it be so. Sir John,
To Master Brook you yet shall hold your word,
For he tonight shall lie with Mistress Ford.

Exeunt.

Love's Labour's Lost

Act 1

Scene 1

The King of Navarre's park.

(King of Navarre; Berowne; Longaville; Dumaine; Constable Dull; Costard)

The King of Navarre has resolved to live an ascetic life of study for three years, away from the court and in the company of his three closest friends, Longaville, Dumaine, and Berowne, though the latter is rather skeptical about the vows they must take, particularly that of seeing no woman — not least because the Princess of France is coming on an embassy, and the King (who had quite forgotten about her visit) will have to see her. Still, he signs the pledge. The lords intend to amuse themselves by keeping around an affected Spaniard, Don Armado, as well as the uneducated peasant Costard. At this point a letter is brought in from Armado, accusing Costard of having infringed the rules about women, which apply to everyone within a mile of the court. Costard does not deny having been caught in flagrante with Jaquenetta, and he is condemned to a week of fasting while being guarded by Armado.

Enter Ferdinand, King of Navarre, Berowne, Longaville, and Dumaine.

Ferdinand, King of Navarre.
Let fame, that all hunt after in their lives,
Live regist'red upon our brazen tombs,
And then grace us in the disgrace of death;
When spite of cormorant devouring Time,
Th' endeavor of this present breath may buy
That honor which shall bate his scythe's keen edge,
And make us heirs of all eternity.
Therefore, brave conquerors—for so you are,
That war against your own affections
And the huge army of the world's desires—
Our late edict shall strongly stand in force:
Navarre shall be the wonder of the world;
Our court shall be a little academe,
Still and contemplative in living art.
You three, Berowne, Dumaine, and Longaville,
Have sworn for three years' term to live with me,
My fellow scholars, and to keep those statutes
That are recorded in this schedule here.
Your oaths are pass'd, and now subscribe your names,
That his own hand may strike his honor down
That violates the smallest branch herein.
If you are arm'd to do, as sworn to do,
Subscribe to your deep oaths, and keep it too.

Longaville.
I am resolved, 'tis but a three years' fast:
The mind shall banquet, though the body pine;
Fat paunches have lean pates; and dainty bits
Make rich the ribs, but bankrupt quite the wits.

Dumaine.
My loving lord, Dumaine is mortified:
The grosser manner of these world's delights
He throws upon the gross world's baser slaves;
To love, to wealth, to pomp, I pine and die,
With all these living in philosophy.

Berowne.
I can but say their protestation over:
So much, dear liege, I have already sworn,
That is, to live and study here three years.
But there are other strict observances:
As not to see a woman in that term,
Which I hope well is not enrolled there;
And one day in a week to touch no food,

And but one meal on every day beside,
The which I hope is not enrolled there;
And then to sleep but three hours in the night,
And not be seen to wink of all the day—
When I was wont to think no harm all night,
And make a dark night too of half the day—
Which I hope well is not enrolled there.
O, these are barren tasks, too hard to keep,
Not to see ladies, study, fast, not sleep.

Ferdinand, King of Navarre.
Your oath is pass'd to pass away from these.

Berowne.
Let me say no, my liege, and if you please:
I only swore to study with your Grace,
And stay here in your court for three years' space.

Longaville.
You swore to that, Berowne, and to the rest.

Berowne.
By yea and nay, sir, then I swore in jest.
What is the end of study, let me know.

Ferdinand, King of Navarre.
Why, that to know which else we should not know.

Berowne.
Things hid and barr'd (you mean) from common sense.

Ferdinand, King of Navarre.
Ay, that is study's godlike recompense.

Berowne.
Com' on then, I will swear to study so,
To know the thing I am forbid to know:
As thus—to study where I well may dine,
When I to feast expressly am forbid;
Or study where to meet some mistress fine,
When mistresses from common sense are hid;
Or having sworn too hard-a-keeping oath,
Study to break it and not break my troth.
If study's gain be thus, and this be so,
Study knows that which yet it doth not know.
Swear me to this, and I will ne'er say no.

Ferdinand, King of Navarre.
These be the stops that hinder study quite,
And train our intellects to vain delight.

Berowne.
Why? All delights are vain, but that most vain
Which, with pain purchas'd, doth inherit pain:
As, painfully to pore upon a book
To seek the light of truth, while truth the while
Doth falsely blind the eyesight of his look.
Light, seeking light, doth light of light beguile;
So ere you find where light in darkness lies,
Your light grows dark by losing of your eyes.
Study me how to please the eye indeed
By fixing it upon a fairer eye,
Who dazzling so, that eye shall be his heed,
And give him light that it was blinded by.
Study is like the heaven's glorious sun,
That will not be deep search'd with saucy looks;
Small have continual plodders ever won,
Save base authority from others' books.
These earthly godfathers of heaven's lights,
That give a name to every fixed star,
Have no more profit of their shining nights
Than those that walk and wot not what they are.
Too much to know is to know nought but fame;
And every godfather can give a name.

Ferdinand, King of Navarre.
How well he's read, to reason against reading!

Dumaine.
Proceeded well, to stop all good proceeding!

Longaville.
He weeds the corn and still lets grow the weeding.

Berowne.
The spring is near when green geese are a-breeding.

Dumaine.
How follows that?

Berowne.
                    Fit in his place and time.

Dumaine.
In reason nothing.

Berowne.
                    Something then in rhyme.

Ferdinand, King of Navarre.
Berowne is like an envious sneaping frost
That bites the first-born infants of the spring.

Berowne.
Well, say I am, why should proud summer boast
Before the birds have any cause to sing?
Why should I joy in any abortive birth?
At Christmas I no more desire a rose
Than wish a snow in May's new-fangled shows;
But like of each thing that in season grows.
So you, to study now it is too late,
Climb o'er the house to unlock the little gate.

Ferdinand, King of Navarre.
Well, sit you out; go home, Berowne; adieu.

Berowne.
No, my good lord, I have sworn to stay with you;
And though I have for barbarism spoke more
Than for that angel knowledge you can say,
Yet, confident, I'll keep what I have sworn,
And bide the penance of each three years' day.
Give me the paper, let me read the same,
And to the strictest decrees I'll write my name.

Ferdinand, King of Navarre.
How well this yielding rescues thee from shame!

Berowne.

Reads.

"Item, That no woman shall come within a mile of my court"—Hath this been proclaim'd?

Longaville.
Four days ago.

Berowne.
Let's see the penalty.

Reads.

"—on pain of losing her tongue." Who devis'd this penalty?

Longaville.
Marry, that did I.

Berowne.
Sweet lord, and why?

Longaville.
To fright them hence with that dread penalty.

Berowne.
A dangerous law against gentility.

Reads.

"Item, If any man be seen to talk with a woman within the term of three years, he shall endure such public shame as the rest of the court can possible devise."
This article, my liege, yourself must break,
For well you know here comes in embassy
The French king's daughter with yourself to speak—
A maid of grace and complete majesty—
About surrender up of Aquitaine
To her decrepit, sick, and bedred father;
Therefore this article is made in vain,
Or vainly comes th' admired Princess hither.

Ferdinand, King of Navarre.
What say you, lords? Why, this was quite forgot.

Berowne.
So study evermore is overshot:
While it doth study to have what it would,
It doth forget to do the thing it should;
And when it hath the thing it hunteth most,
'Tis won as towns with fire—so won, so lost.

Ferdinand, King of Navarre.
We must of force dispense with this decree,
She must lie here on mere necessity.

Berowne.
Necessity will make us all forsworn
Three thousand times within this three years' space;
For every man with his affects is born,
Not by might mast'red, but by special grace.
If I break faith, this word shall speak for me:
I am forsworn "on mere necessity."
So to the laws at large I write my name,

Subscribes.

And he that breaks them in the least degree
Stands in attainder of eternal shame.
Suggestions are to other as to me;
But I believe, although I seem so loath,
I am the last that will last keep his oath.
But is there no quick recreation granted?

Ferdinand, King of Navarre.
Ay, that there is. Our court you know is haunted
With a refined traveler of Spain,
A man in all the world's new fashion planted,
That hath a mint of phrases in his brain;

One who the music of his own vain tongue
Doth ravish like enchanting harmony;
A man of complements, whom right and wrong
Have chose as umpire of their mutiny.
This child of fancy, that Armado hight,
For interim to our studies shall relate,
In high-borne words, the worth of many a knight
From tawny Spain, lost in the world's debate.
How you delight, my lords, I know not, I,
But I protest I love to hear him lie,
And I will use him for my minstrelsy.

Berowne.
Armado is a most illustrious wight,
A man of fire-new words, fashion's own knight.

Longaville.
Costard the swain and he shall be our sport,
And so to study three years is but short.

Enter a Constable Dull with a letter, with Costard.

Dull.
Which is the Duke's own person?

Berowne.
This, fellow. What wouldst?

Dull.
I myself reprehend his own person, for I am his Grace's farborough; but I would see his own person in flesh and blood.

Berowne.
This is he.

Dull.
Signior Arme—Arme—commends you. There's villainy abroad; this letter will tell you more.

Costard.
Sir, the contempts thereof are as touching me.

Ferdinand, King of Navarre.
A letter from the magnificent Armado.

Berowne.
How low soever the matter, I hope in God for high words.

Longaville.
A high hope for a low heaven. God grant us patience!

Berowne.
To hear, or forbear hearing?

Longaville.
To hear meekly, sir, and to laugh moderately; or to forbear both.

Berowne.
Well, sir, be it as the style shall give us cause to climb in the merriness.

Costard.
The matter is to me, sir, as concerning Jaquenetta: the manner of it is, I was taken with the manner.

Berowne.
In what manner?

Costard.
In manner and form following, sir, all those three: I was seen with her in the manor-house, sitting with her upon the form, and taken following her into the park, which, put together, is in manner and form following. Now, sir, for the manner—it is the manner of a man to speak to a woman; for the form—in some form.

Berowne.
For the following, sir?

Costard.
As it shall follow in my correction, and God defend the right!

Ferdinand, King of Navarre.
Will you hear this letter with attention?

Berowne.
As we would hear an oracle.

Costard.
Such is the simplicity of man to hearken after the flesh.

Ferdinand, King of Navarre.

Reads.

"Great deputy, the welkin's viceregent, and sole dominator of Navarre, my soul's earth's god, and body's fost'ring patron"—

Costard.
Not a word of Costard yet.

Ferdinand, King of Navarre.

Reads.

"So it is"—

Costard.
It may be so; but if he say it is so, he is, in telling true—but so.

Ferdinand, King of Navarre.
Peace!

Costard.
—be to me, and every man that dares not fight!

Ferdinand, King of Navarre.
No words!

Costard.
—of other men's secrets, I beseech you.

Ferdinand, King of Navarre.

Reads.

"So it is, besieged with sable-colored melancholy, I did commend the black oppressing humor to the most wholesome physic of thy health-giving air; and as I am a gentleman, betook myself to walk: the time When? About the sixth hour, when beasts most graze, birds best peck, and men sit down to that nourishment which is called supper: so much for the time When. Now for the ground Which? Which, I mean, I walk'd upon: it is ycliped thy park. Then for the place Where? Where, I mean, I did encounter that obscene and most prepost'rous event that draweth from my snow-white pen the ebon-colored ink which here thou viewest, beholdest, surveyest, or seest. But to the place Where? It standeth north-north-east and by east from the west corner of thy curious-knotted garden. There did I see that low-spirited swain, that base minnow of thy mirth"—

Costard.
Me?

Ferdinand, King of Navarre.

Reads.

"that unlettered small-knowing soul"—

Costard.
Me?

Ferdinand, King of Navarre.

Reads.

"that shallow vassal"—

Costard.
Still me?

Ferdinand, King of Navarre.

Reads.

"which, as I remember, hight Costard"—

Costard.
O! Me.

Ferdinand, King of Navarre.

Reads.

"sorted and consorted, contrary to thy established proclaimed edict and continent canon; which with—O, with—but with this I passion to say wherewith"—

Costard.
With a wench.

Ferdinand, King of Navarre.

Reads.

"with a child of our grandmother Eve, a female; or for thy more sweet understanding, a woman. Him I (as my ever-esteemed duty pricks me on) have sent to thee, to receive the meed of punishment, by thy sweet Grace's officer, Anthony Dull, a man of good repute, carriage, bearing, and estimation."

Dull.
Me, an't shall please you: I am Anthony Dull.

Ferdinand, King of Navarre.

Reads.

"For Jaquenetta (so is the weaker vessel called), which I apprehended with the aforesaid swain, I keep her as a vessel of thy law's fury, and shall, at the least of thy sweet notice, bring her to trial. Thine, in all complements of devoted and heart-burning heat of duty, Don Adriano de Armado."

Berowne.
This is not so well as I look'd for, but the best that ever I heard.

Ferdinand, King of Navarre.
Ay, the best for the worst. But, sirrah, what say you to this?

Costard.
Sir, I confess the wench.

Ferdinand, King of Navarre.
Did you hear the proclamation?

Costard.
I do confess much of the hearing it, but little of the marking of it.

Ferdinand, King of Navarre.
It was proclaim'd a year's imprisonment to be taken with a wench.

Costard.
I was taken with none, sir, I was taken with a damsel.

Ferdinand, King of Navarre.
Well, it was proclaim'd damsel.

Costard.
This was no damsel neither, sir, she was a virgin.

Ferdinand, King of Navarre.
It is so varied too, for it was proclaim'd virgin.

Costard.
If it were, I deny her virginity; I was taken with a maid.

Ferdinand, King of Navarre.
This maid will not serve your turn, sir.

Costard.
This maid will serve my turn, sir.

Ferdinand, King of Navarre.
Sir, I will pronounce your sentence: you shall fast a week with bran and water.

Costard.
I had rather pray a month with mutton and porridge.

Ferdinand, King of Navarre.
And Don Armado shall be your keeper.
My Lord Berowne, see him delivered o'er,
And go we, lords, to put in practice that
Which each to other hath so strongly sworn.

Exeunt King, Longaville, and Dumaine.

Berowne.
I'll lay my head to any good man's hat,
These oaths and laws will prove an idle scorn.
Sirrah, come on.

Costard.
I suffer for the truth, sir; for true it is, I was taken with Jaquenetta, and Jaquenetta is a true girl, and therefore welcome the sour cup of prosperity! Affliction may one day smile again, and till then, sit thee down, sorrow!

Exeunt.

Scene 2

The King of Navarre's park.

(Armado; Moth; Clown Costard; Constable Dull; Wench Jaquenetta)

Armado discusses melancholy with his witty page, Moth. Armado confesses that he is in love with the low-born milkmaid, Jaquenetta, however inappropriate this may be. The Constable brings in Costard, while Armado attempts to court Jaquenetta, not very successfully. Having sent Costard to be locked up by Moth, Armado prepares to write a (very long) love letter to the milkmaid.

Enter Armado and Moth, his page.

Don Adriano de Armado.
Boy, what sign is it when a man of great spirit grows melancholy?

Moth.
A great sign, sir, that he will look sad.

Don Adriano de Armado.
Why, sadness is one and the self-same thing, dear imp.

Moth.
No, no, O Lord, sir, no.

Don Adriano de Armado.
How canst thou part sadness and melancholy, my tender juvenal?

Moth.
By a familiar demonstration of the working, my tough signior.

Don Adriano de Armado.
Why tough signior? Why tough signior?

Moth.
Why tender juvenal? Why tender juvenal?

Don Adriano de Armado.
I spoke it tender juvenal as a congruent epitheton appertaining to thy young days, which we may nominate tender.

Moth.
And I tough signior as an appertinent title to your old time, which we may name tough.

Don Adriano de Armado.
Pretty and apt.

Moth.
How mean you, sir? I pretty, and my saying apt? Or I apt, and my saying pretty?

Don Adriano de Armado.
Thou pretty, because little.

Moth.
Little pretty, because little. Wherefore apt?

Don Adriano de Armado.
And therefore apt, because quick.

Moth.
Speak you this in my praise, master?

Don Adriano de Armado.
In thy condign praise.

Moth.
I will praise an eel with the same praise.

Don Adriano de Armado.
What? That an eel is ingenious?

Moth.
That an eel is quick.

Don Adriano de Armado.
I do say thou art quick in answers; thou heat'st my blood.

Moth.
I am answer'd, sir.

Don Adriano de Armado.
I love not to be cross'd.

Moth.
Aside.
He speaks the mere contrary, crosses love not him.

Don Adriano de Armado.
I have promised to study three years with the Duke.

Moth.
You may do it in an hour, sir.

Don Adriano de Armado.
Impossible.

Moth.
How many is one thrice told?

Don Adriano de Armado.
I am ill at reck'ning, it fitteth the spirit of a tapster.

Moth.
You are a gentleman and a gamester, sir.

Don Adriano de Armado.
I confess both, they are both the varnish of a complete man.

Moth.
Then I am sure you know how much the gross sum of deuce-ace amounts to.

Don Adriano de Armado.
It doth amount to one more than two.

Moth.
Which the base vulgar do call three.

Don Adriano de Armado.
True.

Moth.
Why, sir, is this such a piece of study? Now here is three studied ere ye'll thrice wink; and how easy it is to put "years" to the word "three," and study three years in two words, the dancing horse will tell you.

Don Adriano de Armado.
A most fine figure!

Moth.
Aside.
To prove you a cipher.

Don Adriano de Armado.
I will hereupon confess I am in love; and as it is base for a soldier to love, so am I in love with a base wench. If drawing my sword against the humor of affection would deliver me from the reprobate thought of it, I would take Desire prisoner, and ransom him to any French courtier for a new devis'd cur'sy. I think scorn to sigh; methinks I should outswear Cupid. Comfort me, boy: what great men have been in love?

Moth.
Hercules, master.

Don Adriano de Armado.
Most sweet Hercules! More authority, dear boy, name more; and, sweet my child, let them be men of good repute and carriage.

Moth.
Sampson, master; he was a man of good carriage, great carriage, for he carried the town gates on his back like a porter; and he was in love.

Don Adriano de Armado.
O well-knit Sampson, strong-jointed Sampson! I do excel thee in my rapier as much as thou didst me in carrying gates. I am in love too. Who was Sampson's love, my dear Moth?

Moth.
A woman, master.

Don Adriano de Armado.
Of what complexion?

Moth.
Of all the four, or the three, or the two, or one of the four.

Don Adriano de Armado.
Tell me precisely of what complexion.

Moth.
Of the sea-water green, sir.

Don Adriano de Armado.
Is that one of the four complexions?

Moth.
As I have read, sir, and the best of them too.

Don Adriano de Armado.
Green indeed is the color of lovers; but to have a love of that color, methinks Sampson had small reason for it. He surely affected her for her wit.

Moth.
It was so, sir, for she had a green wit.

Don Adriano de Armado.
My love is most immaculate white and red.

Moth.
Most maculate thoughts, master, are mask'd under such colors.

Don Adriano de Armado.
Define, define, well-educated infant.

Moth.
My father's wit and my mother's tongue assist me!

Don Adriano de Armado.
Sweet invocation of a child, most pretty and pathetical!

Moth.
If she be made of white and red,
Her faults will ne'er be known,
For blush in cheeks by faults are bred,
And fears by pale white shown:
Then if she fear, or be to blame,
By this you shall not know,
For still her cheeks possess the same
Which native she doth owe.
A dangerous rhyme, master, against the reason of white and red.

Don Adriano de Armado.
Is there not a ballet, boy, of the King and the Beggar?

Moth.
The world was very guilty of such a ballet some three ages since, but I think now 'tis not to be found; or if it were, it would neither serve for the writing nor the tune.

Don Adriano de Armado.
I will have that subject newly writ o'er, that I may example my digression by some mighty president. Boy, I do love that country girl that I took in the park with the rational hind Costard. She deserves well.

Moth.
Aside.
To be whipt; and yet a better love than my master.

Don Adriano de Armado.
Sing, boy, my spirit grows heavy in love.

Moth.
And that's great marvel, loving a light wench.

Don Adriano de Armado.
I say, sing.

Moth.
Forbear till this company be past.

Enter Clown Costard, Constable Dull, and Wench Jaquenetta.

Dull.
Sir, the Duke's pleasure is that you keep Costard safe, and you must suffer him to take no delight nor no penance, but 'a must fast three days a week. For this damsel, I must keep her at the park; she is allow'd for the dey-woman. Fare you well.

Don Adriano de Armado.
I do betray myself with blushing. Maid.

Jaquenetta.
Man.

Don Adriano de Armado.
I will visit thee at the lodge.

Jaquenetta.
That's hereby.

Don Adriano de Armado.
I know where it is situate.

Jaquenetta.
Lord, how wise you are!

Don Adriano de Armado.
I will tell thee wonders.

Jaquenetta.
With that face?

Don Adriano de Armado.
I love thee.

Jaquenetta.
So I heard you say.

Don Adriano de Armado.
And so farewell.

Jaquenetta.
Fair weather after you!

Dull.
Come, Jaquenetta, away.

Exeunt Dull and Jaquenetta.

Don Adriano de Armado.
Villain, thou shalt fast for thy offenses ere thou be pardoned.

Costard.
Well, sir, I hope when I do it I shall do it on a full stomach.

Don Adriano de Armado.
Thou shalt be heavily punished.

Costard.
I am more bound to you than your fellows, for they are but lightly rewarded.

Don Adriano de Armado.
Take away this villain, shut him up.

Moth.
Come, you transgressing slave, away.

Costard.
Let me not be pent up, sir; I will fast, being loose.

Moth.
No, sir, that were fast and loose; thou shalt to prison.

Costard.
Well, if ever I do see the merry days of desolation that I have seen, some shall see.

Moth.
What shall some see?

Costard.
Nay, nothing, Master Moth, but what they look upon. It is not for prisoners to be too silent in their words, and therefore I will say nothing. I thank God I have as little patience as another man, and therefore I can be quiet.

Exit with Moth.

Don Adriano de Armado.
I do affect the very ground (which is base) where her shoe (which is baser) guided by her foot (which is basest) doth tread. I shall be forsworn (which is a great argument of falsehood) if I love. And how can that be true love, which is falsely attempted? Love is a familiar; Love is a devil; there is no evil angel but Love. Yet was Sampson so tempted, and he had an excellent strength; yet was Salomon so seduced, and he had a very good wit. Cupid's butt-shaft is too hard for Hercules' club, and therefore too much odds for a Spaniard's rapier. The first and second cause will not serve my turn; the passado he respects not, the duello he regards not: his disgrace is to be called boy, but his glory is to subdue men. Adieu, valor, rust, rapier, be still, drum, for your manager is in love; yea, he loveth. Assist me, some extemporal god of rhyme, for I am sure I shall turn sonnet. Devise, wit, write, pen, for I am for whole volumes in folio.

Exit.

Act 2

Scene 1

The King of Navarre's park.

(Princess of France; Rosaline; Maria; Katherine; First French Lord; Second French Lord; Lords; Boyet; King of Navarre; Longaville; Dumaine; Berowne; Attendants)

Lord Boyet, sent to accompany the Princess of France on her embassy to Navarre, reminds her to act as her place demands before going to announce her arrival to Navarre. She and her ladies-in-waiting discuss the King's companions — as it happens, each of them has met one of them before. Boyet returns and informs the Princess that, for the sake of keeping his vow, the King is going to make her sleep in the forest rather than allow her into the palace. The King arrives to welcome her; while he reads the petition she has brought, Berowne and one of the ladies spar. The King insists that he has never received payment for Aquitaine, but the Princess assures him it was sent. As the rest of the diplomatic papers will not arrive until the next day, the men take their leave, but each of the King's three companions sneaks up to Boyet to ask the name of a particular lady. Boyet insists that the King has fallen in love with the Princess.

Enter the Princess of France with three attending Ladies (Rosaline, Maria, Katherine) and three Lords, one named Boyet.

Boyet.
Now, madam, summon up your dearest spirits;
Consider who the King your father sends,
To whom he sends, and what's his embassy:
Yourself, held precious in the world's esteem,
To parley with the sole inheritor
Of all perfections that a man may owe,
Matchless Navarre; the plea of no less weight
Than Aquitaine, a dowry for a queen.
Be now as prodigal of all dear grace
As Nature was in making graces dear,
When she did starve the general world beside
And prodigally gave them all to you.

The Princess of France.
Good Lord Boyet, my beauty, though but mean,
Needs not the painted flourish of your praise:
Beauty is bought by judgment of the eye,
Not utt'red by base sale of chapmen's tongues.
I am less proud to hear you tell my worth
Than you much willing to be counted wise
In spending your wit in the praise of mine.
But now to task the tasker: good Boyet,
You are not ignorant all-telling fame
Doth noise abroad Navarre hath made a vow,
Till painful study shall outwear three years,
No woman may approach his silent court;
Therefore to 's seemeth it a needful course,
Before we enter his forbidden gates,
To know his pleasure; and in that behalf,
Bold of your worthiness, we single you
As our best-moving fair solicitor.
Tell him, the daughter of the King of France,
On serious business craving quick dispatch,
Importunes personal conference with his Grace.
Haste, signify so much, while we attend,
Like humble-visag'd suitors, his high will.

Boyet.
Proud of employment, willingly I go.

Exit Boyet.

The Princess of France.
All pride is willing pride, and yours is so.
Who are the votaries, my loving lords,
That are vow-fellows with this virtuous Duke?

First French Lord.
Lord Longaville is one.

The Princess of France.
                        Know you the man?

Maria.
I know him, madam; at a marriage-feast,
Between Lord Perigort and the beauteous heir
Of Jaques Falconbridge, solemnized
In Normandy, saw I this Longaville,
A man of sovereign parts, peerless esteem'd,
Well fitted in arts, glorious in arms;
Nothing becomes him ill that he would well.
The only soil of his fair virtue's gloss,
If virtue's gloss will stain with any soil,
Is a sharp wit match'd with too blunt a will,
Whose edge hath power to cut, whose will still wills
It should none spare that come within his power.

The Princess of France.
Some merry mocking lord belike, is't so?

Maria.
They say so most that most his humors know.

The Princess of France.
Such short-liv'd wits do wither as they grow.
Who are the rest?

Katherine.
The young Dumaine, a well-accomplish'd youth,
Of all that virtue love for virtue loved;
Most power to do most harm, least knowing ill;
For he hath wit to make an ill shape good,
And shape to win grace though he had no wit.
I saw him at the Duke Alanson's once,
And much too little of that good I saw
Is my report to his great worthiness.

Rosaline.
Another of these students at that time
Was there with him, if I have heard a truth.
Berowne they call him, but a merrier man,
Within the limit of becoming mirth,
I never spent an hour's talk withal.
His eye begets occasion for his wit,
For every object that the one doth catch
The other turns to a mirth-moving jest,
Which his fair tongue, conceit's expositor,
Delivers in such apt and gracious words
That aged ears play truant at his tales,
And younger hearings are quite ravished,
So sweet and voluble is his discourse.

The Princess of France.
God bless my ladies! Are they all in love,
That every one her own hath garnished
With such bedecking ornaments of praise?

First French Lord.
Here comes Boyet.

Enter Boyet.

The Princess of France.
                        Now, what admittance, lord?

Boyet.
Navarre had notice of your fair approach,
And he and his competitors in oath
Were all address'd to meet you, gentle lady,
Before I came. Marry, thus much I have learnt:
He rather means to lodge you in the field,
Like one that comes here to besiege his court,
Than seek a dispensation for his oath,
To let you enter his unpeopled house.

Enter Ferdinand, King of Navarre, Longaville, Dumaine, and Berowne, and Attendants.

Here comes Navarre.

The ladies-in-waiting mask.

Ferdinand, King of Navarre.
Fair Princess, welcome to the court of Navarre.

The Princess of France.
"Fair" I give you back again, and "welcome" I have not yet. The roof of this court is too high to be yours, and welcome to the wide fields too base to be mine.

Ferdinand, King of Navarre.
You shall be welcome, madam, to my court.

The Princess of France.
I will be welcome then—conduct me thither.

Ferdinand, King of Navarre.
Hear me, dear lady: I have sworn an oath.

The Princess of France.
Our Lady help my lord! He'll be forsworn.

Ferdinand, King of Navarre.
Not for the world, fair madam, by my will.

The Princess of France.
Why, will shall break it, will, and nothing else.

Ferdinand, King of Navarre.
Your ladyship is ignorant what it is.

The Princess of France.
Were my lord so, his ignorance were wise,
Where now his knowledge must prove ignorance.
I hear your Grace hath sworn out house-keeping:
'Tis deadly sin to keep that oath, my lord,
And sin to break it.
But pardon me, I am too sudden bold;
To teach a teacher ill beseemeth me.
Vouchsafe to read the purpose of my coming,
And suddenly resolve me in my suit.

Giving a paper.

Ferdinand, King of Navarre.
Madam, I will, if suddenly I may.

The Princess of France.
You will the sooner, that I were away,
For you'll prove perjur'd if you make me stay.

Berowne.
Did not I dance with you in Brabant once?

Rosaline.
Did not I dance with you in Brabant once?

Berowne.
I know you did.

Rosaline.
How needless was it then
To ask the question?

Berowne.
You must not be so quick.

Rosaline.
'Tis long of you that spur me with such questions.

Berowne.
Your wit's too hot, it speeds too fast, 'twill tire.

Rosaline.
Not till it leave the rider in the mire.

Berowne.
What time a' day?

Rosaline.
The hour that fools should ask.

Berowne.
Now fair befall your mask!

Rosaline.
Fair fall the face it covers!

Berowne.
And send you many lovers!

Rosaline.
Amen, so you be none.

Berowne.
Nay then will I be gone.

Ferdinand, King of Navarre.
Madam, your father here doth intimate
The payment of a hundred thousand crowns,
Being but the one half of an entire sum
Disbursed by my father in his wars.
But say that he, or we, as neither have,
Receiv'd that sum, yet there remains unpaid
A hundred thousand more, in surety of the which
One part of Aquitaine is bound to us,
Although not valued to the money's worth.
If then the King your father will restore
But that one half which is unsatisfied,
We will give up our right in Aquitaine,
And hold fair friendship with his Majesty.
But that, it seems, he little purposeth:
For here he doth demand to have repaid
A hundred thousand crowns, and not demands,
On payment of a hundred thousand crowns,
To have his title live in Aquitaine;
Which we much rather had depart withal,
And have the money by our father lent,
Than Aquitaine, so gelded as it is.
Dear Princess, were not his requests so far
From reason's yielding, your fair self should make
A yielding 'gainst some reason in my breast,
And go well satisfied to France again.

The Princess of France.
You do the King my father too much wrong,
And wrong the reputation of your name,
In so unseeming to confess receipt
Of that which hath so faithfully been paid.

Ferdinand, King of Navarre.
I do protest I never heard of it;
And, if you prove it, I'll repay it back,
Or yield up Aquitaine.

The Princess of France.
                        We arrest your word.
Boyet, you can produce acquittances
For such a sum from special officers
Of Charles his father.

Ferdinand, King of Navarre.
                        Satisfy me so.

Boyet.
So please your Grace, the packet is not come
Where that and other specialties are bound:
Tomorrow you shall have a sight of them.

Ferdinand, King of Navarre.
It shall suffice me; at which interview
All liberal reason I will yield unto.
Mean time receive such welcome at my hand
As honor (without breach of honor) may
Make tender of to thy true worthiness.
You may not come, fair Princess, within my gates,
But here without you shall be so receiv'd
As you shall deem yourself lodg'd in my heart,
Though so denied fair harbor in my house.
Your own good thoughts excuse me, and farewell.
Tomorrow shall we visit you again.

The Princess of France.
Sweet health and fair desires consort your Grace!

Ferdinand, King of Navarre.
Thy own wish wish I thee in every place.

Exit with Longaville, Dumaine, and Attendants.

Boyet.
Lady, I will commend you to mine own heart.

Rosaline.
Pray you, do my commendations—I would be glad to see it.

Boyet.
I would you heard it groan.

Rosaline.
Is the fool sick?

Boyet.
Sick at the heart.

Rosaline.
Alack, let it blood.

Boyet.
Would that do it good?

Rosaline.
My physic says ay.

Boyet.
Will you prick't with your eye?

Rosaline.
No point, with my knife.

Boyet.
Now God save thy life!

Rosaline.
And yours from long living!

Berowne.
I cannot stay thanksgiving.

Exit.
Enter Dumaine.

Dumaine.
Sir, I pray you a word. What lady is that same?

Boyet.
The heir of Alanson, Katherine her name.

Dumaine.
A gallant lady. Monsieur, fare you well.

Exit.
Enter Longaville.

Longaville.
I beseech you a word. What is she in the white?

Boyet.
A woman sometimes, and you saw her in the light.

Longaville.
Perchance light in the light. I desire her name.

Boyet.
She hath but one for herself, to desire that were a shame.

Longaville.
Pray you, sir, whose daughter?

Boyet.
Her mother's, I have heard.

Longaville.
God's blessing on your beard!

Boyet.
Good sir, be not offended,
She is an heir of Falconbridge.

Longaville.
Nay, my choler is ended.
She is a most sweet lady.

Boyet.
Not unlike, sir, that may be.

Exit Longaville.
Enter Berowne.

Berowne.
What's her name in the cap?

Boyet.
Rosaline, by good hap.

Berowne.
Is she wedded or no?

Boyet.
To her will, sir, or so.

Berowne.
O, you are welcome, sir, adieu.

Boyet.
Farewell to me, sir, and welcome to you.

Exit Berowne.

Maria.
That last is Berowne, the merry madcap lord.
Not a word with him but a jest.

Boyet.
              And every jest but a word.

The Princess of France.
It was well done of you to take him at his word.

Boyet.
I was as willing to grapple as he was to board.

Katherine.
Two hot sheeps, marry.

Boyet.
              And wherefore not ships?
No sheep, sweet lamb, unless we feed on your lips.

Katherine.
You sheep, and I pasture: shall that finish the jest?

Boyet.
So you grant pasture for me.

Offering to kiss her.

Katherine.
              Not so, gentle beast.
My lips are no common, though several they be.

Boyet.
Belonging to whom?

Katherine.
              To my fortunes and me.

The Princess of France.
Good wits will be jangling, but, gentles, agree:
This civil war of wits were much better used
On Navarre and his book-men, for here 'tis abused.

Boyet.
If my observation (which very seldom lies),
By the heart's still rhetoric, disclosed with eyes,
Deceive me not now, Navarre is infected.

The Princess of France.
With what?

Boyet.
With that which we lovers entitle "affected."

The Princess of France.
Your reason?

Boyet.
Why, all his behaviors did make their retire
To the court of his eye, peeping thorough desire:
His heart like an agot with your print impressed,
Proud with his form, in his eye pride expressed;
His tongue, all impatient to speak and not see,
Did stumble with haste in his eyesight to be;
All senses to that sense did make their repair,
To feel only looking on fairest of fair:
Methought all his senses were lock'd in his eye,
As jewels in crystal for some prince to buy,

Who tend'ring their own worth from where they were glass'd,
Did point you to buy them, along as you pass'd;
His face's own margent did quote such amazes
That all eyes saw his eyes enchanted with gazes.
I'll give you Aquitaine and all that is his,
And you give him for my sake but one loving kiss.

The Princess of France.
Come to our pavilion—Boyet is dispos'd.

Boyet.
But to speak that in words which his eye hath disclos'd.
I only have made a mouth of his eye,
By adding a tongue which I know will not lie.

Maria.
Thou art an old love-monger and speakest skillfully.

Katherine.
He is Cupid's grandfather, and learns news of him.

Rosaline.
Then was Venus like her mother, for her father is but grim.

Boyet.
Do you hear, my mad wenches?

Maria.
No.

Boyet.
What then, do you see?

Maria.
Ay, our way to be gone.

Boyet.
You are too hard for me.

Exeunt omnes.

Act 3

Scene 1

The King of Navarre's park.

(Armado; Moth; Costard; Berowne)

Armado and Moth converse, the page commenting to himself about Armado's foolishness. With Costard, they discuss certain forms of poetry. Armado gives Costard a letter to deliver to Jaquenetta, giving him some money as remuneration; Costard is delighted with this new word. Berowne then pays Costard to deliver a letter to Rosaline. Left alone, Berowne reflects disbelievingly on the fact that he, the great cynic, is in love.

Enter Braggart Armado and his Boy Moth.

Don Adriano de Armado.
Warble, child, make passionate my sense of hearing.

Moth.
Sings the song.
"Concolinel."

Don Adriano de Armado.
Sweet air! Go, tenderness of years, take this key, give enlargement to the swain, bring him festinately hither. I must employ him in a letter to my love.

Moth.
Master, will you win your love with a French brawl?

Don Adriano de Armado.
How meanest thou? Brawling in French?

Moth.
No, my complete master, but to jig off a tune at the tongue's end, canary to it with your feet, humor it with turning up your eyelids, sigh a note and sing a note, sometime through the throat, as if you swallow'd love with singing love, sometime through the nose, as if you snuff'd up love by smelling love; with your hat penthouse-like o'er the shop of your eyes; with your arms cross'd on your thin-bellied doublet like a rabbit on a spit; or your hands in your pocket like a man after the old painting; and keep not too long in one tune, but a snip and away: these are complements, these are humors, these betray nice wenches that would be betray'd without these; and make them men of note—do you note?—men that most are affected to these.

Don Adriano de Armado.
How hast thou purchased this experience?

Moth.
By my penny of observation.

Don Adriano de Armado.
But O—but O—

Moth.
"The hobby-horse is forgot."

Don Adriano de Armado.
Call'st thou my love "hobby-horse"?

Moth.
No, master, the hobby-horse is but a colt,

Aside.

and your love perhaps a hackney.—
But have you forgot your love?

Don Adriano de Armado.
Almost I had.

Moth.
Negligent student, learn her by heart.

Don Adriano de Armado.
By heart and in heart, boy.

Moth.
And out of heart, master; all those three I will prove.

Don Adriano de Armado.
What wilt thou prove?

Moth.
A man, if I live; and this, "by, in, and without," upon the instant: by heart you love her, because your heart cannot come by her; in heart you love her, because your heart is in love with her; and out of heart you love her, being out of heart that you cannot enjoy her.

Don Adriano de Armado.
I am all these three.

Moth.
And three times as much more—

Aside.

and yet nothing at all.

Don Adriano de Armado.
Fetch hither the swain, he must carry me a letter.

Moth.
A message well sympathiz'd—a horse to be ambassador for an ass.

Don Adriano de Armado.
Ha, ha? What sayest thou?

Moth.
Marry, sir, you must send the ass upon the horse, for he is very slow-gaited. But I go.

Don Adriano de Armado.
The way is but short, away!

Moth.
As swift as lead, sir.

Don Adriano de Armado.
The meaning, pretty ingenious?
Is not lead a metal heavy, dull, and slow?

Moth.
Minime, honest master, or rather, master, no.

Don Adriano de Armado.
I say lead is slow.

Moth.
          You are too swift, sir, to say so.
Is that lead slow which is fir'd from a gun?

Don Adriano de Armado.
Sweet smoke of rhetoric!
He reputes me a cannon, and the bullet, that's he;
I shoot thee at the swain.

Moth.
          Thump then, and I flee.

Exit.

Don Adriano de Armado.
A most acute juvenal, volable and free of grace!
By thy favor, sweet welkin, I must sigh in thy face:
Most rude melancholy, valor gives thee place.
My herald is return'd.

Enter Page Moth and Clown Costard.

Moth.
A wonder, master! Here's a costard broken in a shin.

Don Adriano de Armado.
Some enigma, some riddle—come, thy l'envoi—begin.

Costard.
No egma, no riddle, no l'envoi, no salve in the mail, sir. O sir, plantan, a plain plantan; no l'envoi, no l'envoi, no salve, sir, but a plantan!

Don Adriano de Armado.
By virtue thou enforcest laughter—thy silly thought, my spleen; the heaving of my lungs provokes me to ridiculous smiling—O, pardon me, my stars! Doth the inconsiderate take salve for l'envoi, and the word "l'envoi" for a salve?

Moth.
Do the wise think them other? Is not l'envoi a salve?

Don Adriano de Armado.
No, page, it is an epilogue or discourse, to make plain
Some obscure precedence that hath tofore been sain.
I will example it:
The fox, the ape, and the humble-bee
Were still at odds, being but three.
There's the moral. Now the l'envoi.

Moth.
I will add the l'envoi. Say the moral again.

Don Adriano de Armado.
The fox, the ape, and the humble-bee
Were still at odds, being but three.

Moth.
Until the goose came out of door,
And stayed the odds by adding four.
Now will I begin your moral, and do you follow with my l'envoi:
The fox, the ape, and the humble-bee
Were still at odds, being but three.

Don Adriano de Armado.
Until the goose came out of door,
Staying the odds by adding four.

Moth.
A good l'envoi, ending in the goose; would you desire more?

Costard.
The boy hath sold him a bargain, a goose, that's flat.
Sir, your pennyworth is good, and your goose be fat.
To sell a bargain well is as cunning as fast and loose:
Let me see: a fat l'envoi—ay, that's a fat goose.

Don Adriano de Armado.
Come hither, come hither. How did this argument begin?

Moth.
By saying that a costard was broken in a shin.
Then call'd you for the l'envoi.

Costard.
True, and I for a plantan; thus came your argument in;
Then the boy's fat l'envoi, the goose that you bought,
And he ended the market.

Don Adriano de Armado.
But tell me, how was there a costard broken in a shin?

Moth.
I will tell you sensibly.

Costard.
Thou hast no feeling of it, Moth. I will speak that l'envoi:
I, Costard, running out that was safely within,
Fell over the threshold, and broke my shin.

Don Adriano de Armado.
We will talk no more of this matter.

Costard.
Till there be more matter in the shin.

Don Adriano de Armado.
Sirrah Costard, I will enfranchise thee.

Costard.
O, marry me to one Frances! I smell some l'envoi, some goose, in this.

Don Adriano de Armado.
By my sweet soul, I mean setting thee at liberty, enfreedoming thy person: thou wert immured, restrained, captivated, bound.

Costard.
True, true, and now you will be my purgation and let me loose.

Don Adriano de Armado.
I give thee thy liberty, set thee from durance, and in lieu thereof, impose on thee nothing but this: bear this significant

Giving a letter

to the country maid Jaquenetta. There is remuneration, for the best ward of mine honor is rewarding my dependents. Moth, follow.

Act 3, Scene 1

Moth.
Like the sequel, I. Signior Costard, adieu.

Exit Armado, followed by Moth.

Costard.
My sweet ounce of man's flesh, my incony Jew!
Now will I look to his remuneration. Remuneration!
O, that's the Latin word for three farthings: three
farthings—remuneration. "What's the price of this
inkle?"—"One penny."—"No, I'll give you a remuneration": why, it carries it. Remuneration: why, it is a
fairer name than French crown! I will never buy and
sell out of this word.

Enter Berowne.

Berowne.
O, my good knave Costard, exceedingly well met!

Costard.
Pray you, sir, how much carnation ribbon may a man
buy for a remuneration?

Berowne.
O, what is a remuneration?

Costard.
Marry, sir, halfpenny farthing.

Berowne.
O, why then three-farthing worth of silk.

Costard.
I thank your worship, God be wi' you!

Berowne.
O, stay, slave; I must employ thee.
As thou wilt win my favor, good my knave,
Do one thing for me that I shall entreat.

Costard.
When would you have it done, sir?

Berowne.
O, this afternoon.

Costard.
Well, I will do it, sir; fare you well.

Berowne.
O, thou knowest not what it is.

Costard.
I shall know, sir, when I have done it.

Berowne.
Why, villain, thou must know first.

Costard.
I will come to your worship tomorrow morning.

Berowne.
It must be done this afternoon. Hark, slave, it is but
this:
The Princess comes to hunt here in the park,
And in her train there is a gentle lady:
When tongues speak sweetly, then they name her
name,
And Rosaline they call her. Ask for her,
And to her white hand see thou do commend
This seal'd-up counsel. There's thy guerdon; go.

Costard.
Garden, O sweet gardon! Better than remuneration,
eleven-pence-farthing better; most sweet gardon! I
will do it, sir, in print. Gardon! Remuneration!

Exit.

Berowne.
O, and I, forsooth, in love! I, that have been love's
whip,
A very beadle to a humorous sigh,
A critic, nay, a night-watch constable,
A domineering pedant o'er the boy,
Than whom no mortal so magnificent!
This wimpled, whining, purblind, wayward boy,
This senior-junior, giant-dwarf, Dan Cupid,
Regent of love-rhymes, lord of folded arms,
Th' anointed sovereign of sighs and groans,
Liege of all loiterers and malcontents,
Dread prince of plackets, king of codpieces,
Sole imperator and great general
Of trotting paritors (O my little heart!),
And I to be a corporal of his field,
And wear his colors like a tumbler's hoop!
What! I love, I sue, I seek a wife—
A woman, that is like a German clock,
Still a-repairing, ever out of frame,
And never going aright, being a watch,
But being watch'd that it may still go right!
Nay, to be perjur'd, which is worst of all;
And among three to love the worst of all,
A whitely wanton with a velvet brow,

With two pitch-balls stuck in her face for eyes;
Ay, and, by heaven, one that will do the deed
Though Argus were her eunuch and her guard.
And I to sigh for her, to watch for her,
To pray for her, go to! It is a plague
That Cupid will impose for my neglect
Of his almighty dreadful little might.
Well, I will love, write, sigh, pray, sue, groan:
Some men must love my lady, and some Joan.

Exit.

Act 4

Scene 1

The King of Navarre's park.

(Princess of France; Forester; Rosaline; Maria; Katherine; Lords; Boyet; Costard)

The Princess and her ladies are out hunting with bow and arrow. Costard enters to deliver Berowne's letter, but accidentally hands over Armado's instead. The ladies and Boyet mock at the style. The Princess goes off to continue the hunt while Boyet and Rosaline trade barbs.

Enter the Princess, a Forester, her Ladies (Rosaline, Maria, Katherine), and her Lords, among them Boyet.

The Princess of France.
Was that the King that spurr'd his horse so hard
Against the steep-up rising of the hill?

Forester.
I know not, but I think it was not he.

The Princess of France.
Whoe'er 'a was, 'a show'd a mounting mind.
Well, lords, today we shall have our dispatch;
On Saturday we will return to France.
Then, forester, my friend, where is the bush
That we must stand and play the murderer in?

Forester.
Hereby, upon the edge of yonder coppice,
A stand where you may make the fairest shoot.

The Princess of France.
I thank my beauty, I am fair that shoot,
And thereupon thou speak'st the fairest shoot.

Forester.
Pardon me, madam, for I meant not so.

The Princess of France.
What, what? First praise me, and again say no?
O short-liv'd pride! Not fair? Alack for woe!

Forester.
Yes, madam, fair.

The Princess of France.
　　　　　　　Nay, never paint me now;
Where fair is not, praise cannot mend the brow.
Here (good my glass), take this for telling true:

Giving him money.

Fair payment for foul words is more than due.

Forester.
Nothing but fair is that which you inherit.

The Princess of France.
See, see, my beauty will be sav'd by merit.
O heresy in fair, fit for these days!
A giving hand, though foul, shall have fair praise.
But come, the bow: now mercy goes to kill,
And shooting well is then accounted ill.
Thus will I save my credit in the shoot:
Not wounding, pity would not let me do't;
If wounding, then it was to show my skill,
That more for praise than purpose meant to kill.
And out of question so it is sometimes:
Glory grows guilty of detested crimes,
When for fame's sake, for praise, an outward part,
We bend to that the working of the heart;
As I for praise alone now seek to spill
The poor deer's blood, that my heart means no ill.

Boyet.
Do not curst wives hold that self-sovereignty
Only for praise' sake, when they strive to be
Lords o'er their lords?

The Princess of France.
Only for praise—and praise we may afford
To any lady that subdues a lord.

Enter Clown Costard.

Boyet.
Here comes a member of the commonwealth.

Costard.
God dig-you-den all! Pray you, which is the head lady?

The Princess of France.
Thou shalt know her, fellow, by the rest that have no heads.

Costard.
Which is the greatest lady, the highest?

The Princess of France.
The thickest and the tallest.

Costard.
The thickest and the tallest! It is so, truth is truth.
And your waist, mistress, were as slender as my wit,
One a' these maids' girdles for your waist should be fit.
Are not you the chief woman? You are the thickest here.

The Princess of France.
What's your will, sir? What's your will?

Costard.
I have a letter from Monsieur Berowne to one Lady Rosaline.

The Princess of France.
O, thy letter, thy letter! He's a good friend of mine.
Stand aside, good bearer. Boyet, you can carve,
Break up this capon.

Boyet.
     I am bound to serve.
This letter is mistook; it importeth none here.
It is writ to Jaquenetta.

The Princess of France.
     We will read it, I swear.
Break the neck of the wax, and every one give ear.

Boyet.

Reads.

"By heaven, that thou art fair, is most infallible; true, that thou art beauteous; truth itself, that thou art lovely. More fairer than fair, beautiful than beauteous, truer than truth itself, have commiseration on thy heroical vassal! The magnanimous and most illustrate King Cophetua set eye upon the pernicious and indubitate beggar Zenelophon; and he it was that might rightly say, Veni, vidi, vici; which to annothanize in the vulgar—O base and obscure vulgar!—videlicet, He came, saw, and overcame: he came, one; saw, two; overcame, three. Who came? The king. Why did he come? To see. Why did he see? To overcome. To whom came he? To the beggar. What saw he? The beggar. Who overcame he? The beggar. The conclusion is victory; on whose side? The king's. The captive is enrich'd; on whose side? The beggar's. The catastrophe is a nuptial; on whose side? The king's; no, on both in one, or one in both. I am the king, for so stands the comparison; thou the beggar, for so witnesseth thy lowliness. Shall I command thy love? I may. Shall I enforce thy love? I could. Shall I entreat thy love? I will. What shalt thou exchange for rags? Robes; for tittles? Titles; for thyself? Me. Thus expecting thy reply, I profane my lips on thy foot, my eyes on thy picture, and my heart on thy every part. Thine, in the dearest design of industry,
Don Adriano de Armado.
Thus dost thou hear the Nemean lion roar
'Gainst thee, thou lamb, that standest as his prey;
Submissive fall his princely feet before,
And he from forage will incline to play.
But if thou strive, poor soul, what art thou then?
Food for his rage, repasture for his den."

The Princess of France.
What plume of feathers is he that indited this letter?
What vane? What weathercock? Did you ever hear better?

Boyet.
I am much deceived but I remember the style.

The Princess of France.
Else your memory is bad, going o'er it ere-while.

Boyet.
This Armado is a Spaniard that keeps here in court,
A phantasime, a Monarcho, and one that makes sport
To the Prince and his book-mates.

The Princess of France.
     Thou fellow, a word.
Who gave thee this letter?

Costard.
     I told you: my lord.

The Princess of France.
To whom shouldst thou give it?

Costard.
     From my lord to my lady.

The Princess of France.
From which lord to which lady?

Costard.
From my Lord Berowne, a good master of mine,
To a lady of France that he call'd Rosaline.

The Princess of France.
Thou hast mistaken his letter. Come, lords, away.

To Rosaline.

Here, sweet, put up this—'twill be thine another day.

Exeunt Princess, Forester and Train.

Boyet.
Who is the shooter? Who is the shooter?

Rosaline.
Shall I teach you to know?

Boyet.
Ay, my continent of beauty.

Rosaline.
           Why, she that bears the bow.
Finely put off!

Boyet.
My lady goes to kill horns, but if thou marry,
Hang me by the neck if horns that year miscarry.
Finely put on!

Rosaline.
Well then I am the shooter.

Boyet.
           And who is your deer?

Rosaline.
If we choose by the horns, yourself come not near.
Finely put on indeed!

Maria.
You still wrangle with her, Boyet, and she strikes at the brow.

Boyet.
But she herself is hit lower. Have I hit her now?

Rosaline.
Shall I come upon thee with an old saying, that was a man when King Pippen of France was a little boy, as touching the hit it?

Boyet.
So I may answer thee with one as old, that was a woman when Queen Guinover of Britain was a little wench, as touching the hit it.

Rosaline.

Sings.

Thou canst not hit it, hit it, hit it,
Thou canst not hit it, my good man.

Boyet.

Sings.

And I cannot, cannot, cannot,
And I cannot, another can.

Exeunt Rosaline and Katherine.

Costard.
By my troth, most pleasant. How both did fit it!

Maria.
A mark marvelous well shot, for they both did hit it.

Boyet.
A mark! O, mark but that mark! A mark, says my lady!
Let the mark have a prick in't, to mete at, if it may be.

Maria.
Wide a' the bow-hand! I' faith, your hand is out.

Costard.
Indeed 'a must shoot nearer, or he'll ne'er hit the clout.

Boyet.
And if my hand be out, then belike your hand is in.

Costard.
Then will she get the upshoot by cleaving the pin.

Maria.
Come, come, you talk greasily, your lips grow foul.

Costard.
She's too hard for you at pricks, sir, challenge her to bowl.

Boyet.
I fear too much rubbing. Good night, my good owl.

Exeunt Boyet and Maria.

Costard.
By my soul, a swain, a most simple clown!
Lord, Lord, how the ladies and I have put him down!
O' my troth, most sweet jests, most incony vulgar wit!
When it comes so smoothly off, so obscenely as it were, so fit.
Armado a' th' one side—O, a most dainty man!
To see him walk before a lady and to bear her fan!
To see him kiss his hand! And how most sweetly 'a will swear!
And his page a' t' other side, that handful of wit!
Ah, heavens, it is a most pathetical nit!

Shout within.

Sola, sola!

Exit.

Scene 2

The King of Navarre's park.

(Dull; Holofernes; Nathaniel; Jaquenetta; Costard)

Holofernes, the schoolmaster, and Sir Nathaniel, the curate, discuss language as Constable Dull listens. The pedantic, conceited Holofernes politely despises the unlearned; Sir Nathaniel rather worships him as he rattles off his dry knowledge. Jaquenetta and Costard enter, the illiterate girl wanting Holofernes to read her the love letter she's received — which is of course the one Berowne wrote to Rosaline. Holofernes is horrified at the poor style. Discovering the true writer of the letter, he sends Jaquenetta to the King with it. Invited to dinner by a pupil's father, Holofernes invites Nathaniel and Dull to join him.

Enter Dull, Holofernes the Pedant, and Nathaniel from watching the hunt.

Sir Nathaniel.
Very reverent sport truly, and done in the testimony of a good conscience.

Holofernes.
The deer was (as you know) sanguis, in blood, ripe as the pomewater, who now hangeth like a jewel in the ear of caelo, the sky, the welkin, the heaven, and anon falleth like a crab on the face of terra, the soil, the land, the earth.

Sir Nathaniel.
Truly, Master Holofernes, the epithites are sweetly varied, like a scholar at the least; but, sir, I assure ye it was a buck of the first head.

Holofernes.
Sir Nathaniel, haud credo.

Dull.
'Twas not a haud credo, 'twas a pricket.

Holofernes.
Most barbarous intimation! Yet a kind of insinuation, as it were in via, in way, of explication; facere, as it were, replication, or rather ostentare, to show, as it were, his inclination, after his undressed, unpolished, uneducated, unpruned, untrained, or rather unlettered, or ratherest unconfirmed fashion, to insert again my haud credo for a deer.

Dull.
I said the deer was not a haud credo, 'twas a pricket.

Holofernes.
Twice sod simplicity, bis coctus!
O thou monster Ignorance, how deformed dost thou look!

Sir Nathaniel.
Sir, he hath never fed of the dainties that are bred in a book;
He hath not eat paper, as it were; he hath not drunk ink; his intellect is not replenished; he is only an animal, only sensible in the duller parts;
And such barren plants are set before us, that we thankful should be—
Which we of taste and feeling are—for those parts that do fructify in us more than he.
For as it would ill become me to be vain, indiscreet, or a fool,
So were there a patch set on learning, to see him in a school:
But omne bene, say I, being of an old father's mind:
Many can brook the weather that love not the wind.

Dull.
You two are book-men: can you tell me by your wit
What was a month old at Cain's birth, that's not five weeks old as yet?

Holofernes.
Dictynna, goodman Dull, Dictynna, goodman Dull.

Dull.
What is Dictynna?

Sir Nathaniel.
A title to Phoebe, to Luna, to the moon.

Holofernes.
The moon was a month old when Adam was no more,
And raught not to five weeks when he came to five-score.
Th' allusion holds in the exchange.

Dull.
'Tis true indeed, the collusion holds in the exchange.

Holofernes.
God comfort thy capacity! I say, th' allusion holds in the exchange.

Dull.
And I say, the pollution holds in the exchange, for the moon is never but a month old; and I say beside that, 'twas a pricket that the Princess kill'd.

Holofernes.
Sir Nathaniel, will you hear an extemporal epitaph on the death of the deer? And to humor the ignorant, call I the deer the Princess kill'd a pricket.

Sir Nathaniel.
Perge, good Master Holofernes, perge, so it shall please you to abrogate squirility.

Holofernes.
I will something affect the letter, for it argues facility.
The preyful Princess pierc'd and prick'd a pretty pleasing pricket;
Some say a sore, but not a sore, till now made sore with shooting.
The dogs did yell: put l to sore, then sorel jumps from thicket,
Or pricket sore, or else sorel; the people fall a-hooting.
If sore be sore, then L to sore makes fifty sores o' sorel:
Of one sore I an hundred make by adding but one more L.

Sir Nathaniel.
A rare talent!

Dull.
Aside.
If a talent be a claw, look how he claws him with a talent.

Holofernes.
This is a gift that I have, simple; simple, a foolish extravagant spirit, full of forms, figures, shapes, objects, ideas, apprehensions, motions, revolutions. These are begot in the ventricle of memory, nourish'd in the womb of pia mater, and delivered upon the mellowing of occasion. But the gift is good in those in whom it is acute, and I am thankful for it.

Sir Nathaniel.
Sir, I praise the Lord for you, and so may my parishioners, for their sons are well tutor'd by you, and their daughters profit very greatly under you. You are a good member of the commonwealth.

Holofernes.
Mehercle, if their sons be ingenious, they shall want no instruction; if their daughters be capable, I will put it to them: but vir sapit qui pauca loquitur. A soul feminine saluteth us.

Enter Jaquenetta and the Clown Costard.

Jaquenetta.
God give you good morrow, Master Person.

Holofernes.
Master Person, quasi pers-one. And if one should be pierc'd, which is the one?

Costard.
Marry, Master Schoolmaster, he that is likel'est to a hogshead.

Holofernes.
Of piercing a hogshead! A good lustre of conceit in a turf of earth; fire enough for a flint, pearl enough for a swine: 'tis pretty; it is well.

Jaquenetta.
Good Master Person, be so good as read me this letter. It was given me by Costard, and sent me from Don Armado. I beseech you read it.

Holofernes.
Facile, precor gelida quando pecus omne sub umbra ruminat, and so forth. Ah, good old Mantuan! I may speak of thee as the traveler doth of Venice:
Venechia, Venechia,
Che non te vede, che non te prechia.
Old Mantuan, old Mantuan! Who understandeth thee not, loves thee not. Ut, re, sol, la, mi, fa. Under pardon,

sir, what are the contents? Or rather, as Horace says in his—What, my soul, verses?

Sir Nathaniel.
Ay, sir, and very learned.

Holofernes.
Let me hear a staff, a stanze, a verse; lege, domine.

Sir Nathaniel.

Reads.

"If love make me forsworn, how shall I swear to love?
Ah, never faith could hold, if not to beauty vowed!
Though to myself forsworn, to thee I'll faithful prove;
Those thoughts to me were oaks, to thee like osiers bowed.
Study his bias leaves, and makes his book thine eyes,
Where all those pleasures live that art would comprehend.
If knowledge be the mark, to know thee shall suffice;
Well learned is that tongue that well can thee commend,
All ignorant that soul that sees thee without wonder;
Which is to me some praise that I thy parts admire.
Thy eye Jove's lightning bears, thy voice his dreadful thunder,
Which, not to anger bent, is music and sweet fire.
Celestial as thou art, O, pardon love this wrong,
That sings heaven's praise with such an earthly tongue."

Holofernes.
You find not the apostraphus, and so miss the accent. Let me supervise the canzonet.

He takes the letter.

Here are only numbers ratified, but for the elegancy, facility, and golden cadence of poesy, caret. Ovidius Naso was the man. And why indeed "Naso," but for smelling out the odoriferous flowers of fancy, the jerks of invention? Imitari is nothing: so doth the hound his master, the ape his keeper, the tired horse his rider. But, damosella virgin, was this directed to you?

Jaquenetta.
Ay, sir, from one Monsieur Berowne, one of the strange queen's lords.

Holofernes.
I will overglance the superscript: "To the snow-white hand of the most beauteous Lady Rosaline." I will look again on the intellect of the letter, for the nomination of the party

Writing.

to the person written unto: "Your ladyship's in all desired employment, Berowne." Sir Nathaniel, this Berowne is one of the votaries with the King, and here he hath framed a letter to a sequent of the stranger queen's, which accidentally, or by the way of progression, hath miscarried. Trip and go, my sweet, deliver this paper into the royal hand of the King; it may concern much. Stay not thy compliment; I forgive thy duty. Adieu.

Jaquenetta.
Good Costard, go with me. Sir, God save your life!

Costard.
Have with thee, my girl.

Exit with Jaquenetta.

Sir Nathaniel.
Sir, you have done this in the fear of God, very religiously; and as a certain father saith—

Holofernes.
Sir, tell not me of the father, I do fear colorable colors. But to return to the verses: did they please you, Sir Nathaniel?

Sir Nathaniel.
Marvelous well for the pen.

Holofernes.
I do dine today at the father's of a certain pupil of mine, where, if (before repast) it shall please you to gratify the table with a grace, I will, on my privilege I have with the parents of the foresaid child or pupil, undertake your bien venuto; where I will prove those verses to be very unlearned, neither savoring of poetry, wit, nor invention. I beseech your society.

Sir Nathaniel.
And thank you too; for society, saith the text, is the happiness of life.

Holofernes.
And certes the text most infallibly concludes it.

To Dull.

Sir, I do invite you too, you shall not say me nay: pauca verba. Away, the gentles are at their game, and we will to our recreation.

Exeunt.

Scene 3

The King of Navarre's park.

(Berowne; King; Longaville; Dumaine; Jaquenetta; Costard)

Berowne is still considering the fact that he is in love and has written another love letter to Rosaline. Seeing the King coming, he hides, only to overhear the King read out a (rather poor) love poem he has written to the Princess. The King sees Longaville arriving with a paper in hand, and hides; Longaville too reads out a (rather bad) love poem he has written and wonders how to get it to his lady-love. At this point he spies Dumaine arriving and hides. All three overhear this latest arrival agonize and read out his (rather dreadful) love poem. At this point, Longaville jumps out to accuse Dumaine of breaking his vows; the King steps forwards and points out that Longaville is in the same boat; and Berowne, hypocritically vowing to show up hypocrisy, advances to accuse all three of breaking their vow concerning women. Berowne has a fine time being morally superior to the other three, but unfortunately for him Jaquenetta and Costard arrive, bearing his letter to Rosaline, and he too is revealed as a love-sick perjurer. The other three mock him roundly for being in love with an unfashionably dark woman, but he defends her. At their request, Berowne embarks on a hair-splitting rationalization that gets them off the hook for falling in love. The four decide to join together to entertain the ladies, in the hopes of softening their hearts.

Enter Berowne with a paper in his hand, alone.

Berowne.
The King he is hunting the deer: I am coursing myself. They have pitch'd a toil: I am toiling in a pitch—pitch that defiles—defile! A foul word. Well, "set thee down, sorrow!" for so they say the fool said, and so say I, and I the fool: well prov'd, wit! By the Lord, this love is as mad as Ajax. It kills sheep; it kills me, I a sheep: well prov'd again a' my side! I will not love; if I do, hang me; i' faith, I will not. O but her eye—by this light, but for her eye, I would not love her; yes, for her two eyes. Well, I do nothing in the world but lie, and lie in my throat. By heaven, I do love, and it hath taught me to rhyme and to be melancholy; and here is part of my rhyme, and here my melancholy. Well, she hath one a' my sonnets already: the clown bore it, the fool sent it, and the lady hath it: sweet clown, sweeter fool, sweetest lady! By the world, I would not care a pin, if the other three were in. Here comes one with a paper, God give him grace to groan!

He stands aside, climbing into a tree.
The King ent'reth with a paper.

Ferdinand, King of Navarre.
Ay me!

Berowne.

Aside.

Shot, by heaven! Proceed, sweet Cupid, thou hast thump'd him with thy bird-bolt under the left pap. In faith, secrets!

Ferdinand, King of Navarre.

Reads.

"So sweet a kiss the golden sun gives not
To those fresh morning drops upon the rose,
As thy eye-beams, when their fresh rays have smote
The night of dew that on my cheeks down flows;
Nor shines the silver moon one half so bright
Through the transparent bosom of the deep,
As doth thy face through tears of mine give light.
Thou shin'st in every tear that I do weep,
No drop but as a coach doth carry thee;
So ridest thou triumphing in my woe.
Do but behold the tears that swell in me,
And they thy glory through my grief will show.
But do not love thyself, then thou wilt keep
My tears for glasses, and still make me weep.
O queen of queens, how far dost thou excel
No thought can think, nor tongue of mortal tell."
How shall she know my griefs? I'll drop the paper.
Sweet leaves, shade folly. Who is he comes here?

Enter Longaville with a paper. The King steps aside.

What, Longaville, and reading! Listen, ear.

Berowne.

Aside.

Now in thy likeness, one more fool appear!

Act 4, Scene 3

Longaville.
Ay me, I am forsworn!

Berowne.

Aside.

Why, he comes in like a perjure, wearing papers.

Ferdinand, King of Navarre.

Aside.

In love, I hope—sweet fellowship in shame.

Berowne.

Aside.

One drunkard loves another of the name.

Longaville.
Am I the first that have been perjur'd so?

Berowne.

Aside.

I could put thee in comfort: not by two that I know.
Thou makest the triumphery, the corner-cap of society,
The shape of love's Tyburn that hangs up simplicity.

Longaville.
I fear these stubborn lines lack power to move.
O sweet Maria, empress of my love,
These numbers will I tear, and write in prose!

Berowne.

Aside.

O, rhymes are guards on wanton Cupid's hose:
Disfigure not his shop.

Longaville.
              This same shall go.

He reads the sonnet.

"Did not the heavenly rhetoric of thine eye,
'Gainst whom the world cannot hold argument,
Persuade my heart to this false perjury?
Vows for thee broke deserve not punishment.
A woman I forswore, but I will prove,
Thou being a goddess, I forswore not thee.
My vow was earthly, thou a heavenly love;
Thy grace being gain'd cures all disgrace in me.
Vows are but breath, and breath a vapor is;
Then thou, fair sun, which on my earth dost shine,
Exhal'st this vapor-vow; in thee it is.
If broken then, it is no fault of mine:
If by me broke, what fool is not so wise
To lose an oath to win a paradise?"

Berowne.

Aside.

This is the liver-vein, which makes flesh a deity,
A green goose a goddess; pure, pure idolatry.
God amend us, God amend! We are much out a' th' way.

Enter Dumaine with a paper.

Longaville.
By whom shall I send this?—Company? Stay.

Steps aside.

Berowne.

Aside.

"All hid, all hid," an old infant play.
Like a demigod here sit I in the sky,
And wretched fools' secrets heedfully o'er-eye.
More sacks to the mill! O heavens, I have my wish!
Dumaine transformed! Four woodcocks in a dish!

Dumaine.
O most divine Kate!

Berowne.

Aside.

O most profane coxcomb!

Dumaine.
By heaven, the wonder in a mortal eye!

Berowne.

Aside.

By earth, she is not, corporal, there you lie.

Dumaine.
Her amber hairs for foul hath amber coted.

Berowne.

Aside.

An amber-color'd raven was well noted.

Dumaine.
As upright as the cedar.

Berowne.

Aside.

      Stoop, I say,
Her shoulder is with child.

Dumaine.
      As fair as day.

Berowne.

Aside.

Ay, as some days, but then no sun must shine.

Dumaine.
O that I had my wish!

Longaville.

Aside.

      And I had mine!

Ferdinand, King of Navarre.

Aside.

And mine too, good Lord!

Berowne.

Aside.

Amen, so I had mine. Is not that a good word?

Dumaine.
I would forget her, but a fever she
Reigns in my blood, and will rememb'red be.

Berowne.

Aside.

A fever in your blood! Why then incision
Would let her out in saucers. Sweet misprision!

Dumaine.
Once more I'll read the ode that I have writ.

Berowne.

Aside.

Once more I'll mark how love can vary wit.

Dumaine.

Reads his sonnet.

"On a day—alack the day!—
Love, whose month is ever May,
Spied a blossom passing fair
Playing in the wanton air:
Through the velvet leaves the wind,
All unseen, can passage find;
That the lover, sick to death,
Wish'd himself the heavens' breath.
Air, quoth he, thy cheeks may blow;
Air, would I might triumph so!
But, alack, my hand is sworn
ne'er to pluck thee from thy thorn;
Vow, alack, for youth unmeet,
Youth so apt to pluck a sweet.
Do not call it sin in me,
That I am forsworn for thee;
Thou for whom Jove would swear
Juno but an Ethiop were,
And deny himself for Jove,
Turning mortal for thy love."
This will I send and something else more plain
That shall express my true love's fasting pain.
O would the King, Berowne, and Longaville
Were lovers too! Ill, to example ill,
Would from my forehead wipe a perjur'd note:
For none offend where all alike do dote.

Longaville.

Advancing.

Dumaine, thy love is far from charity,
That in love's grief desir'st society:
You may look pale, but I should blush, I know,
To be o'erheard and taken napping so.

Ferdinand, King of Navarre.

Advancing.

Come, sir, you blush; as his your case is such;
You chide at him, offending twice as much.
You do not love Maria? Longaville
Did never sonnet for her sake compile,
Nor never lay his wreathed arms athwart

His loving bosom to keep down his heart.
I have been closely shrouded in this bush
And mark'd you both, and for you both did blush.
I heard your guilty rhymes, observ'd your fashion,
Saw sighs reek from you, noted well your passion.
"Ay me!" says one, "O Jove!" the other cries;
One, her hairs were gold, crystal the other's eyes.

To Longaville.

You would for paradise break faith and troth,

To Dumaine.

And Jove for your love would infringe an oath.
What will Berowne say when that he shall hear
Faith infringed, which such zeal did swear?
How will he scorn! How will he spend his wit!
How will he triumph, leap, and laugh at it!
For all the wealth that ever I did see,
I would not have him know so much by me.

Berowne.
Now step I forth to whip hypocrisy.

Descending and advancing.

Ah, good my liege, I pray thee pardon me!
Good heart, what grace hast thou thus to reprove
These worms for loving, that art most in love?
Your eyes do make no coaches; in your tears
There is no certain princess that appears;
You'll not be perjur'd, 'tis a hateful thing;
Tush, none but minstrels like of sonneting!
But are you not asham'd? Nay, are you not,
All three of you, to be thus much o'ershot?
You found his mote, the King your mote did see;
But I a beam do find in each of three.
O, what a scene of fool'ry have I seen,
Of sighs, of groans, of sorrow, and of teen!
O me, with what strict patience have I sat,
To see a king transformed to a gnat!
To see great Hercules whipping a gig,
And profound Salomon to tune a jig,
And Nestor play at push-pin with the boys,
And critic Timon laugh at idle toys!
Where lies thy grief, O, tell me, good Dumaine?
And, gentle Longaville, where lies thy pain?
And where my liege's? All about the breast!
A caudle ho!

Ferdinand, King of Navarre.
                    Too bitter is thy jest.
Are we betrayed thus to thy over-view?

Berowne.
Not you by me, but I betrayed to you:
I that am honest, I that hold it sin
To break the vow I am engaged in.
I am betrayed by keeping company
With men like you, men of inconstancy.
When shall you see me write a thing in rhyme,
Or groan for Joan, or spend a minute's time
In pruning me? When shall you hear that I
Will praise a hand, a foot, a face, an eye,
A gait, a state, a brow, a breast, a waist,
A leg, a limb—

Ferdinand, King of Navarre.
                    Soft, whither away so fast?
A true man, or a thief, that gallops so?

Berowne.
I post from love; good lover, let me go.

Enter Jaquenetta and Clown Costard.

Jaquenetta.
God bless the King!

Ferdinand, King of Navarre.
                    What present hast thou there?

Costard.
Some certain treason.

Ferdinand, King of Navarre.
                    What makes treason here?

Costard.
Nay, it makes nothing, sir.

Ferdinand, King of Navarre.
                    If it mar nothing neither,
The treason and you go in peace away together.

Jaquenetta.
I beseech your Grace let this letter be read:
Our person misdoubts it; 'twas treason, he said.

Ferdinand, King of Navarre.
Berowne, read it over.

Berowne reads the letter.

                    Where hadst thou it?

Jaquenetta.
Of Costard.

Ferdinand, King of Navarre.
                    Where hadst thou it?

Costard.
Of Dun Adramadio, Dun Adramadio.

Berowne tears the letter.

Ferdinand, King of Navarre.
How now, what is in you? Why dost thou tear it?

Berowne.
A toy, my liege, a toy; your Grace needs not fear it.

Longaville.
It did move him to passion, and therefore let's hear it.

Dumaine.

Gathering up the pieces.

It is Berowne's writing, and here is his name.

Berowne.

To Costard.

Ah, you whoreson loggerhead, you were born to do me shame.
Guilty, my lord, guilty! I confess, I confess.

Ferdinand, King of Navarre.
What?

Berowne.
That you three fools lack'd me fool to make up the mess.
He, he, and you—and you, my liege!—and I,
Are pick-purses in love, and we deserve to die.
O, dismiss this audience, and I shall tell you more.

Dumaine.
Now the number is even.

Berowne.
                    True, true, we are four.
Will these turtles be gone?

Ferdinand, King of Navarre.
                    Hence, sirs, away!

Costard.
Walk aside the true folk, and let the traitors stay.

Exeunt Costard and Jaquenetta.

Berowne.
Sweet lords, sweet lovers, O, let us embrace!
As true we are as flesh and blood can be.
The sea will ebb and flow, heaven show his face;
Young blood doth not obey an old decree.
We cannot cross the cause why we were born;
Therefore of all hands must we be forsworn.

Ferdinand, King of Navarre.
What, did these rent lines show some love of thine?

Berowne.
Did they, quoth you? Who sees the heavenly Rosaline,
That (like a rude and savage man of Inde),
At the first op'ning of the gorgeous east,
Bows not his vassal head, and strucken blind,
Kisses the base ground with obedient breast?
What peremptory eagle-sighted eye
Dares look upon the heaven of her brow,
That is not blinded by her majesty?

Ferdinand, King of Navarre.
What zeal, what fury, hath inspir'd thee now?
My love (her mistress) is a gracious moon,
She (an attending star) scarce seen a light.

Berowne.
My eyes are then no eyes, nor I Berowne.
O, but for my love, day would turn to night!
Of all complexions the cull'd sovereignty
Do meet as at a fair in her fair cheek,
Where several worthies make one dignity,
Where nothing wants that want itself doth seek.
Lend me the flourish of all gentle tongues—
Fie, painted rhetoric! O, she needs it not.
To things of sale a seller's praise belongs:
She passes praise, then praise too short doth blot.
A wither'd hermit, fivescore winters worn,
Might shake off fifty, looking in her eye:
Beauty doth varnish age, as if new born,
And gives the crutch the cradle's infancy.
O, 'tis the sun that maketh all things shine!

Ferdinand, King of Navarre.
By heaven, thy love is black as ebony.

Berowne.
Is ebony like her? O wood divine!
A wife of such wood were felicity.
O, who can give an oath? Where is a book?
That I may swear beauty doth beauty lack,
If that she learn not of her eye to look:
No face is fair that is not full so black.

Ferdinand, King of Navarre.
O paradox! Black is the badge of hell,
The hue of dungeons, and the school of night;
And beauty's crest becomes the heavens well.

Berowne.
Devils soonest tempt, resembling spirits of
O, if in black my lady's brows be deck'd,
It mourns that painting and usurping hair
Should ravish doters with a false aspect:
And therefore is she born to make black fair.
Her favor turns the fashion of the days,
For native blood is counted painting now;
And therefore red, that would avoid dispraise,
Paints itself black, to imitate her brow.

Dumaine.
To look like her are chimney-sweepers black.

Longaville.
And since her time are colliers counted bright.

Ferdinand, King of Navarre.
And Ethiops of their sweet complexion crack.

Dumaine.
Dark needs no candles now, for dark is light.

Berowne.
Your mistresses dare never come in rain,
For fear their colors should be wash'd away.

Ferdinand, King of Navarre.
'Twere good yours did; for, sir, to tell you plain,
I'll find a fairer face not wash'd today.

Berowne.
I'll prove her fair, or talk till doomsday here.

Ferdinand, King of Navarre.
No devil will fright thee then so much as she.

Dumaine.
I never knew man hold vile stuff so dear.

Longaville.
Look, here's thy love,

Showing his boot.

my foot and her face see.

Berowne.
O, if the streets were paved with thine eyes,
Her feet were much too dainty for such tread!

Dumaine.
O vile! Then as she goes what upward lies
The street should see as she walk'd overhead.

Ferdinand, King of Navarre.
But what of this, are we not all in love?

Berowne.
O, nothing so sure, and thereby all forsworn.

Ferdinand, King of Navarre.
Then leave this chat, and, good Berowne, now prove
Our loving lawful, and our faith not torn.

Dumaine.
Ay marry, there—some flattery for this evil.

Longaville.
O, some authority how to proceed;
Some tricks, some quillets, how to cheat the devil.

Dumaine.
Some salve for perjury.

Berowne.
                    O, 'tis more than need.
Have at you then, affection's men-at-arms.
Consider what you first did swear unto:
To fast, to study, and to see no woman—
Flat treason 'gainst the kingly state of youth.
Say, can you fast? Your stomachs are too young,
And abstinence engenders maladies.
(And where that you have vow'd to study, lords,
In that each of you have forsworn his book,
Can you still dream and pore and thereon look?
For when would you, my lord, or you, or you,
Have found the ground of study's excellence
Without the beauty of a woman's face?
From women's eyes this doctrine I derive:
They are the ground, the books, the academes,
From whence doth spring the true Promethean fire.
Why, universal plodding poisons up
The nimble spirits in the arteries,

As motion and long-during action tires
The sinowy vigor of the traveler.
Now for not looking on a woman's face,
You have in that forsworn the use of eyes,
And study too, the causer of your vow.
For where is any author in the world
Teaches such beauty as a woman's eye?
Learning is but an adjunct to ourself,
And where we are, our learning likewise is.
Then when ourselves we see in ladies' eyes,
With ourselves,
Do we not likewise see our learning there?)
O, we have made a vow to study, lords,
And in that vow we have forsworn our books.
For when would you, my liege, or you, or you,
In leaden contemplation have found out
Such fiery numbers as the prompting eyes
Of beauty's tutors have enrich'd you with?
Other slow arts entirely keep the brain;
And therefore, finding barren practicers,
Scarce show a harvest of their heavy toil;
But love, first learned in a lady's eyes,
Lives not alone immured in the brain,
But with the motion of all elements,
Courses as swift as thought in every power,
And gives to every power a double power,
Above their functions and their offices.
It adds a precious seeing to the eye:
A lover's eyes will gaze an eagle blind.
A lover's ear will hear the lowest sound,
When the suspicious head of theft is stopp'd.
Love's feeling is more soft and sensible
Than are the tender horns of cockled snails.
Love's tongue proves dainty Bacchus gross in taste.
For valor, is not Love a Hercules,
Still climbing trees in the Hesperides?
Subtile as Sphinx, as sweet and musical
As bright Apollo's lute, strung with his hair.
And when Love speaks, the voice of all the gods
Make heaven drowsy with the harmony.
Never durst poet touch a pen to write
Until his ink were temp'red with Love's sighs:
O then his lines would ravish savage ears
And plant in tyrants mild humility.
From women's eyes this doctrine I derive:
They sparkle still the right Promethean fire;
They are the books, the arts, the academes,
That show, contain, and nourish all the world,
Else none at all in aught proves excellent.
Then fools you were these women to forswear,
Or keeping what is sworn, you will prove fools.
For wisdom's sake, a word that all men love,
Or for love's sake, a word that loves all men,
Or for men's sake, the authors of these women,
Or women's sake, by whom we men are men,
Let us once lose our oaths to find ourselves,
Or else we lose ourselves to keep our oaths.
It is religion to be thus forsworn:
For charity itself fulfills the law,
And who can sever love from charity?

Ferdinand, King of Navarre.
Saint Cupid, then! And, soldiers, to the field!

Berowne.
Advance your standards, and upon them, lords;
Pell-mell, down with them! But be first advis'd,
In conflict that you get the sun of them.

Longaville.
Now to plain-dealing, lay these glozes by:
Shall we resolve to woo these girls of France?

Ferdinand, King of Navarre.
And win them too; therefore let us devise
Some entertainment for them in their tents.

Berowne.
First, from the park let us conduct them thither;
Then homeward every man attach the hand
Of his fair mistress. In the afternoon
We will with some strange pastime solace them,
Such as the shortness of the time can shape,
For revels, dances, masks, and merry hours
Forerun fair Love, strewing her way with flowers.

Ferdinand, King of Navarre.
Away, away, no time shall be omitted
That will be time, and may by us be fitted.

Berowne.
Allons! Allons!
Sow'd cockle reap'd no corn,
And justice always whirls in equal measure:
Light wenches may prove plagues to men forsworn;
If so, our copper buys no better treasure.

Exeunt.

Act 5

Scene 1

The King of Navarre's park.

(Holofernes; Sir Nathaniel; Dull; Armado; Moth; Costard)

Holofernes rants against changes in pronunciation to Nathaniel. Armado, Costard, and Moth meet up with him and they all get on very well, Moth outpacing Holofernes's brain, though the pedant gets on very well with Armado, whose phraseology he finds admirable. Getting to the point, Armado, insisting that he is very close to the King, explains that he has been asked to present a show to entertain the Princess; needing help, he turns to the schoolmaster and the curate. Holofernes immediately decides that they should present a pageant of the Nine Worthies, even though they do not have nine people to play the roles. Constable Dull, who has been listening all this while, freely admits he hasn't understood a word from the beginning.

Enter the Pedant Holofernes, the Curate Sir Nathaniel, and Dull.

Holofernes.
Satis quid sufficit.

Sir Nathaniel.
I praise God for you, sir. Your reasons at dinner have been sharp and sententious: pleasant without scurrility, witty without affection, audacious without impudency, learned without opinion, and strange without heresy. I did converse this quondam day with a companion of the King's, who is intituled, nominated, or called, Don Adriano de Armado.

Holofernes.
Novi hominem tanquam te. His humor is lofty, his discourse peremptory, his tongue filed, his eye ambitious, his gait majestical, and his general behavior vain, ridiculous, and thrasonical. He is too picked, too spruce, too affected, too odd as it were, too peregrinate, as I may call it.

Sir Nathaniel.
A most singular and choice epithet.

Draw out his table-book.

Holofernes.
He draweth out the thread of his verbosity finer than the staple of his argument. I abhor such fanatical phantasimes, such insociable and point-devise companions, such rackers of orthography, as to speak "dout," fine, when he should say "doubt"; "det," when he should pronounce "debt"—d, e, b, t, not d, e, t: he clepeth a calf, "cauf"; half, "hauf"; neighbor vocatur "nebor"; neigh abbreviated "ne." This is abhominable—which he would call "abbominable"; it insinuateth me of insanie: ne intelligis, domine? To make frantic, lunatic.

Sir Nathaniel.
Laus Deo, bone intelligo.

Holofernes.
Bone? Bone for bene, Priscian a little scratch'd, 'twill serve.

Enter Braggart Armado, Boy Moth, and Costard.

Sir Nathaniel.
Videsne quis venit?

Holofernes.
Video, et gaudeo.

Don Adriano de Armado.

To Moth.

Chirrah!

Holofernes.
Quare. Chirrah, not sirrah?

Don Adriano de Armado.
Men of peace, well encount'red.

Holofernes.
Most military sir, salutation.

Moth.

Aside to Costard

They have been at a great feast of languages, and stol'n the scraps.

Costard.
O, they have liv'd long on the alms-basket of words. I marvel thy master hath not eaten thee for a word, for thou art not so long by the head as honorificabil-

itudinitatibus: thou art easier swallow'd than a flap-dragon.

Moth.
Peace, the peal begins.

Don Adriano de Armado.

To Holofernes.

Monsieur, are you not lett'red?

Moth.
Yes, yes, he teaches boys the horn-book. What is a, b, spell'd backward, with the horn on his head?

Holofernes.
Ba, pueritia, with a horn added.

Moth.
Ba, most silly sheep, with a horn. You hear his learning.

Holofernes.
Quis, quis, thou consonant?

Moth.
The last of the five vowels, if "you" repeat them; or the fift, if I.

Holofernes.
I will repeat them—a, e, I—

Moth.
The sheep: the other two concludes it—o, U.

Don Adriano de Armado.
Now by the salt wave of the Mediterraneum, a sweet touch, a quick venue of wit—snip, snap, quick and home. It rejoiceth my intellect. True wit!

Moth.
Offer'd by a child to an old man: which is wit-old.

Holofernes.
What is the figure? What is the figure?

Moth.
Horns.

Holofernes.
Thou disputes like an infant; go whip thy gig.

Moth.
Lend me your horn to make one, and I will whip about your infamy, manu cita—a gig of a cuckold's horn.

Costard.
And I had but one penny in the world, thou shouldst have it to buy gingerbread. Hold, there is the very remuneration I had of thy master, thou halfpenny purse of wit, thou pigeon-egg of discretion. O, and the heavens were so pleas'd that thou wert but my bastard, what a joyful father wouldest thou make me! Go to, thou hast it ad dunghill, at the fingers' ends, as they say.

Holofernes.
O, I smell false Latin, "dunghill" for unguem.

Don Adriano de Armado.
Arts-man, preambulate, we will be singuled from the barbarous. Do you not educate youth at the charge-house on the top of the mountain?

Holofernes.
Or mons, the hill.

Don Adriano de Armado.
At your sweet pleasure, for the mountain.

Holofernes.
I do, sans question.

Don Adriano de Armado.
Sir, it is the King's most sweet pleasure and affection to congratulate the Princess at her pavilion in the posteriors of this day, which the rude multitude call the afternoon.

Holofernes.
The posterior of the day, most generous sir, is liable, congruent, and measurable for the afternoon. The word is well cull'd, chose, sweet, and apt, I do assure you, sir, I do assure.

Don Adriano de Armado.
Sir, the King is a noble gentleman, and my familiar, I do assure ye, very good friend; for what is inward between us, let it pass. I do beseech thee remember thy courtesy; I beseech thee apparel thy head; and among other importunate and most serious designs, and of great import indeed too—but let that pass; for I must tell thee it will please his Grace (by the world) sometime to lean upon my poor shoulder, and with his royal finger, thus, dally with my excrement, with my mustachio; but, sweet heart, let that pass. By the world, I recount no fable: some certain special honors it pleaseth his greatness to impart to Armado, a soldier, a man of travel, that hath seen the world; but

let that pass. The very all of all is—but, sweet heart, I do implore secrecy—that the King would have me present the Princess (sweet chuck) with some delightful ostentation, or show, or pageant, or antic, or firework. Now, understanding that the curate and your sweet self are good at such eruptions and sudden breaking out of mirth (as it were), I have acquainted you withal, to the end to crave your assistance.

Holofernes.
Sir, you shall present before her the Nine Worthies. Sir Nathaniel, as concerning some entertainment of time, some show in the posterior of this day, to be rend'red by our assistance, the King's command, and this most gallant, illustrate, and learned gentleman, before the Princess, I say none so fit as to present the Nine Worthies.

Sir Nathaniel.
Where will you find men worthy enough to present them?

Holofernes.
Joshua, yourself; myself; and this gallant gentleman, Judas Machabeus; this swain (because of his great limb or joint) shall pass Pompey the Great; the page, Hercules.

Don Adriano de Armado.
Pardon, sir, error: he is not quantity enough for that Worthy's thumb, he is not so big as the end of his club.

Holofernes.
Shall I have audience? He shall present Hercules in minority; his enter and exit shall be strangling a snake; and I will have an apology for that purpose.

Moth.
An excellent device! So if any of the audience hiss, you may cry, "Well done, Hercules, now thou crushest the snake!" That is the way to make an offense gracious, though few have the grace to do it.

Don Adriano de Armado.
For the rest of the Worthies?

Holofernes.
I will play three myself.

Moth.
Thrice-worthy gentleman!

Don Adriano de Armado.
Shall I tell you a thing?

Holofernes.
We attend.

Don Adriano de Armado.
We will have, if this fadge not, an antic. I beseech you follow.

Holofernes.
Via, goodman Dull! Thou hast spoken no word all this while.

Dull.
Nor understood none neither, sir.

Holofernes.
Allons! We will employ thee.

Dull.
I'll make one in a dance, or so; or I will play
On the tabor to the Worthies, and let them dance the hay.

Holofernes.
Most dull, honest Dull! To our sport; away!

Exeunt.

Scene 2

The King of Navarre's park.

(*Princess of France; Maria; Katherine; Rosaline; Boyet; Blackamoors; Moth; King Navarre; Dumaine; Longaville; Costard; Armado; Sir Nathaniel; Holofernes; Berowne; Monsieur Marcade; Hiems, the Winter; Ver, the Spring*)

The Princess shows off a diamond necklace that the King has sent her along with his bad poetry; the other ladies display the gifts they have received, bantering with one another. They resolve to make a mockery of their lovers. Boyet enters, hugely entertained, and warns the ladies that he has overheard the gentlemen planning to visit, disguised as Russians. The Princess, convinced that all this wooing is done in jest, instantly resolves that she and her ladies shall put on masks and therefore make the lovers woo the wrong woman. Moth enters to introduce the Russians, but the ladies behave in such a way that he is forced to modify his text as he goes along to match present circumstances, much to Berowne's annoyance. Each of the men goes to the woman he thinks is his love, judging by which gift they are holding in evidence, and the ladies, who have of course exchanged these gifts, play along. Once the men leave, the ladies compare the oaths they heard. They take up their own gifts in preparation for the men's return, and resolve to tell them about the pack of Russian fools that was just here. The men soon work out that they have been sussed out; Berowne, realizing that it's all over, announces that he will stop trying to woo the traditional way, since it clearly doesn't work. Berowne then works out that they have been made fools of from the start when it is discovered that all of the men pledged their troth to the wrong woman. Costard arrives to announce the pageant of the Nine Worthies; the King realizes that the show is likely to be dreadful and not show off his court well, but the Princess insists it will be even more amusing by being funny without trying. The actors valiantly try to present their show in spite of the running commentary of their audience, the interjections and insults that are thrown at them. Holofernes in the end breaks character and points out that the audience is not behaving like gentlemen. In the middle of Armado's portion of the show, Costard announces to him that Jaquenetta is pregnant by him. Armado threatens to fight Costard for announcing this, but refuses to undo his shirt for the fight, out of fear of losing a cloth of Jaquenetta's that he wears next to his heart. The mockery is silenced when Marcade arrives from France; the Princess immediately realizes that her father must have died and that she is now Queen of France. She immediately prepares to leave. She confesses that she and her ladies believed that the men were merely wooing them to be pleasant, but to their protestations that their feelings are genuine, none of them are receptive. The Queen insists that the King has moved too fast, and tells him that if he will wait a year in a hermitage and emerge with his mind unchanged about her, she will marry him. The other ladies likewise insist on making their men wait a year; Rosaline in particular wishes Berowne to learn a lesson, thinking him too easily mean, and commands him to learn to use his wit to make people happy by spending the year cheering the spirits of dying patients in the hospital. Armado enters, announcing that he is to marry Jaquenetta and that he has promised to work at honest labor for her. He and his companions beg leave to sing the song that was to end their show, and receive it. Then all go their separate ways.

Enter the Ladies: the Princess, Maria, Katherine, and Rosaline.

The Princess of France.
Sweet hearts, we shall be rich ere we depart,
If fairings come thus plentifully in.
A lady wall'd about with diamonds!
Look you what I have from the loving King.

Rosaline.
Madam, came nothing else along with that?

The Princess of France.
Nothing but this? Yes, as much love in rhyme
As would be cramm'd up in a sheet of paper,
Writ a' both sides the leaf, margent and all,
That he was fain to seal on Cupid's name.

Rosaline.
That was the way to make his godhead wax,
For he hath been five thousand year a boy.

Katherine.
Ay, and a shrewd unhappy gallows too.

Rosaline.
You'll ne'er be friends with him, 'a kill'd your sister.

Katherine.
He made her melancholy, sad, and heavy,
And so she died. Had she been light, like you,
Of such a merry, nimble, stirring spirit,
She might 'a' been a grandam ere she died.
And so may you; for a light heart lives long.

Rosaline.
What's your dark meaning, mouse, of this light word?

Katherine.
A light condition in a beauty dark.

Rosaline.
We need more light to find your meaning out.

Katherine.
You'll mar the light by taking it in snuff;
Therefore I'll darkly end the argument.

Rosaline.
Look what you do, you do it still i' th' dark.

Katherine.
So do not you, for you are a light wench.

Rosaline.
Indeed I weigh not you, and therefore light.

Katherine.
You weigh me not? O, that's you care not for me.

Rosaline.
Great reason: for past care is still past cure.

The Princess of France.
Well bandied both, a set of wit well played.
But, Rosaline, you have a favor too?
Who sent it? And what is it?

Rosaline.
      I would you knew.
And if my face were but as fair as yours,
My favor were as great: be witness this.
Nay, I have verses too, I thank Berowne;
The numbers true, and, were the numb'ring too,
I were the fairest goddess on the ground.
I am compar'd to twenty thousand fairs.
O, he hath drawn my picture in his letter!

The Princess of France.
Any thing like?

Rosaline.
Much in the letters, nothing in the praise.

The Princess of France.
Beauteous as ink—a good conclusion.

Katherine.
Fair as a text B in a copy-book.

Rosaline.
Ware pencils ho! Let me not die your debtor,
My red dominical, my golden letter:
O that your face were not so full of o's!

The Princess of France.
A pox of that jest! And I beshrew all shrews.
But, Katherine, what was sent to you from fair Dumaine?

Katherine.
Madam, this glove.

The Princess of France.
      Did he not send you twain?

Katherine.
Yes, madam, and moreover
Some thousand verses of a faithful lover.
A huge translation of hypocrisy,
Vildly compiled, profound simplicity.

Maria.
This, and these pearls, to me sent Longaville.
The letter is too long by half a mile.

The Princess of France.
I think no less. Dost thou not wish in heart
The chain were longer and the letter short?

Maria.
Ay, or I would these hands might never part.

The Princess of France.
We are wise girls to mock our lovers so.

Rosaline.
They are worse fools to purchase mocking so.
That same Berowne I'll torture ere I go.
O that I knew he were but in by th' week!
How I would make him fawn, and beg, and seek,
And wait the season, and observe the times,
And spend his prodigal wits in bootless rhymes,
And shape his service wholly to my device,
And make him proud to make me proud that jests!
So pair-taunt-like would I o'ersway his state
That he should be my fool and I his fate.

The Princess of France.
None are so surely caught, when they are catch'd,
As wit turn'd fool; folly, in wisdom hatch'd,
Hath wisdom's warrant and the help of school,
And wit's own grace to grace a learned fool.

Rosaline.
The blood of youth burns not with such excess
As gravity's revolt to wantonness.

Maria.
Folly in fools bears not so strong a note
As fool'ry in the wise, when wit doth dote,
Since all the power thereof it doth apply
To prove, by wit, worth in simplicity.

Enter Boyet.

The Princess of France.
Here comes Boyet, and mirth is in his face.

Boyet.
O, I am stabb'd with laughter! Where's her Grace?

The Princess of France.
Thy news, Boyet?

Boyet.
                    Prepare, madam, prepare!
Arm, wenches, arm! Encounters mounted are
Against your peace. Love doth approach disguis'd,
Armed in arguments—You'll be surpris'd.
Muster your wits, stand in your own defense,
Or hide your heads like cowards, and fly hence.

The Princess of France.
Saint Denis to Saint Cupid! What are they
That charge their breath against us? Say, scout, say.

Boyet.
Under the cool shade of a sycamore
I thought to close mine eyes some half an hour;
When lo, to interrupt my purpos'd rest,
Toward that shade I might behold address'd
The King and his companions. Warily
I stole into a neighbor thicket by,
And overheard what you shall overhear:
That by and by disguis'd they will be here.
Their herald is a pretty knavish page,
That well by heart hath conn'd his embassage.
Action and accent did they teach him there:
"Thus must thou speak," and "thus thy body bear";
And ever and anon they made a doubt
Presence majestical would put him out;
"For," quoth the King, "an angel shalt thou see;
Yet fear not thou, but speak audaciously."
The boy replied, "An angel is not evil;
I should have fear'd her had she been a devil."
With that all laugh'd, and clapp'd him on the shoulder,
Making the bold wag by their praises bolder.
One rubb'd his elbow thus, and fleer'd, and swore
A better speech was never spoke before.
Another, with his finger and his thumb,
Cried, "Via! We will do't, come what will come."
The third he caper'd, and cried, "All goes well."
The fourth turn'd on the toe, and down he fell.
With that they all did tumble on the ground,
With such a zealous laughter, so profound,
That in this spleen ridiculous appears,
To check their folly, passion's solemn tears.

The Princess of France.
But what, but what, come they to visit us?

Boyet.
They do, they do; and are apparell'd thus,
Like Muscovites or Russians, as I guess.
Their purpose is to parley, to court, and dance,
And every one his love-feat will advance
Unto his several mistress, which they'll know
By favors several which they did bestow.

The Princess of France.
And will they so? The gallants shall be task'd:
For, ladies, we will every one be mask'd,
And not a man of them shall have the grace,
Despite of suit, to see a lady's face.
Hold, Rosaline, this favor thou shalt wear,
And then the King will court thee for his dear.
Hold, take thou this, my sweet, and give me thine,
So shall Berowne take me for Rosaline.
And change you favors too, so shall your loves
Woo contrary, deceiv'd by these removes.

Rosaline.
Come on then, wear the favors most in sight.

Katherine.
But in this changing, what is your intent?

The Princess of France.
The effect of my intent is to cross theirs:
They do it but in mockery merriment,
And mock for mock is only my intent.
Their several counsels they unbosom shall
To loves mistook, and so be mock'd withal
Upon the next occasion that we meet,
With visages display'd, to talk and greet.

Rosaline.
But shall we dance, if they desire us to't?

The Princess of France.
No, to the death we will not move a foot,
Nor to their penn'd speech render we no grace,
But while 'tis spoke each turn away her face.

Boyet.
Why, that contempt will kill the speaker's heart,
And quite divorce his memory from his part.

The Princess of France.
Therefore I do it, and I make no doubt
The rest will ne'er come in, if he be out.
There's no such sport as sport by sport o'erthrown,
To make theirs ours and ours none but our own;
So shall we stay, mocking intended game,

Act 5, Scene 2

And they, well mock'd, depart away with shame.

Sound trumpet within.

Boyet.
The trumpet sounds, be mask'd; the maskers come.

The Ladies mask.
Enter Blackamoors with music, the Boy Moth with a speech, the King and the rest of the Lords disguised as Russians.

Moth.
"All hail, the richest beauties on the earth!"—

Boyet.
Beauties no richer than rich taffeta.

Moth.
"A holy parcel of the fairest dames

The Ladies turn their backs to him.

That ever turn'd their—backs—to mortal views!"

Berowne.
Their "eyes," villain, their "eyes."

Moth.
"That ever turn'd their eyes to mortal views! Out"—

Boyet.
True, out indeed.

Moth.
"Out of your favors, heavenly spirits, vouchsafe Not to behold"—

Berowne.
"Once to behold," rogue.

Moth.
"Once to behold with your sun-beamed eyes, —with your sun-beamed eyes"—

Boyet.
They will not answer to that epithet;
You were best call it "daughter-beamed eyes."

Moth.
They do not mark me, and that brings me out.

Berowne.
Is this your perfectness? Be gone, you rogue!

Exit Moth.

Rosaline.
What would these strangers? Know their minds, Boyet.
If they do speak our language, 'tis our will
That some plain man recount their purposes.
Know what they would.

Boyet.
                    What would you with the Princess?

Berowne.
Nothing but peace, and gentle visitation.

Rosaline.
What would they, say they?

Boyet.
Nothing but peace, and gentle visitation.

Rosaline.
Why, that they have, and bid them so be gone.

Boyet.
She says, you have it, and you may be gone.

Ferdinand, King of Navarre.
Say to her we have measur'd many miles,
To tread a measure with her on this grass.

Boyet.
They say that they have measur'd many a mile
To tread a measure with you on this grass.

Rosaline.
It is not so. Ask them how many inches
Is in one mile: if they have measured many,
The measure then of one is eas'ly told.

Boyet.
If to come hither you have measur'd miles,
And many miles, the Princess bids you tell
How many inches doth fill up one mile.

Berowne.
Tell her, we measure them by weary steps.

Boyet.
She hears herself.

Rosaline.
                    How many weary steps
Of many weary miles you have o'ergone
Are numb'red in the travel of one mile?

Berowne.
We number nothing that we spend for you;
Our duty is so rich, so infinite,
That we may do it still without accompt.
Vouchsafe to show the sunshine of your face,
That we (like savages) may worship it.

Rosaline.
My face is but a moon, and clouded too.

Ferdinand, King of Navarre.
Blessed are clouds, to do as such clouds do!
Vouchsafe, bright moon, and these thy stars, to shine
(Those clouds removed) upon our watery eyne.

Rosaline.
O vain petitioner! Beg a greater matter,
Thou now requests but moonshine in the water.

Ferdinand, King of Navarre.
Then in our measure do but vouchsafe one change.
Thou bid'st me beg; this begging is not strange.

Rosaline.
Play, music, then! Nay, you must do it soon.

Music plays.

Not yet; no dance: thus change I like the moon.

Ferdinand, King of Navarre.
Will you not dance? How come you thus estranged?

Rosaline.
You took the moon at full, but now she's changed.

Ferdinand, King of Navarre.
Yet still she is the moon, and I the man.
The music plays, vouchsafe some motion to it.

Rosaline.
Our ears vouchsafe it.

Ferdinand, King of Navarre.
                    But your legs should do it.

Rosaline.
Since you are strangers, and come here by chance,
We'll not be nice; take hands. We will not dance.

Ferdinand, King of Navarre.
Why take we hands then?

Rosaline.
                    Only to part friends.
Curtsy, sweet hearts—and so the measure ends.

Ferdinand, King of Navarre.
More measure of this measure; be not nice.

Rosaline.
We can afford no more at such a price.

Ferdinand, King of Navarre.
Price you yourselves; what buys your company?

Rosaline.
Your absence only.

Ferdinand, King of Navarre.
                    That can never be.

Rosaline.
Then cannot we be bought; and so, adieu—
Twice to your visor, and half once to you.

Ferdinand, King of Navarre.
If you deny to dance, let's hold more chat.

Rosaline.
In private then.

Ferdinand, King of Navarre.
                  I am best pleas'd with that.

They converse apart.

Berowne.
White-handed mistress, one sweet word with thee.

The Princess of France.
Honey, and milk, and sugar: there is three.

Berowne.
Nay then two treys, and if you grow so nice,
Metheglin, wort, and malmsey; well run, dice!
There's half a dozen sweets.

The Princess of France.
                  Seventh sweet, adieu.
Since you can cog, I'll play no more with you.

Berowne.
One word in secret.

Act 5, Scene 2

The Princess of France.
                Let it not be sweet.

Berowne.
Thou grievest my gall.

The Princess of France.
                Gall! Bitter.

Berowne.
                Therefore meet.

They converse apart.

Dumaine.
Will you vouchsafe with me to change a word?

Maria.
Name it.

Dumaine.
                Fair lady—

Maria.
             Say you so? Fair lord—
Take that for your fair lady.

Dumaine.
                Please it you,
As much in private, and I'll bid adieu.

They converse apart.

Katherine.
What, was your vizard made without a tongue?

Longaville.
I know the reason, lady, why you ask.

Katherine.
O for your reason! Quickly, sir, I long!

Longaville.
You have a double tongue within your mask,
And would afford my speechless vizard half.

Katherine.
"Veal," quoth the Dutchman. Is not veal a calf?

Longaville.
A calf, fair lady!

Katherine.
              No, a fair lord calf.

Longaville.
Let's part the word.

Katherine.
            No, I'll not be your half.
Take all and wean it, it may prove an ox.

Longaville.
Look how you butt yourself in these sharp mocks!
Will you give horns, chaste lady? Do not so.

Katherine.
Then die a calf, before your horns do grow.

Longaville.
One word in private with you ere I die.

Katherine.
Bleat softly then, the butcher hears you cry.

They converse apart.

Boyet.
The tongues of mocking wenches are as keen
As is the razor's edge invisible,
Cutting a smaller hair than may be seen;
Above the sense of sense, so sensible
Seemeth their conference, their conceits have wings
Fleeter than arrows, bullets, wind, thought, swifter things.

Rosaline.
Not one word more, my maids, break off, break off.

Berowne.
By heaven, all dry-beaten with pure scoff!

Ferdinand, King of Navarre.
Farewell, mad wenches, you have simple wits.

Exeunt King, Lords, and Blackamoors.

The Princess of France.
Twenty adieus, my frozen Muscovits.
Are these the breed of wits so wondered at?

Boyet.
Tapers they are, with your sweet breaths puff'd out.

Rosaline.
Well-liking wits they have—gross gross, fat fat.

The Princess of France.
O poverty in wit, kingly-poor flout!
Will they not (think you) hang themselves tonight?
Or ever but in vizards show their faces?
This pert Berowne was out of count'nance quite.

Rosaline.
They were all in lamentable cases!
The King was weeping-ripe for a good word.

The Princess of France.
Berowne did swear himself out of all suit.

Maria.
Dumaine was at my service, and his sword:
"No point," quoth I; my servant straight was mute.

Katherine.
Lord Longaville said I came o'er his heart,
And trow you what he call'd me?

The Princess of France.
                Qualm, perhaps.

Katherine.
Yes, in good faith.

The Princess of France.
                Go, sickness as thou art!

Rosaline.
Well, better wits have worn plain statute-caps.
But will you hear? The King is my love sworn.

The Princess of France.
And quick Berowne hath plighted faith to me.

Katherine.
And Longaville was for my service born.

Maria.
Dumaine is mine, as sure as bark on tree.

Boyet.
Madam, and pretty mistresses, give ear:
Immediately they will again be here
In their own shapes; for it can never be
They will digest this harsh indignity.

The Princess of France.
Will they return?

Boyet.
            They will, they will, God knows,
And leap for joy, though they are lame with blows:
Therefore change favors, and when they repair,
Blow like sweet roses in this summer air.

The Princess of France.
How blow? How blow? Speak to be understood.

Boyet.
Fair ladies mask'd are roses in their bud;
Dismask'd, their damask sweet commixture shown,
Are angels vailing clouds, or roses blown.

The Princess of France.
Avaunt, perplexity! What shall we do,
If they return in their own shapes to woo?

Rosaline.
Good madam, if by me you'll be advis'd,
Let's mock them still, as well known as disguis'd.
Let us complain to them what fools were here,
Disguis'd like Muscovites, in shapeless gear;
And wonder what they were, and to what end
Their shallow shows and prologue vildly penn'd,
And their rough carriage so ridiculous,
Should be presented at our tent to us.

Boyet.
Ladies, withdraw; the gallants are at hand.

The Princess of France.
Whip to our tents, as roes run o'er land.

Exeunt Princess and Ladies.
Enter the King and the rest of the Lords in their proper habits.

Ferdinand, King of Navarre.
Fair sir, God save you! Where's the Princess?

Boyet.
Gone to her tent. Please it your Majesty
Command me any service to her thither?

Ferdinand, King of Navarre.
That she vouchsafe me audience for one word.

Boyet.
I will, and so will she, I know, my lord.

Exit.

Berowne.
This fellow pecks up wit as pigeons pease,
And utters it again when God doth please.
He is wit's pedlar, and retails his wares
At wakes and wassails, meetings, markets, fairs:
And we that sell by gross, the Lord doth know,
Have not the grace to grace it with such show.
This gallant pins the wenches on his sleeve;
Had he been Adam, he had tempted Eve.
'A can carve too, and lisp; why, this is he
That kiss'd his hand away in courtesy;
This is the ape of form, monsieur the nice,
That when he plays at tables chides the dice
In honorable terms; nay, he can sing
A mean most meanly, and in ushering
Mend him who can. The ladies call him sweet;
The stairs as he treads on them kiss his feet.
This is the flow'r that smiles on every one,
To show his teeth as white as whale's bone;
And consciences that will not die in debt
Pay him the due of honey-tongued Boyet.

Ferdinand, King of Navarre.
A blister on his sweet tongue, with my heart,
That put Armado's page out of his part!

Enter the Princess, ushered by Boyet, and her Ladies.

Berowne.
See where it comes! Behavior, what wert thou
Till this madman show'd thee? And what art thou now?

Ferdinand, King of Navarre.
All hail, sweet madam, and fair time of day!

The Princess of France.
"Fair" in "all hail" is foul, as I conceive.

Ferdinand, King of Navarre.
Conster my speeches better, if you may.

The Princess of France.
Then wish me better, I will give you leave.

Ferdinand, King of Navarre.
We came to visit you, and purpose now
To lead you to our court; vouchsafe it then.

The Princess of France.
This field shall hold me, and so hold your vow:
Nor God, nor I, delights in perjur'd men.

Ferdinand, King of Navarre.
Rebuke me not for that which you provoke:
The virtue of your eye must break my oath.

The Princess of France.
You nickname virtue; vice you should have spoke,
For virtue's office never breaks men's troth.
Now by my maiden honor, yet as pure
As the unsallied lily, I protest,
A world of torments though I should endure,
I would not yield to be your house's guest:
So much I hate a breaking cause to be
Of heavenly oaths, vow'd with integrity.

Ferdinand, King of Navarre.
O, you have liv'd in desolation here,
Unseen, unvisited, much to our shame.

The Princess of France.
Not so, my lord, it is not so, I swear;
We have had pastimes here and pleasant game,
A mess of Russians left us but of late.

Ferdinand, King of Navarre.
How, madam? Russians?

The Princess of France.
                    Ay, in truth, my lord;
Trim gallants, full of courtship and of state.

Rosaline.
Madam, speak true. It is not so, my lord.
My lady (to the manner of the days)
In courtesy gives undeserving praise.
We four indeed confronted were with four
In Russian habit; here they stay'd an hour,
And talk'd apace; and in that hour, my lord,
They did not bless us with one happy word.
I dare not call them fools; but this I think,
When they are thirsty, fools would fain have drink.

Berowne.
This jest is dry to me. Gentle sweet,
Your wits makes wise things foolish. When we greet,
With eyes best seeing, heaven's fiery eye,
By light we lose light; your capacity
Is of that nature that to your huge store
Wise things seem foolish, and rich things but poor.

Rosaline.
This proves you wise and rich, for in my eye—

Berowne.
I am a fool, and full of poverty.

Rosaline.
But that you take what doth to you belong,
It were a fault to snatch words from my tongue.

Berowne.
O, I am yours, and all that I possess!

Rosaline.
All the fool mine?

Berowne.
                I cannot give you less.

Rosaline.
Which of the vizards was it that you wore?

Berowne.
Where? When? What vizard? Why demand you this?

Rosaline.
There then, that vizard, that superfluous case,
That hid the worse, and show'd the better face.

Ferdinand, King of Navarre.
Aside.
We were descried, they'll mock us now downright.

Dumaine.
Aside.
Let us confess and turn it to a jest.

The Princess of France.
Amaz'd, my lord? Why looks your Highness sad?

Rosaline.
Help, hold his brows, he'll sound! Why look you pale?
Sea-sick, I think, coming from Muscovy.

Berowne.
Thus pour the stars down plagues for perjury.
Can any face of brass hold longer out?
Here stand I, lady, dart thy skill at me,
Bruise me with scorn, confound me with a flout,
Thrust thy sharp wit quite through my ignorance,
Cut me to pieces with thy keen conceit;
And I will wish thee never more to dance,
Nor never more in Russian habit wait.
O, never will I trust to speeches penn'd,
Nor to the motion of a schoolboy's tongue,
Nor never come in vizard to my friend,
Nor woo in rhyme, like a blind harper's song!
Taffeta phrases, silken terms precise,
Three-pil'd hyperboles, spruce affection,
Figures pedantical—these summer flies
Have blown me full of maggot ostentation.
I do forswear them, and I here protest,
By this white glove (how white the hand, God knows!),
Henceforth my wooing mind shall be express'd
In russet yeas and honest kersey noes.
And to begin, wench, so God help me law!
My love to thee is sound, sans crack or flaw.

Rosaline.
Sans "sans," I pray you.

Berowne.
                Yet I have a trick
Of the old rage. Bear with me, I am sick;
I'll leave it by degrees. Soft, let us see—
Write "Lord have mercy on us" on those three:
They are infected, in their hearts it lies;
They have the plague, and caught it of your eyes.
These lords are visited; you are not free,
For the Lord's tokens on you do I see.

The Princess of France.
No, they are free that gave these tokens to us.

Berowne.
Our states are forfeit, seek not to undo us.

Rosaline.
It is not so, for how can this be true,
That you stand forfeit, being those that sue?

Berowne.
Peace, for I will not have to do with you.

Rosaline.
Nor shall not, if I do as I intend.

Berowne.
Speak for yourselves, my wit is at an end.

Ferdinand, King of Navarre.
Teach us, sweet madam, for our rude transgression
Some fair excuse.

The Princess of France.
                The fairest is confession.
Were not you here but even now, disguis'd?

Ferdinand, King of Navarre.
Madam, I was.

The Princess of France.
              And were you well advis'd?

Ferdinand, King of Navarre.
I was, fair madam.

The Princess of France.
              When you then were here,
What did you whisper in your lady's ear?

Ferdinand, King of Navarre.
That more than all the world I did respect her.

The Princess of France.
When she shall challenge this, you will reject her.

Ferdinand, King of Navarre.
Upon mine honor, no.

The Princess of France.
              Peace, peace, forbear:
Your oath once broke, you force not to forswear.

Ferdinand, King of Navarre.
Despise me when I break this oath of mine.

The Princess of France.
I will, and therefore keep it. Rosaline,
What did the Russian whisper in your ear?

Rosaline.
Madam, he swore that he did hold me dear
As precious eyesight, and did value me
Above this world; adding thereto, moreover,
That he would wed me, or else die my lover.

The Princess of France.
God give thee joy of him! The noble lord
Most honorably doth uphold his word.

Ferdinand, King of Navarre.
What mean you, madam? By my life, my troth,
I never swore this lady such an oath.

Rosaline.
By heaven, you did; and to confirm it plain,
You gave me this: but take it, sir, again.

Ferdinand, King of Navarre.
My faith and this the Princess I did give;
I knew her by this jewel on her sleeve.

The Princess of France.
Pardon me, sir, this jewel did she wear,
And Lord Berowne (I thank him) is my dear.
What? Will you have me, or your pearl again?

Berowne.
Neither of either; I remit both twain.
I see the trick an't; here was a consent,
Knowing aforehand of our merriment,
To dash it like a Christmas comedy.
Some carry-tale, some please-man, some slight zany,
Some mumble-news, some trencher-knight, some Dick,
That smiles his cheek in years and knows the trick
To make my lady laugh when she's dispos'd,
Told our intents before; which once disclos'd,
The ladies did change favors; and then we,
Following the signs, woo'd but the sign of she.
Now, to our perjury to add more terror,
We are again forsworn, in will and error.
Much upon this 'tis;

To Boyet.

              and might not you
Forestall our sport, to make us thus untrue?
Do not you know my lady's foot by th' squier,
And laugh upon the apple of her eye?
And stand between her back, sir, and the fire,
Holding a trencher, jesting merrily?
You put our page out. Go, you are allow'd;
Die when you will, a smock shall be your shroud.
You leer upon me, do you? There's an eye
Wounds like a leaden sword.

Boyet.
              Full merrily
Hath this brave manage, this career, been run.

Berowne.
Lo, he is tilting straight! Peace, I have done.

Enter Clown Costard.

Welcome, pure wit, thou part'st a fair fray.

Costard.
O Lord, sir, they would know
Whether the three Worthies shall come in or no.

Berowne.
What, are there but three?

Costard.
                    No, sir, but it is vara fine,
For every one pursents three.

Berowne.
                    And three times thrice is nine.

Costard.
Not so, sir, under correction, sir, I hope it is not so.
You cannot beg us, sir, I can assure you, sir, we know
what we know.
I hope, sir, three times thrice, sir—

Berowne.
Is not nine.

Costard.
Under correction, sir, we know whereuntil it doth
amount.

Berowne.
By Jove, I always took three threes for nine.

Costard.
O Lord, sir, it were pity you should get your living by
reck'ning, sir.

Berowne.
How much is it?

Costard.
O Lord, sir, the parties themselves, the actors, sir, will
show whereuntil it doth amount. For mine own part,
I am, as they say, but to parfect one man in one poor
man, Pompion the Great, sir.

Berowne.
Art thou one of the Worthies?

Costard.
It pleas'd them to think me worthy of Pompey the
Great; for mine own part, I know not the degree of the
Worthy, but I am to stand for him.

Berowne.
Go bid them prepare.

Costard.
We will turn it finely off, sir; we will take some care.

Exit.

Ferdinand, King of Navarre.
Berowne, they will shame us; let them not approach.

Berowne.
We are shame-proof, my lord; and 'tis some policy
To have one show worse than the King's and his company.

Ferdinand, King of Navarre.
I say they shall not come.

The Princess of France.
Nay, my good lord, let me o'errule you now.
That sport best pleases that doth least know how:
Where zeal strives to content, and the contents
Dies in the zeal of that which it presents.
Their form confounded makes most form in mirth,
When great things laboring perish in their birth.

Berowne.
A right description of our sport, my lord.

Enter Braggart Armado.

Don Adriano de Armado.
Anointed, I implore so much expense of thy royal
sweet breath as will utter a brace of words.

Converses apart with the King, and delivers him a paper.

The Princess of France.
Doth this man serve God?

Berowne.
Why ask you?

The Princess of France.
'A speaks not like a man of God his making.

Don Adriano de Armado.
That is all one, my fair, sweet, honey monarch; for I
protest, the schoolmaster is exceeding fantastical, too
too vain, too too vain: but we will put it (as they say)
to fortuna de la guerra. I wish you the peace of mind,
most royal couplement.

Exit.

Ferdinand, King of Navarre.
Here is like to be a good presence of Worthies: he
presents Hector of Troy; the swain, Pompey the Great;
the parish curate, Alexander; Armado's page, Hercules; the pedant, Judas Machabeus;
And if these four Worthies in their first show thrive,

Act 5, Scene 2

These four will change habits, and present the other five.

Berowne.
There is five in the first show.

Ferdinand, King of Navarre.
You are deceived, 'tis not so.

Berowne.
The pedant, the braggart, the hedge-priest, the fool, and the boy:
Abate throw at novum, and the whole world again
Cannot pick out five such, take each one in his vein.

Ferdinand, King of Navarre.
The ship is under sail, and here she comes amain.

Enter Costard for Pompey.

Costard.
"I Pompey am"—

Berowne.
          You lie, you are not he.

Costard.
"I Pompey am"—

Boyet.
          With libbard's head on knee.

Berowne.
Well said, old mocker. I must needs be friends with thee.

Costard.
"I Pompey am, Pompey surnam'd the Big"—

Dumaine.
"The Great."

Costard.
It is "Great," sir.
"Pompey surnam'd the Great,
That oft in field with targe and shield did make my foe to sweat,
And traveling along this coast, I here am come by chance,
And lay my arms before the legs of this sweet lass of France."
If your ladyship would say, "Thanks, Pompey," I had done.

The Princess of France.
Great thanks, great Pompey.

Costard.
'Tis not so much worth; but I hope I was perfect. I made a little fault in "Great."

Berowne.
My hat to a halfpenny, Pompey proves the best Worthy.

Enter Curate Sir Nathaniel for Alexander.

Sir Nathaniel.
"When in the world I liv'd, I was the world's commander;
By east, west, north, and south, I spread my conquering might.
My scutcheon plain declares that I am Alisander"—

Boyet.
Your nose says, no, you are not; for it stands too right.

Berowne.
Your nose smells "no" in this, most tender-smelling knight.

The Princess of France.
The conqueror is dismay'd. Proceed, good Alexander.

Sir Nathaniel.
"When in the world I liv'd, I was the world's commander"—

Boyet.
Most true, 'tis right; you were so, Alisander.

Berowne.
Pompey the Great—

Costard.
Your servant, and Costard.

Berowne.
Take away the conqueror, take away Alisander.

Costard.
To Nathaniel.

O sir, you have overthrown Alisander the conqueror! You will be scrap'd out of the painted cloth for this. Your lion, that holds his poll-axe sitting on a close-stool, will be given to Ajax; he will be the ninth Worthy. A conqueror, and afeard to speak! Run away for shame, Alisander.

Nathaniel retires.

There an't shall please you, a foolish mild man, an honest man, look you, and soon dash'd. He is a marvelous good neighbor, faith, and a very good bowler; but for Alisander—alas, you see how 'tis—a little o'erparted. But there are Worthies a-coming will speak their mind in some other sort.

The Princess of France.
Stand aside, good Pompey.

Enter Pedant Holofernes for Judas, and the Boy Moth for Hercules.

Holofernes.
"Great Hercules is presented by this imp,
Whose club kill'd Cerberus, that three-headed canus;
And when he was a babe, a child, a shrimp,
Thus did he strangle serpents in his manus.
Quoniam he seemeth in minority,
Ergo I come with this apology."

Aside.
Keep some state in thy exit, and vanish.

Moth retires.

"Judas I am"—

Dumaine.
A Judas!

Holofernes.
Not Iscariot, sir.
"Judas I am, ycliped Machabeus."

Dumaine.
Judas Machabeus clipt is plain Judas.

Berowne.
A kissing traitor. How art thou prov'd Judas?

Holofernes.
"Judas I am"—

Dumaine.
The more shame for you, Judas.

Holofernes.
What mean you, sir?

Boyet.
To make Judas hang himself.

Holofernes.
Begin, sir, you are my elder.

Berowne.
Well follow'd: Judas was hang'd on an elder.

Holofernes.
I will not be put out of countenance.

Berowne.
Because thou hast no face.

Holofernes.
What is this?

Boyet.
A cittern-head.

Dumaine.
The head of a bodkin.

Berowne.
A death's face in a ring.

Longaville.
The face of an old Roman coin, scarce seen.

Boyet.
The pommel of Caesar's falchion.

Dumaine.
The carv'd-bone face on a flask.

Berowne.
Saint George's half-cheek in a brooch.

Dumaine.
Ay, and in a brooch of lead.

Berowne.
Ay, and worn in the cap of a tooth-drawer. And now forward, for we have put thee in countenance.

Holofernes.
You have put me out of countenance.

Berowne.
False, we have given thee faces.

Holofernes.
But you have out-fac'd them all.

Berowne.
And thou wert a lion, we would do so.

Boyet.
Therefore as he is, an ass, let him go. And so adieu, sweet Jude! Nay, why dost thou stay?

Dumaine.
For the latter end of his name.

Berowne.
For the ass to the Jude; give it him. Jud-as, away!

Holofernes.
This is not generous, not gentle, not humble.

Boyet.
A light for Monsieur Judas! It grows dark, he may stumble.

Holofernes retires.

The Princess of France.
Alas, poor Machabeus, how hath he been baited!

Enter Braggart Armado for Hector.

Berowne.
Hide thy head, Achilles, here comes Hector in arms.

Dumaine.
Though my mocks come home by me, I will now be merry.

Ferdinand, King of Navarre.
Hector was but a Troyan in respect of this.

Boyet.
But is this Hector?

Ferdinand, King of Navarre.
I think Hector was not so clean-timber'd.

Longaville.
His leg is too big for Hector's.

Dumaine.
More calf, certain.

Boyet.
No, he is best indu'd in the small.

Berowne.
This cannot be Hector.

Dumaine.
He's a god or a painter, for he makes faces.

Don Adriano de Armado.
"The armipotent Mars, of lances the almighty,
Gave Hector a gift"—

Dumaine.
A gilt nutmeg.

Berowne.
A lemon.

Longaville.
Stuck with cloves.

Dumaine.
No, cloven.

Don Adriano de Armado.
Peace!—
"The armipotent Mars, of lances the almighty,
Gave Hector a gift, the heir of Ilion;
A man so breathed, that certain he would fight, yea,
From morn till night, out of his pavilion.
I am that flower"—

Dumaine.
        That mint.

Longaville.
        That columbine.

Don Adriano de Armado.
Sweet Lord Longaville, rein thy tongue.

Longaville.
I must rather give it the rein, for it runs against Hector.

Dumaine.
Ay, and Hector's a greyhound.

Don Adriano de Armado.
The sweet war-man is dead and rotten, sweet chucks, beat not the bones of the buried. When he breathed, he was a man. But I will forward with my device.

To the Princess.

Sweet royalty, bestow on me the sense of hearing.

Berowne steps forth to whisper to Costard and then returns to his place.

The Princess of France.
Speak, brave Hector, we are much delighted.

Don Adriano de Armado.
I do adore thy sweet Grace's slipper.

Boyet.
Loves her by the foot.

Dumaine.
He may not by the yard.

Don Adriano de Armado.
"This Hector far surmounted Hannibal.
The party is gone"—

Costard.
Fellow Hector, she is gone; she is two months on her way.

Don Adriano de Armado.
What meanest thou?

Costard.
Faith, unless you play the honest Troyan, the poor wench is cast away. She's quick, the child brags in her belly already. 'Tis yours.

Don Adriano de Armado.
Dost thou infamonize me among potentates? Thou shalt die.

Costard.
Then shall Hector be whipt for Jaquenetta that is quick by him, and hang'd for Pompey that is dead by him.

Dumaine.
Most rare Pompey!

Boyet.
Renowned Pompey!

Berowne.
Greater than great, great, great, great Pompey! Pompey the Huge!

Dumaine.
Hector trembles.

Berowne.
Pompey is mov'd. More Ates, more Ates! Stir them on, stir them on!

Dumaine.
Hector will challenge him.

Berowne.
Ay, if 'a have no more man's blood in his belly than will sup a flea.

Don Adriano de Armado.
By the north pole, I do challenge thee.

Costard.
I will not fight with a pole like a Northren man; I'll slash, I'll do it by the sword. I bepray you let me borrow my arms again.

Dumaine.
Room for the incens'd Worthies!

Costard.
I'll do it in my shirt.

Dumaine.
Most resolute Pompey!

Moth.
Master, let me take you a button-hole lower. Do you not see Pompey is uncasing for the combat? What mean you? You will lose your reputation.

Don Adriano de Armado.
Gentlemen and soldiers, pardon me, I will not combat in my shirt.

Dumaine.
You may not deny it; Pompey hath made the challenge.

Don Adriano de Armado.
Sweet bloods, I both may and will.

Berowne.
What reason have you for't?

Don Adriano de Armado.
The naked truth of it is, I have no shirt; I go woolward for penance.

Boyet.
True, and it was enjoin'd him in Rome for want of linen; since when, I'll be sworn he wore none but a dishclout of Jaquenetta's, and that 'a wears next his heart for a favor.

Enter a Messenger, Monsieur Marcade.

Act 5, Scene 2

Marcade.
God save you, madam!

The Princess of France.
                 Welcome, Marcade,
But that thou interruptest our merriment.

Marcade.
I am sorry, madam, for the news I bring
Is heavy in my tongue. The King your father—

The Princess of France.
Dead, for my life!

Marcade.
               Even so: my tale is told.

Berowne.
Worthies, away! The scene begins to cloud.

Don Adriano de Armado.
For mine own part, I breathe free breath. I have seen the day of wrong through the little hole of discretion, and I will right myself like a soldier.

Exeunt Worthies.

Ferdinand, King of Navarre.
How fares your Majesty?

The Princess of France.
Boyet, prepare, I will away tonight.

Ferdinand, King of Navarre.
Madam, not so, I do beseech you stay.

The Princess of France.
Prepare, I say. I thank you, gracious lords,
For all your fair endeavors, and entreat,
Out of a new-sad soul, that you vouchsafe
In your rich wisdom to excuse, or hide,
The liberal opposition of our spirits,
If overboldly we have borne ourselves
In the converse of breath—your gentleness
Was guilty of it. Farewell, worthy lord!
A heavy heart bears not a humble tongue.
Excuse me so, coming too short of thanks
For my great suit so easily obtain'd.

Ferdinand, King of Navarre.
The extreme parts of time extremely forms
All causes to the purpose of his speed,
And often, at his very loose, decides
That which long process could not arbitrate.
And though the mourning brow of progeny
Forbid the smiling courtesy of love
The holy suit which fain it would convince,
Yet since love's argument was first on foot,
Let not the cloud of sorrow justle it
From what it purpos'd; since to wail friends lost
Is not by much so wholesome-profitable
As to rejoice at friends but newly found.

The Princess of France.
I understand you not, my griefs are double.

Berowne.
Honest plain words best pierce the ear of grief,
And by these badges understand the King.
For your fair sakes have we neglected time,
Play'd foul play with our oaths. Your beauty, ladies,
Hath much deformed us, fashioning our humors
Even to the opposed end of our intents;
And what in us hath seem'd ridiculous—
As love is full of unbefitting strains,
All wanton as a child, skipping and vain,
Form'd by the eye and therefore like the eye,
Full of straying shapes, of habits, and of forms,
Varying in subjects as the eye doth roll
To every varied object in his glance;
Which parti-coated presence of loose love
Put on by us, if, in your heavenly eyes,
Have misbecom'd our oaths and gravities,
Those heavenly eyes, that look into these faults,
Suggested us to make. Therefore, ladies,
Our love being yours, the error that love makes
Is likewise yours. We to ourselves prove false,
By being once false forever to be true
To those that make us both—fair ladies, you;
And even that falsehood, in itself a sin,
Thus purifies itself and turns to grace.

The Princess of France.
We have receiv'd your letters full of love;
Your favors, ambassadors of love;
And in our maiden council rated them
At courtship, pleasant jest, and courtesy,
As bombast and as lining to the time;
But more devout than this in our respects
Have we not been, and therefore met your loves
In their own fashion, like a merriment.

Dumaine.
Our letters, madam, show'd much more than jest.

Longaville.
So did our looks.

Rosaline.
                We did not cote them so.

Ferdinand, King of Navarre.
Now at the latest minute of the hour,
Grant us your loves.

The Princess of France.
                A time methinks too short
To make a world-without-end bargain in.
No, no, my lord, your Grace is perjur'd much,
Full of dear guiltiness, and therefore this:
If for my love (as there is no such cause)
You will do aught, this shall you do for me:
Your oath I will not trust, but go with speed
To some forlorn and naked hermitage,
Remote from all the pleasures of the world;
There stay until the twelve celestial signs
Have brought about the annual reckoning.
If this austere insociable life
Change not your offer made in heat of blood;
If frosts and fasts, hard lodging and thin weeds
Nip not the gaudy blossoms of your love
But that it bear this trial, and last love;
Then at the expiration of the year,
Come challenge me, challenge me by these deserts,
And by this virgin palm now kissing thine,
I will be thine; and till that instant shut
My woeful self up in a mourning house,
Raining the tears of lamentation
For the remembrance of my father's death.
If this thou do deny, let our hands part,
Neither intitled in the other's heart.

Ferdinand, King of Navarre.
If this, or more than this, I would deny,
To flatter up these powers of mine with rest,
The sudden hand of death close up mine eye!
Hence hermit then—my heart is in thy breast.

Berowne.
And what to me, my love? And what to me?

Rosaline.
You must be purged too, your sins are rack'd,
You are attaint with faults and perjury:
Therefore if you my favor mean to get,
A twelvemonth shall you spend, and never rest,
But seek the weary beds of people sick.

Dumaine.
But what to me, my love? But what to me?
A wife?

Katherine.
            A beard, fair health, and honesty;
With threefold love I wish you all these three.

Dumaine.
O, shall I say, I thank you, gentle wife?

Katherine.
Not so, my lord, a twelvemonth and a day
I'll mark no words that smooth-fac'd wooers say.
Come when the King doth to my lady come;
Then if I have much love, I'll give you some.

Dumaine.
I'll serve thee true and faithfully till then.

Katherine.
Yet swear not, lest ye be forsworn again.

Longaville.
What says Maria?

Maria.
                At the twelvemonth's end
I'll change my black gown for a faithful friend.

Longaville.
I'll stay with patience, but the time is long.

Maria.
The liker you; few taller are so young.

Berowne.
Studies my lady? Mistress, look on me,
Behold the window of my heart, mine eye,
What humble suit attends thy answer there.
Impose some service on me for thy love.

Rosaline.
Oft have I heard of you, my Lord Berowne,
Before I saw you; and the world's large tongue
Proclaims you for a man replete with mocks,
Full of comparisons and wounding flouts,
Which you on all estates will execute
That lie within the mercy of your wit.
To weed this wormwood from your fructful brain,
And therewithal to win me, if you please,
Without the which I am not to be won,
You shall this twelvemonth term from day to day
Visit the speechless sick, and still converse

With groaning wretches; and your task shall be,
With all the fierce endeavor of your wit,
To enforce the pained impotent to smile.

Berowne.
To move wild laughter in the throat of death?
It cannot be, it is impossible:
Mirth cannot move a soul in agony.

Rosaline.
Why, that's the way to choke a gibing spirit,
Whose influence is begot of that loose grace
Which shallow laughing hearers give to fools.
A jest's prosperity lies in the ear
Of him that hears it, never in the tongue
Of him that makes it; then if sickly ears,
Deaf'd with the clamors of their own dear groans,
Will hear your idle scorns, continue then,
And I will have you and that fault withal;
But if they will not, throw away that spirit,
And I shall find you empty of that fault,
Right joyful of your reformation.

Berowne.
A twelvemonth? Well, befall what will befall,
I'll jest a twelvemonth in an hospital.

The Princess of France.

To the King.

Ay, sweet my lord, and so I take my leave.

Ferdinand, King of Navarre.
No, madam, we will bring you on your way.

Berowne.
Our wooing doth not end like an old play:
Jack hath not Gill. These ladies' courtesy
Might well have made our sport a comedy.

Ferdinand, King of Navarre.
Come, sir, it wants a twelvemonth an' a day,
And then 'twill end.

Berowne.
                    That's too long for a play.

Enter Braggart Armado.

Don Adriano de Armado.
Sweet Majesty, vouchsafe me—

The Princess of France.
Was not that Hector?

Dumaine.
The worthy knight of Troy.

Don Adriano de Armado.
I will kiss thy royal finger, and take leave. I am a votary; I have vow'd to Jaquenetta to hold the plough for her sweet love three year. But, most esteemed greatness, will you hear the dialogue that the two learned men have compiled in praise of the owl and the cuckoo? It should have followed in the end of our show.

Ferdinand, King of Navarre.
Call them forth quickly, we will do so.

Don Adriano de Armado.
Holla! Approach.

Enter all.

This side is Hiems, Winter; this Ver, the Spring; the one maintained by the owl, th' other by the cuckoo. Ver, begin.

The Song

Ver, the Spring.
When daisies pied, and violets blue,
And lady-smocks all silver-white,
And cuckoo-buds of yellow hue
Do paint the meadows with delight,
The cuckoo then on every tree
Mocks married men; for thus sings he, "Cuckoo;
Cuckoo, cuckoo"—O word of fear,
Unpleasing to a married ear!
When shepherds pipe on oaten straws,
And merry larks are ploughmen's clocks;
When turtles tread, and rooks and daws,
And maidens bleach their summer smocks,
The cuckoo then on every tree
Mocks married men; for thus sings he, "Cuckoo;
Cuckoo, cuckoo"—O word of fear,
Unpleasing to a married ear!

Hiems, the Winter.
When icicles hang by the wall,
And Dick the shepherd blows his nail,
And Tom bears logs into the hall,
And milk comes frozen home in pail;
When blood is nipp'd, and ways be foul,

Then nightly sings the staring owl, "Tu-whit, to-who!"—
A merry note,
While greasy Joan doth keel the pot.
When all aloud the wind doth blow,
And coughing drowns the parson's saw,
And birds sit brooding in the snow,
And Marian's nose looks red and raw;
When roasted crabs hiss in the bowl,
Then nightly sings the staring owl, "Tu-whit, to-who!"—
A merry note,
While greasy Joan doth keel the pot.

Don Adriano de Armado.
The words of Mercury are harsh after the songs of Apollo. You that way; we this way.

Exeunt omnes.

Henry V

Prologue

(Prologue)

The Chorus asks the audience to use its imagination to supplement the inadequacies of the stage.

Enter Chorus. CHORUS.

CHORUS.
O for a Muse of fire, that would ascend
The brightest heaven of invention!
A kingdom for a stage, princes to act,
And monarchs to behold the swelling scene!
Then should the warlike Harry, like himself,
Assume the port of Mars, and at his heels
(Leash'd in, like hounds) should famine, sword, and fire
Crouch for employment. But pardon, gentles all,
The flat unraised spirits that hath dar'd
On this unworthy scaffold to bring forth
So great an object. Can this cockpit hold
The vasty fields of France? Or may we cram
Within this wooden O the very casques
That did affright the air at Agincourt?
O, pardon! Since a crooked figure may
Attest in little place a million,
And let us, ciphers to this great accompt,
On your imaginary forces work.
Suppose within the girdle of these walls
Are now confin'd two mighty monarchies,
Whose high, upreared, and abutting fronts
The perilous narrow ocean parts asunder.
Piece out our imperfections with your thoughts;
Into a thousand parts divide one man,
And make imaginary puissance;
Think, when we talk of horses, that you see them
Printing their proud hoofs i' th' receiving earth;
For 'tis your thoughts that now must deck our kings,
Carry them here and there, jumping o'er times,
Turning th' accomplishment of many years
Into an hour-glass: for the which supply,
Admit me Chorus to this history;
Who, Prologue-like, your humble patience pray,
Gently to hear, kindly to judge, our play.

Exit. CHORUS.

Act 1

Scene 1

London. Antechamber in the King's Palace.

(Archbishop of Canterbury; Bishop of Ely)

Canterbury and Ely discuss the great improvement in King Henry's behavior since he inherited the crown. They are concerned about a proposal in parliament to strip the church of a great part of its revenue. Considering Henry's claims to the throne of France, they decide to offer Henry money to fight for France, in return for which they will be allowed to keep the revenue.

Enter the two Bishops, the Archbishop of Canterbury and the Bishop of Ely.

Archbishop of Canterbury
My lord, I'll tell you, that self bill is urg'd
Which in th' eleventh year of the last king's reign
Was like, and had indeed against us pass'd,
But that the scambling and unquiet time

Did push it out of farther question.

Bishop of Ely
But how, my lord, shall we resist it now?

Archbishop of Canterbury
It must be thought on. If it pass against us,
We lose the better half of our possession;
For all the temporal lands, which men devout
By testament have given to the Church,
Would they strip from us; being valu'd thus:
As much as would maintain, to the King's honor,
Full fifteen earls and fifteen hundred knights,
Six thousand and two hundred good esquires;
And to relief of lazars, and weak age
Of indigent faint souls past corporal toil,
A hundred almshouses right well supplied;
And to the coffers of the King beside,
A thousand pounds by th' year. Thus runs the bill.

Bishop of Ely
This would drink deep.

Archbishop of Canterbury
                'Twould drink the cup and all.

Bishop of Ely
But what prevention?

Archbishop of Canterbury
The King is full of grace and fair regard.

Bishop of Ely
And a true lover of the holy Church.

Archbishop of Canterbury
The courses of his youth promis'd it not.
The breath no sooner left his father's body,
But that his wildness, mortified in him,
Seem'd to die too; yea, at that very moment,
Consideration like an angel came
And whipt th' offending Adam out of him,
Leaving his body as a paradise
T' envelop and contain celestial spirits.
Never was such a sudden scholar made;
Never came reformation in a flood
With such a heady currance, scouring faults;
Nor never Hydra-headed willfulness
So soon did lose his seat (and all at once)
As in this king.

Bishop of Ely
                We are blessed in the change.

Archbishop of Canterbury
Hear him but reason in divinity,
And all-admiring, with an inward wish
You would desire the King were made a prelate;
Hear him debate of commonwealth affairs,
You would say it hath been all in all his study;
List his discourse of war, and you shall hear
A fearful battle rend'red you in music;
Turn him to any cause of policy,
The Gordian knot of it he will unloose,
Familiar as his garter; that, when he speaks,
The air, a charter'd libertine, is still,
And the mute wonder lurketh in men's ears
To steal his sweet and honeyed sentences;
So that the art and practic part of life
Must be the mistress to this theoric;
Which is a wonder how his Grace should glean it,
Since his addiction was to courses vain,
His companies unletter'd, rude, and shallow,
His hours fill'd up with riots, banquets, sports;
And never noted in him any study,
Any retirement, any sequestration
From open haunts and popularity.

Bishop of Ely
The strawberry grows underneath the nettle,
And wholesome berries thrive and ripen best
Neighbor'd by fruit of baser quality;
And so the Prince obscur'd his contemplation
Under the veil of wildness, which (no doubt)
Grew like the summer grass, fastest by night,
Unseen, yet crescive in his faculty.

Archbishop of Canterbury
It must be so; for miracles are ceas'd;
And therefore we must needs admit the means
How things are perfected.

Bishop of Ely
                But, my good lord,
How now for mitigation of this bill
Urg'd by the commons? Doth his Majesty
Incline to it, or no?

Archbishop of Canterbury
                He seems indifferent;
Or rather swaying more upon our part
Than cherishing th' exhibitors against us;
For I have made an offer to his Majesty,
Upon our spiritual convocation
And in regard of causes now in hand,

Which I have open'd to his Grace at large,
As touching France, to give a greater sum
Than ever at one time the clergy yet
Did to his predecessors part withal.

Bishop of Ely
How did this offer seem receiv'd, my lord?

Archbishop of Canterbury
With good acceptance of his Majesty;
Save that there was not time enough to hear,
As I perceiv'd his Grace would fain have done,
The severals and unhidden passages
Of his true titles to some certain dukedoms,
And generally to the crown and seat of France,
Deriv'd from Edward, his great-grandfather.

Bishop of Ely
What was th' impediment that broke this off?

Archbishop of Canterbury
The French ambassador upon that instant
Crav'd audience; and the hour, I think, is come
To give him hearing. Is it four a' clock?

Bishop of Ely
It is.

Archbishop of Canterbury
Then go we in, to know his embassy;
Which I could with a ready guess declare,
Before the Frenchman speak a word of it.

Bishop of Ely
I'll wait upon you, and I long to hear it.

Exeunt.

Scene 2

London. Presence Chamber in the King's Palace.

(King; Humphrey Duke of Gloucester; Bedford; Clarence; Warwick; Westmorland; Exeter; Attendants; Archbishop of Canterbury; Bishop of Ely; Ambassadors of France)

King Henry calls on Canterbury to expound on whether there is any bar to Henry's claiming the throne of France. The Archbishop offers a lengthy and somewhat convoluted argument to prove that Henry is in the right; the various lords of the council approve and press Henry to war for his claim. An Ambassador from France brings in a present from the Dauphin, the heir to the throne of France: it is an insulting gift of tennis balls. Angered, Henry tells the Ambassador to warn the French that he will press his claim to the utmost, and that for his insulting behavior the Dauphin will bear the blame.

Enter the King, Humphrey Duke of Gloucester, Bedford, Clarence, Warwick, Westmorland, and Exeter, and other Attendants.

King Henry the Fifth
Where is my gracious Lord of Canterbury?

Duke of Exeter
Not here in presence.

King Henry the Fifth
              Send for him, good uncle.

Earl of Westmorland
Shall we call in th' ambassador, my liege?

King Henry the Fifth
Not yet, my cousin. We would be resolv'd,
Before we hear him, of some things of weight
That task our thoughts, concerning us and France.

Enter two Bishops, the Archbishop of Canterbury and the Bishop of Ely.

Archbishop of Canterbury
God and his angels guard your sacred throne,
And make you long become it!

King Henry the Fifth
              Sure we thank you.
My learned lord, we pray you to proceed,
And justly and religiously unfold
Why the law Salique, that they have in France,
Or should, or should not, bar us in our claim;
And God forbid, my dear and faithful lord,
That you should fashion, wrest, or bow your reading,
Or nicely charge your understanding soul
With opening titles miscreate, whose right
Suits not in native colors with the truth;
For God doth know how many now in health
Shall drop their blood in approbation
Of what your reverence shall incite us to.
Therefore take heed how you impawn our person,
How you awake our sleeping sword of war—
We charge you, in the name of God, take heed;
For never two such kingdoms did contend
Without much fall of blood, whose guiltless drops

Are every one a woe, a sore complaint,
'Gainst him whose wrongs gives edge unto the swords
That makes such waste in brief mortality.
Under this conjuration speak, my lord;
For we will hear, note, and believe in heart,
That what you speak is in your conscience wash'd
As pure as sin with baptism.

Archbishop of Canterbury
Then hear me, gracious sovereign, and you peers,
That owe yourselves, your lives, and services
To this imperial throne. There is no bar
To make against your Highness' claim to France
But this, which they produce from Pharamond:
"In terram Salicam mulieres ne succedant,"
"No woman shall succeed in Salique land";
Which Salique land the French unjustly gloze
To be the realm of France, and Pharamond
The founder of this law and female bar.
Yet their own authors faithfully affirm
That the land Salique is in Germany,
Between the floods of Sala and of Elbe;
Where Charles the Great, having subdu'd the Saxons,
There left behind and settled certain French;
Who holding in disdain the German women
For some dishonest manners of their life,
Establish'd then this law: to wit, no female
Should be inheritrix in Salique land;
Which Salique, as I said, 'twixt Elbe and Sala,
Is at this day in Germany call'd Meisen.
Then doth it well appear the Salique law
Was not devised for the realm of France;
Nor did the French possess the Salique land
Until four hundred one and twenty years
After defunction of King Pharamond,
Idly suppos'd the founder of this law,
Who died within the year of our redemption
Four hundred twenty-six; and Charles the Great
Subdu'd the Saxons, and did seat the French
Beyond the river Sala, in the year
Eight hundred five. Besides, their writers say,
King Pepin, which deposed Childeric,
Did, as heir general, being descended
Of Blithild, which was daughter to King Clothair,
Make claim and title to the crown of France.
Hugh Capet also, who usurp'd the crown
Of Charles the Duke of Lorraine, sole heir male
Of the true line and stock of Charles the Great,
To fine his title with some shows of truth,
Though in pure truth it was corrupt and naught,
Convey'd himself as th' heir to th' Lady Lingare,
Daughter to Charlemain, who was the son
To Lewis the Emperor, and Lewis the son
Of Charles the Great. Also King Lewis the Tenth,
Who was sole heir to the usurper Capet,
Could not keep quiet in his conscience,
Wearing the crown of France, till satisfied
That fair Queen Isabel, his grandmother,
Was lineal of the Lady Ermengare,
Daughter to Charles, the foresaid Duke of Lorraine;
By the which marriage the line of Charles the Great
Was re-united to the crown of France.
So that, as clear as is the summer's sun,
King Pepin's title and Hugh Capet's claim,
King Lewis his satisfaction, all appear
To hold in right and title of the female;
So do the kings of France unto this day.
Howbeit, they would hold up this Salique law
To bar your Highness claiming from the female,
And rather choose to hide them in a net
Than amply to imbar their crooked titles
Usurp'd from you and your progenitors.

King Henry the Fifth
May I with right and conscience make this claim?

Archbishop of Canterbury
The sin upon my head, dread sovereign!
For in the book of Numbers is it writ,
When the man dies, let the inheritance
Descend unto the daughter. Gracious lord,
Stand for your own, unwind your bloody flag,
Look back into your mighty ancestors;
Go, my dread lord, to your great-grandsire's tomb,
From whom you claim; invoke his warlike spirit,
And your great-uncle's, Edward the Black Prince,
Who on the French ground play'd a tragedy,
Making defeat on the full power of France,
Whiles his most mighty father on a hill
Stood smiling to behold his lion's whelp
Forage in blood of French nobility.
O noble English, that could entertain
With half their forces the full pride of France,
And let another half stand laughing by,
All out of work and cold for action!

Bishop of Ely
Awake remembrance of these valiant dead,
And with your puissant arm renew their feats.
You are their heir, you sit upon their throne;
The blood and courage that renowned them

Act 1, Scene 2

Runs in your veins; and my thrice-puissant liege
Is in the very May-morn of his youth,
Ripe for exploits and mighty enterprises.

Duke of Exeter
Your brother kings and monarchs of the earth
Do all expect that you should rouse yourself,
As did the former lions of your blood.

Earl of Westmorland
They know your Grace hath cause, and means, and might;
So hath your Highness. Never King of England
Had nobles richer and more loyal subjects,
Whose hearts have left their bodies here in England,
And lie pavilion'd in the fields of France.

Archbishop of Canterbury
O, let their bodies follow, my dear liege,
With blood and sword and fire, to win your right;
In aid whereof we of the spiritually
Will raise your Highness such a mighty sum
As never did the clergy at one time
Bring in to any of your ancestors.

King Henry the Fifth
We must not only arm t' invade the French,
But lay down our proportions to defend
Against the Scot, who will make road upon us
With all advantages.

Archbishop of Canterbury
They of those marches, gracious sovereign,
Shall be a wall sufficient to defend
Our inland from the pilfering borderers.

King Henry the Fifth
We do not mean the coursing snatchers only,
But fear the main intendment of the Scot,
Who hath been still a giddy neighbor to us;
For you shall read that my great-grandfather
Never went with his forces into France
But that the Scot on his unfurnish'd kingdom
Came pouring like the tide into a breach,
With ample and brim fullness of his force,
Galling the gleaned land with hot assays,
Girding with grievous siege castles and towns;
That England being empty of defense,
Hath shook and trembled at th' ill neighborhood.

Archbishop of Canterbury
She hath been then more fear'd than harm'd, my liege;
For hear her but exampled by herself:
When all her chevalry hath been in France,
And she a mourning widow of her nobles,
She hath herself not only well defended
But taken and impounded as a stray
The King of Scots; whom she did send to France
To fill King Edward's fame with prisoner kings,
And make her chronicle as rich with praise
As is the ooze and bottom of the sea
With sunken wrack and sumless treasuries.

Bishop of Ely
But there's a saying very old and true,
*"If that you will France win,
Then with Scotland first begin."*
For once the eagle (England) being in prey,
To her unguarded nest the weasel (Scot)
Comes sneaking, and so sucks her princely eggs,
Playing the mouse in absence of the cat,
To 'tame and havoc more than she can eat.

Duke of Exeter
It follows then the cat must stay at home,
Yet that is but a crush'd necessity,
Since we have locks to safeguard necessaries,
And pretty traps to catch the petty thieves.
While that the armed hand doth fight abroad,
Th' advised head defends itself at home;
For government, though high, and low, and lower,
Put into parts, doth keep in one consent,
Congreeing in a full and natural close,
Like music.

Archbishop of Canterbury
Therefore doth heaven divide
The state of man in diverse functions,
Setting endeavor in continual motion;
To which is fixed, as an aim or butt,
Obedience; for so work the honey-bees,
Creatures that by a rule in nature teach
The act of order to a peopled kingdom.
They have a king, and officers of sorts,
Where some, like magistrates, correct at home;
Others, like merchants, venter trade abroad;
Others, like soldiers, armed in their stings,
Make boot upon the summer's velvet buds,
Which pillage they with merry march bring home
To the tent-royal of their emperor;
Who busied in his majesty surveys

The singing masons building roofs of gold,
The civil citizens kneading up the honey,
The poor mechanic porters crowding in
Their heavy burdens at his narrow gate,
The sad-ey'd justice, with his surly hum,
Delivering o'er to executors pale
The lazy yawning drone. I this infer,
That many things, having full reference
To one consent, may work contrariously,
As many arrows loosed several ways
Come to one mark; as many ways meet in one town;
As many fresh streams meet in one salt sea;
As many lines close in the dial's center;
So may a thousand actions, once afoot,
End in one purpose, and be all well borne
Without defeat. Therefore to France, my liege!
Divide your happy England into four,
Whereof take you one quarter into France,
And you withal shall make all Gallia shake.
If we, with thrice such powers left at home,
Cannot defend our own doors from the dog,
Let us be worried, and our nation lose
The name of hardiness and policy.

King Henry the Fifth
Call in the messengers sent from the Dauphin.

Exeunt some Attendants.

Now are we well resolv'd, and by God's help
And yours, the noble sinews of our power,
France being ours, we'll bend it to our awe,
Or break it all to pieces. Or there we'll sit,
Ruling in large and ample empery
O'er France and all her (almost) kingly dukedoms,
Or lay these bones in an unworthy urn,
Tombless, with no remembrance over them.
Either our history shall with full mouth
Speak freely of our acts, or else our grave,
Like Turkish mute, shall have a tongueless mouth,
Not worshipp'd with a waxen epitaph.

Enter Ambassadors of France attended.

Now are we well prepar'd to know the pleasure
Of our fair cousin Dauphin; for we hear
Your greeting is from him, not from the King.

Ambassador of France
May't please your Majesty to give us leave
Freely to render what we have in charge?
Or shall we sparingly show you far off
The Dauphin's meaning and our embassy?

King Henry the Fifth
We are no tyrant, but a Christian king,
Unto whose grace our passion is as subject
As is our wretches fett'red in our prisons;
Therefore with frank and with uncurbed plainness
Tell us the Dauphin's mind.

Ambassador of France
                    Thus then in few:
Your Highness, lately sending into France,
Did claim some certain dukedoms, in the right
Of your great predecessor, King Edward the Third.
In answer of which claim, the prince our master
Says that you savor too much of your youth,
And bids you be advis'd: there's nought in France
That can be with a nimble galliard won;
You cannot revel into dukedoms there.
He therefore sends you, meeter for your spirit,
This tun of treasure; and, in lieu of this,
Desires you let the dukedoms that you claim
Hear no more of you. This the Dauphin speaks.

King Henry the Fifth
What treasure, uncle?

Duke of Exeter
                    Tennis-balls, my liege.

King Henry the Fifth
We are glad the Dauphin is so pleasant with us,
His present and your pains we thank you for.
When we have match'd our rackets to these balls,
We will in France, by God's grace, play a set
Shall strike his father's crown into the hazard.
Tell him he hath made a match with such a wrangler
That all the courts of France will be disturb'd
With chaces. And we understand him well,
How he comes o'er us with our wilder days,
Not measuring what use we made of them.
We never valu'd this poor seat of England,
And therefore, living hence, did give ourself
To barbarous license; as 'tis ever common
That men are merriest when they are from home.
But tell the Dauphin I will keep my state,
Be like a king, and show my sail of greatness
When I do rouse me in my throne of France.
For that I have laid by my majesty,
And plodded like a man for working-days;
But I will rise there with so full a glory
That I will dazzle all the eyes of France,

Yea, strike the Dauphin blind to look on us.
And tell the pleasant prince this mock of his
Hath turn'd his balls to gun-stones, and his soul
Shall stand sore charged for the wasteful vengeance
That shall fly with them; for many a thousand widows
Shall this his mock mock out of their dear husbands;
Mock mothers from their sons, mock castles down;
And some are yet ungotten and unborn
That shall have cause to curse the Dauphin's scorn.
But this lies all within the will of God,
To whom I do appeal, and in whose name
Tell you the Dauphin I am coming on
To venge me as I may, and to put forth
My rightful hand in a well-hallow'd cause.
So get you hence in peace; and tell the Dauphin
His jest will savor but of shallow wit,
When thousands weep more than did laugh at it.—
Convey them with safe conduct.—Fare you well.

Exeunt Ambassadors.

Duke of Exeter
This was a merry message.

King Henry the Fifth
We hope to make the sender blush at it.
Therefore, my lords, omit no happy hour
That may give furth'rance to our expedition;
For we have now no thought in us but France,
Save those to God, that run before our business.
Therefore let our proportions for these wars
Be soon collected, and all things thought upon
That may with reasonable swiftness add
More feathers to our wings; for, God before,
We'll chide this Dauphin at his father's door.
Therefore let every man now task his thought,
That this fair action may on foot be brought.

Exeunt.

Act 2

Prologue

(Chorus)

The Chorus tells of the preparations made by both English and French. But all is not well in England: three English knights have agreed to betray the King.

Flourish. Enter Chorus.

Chorus
Now all the youth of England are on fire,
And silken dalliance in the wardrobe lies;
Now thrive the armorers, and honor's thought
Reigns solely in the breast of every man.
They sell the pasture now to buy the horse,
Following the mirror of all Christian kings,
With winged heels, as English Mercuries.
For now sits Expectation in the air,
And hides a sword, from hilts unto the point,
With crowns imperial, crowns and coronets,
Promis'd to Harry and his followers.
The French, advis'd by good intelligence
Of this most dreadful preparation,
Shake in their fear, and with pale policy
Seek to divert the English purposes.
O England! Model to thy inward greatness,
Like little body with a mighty heart,
What mightst thou do, that honor would thee do,
Were all thy children kind and natural!
But see, thy fault France hath in thee found out,
A nest of hollow bosoms, which he fills
With treacherous crowns; and three corrupted men,
One, Richard Earl of Cambridge, and the second,
Henry Lord Scroop of Masham, and the third,
Sir Thomas Grey, knight, of Northumberland,
Have for the gilt of France (O guilt indeed!)
Confirm'd conspiracy with fearful France,
And by their hands this grace of kings must die,
If hell and treason hold their promises,
Ere he take ship for France; and in Southampton.
Linger your patience on, and we'll digest
Th' abuse of distance; force a play:
The sum is paid, the traitors are agreed,
The King is set from London, and the scene
Is now transported, gentles, to Southampton;
There is the playhouse now, there must you sit,
And thence to France shall we convey you safe,
And bring you back, charming the Narrow Seas
To give you gentle pass; for if we may,
We'll not offend one stomach with our play.
But till the King come forth, and not till then,
Unto Southampton do we shift our scene.

Exit.

Scene 1

London. A street in Eastcheap.

(Corporal Nym; Lieutenant Bardolph; Pistol; Hostess Quickly; Boy)

Bardolph wants Nym and Pistol to be friends again so that they can go off to the wars in France, but this will be difficult as Pistol has married Dame Quickly, the Hostess, even though she was promised to Nym. When Pistol and the Hostess come in, he and Nym quickly draw on one another, and Bardolph is hard-pressed to keep the peace. The Boy enters to beg for help for Falstaff, who is very ill. While the Hostess goes to him, Nym and Pistol quarrel again, this time over a small debt. Bardolph makes them friends again. The Hostess requests that they come to Falstaff's side; the three men blame King Henry's bad treatment of the knight for his illness.

Enter Corporal Nym and Lieutenant Bardolph.

Bardolph
Well met, Corporal Nym.

Nym
Good morrow, Lieutenant Bardolph.

Bardolph
What, are Ancient Pistol and you friends yet?

Nym
For my part, I care not; I say little; but when time shall serve, there shall be smiles—but that shall be as it may. I dare not fight, but I will wink and hold out mine iron. It is a simple one, but what though? It will toast cheese, and it will endure cold as another man's sword will; and there's an end.

Bardolph
I will bestow a breakfast to make you friends, and we'll be all three sworn brothers to France. Let't be so, good Corporal Nym.

Nym
Faith, I will live so long as I may, that's the certain of it; and when I cannot live any longer, I will do as I may: that is my rest, that is the rendezvous of it.

Bardolph
It is certain, corporal, that he is married to Nell Quickly, and certainly she did you wrong, for you were troth-plight to her.

Nym
I cannot tell; things must be as they may. Men may sleep, and they may have their throats about them at that time, and some say knives have edges. It must be as it may; though patience be a tir'd mare, yet she will plod—there must be conclusions—well, I cannot tell.

Enter Pistol and Hostess Quickly.

Bardolph
Here comes Ancient Pistol and his wife. Good corporal, be patient here.

Nym
How now, mine host Pistol?

Pistol
Base tike, call'st thou me host?
Now by Gadslugs I swear I scorn the term;
Nor shall my Nell keep lodgers.

Hostess
No, by my troth, not long; for we cannot lodge and board a dozen or fourteen gentlewomen that live honestly by the prick of their needles but it will be thought we keep a bawdy-house straight.

Nym and Pistol draw.

O welliday, Lady, if he be not hewn now, we shall see willful adultery and murder committed.

Bardolph
Good lieutenant! Good corporal! Offer nothing here.

Nym
Pish!

Pistol
Pish for thee, Iceland dog! Thou prick-ear'd cur of Iceland!

Hostess
Good Corporal Nym, show thy valor, and put up your sword.

Nym
Will you shog off? I would have you solus.

Pistol
"Solus," egregious dog? O viper vile!
The "solus" in thy most mervailous face,
The "solus" in thy teeth, and in thy throat,
And in thy hateful lungs, yea, in thy maw, perdy;
And which is worse, within thy nasty mouth!
I do retort the "solus" in thy bowels,
For I can take, and Pistol's cock is up,

Act 2, Scene 1

And flashing fire will follow.

Nym
I am not Barbason, you cannot conjure me. I have an humor to knock you indifferently well. If you grow foul with me, Pistol, I will scour you with my rapier, as I may, in fair terms. If you would walk off, I would prick your guts a little in good terms, as I may, and that's the humor of it.

Pistol
O braggard vile and damned furious wight!
The grave doth gape, and doting death is near,
Therefore exhale.

Bardolph
Hear me, hear me what I say. He that strikes the first stroke, I'll run him up to the hilts, as I am a soldier.

Draws.

Pistol
An oath of mickle might, and fury shall abate.
Give me thy fist, thy fore-foot to me give.
Thy spirits are most tall.

Nym
I will cut thy throat one time or other in fair terms, that is the humor of it.

Pistol
Couple à gorge!
That is the word. I thee defy again.
O hound of Crete, think'st thou my spouse to get?
No, to the spittle go,
And from the powd'ring-tub of infamy
Fetch forth the lazar kite of Cressid's kind,
Doll Tearsheet she by name, and her espouse.
I have, and I will hold, the quondam Quickly
For the only she; and—pauca, there's enough too!
Go to.

Enter the Boy.

Boy
Mine host Pistol, you must come to my master, and your hostess. He is very sick, and would to bed. Good Bardolph, put thy face between his sheets, and do the office of a warming-pan. Faith, he's very ill.

Bardolph
Away, you rogue!

Hostess
By my troth, he'll yield the crow a pudding one of these days. The King has kill'd his heart. Good husband, come home presently.

Exit with Boy.

Bardolph
Come, shall I make you two friends? We must to France together; why the devil should we keep knives to cut one another's throats?

Pistol
Let floods o'erswell, and fiends for food howl on!

Nym
You'll pay me the eight shillings I won of you at betting?

Pistol
Base is the slave that pays.

Nym
That now I will have: that's the humor of it.

Pistol
As manhood shall compound. Push home.

They draw.

Bardolph
By this sword, he that makes the first thrust, I'll kill him; by this sword, I will.

Draws.

Pistol
Sword is an oath, and oaths must have their course.

Bardolph
Corporal Nym, and thou wilt be friends, be friends; and thou wilt not, why then be enemies with me too. Prithee put up.

Nym
I shall have my eight shillings I won of you at betting?

Pistol
A noble shalt thou have, and present pay,
And liquor likewise will I give to thee,
And friendship shall combine, and brotherhood.
I'll live by Nym, and Nym shall live by me.
Is not this just? For I shall sutler be
Unto the camp, and profits will accrue.

Give me thy hand.

Nym
I shall have my noble?

Pistol
In cash, most justly paid.

Nym
Well, then that's the humor of't.

Enter Hostess.

Hostess
As ever you come of women, come in quickly to Sir John. Ah, poor heart! He is so shak'd of a burning quotidian tertian, that it is most lamentable to behold. Sweet men, come to him.

Nym
The King hath run bad humors on the knight, that's the even of it.

Pistol
Nym, thou hast spoke the right.
His heart is fracted and corroborate.

Nym
The King is a good king, but it must be as it may; he passes some humors and careers.

Pistol
Let us condole the knight, for, lambkins, we will live.

Exeunt.

Scene 2

Southampton. A council-chamber.

(Exeter; Bedford; Westmorland; King Henry the Fifth; Scroop; Cambridge; Grey; Attendants)

The three traitors have been discovered, though they are not aware of this. They outrageously flatter King Henry, who talks calmly to them. When the King decides to free a man imprisoned for railing against him, all three counsel against mercy. Henry reveals that he knows of their treason and, using their own arguments against mercy, condemns them all to death. He is particularly bitter at Scroop, who was one of his best friends once. The three confess, expressing gladness that they failed in their plot. Henry rallies his lords for the war.

Enter Exeter, Bedford, and Westmorland.

John, Duke of Bedford
'Fore God, his Grace is bold to trust these traitors.

Duke of Exeter
They shall be apprehended by and by.

Earl of Westmorland
How smooth and even they do bear themselves!
As if allegiance in their bosoms sate
Crowned with faith and constant loyalty.

John, Duke of Bedford
The King hath note of all that they intend,
By interception which they dream not of.

Duke of Exeter
Nay, but the man that was his bedfellow,
Whom he hath dull'd and cloy'd with gracious favors—
That he should, for a foreign purse, so sell
His sovereign's life to death and treachery.

Sound trumpets. Enter the King, Scroop, Cambridge, and Grey, with Attendants.

King Henry the Fifth
Now sits the wind fair, and we will aboard.
My Lord of Cambridge, and my kind Lord of Masham,
And you, my gentle knight, give me your thoughts.
Think you not that the pow'rs we bear with us
Will cut their passage through the force of France,
Doing the execution and the act
For which we have in head assembled them?

Lord Scroop
No doubt, my liege, if each man do his best.

King Henry the Fifth
I doubt not that, since we are well persuaded
We carry not a heart with us from hence
That grows not in a fair consent with ours;
Nor leave not one behind that doth not wish
Success and conquest to attend on us.

Richard, Earl of Cambridge
Never was monarch better fear'd and lov'd
Than is your Majesty. There's not, I think, a subject
That sits in heart-grief and uneasiness
Under the sweet shade of your government.

Sir Thomas Grey
True; those that were your father's enemies
Have steep'd their galls in honey, and do serve you
With hearts create of duty and of zeal.

King Henry the Fifth
We therefore have great cause of thankfulness,
And shall forget the office of our hand
Sooner than quittance of desert and merit,
According to the weight and worthiness.

Lord Scroop
So service shall with steeled sinews toil,
And labor shall refresh itself with hope
To do your Grace incessant services.

King Henry the Fifth
We judge no less. Uncle of Exeter,
Enlarge the man committed yesterday,
That rail'd against our person. We consider
It was excess of wine that set him on,
And on his more advice we pardon him.

Lord Scroop
That's mercy, but too much security.
Let him be punish'd, sovereign, lest example
Breed, by his sufferance, more of such a kind.

King Henry the Fifth
O, let us yet be merciful.

Richard, Earl of Cambridge
So may your Highness, and yet punish too.

Sir Thomas Grey
Sir,
You show great mercy if you give him life
After the taste of much correction.

King Henry the Fifth
Alas, your too much love and care of me
Are heavy orisons 'gainst this poor wretch!
If little faults, proceeding on distemper,
Shall not be wink'd at, how shall we stretch our eye
When capital crimes, chew'd, swallow'd, and digested,
Appear before us? We'll yet enlarge that man,
Though Cambridge, Scroop, and Grey, in their dear care
And tender preservation of our person,
Would have him punish'd. And now to our French causes.
Who are the late commissioners?

Richard, Earl of Cambridge
I one, my lord.
Your Highness bade me ask for it today.

Lord Scroop
So did you me, my liege.

Sir Thomas Grey
And I, my royal sovereign.

King Henry the Fifth
Then, Richard Earl of Cambridge, there is yours;
There yours, Lord Scroop of Masham; and, sir knight,
Grey of Northumberland, this same is yours:
Read them, and know I know your worthiness.
My Lord of Westmorland, and uncle Exeter,
We will aboard tonight.—Why, how now, gentlemen?
What see you in those papers that you lose
So much complexion?—Look ye how they change!
Their cheeks are paper.—Why, what read you there
That have so cowarded and chas'd your blood
Out of appearance?

Richard, Earl of Cambridge
                I do confess my fault,
And do submit me to your Highness' mercy.

Grey and Scroop
To which we all appeal.

King Henry the Fifth
The mercy that was quick in us but late,
By your own counsel is suppress'd and kill'd.
You must not dare (for shame) to talk of mercy,
For your own reasons turn into your bosoms,
As dogs upon their masters, worrying you.
See you, my princes and my noble peers,
These English monsters! My Lord of Cambridge here,
You know how apt our love was to accord
To furnish him with all appertinents
Belonging to his honor; and this man
Hath, for a few light crowns, lightly conspir'd
And sworn unto the practices of France
To kill us here in Hampton. To the which
This knight, no less for bounty bound to us
Than Cambridge is, hath likewise sworn. But O,
What shall I say to thee, Lord Scroop, thou cruel,
Ingrateful, savage, and inhuman creature?
Thou that didst bear the key of all my counsels,
That knew'st the very bottom of my soul,
That (almost) mightst have coin'd me into gold,
Wouldst thou have practic'd on me, for thy use?

May it be possible that foreign hire
Could out of thee extract one spark of evil
That might annoy my finger? 'Tis so strange,
That, though the truth of it stands off as gross
As black and white, my eye will scarcely see it.
Treason and murder ever kept together,
As two yoke-devils sworn to either's purpose,
Working so grossly in a natural cause
That admiration did not hoop at them;
But thou ('gainst all proportion) didst bring in
Wonder to wait on treason and on murder;
And whatsoever cunning fiend it was
That wrought upon thee so preposterously
Hath got the voice in hell for excellence;
And other devils that suggest by treasons
Do botch and bungle up damnation
With patches, colors, and with forms being fetch'd
From glist'ring semblances of piety;
But he that temper'd thee, bade thee stand up,
Gave thee no instance why thou shouldst do treason,
Unless to dub thee with the name of traitor.
If that same demon that hath gull'd thee thus
Should with his lion gait walk the whole world,
He might return to vasty Tartar back,
And tell the legions, "I can never win
A soul so easy as that Englishman's."
O, how hast thou with jealousy infected
The sweetness of affiance! Show men dutiful?
Why, so didst thou. Seem they grave and learned?
Why, so didst thou. Come they of noble family?
Why, so didst thou. Seem they religious?
Why, so didst thou. Or are they spare in diet,
Free from gross passion, or of mirth or anger,
Constant in spirit, not swerving with the blood,
Garnish'd and deck'd in modest complement,
Not working with the eye without the ear,
And but in purged judgment trusting neither?
Such and so finely bolted didst thou seem.
And thus thy fall hath left a kind of blot
To mark the full-fraught man and best indued
With some suspicion. I will weep for thee;
For this revolt of thine, methinks, is like
Another fall of man. Their faults are open,
Arrest them to the answer of the law,
And God acquit them of their practices!

Duke of Exeter
I arrest thee of high treason, by the name of Richard,
Earl of Cambridge.
I arrest thee of high treason, by the name of Henry,
Lord Scroop of Masham.
I arrest thee of high treason, by the name of Thomas
Grey, knight, of Northumberland.

Lord Scroop
Our purposes God justly hath discover'd,
And I repent my fault more than my death,
Which I beseech your Highness to forgive,
Although my body pay the price of it.

Richard, Earl of Cambridge
For me, the gold of France did not seduce,
Although I did admit it as a motive
The sooner to effect what I intended.
But God be thanked for prevention,
Which I in sufferance heartily will rejoice,
Beseeching God, and you, to pardon me.

Sir Thomas Grey
Never did faithful subject more rejoice
At the discovery of most dangerous treason
Than I do at this hour joy o'er myself,
Prevented from a damned enterprise.
My fault, but not my body, pardon, sovereign.

King Henry the Fifth
God quit you in his mercy! Hear your sentence.
You have conspir'd against our royal person,
Join'd with an enemy proclaim'd, and from his coffers
Receiv'd the golden earnest of our death;
Wherein you would have sold your king to slaughter,
His princes and his peers to servitude,
His subjects to oppression and contempt,
And his whole kingdom into desolation.
Touching our person seek we no revenge,
But we our kingdom's safety must so tender,
Whose ruin you have sought, that to her laws
We do deliver you. Get you therefore hence,
Poor miserable wretches, to your death;
The taste whereof God of his mercy give
You patience to endure, and true repentance
Of all your dear offenses! Bear them hence.

Exeunt Cambridge, Scroop, and Grey, guarded.

Now, lords, for France; the enterprise whereof
Shall be to you as us, like glorious.
We doubt not of a fair and lucky war,
Since God so graciously hath brought to light
This dangerous treason lurking in our way
To hinder our beginnings. We doubt not now

But every rub is smoothed on our way.
Then forth, dear countrymen! Let us deliver
Our puissance into the hand of God,
Putting it straight in expedition.
Cheerly to sea! The signs of war advance!
No king of England, if not king of France!

Flourish. Exeunt.

Scene 3

London. Before a tavern in Eastcheap.

(Pistol; Nym; Bardolph; Boy; Hostess)

Pistol, Bardolph, Nym, the Hostess, and the Boy mourn the death of Falstaff. Pistol leaves his wife behind as they head to the wars.

Enter Pistol, Nym, Bardolph, Boy, and Hostess.

Hostess
Prithee, honey-sweet husband, let me bring thee to Staines.

Pistol
No; for my manly heart doth ern.
Bardolph, be blithe; Nym, rouse thy vaunting veins;
Boy, bristle thy courage up; for Falstaff he is dead,
And we must ern therefore.

Bardolph
Would I were with him, wheresome'er he is, either in heaven or in hell!

Hostess
Nay sure, he's not in hell; he's in Arthur's bosom, if ever man went to Arthur's bosom. 'A made a finer end, and went away and it had been any christom child. 'A parted ev'n just between twelve and one, ev'n at the turning o' th' tide; for after I saw him fumble with the sheets, and play with flowers, and smile upon his finger's end, I knew there was but one way; for his nose was as sharp as a pen, and 'a babbl'd of green fields. "How now, Sir John?" quoth I, "what, man? Be a' good cheer." So 'a cried out, "God, God, God!" three or four times. Now I, to comfort him, bid him 'a should not think of God; I hop'd there was no need to trouble himself with any such thoughts yet. So 'a bade me lay more clothes on his feet. I put my hand into the bed and felt them, and they were as cold as any stone; then I felt to his knees, and so up'ard and up'ard, and all was as cold as any stone.

Nym
They say he cried out of sack.

Hostess
Ay, that 'a did.

Bardolph
And of women.

Hostess
Nay, that 'a did not.

Boy
Yes, that 'a did, and said they were dev'ls incarnate.

Hostess
'A could never abide carnation—'twas a color he never lik'd.

Boy
'A said once, the dev'l would have him about women.

Hostess
'A did in some sort, indeed, handle women; but then he was rheumatic, and talk'd of the whore of Babylon.

Boy
Do you not remember, 'a saw a flea stick upon Bardolph's nose, and 'a said it was a black soul burning in hell?

Bardolph
Well, the fuel is gone that maintain'd that fire. That's all the riches I got in his service.

Nym
Shall we shog? The King will be gone from Southampton.

Pistol
Come, let's away. My love, give me thy lips.
Look to my chattels and my moveables.
Let senses rule; the word is "Pitch and pay";
Trust none;
For oaths are straws, men's faiths are wafer-cakes,
And Hold-fast is the only dog, my duck;
Therefore Caveto be thy counsellor.
Go, clear thy crystals. Yoke-fellows in arms,
Let us to France, like horse-leeches, my boys,
To suck, to suck, the very blood to suck!

Boy
And that's but unwholesome food, they say.

Pistol
Touch her soft mouth, and march.

Bardolph
Farewell, hostess.

Kissing her.

Nym
I cannot kiss, that is the humor of it; but adieu.

Pistol
Let huswifery appear. Keep close, I thee command.

Hostess
Farewell; adieu.

Exeunt.

Scene 4

France. An apartment in the King's palace.

(French King; Dauphin; Duke of Berri; Duke of Britain; Constable; French Court Attendant; Lords; Exeter)

The French King prepares his defense. The Dauphin sees little need for this, but is reprimanded for his over-confidence by the other lords. King Henry's uncle Exeter brings the King of France a formal demand that he resign the throne to Henry, on pain of war; he also takes the time to insult the Dauphin in return for his earlier insults. The French King promises an answer the next morning.

Flourish. Enter the French King, the Dauphin, the Dukes of Berri and Britain, the Constable, and others.

Charles the Sixth
Thus comes the English with full power upon us,
And more than carefully it us concerns
To answer royally in our defenses.
Therefore the Dukes of Berri and of Britain,
Of Brabant and of Orléans, shall make forth,
And you, Prince Dauphin, with all swift dispatch,
To line and new repair our towns of war
With men of courage and with means defendant;
For England his approaches makes as fierce
As waters to the sucking of a gulf.
It fits us then to be as provident
As fear may teach us out of late examples
Left by the fatal and neglected English
Upon our fields.

The Dauphin
⸻⸻⸻⸻⸻My most redoubted father,
It is most meet we arm us 'gainst the foe;
For peace itself should not so dull a kingdom
(Though war nor no known quarrel were in question)
But that defenses, musters, preparations,
Should be maintain'd, assembled, and collected,
As were a war in expectation.
Therefore, I say, 'tis meet we all go forth
To view the sick and feeble parts of France;
And let us do it with no show of fear,
No, with no more than if we heard that England
Were busied with a Whitsun morris-dance;
For, my good liege, she is so idly king'd,
Her sceptre so fantastically borne,
By a vain, giddy, shallow, humorous youth,
That fear attends her not.

Constable of France
⸻⸻⸻⸻⸻O, peace, Prince Dauphin,
You are too much mistaken in this king.
Question your Grace the late ambassadors,
With what great state he heard their embassy,
How well supplied with noble counsellors,
How modest in exception, and withal
How terrible in constant resolution,
And you shall find his vanities forespent
Were but the outside of the Roman Brutus,
Covering discretion with a coat of folly,
As gardeners do with ordure hide those roots
That shall first spring and be most delicate.

The Dauphin
Well, 'tis not so, my Lord High Constable;
But though we think it so, it is no matter.
In cases of defense 'tis best to weigh
The enemy more mighty than he seems,
So the proportions of defense are fill'd;
Which, of a weak and niggardly projection,
Doth like a miser spoil his coat with scanting
A little cloth.

Charles the Sixth
⸻⸻⸻⸻⸻Think we King Harry strong;
And, princes, look you strongly arm to meet him.
The kindred of him hath been flesh'd upon us;
And he is bred out of that bloody strain
That haunted us in our familiar paths.
Witness our too much memorable shame
When Cressy battle fatally was struck,
And all our princes captiv'd by the hand

Of that black name, Edward, Black Prince of Wales;
Whiles that his mountain sire, on mountain standing,
Up in the air, crown'd with the golden sun,
Saw his heroical seed, and smil'd to see him,
Mangle the work of nature, and deface
The patterns that by God and by French fathers
Had twenty years been made. This is a stem
Of that victorious stock; and let us fear
The native mightiness and fate of him.

Enter a French Court Attendant.

French Court Attendant
Ambassadors from Harry King of England
Do crave admittance to your Majesty.

Charles the Sixth
We'll give them present audience. Go, and bring them.

Exeunt French Court Attendant and certain Lords.

You see this chase is hotly followed, friends.

The Dauphin
Turn head, and stop pursuit; for coward dogs
Most spend their mouths when what they seem to threaten
Runs far before them. Good my sovereign,
Take up the English short, and let them know
Of what a monarchy you are the head.
Self-love, my liege, is not so vile a sin
As self-neglecting.

Enter Lords with Exeter and Train.

Charles the Sixth
From our brother of England?

Duke of Exeter
From him, and thus he greets your Majesty:
He wills you, in the name of God Almighty,
That you divest yourself, and lay apart
The borrowed glories that by gift of heaven,
By law of nature and of nations, 'longs
To him and to his heirs, namely, the crown,
And all wide-stretched honors that pertain
By custom, and the ordinance of times,
Unto the crown of France. That you may know
'Tis no sinister nor no awkward claim,
Pick'd from the worm-holes of long-vanish'd days,
Nor from the dust of old oblivion rak'd,
He sends you this most memorable line,
In every branch truly demonstrative;

Giving a paper.

Willing you overlook this pedigree;
And when you find him evenly deriv'd
From his most fam'd of famous ancestors,
Edward the Third, he bids you then resign
Your crown and kingdom, indirectly held
From him, the native and true challenger.

Charles the Sixth
Or else what follows?

Duke of Exeter
Bloody constraint; for if you hide the crown
Even in your hearts, there will he rake for it.
Therefore in fierce tempest is he coming,
In thunder and in earthquake, like a Jove,
That if requiring fail he will compel;
And bids you, in the bowels of the Lord,
Deliver up the crown, and to take mercy
On the poor souls for whom this hungry war
Opens his vasty jaws; and on your head
Turning the widows' tears, the orphans' cries,
The dead men's blood, the privy maidens' groans,
For husbands, fathers, and betrothed lovers,
That shall be swallowed in this controversy.
This is his claim, his threat'ning, and my message;
Unless the Dauphin be in presence here,
To whom expressly I bring greeting too.

Charles the Sixth
For us, we will consider of this further.
Tomorrow shall you bear our full intent
Back to our brother of England.

The Dauphin
                For the Dauphin,
I stand here for him. What to him from England?

Duke of Exeter
Scorn and defiance, slight regard, contempt,
And any thing that may not misbecome
The mighty sender, doth he prize you at.
Thus says my King: and if your father's Highness
Do not, in grant of all demands at large,
Sweeten the bitter mock you sent his Majesty,
He'll call you to so hot an answer of it
That caves and womby vaultages of France
Shall chide your trespass and return your mock
In second accent of his ordinance.

The Dauphin
Say: if my father render fair return,
It is against my will; for I desire
Nothing but odds with England. To that end,
As matching to his youth and vanity,
I did present him with the Paris balls.

Duke of Exeter
He'll make your Paris Louvre shake for it,
Were it the mistress court of mighty Europe;
And, be assur'd, you'll find a difference,
As we his subjects have in wonder found,
Between the promise of his greener days
And these he masters now. Now he weighs time
Even to the utmost grain; that you shall read
In your own losses, if he stay in France.

Charles the Sixth
Tomorrow shall you know our mind at full.

Flourish.

Duke of Exeter
Dispatch us with all speed, lest that our King
Come here himself to question our delay;
For he is footed in this land already.

Charles the Sixth
You shall be soon dispatch'd, with fair conditions.
A night is but small breath, and little pause,
To answer matters of this consequence.

Exeunt.

Act 3

Prologue

(Chorus)

The Chorus tells of how the English army crossed into France. The French King offered the princess Katherine and some dukedoms to Henry, but this was not enough for him; instead he has besieged Harfleur.

Flourish. Enter Chorus.

Chorus
Thus with imagin'd wing our swift scene flies
In motion of no less celerity
Than that of thought. Suppose that you have seen
The well-appointed king at Hampton pier
Embark his royalty; and his brave fleet
With silken streamers the young Phoebus fanning.
Play with your fancies: and in them behold
Upon the hempen tackle ship-boys climbing;
Hear the shrill whistle which doth order give
To sounds confus'd; behold the threaden sails,
Borne with th' invisible and creeping wind,
Draw the huge bottoms through the furrowed sea,
Breasting the lofty surge. O, do but think
You stand upon the rivage and behold
A city on th' inconstant billows dancing;
For so appears this fleet majestical,
Holding due course to Harfleur. Follow, follow!
Grapple your minds to sternage of this navy,
And leave your England as dead midnight, still,
Guarded with grandsires, babies, and old women,
Either past or not arriv'd to pith and puissance;
For who is he, whose chin is but enrich'd
With one appearing hair, that will not follow
These cull'd and choice-drawn cavaliers to France?
Work, work your thoughts, and therein see a siege;
Behold the ordinance on their carriages,
With fatal mouths gaping on girded Harfleur.
Suppose th' ambassador from the French comes back,
Tells Harry that the King doth offer him
Katherine his daughter, and with her, to dowry,
Some petty and unprofitable dukedoms.
The offer likes not; and the nimble gunner
With linstock now the devilish cannon touches,

Alarum, and chambers go off.

And down goes all before them. Still be kind,
And eche out our performance with your mind.

Exit.

Scene 1

France. Before Harfleur.

(King Henry the Fifth; Exeter; Bedford; Gloucester; Soldiers)

Henry rouses his men to attack a breach in the walls of Harfleur yet again, even though they have been beaten back from it before.

Enter the King, Exeter, Bedford, and Gloucester. Alarum. Enter Soldiers with scaling-ladders at Harfleur.

King Henry the Fifth
Once more unto the breach, dear friends, once more;
Or close the wall up with our English dead.
In peace there's nothing so becomes a man
As modest stillness and humility;
But when the blast of war blows in our ears,
Then imitate the action of the tiger;
Stiffen the sinews, conjure up the blood,
Disguise fair nature with hard-favor'd rage;
Then lend the eye a terrible aspect;
Let it pry through the portage of the head
Like the brass cannon; let the brow o'erwhelm it
As fearfully as doth a galled rock
O'erhang and jutty his confounded base,
Swill'd with the wild and wasteful ocean.
Now set the teeth and stretch the nostril wide,
Hold hard the breath, and bend up every spirit
To his full height. On, on, you noblest English,
Whose blood is fet from fathers of war-proof!
Fathers that, like so many Alexanders,
Have in these parts from morn till even fought,
And sheath'd their swords for lack of argument.
Dishonor not your mothers; now attest
That those whom you call'd fathers did beget you.
Be copy now to men of grosser blood,
And teach them how to war. And you, good yeomen,
Whose limbs were made in England, show us here
The mettle of your pasture; let us swear
That you are worth your breeding, which I doubt not;
For there is none of you so mean and base
That hath not noble lustre in your eyes.
I see you stand like greyhounds in the slips,
Straining upon the start. The game's afoot!
Follow your spirit; and upon this charge
Cry, "God for Harry, England, and Saint George!"

Exeunt. Alarum, and chambers go off.

Scene 2

France. Before Harfleur.

(Nym; Bardolph; Pistol; Boy; Fluellen; Gower; Macmorris; Captain Jamy)

Bardolph and his band hang back from entering the breach until Fluellen drives them towards it. The Boy has been quite disillusioned about the worth of the three men he serves. The Welsh Fluellen is not particularly happy that King Henry is using mines against Harfleur, and even less that the command of that job has been given to an Irishman, Captain Macmorris. With the English Gower and the Scot Jamy, the four have a discussion over the war.

Enter Nym, Bardolph, Pistol, and Boy.

Bardolph
On, on, on, on, on! To the breach, to the breach!

Nym
Pray thee, corporal, stay. The knocks are too hot; and for mine own part, I have not a case of lives. The humor of it is too hot, that is the very plain-song of it.

Pistol
The plain-song is most just; for humors do abound:
"Knocks go and come; God's vassals drop and die;
And sword and shield,
In bloody field,
Doth win immortal fame."

Boy
Would I were in an alehouse in London, I would give all my fame for a pot of ale and safety.

Pistol
And I:
"If wishes would prevail with me,
My purpose should not fail with me,
But thither would I hie."

Boy
"As duly, but not as truly,
As bird doth sing on bough."

Enter Fluellen.

Fluellen
Up to the breach, you dogs! Avaunt, you cullions!

Driving them forward.

Pistol
Be merciful, great duke, to men of mould.
Abate thy rage, abate thy manly rage,
Abate thy rage, great duke!
Good bawcock, bate thy rage; use lenity, sweet chuck!

Nym
These be good humors! Your honor wins bad humors.

Exit with Bardolph and Pistol.
Fluellen steps aside.

Boy
As young as I am, I have observ'd these three swashers. I am boy to them all three, but all they three, though they would serve me, could not be man to me; for indeed three such antics do not amount to a man. For Bardolph, he is white-liver'd and red-fac'd; by the means whereof 'a faces it out, but fights not. For Pistol, he hath a killing tongue and a quiet sword; by the means whereof 'a breaks words, and keeps whole weapons. For Nym, he hath heard that men of few words are the best men, and therefore he scorns to say his prayers, lest 'a should be thought a coward; but his few bad words are match'd with as few good deeds; for 'a never broke any man's head but his own, and that was against a post when he was drunk. They will steal any thing, and call it purchase. Bardolph stole a lute-case, bore it twelve leagues, and sold it for three half-pence. Nym and Bardolph are sworn brothers in filching, and in Callice they stole a fire-shovel. I knew by that piece of service the men would carry coals. They would have me as familiar with men's pockets as their gloves or their handkerchers; which makes much against my manhood, if I should take from another's pocket to put into mine; for it is plain pocketing up of wrongs. I must leave them, and seek some better service. Their villainy goes against my weak stomach, and therefore I must cast it up.

Exit.
Enter Gower.
Fluellen comes forward.

Gower
Captain Fluellen, you must come presently to the mines; the Duke of Gloucester would speak with you.

Fluellen
To the mines? Tell you the Duke, it is not so good to come to the mines; for look you, the mines is not according to the disciplines of the war; the concavities of it is not sufficient. For look you, th' athversary—you may discuss unto the Duke, look you—is digt himself four yard under the countermines. By Cheshu, I think 'a will plow up all, if there is not better directions.

Gower
The Duke of Gloucester, to whom the order of the siege is given, is altogether directed by an Irishman, a very valiant gentleman, i' faith.

Fluellen
It is Captain Macmorris, is it not?

Gower
I think it be.

Fluellen
By Cheshu, he is an ass, as in the world; I will verify as much in his beard. He has no more directions in the true disciplines of the wars, look you, of the Roman disciplines, than is a puppy-dog.

Enter Macmorris and Captain Jamy.

Gower
Here 'a comes, and the Scots captain, Captain Jamy, with him.

Fluellen
Captain Jamy is a marvelous falorous gentleman, that is certain, and of great expedition and knowledge in th' aunchiant wars, upon my particular knowledge of his directions. By Cheshu, he will maintain his argument as well as any military man in the world, in the disciplines of the pristine wars of the Romans.

Jamy
I say gud day, Captain Fluellen.

Fluellen
God-den to your worship, good Captain James.

Gower
How now, Captain Macmorris, have you quit the mines? Have the pioners given o'er?

Macmorris
By Chrish law, 'tish ill done! The work ish give over, the trompet sound the retreat. By my hand I swear, and my father's soul, the work ish ill done; it ish give over. I would have blowed up the town, so Chrish save me law, in an hour! O, 'tish ill done, 'tish ill done; by my hand 'tish ill done!

Fluellen
Captain Macmorris, I beseech you now, will you vouchsafe me, look you, a few disputations with you, as partly touching or concerning the disciplines of the war, the Roman wars, in the way of argument, look you, and friendly communication; partly to satisfy my opinion, and partly for the satisfaction, look you, of my mind: as touching the direction of the military discipline, that is the point.

Jamy
It sall be vary gud, gud feith, gud captens bath, and I sall quit you with gud leve, as I may pick occasion; that sall I, mary.

Macmorris
It is no time to discourse, so Chrish save me. The day is hot, and the weather, and the wars, and the King, and the Dukes; it is no time to discourse. The town is beseech'd, and the trumpet call us to the breach, and we talk, and be Chrish, do nothing. 'Tis shame for us all. So God sa' me, 'tis shame to stand still, it is shame, by my hand; and there is throats to be cut, and works to be done, and there ish nothing done, so Christ sa' me law!

Jamy
By the mess, ere theise eyes of mine take themselves to slomber, ay'll de gud service, or I'll lig i' th' grund for it; ay, or go to death; and I'll pay't as valorously as I may, that sall I suerly do, that is the breff and the long. Mary, I wad full fain heard some question 'tween you tway.

Fluellen
Captain Macmorris, I think, look you, under your correction, there is not many of your nation—

Macmorris
Of my nation? What ish my nation? Ish a villain, and a basterd, and a knave, and a rascal. What ish my nation? Who talks of my nation?

Fluellen
Look you, if you take the matter otherwise than is meant, Captain Macmorris, peradventure I shall think you do not use me with that affability as in discretion you ought to use me, look you, being as good a man as yourself, both in the disciplines of war, and in the derivation of my birth, and in other particularities.

Macmorris
I do not know you so good a man as myself. So Chrish save me, I will cut off your head.

Gower
Gentlemen both, you will mistake each other.

Jamy
A! That's a foul fault. A parley sounded.

Gower
The town sounds a parley.

Fluellen
Captain Macmorris, when there is more better opportunity to be required, look you, I will be so bold as to tell you I know the disciplines of war; and there is an end.

Exeunt.

Scene 3

France. Before the Harfleur Gates.

(Citizens; King Henry the Fifth; Governor of Harfleur; Exeter)

King Henry gives the townspeople of Harfleur one last chance to surrender before he has them all slaughtered. Having heard that the Dauphin will not be able to rescue them as promised, the citizens choose to hand over the town.

Enter some Citizens on the walls. Enter the King and all his Train before the gates.

King Henry the Fifth
How yet resolves the governor of the town?
This is the latest parle we will admit;
Therefore to our best mercy give yourselves,
Or like to men proud of destruction,
Defy us to our worst; for as I am a soldier,
A name that in my thoughts becomes me best,
If I begin the batt'ry once again,
I will not leave the half-achieved Harfleur
Till in her ashes she lies buried.
The gates of mercy shall be all shut up,
And the flesh'd soldier, rough and hard of heart,
In liberty of bloody hand, shall range,
With conscience wide as hell, mowing like grass
Your fresh fair virgins and your flow'ring infants.
What is it then to me, if impious War,
Arrayed in flames like to the prince of fiends,
Do with his smirch'd complexion all fell feats
Enlink'd to waste and desolation?
What is't to me, when you yourselves are cause,
If your pure maidens fall into the hand
Of hot and forcing violation?
What rein can hold licentious wickedness
When down the hill he holds his fierce career?
We may as bootless spend our vain command

Upon th' enraged soldiers in their spoil,
As send precepts to the leviathan
To come ashore. Therefore, you men of Harfleur,
Take pity of your town and of your people,
Whiles yet my soldiers are in my command,
Whiles yet the cool and temperate wind of grace
O'erblows the filthy and contagious clouds
Of headly murder, spoil, and villainy.
If not—why, in a moment look to see
The blind and bloody soldier with foul hand
Defile the locks of your shrill-shrieking daughters;
Your fathers taken by the silver beards,
And their most reverend heads dash'd to the walls;
Your naked infants spitted upon pikes,
Whiles the mad mothers with their howls confus'd
Do break the clouds, as did the wives of Jewry
At Herod's bloody-hunting slaughter-men.
What say you? Will you yield, and this avoid?
Or guilty in defense, be thus destroy'd?

Enter Governor to the Citizens.

Governor of Harfleur
Our expectation hath this day an end.
The Dauphin, whom of succors we entreated,
Returns us that his powers are yet not ready
To raise so great a siege. Therefore, great King,
We yield our town and lives to thy soft mercy.
Enter our gates, dispose of us and ours,
For we no longer are defensible.

King Henry the Fifth
Open your gates. Come, uncle Exeter,
Go you and enter Harfleur; there remain,
And fortify it strongly 'gainst the French.
Use mercy to them all for us, dear uncle.
The winter coming on, and sickness growing
Upon our soldiers, we will retire to Callice.
Tonight in Harfleur will we be your guest;
Tomorrow for the march are we address'd.

Flourish, and enter the town.

Scene 4
Rouen. A room in the French King's palace.

(Katherine; Alice)

Katherine, who is certain that she'll end up going to England, asks her lady-in-waiting Alice to teach her some English. Unfortunately, Alice does not actually speak the language very well, though both are unaware of this.

Enter Katherine and Alice, an old gentlewoman.

Katherine
Alice, tu as été en Angleterre, et tu bien parles le langage.

Alice
Un peu, madame.

Katherine
Je te prie, m'enseignez; il faut que j'apprenne à parler. Comment appelez-vous la main en Anglois?

Alice
La main? Elle est appelée de hand.

Katherine
De hand. Et les doigts?

Alice
Les doigts? Ma foi, j'oublie les doigts, mais je me souviendrai. Les doigts? Je pense qu'ils sont appelés de fingres, oui, de fingres.

Katherine
La main, de hand; les doigts, de fingres. Je pense que je suis le bon écolier; j'ai gagné deux mots d'Anglois vitement. Comment appelez-vous les ongles?

Alice
Les ongles? Nous les appelons de nailès.

Katherine
De nailès. Écoutez, dites-moi si je parle bien: de hand, de fingres, et de nailès.

Alice
C'est bien dit, madame, il est fort bon Anglois.

Katherine
Dites-moi l'Anglois pour le bras.

Alice
De arma, madame.

Katherine
Et le coude?

Alice
D' elbow.

Katherine
D' elbow. Je m'en fais la répétition de tous les mots que vous m'avez appris dès à présent.

Alice
Il est trop difficile, madame, comme je pense.

Katherine
Excusez-moi, Alice; écoutez: d' hand, de fingre, de nailès, d' arma, de bilbow.

Alice
D' elbow, madame.

Katherine
O Seigneur Dieu, je m'en oublie d' elbow. Comment appelez-vous le col?

Alice
De nick, madame.

Katherine
De nick. Et le menton?

Alice
De chin.

Katherine
De sin. Le col, de nick; le menton, de sin.

Alice
Oui. Sauf votre honneur, en vérité, vous prononcez les mots aussi droit que les natifs d'Angleterre.

Katherine
Je ne doute point d'apprendre, par la grâce de Dieu, et en peu de temps.

Alice
N'avez vous déjà oublié ce que je vous ai enseigné?

Katherine
Non, je réciterai à vous promptement: d' hand, de fingre, de mailès—

Alice
De nailès, madame.

Katherine
De nailès, de arma, de ilbow.

Alice
Sauf votre honneur, d'elbow.

Katherine
Ainsi dis-je; d' elbow, de nick, et de sin. Comment appelez-vous le pied et la robe?

Alice
Le foot, madame, et le count.

Katherine
Le foot et le count! O Seigneur Dieu! Ils sont les mots de son mauvais, corruptible, gros, et impudique, et non pour les dames de honneur d'user. Je ne voudrais prononcer ces mots devant les seigneurs de France pour tout le monde. Foh! Le foot et le count! Néanmoins, je réciterai une autre fois ma leçon ensemble: d' hand, de fingre, de nailès, d' arma, d' elbow, de nick, de sin, de foot, le count.

Alice
Excellent, madame!

Katherine
C'est assez pour une fois: allons-nous à dîner.

Exeunt.

Scene 5

Rouen. Another room in the French King's palace.

(King of France; Dauphin; Duke of Britain; Constable of France)

The French Lords are incensed at the loss of Harfleur and how Henry is moving unopposed through France. They press the French King to send out his armies against the invaders; roused, the King orders a general muster of all forces to exterminate the English.

Enter the King of France, the Dauphin, the Duke of Britain, the Constable of France, and others.

Charles the Sixth
'Tis certain he hath pass'd the river Somme.

Constable of France
And if he be not fought withal, my lord,
Let us not live in France; let us quit all,
And give our vineyards to a barbarous people.

The Dauphin
O Dieu vivant! Shall a few sprays of us,
The emptying of our fathers' luxury,
Our scions, put in wild and savage stock,
Spirt up so suddenly into the clouds

And overlook their grafters?

Duke of Britain
Normans, but bastard Normans, Norman bastards!
Mort Dieu, ma vie! If they march along
Unfought withal, but I will sell my dukedom,
To buy a slobb'ry and a dirty farm
In that nook-shotten isle of Albion.

Constable of France
Dieu de batailles! Where have they this mettle?
Is not their climate foggy, raw, and dull,
On whom, as in despite, the sun looks pale,
Killing their fruit with frowns? Can sodden water,
A drench for sur-rein'd jades, their barley-broth,
Decoct their cold blood to such valiant heat?
And shall our quick blood, spirited with wine,
Seem frosty? O, for honor of our land,
Let us not hang like roping icicles
Upon our houses' thatch, whiles a more frosty people
Sweat drops of gallant youth in our rich fields!
Poor we call them in their native lords!

The Dauphin
By faith and honor,
Our madams mock at us, and plainly say
Our mettle is bred out, and they will give
Their bodies to the lust of English youth
To new-store France with bastard warriors.

Duke of Britain
They bid us to the English dancing-schools,
And teach lavoltas high and swift corantos,
Saying our grace is only in our heels,
And that we are most lofty runaways.

Charles the Sixth
Where is Montjoy the herald? Speed him hence,
Let him greet England with our sharp defiance.
Up, princes, and, with spirit of honor edged
More sharper than your swords, hie to the field!
Charles Delabreth, High Constable of France,
You Dukes of Orléans, Bourbon, and of Berri,
Alanson, Brabant, Bar, and Burgundy,
Jacques Chatillion, Rambures, Vaudemont,
Beaumont, Grandpré, Roussi, and Faulconbridge,
Foix, Lestrake, Bouciqualt, and Charolois;
High dukes, great princes, barons, lords, and knights,
For your great seats now quit you of great shames.
Bar Harry England, that sweeps through our land
With pennons painted in the blood of Harfleur.
Rush on his host, as doth the melted snow
Upon the valleys whose low vassal seat
The Alps doth spit and void his rheum upon.
Go down upon him, you have power enough,
And in a captive chariot into Roan
Bring him our prisoner.

Constable of France
                   This becomes the great.
Sorry am I his numbers are so few,
His soldiers sick and famish'd in their march;
For I am sure, when he shall see our army,
He'll drop his heart into the sink of fear,
And for achievement offer us his ransom.

Charles the Sixth
Therefore, Lord Constable, haste on Montjoy,
And let him say to England that we send
To know what willing ransom he will give.
Prince Dauphin, you shall stay with us in Roan.

The Dauphin
Not so, I do beseech your Majesty.

Charles the Sixth
Be patient, for you shall remain with us.
Now forth, Lord Constable and princes all,
And quickly bring us word of England's fall.

Exeunt.

Scene 6

Picardy. The English camp.

(English Captain; Welsh Captain; Gower; Fluellen; Pistol; King Henry the Fifth; Soldiers; Gloucester; Montjoy)

Pistol asks Gower and Fluellen to help save the life of Bardolph, who has been caught robbing a church and condemned to hang. Fluellen declines, beginning to see what sort of man Bardolph is. King Henry approves of Bardolph's execution, and gives orders that any pillagers should be treated the same way. Montjoy, the French King's herald, enters and presents his master's official defiance to King Henry. Henry respects how Montjoy does his job, but tells him that though the English are weakened by illness, they will stand their ground if attacked.

Enter Captains, English and Welsh, Gower and Fluellen.

Act 3, Scene 6

Gower
How now, Captain Fluellen, come you from the bridge?

Fluellen
I assure you, there is very excellent services committed at the bridge.

Gower
Is the Duke of Exeter safe?

Fluellen
The Duke of Exeter is as magnanimous as Agamemnon, and a man that I love and honor with my soul, and my heart, and my duty, and my live, and my living, and my uttermost power. He is not—God be praised and blessed!—any hurt in the world, but keeps the bridge most valiantly, with excellent discipline. There is an aunchient lieutenant there at the pridge, I think in my very conscience he is as valiant a man as Mark Antony, and he is a man of no estimation in the world, but I did see him do as gallant service.

Gower
What do you call him?

Fluellen
He is call'd Aunchient Pistol.

Gower
I know him not.

Enter Pistol.

Fluellen
Here is the man.

Pistol
Captain, I thee beseech to do me favors.
The Duke of Exeter doth love thee well.

Fluellen
Ay, I praise God, and I have merited some love at his hands.

Pistol
Bardolph, a soldier firm and sound of heart,
And of buxom valor, hath by cruel fate,
And giddy Fortune's furious fickle wheel,
That goddess blind,
That stands upon the rolling restless stone—

Fluellen
By your patience, Aunchient Pistol: Fortune is painted blind, with a muffler afore his eyes, to signify to you that Fortune is blind; and she is painted also with a wheel, to signify to you, which is the moral of it, that she is turning, and inconstant, and mutability, and variation; and her foot, look you, is fixed upon a spherical stone, which rolls, and rolls, and rolls. In good truth, the poet makes a most excellent description of it. Fortune is an excellent moral.

Pistol
Fortune is Bardolph's foe, and frowns on him;
For he hath stol'n a pax, and hanged must 'a be—
A damned death!
Let gallows gape for dog, let man go free,
And let not hemp his windpipe suffocate.
But Exeter hath given the doom of death
For pax of little price.
Therefore go speak, the Duke will hear thy voice;
And let not Bardolph's vital thread be cut
With edge of penny cord and vile reproach.
Speak, captain, for his life, and I will thee requite.

Fluellen
Aunchient Pistol, I do partly understand your meaning.

Pistol
Why then rejoice therefore.

Fluellen
Certainly, aunchient, it is not a thing to rejoice at; for if, look you, he were my brother, I would desire the Duke to use his good pleasure, and put him to execution; for discipline ought to be used.

Pistol
Die and be damn'd! And figo for thy friendship!

Fluellen
It is well.

Pistol
The fig of Spain.

Exit.

Fluellen
Very good.

Gower
Why, this is an arrant counterfeit rascal, I remember him now; a bawd, a cutpurse.

Fluellen
I'll assure you, 'a utt'red as prave words at the pridge as you shall see in a summer's day. But it is very well; what he has spoke to me, that is well, I warrant you, when time is serve.

Gower
Why, 'tis a gull, a fool, a rogue, that now and then goes to the wars, to grace himself at his return into London under the form of a soldier. And such fellows are perfit in the great commanders' names, and they will learn you by rote where services were done—at such and such a sconce, at such a breach, at such a convoy; who came off bravely, who was shot, who disgrac'd, what terms the enemy stood on; and this they con perfitly in the phrase of war, which they trick up with new-tun'd oaths; and what a beard of the general's cut and a horrid suit of the camp will do among foaming bottles and ale-wash'd wits, is wonderful to be thought on. But you must learn to know such slanders of the age, or else you may be marvelously mistook.

Fluellen
I tell you what, Captain Gower: I do perceive he is not the man that he would gladly make show to the world he is. If I find a hole in his coat, I will tell him my mind.

Drum heard.

Hark you, the King is coming, and I must speak with him from the pridge.

Drum and Colors. Enter the King and his poor Soldiers and Gloucester.

God pless your Majesty!

King Henry the Fifth
How now, Fluellen, cam'st thou from the bridge?

Fluellen
Ay, so please your Majesty. The Duke of Exeter has very gallantly maintain'd the pridge. The French is gone off, look you, and there is gallant and most prave passages. Marry, th' athversary was have possession of the pridge, but he is enforced to retire, and the Duke of Exeter is master of the pridge. I can tell your Majesty, the Duke is a prave man.

King Henry the Fifth
What men have you lost, Fluellen?

Fluellen
The perdition of th' athversary hath been very great, reasonable great. Marry, for my part, I think the Duke hath lost never a man, but one that is like to be executed for robbing a church, one Bardolph, if your Majesty know the man. His face is all bubukles, and whelks, and knobs, and flames a' fire, and his lips blows at his nose, and it is like a coal of fire, sometimes plue and sometimes red, but his nose is executed, and his fire's out.

King Henry the Fifth
We would have all such offenders so cut off; and we give express charge that in our marches through the country there be nothing compell'd from the villages; nothing taken but paid for; none of the French upbraided or abus'd in disdainful language; for when lenity and cruelty play for a kingdom, the gentler gamester is the soonest winner.

Tucket. Enter Montjoy.

Montjoy
You know me by my habit.

King Henry the Fifth
Well then, I know thee. What shall I know of thee?

Montjoy
My master's mind.

King Henry the Fifth
Unfold it.

Montjoy
Thus says my King: Say thou to Harry of England, Though we seem'd dead, we did but sleep; advantage is a better soldier than rashness. Tell him we could have rebuk'd him at Harfleur, but that we thought not good to bruise an injury till it were full ripe. Now we speak upon our cue, and our voice is imperial: England shall repent his folly, see his weakness, and admire our sufferance. Bid him therefore consider of his ransom, which must proportion the losses we have borne, the subjects we have lost, the disgrace we have digested; which in weight to re-answer, his pettiness would bow under. For our losses, his exchequer is too poor; for th' effusion of our blood, the muster of his kingdom too faint a number; and for our disgrace,

his own person kneeling at our feet but a weak and worthless satisfaction. To this add defiance; and tell him, for conclusion, he hath betray'd his followers, whose condemnation is pronounc'd. So far my King and master; so much my office.

King Henry the Fifth
What is thy name? I know thy quality.

Montjoy
Montjoy.

King Henry the Fifth
Thou dost thy office fairly. Turn thee back,
And tell thy King I do not seek him now,
But could be willing to march on to Callice
Without impeachment; for to say the sooth,
Though 'tis no wisdom to confess so much
Unto an enemy of craft and vantage,
My people are with sickness much enfeebled,
My numbers lessen'd; and those few I have
Almost no better than so many French;
Who when they were in health, I tell thee, herald,
I thought upon one pair of English legs
Did march three Frenchmen. Yet forgive me, God,
That I do brag thus! This your air of France
Hath blown that vice in me. I must repent.
Go therefore tell thy master here I am;
My ransom is this frail and worthless trunk;
My army but a weak and sickly guard;
Yet, God before, tell him we will come on,
Though France himself and such another neighbor
Stand in our way. There's for thy labor, Montjoy.
Go bid thy master well advise himself.
If we may pass, we will; if we be hind'red,
We shall your tawny ground with your red blood
Discolor; and so, Montjoy, fare you well.
The sum of all our answer is but this:
We would not seek a battle as we are,
Nor, as we are, we say we will not shun it.
So tell your master.

Montjoy
I shall deliver so. Thanks to your Highness.

Exit.

Humphrey, Duke of Gloucester
I hope they will not come upon us now.

King Henry the Fifth
We are in God's hand, brother, not in theirs.
March to the bridge, it now draws toward night;
Beyond the river we'll encamp ourselves,
And on tomorrow bid them march away.

Exeunt.

Scene 7

Agincourt. The French camp.

(Constable of France; Lord Rambures; Duke of Orléans; Dauphin; French Court Attendant)

The self-satisfied and overconfident French lords discuss their armor, their horses, their mistresses, and how many English they shall each kill. They are eager for the morrow's battle.

Enter the Constable of France, the Lord Rambures, Orléans, Dauphin, with others.

Constable of France
Tut, I have the best armor of the world. Would it were day!

Duke of Orléans
You have an excellent armor; but let my horse have his due.

Constable of France
It is the best horse of Europe.

Duke of Orléans
Will it never be morning?

The Dauphin
My Lord of Orléans, and my Lord High Constable, you talk of horse and armor?

Duke of Orléans
You are as well provided of both as any prince in the world.

The Dauphin
What a long night is this! I will not change my horse with any that treads but on four pasterns. Ça, ha! He bounds from the earth, as if his entrails were hairs; le cheval volant, the Pegasus, chez les narines de feu! When I bestride him, I soar, I am a hawk; he trots the air; the earth sings when he touches it; the basest horn of his hoof is more musical than the pipe of Hermes.

Duke of Orléans
He's of the color of the nutmeg.

The Dauphin
And of the heat of the ginger. It is a beast for Perseus. He is pure air and fire; and the dull elements of earth and water never appear in him, but only in patient stillness while his rider mounts him. He is indeed a horse, and all other jades you may call beasts.

Constable of France
Indeed, my lord, it is a most absolute and excellent horse.

The Dauphin
It is the prince of palfreys: his neigh is like the bidding of a monarch, and his countenance enforces homage.

Duke of Orléans
No more, cousin.

The Dauphin
Nay, the man hath no wit that cannot, from the rising of the lark to the lodging of the lamb, vary deserv'd praise on my palfrey. It is a theme as fluent as the sea; turn the sands into eloquent tongues, and my horse is argument for them all. 'Tis a subject for a sovereign to reason on, and for a sovereign's sovereign to ride on; and for the world, familiar to us and unknown, to lay apart their particular functions and wonder at him. I once writ a sonnet in his praise and began thus: "Wonder of nature"—

Duke of Orléans
I have heard a sonnet begin so to one's mistress.

The Dauphin
Then did they imitate that which I compos'd to my courser, for my horse is my mistress.

Duke of Orléans
Your mistress bears well.

The Dauphin
Me well, which is the prescript praise and perfection of a good and particular mistress.

Constable of France
Nay, for methought yesterday your mistress shrewdly shook your back.

The Dauphin
So perhaps did yours.

Constable of France
Mine was not bridled.

The Dauphin
O then belike she was old and gentle, and you rode like a kern of Ireland, your French hose off, and in your strait strossers.

Constable of France
You have good judgment in horsemanship.

The Dauphin
Be warn'd by me then: they that ride so, and ride not warily, fall into foul bogs. I had rather have my horse to my mistress.

Constable of France
I had as lief have my mistress a jade.

The Dauphin
I tell thee, Constable, my mistress wears his own hair.

Constable of France
I could make as true a boast as that, if I had a sow to my mistress.

The Dauphin
"Le chien est retourné à son propre vomissement, et la truie lavée au bourbier." Thou mak'st use of any thing.

Constable of France
Yet do I not use my horse for my mistress, or any such proverb so little kin to the purpose.

Rambures
My Lord Constable, the armor that I saw in your tent tonight, are those stars or suns upon it?

Constable of France
Stars, my lord.

The Dauphin
Some of them will fall tomorrow, I hope.

Constable of France
And yet my sky shall not want.

The Dauphin
That may be, for you bear a many superfluously, and 'twere more honor some were away.

Constable of France
Ev'n as your horse bears your praises, who would trot as well, were some of your brags dismounted.

The Dauphin
Would I were able to load him with his desert! Will it never be day? I will trot tomorrow a mile, and my way shall be pav'd with English faces.

Constable of France
I will not say so, for fear I should be fac'd out of my way. But I would it were morning, for I would fain be about the ears of the English.

Rambures
Who will go to hazard with me for twenty prisoners?

Constable of France
You must first go yourself to hazard, ere you have them.

The Dauphin
'Tis midnight, I'll go arm myself.

Exit.

Duke of Orléans
The Dauphin longs for morning.

Rambures
He longs to eat the English.

Constable of France
I think he will eat all he kills.

Duke of Orléans
By the white hand of my lady, he's a gallant prince.

Constable of France
Swear by her foot, that she may tread out the oath.

Duke of Orléans
He is simply the most active gentleman of France.

Constable of France
Doing is activity, and he will still be doing.

Duke of Orléans
He never did harm, that I heard of.

Constable of France
Nor will do none tomorrow. He will keep that good name still.

Duke of Orléans
I know him to be valiant.

Constable of France
I was told that by one that knows him better than you.

Duke of Orléans
What's he?

Constable of France
Marry, he told me so himself, and he said he car'd not who knew it.

Duke of Orléans
He needs not, it is no hidden virtue in him.

Constable of France
By my faith, sir, but it is; never anybody saw it but his lackey. 'Tis a hooded valor, and when it appears, it will bate.

Duke of Orléans
"Ill will never said well."

Constable of France
I will cap that proverb with "There is flattery in friendship."

Duke of Orléans
And I will take up that with "Give the devil his due."

Constable of France
Well plac'd. There stands your friend for the devil; have at the very eye of that proverb with "A pox of the devil."

Duke of Orléans
You are the better at proverbs, by how much "A fool's bolt is soon shot."

Constable of France
You have shot over.

Duke of Orléans
'Tis not the first time you were overshot.

Enter French Court Attendant.

French Court Attendant
My Lord High Constable, the English lie within fifteen hundred paces of your tents.

Constable of France
Who hath measur'd the ground?

French Court Attendant
The Lord Grandpré.

Constable of France
A valiant and most expert gentleman. Would it were day! Alas, poor Harry of England! He longs not for the dawning as we do.

Duke of Orléans
What a wretched and peevish fellow is this King of England, to mope with his fat-brain'd followers so far out of his knowledge!

Constable of France
If the English had any apprehension, they would run away.

Duke of Orléans
That they lack; for if their heads had any intellectual armor, they could never wear such heavy headpieces.

Rambures
That island of England breeds very valiant creatures; their mastiffs are of unmatchable courage.

Duke of Orléans
Foolish curs, that run winking into the mouth of a Russian bear and have their heads crush'd like rotten apples! You may as well say, that's a valiant flea that dare eat his breakfast on the lip of a lion.

Constable of France
Just, just; and the men do sympathize with the mastiffs in robustious and rough coming on, leaving their wits with their wives; and then give them great meals of beef and iron and steel, they will eat like wolves and fight like devils.

Duke of Orléans
Ay, but these English are shrewdly out of beef.

Constable of France
Then shall we find tomorrow they have only stomachs to eat and none to fight. Now is it time to arm. Come, shall we about it?

Duke of Orléans
It is now two a' clock; but let me see, by ten
We shall have each a hundred Englishmen.

Exeunt.

Act 4

Prologue

(Chorus)

The Chorus asks the audience to imagine the fearful night before the battle, as the two armies, so close together they can almost see each other's faces, ready themselves to fight the next morning. He tells of how King Henry wanders through the camp giving his men heart — and apologizes once again for how little a stage show can truly reproduce so great an event.

Enter Chorus.

Chorus
Now entertain conjecture of a time
When creeping murmur and the poring dark
Fills the wide vessel of the universe.
From camp to camp, through the foul womb of night,
The hum of either army stilly sounds,
That the fix'd sentinels almost receive
The secret whispers of each other's watch.
Fire answers fire, and through their paly flames
Each battle sees the other's umber'd face.
Steed threatens steed, in high and boastful neighs
Piercing the night's dull ear; and from the tents
The armorers, accomplishing the knights,
With busy hammers closing rivets up,
Give dreadful note of preparation.
The country cocks do crow, the clocks do toll,
And the third hour of drowsy morning name.
Proud of their numbers and secure in soul,
The confident and overlusty French
Do the low-rated English play at dice;
And chide the cripple tardy-gaited night,
Who like a foul and ugly witch doth limp
So tediously away. The poor condemned English,
Like sacrifices, by their watchful fires
Sit patiently and inly ruminate
The morning's danger; and their gesture sad,
Investing lank-lean cheeks and war-worn coats,
Presented them unto the gazing moon
So many horrid ghosts. O now, who will behold
The royal captain of this ruin'd band
Walking from watch to watch, from tent to tent,
Let him cry, "Praise and glory on his head!"
For forth he goes, and visits all his host,
Bids them good morrow with a modest smile,
And calls them brothers, friends, and countrymen.
Upon his royal face there is no note

How dread an army hath enrounded him;
Nor doth he dedicate one jot of color
Unto the weary and all-watched night;
But freshly looks, and overbears attaint
With cheerful semblance and sweet majesty;
That every wretch, pining and pale before,
Beholding him, plucks comfort from his looks.
A largess universal, like the sun,
His liberal eye doth give to every one,
Thawing cold fear, that mean and gentle all
Behold, as may unworthiness define,
A little touch of Harry in the night.
And so our scene must to the battle fly;
Where—O for pity!—we shall much disgrace
With four or five most vile and ragged foils
(Right ill dispos'd, in brawl ridiculous)
The name of Agincourt. Yet sit and see,
Minding true things by what their mock'ries be.

Exit.

Scene 1

Agincourt. The English camp.

(King Henry the Fifth; Bedford; Gloucester; Erpingham; Pistol; Fluellen; Gower; Soldiers; John Bates; Alexander Court; Michael Williams)

King Henry discusses the danger the English are in with his brothers, and bids them call a council of war. Wishing to know what the common soldiers are saying, he borrows Sir Thomas Erpingham's cloak to disguise himself. Left alone, he encounters Pistol, who challenges him. Not recognizing Henry, Pistol admits that he is still loyal to the King, despite what happened to Falstaff and Bardolph. Believing Henry to be Welsh, Pistol promises that he will take the leek that Fluellen will wear as a symbol of Welsh pride on St. Davy's Day and hit him around the head with it. When Henry claims to be Fluellen's kinsman, Pistol insults him and walks out. Gower and Fluellen enter, with the latter insisting on great silence even though the enemy knows very well where the English are and they are making a great deal of noise themselves. As the two captains leave, three common soldiers enter. Much less optimistic than the commanders, they would much rather be back home. Henry, still unrecognized, defends the King, arguing that his cause is just, but the soldiers point out that they have no way of knowing that. They suggest that, since they are only obeying orders, if the cause is unjust the King who brought them there will bear all of their deaths on his conscience. Henry insists that this is not so. When Williams suggests that the King has only sworn not to be taken prisoner to make the men fight better, Henry is offended, and the two exchange gloves, promising to meet and fight on the cause if they both survive the battle. Left alone, Henry considers how the commoners can never know what it is to be a king, nor how many things a monarch must think of that they never consider. Erpingham calls him to the conference. Henry prays to God for help, begging that his father's sin of usurpation not be visited on him today.

Enter the King, Bedford, and Gloucester.

King Henry the Fifth
Gloucester, 'tis true that we are in great danger,
The greater therefore should our courage be.
Good morrow, brother Bedford. God Almighty!
There is some soul of goodness in things evil,
Would men observingly distill it out;
For our bad neighbor makes us early stirrers,
Which is both healthful and good husbandry.
Besides, they are our outward consciences
And preachers to us all, admonishing
That we should dress us fairly for our end.
Thus may we gather honey from the weed,
And make a moral of the devil himself.

Enter Erpingham.

Good morrow, old Sir Thomas Erpingham.
A good soft pillow for that good white head
Were better than a churlish turf of France.

Sir Thomas Erpingham
Not so, my liege, this lodging likes me better,
Since I may say, "Now lie I like a king."

King Henry the Fifth
'Tis good for men to love their present pains
Upon example; so the spirit is eased;
And when the mind is quick'ned, out of doubt,
The organs, though defunct and dead before,
Break up their drowsy grave, and newly move
With casted slough and fresh legerity.
Lend me thy cloak, Sir Thomas. Brothers both,
Commend me to the princes in our camp;
Do my good morrow to them, and anon
Desire them all to my pavilion.

Humphrey, Duke of Gloucester
We shall, my liege.

Sir Thomas Erpingham
Shall I attend your Grace?

King Henry the Fifth
                    No, my good knight;
Go with my brothers to my lords of England.
I and my bosom must debate a while,
And then I would no other company.

Sir Thomas Erpingham
The Lord in heaven bless thee, noble Harry!

Exeunt all but the King.

King Henry the Fifth
God-a-mercy, old heart, thou speak'st cheerfully.

Enter Pistol.

Pistol
Qui vous là?

King Henry the Fifth
A friend.

Pistol
Discuss unto me, art thou officer,
Or art thou base, common, and popular?

King Henry the Fifth
I am a gentleman of a company.

Pistol
Trail'st thou the puissant pike?

King Henry the Fifth
Even so. What are you?

Pistol
As good a gentleman as the Emperor.

King Henry the Fifth
Then you are a better than the King.

Pistol
The King's a bawcock, and a heart of gold,
A lad of life, an imp of fame,
Of parents good, of fist most valiant.
I kiss his dirty shoe, and from heart-string
I love the lovely bully. What is thy name?

King Henry the Fifth
Harry le Roy.

Pistol
Le Roy? A Cornish name. Art thou of Cornish crew?

King Henry the Fifth
No, I am a Welshman.

Pistol
Know'st thou Fluellen?

King Henry the Fifth
Yes.

Pistol
Tell him I'll knock his leek about his pate
Upon Saint Davy's day.

King Henry the Fifth
Do not you wear your dagger in your cap that day, lest he knock that about yours.

Pistol
Art thou his friend?

King Henry the Fifth
And his kinsman too.

Pistol
The figo for thee then!

King Henry the Fifth
I thank you. God be with you!

Pistol
My name is Pistol call'd.

Exit.

King Henry the Fifth
It sorts well with your fierceness.

Manet King to one side.
Enter Fluellen and Gower.

Gower
Captain Fluellen!

Fluellen
So! In the name of Jesu Christ, speak fewer. It is the greatest admiration in the universal world, when the true and aunchient prerogatifes and laws of the wars is not kept. If you would take the pains but to examine the wars of Pompey the Great, you shall find, I warrant you, that there is no tiddle taddle nor pibble babble in Pompey's camp. I warrant you, you shall find the ceremonies of the wars, and the cares of it, and the

forms of it, and the sobriety of it, and the modesty of it, to be otherwise.

Gower
Why, the enemy is loud, you hear him all night.

Fluellen
If the enemy is an ass and a fool, and a prating coxcomb, is it meet, think you, that we should also, look you, be an ass and a fool, and a prating coxcomb, in your own conscience now?

Gower
I will speak lower.

Fluellen
I pray you, and beseech you, that you will.

Exit with Gower.

King Henry the Fifth
Though it appear a little out of fashion,
There is much care and valor in this Welshman.

Enter three soldiers, John Bates, Alexander Court, and Michael Williams.

Court
Brother John Bates, is not that the morning which breaks yonder?

Bates
I think it be; but we have no great cause to desire the approach of day.

Williams
We see yonder the beginning of the day, but I think we shall never see the end of it. Who goes there?

King Henry the Fifth
A friend.

Williams
Under what captain serve you?

King Henry the Fifth
Under Sir Thomas Erpingham.

Williams
A good old commander and a most kind gentleman. I pray you, what thinks he of our estate?

King Henry the Fifth
Even as men wrack'd upon a sand, that look to be wash'd off the next tide.

Bates
He hath not told his thought to the King?

King Henry the Fifth
No; nor it is not meet he should. For though I speak it to you, I think the King is but a man, as I am. The violet smells to him as it doth to me; the element shows to him as it doth to me; all his senses have but human conditions. His ceremonies laid by, in his nakedness he appears but a man; and though his affections are higher mounted than ours, yet when they stoop, they stoop with the like wing. Therefore, when he sees reason of fears, as we do, his fears, out of doubt, be of the same relish as ours are; yet in reason, no man should possess him with any appearance of fear, lest he, by showing it, should dishearten his army.

Bates
He may show what outward courage he will; but I believe, as cold a night as 'tis, he could wish himself in Thames up to the neck; and so I would he were, and I by him, at all adventures, so we were quit here.

King Henry the Fifth
By my troth, I will speak my conscience of the King: I think he would not wish himself any where but where he is.

Bates
Then I would he were here alone; so should he be sure to be ransom'd, and a many poor men's lives sav'd.

King Henry the Fifth
I dare say you love him not so ill to wish him here alone, howsoever you speak this to feel other men's minds. Methinks I could not die any where so contented as in the King's company, his cause being just and his quarrel honorable.

Williams
That's more than we know.

Bates
Ay, or more than we should seek after; for we know enough, if we know we are the King's subjects. If his cause be wrong, our obedience to the King wipes the crime of it out of us.

Williams
But if the cause be not good, the King himself hath a heavy reckoning to make, when all those legs, and arms, and heads, chopp'd off in a battle, shall join together at the latter day and cry all, "We died at such a place"—some swearing, some crying for a surgeon, some upon their wives left poor behind them, some upon the debts they owe, some upon their children rawly left. I am afeard there are few die well that die in a battle; for how can they charitably dispose of any thing, when blood is their argument? Now, if these men do not die well, it will be a black matter for the King that led them to it; who to disobey were against all proportion of subjection.

King Henry the Fifth
So, if a son that is by his father sent about merchandise do sinfully miscarry upon the sea, the imputation of his wickedness, by your rule, should be impos'd upon his father that sent him; or if a servant, under his master's command transporting a sum of money, be assail'd by robbers and die in many irreconcil'd iniquities, you may call the business of the master the author of the servant's damnation. But this is not so. The King is not bound to answer the particular endings of his soldiers, the father of his son, nor the master of his servant; for they purpose not their death when they purpose their services. Besides, there is no king, be his cause never so spotless, if it come to the arbitrement of swords, can try it out with all unspotted soldiers. Some, peradventure, have on them the guilt of premeditated and contriv'd murder; some, of beguiling virgins with the broken seals of perjury; some, making the wars their bulwark, that have before gor'd the gentle bosom of peace with pillage and robbery. Now, if these men have defeated the law and outrun native punishment, though they can outstrip men, they have no wings to fly from God. War is his beadle, war is his vengeance; so that here men are punish'd for before-breach of the King's laws in now the King's quarrel. Where they fear'd the death, they have borne life away; and where they would be safe, they perish. Then if they die unprovided, no more is the King guilty of their damnation than he was before guilty of those impieties for the which they are now visited. Every subject's duty is the King's, but every subject's soul is his own. Therefore should every soldier in the wars do as every sick man in his bed, wash every mote out of his conscience; and dying so, death is to him advantage; or not dying, the time was blessedly lost wherein such preparation was gain'd; and in him that escapes, it were not sin to think that making God so free an offer, He let him outlive that day to see His greatness and to teach others how they should prepare.

Williams
'Tis certain, every man that dies ill, the ill upon his own head, the King is not to answer it.

Bates
I do not desire he should answer for me, and yet I determine to fight lustily for him.

King Henry the Fifth
I myself heard the King say he would not be ransom'd.

Williams
Ay, he said so, to make us fight cheerfully; but when our throats are cut, he may be ransom'd, and we ne'er the wiser.

King Henry the Fifth
If I live to see it, I will never trust his word after.

Williams
You pay him then. That's a perilous shot out of an elder-gun, that a poor and a private displeasure can do against a monarch! You may as well go about to turn the sun to ice with fanning in his face with a peacock's feather. You'll never trust his word after! Come, 'tis a foolish saying.

King Henry the Fifth
Your reproof is something too round, I should be angry with you, if the time were convenient.

Williams
Let it be a quarrel between us, if you live.

King Henry the Fifth
I embrace it.

Williams
How shall I know thee again?

King Henry the Fifth
Give me any gage of thine, and I will wear it in my bonnet; then if ever thou dar'st acknowledge it, I will make it my quarrel.

Williams
Here's my glove; give me another of thine.

King Henry the Fifth
There.

Williams
This will I also wear in my cap. If ever thou come to me and say, after tomorrow, "This is my glove," by this hand I will take thee a box on the ear.

King Henry the Fifth
If ever I live to see it, I will challenge it.

Williams
Thou dar'st as well be hang'd.

King Henry the Fifth
Well, I will do it, though I take thee in the King's company.

Williams
Keep thy word; fare thee well.

Bates
Be friends, you English fools, be friends, we have French quarrels now, if you could tell how to reckon.

King Henry the Fifth
Indeed the French may lay twenty French crowns to one they will beat us, for they bear them on their shoulders; but it is no English treason to cut French crowns, and tomorrow the King himself will be a clipper.

Exeunt Soldiers.

Upon the King! Let us our lives, our souls,
Our debts, our careful wives,
Our children, and our sins lay on the King!
We must bear all. O hard condition,
Twin-born with greatness, subject to the breath
Of every fool whose sense no more can feel
But his own wringing! What infinite heart's ease
Must kings neglect, that private men enjoy!
And what have kings, that privates have not too,
Save ceremony, save general ceremony?
And what art thou, thou idol Ceremony?
What kind of god art thou, that suffer'st more
Of mortal griefs than do thy worshippers?
What are thy rents? What are thy comings-in?
O Ceremony, show me but thy worth!
What is thy soul of adoration?
Art thou aught else but place, degree, and form,
Creating awe and fear in other men?
Wherein thou art less happy, being fear'd,
Than they in fearing.
What drink'st thou oft, in stead of homage sweet,
But poison'd flattery? O, be sick, great greatness,
And bid thy ceremony give thee cure!
Thinks thou the fiery fever will go out
With titles blown from adulation?
Will it give place to flexure and low bending?
Canst thou, when thou command'st the beggar's knee,
Command the health of it? No, thou proud dream,
That play'st so subtily with a king's repose.
I am a king that find thee; and I know
'Tis not the balm, the sceptre, and the ball,
The sword, the mace, the crown imperial,
The intertissued robe of gold and pearl,
The farced title running 'fore the king,
The throne he sits on, nor the tide of pomp
That beats upon the high shore of this world—
No, not all these, thrice-gorgeous ceremony,
Not all these, laid in bed majestical,
Can sleep so soundly as the wretched slave;
Who, with a body fill'd and vacant mind,
Gets him to rest, cramm'd with distressful bread,
Never sees horrid night, the child of hell;
But like a lackey, from the rise to set,
Sweats in the eye of Phoebus, and all night
Sleeps in Elysium; next day after dawn,
Doth rise and help Hyperion to his horse,
And follows so the ever-running year
With profitable labor to his grave:
And, but for ceremony, such a wretch,
Winding up days with toil, and nights with sleep,
Had the forehand and vantage of a king.
The slave, a member of the country's peace,
Enjoys it; but in gross brain little wots
What watch the King keeps to maintain the peace,
Whose hours the peasant best advantages.

Enter Erpingham.

Sir Thomas Erpingham
My lord, your nobles, jealous of your absence,
Seek through your camp to find you.

King Henry the Fifth
                Good old knight,
Collect them all together at my tent.
I'll be before thee.

Sir Thomas Erpingham
                I shall do't, my lord.

Exit.

King Henry the Fifth
O God of battles, steel my soldiers' hearts,
Possess them not with fear! Take from them now
The sense of reck'ning, if th' opposed numbers
Pluck their hearts from them. Not today, O Lord,
O, not today, think not upon the fault
My father made in compassing the crown!
I Richard's body have interred new,
And on it have bestowed more contrite tears,
Than from it issued forced drops of blood.
Five hundred poor I have in yearly pay,
Who twice a day their wither'd hands hold up
Toward heaven, to pardon blood; and I have built
Two chauntries, where the sad and solemn priests
Sing still for Richard's soul. More will I do;
Though all that I can do is nothing worth,
Since that my penitence comes after all,
Imploring pardon.

Enter Gloucester.

Humphrey, Duke of Gloucester
My liege!

King Henry the Fifth
My brother Gloucester's voice? Ay;
I know thy errand, I will go with thee.
The day, my friends, and all things stay for me.

Exeunt.

Scene 2

The French camp.

(Dauphin; Duke of Orléans; Rambures; Constable; French Messenger; Grandpré)

The proud French lords mount for battle, scoffing at the wretched condition of the English, and regretting that they will not have better sport.

Enter the Dauphin, Orléans, and Rambures.

Duke of Orléans
The sun doth gild our armor, up, my lords!

The Dauphin
Montez à cheval! My horse, varlot lackey! Ha!

Duke of Orléans
O brave spirit!

The Dauphin
Via! Les eaux et terre.

Duke of Orléans
Rien puis? L'air et feu?

The Dauphin
Cieux! Cousin Orléans.

Enter Constable.

Now, my Lord Constable?

Constable of France
Hark how our steeds for present service neigh!

The Dauphin
Mount them, and make incision in their hides,
That their hot blood may spin in English eyes,
And dout them with superfluous courage, ha!

Rambures
What, will you have them weep our horses' blood?
How shall we then behold their natural tears?

Enter French Messenger.

French Messenger
The English are embattled, you French peers.

Constable of France
To horse, you gallant princes! Straight to horse!
Do but behold yond poor and starved band,
And your fair show shall suck away their souls,
Leaving them but the shales and husks of men.
There is not work enough for all our hands,
Scarce blood enough in all their sickly veins
To give each naked curtle-axe a stain,
That our French gallants shall today draw out,
And sheathe for lack of sport. Let us but blow on them,
The vapor of our valor will o'erturn them.
'Tis positive against all exceptions, lords,
That our superfluous lackeys and our peasants,
Who in unnecessary action swarm
About our squares of battle, were enow
To purge this field of such a hilding foe;
Though we upon this mountain's basis by

Took stand for idle speculation—
But that our honors must not. What's to say?
A very little little let us do,
And all is done. Then let the trumpets sound
The tucket sonance and the note to mount;
For our approach shall so much dare the field,
That England shall crouch down in fear, and yield.

Enter Grandpré.

Grandpré
Why do you stay so long, my lords of France?
Yond island carrions, desperate of their bones,
Ill-favoredly become the morning field.
Their ragged curtains poorly are let loose,
And our air shakes them passing scornfully.
Big Mars seems bankrupt in their beggar'd host,
And faintly through a rusty beaver peeps.
The horsemen sit like fixed candlesticks,
With torch-staves in their hand; and their poor jades
Lob down their heads, dropping the hides and hips,
The gum down-roping from their pale-dead eyes,
And in their pale dull mouths the gimmal'd bit
Lies foul with chaw'd-grass, still and motionless;
And their executors, the knavish crows,
Fly o'er them all, impatient for their hour.
Description cannot suit itself in words
To demonstrate the life of such a battle,
In life so lifeless as it shows itself.

Constable of France
They have said their prayers, and they stay for death.

The Dauphin
Shall we go send them dinners and fresh suits,
And give their fasting horses provender,
And after fight with them?

Constable of France
I stay but for my guidon; to the field!
I will the banner from a trumpet take,
And use it for my haste. Come, come away!
The sun is high, and we outwear the day.

Exeunt.

Scene 3

Agincourt. The English camp.

(Gloucester; Bedford; Exeter; Erpingham; Salisbury; Westmorland; King Henry the Fifth; Montjoy; York)

The English nobles encourage one another, though they are intimidated by the odds against them. King Henry overhears Westmorland wishing that they had more men, and rebukes him, arguing that the fewer they are, the greater the honor when they win, and that every man who lives through this day will look back on it with pride in his old age. Fired up by this speech, Westmorland retracts his wish entirely. Montjoy returns to give Henry one last chance of surrendering, but the King absolutely refuses. The Duke of York begs permission to lead the front lines, which King Henry grants.

Enter Gloucester, Bedford, Exeter, Erpingham with all his host; Salisbury and Westmorland.

Humphrey, Duke of Gloucester
Where is the King?

John, Duke of Bedford
The King himself is rode to view their battle.

Earl of Westmorland
Of fighting men they have full threescore thousand.

Duke of Exeter
There's five to one; besides, they all are fresh.

Earl of Salisbury
God's arm strike with us! 'Tis a fearful odds.
God buy you, princes all; I'll to my charge.
If we no more meet till we meet in heaven,
Then joyfully, my noble Lord of Bedford,
My dear Lord Gloucester, and my good Lord Exeter,
And my kind kinsman, warriors all, adieu!

John, Duke of Bedford
Farewell, good Salisbury, and good luck go with thee!

Duke of Exeter
Farewell, kind lord; fight valiantly today!
And yet I do thee wrong to mind thee of it,
For thou art fram'd of the firm truth of valor.

Exit Salisbury.

John, Duke of Bedford
He is as full of valor as of kindness,
Princely in both.

Enter the King.

Earl of Westmorland
                   O that we now had here
But one ten thousand of those men in England
That do no work today!

King Henry the Fifth
                   What's he that wishes so?
My cousin Westmorland? No, my fair cousin.
If we are mark'd to die, we are enow
To do our country loss; and if to live,
The fewer men, the greater share of honor.
God's will, I pray thee wish not one man more.
By Jove, I am not covetous for gold,
Nor care I who doth feed upon my cost;
It yearns me not if men my garments wear;
Such outward things dwell not in my desires.
But if it be a sin to covet honor,
I am the most offending soul alive.
No, faith, my coz, wish not a man from England.
God's peace, I would not lose so great an honor
As one man more methinks would share from me,
For the best hope I have. O, do not wish one more!
Rather proclaim it, Westmorland, through my host,
That he which hath no stomach to this fight,
Let him depart, his passport shall be made,
And crowns for convoy put into his purse.
We would not die in that man's company
That fears his fellowship to die with us.
This day is call'd the feast of Crispian:
He that outlives this day, and comes safe home,
Will stand a' tiptoe when this day is named,
And rouse him at the name of Crispian.
He that shall see this day, and live old age,
Will yearly on the vigil feast his neighbors,
And say, "Tomorrow is Saint Crispian ."
Then will he strip his sleeve and show his scars,
And say, "These wounds I had on Crispin's day."
Old men forget; yet all shall be forgot,
But he'll remember with advantages
What feats he did that day. Then shall our names,
Familiar in his mouth as household words,
Harry the King, Bedford and Exeter,
Warwick and Talbot, Salisbury and Gloucester,
Be in their flowing cups freshly rememb'red.
This story shall the good man teach his son;
And Crispin Crispian shall ne'er go by,
From this day to the ending of the world,
But we in it shall be remembered—
We few, we happy few, we band of brothers;
For he today that sheds his blood with me
Shall be my brother; be he ne'er so vile,
This day shall gentle his condition;
And gentlemen in England, now a-bed,
Shall think themselves accurs'd they were not here;
And hold their manhoods cheap whiles any speaks
That fought with us upon Saint Crispin's day.

Enter Salisbury.

Earl of Salisbury
My sovereign lord, bestow yourself with speed.
The French are bravely in their battles set,
And will with all expedience charge on us.

King Henry the Fifth
All things are ready, if our minds be so.

Earl of Westmorland
Perish the man whose mind is backward now!

King Henry the Fifth
Thou dost not wish more help from England, coz?

Earl of Westmorland
God's will, my liege, would you and I alone,
Without more help, could fight this royal battle!

King Henry the Fifth
Why, now thou hast unwish'd five thousand men;
Which likes me better than to wish us one.
You know your places. God be with you all!

Tucket. Enter Montjoy.

Montjoy
Once more I come to know of thee, King Harry,
If for thy ransom thou wilt now compound,
Before thy most assured overthrow;
For certainly thou art so near the gulf,
Thou needs must be englutted. Besides, in mercy,
The Constable desires thee thou wilt mind
Thy followers of repentance; that their souls
May make a peaceful and a sweet retire
From off these fields, where (wretches!) their poor bodies
Must lie and fester.

King Henry the Fifth
                   Who hath sent thee now?

Montjoy
The Constable of France.

King Henry the Fifth
I pray thee bear my former answer back:
Bid them achieve me, and then sell my bones.
Good God, why should they mock poor fellows thus?
The man that once did sell the lion's skin
While the beast liv'd, was kill'd with hunting him.
A many of our bodies shall no doubt
Find native graves; upon the which, I trust,
Shall witness live in brass of this day's work.
And those that leave their valiant bones in France,
Dying like men, though buried in your dunghills,
They shall be fam'd; for there the sun shall greet them,
And draw their honors reeking up to heaven,
Leaving their earthly parts to choke your clime,
The smell whereof shall breed a plague in France.
Mark then abounding valor in our English:
That being dead, like to the bullet's crasing,
Break out into a second course of mischief,
Killing in relapse of mortality.
Let me speak proudly: tell the Constable
We are but warriors for the working-day;
Our gayness and our gilt are all besmirch'd
With rainy marching in the painful field;
There's not a piece of feather in our host—
Good argument (I hope) we will not fly—
And time hath worn us into slovenry.
But, by the mass, our hearts are in the trim;
And my poor soldiers tell me, yet ere night,
They'll be in fresher robes, or they will pluck
The gay new coats o'er the French soldiers' heads
And turn them out of service. If they do this—
As, if God please, they shall—my ransom then
Will soon be levied. Herald, save thou thy labor.
Come thou no more for ransom, gentle herald,
They shall have none, I swear, but these my joints;
Which if they have as I will leave 'um them,
Shall yield them little, tell the Constable.

Montjoy
I shall, King Harry. And so fare thee well;
Thou never shalt hear herald any more.

Exit.

King Henry the Fifth
I fear thou wilt once more come again for a ransom.

Enter York.

Duke of York
My lord, most humbly on my knee I beg
The leading of the vaward.

King Henry the Fifth
Take it, brave York. Now, soldiers, march away,
And how thou pleasest, God, dispose the day!

Exeunt.

Scene 4

The field of battle.

(Pistol; French Soldier; Boy)

A French Soldier captured by Pistol begs for his life, though Pistol's poor command of French leaves the situation perilous. Luckily the Boy can interpret, and the Frenchman offers an acceptable ransom. Left alone, the Boy comments on Pistol's cowardice and bravado.

Alarum. Excursions. Enter Pistol, French Soldier, Boy.

Pistol
Yield, cur!

French Soldier
Je pense que vous êtes le gentilhomme de bonne qualité.

Pistol
Qualtitie! Calen o custure me! Art thou a gentleman?
What is thy name? Discuss.

French Soldier
O Seigneur Dieu!

Pistol
O Signieur Dew should be a gentleman.
Perpend my words, O Signieur Dew, and mark:
O Signieur Dew, thou diest on point of fox,
Except, O signieur, thou do give to me
Egregious ransom.

French Soldier
O, prenez miséricorde! Ayez pitié de moi!

Pistol
Moy shall not serve, I will have forty moys,
Or I will fetch thy rim out at thy throat
In drops of crimson blood.

French Soldier
Est-il impossible d'échapper la force de ton bras?

Pistol
Brass, cur?
Thou damned and luxurious mountain goat,
Offer'st me brass?

French Soldier
O, pardonnez moi!

Pistol
Say'st thou me so? Is that a ton of moys?
Come hither, boy, ask me this slave in French
What is his name.

Boy
Écoutez: comment êtes-vous appelé?

French Soldier
Monsieur le Fer.

Boy
He says his name is Master Fer.

Pistol
Master Fer! I'll fer him, and firk him, and ferret him. Discuss the same in French unto him.

Boy
I do not know the French for fer, and ferret, and firk.

Pistol
Bid him prepare, for I will cut his throat.

French Soldier
Que dit-il, monsieur?

Boy
Il me commande à vous dire que vous faites vous prêt; car ce soldat ici est disposé tout à cette heure de couper votre gorge.

Pistol
Owy, cuppele gorge, permafoy,
Peasant, unless thou give me crowns, brave crowns;
Or mangled shalt thou be by this my sword.

French Soldier
O, je vous supplie, pour l'amour de Dieu, me pardonner! Je suis le gentilhomme de bonne maison; gardez ma vie, et je vous donnerai deux cents écus.

Pistol
What are his words?

Boy
He prays you to save his life. He is a gentleman of a good house, and for his ransom he will give you two hundred crowns.

Pistol
Tell him my fury shall abate, and I
The crowns will take.

French Soldier
Petit monsieur, quo dit-il?

Boy
Encore qu'il est contre son jurement de pardonner aucun prisonnier; néanmoins, pour les écus que vous lui promettez, il est content à vous donner la liberté, le franchisement.

French Soldier
Sur mes genoux je vous donne mille remercîments; et je m'estime heureux que je tombe entre les mains d'un chevalier, je pense, le plus brave, vaillant, et très distingué seigneur d'Angleterre.

Pistol
Expound unto me, boy.

Boy
He gives you, upon his knees, a thousand thanks, and he esteems himself happy that he hath fall'n into the hands of one (as he thinks) the most brave, valorous, and thrice-worthy seigneur of England.

Pistol
As I suck blood, I will some mercy show. Follow me!

Boy
Suivez-vous le grand capitaine.

Exeunt Pistol and French Soldier.

I did never know so full a voice issue from so empty a heart; but the saying is true, "The empty vessel makes the greatest sound." Bardolph and Nym had ten times more valor than this roaring devil i' th' old play, that every one may pare his nails with a wooden dagger, and they are both hang'd, and so would this be, if he durst steal any thing adventurously. I must stay with the lackeys with the luggage of our camp. The French might have a good prey of us, if he knew of it, for there is none to guard it but boys.

Exit.

Scene 5

Another part of the battlefield.

(Constable; Duke of Orléans; Bourbon; Dauphin; Rambures)

The French nobles are in confusion at the way the English have broken their ranks, and rally themselves for the defense.

Enter Constable, Orléans, Bourbon, Dauphin, and Rambures.

Constable of France
O diable!

Duke of Orléans
O Seigneur! Le jour est perdu, tout est perdu!

The Dauphin
Mort Dieu, ma vie! All is confounded, all!
Reproach and everlasting shame
Sits mocking in our plumes.

A short alarum.

                    O méchante fortune!
Do not run away.

Constable of France
          Why, all our ranks are broke.

The Dauphin
O perdurable shame! Let's stab ourselves.
Be these the wretches that we play'd at dice for?

Duke of Orléans
Is this the king we sent to for his ransom?

Duke of Bourbon
Shame and eternal shame, nothing but shame!
Let us die! In once more! Back again!
And he that will not follow Bourbon now,
Let him go hence, and with his cap in hand
Like a base pander hold the chamber-door
Whilst by a slave, no gentler than my dog,
His fairest daughter is contaminated.

Constable of France
Disorder, that hath spoil'd us, friend us now!
Let us on heaps go offer up our lives.

Duke of Orléans
We are enow yet living in the field
To smother up the English in our throngs,
If any order might be thought upon.

Duke of Bourbon
The devil take order now! I'll to the throng:
Let life be short, else shame will be too long.

Exeunt.

Scene 6

Another part of the battlefield.

(King Henry the Fifth; Exeter)

Exeter tells of the death of York and Suffolk in each other's arms. Henry sees the French making a new assault and orders that all prisoners be killed.

Alarum. Enter the King and his Train with prisoners; Exeter and others.

King Henry the Fifth
Well have we done, thrice-valiant countrymen,
But all's not done—yet keep the French the field.

Duke of Exeter
The Duke of York commends him to your Majesty.

King Henry the Fifth
Lives he, good uncle? Thrice within this hour
I saw him down; thrice up again, and fighting;
From helmet to the spur all blood he was.

Duke of Exeter
In which array (brave soldier!) doth he lie,
Larding the plain; and by his bloody side
(Yoke-fellow to his honor-owing wounds)
The noble Earl of Suffolk also lies.
Suffolk first died, and York, all haggled over,
Comes to him where in gore he lay insteeped,
And takes him by the beard, kisses the gashes
That bloodily did yawn upon his face.
He cries aloud, "Tarry, my cousin Suffolk!
My soul shall thine keep company to heaven;
Tarry, sweet soul, for mine, then fly abreast,
As in this glorious and well-foughten field
We kept together in our chivalry!"
Upon these words I came and cheer'd him up.
He smil'd me in the face, raught me his hand,
And with a feeble gripe, says, "Dear my lord,
Commend my service to my sovereign."
So did he turn and over Suffolk's neck
He threw his wounded arm, and kiss'd his lips,

And so espous'd to death, with blood he seal'd
A testament of noble-ending love.
The pretty and sweet manner of it forc'd
Those waters from me which I would have stopp'd,
But I had not so much of man in me,
And all my mother came into mine eyes
And gave me up to tears.

King Henry the Fifth
                     I blame you not,
For hearing this, I must perforce compound
With mistful eyes, or they will issue too.

Alarum.

But hark, what new alarum is this same?
The French have reinforc'd their scatter'd men.
Then every soldier kill his prisoners,
Give the word through.

Exeunt.

Scene 7

Another part of the battlefield.

(Fluellen; Gower; King Henry the Fifth; Bourbon; Warwick; Gloucester; Exeter; Heralds; Montjoy; Williams)

Fluellen and Gower discuss the French killing of the boys and Henry's order to kill the prisoners. The Welsh Fluellen is deeply proud that the King was born at Monmouth in Wales, and compares him to Alexander the Great. Montjoy comes to acknowledge the French defeat and asks leave to count the number of French dead. Henry accepts, and decides to name the battle Agincourt, after a nearby castle. Seeing Williams, Henry asks him the meaning of the glove in his cap, and Williams explains about his quarrel the night before. Fluellen tells the King that no matter how noble, Williams's challenger must take up the quarrel should they meet. Williams is sent to fetch his captain, Gower, and Henry gives the glove to Fluellen, telling him it is the glove of a French noble, Alençon, and that anybody that challenges the gage is an enemy to the King. After Fluellen leaves, Henry explains his jest to Warwick and Gloucester the story, and bids them keep watch that the hot-headed Fluellen does not carry things too far.

Enter Fluellen and Gower.

Fluellen
Kill the poys and the luggage! 'Tis expressly against the law of arms. 'Tis as arrant a piece of knavery, mark you now, as can be offert; in your conscience, now, is it not?

Gower
'Tis certain there's not a boy left alive, and the cowardly rascals that ran from the battle ha' done this slaughter. Besides, they have burn'd and carried away all that was in the King's tent; wherefore the King, most worthily, hath caus'd every soldier to cut his prisoner's throat. O, 'tis a gallant king!

Fluellen
Ay, he was porn at Monmouth, Captain Gower. What call you the town's name where Alexander the Pig was born?

Gower
Alexander the Great.

Fluellen
Why, I pray you, is not "pig" great? The pig, or the great, or the mighty, or the huge, or the magnanimous, are all one reckonings, save the phrase is a little variations.

Gower
I think Alexander the Great was born in Macedon. His father was called Philip of Macedon, as I take it.

Fluellen
I think it is in Macedon where Alexander is porn. I tell you, captain, if you look in the maps of the orld, I warrant you sall find, in the comparisons between Macedon and Monmouth, that the situations, look you, is both alike. There is a river in Macedon, and there is also moreover a river at Monmouth. It is call'd Wye at Monmouth; but it is out of my prains what is the name of the other river; but 'tis all one, 'tis alike as my fingers is to my fingers, and there is salmons in both. If you mark Alexander's life well, Harry of Monmouth's life is come after it indifferent well, for there is figures in all things. Alexander, God knows, and you know, in his rages, and his furies, and his wraths, and his cholers, and his moods, and his displeasures, and his indignations, and also being a little intoxicates in his prains, did, in his ales and his angers, look you, kill his best friend, Clytus.

Gower
Our King is not like him in that; he never kill'd any of his friends.

Act 4, Scene 7

Fluellen
It is not well done, mark you now, to take the tales out of my mouth, ere it is made and finished. I speak but in the figures and comparisons of it: as Alexander kill'd his friend Clytus, being in his ales and his cups; so also Harry Monmouth, being in his right wits and his good judgments, turn'd away the fat knight with the great belly doublet. He was full of jests, and gipes, and knaveries, and mocks—I have forgot his name.

Gower
Sir John Falstaff.

Fluellen
That is he. I'll tell you there is good men porn at Monmouth.

Gower
Here comes his Majesty.

Exit.
Alarum. Enter King Harry and Bourbon with other prisoners; Warwick, Gloucester, Exeter, Heralds, and others. Flourish.

King Henry the Fifth
I was not angry since I came to France
Until this instant. Take a trumpet, herald,
Ride thou unto the horsemen on yond hill.
If they will fight with us, bid them come down,
Or void the field; they do offend our sight.
If they'll do neither, we will come to them,
And make them skirr away, as swift as stones
Enforced from the old Assyrian slings;
Besides, we'll cut the throats of those we have,
And not a man of them that we shall take
Shall taste our mercy. Go and tell them so.

Exit a Herald.
Enter Montjoy.

Duke of Exeter
Here comes the herald of the French, my liege.

Humphrey, Duke of Gloucester
His eyes are humbler than they us'd to be.

King Henry the Fifth
How now, what means this, herald? Know'st thou not
That I have fin'd these bones of mine for ransom?
Com'st thou again for ransom?

Montjoy
                No, great King;
I come to thee for charitable license,
That we may wander o'er this bloody field
To book our dead, and then to bury them;
To sort our nobles from our common men.
For many of our princes (woe the while!)
Lie drown'd and soak'd in mercenary blood;
So do our vulgar drench their peasant limbs
In blood of princes, and their wounded steeds
Fret fetlock deep in gore, and with wild rage
Yerk out their armed heels at their dead masters,
Killing them twice. O, give us leave, great King,
To view the field in safety, and dispose
Of their dead bodies!

King Henry the Fifth
                I tell thee truly, herald,
I know not if the day be ours or no,
For yet a many of your horsemen peer
And gallop o'er the field.

Montjoy
                The day is yours.

King Henry the Fifth
Praised be God, and not our strength, for it!
What is this castle call'd that stands hard by?

Montjoy
They call it Agincourt.

King Henry the Fifth
Then call we this the field of Agincourt,
Fought on the day of Crispin Crispianus.

Fluellen
Your grandfather of famous memory, an't please your Majesty, and your great-uncle Edward the Plack Prince of Wales, as I have read in the chronicles, fought a most prave pattle here in France.

King Henry the Fifth
They did, Fluellen.

Fluellen
Your Majesty says very true. If your Majesties is rememb'red of it, the Welshmen did good service in a garden where leeks did grow, wearing leeks in their Monmouth caps, which, your Majesty know, to this hour is an honorable badge of the service; and I do believe your Majesty takes no scorn to wear the leek upon Saint Tavy's day.

King Henry the Fifth
I wear it for a memorable honor;
For I am Welsh, you know, good countryman.

Fluellen
All the water in Wye cannot wash your Majesty's Welsh plood out of your pody, I can tell you that. God pless it, and preserve it, as long as it pleases his Grace, and his Majesty too!

King Henry the Fifth
Thanks, good my countryman.

Fluellen
By Jeshu, I am your Majesty's countryman, I care not who know it. I will confess it to all the orld. I need not to be ashamed of your Majesty, praised be God, so long as your Majesty is an honest man.

King Henry the Fifth
God keep me so!

Enter Williams.

                    Our heralds go with him;
Bring me just notice of the numbers dead
On both our parts. Call yonder fellow hither.

Exeunt Heralds with Montjoy.

Duke of Exeter
Soldier, you must come to the King.

King Henry the Fifth
Soldier, why wear'st thou that glove in thy cap?

Williams
And't please your Majesty, 'tis the gage of one that I should fight withal, if he be alive.

King Henry the Fifth
An Englishman?

Williams
And't please your Majesty, a rascal that swagger'd with me last night; who if alive and ever dare to challenge this glove, I have sworn to take him a box a' th' ear; or if I can see my glove in his cap, which he swore, as he was a soldier, he would wear if alive, I will strike it out soundly.

King Henry the Fifth
What think you, Captain Fluellen? Is it fit this soldier keep his oath?

Fluellen
He is a craven and a villain else, and't please your Majesty, in my conscience.

King Henry the Fifth
It may be his enemy is a gentleman of great sort, quite from the answer of his degree.

Fluellen
Though he be as good a gentleman as the devil is, as Lucifer and Beelzebub himself, it is necessary, look your Grace, that he keep his vow and his oath. If he be perjur'd, see you now, his reputation is as arrant a villain and a Jack sauce, as ever his black shoe trod upon God's ground and His earth, in my conscience law!

King Henry the Fifth
Then keep thy vow, sirrah, when thou meet'st the fellow.

Williams
So I will, my liege, as I live.

King Henry the Fifth
Who serv'st thou under?

Williams
Under Captain Gower, my liege.

Fluellen
Gower is a good captain, and is good knowledge and literatured in the wars.

King Henry the Fifth
Call him hither to me, soldier.

Williams
I will, my liege.

Exit.

King Henry the Fifth
Here, Fluellen, wear thou this favor for me and stick it in thy cap. When Alanson and myself were down together, I pluck'd this glove from his helm. If any man challenge this, he is a friend to Alanson, and an enemy to our person. If thou encounter any such, apprehend him, and thou dost me love.

Fluellen
Your Grace doo's me as great honors as can be desir'd in the hearts of his subjects. I would fain see the man, that has but two legs, that shall find himself aggriev'd

at this glove; that is all. But I would fain see it once, and please God of his grace that I might see.

King Henry the Fifth
Know'st thou Gower?

Fluellen
He is my dear friend, and please you.

King Henry the Fifth
Pray thee go seek him, and bring him to my tent.

Fluellen
I will fetch him.

Exit.

King Henry the Fifth
My Lord of Warwick, and my brother Gloucester,
Follow Fluellen closely at the heels.
The glove which I have given him for a favor
May haply purchase him a box a' th' ear.
It is the soldier's; I by bargain should
Wear it myself. Follow, good cousin Warwick.
If that the soldier strike him, as I judge
By his blunt bearing he will keep his word,
Some sudden mischief may arise of it;
For I do know Fluellen valiant
And touch'd with choler, hot as gunpowder,
And quickly will return an injury.
Follow, and see there be no harm between them.
Go you with me, uncle of Exeter.

Exeunt.

Scene 8

Before King Henry's pavilion.

(Gower; Williams; Fluellen; Warwick; Gloucester; King Henry the Fifth; Exeter; English Herald)

Fluellen and Williams meet, and seeing the gloves start to quarrel. Henry enters and the two contestants tell their conflicting versions of the story. In the end Henry admits to having been Williams's interlocutor the night before; hearing that Williams abused the King, Fluellen demands that he be hanged. When Williams argues that he would never have said any of those things had he known he was talking to the King, Henry likes his answer and rewards him by filling the glove with coins. Fluellen adds a shilling, which Williams at first refuses. The tally of the dead comes, proving that the English have won a crushing victory, having killed ten thousand Frenchmen and lost fewer than thirty themselves. The King praises God for having given the English victory, and gives the order the bury the dead and sail for England.

Enter Gower and Williams.

Williams
I warrant it is to knight you, captain.

Enter Fluellen.

Fluellen
God's will, and his pleasure, captain, I beseech you now, come apace to the King. There is more good toward you peradventure than is in your knowledge to dream of.

Williams
Sir, know you this glove?

Fluellen
Know the glove? I know the glove is a glove.

Williams
I know this, and thus I challenge it.

Strikes him.

Fluellen
'Sblud, an arrant traitor as any's in the universal world, or in France, or in England!

Gower
How now, sir? You villain!

Williams
Do you think I'll be forsworn?

Fluellen
Stand away, Captain Gower, I will give treason his payment into plows, I warrant you.

Williams
I am no traitor.

Fluellen
That's a lie in thy throat. I charge you in his Majesty's name, apprehend him, he's a friend of the Duke Alanson's.

Enter Warwick and Gloucester.

Earl of Warwick
How now, how now, what's the matter?

Fluellen
My Lord of Warwick, here is—praised be God for it!—a most contagious treason come to light, look you, as you shall desire in a summer's day. Here is his Majesty.

Enter King and Exeter.

King Henry the Fifth
How now, what's the matter?

Fluellen
My liege, here is a villain and a traitor, that, look your Grace, has struck the glove which your Majesty is take out of the helmet of Alanson.

Williams
My liege, this was my glove, here is the fellow of it; and he that I gave it to in change promis'd to wear it in his cap. I promis'd to strike him, if he did. I met this man with my glove in his cap, and I have been as good as my word.

Fluellen
Your Majesty hear now, saving your Majesty's manhood, what an arrant, rascally, beggarly, lousy knave it is. I hope your Majesty is pear me testimony and witness, and will avouchment, that this is the glove of Alanson that your Majesty is give me, in your conscience now.

King Henry the Fifth
Give me thy glove, soldier. Look, here is the fellow of it.
'Twas I indeed thou promisedst to strike,
And thou hast given me most bitter terms.

Fluellen
And please your Majesty, let his neck answer for it, if there is any martial law in the world.

King Henry the Fifth
How canst thou make me satisfaction?

Williams
All offenses, my lord, come from the heart. Never came any from mine that might offend your Majesty.

King Henry the Fifth
It was ourself thou didst abuse.

Williams
Your Majesty came not like yourself. You appear'd to me but as a common man; witness the night, your garments, your lowliness; and what your Highness suffer'd under that shape, I beseech you take it for your own fault and not mine; for had you been as I took you for, I made no offense; therefore I beseech your Highness pardon me.

King Henry the Fifth
Here, uncle Exeter, fill this glove with crowns,
And give it to this fellow. Keep it, fellow,
And wear it for an honor in thy cap
Till I do challenge it. Give him the crowns;
And, captain, you must needs be friends with him.

Fluellen
By this day and this light, the fellow has mettle enough in his belly. Hold, there is twelvepence for you, and I pray you to serve God, and keep you out of prawls and prabbles, and quarrels and dissensions, and I warrant you it is the better for you.

Williams
I will none of your money.

Fluellen
It is with a good will; I can tell you it will serve you to mend your shoes. Come, wherefore should you be so pashful? Your shoes is not so good. 'Tis a good silling, I warrant you, or I will change it.

Enter an English Herald.

King Henry the Fifth
Now, herald, are the dead numb'red?

English Herald
Here is the number of the slaught'red French.

Gives a paper.

King Henry the Fifth
What prisoners of good sort are taken, uncle?

Duke of Exeter
Charles Duke of Orléans, nephew to the King,
John Duke of Bourbon, and Lord Bouciqualt:
Of other lords and barons, knights and squires,
Full fifteen hundred, besides common men.

King Henry the Fifth
This note doth tell me of ten thousand French
That in the field lie slain; of princes, in this number,
And nobles bearing banners, there lie dead
One hundred twenty-six; added to these,
Of knights, esquires, and gallant gentlemen,
Eight thousand and four hundred; of the which,
Five hundred were but yesterday dubb'd knights.
So that, in these ten thousand they have lost,
There are but sixteen hundred mercenaries;
The rest are princes, barons, lords, knights, squires,
And gentlemen of blood and quality.
The names of those their nobles that lie dead:
Charles Delabreth, High Constable of France,
Jacques of Chatillion, Admiral of France,
The master of the cross-bows, Lord Rambures,
Great Master of France, the brave Sir Guichard Dauphin,
John Duke of Alanson, Anthony Duke of Brabant,
The brother to the Duke of Burgundy,
And Edward Duke of Bar; of lusty earls,
Grandpré and Roussi, Faulconbridge and Foix,
Beaumont and Marle, Vaudemont and Lestrake.
Here was a royal fellowship of death!
Where is the number of our English dead?

Herald shows him another paper.

Edward the Duke of York, the Earl of Suffolk,
Sir Richard Ketly, Davy Gam, esquire;
None else of name; and of all other men
But five and twenty. O God, thy arm was here;
And not to us, but to thy arm alone,
Ascribe we all! When, without stratagem,
But in plain shock and even play of battle,
Was ever known so great and little loss,
On one part and on th' other? Take it, God,
For it is none but thine!

Duke of Exeter
                    'Tis wonderful!

King Henry the Fifth
Come, go we in procession to the village;
And be it death proclaimed through our host
To boast of this, or take that praise from God
Which is his only.

Fluellen
Is it not lawful, and please your Majesty, to tell how many is kill'd?

King Henry the Fifth
Yes, captain; but with this acknowledgment,
That God fought for us.

Fluellen
Yes, my conscience, he did us great good.

King Henry the Fifth
Do we all holy rites:
Let there be sung Non nobis and Te Deum,
The dead with charity enclos'd in clay;
And then to Callice, and to England then,
Where ne'er from France arriv'd more happy men.

Exeunt.

Act 5

Prologue

(Chorus)

The Chorus relates the return of the King to England and the rejoicing that ensues. He then apologizes for skipping directly to the negotiations for peace.

Enter Chorus.

Chorus
Vouchsafe to those that have not read the story,
That I may prompt them; and of such as have,
I humbly pray them to admit th' excuse
Of time, of numbers, and due course of things,
Which cannot in their huge and proper life
Be here presented. Now we bear the King
Toward Callice; grant him there; there seen,
Heave him away upon your winged thoughts
Athwart the sea. Behold, the English beach
Pales in the flood with men, wives, and boys,
Whose shouts and claps out-voice the deep-mouth'd sea,
Which like a mighty whiffler 'fore the King
Seems to prepare his way. So let him land,
And solemnly see him set on to London.
So swift a pace hath thought that even now
You may imagine him upon Blackheath;
Where that his lords desire him to have borne
His bruised helmet and his bended sword
Before him through the city. He forbids it,
Being free from vainness and self-glorious pride;
Giving full trophy, signal, and ostent
Quite from himself to God. But now behold,

In the quick forge and working-house of thought,
How London doth pour out her citizens!
The Mayor and all his brethren in best sort,
Like to the senators of th' antique Rome,
With the plebeians swarming at their heels,
Go forth and fetch their conqu'ring Caesar in;
As by a lower but by loving likelihood,
Were now the general of our gracious Empress,
As in good time he may, from Ireland coming,
Bringing rebellion broached on his sword,
How many would the peaceful city quit,
To welcome him! Much more, and much more cause,
Did they this Harry. Now in London place him—
As yet the lamentation of the French
Invites the King of England's stay at home;
The Emperor's coming in behalf of France,
To order peace between them—and omit
All the occurrences, what ever chanc'd,
Till Harry's back-return again to France.
There must we bring him; and myself have play'd
The interim, by rememb'ring you 'tis past.
Then brook abridgment, and your eyes advance,
After your thoughts, straight back again to France.

Exit.

Scene 1

France. The English Court of Guard.

(Fluellen; Gower; Pistol)

Gower asks Fluellen why the latter is still wearing his leek in his hat, even though St. Davy's Day is past, and the Welshman explains that he is waiting for Pistol, who insulted him about it the day before. When the braggart appears, Fluellen cudgels him until he eats the leek. Pistol swears revenge, but Fluellen scorns him. Gower points out to Pistol that Fluellen's broken English does not imply anything about his abilities. Left alone, Pistol bemoans his lot, having heard that his wife the Hostess has died of a venereal disease. He plans to return to England and become a pimp, telling stories of his days in the war.

Enter Fluellen and Gower.

Gower
Nay, that's right; but why wear you your leek today? Saint Davy's day is past.

Fluellen
There is occasions and causes why and wherefore in all things. I will tell you asse my friend, Captain Gower: the rascally, scald, beggarly, lousy, pragging knave, Pistol, which you and yourself, and all the world, know to be no petter than a fellow, look you now, of no merits, he is come to me, and prings me pread and salt yesterday, look you, and bid me eat my leek. It was in a place where I could not breed no contention with him; but I will be so bold as to wear it in my cap till I see him once again, and then I will tell him a little piece of my desires.

Enter Pistol.

Gower
Why, here he comes, swelling like a turkey-cock.

Fluellen
'Tis no matter for his swellings nor his turkey-cocks. God pless you, Aunchient Pistol! You scurvy, lousy knave, God pless you!

Pistol
Ha, art thou bedlam? Dost thou thirst, base Troyan,
To have me fold up Parca's fatal web?
Hence! I am qualmish at the smell of leek.

Fluellen
I peseech you heartily, scurvy, lousy knave, at my desires, and my requests, and my petitions, to eat, look you, this leek; because, look you, you do not love it, nor your affections, and your appetites, and your digestions doo's not agree with it, I would desire you to eat it.

Pistol
Not for Cadwallader and all his goats.

Fluellen
There is one goat for you.

Strikes him.

Will you be so good, scald knave, as eat it?

Pistol
Base Troyan, thou shalt die.

Fluellen
You say very true, scald knave, when God's will is. I will desire you to live in the mean time, and eat your victuals. Come, there is sauce for it.

Strikes him.

You call'd me yesterday mountain-squire, but I will make you today a squire of low degree. I pray you fall to; if you can mock a leek, you can eat a leek.

Gower
Enough, captain, you have astonish'd him.

Fluellen
I say, I will make him eat some part of my leek, or I will peat his pate four days. Bite, I pray you, it is good for your green wound and your ploody coxcomb.

Pistol
Must I bite?

Fluellen
Yes, certainly, and out of doubt and out of question too, and ambiguities.

Pistol
By this leek, I will most horribly revenge—I eat and eat—I swear—

Fluellen
Eat, I pray you. Will you have some more sauce to your leek? There is not enough leek to swear by.

Pistol
Quiet thy cudgel, thou dost see I eat.

Fluellen
Much good do you, scald knave, heartily. Nay, pray you throw none away, the skin is good for your broken coxcomb. When you take occasions to see leeks hereafter, I pray you mock at 'em, that is all.

Pistol
Good.

Fluellen
Ay, leeks is good. Hold you, there is a groat to heal your pate.

Pistol
Me a groat?

Fluellen
Yes, verily, and in truth you shall take it, or I have another leek in my pocket, which you shall eat.

Pistol
I take thy groat in earnest of revenge.

Fluellen
If I owe you any thing, I will pay you in cudgels; you shall be a woodmonger, and buy nothing of me but cudgels. God buy you, and keep you, and heal your pate.

Exit.

Pistol
All hell shall stir for this.

Gower
Go, go, you are a counterfeit cowardly knave. Will you mock at an ancient tradition, begun upon an honorable respect, and worn as a memorable trophy of predeceas'd valor, and dare not avouch in your deeds any of your words? I have seen you gleeking and galling at this gentleman twice or thrice. You thought, because he could not speak English in the native garb, he could not therefore handle an English cudgel. You find it otherwise, and henceforth let a Welsh correction teach you a good English condition. Fare ye well.

Exit.

Pistol
Doth Fortune play the huswife with me now?
News have I that my Doll is dead i' th' spittle
Of a malady of France,
And there my rendezvous is quite cut off.
Old I do wax, and from my weary limbs
Honor is cudgell'd. Well, bawd I'll turn,
And something lean to cutpurse of quick hand.
To England will I steal, and there I'll steal;
And patches will I get unto these cudgell'd scars,
And swear I got them in the Gallia wars.

Exit.

Scene 2

France. The French King's apartment in Troyes.

(*King Henry the Fifth; Exeter; Bedford; Gloucester; Warwick; Westmorland; Lords; Queen Isabel; French King; Duke of Burgundy; Katherine; Alice; French Power; English Lords*)

King Henry and the French King meet, protesting their love for one another. The Duke of Burgundy makes an impassioned plea for peace. The French King tells Henry that he has not studied the proposed peace treaty in detail and goes off with the English lords to do so. Left alone with Katherine and Alice, Henry does his best to woo her, which is difficult as her English has not improved since last we saw her and his French is ghastly. Though coy and somewhat taken aback at his bluntness, Katherine is not displeased with his wooing, and in the end permits him to kiss her, at which point the French King and the lords of both countries walk in on them. They announce that the French King has accepted the treaty, under which terms he shall reign until his death, but Henry shall take the throne thereafter. Henry looks forward to his wedding.

Enter, at one door, King Henry, Exeter, Bedford, Gloucester, Warwick, Westmorland, and other Lords; at another, Queen Isabel, the King of France, the Duke of Burgundy, Katherine, Alice, and other French.

King Henry the Fifth
Peace to this meeting, wherefore we are met!
Unto our brother France, and to our sister,
Health and fair time of day; joy and good wishes
To our most fair and princely cousin Katherine;
And as a branch and member of this royalty,
By whom this great assembly is contriv'd,
We do salute you, Duke of Burgundy,
And, princes French, and peers, health to you all!

Charles the Sixth
Right joyous are we to behold your face,
Most worthy brother England, fairly met!
So are you, princes English, every one.

Queen Isabel
So happy be the issue, brother England,
Of this good day and of this gracious meeting,
As we are now glad to behold your eyes—
Your eyes, which hitherto have borne in them
Against the French that met them in their bent
The fatal balls of murdering basilisks.
The venom of such looks we fairly hope
Have lost their quality, and that this day
Shall change all griefs and quarrels into love.

King Henry the Fifth
To cry amen to that, thus we appear.

Queen Isabel
You English princes all, I do salute you.

Duke of Burgundy
My duty to you both, on equal love.
Great Kings of France and England: that I have labor'd
With all my wits, my pains, and strong endeavors
To bring your most imperial Majesties
Unto this bar and royal interview,
Your mightiness on both parts best can witness.
Since then my office hath so far prevail'd,
That face to face, and royal eye to eye,
You have congreeted, let it not disgrace me,
If I demand, before this royal view,
What rub or what impediment there is,
Why that the naked, poor, and mangled Peace,
Dear nurse of arts, plenties, and joyful births,
Should not in this best garden of the world,
Our fertile France, put up her lovely visage?
Alas, she hath from France too long been chas'd,
And all her husbandry doth lie on heaps,
Corrupting in it own fertility.
Her vine, the merry cheerer of the heart,
Unpruned dies; her hedges even-pleach'd,
Like prisoners wildly overgrown with hair,
Put forth disorder'd twigs; her fallow leas
The darnel, hemlock, and rank femetary
Doth root upon, while that the coulter rusts
That should deracinate such savagery;
The even mead, that erst brought sweetly forth
The freckled cowslip, burnet, and green clover,
Wanting the scythe withal, uncorrected, rank,
Conceives by idleness, and nothing teems
But hateful docks, rough thistles, kecksies, burs,
Losing both beauty and utility;
And all our vineyards, fallows, meads, and hedges,
Defective in their natures, grow to wildness.
Even so our houses, and ourselves, and children,
Have lost, or do not learn for want of time,
The sciences that should become our country,
But grow like savages—as soldiers will
That nothing do but meditate on blood—
To swearing and stern looks, defus'd attire,
And every thing that seems unnatural.
Which to reduce into our former favor
You are assembled; and my speech entreats
That I may know the let why gentle Peace
Should not expel these inconveniences,
And bless us with her former qualities.

King Henry the Fifth
If, Duke of Burgundy, you would the peace,
Whose want gives growth to th' imperfections
Which you have cited, you must buy that peace
With full accord to all our just demands,
Whose tenures and particular effects
You have enschedul'd briefly in your hands.

Duke of Burgundy
The King hath heard them; to the which, as yet
There is no answer made.

King Henry the Fifth
                    Well then: the peace,
Which you before so urg'd, lies in his answer.

Charles the Sixth
I have but with a cursitory eye
O'erglanc'd the articles. Pleaseth your Grace
To appoint some of your Council presently
To sit with us once more, with better heed
To re-survey them, we will suddenly
Pass our accept and peremptory answer.

King Henry the Fifth
Brother, we shall. Go, uncle Exeter,
And brother Clarence, and you, brother Gloucester,
Warwick, and Huntington, go with the King,
And take with you free power to ratify,
Augment, or alter, as your wisdoms best
Shall see advantageable for our dignity,
Any thing in or out of our demands,
And we'll consign thereto. Will you, fair sister,
Go with the princes, or stay here with us?

Queen Isabel
Our gracious brother, I will go with them.
Happily a woman's voice may do some good,
When articles too nicely urg'd be stood on.

King Henry the Fifth
Yet leave our cousin Katherine here with us:
She is our capital demand, compris'd
Within the fore-rank of our articles.

Queen Isabel
She hath good leave.

Exeunt omnes. Manent King Henry and Katherine with the gentlewoman Alice.

King Henry the Fifth
Fair Katherine, and most fair,
Will you vouchsafe to teach a soldier terms,
Such as will enter at a lady's ear,
And plead his love-suit to her gentle heart?

Katherine
Your Majesty shall mock at me, I cannot speak your England.

King Henry the Fifth
O fair Katherine, if you will love me soundly with your French heart, I will be glad to hear you confess it brokenly with your English tongue. Do you like me, Kate?

Katherine
Pardonnez-moi, I cannot tell wat is "like me."

King Henry the Fifth
An angel is like you, Kate, and you are like an angel.

Katherine
Que dit-il? Que je suis semblable à les anges?

Alice
Oui, vraiment, sauf votre grâce, ainsi dit-il.

King Henry the Fifth
I said so, dear Katherine, and I must not blush to affirm it.

Katherine
O bon Dieu! Les langues des hommes sont pleines de tromperies.

King Henry the Fifth
What says she, fair one? That the tongues of men are full of deceits?

Alice
Oui, dat de tongeus of de mans is be full of deceits: dat is de Princess.

King Henry the Fifth
The Princess is the better Englishwoman. I' faith, Kate, my wooing is fit for thy understanding. I am glad thou canst speak no better English, for if thou couldst, thou wouldst find me such a plain king that thou wouldst think I had sold my farm to buy my crown. I know no ways to mince it in love, but directly to say "I love you"; then if you urge me farther than to say "Do you in faith?" I wear out my suit. Give me your

answer, i' faith, do, and so clap hands and a bargain. How say you, lady?

Katherine
Sauf votre honneur, me understand well.

King Henry the Fifth
Marry, if you would put me to verses, or to dance for your sake, Kate, why, you undid me: for the one, I have neither words nor measure; and for the other, I have no strength in measure, yet a reasonable measure in strength. If I could win a lady at leap-frog, or by vaulting into my saddle with my armor on my back, under the correction of bragging be it spoken, I should quickly leap into a wife. Or if I might buffet for my love, or bound my horse for her favors, I could lay on like a butcher, and sit like a jack-an-apes, never off. But, before God, Kate, I cannot look greenly, nor gasp out my eloquence, nor I have no cunning in protestation; only downright oaths, which I never use till urg'd, nor never break for urging. If thou canst love a fellow of this temper, Kate, whose face is not worth sunburning, that never looks in his glass for love of any thing he sees there, let thine eye be thy cook. I speak to thee plain soldier. If thou canst love me for this, take me! If not, to say to thee that I shall die, is true; but for thy love, by the Lord, no; yet I love thee too. And while thou liv'st, dear Kate, take a fellow of plain and uncoin'd constancy, for he perforce must do thee right, because he hath not the gift to woo in other places; for these fellows of infinite tongue, that can rhyme themselves into ladies' favors, they do always reason themselves out again. What? A speaker is but a prater, a rhyme is but a ballad; a good leg will fall, a straight back will stoop, a black beard will turn white, a curl'd pate will grow bald, a fair face will wither, a full eye will wax hollow; but a good heart, Kate, is the sun and the moon, or rather the sun and not the moon; for it shines bright and never changes, but keeps his course truly. If thou would have such a one, take me! And take me, take a soldier; take a soldier, take a king. And what say'st thou then to my love? Speak, my fair, and fairly, I pray thee.

Katherine
Is it possible dat I sould love de ennemie of France?

King Henry the Fifth
No, it is not possible you should love the enemy of France, Kate; but in loving me, you should love the friend of France; for I love France so well that I will not part with a village of it; I will have it all mine. And, Kate, when France is mine and I am yours, then yours is France and you are mine.

Katherine
I cannot tell wat is dat.

King Henry the Fifth
No, Kate? I will tell thee in French, which I am sure will hang upon my tongue like a new-married wife about her husband's neck, hardly to be shook off. Je quand sur le possession de France, et quand vous avez le possession de moi—let me see, what then? Saint Denis be my speed!—donc votre est France et vous êtes mienne. It is as easy for me, Kate, to conquer the kingdom as to speak so much more French. I shall never move thee in French, unless it be to laugh at me.

Katherine
Sauf votre honneur, le François que vous parlez, il est meilleur que l'Anglois lequel je parle.

King Henry the Fifth
No, faith, is't not, Kate; but thy speaking of my tongue, and I thine, most truly falsely, must needs be granted to be much at one. But, Kate, dost thou understand thus much English? Canst thou love me?

Katherine
I cannot tell.

King Henry the Fifth
Can any of your neighbors tell, Kate? I'll ask them. Come, I know thou lovest me; and at night, when you come into your closet, you'll question this gentlewoman about me; and I know, Kate, you will to her dispraise those parts in me that you love with your heart. But, good Kate, mock me mercifully, the rather, gentle Princess, because I love thee cruelly. If ever thou beest mine, Kate, as I have a saving faith within me tells me thou shalt, I get thee with scambling, and thou must therefore needs prove a good soldier-breeder. Shall not thou and I, between Saint Denis and Saint George, compound a boy, half French, half English, that shall go to Constantinople and take the Turk by the beard? Shall we not? What say'st thou, my fair flower-de-luce?

Katherine
I do not know dat.

King Henry the Fifth
No; 'tis hereafter to know, but now to promise. Do but now promise, Kate, you will endeavor for your French part of such a boy; and for my English moi'ty, take the word of a king and a bachelor. How answer you, la plus belle Katherine du monde, mon très cher et devin déesse?

Katherine
Your Majestee ave fausse French enough to deceive de most sage demoiselle dat is en France.

King Henry the Fifth
Now fie upon my false French! By mine honor, in true English, I love thee, Kate; by which honor I dare not swear thou lovest me, yet my blood begins to flatter me that thou dost—notwithstanding the poor and untempering effect of my visage. Now beshrew my father's ambition! He was thinking of civil wars when he got me; therefore was I created with a stubborn outside, with an aspect of iron, that when I come to woo ladies, I fright them. But in faith, Kate, the elder I wax, the better I shall appear. My comfort is, that old age, that ill layer-up of beauty, can do no more spoil upon my face. Thou hast me, if thou hast me, at the worst; and thou shalt wear me, if thou wear me, better and better; and therefore tell me, most fair Katherine, will you have me? Put off your maiden blushes, avouch the thoughts of your heart with the looks of an empress, take me by the hand, and say, "Harry of England, I am thine"; which word thou shalt no sooner bless mine ear withal, but I will tell thee aloud, "England is thine, Ireland is thine, France is thine, and Henry Plantagenet is thine"; who, though I speak it before his face, if he be not fellow with the best king, thou shalt find the best king of good fellows. Come, your answer in broken music; for thy voice is music and thy English broken; therefore, queen of all, Katherine, break thy mind to me in broken English—wilt thou have me?

Katherine
Dat is as it shall please de roi mon père.

King Henry the Fifth
Nay, it will please him well, Kate; it shall please him, Kate.

Katherine
Den it sall also content me.

King Henry the Fifth
Upon that I kiss your hand, and I call you my queen.

Katherine
Laissez, mon seigneur, lais sez, laissez! Ma foi, je ne veux point que vous abaissez votre grandeur en baisant la main d'une (Notre Seigneur!) indigne serviteur. Excusez-moi, je vous supplie, mon très puissant seigneur.

King Henry the Fifth
Then I will kiss your lips, Kate.

Katherine
Les dames et demoiselles pour être baisées devant leur noces, il n'est pas la coutume de France.

King Henry the Fifth
Madam my interpreter, what says she?

Alice
Dat it is not be de fashon pour les ladies of France—I cannot tell wat is baiser en Anglish.

King Henry the Fifth
To kiss.

Alice
Your Majestee entendre bettre que moi.

King Henry the Fifth
It is not a fashion for the maids in France to kiss before they are married, would she say?

Alice
Oui, vraiment.

King Henry the Fifth
O Kate, nice customs cur'sy to great kings. Dear Kate, you and I cannot be confin'd within the weak list of a country's fashion. We are the makers of manners, Kate; and the liberty that follows our places stops the mouth of all find-faults, as I will do yours, for upholding the nice fashion of your country in denying me a kiss; therefore patiently and yielding.

Kissing her.

You have witchcraft in your lips, Kate; there is more eloquence in a sugar touch of them than in the tongues of the French council; and they should sooner persuade Harry of England than a general petition of monarchs. Here comes your father.

Enter the French Power and the English Lords.

Duke of Burgundy
God save your Majesty! My royal cousin, teach you our princess English?

King Henry the Fifth
I would have her learn, my fair cousin, how perfectly I love her, and that is good English.

Duke of Burgundy
Is she not apt?

King Henry the Fifth
Our tongue is rough, coz, and my condition is not smooth; so that having neither the voice nor the heart of flattery about me, I cannot so conjure up the spirit of love in her, that he will appear in his true likeness.

Duke of Burgundy
Pardon the frankness of my mirth, if I answer you for that. If you would conjure in her, you must make a circle; if conjure up Love in her in his true likeness, he must appear naked and blind. Can you blame her then, being a maid yet ros'd over with the virgin crimson of modesty, if she deny the appearance of a naked blind boy in her naked seeing self? It were, my lord, a hard condition for a maid to consign to.

King Henry the Fifth
Yet they do wink and yield, as love is blind and enforces.

Duke of Burgundy
They are then excus'd, my lord, when they see not what they do.

King Henry the Fifth
Then, good my lord, teach your cousin to consent winking.

Duke of Burgundy
I will wink on her to consent, my lord, if you will teach her to know my meaning; for maids, well summer'd and warm kept, are like flies at Bartholomew-tide, blind, though they have their eyes, and then they will endure handling, which before would not abide looking on.

King Henry the Fifth
This moral ties me over to time and a hot summer; and so I shall catch the fly, your cousin, in the latter end, and she must be blind too.

Duke of Burgundy
As love is, my lord, before it loves.

King Henry the Fifth
It is so; and you may, some of you, thank love for my blindness, who cannot see many a fair French city for one fair French maid that stands in my way.

Charles the Sixth
Yes, my lord, you see them perspectively: the cities turn'd into a maid; for they are all girdled with maiden walls that war hath never ent'red.

King Henry the Fifth
Shall Kate be my wife?

Charles the Sixth
So please you.

King Henry the Fifth
I am content, so the maiden cities you talk of may wait on her; so the maid that stood in the way for my wish shall show me the way to my will.

Charles the Sixth
We have consented to all terms of reason.

King Henry the Fifth
Is't so, my lords of England?

Earl of Westmorland
The King hath granted every article:
His daughter first; and in sequel, all,
According to their firm proposed natures.

Duke of Exeter
Only he hath not yet subscribed this:
Where your Majesty demands that the King of France, having any occasion to write for matter of grant, shall name your Highness in this form, and with this addition, in French, Notre très cher fils Henri, Roi d'Angleterre, Héritier de France; and thus in Latin, Praeclarissimus filius noster Henricus, Rex Angliae, et Heres Franciae.

Charles the Sixth
Nor this I have not, brother, so denied,
But your request shall make me let it pass.

King Henry the Fifth
I pray you then, in love and dear alliance,
Let that one article rank with the rest,
And thereupon give me your daughter.

Epilogue

Charles the Sixth
Take her, fair son, and from her blood raise up
Issue to me, that the contending kingdoms
Of France and England, whose very shores look pale
With envy of each other's happiness,
May cease their hatred; and this dear conjunction
Plant neighborhood and Christian-like accord
In their sweet bosoms, that never war advance
His bleeding sword 'twixt England and fair France.

English Lords
Amen!

King Henry the Fifth
Now welcome, Kate; and bear me witness all,
That here I kiss her as my sovereign queen.

Flourish.

Queen Isabel
God, the best maker of all marriages,
Combine your hearts in one, your realms in one!
As man and wife, being two, are one in love,
So be there 'twixt your kingdoms such a spousal,
That never may ill office, or fell jealousy,
Which troubles oft the bed of blessed marriage,
Thrust in between the paction of these kingdoms,
To make divorce of their incorporate league;
That English may as French, French Englishmen,
Receive each other. God speak this Amen!

All
Amen!

King Henry the Fifth
Prepare we for our marriage; on which day,
My Lord of Burgundy, we'll take your oath,
And all the peers', for surety of our leagues.
Then shall I swear to Kate, and you to me,
And may our oaths well kept and prosp'rous be!

Sennet. Exeunt.

Epilogue

(Chorus)

The Chorus again apologizes for the inadequacies of the theatre in presenting so great a subject. He reminds the audience that Henry died young, leaving the throne to his infant son, under whose reign all France was lost to England, as the Henry VI plays show.

Enter Chorus as Epilogue.

Chorus
Thus far, with rough and all-unable pen,
Our bending author hath pursu'd the story,
In little room confining mighty men,
Mangling by starts the full course of their glory.
Small time; but in that small most greatly lived
This star of England. Fortune made his sword;
By which the world's best garden he achieved,
And of it left his son imperial lord.
Henry the Sixth, in infant bands crown'd King
Of France and England, did this king succeed;
Whose state so many had the managing,
That they lost France, and made his England bleed;
Which oft our stage hath shown; and for their sake,
In your fair minds let this acceptance take.

Exit.

Measure for Measure

Act 1

Scene 1

Vienna. An apartment in the Duke's palace.

(Duke; Escalus; Lords; Attendants; Angelo)

The Duke is leaving, entrusting the government in his absence to Angelo and Escalus. He slips away from the city, not wishing to be seen by the people. Angelo and Escalus confer, the latter requesting permission to speak freely as they go to find out exactly what powers they have.

Enter Duke, Escalus, Lords, and Attendants.

Vincentio, the Duke.
Escalus.

Escalus.
My lord.

Vincentio, the Duke.
Of government the properties to unfold
Would seem in me t' affect speech and discourse,
Since I am put to know that your own science
Exceeds, in that, the lists of all advice
My strength can give you. Then no more remains
But that, to your sufficiency, as your worth is able,
And let them work. The nature of our people,
Our city's institutions, and the terms
For common justice, y' are as pregnant in
As art and practice hath enriched any
That we remember. There is our commission,
From which we would not have you warp. Call hither,
I say, bid come before us Angelo.

Exit an Attendant.

What figure of us think you he will bear?
For you must know, we have with special soul
Elected him our absence to supply,
Lent him our terror, dress'd him with our love,
And given his deputation all the organs
Of our own pow'r. What think you of it?

Escalus.
If any in Vienna be of worth
To undergo such ample grace and honor,
It is Lord Angelo.

Enter Angelo.

Vincentio, the Duke.
                              Look where he comes.

Angelo.
Always obedient to your Grace's will,
I come to know your pleasure.

Vincentio, the Duke.
                              Angelo:
There is a kind of character in thy life,
That to th' observer doth thy history
Fully unfold. Thyself and thy belongings
Are not thine own so proper as to waste
Thyself upon thy virtues, they on thee.
Heaven doth with us as we with torches do,
Not light them for themselves; for if our virtues
Did not go forth of us, 'twere all alike
As if we had them not. Spirits are not finely touch'd
But to fine issues; nor Nature never lends
The smallest scruple of her excellence,
But like a thrifty goddess, she determines
Herself the glory of a creditor,
Both thanks and use. But I do bend my speech
To one that can my part in him advertise.

Hold therefore, Angelo:
In our remove be thou at full ourself.
Mortality and mercy in Vienna
Live in thy tongue and heart. Old Escalus,
Though first in question, is thy secondary.
Take thy commission.

Angelo.
                    Now, good my lord,
Let there be some more test made of my mettle
Before so noble and so great a figure
Be stamp'd upon it.

Vincentio, the Duke.
                    No more evasion.
We have with a leaven'd and prepared choice
Proceeded to you; therefore take your honors.
Our haste from hence is of so quick condition
That it prefers itself, and leaves unquestion'd
Matters of needful value. We shall write to you,
As time and our concernings shall importune,
How it goes with us, and do look to know
What doth befall you here. So fare you well.
To th' hopeful execution do I leave you
Of your commissions.

Angelo.
                    Yet give leave, my lord,
That we may bring you something on the way.

Vincentio, the Duke.
My haste may not admit it,
Nor need you (on mine honor) have to do
With any scruple. Your scope is as mine own,
So to enforce or qualify the laws
As to your soul seems good. Give me your hand,
I'll privily away. I love the people,
But do not like to stage me to their eyes;
Though it do well, I do not relish well
Their loud applause and aves vehement;
Nor do I think the man of safe discretion
That does affect it. Once more fare you well.

Angelo.
The heavens give safety to your purposes!

Escalus.
Lead forth and bring you back in happiness!

Vincentio, the Duke.
I thank you. Fare you well.

Exit.

Escalus.
I shall desire you, sir, to give me leave
To have free speech with you; and it concerns me
To look into the bottom of my place.
A pow'r I have, but of what strength and nature
I am not yet instructed.

Angelo.
'Tis so with me. Let us withdraw together,
And we may soon our satisfaction have
Touching that point.

Escalus.
                  I'll wait upon your honor.

Exeunt.

Scene 2

Vienna. A street.

(*Lucio; First Gentleman; Second Gentleman; Mistress Overdone; Pompey; Provost; Claudio; Juliet; Officers*)

Lucio is talking to Two Gentlemen, discussing politics and joking. Mistress Overdone, their favorite bawd, approaches. She tells them that Claudio has been arrested and is to be executed for having got Juliet pregnant. The men leave to find out more while Mistress Overdone complains about how poor business is getting. Her servant Pompey arrives to inform her that a new proclamation orders that all houses of prostitution in the suburbs of Vienna will be pulled down. The bawd wonders what will become of her, but Pompey consoles her by pointing out that changing houses does not mean she has to change her job. Claudio, on his way to prison, is met by Lucio and the Two Gentlemen. He explains that he and Juliet were contracted to be married and simply hadn't announced it yet for financial reasons, so their sleeping together wasn't even adultery; but Angelo has revived a forgotten law that sentences him to death. Lucio advises appealing to the Duke, but the latter is nowhere to be found. Claudio's one hope is that his sister Isabella, who is training to become a nun, will plead for him with Angelo; he asks Lucio to visit Isabella and convince her to do so.

Enter Lucio and two other Gentlemen.

Lucio.
If the Duke with the other dukes come not to composition with the King of Hungary, why then all the dukes fall upon the King.

First Gentleman.
Heaven grant us its peace, but not the King of Hungary's!

Second Gentleman.
Amen.

Lucio.
Thou conclud'st like the sanctimonious pirate, that went to sea with the Ten Commandments, but scrap'd one out of the table.

Second Gentleman.
"Thou shalt not steal"?

Lucio.
Ay, that he raz'd.

First Gentleman.
Why, 'twas a commandment to command the captain and all the rest from their functions; they put forth to steal. There's not a soldier of us all, that in the thanksgiving before meat, do relish the petition well that prays for peace.

Second Gentleman.
I never heard any soldier dislike it.

Lucio.
I believe thee; for I think thou never wast where grace was said.

Second Gentleman.
No? A dozen times at least.

First Gentleman.
What? In meter?

Lucio.
In any proportion, or in any language.

First Gentleman.
I think, or in any religion.

Lucio.
Ay, why not? Grace is grace, despite of all controversy; as for example, thou thyself art a wicked villain, despite of all grace.

First Gentleman.
Well; there went but a pair of shears between us.

Lucio.
I grant; as there may between the lists and the velvet. Thou art the list.

First Gentleman.
And thou the velvet—thou art good velvet; thou'rt a three-pil'd piece, I warrant thee. I had as lief be a list of an English kersey as be pil'd, as thou art pil'd, for a French velvet. Do I speak feelingly now?

Lucio.
I think thou dost; and indeed with most painful feeling of thy speech. I will, out of thine own confession, learn to begin thy health; but, whilst I live, forget to drink after thee.

First Gentleman.
I think I have done myself wrong, have I not?

Second Gentleman.
Yes, that thou hast; whether thou art tainted or free.

Enter Bawd Mistress Overdone.

Lucio.
Behold, behold, where Madam Mitigation comes!

First Gentleman.
I have purchas'd as many diseases under her roof as come to—

Second Gentleman.
To what, I pray?

Lucio.
Judge.

Second Gentleman.
To three thousand dolors a year.

First Gentleman.
Ay, and more.

Lucio.
A French crown more.

First Gentleman.
Thou art always figuring diseases in me; but thou art full of error, I am sound.

Act 1, Scene 2

Lucio.
Nay, not (as one would say) healthy; but so sound as things that are hollow.
Thy bones are hollow; impiety has made a feast of thee.

First Gentleman.
How now, which of your hips has the most profound sciatica?

Mistress Overdone.
Well, well; there's one yonder arrested and carried to prison was worth five thousand of you all.

Second Gentleman.
Who's that, I pray thee?

Mistress Overdone.
Marry, sir, that's Claudio, Signior Claudio.

First Gentleman.
Claudio to prison? 'Tis not so.

Mistress Overdone.
Nay, but I know 'tis so. I saw him arrested; saw him carried away; and which is more, within these three days his head to be chopp'd off.

Lucio.
But after all this fooling, I would not have it so. Art thou sure of this?

Mistress Overdone.
I am too sure of it; and it is for getting Madam Julietta with child.

Lucio.
Believe me, this may be. He promis'd to meet me two hours since, and he was ever precise in promise-keeping.

Second Gentleman.
Besides, you know, it draws something near to the speech we had to such a purpose.

First Gentleman.
But most of all agreeing with the proclamation.

Lucio.
Away! Let's go learn the truth of it.

Exit with Gentlemen.

Mistress Overdone.
Thus, what with the war, what with the sweat, what with the gallows, and what with poverty, I am custom-shrunk.

Enter Clown Pompey.

How now? What's the news with you?

Pompey.
Yonder man is carried to prison.

Mistress Overdone.
Well; what has he done?

Pompey.
A woman.

Mistress Overdone.
But what's his offense?

Pompey.
Groping for trouts in a peculiar river.

Mistress Overdone.
What? Is there a maid with child by him?

Pompey.
No; but there's a woman with maid by him. You have not heard of the proclamation, have you?

Mistress Overdone.
What proclamation, man?

Pompey.
All houses in the suburbs of Vienna must be pluck'd down.

Mistress Overdone.
And what shall become of those in the city?

Pompey.
They shall stand for seed. They had gone down too, but that a wise burgher put in for them.

Mistress Overdone.
But shall all our houses of resort in the suburbs be pull'd down?

Pompey.
To the ground, mistress.

Mistress Overdone.
Why, here's a change indeed in the commonwealth! What shall become of me?

Pompey.
Come; fear not you; good counsellors lack no clients. Though you change your place, you need not change your trade; I'll be your tapster still. Courage! There will be pity taken on you. You that have worn your eyes almost out in the service, you will be consider'd.

Mistress Overdone.
What's to do here, Thomas tapster? Let's withdraw.

Pompey.
Here comes Signior Claudio, led by the Provost to prison; and there's Madam Juliet.

Exeunt.
Enter Provost, Claudio, Juliet, Officers.

Claudio.
Fellow, why dost thou show me thus to th' world? Bear me to prison, where I am committed.

Provost.
I do it not in evil disposition,
But from Lord Angelo by special charge.

Claudio.
Thus can the demigod, Authority,
Make us pay down for our offense by weight
The words of heaven: on whom it will, it will;
On whom it will not, so; yet still 'tis just.

Enter Lucio and two Gentlemen.

Lucio.
Why, how now, Claudio? Whence comes this restraint?

Claudio.
From too much liberty, my Lucio, liberty:
As surfeit is the father of much fast,
So every scope by the immoderate use
Turns to restraint. Our natures do pursue,
Like rats that ravin down their proper bane,
A thirsty evil, and when we drink we die.

Lucio.
If I could speak so wisely under an arrest, I would send for certain of my creditors; and yet, to say the truth, I had as lief have the foppery of freedom as the mortality of imprisonment. What's thy offense, Claudio?

Claudio.
What but to speak of would offend again.

Lucio.
What, is't murder?

Claudio.
No.

Lucio.
Lechery?

Claudio.
Call it so.

Provost.
Away, sir, you must go.

Claudio.
One word, good friend. Lucio, a word with you.

Lucio.
A hundred! If they'll do you any good.
Is lechery so look'd after?

Claudio.
Thus stands it with me: upon a true contract
I got possession of Julietta's bed.
You know the lady; she is fast my wife,
Save that we do the denunciation lack
Of outward order. This we came not to,
Only for propagation of a dow'r
Remaining in the coffer of her friends,
From whom we thought it meet to hide our love
Till time had made them for us. But it chances
The stealth of our most mutual entertainment
With character too gross is writ on Juliet.

Lucio.
With child, perhaps?

Claudio.
          Unhappily, even so.
And the new deputy now for the Duke—
Whether it be the fault and glimpse of newness,
Or whether that the body public be
A horse whereon the governor doth ride,
Who, newly in the seat, that it may know
He can command, lets it straight feel the spur;
Whether the tyranny be in his place,
Or in his eminence that fills it up,
I stagger in—but this new governor
Awakes me all the enrolled penalties
Which have, like unscour'd armor, hung by th' wall

So long that nineteen zodiacs have gone round
And none of them been worn; and for a name
Now puts the drowsy and neglected act
Freshly on me—'tis surely for a name.

Lucio.
I warrant it is; and thy head stands so tickle on thy shoulders that a milkmaid, if she be in love, may sigh it off. Send after the Duke, and appeal to him.

Claudio.
I have done so, but he's not to be found.
I prithee, Lucio, do me this kind service:
This day my sister should the cloister enter,
And there receive her approbation.
Acquaint her with the danger of my state;
Implore her, in my voice, that she make friends
To the strict deputy; bid herself assay him.
I have great hope in that; for in her youth
There is a prone and speechless dialect,
Such as move men; beside, she hath prosperous art
When she will play with reason and discourse,
And well she can persuade.

Lucio.
I pray she may; as well for the encouragement of the like, which else would stand under grievous imposition, as for the enjoying of thy life, who I would be sorry should be thus foolishly lost at a game of tick-tack. I'll to her.

Claudio.
I thank you, good friend Lucio.

Lucio.
Within two hours.

Claudio.
                    Come, officer, away!

Exeunt.

Scene 3

Vienna. A monastery.

(Duke; Friar Peter)

The Friar is suspicious that the Duke has hidden himself away to pursue a love affair, but the Duke insists that the real reason is that he is aware that he has been too lenient a ruler, and that therefore Vienna has sunk into depravity. Since he does not think he would be able to suddenly begin enforcing the laws, he has handed over government to Angelo, who is a stickler for the rules. At the same time, the Duke is curious to see how Angelo rules, and whether holding power will corrupt him.

Enter Duke and Friar Peter.

Vincentio, the Duke.
No; holy father, throw away that thought;
Believe not that the dribbling dart of love
Can pierce a complete bosom. Why I desire thee
To give me secret harbor, hath a purpose
More grave and wrinkled than the aims and ends
Of burning youth.

Friar Peter Thomas.
                    May your Grace speak of it?

Vincentio, the Duke.
My holy sir, none better knows than you
How I have ever lov'd the life removed,
And held in idle price to haunt assemblies
Where youth, and cost, witless bravery keeps.
I have deliver'd to Lord Angelo
(A man of stricture and firm abstinence)
My absolute power and place here in Vienna,
And he supposes me travel'd to Poland
(For so I have strew'd it in the common ear,
And so it is receiv'd). Now, pious sir,
You will demand of me why I do this.

Friar Peter Thomas.
Gladly, my lord.

Vincentio, the Duke.
We have strict statutes and most biting laws
(The needful bits and curbs to headstrong weeds),
Which for this fourteen years we have let slip,
Even like an o'ergrown lion in a cave,
That goes not out to prey. Now, as fond fathers,
Having bound up the threat'ning twigs of birch,
Only to stick it in their children's sight
For terror, not to use, in time the rod
Becomes more mock'd than fear'd; so our decrees,
Dead to infliction, to themselves are dead,
And liberty plucks justice by the nose;
The baby beats the nurse, and quite athwart
Goes all decorum.

Friar Peter Thomas.
                    It rested in your Grace
To unloose this tied-up justice when you pleas'd:
And it in you more dreadful would have seem'd

Than in Lord Angelo.

Vincentio, the Duke.
                I do fear—too dreadful;
Sith 'twas my fault to give the people scope,
'Twould be my tyranny to strike and gall them
For what I bid them do; for we bid this be done,
When evil deeds have their permissive pass,
And not the punishment. Therefore indeed, my father,
I have on Angelo impos'd the office,
Who may, in th' ambush of my name, strike home,
And yet my nature never in the fight
To do in slander. And to behold his sway,
I will, as 'twere a brother of your order,
Visit both prince and people; therefore I prithee
Supply me with the habit, and instruct me
How I may formally in person bear
Like a true friar. More reasons for this action
At our more leisure shall I render you;
Only, this one: Lord Angelo is precise;
Stands at a guard with envy; scarce confesses
That his blood flows; or that his appetite
Is more to bread than stone: hence shall we see
If power change purpose: what our seemers be.

Exeunt.

Scene 4

Vienna. A nunnery.

(Isabella; Francisca; Lucio)

Isabella discusses with Sister Francisca the restrictions that the nuns of her order face and wishes they were more stringent. Lucio arrives; as Isabella is still only a novice, she is allowed to speak to the man, while Francisca is not. Lucio explains to Isabella that her brother is in jail and likely to die, and explains the cause; Isabella is not overly sympathetic, though at first thinks that the easiest solution is simply that Claudio and Juliet marry. Lucio agrees that would be the best idea, but explains that the Duke is gone and the punctilious Angelo is ruling instead. Though she doubts she will have any effect, Isabella agrees to plead with Angelo for her brother's life.

Enter Isabel and Francisca, a nun.

Isabella.
And have you nuns no farther privileges?

Francisca.
Are not these large enough?

Isabella.
Yes, truly; I speak not as desiring more,
But rather wishing a more strict restraint
Upon the sisterhood, the votarists of Saint Clare.

Lucio.

Within.

Ho! Peace be in this place!

Isabella.
                Who's that which calls?

Francisca.
It is a man's voice. Gentle Isabella,
Turn you the key, and know his business of him;
You may, I may not; you are yet unsworn.
When you have vow'd, you must not speak with men
But in the presence of the prioress;
Then if you speak, you must not show your face,
Or if you show your face, you must not speak.
He calls again; I pray you answer him.

Exit.

Isabella.
Peace and prosperity! Who is't that calls?

Enter Lucio.

Lucio.
Hail, virgin, if you be, as those cheek-roses
Proclaim you are no less! Can you so stead me
As bring me to the sight of Isabella,
A novice of this place, and the fair sister
To her unhappy brother Claudio?

Isabella.
Why "her unhappy brother"? Let me ask,
The rather for I now must make you know
I am that Isabella, and his sister.

Lucio.
Gentle and fair, your brother kindly greets you.
Not to be weary with you, he's in prison.

Isabella.
Woe me! For what?

Act 1, Scene 4

Lucio.
For that which, if myself might be his judge,
He should receive his punishment in thanks:
He hath got his friend with child.

Isabella.
Sir, make me not your story.

Lucio.
                    'Tis true.
I would not—though 'tis my familiar sin
With maids to seem the lapwing, and to jest,
Tongue far from heart—play with all virgins so.
I hold you as a thing enskied, and sainted,
By your renouncement an immortal spirit,
And to be talk'd with in sincerity,
As with a saint.

Isabella.
You do blaspheme the good in mocking me.

Lucio.
Do not believe it. Fewness and truth, 'tis thus:
Your brother and his lover have embrac'd.
As those that feed grow full, as blossoming time
That from the seedness the bare fallow brings
To teeming foison, even so her plenteous womb
Expresseth his full tilth and husbandry.

Isabella.
Some one with child by him? My cousin Juliet?

Lucio.
Is she your cousin?

Isabella.
Adoptedly, as school-maids change their names
By vain though apt affection.

Lucio.
                    She it is.

Isabella.
O, let him marry her.

Lucio.
                    This is the point.
The Duke is very strangely gone from hence;
Bore many gentlemen (myself being one)
In hand, and hope of action; but we do learn
By those that know the very nerves of state,
His givings-out were of an infinite distance
From his true-meant design. Upon his place,
And with full line of his authority,
Governs Lord Angelo, a man whose blood
Is very snow-broth; one who never feels
The wanton stings and motions of the sense;
But doth rebate and blunt his natural edge
With profits of the mind: study and fast.
He (to give fear to use and liberty,
Which have for long run by the hideous law,
As mice by lions) hath pick'd out an act,
Under whose heavy sense your brother's life
Falls into forfeit; he arrests him on it,
And follows close the rigor of the statute,
To make him an example. All hope is gone,
Unless you have the grace by your fair prayer
To soften Angelo. And that's my pith
Of business 'twixt you and your poor brother.

Isabella.
Doth he so seek his life?

Lucio.
                    H'as censur'd him
Already, and as I hear, the Provost hath
A warrant for 's execution.

Isabella.
Alas, what poor ability's in me
To do him good!

Lucio.
                    Assay the pow'r you have.

Isabella.
My power? Alas, I doubt—

Lucio.
                    Our doubts are traitors,
And makes us lose the good we oft might win,
By fearing to attempt. Go to Lord Angelo,
And let him learn to know, when maidens sue,
Men give like gods; but when they weep and kneel,
All their petitions are as freely theirs
As they themselves would owe them.

Isabella.
I'll see what I can do.

Lucio.
                    But speedily.

Isabella.
I will about it straight;
No longer staying but to give the Mother
Notice of my affair. I humbly thank you.
Commend me to my brother. Soon at night

I'll send him certain word of my success.

Lucio.
I take my leave of you.

Isabella.
      Good sir, adieu.

Exeunt severally.

Act 2

Scene 1

A hall in Angelo's house.

(Angelo; Escalus; Servants; Justice; Provost; Elbow; Froth; Pompey; Officers)

Angelo argues that the laws must be enforced for them to be anything but a mockery, while Escalus pleads that they should not go too far, arguing that Claudio's fault is fairly common. Angelo is adamant, however, pointing out that being tempted and actually going through with the temptation are two different things. Elbow, a constable who has been charged with helping to clean up Vienna, brings in Froth and Pompey, whom he has found in a brothel. In mangled language they argue over the circumstances of the arrest, until Angelo is so bored that he walks out. Escalus, left in charge, resolves the matter kindly, dismissing Froth and threatening Pompey with a whipping if he continues to act as a pimp. Having rid himself of the fools, Escalus continues to meditate on the pity of Claudio's death.

Enter Angelo, Escalus, and Servants, Justice.

Angelo.
We must not make a scarecrow of the law,
Setting it up to fear the birds of prey,
And let it keep one shape, till custom make it
Their perch and not their terror.

Escalus.
      Ay, but yet
Let us be keen, and rather cut a little,
Than fall, and bruise to death. Alas, this gentleman,
Whom I would save, had a most noble father!
Let but your honor know
(Whom I believe to be most strait in virtue)
That in the working of your own affections,
Had time coher'd with place, or place with wishing,
Or that the resolute acting of your blood
Could have attain'd th' effect of your own purpose,
Whether you had not sometime in your life
Err'd in this point which now you censure him,
And pull'd the law upon you.

Angelo.
'Tis one thing to be tempted, Escalus,
Another thing to fall. I not deny
The jury, passing on the prisoner's life,
May in the sworn twelve have a thief or two
Guiltier than him they try. What's open made to justice,
That justice seizes. What knows the laws
That thieves do pass on thieves? 'Tis very pregnant,
The jewel that we find, we stoop and take't,
Because we see it; but what we do not see
We tread upon, and never think of it.
You may not so extenuate his offense
For I have had such faults; but rather tell me,
When I, that censure him, do so offend,
Let mine own judgment pattern out my death,
And nothing come in partial. Sir, he must die.

Enter Provost.

Escalus.
Be it as your wisdom will.

Angelo.
      Where is the Provost?

Provost.
Here, if it like your honor.

Angelo.
      See that Claudio
Be executed by nine tomorrow morning.
Bring him his confessor, let him be prepar'd,
For that's the utmost of his pilgrimage.

Exit Provost.

Escalus.
Well; heaven forgive him! And forgive us all!
Some rise by sin, and some by virtue fall;
Some run from brakes of ice and answer none,
And some condemned for a fault alone.

Enter Elbow, Froth, Clown Pompey, Officers.

Elbow.
Come, bring them away. If these be good people in a commonweal that do nothing but use their abuses in common houses, I know no law. Bring them away.

Angelo.
How now, sir, what's your name? And what's the matter?

Elbow.
If it please your honor, I am the poor Duke's constable, and my name is Elbow. I do lean upon justice, sir, and do bring in here before your good honor two notorious benefactors.

Angelo.
Benefactors? Well; what benefactors are they? Are they not malefactors?

Elbow.
If it please your honor, I know not well what they are; but precise villains they are, that I am sure of, and void of all profanation in the world that good Christians ought to have.

Escalus.
This comes off well. Here's a wise officer.

Angelo.
Go to; what quality are they of? Elbow is your name?

A pause.

Why dost thou not speak, Elbow?

Pompey.
He cannot, sir; he's out at elbow.

Angelo.
What are you, sir?

Elbow.
He, sir! A tapster, sir; parcel-bawd; one that serves a bad woman; whose house, sir, was (as they say) pluck'd down in the suburbs; and now she professes a hot-house; which, I think, is a very ill house too.

Escalus.
How know you that?

Elbow.
My wife, sir, whom I detest before heaven and your honor—

Escalus.
How? Thy wife?

Elbow.
Ay, sir; whom I thank heaven is an honest woman.

Escalus.
Dost thou detest her therefore?

Elbow.
I say, sir, I will detest myself also, as well as she, that this house, if it be not a bawd's house, it is pity of her life, for it is a naughty house.

Escalus.
How dost thou know that, constable?

Elbow.
Marry, sir, by my wife, who, if she had been a woman cardinally given, might have been accus'd in fornication, adultery, and all uncleanliness there.

Escalus.
By the woman's means?

Elbow.
Ay, sir, by Mistress Overdone's means; but as she spit in his face, so she defied him.

Pompey.
Sir, if it please your honor, this is not so.

Elbow.
Prove it before these varlets here, thou honorable man, prove it.

Escalus.
Do you hear how he misplaces?

Pompey.
Sir, she came in great with child; and longing (saving your honors' reverence) for stew'd prunes. Sir, we had but two in the house, which at that very distant time stood, as it were, in a fruit-dish, a dish of some threepence—your honors have seen such dishes; they are not china dishes, but very good dishes.

Escalus.
Go to, go to; no matter for the dish, sir.

Pompey.
No indeed, sir, not of a pin; you are therein in the right. But to the point. As I say, this Mistress Elbow, being (as I say) with child, and being great-bellied, and longing (as I said) for prunes; and having but two in the

dish (as I said), Master Froth here, this very man, having eaten the rest (as I said) and (as I say) paying for them very honestly; for, as you know, Master Froth, I could not give you threepence again.

Froth.
No indeed.

Pompey.
Very well; you being then (if you be rememb'red) cracking the stones of the foresaid prunes—

Froth.
Ay, so I did indeed.

Pompey.
Why, very well; I telling you then (if you be rememb'red) that such a one and such a one were past cure of the thing you wot of, unless they kept very good diet, as I told you—

Froth.
All this is true.

Pompey.
Why, very well then—

Escalus.
Come; you are a tedious fool. To the purpose: what was done to Elbow's wife, that he hath cause to complain of? Come me to what was done to her.

Pompey.
Sir, your honor cannot come to that yet.

Escalus.
No, sir, nor I mean it not.

Pompey.
Sir, but you shall come to it, by your honor's leave. And I beseech you, look into Master Froth here, sir; a man of fourscore pound a year; whose father died at Hallowmas. Was't not at Hallowmas, Master Froth?

Froth.
All-hallond eve.

Pompey.
Why, very well; I hope here be truths. He, sir, sitting (as I say) in a lower chair, sir—'twas in the Bunch of Grapes, where indeed you have a delight to sit, have you not?

Froth.
I have so, because it is an open room and good for winter.

Pompey.
Why, very well then; I hope here be truths.

Angelo.
This will last out a night in Russia
When nights are longest there. I'll take my leave,
And leave you to the hearing of the cause,
Hoping you'll find good cause to whip them all.

Escalus.
I think no less. Good morrow to your lordship.

Exit Angelo.

Now, sir, come on. What was done to Elbow's wife, once more?

Pompey.
Once, sir? There was nothing done to her once.

Elbow.
I beseech you, sir, ask him what this man did to my wife.

Pompey.
I beseech your honor, ask me.

Escalus.
Well, sir, what did this gentleman to her?

Pompey.
I beseech you, sir, look in this gentleman's face. Good Master Froth, look upon his honor; 'tis for a good purpose. Doth your honor mark his face?

Escalus.
Ay, sir, very well.

Pompey.
Nay, I beseech you mark it well.

Escalus.
Well, I do so.

Pompey.
Doth your honor see any harm in his face?

Escalus.
Why, no.

Pompey.
I'll be suppos'd upon a book, his face is the worst thing about him. Good then; if his face be the worst thing about him, how could Master Froth do the constable's wife any harm? I would know that of your honor.

Escalus.
He's in the right, constable. What say you to it?

Elbow.
First, and it like you, the house is a respected house; next, this is a respected fellow; and his mistress is a respected woman.

Pompey.
By this hand, sir, his wife is a more respected person than any of us all.

Elbow.
Varlet, thou liest! Thou liest, wicked varlet! The time is yet to come that she was ever respected with man, woman, or child.

Pompey.
Sir, she was respected with him before he married with her.

Escalus.
Which is the wiser here: Justice or Iniquity? Is this true?

Elbow.
O thou caitiff! O thou varlet! O thou wicked Hannibal! I respected with her before I was married to her? If ever I was respected with her, or she with me, let not your worship think me the poor Duke's officer. Prove this, thou wicked Hannibal, or I'll have mine action of batt'ry on thee.

Escalus.
If he took you a box o' th' ear, you might have your action of slander too.

Elbow.
Marry, I thank your good worship for it. What is't your worship's pleasure I shall do with this wicked caitiff?

Escalus.
Truly, officer, because he hath some offenses in him that thou wouldst discover if thou couldst, let him continue in his courses till thou know'st what they are.

Elbow.
Marry, I thank your worship for it. Thou seest, thou wicked varlet, now, what's come upon thee. Thou art to continue now, thou varlet, thou art to continue.

Escalus.
Where were you born, friend?

Froth.
Here in Vienna, sir.

Escalus.
Are you of fourscore pounds a year?

Froth.
Yes, and't please you, sir.

Escalus.
So.

To Pompey.

What trade are you of, sir?

Pompey.
A tapster, a poor widow's tapster.

Escalus.
Your mistress' name?

Pompey.
Mistress Overdone.

Escalus.
Hath she had any more than one husband?

Pompey.
Nine, sir; Overdone by the last.

Escalus.
Nine? Come hither to me, Master Froth. Master Froth, I would not have you acquainted with tapsters; they will draw you. Master Froth, and you will hang them. Get you gone, and let me hear no more of you.

Froth.
I thank your worship. For mine own part, I never come into any room in a tap-house, but I am drawn in.

Escalus.
Well; no more of it, Master Froth. Farewell.

Exit Froth.

Come you hither to me, Master Tapster. What's your name, Master Tapster?

Pompey.
Pompey.

Escalus.
What else?

Pompey.
Bum, sir.

Escalus.
Troth, and your bum is the greatest thing about you, so that in the beastliest sense you are Pompey the Great. Pompey, you are partly a bawd, Pompey, howsoever you color it in being a tapster, are you not? Come, tell me true, it shall be the better for you.

Pompey.
Truly, sir, I am a poor fellow that would live.

Escalus.
How would you live, Pompey? By being a bawd? What do you think of the trade, Pompey? Is it a lawful trade?

Pompey.
If the law would allow it, sir.

Escalus.
But the law will not allow it, Pompey; nor it shall not be allow'd in Vienna.

Pompey.
Does your worship mean to geld and splay all the youth of the city?

Escalus.
No, Pompey.

Pompey.
Truly, sir, in my poor opinion, they will to't then. If your worship will take order for the drabs and the knaves, you need not to fear the bawds.

Escalus.
There is pretty orders beginning, I can tell you: it is but heading and hanging.

Pompey.
If you head and hang all that offend that way but for ten year together, you'll be glad to give out a commission for more heads. If this law hold in Vienna ten year, I'll rent the fairest house in it after threepence a bay. If you live to see this come to pass, say Pompey told you so.

Escalus.
Thank you, good Pompey; and in requital of your prophecy, hark you: I advise you let me not find you before me again upon any complaint whatsoever; no, not for dwelling where you do. If I do, Pompey, I shall beat you to your tent, and prove a shrewd Caesar to you; in plain-dealing, Pompey, I shall have you whipt. So for this time, Pompey, fare you well.

Pompey.
I thank your worship for your good counsel;

Aside.

but I shall follow it as the flesh and fortune shall better determine.
Whip me? No, no, let carman whip his jade,
The valiant heart's not whipt out of his trade.

Exit.

Escalus.
Come hither to me, Master Elbow; come hither, Master Constable. How long have you been in this place of constable?

Elbow.
Seven year and a half, sir.

Escalus.
I thought, by the readiness in the office, you had continu'd in it some time. You say seven years together?

Elbow.
And a half, sir.

Escalus.
Alas, it hath been great pains to you. They do you wrong to put you so oft upon't. Are there not men in your ward sufficient to serve it?

Elbow.
Faith, sir, few of any wit in such matters. As they are chosen, they are glad to choose me for them. I do it for some piece of money, and go through with all.

Escalus.
Look you bring me in the names of some six or seven, the most sufficient of your parish.

Elbow.
To your worship's house, sir?

Act 2, Scene 2

Escalus.
To my house. Fare you well.

Exit Elbow.

What's a' clock, think you?

Justice.
Eleven, sir.

Escalus.
I pray you home to dinner with me.

Justice.
I humbly thank you.

Escalus.
It grieves me for the death of Claudio,
But there's no remedy.

Justice.
Lord Angelo is severe.

Escalus.
                    It is but needful.
Mercy is not itself, that oft looks so;
Pardon is still the nurse of second woe.
But yet, poor Claudio; there is no remedy.
Come, sir.

Exeunt.

Scene 2

Another room in Angelo's house.

(Provost; Servant; Angelo; Lucio; Isabella)

The Provost, who feels it is a shame that Claudio should die when so many others have committed the same crime, comes to confirm with Angelo that the execution is to go on. He also asks for instructions regarding Juliet, who is close to giving birth. Angelo gives orders that she be treated reasonably well, and he agrees to see Isabella. The novice makes a half-hearted plea for her brother, but Angelo's logical answer defeats her, since she actually agrees with him, and she turns to go. Lucio tells her to plead better, pushing her to be more emotional, and she slowly begins to do so. Angelo is adamant, but Isabella's arguments begin to make some headway and he agrees to see her again the next morning. Left alone, Angelo realizes that he has been captivated by Isabella's modesty and he begins to lust after her.

Enter Provost, Servant.

Servant.
He's hearing of a cause; he will come straight.
I'll tell him of you.

Provost.
                    Pray you do.

Exit Servant.

                    I'll know
His pleasure, may be he will relent. Alas,
He hath but as offended in a dream!
All sects, all ages smack of this vice, and he
To die for't!

Enter Angelo.

Angelo.
                    Now, what's the matter, Provost?

Provost.
Is it your will Claudio shall die tomorrow?

Angelo.
Did not I tell thee yea? Hadst thou not order?
Why dost thou ask again?

Provost.
                    Lest I might be too rash.
Under your good correction, I have seen
When, after execution, judgment hath
Repented o'er his doom.

Angelo.
                    Go to; let that be mine.
Do you your office, or give up your place,
And you shall well be spar'd.

Provost.
                    I crave your honor's pardon.
What shall be done, sir, with the groaning Juliet?
She's very near her hour.

Angelo.
                    Dispose of her
To some more fitter place; and that with speed.

Enter Servant.

Servant.
Here is the sister of the man condemn'd
Desires access to you.

Angelo.
                Hath he a sister?

Provost.
Ay, my good lord, a very virtuous maid,
And to be shortly of a sisterhood,
If not already.

Angelo.
Well; let her be admitted.

Exit Servant.

See you the fornicatress be remov'd.
Let her have needful but not lavish means;
There shall be order for't.

Enter Lucio and Isabella.

Provost.
                'Save your honor!

Angelo.
Stay a little while.

To Isabella.
                Y' are welcome; what's your will?

Isabella.
I am a woeful suitor to your honor,
Please but your honor hear me.

Angelo.
                Well; what's your suit?

Isabella.
There is a vice that most I do abhor,
And most desire should meet the blow of justice;
For which I would not plead, but that I must;
For which I must not plead, but that I am
At war 'twixt will and will not.

Angelo.
                Well; the matter?

Isabella.
I have a brother is condemn'd to die;
I do beseech you let it be his fault,
And not my brother.

Provost.

Aside.

Heaven give thee moving graces!

Angelo.
Condemn the fault, and not the actor of it?
Why, every fault's condemn'd ere it be done.
Mine were the very cipher of a function,
To fine the faults whose fine stands in record,
And let go by the actor.

Isabella.
                O just but severe law!
I had a brother then. Heaven keep your honor!

Lucio.

Aside to Isabella

Give't not o'er so. To him again, entreat him,
Kneel down before him, hang upon his gown;
You are too cold. If you should need a pin,
You could not with more tame a tongue desire it;
To him, I say!

Isabella.
Must he needs die?

Angelo.
                Maiden, no remedy.

Isabella.
Yes; I do think that you might pardon him,
And neither heaven nor man grieve at the mercy.

Angelo.
I will not do't.

Isabella.
                But can you if you would?

Angelo.
Look what I will not, that I cannot do.

Isabella.
But might you do't, and do the world no wrong,
If so your heart were touch'd with that remorse
As mine is to him?

Angelo.
                He's sentenc'd; 'tis too late.

Lucio.

Aside to Isabella

You are too cold.

Isabella.
Too late? Why, no; I that do speak a word
May call it again. Well, believe this,
No ceremony that to great ones 'longs,
Not the king's crown, nor the deputed sword,
The marshal's truncheon, nor the judge's robe,
Become them with one half so good a grace
As mercy does.
If he had been as you, and you as he,
You would have slipp'd like him, but he, like you,
Would not have been so stern.

Angelo.
                    Pray you be gone.

Isabella.
I would to heaven I had your potency,
And you were Isabel! Should it then be thus?
No; I would tell what 'twere to be a judge,
And what a prisoner.

Lucio.

Aside to Isabella.
                    Ay, touch him; there's the vein.

Angelo.
Your brother is a forfeit of the law,
And you but waste your words.

Isabella.
                    Alas, alas!
Why, all the souls that were were forfeit once,
And He that might the vantage best have took
Found out the remedy. How would you be
If He, which is the top of judgment, should
But judge you as you are? O, think on that,
And mercy then will breathe within your lips,
Like man new made.

Angelo.
                    Be you content, fair maid,
It is the law, not I, condemn your brother.
Were he my kinsman, brother, or my son,
It should be thus with him: he must die tomorrow.

Isabella.
Tomorrow? O, that's sudden! Spare him, spare him!
He's not prepar'd for death. Even for our kitchens
We kill the fowl of season. Shall we serve heaven
With less respect than we do minister
To our gross selves? Good, good my lord, bethink you:
Who is it that hath died for this offense?
There's many have committed it.

Lucio.

Aside to Isabella
                    Ay, well said.

Angelo.
The law hath not been dead, though it hath slept.
Those many had not dar'd to do that evil
If the first that did th' edict infringe
Had answer'd for his deed. Now 'tis awake,
Takes note of what is done, and like a prophet
Looks in a glass that shows what future evils,
Either now, or by remissness new conceiv'd,
And so in progress to be hatch'd and born,
Are now to have no successive degrees,
But here they live, to end.

Isabella.
                    Yet show some pity.

Angelo.
I show it most of all when I show justice;
For then I pity those I do not know,
Which a dismiss'd offense would after gall,
And do him right that, answering one foul wrong,
Lives not to act another. Be satisfied;
Your brother dies tomorrow; be content.

Isabella.
So you must be the first that gives this sentence,
And he, that suffers. O, it is excellent
To have a giant's strength; but it is tyrannous
To use it like a giant.

Lucio.

Aside to Isabella
                    That's well said.

Isabella.
Could great men thunder
As Jove himself does, Jove would never be quiet,
For every pelting, petty officer
Would use his heaven for thunder,
Nothing but thunder! Merciful heaven,
Thou rather with thy sharp and sulfurous bolt
Splits the unwedgeable and gnarled oak
Than the soft myrtle; but man, proud man,
Dress'd in a little brief authority,
Most ignorant of what he's most assur'd
(His glassy essence), like an angry ape

Plays such fantastic tricks before high heaven
As makes the angels weep; who, with our spleens,
Would all themselves laugh mortal.

Lucio.

Aside to Isabella

O, to him, to him, wench! He will relent.
He's coming; I perceive't.

Provost.

Aside.
     Pray heaven she win him!

Isabella.
We cannot weigh our brother with ourself.
Great men may jest with saints; 'tis wit in them,
But in the less foul profanation.

Lucio.

Aside to Isabella

Thou'rt i' th' right, girl, more o' that.

Isabella.
That in the captain's but a choleric word,
Which in the soldier is flat blasphemy.

Lucio.

Aside to Isabella

Art avis'd o' that? More on't.

Angelo.
Why do you put these sayings upon me?

Isabella.
Because authority, though it err like others,
Hath yet a kind of medicine in itself,
That skins the vice o' th' top. Go to your bosom,
Knock there, and ask your heart what it doth know
That's like my brother's fault. If it confess
A natural guiltiness such as is his,
Let it not sound a thought upon your tongue
Against my brother's life.

Angelo.

Aside.
     She speaks, and 'tis
Such sense that my sense breeds with it.—Fare you well.

Isabella.
Gentle my lord, turn back.

Angelo.
I will bethink me. Come again tomorrow.

Isabella.
Hark how I'll bribe you. Good my lord, turn back.

Angelo.
How? Bribe me?

Isabella.
Ay, with such gifts that heaven shall share with you.

Lucio.

Aside to Isabella

You had marr'd all else.

Isabella.
Not with fond sicles of the tested gold,
Or stones, whose rate are either rich or poor
As fancy values them; but with true prayers,
That shall be up at heaven, and enter there
Ere sun-rise, prayers from preserved souls,
From fasting maids, whose minds are dedicate
To nothing temporal.

Angelo.
     Well; come to me tomorrow.

Lucio.

Aside to Isabella

Go to; 'tis well. Away!

Isabella.
Heaven keep your honor safe!

Angelo.

Aside.
     Amen!
For I am that way going to temptation,
Where prayers cross.

Isabella.
     At what hour tomorrow
Shall I attend your lordship?

Angelo.
     At any time 'fore noon.

Isabella.
'Save your honor!

Exeunt Isabella, Lucio, and Provost.

Angelo.
                From thee: even from thy virtue.
What's this? What's this? Is this her fault, or mine?
The tempter, or the tempted, who sins most, ha?
Not she; nor doth she tempt; but it is I
That, lying by the violet in the sun,
Do as the carrion does, not as the flow'r,
Corrupt with virtuous season. Can it be
That modesty may more betray our sense
Than woman's lightness? Having waste ground enough,
Shall we desire to raze the sanctuary
And pitch our evils there? O fie, fie, fie!
What dost thou? Or what art thou, Angelo?
Dost thou desire her foully for those things
That make her good? O, let her brother live!
Thieves for their robbery have authority
When judges steal themselves. What, do I love her,
That I desire to hear her speak again?
And feast upon her eyes? What is't I dream on?
O cunning enemy, that to catch a saint,
With saints dost bait thy hook! Most dangerous
Is that temptation that doth goad us on
To sin in loving virtue. Never could the strumpet,
With all her double vigor, art and nature,
Once stir my temper; but this virtuous maid
Subdues me quite. Ever till now,
When men were fond, I smil'd and wond'red how.

Exit.

Scene 3

A room in a prison.

(Duke; Provost; Juliet)

Disguised as a friar, the Duke arrives at the prison and asks the Provost permission to console the prisoners. The Provost tells him about Claudio and Juliet, and the fact that Claudio must die. The Duke speaks with Juliet to find out if she is repentant and whether the crime was mutually committed, then goes to speak with Claudio. Juliet is distraught to hear how soon Claudio will die.

Enter Duke disguised as a friar and Provost, meeting.

Vincentio, the Duke.
Hail to you, Provost! So I think you are.

Provost.
I am the Provost. What's your will, good friar?

Vincentio, the Duke.
Bound by my charity and my blest order,
I come to visit the afflicted spirits
Here in the prison. Do me the common right
To let me see them, and to make me know
The nature of their crimes, that I may minister
To them accordingly.

Provost.
I would do more than that, if more were needful.

Enter Juliet.

Look, here comes one; a gentlewoman of mine,
Who, falling in the flaws of her own youth,
Hath blister'd her report. She is with child,
And he that got it, sentenc'd; a young man
More fit to do another such offense
Than die for this.

Vincentio, the Duke.
When must he die?

Provost.
                As I do think, tomorrow.

To Juliet.

I have provided for you. Stay a while,
And you shall be conducted.

Vincentio, the Duke.
Repent you, fair one, of the sin you carry?

Juliet.
I do; and bear the shame most patiently.

Vincentio, the Duke.
I'll teach you how you shall arraign your conscience,
And try your penitence, if it be sound,
Or hollowly put on.

Juliet.
                I'll gladly learn.

Vincentio, the Duke.
Love you the man that wrong'd you?

Juliet.
Yes, as I love the woman that wrong'd him.

Vincentio, the Duke.
So then it seems your most offenseful act
Was mutually committed?

Juliet.
                        Mutually.

Vincentio, the Duke.
Then was your sin of heavier kind than his.

Juliet.
I do confess it, and repent it, father.

Vincentio, the Duke.
'Tis meet so, daughter, but lest you do repent
As that the sin hath brought you to this shame,
Which sorrow is always toward ourselves, not heaven,
Showing we would not spare heaven as we love it,
But as we stand in fear—

Juliet.
I do repent me as it is an evil,
And take the shame with joy.

Vincentio, the Duke.
                        There rest.
Your partner, as I hear, must die tomorrow,
And I am going with instruction to him.
Grace go with you, Benedicite!

Exit.

Juliet.
Must die tomorrow? O injurious love,
That respites me a life whose very comfort
Is still a dying horror!

Provost.
                        'Tis pity of him.

Exeunt.

Scene 4

A room in Angelo's house.

(Angelo; Servant; Isabella)

Angelo ruminates on how he is fixated on Isabella. When she arrives, he makes her a proposal: if she sleeps with him, he will spare Claudio. Isabella indignantly refuses, and threatens to tell the world, but Angelo points out that no one will believe one little nun against the virtuous ruler. Left alone, Isabella considers the matter and decides that she holds her chastity dearer than her brother's life.

Enter Angelo.

Angelo.
When I would pray and think, I think and pray
To several subjects. Heaven hath my empty words,
Whilst my invention, hearing not my tongue,
Anchors on Isabel; heaven in my mouth,
As if I did but only chew his name,
And in my heart the strong and swelling evil
Of my conception. The state, whereon I studied,
Is like a good thing, being often read,
Grown sere and tedious; yea, my gravity,
Wherein (let no man hear me) I take pride,
Could I, with boot, change for an idle plume,
Which the air beats for vain. O place, O form,
How often dost thou with thy case, thy habit,
Wrench awe from fools, and tie the wiser souls
To thy false seeming! Blood, thou art blood.
Let's write "good angel" on the devil's horn,
'Tis not the devil's crest.

Enter Servant.

                        How now? Who's there?

Servant.
One Isabel, a sister, desires access to you.

Angelo.
Teach her the way.

Exit Servant.

                        O heavens!
Why does my blood thus muster to my heart,
Making both it unable for itself,
And dispossessing all my other parts
Of necessary fitness?
So play the foolish throngs with one that swounds,
Come all to help him, and so stop the air
By which he should revive; and even so
The general subject to a well-wish'd king
Quit their own part, and in obsequious fondness
Crowd to his presence, where their untaught love
Must needs appear offense.

Enter Isabella.

Act 2, Scene 4

How now, fair maid?

Isabella.
I am come to know your pleasure.

Angelo.
That you might know it, would much better please me
Than to demand what 'tis. Your brother cannot live.

Isabella.
Even so. Heaven keep your honor!

Angelo.
Yet may he live a while; and it may be
As long as you or I. Yet he must die.

Isabella.
Under your sentence?

Angelo.
Yea.

Isabella.
When, I beseech you? That in his reprieve,
Longer or shorter, he may be so fitted
That his soul sicken not.

Angelo.
Ha? Fie, these filthy vices! It were as good
To pardon him that hath from nature stol'n
A man already made, as to remit
Their saucy sweetness that do coin heaven's image
In stamps that are forbid. 'Tis all as easy
Falsely to take away a life true made
As to put metal in restrained means
To make a false one.

Isabella.
'Tis set down so in heaven, but not in earth.

Angelo.
Say you so? Then I shall pose you quickly.
Which had you rather, that the most just law
Now took your brother's life, or, to redeem him,
Give up your body to such sweet uncleanness
As she that he hath stain'd?

Isabella.
                Sir, believe this,
I had rather give my body than my soul.

Angelo.
I talk not of your soul; our compell'd sins
Stand more for number than for accompt.

Isabella.
                How say you?

Angelo.
Nay, I'll not warrant that; for I can speak
Against the thing I say. Answer to this:
I (now the voice of the recorded law)
Pronounce a sentence on your brother's life;
Might there not be a charity in sin
To save this brother's life?

Isabella.
                Please you to do't,
I'll take it as a peril to my soul,
It is no sin at all, but charity.

Angelo.
Pleas'd you to do't at peril of your soul,
Were equal poise of sin and charity.

Isabella.
That I do beg his life, if it be sin,
Heaven let me bear it! You granting of my suit,
If that be sin, I'll make it my morn-prayer
To have it added to the faults of mine,
And nothing of your answer.

Angelo.
                Nay, but hear me,
Your sense pursues not mine. Either you are ignorant,
Or seem so craftily; and that's not good.

Isabella.
Let me be ignorant, and in nothing good,
But graciously to know I am no better.

Angelo.
Thus wisdom wishes to appear most bright
When it doth tax itself; as these black masks
Proclaim an enshield beauty ten times louder
Than beauty could, displayed. But mark me:
To be received plain, I'll speak more gross:
Your brother is to die.

Isabella.
So.

Angelo.
And his offense is so, as it appears,
Accountant to the law upon that pain.

Isabella.
True.

Angelo.
Admit no other way to save his life
(As I subscribe not that, nor any other,
But in the loss of question), that you, his sister,
Finding yourself desir'd of such a person,
Whose credit with the judge, or own great place,
Could fetch your brother from the manacles
Of the all-binding law; and that there were
No earthly mean to save him, but that either
You must lay down the treasures of your body
To this supposed, or else to let him suffer—
What would you do?

Isabella.
As much for my poor brother as myself:
That is, were I under the terms of death,
Th' impression of keen whips I'ld wear as rubies,
And strip myself to death, as to a bed
That longing have been sick for, ere I'ld yield
My body up to shame.

Angelo.
                    Then must your brother die.

Isabella.
And 'twere the cheaper way:
Better it were a brother died at once,
Than that a sister, by redeeming him,
Should die forever.

Angelo.
Were not you then as cruel as the sentence
That you have slander'd so?

Isabella.
Ignomy in ransom and free pardon
Are of two houses: lawful mercy
Is nothing kin to foul redemption.

Angelo.
You seem'd of late to make the law a tyrant,
And rather prov'd the sliding of your brother
A merriment than a vice.

Isabella.
O, pardon me, my lord, it oft falls out,
To have what we would have, we speak not what we mean.
I something do excuse the thing I hate,
For his advantage that I dearly love.

Angelo.
We are all frail.

Isabella.
                Else let my brother die,
If not a fedary, but only he,
Owe and succeed thy weakness.

Angelo.
Nay, women are frail too.

Isabella.
Ay, as the glasses where they view themselves,
Which are as easy broke as they make forms.
Women? Help heaven! Men their creation mar
In profiting by them. Nay, call us ten times frail,
For we are soft as our complexions are,
And credulous to false prints.

Angelo.
                I think it well;
And from this testimony of your own sex
(Since I suppose we are made to be no stronger
Than faults may shake our frames), let me be bold.
I do arrest your words. Be that you are,
That is a woman; if you be more, you're none;
If you be one (as you are well express'd
By all external warrants), show it now,
By putting on the destin'd livery.

Isabella.
I have no tongue but one; gentle my lord,
Let me entreat you speak the former language.

Angelo.
Plainly conceive, I love you.

Isabella.
My brother did love Juliet,
And you tell me that he shall die for't.

Angelo.
He shall not, Isabel, if you give me love.

Isabella.
I know your virtue hath a license in't,
Which seems a little fouler than it is,
To pluck on others.

Angelo.   Believe me, on mine honor,
My words express my purpose.

Isabella.
Ha? Little honor to be much believ'd,
And most pernicious purpose! Seeming, seeming!
I will proclaim thee, Angelo, look for't!
Sign me a present pardon for my brother,
Or with an outstretch'd throat I'll tell the world aloud
What man thou art.

Angelo.   Who will believe thee, Isabel?
My unsoil'd name, th' austereness of my life,
My vouch against you, and my place i' th' state,
Will so your accusation overweigh,
That you shall stifle in your own report,
And smell of calumny. I have begun,
And now I give my sensual race the rein.
Fit thy consent to my sharp appetite,
Lay by all nicety and prolixious blushes
That banish what they sue for. Redeem thy brother
By yielding up thy body to my will,
Or else he must not only die the death,
But thy unkindness shall his death draw out
To ling'ring sufferance. Answer me tomorrow,
Or by the affection that now guides me most,
I'll prove a tyrant to him. As for you,
Say what you can: my false o'erweighs your true.

Exit.

Isabella.
To whom should I complain? Did I tell this,
Who would believe me? O perilous mouths,
That bear in them one and the self-same tongue,
Either of condemnation or approof,
Bidding the law make curtsy to their will,
Hooking both right and wrong to th' appetite,
To follow as it draws! I'll to my brother.
Though he hath fall'n by prompture of the blood,
Yet hath he in him such a mind of honor
That had he twenty heads to tender down
On twenty bloody blocks, he'ld yield them up,
Before his sister should her body stoop
To such abhorr'd pollution.
Then, Isabel, live chaste, and, brother, die;
More than our brother is our chastity.
I'll tell him yet of Angelo's request,
And fit his mind to death, for his soul's rest.

Exit.

Act 3

Scene 1

A room in the prison.

(Duke; Claudio; Provost; Isabella)

Still disguised as a friar, the Duke talks with Claudio, encouraging him to not hope for a reprieve and therefore be absolutely ready for death, since in that case whichever way it goes, a reprieve will be all the sweeter, and death less hard. Isabella arrives and the Duke hides himself to eavesdrop on the conversation between brother and sister. Isabella tells Claudio of Angelo's offer, and Claudio is horrified and disgusted; but as he reflects further, and thinks more on his fear of death, he comes to ask Isabella to give in. Isabella rages at him as a coward, and decides that it might be better in the end if he did die quickly. The Duke intervenes. He tells Claudio that Angelo was only testing Isabella, and then speaks to her alone. He informs her that despite his virtuous reputation, Angelo once abandoned his fiancée because she lost her dowry, excusing himself by slandering her. Mariana is still in love with him, however. The Duke suggests that Isabella arrange a rendezvous with Angelo, but that they convince Mariana to take Isabella's place in the dark, thus theoretically solving everyone's problem. Isabella agrees.

Enter Duke disguised as a friar, Claudio, and Provost.

Vincentio, the Duke.
So then you hope of pardon from Lord Angelo?

Claudio.
The miserable have no other medicine
But only hope:
I have hope to live, and am prepar'd to die.

Vincentio, the Duke.
Be absolute for death: either death or life
Shall thereby be the sweeter. Reason thus with life:
If I do lose thee, I do lose a thing
That none but fools would keep. A breath thou art,

Servile to all the skyey influences,
That dost this habitation where thou keep'st
Hourly afflict. Merely, thou art death's fool,
For him thou labor'st by thy flight to shun,
And yet run'st toward him still. Thou art not noble,
For all th' accommodations that thou bear'st
Are nurs'd by baseness. Thou'rt by no means valiant,
For thou dost fear the soft and tender fork
Of a poor worm. Thy best of rest is sleep,
And that thou oft provok'st, yet grossly fear'st
Thy death, which is no more. Thou art not thyself,
For thou exists on many a thousand grains
That issue out of dust. Happy thou art not,
For what thou hast not, still thou striv'st to get,
And what thou hast, forget'st. Thou art not certain,
For thy complexion shifts to strange effects,
After the moon. If thou art rich, thou'rt poor,
For like an ass, whose back with ingots bows,
Thou bear'st thy heavy riches but a journey,
And death unloads thee. Friend hast thou none,
For thine own bowels, which do call thee sire,
The mere effusion of thy proper loins,
Do curse the gout, serpigo, and the rheum
For ending thee no sooner. Thou hast nor youth nor age,
But as it were an after-dinner's sleep,
Dreaming on both, for all thy blessed youth
Becomes as aged, and doth beg the alms
Of palsied eld; and when thou art old and rich,
Thou hast neither heat, affection, limb, nor beauty,
To make thy riches pleasant. What's yet in this
That bears the name of life? Yet in this life
Lie hid more thousand deaths; yet death we fear
That makes these odds all even.

Claudio.
                    I humbly thank you.
To sue to live, I find I seek to die,
And seeking death, find life. Let it come on.

Isabella.

Within.

What ho! Peace here; grace and good company!

Provost.
Who's there? Come in, the wish deserves a welcome.

Vincentio, the Duke.
Dear sir, ere long I'll visit you again.

Claudio.
Most holy sir, I thank you.

Enter Isabella.

Isabella.
My business is a word or two with Claudio.

Provost.
And very welcome. Look, signior, here's your sister.

Vincentio, the Duke.
Provost, a word with you.

Provost.
As many as you please.

Vincentio, the Duke.
Bring me to hear them speak, where I may be conceal'd.

Exeunt Duke and Provost.

Claudio.
Now, sister, what's the comfort?

Isabella.
                    Why,
As all comforts are: most good, most good indeed.
Lord Angelo, having affairs to heaven,
Intends you for his swift ambassador,
Where you shall be an everlasting leiger;
Therefore your best appointment make with speed,
Tomorrow you set on.

Claudio.
                Is there no remedy?

Isabella.
None, but such remedy as, to save a head,
To cleave a heart in twain.

Claudio.
                But is there any?

Isabella.
Yes, brother, you may live;
There is a devilish mercy in the judge,
If you'll implore it, that will free your life,
But fetter you till death.

Claudio.
                Perpetual durance?

Isabella.
Ay, just, perpetual durance, a restraint,
Though all the world's vastidity you had,
To a determin'd scope.

Claudio.
                    But in what nature?

Isabella.
In such a one as, you consenting to't,
Would bark your honor from that trunk you bear,
And leave you naked.

Claudio.
                    Let me know the point.

Isabella.
O, I do fear thee, Claudio, and I quake,
Lest thou a feverous life shouldst entertain,
And six or seven winters more respect
Than a perpetual honor. Dar'st thou die?
The sense of death is most in apprehension,
And the poor beetle that we tread upon
In corporal sufferance finds a pang as great
As when a giant dies.

Claudio.
                    Why give you me this shame?
Think you I can a resolution fetch
From flow'ry tenderness? If I must die,
I will encounter darkness as a bride,
And hug it in mine arms.

Isabella.
There spake my brother; there my father's grave
Did utter forth a voice. Yes, thou must die:
Thou art too noble to conserve a life
In base appliances. This outward-sainted deputy,
Whose settled visage and deliberate word
Nips youth i' th' head, and follies doth enew
As falcon doth the fowl, is yet a devil;
His filth within being cast, he would appear
A pond as deep as hell.

Claudio.
                    The precise Angelo?

Isabella.
O, 'tis the cunning livery of hell,
The damned'st body to invest and cover
In princely guards! Dost thou think, Claudio,
If I would yield him my virginity,
Thou mightst be freed!

Claudio.
                    O heavens, it cannot be.

Isabella.
Yes, he would give't thee, from this rank offense,
So to offend him still. This night's the time
That I should do what I abhor to name,
Or else thou diest tomorrow.

Claudio.
                    Thou shalt not do't.

Isabella.
O, were it but my life,
I'd throw it down for your deliverance
As frankly as a pin.

Claudio.
                    Thanks, dear Isabel.

Isabella.
Be ready, Claudio, for your death tomorrow.

Claudio.
Yes. Has he affections in him,
That thus can make him bite the law by th' nose,
When he would force it? Sure it is no sin,
Or of the deadly seven it is the least.

Isabella.
Which is the least?

Claudio.
If it were damnable, he being so wise,
Why would he for the momentary trick
Be perdurably fin'd? O Isabel!

Isabella.
What says my brother?

Claudio.
                    Death is a fearful thing.

Isabella.
And shamed life a hateful.

Claudio.
Ay, but to die, and go we know not where;
To lie in cold obstruction, and to rot;
This sensible warm motion to become
A kneaded clod; and the delighted spirit
To bathe in fiery floods, or to reside
In thrilling region of thick-ribbed ice;
To be imprison'd in the viewless winds
And blown with restless violence round about

The pendant world; or to be worse than worst
Of those that lawless and incertain thought
Imagine howling—'tis too horrible!
The weariest and most loathed worldly life
That age, ache, penury, and imprisonment
Can lay on nature is a paradise
To what we fear of death.

Isabella.
Alas, alas!

Claudio.
                    Sweet sister, let me live.
What sin you do to save a brother's life,
Nature dispenses with the deed so far,
That it becomes a virtue.

Isabella.
                    O you beast!
O faithless coward! O dishonest wretch!
Wilt thou be made a man out of my vice?
Is't not a kind of incest, to take life
From thine own sister's shame? What should I think?
Heaven shield my mother play'd my father fair!
For such a warped slip of wilderness
Ne'er issu'd from his blood. Take my defiance!
Die, perish! Might but my bending down
Reprieve thee from thy fate, it should proceed.
I'll pray a thousand prayers for thy death,
No word to save thee.

Claudio.
Nay, hear me, Isabel.

Isabella.
                    O fie, fie, fie!
Thy sin's not accidental, but a trade.
Mercy to thee would prove itself a bawd,
'Tis best that thou diest quickly.

Claudio.
                    O, hear me, Isabella!

Enter Duke disguised as a friar.

Vincentio, the Duke.
Vouchsafe a word, young sister, but one word.

Isabella.
What is your will?

Vincentio, the Duke.
Might you dispense with your leisure, I would by and by have some speech with you. The satisfaction I would require is likewise your own benefit.

Isabella.
I have no superfluous leisure; my stay must be stolen out of other affairs; but I will attend you a while.

Walks apart.

Vincentio, the Duke.
Son, I have overheard what hath pass'd between you and your sister. Angelo had never the purpose to corrupt her; only he hath made an assay of her virtue to practice his judgment with the disposition of natures. She (having the truth of honor in her) hath made him that gracious denial which he is most glad to receive. I am confessor to Angelo, and I know this to be true; therefore prepare yourself to death. Do not satisfy your resolution with hopes that are fallible, tomorrow you must die; go to your knees, and make ready.

Claudio.
Let me ask my sister pardon. I am so out of love with life that I will sue to be rid of it.

Vincentio, the Duke.
Hold you there! Farewell.

Exit Claudio.

Provost, a word with you.

Enter Provost.

Provost.
What's your will, father?

Vincentio, the Duke.
That now you are come, you will be gone. Leave me a while with the maid. My mind promises with my habit, no loss shall touch her by my company.

Provost.
In good time.

Exit.

Vincentio, the Duke.

Turning to Isabella.

The hand that hath made you fair hath made you good; the goodness that is cheap in beauty makes beauty brief in goodness; but grace, being the soul of your complexion, shall keep the body of it ever fair. The assault that Angelo hath made to you, fortune hath convey'd to my understanding; and but that frailty hath examples for his falling, I should wonder at Angelo. How will you do to content this substitute, and to save your brother?

Isabella.
I am now going to resolve him. I had rather my brother die by the law than my son should be unlawfully born. But O, how much is the good Duke deceiv'd in Angelo! If ever he return, and I can speak to him, I will open my lips in vain, or discover his government.

Vincentio, the Duke.
That shall not be much amiss; yet, as the matter now stands, he will avoid your accusation: he made trial of you only. Therefore fasten your ear on my advisings: to the love I have in doing good a remedy presents itself. I do make myself believe that you may most uprighteously do a poor wrong'd lady a merited benefit; redeem your brother from the angry law; do no stain to your own gracious person; and much please the absent Duke, if peradventure he shall ever return to have hearing of this business.

Isabella.
Let me hear you speak farther. I have spirit to do any thing that appears not foul in the truth of my spirit.

Vincentio, the Duke.
Virtue is bold, and goodness never fearful. Have you not heard speak of Mariana, the sister of Frederick, the great soldier who miscarried at sea?

Isabella.
I have heard of the lady, and good words went with her name.

Vincentio, the Duke.
She should this Angelo have married; was affianc'd to her by oath, and the nuptial appointed; between which time of the contract and limit of the solemnity, her brother Frederick was wrack'd at sea, having in that perish'd vessel the dowry of his sister. But mark how heavily this befell to the poor gentlewoman: there she lost a noble and renown'd brother, in his love toward her ever most kind and natural; with him, the portion and sinew of her fortune, her marriage-dowry; with both, her combinate-husband, this well-seeming Angelo.

Isabella.
Can this be so? Did Angelo so leave her?

Vincentio, the Duke.
Left her in her tears, and dried not one of them with his comfort; swallow'd his vows whole, pretending in her discoveries of dishonor; in few, bestow'd her on her own lamentation, which she yet wears for his sake; and he, a marble to her tears, is wash'd with them, but relents not.

Isabella.
What a merit were it in death to take this poor maid from the world! What corruption in this life, that it will let this man live! But how out of this can she avail?

Vincentio, the Duke.
It is a rupture that you may easily heal; and the cure of it not only saves your brother, but keeps you from dishonor in doing it.

Isabella.
Show me how, good father.

Vincentio, the Duke.
This forenam'd maid hath yet in her the continuance of her first affection; his unjust unkindness (that in all reason should have quench'd her love) hath (like an impediment in the current) made it more violent and unruly. Go you to Angelo, answer his requiring with a plausible obedience, agree with his demands to the point; only refer yourself to this advantage: first, that your stay with him may not be long; that the time may have all shadow and silence in it; and the place answer to convenience. This being granted in course—and now follows all—we shall advise this wrong'd maid to stead up your appointment, go in your place. If the encounter acknowledge itself hereafter, it may compel him to her recompense; and here, by this is your brother sav'd, your honor untainted, the poor Mariana advantag'd, and the corrupt deputy scal'd. The maid will I frame, and make fit for his attempt. If you think well to carry this as you may, the doubleness of the benefit defends the deceit from reproof. What think you of it?

Isabella.
The image of it gives me content already, and I trust it will grow to a most prosperous perfection.

Vincentio, the Duke.
It lies much in your holding up. Haste you speedily to Angelo; if for this night he entreat you to his bed, give him promise of satisfaction. I will presently to Saint Luke's; there, at the moated grange, resides this dejected Mariana. At that place call upon me, and dispatch with Angelo, that it may be quickly.

Isabella.
I thank you for this comfort. Fare you well, good father.

Exit. Manet Duke.

Scene 2

The street before the prison.

(*Duke; Elbow; Pompey; Officers; Lucio; Escalus; Provost; Mistress Overdone*)

Elbow has arrested Pompey again and is taking him to Escalus for the promised whipping. Seeing Lucio, Pompey is certain that his best client will bail him out, but Lucio merely taunts him instead. The disguised Duke witnesses all this and is not impressed. He talks with Lucio, who points out that nobody knows where the Duke is, slanders Angelo, and implies that the Duke is well-known for having a taste for the ladies himself. The Duke reflects that even the virtuous cannot escape slander. Escalus brings Mistress Overdone off to prison, the bawd protesting all the while that she is being accused by Lucio, who has impregnated one of her ladies and promised to marry her, but is now denying it all. Escalus orders that Lucio be brought before him, and tells the Provost that Claudio is to be executed the next day without fail. The Duke talks with Escalus a little, asking him his opinion of his absent ruler, and Escalus offers an honest assessment. They discuss Claudio's case, and the Duke mentions that if Angelo is going to be so severe, it were best he was absolutely spotless himself.

Enter Elbow, Clown Pompey, and Officers to the Duke.

Elbow.
Nay, if there be no remedy for it but that you will needs buy and sell men and women like beasts, we shall have all the world drink brown and white bastard.

Vincentio, the Duke.
O heavens, what stuff is here?

Pompey.
'Twas never merry world since of two usuries the merriest was put down, and the worser allow'd by order of law; a furr'd gown to keep him warm; and furr'd with fox and lambskins too, to signify that craft, being richer than innocency, stands for the facing.

Elbow.
Come your way, sir. Bless you, good father friar.

Vincentio, the Duke.
And you, good brother father. What offense hath this man made you, sir?

Elbow.
Marry, sir, he hath offended the law; and, sir, we take him to be a thief too, sir, for we have found upon him, sir, a strange picklock, which we have sent to the deputy.

Vincentio, the Duke.
Fie, sirrah, a bawd, a wicked bawd!
The evil that thou causest to be done,
That is thy means to live. Do thou but think
What 'tis to cram a maw or clothe a back
From such a filthy vice; say to thyself,
From their abominable and beastly touches
I drink, I eat, array myself, and live.
Canst thou believe thy living is a life,
So stinkingly depending? Go mend, go mend.

Pompey.
Indeed, it does stink in some sort, sir; but yet, sir, I would prove—

Vincentio, the Duke.
Nay, if the devil have given thee proofs for sin,
Thou wilt prove his. Take him to prison, officer.
Correction and instruction must both work
Ere this rude beast will profit.

Elbow.
He must before the deputy, sir, he has given him warning. The deputy cannot abide a whore-master. If he be a whoremonger, and comes before him, he were as good go a mile on his errand.

Act 3, Scene 2

Vincentio, the Duke.
That we were all, as some would seem to be,
From our faults, as faults from seeming, free!

Enter Lucio.

Elbow.
His neck will come to your waist—a cord, sir.

Pompey.
I spy comfort, I cry bail. Here's a gentleman, and a friend of mine.

Lucio.
How now, noble Pompey? What, at the wheels of Caesar? Art thou led in triumph? What, is there none of Pygmalion's images newly made woman to be had now, for putting the hand in the pocket and extracting it clutch'd? What reply? Ha? What say'st thou to this tune, matter, and method? Is't not drown'd i' th' last rain? Ha? What say'st thou, Trot? Is the world as it was, man? Which is the way? Is it sad, and few words? Or how? The trick of it?

Vincentio, the Duke.
Still thus, and thus; still worse!

Lucio.
How doth my dear morsel, thy mistress? Procures she still? Ha?

Pompey.
Troth, sir, she hath eaten up all her beef, and she is herself in the tub.

Lucio.
Why, 'tis good; it is the right of it; it must be so. Ever your fresh whore and your powder'd bawd, an unshunn'd consequence; it must be so. Art going to prison, Pompey?

Pompey.
Yes, faith, sir.

Lucio.
Why, 'tis not amiss, Pompey. Farewell. Go say I sent thee thither. For debt, Pompey? Or how?

Elbow.
For being a bawd, for being a bawd.

Lucio.
Well, then imprison him. If imprisonment be the due of a bawd, why, 'tis his right. Bawd is he doubtless, and of antiquity too; bawd-born. Farewell, good Pompey. Commend me to the prison, Pompey. You will turn good husband now, Pompey, you will keep the house.

Pompey.
I hope, sir, your good worship will be my bail.

Lucio.
No indeed will I not, Pompey, it is not the wear. I will pray, Pompey, to increase your bondage. If you take it not patiently, why, your mettle is the more. Adieu, trusty Pompey. Bless you, friar.

Vincentio, the Duke.
And you.

Lucio.
Does Bridget paint still, Pompey? Ha?

Elbow.
Come your ways, sir, come.

Pompey.
You will not bail me then, sir?

Lucio.
Then, Pompey, nor now. What news abroad, friar? What news?

Elbow.
Come your ways, sir, come.

Lucio.
Go to kennel, Pompey, go.

Exeunt Elbow, Pompey, and Officers.

What news, friar, of the Duke?

Vincentio, the Duke.
I know none. Can you tell me of any?

Lucio.
Some say he is with the Emperor of Russia; other some, he is in Rome; but where is he, think you?

Vincentio, the Duke.
I know not where; but wheresoever, I wish him well.

Lucio.
It was a mad fantastical trick of him to steal from the state, and usurp the beggary he was never born to. Lord Angelo dukes it well in his absence; he puts transgression to't.

Vincentio, the Duke.
He does well in't.

Lucio.
A little more lenity to lechery would do no harm in him. Something too crabbed that way, friar.

Vincentio, the Duke.
It is too general a vice, and severity must cure it.

Lucio.
Yes, in good sooth, the vice is of a great kindred; it is well allied; but it is impossible to extirp it quite, friar, till eating and drinking be put down. They say this Angelo was not made by man and woman after this downright way of creation. Is it true, think you?

Vincentio, the Duke.
How should he be made then?

Lucio.
Some report a sea-maid spawn'd him; some, that he was begot between two stock-fishes. But it is certain that when he makes water his urine is congeal'd ice, that I know to be true; and he is a motion generative, that's infallible.

Vincentio, the Duke.
You are pleasant, sir, and speak apace.

Lucio.
Why, what a ruthless thing is this in him, for the rebellion of a codpiece to take away the life of a man! Would the Duke that is absent have done this? Ere he would have hang'd a man for the getting a hundred bastards, he would have paid for the nursing a thousand. He had some feeling of the sport; he knew the service, and that instructed him to mercy.

Vincentio, the Duke.
I never heard the absent Duke much detected for women, he was not inclin'd that way.

Lucio.
O, sir, you are deceiv'd.

Vincentio, the Duke.
'Tis not possible.

Lucio.
Who? Not the Duke? Yes, your beggar of fifty; and his use was to put a ducat in her clack-dish. The Duke had crotchets in him. He would be drunk too, that let me inform you.

Vincentio, the Duke.
You do him wrong, surely.

Lucio.
Sir, I was an inward of his. A shy fellow was the Duke, and I believe I know the cause of his withdrawing.

Vincentio, the Duke.
What, I prithee, might be the cause?

Lucio.
No, pardon; 'tis a secret must be lock'd within the teeth and the lips. But this I can let you understand, the greater file of the subject held the Duke to be wise.

Vincentio, the Duke.
Wise? Why, no question but he was.

Lucio.
A very superficial, ignorant, unweighing fellow.

Vincentio, the Duke.
Either this is envy in you, folly, or mistaking. The very stream of his life, and the business he hath helm'd, must, upon a warranted need, give him a better proclamation. Let him be but testimonied in his own bringings-forth, and he shall appear to the envious a scholar, a statesman, and a soldier. Therefore you speak unskillfully; or, if your knowledge be more, it is much dark'ned in your malice.

Lucio.
Sir, I know him, and I love him.

Vincentio, the Duke.
Love talks with better knowledge, and knowledge with dearer love.

Lucio.
Come, sir, I know what I know.

Vincentio, the Duke.
I can hardly believe that, since you know not what you speak. But if ever the Duke return (as our prayers are he may), let me desire you to make your answer

before him. If it be honest you have spoke, you have courage to maintain it. I am bound to call upon you, and I pray you your name?

Lucio.
Sir, my name is Lucio, well known to the Duke.

Vincentio, the Duke.
He shall know you better, sir, if I may live to report you.

Lucio.
I fear you not.

Vincentio, the Duke.
O, you hope the Duke will return no more; or you imagine me too unhurtful an opposite. But indeed I can do you little harm; you'll forswear this again.

Lucio.
I'll be hang'd first; thou art deceiv'd in me, friar. But no more of this. Canst thou tell if Claudio die tomorrow, or no?

Vincentio, the Duke.
Why should he die, sir?

Lucio.
Why? For filling a bottle with a tun-dish. I would the Duke we talk of were return'd again. This ungenitur'd agent will unpeople the province with continency. Sparrows must not build in his house-eaves, because they are lecherous. The Duke yet would have dark deeds darkly answer'd, he would never bring them to light. Would he were return'd! Marry, this Claudio is condemn'd for untrussing. Farewell, good friar, I prithee pray for me. The Duke (I say to thee again) would eat mutton on Fridays. He's now past it, yet (and I say to thee) he would mouth with a beggar, though she smelt brown bread and garlic. Say that I said so. Farewell.

Exit.

Vincentio, the Duke.
No might nor greatness in mortality
Can censure scape; back-wounding calumny
The whitest virtue strikes. What king so strong
Can tie the gall up in the slanderous tongue?
But who comes here?

Enter Escalus, Provost, and Officers with Bawd Mistress Overdone.

Escalus.
Go, away with her to prison.

Mistress Overdone.
Good my lord, be good to me, your honor is accounted a merciful man. Good my lord.

Escalus.
Double and treble admonition, and still forfeit in the same kind! This would make mercy swear and play the tyrant.

Provost.
A bawd of eleven years' continuance, may it please your honor.

Mistress Overdone.
My lord, this is one Lucio's information against me. Mistress Kate Keepdown was with child by him in the Duke's time; he promis'd her marriage. His child is a year and a quarter old come Philip and Jacob. I have kept it myself; and see how he goes about to abuse me!

Escalus.
That fellow is a fellow of much license; let him be call'd before us. Away with her to prison! Go to, no more words.

Exeunt Officers with Mistress Overdone.

Provost, my brother Angelo will not be alter'd, Claudio must die tomorrow. Let him be furnish'd with divines, and have all charitable preparation. If my brother wrought by my pity, it should not be so with him.

Provost.
So please you, this friar hath been with him, and advis'd him for th' entertainment of death.

Escalus.
Good even, good father.

Vincentio, the Duke.
Bliss and goodness on you!

Escalus.
Of whence are you?

Vincentio, the Duke.
Not of this country, though my chance is now
To use it for my time. I am a brother
Of gracious order, late come from the See,
In special business from his Holiness.

Escalus.
What news abroad i' th' world?

Vincentio, the Duke.
None, but that there is so great a fever on goodness, that the dissolution of it must cure it. Novelty is only in request, and, as it is, as dangerous to be ag'd in any kind of course, as it is virtuous to be constant in any undertaking. There is scarce truth enough alive to make societies secure, but security enough to make fellowships accurs'd. Much upon this riddle runs the wisdom of the world. This news is old enough, yet it is every day's news. I pray you, sir, of what disposition was the Duke?

Escalus.
One that, above all other strifes, contended especially to know himself.

Vincentio, the Duke.
What pleasure was he given to?

Escalus.
Rather rejoicing to see another merry, than merry at any thing which profess'd to make him rejoice; a gentleman of all temperance. But leave we him to his events, with a prayer they may prove prosperous, and let me desire to know how you find Claudio prepar'd. I am made to understand that you have lent him visitation.

Vincentio, the Duke.
He professes to have receiv'd no sinister measure from his judge, but most willingly humbles himself to the determination of justice; yet had he fram'd to himself (by the instruction of his frailty) many deceiving promises of life, which I (by my good leisure) have discredited to him, and now is he resolv'd to die.

Escalus.
You have paid the heavens your function, and the prisoner the very debt of your calling. I have labor'd for the poor gentleman to the extremest shore of my modesty, but my brother-justice have I found so severe, that he hath forc'd me to tell him he is indeed Justice.

Vincentio, the Duke.
If his own life answer the straitness of his proceeding, it shall become him well; wherein if he chance to fail, he hath sentenc'd himself.

Escalus.
I am going to visit the prisoner. Fare you well.

Vincentio, the Duke.
Peace be with you!

Exeunt Escalus and Provost.

He who the sword of heaven will bear
Should be as holy as severe;
Pattern in himself to know,
Grace to stand, and virtue go;
More nor less to others paying
Than by self-offenses weighing.
Shame to him whose cruel striking
Kills for faults of his own liking!
Twice treble shame on Angelo,
To weed my vice, and let his grow!
O, what may man within him hide,
Though angel on the outward side!
How may likeness made in crimes,
Making practice on the times,
To draw with idle spiders' strings
Most ponderous and substantial things!
Craft against vice I must apply.
With Angelo tonight shall lie
His old betrothed (but despised);
So disguise shall by th' disguised
Pay with falsehood false exacting,
And perform an old contracting.

Exit.

Act 4
Scene 1
The moated grange at St. Luke's.

(Mariana; Boy; Duke; Isabella)

The Duke comes to visit Mariana, and Isabella joins them. She has made the arrangement for a meeting with Angelo, which is to be brief and conducted entirely in the dark. Mariana agrees to the plan to go in Isabella's place and to remind Angelo to spare Claudio; the Duke reassures her that since she and Angelo were affianced, there is no sin in all this.

Enter Mariana, and Boy singing.
Song.

Boy.
Take, O, take those lips away,
That so sweetly were forsworn,
And those eyes, the break of day,
Lights that do mislead the morn;
But my kisses bring again, bring again,
Seals of love, but seal'd in vain, seal'd in vain.

Enter Duke disguised as a friar.

Mariana.
Break off thy song, and haste thee quick away.
Here comes a man of comfort, whose advice
Hath often still'd my brawling discontent.

Exit Boy.

I cry you mercy, sir, and well could wish
You had not found me here so musical.
Let me excuse me, and believe me so,
My mirth it much displeas'd, but pleas'd my woe.

Vincentio, the Duke.
'Tis good; though music oft hath such a charm
To make bad good, and good provoke to harm.
I pray you tell me, hath any body inquir'd for me here
today? Much upon this time have I promis'd here to
meet.

Mariana.
You have not been inquir'd after. I have sat here all
day.

Enter Isabel.

Vincentio, the Duke.
I do constantly believe you. The time is come even
now. I shall crave your forbearance a little. May be I
will call upon you anon for some advantage to yourself.

Mariana.
I am always bound to you.

Exit.

Vincentio, the Duke.
Very well met, and well come.
What is the news from this good deputy?

Isabella.
He hath a garden circummur'd with brick,
Whose western side is with a vineyard back'd;
And to that vineyard is a planched gate,
That makes his opening with this bigger key.
This other doth command a little door,
Which from the vineyard to the garden leads;
There have I made my promise upon the heavy
Middle of the night to call upon him.

Vincentio, the Duke.
But shall you on your knowledge find this way?

Isabella.
I have ta'en a due and wary note upon't.
With whispering and most guilty diligence,
In action all of precept, he did show me
The way twice o'er.

Vincentio, the Duke.
                    Are there no other tokens
Between you 'greed concerning her observance?

Isabella.
No; none but only a repair i' th' dark,
And that I have possess'd him my most stay
Can be but brief; for I have made him know
I have a servant comes with me along,
That stays upon me, whose persuasion is
I come about my brother.

Vincentio, the Duke.
                    'Tis well borne up.
I have not yet made known to Mariana
A word of this. What ho, within! Come forth!

Enter Mariana.

I pray you be acquainted with this maid,
She comes to do you good.

Isabella.
                    I do desire the like.

Vincentio, the Duke.
Do you persuade yourself that I respect you?

Mariana.
Good friar, I know you do, and have found it.

Vincentio, the Duke.
Take then this your companion by the hand,
Who hath a story ready for your ear.
I shall attend your leisure, but make haste,

The vaporous night approaches.

Mariana.
Will't please you walk aside?

Exit with Isabella.

Vincentio, the Duke.
O place and greatness! Millions of false eyes
Are stuck upon thee. Volumes of report
Run with these false, and most contrarious quest
Upon thy doings; thousand escapes of wit
Make thee the father of their idle dream,
And rack thee in their fancies.

Enter Mariana and Isabella.

Welcome, how agreed?

Isabella.
She'll take the enterprise upon her, father,
If you advise it.

Vincentio, the Duke.
                It is not my consent,
But my entreaty too.

Isabella.
                Little have you to say
When you depart from him, but soft and low,
"Remember now my brother."

Mariana.
                Fear me not.

Vincentio, the Duke.
Nor, gentle daughter, fear you not at all.
He is your husband on a pre-contract:
To bring you thus together 'tis no sin,
Sith that the justice of your title to him
Doth flourish the deceit. Come, let us go,
Our corn's to reap, for yet our tithe's to sow.

Exeunt.

Scene 2

A room in the prison.

(Provost; Pompey; Abhorson; Claudio; Duke; Messenger)

Pompey agrees to act as aid to the hangman, Abhorson, in return for his freedom. Abhorson is not best pleased at having to use a pimp as assistant, afraid this will dishonor the trade of executioner. The Duke arrives, waiting with the Provost for Claudio's reprieve to arrive; instead, a message from Angelo commands that Claudio be beheaded forthwith. The Duke pleads that Barnardine, another prisoner condemned to die that afternoon, should be executed instead and his head sent to Angelo. The Provost does not wish to disobey the direct order he received from Angelo until the Duke shows him a letter, signed and sealed by himself, announcing his return within two days. The Provost then consents.

Enter Provost and Clown Pompey.

Provost.
Come hither, sirrah; can you cut off a man's head?

Pompey.
If the man be a bachelor, sir, I can; but if he be a married man, he's his wive's head, and I can never cut off a woman's head.

Provost.
Come, sir, leave me your snatches, and yield me a direct answer. Tomorrow morning are to die Claudio and Barnardine. Here is in our prison a common executioner, who in his office lacks a helper. If you will take it on you to assist him, it shall redeem you from your gyves; if not, you shall have your full time of imprisonment, and your deliverance with an unpitied whipping, for you have been a notorious bawd.

Pompey.
Sir, I have been an unlawful bawd time out of mind, but yet I will be content to be a lawful hangman. I would be glad to receive some instruction from my fellow partner.

Provost.
What ho, Abhorson! Where's Abhorson there?

Enter Abhorson.

Abhorson.
Do you call, sir?

Provost.
Sirrah, here's a fellow will help you tomorrow in your execution. If you think it meet, compound with him by the year, and let him abide here with you; if not, use him for the present and dismiss him. He cannot plead his estimation with you; for he hath been a bawd.

Abhorson.
A bawd, sir? Fie upon him, he will discredit our mystery.

Provost.
Go to, sir, you weigh equally; a feather will turn the scale.

Exit.

Pompey.
Pray, sir, by your good favor—for surely, sir, a good favor you have, but that you have a hanging look—do you call, sir, your occupation a mystery?

Abhorson.
Ay, sir, a mystery.

Pompey.
Painting, sir, I have heard say, is a mystery; and your whores, sir, being members of my occupation, using painting, do prove my occupation a mystery; but what mystery there should be in hanging, if I should be hang'd, I cannot imagine.

Abhorson.
Sir, it is a mystery.

Pompey.
Proof.

Abhorson.
Every true man's apparel fits your thief. If it be too little for your thief, your true man thinks it big enough; if it be too big for your thief, your thief thinks it little enough; so every true man's apparel fits your thief.

Enter Provost.

Provost.
Are you agreed?

Pompey.
Sir, I will serve him; for I do find your hangman is a more penitent trade than your bawd: he doth oft'ner ask forgiveness.

Provost.
You, sirrah, provide your block and your axe tomorrow, four a' clock.

Abhorson.
Come on, bawd, I will instruct thee in my trade; follow.

Pompey.
I do desire to learn, sir; and I hope, if you have occasion to use me for your own turn, you shall find me yare; for truly, sir, for your kindness, I owe you a good turn.

Provost.
Call hither Barnardine and Claudio.

Exeunt Abhorson and Pompey.

Th' one has my pity; not a jot the other,
Being a murderer, though he were my brother.

Enter Claudio.

Look, here's the warrant, Claudio, for thy death.
'Tis now dead midnight, and by eight tomorrow
Thou must be made immortal. Where's Barnardine?

Claudio.
As fast lock'd up in sleep as guiltless labor
When it lies starkly in the traveler's bones.
He will not wake.

Provost.
                    Who can do good on him?
Well, go, prepare yourself.

Knocking within.

                    But hark, what noise?
Heaven give your spirits comfort!

Exit Claudio.

                    By and by.—
I hope it is some pardon or reprieve
For the most gentle Claudio.

Enter Duke disguised as a friar.

                    Welcome, father.

Vincentio, the Duke.
The best and wholesom'st spirits of the night
Envelop you, good Provost! Who call'd here of late?

Provost.
None since the curfew rung.

Vincentio, the Duke.
Not Isabel?

Provost.
                    No.

Vincentio, the Duke.
          They will then ere't be long.

Provost.
What comfort is for Claudio?

Vincentio, the Duke.
There's some in hope.

Provost.
                It is a bitter deputy.

Vincentio, the Duke.
Not so, not so; his life is parallel'd
Even with the stroke and line of his great justice.
He doth with holy abstinence subdue
That in himself which he spurs on his pow'r
To qualify in others. Were he meal'd with that
Which he corrects, then were he tyrannous,
But this being so, he's just.

Knocking within.
                Now are they come.

Exit Provost.

This is a gentle Provost: seldom when
The steeled jailer is the friend of men.

Knocking within.

How now? What noise? That spirit's possess'd with haste
That wounds th' unsisting postern with these strokes.

Enter Provost.

Provost.
There he must stay until the officer
Arise to let him in; he is call'd up.

Vincentio, the Duke.
Have you no countermand for Claudio yet,
But he must die tomorrow?

Provost.
                None, sir, none.

Vincentio, the Duke.
As near the dawning, Provost, as it is,
You shall hear more ere morning.

Provost.
Happily
You something know, yet I believe there comes
No countermand; no such example have we.
Besides, upon the very siege of justice
Lord Angelo hath to the public ear
Profess'd the contrary.

Enter a Messenger.
                This is his Lordship's man.

Vincentio, the Duke.
And here comes Claudio's pardon.

Messenger.
My lord hath sent you this note, and by me this further charge: that you swerve not from the smallest article of it, neither in time, matter, or other circumstance. Good morrow; for as I take it, it is almost day.

Provost.
I shall obey him.

Exit Messenger.

Vincentio, the Duke.

Aside.

This is his pardon, purchas'd by such sin
For which the pardoner himself is in.
Hence hath offense his quick celerity,
When it is borne in high authority.
When vice makes mercy, mercy's so extended,
That for the fault's love is th' offender friended.
Now, sir, what news?

Provost.
I told you: Lord Angelo (belike) thinking me remiss in mine office, awakens me with this unwonted putting-on, methinks strangely, for he hath not us'd it before.

Vincentio, the Duke.
Pray you let's hear.

Provost.

Reads the letter.

"Whatsoever you may hear to the contrary, let Claudio be executed by four of the clock, and in the afternoon

Barnardine. For my better satisfaction, let me have Claudio's head sent me by five. Let this be duly perform'd, with a thought that more depends on it than we must yet deliver. Thus fail not to do your office, as you will answer it at your peril." What say you to this, sir?

Vincentio, the Duke.
What is that Barnardine who is to be executed in th' afternoon?

Provost.
A Bohemian born; but here nurs'd up and bred, one that is a prisoner nine years old.

Vincentio, the Duke.
How came it that the absent Duke had not either deliver'd him to his liberty or executed him? I have heard it was ever his manner to do so.

Provost.
His friends still wrought reprieves for him; and indeed his fact, till now in the government of Lord Angelo, came not to an undoubtful proof.

Vincentio, the Duke.
It is now apparent?

Provost.
Most manifest, and not denied by himself.

Vincentio, the Duke.
Hath he borne himself penitently in prison? How seems he to be touch'd?

Provost.
A man that apprehends death no more dreadfully but as a drunken sleep, careless, reckless, and fearless of what's past, present, or to come; insensible of mortality, and desperately mortal.

Vincentio, the Duke.
He wants advice.

Provost.
He will hear none. He hath evermore had the liberty of the prison; give him leave to escape hence, he would not. Drunk many times a day, if not many days entirely drunk. We have very oft awak'd him, as if to carry him to execution, and show'd him a seeming warrant for it; it hath not mov'd him at all.

Vincentio, the Duke.
More of him anon. There is written in your brow, Provost, honesty and constancy; if I read it not truly, my ancient skill beguiles me; but in the boldness of my cunning, I will lay myself in hazard. Claudio, whom here you have warrant to execute, is no greater forfeit to the law than Angelo who hath sentenc'd him. To make you understand this in a manifested effect, I crave but four days' respite; for the which you are to do me both a present and a dangerous courtesy.

Provost.
Pray, sir, in what?

Vincentio, the Duke.
In the delaying death.

Provost.
Alack, how may I do it, having the hour limited, and an express command, under penalty, to deliver his head in the view of Angelo? I may make my case as Claudio's, to cross this in the smallest.

Vincentio, the Duke.
By the vow of mine order I warrant you, if my instructions may be your guide. Let this Barnardine be this morning executed, and his head borne to Angelo.

Provost.
Angelo hath seen them both, and will discover the favor.

Vincentio, the Duke.
O, death's a great disguiser, and you may add to it. Shave the head, and tie the beard, and say it was the desire of the penitent to be so bar'd before his death. You know the course is common. If any thing fall to you upon this, more than thanks and good fortune, by the saint whom I profess, I will plead against it with my life.

Provost.
Pardon me, good father, it is against my oath.

Vincentio, the Duke.
Were you sworn to the Duke, or to the deputy?

Provost.
To him, and to his substitutes.

Vincentio, the Duke.
You will think you have made no offense, if the Duke avouch the justice of your dealing?

Provost.
But what likelihood is in that?

Vincentio, the Duke.
Not a resemblance, but a certainty; yet since I see you fearful, that neither my coat, integrity, nor persuasion can with ease attempt you, I will go further than I meant, to pluck all fears out of you. Look you, sir, here is the hand and seal of the Duke; you know the character, I doubt not, and the signet is not strange to you.

Provost.
I know them both.

Vincentio, the Duke.
The contents of this is the return of the Duke. You shall anon over-read it at your pleasure; where you shall find, within these two days he will be here. This is a thing that Angelo knows not, for he this very day receives letters of strange tenor, perchance of the Duke's death, perchance entering into some monastery, but by chance nothing of what is writ. Look, th' unfolding star calls up the shepherd. Put not yourself into amazement how these things should be; all difficulties are but easy when they are known. Call your executioner, and off with Barnardine's head. I will give him a present shrift, and advise him for a better place. Yet you are amaz'd, but this shall absolutely resolve you. Come away, it is almost clear dawn.

Exeunt.

Scene 3

Another room in the prison.

(Pompey; Abhorson; Barnardine; Duke; Provost; Isabella; Lucio)

Pompey comments on how he already knows most of the prisoners, as they used to be clients at Mistress Overdone's. Abhorson orders Pompey to bring out Barnardine for execution, but the prisoner absolutely refuses to be beheaded today. The Provost points out to the Duke that the pirate Ragozine died in prison earlier, and that he looks a lot like Claudio; the Duke quickly agrees that the corpse's head should be chopped off and sent to Angelo instead. The Duke plans to order Angelo to meet him at his public return, so that he can deal with him. Isabella arrives to find out whether her brother has been spared, but the Duke tells her he has been executed. She raves, but he consoles her, promising that the Duke will be returning soon, and telling her to accuse Angelo when he does so. Lucio passes by and tells Isabella he is sorry for Claudio's death. Talking with the disguised Duke, he admits that he did indeed get a wench with child, but denied it to avoid having to marry her.

Enter Clown Pompey.

Pompey.
I am as well acquainted here as I was in our house of profession. One would think it were Mistress Overdone's own house, for here be many of her old customers. First, here's young Master Rash, he's in for a commodity of brown paper and old ginger, ninescore and seventeen pounds, of which he made five marks ready money. Marry, then ginger was not much in request, for the old women were all dead. Then is there here one Master Caper, at the suit of Master Three-pile the mercer, for some four suits of peach-color'd satin, which now peaches him a beggar. Then have we here young Dizzy, and young Master Deep-vow, and Master Copper-spur, and Master Starve-lackey the rapier and dagger man, and young Drop-heir that kill'd lusty Pudding, and Master Forthlight the tilter, and brave Master Shoe-tie the great traveler, and wild Half-can that stabb'd Pots, and I think forty more, all great doers in our trade, and are now "for the Lord's sake."

Enter Abhorson.

Abhorson.
Sirrah, bring Barnardine hither.

Pompey.
Master Barnardine! You must rise and be hang'd, Master Barnardine!

Abhorson.
What ho, Barnardine!

Barnardine.

Within.

A pox o' your throats! Who makes that noise there? What are you?

Pompey.
Your friends, sir, the hangman. You must be so good, sir, to rise, and be put to death.

Barnardine.

Within.

Away, you rogue, away! I am sleepy.

Abhorson.
Tell him he must awake, and that quickly too.

Pompey.
Pray, Master Barnardine, awake till you are executed, and sleep afterwards.

Abhorson.
Go in to him, and fetch him out.

Pompey.
He is coming, sir, he is coming. I hear his straw rustle.

Enter Barnardine.

Abhorson.
Is the axe upon the block, sirrah?

Pompey.
Very ready, sir.

Barnardine.
How now, Abhorson? What's the news with you?

Abhorson.
Truly, sir, I would desire you to clap into your prayers; for look you, the warrant's come.

Barnardine.
You rogue, I have been drinking all night, I am not fitted for't.

Pompey.
O, the better, sir; for he that drinks all night, and is hang'd betimes in the morning, may sleep the sounder all the next day.

Enter Duke disguised as a friar.

Abhorson.
Look you, sir, here comes your ghostly father. Do we jest now, think you?

Vincentio, the Duke.
Sir, induc'd by my charity, and hearing how hastily you are to depart, I am come to advise you, comfort you, and pray with you.

Barnardine.
Friar, not I; I have been drinking hard all night, and I will have more time to prepare me, or they shall beat out my brains with billets. I will not consent to die this day, that's certain.

Vincentio, the Duke.
O sir, you must; and therefore I beseech you
Look forward on the journey you shall go.

Barnardine.
I swear I will not die today for any man's persuasion.

Vincentio, the Duke.
But hear you—

Barnardine.
Not a word. If you have any thing to say to me, come to my ward; for thence will not I today.

Exit.
Enter Provost.

Vincentio, the Duke.
Unfit to live, or die; O gravel heart!
After him, fellows, bring him to the block.

Exeunt Abhorson and Pompey.

Provost.
Now, sir, how do you find the prisoner?

Vincentio, the Duke.
A creature unprepar'd, unmeet for death;
And to transport him in the mind he is
Were damnable.

Provost.
           Here in the prison, father,
There died this morning of a cruel fever
One Ragozine, a most notorious pirate,
A man of Claudio's years; his beard and head
Just of his color. What if we do omit
This reprobate till he were well inclin'd,
And satisfy the deputy with the visage
Of Ragozine, more like to Claudio?

Vincentio, the Duke.
O, 'tis an accident that heaven provides!
Dispatch it presently, the hour draws on
Prefix'd by Angelo. See this be done,
And sent according to command, whiles I
Persuade this rude wretch willingly to die.

Provost.
This shall be done, good father, presently.
But Barnardine must die this afternoon;
And how shall we continue Claudio,
To save me from the danger that might come
If he were known alive?

Vincentio, the Duke.
               Let this be done:
Put them in secret holds, both Barnardine and Claudio.
Ere twice the sun hath made his journal greeting
To yond generation, you shall find
Your safety manifested.

Provost.
I am your free dependent.

Vincentio, the Duke.
Quick, dispatch, and send the head to Angelo.

Exit Provost.

Now will I write letters to Angelo
(The Provost, he shall bear them), whose contents
Shall witness to him I am near at home;
And that by great injunctions I am bound
To enter publicly. Him I'll desire
To meet me at the consecrated fount,
A league below the city; and from thence,
By cold gradation and well-balanc'd form,
We shall proceed with Angelo.

Enter Provost with Ragozine's head.

Provost.
Here is the head, I'll carry it myself.

Vincentio, the Duke.
Convenient is it. Make a swift return,
For I would commune with you of such things
That want no ear but yours.

Provost.
               I'll make all speed.

Exit.

Isabella.

Within.

Peace, ho, be here!

Vincentio, the Duke.
The tongue of Isabel. She's come to know
If yet her brother's pardon be come hither.
But I will keep her ignorant of her good,
To make her heavenly comforts of despair,
When it is least expected.

Enter Isabella.

Isabella.
               Ho, by your leave!

Vincentio, the Duke.
Good morning to you, fair and gracious daughter.

Isabella.
The better, given me by so holy a man.
Hath yet the deputy sent my brother's pardon?

Vincentio, the Duke.
He hath releas'd him, Isabel, from the world,
His head is off, and sent to Angelo.

Isabella.
Nay, but it is not so.

Vincentio, the Duke.
               It is no other.
Show your wisdom, daughter, in your close patience.

Isabella.
O, I will to him, and pluck out his eyes!

Vincentio, the Duke.
You shall not be admitted to his sight.

Isabella.
Unhappy Claudio! Wretched Isabel!
Injurious world! Most damned Angelo!

Vincentio, the Duke.
This nor hurts him, nor profits you a jot.
Forbear it therefore, give your cause to heaven.
Mark what I say, which you shall find
By every syllable a faithful verity.
The Duke comes home tomorrow—nay, dry your eyes—
One of our covent, and his confessor,
Gives me this instance: already he hath carried
Notice to Escalus and Angelo,
Who do prepare to meet him at the gates,
There to give up their pow'r. If you can pace your wisdom
In that good path that I would wish it go,

And you shall have your bosom on this wretch,
Grace of the Duke, revenges to your heart,
And general honor.

Isabella.
                    I am directed by you.

Vincentio, the Duke.
This letter then to Friar Peter give;
'Tis that he sent me of the Duke's return.
Say, by this token, I desire his company
At Mariana's house tonight. Her cause and yours
I'll perfect him withal, and he shall bring you
Before the Duke; and to the head of Angelo
Accuse him home and home. For my poor self,
I am combined by a sacred vow,
And shall be absent. Wend you with this letter.
Command these fretting waters from your eyes
With a light heart; trust not my holy order
If I pervert your course. Who's here?

Enter Lucio.

Lucio.
Good even. Friar, where's the Provost?

Vincentio, the Duke.
Not within, sir.

Lucio.
O pretty Isabella, I am pale at mine heart to see thine eyes so red; thou must be patient. I am fain to dine and sup with water and bran; I dare not for my head fill my belly; one fruitful meal would set me to't. But they say the Duke will be here tomorrow. By my troth, Isabel, I lov'd thy brother. If the old fantastical Duke of dark corners had been at home, he had liv'd.

Exit Isabella.

Vincentio, the Duke.
Sir, the Duke is marvelous little beholding to your reports, but the best is, he lives not in them.

Lucio.
Friar, thou knowest not the Duke so well as I do; he's a better woodman than thou tak'st him for.

Vincentio, the Duke.
Well; you'll answer this one day. Fare ye well.

Lucio.
Nay, tarry, I'll go along with thee. I can tell thee pretty tales of the Duke.

Vincentio, the Duke.
You have told me too many of him already, sir, if they be true; if not true, none were enough.

Lucio.
I was once before him for getting a wench with child.

Vincentio, the Duke.
Did you such a thing?

Lucio.
Yes, marry, did I; but I was fain to forswear it. They would else have married me to the rotten medlar.

Vincentio, the Duke.
Sir, your company is fairer than honest. Rest you well.

Lucio.
By my troth, I'll go with thee to the lane's end. If bawdy talk offend you, we'll have very little of it. Nay, friar, I am a kind of bur, I shall stick.

Exeunt.

Scene 4

A room in Angelo's house.

(Angelo; Escalus)

Angelo and Escalus discuss the Duke's imminent homecoming, somewhat confused about his instructions. Angelo secretly repents of his misdeeds, admitting to himself that he had Claudio executed only out of fear that he would try to revenge his sister's dishonor.

Enter Angelo and Escalus.

Escalus.
Every letter he hath writ hath disvouch'd other.

Angelo.
In most uneven and distracted manner. His actions show much like to madness, pray heaven his wisdom be not tainted! And why meet him at the gates, and redeliver our authorities there?

Escalus.
I guess not.

Angelo.
And why should we proclaim it in an hour before his ent'ring, that if any crave redress of injustice, they should exhibit their petitions in the street?

Escalus.
He shows his reason for that: to have a dispatch of complaints, and to deliver us from devices hereafter, which shall then have no power to stand against us.

Angelo.
Well; I beseech you let it be proclaim'd betimes i' th' morn. I'll call you at your house. Give notice to such men of sort and suit as are to meet him.

Escalus.
I shall, sir. Fare you well.

Angelo.
Good night.

Exit Escalus.

This deed unshapes me quite, makes me unpregnant
And dull to all proceedings. A deflow'red maid!
And by an eminent body that enforc'd
The law against it! But that her tender shame
Will not proclaim against her maiden loss,
How might she tongue me! Yet reason dares her no,
For my authority bears of a credent bulk,
That no particular scandal once can touch
But it confounds the breather. He should have liv'd,
Save that his riotous youth with dangerous sense
Might in the times to come have ta'en revenge,
By so receiving a dishonor'd life
With ransom of such shame. Would yet he had liv'd!
Alack, when once our grace we have forgot,
Nothing goes right—we would, and we would not.

Exit.

Scene 5

Fields without the town.

(Duke; Friar Peter; Varrius)

The Duke, now dressed as himself again, arranges his entrance to Vienna, giving Friar Peter letters that are to be publicly delivered to him at the right moment, and sending him to summon some of his lords.

Enter Duke in his own habit and Friar Peter.

Vincentio, the Duke.
These letters at fit time deliver me.

Giving letters.

The Provost knows our purpose and our plot.
The matter being afoot, keep your instruction,
And hold you ever to our special drift,
Though sometimes you do blench from this to that,
As cause doth minister. Go call at Flavio's house,
And tell him where I stay. Give the like notice
To Valentius, Rowland, and to Crassus,
And bid them bring the trumpets to the gate.
But send me Flavius first.

Friar Peter Thomas.
                  It shall be speeded well.

Exit.
Enter Varrius.

Vincentio, the Duke.
I thank thee, Varrius, thou hast made good haste.
Come, we will walk. There's other of our friends
Will greet us here anon. My gentle Varrius!

Exeunt.

Scene 6

A street near the city gate.

(Isabella; Mariana; Friar Peter)

Mariana and Isabella discuss how they will accuse Angelo. Friar Peter enters to tell them he has found them a good place to stand along the Duke's route, where they cannot miss him.

Enter Isabella and Mariana.

Isabella.
To speak so indirectly I am loath.
I would say the truth, but to accuse him so,
That is your part. Yet I am advis'd to do it,
He says, to veil full purpose.

Mariana.
                Be rul'd by him.

Isabella.
Besides, he tells me that if peradventure
He speak against me on the adverse side,
I should not think it strange, for 'tis a physic

That's bitter to sweet end.

Enter Friar Peter.

Mariana.
I would Friar Peter—

Isabella.
                O, peace, the friar is come.

Friar Peter Thomas.
Come, I have found you out a stand most fit,
Where you may have such vantage on the Duke,
He shall not pass you. Twice have the trumpets sounded;
The generous and gravest citizens
Have hent the gates, and very near upon
The Duke is ent'ring; therefore hence away!

Exeunt.

Act 5

Scene 1

At the city gate.

(Duke; Varrius; Lords; Angelo; Escalus; Lucio; Provost; Officers; Citizens; Friar Peter; Isabella; Mariana; Attendant; Barnardine; Claudio; Julietta)

The Duke returns, meeting Angelo and Escalus and praising them. As he does so, Isabella steps forward and calls for justice against Angelo. Angelo suggests that she has been driven mad by her brother's death. As Isabella tells her tale, Lucio ceaselessly interrupts, despite being told to keep his mouth shut. The Duke pretends that he does not believe Isabella, and threatens to have her sent to prison; she names the Friar who advised her to make this protest, and the Duke orders that he be found. Lucio says that he knows the Friar, and that the latter slandered the Duke, though Friar Peter denies this. Mariana is brought in veiled, promising to free Angelo from the charge of adultery by revealing that in fact, he slept with her, his promised bride. Angelo denies this as well. The Duke leaves Angelo and Escalus in charge of the trial as he slips off on some important business. Disguised as the Friar, he returns. Escalus takes over his interrogation and soon sentences him to jail for slandering the state. The Provost attempts to take the Friar away, but he struggles enough that Lucio must help, in the course of which Lucio pulls off the Friar's hood, revealing that he is in fact the Duke. He immediately takes over the court, warns Lucio that they shall have a chat, forgives Escalus for what he has said, and asks Angelo if he has anything to say for himself. All Angelo can do is beg that he be executed. He is sent off to marry Mariana on admitting that he was contracted to her. In his absence, the Duke apologizes to Isabella for Claudio's death, saying that things went faster than he'd anticipated. When the now-married Angelo and Mariana are brought back, the Duke orders that Angelo be taken away and beheaded at once. Mariana begs for his life, but the Duke is merciless until Mariana manages to convince Isabella to plead for Angelo. The Duke then has the Provost bring in Barnardine, Claudio with a cover around his head, and Juliet. The Duke pardons Barnardine, then has Claudio unmasked; restoring her brother to her, he asks Isabella to marry him. He then turns his attention to Lucio, and while sparing his life, orders that he marry the prostitute he got pregnant. After thanking everybody, the Duke again asks Isabella to marry him. What answer she gives is unknown.

Flourish. Enter Duke, Varrius, Lords, Angelo, Escalus, Lucio, Provost, Officers, Citizens at several doors.

Vincentio, the Duke.
My very worthy cousin, fairly met!
Our old and faithful friend, we are glad to see you.

Both Angelo and Escalus.
Happy return be to your royal Grace!

Vincentio, the Duke.
Many and hearty thankings to you both.
We have made inquiry of you, and we hear
Such goodness of your justice, that our soul
Cannot but yield you forth to public thanks,
Forerunning more requital.

Angelo.
                You make my bonds still greater.

Vincentio, the Duke.
O, your desert speaks loud, and I should wrong it
To lock it in the wards of covert bosom,
When it deserves with characters of brass
A forted residence 'gainst the tooth of time
And razure of oblivion. Give me your hand,
And let the subject see, to make them know
That outward courtesies would fain proclaim
Favors that keep within. Come, Escalus,
You must walk by us on our other hand;
And good supporters are you.

Enter Friar Peter and Isabella.

Friar Peter Thomas.
Now is your time: speak loud, and kneel before him.

Isabella.
Justice, O royal Duke! Vail your regard
Upon a wrong'd—I would fain have said a maid!
O worthy Prince, dishonor not your eye
By throwing it on any other object,
Till you have heard me in my true complaint,
And given me justice, justice, justice, justice!

Vincentio, the Duke.
Relate your wrongs. In what? By whom? Be brief.
Here is Lord Angelo shall give you justice;
Reveal yourself to him.

Isabella.
                    O worthy Duke,
You bid me seek redemption of the devil.
Hear me yourself; for that which I must speak
Must either punish me, not being believ'd,
Or wring redress from you. Hear me, O hear me, here.

Angelo.
My lord, her wits, I fear me, are not firm.
She hath been a suitor to me for her brother,
Cut off by course of justice—

Isabella.
                    By course of justice!

Angelo.
And she will speak most bitterly and strange.

Isabella.
Most strange! But yet most truly will I speak:
That Angelo's forsworn, is it not strange?
That Angelo's a murderer, is't not strange?
That Angelo is an adulterous thief,
An hypocrite, a virgin-violator,
Is it not strange? And strange?

Vincentio, the Duke.
              Nay, it is ten times strange.

Isabella.
It is not truer he is Angelo
Than this is all as true as it is strange;
Nay, it is ten times true, for truth is truth
To th' end of reck'ning.

Vincentio, the Duke.
              Away with her! Poor soul,
She speaks this in th' infirmity of sense.

Isabella.
O Prince, I conjure thee, as thou believ'st
There is another comfort than this world,
That thou neglect me not, with that opinion
That I am touch'd with madness. Make not impossible
That which but seems unlike; 'tis not impossible
But one the wicked'st caitiff on the ground,
May seem as shy, as grave, as just, as absolute
As Angelo. Even so may Angelo,
In all his dressings, caracts, titles, forms,
Be an arch-villain. Believe it, royal Prince,
If he be less, he's nothing, but he's more,
Had I more name for badness.

Vincentio, the Duke.
              By mine honesty,
If she be mad, as I believe no other,
Her madness hath the oddest frame of sense,
Such a dependency of thing on thing,
As e'er I heard in madness.

Isabella.
              O gracious Duke,
Harp not on that; nor do not banish reason
For inequality, but let your reason serve
To make the truth appear, where it seems hid,
And hide the false seems true.

Vincentio, the Duke.
              Many that are not mad
Have sure more lack of reason. What would you say?

Isabella.
I am the sister of one Claudio,
Condemn'd upon the act of fornication
To lose his head, condemn'd by Angelo.
I (in probation of a sisterhood)
Was sent to by my brother; one Lucio
As then the messenger—

Lucio.
              That's I, and't like your Grace.
I came to her from Claudio, and desir'd her
To try her gracious fortune with Lord Angelo,
For her poor brother's pardon.

Isabella.
              That's he indeed.

Vincentio, the Duke.

To Lucio.

You were not bid to speak.

Lucio.
                No, my good lord,
Nor wish'd to hold my peace.

Vincentio, the Duke.
                  I wish you now then.
Pray you take note of it; and when you have
A business for yourself, pray heaven you then
Be perfect.

Lucio.
              I warrant your honor.

Vincentio, the Duke.
The warrant's for yourself; take heed to't.

Isabella.
This gentleman told somewhat of my tale—

Lucio.
Right.

Vincentio, the Duke.
It may be right, but you are i' the wrong
To speak before your time. Proceed.

Isabella.
                    I went
To this pernicious caitiff deputy—

Vincentio, the Duke.
That's somewhat madly spoken.

Isabella.
                  Pardon it,
The phrase is to the matter.

Vincentio, the Duke.
Mended again. The matter; proceed.

Isabella.
In brief, to set the needless process by—
How I persuaded, how I pray'd, and kneel'd,
How he refell'd me, and how I replied
(For this was of much length)—the vild conclusion
I now begin with grief and shame to utter.
He would not, but by gift of my chaste body
To his concupiscible intemperate lust,
Release my brother; and after much debatement,
My sisterly remorse confutes mine honor,
And I did yield to him; but the next morn betimes,
His purpose surfeiting, he sends a warrant
For my poor brother's head.

Vincentio, the Duke.
                This is most likely!

Isabella.
O that it were as like as it is true!

Vincentio, the Duke.
By heaven, fond wretch, thou know'st not what thou speak'st,
Or else thou art suborn'd against his honor
In hateful practice. First, his integrity
Stands without blemish; next, it imports no reason
That with such vehemency he should pursue
Faults proper to himself. If he had so offended,
He would have weigh'd thy brother by himself,
And not have cut him off. Some one hath set you on;
Confess the truth, and say by whose advice
Thou cam'st here to complain.

Isabella.
                And is this all?
Then, O you blessed ministers above,
Keep me in patience, and with ripened time
Unfold the evil which is here wrapp'd up
In countenance! Heaven shield your Grace from woe,
As I, thus wrong'd, hence unbelieved go!

Vincentio, the Duke.
I know you'ld fain be gone. An officer!
To prison with her! Shall we thus permit
A blasting and a scandalous breath to fall
On him so near us? This needs must be a practice.
Who knew of your intent and coming hither?

Isabella.
One that I would were here, Friar Lodowick.

Vincentio, the Duke.
A ghostly father, belike. Who knows that Lodowick?

Lucio.
My lord, I know him, 'tis a meddling friar.
I do not like the man; had he been lay, my lord,
For certain words he spake against your Grace
In your retirement, I had swing'd him soundly.

Vincentio, the Duke.
Words against me? This' a good friar, belike!
And to set on this wretched woman here
Against our substitute! Let this friar be found.

Lucio.
But yesternight, my lord, she and that friar,
I saw them at the prison. A saucy friar,
A very scurvy fellow.

Friar Peter Thomas.
Blessed be your royal Grace!
I have stood by, my lord, and I have heard
Your royal ear abus'd. First, hath this woman
Most wrongfully accus'd your substitute,
Who is as free from touch or soil with her
As she from one ungot.

Vincentio, the Duke.
     We did believe no less.
Know you that Friar Lodowick that she speaks of?

Friar Peter Thomas.
I know him for a man divine and holy,
Not scurvy, nor a temporary meddler,
As he's reported by this gentleman;
And on my trust, a man that never yet
Did (as he vouches) misreport your Grace.

Lucio.
My lord, most villainously, believe it.

Friar Peter Thomas.
Well; he in time may come to clear himself;
But at this instant he is sick, my lord,
Of a strange fever. Upon his mere request,
Being come to knowledge that there was complaint
Intended 'gainst Lord Angelo, came I hither,
To speak as from his mouth, what he doth know
Is true and false; and what he with his oath
And all probation will make up full clear,
Whensoever he's convented. First, for this woman,
To justify this worthy nobleman,
So vulgarly and personally accus'd,
Her shall you hear disproved to her eyes,
Till she herself confess it.

Vincentio, the Duke.
     Good friar, let's hear it.

Isabella is carried off guarded.

Do you not smile at this, Lord Angelo?
O heaven, the vanity of wretched fools!
Give us some seats. Come, cousin Angelo,
In this I'll be impartial. Be you judge
Of your own cause.

Enter Mariana veiled.

     Is this the witness, friar?
First, let her show her face, and after speak.

Mariana.
Pardon, my lord, I will not show my face
Until my husband bid me.

Vincentio, the Duke.
What, are you married?

Mariana.
No, my lord.

Vincentio, the Duke.
Are you a maid?

Mariana.
No, my lord.

Vincentio, the Duke.
A widow then?

Mariana.
Neither, my lord.

Vincentio, the Duke.
Why, you are nothing then: neither maid, widow, nor wife?

Lucio.
My lord, she may be a punk; for many of them are neither maid, widow, nor wife.

Vincentio, the Duke.
Silence that fellow. I would he had some cause
To prattle for himself.

Lucio.
Well, my lord.

Mariana.
My lord, I do confess I ne'er was married,
And I confess besides I am no maid.
I have known my husband, yet my husband
Knows not that ever he knew me.

Lucio.
He was drunk then, my lord, it can be no better.

Vincentio, the Duke.
For the benefit of silence, would thou wert so too!

Lucio.
Well, my lord.

Vincentio, the Duke.
This is no witness for Lord Angelo.

Mariana.
Now I come to't, my lord.
She that accuses him of fornication,
In self-same manner doth accuse my husband,
And charges him, my lord, with such a time
When I'll depose I had him in mine arms
With all th' effect of love.

Angelo.
Charges she more than me?

Mariana.
              Not that I know.

Vincentio, the Duke.
No? You say your husband.

Mariana.
Why, just, my lord, and that is Angelo,
Who thinks he knows that he ne'er knew my body,
But knows he thinks that he knows Isabel's.

Angelo.
This is a strange abuse. Let's see thy face.

Mariana.
My husband bids me, now I will unmask.

Unveiling.

This is that face, thou cruel Angelo,
Which once thou swor'st was worth the looking on;
This is the hand which, with a vow'd contract,
Was fast belock'd in thine; this is the body
That took away the match from Isabel,
And did supply thee at thy garden-house
In her imagin'd person.

Vincentio, the Duke.
              Know you this woman?

Lucio.
Carnally, she says.

Vincentio, the Duke.
              Sirrah, no more!

Lucio.
Enough, my lord.

Angelo.
My lord, I must confess I know this woman,
And five years since there was some speech of marriage
Betwixt myself and her; which was broke off,
Partly for that her promised proportions
Came short of composition, but in chief
For that her reputation was disvalued
In levity. Since which time of five years
I never spake with her, saw her, nor heard from her,
Upon my faith and honor.

Mariana.
              Noble Prince,
As there comes light from heaven, and words from breath,
As there is sense in truth, and truth in virtue,
I am affianc'd this man's wife as strongly
As words could make up vows; and, my good lord,
But Tuesday night last gone, in 's garden-house,
He knew me as a wife. As this is true,
Let me in safety raise me from my knees,
Or else forever be confixed here,
A marble monument!

Angelo.
              I did but smile till now.
Now, good my lord, give me the scope of justice,
My patience here is touch'd. I do perceive
These poor informal women are no more
But instruments of some more mightier member
That sets them on. Let me have way, my lord,
To find this practice out.

Vincentio, the Duke.
              Ay, with my heart,
And punish them to your height of pleasure.
Thou foolish friar, and thou pernicious woman,
Compact with her that's gone, think'st thou thy oaths,
Though they would swear down each particular saint,
Were testimonies against his worth and credit
That's seal'd in approbation? You, Lord Escalus,
Sit with my cousin; lend him your kind pains
To find out this abuse, whence 'tis deriv'd.
There is another friar that set them on,
Let him be sent for.

Friar Peter Thomas.
Would he were here, my lord, for he indeed
Hath set the women on to this complaint.
Your Provost knows the place where he abides,
And he may fetch him.

Vincentio, the Duke.   Go, do it instantly.

Exit Provost.

And you, my noble and well-warranted cousin,
Whom it concerns to hear this matter forth,
Do with your injuries as seems you best,
In any chastisement. I for a while will leave you;
But stir not you till you have well determin'd
Upon these slanderers.

Escalus.   My lord, we'll do it throughly.

Exit Duke.

Signior Lucio, did not you say you knew that Friar
Lodowick to be a dishonest person?

Lucio.
Cucullus non facit monachum: honest in nothing but
in his clothes, and one that hath spoke most villainous speeches of the Duke.

Escalus.
We shall entreat you to abide here till he come, and
enforce them against him. We shall find this friar a
notable fellow.

Lucio.
As any in Vienna, on my word.

Escalus.
Call that same Isabel here once again, I would speak
with her.

Exit an Attendant.

Pray you, my lord, give me leave to question, you shall
see how I'll handle her.

Lucio.
Not better than he, by her own report.

Escalus.
Say you?

Lucio.
Marry, sir, I think if you handled her privately she
would sooner confess; perchance publicly she'll be
asham'd.

Enter Duke in his friar's habit, Provost, Officers with Isabella.

Escalus.
I will go darkly to work with her.

Lucio.
That's the way; for women are light at midnight.

Escalus.
Come on, mistress. Here's a gentlewoman denies all
that you have said.

Lucio.
My lord, here comes the rascal I spoke of, here with
the Provost.

Escalus.
In very good time. Speak not you to him till we call
upon you.

Lucio.
Mum.

Escalus.
Come, sir, did you set these women on to slander Lord
Angelo? They have confess'd you did.

Vincentio, the Duke.
'Tis false.

Escalus.
How! Know you where you are?

Vincentio, the Duke.
Respect to your great place! And let the devil
Be sometime honor'd for his burning throne!
Where is the Duke? 'Tis he should hear me speak.

Escalus.
The Duke's in us; and we will hear you speak:
Look you speak justly.

Vincentio, the Duke.
Boldly, at least. But O, poor souls,
Come you to seek the lamb here of the fox,
Good night to your redress! Is the Duke gone?
Then is your cause gone too. The Duke's unjust
Thus to retort your manifest appeal,

Act 5, Scene 1

And put your trial in the villain's mouth
Which here you come to accuse.

Lucio.
This is the rascal; this is he I spoke of.

Escalus.
Why, thou unreverend and unhallowed friar,
Is't not enough thou hast suborn'd these women
To accuse this worthy man, but in foul mouth,
And in the witness of his proper ear,
To call him villain, and then to glance from him
To th' Duke himself, to tax him with injustice?
Take him hence; to th' rack with him! We'll touze you
Joint by joint, but we will know his purpose.
What? "unjust"?

Vincentio, the Duke.
                    Be not so hot. The Duke
Dare no more stretch this finger of mine than he
Dare rack his own. His subject am I not,
Nor here provincial. My business in this state
Made me a looker-on here in Vienna,
Where I have seen corruption boil and bubble,
Till it o'errun the stew; laws for all faults,
But faults so countenanc'd, that the strong statutes
Stand like the forfeits in a barber's shop,
As much in mock as mark.

Escalus.
                    Slander to th' state!
Away with him to prison.

Angelo.
                    What can you vouch
Against him, Signior Lucio? Is this the man
That you did tell us of?

Lucio.
                    'Tis he, my lord.
Come hither, goodman bald-pate, do you know me?

Vincentio, the Duke.
I remember you, sir, by the sound of your voice; I met you at the prison, in the absence of the Duke.

Lucio.
O, did you so? And do you remember what you said of the Duke?

Vincentio, the Duke.
Most notedly, sir.

Lucio.
Do you so, sir? And was the Duke a flesh-monger, a fool, and a coward, as you then reported him to be?

Vincentio, the Duke.
You must, sir, change persons with me, ere you make that my report. You indeed spoke so of him, and much more, much worse.

Lucio.
O thou damnable fellow! Did not I pluck thee by the nose for thy speeches?

Vincentio, the Duke.
I protest I love the Duke as I love myself.

Angelo.
Hark how the villain would close now, after his treasonable abuses!

Escalus.
Such a fellow is not to be talk'd withal. Away with him to prison! Where is the Provost? Away with him to prison! Lay bolts enough upon him. Let him speak no more. Away with those giglets too, and with the other confederate companion!

The Provost lays hands on the Duke.

Vincentio, the Duke.
Stay, sir, stay a while.

Angelo.
What, resists he? Help him, Lucio.

Lucio.
Come, sir, come, sir, come, sir; foh, sir, why, you bald-pated, lying rascal, you must be hooded, must you? Show your knave's visage, with a pox to you! Show your sheep-biting face, and be hang'd an hour! Will't not off?

Pulls off the friar's hood.

Vincentio, the Duke.
Thou art the first knave that e'er mad'st a duke.
First, Provost, let me bail these gentle three.

To Lucio.

Sneak not away, sir, for the friar and you
Must have a word anon.—Lay hold on him.

Lucio.
This may prove worse than hanging.

Vincentio, the Duke.

To Escalus.

What you have spoke I pardon. Sit you down,
We'll borrow place of him.—Sir, by your leave.

Takes Angelo's seat.

Hast thou or word, or wit, or impudence,
That yet can do thee office? If thou hast,
Rely upon it till my tale be heard,
And hold no longer out.

Angelo.
                   O my dread lord,
I should be guiltier than my guiltiness,
To think I can be undiscernible,
When I perceive your Grace, like pow'r divine,
Hath look'd upon my passes. Then, good Prince,
No longer session hold upon my shame,
But let my trial be mine own confession.
Immediate sentence then, and sequent death,
Is all the grace I beg.

Vincentio, the Duke.
                   Come hither, Mariana.
Say: wast thou e'er contracted to this woman?

Angelo.
I was, my lord.

Vincentio, the Duke.
Go take her hence, and marry her instantly.
Do you the office, friar, which consummate,
Return him here again. Go with him, Provost.

Exeunt Angelo, Mariana, Friar Peter, Provost.

Escalus.
My lord, I am more amaz'd at his dishonor
Than at the strangeness of it.

Vincentio, the Duke.
                   Come hither, Isabel,
Your friar is now your prince. As I was then
Advertising and holy to your business,
Not changing heart with habit, I am still
Attorneyed at your service.

Isabella.
                   O, give me pardon,
That I, your vassal, have employ'd and pain'd
Your unknown sovereignty!

Vincentio, the Duke.
                   You are pardon'd, Isabel;
And now, dear maid, be you as free to us.
Your brother's death I know sits at your heart;
And you may marvel why I obscur'd myself,
Laboring to save his life, and would not rather
Make rash remonstrance of my hidden pow'r
Than let him so be lost. O most kind maid,
It was the swift celerity of his death,
Which I did think with slower foot came on,
That brain'd my purpose. But peace be with him!
That life is better life, past fearing death,
Than that which lives to fear. Make it your comfort,
So happy is your brother.

Enter Angelo, Mariana, Friar Peter, Provost.

Isabella.
                 I do, my lord.

Vincentio, the Duke.
For this new-married man approaching here,
Whose salt imagination yet hath wrong'd
Your well-defended honor, you must pardon
For Mariana's sake; but as he adjudg'd your brother—
Being criminal, in double violation
Of sacred chastity and of promise-breach,
Thereon dependent, for your brother's life—
The very mercy of the law cries out
Most audible, even from his proper tongue,
"An Angelo for Claudio, death for death!"
Haste still pays haste, and leisure answers leisure;
Like doth quit like, and Measure still for Measure.
Then, Angelo, thy fault's thus manifested;
Which though thou wouldst deny, denies thee vantage.
We do condemn thee to the very block
Where Claudio stoop'd to death, and with like haste.
Away with him!

Mariana.
                 O my most gracious lord,
I hope you will not mock me with a husband!

Vincentio, the Duke.
It is your husband mock'd you with a husband.
Consenting to the safeguard of your honor,
I thought your marriage fit; else imputation,
For that he knew you, might reproach your life,
And choke your good to come. For his possessions,
Although by confiscation they are ours,
We do enstate and widow you with all,
To buy you a better husband.

Mariana.
                        O my dear lord,
I crave no other, nor no better man.

Vincentio, the Duke.
Never crave him, we are definitive.

Mariana.

Kneeling.

Gentle my liege—

Vincentio, the Duke.
                    You do but lose your labor.
Away with him to death!

To Lucio.

Now, sir, to you.

Mariana.
O my good lord! Sweet Isabel, take my part!
Lend me your knees, and all my life to come
I'll lend you all my life to do you service.

Vincentio, the Duke.
Against all sense you do importune her.
Should she kneel down in mercy of this fact,
Her brother's ghost his paved bed would break,
And take her hence in horror.

Mariana.
                    Isabel!
Sweet Isabel, do yet but kneel by me.
Hold up your hands, say nothing; I'll speak all.
They say best men are moulded out of faults,
And for the most, become much more the better
For being a little bad; so may my husband.
O Isabel! Will you not lend a knee?

Vincentio, the Duke.
He dies for Claudio's death.

Isabella.

Kneeling

                    Most bounteous sir:
Look, if it please you, on this man condemn'd
As if my brother liv'd. I partly think
A due sincerity governed his deeds,
Till he did look on me. Since it is so,
Let him not die. My brother had but justice,
In that he did the thine for which he died;
For Angelo,
His act did not o'ertake his bad intent,
And must be buried but as an intent
That perish'd by the way. Thoughts are no subjects,
Intents but merely thoughts.

Mariana.
                    Merely, my lord.

Vincentio, the Duke.
Your suit's unprofitable; stand up, I say.
I have bethought me of another fault.
Provost, how came it Claudio was beheaded
At an unusual hour?

Provost.
                  It was commanded so.

Vincentio, the Duke.
Had you a special warrant for the deed?

Provost.
No, my good lord; it was by private message.

Vincentio, the Duke.
For which I do discharge you of your office;
Give up your keys.

Provost.
                  Pardon me, noble lord,
I thought it was a fault, but knew it not,
Yet did repent me, after more advice,
For testimony whereof, one in the prison,
That should by private order else have died,
I have reserv'd alive.

Vincentio, the Duke.
                  What's he?

Provost.
                  His name is Barnardine.

Vincentio, the Duke.
I would thou hadst done so by Claudio.
Go fetch him hither, let me look upon him.

Exit Provost.

Escalus.
I am sorry, one so learned and so wise
As you, Lord Angelo, have still appear'd,
Should slip so grossly, both in the heat of blood
And lack of temper'd judgment afterward.

Angelo.
I am sorry that such sorrow I procure,
And so deep sticks it in my penitent heart
That I crave death more willingly than mercy:
'Tis my deserving, and I do entreat it.

Enter Barnardine and Provost, Claudio muffled, Julietta.

Vincentio, the Duke.
Which is that Barnardine?

Provost.
                    This, my lord.

Vincentio, the Duke.
There was a friar told me of this man.
Sirrah, thou art said to have a stubborn soul
That apprehends no further than this world,
And squar'st thy life according. Thou'rt condemn'd,
But for those earthly faults, I quit them all,
And pray thee take this mercy to provide
For better times to come. Friar, advise him,
I leave him to your hand. What muffled fellow's that?

Provost.
This is another prisoner that I sav'd,
Who should have died when Claudio lost his head,
As like almost to Claudio as himself.

Unmuffles Claudio.

Vincentio, the Duke.

To Isabella.

If he be like your brother, for his sake
Is he pardon'd, and for your lovely sake,
Give me your hand, and say you will be mine,
He is my brother too. But fitter time for that.
By this Lord Angelo perceives he's safe;
Methinks I see a quick'ning in his eye.
Well, Angelo, your evil quits you well.
Look that you love your wife; her worth worth yours.
I find an apt remission in myself;
And yet here's one in place I cannot pardon.

To Lucio.

You, sirrah, that knew me for a fool, a coward,
One all of luxury, an ass, a madman,
Wherein have I so deserv'd of you,
That you extol me thus?

Lucio.
Faith, my lord, I spoke it but according to the trick. If you will hang me for it, you may; but I had rather it would please you I might be whipt.

Vincentio, the Duke.
Whipt first, sir, and hang'd after.
Proclaim it, Provost, round about the city,
If any woman wrong'd by this lewd fellow
(As I have heard him swear himself there's one
Whom he begot with child), let her appear,
And he shall marry her. The nuptial finish'd,
Let him be whipt and hang'd.

Lucio.
I beseech your Highness do not marry me to a whore. Your Highness said even now I made you a duke; good my lord, do not recompense me in making me a cuckold.

Vincentio, the Duke.
Upon mine honor, thou shalt marry her.
Thy slanders I forgive, and therewithal
Remit thy other forfeits. Take him to prison,
And see our pleasure herein executed.

Lucio.
Marrying a punk, my lord, is pressing to death, whipping, and hanging.

Vincentio, the Duke.
Slandering a prince deserves it.

Exeunt Officers with Lucio.

She, Claudio, that you wrong'd, look you restore.
Joy to you, Mariana! Love her, Angelo!
I have confess'd her, and I know her virtue.
Thanks, good friend Escalus, for thy much goodness,
There's more behind that is more gratulate.
Thanks, Provost, for thy care and secrecy,

We shall employ thee in a worthier place.
Forgive him, Angelo, that brought you home
The head of Ragozine for Claudio's,
Th' offense pardons itself. Dear Isabel,
I have a motion much imports your good,
Whereto if you'll a willing ear incline,
What's mine is yours, and what is yours is mine.
So bring us to our palace, where we'll show
What's yet behind, that's meet you all should know.

Exeunt.

The Merchant of Venice

Act 1

Scene 1

Venice. A street.

(Antonio; Salerio; Solanio; Bassanio; Lorenzo; Gratiano)

Antonio cannot put a finger on exactly why he is so sad; none of his friends' suggestions quite hit the mark and their attempts to cheer him up are unsuccessful. His good friend Bassanio joins him. Left alone, Bassanio explains to Antonio that to repair his squandered fortunes, he intends to win the hand of Portia, a wealthy heiress. To make a good show as he woos her, since she is being sought by many suitors from all over the world, he asks Antonio to lend him some money. Antonio agrees, but points out that he has no cash at present, as all his money has been invested in sea ventures that have not yet returned; but his credit is good enough that he believes he will be able to raise the sum.

Enter Antonio, Salerio, and Solanio.

Antonio.
In sooth, I know not why I am so sad;
It wearies me, you say it wearies you;
But how I caught it, found it, or came by it,
What stuff 'tis made of, whereof it is born,
I am to learn;
And such a want-wit sadness makes of me,
That I have much ado to know myself.

Salerio.
Your mind is tossing on the ocean,
There where your argosies with portly sail
Like signiors and rich burghers on the flood,
Or as it were the pageants of the sea,
Do overpeer the petty traffickers
That cur'sy to them, do them reverence,
As they fly by them with their woven wings.

Solanio.
Believe me, sir, had I such venture forth,
The better part of my affections would
Be with my hopes abroad. I should be still
Plucking the grass to know where sits the wind,
Piring in maps for ports and piers and roads;
And every object that might make me fear
Misfortune to my ventures, out of doubt
Would make me sad.

Salerio.
　　　　　　My wind cooling my broth
Would blow me to an ague when I thought
What harm a wind too great might do at sea.
I should not see the sandy hour-glass run
But I should think of shallows and of flats,
And see my wealthy Andrew dock'd in sand,
Vailing her high top lower than her ribs
To kiss her burial. Should I go to church
And see the holy edifice of stone,
And not bethink me straight of dangerous rocks,
Which touching but my gentle vessel's side
Would scatter all her spices on the stream,
Enrobe the roaring waters with my silks,
And in a word, but even now worth this,
And now worth nothing? Shall I have the thought
To think on this, and shall I lack the thought
That such a thing bechanc'd would make me sad?
But tell not me; I know Antonio
Is sad to think upon his merchandise.

Antonio.
Believe me, no. I thank my fortune for it,
My ventures are not in one bottom trusted,
Nor to one place; nor is my whole estate
Upon the fortune of this present year:
Therefore my merchandise makes me not sad.

Solanio.
Why then you are in love.

Antonio.
                Fie, fie!

Solanio.
Not in love neither? Then let us say you are sad
Because you are not merry; and 'twere as easy
For you to laugh and leap, and say you are merry
Because you are not sad. Now by two-headed Janus,
Nature hath fram'd strange fellows in her time:
Some that will evermore peep through their eyes,
And laugh like parrots at a bagpiper;
And other of such vinegar aspect
That they'll not show their teeth in way of smile
Though Nestor swear the jest be laughable.

Enter Bassanio, Lorenzo, and Gratiano.

Here comes Bassanio, your most noble kinsman,
Gratiano, and Lorenzo. Fare ye well,
We leave you now with better company.

Salerio.
I would have stay'd till I had made you merry,
If worthier friends had not prevented me.

Antonio.
Your worth is very dear in my regard.
I take it your own business calls on you,
And you embrace th' occasion to depart.

Salerio.
Good morrow, my good lords.

Bassanio.
Good signiors both, when shall we laugh? Say, when?
You grow exceeding strange. Must it be so?

Salerio.
We'll make our leisures to attend on yours.

Exeunt Salerio and Solanio.

Lorenzo.
My Lord Bassanio, since you have found Antonio,
We two will leave you, but at dinner-time
I pray you have in mind where we must meet.

Bassanio.
I will not fail you.

Gratiano.
You look not well, Signior Antonio,
You have too much respect upon the world.
They lose it that do buy it with much care.
Believe me you are marvelously chang'd.

Antonio.
I hold the world but as the world, Gratiano,
A stage, where every man must play a part,
And mine a sad one.

Gratiano.
                Let me play the fool,
With mirth and laughter let old wrinkles come,
And let my liver rather heat with wine
Than my heart cool with mortifying groans.
Why should a man, whose blood is warm within,
Sit like his grandsire cut in alabaster?
Sleep when he wakes? And creep into the jaundies
By being peevish? I tell thee what, Antonio—
I love thee, and 'tis my love that speaks—
There are a sort of men whose visages
Do cream and mantle like a standing pond,
And do a willful stillness entertain,
With purpose to be dress'd in an opinion
Of wisdom, gravity, profound conceit,
As who should say, "I am Sir Oracle,
And when I ope my lips let no dog bark!"
O my Antonio, I do know of these
That therefore only are reputed wise
For saying nothing; when I am very sure
If they should speak, would almost damn those ears
Which hearing them would call their brothers fools.
I'll tell thee more of this another time;
But fish not with this melancholy bait
For this fool gudgeon, this opinion.
Come, good Lorenzo. Fare ye well a while,
I'll end my exhortation after dinner.

Lorenzo.
Well, we will leave you then till dinner-time.
I must be one of these same dumb wise men,
For Gratiano never lets me speak.

Gratiano.
Well, keep me company but two years more,
Thou shalt not know the sound of thine own tongue.

Antonio.
Fare you well! I'll grow a talker for this gear.

Gratiano.
Thanks, i' faith, for silence is only commendable
In a neat's tongue dried and a maid not vendible.

Exeunt Gratiano and Lorenzo.

Antonio.
It is that—any thing now!

Bassanio.
Gratiano speaks an infinite deal of nothing, more than any man in all Venice. His reasons are as two grains of wheat hid in two bushels of chaff; you shall seek all day ere you find them, and when you have them, they are not worth the search.

Antonio.
Well, tell me now what lady is the same
To whom you swore a secret pilgrimage,
That you today promis'd to tell me of?

Bassanio.
'Tis not unknown to you, Antonio,
How much I have disabled mine estate,
By something showing a more swelling port
Than my faint means would grant continuance.
Nor do I now make moan to be abridg'd
From such a noble rate, but my chief care
Is to come fairly off from the great debts
Wherein my time something too prodigal
Hath left me gag'd. To you, Antonio,
I owe the most in money and in love,
And from your love I have a warranty
To unburden all my plots and purposes
How to get clear of all the debts I owe.

Antonio.
I pray you, good Bassanio, let me know it,
And if it stand, as you yourself still do,
Within the eye of honor, be assur'd
My purse, my person, my extremest means,
Lie all unlock'd to your occasions.

Bassanio.
In my school-days, when I had lost one shaft,
I shot his fellow of the self-same flight
The self-same way with more advised watch
To find the other forth, and by adventuring both
I oft found both. I urge this childhood proof,
Because what follows is pure innocence.
I owe you much, and like a willful youth,
That which I owe is lost, but if you please
To shoot another arrow that self way
Which you did shoot the first, I do not doubt,
As I will watch the aim, or to find both
Or bring your latter hazard back again,
And thankfully rest debtor for the first.

Antonio.
You know me well, and herein spend but time
To wind about my love with circumstance,
And out of doubt you do me now more wrong
In making question of my uttermost
Than if you had made waste of all I have.
Then do but say to me what I should do
That in your knowledge may by me be done,
And I am prest unto it; therefore speak.

Bassanio.
In Belmont is a lady richly left,
And she is fair and, fairer than that word,
Of wondrous virtues. Sometimes from her eyes
I did receive fair speechless messages.
Her name is Portia, nothing undervalu'd
To Cato's daughter, Brutus' Portia.
Nor is the wide world ignorant of her worth,
For the four winds blow in from every coast
Renowned suitors, and her sunny locks
Hang on her temples like a golden fleece,
Which makes her seat of Belmont Colchis' strond,
And many Jasons come in quest of her.
O my Antonio, had I but the means
To hold a rival place with one of them,
I have a mind presages me such thrift
That I should questionless be fortunate!

Antonio.
Thou know'st that all my fortunes are at sea,
Neither have I money nor commodity
To raise a present sum; therefore go forth,
Try what my credit can in Venice do.
That shall be rack'd, even to the uttermost,
To furnish thee to Belmont, to fair Portia.
Go presently inquire, and so will I,

Where money is, and I no question make
To have it of my trust, or for my sake.

Exeunt.

Scene 2

Belmont. A room in Portia's house.

(Portia; Nerissa; Portia's Servant)

Portia laments how she cannot choose her husband for herself, but must accept whichever one chooses the correct casket that her father has left behind after his death. She and her lady-in-waiting Nerissa discuss the various suitors who have come to woo her, none of whom she particularly likes — though she has fond memories of Bassanio. Despite this lack of interest in the possibilities, Portia insists she will obey her father's will. A Servant informs her that four of her suitors have decided not to risk taking the casket test, since if they fail they are bound to never marry, and that the Prince of Morocco will be arriving that evening.

Enter Portia with her waiting-woman, Nerissa.

Portia.
By my troth, Nerissa, my little body is a-weary of this great world.

Nerissa.
You would be, sweet madam, if your miseries were in the same abundance as your good fortunes are; and yet for aught I see, they are as sick that surfeit with too much as they that starve with nothing. It is no mean happiness therefore to be seated in the mean: superfluity comes sooner by white hairs, but competency lives longer.

Portia.
Good sentences, and well pronounc'd.

Nerissa.
They would be better if well follow'd.

Portia.
If to do were as easy as to know what were good to do, chapels had been churches, and poor men's cottages princes' palaces. It is a good divine that follows his own instructions; I can easier teach twenty what were good to be done, than to be one of the twenty to follow mine own teaching. The brain may devise laws for the blood, but a hot temper leaps o'er a cold decree—such a hare is madness the youth, to skip o'er the meshes of good counsel the cripple. But this reasoning is not in the fashion to choose me a husband. O me, the word *choose*! I may neither choose who I would, nor refuse who I dislike; so is the will of a living daughter curb'd by the will of a dead father. Is it not hard, Nerissa, that I cannot choose one, nor refuse none?

Nerissa.
Your father was ever virtuous, and holy men at their death have good inspirations; therefore the lott'ry that he hath devis'd in these three chests of gold, silver, and lead, whereof who chooses his meaning chooses you, will no doubt never be chosen by any rightly but one who you shall rightly love. But what warmth is there in your affection towards any of these princely suitors that are already come?

Portia.
I pray thee over-name them, and as thou namest them, I will describe them; and according to my description level at my affection.

Nerissa.
First, there is the Neapolitan prince.

Portia.
Ay, that's a colt indeed, for he doth nothing but talk of his horse, and he makes it a great appropriation to his own good parts that he can shoe him himself. I am much afeard my lady his mother play'd false with a smith.

Nerissa.
Then is there the County Palentine.

Portia.
He doth nothing but frown, as who should say, "And you will not have me, choose." He hears merry tales and smiles not. I fear he will prove the weeping philosopher when he grows old, being so full of unmannerly sadness in his youth. I had rather be married to a death's-head with a bone in his mouth than to either of these. God defend me from these two!

Nerissa.
How say you by the French lord, Monsieur Le Bon?

Portia.
God made him, and therefore let him pass for a man. In truth, I know it is a sin to be a mocker, but he! Why, he hath a horse better than the Neapolitan's, a better bad habit of frowning than the Count Palen-

tine; he is every man in no man. If a throstle sing, he falls straight a-cap'ring. He will fence with his own shadow. If I should marry him, I should marry twenty husbands. If he would despise me, I would forgive him, for if he love me to madness, I shall never requite him.

Nerissa.
What say you then to Falconbridge, the young baron of England?

Portia.
You know I say nothing to him, for he understands not me, nor I him. He hath neither Latin, French, nor Italian, and you will come into the court and swear that I have a poor pennyworth in the English. He is a proper man's picture, but alas, who can converse with a dumb show? How oddly he is suited! I think he bought his doublet in Italy, his round hose in France, his bonnet in Germany, and his behavior every where.

Nerissa.
What think you of the Scottish lord, his neighbor?

Portia.
That he hath a neighborly charity in him, for he borrow'd a box of the ear of the Englishman, and swore he would pay him again when he was able. I think the Frenchman became his surety and seal'd under for another.

Nerissa.
How like you the young German, the Duke of Saxony's nephew?

Portia.
Very vildly in the morning, when he is sober, and most vildly in the afternoon, when he is drunk. When he is best, he is a little worse than a man, and when he is worst, he is little better than a beast. And the worst fall that ever fell, I hope I shall make shift to go without him.

Nerissa.
If he should offer to choose, and choose the right casket, you should refuse to perform your father's will, if you should refuse to accept him.

Portia.
Therefore for fear of the worst, I pray thee set a deep glass of Rhenish wine on the contrary casket, for if the devil be within, and that temptation without, I know he will choose it. I will do any thing, Nerissa, ere I will be married to a sponge.

Nerissa.
You need not fear, lady, the having any of these lords. They have acquainted me with their determinations, which is indeed to return to their home, and to trouble you with no more suit, unless you may be won by some other sort than your father's imposition depending on the caskets.

Portia.
If I live to be as old as Sibylla, I will die as chaste as Diana, unless I be obtain'd by the manner of my father's will. I am glad this parcel of wooers are so reasonable, for there is not one among them but I dote on his very absence, and I pray God grant them a fair departure.

Nerissa.
Do you not remember, lady, in your father's time, a Venetian, a scholar and a soldier, that came hither in company of the Marquis of Montferrat?

Portia.
Yes, yes, it was Bassanio—as I think, so was he call'd.

Nerissa.
True, madam; he, of all the men that ever my foolish eyes look'd upon, was the best deserving a fair lady.

Portia.
I remember him well, and I remember him worthy of thy praise.

Enter a Servingman.

How now, what news?

Portia's Servant.
The four strangers seek for you, madam, to take their leave; and there is a forerunner come from a fift, the Prince of Morocco, who brings word the Prince his master will be here tonight.

Portia.
If I could bid the fifth welcome with so good heart as I can bid the other four farewell, I should be glad of his approach. If he have the condition of a saint, and the complexion of a devil, I had rather he should shrive me than wive me.
Come, Nerissa. Sirrah, go before.
Whiles we shut the gate upon one wooer, another knocks at the door.

Exeunt.

Scene 3

Venice. A public place.

(Bassanio; Shylock; Antonio)

Bassanio asks the Jewish moneylender Shylock to lend 3000 ducats on Antonio's credit. Shylock points out that all of Antonio's wealth is in risky ventures at present. To himself he considers how much he hates Antonio, who ruins his trade by lending money without interest. Antonio enters, sneering at Shylock for lending at interest; the two loathe one another, Shylock remembering all the times Antonio has insulted him or even spat at him, Antonio showing no remorse. Shylock insists he wants to be friends with Antonio, however, and therefore agrees to make the loan and, as a joke, that they make the penalty for non-repayment a pound of Antonio's flesh. Bassanio will not hear of it, but Antonio brushes off his fears, being utterly certain that his ships will return before the repayment due date.

Enter Bassanio with Shylock the Jew.

Shylock.
Three thousand ducats, well.

Bassanio.
Ay, sir, for three months.

Shylock.
For three months, well.

Bassanio.
For the which, as I told you, Antonio shall be bound.

Shylock.
Antonio shall become bound, well.

Bassanio.
May you stead me? Will you pleasure me? Shall I know your answer?

Shylock.
Three thousand ducats for three months, and Antonio bound.

Bassanio.
Your answer to that.

Shylock.
Antonio is a good man.

Bassanio.
Have you heard any imputation to the contrary?

Shylock.
Ho, no, no, no, no! My meaning in saying he is a good man is to have you understand me that he is sufficient. Yet his means are in supposition: he hath an argosy bound to Tripolis, another to the Indies; I understand moreover upon the Rialto, he hath a third at Mexico, a fourth for England, and other ventures he hath, squand'red abroad. But ships are but boards, sailors but men; there be land-rats and water-rats, water-thieves and land-thieves, I mean pirates, and then there is the peril of waters, winds, and rocks. The man is notwithstanding sufficient. Three thousand ducats; I think I may take his bond.

Bassanio.
Be assur'd you may.

Shylock.
I will be assur'd I may; and that I may be assur'd, I will bethink me. May I speak with Antonio?

Bassanio.
If it please you to dine with us.

Shylock.
Yes, to smell pork, to eat of the habitation which your prophet the Nazarite conjur'd the devil into. I will buy with you, sell with you, talk with you, walk with you, and so following; but I will not eat with you, drink with you, nor pray with you. What news on the Rialto? Who is he comes here?

Enter Antonio.

Bassanio.
This is Signior Antonio.

Shylock.

Aside.

How like a fawning publican he looks!
I hate him for he is a Christian;
But more, for that in low simplicity
He lends out money gratis, and brings down
The rate of usance here with us in Venice.
If I can catch him once upon the hip,
I will feed fat the ancient grudge I bear him.
He hates our sacred nation, and he rails
Even there where merchants most do congregate

On me, my bargains, and my well-won thrift,
Which he calls interest. Cursed be my tribe
If I forgive him!

Bassanio.
               Shylock, do you hear?

Shylock.
I am debating of my present store,
And by the near guess of my memory,
I cannot instantly raise up the gross
Of full three thousand ducats. What of that?
Tubal, a wealthy Hebrew of my tribe,
Will furnish me. But soft, how many months
Do you desire?

To Antonio.

Rest you fair, good signior,
Your worship was the last man in our mouths.

Antonio.
Shylock, albeit I neither lend nor borrow
By taking nor by giving of excess,
Yet to supply the ripe wants of my friend,
I'll break a custom.

To Bassanio.

               Is he yet possess'd
How much ye would?

Shylock.
               Ay, ay, three thousand ducats.

Antonio.
And for three months.

Shylock.
I had forgot—three months—

To Bassanio.

               you told me so.
Well then, your bond; and let me see—but hear you,
Methoughts you said you neither lend nor borrow
Upon advantage.

Antonio.
               I do never use it.

Shylock.
When Jacob graz'd his uncle Laban's sheep—
This Jacob from our holy Abram was
(As his wise mother wrought in his behalf)
The third possessor; ay, he was the third—

Antonio.
And what of him? Did he take interest?

Shylock.
No, not take interest, not as you would say
Directly int'rest. Mark what Jacob did:
When Laban and himself were compromis'd
That all the eanlings which were streak'd and pied
Should fall as Jacob's hire, the ewes being rank
In end of autumn turned to the rams,
And when the work of generation was
Between these woolly breeders in the act,
The skillful shepherd pill'd me certain wands,
And in the doing of the deed of kind,
He stuck them up before the fulsome ewes,
Who then conceiving did in eaning time
Fall parti-color'd lambs, and those were Jacob's.
This was a way to thrive, and he was blest;
And thrift is blessing, if men steal it not.

Antonio.
This was a venture, sir, that Jacob serv'd for,
A thing not in his power to bring to pass,
But sway'd and fashion'd by the hand of heaven.
Was this inserted to make interest good?
Or is your gold and silver ewes and rams?

Shylock.
I cannot tell, I make it breed as fast.
But note me, signior.

Antonio.
               Mark you this, Bassanio,
The devil can cite Scripture for his purpose.
An evil soul producing holy witness
Is like a villain with a smiling cheek,
A goodly apple rotten at the heart.
O, what a goodly outside falsehood hath!

Shylock.
Three thousand ducats—'tis a good round sum.
Three months from twelve; then let me see, the rate—

Antonio.
Well, Shylock, shall we be beholding to you?

Shylock.
Signior Antonio, many a time and oft
In the Rialto you have rated me
About my moneys and my usances.
Still have I borne it with a patient shrug
(For suff'rance is the badge of all our tribe).
You call me misbeliever, cut-throat dog,

And spet upon my Jewish gaberdine,
And all for use of that which is mine own.
Well then, it now appears you need my help.
Go to then, you come to me, and you say,
"Shylock, we would have moneys," you say so—
You, that did void your rheum upon my beard,
And foot me as you spurn a stranger cur
Over your threshold; moneys is your suit.
What should I say to you? Should I not say,
"Hath a dog money? Is it possible
A cur can lend three thousand ducats?" Or
Shall I bend low and in a bondman's key,
With bated breath and whisp'ring humbleness,
Say this:
"Fair sir, you spet on me on Wednesday last,
You spurn'd me such a day, another time
You call'd me dog; and for these courtesies
I'll lend you thus much moneys"?

Antonio.
I am as like to call thee so again,
To spet on thee again, to spurn thee too.
If thou wilt lend this money, lend it not
As to thy friends, for when did friendship take
A breed for barren metal of his friend?
But lend it rather to thine enemy,
Who if he break, thou mayst with better face
Exact the penalty.

Shylock.
                   Why, look you how you storm!
I would be friends with you, and have your love,
Forget the shames that you have stain'd me with,
Supply your present wants, and take no doit
Of usance for my moneys, and you'll not hear me.
This is kind I offer.

Bassanio.
This were kindness.

Shylock.
                   This kindness will I show.
Go with me to a notary, seal me there
Your single bond; and in a merry sport
If you repay me not on such a day,
In such a place, such sum or sums as are
Express'd in the condition, let the forfeit
Be nominated for an equal pound
Of your fair flesh, to be cut off and taken
In what part of your body pleaseth me.

Antonio.
Content, in faith, I'll seal to such a bond,
And say there is much kindness in the Jew.

Bassanio.
You shall not seal to such a bond for me,
I'll rather dwell in my necessity.

Antonio.
Why, fear not, man, I will not forfeit it.
Within these two months, that's a month before
This bond expires, I do expect return
Of thrice three times the value of this bond.

Shylock.
O father Abram, what these Christians are,
Whose own hard dealings teaches them suspect
The thoughts of others! Pray you tell me this:
If he should break his day, what should I gain
By the exaction of the forfeiture?
A pound of man's flesh taken from a man
Is not so estimable, profitable neither,
As flesh of muttons, beefs, or goats. I say,
To buy his favor, I extend this friendship.
If he will take it, so, if not, adieu;
And for my love I pray you wrong me not.

Antonio.
Yes, Shylock, I will seal unto this bond.

Shylock.
Then meet me forthwith at the notary's;
Give him direction for this merry bond,
And I will go and purse the ducats straight,
See to my house, left in the fearful guard
Of an unthrifty knave, and presently
I'll be with you.

Exit.

Antonio.
                   Hie thee, gentle Jew.
The Hebrew will turn Christian, he grows kind.

Bassanio.
I like not fair terms and a villain's mind.

Antonio.
Come on, in this there can be no dismay,
My ships come home a month before the day.

Exeunt.

Act 2

Scene 1

Belmont. A room in Portia's house.

(Prince of Morocco; Followers; Portia; Nerissa)

The bragging Prince of Morocco introduces himself to Portia, who flatters him. He declares his intention of undertaking the choice of caskets, though Portia reminds him that he must vow never to marry if he is unsuccessful. He is determined all the same.

Flourish cornets. Enter the Prince of Morocco, a tawny Moor, all in white, and three or four Followers accordingly, with Portia, Nerissa, and their Train.

The Prince of Morocco.
Mislike me not for my complexion,
The shadowed livery of the burnish'd sun,
To whom I am a neighbor and near bred.
Bring me the fairest creature northward born,
Where Phoebus' fire scarce thaws the icicles,
And let us make incision for your love,
To prove whose blood is reddest, his or mine.
I tell thee, lady, this aspect of mine
Hath fear'd the valiant; by my love, I swear
The best-regarded virgins of our clime
Have lov'd it too. I would not change this hue,
Except to steal your thoughts, my gentle queen.

Portia.
In terms of choice I am not solely led
By nice direction of a maiden's eyes;
Besides, the lott'ry of my destiny
Bars me the right of voluntary choosing.
But if my father had not scanted me,
And hedg'd me by his wit to yield myself
His wife who wins me by that means I told you,
Yourself, renowned Prince, then stood as fair
As any comer I have look'd on yet
For my affection.

The Prince of Morocco.
                    Even for that I thank you;
Therefore I pray you lead me to the caskets
To try my fortune. By this scimitar
That slew the Sophy and a Persian prince
That won three fields of Sultan Solyman,
I would o'erstare the sternest eyes that look,
Outbrave the heart most daring on the earth,
Pluck the young sucking cubs from the she-bear,
Yea, mock the lion when 'a roars for prey,
To win thee, lady. But alas the while!
If Hercules and Lichas play at dice
Which is the better man, the greater throw
May turn by fortune from the weaker hand:
So is Alcides beaten by his rage,
And so may I, blind fortune leading me,
Miss that which one unworthier may attain,
And die with grieving.

Portia.
                    You must take your chance,
And either not attempt to choose at all,
Or swear before you choose, if you choose wrong
Never to speak to lady afterward
In way of marriage; therefore be advis'd.

The Prince of Morocco.
Nor will not. Come bring me unto my chance.

Portia.
First, forward to the temple; after dinner
Your hazard shall be made.

The Prince of Morocco.
                    Good fortune then!
To make me blest or cursed'st among men.

Cornets. Exeunt.

Scene 2

Venice. A street.

(Launcelot Gobbo; Old Gobbo; Bassanio; Followers; Leonardo; Gratiano)

Shylock's servant Launcelot Gobbo wrestles with his conscience over whether to remain a servant to Shylock or not, and finally convinces himself to leave. His blind father comes looking for him and he decides to play a trick on the old man, pretending to be someone else. In the end Launcelot admits to being himself and explains that he intends to run away from Shylock, who starves him, and see if he can get service with Bassanio, who is hiring. Bassanio comes in, giving a flurry of instructions, and the two Gobbos interrupt him and plead for him to take Launcelot into his service, which in the end he does. Gratiano asks Bassanio to let him come along to Belmont with him, and Bassanio agrees on condition he keep a close watch on his sense of humor.

Enter the Clown Launcelot Gobbo alone.

Launcelot Gobbo.
Certainly my conscience will serve me to run from this Jew my master. The fiend is at mine elbow and tempts me, saying to me, "Gobbo, Launcelot Gobbo, good Launcelot," or "good Gobbo," or "good Launcelot Gobbo, use your legs, take the start, run away." My conscience says, "No; take heed, honest Launcelot, take heed, honest Gobbo," or as aforesaid, "honest Launcelot Gobbo, do not run, scorn running with thy heels." Well, the most courageous fiend bids me pack. "Fia!" says the fiend; "away!" says the fiend; "for the heavens, rouse up a brave mind," says the fiend, "and run." Well, my conscience, hanging about the neck of my heart, says very wisely to me, "My honest friend Launcelot, being an honest man's son"—or rather an honest woman's son, for indeed my father did something smack, something grow to, he had a kind of taste—well, my conscience says, "Launcelot, bouge not." "Bouge," says the fiend. "Bouge not," says my conscience. "Conscience," say I, "you counsel well." "Fiend," say I, "you counsel well." To be rul'd by my conscience, I should stay with the Jew my master, who (God bless the mark) is a kind of devil; and to run away from the Jew, I should be rul'd by the fiend, who, saving your reverence, is the devil himself. Certainly the Jew is the very devil incarnation, and in my conscience, my conscience is but a kind of hard conscience, to offer to counsel me to stay with the Jew. The fiend gives the more friendly counsel: I will run, fiend; my heels are at your commandment, I will run.

Enter Old Gobbo with a basket.

Old Gobbo.
Master young man, you, I pray you, which is the way to Master Jew's?

Launcelot Gobbo.

Aside.

O heavens, this is my true-begotten father, who being more than sand-blind, high gravel-blind, knows me not. I will try confusions with him.

Old Gobbo.
Master young gentleman, I pray you, which is the way to Master Jew's?

Launcelot Gobbo.
Turn up on your right hand at the next turning, but at the next turning of all, on your left; marry, at the very next turning, turn of no hand, but turn down indirectly to the Jew's house.

Old Gobbo.
Be God's sonties, 'twill be a hard way to hit. Can you tell me whether one Launcelot, that dwells with him, dwell with him or no?

Launcelot Gobbo.
Talk you of young Master Launcelot?

Aside.

Mark me now, now will I raise the waters.—Talk you of young Master Launcelot?

Old Gobbo.
No master, sir, but a poor man's son. His father, though I say't, is an honest exceeding poor man and, God be thank'd, well to live.

Launcelot Gobbo.
Well, let his father be what 'a will, we talk of young Master Launcelot.

Old Gobbo.
Your worship's friend and Launcelot, sir.

Launcelot Gobbo.
But I pray you, ergo, old man, ergo, I beseech you, talk you of young Master Launcelot.

Old Gobbo.
Of Launcelot, an't please your mastership.

Launcelot Gobbo.
Ergo, Master Launcelot. Talk not of Master Launcelot, father, for the young gentleman, according to Fates and Destinies, and such odd sayings, the Sisters Three, and such branches of learning, is indeed deceas'd, or as you would say in plain terms, gone to heaven.

Old Gobbo.
Marry, God forbid, the boy was the very staff of my age, my very prop.

Launcelot Gobbo.

Aside.

Do I look like a cudgel or a hovel-post, a staff, or a prop?—Do you know me, father?

Old Gobbo.
Alack the day, I know you not, young gentleman, but I pray you tell me, is my boy, God rest his soul, alive or dead?

Launcelot Gobbo.
Do you not know me, father?

Old Gobbo.
Alack, sir, I am sand-blind, I know you not.

Launcelot Gobbo.
Nay, indeed if you had your eyes you might fail of the knowing me; it is a wise father that knows his own child. Well, old man, I will tell you news of your son. Give me your blessing; truth will come to light; murder cannot be hid long; a man's son may, but in the end truth will out.

Old Gobbo.
Pray you, sir, stand up. I am sure you are not Launcelot, my boy.

Launcelot Gobbo.
Pray you let's have no more fooling about it, but give me your blessing. I am Launcelot, your boy that was, your son that is, your child that shall be.

Old Gobbo.
I cannot think you are my son.

Launcelot Gobbo.
I know not what I shall think of that; but I am Launcelot, the Jew's man, and I am sure Margery your wife is my mother.

Old Gobbo.
Her name is Margery indeed. I'll be sworn, if thou be Launcelot, thou art mine own flesh and blood. Lord worshipp'd might he be, what a beard hast thou got! Thou hast got more hair on thy chin than Dobbin my fill-horse has on his tail.

Launcelot Gobbo.
It should seem then that Dobbin's tail grows backward. I am sure he had more hair of his tail than I have of my face when I last saw him.

Old Gobbo.
Lord, how art thou chang'd! How dost thou and thy master agree? I have brought him a present. How 'gree you now?

Launcelot Gobbo.
Well, well; but for mine own part, as I have set up my rest to run away, so I will not rest till I have run some ground. My master's a very Jew. Give him a present! Give him a halter. I am famish'd in his service; you may tell every finger I have with my ribs. Father, I am glad you are come; give me your present to one Master Bassanio, who indeed gives rare new liveries. If I serve not him, I will run as far as God has any ground. O rare fortune, here comes the man. To him, father, for I am a Jew if I serve the Jew any longer.

Enter Bassanio with a follower or two, one of them Leonardo.

Bassanio.
You may do so, but let it be so hasted that supper be ready at the farthest by five of the clock. See these letters deliver'd, put the liveries to making, and desire Gratiano to come anon to my lodging.

Exit one of his men.

Launcelot Gobbo.
To him, father.

Old Gobbo.
God bless your worship!

Bassanio.
Gramercy, wouldst thou aught with me?

Old Gobbo.
Here's my son, sir, a poor boy—

Launcelot Gobbo.
Not a poor boy, sir, but the rich Jew's man, that would, sir, as my father shall specify—

Old Gobbo.
He hath a great infection, sir, as one would say, to serve—

Launcelot Gobbo.
Indeed the short and the long is, I serve the Jew, and have a desire, as my father shall specify—

Old Gobbo.
His master and he (saving your worship's reverence) are scarce cater-cousins—

Launcelot Gobbo.
To be brief, the very truth is that the Jew, having done me wrong, doth cause me, as my father, being I hope an old man, shall frutify unto you—

Old Gobbo.
I have here a dish of doves that I would bestow upon your worship, and my suit is—

Launcelot Gobbo.
In very brief, the suit is impertinent to myself, as your worship shall know by this honest old man, and though I say it, though old man, yet poor man, my father.

Bassanio.
One speak for both. What would you?

Launcelot Gobbo.
Serve you, sir.

Old Gobbo.
That is the very defect of the matter, sir.

Bassanio.
I know thee well, thou hast obtain'd thy suit.
Shylock thy master spoke with me this day,
And hath preferr'd thee, if it be preferment
To leave a rich Jew's service, to become
The follower of so poor a gentleman.

Launcelot Gobbo.
The old proverb is very well parted between my master Shylock and you, sir: you have the grace of God, sir, and he hath enough.

Bassanio.
Thou speak'st it well. Go, father, with thy son.
Take leave of thy old master, and inquire
My lodging out.—Give him a livery
More guarded than his fellows'; see it done.

Launcelot Gobbo.
Father, in. I cannot get a service, no, I have ne'er a tongue in my head, well!

Looking on his palm.

If any man in Italy have a fairer table, which doth offer to swear upon a book, I shall have good fortune. Go to, here's a simple line of life! Here's a small trifle of wives! Alas, fifteen wives is nothing! Eleven widows and nine maids is a simple coming-in for one man. And then to scape drowning thrice, and to be in peril of my life with the edge of a feather-bed, here are simple scapes. Well, if Fortune be a woman, she's a good wench for this gear. Father, come, I'll take my leave of the Jew in the twinkling.

Exit Clown with Old Gobbo.

Bassanio.
I pray thee, good Leonardo, think on this:
These things being bought and orderly bestowed,
Return in haste, for I do feast tonight
My best esteem'd acquaintance. Hie thee, go.

Leonardo.
My best endeavors shall be done herein.

Enter Gratiano.

Gratiano.
Where's your master?

Leonardo.
                    Yonder, sir, he walks.

Exit Leonardo.

Gratiano.
Signior Bassanio!

Bassanio.
Gratiano!

Gratiano.
I have suit to you.

Bassanio.
                    You have obtain'd it.

Gratiano.
You must not deny me; I must go with you to Belmont.

Bassanio.
Why then you must. But hear thee, Gratiano:
Thou art too wild, too rude, and bold of voice—
Parts that become thee happily enough,
And in such eyes as ours appear not faults,
But where thou art not known, why, there they show
Something too liberal. Pray thee take pain
To allay with some cold drops of modesty
Thy skipping spirit, lest through thy wild behavior
I be misconst'red in the place I go to,
And lose my hopes.

Gratiano.
          Signior Bassanio, hear me:
If I do not put on a sober habit,
Talk with respect, and swear but now and then,
Wear prayer-books in my pocket, look demurely,
Nay more, while grace is saying hood mine eyes
Thus with my hat, and sigh and say amen,
Use all the observance of civility,
Like one well studied in a sad ostent
To please his grandam, never trust me more.

Bassanio.
Well, we shall see your bearing.

Gratiano.
Nay, but I bar tonight, you shall not gauge me
By what we do tonight.

Bassanio.
          No, that were pity.
I would entreat you rather to put on
Your boldest suit of mirth, for we have friends
That purpose merriment. But fare you well,
I have some business.

Gratiano.
And I must to Lorenzo and the rest,
But we will visit you at supper-time.

Exeunt.

Scene 3

Venice. A room in Shylock's house.

(Jessica; Launcelot)

Shylock's daughter Jessica expresses her sorrow at Launcelot's leaving, as he was the one distraction from the intense boredom of the household. She gives him a letter for Bassanio's friend Lorenzo, whom she is planning to elope with.

Enter Jessica and the Clown Launcelot.

Jessica.
I am sorry thou wilt leave my father so.
Our house is hell, and thou, a merry devil,
Didst rob it of some taste of tediousness.
But fare thee well, there is a ducat for thee,
And, Launcelot, soon at supper shalt thou see
Lorenzo, who is thy new master's guest.
Give him this letter, do it secretly,
And so farewell. I would not have my father
See me in talk with thee.

Launcelot Gobbo.
Adieu, tears exhibit my tongue. Most beautiful pagan, most sweet Jew! If a Christian do not play the knave and get thee, I am much deceiv'd. But adieu, these foolish drops do something drown my manly spirit. Adieu!

Jessica.
Farewell, good Launcelot.

Exit Launcelot.

Alack, what heinous sin is it in me
To be ashamed to be my father's child!
But though I am a daughter to his blood,
I am not to his manners. O Lorenzo,
If thou keep promise, I shall end this strife,
Become a Christian and thy loving wife.

Exit.

Scene 4

Venice. A street.

(Gratiano; Lorenzo; Salerio; Solanio; Launcelot)

Lorenzo, Gratiano, Salerio, and Solanio discuss the details of the plan to help carry off Jessica. Launcelot delivers Jessica's letter.

Enter Gratiano, Lorenzo, Salerio, and Solanio.

Lorenzo.
Nay, we will slink away in supper-time,
Disguise us at my lodging, and return
All in an hour.

Gratiano.
We have not made good preparation.

Salerio.
We have not spoke us yet of torch-bearers.

Solanio.
'Tis vile, unless it may be quaintly ordered,
And better in my mind not undertook.

Lorenzo.
'Tis now but four of clock, we have two hours
To furnish us.

Enter Launcelot with a letter.

     Friend Launcelot, what's the news?

Launcelot Gobbo.
And it shall please you to break up this, it shall seem to signify.

Lorenzo.
I know the hand; in faith, 'tis a fair hand,
And whiter than the paper it writ on
Is the fair hand that writ.

Gratiano.
     Love-news, in faith.

Launcelot Gobbo.
By your leave, sir.

Lorenzo.
Whither goest thou?

Launcelot Gobbo.
Marry, sir, to bid my old master the Jew to sup tonight with my new master the Christian.

Lorenzo.
Hold here, take this. Tell gentle Jessica
I will not fail her, speak it privately.

Exit Clown.

Go, gentlemen,
Will you prepare you for this masque tonight?
I am provided of a torch-bearer.

Salerio.
Ay, marry, I'll be gone about it straight.

Solanio.
And so will I.

Lorenzo.
     Meet me and Gratiano
At Gratiano's lodging some hour hence.

Salerio.
'Tis good we do so.

Exit with Solanio.

Gratiano.
Was not that letter from fair Jessica?

Lorenzo.
I must needs tell thee all. She hath directed
How I shall take her from her father's house,
What gold and jewels she is furnish'd with,
What page's suit she hath in readiness.
If e'er the Jew her father come to heaven,
It will be for his gentle daughter's sake,
And never dare misfortune cross her foot,
Unless she do it under this excuse,
That she is issue to a faithless Jew.
Come go with me, peruse this as thou goest.
Fair Jessica shall be my torch-bearer.

Exeunt.

Scene 5

Venice. Before Shylock's house.

(Shylock; Launcelot; Jessica)

Shylock bids a grumpy farewell to Launcelot as he prepares to leave for dinner at Bassanio's, predicting that the servant will not find life so easy with another master. He is uneasy and does not particularly wish to go to the meal. Still, he gives Jessica his keys and tells her to bar herself up against the possibility of seeing revelers pass by. He leaves.

Enter Shylock the Jew and his man that was, the Clown Launcelot.

Shylock.
Well, thou shalt see, thy eyes shall be thy judge,
The difference of old Shylock and Bassanio.—
What, Jessica!—Thou shalt not gurmandize,
As thou hast done with me—What, Jessica!—
And sleep and snore, and rend apparel out—
Why, Jessica, I say!

Launcelot Gobbo.
     Why, Jessica!

Shylock.
Who bids thee call? I do not bid thee call.

Launcelot Gobbo.
Your worship was wont to tell me I could do nothing without bidding.

Enter Jessica.

Jessica.
Call you? What is your will?

Shylock.
I am bid forth to supper, Jessica.
There are my keys. But wherefore should I go?
I am not bid for love, they flatter me,
But yet I'll go in hate, to feed upon
The prodigal Christian. Jessica, my girl,
Look to my house. I am right loath to go;
There is some ill a-brewing towards my rest,
For I did dream of money-bags tonight.

Launcelot Gobbo.
I beseech you, sir, go. My young master doth expect your reproach.

Shylock.
So do I his.

Launcelot Gobbo.
And they have conspir'd together. I will not say you shall see a masque, but if you do, then it was not for nothing that my nose fell a-bleeding on Black Monday last at six a' clock i' th' morning, falling out that year on Ash We'n'sday was four year in th' afternoon.

Shylock.
What, are there masques? Hear you me, Jessica:
Lock up my doors, and when you hear the drum
And the vile squealing of the wry-neck'd fife,
Clamber not you up to the casements then,
Nor thrust your head into the public street
To gaze on Christian fools with varnish'd faces;
But stop my house's ears, I mean my casements;
Let not the sound of shallow fopp'ry enter
My sober house. By Jacob's staff I swear
I have no mind of feasting forth tonight;
But I will go. Go you before me, sirrah,
Say I will come.

Launcelot Gobbo.
I will go before, sir. Mistress, look out at window for all this—
         There will come a Christian by,
         Will be worth a Jewess' eye.

Exit.

Shylock.
What says that fool of Hagar's offspring, ha?

Jessica.
His words were "Farewell, mistress!"—nothing else.

Shylock.
The patch is kind enough, but a huge feeder,
Snail-slow in profit, and he sleeps by day
More than the wild-cat. Drones hive not with me,
Therefore I part with him, and part with him
To one that I would have him help to waste
His borrowed purse. Well, Jessica, go in,
Perhaps I will return immediately.
Do as I bid you, shut doors after you;
Fast bind, fast find—
A proverb never stale in thrifty mind.

Exit.

Jessica.
Farewell, and if my fortune be not cross'd,
I have a father, you a daughter, lost.

Exit.

Scene 6

Venice. Before Shylock's house.

(Gratiano; Salerio; Lorenzo; Jessica; Antonio)

Lorenzo's friends wait for him in front of Shylock's house. He arrives and calls out. Jessica, dressed as a boy, throws him a casket of jewels and goes back to find more money, to the general approval of Lorenzo's friends. As they leave, Antonio comes to find Gratiano and remind him that it is past time he were leaving with Bassanio.

Enter two of the masquers, Gratiano and Salerio.

Gratiano.
This is the penthouse under which Lorenzo
Desir'd us to make stand.

Salerio.
         His hour is almost past.

Gratiano.
And it is marvel he out-dwells his hour,
For lovers ever run before the clock.

Salerio.
O, ten times faster Venus' pigeons fly
To seal love's bonds new made, than they are wont
To keep obliged faith unforfeited!

Act 2, Scene 6

Gratiano.
That ever holds. Who riseth from a feast
With that keen appetite that he sits down?
Where is the horse that doth untread again
His tedious measures with the unbated fire
That he did pace them first? All things that are,
Are with more spirit chased than enjoy'd.
How like a younger or a prodigal
The scarfed bark puts from her native bay,
Hugg'd and embraced by the strumpet wind!
How like the prodigal doth she return,
With over-weather'd ribs and ragged sails,
Lean, rent, and beggar'd by the strumpet wind!

Enter Lorenzo.

Salerio.
Here comes Lorenzo, more of this hereafter.

Lorenzo.
Sweet friends, your patience for my long abode;
Not I but my affairs have made you wait.
When you shall please to play the thieves for wives,
I'll watch as long for you then. Approach,
Here dwells my father Jew. Ho! Who's within?

Enter Jessica above in boy's clothes.

Jessica.
Who are you? Tell me for more certainty,
Albeit I'll swear that I do know your tongue.

Lorenzo.
Lorenzo, and thy love.

Jessica.
Lorenzo, certain, and my love indeed,
For who love I so much? And now who knows
But you, Lorenzo, whether I am yours?

Lorenzo.
Heaven and thy thoughts are witness that thou art.

Jessica.
Here, catch this casket, it is worth the pains.
I am glad 'tis night, you do not look on me,
For I am much asham'd of my exchange.
But love is blind, and lovers cannot see
The pretty follies that themselves commit,
For if they could, Cupid himself would blush
To see me thus transformed to a boy.

Lorenzo.
Descend, for you must be my torch-bearer.

Jessica.
What, must I hold a candle to my shames?
They in themselves, good sooth, are too too light.
Why, 'tis an office of discovery, love,
And I should be obscur'd.

Lorenzo.
              So are you, sweet,
Even in the lovely garnish of a boy.
But come at once,
For the close night doth play the runaway,
And we are stay'd for at Bassanio's feast.

Jessica.
I will make fast the doors, and gild myself
With some more ducats, and be with you straight.

Exit above.

Gratiano.
Now by my hood, a gentle, and no Jew.

Lorenzo.
Beshrew me but I love her heartily,
For she is wise, if I can judge of her,
And fair she is, if that mine eyes be true,
And true she is, as she hath prov'd herself;
And therefore, like herself, wise, fair, and true,
Shall she be placed in my constant soul.

Enter Jessica.

What, art thou come? On, gentlemen, away!
Our masquing mates by this time for us stay.

Exit with Jessica and Salerio.
Enter Antonio.

Antonio.
Who's there?

Gratiano.
Signior Antonio!

Antonio.
Fie, fie, Gratiano, where are all the rest?
'Tis nine a' clock—our friends all stay for you.
No masque tonight, the wind is come about,
Bassanio presently will go aboard.
I have sent twenty out to seek for you.

Gratiano.
I am glad on't. I desire no more delight
Than to be under sail, and gone tonight.

Exeunt.

Scene 7

Belmont. A room in Portia's house.

(Portia; Prince of Morocco)

The Prince of Morocco considers the three caskets and finally chooses the golden one, which promises he shall obtain what many men desire. Inside, however, is only a death's head and a moralizing scroll warning him against being taken in by appearances. He leaves at once, to Portia's relief.

Flourish cornets. Enter Portia with the Prince of Morocco and both their Trains.

Portia.
Go, draw aside the curtains and discover
The several caskets to this noble prince.
Now make your choice.

The Prince of Morocco.
This first, of gold, who this inscription bears,
"Who chooseth me shall gain what many men desire";
The second, silver, which this promise carries,
"Who chooseth me shall get as much as he deserves";
This third, dull lead, with warning all as blunt,
"Who chooseth me must give and hazard all he hath."
How shall I know if I do choose the right?

Portia.
The one of them contains my picture, Prince:
If you choose that, then I am yours withal.

The Prince of Morocco.
Some god direct my judgment! Let me see,
I will survey th' inscriptions back again.
What says this leaden casket?
"Who chooseth me must give and hazard all he hath."
Must give—for what? For lead, hazard for lead?
This casket threatens. Men that hazard all
Do it in hope of fair advantages;
A golden mind stoops not to shows of dross.
I'll then nor give nor hazard aught for lead.
What says the silver with her virgin hue?
"Who chooseth me shall get as much as he deserves."
As much as he deserves! Pause there, Morocco,
And weigh thy value with an even hand.
If thou beest rated by thy estimation,
Thou dost deserve enough, and yet enough
May not extend so far as to the lady;
And yet to be afeard of my deserving
Were but a weak disabling of myself.
As much as I deserve! Why, that's the lady.
I do in birth deserve her, and in fortunes,
In graces, and in qualities of breeding;
But more than these, in love I do deserve.
What if I stray'd no farther, but chose here?
Let's see once more this saying grav'd in gold:
"Who chooseth me shall gain what many men desire."
Why, that's the lady, all the world desires her.
From the four corners of the earth they come
To kiss this shrine, this mortal breathing saint.
The Hyrcanian deserts and the vasty wilds
Of wide Arabia are as throughfares now
For princes to come view fair Portia.
The watery kingdom, whose ambitious head
Spets in the face of heaven, is no bar
To stop the foreign spirits, but they come
As o'er a brook to see fair Portia.
One of these three contains her heavenly picture.
Is't like that lead contains her? 'Twere damnation
To think so base a thought; it were too gross
To rib her cerecloth in the obscure grave.
Or shall I think in silver she's immur'd,
Being ten times undervalued to tried gold?
O sinful thought! Never so rich a gem
Was set in worse than gold. They have in England
A coin that bears the figure of an angel
Stamp'd in gold, but that's insculp'd upon;
But here an angel in a golden bed
Lies all within. Deliver me the key.
Here do I choose, and thrive I as I may!

Portia.
There take it, Prince, and if my form lie there,
Then I am yours.

He unlocks the golden casket.

The Prince of Morocco.
                O hell! What have we here?
A carrion Death, within whose empty eye
There is a written scroll! I'll read the writing.

Reads.

"All that glisters is not gold,

*Often have you heard that told;
Many a man his life hath sold
But my outside to behold.
Gilded tombs do worms infold.
Had you been as wise as bold,
Young in limbs, in judgment old,
Your answer had not been inscroll'd.
Fare you well, your suit is cold."
Cold indeed, and labor lost:
Then farewell heat, and welcome frost!
Portia, adieu. I have too griev'd a heart
To take a tedious leave; thus losers part.*

Exit with his Train.

Portia.
A gentle riddance. Draw the curtains, go.
Let all of his complexion choose me so.

Exeunt.

Scene 8

Venice. A street.

(Salerio; Solanio)

Salerio and Solanio discuss Shylock's rage over the loss of his daughter and his money, and how he had the Duke search all over for both. His passion is such that he is being followed and mocked by all the children of Venice. The two realize that Antonio will be in danger from Shylock if he is unable to repay the loan, and Salerio is afraid, as he has heard of a shipwreck that may be of one of Antonio's vessels. They leave to find Antonio and attempt to cheer him up a little.

Enter Salerio and Solanio.

Salerio.
Why, man, I saw Bassanio under sail,
With him is Gratiano gone along;
And in their ship I am sure Lorenzo is not.

Solanio.
The villain Jew with outcries rais'd the Duke,
Who went with him to search Bassanio's ship.

Salerio.
He came too late, the ship was under sail,
But there the Duke was given to understand
That in a gondilo were seen together
Lorenzo and his amorous Jessica.
Besides, Antonio certified the Duke
They were not with Bassanio in his ship.

Solanio.
I never heard a passion so confus'd,
So strange, outrageous, and so variable
As the dog Jew did utter in the streets.
"My daughter! O my ducats! O my daughter!
Fled with a Christian! O my Christian ducats!
Justice! The law! My ducats, and my daughter!
A sealed bag, two sealed bags of ducats,
Of double ducats, stol'n from me by my daughter!
And jewels, two stones, two rich and precious stones,
Stol'n by my daughter! Justice! Find the girl,
She hath the stones upon her, and the ducats."

Salerio.
Why, all the boys in Venice follow him,
Crying, his stones, his daughter, and his ducats.

Solanio.
Let good Antonio look he keep his day,
Or he shall pay for this.

Salerio.
                    Marry, well rememb'red.
I reason'd with a Frenchman yesterday,
Who told me, in the Narrow Seas that part
The French and English, there miscarried
A vessel of our country richly fraught.
I thought upon Antonio when he told me,
And wish'd in silence that it were not his.

Solanio.
You were best to tell Antonio what you hear,
Yet do not suddenly, for it may grieve him.

Salerio.
A kinder gentleman treads not the earth.
I saw Bassanio and Antonio part:
Bassanio told him he would make some speed
Of his return; he answered, "Do not so,
Slubber not business for my sake, Bassanio,
But stay the very riping of the time;
And for the Jew's bond which he hath of me,
Let it not enter in your mind of love.
Be merry, and employ your chiefest thoughts
To courtship, and such fair ostents of love
As shall conveniently become you there."
And even there, his eye being big with tears,
Turning his face, he put his hand behind him,
And with affection wondrous sensible

He wrung Bassanio's hand, and so they parted.

Solanio.
I think he only loves the world for him.
I pray thee let us go and find him out
And quicken his embraced heaviness
With some delight or other.

Salerio.
                    Do we so.

Exeunt.

Scene 9

Belmont. A room in Portia's house.

(Nerissa; Servitor; Prince of Arragon; Portia; Stephano)

The pretentious Prince of Aragon comes to make his choice of the caskets. He chooses the silver, who only contains a fool's head and a scroll calling him an idiot. He leaves, and Portia's servant Stephano announces the arrival of a contender from Venice, whom he praises to the skies. Portia is excited and Nerissa hopes that it will prove to be Bassanio.

Enter Nerissa and a servant.

Nerissa.
Quick, quick, I pray thee, draw the curtain straight;
The Prince of Arragon hath ta'en his oath,
And comes to his election presently.

Flourish cornets. Enter the Prince of Arragon, his Train, and Portia.

Portia.
Behold, there stand the caskets, noble Prince
If you choose that wherein I am contain'd,
Straight shall our nuptial rites be solemniz'd;
But if you fail, without more speech, my lord,
You must be gone from hence immediately.

The Prince of Arragon.
I am enjoin'd by oath to observe three things:
First, never to unfold to any one
Which casket 'twas I chose; next, if I fail
Of the right casket, never in my life
To woo a maid in way of marriage;
Lastly,
If I do fail in fortune of my choice,
Immediately to leave you, and be gone.

Portia.
To these injunctions every one doth swear
That comes to hazard for my worthless self.

The Prince of Arragon.
And so have I address'd me. Fortune now
To my heart's hope! Gold, silver, and base lead.
"Who chooseth me must give and hazard all he hath."
You shall look fairer ere I give or hazard.
What says the golden chest? Ha, let me see:
"Who chooseth me shall gain what many men desire."
What many men desire! That many may be meant
By the fool multitude that choose by show,
Not learning more than the fond eye doth teach,
Which pries not to th' interior, but like the martlet
Builds in the weather on the outward wall,
Even in the force and road of casualty.
I will not choose what many men desire,
Because I will not jump with common spirits,
And rank me with the barbarous multitudes.
Why then to thee, thou silver treasure house,
Tell me once more what title thou dost bear:
"Who chooseth me shall get as much as he deserves."
And well said too; for who shall go about
To cozen fortune, and be honorable
Without the stamp of merit? Let none presume
To wear an undeserved dignity.
O that estates, degrees, and offices
Were not deriv'd corruptly, and that clear honor
Were purchas'd by the merit of the wearer!
How many then should cover that stand bare?
How many be commanded that command?
How much low peasantry would then be gleaned
From the true seed of honor? And how much honor
Pick'd from the chaff and ruin of the times
To be new varnish'd? Well, but to my choice:
"Who chooseth me shall get as much as he deserves."
I will assume desert. Give me a key for this,
And instantly unlock my fortunes here.

He unlocks the silver casket.

Portia.
Too long a pause for that which you find there.

The Prince of Arragon.
What's here? The portrait of a blinking idiot,
Presenting me a schedule! I will read it.
How much unlike art thou to Portia!
How much unlike my hopes and my deservings!

"Who chooseth me shall have as much as he deserves"!
Did I deserve no more than a fool's head?
Is that my prize? Are my deserts no better?

Portia.
To offend and judge are distinct offices,
And of opposed natures.

The Prince of Arragon.   What is here?

Reads.

"The fire seven times tried this:
Seven times tried that judgment is,
That did never choose amiss.
Some there be that shadows kiss,
Such have but a shadow's bliss.
There be fools alive, iwis,
Silver'd o'er, and so was this.
Take what wife you will to bed,
I will ever be your head.
So be gone, you are sped."
Still more fool I shall appear
By the time I linger here.
With one fool's head I came to woo,
But I go away with two.
Sweet, adieu. I'll keep my oath,
Patiently to bear my wroth.

Exit with his Train.

Portia.
Thus hath the candle sing'd the moth.
O, these deliberate fools, when they do choose,
They have the wisdom by their wit to lose.

Nerissa.
The ancient saying is no heresy,
Hanging and wiving goes by destiny.

Portia.
Come draw the curtain, Nerissa.

Enter Stephano.

Stephano.
Where is my lady?

Portia.
                Here; what would my lord?

Stephano.
Madam, there is alighted at your gate
A young Venetian, one that comes before
To signify th' approaching of his lord,
From whom he bringeth sensible regreets:
To wit (besides commends and courteous breath),
Gifts of rich value. Yet I have not seen
So likely an ambassador of love.
A day in April never came so sweet,
To show how costly summer was at hand,
As this fore-spurrer comes before his lord.

Portia.
No more, I pray thee. I am half afeard
Thou wilt say anon he is some kin to thee,
Thou spend'st such high-day wit in praising him.
Come, come, Nerissa, for I long to see
Quick Cupid's post that comes so mannerly.

Nerissa.
Bassanio, Lord Love, if thy will it be!

Exeunt.

Act 3

Scene 1

Venice. A street.

(Solanio; Salerio; Shylock; Antonio's Servant; Tubal)

Salerio and Solanio discuss Antonio's growing losses at sea. Shylock bitterly reproaches them for having known about his daughter's flight, and they both admit to it and mock him on the subject. To their shock, the moneylender insists that he will have the pound of flesh he has been promised if Antonio cannot pay him back. Shylock's acquaintance Tubal, who has been searching for Jessica, arrives to tell Shylock of how she has been seen all over Italy and has been extravagantly spending the stolen money, even giving away a ring her mother gave her father for the sake of a monkey. Tubal also tells Shylock that Antonio is almost certain to go bankrupt, and Shylock swears to cut out the merchant's heart.

Enter Solanio and Salerio.

Solanio.
Now what news on the Rialto?

Salerio.
Why, yet it lives there uncheck'd that Antonio hath a ship of rich lading wrack'd on the Narrow Seas; the Goodwins I think they call the place, a very dangerous flat, and fatal, where the carcasses of many a tall ship lie buried, as they say, if my gossip Report be an honest woman of her word.

Solanio.
I would she were as lying a gossip in that as ever knapp'd ginger or made her neighbors believe she wept for the death of a third husband. But it is true, without any slips of prolixity, or crossing the plain highway of talk, that the good Antonio, the honest Antonio—O that I had a title good enough to keep his name company!—

Salerio.
Come, the full stop.

Solanio.
Ha, what sayest thou? Why, the end is, he hath lost a ship.

Salerio.
I would it might prove the end of his losses.

Solanio.
Let me say amen betimes, lest the devil cross my prayer, for here he comes in the likeness of a Jew.

Enter Shylock.

How now, Shylock, what news among the merchants?

Shylock.
You knew, none so well, none so well as you, of my daughter's flight.

Salerio.
That's certain. I for my part knew the tailor that made the wings she flew withal.

Solanio.
And Shylock for his own part knew the bird was fledge, and then it is the complexion of them all to leave the dam.

Shylock.
She is damn'd for it.

Salerio.
That's certain, if the devil may be her judge.

Shylock.
My own flesh and blood to rebel!

Solanio.
Out upon it, old carrion, rebels it at these years?

Shylock.
I say, my daughter is my flesh and my blood.

Salerio.
There is more difference between thy flesh and hers than between jet and ivory, more between your bloods than there is between red wine and Rhenish. But tell us, do you hear whether Antonio have had any loss at sea or no?

Shylock.
There I have another bad match. A bank-rout, a prodigal, who dare scarce show his head on the Rialto; a beggar, that was us'd to come so smug upon the mart: let him look to his bond. He was wont to call me usurer, let him look to his bond. He was wont to lend money for a Christian cur'sy, let him look to his bond.

Salerio.
Why, I am sure if he forfeit thou wilt not take his flesh. What's that good for?

Shylock.
To bait fish withal—if it will feed nothing else, it will feed my revenge. He hath disgrac'd me, and hind'red me half a million, laugh'd at my losses, mock'd at my gains, scorn'd my nation, thwarted my bargains, cool'd my friends, heated mine enemies; and what's his reason? I am a Jew. Hath not a Jew eyes? Hath not a Jew hands, organs, dimensions, senses, affections, passions; fed with the same food, hurt with the same weapons, subject to the same diseases, heal'd by the same means, warm'd and cool'd by the same winter and summer, as a Christian is? If you prick us, do we not bleed? If you tickle us, do we not laugh? If you poison us, do we not die? And if you wrong us, shall we not revenge? If we are like you in the rest, we will resemble you in that. If a Jew wrong a Christian, what is his humility? Revenge. If a Christian wrong a Jew, what should his sufferance be by Christian example? Why, revenge. The villainy you teach me, I will execute, and it shall go hard but I will better the instruction.

Enter a Servingman from Antonio.

Antonio's Servant.
Gentlemen, my master Antonio is at his house, and desires to speak with you both.

Salerio.
We have been up and down to seek him.

Enter Tubal.

Solanio.
Here comes another of the tribe; a third cannot be match'd, unless the devil himself turn Jew.

Exeunt Gentlemen Solanio and Salerio, with Servingman.

Shylock.
How now, Tubal, what news from Genoa? Hast thou found my daughter?

Tubal.
I often came where I did hear of her, but cannot find her.

Shylock.
Why, there, there, there, there! A diamond gone, cost me two thousand ducats in Frankford! The curse never fell upon our nation till now, I never felt it till now. Two thousand ducats in that, and other precious, precious jewels. I would my daughter were dead at my foot, and the jewels in her ear! Would she were hears'd at my foot, and the ducats in her coffin! No news of them? Why, so—and I know not what's spent in the search. Why, thou loss upon loss! The thief gone with so much, and so much to find the thief, and no satisfaction, no revenge, nor no ill luck stirring but what lights a' my shoulders, no sighs but a' my breathing, no tears but a' my shedding.

Tubal.
Yes, other men have ill luck too. Antonio, as I heard in Genoa—

Shylock.
What, what, what? Ill luck, ill luck?

Tubal.
Hath an argosy cast away, coming from Tripolis.

Shylock.
I thank God, I thank God. Is it true, is it true?

Tubal.
I spoke with some of the sailors that escap'd the wrack.

Shylock.
I thank thee, good Tubal, good news, good news! Ha, ha! Heard in Genoa?

Tubal.
Your daughter spent in Genoa, as I heard, one night fourscore ducats.

Shylock.
Thou stick'st a dagger in me. I shall never see my gold again. Fourscore ducats at a sitting, fourscore ducats!

Tubal.
There came diverse of Antonio's creditors in my company to Venice that swear he cannot choose but break.

Shylock.
I am very glad of it. I'll plague him, I'll torture him. I am glad of it.

Tubal.
One of them show'd me a ring that he had of your daughter for a monkey.

Shylock.
Out upon her! Thou torturest me, Tubal. It was my turkis, I had it of Leah when I was a bachelor. I would not have given it for a wilderness of monkeys.

Tubal.
But Antonio is certainly undone.

Shylock.
Nay, that's true, that's very true. Go, Tubal, fee me an officer; bespeak him a fortnight before. I will have the heart of him if he forfeit, for were he out of Venice I can make what merchandise I will. Go, Tubal, and meet me at our synagogue; go, good Tubal, at our synagogue, Tubal.

Exeunt.

Scene 2

Belmont. A room in Portia's house.

(Bassanio; Portia; Gratiano; Nerissa; Lorenzo; Jessica; Salerio; Singer)

Portia, who is enjoying Bassanio's company greatly and fears losing him should he make the wrong choice of casket, tries to convince him to wait a few days before making the test, but he insists on going through with it. After a long consideration, Bassanio chooses the lead casket, which contains a portrait of Portia. Both are overjoyed — as is Gratiano, who has been wooing Nerissa without their noticing, and now asks permission to marry her. Lorenzo, Jessica, and Salerio arrive and interrupt the joyfulness — Salerio bears a letter from Antonio informing Bassanio that he cannot repay the loan and will therefore be submitting to Shylock's craving for a pound of his flesh. Salerio informs the horrified Bassanio that it seems Shylock would not take the money now even if Antonio had it, and Jessica confirms the likelihood of this. The supremely rich Portia offers to pay the debt many times over, and sends Bassanio on his way to save Antonio.

Enter Bassanio, Portia, Gratiano, Nerissa, and all their Trains.

Portia.
I pray you tarry, pause a day or two
Before you hazard, for in choosing wrong
I lose your company; therefore forbear a while.
There's something tells me (but it is not love)
I would not lose you, and you know yourself,
Hate counsels not in such a quality.
But lest you should not understand me well—
And yet a maiden hath no tongue but thought—
I would detain you here some month or two
Before you venture for me. I could teach you
How to choose right, but then I am forsworn.
So will I never be, so may you miss me,
But if you do, you'll make me wish a sin,
That I had been forsworn. Beshrew your eyes,
They have o'erlook'd me and divided me:
One half of me is yours, the other half yours—
Mine own, I would say; but if mine, then yours,
And so all yours. O, these naughty times
Puts bars between the owners and their rights!
And so though yours, not yours. Prove it so,
Let fortune go to hell for it, not I.
I speak too long, but 'tis to peize the time,
To eche it, and to draw it out in length,
To stay you from election.

Bassanio.
                    Let me choose,
For as I am, I live upon the rack.

Portia.
Upon the rack, Bassanio! Then confess
What treason there is mingled with your love.

Bassanio.
None but that ugly treason of mistrust,
Which makes me fear th' enjoying of my love;
There may as well be amity and life
'Tween snow and fire, as treason and my love.

Portia.
Ay, but I fear you speak upon the rack,
Where men enforced do speak any thing.

Bassanio.
Promise me life, and I'll confess the truth.

Portia.
Well then, confess and live.

Bassanio.
                    Confess and love
Had been the very sum of my confession.
O happy torment, when my torturer
Doth teach me answers for deliverance!
But let me to my fortune and the caskets.

Portia.
Away then! I am lock'd in one of them;
If you do love me, you will find me out.
Nerissa and the rest, stand all aloof.
Let music sound while he doth make his choice;
Then if he lose he makes a swan-like end,
Fading in music. That the comparison
May stand more proper, my eye shall be the stream
And wat'ry death-bed for him. He may win,
And what is music then? Then music is
Even as the flourish when true subjects bow
To a new-crowned monarch; such it is
As are those dulcet sounds in break of day
That creep into the dreaming bridegroom's ear,
And summon him to marriage. Now he goes,
With no less presence, but with much more love,
Than young Alcides, when he did redeem
The virgin tribute paid by howling Troy
To the sea-monster. I stand for sacrifice;
The rest aloof are the Dardanian wives,
With bleared visages, come forth to view
The issue of th' exploit. Go, Hercules,
Live thou, I live; with much, much more dismay
I view the fight than thou that mak'st the fray.

Here music.

A song, the whilst Bassanio comments on the caskets to himself.

Singer.
Tell me where is fancy bred,
Or in the heart or in the head?
How begot, how nourished?

All.
Reply, reply.

Singer.
It is engend'red in the eyes,
With gazing fed, and fancy dies
In the cradle where it lies.
Let us all ring fancy's knell.
I'll begin it. Ding, dong, bell.

All.
Ding, dong, bell.

Bassanio.
So may the outward shows be least themselves—
The world is still deceiv'd with ornament.
In law, what plea so tainted and corrupt
But, being season'd with a gracious voice,
Obscures the show of evil? In religion,
What damned error but some sober brow
Will bless it, and approve it with a text,
Hiding the grossness with fair ornament?
There is no vice so simple but assumes
Some mark of virtue on his outward parts.
How many cowards, whose hearts are all as false
As stairs of sand, wear yet upon their chins
The beards of Hercules and frowning Mars,
Who inward search'd, have livers white as milk,
And these assume but valor's excrement
To render them redoubted! Look on beauty,
And you shall see 'tis purchas'd by the weight,
Which therein works a miracle in nature,
Making them lightest that wear most of it.
So are those crisped snaky golden locks,
Which make such wanton gambols with the wind
Upon supposed fairness, often known
To be the dowry of a second head,
The skull that bred them in the sepulchre.
Thus ornament is but the guiled shore
To a most dangerous sea; the beauteous scarf
Veiling an Indian beauty; in a word,
The seeming truth which cunning times put on
To entrap the wisest. Therefore then, thou gaudy gold,
Hard food for Midas, I will none of thee;
Nor none of thee, thou pale and common drudge
'Tween man and man; but thou, thou meager lead,
Which rather threaten'st than dost promise aught,
Thy paleness moves me more than eloquence,
And here choose I. Joy be the consequence!

Portia.

Aside.

How all the other passions fleet to air,
As doubtful thoughts, and rash-embrac'd despair,
And shudd'ring fear, and green-eyed jealousy!
O love, be moderate, allay thy ecstasy,
In measure rain thy joy, scant this excess!
I feel too much thy blessing; make it less,
For fear I surfeit.

Bassanio.
                    What find I here?

Opening the leaden casket.

Fair Portia's counterfeit! What demigod
Hath come so near creation? Move these eyes?
Or whether, riding on the balls of mine,
Seem they in motion? Here are sever'd lips,
Parted with sugar breath; so sweet a bar
Should sunder such sweet friends. Here in her hairs
The painter plays the spider, and hath woven
A golden mesh t' entrap the hearts of men
Faster than gnats in cobwebs. But her eyes—
How could he see to do them? Having made one,
Methinks it should have power to steal both his
And leave itself unfurnish'd. Yet look how far
The substance of my praise doth wrong this shadow
In underprizing it, so far this shadow
Doth limp behind the substance. Here's the scroll,
The continent and summary of my fortune.

Reads.

"You that choose not by the view,
Chance as fair, and choose as true:
Since this fortune falls to you,
Be content, and seek no new.
If you be well pleas'd with this,
And hold your fortune for your bliss,
Turn you where your lady is,
And claim her with a loving kiss."

A gentle scroll. Fair lady, by your leave,
I come by note, to give and to receive.
Like one of two contending in a prize,
That thinks he hath done well in people's eyes,
Hearing applause and universal shout,
Giddy in spirit, still gazing in a doubt
Whether those peals of praise be his or no,
So, thrice-fair lady, stand I, even so,
As doubtful whether what I see be true,
Until confirm'd, sign'd, ratified by you.

Portia.
You see me, Lord Bassanio, where I stand,
Such as I am. Though for myself alone
I would not be ambitious in my wish
To wish myself much better, yet for you,
I would be trebled twenty times myself,
A thousand times more fair, ten thousand times more rich,
That only to stand high in your account,
I might in virtues, beauties, livings, friends,
Exceed account. But the full sum of me
Is sum of something; which, to term in gross,
Is an unlesson'd girl, unschool'd, unpractic'd,
Happy in this, she is not yet so old
But she may learn; happier than this,
She is not bred so dull but she can learn;
Happiest of all, is that her gentle spirit
Commits itself to yours to be directed,
As from her lord, her governor, her king.
Myself, and what is mine, to you and yours
Is now converted. But now I was the lord
Of this fair mansion, master of my servants,
Queen o'er myself; and even now, but now,
This house, these servants, and this same myself
Are yours—my lord's!—I give them with this ring,
Which when you part from, lose, or give away,
Let it presage the ruin of your love,
And be my vantage to exclaim on you.

Bassanio.
Madam, you have bereft me of all words,
Only my blood speaks to you in my veins,
And there is such confusion in my powers,
As after some oration fairly spoke
By a beloved prince, there doth appear
Among the buzzing pleased multitude,
Where every something, being blent together,
Turns to a wild of nothing, save of joy
Express'd and not express'd. But when this ring
Parts from this finger, then parts life from hence;
O then be bold to say Bassanio's dead!

Nerissa.
My lord and lady, it is now our time,
That have stood by and seen our wishes prosper,
To cry good joy. Good joy, my lord and lady!

Gratiano.
My Lord Bassanio and my gentle lady,
I wish you all the joy that you can wish;
For I am sure you can wish none from me;
And when your honors mean to solemnize
The bargain of your faith, I do beseech you
Even at that time I may be married too.

Bassanio.
With all my heart, so thou canst get a wife.

Gratiano.
I thank your lordship, you have got me one.
My eyes, my lord, can look as swift as yours:
You saw the mistress, I beheld the maid;
You lov'd, I lov'd; for intermission
No more pertains to me, my lord, than you;
Your fortune stood upon the caskets there,
And so did mine too as the matter falls;
For wooing here until I sweat again,
And swearing till my very roof was dry
With oaths of love, at last, if promise last,
I got a promise of this fair one here
To have her love—provided that your fortune
Achiev'd her mistress.

Portia.
              Is this true, Nerissa?

Nerissa.
Madam, it is, so you stand pleas'd withal.

Bassanio.
And do you, Gratiano, mean good faith?

Gratiano.
Yes, faith, my lord.

Bassanio.
Our feast shall be much honored in your marriage.

Gratiano.
We'll play with them the first boy for a thousand ducats.

Nerissa.
What, and stake down?

Gratiano.
No, we shall ne'er win at that sport, and stake down.
But who comes here? Lorenzo and his infidel?
What, and my old Venetian friend Salerio?

Enter Lorenzo, Jessica, and Salerio, a messenger from Venice.

Bassanio.
Lorenzo and Salerio, welcome hither,
If that the youth of my new int'rest here
Have power to bid you welcome. By your leave,
I bid my very friends and countrymen,
Sweet Portia, welcome.

Portia.
                So do I, my lord,
They are entirely welcome.

Lorenzo.
I thank your honor. For my part, my lord,
My purpose was not to have seen you here,
But meeting with Salerio by the way,
He did entreat me, past all saying nay,
To come with him along.

Salerio.
              I did, my lord,
And I have reason for it. Signior Antonio
Commends him to you.

Gives Bassanio a letter.

Bassanio.
              Ere I ope his letter,
I pray you tell me how my good friend doth.

Salerio.
Not sick, my lord, unless it be in mind,
Nor well, unless in mind. His letter there
Will show you his estate.

Bassanio opens the letter.

Gratiano.
Nerissa, cheer yond stranger, bid her welcome.
Your hand, Salerio. What's the news from Venice?
How doth that royal merchant, good Antonio?
I know he will be glad of our success;
We are the Jasons, we have won the fleece.

Salerio.
I would you had won the fleece that he hath lost.

Portia.
There are some shrewd contents in yond same paper
That steals the color from Bassanio's cheek—
Some dear friend dead, else nothing in the world
Could turn so much the constitution
Of any constant man. What, worse and worse!
With leave, Bassanio, I am half yourself,
And I must freely have the half of any thing
That this same paper brings you.

Bassanio.
              O sweet Portia,
Here are a few of the unpleasant'st words
That ever blotted paper! Gentle lady,
When I did first impart my love to you,
I freely told you all the wealth I had
Ran in my veins: I was a gentleman;
And then I told you true. And yet, dear lady,
Rating myself at nothing, you shall see
How much I was a braggart: when I told you
My state was nothing, I should then have told you
That I was worse than nothing; for indeed
I have engag'd myself to a dear friend,
Engag'd my friend to his mere enemy,
To feed my means. Here is a letter, lady,
The paper as the body of my friend,
And every word in it a gaping wound
Issuing life-blood. But is it true, Salerio?
Hath all his ventures fail'd? What, not one hit?
From Tripolis, from Mexico, and England,
From Lisbon, Barbary, and India,
And not one vessel scape the dreadful touch
Of merchant-marring rocks?

Salerio.
              Not one, my lord.
Besides, it should appear, that if he had
The present money to discharge the Jew,
He would not take it. Never did I know
A creature that did bear the shape of man
So keen and greedy to confound a man.
He plies the Duke at morning and at night,
And doth impeach the freedom of the state,
If they deny him justice. Twenty merchants,
The Duke himself, and the magnificoes
Of greatest port, have all persuaded with him,
But none can drive him from the envious plea
Of forfeiture, of justice, and his bond.

Jessica.
When I was with him I have heard him swear
To Tubal and to Chus, his countrymen,
That he would rather have Antonio's flesh
Than twenty times the value of the sum
That he did owe him; and I know, my lord,
If law, authority, and power deny not,
It will go hard with poor Antonio.

Portia.
Is it your dear friend that is thus in trouble?

Bassanio.
The dearest friend to me, the kindest man,
The best-condition'd and unwearied spirit
In doing courtesies, and one in whom
The ancient Roman honor more appears
Than any that draws breath in Italy.

Portia.
What sum owes he the Jew?

Bassanio.
For me, three thousand ducats.

Portia.
                    What, no more?
Pay him six thousand, and deface the bond;
Double six thousand, and then treble that,
Before a friend of this description
Shall lose a hair through Bassanio's fault.
First go with me to church and call me wife,
And then away to Venice to your friend;
For never shall you lie by Portia's side
With an unquiet soul. You shall have gold
To pay the petty debt twenty times over.
When it is paid, bring your true friend along.
My maid Nerissa and myself mean time
Will live as maids and widows. Come away!
For you shall hence upon your wedding-day.
Bid your friends welcome, show a merry cheer—
Since you are dear bought, I will love you dear.
But let me hear the letter of your friend.

Bassanio.

Reads.

"Sweet Bassanio, my ships have all miscarried, my creditors grow cruel, my estate is very low, my bond to the Jew is forfeit; and since in paying it, it is impossible I should live, all debts are clear'd between you and I, if I might but see you at my death. Notwithstanding, use your pleasure; if your love do not persuade you to come, let not my letter."

Portia.
O love! Dispatch all business and be gone.

Bassanio.
Since I have your good leave to go away,
I will make haste; but till I come again,
No bed shall e'er be guilty of my stay,
Nor rest be interposer 'twixt us twain.

Exeunt.

Scene 3

Venice. A street.

(Shylock; Solanio; Antonio; Jailer)

Antonio, guarded by a Jailer, attempts to speak to Shylock, but the latter refuses to hear him and insists that he will have the promised forfeit. To Solanio's reassurance that the Duke will never let Shylock get away with it, Antonio points out that he will have no choice, as Venice's whole economy would collapse if the Duke simply disregards a lawful bond simply because he doesn't like it.

Enter Shylock the Jew and Solanio and Antonio and the Jailer.

Shylock.
Jailer, look to him, tell not me of mercy.
This is the fool that lent out money gratis.
Jailer, look to him.

Antonio.
                    Hear me yet, good Shylock.

Shylock.
I'll have my bond, speak not against my bond,
I have sworn an oath that I will have my bond.
Thou call'dst me dog before thou hadst a cause,
But since I am a dog, beware my fangs.
The Duke shall grant me justice. I do wonder,
Thou naughty jailer, that thou art so fond
To come abroad with him at his request.

Antonio.
I pray thee hear me speak.

Shylock.
I'll have my bond; I will not hear thee speak.
I'll have my bond, and therefore speak no more.
I'll not be made a soft and dull-ey'd fool
To shake the head, relent, and sigh, and yield
To Christian intercessors. Follow not,
I'll have no speaking, I will have my bond.

Exit Jew.

Solanio.
It is the most impenetrable cur
That ever kept with men.

Antonio.
                            Let him alone,
I'll follow him no more with bootless prayers.
He seeks my life; his reason well I know:
I oft deliver'd from his forfeitures
Many that have at times made moan to me;
Therefore he hates me.

Solanio.
                            I am sure the Duke
Will never grant this forfeiture to hold.

Antonio.
The Duke cannot deny the course of law;
For the commodity that strangers have
With us in Venice, if it be denied,
Will much impeach the justice of the state,
Since that the trade and profit of the city
Consisteth of all nations. Therefore go.
These griefs and losses have so bated me
That I shall hardly spare a pound of flesh
Tomorrow to my bloody creditor.
Well, jailer, on. Pray God Bassanio come
To see me pay his debt, and then I care not!

Exeunt.

Scene 4

Belmont. A room in Portia's house.

(Portia; Nerissa; Lorenzo; Jessica; Balthazar)

As Lorenzo praises Portia for offering to get Antonio out of trouble, the lady insists that it is nothing. She entrusts Belmont to Lorenzo and Jessica as she and Nerissa have decided to spend the time of their husbands' absence in a nearby monastery. Actually, Portia has a completely different plan in mind. She sends a letter to an old family friend, the noted lawyer Bellario, while she and Nerissa leave for Venice, planning to arrive there dressed as men.

Enter Portia, Nerissa, Lorenzo, Jessica, and Balthazar, a man of Portia's.

Lorenzo.
Madam, although I speak it in your presence,
You have a noble and a true conceit
Of godlike amity, which appears most strongly
In bearing thus the absence of your lord.
But if you knew to whom you show this honor,
How true a gentleman you send relief,
How dear a lover of my lord your husband,
I know you would be prouder of the work
Than customary bounty can enforce you.

Portia.
I never did repent for doing good,
Nor shall not now: for in companions
That do converse and waste the time together,
Whose souls do bear an egall yoke of love,
There must be needs a like proportion
Of lineaments, of manners, and of spirit;
Which makes me think that this Antonio,
Being the bosom lover of my lord,
Must needs be like my lord. If it be so,
How little is the cost I have bestowed
In purchasing the semblance of my soul,
From out the state of hellish cruelty.
This comes too near the praising of myself,
Therefore no more of it. Hear other things:
Lorenzo, I commit into your hands
The husbandry and manage of my house
Until my lord's return. For mine own part,
I have toward heaven breath'd a secret vow
To live in prayer and contemplation,
Only attended by Nerissa here,
Until her husband and my lord's return.
There is a monast'ry two miles off,
And there we will abide. I do desire you
Not to deny this imposition,
The which my love and some necessity
Now lays upon you.

Lorenzo.
                            Madam, with all my heart,
I shall obey you in all fair commands.

Portia.
My people do already know my mind,
And will acknowledge you and Jessica
In place of Lord Bassanio and myself.
So fare you well till we shall meet again.

Lorenzo.
Fair thoughts and happy hours attend on you!

Jessica.
I wish your ladyship all heart's content.

Portia.
I thank you for your wish, and am well pleas'd
To wish it back on you. Fare you well, Jessica.

Exeunt Jessica and Lorenzo.

Now, Balthazar,
As I have ever found thee honest-true,
So let me find thee still. Take this same letter,
And use thou all th' endeavor of a man
In speed to Padua. See thou render this
Into my cousin's hands, Doctor Bellario,
And look what notes and garments he doth give thee,
Bring them, I pray thee, with imagin'd speed
Unto the traject, to the common ferry
Which trades to Venice. Waste no time in words,
But get thee gone. I shall be there before thee.

Balthazar.
Madam, I go with all convenient speed.

Exit.

Portia.
Come on, Nerissa, I have work in hand
That you yet know not of. We'll see our husbands
Before they think of us.

Nerissa.
                    Shall they see us?

Portia.
They shall, Nerissa; but in such a habit
That they shall think we are accomplished
With that we lack. I'll hold thee any wager,
When we are both accoutered like young men,
I'll prove the prettier fellow of the two,
And wear my dagger with the braver grace,
And speak between the change of man and boy
With a reed voice, and turn two mincing steps
Into a manly stride; and speak of frays
Like a fine bragging youth, and tell quaint lies,
How honorable ladies sought my love,
Which I denying, they fell sick and died.
I could not do withal. Then I'll repent,
And wish, for all that, that I had not kill'd them;
And twenty of these puny lies I'll tell,
That men shall swear I have discontinued school
Above a twelvemonth. I have within my mind
A thousand raw tricks of these bragging Jacks,
Which I will practice.

Nerissa.
                Why, shall we turn to men?

Portia.
Fie, what a question's that,
If thou wert near a lewd interpreter!
But come, I'll tell thee all my whole device
When I am in my coach, which stays for us
At the park-gate; and therefore haste away,
For we must measure twenty miles today.

Exeunt.

Scene 5

Belmont. A garden at Portia's house.

(Launcelot; Jessica; Lorenzo)

Launcelot and Jessica meet again and trade barbs, the servant insisting that she is damned for not being a Christian. Lorenzo enters and joins in the fun, though in the end he dismisses Launcelot to his work. They are all in a merry mood. Jessica praises Portia, and Lorenzo assures her that he is as good a man as Portia is a good woman, a claim Jessica does not take overly seriously.

Enter Clown Launcelot and Jessica.

Launcelot Gobbo.
Yes, truly, for look you, the sins of the father are to be laid upon the children; therefore, I promise you, I fear you. I was always plain with you, and so now I speak my agitation of the matter; therefore be a' good cheer, for truly I think you are damn'd. There is but one hope in it that can do you any good, and that is but a kind of bastard hope neither.

Jessica.
And what hope is that, I pray thee?

Launcelot Gobbo.
Marry, you may partly hope that your father got you not, that you are not the Jew's daughter.

Jessica.
That were a kind of bastard hope indeed; so the sins of my mother should be visited upon me.

Launcelot Gobbo.
Truly then I fear you are damn'd both by father and mother; thus when I shun Scylla, your father, I fall into Charybdis, your mother. Well, you are gone both ways.

Jessica.
I shall be sav'd by my husband, he hath made me a Christian!

Launcelot Gobbo.
Truly, the more to blame he; we were Christians enow before, e'en as many as could well live one by another. This making of Christians will raise the price of hogs. If we grow all to be pork-eaters, we shall not shortly have a rasher on the coals for money.

Enter Lorenzo.

Jessica.
I'll tell my husband, Launcelot, what you say. Here he comes.

Lorenzo.
I shall grow jealous of you shortly, Launcelot, if you thus get my wife into corners!

Jessica.
Nay, you need not fear us, Lorenzo, Launcelot and I are out. He tells me flatly there's no mercy for me in heaven because I am a Jew's daughter; and he says you are no good member of the commonwealth, for in converting Jews to Christians, you raise the price of pork.

Lorenzo.
I shall answer that better to the commonwealth than you can the getting up of the Negro's belly; the Moor is with child by you, Launcelot.

Launcelot Gobbo.
It is much that the Moor should be more than reason; but if she be less than an honest woman, she is indeed more than I took her for.

Lorenzo.
How every fool can play upon the word! I think the best grace of wit will shortly turn into silence, and discourse grow commendable in none only but parrots. Go in, sirrah, bid them prepare for dinner.

Launcelot Gobbo.
That is done, sir, they have all stomachs!

Lorenzo.
Goodly Lord, what a wit-snapper are you! Then bid them prepare dinner.

Launcelot Gobbo.
That is done too, sir, only "cover" is the word.

Lorenzo.
Will you cover then, sir?

Launcelot Gobbo.
Not so, sir, neither, I know my duty.

Lorenzo.
Yet more quarreling with occasion! Wilt thou show the whole wealth of thy wit in an instant? I pray thee understand a plain man in his plain meaning: go to thy fellows, bid them cover the table, serve in the meat, and we will come in to dinner.

Launcelot Gobbo.
For the table, sir, it shall be serv'd in; for the meat, sir, it shall be cover'd; for your coming in to dinner, sir, why, let it be as humors and conceits shall govern.

Exit Clown.

Lorenzo.
O dear discretion, how his words are suited!
The fool hath planted in his memory
An army of good words, and I do know
A many fools, that stand in better place,
Garnish'd like him, that for a tricksy word
Defy the matter. How cheer'st thou, Jessica?
And now, good sweet, say thy opinion,
How dost thou like the Lord Bassanio's wife?

Jessica.
Past all expressing. It is very meet
The Lord Bassanio live an upright life,
For having such a blessing in his lady,
He finds the joys of heaven here on earth,
And if on earth he do not merit it,
In reason he should never come to heaven!

Why, if two gods should play some heavenly match,
And on the wager lay two earthly women,
And Portia one, there must be something else
Pawn'd with the other, for the poor rude world
Hath not her fellow.

Lorenzo.
　　　　　　　Even such a husband
Hast thou of me as she is for a wife.

Jessica.
Nay, but ask my opinion too of that.

Lorenzo.
I will anon, first let us go to dinner.

Jessica.
Nay, let me praise you while I have a stomach.

Lorenzo.
No, pray thee, let it serve for table-talk;
Then howsome'er thou speak'st, 'mong other things
I shall digest it.

Jessica.
　　　　　　　Well, I'll set you forth.

Exeunt.

Act 4

Scene 1

Venice. A court of justice.

(Duke; Magnificoes; Antonio; Bassanio; Salerio; Gratiano; Shylock; Nerissa; Portia)

The Duke of Venice tells Antonio how sorry he is about all this, but Antonio insists that he would rather suffer than see the law diminished. The Duke tells Shylock how he expects the moneylender to relent, but Shylock insists he will have his pound of flesh, predicting the downfall of all that sustains the state if he is refused. Bassanio offers him twice the amount of money he paid, but Shylock still refuses, while Antonio tells his friends that there is no point in trying to argue. The Duke threatens to dismiss the court unless the lawyer Bellario arrives, as Gratiano hurls insults on Shylock to no effect. In Bellario's place come Portia and Nerissa, disguised as a lawyer and his clerk. After assessing the case, Portia concludes that nothing can stop Shylock other than his granting mercy, which she asks him to do, but he refuses. She reads the contract between Antonio and Shylock and insists that it must be followed to the letter. Antonio prepares to die. But just at the moment that Shylock is going to take his pound of flesh, Portia warns him that the contract does not allow him to take any of Antonio's blood. Flummoxed, Shylock agrees to take the money he was offered, but now Portia is as inflexible as he was, insisting that he only take a pound of flesh, no more nor less, and without spilling any blood, on pain of being convicted of trying to murder a citizen of Venice. Bassanio is ready to pay Shylock back his money, but Portia rules that it is too late for that. Shylock gives up his claim, but now Portia tells him that for having attempted to kill a citizen, his goods are forfeited to Antonio and the state, and he himself is under sentence of death. To show off his mercy, the Duke immediately pardons the moneylender his life. Shylock protests that without his money, he is no longer anything. Antonio returns his goods to him, on condition that he swear to leave his money to Jessica and Lorenzo and that he become a Christian. Forced to agree, Shylock begs leave to return home, swearing he will sign all the promises there. He does not feel well. Antonio and Bassanio thank the lawyer, asking permission to pay "him", but Portia insists she will accept nothing. To test her husband, she asks only for the ring he is wearing. He tries to refuse it, as he received it from his wife and swore to her he would not take it off, but in the end he sends Gratiano after the lawyer with the ring.

Enter the Duke, the Magnificoes, Antonio, Bassanio, Salerio, and Gratiano with others.

The Duke of Venice.
What, is Antonio here?

Antonio.
Ready, so please your Grace.

The Duke of Venice.
I am sorry for thee. Thou art come to answer
A stony adversary, an inhuman wretch,
Uncapable of pity, void and empty
From any dram of mercy.

Antonio.
　　　　　　　I have heard
Your Grace hath ta'en great pains to qualify
His rigorous course; but since he stands obdurate,
And that no lawful means can carry me
Out of his envy's reach, I do oppose
My patience to his fury, and am arm'd
To suffer, with a quietness of spirit,
The very tyranny and rage of his.

Act 4, Scene 1

The Duke of Venice.
Go one, and call the Jew into the court.

Salerio.
He is ready at the door; he comes, my lord.

Enter Shylock.

The Duke of Venice.
Make room, and let him stand before our face.
Shylock, the world thinks, and I think so too,
That thou but leadest this fashion of thy malice
To the last hour of act, and then 'tis thought
Thou'lt show thy mercy and remorse more strange
Than is thy strange apparent cruelty;
And where thou now exacts the penalty,
Which is a pound of this poor merchant's flesh,
Thou wilt not only loose the forfeiture,
But touch'd with humane gentleness and love,
Forgive a moi'ty of the principal,
Glancing an eye of pity on his losses,
That have of late so huddled on his back,
Enow to press a royal merchant down,
And pluck commiseration of his state
From brassy bosoms and rough hearts of flints,
From stubborn Turks, and Tartars never train'd
To offices of tender courtesy.
We all expect a gentle answer, Jew!

Shylock.
I have possess'd your Grace of what I purpose,
And by our holy Sabbath have I sworn
To have the due and forfeit of my bond.
If you deny it, let the danger light
Upon your charter and your city's freedom!
You'll ask me why I rather choose to have
A weight of carrion flesh than to receive
Three thousand ducats. I'll not answer that;
But say it is my humor, is it answer'd?
What if my house be troubled with a rat,
And I be pleas'd to give ten thousand ducats
To have it ban'd? What, are you answer'd yet?
Some men there are love not a gaping pig;
Some that are mad if they behold a cat;
And others, when the bagpipe sings i' th' nose,
Cannot contain their urine: for affection,
Mistress of passion, sways it to the mood
Of what it likes or loathes. Now for your answer:
As there is no firm reason to be rend'red
Why he cannot abide a gaping pig;
Why he, a harmless necessary cat;
Why he, a woollen bagpipe, but of force
Must yield to such inevitable shame
As to offend, himself being offended;
So can I give no reason, nor I will not,
More than a lodg'd hate and a certain loathing
I bear Antonio, that I follow thus
A losing suit against him. Are you answered?

Bassanio.
This is no answer, thou unfeeling man,
To excuse the current of thy cruelty.

Shylock.
I am not bound to please thee with my answers.

Bassanio.
Do all men kill the things they do not love?

Shylock.
Hates any man the thing he would not kill?

Bassanio.
Every offense is not a hate at first.

Shylock.
What, wouldst thou have a serpent sting thee twice?

Antonio.
I pray you think you question with the Jew:
You may as well go stand upon the beach
And bid the main flood bate his usual height;
You may as well use question with the wolf
Why he hath made the ewe bleak for the lamb;
You may as well forbid the mountain pines
To wag their high tops, and to make no noise
When they are fretten with the gusts of heaven;
You may as well do any thing most hard
As seek to soften that—than which what's harder?—
His Jewish heart! Therefore I do beseech you
Make no more offers, use no farther means,
But with all brief and plain conveniency
Let me have judgment and the Jew his will.

Bassanio.
For thy three thousand ducats here is six.

Shylock.
If every ducat in six thousand ducats
Were in six parts, and every part a ducat,
I would not draw them, I would have my bond.

The Duke of Venice.
How shalt thou hope for mercy, rend'ring none?

Shylock.
What judgment shall I dread, doing no wrong?
You have among you many a purchas'd slave,
Which like your asses, and your dogs and mules,
You use in abject and in slavish parts,
Because you bought them. Shall I say to you,
"Let them be free! Marry them to your heirs!
Why sweat they under burdens? Let their beds
Be made as soft as yours, and let their palates
Be season'd with such viands?" You will answer,
"The slaves are ours." So do I answer you:
The pound of flesh which I demand of him
Is dearly bought as mine, and I will have it.
If you deny me, fie upon your law!
There is no force in the decrees of Venice.
I stand for judgment. Answer—shall I have it?

The Duke of Venice.
Upon my power I may dismiss this court,
Unless Bellario, a learned doctor,
Whom I have sent for to determine this,
Come here today.

Salerio.
                My lord, here stays without
A messenger with letters from the doctor,
New come from Padua.

The Duke of Venice.
Bring us the letters; call the messenger.

Bassanio.
Good cheer, Antonio! What, man, courage yet!
The Jew shall have my flesh, blood, bones, and all,
Ere thou shalt lose for me one drop of blood.

Antonio.
I am a tainted wether of the flock,
Meetest for death; the weakest kind of fruit
Drops earliest to the ground, and so let me.
You cannot better be employ'd, Bassanio,
Than to live still and write mine epitaph.

Enter Nerissa dressed like a lawyer's clerk.

The Duke of Venice.
Came you from Padua, from Bellario?

Nerissa.
From both, my lord. Bellario greets your Grace.

Presenting a letter.

Bassanio.
Why dost thou whet thy knife so earnestly?

Shylock.
To cut the forfeiture from that bankrupt there.

Gratiano.
Not on thy sole, but on thy soul, harsh Jew,
Thou mak'st thy knife keen; but no metal can,
No, not the hangman's axe, bear half the keenness
Of thy sharp envy. Can no prayers pierce thee?

Shylock.
No, none that thou hast wit enough to make.

Gratiano.
O, be thou damn'd, inexecrable dog!
And for thy life let justice be accus'd.
Thou almost mak'st me waver in my faith
To hold opinion with Pythagoras,
That souls of animals infuse themselves
Into the trunks of men. Thy currish spirit
Govern'd a wolf, who hang'd for human slaughter,
Even from the gallows did his fell soul fleet,
And whilst thou layest in thy unhallowed dam,
Infus'd itself in thee; for thy desires
Are wolvish, bloody, starv'd, and ravenous.

Shylock.
Till thou canst rail the seal from off my bond,
Thou but offend'st thy lungs to speak so loud.
Repair thy wit, good youth, or it will fall
To cureless ruin. I stand here for law.

The Duke of Venice.
This letter from Bellario doth commend
A young and learned doctor to our court.
Where is he?

Nerissa.
                He attendeth here hard by
To know your answer, whether you'll admit him.

The Duke of Venice.
With all my heart. Some three or four of you
Go give him courteous conduct to this place.
Mean time the court shall hear Bellario's letter.

Reads.

"Your Grace shall understand that at the receipt of your letter I am very sick, but in the instant that your messenger came, in loving visitation was with me a young doctor of Rome. His name is Balthazar. I acquainted him

Act 4, Scene 1

with the cause in controversy between the Jew and Antonio the merchant. We turn'd o'er many books together. He is furnish'd with my opinion, which better'd with his own learning, the greatness whereof I cannot enough commend, comes with him, at my importunity, to fill up your Grace's request in my stead. I beseech you let his lack of years be no impediment to let him lack a reverend estimation, for I never knew so young a body with so old a head. I leave him to your gracious acceptance, whose trial shall better publish his commendation."

Enter Portia for Balthazar.

You hear the learn'd Bellario, what he writes,
And here I take it is the doctor come.
Give me your hand. Come you from old Bellario?

Portia.
I did, my lord.

The Duke of Venice.
                    You are welcome, take your place.
Are you acquainted with the difference
That holds this present question in the court?

Portia.
I am informed throughly of the cause.
Which is the merchant here? And which the Jew?

The Duke of Venice.
Antonio and old Shylock, both stand forth.

Portia.
Is your name Shylock?

Shylock.
                    Shylock is my name.

Portia.
Of a strange nature is the suit you follow,
Yet in such rule that the Venetian law
Cannot impugn you as you do proceed.—
You stand within his danger, do you not?

Antonio.
Ay, so he says.

Portia.
                    Do you confess the bond?

Antonio.
I do.

Portia.
Then must the Jew be merciful.

Shylock.
On what compulsion must I? Tell me that.

Portia.
The quality of mercy is not strain'd,
It droppeth as the gentle rain from heaven
Upon the place beneath. It is twice blest:
It blesseth him that gives and him that takes.
'Tis mightiest in the mightiest, it becomes
The throned monarch better than his crown.
His sceptre shows the force of temporal power,
The attribute to awe and majesty,
Wherein doth sit the dread and fear of kings;
But mercy is above this sceptred sway,
It is enthroned in the hearts of kings,
It is an attribute to God himself;
And earthly power doth then show likest God's
When mercy seasons justice. Therefore, Jew,
Though justice be thy plea, consider this,
That in the course of justice, none of us
Should see salvation. We do pray for mercy,
And that same prayer doth teach us all to render
The deeds of mercy. I have spoke thus much
To mitigate the justice of thy plea,
Which if thou follow, this strict court of Venice
Must needs give sentence 'gainst the merchant there.

Shylock.
My deeds upon my head! I crave the law,
The penalty and forfeit of my bond.

Portia.
Is he not able to discharge the money?

Bassanio.
Yes, here I tender it for him in the court,
Yea, twice the sum. If that will not suffice,
I will be bound to pay it ten times o'er,
On forfeit of my hands, my head, my heart.
If this will not suffice, it must appear
That malice bears down truth.

To the Duke.
                    And I beseech you
Wrest once the law to your authority:
To do a great right, do a little wrong,
And curb this cruel devil of his will.

Portia.
It must not be, there is no power in Venice
Can alter a decree established.
'Twill be recorded for a precedent,
And many an error by the same example
Will rush into the state. It cannot be.

Shylock.
A Daniel come to judgment! Yea, a Daniel!
O wise young judge, how I do honor thee!

Portia.
I pray you let me look upon the bond.

Shylock.
Here 'tis, most reverend doctor, here it is.

Portia.
Shylock, there's thrice thy money off'red thee.

Shylock.
An oath, an oath, I have an oath in heaven!
Shall I lay perjury upon my soul?
No, not for Venice.

Portia.
           Why, this bond is forfeit,
And lawfully by this the Jew may claim
A pound of flesh, to be by him cut off
Nearest the merchant's heart. Be merciful,
Take thrice thy money, bid me tear the bond.

Shylock.
When it is paid according to the tenure.
It doth appear you are a worthy judge;
You know the law, your exposition
Hath been most sound. I charge you by the law,
Whereof you are a well-deserving pillar,
Proceed to judgment. By my soul I swear
There is no power in the tongue of man
To alter me: I stay here on my bond.

Antonio.
Most heartily I do beseech the court
To give the judgment.

Portia.
           Why then thus it is:
You must prepare your bosom for his knife—

Shylock.
O noble judge, O excellent young man!

Portia.
For the intent and purpose of the law
Hath full relation to the penalty,
Which here appeareth due upon the bond.

Shylock.
'Tis very true. O wise and upright judge!
How much more elder art thou than thy looks!

Portia.
Therefore lay bare your bosom.

Shylock.
           Ay, his breast,
So says the bond, doth it not, noble judge?
"Nearest his heart," those are the very words.

Portia.
It is so. Are there balance here to weigh
The flesh?

Shylock.
           I have them ready.

Portia.
Have by some surgeon, Shylock, on your charge,
To stop his wounds, lest he do bleed to death.

Shylock.
Is it so nominated in the bond?

Portia.
It is not so express'd, but what of that?
'Twere good you do so much for charity.

Shylock.
I cannot find it, 'tis not in the bond.

Portia.
You, merchant, have you any thing to say?

Antonio.
But little; I am arm'd and well prepar'd.
Give me your hand, Bassanio, fare you well.
Grieve not that I am fall'n to this for you;
For herein Fortune shows herself more kind
Than is her custom. It is still her use
To let the wretched man outlive his wealth,
To view with hollow eye and wrinkled brow
An age of poverty; from which ling'ring penance
Of such misery doth she cut me off.
Commend me to your honorable wife,
Tell her the process of Antonio's end,
Say how I lov'd you, speak me fair in death;

And when the tale is told, bid her be judge
Whether Bassanio had not once a love.
Repent but you that you shall lose your friend,
And he repents not that he pays your debt;
For if the Jew do cut but deep enough,
I'll pay it instantly with all my heart.

Bassanio.
Antonio, I am married to a wife
Which is as dear to me as life itself,
But life itself, my wife, and all the world,
Are not with me esteem'd above thy life.
I would lose all, ay, sacrifice them all
Here to this devil, to deliver you.

Portia.
Your wife would give you little thanks for that
If she were by to hear you make the offer.

Gratiano.
I have a wife who I protest I love;
I would she were in heaven, so she could
Entreat some power to change this currish Jew.

Nerissa.
'Tis well you offer it behind her back,
The wish would make else an unquiet house.

Shylock.

Aside.

These be the Christian husbands. I have a daughter—
Would any of the stock of Barrabas
Had been her husband rather than a Christian!
—We trifle time. I pray thee pursue sentence.

Portia.
A pound of that same merchant's flesh is thine,
The court awards it, and the law doth give it.

Shylock.
Most rightful judge!

Portia.
And you must cut this flesh from off his breast,
The law allows it, and the court awards it.

Shylock.
Most learned judge, a sentence! Come prepare!

Portia.
Tarry a little, there is something else.
This bond doth give thee here no jot of blood;
The words expressly are 'a pound of flesh.'
Take then thy bond, take thou thy pound of flesh,
But in the cutting it, if thou dost shed
One drop of Christian blood, thy lands and goods
Are by the laws of Venice confiscate
Unto the state of Venice.

Gratiano.
O upright judge! Mark, Jew. O learned judge!

Shylock.
Is that the law?

Portia.
                    Thyself shalt see the act;
For as thou urgest justice, be assur'd
Thou shalt have justice more than thou desir'st.

Gratiano.
O learned judge! Mark, Jew, a learned judge!

Shylock.
I take this offer then; pay the bond thrice
And let the Christian go.

Bassanio.
                    Here is the money.

Portia.
Soft,
The Jew shall have all justice. Soft, no haste.
He shall have nothing but the penalty.

Gratiano.
O Jew! An upright judge, a learned judge!

Portia.
Therefore prepare thee to cut off the flesh.
Shed thou no blood, nor cut thou less nor more
But just a pound of flesh. If thou tak'st more
Or less than a just pound, be it but so much
As makes it light or heavy in the substance
Or the division of the twentith part
Of one poor scruple, nay, if the scale do turn
But in the estimation of a hair,
Thou diest, and all thy goods are confiscate.

Gratiano.
A second Daniel! A Daniel, Jew!
Now, infidel, I have you on the hip.

Portia.
Why doth the Jew pause? Take thy forfeiture.

Shylock.
Give me my principal, and let me go.

Bassanio.
I have it ready for thee, here it is.

Portia.
He hath refus'd it in the open court;
He shall have merely justice and his bond.

Gratiano.
A Daniel, still say I, a second Daniel!
I thank thee, Jew, for teaching me that word.

Shylock.
Shall I not have barely my principal?

Portia.
Thou shalt have nothing but the forfeiture,
To be so taken at thy peril, Jew.

Shylock.
Why then the devil give him good of it!
I'll stay no longer question.

Portia.
                    Tarry, Jew,
The law hath yet another hold on you.
It is enacted in the laws of Venice,
If it be proved against an alien,
That by direct or indirect attempts
He seek the life of any citizen,
The party 'gainst the which he doth contrive
Shall seize one half his goods; the other half
Comes to the privy coffer of the state,
And the offender's life lies in the mercy
Of the Duke only, 'gainst all other voice:
In which predicament I say thou stand'st;
For it appears, by manifest proceeding,
That indirectly, and directly too,
Thou hast contrived against the very life
Of the defendant; and thou hast incurr'd
The danger formerly by me rehears'd.
Down therefore, and beg mercy of the Duke.

Gratiano.
Beg that thou mayst have leave to hang thyself,
And yet thy wealth being forfeit to the state,
Thou hast not left the value of a cord;
Therefore thou must be hang'd at the state's charge.

The Duke of Venice.
That thou shalt see the difference of our spirit,
I pardon thee thy life before thou ask it.
For half thy wealth, it is Antonio's;
The other half comes to the general state,
Which humbleness may drive unto a fine.

Portia.
Ay, for the state, not for Antonio.

Shylock.
Nay, take my life and all, pardon not that:
You take my house when you do take the prop
That doth sustain my house; you take my life
When you do take the means whereby I live.

Portia.
What mercy can you render him, Antonio?

Gratiano.
A halter gratis—nothing else, for God sake.

Antonio.
So please my lord the Duke and all the court
To quit the fine for one half of his goods,
I am content; so he will let me have
The other half in use, to render it
Upon his death unto the gentleman
That lately stole his daughter.
Two things provided more, that for this favor
He presently become a Christian;
The other, that he do record a gift,
Here in the court, of all he dies possess'd
Unto his son Lorenzo and his daughter.

The Duke of Venice.
He shall do this, or else I do recant
The pardon that I late pronounced here.

Portia.
Art thou contented, Jew? What dost thou say?

Shylock.
I am content.

Portia.
                    Clerk, draw a deed of gift.

Shylock.
I pray you give me leave to go from hence,
I am not well. Send the deed after me,
And I will sign it.

The Duke of Venice.
                    Get thee gone, but do it.

Gratiano.
In christ'ning shalt thou have two god-fathers:
Had I been judge, thou shouldst have had ten more,
To bring thee to the gallows, not to the font.

Exit Shylock.

The Duke of Venice.
Sir, I entreat you home with me to dinner.

Portia.
I humbly do desire your Grace of pardon,
I must away this night toward Padua,
And it is meet I presently set forth.

The Duke of Venice.
I am sorry that your leisure serves you not.
Antonio, gratify this gentleman,
For in my mind you are much bound to him.

Exeunt Duke and his Train.

Bassanio.
Most worthy gentleman, I and my friend
Have by your wisdom been this day acquitted
Of grievous penalties, in lieu whereof
Three thousand ducats, due unto the Jew,
We freely cope your courteous pains withal.

Antonio.
And stand indebted, over and above,
In love and service to you evermore.

Portia.
He is well paid that is well satisfied,
And I, delivering you, am satisfied,
And therein do account myself well paid.
My mind was never yet more mercenary.
I pray you know me when we meet again;
I wish you well, and so I take my leave.

Bassanio.
Dear sir, of force I must attempt you further.
Take some remembrance of us as a tribute,
Not as fee. Grant me two things, I pray you,
Not to deny me, and to pardon me.

Portia.
You press me far, and therefore I will yield.

To Antonio.

Give me your gloves, I'll wear them for your sake,

To Bassanio.

And for your love I'll take this ring from you.
Do not draw back your hand, I'll take no more,
And you in love shall not deny me this!

Bassanio.
This ring, good sir, alas, it is a trifle!
I will not shame myself to give you this.

Portia.
I will have nothing else but only this,
And now methinks I have a mind to it.

Bassanio.
There's more depends on this than on the value.
The dearest ring in Venice will I give you,
And find it out by proclamation;
Only for this, I pray you pardon me.

Portia.
I see, sir, you are liberal in offers.
You taught me first to beg, and now methinks
You teach me how a beggar should be answer'd.

Bassanio.
Good sir, this ring was given me by my wife,
And when she put it on, she made me vow
That I should neither sell, nor give, nor lose it.

Portia.
That 'scuse serves many men to save their gifts,
And if your wife be not a mad woman,
And know how well I have deserv'd this ring,
She would not hold out enemy forever
For giving it to me. Well, peace be with you!

Exeunt Portia and Nerissa.

Antonio.
My Lord Bassanio, let him have the ring.
Let his deservings and my love withal
Be valued 'gainst your wive's commandment.

Bassanio.
Go, Gratiano, run and overtake him;
Give him the ring, and bring him, if thou canst,
Unto Antonio's house. Away, make haste.

Exit Gratiano.

Come, you and I will thither presently,
And in the morning early will we both
Fly toward Belmont. Come, Antonio.

Exeunt.

Scene 2

Venice. A street.

(Portia; Nerissa; Gratiano)

Gratiano catches up with Portia and Nerissa as they search for Shylock's house. Portia receives the ring with thanks while Nerissa plans to get the ring off her husband's finger as well.

Enter Portia and Nerissa disguised as before.

Portia.
Inquire the Jew's house out, give him this deed,
And let him sign it. We'll away tonight,
And be a day before our husbands home.
This deed will be well welcome to Lorenzo.

Enter Gratiano.

Gratiano.
Fair sir, you are well o'erta'en.
My Lord Bassanio upon more advice
Hath sent you here this ring, and doth entreat
Your company at dinner.

Portia.
                        That cannot be.
His ring I do accept most thankfully,
And so I pray you tell him; furthermore,
I pray you show my youth old Shylock's house.

Gratiano.
That will I do.

Nerissa.
              Sir, I would speak with you.

Aside to Portia.

I'll see if I can get my husband's ring,
Which I did make him swear to keep forever.

Portia.

Aside to Nerissa

Thou mayst, I warrant. We shall have old swearing
That they did give the rings away to men;
But we'll outface them, and outswear them too.—
Away, make haste. Thou know'st where I will tarry.

Nerissa.
Come, good sir, will you show me to this house?

Exeunt.

Act 5

Scene 1

Belmont. Outside Portia's house.

(Lorenzo; Jessica; Stephano; Launcelot; Musicians; Portia; Nerissa; Bassanio; Antonio; Gratiano; Followers)

Lorenzo and Jessica have a mock quarrel, comparing themselves to great lovers of the past. Stephano announces that Portia and Nerissa are on their way back, and Launcelot informs them that Bassanio is also returning. Lorenzo calls for music, and he and Jessica listen until Portia and Nerissa arrive. Portia tells them to make sure that no one tells Bassanio she has been away. Bassanio and Gratiano arrive, along with Antonio, who is introduced to Portia. Peace is broken when Gratiano and Nerissa begin a furious quarrel over the ring he gave to the lawyer's clerk. Portia announces her confidence that Bassanio would not have done so, but her husband is forced to admit that he did. Antonio attempts to reconcile the couples, seeing this all as his fault. Portia finally admits the whole story, to widespread wide-eyed amazement. She is also able to tell Antonio that some of his ships have made it back, and that he is therefore not ruined after all, while Nerissa informs Lorenzo and Jessica of how they will inherit all Shylock's goods on his death. As Gratiano makes bawdy comments, everyone goes into the house to unravel the whole story.

Enter Lorenzo and Jessica.

Lorenzo.
The moon shines bright. In such a night as this,
When the sweet wind did gently kiss the trees,
And they did make no noise, in such a night
Troilus methinks mounted the Troyan walls,

And sigh'd his soul toward the Grecian tents,
Where Cressid lay that night.

Jessica.
                    In such a night
Did Thisby fearfully o'ertrip the dew,
And saw the lion's shadow ere himself,
And ran dismayed away.

Lorenzo.
                    In such a night
Stood Dido with a willow in her hand
Upon the wild sea-banks, and waft her love
To come again to Carthage.

Jessica.
                    In such a night
Medea gathered the enchanted herbs
That did renew old Aeson.

Lorenzo.
                    In such a night
Did Jessica steal from the wealthy Jew,
And with an unthrift love did run from Venice,
As far as Belmont.

Jessica.
                    In such a night
Did young Lorenzo swear he lov'd her well,
Stealing her soul with many vows of faith,
And ne'er a true one.

Lorenzo.
                    In such a night
Did pretty Jessica (like a little shrew)
Slander her love, and he forgave it her.

Jessica.
I would out-night you, did nobody come;
But hark, I hear the footing of a man.

Enter Stephano.

Lorenzo.
Who comes so fast in silence of the night?

Stephano.
A friend.

Lorenzo.
A friend! What friend? Your name, I pray you, friend?

Stephano.
Stephano is my name, and I bring word
My mistress will before the break of day
Be here at Belmont. She doth stray about
By holy crosses, where she kneels and prays
For happy wedlock hours.

Lorenzo.
                    Who comes with her?

Stephano.
None but a holy hermit and her maid.
I pray you, is my master yet return'd?

Lorenzo.
He is not, nor we have not heard from him.
But go we in, I pray thee, Jessica,
And ceremoniously let us prepare
Some welcome for the mistress of the house.

Enter Clown Launcelot.

Launcelot Gobbo.
Sola, sola! Wo ha, ho! Sola, sola!

Lorenzo.
Who calls?

Launcelot Gobbo.
Sola! Did you see Master Lorenzo? Master Lorenzo, sola, sola!

Lorenzo.
Leave hollowing, man—here.

Launcelot Gobbo.
Sola! Where, where?

Lorenzo.
Here!

Launcelot Gobbo.
Tell him there's a post come from my master, with his horn full of good news. My master will be here ere morning.

Exit.

Lorenzo.
Sweet soul, let's in, and there expect their coming.
And yet no matter; why should we go in?
My friend Stephano, signify, I pray you,
Within the house, your mistress is at hand,
And bring your music forth into the air.

Exit Stephano.

How sweet the moonlight sleeps upon this bank!
Here will we sit, and let the sounds of music
Creep in our ears. Soft stillness and the night
Become the touches of sweet harmony.
Sit, Jessica. Look how the floor of heaven
Is thick inlaid with patens of bright gold.
There's not the smallest orb which thou behold'st
But in his motion like an angel sings,
Still quiring to the young-ey'd cherubins;
Such harmony is in immortal souls,
But whilst this muddy vesture of decay
Doth grossly close it in, we cannot hear it.

Enter Musicians.

Come ho, and wake Diana with a hymn,
With sweetest touches pierce your mistress' ear,
And draw her home with music.

Play Music.

Jessica.
I am never merry when I hear sweet music.

Lorenzo.
The reason is, your spirits are attentive;
For do but note a wild and wanton herd
Or race of youthful and unhandled colts,
Fetching mad bounds, bellowing and neighing loud,
Which is the hot condition of their blood,
If they but hear perchance a trumpet sound,
Or any air of music touch their ears,
You shall perceive them make a mutual stand,
Their savage eyes turn'd to a modest gaze,
By the sweet power of music; therefore the poet
Did feign that Orpheus drew trees, stones, and floods;
Since nought so stockish, hard, and full of rage,
But music for the time doth change his nature.
The man that hath no music in himself,
Nor is not moved with concord of sweet sounds,
Is fit for treasons, stratagems, and spoils;
The motions of his spirit are dull as night,
And his affections dark as Erebus
Let no such man be trusted. Mark the music.

Enter Portia and Nerissa.

Portia.
That light we see is burning in my hall.
How far that little candle throws his beams!
So shines a good deed in a naughty world.

Nerissa.
When the moon shone, we did not see the candle.

Portia.
So doth the greater glory dim the less:
A substitute shines brightly as a king
Until a king be by, and then his state
Empties itself, as doth an inland brook
Into the main of waters. Music, hark!

Nerissa.
It is your music, madam, of the house.

Portia.
Nothing is good, I see, without respect;
Methinks it sounds much sweeter than by day.

Nerissa.
Silence bestows that virtue on it, madam.

Portia.
The crow doth sing as sweetly as the lark
When neither is attended; and I think
The nightingale, if she should sing by day
When every goose is cackling, would be thought
No better a musician than the wren.
How many things by season season'd are
To their right praise and true perfection!
Peace ho! The Moon sleeps with Endymion,
And would not be awak'd.

Music ceases.

Lorenzo.
                That is the voice,
Or I am much deceiv'd, of Portia.

Portia.
He knows me as the blind man knows the cuckoo,
By the bad voice!

Lorenzo.
                Dear lady, welcome home!

Portia.
We have been praying for our husbands' welfare,
Which speed we hope the better for our words.
Are they return'd?

Lorenzo.
               Madam, they are not yet;
But there is come a messenger before,
To signify their coming.

Portia.
               Go in, Nerissa.
Give order to my servants that they take
No note at all of our being absent hence—
Nor you, Lorenzo—Jessica, nor you.

A tucket sounds.

Lorenzo.
Your husband is at hand, I hear his trumpet.
We are no tell-tales, madam, fear you not.

Portia.
This night methinks is but the daylight sick,
It looks a little paler. 'Tis a day,
Such as the day is when the sun is hid.

Enter Bassanio, Antonio, Gratiano, and their Followers.

Bassanio.
We should hold day with the Antipodes,
If you would walk in absence of the sun.

Portia.
Let me give light, but let me not be light,
For a light wife doth make a heavy husband,
And never be Bassanio so for me—
But God sort all! You are welcome home, my lord.

Bassanio.
I thank you, madam. Give welcome to my friend;
This is the man, this is Antonio,
To whom I am so infinitely bound.

Portia.
You should in all sense be much bound to him,
For as I hear he was much bound for you.

Antonio.
No more than I am well acquitted of.

Portia.
Sir, you are very welcome to our house.
It must appear in other ways than words,
Therefore I scant this breathing courtesy.

Gratiano.

To Nerissa.

By yonder moon I swear you do me wrong;
In faith, I gave it to the judge's clerk.
Would he were gelt that had it, for my part,
Since you do take it, love, so much at heart.

Portia.
A quarrel ho already! What's the matter?

Gratiano.
About a hoop of gold, a paltry ring
That she did give me, whose posy was
For all the world like cutler's poetry
Upon a knife, "Love me, and leave me not."

Nerissa.
What talk you of the posy or the value?
You swore to me, when I did give it you,
That you would wear it till your hour of death,
And that it should lie with you in your grave.
Though not for me, yet for your vehement oaths,
You should have been respective and have kept it.
Gave it a judge's clerk! No, God's my judge,
The clerk will ne'er wear hair on 's face that had it.

Gratiano.
He will, and if he live to be a man.

Nerissa.
Ay, if a woman live to be a man.

Gratiano.
Now, by this hand, I gave it to a youth,
A kind of boy, a little scrubbed boy,
No higher than thyself, the judge's clerk,
A prating boy, that begg'd it as a fee.
I could not for my heart deny it him.

Portia.
You were to blame, I must be plain with you,
To part so slightly with your wive's first gift,
A thing stuck on with oaths upon your finger,
And so riveted with faith unto your flesh.
I gave my love a ring, and made him swear
Never to part with it, and here he stands.
I dare be sworn for him he would not leave it,
Nor pluck it from his finger, for the wealth
That the world masters. Now, in faith, Gratiano,
You give your wife too unkind a cause of grief;
And 'twere to me I should be mad at it.

Bassanio.

Aside.

Why, I were best to cut my left hand off,
And swear I lost the ring defending it.

Gratiano.
My Lord Bassanio gave his ring away
Unto the judge that begg'd it, and indeed
Deserv'd it too; and then the boy, his clerk,
That took some pains in writing, he begg'd mine,
And neither man nor master would take aught
But the two rings.

Portia.
              What ring gave you, my lord?
Not that, I hope, which you receiv'd of me.

Bassanio.
If I could add a lie unto a fault,
I would deny it; but you see my finger
Hath not the ring upon it, it is gone.

Portia.
Even so void is your false heart of truth.
By heaven, I will ne'er come in your bed
Until I see the ring!

Nerissa.
              Nor I in yours
Till I again see mine!

Bassanio.
              Sweet Portia,
If you did know to whom I gave the ring,
If you did know for whom I gave the ring,
And would conceive for what I gave the ring,
And how unwillingly I left the ring,
When nought would be accepted but the ring,
You would abate the strength of your displeasure.

Portia.
If you had known the virtue of the ring,
Or half her worthiness that gave the ring,
Or your own honor to contain the ring,
You would not then have parted with the ring.
What man is there so much unreasonable,
If you had pleas'd to have defended it
With any terms of zeal, wanted the modesty
To urge the thing held as a ceremony?
Nerissa teaches me what to believe—
I'll die for't but some woman had the ring!

Bassanio.
No, by my honor, madam, by my soul,
No woman had it, but a civil doctor,
Which did refuse three thousand ducats of me,
And begg'd the ring, the which I did deny him,
And suffer'd him to go displeas'd away—
Even he that had held up the very life
Of my dear friend. What should I say, sweet lady?
I was enforc'd to send it after him,
I was beset with shame and courtesy,
My honor would not let ingratitude
So much besmear it. Pardon me, good lady,
For by these blessed candles of the night,
Had you been there, I think you would have begg'd
The ring of me to give the worthy doctor.

Portia.
Let not that doctor e'er come near my house.
Since he hath got the jewel that I loved,
And that which you did swear to keep for me,
I will become as liberal as you,
I'll not deny him any thing I have,
No, not my body nor my husband's bed.
Know him I shall, I am well sure of it.
Lie not a night from home. Watch me like Argus;
If you do not, if I be left alone,
Now by mine honor, which is yet mine own,
I'll have that doctor for my bedfellow.

Nerissa.
And I his clerk; therefore be well advis'd
How you do leave me to mine own protection.

Gratiano.
Well, do you so; let not me take him then,
For if I do, I'll mar the young clerk's pen.

Antonio.
I am th' unhappy subject of these quarrels.

Portia.
Sir, grieve not you, you are welcome notwithstanding.

Bassanio.
Portia, forgive me this enforced wrong,
And in the hearing of these many friends
I swear to thee, even by thine own fair eyes,
Wherein I see myself—

Portia.
                Mark you but that!
In both my eyes he doubly sees himself,
In each eye, one. Swear by your double self,
And there's an oath of credit.

Bassanio.
               Nay, but hear me.
Pardon this fault, and by my soul I swear
I never more will break an oath with thee.

Antonio.
I once did lend my body for his wealth,
Which but for him that had your husband's ring
Had quite miscarried. I dare be bound again,
My soul upon the forfeit, that your lord
Will never more break faith advisedly.

Portia.
Then you shall be his surety. Give him this,
And bid him keep it better than the other.

Antonio.
Here, Lord Bassanio, swear to keep this ring.

Bassanio.
By heaven, it is the same I gave the doctor!

Portia.
I had it of him. Pardon me, Bassanio,
For by this ring, the doctor lay with me.

Nerissa.
And pardon me, my gentle Gratiano,
For that same scrubbed boy, the doctor's clerk,
In lieu of this last night did lie with me.

Gratiano.
Why, this is like the mending of highways
In summer, where the ways are fair enough.
What, are we cuckolds ere we have deserv'd it?

Portia.
Speak not so grossly, you are all amaz'd.
Here is a letter, read it at your leisure.
It comes from Padua, from Bellario.
There you shall find that Portia was the doctor,
Nerissa there her clerk. Lorenzo here
Shall witness I set forth as soon as you,
And even but now return'd; I have not yet
Enter'd my house. Antonio, you are welcome,
And I have better news in store for you
Than you expect. Unseal this letter soon;
There you shall find three of your argosies
Are richly come to harbor suddenly.
You shall not know by what strange accident
I chanced on this letter.

Antonio.
                I am dumb.

Bassanio.
Were you the doctor, and I knew you not?

Gratiano.
Were you the clerk that is to make me cuckold?

Nerissa.
Ay, but the clerk that never means to do it,
Unless he live until he be a man.

Bassanio.
Sweet doctor, you shall be my bedfellow—
When I am absent, then lie with my wife.

Antonio.
Sweet lady, you have given me life and living,
For here I read for certain that my ships
Are safely come to road.

Portia.
              How now, Lorenzo?
My clerk hath some good comforts too for you.

Nerissa.
Ay, and I'll give them him without a fee.
There do I give to you and Jessica,
From the rich Jew, a special deed of gift,
After his death, of all he dies possess'd of.

Lorenzo.
Fair ladies, you drop manna in the way
Of starved people.

Portia.
               It is almost morning,
And yet I am sure you are not satisfied
Of these events at full. Let us go in,
And charge us there upon inter'gatories,
And we will answer all things faithfully.

Gratiano.
Let it be so. The first inter'gatory
That my Nerissa shall be sworn on is,
Whether till the next night she had rather stay,
Or go to bed now, being two hours to day.
But were the day come, I should wish it dark

Till I were couching with the doctor's clerk. *Exeunt.*
Well, while I live I'll fear no other thing
So sore, as keeping safe Nerissa's ring.